"A very important guide. Gives a very clear, very factual picture.
I must admit that I carry and use the book like a bible and refer to it
often. Thank you *Billboard* and thank you Joel."

Hy Lit
Program Director
WSNI, RADIO, Philadelphia

"For a number of years I have used a review of music from a specific
year as a specialty on my radio show. In those years I've been
nicknamed "The Professor" for my history lessons on music. One of
my choice sources of information has been Joel Whitburn's books.
Thanks."

Scott Muni
WNEW-FM, New York

"There's nothing else like it—only Joel Whitburn could accurately
track 9,311 records of the rock era. *The Billboard Book of Top 40 Hits* is
worth its weight in solid gold!"

Arnie "WooWoo' Ginsburg
WXKS-FM, Boston

"Don't stay home without it!"

Bruce Bradley
WYNY-FM, New York

The Billboard Book of

TOP 40

REVISED AND ENLARGED 6TH EDITION

HITS

BILLBOARD BOOKS
An imprint of
Watson-Guptill
Publications/New York

JOEL WHITBURN

Edited by Amy Handy
Photo captions by Dave DiMartino
Picture sleeves selected from Joel Whitburn's personal collection
Book and cover design by Bob Fillie, Graphiti Graphics
Graphic production by Hector Campbell

First published 1996 by Billboard Publications, Inc.

1515 Broadway, New York, NY 10036.
ISBN 8230-7632-6

Library of Congress Cataloging-in-Publication Data
Whitburn, Joel
    The Billboard book of top 40 hits/Joel Whitburn.—6th ed.
        p.   cm.
    ISBN 0-8230-7632-6 :
1. Popular music—United States—Discography. 2. Popular music—
United States—Statistics. I. Billboard. II. Title. III. Title:
Billboard book of top 40 hits. IV. Title: Top 40 hits.
ML156242P6W44   1992
016.78164'026'6—dc20   91-45488
                                              CIP
                                              MN

Manufactured in the United States of America

First printing, 1996

3 4 5 6 7 8 9 10 / 99 98

This book is dedicated to the Top 40 radio format of days passed.
I remember tuning my radio dial to 920 AM in Milwaukee on summer evenings
in 1962 and hearing the hits of Elvis Presley, Ray Charles, Kenny Ball and His Jazzmen,
Gene Chandler, David Rose and His Orchestra, Walter Brennan, Booker T. & The MG's,
The Orlons, Jimmy Dean, Tony Bennett, Tommy Roe and Peter, Paul & Mary.
What a great mix!

The author wishes to give thanks
to the staff of Record Research:

Bill Hathaway
Kim Bloxdorf
Fran Whitburn
Brent Olynick
Joanne Wagner
Troy Kluess
Jeanne Olynick
Paul Haney
Oscar Vidotto
Bobby DeSai

CONTENTS

AUTHOR'S NOTE

As a teenager in the 1950s, I remember listening to Milwaukee's WOKY and WRIT, and Chicago's WLS and WJJD. The DJs of these Top 40 AM radio stations played all of the hits. In a single hour I would hear the hits of Ricky Nelson, Perez Prado, The Elegants, Johnny Cash, Patti Page, Jerry Butler and the Impressions, Johnny Mathis, Perry Como, Chuck Berry and Marty Robbins. I was treated to a variety of musical genres — rock 'n' roll, R&B, Country and Easy Listening.

The nightly airwaves buzzed with activity. Taking requests and dedications, the colorful DJs had an ongoing open line with a massive teen audience. Between songs, callers would tell listeners who won the Watertown vs. Hartford high school basketball game or report a "hot happening" around town. Top 40 radio provided an immediate connection to the world beyond my community.

More than anything, Top 40 radio fed my passion for record collecting. Every night, I was guaranteed to hear one brand new release. I wondered if it would be something new from Buddy Holly or Duane Eddy, or maybe the latest from Connie Francis or The Platters. At the end of the week, I'd head down to the local "mom & pop" record shop. Along with my purchase, I'd pick up one of the colored cards distributed by the local radio stations that featured their playlists, "pick of the week" and occasionally a DJ profile.

The '50s and '60s marked my golden years of Top 40 radio listening, perhaps because I was in my teens and twenties. However, I like to think that it was the tremendous mix of styles and the energetic DJs.

As it had done for me, Top 40 radio continued over the decades to foster many new record collectors. The advent of weekly Top 40 radio countdowns in the 1970s, beginning with American Top 40, encouraged many loyal listeners to follow the charts.

By the end of the 1980s, Top 40 radio splintered into Top 40 Urban, Top 40 Adult, Top 40 Rock, etc. To ensure advertising revenue, stations began to cater to well-defined niches. Playing all of the Top 40 hits was too broad. The days of a radio station playing the complete Top 40 of *Billboard*'s Hot 100 chart seem long gone. Today, stations are more likely to change formats rather than introduce a mix of styles into their rotations. If a DJ dared to follow TLC with Alan Jackson, hordes of listeners might immediately hit the scan button. But, they might not.

Imagine a radical Top 40 station that could afford to experiment for one week and play all of the Top 40 of *Billboard*'s Hot 100. No automation. A live DJ would announce Coolio's latest release followed by Celine Dion, Smashing Pumpkins and a request for Shania Twain's recent hit.

In reality, with hot competition for rating points, such an experiment goes against today's business practices. It would be risky, but I think that listeners of all ages would find such a station invigorating.

For now, this book may be one of the few places that you'll find Conway Twitty next to Twisted Sister.

JOEL WHITBURN

ABOUT THE AUTHOR

When Joel Whitburn spun his first 78 rpm single back in 1950, little did he know that his part-time passion would spin off into a lifelong career and the uncontested title of "The World's #1 Chart Authority."

From a few chart facts scribbled on 3x5 note cards as a hobby to help organize his personal record collection, to a vast computerized database encompassing over a century of charted music, Joel's research has developed a richness and diversity rivaling that of the music it documents.

Joel published his first book—a slim, 104-page volume on Pop music singles—in 1970. The first edition of *Top 40 Hits* was released in 1983; the book you now hold in your hands is the sixth edition of this title. With over 60 Record Research volumes published to date, Joel has proven himself to be a prolific compiler of chart research books. He has also delved into *Billboard*'s charts covering Pop albums, Country singles, R&B singles, Adult Contemporary singles, and Album Rock and Modern Rock tracks. His research on the music charts stretches back to 1890, and his book formats run the gamut from yearly record rankings to artist-by-artist compilations of charted record data to reproductions of the original charts themselves.

Joel's ongoing collaborations with Rhino Records have also produced well over 100 yearly CD compilations featuring his personal picks of *Billboard*'s top R&B, Rock 'n' Roll, Pop, Country, Dance, and Christmas hits.

RESEARCHING THE CHARTS

The majority of the research within this book was compiled from *Billboard* magazine's Hot 100 chart. The Hot 100 made its debut on August 4, 1958, and it has long been regarded as the definitive weekly ranking of America's most popular singles in sales and radio airplay.

The pop chart research for this book began with the January 1, 1955, issue of *Billboard*. At this time, *Billboard* was publishing the forerunners to the Hot 100 chart. These charts appeared in the magazine weekly and each focused on specific areas of the music trade. The most obvious antecedent of the Hot 100 was the Top 100 chart which *Billboard* debuted in November of 1955. By October of 1958, all of these charts were discontinued in favor of the all-encompassing Hot 100.

The *Billboard* pop charts researched for this book:

Chart Title	Dates Researched	# of Positions
Best Sellers In Stores	1/1/55–10/13/58 (chart ended)	25–50
Most Played By Jockeys	1/1/55–7/28/58 (chart ended)	20–25
Most Played In Juke Boxes	1/1/55–6/17/57 (chart ended)	20
Top 100	11/12/55–7/28/58 (chart ended)	100
Hot 100	8/4/58–12/30/95	100

A chart-by-chart breakdown of the highest position a single attained on any of the above 1955–1958 *Billboard* Pop charts is listed below the title. Total weeks at the #1 position are shown in parentheses after the peak position. If a single hit only the Top 100 or Hot 100, no chart information is shown below that title.

pre   If a single enters a newly published chart well after the single's height of popularity, the word **pre** is shown after the position. Had the chart been published earlier, the single would, most likely, have scored higher on that chart.

end   If a single had not yet peaked on a chart that was terminated, the word **end** is shown after the position. Had the chart continued, the still-climbing single would probably have reached a higher position.

DATE: *Billboard*'s actual issue date from the chart on which the single first reached the Top 40. It is not the "week ending" date which *Billboard* published on their various charts. The issue and week ending dates were different until January 13, 1962, when *Billboard* began using one date system for both the issue and the charts inside.

POS: The single's highest position is taken from the chart on which it achieved its highest ranking. (The total weeks a single held the #1 or #2 position is shown in parentheses after the peak position, and is taken from the chart on which it achieved its highest total.)

WKS: Total weeks charted in the Top 40.

LABEL & NO.: The original label and its catalog number at the time each single charted.

NOTES: Directly under nearly every artist name are brief notes about the artist.

Directly under some song titles are brief notes that may be of special interest, such as a single that may have first charted on the Hot 100 at an earlier date, but did not reach the Top 40, or one that may feature a famous singer providing background vocals. If the song is featured in a Broadway musical or a movie, the title of the show or movie and the leading actor(s) are listed under the title of the single.

HOT 100 SALES & AIRPLAY CHARTS

The peak positions attained on the Hot 100 Sales and Airplay charts are included for the first time in this edition. *Billboard* began publishing a 30-position Hot 100 Sales chart and Hot 100 Airplay chart on October 20, 1984. These charts were expanded to 40 positions on May 31, 1986, and on June 6, 1991, they were expanded to their present size of 75 positions. Most singles that made these charts also charted on the Hot 100 and many reached the Top 40. The peak positions attained on the Sales and Airplay charts by a Top 40 single are noted below its listing (ex.: Sales #2 / Airplay #5).

If a single peaked at #1, the total weeks charted at #1 are shown in parentheses after the peak position.

#1 HITS ON OTHER CHARTS
Singles that peaked at #1 on the Adult Contemporary, R&B or Country charts are indicated in the titles notes, along with each single's total weeks at #1.

FOUR OR MORE HITS FROM AN ALBUM
If an artist charted four or more Top 40 singles from an album, the album title is shown in the title notes. These title notes are generally applicable to singles that charted after 1963. Prior to 1963, singles greatly outsold albums. The arrival of The Beatles on the music scene in 1964 ushered in the rock album era. Album sales exploded thereafter and eventually outpaced the sales of singles.

THE ARTISTS

HOW TO USE THIS SECTION

This section lists, alphabetically by artist name, every single that charted in the Top 40 on *Billboard*'s pop singles charts from January 1, 1955, through December 30, 1995.

Each artist's Top 40 hits are listed in chronological order. A sequential number is shown in front of each song title to indicate that artist's number of Top 40 hits. All Top 10 hits are highlighted in dark type.

EXPLANATION OF COLUMNAR HEADINGS

DATE: Date single debuted in the Top 40

POS: Single's highest charted position (highlighted in bold type)

WKS: Total weeks charted in the Top 40

LABEL & NO.: Original label and catalog number at the time single charted

EXPLANATION OF SYMBOLS

(1) Number in parentheses to the right of a #1 or #2 peak position is the total weeks the single held that position

+   Indicates single peaked in the year after it first charted (symbol shown next to date)

●   Gold single*

▲   Platinum single* (additional million units sold are indicated by a numeral following the symbol)

> *The primary source used to determine gold and platinum singles is the Recording Industry Association of America (RIAA), which began certifying gold singles in 1958 and platinum singles in 1976. From 1958 through 1988, RIAA required sales of one million units for a gold single and two million units for a platinum single; however, as of January 1, 1989, RIAA lowered the certification requirements for gold singles to sales of 500,000 units and for platinum to one million units. Please keep in mind that some record labels have never requested RIAA certifications for their hits. In order to fill in the gaps, especially during the period prior to 1958, various other trade publications and reports were used to supplement RIAA's certifications.

/	Divides a two-sided hit. Complete chart data (date, peak position, etc.) is shown for both sides if each side achieved its own peak position. If a title was shown only as the B-side, then only the weeks it was shown as a "tag along" are listed.
↑	Indicates the weeks charted data is subject to change since the single was still charted as of the 4/13/96 cut-off date

LETTER(S) IN BRACKETS AFTER TITLES

[I]   instrumental recording

[N]   novelty recording

[C]   comedy recording

[S]   spoken recording

[F]   foreign language recording

[X]   Christmas recording

[R]   re-entry, reissue, remix or re-recording of a previous hit by that artist

See RESEARCHING THE CHARTS for an explanation of the chart names listed below titles from 1955 to 1958 and from 1984 to 1995.

DATE	POS	WKS	ARTIST–RECORD TITLE	LABEL & NO.

A

AALIYAH

Aaliyah (pronounced: ah-lee-yah) Haughton. Female singer from Detroit. Fifteen years old in 1994. Married singer/producer R. Kelly on 8/31/94.

DATE	POS	WKS	ARTIST–RECORD TITLE	LABEL & NO.
5/7/94	5	21	● 1. **Back & Forth** Sales #3 / Airplay #7; written and produced with rap by R. Kelly; #1 R&B hit (3 weeks)	Jive 42174
9/10/94	6	14	● 2. **At Your Best (You Are Love)** Sales #4 / Airplay #11; written by The Isley Brothers (from their 1976 album *Harvest For The World*); produced by R. Kelly	Jive 42239

ABBA

Pop quartet formed in Stockholm, Sweden, in 1970, using their first initials as an acronym. Consisted of Anni-Frid "Frida" Lyngstad and Agnetha Fältskog (vocals), Bjorn Ulvaeus (guitar) and Benny Andersson (keyboards). Benny and Bjorn recorded together in 1966. Bjorn and Agnetha married in 1971, divorced in 1979. Benny and Frida married in 1978, divorced in 1981. Disbanded in the early 1980s. Bjorn and Benny co-wrote the musical *Chess* with Tim Rice.

DATE	POS	WKS	ARTIST–RECORD TITLE	LABEL & NO.
6/22/74	6	12	1. **Waterloo** **ABBA (Bjorn, Benny, Anna & Frida)**	Atlantic 3035
10/12/74	27	4	2. Honey, Honey	Atlantic 3209
10/11/75	15	8	3. SOS only chart hit where both title and artist are palindromes	Atlantic 3265
3/27/76	15	8	4. I Do, I Do, I Do, I Do, I Do	Atlantic 3310
6/19/76	32	4	5. Mamma Mia	Atlantic 3315
9/25/76	13	11	6. Fernando #1 Adult Contemporary hit (2 weeks)	Atlantic 3346
1/22/77	1 (1)	15	● 7. **Dancing Queen**	Atlantic 3372
6/4/77	14	10	8. Knowing Me, Knowing You	Atlantic 3387
1/28/78	12	9	9. The Name Of The Game	Atlantic 3449
5/6/78	3	14	● 10. **Take A Chance On Me**	Atlantic 3457
6/9/79	19	10	11. Does Your Mother Know	Atlantic 3574
12/8/79+	29	6	12. Chiquitita Spanish version released on Atlantic 3630	Atlantic 3629
12/27/80+	8	16	13. **The Winner Takes It All** #1 Adult Contemporary hit (2 weeks)	Atlantic 3776
2/6/82	27	8	14. When All Is Said And Done all of above written and produced by Benny & Bjorn	Atlantic 3889

ABBOTT, Gregory

Soul singer/songwriter from New York. At age eight, member of St. Patrick's Cathedral Choir. Psychology major at Boston University and Stanford; taught English at Berkeley.

DATE	POS	WKS	ARTIST–RECORD TITLE	LABEL & NO.
11/8/86+	1 (1)	16	▲ 1. **Shake You Down** Airplay #1(1) / Sales #2; #1 R&B hit (2 weeks)	Columbia 06191

DATE	POS	WKS	ARTIST–RECORD TITLE	LABEL & NO.
			ABC	
			Electro-pop group formed in 1980 in Sheffield, England: Martin Fry (vocals), Mark White (guitar) and Stephen Singleton (saxophone; left in 1984).	
10/30/82+	**18**	13	1. The Look Of Love (Part One)	Mercury 76168
2/26/83	**25**	8	2. Poison Arrow	Mercury 810340
9/28/85	**9**	11	3. **Be Near Me**	Mercury 880626
			Sales #10 / Airplay #10	
2/15/86	**20**	7	4. (How To Be A) Millionaire	Mercury 884382
			Sales #17 / Airplay #26	
8/1/87	**5**	12	5. **When Smokey Sings**	Mercury 888604
			Sales #5 / Airplay #6; a tribute to Smokey Robinson	
			ABDUL, Paula	
			Born on 6/19/62 of Brazilian and French Canadian parentage. Los Angeles singer/choreographer. While still a teen, was the choreographer and member of the Los Angeles Lakers cheerleaders. Choreographed Janet Jackson's *Control* videos and TV's "The Tracey Ullman Show." Married actor Emilio Estevez on 4/29/92; split on 5/10/94.	
12/24/88+	**1 (3)**	16	▲ 1. **Straight Up**	Virgin 99256
			Airplay #1(3) / Sales #1(1)	
4/1/89	**1 (2)**	14	● 2. **Forever Your Girl**	Virgin 99230
			Airplay #1(2) / Sales #2	
7/8/89	**1 (1)**	15	● 3. **Cold Hearted**	Virgin 99196
			Sales #1(1) / Airplay #1(1); also the original B-side of #1 above	
10/7/89	**3**	14	4. (It's Just) The Way That You Love Me [R]	Virgin 99282
			Airplay #2 / Sales #4; originally charted in 1988 at #88	
1/6/90	**1 (3)**	14	● 5. **Opposites Attract**	Virgin 99158
			PAULA ABDUL With The Wild Pair (Marv Gunn & Bruce Christian)	
			Airplay #1(4) / Sales #1(3); all of above from the album *Forever Your Girl*	
5/11/91	**1 (5)**	15	● 6. **Rush, Rush**	Virgin 98828
			Airplay #1(8) / Sales #3; #1 Adult Contemporary hit (5 weeks)	
7/20/91	**1 (1)**	13	7. **The Promise Of A New Day**	Virgin 98752
			Airplay #5 / Sales #25	
10/26/91	**6**	14	8. **Blowing Kisses In The Wind**	Virgin 98683
			Airplay #5 / Sales #15	
2/1/92	**16**	7	9. Vibeology	Virgin 98737
			Airplay #16 / Sales #22	
4/18/92	**19**	8	10. Will You Marry Me?	Virgin 98584
			Airplay #13 / Sales #61; Sandra St. Victor (backing vocal); Stevie Wonder (harmonica); above 5 from the album *Spellbound*	
6/17/95	**28**	6	11. My Love Is For Real	Captive/Virgin 38493
			Sales #24 / Airplay #44; Ofra Haza (backing vocal)	
			AC/DC	
			Hard-rock band formed in Sydney, Australia, in 1974. Consisted of brothers Angus and Malcolm Young (guitars), Ron Belford "Bon" Scott (lead singer), Phil Rudd (drums) and Mark Evans (bass). Cliff Williams replaced Evans in 1977. Bon Scott died on 2/19/80 (age 33) from alcohol abuse and was replaced by Brian Johnson. Simon Wright replaced Rudd in 1985. Wright joined Dio in 1989, replaced by Chris Slade of The Firm. Rudd returned in 1995. Angus and Malcolm are the younger brothers of George Young of The Easybeats.	
10/25/80	**35**	3	1. You Shook Me All Night Long	Atlantic 3761
2/7/81	**37**	5	2. Back In Black	Atlantic 3787

DATE	POS	WKS	ARTIST–RECORD TITLE	LABEL & NO.
1/26/91	23	5	3. Moneytalks Sales #16 / Airplay #30	Atco 98881

ACE

Pub-rock quintet from Sheffield, England, led by vocalist Paul Carrack. Disbanded in 1977. Carrack joined Squeeze in 1981, then Mike + The Mechanics in 1985.

DATE	POS	WKS	ARTIST–RECORD TITLE	LABEL & NO.
4/5/75	3	11	1. **How Long**	Anchor 21000

ACE, Johnny

Born John Marshall Alexander, Jr., on 6/9/29 in Memphis. Killed playing Russian Roulette backstage at the City Auditorium in Houston on 12/24/54. R&B vocalist/pianist/organist/composer. Worked with the B.B. King band, then formed The Beale Streeters with Bobby Bland and Earl Forrest before going solo.

DATE	POS	WKS	ARTIST–RECORD TITLE	LABEL & NO.
2/19/55	17	9	1. Pledging My Love Best Seller #17 / Juke Box #17 / Jockey #19; Johnny Board (orch.); #1 R&B hit (10 weeks)	Duke 136

ACE OF BASE

Pop quartet from Gothenburg, Sweden: vocalists/sisters Jenny and Linn Berggren with keyboardists Jonas "Joker" Berggren (their brother) and Ulf "Buddha" Ekberg.

DATE	POS	WKS	ARTIST–RECORD TITLE	LABEL & NO.
10/9/93	2 (3)	30	▲ 1. **All That She Wants** Sales #1(3) / Airplay #2	Arista 12614
1/22/94	1 (6)	33	▲ 2. **The Sign** Airplay #1(13) / Sales #2	Arista 12653
5/14/94	4	28	● 3. **Don't Turn Around** Airplay #1(2) / Sales #6; #19 Adult Contemporary hit for Neil Diamond in 1992; #55 R&B hit for Luther Ingram in 1987; #45 R&B hit for Aswad in 1988	Arista 12691
10/29/94	20	13	4. Living In Danger Airplay #16 / Sales #42; all of above from the album *The Sign*	Arista 12754
11/11/95	15	13	5. Beautiful Life Sales #11 / Airplay #21	Arista 12889

ACKLIN, Barbara

Born on 2/28/44 in Chicago. R&B singer/songwriter. Cousin to Monk Higgins, who produced her first sessions for Special Agent in 1966 (as Barbara Allen). Backup vocalist at Chess Records in the mid-1960s. Married Eugene Record of The Chi-Lites.

DATE	POS	WKS	ARTIST–RECORD TITLE	LABEL & NO.
8/10/68	15	8	1. Love Makes A Woman	Brunswick 55379

ADAM & THE ANTS—see ANT, Adam

ADAMS, Bryan

Born on 11/5/59 in Kingston, Ontario. Rock singer/songwriter/guitarist based in Vancouver, Canada. Lead singer of Sweeney Todd in 1976. Teamed with Jim Vallance in 1977 in songwriting partnership. Cameo appearance in the movie *Pink Cadillac*.

DATE	POS	WKS	ARTIST–RECORD TITLE	LABEL & NO.
4/16/83	10	11	1. **Straight From The Heart**	A&M 2536
6/25/83	15	8	2. Cuts Like A Knife "live" version is on the B-side of #17 below	A&M 2553
10/1/83	24	6	3. This Time	A&M 2574

DATE	POS	WKS	ARTIST–RECORD TITLE	LABEL & NO.
11/24/84+	6	12	4. **Run To You** Airplay #6 / Sales #7	A&M 2686
2/23/85	11	10	5. Somebody Airplay #10 / Sales #14	A&M 2701
4/27/85	1 (2)	14	6. **Heaven** Sales #1(2) / Airplay #2	A&M 2729
7/13/85	5	12	7. **Summer Of '69** Airplay #4 / Sales #5; "live" version is on the B-side of #16 below	A&M 2739
9/28/85	13	9	8. One Night Love Affair Airplay #10 / Sales #15	A&M 2770
12/7/85+	15	9	9. It's Only Love **BRYAN ADAMS/TINA TURNER** Airplay #14 / Sales #16; above 6 from the album *Reckless*	A&M 2791
4/11/87	6	10	10. **Heat Of The Night** Sales #4 / Airplay #6; "live" version is on the B-side of #15 below	A&M 2921
7/4/87	26	6	11. Hearts On Fire Sales #23 / Airplay #26	A&M 2948
9/12/87	32	5	12. Victim Of Love Sales #29 / Airplay #30; all of above produced by Bryan Adams and Bob Clearmountain	A&M 2964
7/6/91	1 (7)	17	▲³ 13. **(Everything I Do) I Do It For You** Sales #1(17) / Airplay #1(8); from the movie *Robin Hood: Prince Of Thieves* starring Kevin Costner; longer version is on the B-side of #14 below; #1 Adult Contemporary hit (8 weeks)	A&M 1567
9/21/91	2 (1)	19	● 14. **Can't Stop This Thing We Started** Sales #11 / Airplay #14; "live" version is on the B-side of #18 below	A&M 1576
2/1/92	31	4	15. There Will Never Be Another Tonight Airplay #48 / Sales #72	A&M 1588
4/4/92	13	13	16. Thought I'd Died And Gone To Heaven Airplay #14 / Sales #24	A&M 1592
8/15/92	11	15	17. Do I Have To Say The Words? Airplay #10 / Sales #29; above 5 from the album *Waking Up The Neighbours*	A&M 1611
11/6/93	7	26	18. **Please Forgive Me** Airplay #3 / Sales #8	A&M 0422
12/4/93+	1 (3)	20	▲ 19. **All For Love** **BRYAN ADAMS ROD STEWART STING** Sales #1(5) / Airplay #3; from the movie *The Three Musketeers* starring Kiefer Sutherland and Charlie Sheen	A&M 0476
4/22/95	1 (5)	20	20. **Have You Ever Really Loved A Woman?** Sales #1(1) / Airplay #3; from the movie *Don Juan DeMarco* starring Johnny Depp; Paco de Lucia (acoustic guitar); #1 Adult Contemporary hit (5 weeks)	A&M 1028
			## ADAMS, Johnny Born Lathan John Adams on 1/5/32 in New Orleans. Soul singer nicknamed "The Tan Canary." First recorded on the RIC label in 1959.	
7/26/69	28	4	1. Reconsider Me	SSS Int'l. 770
			## ADAMS, Oleta Native of Yakima, Washington. Discovered by Tears For Fears in Kansas City; backing singer on their *Seeds Of Love* album and tour.	
2/9/91	5	10	1. **Get Here** Sales #2 / Airplay #13	Fontana 878476

DATE	POS	WKS	ARTIST–RECORD TITLE	LABEL & NO.
			ADDERLEY, "Cannonball"	
			Born Julian Edwin Adderley on 9/15/28 in Tampa. Died on 8/8/75 in Gary, Indiana. Nickname derived from "cannibal," in tribute to his love of eating. Alto saxophonist/leader of own jazz combo.	
1/28/67	**11**	8	1. Mercy, Mercy, Mercy　　　　　　　　　　　　[I]	Capitol 5798
			ADDRISI BROTHERS, The	
			Pop singing/songwriting duo: Dick (born 7/4/41) and Don (born 12/14/38; died 11/13/84) Addrisi, from Winthrop, Massachusetts. Wrote "Never My Love."	
2/26/72	**25**	7	1. We've Got To Get It On Again	Columbia 45521
5/14/77	**20**	8	2. Slow Dancin' Don't Turn Me On	Buddah 566
			AD LIBS, The	
			Newark, New Jersey, quintet: Mary Ann Thomas (lead singer), Hugh Harris, Danny Austin, Norman Donegan and Dave Watt.	
2/6/65	**8**	7	1. **The Boy From New York City**	Blue Cat 102
			ADVENTURES OF STEVIE V	
			Dance outfit assembled by Stevie Vincent, a native of Bedfordshire, England. Includes singer Melodie Washington and multi-instrumentalist Mick Walsh.	
8/25/90	**25**	8	1. Dirty Cash (Money Talks)　　　 Sales #13 / Airplay #31	Mercury 875802
			AEROSMITH	
			Hard-rock band formed in Sunapee, New Hampshire, in 1970. Consisted of Steven Tyler (lead singer; born Steven Tallarico), Joe Perry and Brad Whitford (guitars), Tom Hamilton (bass) and Joey Kramer (drums). Perry left for own Joe Perry Project in 1979; replaced by Jimmy Crespo. Whitford left in 1981; replaced by Rick Dufay. Original band reunited in April 1984. Tyler's daughter model/actress Liv acted in the movie *Silent Fall*.	
7/12/75	**36**	3	1. Sweet Emotion	Columbia 10155
2/14/76	**6**	11	2. **Dream On**　　　　　　　　　　　　　[R] 　originally charted in 1973 at #59	Columbia 10278
6/26/76	**21**	10	3. Last Child	Columbia 10359
12/18/76+	**10**	11	4. **Walk This Way** 　revived in 1986 as a "rap" hit by Run-D.M.C. (with Tyler & Perry)	Columbia 10449
5/7/77	**38**	2	5. Back In The Saddle	Columbia 10516
9/2/78	**23**	7	6. Come Together 　from the movie *Sgt. Pepper's Lonely Hearts Club Band* starring Peter Frampton and The Bee Gees	Columbia 10802
11/14/87	**14**	10	7. Dude (Looks Like A Lady) 　Sales #10 / Airplay #15	Geffen 28240
2/27/88	**3**	15	8. **Angel** 　Sales #2 / Airplay #4	Geffen 28249
7/9/88	**17**	8	9. Rag Doll 　Sales #15 / Airplay #20	Geffen 27915
9/16/89	**5**	11	● 10. **Love In An Elevator** 　Sales #2 / Airplay #7	Geffen 22845
12/16/89+	**4**	13	11. **Janie's Got A Gun** 　Sales #3 / Airplay #7	Geffen 22727
3/31/90	**9**	10	12. **What It Takes** 　Sales #7 / Airplay #10	Geffen 19944

DATE	POS	WKS	ARTIST–RECORD TITLE	LABEL & NO.
7/21/90	**22**	7	13. The Other Side Airplay #19 / Sales #24; above 4 from the album *Pump*	Geffen 19927
4/24/93	**18**	11	14. Livin' On The Edge Sales #16 / Airplay #38	Geffen 19149
8/28/93	**12**	20	● 15. Cryin' Sales #9 / Airplay #23	Geffen 19256
1/1/94	**24**	16	16. Amazing Sales #24 / Airplay #26	Geffen 19264
6/18/94	**17**	16	17. Crazy Airplay #18 / Sales #21; above 4 from the album *Get A Grip*; above 11 produced by Bruce Fairbairn	Geffen 19267

AFTERNOON DELIGHTS, The

Female studio vocal quartet from Boston: Rebecca Hall, Suzanne Boucher, Janet Powell and Robalee Barnes.

9/12/81	**33**	5	1. General Hospi-Tale [N] parody of the TV soap "General Hospital"	MCA 51148

AFTER 7

Indianapolis R&B vocal trio: Keith Mitchell with brothers Kevon and Melvin Edmonds. Keith is the cousin of L.A. Reid. Kevon and Melvin are the brothers of Babyface.

4/28/90	**7**	13	● 1. **Ready Or Not** Sales #5 / Airplay #9; #1 R&B hit (2 weeks)	Virgin 98995
8/25/90	**6**	15	● 2. **Can't Stop** Airplay #6 / Sales #10; #1 R&B hit (1 week)	Virgin 98961
1/26/91	**19**	5	3. Heat Of The Moment [R] Airplay #18 / Sales #20; originally charted in 1989 at #74	Virgin 99204
7/6/91	**24**	5	4. Nights Like This Sales #36 / Airplay #36; from the movie *The Five Heartbeats* starring Robert Townsend	Virgin 98798
9/2/95	**31**	11	5. 'Til You Do Me Right Sales #20 / Airplay #59	Virgin 38494

AFTER THE FIRE

English rock band: Andy Piercy, Peter Banks (ex-Yes, ex-Flash), John Russell and Pete King.

3/5/83	**5**	14	1. **Der Kommissar** Kommissar is German for "government official."	Epic 03559

A-HA

Pop trio formed in Oslo, Norway: Morten Harket (vocals), Pal Waaktaar (guitar) and Magne "Mags" Furuholmen (keyboards).

8/24/85	**1 (1)**	15	1. **Take On Me** Airplay #1(2) / Sales #3	Warner 29011
1/11/86	**20**	8	2. The Sun Always Shines On T.V. Airplay #17 / Sales #21	Warner 28846

AHMAD

Ahmad Ali Lewis. Rapper from Los Angeles.

6/25/94	**26**	12	● 1. Back In The Day Sales #13 / Airplay #39; samples Curtis Mayfield's composition "Let's Do It Again"	Giant 18217

DATE	POS	WKS	ARTIST–RECORD TITLE	LABEL & NO.
			AIR SUPPLY	
			Vocal group from Melbourne, Australia, featuring Russell Hitchcock (born on 6/15/49 in Melbourne) and Graham Russell (born on 6/1/50 in Nottingham, England). Disbanded in 1988. Hitchcock and Russell reunited in 1991.	
3/8/80	3	17	1. **Lost In Love**	Arista 0479
			#1 Adult Contemporary hit (6 weeks)	
7/19/80	2 (4)	17	● 2. **All Out Of Love**	Arista 0520
11/15/80+	5	17	3. **Every Woman In The World**	Arista 0564
5/23/81	1 (1)	14	● 4. **The One That You Love**	Arista 0604
10/3/81	5	15	5. **Here I Am (Just When I Thought I Was Over You)**	Arista 0626
			#1 Adult Contemporary hit (3 weeks)	
1/9/82	5	15	6. **Sweet Dreams**	Arista 0655
6/26/82	5	13	7. **Even The Nights Are Better**	Arista 0692
			#1 Adult Contemporary hit (4 weeks)	
10/23/82	38	2	8. Young Love	Arista 1005
12/25/82+	38	5	9. Two Less Lonely People In The World	Arista 1004
8/13/83	2 (3)	17	● 10. **Making Love Out Of Nothing At All**	Arista 9056
6/8/85	19	10	11. Just As I Am	Arista 9353
			Sales #16 / Airplay #22	
			AKENS, Jewel	
			Born on 9/12/40 in Houston. Black male vocalist/producer. Recorded with Eddie Daniels as Jewel and Eddie on the Silver label in 1960.	
2/6/65	3	12	1. **The Birds And The Bees**	Era 3141
			ALABAMA	
			Country quartet from Fort Payne, Alabama: Randy Owen (vocals, guitar), Jeff Cook (keyboards, fiddle), Teddy Gentry (bass, vocals) and Mark Herndon (drums, vocals). Randy, Jeff and Teddy are cousins.	
7/25/81	20	8	1. **Feels So Right**	RCA 12236
			#1 Country hit (2 weeks)	
1/16/82	15	10	2. Love In The First Degree	RCA 12288
			#1 Country hit (2 weeks)	
6/5/82	18	8	3. Take Me Down	RCA 13210
			#1 Country hit (1 week)	
6/4/83	38	3	4. The Closer You Get	RCA 13524
			#1 Country hit (1 week)	
			ALBERT, Morris	
			Born Morris Albert Kaisermann in Brazil. Singer/songwriter.	
8/23/75	6	16	● 1. **Feelings**	RCA 10279
			AL B. SURE!	
			Born Al Brown in Boston; raised in Mt. Vernon, New York. R&B singer. Turned down a football scholarship to the University of Iowa in order to pursue music career.	
5/14/88	7	13	1. **Nite And Day**	Warner 28192
			Sales #6 / Airplay #8; French version is on the B-side; #1 R&B hit (3 weeks)	

DATE	POS	WKS	ARTIST–RECORD TITLE	LABEL & NO.
4/7/90	31	4	● 2. The Secret Garden (Sweet Seduction Suite) **QUINCY JONES/Al B. Sure!/James Ingram/El DeBarge/Barry White** Sales #20	Qwest 19992
			## ALEXANDER, Arthur	
			Born on 5/10/40 in Florence, Alabama. Died on 6/9/93 from a heart attack. Influential soul singer/songwriter. Teamed with Rick Hall in studio work at Muscle Shoals. First recorded for Judd in 1960. Retired from music business from 1975 until his comeback in 1993; worked as a bus driver for Cleveland's Center For Human Services, 1981–93. Only rock-era artist to have his compositions recorded by The Beatles, The Rolling Stones and Bob Dylan.	
3/31/62	24	6	1. You Better Move On	Dot 16309
			## ALIAS	
			Rock quintet formed in Los Angeles by former Sheriff bandmates Freddy Curci (vocals) and Steve DeMarchi (guitar), with former Heart members Roger Fisher (guitar), Steve Fossen (bass) and Mike Derosier (drums).	
9/29/90	2 (1)	15	1. **More Than Words Can Say** Airplay #3 / Sales #4	EMI 50324
2/2/91	13	9	2. Waiting For Love Airplay #13 / Sales #20	EMI 50337
			## ALIVE AND KICKING	
			New York City-based, five-man, one-woman, pop-rock group led by singers Pepe Cardona and Sandy Toder.	
7/4/70	7	10	1. **Tighter, Tighter**	Roulette 7078
			## ALLAN, Davie, And The Arrows	
			Allan, born in Los Angeles, began as a session guitarist for Mike Curb. While in high school at Van Nuys, California, formed The Arrows, consisting of Allan (Fender lead guitar), Drew Bennett (bass), Jared Hendler (keyboards) and Larry Brown (drums).	
9/9/67	37	3	1. Blues' Theme [I] from the movie *The Wild Angels* starring Peter Fonda	Tower 295
			## ALLEN, Deborah	
			Born Deborah Lynn Thurmond on 9/30/53 in Memphis. Country singer/songwriter.	
12/24/83+	26	7	1. Baby I Lied	RCA 13600
			## ALLEN, Donna	
			Born in Key West and raised in Tampa. Soul singer. Former cheerleader for the Tampa Bay Buccaneers.	
3/28/87	21	9	1. Serious Airplay #19 / Sales #21	21 Records 99497
			## ALLEN, Rex	
			Born on 12/31/20 in Wilcox, Arizona. Singer/guitarist/actor. Starred in 35 Western movies in the 1950s. Narrator for Walt Disney documentaries during the 1960s and 1970s.	
10/6/62	17	4	1. Don't Go Near The Indians The Merry Melody Singers (backing vocals)	Mercury 71997

DATE	POS	WKS	ARTIST–RECORD TITLE	LABEL & NO.
			ALLEN, Steve	
			Born on 12/26/21 in New York City. Comedian/actor/songwriter/author. In 1954, became the first host of TV's "Tonight Show." Played title role in the 1956 movie *The Benny Goodman Story*. Hosted own variety and talk shows, 1956–80. Married to actress Jayne Meadows.	
12/3/55	35	2	1. Autumn Leaves [I] **STEVE ALLEN with GEORGE CATES And His Orchestra & Chorus**	Coral 61485
			ALL-4-ONE	
			Male vocal quartet based in Southern California: Jamie Jones, Delious Kennedy, Alfred Nevarez and Tony Borowiak.	
1/22/94	5	19	● 1. **So Much In Love** Sales #4 / Airplay #6; originally released on Blitzz 15001	Blitzz/Atl. 87271
4/30/94	1 (11)	26	▲ 2. **I Swear** Airplay #1(9) / Sales #1(7); #1 Country hit for John Michael Montgomery in 1994	Blitzz/Atl. 87243
6/17/95	5	28	● 3. **I Can Love You Like That** Airplay #3 / Sales #10; #1 Country hit for John Michael Montgomery in 1995	Blitzz/Atl. 87134
			ALLISON, Gene	
			Born on 8/29/34 in Nashville. R&B singer. First recorded for Calvert in 1956.	
3/10/58	36	1	1. You Can Make It If You Try Best Seller #36 / Top 100 #37	Vee-Jay 256
			ALLMAN, Gregg	
			Born on 12/8/47 in Nashville; raised in Daytona Beach, Florida. Keyboardist/vocalist. In 1965, Greg and brother Duane formed The Allman Joys, which evolved into The Allman Brothers Band by 1969. Married to Cher, 1975–77. Acted in the movie *Rush*.	
1/19/74	19	8	1. Midnight Rider originally released by the Allman Brothers Band on the 1970 album *Idlewild South*	Capricorn 0035
			ALLMAN BROTHERS BAND, The	
			Southern-rock band formed in Macon, Georgia, in 1969. Consisted of brothers Duane (lead guitar) and Gregg Allman (keyboards), Dickey Betts (guitar), Berry Oakley (bass), and the drum duo of Butch Trucks and Jai Johnny Johanson (pronounced: Jay Johnny Johnson). Duane and Gregg known earlier as The Allman Joys and Hour Glass. Duane was the top session guitarist at Muscle Shoals studio; killed in a motorcycle crash on 10/29/71 (age 24). Oakley died in another cycle accident on 11/11/72 (age 24); replaced by Lamar Williams (died 1/25/83). Chuck Leavell (keyboards) added in 1972. Group split up in 1976. Gregg formed the Gregg Allman Band. Betts formed Great Southern. Leavell, Williams and Johanson formed the fusion-rock band Sea Level. Allman and Betts reunited with a new Allman Brothers' lineup in 1978. Disbanded in 1981. Allman, Betts, Trucks and Johanson regrouped with Warren Haynes (guitar), Allen Woody (bass) and Johnny Neel (keyboards) in 1989. Neel left in 1990, replaced by Mark Quinones. Group inducted into the Rock and Roll Hall of Fame in 1995.	
9/8/73	2 (1)	13	1. **Ramblin Man**	Capricorn 0027
4/7/79	29	5	2. Crazy Love	Capricorn 0320
9/19/81	39	2	3. Straight From The Heart	Arista 0618

DATE	POS	WKS	ARTIST—RECORD TITLE	LABEL & NO.
			## ALPERT, Herb, & The Tijuana Brass	
			Alpert, born on 3/31/35 in Los Angeles, played trumpet since age eight. Producer/composer/trumpeter/bandleader. A&R for Keen Records. Produced first Jan & Dean session. Wrote "Wonderful World" hit for Sam Cooke. Recorded as Dore Alpert in 1962. Formed A&M Records with Jerry Moss in 1962. Used studio musicians until early 1965, then formed own band. Alpert and Moss formed the Almo Sounds label in 1994.	
11/10/62	6	11	1. **The Lonely Bull (El Solo Torro)** [I] **THE TIJUANA BRASS Featuring Herb Alpert** crowd noises dubbed in from bullring in Tijuana, Mexico	A&M 703
10/16/65	7	13	2. **Taste Of Honey** [I] #1 Adult Contemporary hit (5 weeks); tune introduced by Bobby Scott in the 1960 Broadway show *A Taste of Honey*	A&M 775
1/22/66	11	7	3. **Zorba The Greek/** [I] title song from the movie starring Anthony Quinn	
2/5/66	38	2	4. Tijuana Taxi [I]	A&M 787
4/9/66	24	5	5. What Now My Love/ [I] written in France in 1962 by Gilbert Becaud as "Et Maintenant"	
4/9/66	27	4	6. Spanish Flea [I] theme song from TV's "The Dating Game"	A&M 792
7/9/66	18	6	7. The Work Song [I] written in 1960 by jazz artist Nat Adderley	A&M 805
9/17/66	28	4	8. Flamingo [I] #13 hit for Duke Ellington in 1941	A&M 813
12/3/66	19	6	9. Mame title song from the Broadway musical starring Angela Lansbury	A&M 823
4/1/67	37	2	10. Wade In The Water [I]	A&M 840
4/29/67	27	6	11. Casino Royale [I] title song from the movie starring David Niven and Peter Sellers; #1 Adult Contemporary hit (2 weeks)	A&M 850
7/22/67	32	3	12. The Happening [I] title song from the movie starring Anthony Quinn	A&M 860
9/30/67	35	3	13. A Banda (Ah Bahn-da) [I] #1 Adult Contemporary hit (2 weeks)	A&M 870
			HERB ALPERT:	
5/25/68	1 (4)	12	● 14. **This Guy's In Love With You** #1 Adult Contemporary hit (10 weeks)	A&M 929
8/25/79	1 (2)	15	● 15. **Rise** [I] #1 Adult Contemporary hit (1 week)	A&M 2151
12/22/79+	30	6	16. Rotation [I]	A&M 2202
7/31/82	37	4	17. Route 101 [I]	A&M 2422
5/2/87	5	12	18. **Diamonds** Sales #5 / Airplay #7; Janet Jackson and Lisa Keith (vocals); #1 R&B hit (2 weeks)	A&M 2929
8/29/87	35	3	19. Making Love In The Rain Sales #35 / Airplay #39; Lisa Keith (vocal)	A&M 2949
			## AMAZING RHYTHM ACES, The	
			Memphis country-rock group: Russell Smith (lead vocals, guitar), Barry "Byrd" Burton (guitar, dobro), Billy Earhart III (keyboards), Jeff Davis (bass) and Butch McDade (drums). Disbanded in 1980.	
7/26/75	14	9	1. Third Rate Romance	ABC 12078

DATE	POS	WKS	ARTIST—RECORD TITLE	LABEL & NO.
			AMBOY DUKES, The	
			Detroit rock group led by Ted Nugent. After group split in 1975, Nugent embarked on prolific solo career before forming Damn Yankees in 1989.	
7/27/68	16	7	1. Journey To The Center Of The Mind	Mainstream 684
			AMBROSIA	
			Los Angeles-based pop group. Lead singers David Pack and Joe Puerta with Burleigh Drummond and Christopher North (left in 1977).	
7/19/75	17	8	1. Holdin' On To Yesterday	20th Century 2207
4/2/77	39	2	2. Magical Mystery Tour	20th Century 2327
			featuring the London Symphony Orchestra and the Royal Philharmonic Orchestra; from the documentary movie *All This And World War II*	
9/30/78	3	14	3. **How Much I Feel**	Warner 8640
4/19/80	3	14	4. **Biggest Part Of Me**	Warner 49225
8/2/80	13	10	5. You're The Only Woman (You & I)	Warner 49508
			AMERICA	
			Trio formed in London in 1969. Consisted of Americans Dan Peek and Gerry Beckley, with Englishman Dewey Bunnell. Met at U.S. Air Force base. All played guitars. Members of Daze in 1970. Moved to the U.S. in February 1972. Won the 1972 Best New Artist Grammy Award. Peek left in 1976 and became a popular Contemporary Christian artist.	
3/4/72	1 (3)	12	● 1. **A Horse With No Name**	Warner 7555
5/27/72	9	9	2. **I Need You**	Warner 7580
11/4/72	8	9	3. **Ventura Highway**	Warner 7641
2/24/73	35	2	4. Don't Cross The River	Warner 7670
9/21/74	4	11	5. **Tin Man**	Warner 7839
			#1 Adult Contemporary hit (1 week)	
1/18/75	5	10	6. **Lonely People**	Warner 8048
			#1 Adult Contemporary hit (1 week)	
4/26/75	1 (1)	12	7. **Sister Golden Hair**	Warner 8086
8/16/75	20	7	8. Daisy Jane	Warner 8118
6/12/76	23	6	9. Today's The Day	Warner 8212
			#1 Adult Contemporary hit (2 weeks); above 5 produced by George Martin (Beatles' producer)	
8/21/82	8	15	10. **You Can Do Magic**	Capitol 5142
7/16/83	33	6	11. The Border	Capitol 5236
			AMERICAN BREED, The	
			Interracial rock quartet from Cicero, Illinois, led by Gary Loizzo. Drummer Andre Fischer and keyboardist Kevin Murphy were later members of Rufus.	
7/8/67	24	4	1. Step Out Of Your Mind	Acta 804
12/16/67+	5	12	● 2. **Bend Me, Shape Me**	Acta 811
3/16/68	39	3	3. Green Light	Acta 821
			AMES, Ed	
			Born Ed Urick on 7/9/27 in Malden, Massachusetts. One of The Ames Brothers. Played the Indian Mingo on the "Daniel Boone" TV series.	
2/11/67	8	10	1. **My Cup Runneth Over**	RCA 9002
			from the Broadway musical *I Do, I Do* starring Mary Martin and Robert Preston; #1 Adult Contemporary hit (4 weeks)	

DATE	POS	WKS	ARTIST–RECORD TITLE	LABEL & NO.
12/30/67+	19	4	2. Who Will Answer?	RCA 9400

AMES BROTHERS, The

Pop vocal group from Malden, Massachusetts. Formed in 1947. Family name Urick. Consisted of lead singer Ed Ames (born 7/9/27) and his brothers Gene (born 2/13/25), Joe (born 5/3/24) and Vic (born 5/20/26; died 1/23/78). Own TV series in 1955. Ed recorded solo and acted on Broadway and TV.

DATE	POS	WKS	ARTIST–RECORD TITLE	LABEL & NO.
11/20/54+	3	15	● 1. **The Naughty Lady Of Shady Lane** Best Seller #3 / Jockey #3 / Juke Box #3	RCA 5897
9/24/55	11	11	2. My Bonnie Lassie Best Seller #11 / Top 100 #11 / Jockey #14 / Juke Box #16; melody written in Scotland in 1952 as "Scotland The Brave"	RCA 6208
3/24/56	35	3	3. Forever Darling title song from the movie starring Lucille Ball and Desi Arnaz	RCA 6400
5/19/56	11	20	4. It Only Hurts For A Little While Juke Box #11 / Top 100 #15 / Jockey #15 / Best Seller #16	RCA 6481
7/22/57	5	16	5. **Tammy** Jockey #5 / Best Seller #24 / Top 100 #29; from the movie *Tammy and The Bachelor* starring Debbie Reynolds	RCA 6930
10/7/57	5	14	6. **Melodie D'Amour (Melody Of Love)** Jockey #5 / Best Seller #12 / Top 100 #12	RCA 7046
3/31/58	23	2	7. A Very Precious Love Jockey #23 / Top 100 #65; from the movie *Marjorie Morningstar* starring Natalie Wood	RCA 7167
9/29/58	17	10	8. Pussy Cat Hot 100 #17 / Best Seller #20 end	RCA 7315
1/19/59	37	4	9. Red River Rose Hugo Winterhalter (orch., all of above - except #4)	RCA 7413
2/22/60	38	2	10. China Doll	RCA 7655

ANDERSON, Bill

Born James William Anderson III on 11/1/37 in Columbia, South Carolina. Country singer/songwriter/actor. Hosted Nashville Network's TV game show "Fandango." Member of the *Grand Ole Opry* since 1961. Known as "Whispering Bill."

DATE	POS	WKS	ARTIST–RECORD TITLE	LABEL & NO.
5/11/63	8	11	1. **Still** #1 Country hit (7 weeks)	Decca 31458

ANDERSON, Carl—see LORING, Gloria

ANDERSON, Lynn

Born on 9/26/47 in Grand Forks, North Dakota; raised in Sacramento. Country singer. Daughter of country singer Liz Anderson. An accomplished equestrian, Lynn was the California Horse Show Queen in 1966.

DATE	POS	WKS	ARTIST–RECORD TITLE	LABEL & NO.
12/19/70+	3	14	● 1. **Rose Garden**	Columbia 45252

ANDREWS, Lee, And The Hearts

Andrews was born Arthur Lee Andrew Thompson in Goldsboro, North Carolina. Moved to Philadelphia at age two. Formed vocal group The Hearts in 1952. First recorded for Rainbow in 1954. Group on Chess included Thomas "Butch" Curry, Ted Weems, Roy and Wendell Calhoun.

DATE	POS	WKS	ARTIST–RECORD TITLE	LABEL & NO.
12/9/57	20	10	1. Tear Drops Best Seller #20 / Top 100 #20 / Jockey #21	Chess 1675

DATE	POS	WKS	ARTIST–RECORD TITLE	LABEL & NO.
6/16/58	**33**	1	2. Try The Impossible Best Seller #33 / Top 100 #33; first released on Casino 452 in 1958	United Art. 123
			ANGELICA	
11/30/91+	**29**	7	Born Angelica Garcia on 5/21/72 in El Monte, California. 1. Angel Baby Sales #19 / Airplay #40	Quality 15171
			ANGELS, The	
			Female pop trio from Orange, New Jersey. Formed as The Starlets with sisters Phyllis "Jiggs" & Barbara Allbut, and Linda Jansen (lead singer). Jansen was replaced by Peggy Santiglia in 1962. Studio backing vocalists for Lou Christie and others in the mid-1960s. Disbanded in 1967.	
12/4/61+	**14**	7	1. 'Til	Caprice 107
4/7/62	**38**	1	2. Cry Baby Cry· Hutch Davie (orch., above 2)	Caprice 112
8/10/63	**1 (3)**	12	3. **My Boyfriend's Back**	Smash 1834
11/9/63	**25**	5	4. I Adore Him	Smash 1854
			ANIMALS, The	
			Rock group formed in Newcastle, England, in 1958 as the Alan Price Combo. Consisted of Eric Burdon (vocals), Alan Price (keyboards), Bryan "Chas" Chandler (bass), Hilton Valentine (guitar) and John Steel (drums). Price left in May 1965, replaced by Dave Rowberry. Chandler pursued a management career and discovered Jimi Hendrix in 1966. Steel left in 1966, replaced by Barry Jenkins. Group disbanded in July 1968. After a period with War, Burdon and the other originals reunited in 1976 and again in 1983. Inducted into the Rock and Roll Hall of Fame in 1994.	
8/15/64	**1 (3)**	10	1. **The House Of The Rising Sun**	MGM 13264
10/17/64	**19**	6	2. I'm Crying	MGM 13274
3/6/65	**15**	6	3. Don't Let Me Be Misunderstood	MGM 13311
5/29/65	**32**	4	4. Bring It On Home To Me	MGM 13339
9/4/65	**13**	8	5. We Gotta Get Out Of This Place	MGM 13382
12/4/65+	**23**	8	6. It's My Life all of above produced by Mickie Most; above 4 from the album Animal Tracks	MGM 13414
4/2/66	**34**	1	7. Inside-Looking Out	MGM 13468
6/4/66	**12**	8	8. Don't Bring Me Down	MGM 13514
			ERIC BURDON & THE ANIMALS:	
10/1/66	**10**	7	9. **See See Rider** #14 hit for Ma Rainey in 1925 (as "See See Rider Blues")	MGM 13582
12/31/66	**29**	4	10. Help Me Girl	MGM 13636
4/22/67	**15**	6	11. When I Was Young	MGM 13721
8/19/67	**9**	8	12. **San Franciscan Nights**	MGM 13769
12/30/67+	**15**	6	13. Monterey story-in-song of the famed Monterey International Pop Festival, June 1967	MGM 13868
6/22/68	**14**	10	14. Sky Pilot (Part One) above 8 produced by Tom Wilson	MGM 13939

DATE	POS	WKS	ARTIST—RECORD TITLE	LABEL & NO.
			ANIMOTION	
			Techno-pop quintet led by Astrid Plane and Bill Wadhams. Four of five members replaced in 1988, including Plane and Wadhams. New vocalists include Paul Engemann (formerly of Device) and actress/dancer Cynthia Rhodes (appeared in the movies *Staying Alive* and *Dirty Dancing*; married Richard Marx on 1/8/89). Plane married group's founding bassist, Charles Ottavio, on 10/13/90.	
3/2/85	6	14	1. **Obsession** Sales #5 / Airplay #5	Mercury 880266
7/27/85	39	1	2. Let Him Go	Mercury 880737
3/11/89	9	11	3. **Room To Move** Airplay #9 / Sales #12; from the movie *My Stepmother Is An Alien* starring Dan Aykroyd and Kim Basinger	Polydor 871418
			ANKA, Paul	
			Born on 7/30/41 in Ottawa, Canada. Performer since age 12. Father financed first recording, "I Confess," on RPM 472 in 1956. Wrote "She's A Lady" for Tom Jones and the English lyrics to "My Way" for Frank Sinatra. Also wrote theme for TV's "Tonight Show." Own variety show in 1973. Cameo appearances in the 1962 movie *The Longest Day* and the 1992 movie *Captain Ron*. Longtime popular entertainer in Las Vegas.	
7/29/57	1 (1)	18	● 1. **Diana** Best Seller #1 / Top 100 #2 / Jockey #2; Diana was the Anka family's babysitter; #1 R&B hit (2 weeks)	ABC-Para. 9831
2/3/58	7	11	2. **You Are My Destiny** Top 100 #7 / Best Seller #9 / Jockey #9	ABC-Para. 9880
4/28/58	15	10	3. Crazy Love/ Best Seller #15 / Top 100 #19	
4/28/58	16	10	4. Let The Bells Keep Ringing Best Seller #16 / Jockey #18 / Top 100 #30	ABC-Para. 9907
12/15/58+	29	5	5. The Teen Commandments [S] **PAUL ANKA-GEO. HAMILTON IV-JOHNNY NASH** inspirational talk from the 3 ABC-Paramount artists	ABC-Para. 9974
1/5/59	15	13	6. (All of a Sudden) My Heart Sings #7 hit for Johnnie Johnston in 1945	ABC-Para. 9987
4/20/59	33	3	7. I Miss You So #20 hit for The Cats and the Fiddle in 1940	ABC-Para. 10011
6/8/59	1 (4)	14	● 8. **Lonely Boy** from the movie *Girls Town* starring Anka and Mamie Van Doren	ABC-Para. 10022
9/14/59	2 (3)	14	9. **Put Your Head On My Shoulder** Don Costa (orch., all of above)	ABC-Para. 10040
11/30/59	4	12	10. **It's Time To Cry**	ABC-Para. 10064
3/7/60	2 (2)	11	11. **Puppy Love**	ABC-Para. 10082
6/6/60	8	9	12. **My Home Town**	ABC-Para. 10106
8/22/60	23	6	13. Hello Young Lovers/ from the musical *The King And I* starring Yul Brynner	
9/12/60	40	1	14. I Love You In The Same Old Way	ABC-Para. 10132
10/10/60	11	7	15. Summer's Gone	ABC-Para. 10147
2/6/61	16	5	16. The Story Of My Love	ABC-Para. 10168
3/27/61	13	8	17. Tonight My Love, Tonight melody adapted from "Caro Nome" from Verdi's opera *Rigoletto*	ABC-Para. 10194
6/12/61	10	7	18. **Dance On Little Girl**	ABC-Para. 10220
9/11/61	35	1	19. Kissin' On The Phone	ABC-Para. 10239
3/17/62	12	9	20. Love Me Warm And Tender	RCA 7977
6/16/62	13	7	21. A Steel Guitar And A Glass Of Wine	RCA 8030

DATE	POS	WKS	ARTIST–RECORD TITLE	LABEL & NO.
11/24/62	19	5	22. Eso Beso (That Kiss!)	RCA 8097
2/9/63	26	4	23. Love (Makes the World Go 'Round)	RCA 8115
5/25/63	39	1	24. Remember Diana	RCA 8170
2/1/69	27	6	25. Goodnight My Love	RCA 9648
			#7 R&B hit for Jesse Belvin in 1956	
7/27/74	1 (3)	11	● 26. **(You're) Having My Baby**	United Art. 454
11/30/74+	7	11	27. **One Man Woman/One Woman Man**	United Art. 569
			PAUL ANKA with ODIA COATES	
4/5/75	8	10	28. **I Don't Like To Sleep Alone**	United Art. 615
8/16/75	15	8	29. **(I Believe) There's Nothing Stronger Than Our Love**	United Art. 685
			PAUL ANKA with Odia Coates (Odia also has vocals on #26 & 28 above)	
11/29/75+	7	12	30. **Times Of Your Life**	United Art. 737
			#1 Adult Contemporary hit (1 week); tune adapted from a Kodak jingle	
5/1/76	33	3	31. **Anytime (I'll Be There)**	United Art. 789
11/18/78	35	3	32. This Is Love	RCA 11395
9/3/83	40	2	33. Hold Me 'Til The Mornin' Comes	Columbia 03897
			Peter Cetera (backing vocal); Anka wrote all of his hits (except #5–7, 13, 19, 22, 25, 33)	

ANNETTE with the Afterbeats

Born Annette Funicello on 10/22/42 in Utica, New York. Became a Mousekateer in 1955. Acted in several teen movies in the early '60s. Co-starred with Frankie Avalon in the 1987 movie *Back To The Beach*. Diagnosed with multiple sclerosis in 1987.

DATE	POS	WKS	ARTIST–RECORD TITLE	LABEL & NO.
2/2/59	7	9	1. **Tall Paul**	Disneyland 118
12/14/59+	20	10	2. First Name Initial	Buena Vista 349
3/7/60	10	8	3. **O Dio Mio**	Buena Vista 354
			ANNETTE	
6/20/60	36	3	4. Train Of Love	Buena Vista 359
			written by Paul Anka	
9/5/60	11	9	5. Pineapple Princess	Buena Vista 362

ANN-MARGRET

Born Ann-Margret Olsson on 4/28/41 in Stockholm, Sweden. Actress/dancer/singer. Moved to Wilmette, Illinois, in 1946. Starred with Elvis Presley in *Viva Las Vegas* and in several other movies and Broadway shows.

DATE	POS	WKS	ARTIST–RECORD TITLE	LABEL & NO.
8/21/61	17	6	1. I Just Don't Understand	RCA 7894

ANOTHER BAD CREATION

Pre-teen R&B/rap vocal quintet managed and produced by Michael Bivins of Bell Biv DeVoe. Made up of Atlanta natives: Chris Sellers, Dave Shelton, Romell Chapman, with brothers Marliss and Demetrius Pugh. Appeared in the movie *The Meteor Man*.

DATE	POS	WKS	ARTIST–RECORD TITLE	LABEL & NO.
2/2/91	9	15	● 1. **Iesha**	Motown 2070
			Sales #2 / Airplay #18; Michael Bivins (rap)	
5/18/91	10	10	2. **Playground**	Motown 2088
			Sales #9 / Airplay #27; Boyz II Men (backing vocals, above 2)	

DATE	POS	WKS	ARTIST–RECORD TITLE	LABEL & NO.
			ANT, Adam	
			Born Stuart Goddard on 11/3/54 in London. Formed romantic-punk group Adam And The Ants in 1976. Three original Ants left to join Bow Wow Wow and Ant headed new lineup in 1980. Ant went solo in 1982. Acted in the movies *World Gone Wild* and *Slam Dance*, and several TV shows, including "The Equalizer."	
12/11/82+	12	14	1. Goody Two Shoes	Epic 03367
4/7/90	17	8	2. Room At The Top	MCA 53679
			Sales #15 / Airplay #16	
5/27/95	39	2	3. Wonderful	Capitol 58239
			. Airplay #37 / Sales #69	
			ANTHONY, Ray	
			Born Raymond Antonini on 1/20/22 in Bentleyville, Pennsylvania; raised in Cleveland. Big band leader/trumpeter. Joined Al Donahue in 1939, then with Glenn Miller and Jimmy Dorsey, 1940–42. Led U.S. Army band. Own band in 1946. Own TV series in the '50s. Appeared in the movie *Daddy Long Legs* with Fred Astaire in 1955. Wrote "Bunny Hop." Married for a time to actress Mamie Van Doren.	
1/22/55	19	4	1. Melody Of Love	Capitol 3018
			FRANK SINATRA AND RAY ANTHONY AND HIS ORCHESTRA	
			Jockey #19; music written in 1903, lyrics added in 1954 by Tom Glazer	
1/19/59	8	13	2. **Peter Gunn** [I]	Capitol 4041
			title song from the TV series starring Craig Stevens	
			ANTON, Susan—see KNOBLOCK, Fred	
			APOLLO 100	
			English studio band featuring keyboardist Tom Parker.	
1/22/72	6	10	1. **Joy** [I]	Mega 0050
			adaptation of Bach's *Jesu, Joy of Man's Desiring*	
			APPLEJACKS, The	
			Studio band led by Dave Appell (born 3/24/22 in Philadelphia).	
10/6/58	16	9	1. Mexican Hat Rock [I]	Cameo 149
			Hot 100 #16 / Best Seller #29 end; adaptation of the 1919 song "Mexican Hat Dance"	
1/12/59	38	3	2. Rocka-Conga	Cameo 155
			early pressings issued as "Rocka-Tonga"	
			APRIL WINE	
			Rock quintet formed in Montreal in 1970: Myles Goodwin (vocals, guitar), Brian Greenway and Gary Moffet (guitars), Steve Lang (bass) and Jerry Mercer (drums). Lang, Moffet and Mercer replaced by Daniel Barbe (keyboards), Jean Pellerin (bass) and Marty Simon (drums) in 1985.	
4/29/72	32	5	1. You Could Have Been A Lady	Big Tree 133
4/14/79	34	4	2. Roller	Capitol 4660
3/14/81	21	7	3. Just Between You And Me	Capitol 4975

DATE	POS	WKS	ARTIST–RECORD TITLE	LABEL & NO.
			AQUATONES, The	
			Group formed in Valley Stream, Long Island, New York, in 1957. Consisted of Lynn Nixon and Larry Vannata (lead singers), David Goddard and Eugene McCarthy.	
5/5/58	21	8	1. You	Fargo 1001
			Top 100 #21 / Best Seller #24	
			ARBORS, The	
			Pop vocal group formed at the University of Michigan in Ann Arbor by two pairs of brothers: Edward and Fred Farran, and Scott and Tom Herrick.	
4/5/69	20	3	1. The Letter	Date 1638
			ARCADIA	
			English group featuring Duran Duran's Simon LeBon, Nick Rhodes and Roger Taylor.	
11/2/85	6	12	1. **Election Day**	Capitol 5501
			Sales #4 / Airplay #6; Grace Jones (narration)	
3/1/86	33	3	2. Goodbye Is Forever	Capitol 5542
			Sales #29	
			ARCHER, Tasmin	
			Native of Bradford, England. Female singer of Jamaican parentage.	
5/29/93	32	5	1. Sleeping Satellite	SBK 50426
			Airplay #29 / Sales #73	
			ARCHIES, The	
			Studio group created by Don Kirshner; based on the Saturday morning cartoon television series. Lead vocalist Ron Dante (born Carmine Granito on 8/22/45 in Staten Island, New York) was also the ghost voice of The Cuff Links and co-producer of many of Barry Manilow's hits. All tunes written and produced by Jeff Barry, who was half of a prolific hit-writing partnership with his then-wife Ellie Greenwich.	
11/2/68	22	8	1. Bang-Shang-A-Lang	Calendar 1006
8/16/69	1 (4)	18	● 2. **Sugar, Sugar**	Calendar 1008
12/20/69+	10	10	● 3. **Jingle Jangle**	Kirshner 5002
3/28/70	40	2	4. Who's Your Baby?	Kirshner 5003
			ARDEN, Toni	
			Vocalist from New York City. Real name: Antoinette Aroizzone. Sang with Al Trace in 1945 and Joe Reichman in 1946.	
6/2/58	13	11	1. Padre	Decca 30628
			Jockey #13 / Top 100 #18 / Best Seller #19; Jack Pleis (orch.)	
			ARGENT	
			British rock quartet. Consisted of ex-Zombies member Rod Argent (vocals, keyboards), Jim Rodford (bass; Argent's cousin), Robert Henrit (drums) and Russ Ballard (guitar; later a successful songwriter).	
7/8/72	5	11	1. **Hold Your Head Up**	Epic 10852

DATE	POS	WKS	ARTIST—RECORD TITLE	LABEL & NO.
			## ARMS, Russell	
			Born on 2/3/29 in Berkeley, California. One of the regulars on TV's "Your Hit Parade," 1952-57.	
2/2/57	22	8	1. Cinco Robles (Five Oaks) Best Seller #22 / Top 100 #23 / Jockey #23; Pete King (orch.)	Era 1026
			## ARMSTRONG, Louis	
			Born Daniel Louis Armstrong in New Orleans on 8/4/01 (not 7/4/1900, as Armstrong claimed). Died on 7/6/71 in New York. Nickname: "Satchmo." Joined the legendary band of Joe "King" Oliver in Chicago in 1922. By 1929, had become the most widely known black musician in the world. Influenced dozens of singers and trumpet players, both black and white. Numerous appearances on radio, TV and in movies. Awarded a Lifetime Achievement Grammy in 1972. Inducted into the Rock and Roll Hall of Fame in 1990 as a forefather of rock music.	
2/25/56	20	7	1. A Theme From The Threepenny Opera (Mack The Knife) **LOUIS ARMSTRONG & HIS ALL-STARS**	Columbia 40587
12/15/56	29	1	2. Blueberry Hill **LOUIS ARMSTRONG AND GORDON JENKINS AND HIS ORCHESTRA AND CHORUS** recorded in 1949; B-side "That Lucky Old Sun" was a #19 hit in 1949; both were on Decca 24752	Decca 30091
2/29/64	1 (1)	19	3. **Hello, Dolly!** **LOUIS ARMSTRONG AND THE ALL STARS** title song from the Broadway musical starring Carol Channing; #1 Adult Contemporary hit (9 weeks); a court ruling found this song to be based on the 1949 hit "Sunflower"	Kapp 573
3/19/88	32	3	4. What A Wonderful World Sales #29 / Airplay #38; featured in the movie *Good Morning, Vietnam* starring Robin Williams; originally hit the Adult Contemporary charts in 1967 at #12; B-side is Wayne Fontana & The Mindbenders' 1965 hit "Game Of Love"	A&M 3010
			## ARNOLD, Eddy	
			Born Richard Edward Arnold on 5/15/18 near Henderson, Tennessee. Ranked as the #1 artist in the book *Joel Whitburn's Top Country Singles 1944–1993*. Became popular on Nashville's *Grand Ole Opry* as a singer with Pee Wee King, 1940-43.	
12/1/56	22	1	1. I Wouldn't Know Where To Begin Jockey #22 / Top 100 #64	RCA 6699
11/13/65	6	10	2. **Make The World Go Away** #1 Adult Contemporary hit (4 weeks); #1 Country hit (3 weeks)	RCA 8679
3/12/66	36	5	3. I Want To Go With You #1 Country hit (6 weeks); #1 Adult Contemporary hit (3 weeks)	RCA 8749
6/18/66	40	1	4. The Last Word In Lonesome Is Me written by Roger Miller; all of above produced by Chet Atkins	RCA 8818
			## ARRESTED DEVELOPMENT	
			Coed rap outfit from Georgia led by Milwaukee-born, Tennessee-raised Todd "Speech" Thomas. Includes his cousin Aerlee Taree (pronounced Early Ta-Ree), Tim "Headliner" Barnwell, Montsho Eshe, Rasa Don and Baba Oje. Won the 1992 Best New Artist Grammy Award. Thomas's parents publish the *Milwaukee Community Journal*.	
4/25/92	6	17	● 1. **Tennessee** Sales #4 / Airplay #10; #1 R&B hit (1 week)	Chrysalis 23829
8/29/92	8	18	● 2. **People Everyday** Sales #5 / Airplay #10; contains chorus to Sly & The Family Stone's "Everyday People"	Chrysalis 50397

DATE	POS	WKS	ARTIST–RECORD TITLE	LABEL & NO.
1/9/93	6	20	● 3. **Mr. Wendal** *Airplay #6 / Sales #7*	Chrysalis 24810
			ARROWS, The—see ALLAN, Davie	
			ARTISTS UNITED AGAINST APARTHEID	
			Benefit group of 49 superstar artists formed to protest the South African apartheid government; proceeds went to political prisoners in South Africa. Organized by Little Steven and Arthur Baker. Featuring Pat Benatar, Bono (U2), Jackson Browne, Jimmy Cliff, Bob Dylan, Peter Gabriel, Bonnie Raitt, Lou Reed, Bruce Springsteen and many others.	
12/7/85	38	3	1. Sun City *Sales #25*	Manhattan 50017
			ART OF NOISE, The	
			British techno-pop trio: Anne Dudley (keyboards), J.J. Jeczalik (keyboards, programmer) and Gary Langan (engineer). All three were part of Trevor Horn's production team in the early 1980s. Worked with ABC, Frankie Goes To Hollywood and others. Disbanded in mid-1990.	
9/20/86	34	4	1. Paranoimia **THE ART OF NOISE with MAX HEADROOM** *Airplay #33 / Sales #37; Max Headroom is a British "computer-generated" celebrity played by actor Matt Frewer*	China 43002
12/24/88+	31	6	2. Kiss **THE ART OF NOISE Featuring Tom Jones** *Sales #23 / Airplay #35*	China 871038
			ASHFORD & SIMPSON	
			Husband-and-wife R&B vocal/songwriting duo: Nickolas Ashford (born 5/4/42, Fairfield, South Carolina) and Valerie Simpson (born 8/26/46, New York City). Recorded as Valerie & Nick in 1964 ("Bubbled Under"). Team wrote for Chuck Jackson and Maxine Brown. Joined staff at Motown and wrote and produced for many of the label's top stars. Valerie recorded solo in 1972. They married in 1974. Valerie's brother, Ray Simpson, was the lead singer of Village People.	
10/13/79	36	2	1. Found A Cure	Warner 8870
1/5/85	12	11	2. Solid *Sales #8 / Airplay #15; #1 R&B hit (3 weeks)*	Capitol 5397
			ASHTON, GARDNER & DYKE	
			British pop trio: Tony Ashton, Kim Gardner and Roy Dyke. Keyboardist Ashton and drummer Dyke later joined Medicine Head.	
8/7/71	40	1	1. Resurrection Shuffle	Capitol 3060
			ASIA	
			British rock supergroup: guitarist Steve Howe (Yes), drummer Carl Palmer (Emerson, Lake & Palmer, Atomic Rooster), keyboardist Geoff Downes (Buggles, Yes) and vocalist/bassist John Wetton (King Crimson, Uriah Heep, U.K.). Howe replaced by Mandy Meyer (Krokus) in 1985. Meyer replaced in 1990 by Oakland, California native Pat Thrall (Automatic Man, Pat Travers Band, Hughes/Thrall).	
5/1/82	4	12	1. **Heat Of The Moment**	Geffen 50040
8/14/82	17	8	2. Only Time Will Tell	Geffen 29970
8/6/83	10	11	3. **Don't Cry**	Geffen 29571
11/12/83	34	5	4. The Smile Has Left Your Eyes	Geffen 29475

DATE	POS	WKS	ARTIST–RECORD TITLE	LABEL & NO.
			ASSEMBLED MULTITUDE, The	
			Philadelphia-based studio group arranged and conducted by Tom Sellers (died 3/9/88 in a fire in his hometown of Wayne, Pennsylvania, at age 39).	
8/1/70	16	7	1. Overture From Tommy (A Rock Opera) [I]	Atlantic 2737
			ASSOCIATION, The	
			Group formed in Los Angeles in 1965. Consisted of Terry Kirkman (plays 23 wind, reed and percussion instruments), Gary "Jules" Alexander (guitar), Brian Cole (bass), Jim Yester (guitar), Ted Bluechel, Jr. (drums) and Russ Giguere (percussion). Larry Ramos, Jr., joined in early 1968. Cole died on 8/2/72 of a heroin overdose.	
6/25/66	7	8	1. **Along Comes Mary**	Valiant 741
9/3/66	1 (3)	12	● 2. **Cherish**	Valiant 747
12/17/66	35	3	3. Pandora's Golden Heebie Jeebies	Valiant 755
			title refers to the Sunset Strip nightclub Pandora's Box	
6/3/67	1 (4)	13	● 4. **Windy**	Warner 7041
9/9/67	2 (2)	11	● 5. **Never My Love**	Warner 7074
			written by the Addrisi Brothers	
2/10/68	10	8	6. **Everything That Touches You**	Warner 7163
6/22/68	39	2	7. Time For Livin'	Warner 7195
			ASTLEY, Rick	
			Born on 2/6/66 in Warrington and raised in Manchester, England. Pop singer/guitarist.	
1/23/88	1 (2)	14	● 1. **Never Gonna Give You Up**	RCA 5347
			Sales #1(1) / Airplay #1(1); #1 Adult Contemporary hit (3 weeks)	
4/30/88	1 (1)	12	2. **Together Forever**	RCA 8319
			Sales #1(1) / Airplay #1(1)	
8/6/88	10	10	3. **It Would Take A Strong Strong Man**	RCA 8663
			Sales #8 / Airplay #12; #1 Adult Contemporary hit (1 week)	
1/7/89	6	10	4. **She Wants To Dance With Me**	RCA 8838
			Sales #6 / Airplay #6	
5/27/89	38	1	5. Giving Up On Love	RCA 8872
			Sales #34 / Airplay #40	
3/9/91	7	12	6. **Cry For Help**	RCA 2774
			Airplay #7 / Sales #7; #1 Adult Contemporary hit (1 week)	
10/2/93	28	6	7. Hopelessly	RCA 62597
			Airplay #21 / Sales #64	
			ATLANTA RHYTHM SECTION	
			Group formed by musicians from Studio One, Doraville, Georgia, in 1971. Consisted of Rodney Justo (vocals), Barry Bailey and J.R. Cobb (guitars), Paul Goddard (bass), Dean Daughtry (keyboards) and Robert Nix (drums). Justo, Daughtry and Nix were with Roy Orbison's band, The Candymen. Cobb, Daughtry and band manager/producer Buddy Buie were with the Classics IV. Justo left after first album, replaced by Ronnie Hammond.	
11/9/74	35	2	1. Doraville	Polydor 14248
2/26/77	7	14	2. **So In To You**	Polydor 14373
3/25/78	7	12	3. **Imaginary Lover**	Polydor 14459
7/8/78	14	7	4. I'm Not Gonna Let It Bother Me Tonight	Polydor 14484
6/16/79	19	9	5. Do It Or Die	Polydor 14568
9/8/79	17	8	6. Spooky	Polydor 2001

DATE	POS	WKS	ARTIST–RECORD TITLE	LABEL & NO.
10/10/81	**29**	4	7. Alien all of above co-written and produced by Buddy Buie	Columbia 02471

ATLANTIC STARR

Soul band formed in 1976 in White Plains, New York, by brothers Wayne, David and Jonathan Lewis. Wayne and David on vocals with Sharon Bryant. In 1984, reduced to a quintet; Barbara Weathers replaced Bryant. Porscha Martin replaced Weathers in 1989. Rachel Oliver replaced Martin in 1991. By 1994, Aisha Tanner replaced Oliver.

DATE	POS	WKS	ARTIST–RECORD TITLE	LABEL & NO.
5/15/82	**38**	3	1. Circles	A&M 2392
1/25/86	**3**	14	2. **Secret Lovers** Sales #2 / Airplay #2; #1 Adult Contemporary hit (1 week)	A&M 2788
4/25/87	**1** (1)	14	3. **Always** Airplay #1(1) / Sales #2; #1 R&B hit (2 weeks); #1 Adult Contemporary hit (2 weeks)	Warner 28455
2/1/92	**3**	19	● 4. **Masterpiece** Airplay #4 / Sales #6; written by Kenny Nolan	Reprise 19076

AUGUST, Jan—see HAYMAN, Richard

AUSTIN, Patti

Born on 8/10/48 in New York City. Backup work in New York. Goddaughter of Quincy Jones. Made debut at Harlem's Apollo Theatre at age four. Appeared in the 1988 movie *Tucker*.

DATE	POS	WKS	ARTIST–RECORD TITLE	LABEL & NO.
12/4/82+	**1** (2)	18	● 1. **Baby, Come To Me** **PATTI AUSTIN with James Ingram** #1 Adult Contemporary hit (3 weeks)	Qwest 50036

AUSTIN, Sil

Born Sylvester Austin on 9/17/29 in Donellon, Florida. R&B tenor saxophonist. Played with Tiny Bradshaw Band before forming own group.

DATE	POS	WKS	ARTIST–RECORD TITLE	LABEL & NO.
11/24/56	**17**	7	1. Slow Walk　　　　　　　　[I] Juke Box #17 / Top 100 #19 / Best Seller #20	Mercury 70963

AUTOGRAPH

Los Angeles-based rock quintet: Steve Plunkett (vocals, guitar), Steve Lynch (guitar), Steven Isham (keyboards), Randy Rand (bass) and Keni Richards (drums).

DATE	POS	WKS	ARTIST–RECORD TITLE	LABEL & NO.
2/23/85	**29**	5	1. Turn Up The Radio Sales #25	RCA 13953

AVALON, Frankie

Born Francis Avallone on 9/18/39 in Philadelphia. Teen idol managed by Bob Marcucci. Worked in bands in Atlantic City, New Jersey, in 1953. Radio and TV with Paul Whiteman, mid-1950s. Singer/trumpet player in 1957 with Rocco & His Saints, which included Bobby Rydell. Co-starred in many movies with Annette. Appeared in the movies *Jamboree!* (1957), *Guns Of The Timberland* (1960), *The Alamo* (1960) and *Back To The Beach* (1987).

DATE	POS	WKS	ARTIST–RECORD TITLE	LABEL & NO.
1/27/58	**7**	11	1. **Dede Dinah** Top 100 #7 / Best Seller #9 / Jockey #24	Chancellor 1011
7/28/58	**9**	12	2. **Ginger Bread** Hot 100 #9 / Best Seller #11; The Four Dates (backing vocals)	Chancellor 1021
11/17/58	**15**	10	3. I'll Wait For You	Chancellor 1026
2/23/59	**1** (5)	14	● 4. **Venus**	Chancellor 1031

DATE	POS	WKS	ARTIST–RECORD TITLE	LABEL & NO.
6/1/59	8	10	5. **Bobby Sox To Stockings/**	
6/15/59	10	9	6. **A Boy Without A Girl**	Chancellor 1036
9/14/59	7	11	7. **Just Ask Your Heart**	Chancellor 1040
12/7/59	1 (1)	12	8. **Why/**	
1/4/60	39	1	9. Swingin' On A Rainbow	Chancellor 1045
3/28/60	22	6	10. Don't Throw Away All Those Teardrops	Chancellor 1048
8/1/60	32	4	11. Where Are You	Chancellor 1052
			all of above arranged and conducted by Peter De Angelis	
10/17/60	26	7	12. Togetherness	Chancellor 1056
5/5/62	26	4	13. You Are Mine	Chancellor 1107

AVANT-GARDE, The

Duo of Chuck Woolery and Elkin "Bubba" Fowler. Woolery was the orignal host of TV's "Wheel of Fortune" and is the current host of "Love Connection."

DATE	POS	WKS	ARTIST–RECORD TITLE	LABEL & NO.
10/26/68	40	1	1. Naturally Stoned	Columbia 44590

AWB (AVERAGE WHITE BAND)

Vocal/instrumental group formed in Scotland in 1972. Consisted of Alan Gorrie (of Forever More; vocals, bass), Hamish Stuart (vocals, guitar), Onnie McIntyre (vocal, guitar), Malcolm Duncan (saxophone), Roger Ball (keyboards, saxophone) and Robbie McIntosh (drums). McIntosh died of drug poisoning on 9/23/74, replaced by Steve Ferrone. McIntosh and Ferrone were members of Brian Auger's Oblivion Express.

AWB:

DATE	POS	WKS	ARTIST–RECORD TITLE	LABEL & NO.
12/21/74+	1 (1)	13	● 1. **Pick Up The Pieces** [I]	Atlantic 3229
4/26/75	10	12	2. **Cut The Cake**	Atlantic 3261
9/27/75	39	2	3. If I Ever Lose This Heaven	Atlantic 3285
12/20/75	33	3	4. School Boy Crush	Atlantic 3304

AVERAGE WHITE BAND:

DATE	POS	WKS	ARTIST–RECORD TITLE	LABEL & NO.
10/16/76	40	1	5. Queen Of My Soul	Atlantic 3354
			all of above produced by Arif Mardin	

AZ The Visualiza

Born Anthony Cruz in Brooklyn. Male rapper. Former member of Five Percent Nation, under the name Asiatic.

DATE	POS	WKS	ARTIST–RECORD TITLE	LABEL & NO.
8/12/95	25	13	● 1. Sugar Hill	EMI 58407
			Sales #11 / Airplay #64; rap version of "Sugar Free" by Juicy; missjones (female vocal)	

B

BABYFACE

Vocalist/instrumentalist Kenneth Edmonds, formerly with Manchild and The Deele. Brother of Kevon and Melvin Edmonds of After 7. Prolific writing/production duo with L.A. Reid.

DATE	POS	WKS	ARTIST–RECORD TITLE	LABEL & NO.
9/9/89	7	10	1. **It's No Crime**	Solar 68966
			Airplay #7 / Sales #8; #1 R&B hit (2 weeks)	
12/23/89+	14	9	2. Tender Lover	Solar 74003
			Sales #8 / Airplay #18; #1 R&B hit (1 week)	

DATE	POS	WKS	ARTIST–RECORD TITLE	LABEL & NO.
3/17/90	6	11	3. **Whip Appeal** Airplay #6 / Sales #6	Solar 74007
7/21/90	30	5	4. My Kinda Girl Airplay #24 / Sales #38; above 4 from the album *Tender Lover*	Solar 74515
8/22/92	29	6	5. Give U My Heart **BABYFACE (Featuring Toni Braxton)** Airplay #29 / Sales #39; from the movie *Boomerang* starring Eddie Murphy	LaFace 24026
11/27/93+	15	16	6. Never Keeping Secrets Airplay #15 / Sales #18	Epic 77264
4/2/94	21	10	7. And Our Feelings Airplay #26 / Sales #29; After 7 (backing vocals)	Epic 77394
7/9/94	4	30	● 8. **When Can I See You** Airplay #4 / Sales #9	Epic 77550
5/27/95	10	22	9. **Someone To Love** **JON B. featuring BABYFACE** Sales #9 / Airplay #16; from the movie *Bad Boys* starring Martin Lawrence and Will Smith	Yab Yum 77895

BABYS, The

British rock group: John Waite (vocals), Walt Stocker, Mike Corby and Tony Brock. By 1980, keyboardist Jonathan Cain (later of Journey) had replaced Corby, and bassist Ricky Phillips joined group. In 1989, Waite formed Bad English with Phillips and Cain.

DATE	POS	WKS	ARTIST–RECORD TITLE	LABEL & NO.
10/29/77	13	11	1. Isn't It Time	Chrysalis 2173
2/3/79	13	10	2. Every Time I Think Of You	Chrysalis 2279
3/8/80	33	3	3. Back On My Feet Again	Chrysalis 2398

BACHELORS, The

Pop vocal trio from Dublin, Ireland: brothers Declan and Con Cluskey, with John Stokes. Formed as a harmonica instrumental trio known as the Harmonichords.

DATE	POS	WKS	ARTIST–RECORD TITLE	LABEL & NO.
5/16/64	10	8	1. **Diane** #2 hit for the Nat Shilkret Orchestra in 1928	London 9639
8/1/64	33	2	2. I Believe #2 hit for Frankie Laine in 1953	London 9672
1/30/65	27	4	3. No Arms Can Ever Hold You	London 9724
7/3/65	15	7	4. Marie #1 hit for Tommy Dorsey in 1937	London 9762
11/6/65	32	3	5. Chapel In The Moonlight #1 hit for Shep Fields in 1936	London 9793
5/14/66	38	2	6. Love Me With All Of Your Heart	London 9828

BACHMAN-TURNER OVERDRIVE

Hard-rock group formed in Vancouver, Canada, in 1972. Brothers Randy (vocals, guitar), Tim (guitar) and Robbie Bachman (drums), with C. Fred Turner (vocals, bass). Originally known as Brave Belt. Randy had been in The Guess Who and recorded solo. Tim left in 1973, replaced by Blair Thornton. Randy left in 1977 to form Ironhorse. Randy and Tim regrouped with C.F. Turner in 1984.

DATE	POS	WKS	ARTIST–RECORD TITLE	LABEL & NO.
3/23/74	23	9	1. Let It Ride	Mercury 73457
6/29/74	12	10	2. Takin' Care Of Business	Mercury 73487
10/5/74	1 (1)	12	● 3. **You Ain't Seen Nothing Yet/**	Mercury 73622
		3	4. Free Wheelin' [I] dedicated to Duane Allman	

DATE	POS	WKS	ARTIST–RECORD TITLE	LABEL & NO.
2/1/75	**14**	7	5. Roll On Down The Highway	Mercury 73656
6/7/75	**21**	7	6. Hey You	Mercury 73683
2/28/76	**33**	3	7. Take It Like A Man Little Richard (backing vocal)	Mercury 73766

BACKUS, Jim, and Friend

Born on 2/25/13 in Cleveland. Died of pneumonia on 7/3/89. Actor, starred in dozens of movies. Played Thurston Howell III on TV's "Gilligan's Island." Also famous as the voice of Mr. Magoo in the cartoon series. Label misspelled last name as Bakus on some pressings. The "Friend" is actress Hermione Gingold (born 12/9/1897, London; died 4/30/87).

DATE	POS	WKS	ARTIST–RECORD TITLE	LABEL & NO.
7/21/58	**40**	2	1. Delicious! [N] Best Seller #40 / Top 100 #42; Appleknocker And His Group (instrumental backing)	Jubilee 5330

BAD COMPANY

British rock band formed in 1973: Paul Rodgers (vocals), Mick Ralphs (guitar), Raymond "Boz" Burrell (bass) and Simon Kirke (drums). Rodgers and Kirke from Free; Ralphs from Mott The Hoople; and Burrell from King Crimson. Rodgers, who left group in late 1982, was a member of The Firm (1984–86) and The Law (in 1991). Vocalist Brian Howe joined in 1986. Burrell left in 1987. Dave "Bucket" Colwell (guitar) and Rick Wills (of Foreigner; bass) joined in late 1992. Howe left in early 1995, replaced by Robert Hart. Band named after a 1972 Jeff Bridges movie.

DATE	POS	WKS		ARTIST–RECORD TITLE	LABEL & NO.
8/31/74	**5**	11		1. **Can't Get Enough**	Swan Song 70015
2/8/75	**19**	6		2. Movin' On	Swan Song 70101
5/31/75	**36**	2		3. Good Lovin' Gone Bad	Swan Song 70103
7/26/75	**10**	11		4. **Feel Like Makin' Love**	Swan Song 70106
4/24/76	**20**	7		5. Young Blood	Swan Song 70108
4/14/79	**13**	12	●	6. Rock 'N' Roll Fantasy	Swan Song 70119
1/26/91	**16**	8		7. If You Needed Somebody Airplay #14 / Sales #18	Atco 98914
9/28/91	**28**	5		8. Walk Through Fire Airplay #54	Atco 98748
10/31/92	**38**	2		9. How About That Airplay #55	Atco 98509

BAD ENGLISH

Rock supergroup: John Waite (vocals), Ricky Phillips (bass), Jonathan Cain (keyboards), Neal Schon (guitar) and Deen Castronovo (drums). Waite, Phillips and Cain were members of The Babys. Cain and Schon (ex-Santana) were members of Journey. Schon and Castronovo with Hardline in 1992.

DATE	POS	WKS		ARTIST–RECORD TITLE	LABEL & NO.
9/30/89	**1 (2)**	15	●	1. **When I See You Smile** Sales #1(2) / Airplay #1(2)	Epic 69082
1/20/90	**5**	11		2. **Price Of Love** Airplay #5 / Sales #7	Epic 73094
7/14/90	**21**	8		3. Possession Airplay #14 / Sales #34	Epic 73398

DATE	POS	WKS	ARTIST–RECORD TITLE	LABEL & NO.
			BADFINGER	
			Welsh rock quartet originally known as The Iveys. Consisted of Pete Ham (guitar), Tom Evans (bass), Joey Molland (guitar; joined in late 1968, after band's first hit single "Maybe Tomorrow") and Mike Gibbins (drums). All but Gibbins share vocals. Ham (born 4/27/47) committed suicide on 4/23/75. Group disbanded from 1976 to 1978. Molland and Evans re-grouped in 1979. Evans committed suicide on 11/23/83 (age 36).	
3/7/70	7	11	1. **Come And Get It** written by Paul McCartney; from the movie *The Magic Christian* starring Peter Sellers	Apple 1815
11/21/70	8	9	2. **No Matter What**	Apple 1822
12/18/71+	4	12	● 3. **Day After Day** produced by George Harrison	Apple 1841
4/8/72	14	7	4. Baby Blue produced by Todd Rundgren	Apple 1844
			BAEZ, Joan	
			Born Joan Chandos Baez in Staten Island, New York, on 1/9/41 to a Mexican father and British mother. Preeminent folk song stylist. Became a political activist while attending Boston University in the late 1950s. Made her professional debut in July 1959 at the first Newport Folk Festival. Orientation changed from traditional to popular folk songs in the early '60s. Influential in fostering career of Bob Dylan.	
8/28/71	3	13	● 1. **The Night They Drove Old Dixie Down** written by Robbie Robertson (leader of The Band); #1 Adult Contemporary hit (5 weeks)	Vanguard 35138
11/8/75	35	2	2. Diamonds And Rust autobiographical song about Baez and Bob Dylan	A&M 1737
			BAILEY, Philip	
			Born on 5/8/51 in Denver. R&B percussionist/co-lead vocalist with Earth, Wind & Fire since 1971.	
12/8/84+	2 (2)	16	● 1. **Easy Lover** **PHILIP BAILEY with Phil Collins** Sales #1(1) / Airplay #2	Columbia 04679
			BAIRD, Dan	
			Born on 12/12/53 in San Diego; moved to Atlanta at age two. Former lead singer of the Georgia Satellites.	
1/16/93	26	5	1. I Love You Period. Sales #36 / Airplay #46	Def Amer. 18724
			BAKER, Anita	
			Born on 1/26/58 in Toledo, Ohio; raised in Detroit. Soul singer. Female lead singer of Chapter 8, 1976-83.	
9/13/86	8	11	1. **Sweet Love** Sales #6 / Airplay #9	Elektra 69557
2/7/87	37	2	2. Caught Up In The Rapture Sales #37 / Airplay #40	Elektra 69511
10/22/88	3	15	3. **Giving You The Best That I Got** Sales #2 / Airplay #3; #1 R&B hit (2 weeks); #1 Adult Contemporary hit (1 week)	Elektra 69371
2/4/89	14	11	4. Just Because Airplay #11 / Sales #14; #1 R&B hit (1 week)	Elektra 69327

Aaliyah holds two impressive chart distinctions. First, her 1994 single "Back & Forth" was a smash No. 5 hit. Secondly, of all artists to ever appear in the Top 100, she is the first...alphabetically speaking.

Paula Abdul's 1989 single "Knocked Out" lived up to its name: despite five other Top 5 hits from her debut album *Forever Your Girl*, that track was "knocked out" of the running and peaked disappointingly at No. 41.

AC/DC's comparatively weak showing on the singles chart—1991's "Moneytalks" peaked at No. 23 and was their biggest hit—belies their enormous success and continued staying power as top-ranking album artists.

Bryan Adams's second major hit—1983's "Cuts Like A Knife"—reached No. 15 and served as the title track of his second A&M album. Ten years later, the Canadian rocker teamed with fellow hitmakers Sting and Rod Stewart on "All For Love" from the film *The Three Musketeers*.

Aerosmith's career turnaround in 1987 was one of pop music's greatest surprises. The former Columbia act, who'd last seen the Top 40 with 1978's Beatle cover "Come Together," recorded with rappers Run-D.M.C., signed to Geffen and scored big with such hits as 1988's Top 20 "Rag Doll."

After 7's entree into stardom came courtesy of talent and bloodlines: trio members Keith Mitchell and Kevon and Melvin Edwards are relatives of R&B production titans L.A. & Babyface. "Heat Of The Moment" shot to the Top 20 in 1991.

All-4-One followed Boyz II Men's lead and helped propel old-school vocal harmonies back to the top of the charts. The Southern California band's "I Swear" was a No. 1 hit in 1994.

Herb Alpert & The Tijuana Brass looked to be on the career decline by February 1968, when the instrumental "Carmen" peaked at No. 51 and "The Lonely Bull" was just a memory. Three months later, the trumpeter scored his first No. 1 single with a vocal, "This Guy's In Love With You."

Paul Anka's hot streak of five Top 10 singles began with 1959's "Lonely Boy" and ended the next year with "My Home Town." Though his "Hello Young Lovers" only reached No. 23, its B-side, "I Love You In The Same Old Way," also climbed to No. 40.

Annette's follow-up to her final Top 40 hit "Pineapple Princess," 1961's "Dream Boy," peaked at No. 80 and dropped off the charts after two weeks.

Ann-Margret's singing career includes just one Top 40 single—1961's "I Just Don't Understand"—and a memorable appearance on RCA's *Bye Bye Birdie* film soundtrack, which reached No. 2 in 1963.

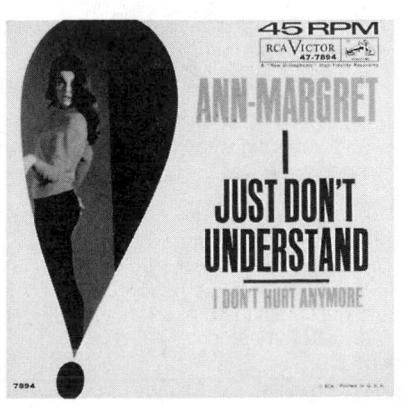

DATE	POS	WKS	ARTIST–RECORD TITLE	LABEL & NO.
9/17/94	36	7	5. Body & Soul *Sales #19 / Airplay #52*	Elektra 64520
			### BAKER, George, Selection	
			Baker is Johannes Bouwens (born 12/9/44). Pop vocalist/guitarist/ keyboardist of Dutch group.	
4/11/70	21	10	1. Little Green Bag	Colossus 112
1/10/76	26	5	2. Paloma Blanca *#1 Adult Contemporary hit (1 week)*	Warner 8115
			### BAKER, LaVern	
			Born Delores Williams on 11/11/29 in Chicago. Recorded as "Little Miss Share Cropper" and "Bea Baker." After working with the Todd Rhodes Orchestra, 1952–53, toured Europe, solo. Returned to work for Atlantic Records and became one of the most popular female R&B singers in the early rock era. Backing group: The Gliders. Inducted into the Rock and Roll Hall of Fame in 1991.	
1/15/55	14	11	1. Tweedlee Dee **LaVERN BAKER AND THE GLIDERS** *Juke Box #14 / Best Seller #22*	Atlantic 1047
10/13/56	22	2	2. I Can't Love You Enough *Jockey #22 / Top 100 #48*	Atlantic 1104
12/29/56+	17	14	3. Jim Dandy **LaVERN BAKER AND THE GLIDERS** *Best Seller #17 / Jockey #20 / Top 100 #22; #1 R&B hit (1 week)*	Atlantic 1116
12/28/58+	6	15	● 4. **I Cried A Tear**	Atlantic 2007
6/1/59	33	2	5. I Waited Too Long *written by Neil Sedaka*	Atlantic 2021
5/1/61	37	3	6. Saved	Atlantic 2099
1/5/63	34	3	7. See See Rider *#14 hit for Ma Rainey in 1925 (as "See See Rider Blues")*	Atlantic 2167
			### BALANCE	
			New York City-based rock trio led by Illinois native Peppy Castro (vocals; founder of the Blues Magoos). With guitarist Bob Kulick (brother of Bruce Kulick of Kiss) and keyboardist Doug Katsaros.	
8/15/81	22	9	1. Breaking Away	Portrait 02177
			### BALIN, Marty	
			Born Martyn Buchwald on 1/30/43 in Cincinnati. Co-founder of Jefferson Airplane/Jefferson Starship/KBC Band.	
6/13/81	8	13	1. **Hearts**	EMI America 8084
10/10/81	27	5	2. Atlanta Lady (Something About Your Love)	EMI America 8093
			### BALL, David	
			Born on 7/9/53 in Rock Hill, South Carolina. Country singer.	
7/23/94	40	1	1. Thinkin' Problem *Sales #18*	Warner 18250

DATE	POS	WKS	ARTIST–RECORD TITLE	LABEL & NO.
			### BALL, Kenny, and his Jazzmen	
2/17/62	**2** (1)	12	Born on 5/22/30 in Ilford, England. Leader of English Dixieland jazz band formed in 1958. 1. **Midnight In Moscow** [I] original Russian title: "Padmeskoveeye Vietchera"; #1 Adult Contemporary hit (3 weeks)	Kapp 442
			### BALLARD, Hank, And The Midnighters	
			R&B vocal group from Detroit, formed in 1952 as The Royals: Henry Booth, Charles Sutton, Lawson Smith and Sonny Woods. In late 1953, Henry "Hank" Ballard (born 11/18/36, Detroit) replaced Smith and became lead singer. Name changed to Midnighters in 1954. Had the original recording of "The Twist," written by Ballard, who is still active as a solo artist. After group disbanded in 1965, re-formed with Frank Stadford, Walter Miller and Wesley Hargrove. Worked in the James Brown Revue. Ballard inducted into the Rock and Roll Hall of Fame in 1990.	
7/18/60	**7**	13	1. **Finger Poppin' Time**	King 5341
8/29/60	**28**	6	2. The Twist B-side of Ballard's first *Hot 100* hit "Teardrops On Your Letter" (1959)	King 5171
10/17/60	**6**	11	3. **Let's Go, Let's Go, Let's Go** #1 R&B hit (3 weeks)	King 5400
1/16/61	**23**	4	4. The Hoochi Coochi Coo	King 5430
3/20/61	**39**	1	5. Let's Go Again (Where We Went Last Night)	King 5459
5/1/61	**33**	3	6. The Continental Walk	King 5491
7/17/61	**26**	4	7. The Switch-A-Roo	King 5510
			### BALLOON FARM, The	
3/16/68	**37**	4	New York flower-pop quintet. A Hugo & Luigi production. 1. A Question Of Temperature	Laurie 3405
			### BALTIMORA	
1/11/86	**13**	10	Born Jimmy McShane on 5/23/57 in Londonderry, Northern Ireland. 1. **Tarzan Boy** Sales #11 / Airplay #17	Manhattan 50018
			### BANANARAMA	
			Female pop-rock trio from London: Sarah Dallin, Keren Woodward and Siobhan Fahey. Group name is a combination of the children's TV show "The Banana Splits" and the Roxy Music song "Pyjamarama." Fahey married Dave Stewart (Eurythmics) on 8/1/87; left group in early 1988, replaced by Jacqui O'Sullivan (who left in mid-1991). Fahey later formed duo Shakespear's Sister.	
8/11/84	**9**	11	1. **Cruel Summer** Sales #17 pre	London 810127
7/19/86	**1** (1)	12	2. **Venus** Sales #1(2) / Airplay #3	London 886056
8/15/87	**4**	12	3. **I Heard A Rumour** Sales #3 / Airplay #5; from the movie *Disorderlies* starring The Fat Boys and Ralph Bellamy	London 886165

DATE	POS	WKS	ARTIST—RECORD TITLE	LABEL & NO.

BAND, The

Rock group formed in Woodstock, New York, in 1967: Robbie Robertson (guitar), Levon Helm (drums), Rick Danko (bass), Richard Manuel and Garth Hudson (keyboards). All from Canada (except Helm from Arkansas) and all were with Ronnie Hawkins' Hawks. Group's "farewell concert" on Thanksgiving Day in 1976 was documented in the Martin Scorcese movie *The Last Waltz*. Manuel committed suicide on 3/4/86 (age 42). Helm, Danko and Hudson reunited in 1993 with Jim Weider (guitar), Richard Bell (piano) and Randy Ciarlante (drums). Inducted into the Rock and Roll Hall of Fame in 1994.

DATE	POS	WKS	ARTIST—RECORD TITLE	LABEL & NO.
11/29/69+	25	7	1. Up On Cripple Creek B-side is the original version of "The Night They Drove Old Dixie Down"	Capitol 2635
10/14/72	34	6	2. Don't Do It "live" recording	Capitol 3433

BAND AID

A benefit recording to assist famine relief in Ethiopia. All-star group organized by Bob Geldof of The Boomtown Rats.

DATE	POS	WKS	ARTIST—RECORD TITLE	LABEL & NO.
1/5/85+	13	4	● 1. Do They Know It's Christmas? [X] Sales #6; with Paul Young, Boy George & Jon Moss (Culture Club), George Michael, Sting, Phil Collins, Duran Duran, Bananarama, Spandau Ballet, Paul Weller (Style Council), Boomtown Rats and members of Kool & The Gang, U2, Ultravox, Status Quo and Heaven 17	Columbia 04749

BANGLES

Female pop-rock quartet formed in Los Angeles in January 1981. Consisted of sisters Vicki (lead guitar) and Debbi Peterson (drums), Michael Steele (bass) and Susanna Hoffs (guitar). Originally named The Bangs. Steele was previously in The Runaways. Hoffs starred in the 1987 movie *The Allnighter*. Disbanded in October 1989. Hoffs recorded solo in 1991.

DATE	POS	WKS	ARTIST—RECORD TITLE	LABEL & NO.
2/22/86	2 (1)	14	1. **Manic Monday** Sales #3 / Airplay #4; written by Prince under the pseudonym "Christopher"	Columbia 05757
6/14/86	29	5	2. If She Knew What She Wants Airplay #27 / Sales #29	Columbia 05886
11/1/86	1 (4)	15	● 3. **Walk Like An Egyptian** Sales #1(4) / Airplay #1(4)	Columbia 06257
3/14/87	11	9	4. Walking Down Your Street Sales #9 / Airplay #10; above 4 from the album *Different Light*	Columbia 06674
12/5/87+	2 (1)	14	5. **Hazy Shade Of Winter** Sales #2 / Airplay #3; from the movie *Less Than Zero* starring Andrew McCarthy; B-side is "She Lost You" by Joan Jett & The Blackhearts	Def Jam 07630
11/12/88+	5	12	6. **In Your Room** Sales #4 / Airplay #9	Columbia 08090
2/11/89	1 (1)	14	● 7. **Eternal Flame** Airplay #1(1) / Sales #2; #1 Adult Contemporary hit (2 weeks)	Columbia 68533
6/3/89	30	5	8. Be With You Sales #29 / Airplay #29	Columbia 68744

BANKS, Darrell

Born Darrell Eubanks in 1938 in Buffalo. Soul singer. Killed by a gunshot wound in Detroit, March 1970.

DATE	POS	WKS	ARTIST—RECORD TITLE	LABEL & NO.
9/10/66	27	4	1. Open The Door To Your Heart	Revilot 201

DATE	POS	WKS	ARTIST–RECORD TITLE	LABEL & NO.
			BARBER('S), Chris, Jazz Band	
			Trombonist/leader Barber was born on 4/17/30 in Welwyn Garden City, England. Dixieland-styled band, formed in 1949, featuring Monty Sunshine on clarinet.	
2/2/59	**5**	10	● 1. **Petite Fleur (Little Flower)** [I] written in 1952 by jazz great Sidney Bechet	Laurie 3022
			BARBOUR, Keith	
			Born on 1/21/41 in New York City. Pop singer/songwriter. Formerly with The New Christy Minstrels. Married to TV actress Deidre Hall ("Our House" and "Days of Our Lives"), 1971–78.	
11/1/69	**40**	2	1. Echo Park	Epic 10486
			BARBUSTERS, The—see JETT, Joan	
			BARCLAY, Eddie, and His Orch.	
			Born on 1/26/21 in Paris. Head of the French recording company Compagnie Phonographique Française and own Barclay label.	
7/16/55	**18**	1	1. The Bandit (O'Cangaceiro) [I] Juke Box #18; theme from the Brazilian movie *O Cangaceiro*	Tico 249
			BARDEUX	
			Los Angeles female dance duo: Stacy "Acacia" Smith and Jazz (replaced by Melanie Taylor in 1989).	
5/28/88	**36**	3	1. When We Kiss Airplay #32 / Sales #40	Synthicide 75018
			BARE, Bobby	
			Born Robert Joseph Bare on 4/7/35 in Ironton, Ohio. Prominent country singer/songwriter/guitarist. Drafted by the Army in 1958; left a demo tape of "The All American Boy" with Fraternity Records. The song was released erroneously as by Bill Parsons. Wrote songs for the movie *Teenage Millionaire* and acted in the movie *A Distant Trumpet* in 1964. Own TV series in the mid-1980s.	
12/28/58+	**2 (1)**	13	1. **The All American Boy** [N] **BILL PARSONS**	Fraternity 835
8/18/62	**23**	7	2. Shame On Me	RCA 8032
6/29/63	**16**	9	3. Detroit City written by Mel Tillis	RCA 8183
10/26/63	**10**	7	4. **500 Miles Away From Home** traditional folk ballad written by Hedy West as "500 Miles"	RCA 8238
3/7/64	**33**	2	5. Miller's Cave	RCA 8294
			BAR-KAYS	
			R&B vocal/instrumental combo: Jimmy King (guitar), Ronnie Caldwell (organ), James Alexander (bass), Carl Cunningham (drums), Phalon Jones (saxophone) and Ben Cauley (trumpet). Formed by Al Jackson, drummer with Booker T. & The MG's. The plane crash that killed Otis Redding (12/10/67) also claimed the lives of all the Bar-Kays except Alexander (not on the plane) and Cauley (survived the crash). Alexander re-formed the band. Appeared in the movie *Wattstax*; much session work at Stax. Alexander's son Phalon began solo career in 1990.	
7/1/67	**17**	9	● 1. Soul Finger [I]	Volt 148
12/4/76+	**23**	8	2. Shake Your Rump To The Funk	Mercury 73833

DATE	POS	WKS	ARTIST–RECORD TITLE	LABEL & NO.
			BARNUM, H.B.	
			Born on 7/15/36 in Houston. Member of The Dyna-Sores.	
2/6/61	35	1	1. Lost Love [I]	Eldo 111
			BARRETTO, Ray	
			Born in Brooklyn in April 1939. Latin percussionist. With Tito Puente and Herbie Mann before forming his own group, Charanga Moderna.	
5/11/63	17	7	1. El Watusi [F-N]	Tico 419
			BARRY, Joe	
			Born Joe Barrios in Cut Off, Louisiana. Singer/guitarist.	
5/29/61	24	5	1. I'm A Fool To Care first released on JIN 144 in 1961; #1 hit for Les Paul & Mary Ford in 1954	Smash 1702
			BARRY, Len	
			Born Leonard Borisoff on 12/6/42 in Philadelphia. Lead singer of The Dovells from 1957-63.	
10/23/65	2 (1)	10	1. **1-2-3**	Decca 31827
1/22/66	27	5	2. Like A Baby	Decca 31889
4/9/66	26	5	3. Somewhere from the musical *West Side Story*	Decca 31923
			BARRY And The TAMERLANES	
			California pop trio led by Barry DeVorzon and arranged by Perry Botkin, Jr. Songwriters Terry Smith and Bodie Chandler were The Tamerlanes. DeVorzon founded the Valiant label and began his ongoing prolific songwriting career in the mid-1950s.	
11/16/63	21	5	1. I Wonder What She's Doing Tonight	Valiant 6034
			BARTLEY, Chris	
			Born on 4/17/49 in New York City. Soul singer/guitarist. Sang with the Soulful Inspirations and own group, the Mindbenders, in the mid-1960s.	
8/19/67	32	2	1. The Sweetest Thing This Side Of Heaven written and produced by Van McCoy	Vando 101
			BASIA	
			Born Basia Trzetrzelewska (pronounced: Basha Tshet-shel-ev-ska) on 9/30/59 in Jaworzno, Poland. Pop-jazz singer/composer. Former vocalist of the British group Matt Bianco.	
9/24/88	26	7	1. Time And Tide Sales #21 / Airplay #28	Epic 07730
5/12/90	29	4	2. Cruising For Bruising Airplay #27 / Sales #34	Epic 73239

DATE	POS	WKS	ARTIST–RECORD TITLE	LABEL & NO.

BASIE, Count

Born William Basie on 8/21/04 in Red Bank, New Jersey. Died on 4/26/84 of pancreatic cancer. World-renowned jazz, big-band leader/pianist/organist. Learned music and piano from mother, organ from Fats Waller. First recorded with own band in 1937 for Decca. Appeared in many movies and toured into the '70s. His best-known recording, "One O'Clock Jump" (1937), is in the Grammy Hall of Fame. Won the Grammy's Trustees Award in 1981.

DATE	POS	WKS	ARTIST–RECORD TITLE	LABEL & NO.
2/4/56	**28**	3	1. April In Paris [I] written in 1932; Grammy Hall of Fame Award winner in 1985	Clef 89162

BASIL, Toni

Born in 1950 in Los Angeles. Choreographer/actress/video director. Worked on TV shows "Shindig" and "Hullabaloo." Choreographed the movie *American Graffiti*. Appeared in the movie *Easy Rider* and others.

DATE	POS	WKS	ARTIST–RECORD TITLE	LABEL & NO.
10/9/82	**1** (1)	18	▲ 1. **Mickey** cheering provided by the 1981 Dorsey High School cheerleaders	Chrysalis 2638

BASS, Fontella

Born on 7/3/40 in St. Louis. Soul vocalist/pianist/organist. Mother was a member of Clara Ward Gospel Troupe. Sang in church choirs; with Oliver Sain band, St. Louis; with Little Milton blues show to 1964. Married to trumpet player Lester Bowie.

DATE	POS	WKS	ARTIST–RECORD TITLE	LABEL & NO.
3/27/65	**33**	3	1. Don't Mess Up A Good Thing **FONTELLA BASS & BOBBY McCLURE**	Checker 1097
10/23/65	**4**	10	2. **Rescue Me** #1 R&B hit (4 weeks)	Checker 1120
1/29/66	**37**	1	3. Recovery	Checker 1131

BASSEY, Shirley

Born on 1/8/37 in Cardiff, Wales. Soul songstress. Began professional career at age 16 as a member of the touring show *Memories Of Al Jolson*. Became a popular club attraction in America in 1961.

DATE	POS	WKS	ARTIST–RECORD TITLE	LABEL & NO.
2/27/65	**8**	8	1. **Goldfinger** John Barry (orch.)	United Art. 790

BAXTER, Les

Born on 3/14/22 in Mexia, Texas. Died on 1/15/96. Orchestra leader/arranger. Began as a conductor on radio shows in the 1930s. Member of Mel Torme's vocal group, the Mel-Tones. Musical arranger for Capitol Records (Nat King Cole, Margaret Whiting and others) in the 1950s. Composed over 100 movie scores.

DATE	POS	WKS	ARTIST–RECORD TITLE	LABEL & NO.
4/9/55	**1** (2)	21	1. **Unchained Melody/** Jockey #1 / Best Seller #2 / Juke Box #3; from the movie *Unchained* starring football star Elroy "Crazylegs" Hirsch	
		1	2. Medic [I] Best Seller flip; theme from the TV series "Medic" starring Richard Boone; song better known as "Blue Star"	Capitol 3055
8/13/55	**5**	12	3. **Wake The Town And Tell The People** Jockey #5 / Juke Box #8 / Best Seller #10 / Top 100 #24 pre; The Notables (vocals)	Capitol 3120
2/18/56	**1** (6)	20	● 4. **The Poor People Of Paris** [I] Top 100 #1(6) / Jockey #1(6) / Best Seller #1(4) / Juke Box #1(3); French song written in 1954 as "Le Goualante De Pauvre Jean"	Capitol 3336

DATE	POS	WKS	ARTIST–RECORD TITLE	LABEL & NO.
			BAY CITY ROLLERS	
			Rock group formed in 1967 in Edinburgh, Scotland, as the Saxons. Original members: brothers Alan and Derek Longmuir, Les McKeoun (lead singer), Eric Faulkner and Stuart "Woody" Wood.	
11/8/75+	**1** (1)	12	● 1. **Saturday Night**	Arista 0149
2/14/76	**9**	11	2. **Money Honey**	Arista 0170
5/22/76	**28**	4	3. Rock And Roll Love Letter	Arista 0185
9/18/76	**12**	12	4. I Only Want To Be With You	Arista 0205
6/25/77	**10**	12	5. **You Made Me Believe In Magic**	Arista 0256
11/19/77+	**24**	9	6. The Way I Feel Tonight	Arista 0272
			BAZUKA	
			Instrumental studio group assembled by producer Tony Camillo, who was earlier with Cecil Holmes Soulful Sounds.	
6/7/75	**10**	11	1. **Dynomite-Part I** [I]	A&M 1666
			Tony Camillo's BAZUKA	
			song inspired by phrase used on TV series *Good Times* by J.J. Walker	
			B. BUMBLE & THE STINGERS	
			Los Angeles sessionmen Plas Johnson, Rene Hall, Earl Palmer and Al Hassan comprised recording group with Ernie Freeman (B. Bumble) playing piano on first two recordings and pianist Lincoln Mayorga on "Nut Rocker." Pianist R.C. Gamble toured as B. Bumble.	
4/24/61	**21**	5	1. Bumble Boogie [I]	Rendezvous 140
			adaptation of Rimsky-Korsakov's *Flight Of The Bumble Bee*; #7 hit for Freddy Martin in 1946	
3/31/62	**23**	7	2. Nut Rocker [I]	Rendezvous 166
			adapted from Tchaikovsky's *The Nutcracker* ballet	
			BEACH BOYS, The	
			Group formed in Hawthorne, California, in 1961. Consisted of brothers Brian Wilson (keyboards, bass), Carl Wilson (guitar) and Dennis Wilson (drums); their cousin Mike Love (lead vocals, saxophone; formed the group Celebration in 1978), and Al Jardine (guitar). Known in high school as Kenny & The Cadets, Carl & The Passions, then The Pendletones. First recorded for X/Candix in 1961. Jardine replaced by David Marks from March 1962 to March 1963. Brian quit touring with group in December 1964, replaced briefly by Glen Campbell until Bruce Johnston (of Bruce & Terry) joined permanently in April 1965. Johnston and Campbell also recorded in the studio band Sagittarius in 1967. Brian continued to write for and produce group, returned to stage in 1983. Daryl Dragon (of Captain & Tennille) was a keyboardist in their stage band. Dennis Wilson drowned on 12/28/83 (age 39). Lineup of Carl, Brian, Mike, Alan and Bruce continues to perform today. Carnie and Wendy Wilson, daughters of Brian Wilson, are members of Wilson Phillips. Group was inducted into the Rock and Roll Hall of Fame in 1988.	
9/15/62	**14**	10	1. Surfin' Safari	Capitol 4777
4/13/63	**3**	13	2. **Surfin' U.S.A.**/	
			also see #28 below	
5/25/63	**23**	8	3. Shut Down	Capitol 4932
8/17/63	**7**	11	4. **Surfer Girl**/	
9/7/63	**15**	7	5. Little Deuce Coupe	Capitol 5009
11/23/63	**6**	8	6. **Be True To Your School**/	
			featuring cheerleading by The Honeys, and the march "On Wisconsin"	

DATE	POS	WKS		ARTIST–RECORD TITLE	LABEL & NO.
11/30/63	**23**	6		7. In My Room	Capitol 5069
2/22/64	**5**	9		8. **Fun, Fun, Fun**	Capitol 5118
6/6/64	**1 (2)**	13	●	9. **I Get Around/**	
6/27/64	**24**	6		10. Don't Worry Baby	Capitol 5174
9/19/64	**9**	8		11. **When I Grow Up (To Be A Man)**	Capitol 5245
11/21/64	**8**	8		12. **Dance, Dance, Dance**	Capitol 5306
3/13/65	**12**	6		13. Do You Wanna Dance?	Capitol 5372
5/1/65	**1 (2)**	11		14. **Help Me, Rhonda**	Capitol 5395
				above 4 from the album The Beach Boys Today!	
8/7/65	**3**	9		15. **California Girls**	Capitol 5464
12/11/65+	**20**	5		16. The Little Girl I Once Knew	Capitol 5540
1/15/66	**2 (2)**	9		17. **Barbara Ann**	Capitol 5561
				Dean Torrence (of Jan & Dean; vocals)	
4/9/66	**3**	10		18. **Sloop John B**	Capitol 5602
				originally a folk song originating from the West Indies in 1927	
4/23/66	**32**	3		19. Caroline, No	Capitol 5610
				BRIAN WILSON	
8/20/66	**8**	7		20. **Wouldn't It Be Nice/**	
9/17/66	**39**	2		21. God Only Knows	Capitol 5706
				above 4 from the album Pet Sounds	
10/29/66	**1 (1)**	12	●	22. **Good Vibrations**	Capitol 5676
8/12/67	**12**	5		23. Heroes And Villains	Brother 1001
11/18/67	**31**	4		24. Wild Honey	Capitol 2028
1/13/68	**19**	6		25. Darlin'	Capitol 2068
8/17/68	**20**	7		26. Do It Again	Capitol 2239
4/5/69	**24**	6		27. I Can Hear Music	Capitol 2432
9/28/74	**36**	1		28. Surfin' U.S.A. [R]	Capitol 3924
				song now credited as written by Chuck Berry ("Sweet Little Sixteen")	
6/19/76	**5**	13		29. **Rock And Roll Music**	Brother 1354
9/18/76	**29**	4		30. It's O.K.	Brother 1368
6/9/79	**40**	1		31. Good Timin'	Caribou 9029
8/15/81	**12**	11		32. The Beach Boys Medley	Capitol 5030
				Good Vibrations/Help Me, Rhonda/I Get Around/Shut Down/Surfin' Safari/Barbara Ann/Survin' USA/Fun, Fun, Fun; B-side is a reissue of the group's 1966 hit "God Only Knows"	
12/19/81+	**18**	8		33. Come Go With Me	Caribou 02633
6/8/85	**26**	7		34. Getcha Back	Caribou 04913
				Airplay #24 / Sales #29	
8/8/87	**12**	11		35. Wipeout	Tin Pan 885960
				FAT BOYS (with The Beach Boys)	
				Sales #4 / Airplay #20	
9/24/88	**1 (1)**	15	▲	36. **Kokomo**	Elektra 69385
				Airplay #1(2) / Sales #1(1); from the movie Cocktail starring Tom Cruise; B-side is the original version of "Tutti Frutti" by Little Richard	

DATE	POS	WKS	ARTIST—RECORD TITLE	LABEL & NO.

BEASTIE BOYS

New York white rap trio formed in 1981. Consists of King Ad-Rock (Adam Horovitz, son of playwright Israel Horovitz), MCA (Adam Yauch) and Mike D (Michael Diamond). Horovitz starred in the movie *Lost Angels* and married actress Ione Skye (daughter of Donovan). Their DJ, Doctor Dre, became co-host of "Yo! MTV Raps." Beastie stands for Boys Entering Anarchistic States Towards Internal Excellence.

DATE	POS	WKS	ARTIST—RECORD TITLE	LABEL & NO.
1/24/87	7	10	1. **(You Gotta) Fight For Your Right (To Party)!** Sales #4 / Airplay #9	Def Jam 06595
8/26/89	36	2	2. Hey Ladies Sales #25	Capitol 44454

BEATLES, The

The world's #1 rock group was formed in Liverpool, England, in the late 1950s. Known in early forms as The Quarrymen, Johnny & the Moondogs, The Rainbows, and the Silver Beatles. Named The Beatles in 1960. Originally consisted of John Lennon, Paul McCartney, George Harrison (guitars), Stu Sutcliffe (bass) and Pete Best (drums). Sutcliffe left in April 1961 (died on 4/10/62 of a brain hemorrhage); McCartney moved to bass. Best replaced by Ringo Starr in August 1962. Group managed by Brian Epstein (died on 8/27/67 of sleeping-pill overdose) and produced by George Martin. First U.S. tour in February 1964. Won the 1964 Best New Artist Grammy Award. Group starred in the movies *A Hard Day's Night* (1964), *Help* (1965), *Magical Mystery Tour* (1967) and *Let It Be* (1970); contributed soundtrack to the animated movie *Yellow Submarine* (1968). Own Apple label in 1968. McCartney publicly announced group's dissolution on 4/10/70. Won the Grammy's Trustees Award in 1972. Lennon was shot to death on 12/8/80. Inducted into the Rock and Roll Hall of Fame in 1988.

DATE	POS	WKS	ARTIST—RECORD TITLE	LABEL & NO.
1/25/64	1 (7)	14	● 1. **I Want To Hold Your Hand/**	
1/25/64	14	8	2. I Saw Her Standing There	Capitol 5112
2/1/64	1 (2)	14	3. **She Loves You**	Swan 4152
2/22/64	3	10	4. **Please Please Me** recorded November 1962	Vee-Jay 581
3/7/64	26	2	5. My Bonnie (My Bonnie Lies Over The Ocean) **THE BEATLES with TONY SHERIDAN**	MGM 13213
3/21/64	2 (4)	9	6. **Twist And Shout** song first recorded by the Top Notes in 1961 (Atlantic 2115)	Tollie 9001
3/28/64	1 (5)	9	● 7. **Can't Buy Me Love**	Capitol 5150
4/11/64	2 (1)	9	8. **Do You Want To Know A Secret/**	
4/25/64	35	3	9. Thank You Girl	Vee-Jay 587
5/2/64	1 (1)	11	10. **Love Me Do/**	
5/16/64	10	7	11. **P.S. I Love You** above 2 recorded September 1962 (with Andy White on drums, Ringo on tambourine); #2, 4, 6, 8, 10, 11 from the album *Introducing...The Beatles*	Tollie 9008
7/18/64	1 (2)	12	● 12. **A Hard Day's Night**	Capitol 5222
8/1/64	19	7	13. Ain't She Sweet recorded May 1961 (Pete Best, Lennon, McCartney, Harrison); #1 hit for Ben Bernie in 1927	Atco 6308
8/8/64	12	7	14. And I Love Her	Capitol 5235
8/15/64	25	5	15. I'll Cry Instead #12, 14, 15: from the movie *A Hard Day's Night*	Capitol 5234
9/19/64	17	5	16. Matchbox/ written by Carl Perkins	
9/26/64	25	4	17. Slow Down written by Larry Williams; above 4 from the album *Something New*	Capitol 5255

DATE	POS	WKS	ARTIST–RECORD TITLE	LABEL & NO.
12/5/64	**1** (3)	11	● 18. **I Feel Fine/**	
12/12/64	**4**	8	19. **She's A Woman**	Capitol 5327
2/27/65	**1** (2)	9	● 20. **Eight Days A Week/**	
3/20/65	**39**	1	21. I Don't Want To Spoil The Party	Capitol 5371
5/1/65	**1** (1)	9	22. **Ticket To Ride**	Capitol 5407
8/14/65	**1** (3)	12	● 23. **Help!**	Capitol 5476
			above 2 from the movie *Help* (originally *Eight Arms to Hold You*)	
10/2/65	**1** (4)	9	● 24. **Yesterday**	Capitol 5498
			there have been more than 2500 recorded versions of this song; the first 5-million performance song (25,000 hours of U.S. radio and TV play)	
12/18/65+	**1** (3)	11	● 25. **We Can Work It Out/**	
12/25/65+	**5**	8	26. **Day Tripper**	Capitol 5555
3/5/66	**3**	9	● 27. **Nowhere Man**	Capitol 5587
6/11/66	**1** (2)	10	● 28. **Paperback Writer/**	
6/25/66	**23**	5	29. Rain	Capitol 5651
8/27/66	**2** (1)	8	● 30. **Yellow Submarine/**	
			title song of The Beatles' animated movie, released in 1968	
9/10/66	**11**	6	31. Eleanor Rigby	Capitol 5715
3/4/67	**1** (1)	9	● 32. **Penny Lane/**	
3/11/67	**8**	7	33. **Strawberry Fields Forever**	Capitol 5810
7/29/67	**1** (1)	9	● 34. **All You Need Is Love/**	
8/12/67	**34**	2	35. Baby You're A Rich Man	Capitol 5964
12/9/67	**1** (3)	10	● 36. **Hello Goodbye**	Capitol 2056
3/23/68	**4**	10	● 37. **Lady Madonna**	Capitol 2138
9/14/68	**1** (9)	19	● 38. **Hey Jude/**	
9/14/68	**12**	11	39. Revolution	Apple 2276
5/10/69	**1** (5)	12	● 40. **Get Back/**	
5/10/69	**35**	3	41. Don't Let Me Down	Apple 2490
			THE BEATLES with Billy Preston (above 2)	
6/21/69	**8**	8	● 42. **The Ballad Of John And Yoko**	Apple 2531
			#28, 29, 37, 38, 39, 41, 42 from the album *Hey Jude*	
10/18/69	**1** (1)	16	● 43. **Come Together/**	
10/18/69	**3**	16	● 44. **Something**	Apple 2654
3/21/70	**1** (2)	13	● 45. **Let It Be**	Apple 2764
			#1 Adult Contemporary hit (4 weeks)	
5/23/70	**1** (2)	10	46. **The Long And Winding Road/**	
		10	47. For You Blue	Apple 2832
			above 3 songs from The Beatles' documentary movie *Let It Be*; above 3 from the album *Let It Be* (also #40 above)	
6/19/76	**7**	11	48. **Got To Get You Into My Life**	Capitol 4274
			from the 1966 album *Revolver*	
4/10/82	**12**	8	49. The Beatles' Movie Medley	Capitol 5107
			Magical Mystery Tour/All You Need Is Love/You've Got To Hide Your Love Away/I Should Have Known Better/A Hard Day's Night/Ticket To Ride/Get Back	
8/30/86	**23**	7	50. Twist And Shout [R]	Capitol 5624
			revived through inclusion in movies *Ferris Bueller's Day Off* and *Back to School*	
12/30/95+	**6**	4	51. **Free As A Bird**	Apple 58497
			Sales #5 / Airplay #60; original demo recorded by John Lennon in 1977, with new vocals and instrumentation by the other Beatles; produced by Jeff Lynne	

DATE	POS	WKS	ARTIST—RECORD TITLE	LABEL & NO.
			BEAU, Toby—see TOBY	
			BEAU BRUMMELS, The	
			Rock group formed in 1964 in San Francisco. Led by Sal Valentino (born Sal Spaminato on 9/8/42, San Francisco; vocals) and Ron Elliott (born 10/21/43, Haddsburg, California; guitar).	
1/30/65	15	8	1. Laugh, Laugh	Autumn 8
5/8/65	8	9	2. **Just A Little**	Autumn 10
8/28/65	38	1	3. You Tell Me Why	Autumn 16
			BECK	
			Born Beck Hansen on 7/8/70 near Kansas City; raised in Los Angeles. Male singer/songwriter/guitarist.	
3/5/94	10	15	● 1. **Loser**	DGC 19270
			Sales #3 / Airplay #31; samples "I Walk On Guilded Splinters" by Dr. John	
			BECK, Jeff—see DONOVAN	
			BECKHAM, Bob	
			Born on 7/8/27 in Stratford, Oklahoma. Pop-country singer. Moved to Nashville in 1959.	
10/12/59	32	10	1. Just As Much As Ever	Decca 30861
2/29/60	36	1	2. Crazy Arms	Decca 31029
			BEE GEES	
			Trio of brothers from Manchester, England: Barry Gibb (born 9/1/47) and twins Maurice and Robin Gibb (born 12/22/49). First performed December 1955. To Australia in 1958, performed as The Gibbs, later as BG's, finally The Bee Gees. First recorded for Leedon/Festival in 1963. Returned to England in February 1967, with guitarist Vince Melouney and drummer Colin Peterson. Toured Europe and the U.S. in 1968. Melouney left in December 1968; Robin left for solo career in 1969. When Peterson left in August 1969, Barry and Maurice went solo. After eight months, the brothers reunited. Composed soundtracks for *Saturday Night Fever* and *Staying Alive*. Acted in the movie *Sgt. Pepper's Lonely Hearts Club Band*. Youngest brother Andy Gibb was a successful solo singer (died 3/10/88).	
6/10/67	14	4	1. New York Mining Disaster 1941 (Have You Seen My Wife, Mr. Jones)	Atco 6487
7/29/67	17	7	2. To Love Somebody	Atco 6503
10/21/67	16	5	3. Holiday	Atco 6521
11/25/67	11	6	4. (The Lights Went Out In) Massachusetts	Atco 6532
2/10/68	15	8	5. Words	Atco 6548
			"live" version is on the B-side of #20 below	
9/7/68	8	10	6. **I've Gotta Get A Message To You**	Atco 6603
1/4/69	6	9	7. **I Started A Joke**	Atco 6639
4/12/69	37	3	8. First Of May	Atco 6657
12/26/70+	3	10	● 9. **Lonely Days**	Atco 6795
7/3/71	1 (4)	14	● 10. **How Can You Mend A Broken Heart**	Atco 6824
2/5/72	16	7	11. My World	Atco 6871
8/26/72	16	7	12. Run To Me	Atco 6896
12/2/72	34	4	13. Alive	Atco 6909

DATE	POS	WKS	ARTIST–RECORD TITLE	LABEL & NO.
6/28/75	**1 (2)**	12	● 14. **Jive Talkin'**	RSO 510
10/18/75	**7**	13	15. **Nights On Broadway**	RSO 515
1/17/76	**12**	12	16. Fanny (Be Tender With My Love)	RSO 519
7/17/76	**1 (1)**	12	● 17. **You Should Be Dancing**	RSO 853
10/2/76	**3**	16	● 18. **Love So Right**	RSO 859
1/29/77	**12**	9	19. **Boogie Child**	RSO 867
8/13/77	**26**	5	20. Edge Of The Universe	RSO 880
			"live" recording; studio version is on the B-side of #15 above	
10/8/77	**1 (3)**	26	● 21. **How Deep Is Your Love**	RSO 882
			#1 Adult Contemporary hit (6 weeks)	
12/24/77+	**1 (4)**	22	▲ 22. **Stayin' Alive**	RSO 885
			also on the B-side of #28 below; B-side is Bee Gees' original version of Yvonne Elliman's hit "If I Can't Have You"	
2/11/78	**1 (8)**	18	▲ 23. **Night Fever**	RSO 889
			above 3 from the album and movie Saturday Night Fever starring John Travolta	
11/18/78+	**1 (2)**	17	▲ 24. **Too Much Heaven**	RSO 913
2/10/79	**1 (2)**	13	▲ 25. **Tragedy**	RSO 918
4/21/79	**1 (1)**	13	● 26. **Love You Inside Out**	RSO 925
10/10/81	**30**	4	27. He's A Liar	RSO 1066
5/28/83	**24**	6	28. The Woman In You	RSO 813173
			from the movie Staying Alive starring John Travolta	
8/12/89	**7**	10	29. **One**	Warner 22899
			Sales #8 / Airplay #9; #1 Adult Contemporary hit (2 weeks)	

BEGINNING OF THE END, The

Bahamas quartet consisting of brothers Raphael "Ray" (organ), Liroy "Roy" (guitar) and Frank "Bud" Munnings (drums), with Fred Henfield (bass).

DATE	POS	WKS	ARTIST–RECORD TITLE	LABEL & NO.
6/5/71	**15**	10	1. Funky Nassau-Part I	Alston 4595

BELAFONTE, Harry

Born Harold George Belafonte, Jr., on 3/1/27 in Harlem to a Jamaican mother and a West Indian father. Actor in American Negro Theater, Drama Workshop, mid-1940s. Started career as a "straight pop" singer. Recorded for Jubilee Records in 1949, shortly afterward began specializing in folk music. Rode the crest of the calypso craze to worldwide stardom. Starred in eight movies from 1953 to 1974. Replaced Danny Kaye in 1987 as UNICEF goodwill ambassador. Father of actress Shari Belafonte.

DATE	POS	WKS	ARTIST–RECORD TITLE	LABEL & NO.
11/24/56+	**14**	16	1. Jamaica Farewell	RCA 6663
			Jockey #14 / Best Seller #17 / Top 100 #17 / Juke Box #17; adaptation of a West Indian folk song	
12/29/56	**12**	3	2. Mary's Boy Child [X]	RCA 6735
			Best Seller #12 / Jockey #12 / Top 100 #15; William Lorin (orch., above 2)	
1/12/57	**5**	17	● 3. **Banana Boat (Day-O)**	RCA 6771
			Best Seller #5 / Top 100 #5 / Jockey #5 / Juke Box #5; Tony Scott (orch. and chorus); based on a Jamaican folk song brought to the U.S. in the late 1940s	
3/23/57	**11**	10	4. Mama Look At Bubu	RCA 6830
			Best Seller #11 / Top 100 #13 / Jockey #14 / Juke Box #18	
7/8/57	**25**	3	5. Cocoanut Woman/	
			Best Seller #25 / Top 100 #48	
7/8/57	**30**	3	6. Island In The Sun	RCA 6885
			Best Seller #30 / Top 100 #42; title song from the movie starring Belafonte; Bob Corman (orch., above 3)	

DATE	POS	WKS	ARTIST—RECORD TITLE	LABEL & NO.
			### BELL, Archie, & The Drells	
			Bell was born on 9/1/44 in Henderson, Texas. Lead singer of the Drells, R&B vocal group from Leo Smith Junior High School in Houston. First recorded for Ovid in 1967. Recorded "Tighten Up" with group consisting of Bell, Huey "Billy" Butler, Joe Cross and James Wise. Bell was in U.S. Army at time of hit. Later recordings consisted of Bell, Wise, Lee Bell and Willie Parnell. Still active in "beach music" scene.	
4/13/68	**1** (2)	13	● 1. **Tighten Up** #1 R&B hit (2 weeks)	Atlantic 2478
8/3/68	**9**	8	2. **I Can't Stop Dancing**	Atlantic 2534
1/4/69	**21**	8	3. There's Gonna Be A Showdown	Atlantic 2583
			### BELL, Benny	
			Jewish risque singer/songwriter from Brooklyn. Real name: Ben Samberg. Revived popularity due to exposure on radio's Dr. Demento program.	
4/19/75	**30**	4	1. Shaving Cream [N] Paul Wynn (vocal); originally released on the Cocktail Party Songs label in 1946	Vanguard 35183
			### BELL, Madeline	
			In cast of *Black Nativity*; toured England in the mid-1960s and remained there. Formed group Blue Mink, 1969–73. Commercial jingle singer since then.	
3/9/68	**26**	5	1. I'm Gonna Make You Love Me	Philips 40517
			### BELL, Vincent	
			Born Vincent Gambella on 7/28/35 in Brooklyn. Veteran studio guitarist. Formerly with the East Coast vocal group The Gallahads. His "water sound" guitar was featured in Ferrante & Teicher's hit "Midnight Cowboy." Not to be confused with Vincent Lee Bell of The Ramrods.	
4/25/70	**31**	5	1. Airport Love Theme (Gwen And Vern) [I] from the movie *Airport* starring Burt Lancaster	Decca 32659
			### BELL, William	
			Born William Yarborough on 7/16/39 in Memphis. R&B singer.	
3/12/77	**10**	9	● 1. **Tryin' To Love Two** #1 R&B hit (1 week)	Mercury 73839
			### BELLAMY BROTHERS	
			Country duo from Darby, Florida: brothers Howard (born 2/2/46; guitar) and David Bellamy (born 9/16/50; guitar, keyboards). Made their professional debut in 1958. David wrote "Spiders And Snakes" hit for Jim Stafford. Moved to Los Angeles in 1973.	
3/6/76	**1** (1)	12	1. **Let Your Love Flow**	Warner/Curb 8169
7/14/79	**39**	2	2. If I Said You Have A Beautiful Body Would You Hold It Against Me #1 Country hit (3 weeks)	Warner/Curb 8790
			### BELL & JAMES	
			R&B duo of Leroy Bell and Casey James. Began as songwriting team for Bell's uncle, producer Thom Bell.	
3/10/79	**15**	8	● 1. Livin' It Up (Friday Night)	A&M 2069

DATE	POS	WKS	ARTIST–RECORD TITLE	LABEL & NO.
			BELL BIV DeVOE	
			Trio of New Edition members: Ricky Bell, Michael Bivins and Ronnie DeVoe. Bivins produced Another Bad Creation, Boyz II Men and M.C. Brains, formed own record label, Biv 10, and assembled East Coast Family.	
4/14/90	**3**	17	▲ 1. **Poison**	MCA 53772
			Sales #1(3) / Airplay #3; #1 R&B hit (2 weeks)	
7/21/90	**3**	16	2. **Do Me!**	MCA 79045
			Sales #1(1) / Airplay #4	
11/10/90	**26**	5	3. **B.B.D. (I Thought It Was Me)?**	MCA 53897
			Sales #18 / Airplay #39; #1 R&B hit (1 week)	
5/30/92	**10**	18	4. **The Best Things In Life Are Free**	Perspective 0010
			LUTHER VANDROSS and JANET JACKSON with BBD and Ralph Tresvant	
			Airplay #5 / Sales #16; from the movie *Mo' Money* starring Damon and Marlon Wayans; #1 R&B hit (1 week)	
11/28/92+	**21**	8	5. **Gangsta**	MCA 54555
			Sales #10 / Airplay #29	
10/9/93	**38**	2	6. **Something In Your Eyes**	MCA 54725
			Sales #26 / Airplay #54	
			BELLE, Regina—see BRYSON, Peabo	
			BELLE STARS, The	
			English female band formed as The Bodysnatchers in 1981. Changed name to The Belle Stars in 1983. Features Jennie McKeown (vocals) and Sarah-Jane Owen (guitar).	
4/1/89	**14**	10	1. **Iko Iko**	Capitol 44343
			Sales #6 / Airplay #18; from the movie *Rain Man* starring Dustin Hoffman and Tom Cruise; earlier version featured on their 1983 album *The Belle Stars*	
			BELL NOTES, The	
			Quintet from Long Island, New York: Carl Bonura (sax), Ray Ceroni (guitar), Lenny Giamblavo (bass), Peter Kane (piano) and John Casey (drums).	
2/9/59	**6**	11	1. **I've Had It**	Time 1004
			BELLS, The	
			Canadian pop quintet. Jacki Ralph and Cliff Edwards, lead singers.	
3/27/71	**7**	11	● 1. **Stay Awhile**	Polydor 15023
			BELLUS, Tony	
			Born Anthony Bellusci on 4/17/36 in Chicago. Pop singer/accordionist. First recorded for Shi-Fi in 1958.	
6/29/59	**25**	11	1. **Robbin' The Cradle**	NRC 023
			BELMONTS, The	
			Angelo D'Aleo, Fred Milano and Carlo Mastrangelo. Sang with Dion, 1957–60. Named after Belmont Avenue in the Bronx. Frank Lyndon replaced Mastrangelo in May 1962.	
6/19/61	**18**	6	1. **Tell Me Why**	Sabrina 500
			first released on Surprise 1000 in 1961	
8/25/62	**28**	8	2. **Come On Little Angel**	Sabina 505

DATE	POS	WKS	ARTIST–RECORD TITLE	LABEL & NO.
			BELVIN, Jesse	
			Born Jessie Lorenzo Belvin on 12/15/32 in San Antonio, Texas. Jesse and his wife were killed in an auto accident on 2/6/60. Recorded with Marvin Phillips as "Jesse & Marvin." A pivotal figure in the development of the R&B sound on the West Coast. Co-wrote "Earth Angel" with Curtis Williams of The Penguins. Also see The Shields.	
4/13/59	31	9	1. Guess Who written by Jesse's wife, Jo Anne Belvin; Shorty Rogers (orch. and chorus)	RCA 7469
			BENATAR, Pat	
			Born Patricia Andrzejewski on 1/10/53 in Lindenhurst, Long Island, New York. Rock singer. Married her producer/guitarist Neil Giraldo on 2/20/82. Acted in the movie *Union City* and the 1989 ABC afterschool TV special "Torn Between Two Fathers."	
2/9/80	23	10	1. Heartbreaker	Chrysalis 2395
5/17/80	27	6	2. We Live For Love	Chrysalis 2419
10/18/80	9	15	● 3. **Hit Me With Your Best Shot**	Chrysalis 2464
1/31/81	18	10	4. Treat Me Right	Chrysalis 2487
8/1/81	17	9	5. Fire And Ice	Chrysalis 2529
10/31/81	38	2	6. Promises In The Dark	Chrysalis 2555
11/6/82	13	10	7. Shadows Of The Night	Chrysalis 2647
3/5/83	20	7	8. Little Too Late	Chrysalis 03536
5/21/83	39	3	9. Looking For A Stranger	Chrysalis 42688
10/15/83	5	14	● 10. **Love Is A Battlefield**	Chrysalis 42732
11/3/84+	5	14	11. **We Belong** Airplay #2 / Sales #3	Chrysalis 42826
2/9/85	36	3	12. Ooh Ooh Song	Chrysalis 42843
7/27/85	10	11	13. **Invincible** Sales #9 / Airplay #9; theme from the movie *Legend of Billie Jean* starring Helen Slater	Chrysalis 42877
12/14/85+	28	7	14. Sex As A Weapon Airplay #28	Chrysalis 42927
7/30/88	19	8	15. All Fired Up Sales #11 / Airplay #30	Chrysalis 43268
			BENNETT, Boyd, And His Rockets	
			Bennett was born in Muscle Shoals, Alabama, on 12/7/24. Attended high school in Tennessee; formed first band there. Later became a DJ in Kentucky.	
7/9/55	5	17	1. **Seventeen** Best Seller #5 / Juke Box #8 / Jockey #9 / Top 100 #28 pre	King 1470
11/12/55	39	1	2. My Boy-Flat Top Big Moe (vocal, above 2)	King 1494
			BENNETT, Joe, and The Sparkletones	
			Teenage band from Spartanburg, South Carolina. Consisted of Joe Bennett (vocals, guitar), Howard Childress (guitar), Wayne Arthur (bass) and Irving Denton (drums).	
9/23/57	17	9	1. Black Slacks Top 100 #17 / Best Seller #18 / Jockey #21	ABC-Para. 9837

DATE	POS	WKS	ARTIST–RECORD TITLE	LABEL & NO.

BENNETT, Tony

Born Anthony Dominick Benedetto on 8/13/26 in Queens, New York. One of the top jazz vocalists of the past 40 years. Worked local clubs while in high school, sang in U.S. Army bands. Breakthrough in 1949 with Bob Hope, who suggested that he change his then-stage name, Joe Bari, to Tony Bennett. Audition record of "Boulevard Of Broken Dreams" earned a Columbia contract in 1950. Appeared in the movie *The Oscar*.

DATE	POS	WKS	ARTIST–RECORD TITLE	LABEL & NO.
5/5/56	**16**	11	1. Can You Find It In Your Heart Best Seller #16 / Juke Box #18 / Top 100 #19 / Jockey #20	Columbia 40667
8/18/56	11	7	2. From The Candy Store On The Corner To The Chapel On The Hill/ Jockey #11 / Top 100 #33; Lois Winter (female vocal)	
10/6/56	**38**	2	3. Happiness Street (Corner Sunshine Square)	Columbia 40726
11/17/56	**18**	4	4. The Autumn Waltz Jockey #18 / Top 100 #41	Columbia 40770
8/12/57	**9**	14	5. **In The Middle Of An Island** Best Seller #9 / Top 100 #9 / Jockey #13	Columbia 40965
11/18/57	**22**	1	6. Ca, C'est L'amour Jockey #22 / Top 100 #96; from the movie *Les Girls* starring Gene Kelly	Columbia 41032
6/30/58	**23**	1	7. Young And Warm And Wonderful Jockey #23 / Best Seller #42 / Top 100 #57	Columbia 41172
9/22/58	**20**	8	8. Firefly Hot 100 #20 / Best Seller #45 end	Columbia 41237
9/29/62	**19**	10	9. I Left My Heart In San Francisco new lyrics to this song written in 1954	Columbia 42332
2/16/63	**14**	10	10. I Wanna Be Around	Columbia 42634
6/1/63	**18**	6	11. The Good Life	Columbia 42779
10/31/64	**33**	6	12. Who Can I Turn To (When Nobody Needs Me) from the Broadway musical *The Roar of the Greasepaint* starring Anthony Newley	Columbia 43141
3/20/65	**34**	4	13. If I Ruled The World from the Broadway musical *Pickwick* starring Harry Secombe; The Will Bronson Chorus (backing vocals)	Columbia 43220

BENSON, George

Born on 3/22/43 in Pittsburgh. R&B-jazz guitarist. Played guitar from age eight. Played in Brother Jack McDuff's trio in 1963. House musician at CTI Records to early '70s. Influenced by Wes Montgomery. Member of Fuse One.

DATE	POS	WKS	ARTIST–RECORD TITLE	LABEL & NO.
7/17/76	**10**	11	1. **This Masquerade** written by Leon Russell	Warner 8209
9/3/77	**24**	7	2. The Greatest Love Of All from the movie *The Greatest* starring Muhammad Ali	Arista 0251
4/22/78	**7**	10	3. **On Broadway** "live" recording	Warner 8542
3/24/79	**18**	8	4. Love Ballad	Warner 8759
8/2/80	**4**	14	5. **Give Me The Night** #1 R&B hit (3 weeks)	Warner 49505
11/21/81+	**5**	16	6. **Turn Your Love Around** #1 R&B hit (1 week)	Warner 49846
8/27/83	**30**	6	7. Lady Love Me (One More Time)	Warner 29563

DATE	POS	WKS	ARTIST—RECORD TITLE	LABEL & NO.
			BENSON, Jo Jo—see SCOTT, Peggy	
			BENTON, Brook	
			Born Benjamin Franklin Peay on 9/19/31 in Camden, South Carolina. Died on 4/9/88 of complications from spinal meningitis. R&B singer/songwriter. In The Camden Jubilee Singers. To New York in 1948, joined Bill Langford's Langfordaires. With Jerusalem Stars in 1951. First recorded under own name for Okeh in 1953. Wrote "Looking Back," "A Lover's Question," "The Stroll," "It's Just A Matter Of Time" and "Endlessly."	
2/9/59	3	14	● 1. **It's Just A Matter Of Time** #1 R&B hit (9 weeks)	Mercury 71394
5/4/59	12	9	2. Endlessly/	
6/8/59	38	1	3. So Close	Mercury 71443
8/3/59	16	9	4. Thank You Pretty Baby #1 R&B hit (4 weeks)	Mercury 71478
10/26/59	6	13	5. **So Many Ways** #1 R&B hit (3 weeks)	Mercury 71512
2/8/60	5	12	● 6. **Baby (You've Got What It Takes)** **DINAH WASHINGTON & BROOK BENTON** #1 R&B hit (10 weeks)	Mercury 71565
5/9/60	37	1	7. The Ties That Bind	Mercury 71566
6/6/60	7	10	8. **A Rockin' Good Way (To Mess Around** **And Fall In Love)** **DINAH WASHINGTON & BROOK BENTON** #1 R&B hit (4 weeks); tune first recorded by The Spaniels in 1958	Mercury 71629
8/22/60	7	13	9. **Kiddio/** #1 R&B hit (9 weeks); tune introduced by Teddy Randazzo in the 1957 movie *Mr. Rock And Roll* starring Alan Freed	
8/29/60	16	10	10. The Same One	Mercury 71652
11/21/60	24	7	11. Fools Rush In (Where Angels Fear To Tread) #3 hit for Glenn Miller in 1940	Mercury 71722
2/27/61	11	9	12. Think Twice/	
3/20/61	28	1	13. For My Baby	Mercury 71774
6/5/61	2 (3)	12	14. **The Boll Weevil Song** [N] adaptation of a traditional American folk song; The Mike Stewart Singers (backing vocals); #1 Adult Contemporary hit (3 weeks)	Mercury 71820
9/4/61	20	4	15. Frankie And Johnny version of mid-19th century traditional folk song	Mercury 71859
12/18/61+	15	5	16. Revenge	Mercury 71903
1/27/62	19	5	17. Shadrack written in 1931 as "Shadrack Meshack, Abednigo"	Mercury 71912
9/15/62	13	6	18. Lie To Me	Mercury 72024
12/8/62+	3	10	19. **Hotel Happiness**	Mercury 72055
4/6/63	28	4	20. I Got What I Wanted	Mercury 72099
7/13/63	22	4	21. My True Confession	Mercury 72135
10/5/63	32	5	22. Two Tickets To Paradise	Mercury 72177
2/15/64	35	3	23. Going Going Gone	Mercury 72230
1/31/70	4	12	● 24. **Rainy Night In Georgia** written by Tony Joe White; #1 R&B hit (1 week)	Cotillion 44057

DATE	POS	WKS	ARTIST—RECORD TITLE	LABEL & NO.
			BERLIN	
			Los Angeles electro-pop group. In 1985 went from a sextet to a trio featuring Terri Nunn (vocals), John Crawford (bass) and Rob Brill (drums). Nunn, who as a teen acted on "Lou Grant" and several other TV shows, left band in 1987 and had an adult contemporary hit with Paul Carrack in 1989, "Romance."	
4/7/84	23	8	1. No More Words also on the B-side of "Crazy For You" by Madonna	Geffen 29360
7/19/86	1 (1)	13	● 2. **Take My Breath Away** Sales #1(1) / Airplay #2; love theme from the movie *Top Gun* starring Tom Cruise	Columbia 05903
			BERNARD, Rod	
			Born on 8/12/40 in Opelousas, Louisiana. R&B singer/guitarist. On local radio since age 10. DJ for KSLO in 1957. First recorded for Carl in 1957. Program director for KVOL-Lafayette, Louisiana, in the '60s.	
3/23/59	20	9	1. This Should Go On Forever first released on JIN 105 in 1958	Argo 5327
			BERNSTEIN, Elmer, and Orchestra	
			Born on 4/4/22 in New York City. Composer/conductor for over 60 movie soundtracks.	
4/7/56	16	9	1. Main Title From "The Man With The Golden Arm" [I] Best Seller #16 / Top 100 #32; title song from the movie starring Frank Sinatra; Shelly Manne (drums)	Decca 29869
			BERRY, Chuck	
			Born Charles Edward Anderson Berry on 10/18/26 in San Jose, California. Grew up in St. Louis. Muddy Waters introduced Chuck to Leonard Chess (Chess Records) in Chicago. First recording, "Maybellene," was an instant success. Appeared in the movie *Rock, Rock, Rock* in 1956, and several others. Won Lifetime Achievement Grammy in 1984. Inducted into the Rock and Roll Hall of Fame in 1986. Movie documentary/concert tribute to Chuck, *Hail! Hail! Rock 'N' Roll*, released in 1987. Acclaimed as one of rock and roll's most influential artists.	
8/20/55	5	11	1. **Maybellene** Best Seller #5 / Juke Box #6 / Jockey #13 / Top 100 #42 pre; Grammy Hall of Fame Award winner in 1988; #1 R&B hit (11 weeks)	Chess 1604
6/30/56	29	1	2. Roll Over Beethoven **CHUCK BERRY and His Combo** (above 2) Grammy Hall of Fame Award winner in 1989	Chess 1626
4/20/57	3	15	3. **School Day** Best Seller #3 / Top 100 #5 / Jockey #6 / Juke Box #7; #1 R&B hit (5 weeks)	Chess 1653
11/11/57	8	13	4. **Rock & Roll Music** Top 100 #8 / Best Seller #9	Chess 1671
2/24/58	2 (3)	11	5. **Sweet Little Sixteen** Best Seller #2 / Top 100 #2 / Jockey #5; #1 R&B hit (3 weeks)	Chess 1683
5/5/58	8	11	6. **Johnny B. Goode** Top 100 #8 / Best Seller #9 / Jockey #16; "live" version is on the B-side of #13 below	Chess 1691
9/15/58	18	5	7. Carol Hot 100 #18 / Best Seller #29	Chess 1700
4/20/59	32	7	8. Almost Grown	Chess 1722
7/13/59	37	1	9. Back In The U.S.A. B-side is the original version of "Memphis, Tennessee"	Chess 1729

DATE	POS	WKS	ARTIST–RECORD TITLE	LABEL & NO.
4/4/64	23	5	10. Nadine (Is It You?)	Chess 1883
6/13/64	10	7	11. **No Particular Place To Go**	Chess 1898
8/22/64	14	5	12. You Never Can Tell	Chess 1906
9/9/72	1 (2)	12	● 13. **My Ding-A-Ling** [N] originally recorded by Berry in 1966 as "My Tambourine"	Chess 2131
1/6/73	27	7	14. Reelin' & Rockin' above 2 recorded "live" in Manchester, England; original version of "Reelin' & Rockin'" was the B-side of "Sweet Little Sixteen"	Chess 2136

BETTER THAN EZRA

Rock trio from Louisiana: Kevin Griffin (vocals, guitar), Tom Drummond (bass) and Cary Bonnecaze (drums).

DATE	POS	WKS	ARTIST–RECORD TITLE	LABEL & NO.
7/1/95	30	11	1. Good Airplay #21 / Sales #40	Elektra 64428

B-52's, The

Formed in 1977 in Athens, Georgia, as a new wave dance band: Cindy Wilson (guitar, vocals) and her brother Ricky Wilson (guitar; died of AIDS on 10/12/85), Kate Pierson (organ, vocals), Fred Schneider (keyboards, vocals) and Keith Strickland (drums; moved to guitar after Ricky's death). Cindy left in 1991, replaced on tour by Julee Cruise. Appeared as The B.C. 52's in the movie *The Flintstones*. B-52 is slang for the bouffant hairstyle worn by Kate and Cindy.

DATE	POS	WKS	ARTIST–RECORD TITLE	LABEL & NO.
9/30/89	3	17	● 1. **Love Shack** Sales #2 / Airplay #6	Reprise 22817
1/20/90	3	13	● 2. **Roam** Airplay #2 / Sales #2	Reprise 22667
5/19/90	30	4	3. Deadbeat Club Airplay #25	Reprise 19938
7/4/92	28	7	4. Good Stuff Airplay #25 / Sales #46	Reprise 18895
6/11/94	33	1	5. (Meet) The Flintstones [N] **THE B.C. 52's** Airplay #32 / Sales #50; from the movie *The Flintstones* starring John Goodman, Elizabeth Perkins, Rick Moranis and Rosie O'Donnell	MCA 54839

BIG AUDIO DYNAMITE II

Mick Jones, leader/guitarist/vocalist of British group Big Audio Dynamite, revives band with all new members. Includes Nick Hawkins (guitar; ex-Sigue Sigue Sputnik), Gary Stonadge (bass) and Chris Kavanagh (drums). Jones was co-founder of The Clash; not to be confused with Mick Jones of Foreigner. By 1994, group simply known as Big Audio.

DATE	POS	WKS	ARTIST–RECORD TITLE	LABEL & NO.
11/2/91	32	4	1. Rush Sales #53 / Airplay #75; borrows organ riff from The Who's "Baba O'Reilly"	Columbia 73987

BIG BOPPER

Born Jiles Perry Richardson on 10/24/30 in Sabine Pass, Texas. DJ at KTRM in Beaumont, Texas. Wrote "Running Bear" for Johnny Preston. Died with Buddy Holly and Ritchie Valens in the 2/3/59 plane crash.

DATE	POS	WKS	ARTIST–RECORD TITLE	LABEL & NO.
8/4/58	6	22	1. **Chantilly Lace** [N] Hot 100 #6 / Best Seller #13 end; first released on "D" 1008 in 1958	Mercury 71343
12/22/58	38	1	2. Big Bopper's Wedding [N]	Mercury 71375

DATE	POS	WKS	ARTIST–RECORD TITLE	LABEL & NO.
			BIG BROTHER AND THE HOLDING COMPANY	
			Rock group formed in San Francisco in 1965. Janis Joplin joined as lead singer in 1966. Other members: Peter Albin (bass), James Gurley (guitar), Sam Andrew (guitar) and David Getz (drums). Sensation at the Monterey Pop Festival in 1967. Disbanded in 1972.	
9/28/68	**12**	8	1. Piece Of My Heart	Columbia 44626
			BIG COUNTRY	
			Pop-rock quartet formed in Dunfermline, Scotland: Stuart Adamson (vocals, guitar), Bruce Watson (guitar), Tony Butler (bass) and Mark Brzezicki (drums).	
11/12/83	**17**	9	1. In A Big Country	Mercury 814467
			BIG MOUNTAIN	
			Multi-cultural reggae band from San Diego: Quino (vocals, rhythm guitar), Jerome Cruz, Manfred Reinke, Gregory Blakney, Lance Rhodes and Lynn Copeland.	
3/19/94	**6**	24	● 1. **Baby, I Love Your Way** Airplay #2 / Sales #12; from the movie *Reality Bites* starring Winona Ryder	RCA 62780
			BILK, Mr. Acker	
			Born Bernard Stanley Bilk on 1/28/29 in Somerset, England. Clarinetist/composer.	
4/7/62	**1** (1)	15	● 1. **Stranger On The Shore** [I] #1 Adult Contemporary hit (7 weeks); title song from the British TV show; originally titled "Jenny"	Atco 6217
			BILLY & LILLIE	
			Vocal duo of Billy Ford (born 3/9/25, Bloomfield, New Jersey) and Lillie Bryant (born 2/14/40, Newburg, New York). Backing group: Billy Ford and the Thunderbirds.	
1/13/58	**9**	10	1. **La Dee Dah** Top 100 #9 / Best Seller #10 / Jockey #23	Swan 4002
1/5/59	**14**	8	2. Lucky Ladybug	Swan 4020
			BILLY & THE BEATERS—see VERA, Billy	
			BILLY JOE & THE CHECKMATES	
			Born Louis Bideu on 3/21/19 in El Paso, Texas. Worked as a comedian. Hosted own local "Lew Bedell Show" in New York. Dubbed himself Billy Joe Hunter in the early 1960s.	
2/17/62	**10**	7	1. **Percolator (Twist)** [I] based on the "perky" tune used in a Maxwell House coffee jingle	Dore 620
			BINGOBOYS	
			Dance trio of DJs from Vienna, Austria: Klaus Biedermann, Paul Pfab and Helmut Wolfgruber. Princessa is a female rapper from New York.	
3/16/91	**25**	6	1. How To Dance **BINGOBOYS Featuring Princessa** Sales #23 / Airplay #31; samples Chic's "Dance, Dance, Dance," Sylvester's "Dance (Disco Heat)" and Art Of Noise/Tom Jones's "Kiss"	Atlantic 87756

DATE	POS	WKS	ARTIST—RECORD TITLE	LABEL & NO.
			BISHOP, Elvin	
			Born on 10/21/42 in Tulsa, Oklahoma. Lead guitarist with The Paul Butterfield Blues Band, 1965-68.	
4/3/76	3	12	● 1. **Fooled Around And Fell In Love** Mickey Thomas (of Starship; lead vocal)	Capricorn 0252
			BISHOP, Stephen	
			Born on 11/14/51 in San Diego. Pop-rock singer/songwriter. Wrote theme for the movie *The China Syndrome*. Cameo role as the "Charming Guy With Guitar" in *National Lampoon's Animal House*.	
1/22/77	22	7	1. Save It For A Rainy Day Eric Clapton (guitar solo); Chaka Khan (background vocal)	ABC 12232
7/23/77	11	15	2. On And On	ABC 12260
10/28/78	32	5	3. Everybody Needs Love	ABC 12406
4/2/83	25	8	4. It Might Be You theme from the movie *Tootsie* starring Dustin Hoffman; #1 Adult Contemporary hit (2 weeks)	Warner 29791
			BIZ MARKIE	
			Born Marcel Hall on 4/8/64 in Harlem. Rapper/actor. Appeared in the movie *The Meteor Man*.	
2/10/90	9	11	▲ 1. **Just A Friend** Sales #5 / Airplay #19	Cold Chillin' 22784
			BLACK('s), Bill, Combo	
			Black was born on 9/17/26 in Memphis; died of a brain tumor on 10/21/65. Bass guitarist. Session work in Memphis; backed Elvis Presley (with Scotty Moore, guitar; D.J. Fontana, drums) on most of his early records. Formed own band in 1959. Labeled "The Untouchable Sound."	
12/21/59+	17	8	● 1. Smokie — Part 2 [I] #1 R&B hit (4 weeks)	Hi 2018
3/21/60	9	11	● 2. **White Silver Sands** [I] #1 R&B hit (4 weeks)	Hi 2021
7/4/60	18	8	● 3. Josephine [I] #3 hit for Wayne King's Orchestra in 1937	Hi 2022
10/3/60	11	9	4. Don't Be Cruel [I] Black played bass on Elvis Presley's original hit	Hi 2026
12/12/60	16	7	5. Blue Tango [I] #1 hit for Leroy Anderson in 1952	Hi 2027
3/6/61	20	4	6. Hearts Of Stone [I]	Hi 2028
6/26/61	25	4	7. Ole Buttermilk Sky [I] written and popularized in 1946 by Hoagy Carmichael	Hi 2036
1/20/62	26	4	8. Twist-Her [I]	Hi 2042
			BLACK, Cilla	
			Born Priscilla White on 5/27/43 in Liverpool, England. Discovered by The Beatles' manager Brian Epstein while she was working as a coat checker/singer at Liverpool's Cavern Club.	
7/25/64	26	4	1. You're My World	Capitol 5196

DATE	POS	WKS	ARTIST–RECORD TITLE	LABEL & NO.
			BLACK, Jeanne	
			Born Gloria Jeanne Black on 10/25/37 in Pomona, California. Appearances on local TV show "Hometown Jamboree." Discovered by Cliffie Stone.	
5/2/60	4	10	● 1. **He'll Have To Stay** answer song to Jim Reeves's "He'll Have To Go"	Capitol 4368
			BLACK BOX	
			Male Italian dance trio of producer Daniele Davoli and musicians Mirko Limoni and Valerio Semplici. Videos feature French model Katrin Quinol as lead singer; however, Martha Wash (The Weather Girls) is the uncredited lead vocalist on all of the group's hits.	
9/1/90	8	12	1. **Everybody Everybody** Sales #5 / Airplay #15	RCA 2628
1/19/91	23	4	2. I Don't Know Anybody Else Sales #15	RCA 2735
4/27/91	8	12	3. **Strike It Up** Airplay #10 / Sales #14	RCA 2794
			BLACKBYRDS, The	
			Soul group founded in 1973 by Donald Byrd (born 12/9/32, Detroit) while teaching jazz at Howard University in Washington, D.C.	
3/15/75	6	12	1. **Walking In Rhythm**	Fantasy 736
4/17/76	19	6	2. Happy Music	Fantasy 762
			BLACK CROWES, The	
			Rock group from Atlanta, led by brothers Chris (vocals) and Rich (guitar) Robinson. Includes Jeff Cease (guitar), Johnny Colt (bass) and Steve Gorman (drums). Cease left in late 1991, replaced by Marc Ford (ox Burning Tree). By 1994, Eddie Harsch (keyboards) joined.	
4/20/91	30	7	1. She Talks To Angels Airplay #28 / Sales #33	Def Amer. 19403
7/20/91	26	6	2. Hard To Handle [R] Airplay #26 / Sales #36; originally charted in 1990 at #45	Def Amer. 19245
			BLACKFOOT	
			Rock band formed in Jacksonville, Florida, in 1971: Rick Medlocke (vocals), Charlie Hargrett (guitar), Greg Walker (bass) and Jakson Spires (drums). Hargrett left in 1983. Ken Hensley (keyboards; ex-Uriah Heep) joined in early 1984.	
8/4/79	26	6	1. Highway Song	Atco 7104
12/22/79	38	4	2. Train, Train	Atco 7207
			BLACK OAK ARKANSAS	
			Southern-rock sextet led by Jim "Dandy" Mangrum (born 3/30/48; vocals). Extensive touring group, named after their hometown.	
1/26/74	25	6	1. Jim Dandy Ruby Starr (background vocal; born Constance Mierzwiak; died 1/14/95 [age 44] of lung and brain cancer in Toledo, Ohio)	Atco 6948

DATE	POS	WKS	ARTIST—RECORD TITLE	LABEL & NO.
			BLACKstreet	
			Hip-hop quartet: Teddy Riley (vocals), Chauncey Hannibal, Levi Little and David Hollister. Riley, a prolific producer (Michael Jackson, Wreckx-N-Effect, Bobby Brown and more) and originator of the "new jack swing" sound, was a member of Guy and Kids At Work. Hollister is the cousin of JoJo and K-Ci Hailey of Jodeci.	

8/13/94	34	2	1. Booti Call
			   Sales #21 / Airplay #71; samples "Atomic Dog" by George
			   Clinton and "Heartbreaker" by Zapp
				Interscope 98255

11/19/94+	7	21	2. **Before I Let You Go** Sales #5 / Airplay #14	Interscope 98211
			BLANCHARD, Jack, & Misty Morgan	
			Husband-and-wife country duo. Both born in Buffalo. Jack (born 5/8/42) plays saxophone and keyboards. Misty (born 5/23/45) plays keyboards. Met and married while working in Florida.	
3/28/70	23	8	1. Tennessee Bird Walk [N] #1 Country hit (2 weeks)	Wayside 010
			BLAND, Billy	
			Born on 4/5/32 in Wilmington, North Carolina. R&B singer; formed group, the Four Bees, in 1954. First recorded solo for Old Town in 1955.	
3/28/60	7	13	1. **Let The Little Girl Dance**	Old Town 1076
			BLAND, Bobby	
			Born Robert Calvin Bland on 1/27/30 in Rosemark, Tennessee. Nicknamed "Blue." Sang in gospel group The Miniatures in Memphis, late '40s. Member of the Beale Streeters, which included Johnny Ace, B.B. King, Rosco Gordon, Earl Forest and Willie Nix in 1949. Driver and valet for B.B. King; appeared in the Johnny Ace Revue, early '50s. First recorded in 1952 for the Modern label.	
1/20/62	28	3	1. Turn On Your Love Light	Duke 344
2/2/63	22	7	2. Call On Me/	
2/9/63	33	5	3. That's The Way Love Is #1 R&B hit (2 weeks)	Duke 360
3/28/64	20	6	4. Ain't Nothing You Can Do	Duke 375
			BLANE, Marcie	
			Born on 5/21/44 in Brooklyn, New York.	
11/10/62	3	13	1. **Bobby's Girl**	Seville 120
			BLESSID UNION OF SOULS	
			Pop vocal group from Cincinnati: Eliot Sloan, Jeff Pence, Eddie Hedges and C.P. Roth.	
3/25/95	8	23	1. **I Believe** Airplay #3 / Sales #14	EMI 58320
9/23/95	29	10	2. Let Me Be The One Airplay #28 / Sales #66	EMI 58443

DATE	POS	WKS	ARTIST–RECORD TITLE	LABEL & NO.

BLEYER, Archie

Born on 6/12/09 in Corona, New York. Died on 3/20/89 of Parkinson's disease. Arranger/music director for the radio and TV show "Arthur Godfrey and His Friends," 1949–54. Founded Cadence Records. Married Chordettes member Janet Ertel in 1954.

DATE	POS	WKS	ARTIST–RECORD TITLE	LABEL & NO.
12/4/54+	17	6	1. The Naughty Lady Of Shady Lane Jockey #17 / Juke Box #20 / Best Seller #26	Cadence 1254

BLIGE, Mary J.

Born in Atlanta and raised in Yonkers, New York. R&B singer.

DATE	POS	WKS	ARTIST–RECORD TITLE	LABEL & NO.
8/1/92	29	6	● 1. You Remind Me Sales #17 / Airplay #37; from the movie *Strictly Business* starring Tommy Davidson; #1 R&B hit (1 week)	Uptown/MCA 54327
9/26/92	7	23	● 2. **Real Love** Airplay #4 / Sales #12; #1 R&B hit (2 weeks)	Uptown/MCA 54455
2/20/93	28	9	3. Sweet Thing Airplay #16 / Sales #43	Uptown/MCA 54586
12/3/94	29	8	4. Be Happy Sales #21 / Airplay #48; samples "You're Too Good To Me" by Curtis Mayfield	Uptown/MCA 54927
4/15/95	22	6	5. I'm Goin' Down Sales #11 / Airplay #22; #70 hit for Rose Royce in 1977	Uptown/MCA 55008
5/13/95	3	13	6. **I'll Be There For You/You're All I Need To Get By** **METHOD MAN featuring Mary J. Blige** Sales #1(1) / Airplay #33; medley of songs written by Ashford & Simpson; Method Man raps to "I'll Be There For You" (#2 R&B hit for Ashford & Simpson in 1989) and Blige sings chorus of "You're All I Need To Get By"; #1 R&B hit (3 weeks)	Def Jam/RAL 1878

BLIND MELON

Male rock band formed in Los Angeles in 1990: Shannon Hoon (vocals), Rogers Stevens and Christopher Thorn (guitars), Brad Smith (bass) and Glen Graham (drums). Stevens, Smith and Graham are from West Point, Mississippi. Hoon died on 10/21/95 (age 28).

DATE	POS	WKS	ARTIST–RECORD TITLE	LABEL & NO.
10/9/93	20	11	1. No Rain Airplay #16 / Sales #66	Capitol 44939

BLONDIE

New York City techno-pop sextet formed in 1975. Consisted of Debbie Harry (lead singer), Chris Stein and Frank Infante (guitars), Jimmy Destri (keyboards), Nigel Harrison (bass) and Clem Burke (drums). Harry had been in the folk-rock group Wind In The Willows. Blondie disbanded in 1983.

DATE	POS	WKS	ARTIST–RECORD TITLE	LABEL & NO.
3/17/79	1 (1)	14	● 1. **Heart Of Glass**	Chrysalis 2295
6/30/79	24	7	2. One Way Or Another	Chrysalis 2336
11/3/79	27	6	3. Dreaming	Chrysalis 2379
3/8/80	1 (6)	19	● 4. **Call Me** theme from the movie *American Gigolo* starring Richard Gere	Chrysalis 2414
6/21/80	39	3	5. Atomic	Chrysalis 2410
11/29/80+	1 (1)	17	● 6. **The Tide Is High**	Chrysalis 2465
2/14/81	1 (2)	14	● 7. **Rapture**	Chrysalis 2485
6/26/82	37	3	8. Island Of Lost Souls all of above produced by Mike Chapman (except #4: Giorgio Moroder)	Chrysalis 2603

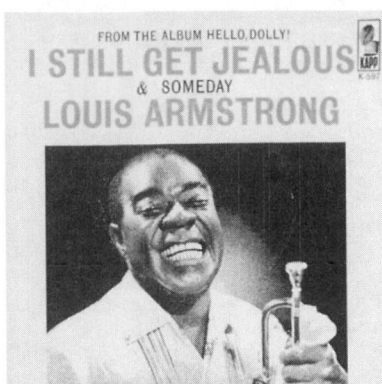

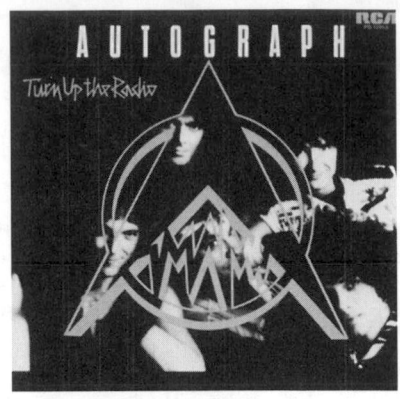

Louis Armstrong's stature as the founding father of jazz by no means hurt his chances on the pop charts. Following his No. 1 pop hit "Hello, Dolly!" was "I Still Get Jealous," which peaked at No. 45 in 1964. His next Top 40 hit? "What A Wonderful World" in 1988.

Rick Astley's triumphant 1988 No. 1 "Together Forever" led many to wonder whether the British songwriting/production team of Stock, Aitken & Waterman might duplicate their overseas success Stateside. For the most part, they didn't.

Autograph's major chart accomplishment? Getting their metal-leaning hard rock played on Top 40 radio. "Turn Up The Radio," which hit No. 29 in 1985, was wisely named: if listeners didn't heed that advice, they'd never hear Autograph again.

Frankie Avalon's second-to-last Top 40 hit "Togetherness" peaked at No. 26 in 1960, though the Philadelphia-born singer's career was by no means over. Along with Annette Funicello, the singer—who'd already starred in films—smoothly began a recurring role in several Beach Party films of the era.

Babyface—real name Kenneth Edmonds—initially rose to prominence partnered with L.A. Reid, though his booming solo career soon made his name alone equally recognizable to most pop fans. His 1990 single "Whip Appeal" was a No. 6 hit.

Anita Baker's classy mixture of soulfulness and balladry won a massive American audience in the late '80s. Her last appearance in the Top 40, "Just Because," climbed into the Top 20 in late '89.

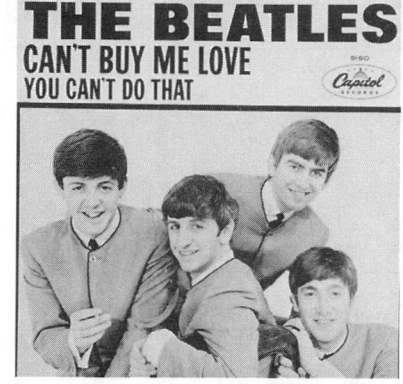

The Beach Boys' fourth Top 10 single, "Fun Fun Fun," would be swiftly followed up with their first-ever No. 1, 1964's certified-gold smash "I Get Around."

The Beatles' third No. 1 single, 1964's "Can't Buy Me Love," as well as its well-known flipside, "You Can't Do That," showed up in alternate-take form on 1995's No. 1 album *Anthology I*.

Pat Benatar dominated the "female rocker" category throughout most of the early '80s, thanks largely to her accessible blend of hard rock and melodicism, displayed ably on her 1983 Top 20 hit "Little Too Late." In 1991 she stunned audiences by recording a straight blues album.

Tony Bennett's signature song, 1962's "I Left My Heart In San Francisco," was outranked chartwise by five other of his hits between 1956 and 1963. Always highly regarded by other singers, Bennett reached a whole new pop audience via his "MTV Unplugged" gig in the mid-'90s.

George Benson's mid-'70s pop success surprised many jazz fans, but longtime fans knew the guitarist had sung early in his career. "Give Me The Night" was his biggest pop hit—reaching No. 4 in 1980, four full years after his multi-platinum album crossover hit, "Breezin'."

Brook Benton enjoyed eight Top 10 hits between 1959 and 1970, of which 1962's "Hotel Happiness" was the seventh. Ironically, the singer's last hit, 1970's "Rainy Night In Georgia," was his first official gold single.

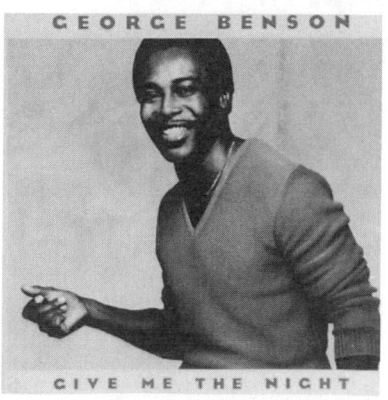

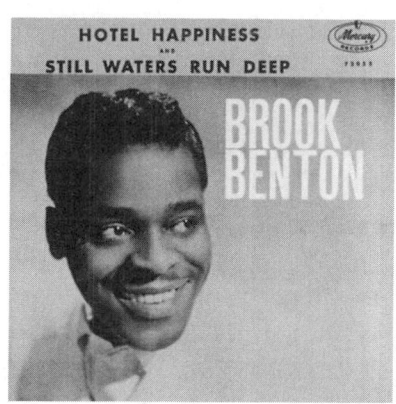

DATE	POS	WKS	ARTIST—RECORD TITLE	LABEL & NO.
			## BLOODROCK	
			Rock group from Fort Worth, Texas. Jim Rutledge, lead vocals. Rutledge headed own production company in the 1970s; produced Meri Wilson's "Telephone Man."	
2/27/71	36	2	1. D.O.A.	Capitol 3009
			## BLOODSTONE	
			Soul group from Kansas City, Missouri. Formed in 1962 as the Sinceres. Consisted of Charles McCormick, Willis Draffen, Charles Love, Henry Williams and Roger Durham (died 1973, age 27).	
6/9/73	10	12	● 1. **Natural High**	London 1046
4/6/74	34	4	2. Outside Woman	London 1052
			## BLOOD, SWEAT & TEARS	
			Pop-jazz group formed by Al Kooper (Royal Teens, Blues Project) in 1968. Nucleus consisted of Kooper (keyboards), Steve Katz (guitar; Blues Project), Bobby Colomby (drums) and Jim Fielder (bass). Kooper replaced by lead singer David Clayton-Thomas in 1969. Clayton-Thomas replaced by Jerry Fisher in 1972. Katz left in 1973. Clayton-Thomas rejoined in 1974. Colomby later worked as a television music reporter and an executive with Epic, Capitol, EMI and CBS.	
3/15/69	2 (3)	11	● 1. **You've Made Me So Very Happy**	Columbia 44776
6/7/69	2 (3)	12	● 2. **Spinning Wheel** #1 Adult Contemporary hit (2 weeks)	Columbia 44871
10/25/69	2 (1)	12	● 3. **And When I Die** written by Laura Nyro	Columbia 45008
8/15/70	14	6	4. Hi-De-Ho	Columbia 45204
10/10/70	29	6	5. Lucretia Mac Evil	Columbia 45235
8/14/71	32	5	6. Go Down Gamblin'	Columbia 45427
			## BLOOM, Bobby	
			Pop singer/songwriter, much session work in the '60s. Died from an accidental shooting on 2/28/74.	
10/17/70	8	11	1. **Montego Bay**	L&R/MGM 157
			## BLOW MONKEYS, The	
			British quartet led by Dr. Robert (Robert Howard). Includes: Mick Anker, Neville Henry and Tony Kiley.	
6/14/86	14	10	1. Digging Your Scene Sales #12 / Airplay #16	RCA 14325
			## BLUE-BELLES, The—see STARLETS, and LaBELLE, Patti	
			## BLUE CHEER	
			San Francisco hard-rock group: Dickie Peterson (vocals, bass), Leigh Stephens (guitar) and Paul Whaley (drums).	
3/23/68	14	10	1. Summertime Blues	Philips 40516

DATE	POS	WKS	ARTIST–RECORD TITLE	LABEL & NO.
			BLUE HAZE	
			British male group.	
12/23/72+	27	7	1. Smoke Gets In Your Eyes	A&M 1357
			#1 hit for Paul Whiteman in 1934 (from the 1933 musical *Roberta* starring Bob Hope)	
			BLUE JAYS, The	
			Los Angeles R&B vocal quartet: Leon Peels (lead), Van Richardson, Alex Manigo and Leonard Davidson.	
9/4/61	31	4	1. Lover's Island	Milestone 2008
			BLUE MAGIC	
			Soul vocal group from Philadelphia. Consisted of Theodore Mills (lead vocals), Vernon Sawyer, Wendell Sawyer, Keith Beaton and Richard Pratt.	
6/8/74	8	15	● 1. **Sideshow**	Atco 6961
			#1 R&B hit (1 week)	
11/23/74	36	2	2. Three Ring Circus	Atco 7004
			BLUE ÖYSTER CULT	
			Hard-rock quintet formed in Long Island, New York, in 1970: Eric Bloom (vocals), Donald "Buck Dharma" Roeser (guitar), Allen Lanier (keyboards) and brothers Joe (bass) and Albert (drums) Bouchard. Rick Downey replaced Albert Bouchard in 1982. Downey left in 1984. Tommy Zvoncheck (keyboards) and Jimmy Wilcox (drums) joined in 1985. Original lineup reunited in 1988.	
9/4/76	12	14	1. (Don't Fear) The Reaper	Columbia 10384
10/3/81	40	3	2. Burnin' For You	Columbia 02415
			BLUE RIDGE RANGERS—see FOGERTY, John	
			BLUES BROTHERS	
			Joliet "Jake" (John Belushi; born 1/24/49, Wheaton, Illinois; died 3/5/82) and Elwood Blues (Dan Aykroyd; born 7/1/52, Ottawa, Ontario); originally created for TV's "Saturday Night Live."	
1/6/79	14	9	1. Soul Man	Atlantic 3545
3/31/79	37	3	2. Rubber Biscuit [N]	Atlantic 3564
			gibberish tune introduced by the Chips in 1956 (Josie 803)	
6/21/80	18	8	3. Gimme Some Lovin'	Atlantic 3666
			from the soundtrack *The Blues Brothers*	
1/31/81	39	2	4. Who's Making Love	Atlantic 3785
			BLUES IMAGE	
			Tampa, Florida, rock quintet led by Mike Pinera, a featured guitarist with Iron Butterfly in 1970.	
5/23/70	4	12	● 1. **Ride Captain Ride**	Atco 6746
			BLUES MAGOOS	
			Bronx, New York, psychedelic rock quintet led by singer/guitarist Peppy Castro (real name: Emil Thielhelm). Originally known as the Bloos Magoos. Castro later became lead singer of Balance.	
1/7/67	5	10	1. (We Ain't Got) Nothin' Yet	Mercury 72622

DATE	POS	WKS	ARTIST–RECORD TITLE	LABEL & NO.
			BLUE STARS	
			Four-man, four-woman, pop-jazz group from Paris, led by Blossom Dearie, former big band vocalist (born 4/28/26, East Durham, New York); sang with King Pleasure on his 1952 R&B hit "Moody Mood For Love."	
2/4/56	**16**	7	1. Lullaby Of Birdland [F]	Mercury 70742
			Jockey #16 / Best Seller #20 / Top 100 #20; arranged by Michel Legrand; composed by George Shearing in 1952	
			BLUE SWEDE	
			Swedish pop sextet. Bjorn Skifs, lead singer.	
3/2/74	**1** (1)	14	● 1. **Hooked On A Feeling**	EMI 3627
			also released on Capitol 3627 in 1974; "oogachuga" arrangement borrowed from Jonathan King's 1971 hit of the same title	
9/7/74	**7**	8	2. **Never My Love**	EMI 3938
			BLUES TRAVELER	
			Blues-rock band from New York City: John Popper (vocals, harmonica), Chan Kinchla (guitar), Bobby Sheehan (bass) and Brendan Hill (drums).	
5/20/95	**8**	36	1. **Run-Around**	A&M 0982
			Airplay #3 / Sales #27	
12/30/95+	**23**	15↑	2. Hook	A&M 1176
			Airplay #18 / Sales #50	
			B.M.U. (BLACK MEN UNITED)	
			All-star gathering of top R&B stars: R. Kelly, Tevin Campbell, Aaron Hall, Brian McKnight, Boyz II Men, Tony Toni Tone, Silk, Keith Sweat, Stokley (Mint Condition), H-Town, Christopher Williams, Portrait, Gerald Levert, Al B. Sure!, Damion Hall, Lil' Joe (Rude Boys), Intro, D.R.S., El DeBarge, After 7, Usher, Sovory, Joe, D'Angelo and Lenny Kravitz (guitar).	
11/5/94	**28**	6	1. U Will Know	Mercury 856200
			Sales #12; from the movie *Jason's Lyric* starring Forest Whitaker	
			BOBBETTES, The	
			Female doo-wop quintet (ages 11–13 in '57) from New York City. Consisted of sisters Emma and Janice Pought, Laura Webb, Helen Gathers and Reather Dixon. Originally called the Harlem Queens.	
8/12/57	**6**	14	1. **Mr. Lee**	Atlantic 1144
			Top 100 #6 / Jockey #6 / Best Seller #7; song inspired by group's 5th grade teacher; #1 R&B hit (4 weeks)	
			BOB B. SOXX And The Blue Jeans	
			Bobby Sheen with Darlene Love and Fanita James (both formerly with The Blossoms). Love and James later replaced by Gloria Jones (also with The Blossoms) and Carolyn Willis.	
12/8/62+	**8**	9	1. **Zip-A-Dee Doo-Dah**	Philles 107
			Academy Award-winning song introduced in the 1947 Disney movie *Song of the South*	
3/23/63	**38**	3	2. Why Do Lovers Break Each Other's Heart?	Philles 110

DATE	POS	WKS	ARTIST–RECORD TITLE	LABEL & NO.
			BOLTON, Michael	
			Born Michael Bolotin on 2/26/54 in New Haven, Connecticut. First recorded for Epic in 1969. Lead singer of Blackjack in the late '70s. Began recording as Michael Bolton in 1983.	
11/7/87	**19**	10	1. That's What Love Is All About Airplay #17 / Sales #18; also on the B-side of #5 & 9 below	Columbia 7322
2/13/88	**11**	10	2. (Sittin' On) The Dock Of The Bay Sales #7 / Airplay #12	Columbia 07680
8/12/89	**17**	7	3. Soul Provider Sales #18 / Airplay #21; also on the B-side of #8 & 13 below	Columbia 68909
11/25/89+	**1 (3)**	16	4. **How Am I Supposed To Live Without You** Airplay #1(2) / Sales #1(1); #1 Adult Contemporary hit (2 weeks)	Columbia 73017
3/17/90	**3**	12	5. **How Can We Be Lovers** Airplay #3 / Sales #4	Columbia 73318
6/9/90	**7**	11	6. **When I'm Back On My Feet Again** Airplay #5 / Sales #14; #1 Adult Contemporary hit (3 weeks)	Columbia 73342
10/6/90	**36**	2	7. Georgia On My Mind Airplay #30 / Sales #39; sax solo by Kenny G on single version, Michael Brecker (of The Brecker Brothers) on album version; tune written in 1930 by Hoagy Carmichael; above 5 from the album *Soul Provider*	Columbia 73490
4/20/91	**4**	13	8. **Love Is A Wonderful Thing** Airplay #2 / Sales #11; a 1994 court ruling found that Bolton took "significant" elements from The Isley Brothers' same-named song of 1966; #1 Adult Contemporary hit (4 weeks)	Columbia 73719
7/27/91	**7**	13	9. **Time, Love And Tenderness** Airplay #15 / Sales #39; #1 Adult Contemporary hit (2 weeks)	Columbia 73889
10/19/91	**1 (1)**	16	10. **When A Man Loves A Woman** Airplay #1(3) / Sales #8; #1 Adult Contemporary hit (4 weeks)	Columbia 74020
2/8/92	**12**	12	11. Missing You Now **MICHAEL BOLTON Featuring Kenny G** Airplay #10 / Sales #33; #1 Adult Contemporary hit (3 weeks); above 4 from the album *Time, Love & Tenderness*	Columbia 74184
11/7/92	**11**	14	12. To Love Somebody Airplay #13 / Sales #16; #1 Adult Contemporary hit (5 weeks)	Columbia 74733
11/13/93+	**6**	20	● 13. **Said I Loved You...But I Lied** Airplay #7 / Sales #10; #1 Adult Contemporary hit (12 weeks)	Columbia 77260
4/16/94	**32**	4	14. Completely Airplay #32 / Sales #51	Columbia 77376
9/9/95	**27**	6	15. Can I Touch You...There? Sales #26 / Airplay #36	Columbia 77991
			BOND, Johnny	
			Country singer/songwriter/actor/author; worked on radio from age 19. Appeared with Jimmy Wakely in 1937 and joined *Gene Autry's Melody Ranch* in 1940. Appeared in over 50 movies.	
8/22/60	**26**	7	1. Hot Rod Lincoln [N] original version by Tiny Hill charted in 1951	Republic 2005
			BONDS, Gary (U.S.)	
			Born Gary Anderson on 6/6/39 in Jacksonville, Florida. To Norfolk, Virginia, in the mid-1950s. Signed to Legrand by Frank Guida. Wrote "She's All I Got" hit for Johnny Paycheck in 1971.	
10/31/60	**6**	11	1. **New Orleans** **BY-U.S. BONDS**	Legrand 1003

DATE	POS	WKS	ARTIST–RECORD TITLE	LABEL & NO.
6/5/61	1 (2)	12	● 2. **Quarter To Three** **U.S. BONDS** melody same as The Church Street Five's "A Night With Daddy G" (Bubbled Under in 1961 at #111)	Legrand 1008
7/31/61	5	9	3. **School Is Out**	Legrand 1009
11/6/61	28	2	4. School Is In	Legrand 1012
1/13/62	9	11	5. **Dear Lady Twist**	Legrand 1015
4/7/62	9	9	6. **Twist, Twist Senora** inspired by the calypso song "Shake Shake Senora (Jump In The Line)"	Legrand 1018
7/7/62	27	4	7. **Seven Day Weekend** from the movie *It's Trad-Dad* starring Helen Shapiro	Legrand 1019
5/2/81	11	13	8. This Little Girl	EMI America 8079
7/10/82	21	9	9. Out Of Work Clarence Clemons (sax solo); above 2 produced by Bruce Springsteen and Miami Steve Van Zandt	EMI America 8117

BONE THUGS-N-HARMONY

Male rap quintet from Cleveland: Krayzie Bone, Layzie Bone, Bizzy Bone, Wish Bone and Flesh-N-Bone. Discovered by Eazy-E.

DATE	POS	WKS	ARTIST–RECORD TITLE	LABEL & NO.
10/8/94	22	15	● 1. thuggish-ruggish-Bone Sales #10 / Airplay #53; Shatasha Williams (female vocal)	Ruthless 5527
9/2/95	14	10	● 2. 1st Of Tha Month Sales #9 / Airplay #35	Ruthless 6331

BONEY M

Vocal group assembled in Germany by producer/composer Frank Farian. Farian created the Far Corporation in 1986 and Milli Vanilli in 1988.

DATE	POS	WKS	ARTIST–RECORD TITLE	LABEL & NO.
7/22/78	30	6	1. Rivers Of Babylon	Sire 1027

BON JOVI

Hard-rock quintet formed in Sayreville, New Jersey, in 1983: Jon Bon Jovi (born 3/2/62; original spelling: Bongiovi; lead vocals), Richie Sambora (born 7/11/59; guitar), Dave Bryan (born 2/7/62; keyboards), Alec John Such (born 11/14/56; bass) and Tico Torres (born 10/7/53; drums). Such left in November 1994. Jon starred in the 1995 movie *Moonlight and Valentino*.

DATE	POS	WKS	ARTIST–RECORD TITLE	LABEL & NO.
4/21/84	39	1	1. Runaway "live" version is on the B-side of #8 below	Mercury 818309
10/11/86	1 (1)	14	2. **You Give Love A Bad Name** Sales #1(2) / Airplay #5	Mercury 884953
1/10/87	1 (4)	13	3. **Livin' On A Prayer** Airplay #1(4) / Sales #1(3)	Mercury 888184
4/25/87	7	12	4. **Wanted Dead Or Alive** Sales #6 / Airplay #6	Mercury 888467
10/1/88	1 (2)	12	5. **Bad Medicine** Sales #2 / Airplay #2	Mercury 870657
12/17/88+	3	13	6. **Born To Be My Baby** Airplay #2 / Sales #3	Mercury 872156
3/18/89	1 (1)	13	7. **I'll Be There For You** Sales #1(1) / Airplay #1(1)	Mercury 872564
6/17/89	7	11	8. **Lay Your Hands On Me** Sales #7 / Airplay #7; "live" version is on the B-side of #13 below	Mercury 874452

DATE	POS	WKS	ARTIST–RECORD TITLE	LABEL & NO.
10/28/89	9	12	9. **Living In Sin** Airplay #9 / Sales #10; above 5 from the album *New Jersey*	Mercury 876070
7/28/90	1 (1)	14	▲ 10. **Blaze Of Glory** **JON BON JOVI** Sales #1(3) / Airplay #2; with Jeff Beck and Aldo Nova (guitars) and Randy Jackson (bass)	Mercury 875896
11/10/90	12	11	11. Miracle **JON BON JOVI** Sales #11 / Airplay #12; above 2 from the movie *Young Guns II* starring Emilio Estevez and Kiefer Sutherland	Mercury 878392
10/31/92	29	9	12. Keep The Faith Sales #31 / Airplay #39	Jambco 864432
2/6/93	10	15	13. **Bed Of Roses** Sales #10 / Airplay #20	Jambco 864852
5/29/93	27	7	14. In These Arms Airplay #27 / Sales #46	Jambco 862088
10/8/94	4	29	▲ 15. **Always** Sales #2 / Airplay #3	Mercury 856227
6/10/95	14	13	16. This Ain't A Love Song Sales #15 / Airplay #27	Mercury 856824

BONNIE LOU

Born Bonnie Lou Kath on 10/27/24 in Talawanda, Illinois. Worked on radio KMBC-Kansas City and WLW-Cincinnati. On *Midwestern Hayride* for over 20 years.

DATE	POS	WKS	ARTIST–RECORD TITLE	LABEL & NO.
11/26/55	14	3	1. Daddy-O Juke Box #14 / Best Seller #25 / Top 100 #28	King 4835

BONNIE SISTERS

Pat, Jean and Sylvia Bonnie from New York City. All were nurses at Bellevue Hospital.

DATE	POS	WKS	ARTIST–RECORD TITLE	LABEL & NO.
2/25/56	18	3	1. Cry Baby Best Seller #18 / Top 100 #35	Rainbow 328

BONOFF, Karla

Born on 12/27/51 in Los Angeles. Pop singer/songwriter/pianist.

DATE	POS	WKS	ARTIST–RECORD TITLE	LABEL & NO.
6/5/82	19	12	1. Personally	Columbia 02805

BOOKER T. & THE MG'S

Band formed by sessionmen from Stax Records, Memphis, in 1962. Consisted of Booker T. Jones (born 11/12/44, Memphis; keyboards), Steve Cropper (born 10/21/42, Ozark Mountains, Missouri; guitar), Donald "Duck" Dunn (born 11/24/41, Memphis; bass) and Al Jackson, Jr. (born 11/27/34, Memphis; murdered 10/1/75; drums). MG stands for Memphis Group. Group disbanded in 1971; reorganized for a short time in 1973. Jones produced Willie Nelson's *Stardust* album. Cropper and Dunn joined the Blues Brothers. Group inducted into the Rock and Roll Hall of Fame in 1992.

DATE	POS	WKS	ARTIST–RECORD TITLE	LABEL & NO.
9/1/62	3	12	● 1. **Green Onions** [I] #1 R&B hit (4 weeks)	Stax 127
5/20/67	37	3	2. Hip Hug-Her [I]	Stax 211
9/2/67	21	7	3. Groovin' [I]	Stax 224
8/3/68	17	7	4. Soul-Limbo [I]	Stax 0001
12/28/68+	9	11	5. **Hang 'Em High** [I] title song from the movie starring Clint Eastwood	Stax 0013

DATE	POS	WKS	ARTIST—RECORD TITLE	LABEL & NO.
4/5/69	6	10	6. **Time Is Tight** [I] from the movie *Up Tight* starring Ruby Dee	Stax 0028
7/5/69	37	3	7. Mrs. Robinson [I] from the movie *The Graduate* starring Dustin Hoffman	Stax 0037

BOONE, Daniel

English singer/songwriter. Real name: Peter Lee Stirling.

DATE	POS	WKS	ARTIST—RECORD TITLE	LABEL & NO.
8/5/72	15	11	1. Beautiful Sunday	Mercury 73281

BOONE, Debby

Born on 9/22/56 in Hackensack, New Jersey. Third daughter of Shirley and Pat Boone and granddaughter of Red Foley. Worked with the Boone Family from 1969, sang with sisters in the Boones' gospel quartet. Went solo in 1977. Winner of three Grammys including Best New Artist of 1977. Popular Contemporary Christian artist. Married Gabriel Ferrer, son of Rosemary Clooney and Jose Ferrer, in 1982.

DATE	POS	WKS	ARTIST—RECORD TITLE	LABEL & NO.
9/17/77	1 (10)	21	▲ 1. **You Light Up My Life** title song from the movie starring Didi Conn; originally released on Warner 8446; #1 Adult Contemporary hit (1 week)	Warner/Curb 8455

BOONE, Pat

Born Charles Eugene Boone on 6/1/34 in Jacksonville, Florida. To Tennessee in 1936. Direct descendant of Daniel Boone. Married country singer Red Foley's daughter, Shirley, on 11/7/53. Won on "Ted Mack's Amateur Hour" and "Arthur Godfrey's Talent Scouts" in 1954. First recorded for Republic Records in 1954. Graduated from New York's Columbia University in 1958. Hosted own TV show, "The Pat Boone-Chevy Showroom," 1957–60. Appeared in 15 movies. Toured with wife and daughters Cherry, Linda, Laura and Debby Boone in the mid-1960s. Recording artist Nick Todd is his younger brother. Pat's trademark: white buck shoes.

DATE	POS	WKS	ARTIST—RECORD TITLE	LABEL & NO.
4/2/55	16	12	1. Two Hearts Best Seller #16 / Juke Box #16; #8 R&B hit for The Charms in 1955; Lew Douglas (orch.)	Dot 15338
7/9/55	1 (2)	20	● 2. **Ain't That A Shame** Juke Box #1 / Best Seller #2 / Jockey #2 / Top 100 #21 pre	Dot 15377
10/29/55	7	10	3. **At My Front Door (Crazy Little Mama)/** Top 100 #7 / Juke Box #7 / Best Seller #8 / Jockey #10	
11/19/55	26	5	4. No Other Arms tune better known as "No Arms Can Ever Hold You"	Dot 15422
12/24/55+	19	5	5. Gee Whittakers! Juke Box #19 / Top 100 #27; #14 R&B hit for The Five Keys in 1956	Dot 15435
2/4/56	4	18	● 6. **I'll Be Home/** Jockey #4 / Juke Box #4 / Top 100 #5 / Best Seller #6; #5 R&B hit for The Flamingos in 1956	
2/4/56	12	10	7. Tutti' Frutti Top 100 #12 / Juke Box #13 / Best Seller #15 / Jockey #15	Dot 15443
4/28/56	8	9	8. **Long Tall Sally** Juke Box #8 / Top 100 #18 / Best Seller #23 / Jockey #23	Dot 15457
6/9/56	1 (4)	19	● 9. **I Almost Lost My Mind** Juke Box #1(4) / Top 100 #1(2) / Best Seller #2 / Jockey #2; #1 R&B hit for Ivory Joe Hunter in 1950	Dot 15472
9/22/56	5	17	● 10. **Friendly Persuasion (Thee I Love)/** Jockey #5 / Top 100 #8 / Juke Box #8 / Best Seller #9; from the movie *Friendly Persuasion* starring Gary Cooper	

DATE	POS	WKS	ARTIST–RECORD TITLE	LABEL & NO.
9/29/56	**10**	8	11. **Chains Of Love** Juke Box #10 / Best Seller #15 / Top 100 #20; #2 R&B hit for Joe Turner in 1951	Dot 15490
12/22/56+	**1** (1)	19	● 12. **Don't Forbid Me/** Top 100 #1(1) / Juke Box #1(1) / Jockey #2 / Best Seller #3	
1/26/57	**37**	2	13. Anastasia title song from the movie starring Ingrid Bergman	Dot 15521
3/23/57	**5**	13	● 14. **Why Baby Why/** Best Seller #5 / Top 100 #6 / Jockey #7 / Juke Box #7	
3/23/57	**27**	5	15. I'm Waiting Just For You #2 R&B hit for Lucky Millinder in 1951	Dot 15545
5/13/57	**1** (7)	24	● 16. **Love Letters In The Sand/** Jockey #1(7) / Best Seller #1(5) / Top 100 #1(5) / Juke Box #2 end; #6 hit for Ted Black & His Orchestra in 1931	
5/20/57	**14**	13	17. Bernardine Jockey #14 / Top 100 #23; above 2 from the movie *Bernardine* starring Boone	Dot 15570
8/12/57	**6**	14	● 18. **Remember You're Mine/** Jockey #6 / Best Seller #10 / Top 100 #20	
8/19/57	**14**	11	19. There's A Gold Mine In The Sky Best Seller #14 / Jockey #20 / Top 100 #28; #5 hit for Horace Heidt in 1938	Dot 15602
10/28/57	**1** (6)	19	● 20. **April Love** Jockey #1(6) / Best Seller #1(2) / Top 100 #1(1); title song from the movie starring Boone and Shirley Jones	Dot 15660
2/17/58	**4**	15	● 21. **A Wonderful Time Up There/** Best Seller #4 / Jockey #7 / Top 100 #10; originally titled "Gospel Boogie" (1947)	
2/17/58	**4**	15	22. **It's Too Soon To Know** Best Seller #4 / Jockey #11 / Top 100 #13; #1 R&B hit for The Orioles in 1948	Dot 15690
5/12/58	**5**	12	23. **Sugar Moon** Jockey #5 / Best Seller #10 / Top 100 #11	Dot 15750
7/14/58	**7**	10	24. **If Dreams Came True/** Jockey #7 / Best Seller #11 / Hot 100 #12	
8/4/58	**39**	1	25. That's How Much I Love You #10 hit for Frank Sinatra in 1947	Dot 15785
9/22/58	**23**	4	26. For My Good Fortune/ Hot 100 #23 / Best Seller #29	
10/6/58	**21**	2	27. Gee, But It's Lonely Best Seller #21 / Hot 100 #31; written by Phil Everly	Dot 15825
11/17/58	**34**	5	28. I'll Remember Tonight from the movie *Mardi Gras* starring Boone	Dot 15840
1/26/59	**21**	8	29. With The Wind And The Rain In Your Hair Top 10 hit in 1940 for both Bob Crosby and Kay Kyser	Dot 15888
4/6/59	**23**	7	30. For A Penny Billy Vaughn (orch., all of above except #1)	Dot 15914
6/29/59	**17**	6	31. Twixt Twelve And Twenty also the title of Boone's best-selling book	Dot 15955
9/28/59	**29**	4	32. Fools Hall Of Fame	Dot 15982
3/7/60	**18**	7	33. (Welcome) New Lovers Mort Lindsey (orch.: #31 & 33)	Dot 16048
5/22/61	**1** (1)	12	34. **Moody River**	Dot 16209
9/4/61	**19**	5	35. Big Cold Wind Milt Rogers (orch.)	Dot 16244
12/25/61+	**35**	3	36. Johnny Will	Dot 16284

DATE	POS	WKS	ARTIST—RECORD TITLE	LABEL & NO.
2/24/62	32	3	37. I'll See You In My Dreams 4 versions of this tune hit the Top 10 in 1925; Billy Vaughn (orch.: #34, 36, 37)	Dot 16312
6/30/62	6	10	38. **Speedy Gonzales** [N] featuring the voice of Mel Blanc as "Speedy Gonzales"; Jimmie Haskell (orch.)	Dot 16368

BOSTON

Rock group from Boston, spearheaded by Tom Scholz (guitars, keyboards) and Brad Delp (lead vocals). Group also included Barry Goudreau (guitar), Fran Sheehan (bass) and Sib Hashian (drums). Goudreau formed Orion The Hunter. After a long absence from the charts, Boston returned in 1986 as a duo: Scholz and Delp. Delp and Goudreau spearheaded RTZ in 1991. Scholz's 1994 Boston lineup: Fran Cosmo and Tommy Funderburk (vocals), Gary Pihl (guitar), David Sikes (bass) and Doug Huffman (drums).

DATE	POS	WKS	ARTIST—RECORD TITLE	LABEL & NO.
10/16/76	5	14	1. **More Than A Feeling**	Epic 50266
2/12/77	22	6	2. Long Time	Epic 50329
6/18/77	38	2	3. Peace Of Mind	Epic 50381
8/26/78	4	10	4. **Don't Look Back**	Epic 50590
12/23/78+	31	5	5. A Man I'll Never Be	Epic 50638
10/4/86	1 (2)	12	6. **Amanda** Airplay #1(3) / Sales #1(2)	MCA 52756
12/27/86+	9	10	7. **We're Ready** Sales #8 / Airplay #9	MCA 52985
3/28/87	20	5	8. Can'tcha Say (You Believe In Me)/Still In Love Sales #20 / Airplay #24	MCA 53029

BOTKIN, Perry Jr.—see DeVORZON, Barry

BOURGEOIS, Brent

Born in New Orleans; raised in New Jersey and Dallas. Former member of Bourgeois Tagg.

DATE	POS	WKS	ARTIST—RECORD TITLE	LABEL & NO.
6/9/90	32	3	1. Dare To Fall In Love Airplay #25	Charisma 98971

BOURGEOIS TAGG

West Coast rock quintet formed in 1984 and led by Brent Bourgeois and Larry Tagg.

DATE	POS	WKS	ARTIST—RECORD TITLE	LABEL & NO.
12/5/87	38	2	1. I Don't Mind At All Sales #35; produced by Todd Rundgren	Island 99409

BOWEN, Jimmy, with the Rhythm Orchids

Born on 11/30/37 in Santa Rita, New Mexico. Formed The Rhythm Orchids at West Texas State University with Buddy Knox, Don Lanier and Dave "Dicky Doo" Alldred. Jimmy became a producer and top record executive on the West Coast. Produced 20 of Dean Martin's hits, 1964–69. In 1977, moved to Nashville. In 1984, became president of MCA Records in Nashville (renamed Universal Records in 1988).

DATE	POS	WKS	ARTIST—RECORD TITLE	LABEL & NO.
3/9/57	14	12	1. I'm Stickin' With You Top 100 #14 / Juke Box #15 / Best Seller #16 / Jockey #20; originally on Triple-D 798 in 1956 (B-side: "Party Doll" by Buddy Knox)	Roulette 4001

DATE	POS	WKS	ARTIST–RECORD TITLE	LABEL & NO.

BOWIE, David

Born David Robert Jones on 1/8/47 in London. First recorded as David Jones & the King Bees, Lower Third, and Manish Boys in 1963. Brought highly theatrical values to rock through work with Lindsay Kemp Mime Troupe. Periods of reclusiveness heightened his appeal. Appeared in the movies *The Man Who Fell To Earth* (1976), *Labyrinth* (1986), *Absolute Beginners* (1986) and others, and in the Broadway play *The Elephant Man* (1980). Married to Angie Barnet (the subject of The Rolling Stones' song "Angie"), 1970–80. Formed the group Tin Machine in 1988. Married Somalian actress/supermodel Iman on 4/24/92. Inducted into the Rock and Roll Hall of Fame in 1996.

DATE	POS	WKS	ARTIST–RECORD TITLE	LABEL & NO.
2/24/73	**15**	10	1. Space Oddity	RCA 0876
			first released on Mercury 72949 in 1969; with Rick Wakeman (Yes) on piano	
4/19/75	**28**	4	2. Young Americans	RCA 10152
			David Sanborn (saxophone)	
8/2/75	**1** (2)	14	● 3. **Fame**	RCA 10320
			John Lennon (backing vocal and song's co-writer)	
1/10/76	**10**	16	4. **Golden Years**	RCA 10441
12/5/81+	**29**	8	5. Under Pressure	Elektra 47235
			QUEEN & DAVID BOWIE	
4/9/83	**1** (1)	14	● 6. **Let's Dance**	EMI America 8158
7/9/83	**10**	11	7. **China Girl**	EMI America 8165
10/1/83	**14**	9	8. Modern Love	EMI America 8177
			Stevie Ray Vaughan (guitar, above 3)	
9/29/84	**8**	10	9. **Blue Jean**	EMI America 8231
			Sales #7 / Airplay #10	
3/9/85	**32**	4	10. This Is Not America	EMI America 8251
			DAVID BOWIE/PAT METHENY GROUP	
			Sales #27; theme from the movie *The Falcon And The Snowman* starring Timothy Hutton and Sean Penn	
9/7/85	**7**	9	11. **Dancing In The Street**	EMI America 8288
			MICK JAGGER/DAVID BOWIE	
			Sales #5 / Airplay #8; all proceeds donated to Live-Aid	
4/25/87	**21**	7	12. Day-In Day-Out	EMI America 8380
			Sales #17 / Airplay #24	
9/5/87	**27**	5	13. Never Let Me Down	EMI America 43031
			Sales #23 / Airplay #32	

BOX TOPS, The

Pop-rock group formed in Memphis in 1966. Included Alex Chilton (born 12/28/50, Memphis; lead singer, guitar, bass, harmonica), Bill Cunningham (born 1/23/50, Memphis; keyboards) and Gary Talley (born 8/17/47, Memphis; guitar, bass). Reorganized after first hit to include Tom Boggs, drums; and Rick Allen, organ. Disbanded in 1970. Chilton later formed the power pop band Big Star. Cunningham is the brother of B.B. Cunningham of The Hombres.

DATE	POS	WKS	ARTIST–RECORD TITLE	LABEL & NO.
8/26/67	**1** (4)	13	● 1. **The Letter**	Mala 565
12/2/67	**24**	5	2. Neon Rainbow	Mala 580
3/16/68	**2** (2)	12	● 3. **Cry Like A Baby**	Mala 593
6/8/68	**26**	6	4. Choo Choo Train	Mala 12005
10/12/68	**37**	1	5. I Met Her In Church	Mala 12017
2/8/69	**28**	9	6. Sweet Cream Ladies, Forward March	Mala 12035
8/23/69	**18**	7	7. Soul Deep	Mala 12040

DATE	POS	WKS	ARTIST–RECORD TITLE	LABEL & NO.
			### BOYCE, Tommy, & Bobby Hart	
			Songwriting/singing/production duo. Boyce was born on 9/29/44 in Charlottesville, Virginia; died of a self-inflicted gunshot wound on 11/23/94. Phoenix native Hart was born in 1944.	
8/5/67	39	2	1. Out & About	A&M 858
1/20/68	8	9	2. **I Wonder What She's Doing Tonite**	A&M 893
8/3/68	27	6	3. Alice Long (You're Still My Favorite Girlfriend)	A&M 948
			### BOY GEORGE	
			Born George O'Dowd on 6/14/61 in Bexleyheath, England. Former lead singer of Culture Club. Brief stint as Lieutenant Lush, a backing singer with Bow Wow Wow.	
2/20/88	40	1	1. Live My Life Sales #37 / Airplay #39; from the movie *Hiding Out* starring Jon Cryer	Virgin 99390
4/3/93	15	9	2. The Crying Game Sales #18 / Airplay #22; title song from the movie starring Stephen Rea; produced by the Pet Shop Boys	SBK 50437
			### BOY KRAZY	
			Pop female vocal quartet formed in New York: Kimberly Blake, Johnna Lee Cummings, Josselyne Jones and Ruth Ann Roberts (a former Miss Junior America).	
2/13/93	18	16	1. That's What Love Can Do Airplay #11 / Sales #40	Next Plat. 857024
			### BOY MEETS GIRL	
			Seattle songwriting/recording duo: Shannon Rubicam and George Merrill. Wrote Whitney Houston's hits "How Will I Know" and "I Wanna Dance With Somebody." Married in 1988.	
5/25/85	39	1	1. Oh Girl	A&M 2713
10/15/88	5	16	2. **Waiting For A Star To Fall** Sales #4 / Airplay #6; #1 Adult Contemporary hit (1 week)	RCA 8691
			### BOYS, The	
			Quartet of brothers, ages 9–14 in 1988, from Northridge, California: Khiry (lead), Hakeem, Tajh and Bilal Samad. All are members of performing gymnastic troupes.	
1/14/89	13	9	1. Dial My Heart Sales #11 / Airplay #17; #1 R&B hit (1 week)	Motown 53301
9/8/90	29	8	2. Crazy Sales #17; #1 R&B hit (1 week)	Motown 924
			### BOYS CLUB	
			Duo formed in Minneapolis: vocalists Joe Pasquale and Gene Hunt (real name: Eugene Wolfgramm, formerly with his family group, The Jets).	
11/19/88+	8	12	1. **I Remember Holding You** Sales #6 / Airplay #11	MCA 53430
			### BOYS DON'T CRY	
			British quintet. Nick Richards, lead singer.	
5/17/86	12	9	1. I Wanna Be A Cowboy Sales #11 / Airplay #11	Profile 5084

DATE	POS	WKS	ARTIST–RECORD TITLE	LABEL & NO.
			BOYZ II MEN	
			R&B vocal quartet formed in 1988 at Philadelphia's High School of Creative and Performing Arts: Wanya Morris, Michael McCary, Shawn Stockman and Nathan Morris. Discovered by Michael Bivins (New Edition, Bell Biv DeVoe). Appeared in the 1992 TV mini-series "The Jacksons: An American Dream."	
7/6/91	3	18	▲ 1. **Motownphilly** Sales #2 / Airplay #3; Michael Bivins (rap)	Motown 2090
10/12/91	2 (4)	19	● 2. **It's So Hard To Say Goodbye To Yesterday** Sales #2 / Airplay #5; #1 R&B hit (1 week)	Motown 2136
1/18/92	16	14	3. Uhh Ahh Sales #14 / Airplay #19; #1 R&B hit (1 week)	Motown 2141
7/25/92	1 (13)	28	▲ 4. **End of the Road** Airplay #1(13) / Sales #1(12); from the movie *Boomerang* starring Eddie Murphy; #1 R&B hit (4 weeks)	Motown 2178
11/28/92+	3	17	▲ 5. **In The Still Of The Nite (I'll Remember)** Airplay #2 / Sales #3; from the TV mini-series "The Jacksons: An American Dream"	Motown 2193
1/8/94	32	1	6. Let It Snow [X] Sales #27 / Airplay #40; Brian McKnight (guest vocal/co-writer/co-producer)	Motown 2218
8/13/94	1 (14)	31	▲ 7. **I'll Make Love To You** Airplay #1(12) / Sales #1(11); #1 R&B hit (9 weeks); #1 Adult Contemporary hit (3 weeks)	Motown 2257
11/19/94	1 (6)	25	▲ 8. **On Bended Knee** Airplay #1(11) / Sales #2	Motown 0244
3/4/95	21	10	9. Thank You Sales #21 / Airplay #28; samples "La-Di-Da-Di" by Doug E. Fresh	Motown 0274
4/29/95	2 (1)	25	● 10. **Water Runs Dry** Airplay #1(1) / Sales #8; above 4 from the album *II*	Motown 0358
12/2/95	1 (16)	20↑	▲² 11. **One Sweet Day** **MARIAH CAREY & BOYZ II MEN** Airplay #1(13) / Sales #1(11); the #1 hit in *Hot 100* history; #1 Adult Contemporary hit (13 weeks)	Columbia 78074
			BRADLEY, Jan	
			Born Addie Bradley on 7/6/43 in Byhalia, Mississippi; raised in Robbins, Illinois. Soul singer. First recorded for Formal in 1961. Became a social worker in 1976.	
2/2/63	14	9	1. Mama Didn't Lie first released on Formal 1044 in 1962	Chess 1845
			BRADLEY, Owen, Quintet	
			Born on 10/21/15 in Westmoreland, Tennessee. Band leader/producer/organist/combo leader. Country A&R director for Decca, 1958–68. Vice president of MCA from 1968. Elected to the Country Music Hall of Fame in 1974.	
7/29/57	18	4	1. White Silver Sands Jockey #18 / Top 100 #68; Anita Kerr Quartet (vocals)	Decca 30363
			BRAM TCHAIKOVSKY	
			Rock quartet formed in Lincolnshire, England. Led by Peter Bramall (earlier with The Motors).	
8/18/79	37	3	1. Girl Of My Dreams	Polydor 14575

DATE	POS	WKS	ARTIST–RECORD TITLE	LABEL & NO.
			BRANDY	
			Born Brandy Norwood on 2/11/79 in McComb, Mississippi; raised in California. Singer/actress. Regular on TV's "Thea."	
10/8/94	6	25	● 1. **I Wanna Be Down** Sales #4 / Airplay #10; #1 R&B hit (4 weeks); remix is on B-side of #2 below	Atlantic 87225
2/11/95	4	18	▲ 2. **Baby** Sales #1(5) / Airplay #19; #1 R&B hit (4 weeks)	Atlantic 87173
7/1/95	34	6	3. Best Friend Sales #25 / Airplay #51	Atlantic 87148
9/9/95	9	14	● 4. **Brokenhearted** Sales #5 / Airplay #21; Wanya Morris from Boyz II Men (male vocal); all of above from the album *Brandy*	Atlantic 87150
			BRANIGAN, Laura	
			Born on 7/3/57 in Brewster, New York. Former backing vocalist with Leonard Cohen. Guest-starred on the TV show "CHiPs" and appeared in the 1984 movie *Mugsy's Girl*.	
9/4/82	2 (3)	22	▲ 1. **Gloria** tune first popularized in Italy in 1979 by the song's composer, Umberto Tozzi	Atlantic 4048
4/2/83	7	13	2. **Solitaire**	Atlantic 89868
8/13/83	12	12	3. How Am I Supposed To Live Without You #1 Adult Contemporary hit (3 weeks)	Atlantic 89805
5/5/84	4	15	4. **Self Control**	Atlantic 89676
8/25/84	20	8	5. The Lucky One from the TV program "An Uncommon Love"	Atlantic 89636
9/7/85	40	2	6. Spanish Eddie	Atlantic 89531
11/28/87+	26	9	7. Power Of Love Sales #19 / Airplay #32	Atlantic 89191
			BRASS CONSTRUCTION	
			Nine-man, multi-ethnic disco ensemble. Formed in Brooklyn in 1968 as Dynamic Soul by Guyana-born vocalist Randy Muller. Randy also organized the band Skyy.	
5/8/76	14	9	1. Movin' [I] #1 R&B hit (1 week)	United Art. 775
			BRASS RING, The	
			New York studio band headed by producer/arranger/saxophonist Phil Bodner (born 6/13/21).	
4/16/66	32	4	1. The Phoenix Love Theme (Senza Fine) [I] from the movie *The Flight Of The Phoenix* starring James Stewart	Dunhill 4023
3/4/67	36	2	2. The Dis-Advantages Of You [I] melody taken from a Benson & Hedges cigarette jingle	Dunhill 4065
			BRAT PACK, The	
			Male vocal duo from New Jersey: Patrick J. Donovan and Ray-Ray Frazier. Donovan was a member of gospel artist CeCe Roger's stage band.	
3/17/90	36	3	1. You're The Only Woman Airplay #33	Vendetta 1447

DATE	POS	WKS	ARTIST–RECORD TITLE		LABEL & NO.
			BRAUN, Bob		
			Born Robert Earl Brown on 4/20/29 in Ludlow, Kentucky. Hosted TV show in Cincinnati.		
8/18/62	26	4	1. Till Death Do Us Part	[S]	Decca 31355
			BRAXTON, Toni		
			Female singer born in Severn, Maryland. Recorded in 1990 with her younger sisters as The Braxtons. Won the 1993 Best New Artist Grammy Award.		
8/22/92	29	6	1. Give U My Heart **BABYFACE (Featuring Toni Braxton)** Airplay #29 / Sales #39		LaFace 24026
1/9/93	33	2	2. Love Shoulda Brought You Home Sales #25 / Airplay #36; above 2 from the movie *Boomerang* starring Eddie Murphy		LaFace 24035
8/14/93	7	18	● 3. **Another Sad Love Song** Airplay #8 / Sales #14		LaFace 24047
10/30/93+	3	33	● 4. **Breathe Again** Airplay #1(1) / Sales #6		LaFace 24054
4/16/94	7	28	● 5. **You Mean The World To Me** Airplay #3 / Sales #14		LaFace 24064
11/26/94+	28	11	6. I Belong To You/ Sales #31 / Airplay #35		
11/12/94	35	13	7. How Many Ways Sales #2/ / Airplay #54; remix by R. Kelly		LaFace 24081
			BREAD		
			Formed in Los Angeles in 1969. Consisted of leader David Gates (vocals, guitar, keyboards), James Griffin (guitar), Robb Royer (guitar) and Jim Gordon (drums). Originally called Pleasure Faire. Griffin and Royer co-wrote the award-winning hit "For All We Know" with Fred Karlin in 1969. Mike Botts replaced Gordon after first album. Royer replaced by Larry Knechtel (top sessionman, member of Duane Eddy's Rebels) in 1971. Disbanded in 1973, reunited briefly in 1976. All songs written and produced by David Gates.		
7/11/70	1 (1)	13	● 1. **Make It With You**		Elektra 45686
10/10/70	10	9	2. **It Don't Matter To Me**		Elektra 45701
1/30/71	28	4	3. Let Your Love Go		Elektra 45711
4/3/71	4	11	4. **If** #1 Adult Contemporary hit (3 weeks)		Elektra 45720
8/14/71	37	2	5. Mother Freedom		Elektra 45740
11/6/71	3	10	● 6. **Baby I'm-A Want You** #1 Adult Contemporary hit (1 week)		Elektra 45751
2/5/72	5	11	7. **Everything I Own**		Elektra 45765
5/6/72	15	8	8. Diary above 4 from the album *Baby I'm-A Want You*		Elektra 45784
8/5/72	11	9	9. The Guitar Man #1 Adult Contemporary hit (1 week)		Elektra 45803
11/18/72	15	8	10. Sweet Surrender #1 Adult Contemporary hit (2 weeks)		Elektra 45818
2/17/73	15	8	11. Aubrey		Elektra 45832
12/4/76+	9	13	12. **Lost Without Your Love**		Elektra 45365

DATE	POS	WKS	ARTIST–RECORD TITLE	LABEL & NO.
			BREAKFAST CLUB	
			New York-based quartet. Madonna was with the group for a short time in the early '80s. Member Steve Bray co-produced Madonna's *True Blue* album.	
4/11/87	7	11	1. **Right On Track** Sales #5 / Airplay #12	MCA 52954
			BREATHE	
			Pop group from suburban London: David Glasper (born 1/4/66; vocals), Ian "Spike" Spice, Marcus Lillington and Michael Delahunty (who left in 1988).	
6/11/88	2 (2)	16	1. **Hands To Heaven** Sales #1(2) / Airplay #2	A&M 2991
10/1/88	3	16	2. **How Can I Fall?** Sales #1(1) / Airplay #3; #1 Adult Contemporary hit (2 weeks)	A&M 1224
1/28/89	10	10	3. **Don't Tell Me Lies** Airplay #9 / Sales #13	A&M 1267
9/15/90	21	8	4. Say A Prayer Airplay #15 / Sales #30	A&M 1519
1/5/91	34	3	5. Does She Love That Man? **BREATHE featuring DAVID GLASPER** Airplay #32	A&M 1535
			BREMERS, Beverly	
			Chicago-born actress/singer.	
1/22/72	15	10	1. Don't Say You Don't Remember	Scepter 12315
7/22/72	40	2	2. We're Free	Scepter 12348
			BRENDA & THE TABULATIONS	
			R&B group from Philadelphia, formed in 1966, with Brenda Payton, Jerry Jones, Eddie Jackson and Maurice Coates. Bernard Murphy was added in 1969. Reorganized in 1970 with vocalists Brenda Payton, Pat Mercer and Deborah Martin. Payton died on 6/14/92.	
3/25/67	20	6	1. Dry Your Eyes	Dionn 500
5/1/71	23	9	2. Right On The Tip Of My Tongue	Top & Bottom 407
			BRENNAN, Walter	
			Born on 7/25/1894 in Swampscott, Massachusetts. Died on 9/21/74. Beloved character actor. First movie role in 1924. Three-time Oscar winner. Played Grandpa on "The Real McCoys" TV series.	
5/30/60	30	3	1. **Dutchman's Gold** [S] **WALTER BRENNAN With BILLY VAUGHN and His Orchestra**	Dot 16066
4/21/62	5	9	2. **Old Rivers** [S]	Liberty 55436
12/1/62	38	1	3. Mama Sang A Song [S] The Johnny Mann Singers (backing vocals, above 2)	Liberty 55508
			BREWER, Teresa	
			Born Theresa Breuer on 5/7/31 in Toledo, Ohio. Debuted on "Major Bowes Amateur Hour" at age five, toured with show until age 12. Appeared on "Pick & Pat" radio show. First recorded for London in 1949. Appeared in the movie *Those Redheads From Seattle* (1953).	
12/18/54+	6	12	1. **Let Me Go, Lover!** **TERESA BREWER with The Lancers** Juke Box #6 / Jockey #7 / Best Seller #8	Coral 61315

DATE	POS	WKS	ARTIST–RECORD TITLE	LABEL & NO.
3/19/55	17	3	2. Pledging My Love/ Jockey #17 / Juke Box #18 / Best Seller #30	
		1	3. How Important Can It Be? Juke Box flip	Coral 61362
6/4/55	20	1	4. Silver Dollar Juke Box #20; Jack Pleis (orch., all of above)	Coral 61394
7/30/55	15	4	5. The Banjo's Back In Town Juke Box #15	Coral 61448
3/3/56	5	17	6. **A Tear Fell/** Juke Box #5 / Top 100 #7 / Best Seller #9 / Jockey #9; #15 R&B hit for Ivory Joe Hunter in 1956	
3/10/56	17	10	7. Bo Weevil Top 100 #17 / Jockey #20	Coral 61590
6/16/56	7	16	8. **A Sweet Old Fashioned Girl** Juke Box #7 / Top 100 #9 / Jockey #11 / Best Seller #12	Coral 61636
11/17/56	21	8	9. Mutual Admiration Society Top 100 #21 / Best Seller #24 / Jockey #24; from the musical *Happy Hunting* starring Ethel Merman	Coral 61737
4/27/57	13	9	10. Empty Arms Juke Box #13 / Top 100 #18 / Jockey #19 / Best Seller #23	Coral 61805
11/11/57	8	11	11. **You Send Me** Jockey #8 / Best Seller #27 / Top 100 #31	Coral 61898
10/20/58	38	1	12. The Hula Hoop Song	Coral 62033
4/6/59	40	1	13. Heavenly Lover	Coral 62084
9/12/60	31	6	14. Anymore Dick Jacobs (orch.: #5-14)	Coral 62219

BREWER & SHIPLEY

Folk-rock duo formed in Los Angeles: Mike Brewer (born 1944, Oklahoma City) and Tom Shipley (born 1942, Mineral Ridge, Ohio).

DATE	POS	WKS	ARTIST–RECORD TITLE	LABEL & NO.
3/13/71	10	10	1. **One Toke Over The Line**	Kama Sutra 516

BRICK

Disco-jazz group formed in Atlanta in 1972. Consisted of Jimmy Brown (vocals), Ray Ransom, Donald Nevins, Reggie Hargis and Eddie Irons. Session work in the early 1970s.

DATE	POS	WKS	ARTIST–RECORD TITLE	LABEL & NO.
11/20/76+	3	15	1. **Dazz** #1 R&B hit (4 weeks)	Bang 727
10/1/77	18	10	2. Dusic	Bang 734

BRICKELL, Edie, & New Bohemians

Vocalist Brickell joined the Dallas-based band in 1985. Varying personnel since then. Brickell was born in Oak Cliff, Texas; her father, Eddie, is a pro bowler. Bohemians' lineup: Kenny Withrow (guitar), Brad Houser (bass) and John Bush (drums). Joining the band by 1990 were Wes Burt-Martin (guitar) and Matt Chamberlain (drums). Brickell married Paul Simon on 5/30/92.

DATE	POS	WKS	ARTIST–RECORD TITLE	LABEL & NO.
1/14/89	7	10	1. **What I Am** Sales #4 / Airplay #9	Geffen 27696

BRIDGES, Alicia

Born on 7/15/53 in Lawndale, North Carolina. Disco singer/songwriter.

DATE	POS	WKS	ARTIST–RECORD TITLE	LABEL & NO.
9/9/78	5	19	● 1. **I Love The Nightlife (Disco 'Round)**	Polydor 14483

DATE	POS	WKS	ARTIST—RECORD TITLE	LABEL & NO.

9/17/55	18	3	**BRIGGS, Lillian**
			Pop singer/trombonist from Philadelphia. Discovered by Alan Freed while working in Joy Cayler's All-Girl Orchestra in New York City.
			    1. I Want You To Be My Baby
			        Jockey #18 / Juke Box #19 / Best Seller #23 / Top 100 #53 pre;
			        O.B. Masingill (orch.)
				Epic 9115

1/6/73	16	8	**BRIGHTER SIDE OF DARKNESS** R&B group formed at Calumet High School, Chicago, in 1971; featuring 12-year-old lead singer Darryl Lamont, Ralph Eskridge, Randolph Murph and Larry Washington. ● 1. Love Jones	20th Century 2002
7/16/83	36	3	**BRILEY, Martin** British session musician/songwriter. Moved to New York City in 1977. 1. The Salt In My Tears	Mercury 812165
7/20/74	8	13	**BRISTOL, Johnny** Born on 2/3/39 in Morganton, North Carolina. Soul vocalist/composer/producer. Teamed with Jackie Beaver, recorded as Johnny & Jackie for Tri-Phi, 1961. Teamed with Harvey Fuqua as Motown producers until 1973. 1. **Hang On In There Baby**	MGM 14715
9/1/79	35	3	**BROOD, Herman** Born on 11/5/46 in Zwolle, Holland. Leader of rock band from the Netherlands. 1. Saturdaynight	Ariola Am. 7754
1/4/69	3	10	**BROOKLYN BRIDGE** Outfit from Long Island, New York, led by vocalist Johnny Maestro (of The Crests). The Del-Satins, a vocal quartet led by Maestro, and The Rhythm Method, a seven-piece band, united as Brooklyn Bridge in 1967. ● 1. **Worst That Could Happen**	Buddah 75
			BROOKLYN DREAMS—see SUMMER, Donna	

7/11/60
12/26/60
	7
	31
		15
		3
			BROOKS, Donnie
			Born John Abahosh in Dallas; raised in Ventura, California, as John Faircloth. Early recording names: Johnny Faire, Dick Bush and Johnny Jordan.
			    1. **Mission Bell**
			    2. Doll House
				Era 3018
				Era 3028

8/11/90	27	4	**BROTHER BEYOND**
			British pop quartet: Nathan Moore (vocals), David White, Carl Fysh and Steve Alexander.
			    1. The Girl I Used To Know
			        Sales #26 / Airplay #28
				EMI 50287

DATE	POS	WKS	ARTIST–RECORD TITLE	LABEL & NO.
			BROTHERHOOD OF MAN, The	
			British studio group featuring Tony Burrows, Johnny Goddison and Sunny (female singer). Burrows was lead singer of Edison Lighthouse, First Class, The Pipkins and White Plains. 1976 hit featured new members: Nicky Stevens, Sandra Stevens, Martin Lee and Lee Sheridan.	
5/23/70	13	10	1. United We Stand	Deram 85059
6/19/76	27	4	2. Save Your Kisses For Me	Pye 71066
			#1 Adult Contemporary hit (1 week)	
			BROTHERS FOUR, The	
			Folk-pop quartet: Dick Foley, Bob Flick, John Paine and Mike Kirkland. Formed while Phi Gamma Delta fraternity brothers at the University of Washington.	
3/21/60	2 (4)	15	1. **Greenfields**	Columbia 41571
			written in 1956 by Terry Gilkyson & The Easy Riders	
4/24/61	32	3	2. Frogg　　　　　　　　　　　　　　　　　　[N]	Columbia 41958
			new version of tune written back in 1580 as "Frog Went A-Courtin'"	
			BROTHERS JOHNSON, The	
			Los Angeles R&B-funk duo of brothers George (born 5/17/53) and Louis (born 4/13/55) Johnson. Own band, The Johnson Three + 1, with brother Tommy and cousin Alex Weir. With Billy Preston's band to 1975.	
5/22/76	3	12	● 1. **I'll Be Good To You**	A&M 1806
			#1 R&B hit (1 week)	
9/18/76	30	6	2. Get The Funk Out Ma Face	A&M 1851
7/30/77	5	13	● 3. **Strawberry Letter 23**	A&M 1949
			Lee Ritenour (guitar solo); #1 R&B hit (1 week)	
4/12/80	7	13	4. **Stomp!**	A&M 2216
			#1 R&B hit (2 weeks)	
			BROWN('s), Al, Tunetoppers featuring Cookie Brown	
			Al was born on 5/22/30 in Fairmont, West Virginia. Tunetoppers formed in 1953.	
5/2/60	23	5	1. The Madison	Amy 804
			BROWN, Arthur, The Crazy World Of	
			Born Arthur Wilton on 6/24/44 in Whitby, England. Theatrical rock singer. Band included drummer Carl Palmer, later of Atomic Rooster, Emerson, Lake & Palmer and Asia. Since 1992, has been a partner in a music therapy practice Healing Songs Therapy.	
9/21/68	2 (1)	11	● 1. **Fire**	Atlantic 2556
			BROWN, Bobby	
			Born on 2/5/69 in Boston. Former member of the teen R&B-pop group New Edition. Had a bit part in the movie *Ghostbusters II*. Established own Bosstown recording studio and label in Atlanta in 1991. Married Whitney Houston on 7/18/92.	
8/20/88	8	14	● 1. **Don't Be Cruel**	MCA 53327
			Sales #3 / Airplay #13; #1 R&B hit (2 weeks)	
11/12/88+	1 (1)	15	● 2. **My Prerogative**	MCA 53383
			Sales #1(1) / Airplay #2; #1 R&B hit (2 weeks)	

DATE	POS	WKS	ARTIST—RECORD TITLE	LABEL & NO.
1/28/89	**3**	11	3. **Roni** Airplay #3 / Sales #4	MCA 53463
4/15/89	**3**	13	● 4. **Every Little Step** Sales #2 / Airplay #3; #1 R&B hit (1 week)	MCA 53618

7/1/89	**2 (3)**	13	▲ 5. **On Our Own**
			       Sales #1(2) / Airplay #2; from the movie *Ghostbusters II* starring
			       Bill Murray and Dan Aykroyd; #1 R&B hit (1 week)
				MCA 53662

9/16/89	**7**	11	● 6. **Rock Wit'cha**
			       Airplay #6 / Sales #8; all of above (except #5) from the album
			       Don't Be Cruel
				MCA 53652

5/26/90	**1 (2)**	14	● 7. **She Ain't Worth It**
			       GLENN MEDEIROS Featuring Bobby Brown
			       Airplay #1(3) / Sales #4
				MCA 79047

8/8/92	**3**	17	● 8. **Humpin' Around** Sales #4 / Airplay #4; #1 R&B hit (2 weeks)	MCA 54342
10/24/92	**7**	21	● 9. **Good Enough** Airplay #5 / Sales #7	MCA 54517
1/30/93	**14**	10	10. **Get Away** Sales #15 / Airplay #18	MCA 54511
			## BROWN, Boots, And His Blockbusters Brown was born Milton "Shorty" Rogers on 4/14/24 in Lee, Massachusetts. Jazz trumpeter/bandleader.	

9/15/58	**23**	3	1. **Cerveza** [I]
			       Best Seller #23 / Hot 100 #62; tune is very similar to The Champs'
			       "Tequila"
				RCA 7269

			## BROWN, Buster Born on 8/15/11 in Cordele, Georgia. Died on 1/31/76. R&B vocalist/harmonica player.	
3/28/60	**38**	3	1. **Fannie Mae** #1 R&B hit (1 week)	Fire 1008
			## BROWN, Chuck, & The Soul Searchers Washington, D.C., group formed in 1968 as The Soul Searchers.	
3/17/79	**34**	5	● 1. **Bustin' Loose Part 1** #1 R&B hit (4 weeks)	Source 40967
			## BROWN, James Born on 5/3/28 in Macon, Georgia; raised in Augusta. Formed own vocal group, the Famous Flames. Cut a demo record of own composition "Please Please Please" in November 1955, at radio station WIBB in Macon. Signed to King/Federal Records in January 1956 and re-recorded the song. Cameo appearances in the movies *The Blues Brothers* and *Rocky IV*. One of the originators of "Soul" music, variously billed on Polydor hits as "Soul I," "The Creator," "The Godfather of Soul," "The Hit Man" and "Minister of New New Super Heavy Funk." His backing group, The JB's, featured various personnel, including Nat Kendrick, Bootsy Collins, Maceo Parker and Fred Wesley. Inducted into the Rock and Roll Hall of Fame in 1986. On 12/15/88, received a six-year prison sentence after leading police on an interstate car chase; released from prison on 2/27/91. Won Lifetime Achievement Grammy in 1992. Ranked as the #1 artist in the book *Joel Whitburn's Top R&B Singles*.	
5/30/60	**33**	2	1. **Think**	Federal 12370
4/3/61	**40**	2	2. **Bewildered**	King 5442

DATE	POS	WKS	ARTIST—RECORD TITLE	LABEL & NO.
5/19/62	35	4	3. Night Train #27 hit for Buddy Morrow in 1952	King 5614
5/18/63	18	7	4. Prisoner Of Love #1 hit for Perry Como in 1946	King 5739
2/15/64	23	7	5. Oh Baby Don't You Weep (Part 1)	King 5842
9/12/64	24	5	6. Out Of Sight **JAMES BROWN And His Orchestra**	Smash 1919
8/7/65	8	9	7. **Papa's Got A Brand New Bag Part I** #1 R&B hit (8 weeks)	King 5999
11/20/65	3	10	8. **I Got You (I Feel Good)** #1 R&B hit (6 weeks)	King 6015
5/7/66	8	8	9. **It's A Man's Man's Man's World** #1 R&B hit (2 weeks)	King 6035
1/28/67	29	4	10. Bring It Up	King 6071
8/12/67	7	8	11. **Cold Sweat - Part 1** #1 R&B hit (3 weeks)	King 6110
11/25/67	40	1	12. Get It Together (Part 1)	King 6122
12/30/67+	28	5	13. I Can't Stand Myself (When You Touch Me)/	
2/17/68	36	4	14. There Was A Time	King 6144
3/23/68	6	10	15. **I Got The Feelin'** #1 R&B hit (2 weeks)	King 6155
6/1/68	14	7	16. Licking Stick - Licking Stick (Part 1) **JAMES BROWN And The Famous Flames** (all of above King titles)	King 6166
9/14/68	10	10	17. **Say It Loud - I'm Black And I'm Proud (Part 1)** #1 R&B hit (6 weeks)	King 6187
12/7/68	31	2	18. Goodbye My Love	King 6198
2/8/69	15	7	19. Give It Up Or Turnit A Loose #1 R&B hit (2 weeks)	King 6213
4/19/69	20	6	20. I Don't Want Nobody To Give Me Nothing (Open Up The Door, I'll Get It Myself)	King 6224
6/21/69	11	10	21. Mother Popcorn (You Got To Have A Mother For Me) Part 1 #1 R&B hit (2 weeks)	King 6245
6/28/69	30	5	22. The Popcorn [I]	King 6240
9/27/69	37	2	23. World (Part 1)	King 6258
11/1/69	21	5	24. Let A Man Come In And Do The Popcorn Part One	King 6255
12/13/69+	24	8	25. Ain't It Funky Now (Part 1) [I]	King 6280
1/24/70	40	2	26. Part Two (Let A Man Come In And Do The Popcorn)	King 6275
2/28/70	32	6	27. It's A New Day (Part 1)	King 6292
5/23/70	32	2	28. Brother Rapp (Part 1)	King 6310
8/1/70	15	7	29. Get Up (I Feel Like Being Like A) Sex Machine (Part 1)	King 6318
10/17/70	13	8	30. Super Bad (Part 1 & Part 2) #1 R&B hit (2 weeks)	King 6329
1/16/71	34	5	31. Get Up, Get Into It, Get Involved Pt. 1	King 6347
3/13/71	29	6	32. Soul Power Pt. 1	King 6368
6/26/71	35	3	33. Escape-ism (Part 1) [S]	People 2500
7/17/71	15	9	34. Hot Pants Pt. 1 (She Got To Use What She Got To Get What She Wants) #1 R&B hit (1 week)	People 2501

DATE	POS	WKS	ARTIST–RECORD TITLE	LABEL & NO.
9/11/71	22	6	35. Make It Funky (Part 1) #1 R&B hit (2 weeks)	Polydor 14088
12/4/71	35	3	36. I'm A Greedy Man - Part I	Polydor 14100
2/26/72	27	4	37. Talking Loud And Saying Nothing - Part I #1 R&B hit (1 week)	Polydor 14109
4/1/72	40	2	38. King Heroin [S]	Polydor 14116
9/9/72	18	8	● 39. Get On The Good Foot-Part 1 #1 R&B hit (4 weeks)	Polydor 14139
2/10/73	27	4	40. I Got Ants In My Pants - Part 1 (and i want to dance)	Polydor 14162
4/13/74	26	9	● 41. The Payback - Part I #1 R&B hit (2 weeks)	Polydor 14223
8/3/74	29	4	42. My Thang #1 R&B hit (2 weeks)	Polydor 14244
9/21/74	31	3	43. Papa Don't Take No Mess Part I #1 R&B hit (1 week)	Polydor 14255
1/11/86	4	11	44. **Living In America** Sales #4 / Airplay #6; from the movie *Rocky IV* starring Sylvester Stallone	Scotti Br. 05682
			## BROWN, Maxine	
			Born in Kingstree, South Carolina. R&B singer. With gospel groups Manhattans and Royaltones in New York City in the late 1950s.	
1/30/61	19	6	1. All In My Mind	Nomar 103
4/24/61	25	5	2. Funny	Nomar 106
12/5/64+	24	7	3. Oh No Not My Baby	Wand 162
			## BROWN, Nappy	
			Born Napoleon Brown Culp on 10/12/29 in Charlotte, North Carolina. R&B-gospel singer.	
4/30/55	25	4	1. Don't Be Angry Best Seller #25	Savoy 1155
			## BROWN, Peter	
			Born on 7/11/53 in Blue Island, Illinois. R&B vocalist/keyboardist/producer.	
10/8/77	18	8	1. Do Ya Wanna Get Funky With Me Wildflower (backing vocals)	Drive 6258
5/6/78	8	14	2. **Dance With Me** **PETER BROWN with Betty Wright**	Drive 6269
			## BROWN, Polly	
			Born on 4/18/47 in Birmingham, England. White soul singer. Lead vocalist of Pickettywitch and Sweet Dreams.	
2/8/75	16	7	1. Up In A Puff Of Smoke	GTO 1002
			## BROWN, Roy	
			Born on 9/10/25 in New Orleans. Died of a heart attack on 5/25/81 in Los Angeles. R&B vocalist/pianist. One of the originators of the New Orleans R&B sound. Wrote "Good Rocking Tonight."	
7/1/57	29	1	1. Let The Four Winds Blow Best Seller #29 / Top 100 #38	Imperial 5439

DATE	POS	WKS	ARTIST–RECORD TITLE	LABEL & NO.
			BROWN, Ruth	
			Born on 1/12/28 in Portsmouth, Virginia, as Ruth Weston. R&B pioneer. Married singer/trumpeter Jimmy Brown in 1945. In late 1946, sang for one month with Lucky Millinder's band, then fired. Later heard by Duke Ellington, who alerted Herb Abramson of the then-new Atlantic Records. Abramson signed her to a contract. Became Atlantic Records' top-selling artist of the 1950s. Married for a time to Willis Jackson. In later years, had acting roles in the TV shows "Hello, Larry" and "Checking In," plus several Broadway and Las Vegas musicals. Appeared in the movies *Under The Rainbow* (1981) and *Hairspray* (1988). Starred in the 1988 musical *Black And Blue*. Inducted into the Rock and Roll Hall of Fame in 1993.	
3/2/57	25	5	1. Lucky Lips Best Seller #25 / Jockey #25 / Top 100 #26	Atlantic 1125
10/13/58	24	2	2. This Little Girl's Gone Rockin' King Curtis (sax solo)	Atlantic 1197
			BROWN, Shirley	
			Born on 1/6/47 in West Memphis, Arkansas; raised in East St. Louis. Soul vocalist.	
11/23/74	22	6	1. Woman To Woman #1 R&B hit (2 weeks)	Truth 3206
			BROWNE, Jackson	
			Born on 10/9/48 in Heidelberg, Germany. Rock singer/guitarist/pianist/composer. To Los Angeles in 1951. With Tim Buckley and Nico in 1967 in New York City. Returned to Los Angeles, concentrated on songwriting. His songs were recorded by Linda Ronstadt, Tom Rush, Joe Cocker, The Byrds, Johnny Rivers, Bonnie Raitt and many others. Worked with the Eagles. Produced Warren Zevon's first album. Wife, Phyllis, committed suicide on 3/25/76. A prominent activist against nuclear power.	
4/8/72	8	9	1. **Doctor My Eyes**	Asylum 11004
2/19/77	23	6	2. Here Come Those Tears Again John Hall (of Orleans; guitar solo); Bonnie Raitt (harmony vocal)	Asylum 45379
3/4/78	11	12	3. Running On Empty	Asylum 45460
7/8/78	20	7	4. Stay/ David Lindley (falsetto vocal); Rosemary Butler (female vocal)	
		4	5. The Load-Out originally issued with "Rosie" as the B-side of "Stay"	Asylum 45485
7/26/80	19	10	6. Boulevard	Asylum 47003
10/18/80	22	5	7. That Girl Could Sing	Asylum 47036
8/21/82	7	12	8. **Somebody's Baby** from the movie *Fast Times At Ridgemont High* starring Sean Penn	Asylum 69982
7/16/83	13	12	9. Lawyers In Love	Asylum 69826
10/22/83	25	7	10. Tender Is The Night	Asylum 69791
11/23/85+	18	12	11. You're A Friend Of Mine **CLARENCE CLEMONS And Jackson Browne** Airplay #17 / Sales #20; includes vocals by actress Daryl Hannah (Browne's then-girlfriend)	Columbia 05660
3/29/86	30	5	12. For America Airplay #27	Asylum 69566

DATE	POS	WKS	ARTIST–RECORD TITLE	LABEL & NO.
			BROWNS, The	
			Family trio: Jim Ed Brown (born 4/1/34, Sparkman, Arkansas) and his sisters Maxine (born 4/27/32, Sampti, Louisiana) and Bonnie (born 7/31/37, Sparkman, Arkansas).	
8/3/59	**1 (4)**	14	● 1. **The Three Bells** French tune written in 1946; #1 Country hit (10 weeks); #14 hit for Les Compagnons De La Chanson in 1952	RCA 7555
11/23/59	**13**	9	2. Scarlet Ribbons (For Her Hair) #14 hit for Jo Stafford in 1950	RCA 7614
3/28/60	**5**	12	3. **The Old Lamplighter** **THE BROWNS featuring Jim Edward Brown** #1 hit for Sammy Kaye's Orchestra in 1946	RCA 7700
			BROWNSTONE	
			Los Angeles-based female vocal trio: Mimi, Nicci and Maxee. Mimi left group for health reasons in 1995, replaced by Kina Cosper.	
1/7/95	**8**	22	● 1. **If You Love Me** Sales #5 / Airplay #9; samples "Spellbound" by K-Solo	MJJ Music 77732
			BROWNSVILLE STATION	
			Rock trio from Ann Arbor, Michigan: Michael "Cub" Koda (guitar), Michael Lutz (vocals) and Henry Weck (drums). Koda writes a column for the record collector's magazine *Goldmine*.	
12/8/73+	**3**	13	● 1. **Smokin' In The Boy's Room**	Big Tree 16011
10/5/74	**31**	3	2. Kings Of The Party	Big Tree 16001
			BRUBECK, Dave, Quartet	
			Born David Warren on 12/6/20 in Concord, California. Leader of jazz quartet consisting of Brubeck (piano), Paul Desmond (alto sax), Joe Morello (drums) and Eugene Wright (bass). One of America's all-time most popular jazz groups on college campuses.	
9/25/61	**25**	7	1. Take Five [I] trend-setting jazz classic played in 5/4 time	Columbia 41479
			BRYANT, Anita	
			Born on 3/25/40 in Barnsdale, Oklahoma. As Miss Oklahoma, she was 2nd runner-up to Miss America in 1958.	
7/27/59	**30**	7	1. Till There Was You from the Broadway musical *The Music Man* starring Robert Preston	Carlton 512
5/2/60	**5**	12	2. **Paper Roses** Monty Kelly (orch., above 2)	Carlton 528
8/8/60	**10**	9	3. **In My Little Corner Of The World**	Carlton 530
12/26/60+	**18**	6	4. Wonderland By Night Lew Douglas (orch.)	Carlton 537
			BRYANT, Ray, Combo	
			Bryant was born Raphael Bryant on 12/24/31 in Philadelphia. R&B-jazz pianist/bandleader. Uncle of jazz guitarist Kevin Eubanks.	
5/9/60	**30**	4	1. The Madison Time - Part I [I-S] dance calls: Eddie Morrison (died on 2/28/87 in Chicago)	Columbia 41628

DATE	POS	WKS	ARTIST–RECORD TITLE	LABEL & NO.
			BRYANT, Sharon	
			Lead singer of Atlantic Starr, 1976–84. Native of White Plains, New York. Married Rick Gallwey (former percussionist with the group Change) in 1984.	
9/30/89	34	4	1. Let Go Sales #32 / Airplay #35	Wing 871722
			BRYSON, Peabo	
			Born Robert Peabo Bryson on 4/13/51 in Greenville, South Carolina. R&B singer/producer. First solo recording for Bang in 1970. Married Juanita Leonard, former wife of boxer Sugar Ray Leonard, in 1992.	
9/3/83	16	15	1. Tonight, I Celebrate My Love **PEABO BRYSON/ROBERTA FLACK**	Capitol 5242
6/30/84	10	13	2. If Ever You're In My Arms Again #1 Adult Contemporary hit (4 weeks)	Elektra 69728
2/22/92	9	14	▲ 3. Beauty And The Beast **CELINE DION and PEABO BRYSON** Sales #8 / Airplay #17; title song from the Disney animated movie	Epic 74090
1/2/93	1 (1)	18	● 4. A Whole New World (Aladdin's Theme) **PEABO BRYSON and REGINA BELLE** Airplay #1(4) / Sales #2; from the Disney animated movie *Aladdin*; #1 Adult Contemporary hit (6 weeks)	Columbia 74751
6/19/93	25	7	5. By The Time This Night Is Over **KENNY G (with Peabo Bryson)** Airplay #24 / Sales #57; #1 Adult Contemporary hit (2 weeks)	Arista 12565
			B.T. EXPRESS	
			Brooklyn, New York R&B-disco outfit earlier known as Brooklyn Trucking Express. Keyboardist Michael Jones, who joined group at age 15, later recorded solo as techno-funk musician Kashif.	
10/5/74	2 (2)	14	● 1. Do It ('Til You're Satisfied) #1 R&B hit (1 week)	Roadshow 12395
2/8/75	4	11	● 2. Express [I] #1 R&B hit (1 week)	Roadshow 7001
9/13/75	31	4	3. Peace Pipe/	
9/6/75	40	2	4. Give It What You Got	Roadshow 7003
			BUBBLE PUPPY, The	
			Psychedelic rock quartet from Houston: Rod Price, Roy Cox, Todd Potter and David Fore. Later recorded as Demian.	
3/15/69	14	7	1. Hot Smoke & Sasafrass	Int. Artists 128
			BUCHANAN & GOODMAN—see GOODMAN, Dickie	
			BUCHANAN BROTHERS	
			Producers Terry Cashman, Gene Pistilli and Tommy West.	
5/31/69	22	7	1. Medicine Man (Part I)	Event 3302

The Black Crowes drew equal parts praise and criticism for bringing the sound of '70s rockers such as Faces, Free and Humble Pie back into the early '90s pop scene. The Atlanta-based combo's single "Remedy" came from their album *The Southern Harmony And Musical Companion*, which reached No. 1 in 1992.

The Blues Brothers' comedic '60s R&B covers featured professional non-singers Dan Aykroyd and John Belushi being backed by many of the same musicians that had played on the original hits—including stellar Stax Records guitarist Steve Cropper. Ironically, 1980's "Gimme Some Lovin'" was a Spencer Davis Group cover.

Michael Bolton's booming, blue-eyed soul style was a natural to cover well-known soul standards. Among them were 1988's "(Sittin' On) The Dock Of The Bay" and 1990's "Georgia On My Mind," sung first by Otis Redding and then Ray Charles.

Gary U.S. Bonds's second biggest single—1961's "School Is Out"—entered the charts just a month after its No. 1 predecessor, "Quarter To Three." In 1981, Bonds recorded an album co-produced by fans Bruce Springsteen and Miami Steve Van Zandt.

Bon Jovi's massive commerical success in the late '80s—as displayed via such singles as 1989's Top 10 hit "Lay Your Hands On Me"—allowed the five-piece Jersey band to follow other artistic pursuits, including solo albums, acting, film scoring and the visual arts.

Pat Boone's "Spring Rain" peaked at No. 50 in 1960, a year before his last No. 1, "Moody River." In 1996, Boone was recording a new album of—incredibly—heavy metal cover songs for Rhino Records.

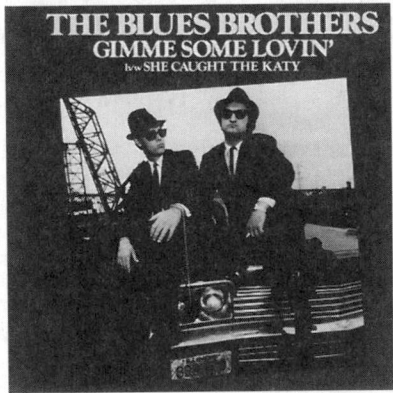

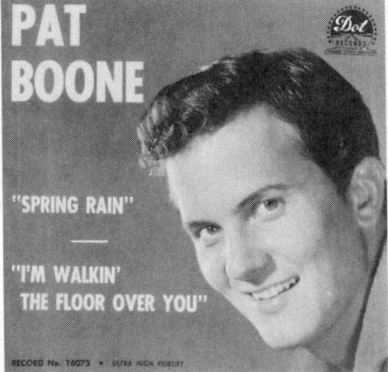

David Bowie and Mick Jagger caused a stir in 1985 with their unlikely duet version of Martha & The Vandellas' "Dancing In The Street " at Live-Aid. Ironically for Rolling Stone Jagger, the seeming throwaway reached No. 7 and became the highest-charting single ever released under his own name.

Tommy Boyce & Bobby Hart became best known in the '60s as the writing source of much of The Monkees' best early material. Of their own recordings, 1968's "I Wonder What She's Doing Tonight?" reached No. 8 and became their biggest single.

Boy Meets Girl's Top 5 1988 hit, "Waiting For A Star To Fall," was the work of husband/wife songwriting team Shannon Rubicam and George Merill, who'd garnered considerable acclaim for providing hitmaking material to Whitney Houston.

Boyz II Men's record-shattering No. 1 single "I'll Make Love To You" signaled that the Philly-based vocal quartet was one of the true pop phenomenons of the '90s. The Motown group would ring out 1995 with another record-breaker via a No. 1 duet with Columbia's Mariah Carey.

Laura Branigan's hit "Solitaire" was her second of three Top 10 hits, reaching No. 7 in 1983. Branigan later became one of the select few artists the Warner Music Group utilized to display the then-cutting-edge (and since failed) CD+Graphics format.

DATE	POS	WKS	ARTIST–RECORD TITLE	LABEL & NO.

BUCKINGHAM, Lindsey

Born on 10/3/47 in Palo Alto, California. Rock guitarist/vocalist/songwriter. In group Fritz, 1967–71; with Stevie Nicks (Fritz lead singer) formed duo, Buckingham Nicks, in early '70s. Both joined Fleetwood Mac in 1975. Buckingham left Fleetwood Mac in 1987. His grandfather founded Keystone Coffee; his father founded Alta Coffee. Buckingham's brother Gregg won a silver medal in swimming in the 1968 Olympics.

DATE	POS	WKS	ARTIST–RECORD TITLE	LABEL & NO.
11/7/81+	9	14	1. **Trouble**	Asylum 47223
8/25/84	23	9	2. Go Insane	Elektra 69714

BUCKINGHAMS, The

Chicago rock quintet: Dennis Tufano (lead singer), Carl Giammarese, Nick Fortune, Jon Paulos and Dennis Miccoli. Martin Grebb replaced Miccoli in 1967. Paulos died of a drug overdose on 3/26/80 (age 32). Tufano and Giammarese recorded as a duo in 1973. Grebb formed The Fabulous Rhinestones.

DATE	POS	WKS	ARTIST–RECORD TITLE	LABEL & NO.
1/21/67	1 (2)	10	1. **Kind Of A Drag**	U.S.A. 860
4/8/67	6	10	2. **Don't You Care**	Columbia 44053
7/1/67	5	10	3. **Mercy, Mercy, Mercy**	Columbia 44182
9/30/67	12	7	4. Hey Baby (They're Playing Our Song)	Columbia 44254
12/23/67+	11	10	5. Susan	Columbia 44378

BUCKNER & GARCIA

Atlanta-based duo: Jerry Buckner and Gary Garcia.

DATE	POS	WKS	ARTIST–RECORD TITLE	LABEL & NO.
1/30/82	9	14	● 1. **Pac-Man Fever** [N]	Columbia 02673
			inspired by the all-time #1 video game "Pac-Man"; originally released on BGO 1001 in 1981	

BUFFALO SPRINGFIELD, The

Superstar group formed in Los Angeles in 1966: Stephen Stills, Neil Young, Richie Furay, Dewey Martin and Bruce Palmer (replaced by Jim Messina after first two albums). Disbanded in 1968. Stills and Young formed Crosby, Stills, Nash & Young. Furay and Messina formed Poco.

DATE	POS	WKS	ARTIST–RECORD TITLE	LABEL & NO.
2/18/67	7	11	1. **For What It's Worth (Stop, Hey What's That Sound)**	Atco 6459

BUFFETT, Jimmy

Born on 12/25/46 in Mobile, Alabama. Has BS degree in history and journalism from the University of Southern Mississippi. After working in New Orleans, moved to Nashville in 1969. Staff reporter at *Billboard*, 1969–70. Settled in Key West in 1971. Owns a store called Margaritaville and has his own line of tropical clothing.

DATE	POS	WKS	ARTIST–RECORD TITLE	LABEL & NO.
6/29/74	30	5	1. Come Monday	Dunhill 4385
5/7/77	8	15	2. **Margaritaville**	ABC 12254
			#1 Adult Contemporary hit (1 week)	
10/22/77	37	3	3. Changes In Latitudes, Changes In Attitudes	ABC 12305
5/27/78	32	4	4. Cheeseburger In Paradise [N]	ABC 12358
10/20/79	35	3	5. Fins	MCA 41109

BUGGLES, The

English rock duo: Geoff Downes and Trevor Horn. Both joined the group Yes in 1980. Downes joined Asia in 1981. Horn became a prolific producer.

DATE	POS	WKS	ARTIST–RECORD TITLE	LABEL & NO.
12/15/79	40	1	1. Video Killed The Radio Star	Island 49114
			the premiere video on MTV's first show (8/1/81)	

DATE	POS	WKS	ARTIST–RECORD TITLE	LABEL & NO.
			BULL & THE MATADORS	
			Three-man group from St. Louis: JaMell "Bull" Parks (born 6/7/45), Milton Hardy and James Otis Love.	
11/16/68	39	1	1. The Funky Judge	Toddlin' Town 108
			BULLET	
			London-based duo of former Atomic Rooster members: John Cann (vocals) and Paul Hammond (drums).	
12/25/71+	28	5	1. White Lies, Blue Eyes	Big Tree 123
			BUOYS, The	
			Rock quintet from northeastern Pennsylvania led by vocalist Bill Kelly. Included Fran Brozena, Jerry Hludzik, Carl Siracuse and Chris Hanlon. Rupert Holmes was their composer/arranger.	
4/17/71	17	8	1. Timothy	Scepter 12275
			BURDON, Eric, And War	
			Burdon was born on 5/11/41 in Newcastle-On-Tyne, England. After leaving The Animals, Burdon teamed up with the funk band War for two albums. Starred in the 1982 movie *Comeback* and made a cameo appearance in *The Doors* (1991).	
7/11/70	3	13	● 1. **Spill The Wine**	MGM 14118
			BURKE, Solomon	
			Born in 1936 in Philadelphia. Soul singer. Preached and broadcasted from own church, "Solomon's Temple," in Philadelphia, 1945–55, as the "Wonder Boy Preacher." Church was founded for him by his grandmother. First recorded for Apollo in 1954. Left music to attend mortuary school, returned in 1960.	
11/13/61	24	7	1. Just Out Of Reach (Of My Two Open Arms)	Atlantic 2114
5/25/63	37	2	2. If You Need Me	Atlantic 2185
5/23/64	33	4	3. Goodbye Baby (Baby Goodbye)	Atlantic 2226
4/3/65	22	5	4. Got To Get You Off My Mind	Atlantic 2276
			#1 R&B hit (3 weeks)	
7/3/65	28	5	5. Tonight's The Night	Atlantic 2288
			BURNETTE, Dorsey	
			Born on 12/28/32 in Memphis. Died of a heart attack on 8/19/79 in Canoga Park, California. Older brother of Johnny Burnette and father of Billy Burnette.	
2/22/60	23	9	1. (There Was A) Tall Oak Tree	Era 3012
			BURNETTE, Johnny	
			Born on 3/25/34 in Memphis. Died on 8/1/64 in a boating accident on Clear Lake in California. Johnny, brother Dorsey Burnette and Paul Burlison formed the Johnny Burnette Rock 'N Roll Trio, 1953–57. Father of Rocky Burnette.	
8/15/60	11	11	1. Dreamin'	Liberty 55258
11/21/60	8	11	2. **You're Sixteen**	Liberty 55285
2/20/61	17	6	3. Little Boy Sad	Liberty 55298
11/6/61	18	4	4. God, Country And My Baby	Liberty 55379
			Johnny Mann Singers (backing vocals)	

DATE	POS	WKS	ARTIST–RECORD TITLE	LABEL & NO.
			BURNETTE, Rocky	
			Born on 6/12/53 in Memphis. Son of Johnny Burnette, nephew of Dorsey Burnette and cousin of Billy Burnette (of Fleetwood Mac).	
6/7/80	8	12	1. **Tired Of Toein' The Line**	EMI America 8043
			BUSCH, Lou, and His Orchestra	
			Born on 7/18/10 in Louisville. Died on 9/19/79. Pianist/orchestra leader. Also recorded as Joe "Fingers" Carr.	
3/24/56	35	2	1. 11th Hour Melody	Capitol 3349
6/16/56	19	10	2. Portuguese Washerwomen [I]	Capitol 3418
			JOE "FINGERS" CARR	
			Jockey #19 / Best Seller #25 / Top 100 #25	
			BUSH	
			Rock quartet from London: Gavin Rossdale (vocals, guitar), Nigel Pulsford (guitar), Dave Parsons (bass) and Robin Goodridge (drums).	
10/14/95	30	7	1. Comedown	Trauma/Intersc. 98134
			Airplay #25 / Sales #68	
			BUSH, Kate	
			Born on 7/30/58 in Bexleyheath, Kent, England. Discovered by David Gilmour of Pink Floyd. Signed to EMI at age 16 while still at St. Joseph's Convent Grammar School. In 1993, directed the movie *The Line, The Curve and The Cross*, which was based on six songs from her album *The Red Shoes*.	
11/9/85	30	4	1. Running Up That Hill	EMI America 8285
			Sales #26	
			BUSTERS, The	
			Western Massachusetts rock group. Originally known as the Northern Lights, recorded "Typhoid," which was released as "Bust Out" by The Busters. Members Jack Baker (sax) and Fran Parda (drums) put together new touring group known as The Busters.	
9/28/63	25	5	1. Bust Out [I]	Arlen 735
			BUTLER, Jerry	
			Born on 12/8/39 in Sunflower, Mississippi. Older brother of Billy Butler. Sang in the Northern Jubilee Gospel Singers, with Curtis Mayfield. Later with the Quails. In 1957, Butler and Mayfield joined the Roosters with Sam Gooden and brothers Arthur & Richard Brooks. Changed name to The Impressions in 1957. Left for solo career in autumn of 1958. Also worked as the Cook County Commissioner in Illinois. Dubbed "The Ice Man."	
6/16/58	11	9	1. For Your Precious Love	Abner 1013
			JERRY BUTLER AND THE IMPRESSIONS	
			Best Seller #11 / Top 100 #11 / Jockey #25; released first on Falcon 1013, then on Abner 1013 (also on Vee-Jay 280)	
11/7/60	7	13	2. **He Will Break Your Heart**	Vee-Jay 354
			#1 R&B hit (7 weeks)	
4/3/61	27	4	3. Find Another Girl	Vee-Jay 375
8/7/61	25	4	4. I'm A Telling You	Vee-Jay 390
10/30/61	11	11	5. Moon River	Vee-Jay 405
			from the movie *Breakfast at Tiffany's* starring Audrey Hepburn	
8/18/62	20	4	6. Make It Easy On Yourself	Vee-Jay 451
12/28/63+	31	5	7. Need To Belong	Vee-Jay 567

DATE	POS	WKS	ARTIST–RECORD TITLE	LABEL & NO.
9/19/64	5	11	8. **Let It Be Me** **BETTY EVERETT & JERRY BUTLER**	Vee-Jay 613
11/25/67	38	2	9. Mr. Dream Merchant	Mercury 72721
6/8/68	20	9	10. Never Give You Up	Mercury 72798
10/5/68	16	8	11. Hey, Western Union Man #1 R&B hit (1 week)	Mercury 72850
1/18/69	39	2	12. Are You Happy	Mercury 72876
3/8/69	4	12	● 13. **Only The Strong Survive** #1 R&B hit (2 weeks)	Mercury 72898
6/21/69	24	7	14. Moody Woman	Mercury 72929
9/6/69	20	9	15. What's The Use Of Breaking Up	Mercury 72960
2/5/72	21	10	● 16. Ain't Understanding Mellow **JERRY BUTLER and BRENDA LEE EAGER**	Mercury 73255

BUTLER, Jonathan

Born in Capetown, South Africa. Soul guitarist/singer/songwriter. Migrated to London, 1984 (age 21).

DATE	POS	WKS	ARTIST–RECORD TITLE	LABEL & NO.
8/15/87	27	5	1. Lies Sales #21 / Airplay #30	Jive 1038

BYRD, Charlie—see GETZ, Stan

BYRDS, The

Folk-rock group formed in Los Angeles in 1964. Consisted of James "Roger" McGuinn (12-string guitar), David Crosby (guitar), Gene Clark (percussion), Chris Hillman (bass) and Mike Clarke (drums). McGuinn, who changed his name to Roger in 1968, had been with Bobby Darin and the Chad Mitchell Trio. Clark had been with the New Christy Minstrels. All except Clarke had folk music background. First recorded as the Beefeaters for Elektra in 1964. Also recorded as the Jet Set. Professional debut in March 1965. Clark left after "Eight Miles High." Crosby left in late 1967 to form Crosby, Stills & Nash. Re-formed in 1968 with McGuinn, Hillman, Kevin Kelly (drums) and Gram Parsons (guitar). Hillman and Parsons left that same year to form the Flying Burrito Brothers. McGuinn again re-formed with Clarence White (guitar), John York (bass) and Gene Parsons (drums). Reunions with original members in 1973 and 1979. Gram Parsons died on 9/19/73 (age 26) of a heroin overdose. McGuinn, Clark & Hillman later recorded as a trio. In 1986, Hillman formed popular country group, The Desert Rose Band. McGuinn, Crosby and Hillman reunited on stage on 2/24/90 for a Roy Orbison tribute. Gene Clark died on 5/24/91 (age 46) of natural causes. Mike Clarke, also with the Flying Burrito Brothers and Firefall, died of liver failure on 12/19/93 (age 49). Group inducted into the Rock and Roll Hall of Fame in 1991.

DATE	POS	WKS	ARTIST–RECORD TITLE	LABEL & NO.
6/5/65	1 (1)	10	1. **Mr. Tambourine Man**	Columbia 43271
8/21/65	40	1	2. All I Really Want To Do	Columbia 43332
11/6/65	1 (3)	11	3. **Turn! Turn! Turn! (To Everything There Is A Season)** lyrics adapted by Pete Seeger from the Book of Ecclesiastes	Columbia 43424
4/30/66	14	6	4. Eight Miles High	Columbia 43578
10/22/66	36	2	5. Mr. Spaceman	Columbia 43766
2/18/67	29	3	6. So You Want To Be A Rock 'N' Roll Star	Columbia 43987
4/29/67	30	3	7. My Back Pages #1, 2, 7: written by Bob Dylan	Columbia 44054

DATE	POS	WKS	ARTIST—RECORD TITLE	LABEL & NO.
			BYRNES, Edward	
			Born Edward Breitenberger on 7/30/33 in New York City. Best known as Kookie on TV's "77 Sunset Strip."	
4/27/59	4	11	● 1. **Kookie, Kookie (Lend Me Your Comb)** [N] **EDWARD BYRNES And CONNIE STEVENS**	Warner 5047
			C	
			CADETS, The	
			Los Angeles R&B quintet: Aaron Collins (lead singer), Ted Taylor, William "Dub" Jones (bass man for The Coasters), Willie Davis and Lloyd McCraw. Also recorded as The Jacks on RPM with Davis as lead. Collins and Davis later joined The Flares. Collins's sisters, Betty and Rosie, recorded as The Teen Queens.	
7/21/56	15	7	1. Stranded In The Jungle [N] Best Seller #15 / Jockey #16 / Juke Box #16 / Top 100 #18	Modern 994
			CADILLACS, The	
			R&B vocal group formed at P.S. 139 in Harlem in 1953 as the Carnations. The first R&B vocal group to use choreography extensively in their stage routines. Lead vocalist Earl "Speedoo" Carroll left in 1958 to join The Coasters.	
2/4/56	17	5	1. Speedoo Best Seller #17 / Top 100 #30; song's title is lead singer Earl Carroll's nickname; Jesse Powell (orch.)	Josie 785
1/12/59	28	3	2. Peek-A-Boo Osie Johnson (orch.)	Josie 846
			CAFFERTY, John, And The Beaver Brown Band	
			Rock sextet formed in Narragansett, Rhode Island, in 1972: John Cafferty (vocals, guitar), Gary Gramolini (guitar), Robert Cotoia (keyboards), Michael Antunes (saxophone), Pat Lupo (bass) and Kenny Jo Silva (drums). Wrote and recorded the music for the soundtrack *Eddie And The Cruisers*.	
9/15/84	7	11	1. **On The Dark Side** [R] Airplay #6 / Sales #11; originally charted in 1983 at #64	Scotti Br. 04594
12/8/84+	31	7	2. Tender Years [R] Airplay #28 / Sales #28; originally charted in 1984 at #78; above 2 from the movie *Eddie and the Cruisers* starring Tom Berenger	Scotti Br. 04682
6/1/85	22	8	3. Tough All Over Airplay #13 / Sales #26	Scotti Br. 04891
8/31/85	18	8	4. C-I-T-Y Sales #19 / Airplay #19	Scotti Br. 05452
			CAIN, Tane	
			Born and raised in Hawaii. (First name pronounced: tawnee.) Former wife of Jonathan Cain (of The Babys, Journey and Bad English). Daughter of actor Doug McClure.	
9/18/82	37	3	1. Holdin' On	RCA 13287

DATE	POS	WKS	ARTIST—RECORD TITLE	LABEL & NO.
			CAIOLA, Al, And His Orchestra	
			Born on 9/7/20 in Jersey City, New Jersey. Guitarist/composer/bandleader. First recorded for Savoy in 1955. Prolific studio work.	
1/16/61	35	4	1. The Magnificent Seven [I] title song from the movie starring Yul Brynner	United Art. 261
5/1/61	19	5	2. Bonanza [I] title song from the TV series starring Lorne Greene	United Art. 302
			CALDWELL, Bobby	
			Born on 8/15/51 in New York City; raised in Florida. Multi-instrumentalist/ songwriter. Percussionist with Johnny Winter, Rick Derringer, Captain Beyond and Armageddon. Wrote tracks for "New Mickey Mouse Club" TV show, commercials, and Peter Cetera and Amy Grant's "The Next Time I Fall."	
2/3/79	9	12	1. **What You Won't Do For Love**	Clouds 11
			CALE, J.J.	
			Born Jean Jacques Cale on 12/5/38 in Oklahoma City. Rock singer/songwriter/guitarist. Wrote Eric Clapton's "After Midnight" and "Cocaine." In high school bands with Leon Russell. Worked with Phil Spector and Delaney & Bonnie. Session work with Art Garfunkel, Bob Seger and Neil Young.	
3/11/72	22	8	1. Crazy Mama	Shelter 7314
			CALLOWAY	
			R&B duo of brothers Reggie and Vincent Calloway from Cincinnati. Both founded Midnight Star.	
3/10/90	2 (1)	15	● 1. **I Wanna Be Rich** Sales #2 / Airplay #2	Solar 74005
			CAMEO	
			New York City soul-funk group, founded in 1974 as The New York City Players by Larry Blackmon (drums), with Gregory "Straps" Johnson (keyboards). Vocals by Wayne Cooper and Tomi "Tee" Jenkins. By 1985, group pared down to a trio of Blackmon, Jenkins and Nathan Leftenant.	
10/4/86	6	14	1. **Word Up** Sales #2 / Airplay #8; #1 R&B hit (3 weeks)	Atl. Art. 884933
2/14/87	21	7	2. Candy Sales #19 / Airplay #28; #1 R&B hit (2 weeks)	Atl. Art. 888193
			CAMILLO, Tony—see BAZUKA	
			CAMPBELL, Glen	
			Born on 4/22/36 in Billstown, Arkansas. Vocalist/guitarist/composer. With his uncle Dick Bills's band, 1954–58. To Los Angeles; recorded with The Champs in 1960. Became prolific studio musician; with The Hondells in 1964, The Beach Boys in 1965 and Sagittarius in 1967. Own TV show "The Glen Campbell Goodtime Hour," 1968–72. Appeared in the movies *True Grit, Norwood* and *Strange Homecoming*; voice in the animated movie *Rock-A-Doodle*.	
11/25/67	26	7	1. By The Time I Get To Phoenix	Capitol 2015
5/25/68	36	2	2. I Wanna Live #1 Country hit (3 weeks)	Capitol 2146
8/3/68	32	3	3. Dreams Of The Everyday Housewife	Capitol 2224
11/2/68	39	1	4. Gentle On My Mind [R] originally charted in 1967 at #62	Capitol 5939

DATE	POS	WKS	ARTIST–RECORD TITLE	LABEL & NO.
11/16/68+	**3**	13	● 5. **Wichita Lineman** #1 Adult Contemporary hit (6 weeks); #1 Country hit (2 weeks)	Capitol 2302
3/8/69	**36**	1	6. Let It Be Me **GLEN CAMPBELL AND BOBBIE GENTRY**	Capitol 2387
3/15/69	**4**	10	● 7. **Galveston** #1 Adult Contemporary hit (6 weeks); #1 Country hit (3 weeks)	Capitol 2428
5/17/69	**26**	5	8. Where's The Playground Susie	Capitol 2494
8/23/69	**35**	2	9. True Grit title song from the movie starring John Wayne and Campbell	Capitol 2573
11/1/69	**23**	7	10. Try A Little Kindness #1 Adult Contemporary hit (1 week)	Capitol 2659
1/31/70	**19**	7	11. Honey Come Back #1, 5, 7, 8, 11: written by Jimmy Webb	Capitol 2718
3/14/70	**27**	6	12. All I Have To Do Is Dream **BOBBIE GENTRY & GLEN CAMPBELL**	Capitol 2745
5/9/70	**40**	2	13. Oh Happy Day	Capitol 2787
9/26/70	**10**	9	14. **It's Only Make Believe**	Capitol 2905
3/27/71	**31**	4	15. Dream Baby (How Long Must I Dream)	Capitol 3062
6/21/75	**1 (2)**	18	● 16. **Rhinestone Cowboy** #1 Country hit (3 weeks); #1 Adult Contemporary hit (1 week); #24 Adult Contemporary hit for Larry Weiss (song's writer) in 1974	Capitol 4095
11/22/75+	**11**	11	17. Country Boy (You Got Your Feet In L.A.) #1 Adult Contemporary hit (1 week)	Capitol 4155
4/17/76	**27**	5	18. Don't Pull Your Love/Then You Can Tell Me Goodbye #1 Adult Contemporary hit (1 week)	Capitol 4245
3/5/77	**1 (1)**	15	● 19. **Southern Nights** #1 Adult Contemporary hit (4 weeks); #1 Country hit (2 weeks)	Capitol 4376
8/13/77	**39**	2	20. Sunflower written by Neil Diamond; #1 Adult Contemporary hit (1 week)	Capitol 4445
12/9/78	**38**	2	21. Can You Fool originally released earlier in 1978 on Capitol 4584	Capitol 4638
			CAMPBELL, Jo Ann	
			Born on 7/20/38 in Jacksonville, Florida. First recorded for El Dorado in 1957. Appeared in the movies *Johnny Melody*, *Go Johnny Go* and *Hey, Let's Twist*. Married country singer Troy Seals (cousin of Dan Seals) in the early 1960s; recorded together as Jo Ann & Troy in 1964.	
9/8/62	**38**	3	1. (I'm The Girl On) Wolverton Mountain answer song to Claude King's "Wolverton Mountain"; some pressings titled as: "I'm The Girl From Wolverton Mountain"	Cameo 223
			CAMPBELL, Tevin	
			Born on 11/12/78 in Waxahachie, Texas. Won role in 1988 for the TV show "Wally & The Valentines." Discovered by Quincy Jones. Appeared in the movie *Graffiti Bridge*.	
2/9/91	**12**	13	● 1. Round And Round Airplay #12 / Sales #13; written and produced by Prince; from the movie *Graffiti Bridge* starring Prince	Paisley P. 21740
12/7/91+	**6**	20	● 2. **Tell Me What You Want Me To Do** Airplay #6 / Sales #8; #1 R&B hit (1 week)	Qwest 19131
10/23/93+	**9**	23	● 3. **Can We Talk** Airplay #9 / Sales #9; #1 R&B hit (3 weeks)	Qwest 18346
3/26/94	**9**	18	4. **I'm Ready** Airplay #8 / Sales #15; written and co-produced by Babyface	Qwest 18264

DATE	POS	WKS	ARTIST–RECORD TITLE	LABEL & NO.
7/9/94	**20**	10	5. Always In My Heart Airplay #22 / Sales #24	Qwest 18260

C & C MUSIC FACTORY

Dance outfit led by producers/songwriters Robert Clivilles (New York native; percussion) & David Cole (Tennessee native; keyboards). Featured vocalists include Freedom Williams and Deborah Cooper (Fatback, Change). Martha Wash (Two Tons O' Fun, The Weather Girls) is the actual vocalist of "Gonna Make You Sweat," lip-synched in video by Liberian-born Zelma Davis. Cole died of spinal meningitis on 1/25/95 (age 32).

DATE	POS	WKS	ARTIST–RECORD TITLE	LABEL & NO.
12/15/90+	**1 (2)**	17	▲ 1. **Gonna Make You Sweat (Everybody Dance Now)** **C & C MUSIC FACTORY Featuring Freedom Williams** (see bio note) Sales #1(4) / Airplay #3; #1 R&B hit (1 week)	Columbia 73604
3/23/91	**3**	14	● 2. **Here We Go** **C + C MUSIC FACTORY Presents Freedom Williams and Zelma Davis** Sales #3 / Airplay #5	Columbia 73690
7/27/91	**4**	12	● 3. **Things That Make You Go Hmmmm...** **C + C MUSIC FACTORY featuring Freedom Williams** Airplay #10 / Sales #12	Columbia 73687
9/10/94	**40**	2	4. Do You Wanna Get Funky Sales #21 / Airplay #47	Columbia 77582

CANDLEBOX

Seattle-based rock band: Kevin Martin (vocals), Peter Klett (guitar), Bardi Martin (bass) and Scott Mercado (drums). The Martins are not related.

DATE	POS	WKS	ARTIST–RECORD TITLE	LABEL & NO.
9/3/94	**18**	15	1. Far Behind Sales #13 / Airplay #23	Maverick/Sire 18118

CANDYMAN

Born on 6/25/68. Rapper from Los Angeles. Backing rapper/dancer with Tone Loc.

DATE	POS	WKS	ARTIST–RECORD TITLE	LABEL & NO.
10/13/90	**9**	12	▲ 1. **Knockin' Boots** Sales #2 / Airplay #28; samples Rose Royce's "Ooh Boy" and Betty Wright's "Tonight Is The Night"	Epic 73450

CANNED HEAT

Blues-rock band formed in Los Angeles in 1966. Consisted of Bob "The Bear" Hite (vocals, harmonica), Alan "Blind Owl" Wilson (guitar, harmonica, vocals), Henry Vestine (guitar), Larry Taylor (bass) and Frank Cook (drums). Cook replaced by Fito de la Parra in 1968. Vestine replaced by Harvey Mandel in 1969. Wilson died of a drug overdose on 9/3/70 (age 27). Hite died of a drug-related heart attack on 4/6/81 (age 36).

DATE	POS	WKS	ARTIST–RECORD TITLE	LABEL & NO.
9/7/68	**16**	7	1. On The Road Again	Liberty 56038
12/21/68+	**11**	9	2. Going Up The Country	Liberty 56077
11/7/70	**26**	6	3. Let's Work Together	Liberty 56151

CANNIBAL and THE HEADHUNTERS

Four Mexican-American youths based in Los Angeles; led by Frankie "Cannibal" Garcia (died on 1/21/96, age 49).

DATE	POS	WKS	ARTIST–RECORD TITLE	LABEL & NO.
4/17/65	**30**	6	1. Land Of 1000 Dances	Rampart 642

DATE	POS	WKS	ARTIST–RECORD TITLE	LABEL & NO.
			CANNON, Ace	
			Born on 5/5/34 in Grenada, Mississippi. Saxophonist since age 10. Worked with Bill Black's Combo.	
1/27/62	17	10	1. Tuff [I]	Hi 2040
5/19/62	36	1	2. Blues (Stay Away From Me) [I]	Hi 2051
			#11 hit for Owen Bradley in 1949	
			CANNON, Freddy	
			Born Frederick Picariello on 12/4/39 in Lynn, Massachusetts. Local work with own band, Freddy Karmon & The Hurricanes. Nickname "Boom Boom" came from big bass drum-sound on his records. Band arrangements by Frank Slay on all Swan recordings.	
5/25/59	6	10	1. **Tallahassee Lassie**	Swan 4031
			written by Cannon's mother	
12/7/59+	3	11	● 2. **Way Down Yonder In New Orleans**	Swan 4043
			FREDDIE CANNON	
			jazz song written in 1922	
3/7/60	34	3	3. Chattanooga Shoe Shine Boy	Swan 4050
			#1 hit for Red Foley in 1950	
5/30/60	28	4	4. Jump Over	Swan 4053
9/4/61	35	1	5. Transistor Sister	Swan 4078
5/26/62	3	12	6. **Palisades Park**	Swan 4106
			written by Chuck Barris (host of TV's "The Gong Show")	
2/15/64	16	6	7. Abigail Beecher	Warner 5409
			all of above produced by Frank Slay	
8/28/65	13	6	8. Action	Warner 5645
			from Dick Clark's TV show "Where the Action Is"	
			CAPALDI, Jim	
			Born on 8/24/44 in Evesham, England. Drummer with Traffic.	
5/28/83	28	5	1. That's Love	Atlantic 89849
			CAPITOLS, The	
			R&B vocal trio from Detroit. Consisted of lead singer Sam George (murdered on 3/17/82, age 39), "Donald Norman" Storball and "Richard Mitchell" McDougall.	
5/21/66	7	11	1. **Cool Jerk**	Karen 1524
			CAPRIS, The	
			Italian vocal group from Queens, New York, formed in 1958. Consisted of Nick Santamaria (lead), Vinny Narcardo (baritone), Mike Mincelli (1st tenor), Frank Reina (2nd tenor) and John Cassese (bass). Group disbanded in 1959, re-formed when song "There's A Moon Out Tonight" was reissued on Lost Nite in 1960 and became a hit in 1961.	
1/23/61	3	10	1. **There's A Moon Out Tonight**	Old Town 1094
			originally released on Planet 1010 in 1959	

DATE	POS	WKS	ARTIST–RECORD TITLE	LABEL & NO.
			CAPTAIN & TENNILLE	
			Daryl "The Captain" Dragon (born 8/27/42, Los Angeles) and his wife, Toni Tennille (born 5/8/43, Montgomery, Alabama). Dragon is the son of noted conductor Carmen Dragon. Keyboardist with The Beach Boys, nicknamed "The Captain" by Mike Love. Duo had own TV show on ABC, 1976–77.	
5/24/75	1 (4)	16	● 1. **Love Will Keep Us Together** #1 Adult Contemporary hit (1 week)	A&M 1672
10/4/75	4	14	● 2. **The Way I Want To Touch You** first released on Butterscotch Castle 001, then on Joyce 101, then on A&M 1624, all in 1974; #1 Adult Contemporary hit (2 weeks)	A&M 1725
2/7/76	3	13	● 3. **Lonely Night (Angel Face)** #1 Adult Contemporary hit (1 week)	A&M 1782
5/8/76	4	12	● 4. **Shop Around** #1 Adult Contemporary hit (1 week)	A&M 1817
10/9/76	4	15	● 5. **Muskrat Love** #1 Adult Contemporary hit (4 weeks)	A&M 1870
4/2/77	13	8	6. **Can't Stop Dancin'** written by Ray Stevens	A&M 1912
9/9/78	10	14	7. **You Never Done It Like That** #1,3,7: written by Neil Sedaka	A&M 2063
1/27/79	40	1	8. You Need A Woman Tonight	A&M 2106
11/10/79+	1 (1)	22	● 9. **Do That To Me One More Time**	Casablanca 2215
			CAPTAIN HOLLYWOOD PROJECT	
			Captain Hollywood is Tony Harrison. Born in Newark, New Jersey; raised in Detroit. While in the Army, was stationed in Nuremburg, Germany, where he began entertainment career as a choreographer.	
5/22/93	17	12	1. More And More Airplay #12 / Sales #21; Nina (lead vocal)	Imago 25029
			CARA, Irene	
			Born on 3/18/59 in New York City. Vocalist/actress/dancer/pianist. Professional debut at age seven. Won Obie Award for *The Me Nobody Knows* in 1970. Much TV work, including "Electric Company" and "Roots 2"; appeared in the movies *Fame*, *D.C. Cab* and *The Cotton Club*.	
7/26/80	4	12	1. **Fame**	RSO 1034
9/27/80	19	9	2. Out Here On My Own co-written by Lesley Gore; above 2 from the movie *Fame* starring Cara	RSO 1048
4/16/83	1 (6)	20	● 3. **Flashdance...What A Feeling** from the movie *Flashdance* starring Jennifer Beals	Casablanca 811440
11/5/83	13	10	4. Why Me?	Geffen 29464
1/28/84	37	3	5. The Dream (Hold On To Your Dream) from the movie *D.C. Cab* starring Cara and Mr. T.	Geffen 29396
4/14/84	8	11	6. **Breakdance**	Geffen 29328
			CARAVELLES, The	
			English pop duo: Andrea Simpson and Lois Wilkinson.	
11/23/63	3	10	1. **You Don't Have To Be A Baby To Cry** #10 Country hit for Ernest Tubb in 1950	Smash 1852

DATE	POS	WKS	ARTIST–RECORD TITLE	LABEL & NO.
			CAREFREES, The	
4/11/64	39	1	British trio: Lyn Cornell, Betty Prescott and Barbara Kay. 1. We Love You Beatles [N] new lyrics to "We Love You Conrad" from the musical *Bye Bye Birdie* starring Chita Rivera	London Int. 10614
			CAREY, Mariah	
			Born on 3/27/70 of Irish-American and Black-Venezuelan parentage. Native of Long Island, New York. Her mother is Patricia Carey, former singer with the New York City Opera. Mariah sang backup for Brenda K. Starr. Won the 1990 Best New Artist Grammy Award. Married Tommy Mottola, president of Sony Music Entertainment, on 6/5/93.	
6/16/90	1 (4)	17	● 1. **Vision Of Love** Airplay #1(3) / Sales #1(2); #1 Adult Contemporary hit (3 weeks); #1 R&B hit (2 weeks)	Columbia 73348
9/29/90	1 (3)	18	● 2. **Love Takes Time** Sales #1(2) / Airplay #1(2); #1 Adult Contemporary hit (1 week); #1 R&B hit (1 week)	Columbia 73455
1/19/91	1 (2)	15	● 3. **Someday** Airplay #1(4) / Sales #2	Columbia 73561
4/13/91	1 (2)	14	4. **I Don't Wanna Cry** Airplay #1(2) / Sales #3; #1 Adult Contemporary hit (1 week); above 4 from the album *Mariah Carey*	Columbia 73743
8/31/91	1 (3)	20	● 5. **Emotions** Airplay #1(4) / Sales #10; #1 R&B hit (1 week); different version on the B-side of #7 below	Columbia 73977
11/23/91+	2 (1)	17	6. **Can't Let Go** Airplay #2 / Sales #8; #1 Adult Contemporary hit (3 weeks)	Columbia 74088
3/7/92	5	16	7. **Make It Happen** Airplay #2 / Sales #18	Columbia 74239
5/30/92	1 (2)	14	8. **I'll Be There** Airplay #1(8) / Sales #3; recorded on MTV's *Unplugged*; Trey Lorenz (male vocal); #1 Adult Contemporary hit (2 weeks)	Columbia 74330
8/7/93	1 (8)	26	▲ 9. **Dreamlover** Airplay #1(11) / Sales #2; samples "Blind Alley" (from The Emotions' album *Untouched*)	Columbia 77080
11/6/93	1 (4)	25	▲ 10. **Hero** Airplay #1(10) / Sales #2	Columbia 77224
2/5/94	3	21	● 11. **Without You/** Airplay #2 / Sales #3; written by Badfinger's Pete Ham and Tom Evans	
		20	12. Never Forget You	Columbia 77358
6/4/94	12	18	13. Anytime You Need A Friend Airplay #8 / Sales #19; above 5 from the album *Music Box*	Columbia 77499
9/10/94	2 (1)	13	● 14. **Endless Love** **LUTHER VANDROSS & MARIAH CAREY** Sales #2 / Airplay #5	Columbia 77629
9/30/95	1 (8)	23	▲² 15. **Fantasy** Airplay #1(7) / Sales #1(5); samples "Genius Of Love" by Tom Tom Club; side 2 remix features rap by Ol' Dirty Bastard; #1 R&B hit (6 weeks)	Columbia 78043
12/2/95	1 (16)	20↑	▲² 16. **One Sweet Day** **MARIAH CAREY & BOYZ II MEN** Airplay #1(13) / Sales #1(11); the #1 hit in *Hot 100* history; #1 Adult Contemporary hit (13 weeks)	Columbia 78074

DATE	POS	WKS	ARTIST—RECORD TITLE	LABEL & NO.
			CAREY, Tony	
			Born on 10/16/53 in Fresno, California. Later settled in West Germany. Ex-keyboardist with Rainbow and lead singer of Planet P.	
3/31/84	22	8	1. A Fine Fine Day	MCA 52343
7/14/84	33	2	2. The First Day Of Summer	MCA 52388
			CARGILL, Henson	
			Born on 2/5/41 in Oklahoma City. Country singer.	
1/20/68	25	7	1. Skip A Rope #1 Country hit (5 weeks)	Monument 1041
			CARLISLE, Belinda	
			Born on 8/17/58 in Hollywood. Lead singer of the Go-Go's, 1978–84. Married to Morgan Mason, son of late actor James Mason.	
6/21/86	3	14	1. **Mad About You** Sales #2 / Airplay #4; Andy Taylor (of Duran Duran; guitar solo)	I.R.S. 52815
10/10/87	1 (1)	15	2. **Heaven Is A Place On Earth** Sales #1(2) / Airplay #1(1)	MCA 53181
1/23/88	2 (1)	13	3. **I Get Weak** Sales #1(1) / Airplay #3	MCA 53242
5/7/88	7	10	4. **Circle In The Sand** Sales #6 / Airplay #9	MCA 53308
10/28/89	11	10	5. **Leave A Light On** Sales #11 / Airplay #13; George Harrison (slide guitar solo)	MCA 53706
2/17/90	30	5	6. Summer Rain Sales #23 / Airplay #35	MCA 53783
			CARLTON, Carl	
			Born in 1952 in Detroit. Soul singer. First recorded for Lando Records in 1964.	
10/12/74	6	10	1. **Everlasting Love**	Back Beat 27001
9/26/81	22	7	● 2. **She's A Bad Mama Jama (She's Built, She's Stacked)**	20th Century 2488
			CARMEN, Eric	
			Born on 8/11/49 in Cleveland. Classical training at Cleveland Institute of Music from early years to mid-teens. Lead singer of the Raspberries, 1970–74.	
1/17/76	2 (3)	14	● 1. **All By Myself** melody based on Rachmaninov's "Piano Concerto No.2"	Arista 0165
5/22/76	11	10	2. Never Gonna Fall In Love Again #1 Adult Contemporary hit (1 week); melody based on Rachmaninov's *Second Symphony*	Arista 0184
9/18/76	34	3	3. Sunrise	Arista 0200
9/24/77	23	8	4. She Did It	Arista 0266
10/28/78	19	7	5. Change Of Heart	Arista 0354
2/9/85	35	4	6. I Wanna Hear It From Your Lips	Geffen 29118
12/12/87+	4	16	7. **Hungry Eyes** Sales #4 / Airplay #4; from the movie *Dirty Dancing* starring Patrick Swayze	RCA 5315
6/18/88	3	13	8. **Make Me Lose Control** Sales #1(1) / Airplay #4; #1 Adult Contemporary hit (3 weeks)	Arista 9686

DATE	POS	WKS	ARTIST—RECORD TITLE	LABEL & NO.
			CARNES, Kim	
			Born on 7/20/45 in Los Angeles. Vocalist/pianist/composer. Member of The New Christy Minstrels with husband/co-writer Dave Ellingson and Kenny Rogers, late 1960s. Wrote for and performed in commercials. Co-wrote "Love Comes From Unexpected Places," which won the American Song Festival in 1977 and was later recorded by Barbra Streisand.	
8/5/78	36	3	1. You're A Part Of Me **GENE COTTON with Kim Carnes** Carnes's solo version made the Adult Contemporary charts in 1976 on A&M 1767 (#32)	Ariola Am. 7704
4/12/80	4	14	2. **Don't Fall In Love With A Dreamer** **KENNY ROGERS with KIM CARNES**	United Art. 1345
6/14/80	10	15	3. **More Love**	EMI America 8045
4/11/81	1 (9)	20	● 4. **Bette Davis Eyes** written by Jackie DeShannon and Donna Weiss	EMI America 8077
8/29/81	28	6	5. Draw Of The Cards	EMI America 8087
9/11/82	29	6	6. Voyeur	EMI America 8127
12/25/82+	36	4	7. Does It Make You Remember	EMI America 8147
11/26/83	40	2	8. Invisible Hands	EMI America 8181
10/13/84	15	9	9. What About Me? **KENNY ROGERS with KIM CARNES and JAMES INGRAM** Airplay #14 / Sales #16 / #1 Adult Contemporary hit (2 weeks)	RCA 13899
6/1/85	15	9	10. Crazy In The Night (Barking At Airplanes) Sales #14 / Airplay #20	EMI America 8267
			CAROSONE, Renato	
			Born on 1/2/20 in Naples, Italy. Male vocalist.	
5/12/58	18	9	1. Torero [F] Jockey #18 / Top 100 #19 / Best Sellers #20	Capitol 71080
			CARPENTERS	
			Richard Carpenter (born 10/15/46) and sister Karen (born 3/2/50; died 2/4/83 of heart failure due to anorexia nervosa). From New Haven, Connecticut. Richard played piano from age nine. To Downey, California, in 1963. Karen played drums in group with Richard and bass player Wes Jacobs in 1965. The trio recorded for RCA in 1966. After a period with the band Spectrum, the Carpenters recorded as a duo for A&M in 1969. Won the 1970 Best New Artist Grammy Award. Hosts of the TV variety show "Make Your Own Kind Of Music" in 1971. 1988 TV movie "The Karen Carpenter Story" was based on Karen's life.	
6/27/70	1 (4)	15	● 1. **(They Long To Be) Close To You** #1 Adult Contemporary hit (6 weeks)	A&M 1183
10/3/70	2 (4)	14	● 2. **We've Only Just Begun** adapted from an insurance commercial jingle; #1 Adult Contemporary hit (7 weeks)	A&M 1217
2/13/71	3	12	● 3. **For All We Know** from the movie *Lovers and Other Strangers* starring Bea Arthur; written by James Griffin and Robb Royer of Bread under the pseudonyms Arther James and Robb Wilson; #1 Adult Contemporary hit (3 weeks)	A&M 1243
5/22/71	2 (2)	11	● 4. **Rainy Days And Mondays** #1 Adult Contemporary hit (4 weeks)	A&M 1260
9/11/71	2 (2)	12	● 5. **Superstar** written by Leon Russell and Bonnie Bramlett (of Delaney & Bonnie); #1 Adult Contemporary hit (2 weeks)	A&M 1289

DATE	POS	WKS	ARTIST–RECORD TITLE	LABEL & NO.
1/22/72	2 (2)	11	● 6. **Hurting Each Other** #1 Adult Contemporary hit (2 weeks)	A&M 1322
5/13/72	12	8	7. It's Going To Take Some Time written by Carole King	A&M 1351
7/22/72	7	9	8. **Goodbye To Love**	A&M 1367
3/10/73	3	11	● 9. **Sing** featured on the "Sesame Street" TV show; #1 Adult Contemporary hit (2 weeks)	A&M 1413
6/16/73	2 (1)	12	● 10. **Yesterday Once More** #1 Adult Contemporary hit (3 weeks)	A&M 1446
10/20/73	1 (2)	16	● 11. **Top Of The World**	A&M 1468
4/27/74	11	9	12. I Won't Last A Day Without You #1 Adult Contemporary hit (1 week); #2, 4, 12: written by Paul Williams and Roger Nichols	A&M 1521
12/7/74+	1 (1)	12	● 13. **Please Mr. Postman** #1 Adult Contemporary hit (1 week)	A&M 1646
4/12/75	4	9	14. **Only Yesterday** #1 Adult Contemporary hit (1 week)	A&M 1677
8/16/75	17	7	15. Solitaire written by Neil Sedaka; #1 Adult Contemporary hit (1 week)	A&M 1721
3/13/76	12	8	16. There's A Kind Of Hush (All Over The World) #1 Adult Contemporary hit (2 weeks)	A&M 1800
7/4/76	25	5	17. I Need To Be In Love #1 Adult Contemporary hit (1 week)	A&M 1828
6/18/77	35	3	18. All You Get From Love Is A Love Song	A&M 1940
11/5/77	32	4	19. Calling Occupants Of Interplanetary Craft (The Recognized Anthem of World Contact Day)	A&M 1978
7/4/81	16	8	20. Touch Me When We're Dancing #1 Adult Contemporary hit (2 weeks)	A&M 2344
			CARR, Cathy	
			Born Angela Helen Catherine Cordovano on 6/28/36 in the Bronx. Died in November 1988.	
4/7/56	2 (1)	18	1. **Ivory Tower** Juke Box #2 / Top 100 #6 / Best Seller #7 / Jockey #9	Fraternity 734
			CARR, Joe "Fingers"—see BUSCH, Lou	
			CARR, Valerie	
			Black vocalist born in 1936 in New York.	
6/9/58	19	2	1. When The Boys Talk About The Girls Jockey #19 / Top 100 #84; Hugo Peretti (of Hugo & Luigi; orch.); B-side is Carr's version of Toni Arden's hit "Padre"	Roulette 4066
			CARR, Vikki	
			Born Florencia Martinez Cardona on 7/19/41 in El Paso, Texas. Regular on TV's "Ray Anthony Show," 1962.	
9/30/67	3	11	1. **It Must Be Him** #1 Adult Contemporary hit (3 weeks)	Liberty 55986
1/27/68	34	1	2. The Lesson #1 Adult Contemporary hit (1 week)	Liberty 56012
6/28/69	35	4	3. With Pen In Hand	Liberty 56092

DATE	POS	WKS	ARTIST—RECORD TITLE	LABEL & NO.
			CARRACK, Paul	
			Born on 4/22/51 in Sheffield, England. Lead singer of Ace (1973–76), Squeeze (1981, 1993) and Mike + The Mechanics (1985–92). Keyboardist with Roxy Music (1978–80).	
10/30/82	37	2	1. I Need You	Epic 03146
12/19/87+	9	13	2. **Don't Shed A Tear** Sales #6 / Airplay #9	Chrysalis 43164
4/23/88	28	5	3. One Good Reason Sales #25 / Airplay #25	Chrysalis 43204
11/25/89	31	4	4. I Live By The Groove Sales #28 / Airplay #31	Chrysalis 23427
			CARRADINE, Keith	
			Born on 8/8/49 in San Mateo, California. Leading actor in dozens of movies, including *Pretty Baby*, *Nashville* and *The Long Riders*. Son of actor John Carradine; half-brother of David Carradine.	
6/12/76	17	12	1. I'm Easy from the movie *Nashville* starring Carradine; #1 Adult Contemporary hit (1 week)	ABC 12117
			CARROLL, David, And His Orchestra	
			Born Nook Schrier on 10/15/13 in Chicago. Arranger/conductor since 1951 for many top Mercury artists.	
1/8/55	8	17	1. **Melody Of Love** [I] Jockey #8 / Best Seller #9 / Juke Box #12; music written in 1903, lyrics added in 1954 by Tom Glazer; narrative (Paul Tremaine) version on Mercury 70521	Mercury 70516
12/17/55	20	1	2. It's Almost Tomorrow Jockey #20 / Top 100 #34; Jack Halloran Singers (vocals)	Mercury 70717
			CARS, The	
			Rock group formed in Boston in 1976. Consisted of Ric Ocasek (lead vocals, guitar), Benjamin Orr (bass, vocals), Elliot Easton (guitar), Greg Hawkes (keyboards) and David Robinson (drums). Ocasek, Orr and Hawkes had been in trio in the early 1970s. Group named by Robinson, got start at the Rat Club in Boston. Disbanded in 1988.	
8/12/78	27	7	1. Just What I Needed also on the B-side of #11 below	Elektra 45491
12/9/78	35	5	2. My Best Friend's Girl	Elektra 45537
7/28/79	14	9	3. Let's Go	Elektra 46063
10/11/80	37	3	4. Touch And Go	Elektra 47039
12/12/81+	4	17	5. **Shake It Up**	Elektra 47250
3/24/84	7	11	6. **You Might Think**	Elektra 69744
5/26/84	12	11	7. Magic	Elektra 69724
8/11/84	3	14	8. **Drive** Sales #3 / Airplay #8 pre; #1 Adult Contemporary hit (3 weeks)	Elektra 69706
11/10/84	20	10	9. Hello Again Airplay #17 / Sales #17	Elektra 69681
3/9/85	33	5	10. Why Can't I Have You Airplay #28; above 5 from the album *Heartbeat City*	Elektra 69657
11/16/85+	7	12	11. **Tonight She Comes** Airplay #7 / Sales #10	Elektra 69589

DATE	POS	WKS	ARTIST–RECORD TITLE	LABEL & NO.
3/8/86	**32**	4	12. I'm Not The One Airplay #30	Elektra 69569
9/12/87	**17**	9	13. You Are The Girl Airplay #16 / Sales #19	Elektra 69446

CARSON, Kit

Real name: Liza Morrow. Vocalist on Benny Goodman's 1946 #2 hit "Symphony."

DATE	POS	WKS	ARTIST–RECORD TITLE	LABEL & NO.
12/31/55+	**11**	11	1. Band Of Gold Jockey #11 / Top 100 #17; Dick Hyman (orch.)	Capitol 3283

CARSON, Mindy

Born on 7/16/27 in New York City. Sang with Paul Whiteman in the 1940s.

DATE	POS	WKS	ARTIST–RECORD TITLE	LABEL & NO.
8/27/55	**13**	8	1. Wake The Town And Tell The People Jockey #13 / Juke Box #13 / Best Seller #20 / Top 100 #33 pre; Norman Leyden (orch.)	Columbia 40537
1/5/57	**34**	2	2. Since I Met You Baby	Columbia 40789

CARTER, Carlene—see ORRALL, Robert Ellis

CARTER, Clarence

Born in 1936 in Montgomery, Alabama. R&B vocalist/guitarist. Blind since age one; self-taught on guitar at age 11. Teamed with vocalist/pianist Calvin Scott as Clarence & Calvin, recorded for Fairlane in the early 1960s. Carter went solo in 1966. Married for a time to Candi Staton.

DATE	POS	WKS	ARTIST–RECORD TITLE	LABEL & NO.
8/17/68	**6**	11	● 1. **Slip Away**	Atlantic 2508
11/30/68+	**13**	11	● 2. Too Weak To Fight	Atlantic 2569
3/29/69	**31**	5	3. Snatching It Back	Atlantic 2605
8/1/70	**4**	12	● 4. **Patches**	Atlantic 2748

CARTER, June—see CASH, Johnny

CARTER, Mel

Born on 4/22/39 in Cincinnati. Soul vocalist/actor. Sang on local radio from age four; with Lionel Hampton on stage show at age nine. With Paul Gayten, Jimmy Scott bands. Joined Raspberry Singers gospel group in the early '50s. With his mother's gospel group, The Carvetts, in the mid-1950s. Named Top Gospel Tenor in 1957. Recorded in late '50s for Tri-State, Arwin, then Mercury. With Gospel Pearls in the early '60s. Acted on TV's "Quincy," "Sanford And Son," "Marcus Welby, MD" and "Magnum P.I."

DATE	POS	WKS	ARTIST–RECORD TITLE	LABEL & NO.
7/24/65	**8**	11	1. **Hold Me, Thrill Me, Kiss Me** #1 Adult Contemporary hit (1 week); #5 hit for Karen Chandler in 1953	Imperial 66113
11/27/65	**38**	2	2. (All Of A Sudden) My Heart Sings #7 hit for Johnnie Johnston in 1945	Imperial 66138
5/21/66	**32**	2	3. Band Of Gold #1 Adult Contemporary hit (2 weeks)	Imperial 66165

CASCADES, The

Pop group from San Diego consisting of John Gummoe (lead vocals), Eddie Snyder, David Stevens, David Wilson and David Zabo.

DATE	POS	WKS	ARTIST–RECORD TITLE	LABEL & NO.
1/26/63	**3**	13	1. **Rhythm Of The Rain** #1 Adult Contemporary hit (2 weeks)	Valiant 6026

DATE	POS	WKS	ARTIST–RECORD TITLE	LABEL & NO.

CASH, Alvin, & The Crawlers

Cash was born on 2/15/39 in St. Louis. Singer/dancer. Formed song/dance troupe, The Crawlers, in 1960, with brothers Robert, Arthur and George (ages eight to 10). They never sang on any of Alvin's hits. Alvin moved to Chicago in 1963. First recorded for Mar-V-Lus in 1964. Cut "Twine Time" with backing band the Nightlighters from Louisville, who changed their name to the Registers.

DATE	POS	WKS	ARTIST–RECORD TITLE	LABEL & NO.
1/30/65	14	7	1. Twine Time [I]	Mar-V-Lus 6002

CASH, Johnny

Born on 2/26/32 in Kingsland, Arkansas. To Dyess, Arkansas, at age three. Brother Roy led the Dixie Rhythm Ramblers band in late 1940s. In U.S. Air Force, 1950–54. Formed trio with Luther Perkins (guitar) and Marshall Grant (bass) in 1955. First recorded for Sun in 1955. On "Louisiana Hayride" and "Grand Ole Opry" in 1957. Own TV show for ABC, 1969–71. Worked with June Carter from 1961, married her in March 1968. Ranks within the top three male vocalists of the country charts. Daughter Rosanne Cash and stepdaughter Carlene Carter currently enjoying successful singing careers. Elected to the Country Music Hall of Fame in 1980. Won Grammy's Living Legends Award in 1990.

DATE	POS	WKS	ARTIST–RECORD TITLE	LABEL & NO.
10/20/56	17	11	1. I Walk The Line Best Seller #17 / Juke Box #17 / Top 100 #19 / Jockey #25; #1 Country hit (6 weeks)	Sun 241
2/10/58	14	13	2. Ballad Of A Teenage Queen/ Jockey #14 / Best Seller #16 / Top 100 #16; #1 Country hit (10 weeks)	
		7	3. Big River Best Seller flip	Sun 283
6/9/58	11	13	4. Guess Things Happen That Way Best Seller #11 / Top 100 #11 / Jockey #18; #1 Country hit (8 weeks)	Sun 295
9/1/58	24	6	5. The Ways Of A Woman In Love/ Hot 100 #24 / Best Seller #26	
		5	6. You're The Nearest Thing To Heaven	Sun 302
11/10/58	38	1	7. All Over Again	Columbia 41251
2/2/59	32	6	8. Don't Take Your Guns To Town #1 Country hit (6 weeks)	Columbia 41313
6/22/63	17	10	9. Ring Of Fire #1 Country hit (7 weeks)	Columbia 42788
3/14/64	35	3	10. Understand Your Man #1 Country hit (6 weeks)	Columbia 42964
6/29/68	32	6	11. Folsom Prison Blues recorded "live" at Folsom Prison; #1 Country hit (4 weeks)	Columbia 44513
8/2/69	2 (3)	11	● 12. **A Boy Named Sue** [N] recorded "live" at San Quentin prison; #1 Country hit (5 weeks); #1 Adult Contemporary hit (2 weeks)	Columbia 44944
2/21/70	36	2	13. If I Were A Carpenter **JOHNNY CASH & JUNE CARTER**	Columbia 45064
4/25/70	19	6	14. What Is Truth [S]	Columbia 45134
5/15/76	29	3	15. One Piece At A Time [N] **JOHNNY CASH And The Tennessee Three** #1 Country hit (2 weeks)	Columbia 10321

DATE	POS	WKS	ARTIST–RECORD TITLE	LABEL & NO.
			CASH, Rosanne	
			Born on 5/24/55 in Memphis. Daughter of Johnny Cash and Vivian Liberto. Raised by her mother in California, then moved to Nashville after high school graduation. Worked in the Johnny Cash Road Show. Married to Rodney Crowell, 1979–92.	
6/13/81	22	7	1. Seven Year Ache	Columbia 11426
			#1 Country hit (1 week)	
			CASHMAN & WEST	
			Duo of pop record producers/songwriters/singers Dennis "Terry Cashman" Minogue (born 7/5/41) and Thomas "Tommy West" Picardo, Jr. (born 8/17/42). Produced all of Jim Croce's recordings. Also see Buchanan Brothers.	
10/21/72	27	7	1. American City Suite	Dunhill 4324
			Sweet City Song/All Around The Town/A Friend Is Dying	
			CASINOS, The	
			Nine-man pop group from Cincinnati formed by Gene Hughes (lead singer).	
1/28/67	6	10	1. **Then You Can Tell Me Goodbye**	Fraternity 977
			CASSIDY, David	
			Born on 4/12/50 in New York City. Son of actor Jack Cassidy and actress Evelyn Ward. Played Keith Partridge, the lead singer of TV's "The Partridge Family." Married to actress Kay Lenz, 1977–81. Co-starred with his half-brother Shaun Cassidy in Broadway's *Blood Brothers* in 1993.	
11/13/71	9	11	● 1. **Cherish**	Bell 45150
			#1 Adult Contemporary hit (1 week)	
3/25/72	37	2	2. Could It Be Forever	Bell 45187
6/10/72	25	5	3. How Can I Be Sure	Bell 45220
10/14/72	38	2	4. Rock Me Baby	Bell 45260
10/27/90	27	5	5. Lyin' To Myself	Enigma 75084
			Sales #26 / Airplay #26	
			CASSIDY, Shaun	
			Born on 9/27/59 in Los Angeles. Son of actor Jack Cassidy and actress Shirley Jones of TV's "The Partridge Family." Played Joe Hardy on TV's "The Hardy Boys." Shaun and David Cassidy are half-brothers. Cast member of the TV soap "General Hospital" in 1987. Married to model Ann Pennington, 1979–91.	
6/4/77	1 (1)	12	● 1. **Da Doo Ron Ron**	Warner/Curb 8365
8/20/77	3	15	● 2. **That's Rock 'N' Roll**	Warner/Curb 8423
11/26/77+	7	12	● 3. **Hey Deanie**	Warner/Curb 8488
			above 2 written by Eric Carmen	
4/22/78	31	5	4. Do You Believe In Magic	Warner/Curb 8533
			CASTAWAYS, The	
			Teen quintet formed in Richfield, Minnesota. Nucleus of group: Denny Craswell (drums), Dick Roby (bass) and Roy Hensley (guitar). Craswell later joined Crow.	
9/18/65	12	9	1. Liar, Liar	Soma 1433

DATE	POS	WKS	ARTIST–RECORD TITLE	LABEL & NO.
			CASTELLS, The	
			Santa Rosa, California quartet: Bob Ussery, Tom Hicks, Joe Kelly and Chuck Girard (both later with The Hondells).	
7/3/61	20	7	1. Sacred	Era 3048
5/26/62	21	5	2. So This Is Love	Era 3073
			CASTLEMAN, Boomer	
			Owen "Boomer" Clarke of The Lewis & Clarke Expedition. Originally from Farmers Branch, Texas.	
5/31/75	33	3	1. Judy Mae	Mums 6038
			CASTOR, Jimmy	
			Born on 6/2/43 in New York City. R&B singer/saxophonist/composer/arranger. Formed the Jimmy Castor Bunch in 1972, with Gerry Thomas (keyboards), Doug Gibson (bass), Harry Jensen (guitar), Lenny Fridie, Jr. (congas) and Bobby Manigault (drums).	
2/4/67	31	3	1. Hey, Leroy, Your Mama's Callin' You [I]	Smash 2069
			THE JIMMY CASTOR BUNCH:	
5/27/72	6	10	● 2. **Troglodyte (Cave Man)** [N]	RCA 1029
3/22/75	16	8	3. The Bertha Butt Boogie-Part 1 [N]	Atlantic 3232
			CATE BROS.	
			Pop duo of twins Ernie (vocals, piano) and Earl (guitar) Cate, born on 12/26/42 in Fayetteville, Arkansas.	
4/17/76	24	8	1. Union Man	Asylum 45294
			CATES, George, And His Orchestra	
			Born on 10/19/11 in New York City. Arranger for Bing Crosby, Teresa Brewer, The Andrews Sisters and others. Musical director of TV's "Lawrence Welk Show" for 25 years.	
12/3/55	35	2	1. Autumn Leaves [I] STEVE ALLEN with GEORGE CATES And His Orchestra & Chorus	Coral 61485
4/21/56	4	19	2. **Moonglow And Theme From "Picnic"** [I] Top 100 #4 / Jockey #4 / Best Seller #5 / Juke Box #7; featuring The Stan Wrightsman Quartet; from the movie *Picnic* starring William Holden; 4 Top 10 versions of "Moonglow" charted in 1934	Coral 61618
			CATHY JEAN and The Roommates	
			Cathy was born on 9/8/45 in Brooklyn. The Roommates were a male teen-age vocal quartet from Queens, New York.	
3/6/61	12	10	1. Please Love Me Forever	Valmor 007
			CAT MOTHER and the ALL NIGHT NEWS BOYS	
			New York rock quintet produced by Jimi Hendrix: Charley Chin, Roy "Bones" Michaels, Bob Smith, Michael Equine and Larry Israel Packer.	
7/12/69	21	6	1. Good Old Rock 'N Roll Sweet Little Sixteen/Long Tall Sally/Chantilly Lace/Whole Lotta Shakin' Goin On/Blue Suede Shoes/Party Doll	Polydor 14002

DATE	POS	WKS	ARTIST–RECORD TITLE	LABEL & NO.
			CAUSE & EFFECT	
			Northern California-based duo: Sean Rowley (keyboards) and British-born Robert Rowe (vocals, guitar). Joined on tour by drummer Evan Parandes, then Richard Shepherd. Rowley died of asthma-related cardiac arrest on 11/12/92 (age 23). Rowe, Shepard and Keith David Milo continued as a trio.	
5/9/92	38	2	1. You Think You Know Her Airplay #33	SRC 14025
			CAVALIERE, Felix	
			Born on 11/29/43 in Pelham, New York. Lead singer of The Rascals after a stint with Joey Dee's band.	
4/12/80	36	3	1. Only A Lonely Heart Sees	Epic 50829
			C COMPANY Featuring TERRY NELSON	
			Group of studio musicians led by DJ/singer Terry Nelson from Russellville, Alabama.	
5/1/71	37	3	● 1. Battle Hymn Of Lt. Calley [S] Lt. William Calley Jr. was court-martialed for the massacre of unarmed civilians in My Lai, Vietnam, committed by his Army company	Plantation 73
			CELEBRATION featuring MIKE LOVE	
			Pop quartet formed in 1977: Mike Love (of The Beach Boys), Ron Altback, Charles Lloyd and Dave "Doc" Robinson. Altback and Robinson were members of King Harvest.	
6/3/78	28	4	1. Almost Summer title song from the movie starring Bruno Kirby	MCA 40891
			CERRONE	
			Born Jean-Marc Cerrone in France in 1952. Composer/producer/drummer.	
3/26/77	36	3	1. Love In 'C' Minor - Pt. I [I]	Cotillion 44215
			CETERA, Peter	
			Born on 9/13/44 in Chicago. Lead singer/bass guitarist of Chicago, 1967–85.	
6/21/86	1 (2)	14	1. Glory Of Love Airplay #1(2) / Sales #2; theme from the movie The Karate Kid Part II starring Ralph Macchio; #1 Adult Contemporary hit (5 weeks)	Full Moon 28662
10/11/86	1 (1)	15	2. The Next Time I Fall PETER CETERA w/AMY GRANT Airplay #2 / Sales #3; #1 Adult Contemporary hit (2 weeks)	Full Moon 28597
8/6/88	4	13	3. One Good Woman Airplay #3 / Sales #6; #1 Adult Contemporary hit (4 weeks)	Full Moon 27824
4/1/89	6	11	● 4. After All CHER and PETER CETERA Sales #4 / Airplay #9; love theme from the movie Chances Are starring Cybill Shepherd and Robert Downey, Jr.; #1 Adult Contemporary hit (4 weeks)	Geffen 27529
8/29/92	35	4	5. Restless Heart Airplay #30 / Sales #48; #1 Adult Contemporary hit (2 weeks)	Warner 18897

DATE	POS	WKS	ARTIST–RECORD TITLE	LABEL & NO.
			CHAD & JEREMY	
			Folk-rock duo formed in the early 1960s: Chad Stuart (born 12/10/43, England) and Jeremy Clyde (born 3/22/44, England). Broke up in 1967. Re-formed briefly in 1982.	
			CHAD STUART AND JEREMY CLYDE:	
6/13/64	21	6	1. Yesterday's Gone	World Art. 1021
9/19/64	7	9	2. **A Summer Song**	World Art. 1027
			CHAD & JEREMY:	
12/12/64+	15	8	3. Willow Weep For Me	World Art. 1034
			#1 Adult Contemporary hit (1 week); #2 hit for Paul Whiteman in 1933	
3/13/65	23	5	4. If I Loved You	World Art. 1041
			from the musical *Carousel*	
5/29/65	17	6	5. Before And After	Columbia 43277
8/28/65	35	3	6. I Don't Wanna Lose You Baby	Columbia 43339
8/13/66	30	2	7. Distant Shores	Columbia 43682
			CHAIRMEN OF THE BOARD	
			Soul vocal group formed in Detroit in 1969. Consisted of General Norman Johnson, Danny Woods, Harrison Kennedy and Eddie Curtis. First recorded for Invictus in 1969. Johnson was leader of The Showmen, 1961–67; wrote "Patches," hit for Clarence Carter. Johnson went solo in 1976.	
2/7/70	3	12	● 1. **Give Me Just A Little More Time**	Invictus 9074
6/6/70	38	2	2. (You've Got Me) Dangling On A String	Invictus 9078
9/12/70	38	2	3. Everything's Tuesday	Invictus 9079
			CHAIRMAN OF THE BOARD	
12/12/70+	13	9	4. Pay To The Piper	Invictus 9081
			CHAKACHAS, The	
			Band led by the fictional Gaston Boogaerts. Actually was a sextet of Belgian studio musicians. Barrio, a New York Latino group, posed as The Chakachas on tour.	
2/19/72	8	10	● 1. **Jungle Fever** [I]	Polydor 15030
			CHAMBERLAIN, Richard	
			Born on 3/31/35 in Los Angeles. Leading movie, theater and TV actor. Played lead role in TV's "Dr. Kildare," 1961–66.	
6/23/62	10	10	1. Theme From Dr. Kildare (Three Stars Will Shine Tonight)	MGM 13075
10/27/62	21	5	2. Love Me Tender	MGM 13097
			adapted from the 1861 tune "Aura Lee"	
3/9/63	14	7	3. All I Have To Do Is Dream	MGM 13121
			CHAMBERS BROTHERS, The	
			Four Mississippi-born brothers: George (bass), Willie (guitar), Lester (harmonica) and Joe Chambers (guitar). Formed as a gospel group in Los Angeles in 1954. Drummer Brian Keenan added in 1965.	
9/14/68	11	9	1. Time Has Come Today	Columbia 44414
12/21/68	37	2	2. I Can't Turn You Loose	Columbia 44679
			written by Otis Redding	

DATE	POS	WKS	ARTIST–RECORD TITLE	LABEL & NO.
			CHAMPAIGN	
			Interracial sextet from Champaign, Illinois. Pauli Carman and Rena Jones, lead singers. Reduced to a duo of Pauli Carman and Rena Jones.	
3/28/81	**12**	13	1. How 'Bout Us #1 Adult Contemporary hit (2 weeks)	Columbia 11433
5/14/83	**23**	9	2. Try Again	Columbia 03563
			CHAMPS, The	
			Instrumental combo from Los Angeles. Named after Gene Autry's horse, Champ. Originally consisted of studio musicians Dave Burgess (rhythm guitar), Buddy Bruce (lead guitar), Danny Flores (sax; later changed name to Chuck Rio), Cliff Hils (bass) and Gene Alden (drums). Shortly after "Tequila" became a hit, Bruce and Hils were replaced by Dale Norris and Joe Burnas. Eight months after recording "Tequila," Flores and Alden left; replaced by Jimmy Seals (sax) & Dash Crofts (drums), later a hit recording duo. Other personnel changes followed; in 1960, guitarist Glen Campbell spent some time in the group.	
3/3/58	**1** (5)	16	● 1. **Tequila** [I] Best Seller #1(5) / Top 100 #1(5) / Jockey #1(2); #1 R&B hit (4 weeks)	Challenge 1016
6/2/58	**30**	5	2. El Rancho Rock [I] Top 100 #30 / Best Seller #31; based on the 1934 tune "Alla En El Rancho Grande"; #6 hit for Bing Crosby in 1939	Challenge 59007
2/8/60	**30**	5	3. Too Much Tequila [I]	Challenge 59063
7/14/62	**40**	1	4. Limbo Rock [I]	Challenge 9131
			CHANDLER, Gene	
			Born Eugene Dixon on 7/6/37 in Chicago. R&B singer/producer. Formed the Gaytones at Englewood High School in 1955. Joined The Dukays vocal group in 1957. Served in U.S. Army in Germany, 1957–60. Rejoined The Dukays in 1960; they first recorded for Nat in 1961. Group then recorded "Duke Of Earl" for Vee-Jay. Due to contract conflicts with Nat, Dixon left the group, changed his name to Gene Chandler and promoted "Duke Of Earl." Own label, Mr. Chand, 1969–73.	
1/27/62	**1** (3)	11	● 1. **Duke Of Earl** #1 R&B hit (5 weeks)	Vee-Jay 416
8/1/64	**19**	7	2. Just Be True	Constellation 130
11/14/64	**39**	1	3. Bless Our Love	Constellation 136
1/16/65	**40**	1	4. What Now	Constellation 141
5/22/65	**18**	6	5. Nothing Can Stop Me #2, 4, 5: written by Curtis Mayfield	Constellation 149
8/8/70	**12**	11	● 6. Groovy Situation	Mercury 73083
			CHANGE	
			European-American studio group formed by Italian producer Jacques Fred Petrus.	
7/19/80	**40**	1	1. A Lover's Holiday	RFC 49208
			CHANGING FACES	
			Female vocal duo: Bronx-born Charisse Rose and Manhattan-born Cassandra Lucas.	
8/6/94	**3**	18	▲ 1. **Stroke You Up** Sales #2 / Airplay #12	Big Beat 98279
2/4/95	**38**	2	2. Foolin' Around Sales #19 / Airplay #68; above 2 written and produced by R. Kelly	Big Beat 98207

DATE	POS	WKS	ARTIST–RECORD TITLE	LABEL & NO.
			CHANNEL, Bruce	
			Born on 11/28/40 in Jacksonville, Texas. Appeared on "Louisiana Hayride" in 1958.	
2/10/62	**1** (3)	12	● **1.** **Hey! Baby** Delbert McClinton (harmonica player); first released on Le Cam 953 in 1961	Smash 1731
			CHANSON	
			Studio disco band. Lead vocals by James Jamerson, Jr., and David Williams. Jamerson's father was a prominent Motown bassist.	
12/16/78+	**21**	9	**1.** Don't Hold Back	Ariola Am. 7717
			CHANTAY'S	
			Teenage surf-rock quintet from Santa Ana, California: Bob Spickard (lead guitar), Brian Carman (rhythm guitar), Rob Marshall (piano), Warren Waters (bass) and Bob Welsh (drums).	
4/6/63	**4**	11	**1.** **Pipeline** [I] Pipeline is a surfing term for the curl of the wave before it breaks; first released on Downey 104 in 1962	Dot 16440
			CHANTELS, The	
			R&B vocal group from the Bronx. Formed in high school, with lead Arlene Smith, Sonia Goring, Rene Minus, Jackie Landry and Lois Harris. Group name taken from that of a rival school, St. Francis de Chantelle. Auditioned for Richard Barrett, who became their manager and obtained a contract with Gone/End Records.	
1/27/58	**15**	12	**1.** Maybe Top 100 #15 / Best Seller #16	End 1005
4/7/58	**39**	3	**2.** Every Night (I Pray) Best Seller #39 / Top 100 #40	End 1015
9/11/61	**14**	8	**3.** Look In My Eyes	Carlton 555
12/11/61	**29**	3	**4.** Well, I Told You answer song to Ray Charles's "Hit The Road Jack"	Carlton 564
			CHAPIN, Harry	
			Born on 12/7/42 in New York City. Died in an auto accident on 7/16/81. Folk-rock balladeer. As a child, was a member of the Brooklyn Heights Boys Choir. Documentary moviemaker in the '60s. Signed to Elektra in 1971.	
4/22/72	**24**	9	**1.** Taxi	Elektra 45770
3/16/74	**36**	2	**2.** WOLD	Elektra 45874
11/2/74	**1** (1)	12	● **3.** **Cat's In The Cradle** lyrics from a poem by Harry's wife, Sandy	Elektra 45203
11/22/80	**23**	7	**4.** Sequel sequel to 1972's "Taxi"	Boardwalk 5700
			CHAPMAN, Tracy	
			Born on 3/30/64 in Cleveland. Singer/songwriter. Graduated from Tufts University in 1986 with an anthropology degree. Won the 1988 Best New Artist Grammy Award.	
7/16/88	**6**	12	**1.** **Fast Car** Sales #4 / Airplay #7	Elektra 69412

DATE	POS	WKS	ARTIST–RECORD TITLE	LABEL & NO.
			CHARLENE	
			Pop singer Charlene Duncan (née: D'Angelo). Born on 6/1/50 in Hollywood.	
3/27/82	3	14	1. **I've Never Been To Me** [R]	Motown 1611
			originally charted in 1977 (at #97)	
			CHARLES, Jimmy	
			Born in 1942 in Paterson, New Jersey. R&B singer. Won Apollo Amateur Contest in 1958.	
9/5/60	5	11	1. **A Million To One**	Promo 1002
			The Revelletts (backing vocals)	
			CHARLES, Ray	
			Born Ray Charles Robinson on 9/23/30 in Albany, Georgia. To Greenville, Florida, while still an infant. Partially blind at age five, completely blind at seven (glaucoma). Studied classical piano and clarinet at State School for Deaf and Blind Children, St. Augustine, Florida, 1937–45. With local Florida bands; moved to Seattle in 1948. Formed the McSon Trio (also known as the Maxim Trio and the Maxine Trio) with Gossady McGhee (guitar) and Milton Garred (bass). First recordings were very much in the King Cole Trio style. Formed own band in 1954. The 1950s female vocal group, The Cookies, became his backing group, The Raeletts. Inducted into the Rock and Roll Hall of Fame in 1986. Recipient of the Grammy Lifetime Achievement Award in 1987. Popular performer with many TV and movie appearances.	
11/25/57	34	1	1. Swanee River Rock (Talkin' 'Bout That River)	Atlantic 1154
			Best Seller #34 / Top 100 #42; based on Stephen Foster's "Old Folks At Home"	
7/20/59	6	11	2. **What'd I Say (Part I)**	Atlantic 2031
			#1 R&B hit (1 week)	
12/14/59	40	1	3. I'm Movin' On	Atlantic 2043
			#1 Country hit (21 weeks) for Hank Snow in 1950	
8/8/60	40	1	4. Sticks And Stones	ABC-Para. 10118
10/10/60	1 (1)	10	5. **Georgia On My Mind**	ABC-Para. 10135
			Ralph Burns (orch.); #10 hit for Frankie Trumbauer in 1931	
12/12/60	28	5	6. Ruby	ABC-Para. 10164
			there were 4 Top 30 versions of this tune in 1953; from the movie *Ruby Gentry* starring Charlton Heston	
3/27/61	8	9	7. **One Mint Julep** [I]	Impulse 200
			#1 R&B hit (1 week); #2 R&B hit for The Clovers in 1952	
9/18/61	1 (2)	11	8. **Hit The Road Jack**	ABC-Para. 10244
			#1 R&B hit (5 weeks)	
12/4/61+	9	10	9. **Unchain My Heart**	ABC-Para. 10266
			#1 R&B hit (2 weeks)	
4/21/62	20	4	10. Hide 'Nor Hair	ABC-Para. 10314
5/19/62	1 (5)	14	● 11. **I Can't Stop Loving You**	ABC-Para. 10330
			#1 R&B hit (10 weeks); #1 Adult Contemporary hit (5 weeks)	
8/4/62	2 (1)	9	12. **You Don't Know Me**	ABC-Para. 10345
			#1 Adult Contemporary hit (3 weeks)	
12/1/62	7	9	13. **You Are My Sunshine/**	
			#1 R&B hit (3 weeks); #20 hit for Bing Crosby in 1941	
12/8/62	29	5	14. Your Cheating Heart	ABC-Para. 10375
			#1 Country hit for Hank Williams in 1953	
3/16/63	20	4	15. Don't Set Me Free	ABC-Para. 10405
4/27/63	8	8	16. **Take These Chains From My Heart**	ABC-Para. 10435
			Jack Halloran Singers (backing vocals); #1 Country hit for Hank Williams in 1953	

Bobby Brown was one of several chart-topping alumni of '80s R&B sensations New Edition; other members included singers Ralph Tresvant, Johnny Gill and Bell Biv DeVoe. Brown's No. 3 hit "Roni" came from his enormously successful 1988 album *Don't Be Cruel*.

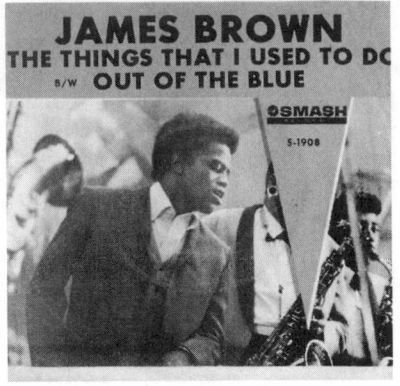

James Brown's masterful grasp of the Top 40 charts during the '60s didn't extend to much of his material on the Smash label—the release of which greatly disturbed King Records, to whom Brown was still signed. His blues cover "The Things That I Used To Do" spent only a week on the chart in 1964.

Maxine Brown's 1964 Wand single "Ask Me" stalled at No. 75 on the charts and again failed to match her earlier successes "All In My Mind" and "Funny." Within a year, however, her "Oh No Not My Baby" climbed to No. 24.

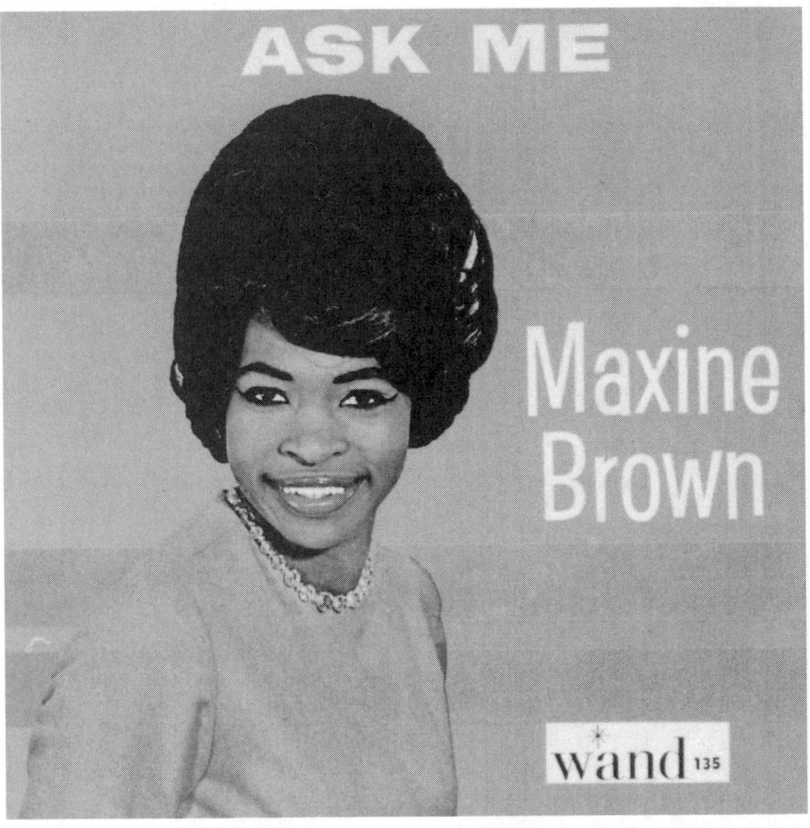

Jackson Browne's 1978 version of the pop chestnut "Stay" managed a surprising showing at No. 11 in 1978—thus beating The 4 Seasons' 1964 cover version (which reached No. 16), but not the original 1960 chart-topper by Maurice Williams & The Zodiacs.

The Buckinghams' "Mercy Mercy Mercy" took a recent Cannonball Adderley hit (penned by pianist Joe Zawinul), added a rock sound, and then shot upward to the Top 5 in 1967—six slots higher than the original Adderley hit.

Johnny Burnette's influence on rock and roll extends beyond a mere four Top 20 singles, including 1961's "Little Boy Sad." His renowned partnership with brother Dorsey and Paul Burlison in his earlier Rock 'N Roll Trio grows in critical stature every year.

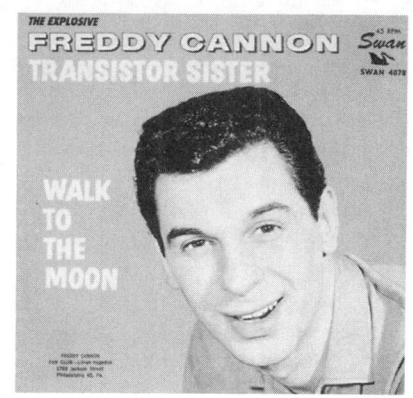

Jonathan Butler's hit "Lies," which climbed to No. 27 in 1987, displayed but one aspect of his talent. The South African singer/songwriter's guitar-playing abilities drew many comparisons to George Benson at the time.

Tevin Campbell's discovery by Quincy Jones led the youthful singer to score his first Top 10 hit—1992's "Tell Me What You Want Me To Do"—before he was 14.

Freddy Cannon was better known as "Boom Boom" to teen fans of the early '60s—who often enjoyed hearing his hits on their own transistor radios. How could 1962's "Transistor Sister"—which climbed to No. 35—fail to find an audience?

Mariah Carey's chart career started off with the loudest possible bang: Her self-titled 1990 debut album bore four No. 1 singles, beginning with "Vision Of Love." She would later marry Sony Music topper Tommy Mottola.

Belinda Carlisle's stint as lead singer in The Go-Go's took her to the Top 10 twice in 1982; as a solo artist, such tracks as 1988's "I Get Weak" took her there again four additional times. The pioneering all-girl group re-formed sporadically on several occasions during the '90s.

The Carpenters' "We've Only Just Begun" held the No. 2 slot for four weeks in Fall 1970 and became the class song of countless Classes of 1971 around the country. A&M Records released an all-star Carpenters tribute album in 1994.

DATE	POS	WKS	ARTIST–RECORD TITLE	LABEL & NO.
7/6/63	21	5	17. No One/	
7/6/63	29	4	18. Without Love (There Is Nothing)	ABC-Para. 10453
9/14/63	4	11	19. **Busted**	ABC-Para. 10481
12/21/63+	20	7	20. That Lucky Old Sun	ABC-Para. 10509
			#1 hit for Frankie Laine in 1949	
3/21/64	38	2	21. My Heart Cries For You/	
			there were 8 Top 30 versions of this tune in 1951	
3/21/64	39	1	22. Baby, Don't You Cry (The New Swingova Rhythm)	ABC-Para. 10530
1/15/66	6	9	23. **Crying Time**	ABC-Para. 10739
			Jack Halloran Singers (backing vocals); #1 Adult Contemporary hit (3 weeks)	
4/16/66	19	5	24. Together Again	ABC-Para. 10785
			#1 Adult Contemporary hit (3 weeks); above 2 written by Buck Owens	
6/25/66	31	4	25. Let's Go Get Stoned	ABC 10808
			#1 R&B hit (1 week)	
10/1/66	32	2	26. I Chose To Sing The Blues	ABC 10840
			The Raeletts (backing vocals: #4, 8, 9, 13, 15, 17, 23, 25, 26)	
6/10/67	15	9	27. Here We Go Again	ABC/TRC 10938
9/23/67	33	3	28. In The Heat Of The Night	ABC/TRC 10970
			title song from the movie starring Sidney Poitier	
12/2/67	25	3	29. Yesterday	ABC/TRC 11009
7/20/68	35	3	30. Eleanor Rigby	ABC/TRC 11090
4/17/71	36	4	31. Don't Change On Me	ABC/TRC 11291
5/15/71	36	2	32. Booty Butt [I]	Tangerine 1015
			THE RAY CHARLES ORCHESTRA	
12/16/89+	18	8	33. I'll Be Good To You	Qwest 22697
			QUINCY JONES Featuring Ray Charles and Chaka Khan Sales #13 / Airplay #26; #1 R&B hit (2 weeks)	

CHARLES, Ray, Singers

			Born Charles Raymond Offenberg on 9/13/18 in Chicago. Arranger/conductor for many TV shows including the "Perry Como Show," "Glen Campbell Goodtime Hour" and "Sha-Na-Na." Winner of two Emmys.	
5/2/64	3	12	1. **Love Me With All Your Heart (Cuando Calienta El Sol)**	Command 4046
			#1 Adult Contemporary hit (4 weeks)	
7/25/64	29	4	2. Al-Di-La	Command 4049
			from the movie *Rome Adventure* starring Troy Donahue	
12/19/64+	32	5	3. One More Time	Command 4057

CHARLES, Sonny/Checkmates, Ltd.

			Former lead singer of The Checkmates, Ltd., an integrated quintet from Ft. Wayne, Indiana. Consisted of Sonny, Bobby Stevens, Harvey Trees, Bill Van Buskirk and Marvin Smith.	
5/31/69	13	10	1. Black Pearl	A&M 1053
			SONNY CHARLES and THE CHECKMATES, LTD.	
1/22/83	40	2	2. Put It In A Magazine	Highrise 2001
			SONNY CHARLES	

DATE	POS	WKS	ARTIST—RECORD TITLE	LABEL & NO.
			CHARLES & EDDIE	
			Soul vocal duo of Charles Pettigrew (from Philadelphia) and Eddie Chacon (from Oakland, California).	
9/19/92	**13**	20	1. Would I Lie To You? Airplay #14 / Sales #15	Capitol 44809
			CHARLIE	
			British rock quintet formed in 1972: Terry Slesser (vocals), Terry Thomas (guitar), John Anderson (bass), and Bob Henrit and Steve Gadd (drums). Henrit joined The Kinks in 1987.	
8/6/83	**38**	2	1. It's Inevitable	Mirage 99862
			CHARMS, The	
			R&B vocal group from Cincinnati consisting of Otis Williams, Richard Parker, Donald Peak, Joe Penn and Rolland Bradley. Group first recorded for Rockin' in 1953. Otis (not to be confused with the same-named member of The Temptations) later recorded country music.	
11/27/54+	**15**	15	1. Hearts Of Stone Best Seller #15 / Juke Box #15 / Jockey #20; #1 R&B hit (9 weeks)	DeLuxe 6062
1/15/55	**26**	3	2. Ling, Ting, Tong Best Seller #26	DeLuxe 6076
4/14/56	**11**	15	3. Ivory Tower **OTIS WILLIAMS And His CHARMS** Jockey #11 / Top 100 #12 / Best Seller #13 / Juke Box #19	DeLuxe 6093
			CHARTBUSTERS, The	
			Washington, D.C., rock quartet.	
8/15/64	**33**	3	1. She's The One	Mutual 502
			CHASE	
			Jazz-rock band organized by trumpeter Bill Chase (formerly with Woody Herman and Stan Kenton). Chase and three other members were killed in a plane crash on 8/9/74.	
6/26/71	**24**	8	1. Get It On	Epic 10738
			CHEAP TRICK	
			Rock quartet formed in Rockford, Illinois, in 1972: Robin Zander (vocals), Rick Nielsen (guitar), Tom Petersson (bass) and Bun E. Carlos (real name: Brad Carlson; drums). Discovered by Aerosmith's producer Jack Douglas. Petersson replaced by Jon Brant in 1980; returned in 1988, replacing Brant.	
5/26/79	**7**	13	● 1. **I Want You To Want Me** "live" version of tune from the 1977 album *In Color*	Epic 50680
9/15/79	**35**	3	2. Ain't That A Shame above 2 recorded "live" at Budokan concert hall in Japan	Epic 50743
10/27/79	**26**	5	3. Dream Police	Epic 50774
1/19/80	**32**	3	4. Voices	Epic 50814
5/21/88	**1** (2)	14	5. **The Flame** Airplay #1(2) / Sales #1(1)	Epic 07745
8/20/88	**4**	12	6. **Don't Be Cruel** Sales #3 / Airplay #4	Epic 07965
12/17/88	**33**	5	7. Ghost Town Airplay #32 / Sales #34	Epic 08097

DATE	POS	WKS	ARTIST–RECORD TITLE	LABEL & NO.
8/18/90	12	7	8. Can't Stop Fallin' Into Love Airplay #13 / Sales #15	Epic 73444

CHECKER, Chubby

Born Ernest Evans on 10/3/41 in Philadelphia. Did impersonations of famous singers. First recorded for Parkway in 1959. Dick Clark's then-wife Bobbie suggested that Evans change his name to Chubby Checker due to his resemblance to a teenage Fats Domino. Cover version of Hank Ballard's "The Twist" started worldwide dance craze. On 4/12/64, married Dutch-born Catharina Lodders, Miss World 1962 ("Loddy Lo" written for her). Appeared in the movies *Don't Knock The Twist* and *Twist Around The Clock*.

DATE	POS	WKS	ARTIST–RECORD TITLE	LABEL & NO.
6/15/59	38	2	1. The Class [N] imitations of Fats Domino, The Coasters, Elvis Presley and The Chipmunks	Parkway 804
8/8/60	1 (1)	15	● 2. **The Twist**	Parkway 811
10/31/60	14	9	3. The Hucklebuck written in 1949; #5 hit for Tommy Dorsey; #10 for Frank Sinatra	Parkway 813
1/30/61	1 (3)	14	4. **Pony Time** tune is similar to The Midnighters' 1954 R&B hit "Sexy Ways"; #1 R&B hit (2 weeks)	Parkway 818
5/1/61	24	4	5. (Dance The) Mess Around remake of Richard Berry's "The Mess Around" (1958-Flip 336)	Parkway 822
7/3/61	8	15	● 6. **Let's Twist Again** originally charted for 9 weeks; re-entered on 11/20/61 (POS 22)	Parkway 824
10/2/61	7	11	7. **The Fly**	Parkway 830
11/20/61+	1 (2)	18	● 8. **The Twist** [R] except for Bing Crosby's "White Christmas," "The Twist" is the only record in history to re-enter the charts and return to the #1 position	Parkway 811
12/25/61	21	3	9. Jingle Bell Rock [X] **BOBBY RYDELL CHUBBY CHECKER**	Cameo 205
3/10/62	3	12	10. **Slow Twistin'** **CHUBBY CHECKER (with Dee Dee Sharp)**	Parkway 835
7/7/62	12	7	11. Dancin' Party	Parkway 842
9/29/62	2 (2)	17	● 12. **Limbo Rock/**	Parkway 849
9/29/62	10	9	13. **Popeye (The Hitchhiker)**	
2/23/63	20	8	14. Let's Limbo Some More/	Parkway 862
3/23/63	15	7	15. Twenty Miles	
6/1/63	12	7	16. Birdland remake of Huey "Piano" Smith's "We Like Birdland" (1958-Ace 548)	Parkway 873
8/3/63	25	5	17. Twist It Up	Parkway 879
11/23/63	12	9	18. Loddy Lo/ adapted from the Bahamian folk song "Hey Li-Lee, Hey Li-Lee Lo"	
1/11/64	17	8	19. Hooka Tooka	Parkway 890
4/4/64	23	5	20. Hey, Bobba Needle	Parkway 907
7/11/64	40	1	21. Lazy Elsie Molly	Parkway 920
5/22/65	40	1	22. Let's Do The Freddie many of above hits written by Kal Mann and Dave Appell (The Applejacks)	Parkway 949
7/9/88	16	8	23. The Twist (Yo, Twist!) [R] **FAT BOYS (with Chubby Checker)** Sales #12 / Airplay #17	Tin Pan 887571

DATE	POS	WKS	ARTIST—RECORD TITLE	LABEL & NO.
			CHECKMATES, LTD., The—see CHARLES, Sonny	
			CHEECH & CHONG	
			Comedians Richard "Cheech" Marin (born 7/13/46, Watts, California) and Thomas Chong (born 5/24/38, Edmonton, Alberta, Canada). Starred in movies since 1978. Chong, the father of actress Rae Dawn Chong, was the guitarist of Bobby Taylor & The Vancouvers. Cheech was a cast member of TV's "Golden Palace."	
9/29/73	15	7	1. Basketball Jones Featuring Tyrone Shoelaces [N] parody of "Love Jones" by Brighter Side Of Darkness; all-star band includes George Harrison, Carole King, Billy Preston and Tom Scott, with Darlene Love and Michelle Phillips (The Mamas & The Papas) as cheerleaders	Ode 66038
12/29/73+	24	5	2. Sister Mary Elephant (Shudd-Up!) [C]	Ode 66041
8/31/74	9	8	3. **Earache My Eye (Featuring Alice Bowie)** [C]	Ode 66102
			CHEERS, The	
			Vocal trio from Los Angeles consisting of TV actor Bert Convy (died on 7/15/91 of a brain tumor), Gil Garfield and Sue Allen.	
9/24/55	6	11	1. **Black Denim Trousers** Best Seller #6 / Jockey #6 / Top 100 #13 / Juke Box #20; Les Baxter (orch. and chorus)	Capitol 3219
			CHER	
			Born Cherilyn LaPierre on 5/20/46 in El Centro, California. Worked as backup singer for Phil Spector. Recorded as "Bonnie Jo Mason" and "Cherilyn" in 1964. Recorded with Sonny Bono as "Caesar & Cleo" in 1963, then as Sonny & Cher, 1965–73. Married to Gregg Allman, 1975–77. Own TV series with Bono, 1971–77. Member of the group Black Rose in 1980. Acclaimed movie actress (won Best Actress Oscar in 1987 for *Moonstruck*).	
8/7/65	15	6	1. All I Really Want To Do	Imperial 66114
11/6/65	25	3	2. Where Do You Go	Imperial 66136
3/26/66	2 (1)	9	3. **Bang Bang (My Baby Shot Me Down)**	Imperial 66160
8/20/66	32	3	4. Alfie title song from the movie starring Michael Caine	Imperial 66192
11/18/67	9	9	5. **You Better Sit Down Kids** all of above produced by Sonny Bono	Imperial 66261
10/2/71	1 (2)	14	● 6. **Gypsys, Tramps & Thieves**	Kapp 2146
2/12/72	7	10	7. **The Way Of Love**	Kapp 2158
6/3/72	22	6	8. Living In A House Divided	Kapp 2171
9/1/73	1 (2)	14	● 9. **Half-Breed**	MCA 40102
2/2/74	1 (1)	12	● 10. **Dark Lady**	MCA 40161
6/15/74	27	4	11. Train Of Thought	MCA 40245
3/17/79	8	11	● 12. **Take Me Home**	Casablanca 965
1/16/88	10	12	13. **I Found Someone**	Geffen 28191
4/30/88	14	9	14. We All Sleep Alone Airplay #12 / Sales #14; co-written and co-produced by Jon Bon Jovi	Geffen 27986
4/1/89	6	11	● 15. **After All** **CHER and PETER CETERA** Sales #4 / Airplay #9; love theme from the movie *Chances Are* starring Cybill Shepherd and Robert Downey, Jr.; #1 Adult Contemporary hit (4 weeks)	Geffen 27529

DATE	POS	WKS	ARTIST–RECORD TITLE	LABEL & NO.
8/5/89	3	14	● 16. **If I Could Turn Back Time** Sales #2 / Airplay #4; #1 Adult Contemporary hit (1 week)	Geffen 22886
11/18/89	8	11	17. **Just Like Jesse James** Sales #6 / Airplay #11	Geffen 22844
3/24/90	20	6	18. Heart Of Stone	Geffen 19953
1/19/91	33	2	19. The Shoop Shoop Song (It's In His Kiss) Sales #23; from the movie *Mermaids* starring Cher	Geffen 19659
6/29/91	17	9	20. Love And Understanding Airplay #38 / Sales #45	Geffen 19023
12/21/91+	37	4	21. Save Up All Your Tears Airplay #40 / Sales #59	Geffen 19105

CHERI

Canadian duo: Rosalind Milligan Hunt and Lyn Cullerier.

DATE	POS	WKS	ARTIST–RECORD TITLE	LABEL & NO.
6/5/82	39	2	1. Murphy's Law　　　　　　　　　　　　　[N]	Venture 149

CHERRELLE

Born Cheryl Norton in Los Angeles. Soul vocalist/drummer. Cousin of vocalist Pebbles. Moved to Detroit in 1979. Discovered by Michael Henderson.

DATE	POS	WKS	ARTIST–RECORD TITLE	LABEL & NO.
3/29/86	26	6	1. Saturday Love **CHERRELLE with ALEXANDER O'NEAL** Sales #19	Tabu 05767
3/5/88	28	6	2. Never Knew Love Like This **ALEXANDER O'NEAL featuring Cherrelle** Airplay #26 / Sales #28	Tabu 07646

CHERRY, Don

Born on 1/11/24 in Wichita Falls, Texas. Studied voice after military service in mid-1940s. Vocalist with Jan Garber band in the late '40s. Accomplished professional golfer.

DATE	POS	WKS	ARTIST–RECORD TITLE	LABEL & NO.
12/10/55+	4	18	1. **Band Of Gold** Jockey #4 / Best Seller #5 / Top 100 #5 / Juke Box #5	Columbia 40597
4/14/56	29	6	2. Wild Cherry	Columbia 40665
8/11/56	22	6	3. Ghost Town Jockey #22 / Top 100 #26; Ray Conniff (orch., above 3)	Columbia 40705

CHERRY, Neneh

Born on 8/10/64 in Stockholm, of Swedish and West African parentage; raised in New York City. London-based R&B singer. Stepdaughter of jazz trumpeter Don Cherry.

DATE	POS	WKS	ARTIST–RECORD TITLE	LABEL & NO.
5/6/89	3	14	● 1. **Buffalo Stance** Sales #1(2) / Airplay #4; from the movie *Slaves Of New York* starring Bernadette Peters	Virgin 99231
8/19/89	8	8	2. **Kisses On The Wind** Sales #9 / Airplay #10	Virgin 99183

DATE	POS	WKS	ARTIST—RECORD TITLE	LABEL & NO.

CHIC

R&B-disco group formed in New York City by prolific producers Bernard Edwards (bass) and Nile Rodgers (guitar). Vocalists: Norma Jean Wright (replaced by Alfa Anderson) and Luci Martin; drums: Tony Thompson. Wright began solo career in 1978 as Norma Jean. Edwards recorded with the studio group Roundtree in 1978. Rodgers joined The Honeydrippers in 1984. Thompson joined the Power Station in 1985 and Edwards became their producer. Wright, along with supporting Chic member Raymond Jones, formed State Of Art in 1991. Rodgers and Edwards regrouped as Chic in 1992 with female lead vocalists Sylvester Logan Sharp and Jenn Thomas (both South Carolina natives).

DATE	POS	WKS	ARTIST—RECORD TITLE	LABEL & NO.
12/10/77+	6	17	● 1. **Dance, Dance, Dance (Yowsah, Yowsah, Yowsah)** first released on Buddah 583 in 1977	Atlantic 3435
6/17/78	38	1	2. Everybody Dance Luther Vandross (backing vocal, above 2)	Atlantic 3469
11/18/78	1 (6)	19	▲ 3. **Le Freak** #1 R&B hit (5 weeks)	Atlantic 3519
3/10/79	7	12	● 4. **I Want Your Love**	Atlantic 3557
7/7/79	1 (1)	14	● 5. **Good Times** #1 R&B hit (6 weeks)	Atlantic 3584

CHICAGO

Jazz-oriented rock group formed in Chicago in 1967. Consisted of Peter Cetera (lead singer, bass guitar), Robert Lamm (keyboards), James Pankow (trombone), Lee Loughnane (trumpet), Terry Kath (guitar; died 1/23/78, age 31, of accidental self-inflicted gunshot), Walt Parazaider (reeds) and Danny Seraphine (drums). Originally called The Big Thing, later Chicago Transit Authority. To Los Angeles in the late '60s. Kath replaced by Donnie Dacus (left in 1979). Bill Champlin (keyboards) joined in 1982. Cetera left in 1985, replaced by Jason Scheff. Seraphine left in 1989; guitarist DaWayne Bailey added.

DATE	POS	WKS	ARTIST—RECORD TITLE	LABEL & NO.
4/25/70	9	11	1. **Make Me Smile**	Columbia 45127
8/1/70	4	11	2. **25 Or 6 To 4**	Columbia 45194
11/21/70+	7	11	3. **Does Anybody Really Know What Time It Is?**	Columbia 45264
3/6/71	20	6	4. Free	Columbia 45331
5/29/71	35	4	5. Lowdown	Columbia 45370
7/10/71	7	11	6. **Beginnings/** #1 Adult Contemporary hit (1 week); originally released on Columbia 45011 in 1969	
		11	7. Colour My World first released as the B-side of "Make Me Smile"	Columbia 45417
10/30/71	24	6	8. Questions 67 And 68 [R] originally charted in 1969 at #71	Columbia 45467
8/12/72	3	10	● 9. **Saturday In The Park**	Columbia 45657
11/18/72	24	6	10. Dialogue (Part I & II)	Columbia 45717
7/7/73	10	12	11. **Feelin' Stronger Every Day**	Columbia 45880
10/20/73	4	14	● 12. **Just You 'N' Me**	Columbia 45933
4/6/74	9	12	13. (I've Been) Searchin' So Long	Columbia 46020
7/13/74	6	8	14. **Call On Me** #1 Adult Contemporary hit (1 week)	Columbia 46062
10/26/74	11	10	15. Wishing You Were Here The Beach Boys (backing vocals); #1 Adult Contemporary hit (1 week)	Columbia 10049
3/8/75	13	7	16. Harry Truman	Columbia 10092
5/10/75	5	7	17. **Old Days**	Columbia 10131
7/17/76	32	4	18. Another Rainy Day In New York City	Columbia 10360

DATE	POS	WKS	ARTIST–RECORD TITLE	LABEL & NO.
8/21/76	1 (2)	17	● 19. **If You Leave Me Now** #1 Adult Contemporary hit (1 week)	Columbia 10390
10/15/77	4	12	20. **Baby, What A Big Surprise** all of above produced by James William Guercio	Columbia 10620
10/28/78	14	8	21. Alive Again	Columbia 10845
1/13/79	14	9	22. No Tell Lover	Columbia 10879
6/26/82	1 (2)	18	● 23. **Hard To Say I'm Sorry** from the movie *Summer Lovers* starring Daryl Hannah; #1 Adult Contemporary hit (3 weeks)	Full Moon 29979
10/23/82	22	8	24. Love Me Tomorrow	Full Moon 29911
5/12/84	16	10	25. Stay The Night	Warner 29306
8/25/84	3	15	26. **Hard Habit To Break** Airplay #2 / Sales #3	Warner 29214
12/1/84+	3	14	27. **You're The Inspiration** Airplay #1(1) / Sales #5; #1 Adult Contemporary hit (2 weeks)	Warner 29126
3/9/85	14	10	28. **Along Comes A Woman** Airplay #7 / Sales #25	Warner 29082
12/27/86+	3	13	29. **Will You Still Love Me?** Airplay #2 / Sales #4	Warner 28512
4/25/87	17	8	30. **If She Would Have Been Faithful...** Airplay #11 / Sales #22	Warner 28424
7/2/88	3	13	31. **I Don't Wanna Live Without Your Love** Airplay #2 / Sales #3	Reprise 27855
10/15/88	1 (2)	16	● 32. **Look Away** Airplay #1(3) / Sales #1(1); #1 Adult Contemporary hit (1 week)	Reprise 27766
2/4/89	10	10	33. **You're Not Alone** Airplay #8 / Sales #13	Reprise 27757
12/23/89+	5	12	34. **What Kind Of Man Would I Be?**	Reprise 22741
3/9/91	39	2	35. **Chasin' The Wind** Sales #37 / Airplay #38	Reprise 19466
			CHICAGO LOOP, The	
			Chicago rock band featuring guitarist Stefan Grossman.	
11/26/66	37	3	1. (When She Needs Good Lovin') She Comes To Me some pressings titled as: "(When She Wants Good Lovin') My Baby Comes To Me"	DynoVoice 226
			CHIFFONS, The	
			Black female vocal group from the Bronx. Formed while high school classmates; worked as backup singers in 1960. Consisted of Judy Craig, Barbara Lee Jones (died 5/15/92, age 48, of a heart attack), Patricia Bennett and Sylvia Peterson. Also recorded as The Four Pennies on the Rust label.	
3/9/63	1 (4)	12	1. **He's So Fine** #1 R&B hit (4 weeks); a 1976 court ruling found George Harrison guilty of "subconscious plagiarism" of song when writing "My Sweet Lord"	Laurie 3152
6/8/63	5	9	2. **One Fine Day**	Laurie 3179
10/19/63	40	1	3. A Love So Fine	Laurie 3195
1/4/64	36	1	4. I Have A Boyfriend	Laurie 3212
5/28/66	10	7	5. **Sweet Talkin' Guy**	Laurie 3340

DATE	POS	WKS	ARTIST–RECORD TITLE	LABEL & NO.
			CHILD, Desmond	
			Born John Charles Barrett, Jr., on 10/28/53 in Miami to a Cuban mother and a Hungarian father. Prolific producer/songwriter. Formed vocal group Rouge with Diane Grasselli, Myriam Valle and Maria Vidal in 1974. Wrote "We All Sleep Alone," "Livin' On A Prayer" and "Dude (Looks Like A Lady)."	
8/17/91	40	1	1. Love On A Rooftop Airplay #66	Elektra 64883
			CHILD, Jane	
			Toronto native. Member of the Children's Chorus of the Canadian Opera Company at age 12. Studied piano at the Royal Conservatory of Music.	
3/3/90	2 (3)	14	● 1. **Don't Wanna Fall In Love** Airplay #1(2) / Sales #3	Warner 19933
			CHI-LITES, The	
			R&B vocal group from Chicago. Consisted of Eugene Record (lead vocals), Robert "Squirrel" Lester (tenor), Marshall Thompson (baritone) and Creadel "Red" Jones (bass). First recorded as the Hi-Lites on Daran in 1963. Eugene Record (husband of Barbara Acklin) went solo in 1976.	
5/8/71	26	6	1. (For God's Sake) Give More Power To The People	Brunswick 55450
10/30/71	3	13	2. **Have You Seen Her** #1 R&B hit (2 weeks)	Brunswick 55462
4/15/72	1 (1)	14	3. **Oh Girl** #1 R&B hit (2 weeks)	Brunswick 55471
3/24/73	33	5	4. A Letter To Myself	Brunswick 55491
9/1/73	30	5	5. Stoned Out Of My Mind	Brunswick 55500
			CHILLIWACK	
			Canadian rock band formed in Vancouver in 1969: Bill Henderson (vocals, guitar), Ab Bryant (bass) and Brian MacLeod (drums).	
10/31/81	22	11	1. My Girl (Gone, Gone, Gone)	Millennium 11813
2/27/82	33	3	2. I Believe	Millennium 13102
			CHIMES, The	
			Brooklyn-based vocal quintet led by Leonard Cocco.	
1/16/61	11	6	1. Once In Awhile #1 hit for Tommy Dorsey in 1937	Tag 444
5/15/61	38	1	2. I'm In The Mood For Love #1 hit for Little Jack Little in 1935	Tag 445
			CHIPMUNKS, The	
			Characters created by Ross Bagdasarian ("David Seville") who named Alvin, Simon and Theodore after Liberty executives Alvin Bennett, Simon Waronker and Theodore Keep. The Chipmunks starred in own prime-time animated TV show in the early 1960s and a Saturday morning cartoon series in the mid-1980s. Bagdasarian died on 1/16/72 (age 52). His son, Ross, Jr., resurrected the act in 1980.	
			THE CHIPMUNKS WITH THE MUSIC OF DAVID SEVILLE:	
12/8/58	1 (4)	11	● 1. **The Chipmunk Song** [X-N]	Liberty 55168

DATE	POS	WKS	ARTIST–RECORD TITLE	LABEL & NO.
			DAVID SEVILLE AND THE CHIPMUNKS:	
2/23/59	3	9	● 2. Alvin's Harmonica [N]	Liberty 55179
7/13/59	16	6	3. Ragtime Cowboy Joe [N]	Liberty 55200
			#1 hit for Bob Roberts in 1912	
3/7/60	33	2	4. Alvin's Orchestra [N]	Liberty 55233
12/26/60	21	1	5. Rudolph The Red Nosed Reindeer [X-N]	Liberty 55289
			THE CHIPMUNKS WITH DAVID SEVILLE:	
3/31/62	40	1	6. The Alvin Twist [N]	Liberty 55424
1/6/62+	39	1	7. The Chipmunk Song (Christmas Don't Be Late) [X-R]	Liberty 55250
12/29/62	40	1	8. The Chipmunk Song (Christmas Don't Be Late) [X-R]	Liberty 55250

CHORDETTES, The

Female vocal group from Sheboygan, Wisconsin, formed in 1946; initially recorded as a barbershop quartet for Columbia Records. Consisted of Janet Ertel (née: Buschman; bass), her sister-in-law Carol Buschman (baritone), Lynn Evans (lead singer; replaced Dorothy Schwartz [née: Hummitzsch], 1953) and Margie Needham (tenor; replaced Jinny Lockard, 1953). With Arthur Godfrey, 1949–53. Ertel married Cadence owner Archie Bleyer in 1954; her daughter Jackie was married to Phil Everly of The Everly Brothers. Janet died of cancer on 11/22/88.

DATE	POS	WKS	ARTIST–RECORD TITLE	LABEL & NO.
3/10/56	14	9	1. Eddie My Love	Cadence 1284
			Jockey #14 / Best Seller #17 / Top 100 #18	
6/2/56	5	17	2. **Born To Be With You**	Cadence 1291
			Top 100 #5 / Jockey #5 / Juke Box #5 / Best Seller #7	
10/13/56	16	10	3. Lay Down Your Arms	Cadence 1299
			Top 100 #16 / Juke Box #16 / Best Seller #18 / Jockey #20	
9/16/57	8	8	4. **Just Between You And Me**	Cadence 1330
			Jockey #8 / Best Seller #15 / Top 100 #19	
3/10/58	2 (2)	12	5. **Lollipop**	Cadence 1345
			Best Seller #2 / Top 100 #2 / Jockey #2	
5/26/58	17	7	6. Zorro	Cadence 1349
			Top 100 #17 / Best Seller #18 / Jockey #22; theme from the Disney TV series starring Guy Williams	
3/30/59	27	4	7. No Other Arms, No Other Lips	Cadence 1361
7/3/61	13	8	8. Never On Sunday	Cadence 1402
			Archie Bleyer (orch., all of above)	

CHRISTIAN, Chris

Born on 2/7/51. Guitarist/songwriter/producer. With the trio Cotton, Lloyd and Christian.

DATE	POS	WKS	ARTIST–RECORD TITLE	LABEL & NO.
11/14/81	37	3	1. I Want You, I Need You	Boardwalk 126

CHRISTIE

English rock trio: Jeff Christie, Vic Elms and Mike Blakely (brother of Alan Blakely of The Tremeloes).

DATE	POS	WKS	ARTIST–RECORD TITLE	LABEL & NO.
10/24/70	23	8	1. Yellow River	Epic 10626

DATE	POS	WKS	ARTIST–RECORD TITLE	LABEL & NO.
			CHRISTIE, Lou	
			Born Lugee Sacco on 2/19/43 in Glen Willard, Pennsylvania. Joined vocal group The Classics; first recorded for Starr in 1960. Started long association with songwriter Twyla Herbert. Recorded as Lugee & The Lions for Robbee in 1961. Sang lead for The Cantina Band in 1981.	
2/16/63	24	6	1. The Gypsy Cried	Roulette 4457
			first released on C&C 102 in 1962	
4/27/63	6	10	2. **Two Faces Have I**	Roulette 4481
1/22/66	1 (1)	10	● 3. **Lightnin' Strikes**	MGM 13412
4/23/66	16	4	4. Rhapsody In The Rain	MGM 13473
			includes the lyrics "we were makin' out in the rain"; reissued as "we fell in love in the rain"; melody inspired by Tchaikovsky's *Romeo and Juliet*	
9/13/69	10	9	5. **I'm Gonna Make You Mine**	Buddah 116
			CHRISTOPHER, Gavin	
			Chicago-born soul singer/composer/producer. His sister is singer Shawn Christopher.	
7/12/86	22	7	1. One Step Closer To You	Manhattan 50028
			Sales #18 / Airplay #27	
			CHURCH, Eugene	
			Born on 1/23/38 in St. Louis and raised in Los Angeles. Died on 4/16/93 from AIDS. Recorded with Jesse Belvin as The Cliques. Later worked in Texas as a beautician and sang gospel music.	
2/23/59	36	2	1. Pretty Girls Everywhere	Class 235
			EUGENE CHURCH and The Fellows	
			Bobby Day (backing vocal)	
			CHURCH, The	
			Australian folk-rock quartet: Steve Kilbey (vocals, bass), Peter Koppes and Marty Willson-Piper (guitars), and Richard Ploog (drums). Ploog left in 1991, replaced by Jay Dee Daugherty.	
5/28/88	24	5	1. Under The Milky Way	Arista 9673
			Sales #19 / Airplay #29	
			CINDERELLA	
			Pennsylvania-based, hard-rock band consisting of Tom Keifer (vocals, guitar), Jeff LaBar (guitar), Eric Brittingham (bass) and Fred Coury (drums; left in 1992 and formed Arcade).	
1/17/87	13	8	1. Nobody's Fool	Mercury 884851
			Sales #11 / Airplay #22	
10/1/88	12	11	2. Don't Know What You Got (Till It's Gone)	Mercury 870644
			Sales #9 / Airplay #16	
2/25/89	36	2	3. The Last Mile	Mercury 872148
			Sales #34 / Airplay #39	
5/20/89	20	7	4. Coming Home	Mercury 872982
			Sales #18 / Airplay #20	
1/26/91	36	2	5. Shelter Me	Mercury 878700
			Airplay #35 / Sales #37	

DATE	POS	WKS	ARTIST–RECORD TITLE	LABEL & NO.
			CITY BOY	
			British rock sextet. Lol Mason, lead singer.	
9/9/78	27	6	1. 5.7.0.5.	Mercury 73999
			C.J. & CO.	
			Detroit group assembled by Dennis Coffey. Consisted of Cornelius Brown, Jr., Curtis Durden, Joni Tolbert, Connie Durden and Charles Clark.	
7/9/77	36	2	1. Devil's Gun	Westbound 55400
			CLANTON, Jimmy	
			Born on 9/2/40 in Baton Rouge, Louisiana. Played in local bands, discovered by Ace Records while making a demo at Cosimo Matassa's studio in New Orleans. Recorded with famous New Orleans sessionmen, including Huey "Piano" Smith, Earl King (guitar) and Lee Allen (tenor sax). Toured with Dick Clark's Caravan Of Stars. Starred in the 1958 movie *Go, Johnny, Go!* DJ in Lancaster, Pennsylvania, 1972–76.	
7/21/58	4	15	1. **Just A Dream** **JIMMY CLANTON AND HIS ROCKETS** Hot 100 #4 / Best Seller #4; #1 R&B hit (1 week)	Ace 546
11/17/58	25	5	2. A Letter To An Angel/	
12/1/58	38	2	3. A Part Of Me	Ace 551
8/17/59	33	6	4. My Own True Love melody is "Tara's Theme" from *Gone With The Wind*	Ace 567
12/21/59+	5	11	5. **Go, Jimmy, Go**	Ace 575
5/30/60	22	6	6. Another Sleepless Night	Ace 585
9/1/62	7	10	7. **Venus In Blue Jeans** above 2 written by Neil Sedaka	Ace 8001
			CLAPTON, Eric	
			Born Eric Patrick Clapp on 3/30/45 in Ripley, England. Prolific rock-blues guitarist/vocalist. With The Roosters, 1963; The Yardbirds, 1963–65; and John Mayall's Bluesbreakers, 1965–66. Formed Cream with Jack Bruce and Ginger Baker in 1966. Formed Blind Faith in 1968; worked with John Lennon's Plastic Ono Band, and Delaney & Bonnie. Formed Derek and The Dominos in 1970. After two years of reclusion (1971–72), Clapton performed his comeback concert at London's Rainbow Theatre in January 1973. Began actively recording and touring again in 1974. Nicknamed "Slowhand" in 1964 while with The Yardbirds.	
11/14/70	18	8	1. After Midnight	Atco 6784
6/17/72	10	10	2. **Layla** [R] **DEREK AND THE DOMINOS** originally charted in 1971 at #51; 1971 version: 2:43; 1972 version: 7:10; also see #16 below	Atco 6809
8/3/74	1 (1)	10	● 3. **I Shot The Sheriff** written by Bob Marley; Yvonne Elliman (female vocal); also released on RSO 500	RSO 409
11/23/74	26	5	4. Willie And The Hand Jive	RSO 503
11/13/76	24	6	5. Hello Old Friend	RSO 861
2/4/78	3	17	● 6. **Lay Down Sally**	RSO 886
6/10/78	16	7	7. Wonderful Tonight written for Clapton's wife, Patti; Yvonne Elliman and Marcy Levy (backing vocals, above 3)	RSO 895
			ERIC CLAPTON AND HIS BAND:	
11/25/78+	9	11	8. **Promises/**	

DATE	POS	WKS	ARTIST–RECORD TITLE	LABEL & NO.
3/24/79	40	2	9. Watch Out For Lucy	RSO 910
7/26/80	30	5	10. Tulsa Time/	
			"live" version of tune from the 1978 *Backless* album; #1 Country hit for Don Williams in 1978	
		5	11. Cocaine	RSO 1039
			"live" version of tune from the 1977 *Slowhand* album	
3/14/81	10	12	12. **I Can't Stand It**	RSO 1060
			ERIC CLAPTON:	
2/19/83	18	10	13. I've Got A Rock N' Roll Heart	Duck 29780
3/30/85	26	6	14. Forever Man	Duck 29081
			Airplay #20 / Sales #30	
2/15/92	2 (4)	23	▲ 15. **Tears In Heaven**	Reprise 19038
			Sales #1(3) / Airplay #3; #1 Adult Contemporary hit (3 weeks); from the movie *Rush* starring Jason Patric and Jennifer Jason Leigh; Clapton wrote this for his son, Conor, who fell to his death from a New York apartment window on 3/20/91 (age 4)	
10/17/92	12	14	16. Layla [R]	Duck 18787
			Airplay #12 / Sales #16; "live" acoustic version	

CLARK, Claudine

Born on 4/26/41 in Macon, Georgia. Moved to Philadelphia when very young. First recorded for Herald in 1958. Also recorded for Swan as Joy Dawn.

DATE	POS	WKS	ARTIST–RECORD TITLE	LABEL & NO.
7/21/62	5	10	1. **Party Lights**	Chancellor 1113

CLARK, Dave, Five

Rock group formed in Tottenham, England, in 1960 by Dave Clark to raise money for his soccer team, the Tottenham Hotspurs. (Clark had been a movie stuntman.) Consisted of Clark (drums), Mike Smith (lead singer, keyboards), Lenny Davidson (guitar), Denny Payton (sax) and Rick Huxley (bass). First recorded for Ember/Pye in 1962. Appeared on "The Ed Sullivan Show" in March 1964, and in the movie *Having A Wild Weekend* in 1965. Disbanded in 1973. Clark wrote the 1986 London stage musical *Time*.

DATE	POS	WKS	ARTIST–RECORD TITLE	LABEL & NO.
3/7/64	6	11	1. **Glad All Over**	Epic 9656
4/11/64	4	10	2. **Bits And Pieces**	Epic 9671
5/9/64	11	9	3. Do You Love Me	Epic 9678
6/20/64	4	9	4. **Can't You See That She's Mine**	Epic 9692
8/8/64	3	9	5. **Because**	Epic 9704
10/17/64	15	6	6. Everybody Knows (I Still Love You)	Epic 9722
12/5/64+	14	9	7. Any Way You Want It	Epic 9739
2/27/65	14	6	8. Come Home	Epic 9763
5/8/65	23	5	9. Reelin' And Rockin'	Epic 9786
7/10/65	7	8	10. **I Like It Like That**	Epic 9811
9/4/65	4	9	11. **Catch Us If You Can**	Epic 9833
			from the movie *Having a Wild Weekend* (originally titled *Catch Us If You Can*)	
11/20/65	1 (1)	11	12. **Over And Over**	Epic 9863
2/19/66	18	5	13. At The Scene	Epic 9882
4/23/66	12	5	14. Try Too Hard	Epic 10004
7/2/66	28	4	15. Please Tell Me Why	Epic 10031
4/15/67	7	7	16. **You Got What It Takes**	Epic 10144
7/1/67	35	2	17. You Must Have Been A Beautiful Baby	Epic 10179

DATE	POS	WKS	ARTIST–RECORD TITLE	LABEL & NO.
			CLARK, Dee	
			Born Delecta Clark on 11/7/38 in Blytheville, Arkansas. Died on 12/7/90 of a heart attack. To Chicago in 1941. In Hambone Kids with Sammy McGrier and Ronny Strong; first recorded for Okeh in 1952. Joined R&B vocal group the Goldentones in 1953. Group became the Kool Gents; billed as The Delegates for Vee-Jay recording in 1956. First solo recording for Falcon in 1957.	
1/12/59	21	6	1. Nobody But You	Abner 1019
5/25/59	18	9	2. Just Keep It Up	Abner 1026
9/14/59	20	9	3. Hey Little Girl	Abner 1029
1/4/60	33	5	4. How About That	Abner 1032
3/6/61	34	4	5. Your Friends	Vee-Jay 372
5/22/61	2 (1)	12	6. **Raindrops**	Vee-Jay 383
			CLARK, Petula	
			Born on 11/15/32 in Epsom, England. Pop singer/actress. On radio at age nine; own show "Pet's Parlour" at age 11. TV series in England in 1950. First U.S. record release for Coral in 1953. Appeared in over 20 British movies, 1944–57; revived her movie career in the late 1960s, starring in *Finian's Rainbow* and *Goodbye Mr. Chips*.	
1/2/65	1 (2)	13	● 1. **Downtown**	Warner 5494
4/3/65	3	9	2. **I Know A Place**	Warner 5612
7/31/65	22	5	3. You'd Better Come Home	Warner 5643
10/30/65	21	4	4. Round Every Corner	Warner 5661
1/15/66	1 (2)	9	5. **My Love**	Warner 5684
4/2/66	11	7	6. A Sign Of The Times	Warner 5802
7/30/66	9	7	7. **I Couldn't Live Without Your Love** #1 Adult Contemporary hit (1 week)	Warner 5835
10/29/66	21	6	8. Who Am I	Warner 5863
12/31/66+	16	7	9. Color My World all of above written and produced by Tony Hatch	Warner 5882
3/18/67	3	9	10. **This Is My Song** from the movie *A Countess from Hong Kong* starring Marlon Brando	Warner 7002
6/17/67	5	7	11. **Don't Sleep In The Subway** #1 Adult Contemporary hit (3 weeks)	Warner 7049
9/16/67	26	4	12. The Cat In The Window (The Bird In The Sky)	Warner 7073
12/30/67	31	2	13. The Other Man's Grass Is Always Greener	Warner 7097
3/2/68	15	9	14. Kiss Me Goodbye	Warner 7170
8/24/68	37	1	15. Don't Give Up	Warner 7216
			CLARK, Roy	
			Born on 4/15/33 in Meherrin, Virginia. Superb guitar, banjo and fiddle player. With the TV series "Hee Haw" from the first show in 1969.	
7/12/69	19	6	1. Yesterday, When I Was Young	Dot 17246
			CLARK, Sanford	
			Born in 1935 in Tulsa, Oklahoma. Moved to Phoenix in his teens.	
8/11/56	7	15	1. **The Fool** Best Seller #7 / Juke Box #7 / Top 100 #9 / Jockey #16; first released on MCI 1003 in 1956; Al Casey (guitar)	Dot 15481

DATE	POS	WKS	ARTIST–RECORD TITLE	LABEL & NO.
			CLARKE, Stanley	
			Born on 6/30/51 in Philadelphia. R&B-jazz bassist/violinist/cellist. With Chick Corea in Return To Forever in 1973. Much session work, solo debut in 1974. Member of Fuse One in 1982 and Animal Logic in 1989.	
6/13/81	**19**	9	1. Sweet Baby **STANLEY CLARKE/GEORGE DUKE**	Epic 01052
			CLARKE, Tony	
			Born in New York City; raised in Detroit. Died in Detroit in 1970. Soul singer/songwriter. Acted in the movie *They Call Me Mr. Tibbs*.	
5/8/65	**31**	2	1. The Entertainer	Chess 1924
			CLASH, The	
			Eclectic new wave rock group formed in London in 1976. Consisted of John "Joe Strummer" Mellor (vocals), Mick Jones (guitar), Paul Simonon (bass) and Nicky "Topper" Headon (drums). Political activists, they wrote songs protesting racism and oppression. Headon left in May 1983; replaced by Peter Howard. Jones (not to be confused with Mick Jones of Foreigner) left band in 1984 to form Big Audio Dynamite. Strummer disbanded The Clash in early 1986, and appeared in the 1987 movie *Straight To Hell*.	
4/26/80	**23**	7	1. Train In Vain (Stand By Me)	Epic 50851
11/13/82+	**8**	15	2. **Rock The Casbah**	Epic 03245
			CLASSICS, The	
			White vocal quartet from Brooklyn, formed in 1958. Consisted of Emil Stucchio (lead), Johnny Gambale, Tony Victor and Jamie Troy.	
7/20/63	**20**	5	1. Till Then #8 hit for The Mills Brothers in 1944; #10 hit for The Hilltoppers in 1954	Musicnote 1116
			CLASSICS IV	
			Quintet formed in Jacksonville, Florida. Consisted of Dennis Yost (vocals), J.R. Cobb (lead guitar), Wally Eaton (rhythm guitar), Joe Wilson (bass; replaced by Dean Daughtry) and Kim Venable (drums). Cobb, Daughtry and producer Buddy Buie joined the Atlanta Rhythm Section in 1974.	
1/13/68	**3**	12	1. **Spooky**	Imperial 66259
			CLASSICS IV FEATURING DENNIS YOST:	
11/16/68	**5**	12	● 2. **Stormy**	Imperial 66328
2/22/69	**2** (1)	10	3. **Traces**	Imperial 66352
5/31/69	**19**	7	4. Everyday With You Girl	Imperial 66378
			DENNIS YOST AND THE CLASSICS IV:	
12/9/72	**39**	3	5. What Am I Crying For?	MGM South 7002
			CLAY, Judy—see VERA, Billy	
			CLAY, Tom	
			Clay was a substitute DJ at KGBS-Los Angeles when he created this recording. Died on 11/22/95 (age 66).	
7/24/71	**8**	7	1. **What The World Needs Now Is Love/Abraham, Martin and John** [S] The Blackberries (vocal accompaniment)	Mowest 5002

DATE	POS	WKS	ARTIST–RECORD TITLE	LABEL & NO.
			CLEFTONES, The	
			Black doo-wop group from Queens, New York, formed at Jamaica High School in 1955. Consisted of Herbie Cox (lead), Charlie James (first tenor), Berman Patterson (second tenor), William McClain (baritone) and Warren Corbin (bass). Originally called the Silvertones.	
6/19/61	**18**	4	1. Heart And Soul	Gee 1064
			#1 hit for Larry Clinton in 1938	
			CLEMONS, Clarence	
			Born on 1/11/42 in Norfolk, Virginia. Saxophonist in Bruce Springsteen's E Street Band, 1973–89.	
11/23/85+	**18**	12	1. You're A Friend Of Mine	Columbia 05660
			CLARENCE CLEMONS And Jackson Browne	
			Airplay #17 / Sales #20; includes vocals by actress Daryl Hannah (Browne's then-girlfriend)	
			CLIFF, Jimmy	
			Born James Chambers in 1948. Jamaican reggae singer/composer. Starred in the movies *The Harder They Come* (1975) and *Club Paradise* (1986).	
12/27/69+	**25**	7	1. Wonderful World, Beautiful People	A&M 1146
12/4/93+	**18**	14	2. I Can See Clearly Now	Chaos 77207
			Airplay #11 / Sales #33; from the movie *Cool Runnings* starring John Candy	
			CLIFFORD, Buzz	
			Born Reese Francis Clifford III on 10/8/42 in Berwyn, Illinois.	
1/30/61	**6**	10	1. **Baby Sittin' Boogie** [N]	Columbia 41876
			babies' voices are by the children (boy and girl) of the producer; originally titled "Baby Sitter Boogie"	
			CLIFFORD, Mike	
			Born on 11/6/43 in Los Angeles. In the 1970s Broadway production of *Grease*.	
10/13/62	**12**	8	1. Close To Cathy	United Art. 489
			CLIMAX	
			Los Angeles-based pop quintet featuring lead singer Sonny Geraci (formerly with The Outsiders).	
1/22/72	**3**	12	● 1. **Precious And Few**	Rocky Road 30055
			originally released on Carousel 30055	
			CLIMAX BLUES BAND	
			Blues-rock band formed in Stafford, England. Nucleus consisted of Colin Cooper (sax, vocals), Peter Haycock (guitar, vocals), Derek Holt (bass) and John Cuffley (drums).	
3/26/77	**3**	14	1. **Couldn't Get It Right**	Sire 736
4/4/81	**12**	17	2. I Love You	Warner 49669

DATE	POS	WKS	ARTIST–RECORD TITLE	LABEL & NO.
			CLIMIE FISHER	
			U.K.-based pop/rock duo: Simon Climie (vocals) and Rob Fisher (keyboards). Fisher was a member of Naked Eyes. Chrysalis songwriter Climie wrote Pat Benatar's "Invincible" and "I Knew You Were Waiting (For Me)" by Aretha Franklin and George Michael.	
7/2/88	23	6	1. Love Changes (Everything) Sales #22 / Airplay #24	Capitol 44137
			CLINE, Patsy	
			Born Virginia Patterson Hensley on 9/8/32 in Winchester, Virginia. Killed in a plane crash with Cowboy Copas and Hawkshaw Hawkins on 3/5/63 near Camden, Tennessee. Elected to the Country Music Hall of Fame in 1973. Jessica Lange played Cline in the 1985 biographical movie *Sweet Dreams*.	
3/2/57	12	11	1. Walkin' After Midnight Juke Box #12 / Top 100 #17 / Best Seller #21 / Jockey #22	Decca 30221
7/24/61	12	10	2. I Fall To Pieces #1 Country hit (2 weeks)	Decca 31205
11/6/61	9	7	3. **Crazy** written by Willie Nelson	Decca 31317
2/24/62	14	8	4. She's Got You #1 Country hit (5 weeks)	Decca 31354
			CLIQUE, The	
			Pop-rock quintet from Texas led by Randy Shaw.	
9/20/69	22	7	1. Sugar On Sunday written by Tommy James	White Whale 323
			CLOONEY, Rosemary	
			Born on 5/23/28 in Maysville, Kentucky. One of the most popular singers of the 1950s, Rosemary and sister Betty sang with the Tony Pastor band in the late '40s before her solo career was launched. Rosemary was featured in *White Christmas* and several other '50s movies. After a period of personal difficulties, she re-emerged in the late '70s as a successful jazz and ballad singer. Married for a time to actor Jose Ferrer; their son Gabriel married Debby Boone.	
3/17/56	20	1	1. Memories Of You **THE BENNY GOODMAN TRIO with ROSEMARY CLOONEY** Juke Box #20 / Top 100 #52; from the movie *The Benny Goodman Story* starring Steve Allen (originally from the 1930 all-black revue *Blackbirds*)	Columbia 40616
4/13/57	10	9	2. **Mangos** Jockey #10 / Best Seller #23 / Top 100 #25; Frank Comstock (orch.); from the musical revue *Ziegfeld Follies 1957*	Columbia 40835
			CLOVERS, The	
			R&B group from Washington, D.C. By 1949, personnel lineup included John "Buddy" Bailey (lead), Matthew McQuater, Harold Lucas, Harold Winely and Bill Harris. Bailey entered the Army in 1952, replaced by Billy Mitchell. Upon Bailey's return, Mitchell stayed in the group. Group had 13 consecutive Top 10 R&B hits, 1951–54. Harris died of pancreatic cancer on 12/10/88 (age 63). A Clovers unit with Lucas performed until 1992. Lucas died of cancer on 1/6/94 (age 61).	
7/28/56	30	3	1. Love, Love, Love	Atlantic 1094
11/2/59	23	5	2. Love Potion No. 9	United Art. 180

DATE	POS	WKS	ARTIST–RECORD TITLE	LABEL & NO.
			CLUB NOUVEAU	
			Sacramento-based dance-disco group formed and fronted by Jay King (producer/owner of King Jay Records; produced the Timex Social Club). Early lineup: vocalists Valerie Watson and Samuelle Prater with Denzil Foster and Thomas McElroy. Prater, Foster and McElroy left in 1988, replaced by David Agent and Kevin Irving. Agent left in 1989. Foster and McElroy formed a prolific production duo and also recorded as FMob.	
2/21/87	**1** (2)	12	● 1. **Lean On Me**	King Jay/War. 28430
			Airplay #1(2) / Sales #1(1); King Jay/Warner 7" sold 600,000 units; Tommy Boy 12" sold 400,000	
7/18/87	39	1	2. Why You Treat Me So Bad	King Jay/War. 28360
			Sales #37	
			COASTERS, The	
			R&B group formed in Los Angeles in late 1955 from elements of The Robins. Originally consisted of Carl Gardner (ex-Robins; lead), Leon Hughes (tenor), Billy Guy (baritone lead), Bobby Nunn (ex-Robins; bass) and Adolph Jacobs (guitar). Noted for serio-comic recordings, primarily of Leiber & Stoller songs. Cornelius Gunter (early member of The Flairs, brother of Shirley Gunter) joined in 1957, left in 1961. Will "Dub" Jones (ex-Cadets) replaced Nunn in late 1958 and is heard on "Charlie Brown" and "Along Came Jones." Earl "Speedoo" Carroll (ex-Cadillacs) joined group in 1961. Bobby Nunn died of a heart attack on 11/5/86 (age 61). Gunter was shot to death on 2/26/90 (age 51). Today there are two or three "Coasters" groups still working, some of which contain one or two original members. Inducted into the Rock and Roll Hall of Fame in 1987.	
5/20/57	3	22	● 1. **Searchin'/**	
			Best Seller #3 / Top 100 #5 / Jockey #6 / Juke Box #10 end; #1 R&B hit (13 weeks)	
5/20/57	8	11	2. **Young Blood**	Atco 6087
			Top 100 #8 / Jockey #10 / Juke Box #12 / Best Seller #14; #1 R&B hit (1 week)	
6/9/58	**1** (1)	15	● 3. **Yakety Yak**	Atco 6116
			Top 100 #1 / Best Seller #2 / Jockey #2; #1 R&B hit (7 weeks)	
2/9/59	**2** (3)	12	● 4. **Charlie Brown** [N]	Atco 6132
			King Curtis (saxophone, above 2)	
6/1/59	9	8	5. **Along Came Jones** [N]	Atco 6141
9/7/59	7	11	● 6. **Poison Ivy/**	
			#1 R&B hit (4 weeks)	
9/21/59	38	1	7. I'm A Hog For You	Atco 6146
1/25/60	36	1	8. Run Red Run	Atco 6153
2/27/61	37	2	9. Wait A Minute	Atco 6186
			written by Bobby Darin and Don Kirshner	
5/29/61	23	6	10. Little Egypt (Ying-Yang) [N]	Atco 6192
			all of above (except #9) written by Leiber and Stoller	
			COATES, Odia—see ANKA, Paul	
			COCHRAN, Eddie	
			Born Edward Ray Cochrane on 10/3/38 in Oklahoma City, Oklahoma; raised in Albert Lea, Minnesota. Influential rock and roll singer/guitarist. Moved to Bell Gardens, California in 1953. Teamed with Hank Cochran (no relation) as the Cochran Brothers; first recorded as country act for Ekko Records in 1954. Appeared in movies *The Girl Can't Help It*, *Untamed Youth* and *Go, Johnny, Go!*. Killed in a car accident in Chippenham, Wiltshire, England, on 4/17/60. Accident also injured Gene Vincent. Inducted into the Rock and Roll Hall of Fame in 1987.	
3/30/57	18	8	1. Sittin' In The Balcony	Liberty 55056
			Top 100 #18 / Jockey #18 / Juke Box #20 / Best Seller #22	

DATE	POS	WKS	ARTIST–RECORD TITLE	LABEL & NO.
8/25/58	8	12	2. **Summertime Blues** Hot 100 #8 / Best Seller #13 end	Liberty 55144
1/5/59	35	1	3. C'mon Everybody	Liberty 55166

COCHRANE, Tom

Born on 5/13/53 in Lynn Lake, Manitoba, Canada. Toronto-based rock singer/songwriter. Formed rock group Red Rider in 1980.

DATE	POS	WKS	ARTIST–RECORD TITLE	LABEL & NO.
6/6/92	6	20	● 1. **Life Is A Highway** Sales #7 / Airplay #7	Capitol 44815

COCKBURN, Bruce

Cockburn (pronounced: CO-burn) was born on 5/27/45 in Canada. Pop-rock singer/songwriter.

DATE	POS	WKS	ARTIST–RECORD TITLE	LABEL & NO.
5/3/80	21	9	1. Wondering Where The Lions Are	Millennium 11786

COCKER, Joe

Born John Robert Cocker on 5/20/44 in Sheffield, England. Own skiffle band, the Cavaliers, late 1950s, later reorganized as Vance Arnold & The Avengers. Assembled the Grease Band in the mid-1960s. Performed at Woodstock in 1969. Successful tour with 43-piece revue, Mad Dogs & Englishmen, in 1970. Notable spastic stage antics were based on Ray Charles's movements at the piano.

DATE	POS	WKS	ARTIST–RECORD TITLE	LABEL & NO.
1/10/70	30	7	1. She Came In Through The Bathroom Window written by John Lennon and Paul McCartney	A&M 1147
5/9/70	7	9	2. **The Letter** **JOE COCKER with Leon Russell & The Shelter People** "live" recording	A&M 1174
10/24/70	11	7	3. Cry Me A River recorded "live" at Fillmore East, New York, on 3/27/70	A&M 1200
6/19/71	22	6	4. High Time We Went/	
		6	5. Black-Eyed Blues	A&M 1258
1/29/72	33	5	6. Feeling Alright [R] originally charted in 1969 at #69	A&M 1063
10/7/72	27	5	7. Midnight Rider **JOE COCKER and The Chris Stainton Band**	A&M 1370
2/15/75	5	10	8. **You Are So Beautiful** co-written by Billy Preston	A&M 1641
10/2/82	1 (3)	15	▲ 9. **Up Where We Belong** **JOE COCKER and JENNIFER WARNES** love theme from the movie *An Officer and a Gentleman* starring Richard Gere	Island 99996
12/2/89+	11	11	10. When The Night Comes Airplay #9 / Sales #15	Capitol 44437

COCK ROBIN

Pop quartet from Los Angeles: Peter Kingsbery (vocals, bass), Anna LaCazio (vocals, keyboards), Clive Wright (guitars) and Louis Molino III (drums).

DATE	POS	WKS	ARTIST–RECORD TITLE	LABEL & NO.
8/17/85	35	3	1. When Your Heart Is Weak	Columbia 04875

DATE	POS	WKS	ARTIST—RECORD TITLE	LABEL & NO.
			COFFEY, Dennis, And The Detroit Guitar Band	
			Detroit native Coffey was a session guitarist for The Temptations, The Jackson 5 and others. Coffey later formed C.J. & Co.	
11/13/71+	6	15	● 1. **Scorpio** [I]	Sussex 226
3/11/72	18	8	2. Taurus [I]	Sussex 233
			COHN, Marc	
			Born on 7/5/59 in Cleveland. Formed a 14-piece band in New York, the Supreme Court, which was discovered by Carly Simon and played at Caroline Kennedy's wedding. Won the 1991 Best New Artist Grammy Award.	
5/25/91	13	10	1. Walking In Memphis Airplay #27 / Sales #30	Atlantic 87747
			COLE, Cozy	
			Born William Randolph Cole on 10/17/09 in East Orange, New Jersey. Died of cancer on 1/29/81. Lead drummer for many swing bands, including Benny Carter, Willie Bryant, Cab Calloway and Louis Armstrong.	
9/29/58	3	14	● 1. **Topsy II/** [I] Hot 100 #3 / Best Seller #10 end; #1 R&B hit (6 weeks); #14 hit for Benny Goodman in 1938	
10/27/58	27	3	2. Topsy I [I] Hot 100 #27 / Best Seller #45	Love 5004
12/28/58	36	1	3. Turvy II [I]	Love 5014
			COLE, Jude	
			Native of East Moline, Illinois. Male guitarist/vocalist of Moon Martin's band. Touring guitarist with Billy Thorpe, Del Shannon and Dwight Twilley.	
5/5/90	16	10	1. Baby, It's Tonight Airplay #12 / Sales #21	Reprise 19869
9/22/90	32	4	2. Time For Letting Go Airplay #26	Reprise 19743
			COLE, Natalie	
			Born on 2/6/50 in Los Angeles. Daughter of Nat "King" Cole. Professional debut at age 11. Married for a time to her producer, Marvin Yancey, Jr. Later married Andre Fischer, former drummer of Rufus and producer for Brenda Russell, Michael Franks and Andre Crouch, until 1992. Natalie won the 1975 Best New Artist Grammy Award. Hosted own syndicated variety TV show "Big Break" in 1990.	
10/4/75	6	11	1. **This Will Be** #1 R&B hit (2 weeks)	Capitol 4109
2/28/76	32	5	2. Inseparable #1 R&B hit (1 week)	Capitol 4193
6/26/76	25	7	3. Sophisticated Lady (She's A Different Lady) #1 R&B hit (1 week)	Capitol 4259
2/26/77	5	14	● 4. **I've Got Love On My Mind** #1 R&B hit (5 weeks)	Capitol 4360
2/11/78	10	15	● 5. **Our Love** #1 R&B hit (2 weeks)	Capitol 4509
8/9/80	21	9	6. Someone That I Used To Love	Capitol 4869
8/22/87	13	10	7. Jump Start Sales #12 / Airplay #16	Manhattan 50073

DATE	POS	WKS	ARTIST–RECORD TITLE	LABEL & NO.
12/19/87+	**13**	11	8. I Live For Your Love Sales #11 / Airplay #17	Manhattan 50094
3/19/88	**5**	12	9. **Pink Cadillac** Sales #2 / Airplay #6; written and recorded by Bruce Springsteen in 1984 (B-side of his pop hit "Dancing In The Dark")	EMI-Man. 50117
5/13/89	**7**	13	10. **Miss You Like Crazy** Sales #5 / Airplay #8; #1 R&B hit (1 week); #1 Adult Contemporary hit (1 week)	EMI 50185
3/31/90	**34**	3	11. **Wild Women Do** Sales #25; from the movie *Pretty Woman* starring Richard Gere and Julia Roberts	EMI 50275
7/27/91	**14**	10	● 12. Unforgettable **NATALIE COLE with Nat "King" Cole** Sales #9 / Airplay #37; Nat's vocals are dubbed in from his original 1952 hit (at #12)	Elektra 64875

COLE, Nat "King"

Born Nathaniel Adams Coles on 3/17/17 in Montgomery, Alabama; raised in Chicago. Died of lung cancer on 2/15/65 in Santa Monica, California. Own band, the Royal Dukes, at age 17. First recorded in 1936 in band led by brother Eddie. Toured with "Shuffle Along" musical revue, lived in Los Angeles. Formed The King Cole Trio in 1939: Nat (piano), Oscar Moore (guitar; later joined brother's group, Johnny Moore's Three Blazers) and Wesley Prince (bass; replaced several years later by Johnny Miller). Long series of top-selling records led to his solo career in 1950. In movies *St. Louis Blues*, *Cat Ballou*, and many other movie appearances. First major black performer to star in a network (NBC) TV variety series (1956–57). Stopped performing in 1964 due to ill health. His daughter Natalie Cole is a recording star. Won Lifetime Achievement Grammy in 1990.

DATE	POS	WKS	ARTIST–RECORD TITLE	LABEL & NO.
3/5/55	**7**	16	1. **Darling Je Vous Aime Beaucoup/** Jockey #7 / Best Seller #10 / Juke Box #14; #21 hit for Hildegarde in 1943 (her theme song)	
3/5/55	**23**	13	2. The Sand And The Sea Best Seller #23	Capitol 3027
5/7/55	**2 (1)**	20	3. **A Blossom Fell/** Best Seller #2 / Juke Box #2 / Jockey #3	
5/21/55	**8**	10	4. **If I May** **NAT "KING" COLE AND THE FOUR KNIGHTS** Jockey #8	Capitol 3095
7/16/55	**24**	2	5. My One Sin Best Seller #24	Capitol 3136
10/22/55	**13**	8	6. Forgive My Heart/ Best Seller #13 / Top 100 #21	
10/22/55	**13**	8	7. Someone You Love Best Seller #13 / Jockey #19 / Top 100 #21	Capitol 3234
3/3/56	**18**	3	8. Ask Me Jockey #18 / Top 100 #25	Capitol 3328
4/21/56	**21**	6	9. Too Young To Go Steady Jockey #21 / Top 100 #31; from the musical *Strip for Action*	Capitol 3390
7/21/56	**16**	12	10. That's All There Is To That **NAT "KING" COLE AND THE FOUR KNIGHTS** Juke Box #16 / Best Seller #17 / Top 100 #18 / Jockey #18	Capitol 3456
11/3/56	**11**	10	11. Night Lights/ Jockey #11 / Top 100 #16 / Best Seller #17	
11/10/56	**25**	2	12. To The Ends Of The Earth Best Seller #25 / Jockey #25 / Top 100 #39	Capitol 3551

DATE	POS	WKS	ARTIST–RECORD TITLE	LABEL & NO.
2/23/57	**18**	5	13. Ballerina Jockey #18 / Top 100 #36; #1 hit for Vaughn Monroe in 1947; Nelson Riddle (orch., all of above)	Capitol 3619
7/1/57	**6**	18	14. **Send For Me/** Best Seller #6 / Top 100 #7 / Jockey #9; #1 R&B hit (2 weeks)	
8/5/57	**21**	2	15. My Personal Possession **NAT "KING" COLE AND THE FOUR KNIGHTS** Jockey #21 / Top 100 #63	Capitol 3737
10/21/57	**30**	4	16. With You On My Mind/ Best Seller #30 / Top 100 #33; McCoy's Boys (backing vocals: #14 & 16); Billy May (orch.: #14 & 16)	
		3	17. (The Song Of) Raintree County Best Seller flip; from the movie Raintree County starring Elizabeth Taylor; Johnny Green (MGM Studio Orch.)	Capitol 3782
2/24/58	**33**	3	18. Angel Smile Best Seller #33 / Top 100 #35	Capitol 3860
4/14/58	**5**	16	19. **Looking Back** Best Seller #5 / Top 100 #5 / Jockey #9	Capitol 3939
7/28/58	**38**	2	20. Come Closer To Me (Acercate Mas) Best Seller #38 / Top 100 #41; Armando Romeu, Jr. (orch.; 1940 Mexican song)	Capitol 4004
2/15/60	**30**	3	21. Time And The River	Capitol 4325
8/18/62	**2** (2)	13	● 22. **Ramblin' Rose** #1 Adult Contemporary hit (5 weeks)	Capitol 4804
12/1/62	**13**	8	23. Dear Lonely Hearts	Capitol 4870
5/25/63	**6**	9	24. **Those Lazy-Hazy-Crazy Days Of Summer**	Capitol 4965
9/28/63	**12**	9	25. That Sunday, That Summer	Capitol 5027
5/16/64	**22**	6	26. I Don't Want To Be Hurt Anymore	Capitol 5155
10/24/64	**34**	4	27. I Don't Want To See Tomorrow	Capitol 5261
7/27/91	**14**	10	● 28. **Unforgettable** **NATALIE COLE with Nat "King" Cole** Sales #9 / Airplay #37; Nat's vocals are dubbed in from his original 1952 hit (at #12)	Elektra 64875
			COLLECTIVE SOUL	
			Rock quintet from Stockbridge, Georgia: brothers Ed (vocals) and Dean (guitar) Roland with Ross Childress (guitar), Will Turpin (bass) and Shane Evans (drums). Group name taken from a reference in Ayn Rand's novel The Fountainhead.	
6/4/94	**11**	23	● 1. Shine Airplay #8 / Sales #11	Atlantic 87237
6/3/95	**20**	30	2. December Airplay #11 / Sales #57	Atlantic 87157
12/23/95+	**19**	17↑	3. The World I Know Airplay #10 / Sales #51	Atlantic 87088
			COLLINS, Dave And Ansil	
			Jamaican duo. By 1983, known as Clint Eastwood & General Saint.	
7/3/71	**22**	8	1. Double Barrel	Big Tree 115

DATE	POS	WKS	ARTIST–RECORD TITLE	LABEL & NO.
			COLLINS, Dorothy	
			Born Marjorie Chandler on 11/18/26 in Windsor, Ontario. Died on 7/21/94 of a heart attack. Star of TV's "Your Hit Parade." Married to orchestra leader Raymond Scott, 1952–mid 1960s.	
12/3/55	**16**	3	1. My Boy-Flat Top Juke Box #16 / Top 100 #22	Coral 61510
2/11/56	**17**	2	2. Seven Days Juke Box #17 / Top 100 #25; Dick Jacobs (orch., above 2)	Coral 61562
			COLLINS, Edwyn	
			Singer/songwriter from Scotland. Former lead singer of Scottish pop group Orange Juice.	
11/4/95	**32**	3	1. A Girl Like You Airplay #31; from the movie *Empire Records* starring Anthony LaPaglia	Bar None 1234
			COLLINS, Judy	
			Born on 5/1/39 in Seattle. Contemporary folk singer/songwriter. Began studying classical piano at age five. Moved to Los Angeles, then to Denver at age nine, where her father, Chuck Collins, was a radio personality. Classical debut at 13, playing with the Denver Businessmen's Symphony Orchestra. Discovered folk music at 15. Signed to Elektra in 1961. Her cover versions gave exposure to then-unknown songwriters Leonard Cohen, Joni Mitchell, Randy Newman and Sandy Denny. Stephen Stills wrote "Suite: Judy Blue Eyes" for her. Appeared in the New York Shakespeare Festival's production of *Peer Gynt*. Nominated for a 1974 Academy Award for co-directing *Antonia: A Portrait of the Woman*, a documentary about Judy's former classical mentor and a pioneer female orchestra conductor, Dr. Antonia Brico.	
11/23/68	**8**	9	1. **Both Sides Now** written by Joni Mitchell	Elektra 45639
1/9/71	**15**	11	2. Amazing Grace recorded at St. Paul's Chapel, Columbia University; Rev. John Newton wrote the words in 1779; William Walker composed the melody in 1844	Elektra 45709
3/17/73	**32**	5	3. Cook With Honey	Elektra 45831
7/26/75	**36**	3	4. Send In The Clowns from the Broadway musical *A Little Night Music* starring Glynis Johns	Elektra 45253
10/15/77	**19**	8	5. Send In The Clowns [R]	Elektra 45253
			COLLINS, Phil	
			Born on 1/30/51 in London. Pop vocalist/multi-instrumentalist/composer. Stage actor as a young child; played the Artful Dodger in the London production of *Oliver*. With group Flaming Youth in 1969. Joined Genesis as its drummer in 1970, became lead singer in 1975. Also with jazz-rock group Brand X. First solo album in 1981. Starred in the 1988 movie *Buster* and appeared in *Hook* and *Frauds*.	
4/11/81	**19**	9	1. I Missed Again	Atlantic 3790
7/11/81	**19**	8	● 2. In The Air Tonight	Atlantic 3824
11/27/82+	**10**	16	3. **You Can't Hurry Love**	Atlantic 89933
3/26/83	**39**	3	4. I Don't Care Anymore	Atlantic 89877
3/10/84	**1** (3)	16	● 5. **Against All Odds (Take A Look At Me Now)** title song from the movie *Against All Odds* starring Jeff Bridges	Atlantic 89700
12/8/84+	**2** (2)	16	● 6. **Easy Lover** **PHILIP BAILEY with PHIL COLLINS** Sales #1(1) / Airplay #2	Columbia 04679

DATE	POS	WKS	ARTIST–RECORD TITLE	LABEL & NO.
2/23/85	1 (2)	12	● 7. **One More Night** Airplay #1(2) / Sales #1(1); #1 Adult Contemporary hit (3 weeks)	Atlantic 89588
5/11/85	1 (1)	14	● 8. **Sussudio** Airplay #1(4) / Sales #2	Atlantic 89560
7/27/85	4	13	9. **Don't Lose My Number** Airplay #2 / Sales #7	Atlantic 89536
10/12/85	1 (1)	16	10. **Separate Lives** **PHIL COLLINS and MARILYN MARTIN** Airplay #1(2) / Sales #2; love theme from the movie *White Nights* starring Mikhail Baryshnikov; #1 Adult Contemporary hit (3 weeks)	Atlantic 89498
3/29/86	7	11	11. **Take Me Home** Airplay #3 / Sales #10; Peter Gabriel and Sting (backing vocals); above 5 (except #10) from the album *No Jacket Required*	Atlantic 89472
9/17/88	1 (2)	13	● 12. **Groovy Kind Of Love** Airplay #1(2) / Sales #1(1); #1 Adult Contemporary hit (3 weeks)	Atlantic 89017
11/26/88+	1 (2)	13	13. **Two Hearts** Airplay #1(3) / Sales #1(1); #1 Adult Contemporary hit (5 weeks); above 2 from the movie *Buster* starring Collins	Atlantic 88980
11/11/89	1 (4)	14	● 14. **Another Day In Paradise** Airplay #1(5) / Sales #2; David Crosby (backing vocal); #1 Adult Contemporary hit (5 weeks)	Atlantic 88774
2/17/90	3	11	15. **I Wish It Would Rain Down** Airplay #3 / Sales #4; Eric Clapton (guitar); also on the B-side of #16 below (without guitar)	Atlantic 88738
5/5/90	4	13	16. **Do You Remember?** Airplay #4 / Sales #9; #1 Adult Contemporary hit (5 weeks); demo version is on the B-side of #17 below	Atlantic 87955
8/18/90	4	12	17. **Something Happened On The Way To Heaven** Airplay #1(2) / Sales #10	Atlantic 87885
12/8/90+	23	7	18. Hang In Long Enough Airplay #24 / Sales #26; above 5 from the album *...But Seriously*	Atlantic 87800
11/13/93	25	7	19. Both Sides Of The Story Airplay #22	Atlantic 87299
2/12/94	24	13	20. Everyday Airplay #16	Atlantic 87300
			COLLINS, Tyler	
			Born in Harlem; raised in Detroit. Female R&B singer.	
6/2/90	6	13	1. **Girls Nite Out** Airplay #3 / Sales #9	RCA 2630
			COLOR ME BADD	
			New York City-based dance/vocal quartet: Bryan Abrams, Sam Watters, Mark Calderon and Kevin Thornton. Formed while in high school in Oklahoma City.	
4/27/91	2 (4)	16	▲² 1. **I Wanna Sex You Up** Sales #1(3) / Airplay #2; from the movie *New Jack City* starring Wesley Snipes and Ice-T; #1 R&B hit (2 weeks)	Giant 19382
8/10/91	1 (2)	14	● 2. **I Adore Mi Amor** Airplay #1(3) / Sales #4; #1 R&B hit (1 week)	Giant 19204
11/9/91+	1 (1)	25	● 3. **All 4 Love** Airplay #1(4) / Sales #4	Giant 19236
2/15/92	16	12	4. Thinkin' Back Airplay #15 / Sales #33	Giant 19074

DATE	POS	WKS	ARTIST–RECORD TITLE	LABEL & NO.
5/23/92	**18**	12	5. Slow Motion Airplay #12 / Sales #43; samples "Spinning Wheel" by Blood, Sweat & Tears; above 5 from the album *C.M.B.*	Giant 18908
9/26/92	**15**	10	6. Forever Love Airplay #9 / Sales #16; from the movie *Mo' Money* starring Damon and Marlon Wayans	Giant 18727
11/20/93	**23**	9	7. Time And Chance Sales #19 / Airplay #44; samples "My Philosophy" by Boogie Down Productions	Giant 18339
1/22/94	**23**	9	8. Choose Airplay #20 / Sales #42	Giant 18270

COLTER, Jessi

Born Miriam Johnson on 5/25/47 in Phoenix. Country singer/songwriter. Married to Duane Eddy, 1962-68. Married Waylon Jennings in October 1969.

DATE	POS	WKS	ARTIST–RECORD TITLE	LABEL & NO.
4/26/75	**4**	14	1. **I'm Not Lisa** #1 Country hit (1 week)	Capitol 4009

COLTRANE, Chi

Born on 11/16/48 in Racine, Wisconsin. Female vocalist/pianist. (Chi pronounced: shy.)

DATE	POS	WKS	ARTIST–RECORD TITLE	LABEL & NO.
9/30/72	**17**	9	1. Thunder And Lightning	Columbia 45640

COMMANDER CODY And His Lost Planet Airmen

Group formed while Cody (George Frayne) attended the University of Michigan. To San Francisco in 1968.

DATE	POS	WKS	ARTIST–RECORD TITLE		LABEL & NO.
4/15/72	**9**	11	1. **Hot Rod Lincoln** original version by Tiny Hill charted in 1951	[N]	Paramount 0146

COMMODORES

R&B group formed in Tuskegee, Alabama, in 1970. Consisted of Lionel Richie (vocals, saxophone), William King (trumpet), Thomas McClary (guitar), Milan Williams (keyboards), Ronald LaPread (bass) and Walter "Clyde" Orange (drums). First recorded for Motown in 1972. In the movie *Thank God It's Friday*. Richie began solo work in 1981, left group in 1982.

DATE	POS	WKS	ARTIST–RECORD TITLE		LABEL & NO.
7/6/74	**22**	6	1. Machine Gun	[I]	Motown 1307
6/28/75	**19**	7	2. Slippery When Wet #1 R&B hit (1 week)		Motown 1338
2/14/76	**5**	14	3. **Sweet Love**		Motown 1381
10/9/76	**7**	11	4. **Just To Be Close To You** #1 R&B hit (2 weeks)		Motown 1402
2/19/77	**39**	1	5. Fancy Dancer		Motown 1408
6/25/77	**4**	13	6. **Easy** #1 R&B hit (1 week)		Motown 1418
9/17/77	**5**	11	7. **Brick House**		Motown 1425
1/14/78	**24**	7	8. Too Hot Ta Trot #1 R&B hit (1 week)		Motown 1432
7/8/78	**1 (2)**	16	9. **Three Times A Lady** #1 Adult Contemporary hit (3 weeks); #1 R&B hit (2 weeks)		Motown 1443
11/4/78	**38**	2	10. Flying High		Motown 1452
8/18/79	**4**	12	11. **Sail On**		Motown 1466

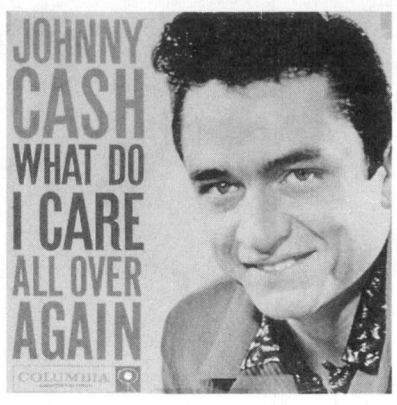

Johnny Cash's first hit for Columbia Records, following his reputable stretch at the pioneering Sun label, was the 1958 single "All Over Again." Cash later recorded for Rick Rubin's American label in the early '90s.

Shaun Cassidy's stint as a best-selling teen idol came six years after his brother David's first solo Top 10 hit. Top 10 sibling score: David, one (1971's "Cherish"), Shaun, three (1977's trio of "Da Doo Ron Ron," "That's Rock 'N' Roll," and "Hey Deanie").

Chad & Jeremy's take on the pop standard "Willow Weep For Me" gave the British duo a No. 15 hit in early 1965. The pair's later, critically praised work on Columbia was reissued as *Painted Dayglow Smile* by Sony Legacy in 1992.

Chubby Checker's nonstop string of early '60s dance songs—celebrating the Twist, the Pony, the Hucklebuck, the Fly, and the Limbo—was briefly interrupted for, perhaps predictably, "Dancin' Party," a No. 12 hit in 1962.

Cheech & Chong's wacky '70s comedy style saw Top 40 exposure with "Sister Mary Elephant (Shudd-Up!)," issued by Ode Records in 1973. The duo's not-ready-for-airtime style produced only two other Top 40 hits.

Chic's mesmerizing brand of sophisticated dance-pop produced four Top 10 records during the late '70s, including the impeccably produced 1979 hit "I Want Your Love." The group's music would be further immortalized as part of the Sony Playstation videogame "Krazy Ivan" in 1996.

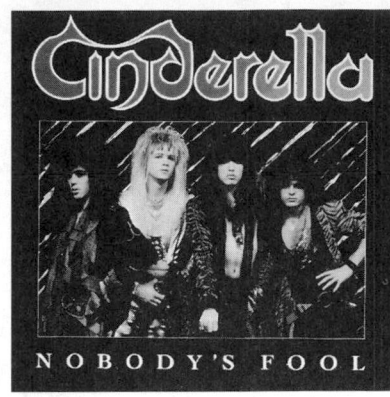

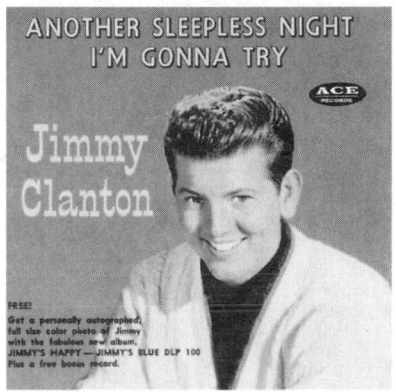

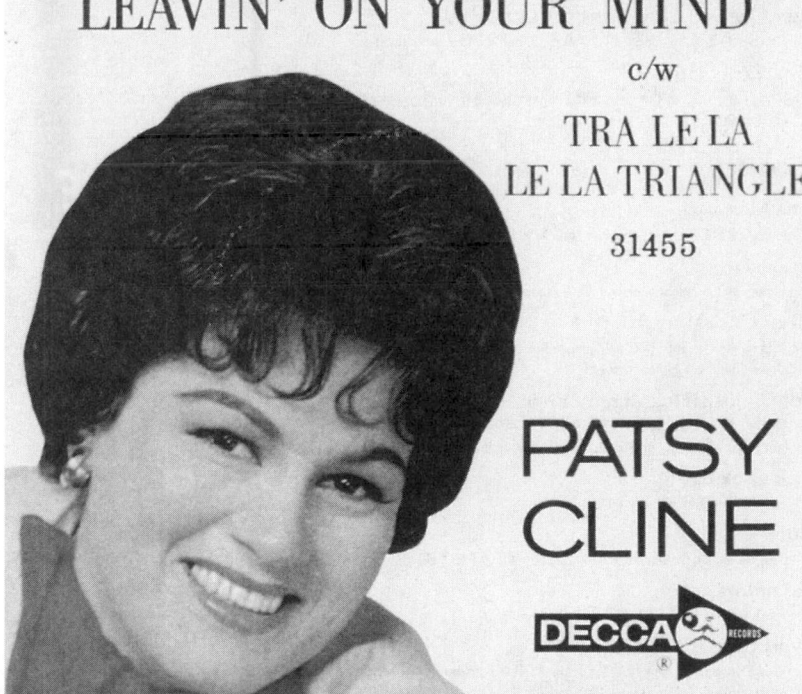

The Chipmunks' sole No. 1 hit, "The Chipmunk Song," held the top spot for four weeks in 1958. The timeless animated group visited such genres as punk and country music as later decades unfolded.

Lou Christie's MGM Records hit "Lightnin' Strikes" reached No. 1 in early 1966, which might be why Colpix Records decided to release their own Christie single four weeks later. Despite its title, "Big Time" stayed on the chart for only one week.

Cinderella's late-'80s rise to pop prominence must have seemed like a fairy tale to the band. The hard-rocking Pennsylvanian quartet's Top 40 debut "Nobody's Fool" reached No. 13 in in 1987, and four additional hits followed.

Jimmy Clanton starred in the first rock and roll film to reach the home video market in the mid-'80s, 1959's *Go, Johnny, Go*. His second-to-last Top 40 hit, "Another Sleepless Night," reached No. 22 in 1960.

The Dave Clark Five's steady stream of early '60s hits resulted in only one No. 1 hit—1965's "Over And Over." The group's vast catalog was one of the very last major repertoires to see CD reissue in the early '90s.

Patsy Cline's ironically titled "Leavin' On Your Mind" peaked at No. 83 and fell off the pop chart the last week of February 1963. A week later, she was tragically killed in a plane crash.

DATE	POS	WKS	ARTIST–RECORD TITLE	LABEL & NO.
10/13/79	1 (1)	15	12. **Still** #1 R&B hit (1 week)	Motown 1474
1/26/80	25	6	13. Wonderland	Motown 1479
7/12/80	20	11	14. Old-Fashion Love	Motown 1489
7/11/81	8	15	15. **Lady (You Bring Me Up)**	Motown 1514
10/10/81	4	15	16. **Oh No** Lionel Richie's last song as lead singer	Motown 1527
3/2/85	3	13	17. **Nightshift** Sales #3 / Airplay #4; a tribute to Marvin Gaye and Jackie Wilson; #1 R&B hit (4 weeks)	Motown 1773

COMMUNARDS

British rock duo consisting of Bronski Beat vocalist Jimmy Somerville and multi-instrumentalist Richard Coles.

DATE	POS	WKS	ARTIST–RECORD TITLE	LABEL & NO.
3/7/87	40	1	1. Don't Leave Me This Way Sales #31	MCA 52928

COMO, Perry

Born Pierino Como on 5/18/12 in Canonsburg, Pennsylvania. Owned barbershop in hometown. With Freddy Carlone band in 1933; with Ted Weems, 1936–42. Appeared in the movies *Something For The Boys, Doll Face, If I'm Lucky* and *Words And Music*, 1944–48. Own "Supper Club" radio series to late 1940s. Television shows (15 minutes), 1948–55. Host of hourly TV shows, 1955–63. Winner of five Emmys. One of the most popular singers of the past 50 years.

DATE	POS	WKS	ARTIST–RECORD TITLE	LABEL & NO.
2/5/55	2 (3)	14	1. **Ko Ko Mo (I Love You So)** Jockey #2 / Best Seller #4 / Juke Box #5; #6 R&B hit for Gene & Eunice in 1955	RCA 5994

PERRY COMO AND JAYE P. MORGAN:

DATE	POS	WKS	ARTIST–RECORD TITLE	LABEL & NO.
6/11/55	12	5	2. Chee Chee-oo Chee (Sang the Little Bird)/ Jockey #12 / Juke Box #14 / Best Seller #24; Italian song	
6/25/55	18	1	3. Two Lost Souls Jockey #18; from the Broadway musical *Damn Yankees* starring Gwen Verdon	RCA 6137

PERRY COMO:

DATE	POS	WKS	ARTIST–RECORD TITLE	LABEL & NO.
8/13/55	5	14	4. **Tina Marie/** Jockey #5 / Best Seller #6 / Juke Box #8 / Top 100 #12 pre	
8/20/55	20	1	5. Fooled Jockey #20; melody based on a classical theme by Franz Lehar	RCA 6192
11/19/55+	11	11	6. All At Once You Love Her Jockey #11 / Top 100 #24; from the Broadway musical *Pipe Dream* starring Helen Traubel	RCA 6294
3/10/56	1 (1)	20	● 7. **Hot Diggity (Dog Ziggity Boom)/** Jockey #1 / Best Seller #2 / Top 100 #2 / Juke Box #2; adapted from the 1883 *Espana Rhapsody* by French composer Chabrier	
3/10/56	10	10	8. **Juke Box Baby** Top 100 #10 / Jockey #11	RCA 6427
6/16/56	4	14	9. **More/** Best Seller #4 / Juke Box #6 / Jockey #8 / Top 100 #9	
6/23/56	8	12	10. **Glendora** Jockey #8 / Top 100 #14	RCA 6554
8/25/56	18	3	11. Somebody Up There Likes Me Juke Box #18 / Jockey #22 / Top 100 #26; title song from the movie starring Paul Newman	RCA 6590

DATE	POS	WKS	ARTIST–RECORD TITLE	LABEL & NO.
3/2/57	**1** (2)	19	● 12. **Round And Round** Jockey #1(2) / Best Seller #1(1) / Top 100 #1(1) / Juke Box #3	RCA 6815
5/27/57	**13**	6	13. The Girl With The Golden Braids Jockey #13 / Top 100 #15 / Best Seller #26	RCA 6904
10/14/57	**12**	14	14. Just Born (To Be Your Baby)/ Best Seller #12 / Jockey #13 / Top 100 #19	
10/21/57	**18**	8	15. Ivy Rose Jockey #18 / Top 100 #32	RCA 7050
1/13/58	**1** (1)	16	● 16. **Catch A Falling Star/** Jockey #1 / Best Seller #3 / Top 100 #9	
1/20/58	**4**	12	17. **Magic Moments** Jockey #4 / Top 100 #27 / Best Seller #42	RCA 7128
4/21/58	**6**	11	18. **Kewpie Doll/** Jockey #6 / Best Seller #12 / Top 100 #12	
5/5/58	**19**	1	19. Dance Only With Me Jockey #19; from the Broadway musical *Say Darling* starring David Wayne	RCA 7202
8/4/58	**28**	6	20. Moon Talk Best Seller #28 / Hot 100 #29	RCA 7274
11/17/58	**33**	2	21. Love Makes The World Go 'Round	RCA 7353
3/23/59	**29**	3	22. Tomboy	RCA 7464
2/22/60	**22**	6	23. Delaware [N]	RCA 7670
4/28/62	**23**	6	24. Caterina	RCA 8004
7/20/63	**39**	1	25. (I Love You) Don't You Forget It Mitchell Ayres (orch., all of above); Ray Charles Singers (backing vocals, all of above - except #3, 5, 13)	RCA 8186
5/1/65	**25**	6	26. Dream On Little Dreamer	RCA 8533
5/31/69	**38**	1	27. Seattle from the TV series "Here Come The Brides" starring Bobby Sherman	RCA 9722
12/5/70+	**10**	13	28. **It's Impossible** #1 Adult Contemporary hit (4 weeks)	RCA 0387
5/19/73	**29**	8	29. And I Love You So written by Don McLean; #1 Adult Contemporary hit (1 week)	RCA 0906

COMPANY B

Miami-based dance trio founded and produced by Foxy leader Ish Ledesma. Consisted of Lori L, Lezlee Livrano and Susan Johnson.

DATE	POS	WKS	ARTIST–RECORD TITLE	LABEL & NO.
5/9/87	**21**	8	1. Fascinated Sales #17 / Airplay #27	Atlantic 89294

CONCRETE BLONDE

Rock group formed in Los Angeles in 1982: Johnette Napolitano (vocals, bass), James Andrew Mankey (guitar) and Harry Rushakoff (drums). Paul Thompson replaced Rushakoff in early 1990; Rushakoff returned in late 1991, replacing Thompson. Group originally known as Dream 6, renamed by Michael Stipe of R.E.M.

DATE	POS	WKS	ARTIST–RECORD TITLE	LABEL & NO.
10/6/90	**19**	8	1. Joey Sales #14 / Airplay #30	I.R.S. 73014

DATE	POS	WKS	ARTIST–RECORD TITLE	LABEL & NO.
			CON FUNK SHUN	
			Soul band formed as Project Soul in Vallejo, California, in 1968 by high school classmates Michael Cooper (lead vocals, guitar) and Louis McCall (drums). Moved to Memphis in 1972, changed name to Con Funk Shun.	
1/21/78	23	6	1. Ffun	Mercury 73959
			#1 R&B hit (2 weeks)	
2/28/81	40	1	2. Too Tight	Mercury 76089
			CONLEY, Arthur	
			Soul singer, born on 1/4/46 in Atlanta. Discovered by Otis Redding in 1965. First recorded for NRC as Arthur & The Corvets.	
4/1/67	2 (1)	11	● 1. **Sweet Soul Music**	Atco 6463
			originally written by Sam Cooke as "Yeah Man"	
7/1/67	31	3	2. Shake, Rattle & Roll	Atco 6494
			#1 R&B hit (3 weeks) for Joe Turner in 1954	
4/6/68	14	9	3. Funky Street	Atco 6563
			CONNIFF, Ray	
			Born on 11/6/16 in Attleboro, Massachusetts. Trombonist/arranger with Bunny Berigan, Bob Crosby, Harry James, Vaughn Monroe and Artie Shaw bands. Long string of hit albums beginning in 1957. Arranger/conductor for many of Columbia Records' top vocalists during the '50s and '60s (Guy Mitchell, Johnny Mathis, Marty Robbins and others).	
7/9/66	9	9	1. **Somewhere, My Love** **RAY CONNIFF And The Singers** Lara's Theme from the movie *Dr. Zhivago* starring Omar Sharif; #1 Adult Contemporary hit (4 weeks)	Columbia 43626
			CONNOR, Chris	
			Born on 11/8/27 in Kansas City, Missouri. Female jazz-styled singer; with Stan Kenton, 1952-53.	
2/16/57	34	3	1. I Miss You So	Atlantic 1105
			#20 hit for The Cats and the Fiddle in 1940	
			CONNORS, Norman	
			Born on 3/1/48 in Philadelphia. Jazz drummer with Archie Shepp, John Coltrane, Pharoah Sanders and others. Own group on Buddah in 1972.	
10/2/76	27	10	1. You Are My Starship	Buddah 542
			Michael Henderson (vocal)	
			CONTI, Bill	
			Born on 4/13/42 in Providence, Rhode Island. Composer/conductor for the first three *Rocky* movies; also for *The Karate Kid*, *Private Benjamin*, *For Your Eyes Only* and Oscar-winning score for *The Right Stuff*.	
5/7/77	1 (1)	13	● 1. **Gonna Fly Now** [I]	United Art. 940
			theme from the movie *Rocky* starring Sylvester Stallone	
			CONTOURS, The	
			R&B vocal group formed in Detroit: Billy Gordon, Billy Hoggs, Joe Billingslea, Sylvester Potts, Huey Davis (guitar) and Hubert Johnson (died 7/11/81). Dennis Edwards, a member in 1967, joined The Temptations in 1968. Gordon was married to Georgeanna Tillman of The Marvelettes. Johnson was the cousin of Jackie Wilson.	

DATE	POS	WKS	ARTIST–RECORD TITLE	LABEL & NO.
9/22/62	3	11	● 1. **Do You Love Me** #1 R&B hit (3 weeks)	Gordy 7005
7/2/88	11	8	2. Do You Love Me [R] Airplay #7 / Sales #15; featured in the movie *Dirty Dancing* starring Patrick Swayze; label is Motown's Yesteryear series	Motown Yest. 448

COOKE, Sam

Born on 1/2/31 in Clarksdale, Mississippi; raised in Chicago. Died from a gunshot wound on 12/11/64 in Los Angeles; shot by a female motel manager under mysterious circumstances. Son of a Baptist minister. Sang in choir from age six. Joined gospel group the Highway Q.C.'s. Lead singer of the Soul Stirrers, 1950-56. First recorded secular songs in 1956 as "Dale Cook" on Specialty. String of hits on Keen label led to contract with RCA. Nephew is singer R.B. Greaves. Inducted into the Rock and Roll Hall of Fame in 1986. Revered as the definitive soul singer.

DATE	POS	WKS	ARTIST–RECORD TITLE	LABEL & NO.
10/28/57	1 (3)	17	● 1. **You Send Me** Top 100 #1(3) / Best Seller #1(2) / Jockey #1(1); written by Sam's brother, Charles "L.C." Cooke; #1 R&B hit (6 weeks)	Keen 34013
12/23/57+	18	10	2. I'll Come Running Back To You Best Seller #18 / Top 100 #22; #1 R&B hit (1 week)	Specialty 619
1/6/58	17	7	3. (I Love You) For Sentimental Reasons Best Seller #17 / Top #43	Keen 4002
3/24/58	26	5	4. Lonely Island/ Best Seller #26 / Top 100 #39	
3/24/58	27	5	5. You Were Made For Me Best Seller #27 / Top 100 #39	Keen 4009
9/8/58	22	6	6. Win Your Love For Me Best Seller #22 / Hot 100 #33	Keen 2006
12/15/58	26	7	7. Love You Most Of All Bumps Blackwell (orch.: #1,4,5,7)	Keen 2008
3/30/59	31	5	8. Everybody Likes To Cha Cha Cha	Keen 2018
7/6/59	28	4	9. Only Sixteen	Keen 2022
5/23/60	12	11	10. Wonderful World	Keen 2112
8/29/60	2 (2)	13	11. **Chain Gang** Glenn Osser (orch.)	RCA 7783
12/19/60	29	4	12. Sad Mood	RCA 7816
3/20/61	31	4	13. That's It-I Quit-I'm Movin' On Sammy Lowe (orch., above 2)	RCA 7853
6/26/61	17	9	14. Cupid	RCA 7883
2/17/62	9	13	15. **Twistin' The Night Away** #1 R&B hit (3 weeks)	RCA 7983
8/4/62	13	5	16. Bring It On Home To Me/	
6/16/62	17	9	17. Having A Party Lou Rawls (backing vocal, above 2)	RCA 8036
10/20/62	12	8	18. Nothing Can Change This Love	RCA 8088
2/2/63	13	8	19. Send Me Some Lovin'	RCA 8129
5/4/63	10	9	20. **Another Saturday Night** #1 R&B hit (1 week)	RCA 8164
8/17/63	14	7	21. Frankie And Johnny version of mid-19th century traditional folk song; Ralph Burns (orch.)	RCA 8215
11/9/63	11	8	22. Little Red Rooster	RCA 8247
2/15/64	11	7	23. Good News	RCA 8299
6/27/64	11	7	24. Good Times/	

DATE	POS	WKS	ARTIST–RECORD TITLE	LABEL & NO.
7/4/64	35	4	25. Tennessee Waltz *#1 hit (13 weeks) for Patti Page in 1950; Hugo & Luigi produced all of above RCA recordings*	RCA 8368
10/24/64	31	4	26. Cousin Of Mine	RCA 8426
1/16/65	7	9	27. **Shake/**	
2/13/65	31	4	28. A Change Is Gonna Come *written by Sam in response to Bob Dylan's "Blowin' In The Wind"*	RCA 8486
8/28/65	32	3	29. Sugar Dumpling	RCA 8631

COOKIES, The

R&B vocal trio from New York with varying membership. Backup work for Neil Sedaka, Carole King and Little Eva. One member, Ethel "Earl-Jean" McCrea, later went solo. The 1950s lineup of The Cookies became Ray Charles' vocal backing trio, The Raelettes.

DATE	POS	WKS	ARTIST–RECORD TITLE	LABEL & NO.
12/1/62	17	8	1. Chains	Dimension 1002
3/23/63	7	9	2. **Don't Say Nothin' Bad (About My Baby)**	Dimension 1008
1/18/64	33	4	3. Girls Grow Up Faster Than Boys	Dimension 1020

COOLEY, Eddie, And The Dimples

Cooley, a New York songwriter, wrote "Fever" (hit for Little Willie John, Peggy Lee and The McCoys). The Dimples were a female trio.

DATE	POS	WKS	ARTIST–RECORD TITLE	LABEL & NO.
11/24/56	20	8	1. Priscilla *Best Seller #20 / Juke Box #20 / Top 100 #26*	Royal Roost 621

COOLIDGE, Rita

Born on 5/1/44 in Nashville. Had own group, R.C. and the Moonpies, at Florida State University. Moved to Los Angeles in the late '60s. Did backup work for Delaney & Bonnie, Leon Russell, Joe Cocker and Eric Clapton. With Kris Kristofferson from 1971; married to him, 1973-80. Known as "The Delta Lady," for whom Leon Russell wrote the song of the same name. Appeared in the 1983 movie *Club Med.*

DATE	POS	WKS	ARTIST–RECORD TITLE	LABEL & NO.
6/11/77	2 (1)	17	● 1. **(Your Love Has Lifted Me) Higher And Higher**	A&M 1922
10/15/77	7	13	● 2. **We're All Alone** *written by Boz Scaggs; #1 Adult Contemporary hit (1 week)*	A&M 1965
2/4/78	20	7	3. The Way You Do The Things You Do	A&M 2004
7/29/78	25	6	4. You	A&M 2058
1/5/80	38	2	5. I'd Rather Leave While I'm In Love	A&M 2199
8/6/83	36	4	6. All Time High *from the James Bond movie Octopussy starring Roger Moore; #1 Adult Contemporary hit (4 weeks)*	A&M 2551

COOLIO

Coolio is Artis Ivey, a rapper from Compton, California. His DJ partner is Bryan "Wino" Dobbs. Coolio is a member of WC and the MAAD Circle.

DATE	POS	WKS	ARTIST–RECORD TITLE	LABEL & NO.
6/25/94	3	21	▲ 1. **Fantastic Voyage** *Sales #1(4) / Airplay #11*	Tommy Boy 7617
8/19/95	1 (3)	35↑	▲³ 2. **Gangsta's Paradise** **COOLIO FEATURING L.V.** *Sales #1(7) / Airplay #7; rap version of "Pastime Paradise" by Stevie Wonder (from his 1976 album "Songs In The Key Of Life"); from the movie Dangerous Minds starring Michelle Pfeiffer*	MCA 55104
12/16/95+	24	5	3. Too Hot *Sales #13*	Tommy Boy 7718

DATE	POS	WKS	ARTIST–RECORD TITLE	LABEL & NO.
			COOPER, Alice	
			Born Vincent Furnier on 2/4/48 in Detroit. Formed rock group in Phoenix in 1965; adopted his stage name in 1966 from a 16th-century witch. To Los Angeles in 1968, then to Detroit in 1969. Known primarily for his bizarre stage antics. Appeared in the movies *Prince Of Darkness* and *Wayne's World*, among others.	
3/20/71	21	8	1. Eighteen	Warner 7499
6/24/72	7	10	2. **School's Out**	Warner 7596
10/21/72	26	6	3. Elected	Warner 7631
3/10/73	35	3	4. Hello Hurray	Warner 7673
5/12/73	25	8	5. No More Mr. Nice Guy	Warner 7691
5/3/75	12	11	6. Only Women	Atlantic 3254
10/30/76+	12	14	● 7. I Never Cry	Warner 8228
6/11/77	9	13	8. **You And Me**	Warner 8349
11/11/78	12	11	9. How You Gonna See Me Now	Warner 8695
7/5/80	40	1	10. Clones (We're All)	Warner 49204
10/14/89	7	10	● 11. **Poison**	Epic 68958
			Sales #5 / Airplay #12	
			COOPER, Les, and the Soul Rockers	
			Cooper was born on 3/15/31 in Norfolk, Virginia. Pianist/singer/arranger/leader.	
11/17/62+	22	11	1. Wiggle Wobble [I]	Everlast 5019
			Joe Grier (former lead singer of The Charts; tenor sax solo)	
			COPELAND, Ken	
			Born in 1937 in Texas. Currently a televangelist with own Kenneth Copeland Ministries, based in Fort Worth, Texas. Also records inspirational albums.	
4/20/57	12	8	1. Pledge Of Love	Imperial 5432
			Jockey #12 / Top 100 #17 / Best Seller #23; first released on LIN 5007 in 1957; B-side is "Night Air" by The Mints	
			COREY, Jill	
			Born Norma Jean Speranza on 9/30/35. Married major league baseball player Don Hoak. Regular on TV's "Your Hit Parade," 1957-58.	
2/2/57	21	5	1. I Love My Baby (My Baby Loves Me)	Columbia 40794
			Jockey #21 / Top 100 #28; #6 hit for Fred Waring's Pennsylvanians in 1926	
8/5/57	11	9	2. Love Me To Pieces	Columbia 40955
			Best Seller #11 / Jockey #11 / Top 100 #18; performed by Jill on the 7/15/57 "Studio One Summer Theatre" TV production of "Love Me To Pieces"; Jimmy Carroll (orch., all of above)	
			CORINA	
			Manhattan-born, Bronx-raised dance singer. Placed second in the Miss Puerto Rico pageant in 1983.	
6/22/91	6	13	1. **Temptation**	Atco 98775
			Airplay #2 / Sales #24	

DATE	POS	WKS	ARTIST–RECORD TITLE	LABEL & NO.
			CORNELIUS BROTHERS & SISTER ROSE	
			Family group from Dania, Florida. Consisted of Edward, Carter and Rose. Billie Jo was added in 1973. All 15 Cornelius children play instruments or sing. Carter died on 11/7/91 (age 43).	
5/15/71	3	13	● 1. **Treat Her Like A Lady**	United Art. 50721
			first released on Platinum 105 in 1970	
6/17/72	2 (2)	11	● 2. **Too Late To Turn Back Now**	United Art. 50910
9/23/72	23	7	3. Don't Ever Be Lonely (A Poor Little Fool Like Me)	United Art. 50954
2/3/73	37	2	4. I'm Never Gonna Be Alone Anymore	United Art. 50996
			CORNELL, Don	
			Born on 4/21/19 in New York City. Popular singer/guitarist. From the late 1930s, worked with Al Kavelin and Red Nichols. Achieved greatest success with Sammy Kaye, charting 14 hits, 1942-50.	
5/14/55	14	6	1. Most Of All/	
			Jockey #14 / Best Seller #20; #5 R&B hit for The Moonglows in 1955	
		2	2. The Door Is Still Open To My Heart	Coral 61393
			Best Seller flip; written by Chuck Willis; #4 R&B hit for The Cardinals in 1955	
9/10/55	7	13	3. **The Bible Tells Me So/**	
			Best Seller #7 / Juke Box #8 / Jockey #18 / Top 100 #31 pre; written by Roy Rogers' wife, Dale Evans	
11/5/55	26	3	4. Love Is A Many-Splendored Thing	Coral 61467
			Carretta (orch.); title song from the movie starring William Holden	
11/12/55	25	1	5. Young Abe Lincoln	Coral 61521
			Dick Jacobs (orch., all of above - except #4)	
			CORONA	
			Studio creation of Italian producers Checco and Soul Train. Group name is Spanish for crown.	
12/17/94+	11	20	1. The Rhythm Of The Night	EastWest 98192
			Airplay #10 / Sales #18	
			CORSAIRS Featuring JAY "BIRD" UZZELL	
			R&B vocal quartet from La Grange, North Carolina, consisting of brothers Jay "Bird" (lead singer), James and Moses Uzzell, with cousin George Wooten.	
1/27/62	12	10	1. Smoky Places	Tuff 1808
			CORTEZ, Dave "Baby"	
			Born David Cortez Clowney on 8/13/38 in Detroit. Black keyboardist/composer. Played organ and sang with vocal group The Pearls, 1955-57; also with the Valentines, which included Richard Barrett and Ronnie Bright (of "Mr. Bass Man" fame), 1956-57. Frequent session work in New York. First recorded (as David Clooney) for Ember in 1956.	
3/30/59	1 (1)	14	1. **The Happy Organ** [I]	Clock 1009
8/11/62	10	9	2. **Rinky Dink** [I]	Julia/Chess 1829
			COSBY, Bill	
			Born on 7/12/38 in Philadelphia. Top comedian who has appeared in nightclubs, movies and on TV. His first seven comedy albums were all million sellers. Played Alexander Scott on TV series "I Spy." Star of the highly rated NBC-TV series "The Cosby Show." Winner of five Emmys and nine Grammys.	
9/16/67	4	8	1. **Little Ole Man** (Uptight-Everything's Alright) [N]	Warner 7072

DATE	POS	WKS	ARTIST–RECORD TITLE	LABEL & NO.
			COSTA, Don, And His Orchestra And Chorus	
			Costa was born on 6/10/25 in Boston. Died on 1/19/83. Arranger for Vaughn Monroe, Frank Sinatra, Vic Damone, The Ames Brothers and many more. A&R director of ABC–Paramount Records, then for United Artists Records.	
6/27/60	27	4	1. Theme From "The Unforgiven" (The Need For Love)[I] from the movie *The Unforgiven* starring Burt Lancaster and Audrey Hepburn	United Art. 221
8/29/60	19	14	2. Never On Sunday [I] title song from the movie starring Melina Mercouri; originally charted for 11 weeks; re-entered on 5/14/61 at #37	United Art. 234
			COSTELLO, Elvis	
			Born Declan McManus in Liverpool, England, on 8/25/54. Leading eclectic rock singer. Changed name to Elvis Costello in 1976; Costello is his mother's maiden name. Formed backing band The Attractions (Steve Nieve, Bruce Thomas and Peter Thomas) in 1977. Appeared in the 1987 movie *Straight To Hell*. Married Cait O'Riordan, former bassist with The Pogues, on 5/16/86.	
10/15/83	36	2	1. Everyday I Write The Book **ELVIS COSTELLO & THE ATTRACTIONS**	Columbia 04045
5/27/89	19	6	2. Veronica Sales #15 / Airplay #28; Paul McCartney (co-writer, bass guitar)	Warner 22981
			COTTON, Gene	
			Born on 6/30/44 in Columbus, Ohio. Attended Ohio State University. Recording since 1967.	
1/22/77	33	3	1. You've Got Me Runnin'	ABC 12227
3/4/78	23	7	2. Before My Heart Finds Out	Ariola Am. 7675
8/5/78	36	3	3. You're A Part Of Me **GENE COTTON with Kim Carnes**	Ariola Am. 7704
11/11/78	40	2	4. Like A Sunday In Salem (The Amos & Andy Song) originally released as the B-side of #2 above	Ariola Am. 7723
			COUGAR, John—see MELLENCAMP	
			COUNT FIVE	
			Psychedelic garage rock quintet of teenagers from San Jose, California. Kenn Ellner, lead singer.	
9/24/66	5	9	1. **Psychotic Reaction**	Double Shot 104
			COVAY, Don	
			Born in March 1938 in Orangeburg, South Carolina. R&B singer/songwriter. Member of the Rainbows in 1955. Recorded as "Pretty Boy" with Little Richard's band for Atlantic in 1957. Formed The Goodtimers in 1960.	
10/3/64	35	5	1. Mercy, Mercy **DON COVAY & THE GOODTIMERS**	Rosemart 801
8/11/73	29	5	2. I Was Checkin' Out She Was Checkin' In	Mercury 73385
			COVEN	
			Pop quintet featuring the voice of Jinx Dawson.	
10/30/71	26	6	1. One Tin Soldier (The Legend of Billy Jack) from the movie *Billy Jack* starring Tom Laughlin	Warner 7509

DATE	POS	WKS	ARTIST–RECORD TITLE	LABEL & NO.
			COVER GIRLS, The	
			New York City-based female dance trio: Louise "Angel" Sabater, Caroline Jackson and Sunshine Wright (replaced by Margo Urban in 1989). 1992 lineup: Jackson, Evelyn Escalera and Michelle Valentine.	
1/30/88	27	8	1. Because Of You Sales #24 / Airplay #28	Fever 1914
5/21/88	40	1	2. Promise Me Sales #33	Fever 1917
10/21/89	38	2	3. My Heart Skips A Beat Sales #36	Capitol 44436
1/13/90	8	11	4. **We Can't Go Wrong** Airplay #7 / Sales #9	Capitol 44498
6/6/92	9	14	5. **Wishing On A Star** Airplay #2 / Sales #16	Epic 74343
			COWBOY CHURCH SUNDAY SCHOOL, The	
			Producer Stuart Hamblen's family: his daughters Veeva Susanne (age 18) and Obee Jane "Lisa" (age 16) with his wife, Suzy, plus two of the girls' friends. Recorded at 33 1/3 rpm so that the record sounds like children's voices at 45 rpm.	
1/1/55	8	21	1. **Open Up Your Heart (And Let The Sunshine In)** Best Seller #8 / Jockey #18 / Juke Box #19	Decca 29367
			COWSILLS, The	
			Family pop group from Newport, Rhode Island. Consisted of five brothers (Bill, Bob, Paul, Barry and John), with their younger sister (Susan) and mother (Barbara, died 1/31/85, age 56). Bob, Paul, John and Susan reunited for touring in 1990. Susan married Peter Holsapple of The dB's on 4/18/93. Group was the inspiration for TV's "The Partridge Family."	
10/21/67	2 (2)	12	● 1. **The Rain, The Park & Other Things**	MGM 13810
2/3/68	21	6	2. **We Can Fly**	MGM 13886
6/22/68	10	9	3. **Indian Lake**	MGM 13944
3/29/69	2 (2)	13	● 4. **Hair** from the rock musical *Hair* starring Steve Curry	MGM 14026
			COX, Deborah	
			Born on 7/13/74 in Toronto. Female singer/songwriter.	
10/21/95	27	8	1. Sentimental Sales #9	Arista 12852
			CRABBY APPLETON	
			West Coast rock quintet led by Michael Fennelly.	
6/27/70	36	5	1. Go Back	Elektra 45687
			CRADDOCK, Billy "Crash"	
			Born on 6/16/39 in Greensboro, North Carolina. Country-rock singer. First recorded for Colonial in 1957. Nickname "Crash" came from his stock car racing hobby.	
7/27/74	16	9	1. Rub It In #1 Country hit (2 weeks)	ABC 12013
12/28/74+	33	2	2. Ruby, Baby #1 Country hit (1 week)	ABC 12036

DATE	POS	WKS	ARTIST—RECORD TITLE	LABEL & NO.

CRAMER, Floyd

Born on 10/27/33 in Samti, Louisiana; raised in Huttig, Arkansas. Nashville's top session pianist. Played piano from age five. Moved to Nashville in 1955. Worked with Elvis Presley, Johnny Cash, Perry Como and Chet Atkins.

DATE	POS	WKS	ARTIST—RECORD TITLE	LABEL & NO.
10/31/60	2 (4)	15	● 1. **Last Date** [I]	RCA 7775
3/13/61	4	11	2. **On The Rebound** [I]	RCA 7840
6/26/61	8	8	3. **San Antonio Rose** [I] written by Bob Wills in 1938	RCA 7893
2/24/62	36	2	4. Chattanooga Choo Choo · [I] #1 hit for Glenn Miller in 1941; from the movie *Sun Valley Serenade* starring Sonja Henie	RCA 7978

CRANBERRIES, The

Band from Limerick, Ireland: Dolores O'Riordan (vocals), brothers Noel (guitar) and Mike (bass) Hogan, and Fergal Lawler (drums). Group formed in 1990 as The Cranberry Saw Us. O'Riordan joined in 1991 and group shortened name to The Cranberries. O'Riordan married Don Burton, assistant tour manager for Duran Duran, on 7/18/94.

DATE	POS	WKS	ARTIST—RECORD TITLE	LABEL & NO.
11/20/93+	8	19	● 1. **Linger** Airplay #14 / Sales #16	Island 862800

CRANE, Les

Born in San Francisco in 1935. Hosted TV talk show "ABC's Nightlife" in 1964. Formerly married to actress Tina Louise.

DATE	POS	WKS	ARTIST—RECORD TITLE	LABEL & NO.
10/23/71	8	10	1. **Desiderata** [S] originally a piece of prose, written in 1906 by Max Ehrmann	Warner 7520

CRASH TEST DUMMIES

Band from Winnipeg, Canada: Brad Roberts (lead vocals) and his younger brother Dan (bass) with Ellen Reid (keyboards) and Benjamin Darvill (harmonica). Mitch Dorge (drums) joined after group's first album.

DATE	POS	WKS	ARTIST—RECORD TITLE	LABEL & NO.
3/5/94	4	18	● 1. **Mmm Mmm Mmm Mmm** Sales #2 / Airplay #15	Arista 12654

CRAWFORD, Johnny

Born on 3/26/46 in Los Angeles. One of the original Mouseketeers. Played Chuck Connors's son (Mark McCain) in the TV series "The Rifleman," 1958–63.

DATE	POS	WKS	ARTIST—RECORD TITLE	LABEL & NO.
6/2/62	8	9	1. **Cindy's Birthday**	Del-Fi 4178
8/25/62	14	6	2. Your Nose Is Gonna Grow	Del-Fi 4181
11/24/62	12	7	3. Rumors	Del-Fi 4188
1/26/63	29	4	4. Proud	Del-Fi 4193

CRAWFORD, Randy—see CRUSADERS, The

CRAY, Robert, Band

Cray was born on 8/1/53 in Columbus, Georgia. Blues guitarist/vocalist. Played bass with fictional band, Otis Day & The Knights, in the movie *Animal House*. Band formed in 1974 as backing tour group for Albert Collins.

DATE	POS	WKS	ARTIST—RECORD TITLE	LABEL & NO.
3/21/87	22	6	1. Smoking Gun Sales #21 / Airplay #33	Mercury 888343

DATE	POS	WKS	ARTIST–RECORD TITLE	LABEL & NO.
			## CRAZY ELEPHANT	
			Bubblegum studio concoction of producers Jerry Kasenetz and Jeff Katz. Robert Spencer (The Cadillacs) on lead vocals; Joey Levine (Ohio Express, Reunion) on backing vocals. Touring group formed later.	
4/5/69	12	8	1. Gimme Gimme Good Lovin' first released on Sphere Sound 77005 in 1968	Bell 763
			## CRAZY OTTO	
			Born Fritz Schulz-Reichel on 7/4/12 in Germany. Honky-tonk pianist. Wrote original German version of 1954 hit "The Man With The Banjo." Also see Johnny Maddox's 1955 hit "The Crazy Otto."	
2/26/55	19	5	1. Glad Rag Doll/ [I] Best Seller #19; #10 hit for Ted Lewis in 1929	
2/26/55	21	3	2. Smiles [I] Best Seller #21; #1 hit for Joseph C. Smith's Orchestra in 1918	Decca 29403
			## CREAM	
			British rock supergroup: Eric Clapton (guitar), Ginger Baker (drums) and Jack Bruce (bass). Baker and Bruce had been in Alexis Korner's Blues Inc. and the Graham Bond Organization. Clapton and Bruce were in John Mayall's Bluesbreakers. After Cream disbanded, Clapton and Baker formed Blind Faith. Cream inducted into the Rock and Roll Hall of Fame in 1993.	
2/24/68	5	12	● 1. **Sunshine Of Your Love** originally charted for 2 weeks at #36; re-entered on 7/6/68	Atco 6544
10/19/68	6	9	2. **White Room**	Atco 6617
2/8/69	28	6	3. Crossroads recorded "live" at the Fillmore Auditorium in San Francisco	Atco 6646
			## CREEDENCE CLEARWATER REVIVAL	
			Rock group formed while members attended high school at El Cerrito, California. Consisted of John Fogerty (vocals, guitar), brother Tom Fogerty (guitar), Stu Cook (keyboards, bass) and Doug Clifford (drums). First recorded as the Blue Velvets for the Orchestra label in 1959. Recorded as the Golliwogs for Fantasy in 1964. Renamed Creedence Clearwater Revival in 1967. Tom Fogerty left for a solo career in 1971 and group disbanded in October 1972. Tom Fogerty died on 9/6/90 (age 48) of respiratory failure. Group inducted into the Rock and Roll Hall of Fame in 1993.	
9/28/68	11	9	● 1. Suzie Q. (Part One)	Fantasy 616
2/8/69	2 (3)	12	▲ 2. **Proud Mary**	Fantasy 619
5/17/69	2 (1)	12	▲ 3. **Bad Moon Rising**	Fantasy 622
8/9/69	2 (1)	11	● 4. **Green River/**	
8/9/69	30	7	5. Commotion above 4 from the album *Green River*	Fantasy 625
11/8/69	3	13	▲ 6. **Down On The Corner/**	
11/8/69	14	13	7. Fortunate Son	Fantasy 634
2/7/70	2 (2)	9	▲ 8. **Travelin' Band/**	
		9	9. Who'll Stop The Rain	Fantasy 637
5/2/70	4	10	● 10. **Up Around The Bend/**	
		10	● 11. **Run Through The Jungle**	Fantasy 641
8/15/70	2 (1)	12	▲ 12. **Lookin' Out My Back Door/**	
		12	13. Long As I Can See The Light above 6 from the album *Cosmo's Factory*	Fantasy 645

DATE	POS	WKS	ARTIST–RECORD TITLE	LABEL & NO.
2/6/71	8	9	● 14. **Have You Ever Seen The Rain/**	Fantasy 655
		4	15. Hey Tonight	
7/24/71	6	8	● 16. **Sweet Hitch-Hiker**	Fantasy 665
5/20/72	25	5	17. Someday Never Comes	Fantasy 676
			all of above written (except #1), produced and arranged by John Fogerty	

CRENSHAW, Marshall

Born on 11/11/53 in Detroit. Rockabilly singer/guitarist. Played John Lennon in the road show of *Beatlemania* in 1976. Appeared in the movie *Peggy Sue Got Married* and portrayed Buddy Holly in the 1987 movie *La Bamba*.

DATE	POS	WKS	ARTIST–RECORD TITLE	LABEL & NO.
8/14/82	36	4	1. Someday, Someway	Warner 29974

CRESCENDOS, The

Vocal group from Nashville. Formed as The Spades in high school with George Lanuis (lead singer), his cousin James Lanuis, Ken Brigham, Tom Fortner and Jim Hall.

DATE	POS	WKS	ARTIST–RECORD TITLE	LABEL & NO.
1/20/58	5	14	1. **Oh Julie**	Nasco 6005
			Top 100 #5 / Best Seller #6 / Jockey #7; Janice Green (female vocal)	

CRESTS, The

Formed as a black quartet in 1955 at a Manhattan junior high school, consisting of Brooklyn-born white singer Johnny Maestro (shown as Mastro on all The Crests' hits; joined as lead singer in 1956), Harold Torres, Talmadge Gough, J.T. Carter and Patricia Van Dross. Van Dross left group in 1958. Mastrangelo left for solo work as Johnny Maestro in 1960, replaced by James Ancrum. Maestro later formed Brooklyn Bridge.

DATE	POS	WKS	ARTIST–RECORD TITLE	LABEL & NO.
12/22/58+	2 (2)	14	1. **16 Candles**	Coed 506
4/13/59	28	7	2. Six Nights A Week	Coed 509
9/14/59	22	9	3. The Angels Listened In	Coed 515
4/4/60	14	8	4. Step By Step	Coed 525
7/18/60	20	8	5. Trouble In Paradise	Coed 531

CREW-CUTS, The

Vocal group from Toronto formed in 1952. Consisted of John Perkins (lead), his brother Ray Perkins (bass), Pat Barrett (tenor) and Rudi Maugeri (baritone). First called the Canadaires, changed name in 1954. Maugeri did vocal arrangements for the group. Their huge #1 hit (9 weeks) in the summer of 1954, "Sh-Boom," helped to usher in the rock 'n' roll era. Disbanded in 1963.

DATE	POS	WKS	ARTIST–RECORD TITLE	LABEL & NO.
1/29/55	3	13	1. **Earth Angel/**	Mercury 70529
			Jockey #3 / Juke Box #8 / Best Seller #8	
1/29/55	6	14	2. **Ko Ko Mo (I Love You So)**	
			Juke Box #6 / Best Seller #10 / Jockey #11; #6 R&B hit for Gene & Eunice in 1955	
4/30/55	14	8	3. Don't Be Angry/	Mercury 70597
			Best Seller #14 / Jockey #14 / Juke Box #19	
		8	4. Chop Chop Boom	
			Best Seller flip; #10 R&B hit for The Danderliers in 1955	
6/25/55	16	7	5. A Story Untold	Mercury 70634
			Best Seller #16; #2 R&B hit for The Nutmegs in 1955	
8/27/55	10	8	6. **Gum Drop**	Mercury 70668
			Best Seller #10 / Jockey #14 / Juke Box #20 / Top 100 #80 pre; recorded by the R&B group The Charms in 1955	

DATE	POS	WKS	ARTIST—RECORD TITLE	LABEL & NO.
12/17/55+	11	15	7. Angels In The Sky/ Best Seller #11 / Top 100 #13 / Juke Box #13 / Jockey #16; song first recorded in 1954 by Tony Martin (RCA 5757)	
1/7/56	31	8	8. Mostly Martha based on "M'Appari" from the Flotow opera Martha; #2 hit for Larry Clinton in 1938	Mercury 70741
2/18/56	18	5	9. Seven Days Jockey #18 / Top 100 #20	Mercury 70782
1/26/57	17	3	10. Young Love Jockey #17 / Juke Box #17 / Top 100 #24; David Carroll (orch., all of above)	Mercury 71022
			CREWE, Bob	
			Born on 11/12/37 in Newark, New Jersey. Wrote many hit songs beginning with "Silhouettes" in 1957. One of the top producers of the 1960s. Wrote and produced most of the hits by The 4 Seasons. Head of several labels, publishing and production companies. Assembled The Bob Crewe Generation, an aggregation of studio musicians.	
1/21/67	15	7	1. Music To Watch Girls By [I] tune used in a Diet Pepsi commercial	DynoVoice 229
			CRICKETS, The—see HOLLY, Buddy	
			CRITTERS, The	
			New Jersey pop quintet originally known as The Vibratones. Consisted of Don Ciccone (lead singer/guitarist), Chris Darway, Kenny Gorka, Bob Podstawski and Jack Decker. Ciccone later joined The 4 Seasons.	
9/3/66	17	8	1. Mr. Dieingly Sad	Kapp 769
8/5/67	39	3	2. Don't Let The Rain Fall Down On Me	Kapp 838
			CROCE, Jim	
			Born on 1/10/43 in Philadelphia. Killed in a plane crash on 9/20/73 in Natchitoches, Louisiana. Vocalist/guitarist/composer. Recorded with his wife, Ingrid, for Capitol in 1968. Maury Muehleisen, lead guitarist on Croce's hits, was killed in the same crash.	
7/22/72	8	10	1. **You Don't Mess Around With Jim**	ABC 11328
11/4/72	17	8	2. Operator (That's Not the Way it Feels)	ABC 11335
3/17/73	37	3	3. One Less Set Of Footsteps	ABC 11346
6/2/73	1 (2)	16	● 4. **Bad, Bad Leroy Brown**	ABC 11359
10/13/73	10	13	5. **I Got A Name** from the movie The Last American Hero starring Jeff Bridges	ABC 11389
12/1/73	1 (2)	12	● 6. **Time In A Bottle** #1 Adult Contemporary hit (2 weeks)	ABC 11405
3/16/74	9	11	7. **I'll Have To Say I Love You In A Song** #1 Adult Contemporary hit (1 week)	ABC 11424
6/29/74	32	6	8. Workin' At The Car Wash Blues	ABC 11447

DATE	POS	WKS	ARTIST—RECORD TITLE	LABEL & NO.

CROSBY, Bing

One of the most popular entertainers of the 20th century. Born Harry Lillis Crosby on 5/3/03 in Tacoma, Washington. Died of a heart attack on 10/14/77 on a golf course near Madrid, Spain. Bing and singing partner Al Rinker were hired in 1926 by Paul Whiteman; with Harry Barris they became the Rhythm Boys and gained an increasing following. The trio split from Whiteman in 1930, and Bing sang briefly with Gus Arnheim's band. It was his early 1931 smash with Arnheim, "I Surrender, Dear," which earned Bing a CBS radio contract and launched an unsurpassed solo career. Over the next three decades the resonant Crosby baritone and breezy persona sold more than 300 million records and were featured in over 50 movies (won Academy Award for *Going My Way*, 1944). Won the Lifetime Achievement Grammy in 1962. Ranked as the #1 artist in the book *Joel Whitburn's Pop Memories 1890–1954*, Bing had over 150 hits from 1931 to 1939. Married to actress Dixie Lee from 1930 until her death in 1952; their son Gary began recording in 1950. Married to actress Kathryn Grant from 1957 until his death; their daughter Mary became an actress. Bing's youngest brother, Bob Crosby, was a popular swing-era bandleader.

DATE	POS	WKS	ARTIST—RECORD TITLE	LABEL & NO.
12/31/55	7	2	● 1. **White Christmas** [X-R] Jockey #7 / Top 100 #18; with the Ken Darby Singers and John Scott Trotter's Orchestra; original version hit #1 in October 1942; new version recorded in 1947; made pop charts for 20 Christmas seasons; the best-selling single of all-time (combined versions)	Decca 23778
10/6/56	3	22	● 2. **True Love** **BING CROSBY and GRACE KELLY** (died in an auto accident on 9/14/82) Jockey #3 / Top 100 #4 / Best Seller #5 / Juke Box #6	Capitol 3507
10/21/57	25	1	3. Around The World Best Seller #25 / Top 100 #54; from Michael Todd's movie *Around The World In 80 Days*; B-side is Victor Young's hit instrumental version	Decca 30262
1/6/58	34	2	4. White Christmas [X-R] Top 100 #34 / Best Seller #36	Decca 23778
12/19/60	26	2	5. White Christmas [X-R]	Decca 23778
12/18/61	12	3	6. White Christmas [X-R]	Decca 23778
12/29/62	38	1	7. White Christmas [X-R]	Decca 23778

CROSBY, David—see NASH, Graham

CROSBY, STILLS & NASH (& YOUNG)

Trio formed in Laurel Canyon, California, in 1968. Consisted of David Crosby (guitar), Stephen Stills (guitar, keyboards, bass) and Graham Nash (guitar). Crosby had been in The Byrds, Stills had been in Buffalo Springfield, and Nash was with The Hollies. Won the 1969 Best New Artist Grammy Award. Neil Young (guitar), formerly with Buffalo Springfield, joined group in 1969, left in 1974. Reunion in 1988.

CROSBY, STILLS & NASH:

DATE	POS	WKS	ARTIST—RECORD TITLE	LABEL & NO.
8/2/69	28	6	1. Marrakesh Express	Atlantic 2652
10/25/69	21	9	2. Suite: Judy Blue Eyes written by Stephen Stills for Judy Collins	Atlantic 2676

CROSBY, STILLS, NASH & YOUNG:

DATE	POS	WKS	ARTIST—RECORD TITLE	LABEL & NO.
4/4/70	11	10	3. Woodstock written by Joni Mitchell about the legendary 1969 rock festival	Atlantic 2723
6/20/70	16	9	4. Teach Your Children Jerry Garcia (of Grateful Dead; steel guitar)	Atlantic 2735
7/11/70	14	7	5. Ohio written by Neil Young after four students were killed at Kent State University by National Guardsmen during an antiwar demonstration on 5/18/70	Atlantic 2740

DATE	POS	WKS	ARTIST–RECORD TITLE	LABEL & NO.
10/10/70	30	6	6. Our House	Atlantic 2760
			CROSBY, STILLS & NASH:	
7/2/77	7	12	7. **Just A Song Before I Go**	Atlantic 3401
7/3/82	9	12	8. **Wasted On The Way**	Atlantic 4058
10/9/82	18	9	9. Southern Cross	Atlantic 89969

CROSS, Christopher

Born Christopher Geppert on 5/3/51 in San Antonio, Texas. Formed own group with Rob Meurer (keyboards), Andy Salmon (bass) and Tommy Taylor (drums) in 1973. Won the 1980 Best New Artist Grammy Award.

DATE	POS	WKS	ARTIST–RECORD TITLE	LABEL & NO.
3/1/80	2 (4)	17	1. **Ride Like The Wind** Michael McDonald (backing vocal)	Warner 49184
7/5/80	1 (1)	13	2. **Sailing**	Warner 49507
10/25/80	15	12	3. Never Be The Same #1 Adult Contemporary hit (2 weeks)	Warner 49580
4/25/81	20	7	4. Say You'll Be Mine Nicolette Larson (backing vocal); above 4 from the album *Christopher Cross*	Warner 49705
8/29/81	1 (3)	17	● 5. **Arthur's Theme (Best That You Can Do)** from the movie *Arthur* starring Dudley Moore; #1 Adult Contemporary hit (4 weeks)	Warner 49787
1/22/83	12	13	6. All Right	Warner 29843
5/21/83	33	5	7. No Time For Talk	Warner 29662
12/24/83+	9	11	8. **Think Of Laura** popularized through play on TV's "General Hospital"; #1 Adult Contemporary hit (4 weeks); all of above produced by Michael Omartian	Warner 29658

CROSS COUNTRY

Jay Siegel, Mitch and Phil Margo; all formerly with The Tokens.

DATE	POS	WKS	ARTIST–RECORD TITLE	LABEL & NO.
9/22/73	30	4	1. In The Midnight Hour	Atco 6934

CROW

Rock-blues quintet from Minneapolis. Dave Wagner, lead singer. Drummer Denny Craswell was a member of The Castaways.

DATE	POS	WKS	ARTIST–RECORD TITLE	LABEL & NO.
11/29/69+	19	10	1. Evil Woman Don't Play Your Games With Me	Amaret 112

CROW, Sheryl

Born on 2/11/63 in Kennett, Missouri. After attending the University of Missouri, worked as a grade school music teacher, until moving to Los Angeles in 1986. Worked as backing singer for Michael Jackson, Don Henley, George Harrison and others. Crow's compositions covered by Eric Clapton and Wynonna Judd. Won the 1994 Best New Artist Grammy Award.

DATE	POS	WKS	ARTIST–RECORD TITLE	LABEL & NO.
8/27/94	2 (6)	27	● 1. **All I Wanna Do** Airplay #2 / Sales #7; #1 Adult Contemporary hit (8 weeks)	A&M 0702
1/28/95	5	21	2. **Strong Enough** Airplay #2 / Sales #11	A&M 0798
8/5/95	36	6	3. Can't Cry Anymore Airplay #30 / Sales #69	A&M 0638

DATE	POS	WKS	ARTIST–RECORD TITLE	LABEL & NO.
			CROWDED HOUSE	
			New Zealand/Australian pop trio formed in 1986 by former Split Enz members Neil Finn (vocals, guitar, piano) and Paul Hester (drums), with Nick Seymour (bass). Neil's brother, Tim Finn (also of Split Enz), joined band in 1991; left in 1993, replaced by Mark Hart. Hester left band in April 1994.	
2/21/87	**2** (1)	15	1. **Don't Dream It's Over** Sales #2 / Airplay #2	Capitol 5614
5/30/87	**7**	11	2. **Something So Strong** Sales #7 / Airplay #7	Capitol 5695
			CROWELL, Rodney	
			Born on 8/7/50 in Houston. Country singer/songwriter/guitarist. Married to Rosanne Cash, 1979–92. Wrote the Dirt Band's "American Dream" and many other country hits.	
6/28/80	**37**	2	1. Ashes By Now	Warner 49224
			CRUSADERS, The	
			Instrumental jazz-oriented group formed in Houston. 1979 lineup: Joe Sample (keyboards), Wilton Felder (reeds) and Nesbert "Stix" Hooper (drums). Sample and Felder reunited with a new lineup in 1991.	
10/27/79	**36**	3	1. Street Life Randy Crawford (vocal)	MCA 41054
			CRYSTALS, The	
			Female vocal group (ages 16–18 in 1961) from Brooklyn. Consisted of Barbara Alston, Delores Kennibrew, Mary Thomas, Pattie Wright and Merna Girard. Discovered by producer Phil Spector. La La Brooks replaced Merna in 1962. Mary left in 1962 and Patricia was replaced by Frances Collins in 1964.	
12/11/61+	**20**	7	1. There's No Other (Like My Baby)	Philles 100
4/28/62	**13**	8	2. Uptown Barbara Alston (lead vocal, above 2)	Philles 102
10/6/62	**1** (2)	12	3. **He's A Rebel** written by Gene Pitney	Philles 106
1/19/63	**11**	8	4. He's Sure The Boy I Love above 2 actually recorded by The Blossoms; Darlene Love (lead vocal)	Philles 109
5/11/63	**3**	10	5. **Da Doo Ron Ron (When He Walked Me Home)**	Philles 112
8/31/63	**6**	9	6. **Then He Kissed Me** La La Brooks (lead vocal, above 2); all of above produced by Phil Spector	Philles 115
			CUFF LINKS, The	
			Group is actually the overdubbed voices of Ron Dante (The Archies).	
10/4/69	**9**	9	1. **Tracy**	Decca 32533
			CULTURE BEAT	
			Dance outfit assembled by Germans Torsten Fenslau (DJ/producer; died in a car accident on 11/6/93, age 29), Juergen "Nosie" Katzmann (composer/guitarist) and Peter Zweier (composer/engineer). Includes London vocalist Tania Evans and New Jersey rapper Jay Supreme.	
11/27/93+	**17**	13	● 1. Mr. Vain Airplay #17 / Sales #19	550 Music 77259

DATE	POS	WKS	ARTIST–RECORD TITLE	LABEL & NO.
			CULTURE CLUB	
			Formed in London in 1981. Consisted of George "Boy George" O'Dowd (born 6/14/61; vocals), Roy Hay (guitar, keyboards), Michael Craig (bass) and Jon Moss (drums). Designer Sue Clowes originated distinctive costuming for the group. Won the 1983 Best New Artist Grammy Award. Boy George went solo in 1987.	
1/15/83	**2** (3)	18	1. **Do You Really Want To Hurt Me**	Epic 03368
4/30/83	**2** (2)	13	2. **Time (Clock Of The Heart)**	Epic 03796
7/16/83	**9**	12	3. **I'll Tumble 4 Ya**	Epic 03912
10/29/83	**10**	12	4. **Church Of The Poison Mind**	Epic 04144
12/10/83+	**1** (3)	16	● 5. **Karma Chameleon**	Virgin 04221
3/3/84	**5**	12	6. **Miss Me Blind**	Virgin 04388
			Jermaine Stewart (backing vocal)	
5/19/84	**13**	8	7. **It's A Miracle**	Virgin 04457
			above 4 from the album Colour By Numbers	
10/20/84	**17**	7	8. **The War Song**	Virgin 04638
			Sales #18 / Airplay #18	
1/12/85	**33**	5	9. **Mistake No. 3**	Virgin 04727
			Airplay #29	
4/19/86	**12**	10	10. **Move Away**	Virgin 05847
			Sales #11 / Airplay #14	
			CUMMINGS, Burton	
			Born on 12/31/47 in Winnipeg, Canada. Lead singer of The Guess Who.	
11/6/76+	**10**	15	● 1. **Stand Tall**	Portrait 70001
10/24/81	**37**	2	2. **You Saved My Soul**	Alfa 7008
			CURB, Mike, Congregation	
			Curb was born on 12/24/44 in Savannah, Georgia. Pop music mogul and politician. President of MGM Records, 1969–73. Elected lieutenant governor of California in 1978; served as governor of California, 1980. Formed own company, Sidewalk Records, in 1964; became Curb Records in 1974. Currently resides in Nashville.	
2/27/71	**34**	4	1. **Burning Bridges**	MGM 14151
			from the movie Kelly's Heroes starring Clint Eastwood	
4/15/72	**1** (3)	16	● 2. **The Candy Man**	MGM 14320
			SAMMY DAVIS, JR., With The Mike Curb Congregation *from the movie Willy Wonka and the Chocolate Factory starring Gene Wilder; originally recorded as by The Mike Curb Congregation; Davis's vocals dubbed in later; #1 Adult Contemporary hit (2 weeks)*	
			CURE, The	
			British techno-rock group formed in 1977 by Robert Smith (born 4/21/59; vocals, guitar) and Laurence "Lol" Tolhurst (drums). Since 1983, members have included Smith, Tolhurst (until 1990), Porl Thompson, Simon Gallup, Andy Anderson (1984), Boris Williams and Roger O'Donnell (1989). Perry Bamonte joined in 1992. Smith was also a touring member of Siouxsie And The Banshees in the early '80s.	
1/9/88	**40**	1	1. **Just Like Heaven**	Elektra 69443
			Airplay #37	
8/26/89	**2** (1)	12	2. **Love Song**	Elektra 69280
			Sales #3 / Airplay #7	
6/20/92	**18**	14	3. **Friday I'm In Love**	Fiction 64742
			Airplay #16 / Sales #28	

DATE	POS	WKS	ARTIST—RECORD TITLE	LABEL & NO.
			CURTIS—see KING CURTIS	
			CUTTING CREW	
			British rock group led by singer Nick Van Eede, with Kevin Scott MacMichael (guitar; from Canada), Colin Farley (bass) and Martin Beedle (drums).	
3/21/87	**1** (2)	13	1. **(I Just) Died In Your Arms**	Virgin 99481
			Airplay #1(2) / Sales #2	
7/18/87	**38**	2	2. One For The Mockingbird	Virgin 99464
			Airplay #32	
10/3/87	**9**	11	3. **I've Been In Love Before**	Virgin 99425
			Airplay #8 / Sales #11	
			CYMARRON	
			Male pop vocal trio formed in Memphis: Richard Mainegra, Rick Yancey and Sherrill Parks.	
7/17/71	**17**	7	1. Rings	Entrance 7500
			CYMBAL, Johnny	
			Born on 2/3/45 in Ochitree, Scotland. Died on 3/16/93 of a heart attack. Singer/songwriter/producer. Moved to Goderich, Ontario, in 1952. Moved to Cleveland in 1960. Also recorded as Derek.	
3/16/63	**16**	8	1. Mr. Bass Man [N]	Kapp 503
			Ronnie Bright (bass singer; member of the Valentines)	
11/23/68+	**11**	11	2. Cinnamon	Bang 558
			DEREK	
			CYPRESS HILL	
			Rap trio based in Los Angeles: Sen "Sen Dog" Reyes (Cuban-born; older brother of Mellow Man Ace), Louis "B-Real" Freeze and Lawrence "Mixmaster Muggs" Muggerud (former member of The 7A3). Band named for Cypress Street in the Southgate section of Los Angeles. Appeared in the movie *The Meteor Man*.	
7/24/93	**19**	15	● 1. Insane In The Brain	Ruffhouse 77135
			Sales #10 / Airplay #35	
			CYRKLE, The	
			Pop group formed while members attended Lafayette College in Easton, Pennsylvania. Signed to Columbia Records and managed by The Beatles' Brian Epstein; named by John Lennon. Featured vocalists are Don Dannemann and Tom Dawes.	
6/4/66	**2** (1)	11	1. **Red Rubber Ball**	Columbia 43589
			written by Paul Simon and Bruce Woodley (of The Seekers)	
8/27/66	**16**	5	2. Turn-Down Day	Columbia 43729
			CYRUS, Billy Ray	
			Born on 8/25/61 in Flatwoods, Kentucky. Country singer.	
5/23/92	**4**	22	▲ 1. **Achy Breaky Heart**	Mercury 866522
			Sales #2 / Airplay #38; recorded by The Marcy Brothers in 1991 as "Don't Tell My Heart"; #1 Country hit (5 weeks)	

DATE	POS	WKS	ARTIST–RECORD TITLE	LABEL & NO.

D

DA BRAT

Female rapper Shawntae Harris. Began professional career after winning a rap contest at a Kris Kross concert in Chicago.

DATE	POS	WKS	ARTIST–RECORD TITLE	LABEL & NO.
6/18/94	6	17	▲ 1. **Funkdafied** Sales #3 / Airplay #17; samples "Between The Sheets" by The Isley Brothers	So So Def 77532
11/26/94	37	4	2. Fa All Y'all Sales #20	So So Def 77594
4/22/95	26	11	● 3. Give It 2 You Sales #15 / Airplay #43; Trey Lorenz (backing vocal)	So So Def 77836

DADDY DEWDROP

Cleveland singer Richard Monda.

4/10/71	9	11	1. **Chick-A-Boom (Don't Ya Jes' Love It)**　　[N]	Sunflower 105

DADDY-O'S, The

Produced by guitarist Billy Mure.

6/23/58	39	3	1. **Got A Match?**　　[I] Best Seller #39 / Top 100 #40	Cabot 122

DALE, Alan

Born Aldo Sigiamundi on 7/9/25 in Brooklyn. Baritone singer formerly with Carmen Cavallaro. Hosted his own TV show in 1951. Starred in the 1956 rock and roll movie *Don't Knock The Rock*.

4/30/55	14	7	1. Cherry Pink (And Apple Blossom White) Juke Box #14 / Jockey #19 / Best Seller #27; from the movie *Underwater!* starring Jane Russell	Coral 61373
7/2/55	10	7	2. **Sweet And Gentle** Jockey #10 / Best Seller #12 / Juke Box #14; Cuban song ("Me Lo Dijo Adela"); Dick Jacobs (orch., above 2)	Coral 61435

DALE & GRACE

Pop vocal duo: Dale Houston (of Ferriday, Louisiana) and Grace Broussard (of Prairieville, Louisiana).

10/26/63	1 (2)	12	1. **I'm Leaving It Up To You** #1 Adult Contemporary hit (2 weeks); first recorded by Don & Dewey in 1957	Montel 921
2/8/64	8	7	2. **Stop And Think It Over** above 2 first released on Michelle 921 and 923, respectively	Montel 922

DALTREY, Roger

Born on 3/1/44 in London. Formed band The Detours, which later became The Who. Daltrey was The Who's lead singer and starred in the movies *Tommy*, *Lisztomania*, *The Legacy* and *McVicar*.

10/25/80	20	8	1. Without Your Love from the movie *McVicar* starring Daltrey	Polydor 2121

DATE	POS	WKS	ARTIST–RECORD TITLE	LABEL & NO.
			DAMIAN, Michael	
			Born Michael Weir on 4/26/62 in San Diego. Discovered by the producers of "The Young & The Restless" while performing on "American Bandstand"; has played Danny Romalotti on that TV soap since 1981.	Cypress 1420
4/8/89	**1** (1)	13	● 1. **Rock On** Airplay #1(1) / Sales #2; from the movie *Dream A Little Dream* starring Corey Feldman	
7/29/89	**31**	4	2. Cover Of Love Airplay #29 / Sales #34	Cypress 1430
12/23/89+	**24**	9	3. Was It Nothing At All Sales #22 / Airplay #22	Cypress 1451
			DAMN YANKEES	
			Superstar rock group: guitarist Ted Nugent (Amboy Dukes), bassist/vocalist Jack Blades (Night Ranger), guitarist/vocalist Tommy Shaw (Styx) and drummer Michael Cartellone. Shaw and Blades recorded as duo in 1995.	
11/3/90+	**3**	18	● 1. **High Enough** Sales #2 / Airplay #4	Warner 19595
11/7/92	**20**	11	2. Where You Goin' Now Airplay #28 / Sales #37	Warner 18728
			DAMON('S), Liz, Orient Express	
			Damon is the leader of the three-woman, six-man vocal/instrumental group from Hawaii.	
1/30/71	**33**	3	1. 1900 Yesterday	White Whale 368
			DAMONE, Vic	
			Born Vito Farinola on 6/12/28 in Brooklyn. Damone is among the most popular of postwar ballad singers. Appeared in the movies *Kismet, Meet Me In Las Vegas* and *Hell To Eternity*. Hosted own TV series, 1956–57. Married actress Diahann Carroll on 1/3/87.	
6/2/56	**4**	16	1. **On The Street Where You Live** Jockey #4 / Best Seller #8 / Top 100 #8 / Juke Box #13; from the Broadway musical *My Fair Lady* starring Julie Andrews	Columbia 40654
9/30/57	**16**	4	2. An Affair To Remember (Our Love Affair) Jockey #16 / Top 100 #35; from the movie *An Affair To Remember* starring Cary Grant and Deborah Kerr; Percy Faith (orch., above 2)	Columbia 40945
5/22/65	**30**	4	3. You Were Only Fooling (While I Was Falling In Love) Ernie Freeman (orch.); #8 hit for the Ink Spots in 1949	Warner 5616
			DANA, Vic	
			Born on 8/26/42 in Buffalo, New York. Moved to California as a teen. Adult Contemporary artist.	
4/25/64	**27**	5	1. Shangri-La	Dolton 92
3/6/65	**10**	8	2. **Red Roses For A Blue Lady** #3 hit for Vaughn Monroe in 1949	Dolton 304
6/4/66	**30**	4	3. I Love You Drops #4 Country hit for Bill Anderson in 1966	Dolton 319
			DANCER, PRANCER AND NERVOUS	
			Novelty production featuring Russ Regan.	
12/28/59	**34**	1	1. The Happy Reindeer [X-N]	Capitol 4300

DATE	POS	WKS	ARTIST–RECORD TITLE	LABEL & NO.
			D'ANGELO	
			Born Michael D'Angelo Archer in Richmond, Virginia. Singer/songwriter.	EMI 58360
7/29/95	27	11	1. Brown Sugar Sales #16 / Airplay #63	
			DANIELS, Charlie, Band	
			Daniels (born 10/28/36, Wilmington, North Carolina; vocals, guitar, fiddle) formed band in Nashville in 1971. Included Tom Crain (guitar), Joe "Taz" DiGregorio (keyboards), Charles Hayward (bass), and James W. Marshall and Fred Edwards (drums). Marshall and Edwards left in 1986; replaced by Jack Gavin. Daniels led the Jaguars, 1958–67. Went solo in 1968 and worked as a session musician in Nashville. Played on Bob Dylan's *Nashville Skyline* hit album. Appeared in the movie *Urban Cowboy*.	
7/21/73	9	9	1. **Uneasy Rider** [N] **CHARLIE DANIELS**	Kama Sutra 576
3/15/75	29	3	2. The South's Gonna Do It	Kama Sutra 598
7/21/79	3	12	▲ 3. **The Devil Went Down To Georgia** #1 Country hit (1 week)	Epic 50700
6/28/80	11	8	4. In America	Epic 50888
9/27/80	31	4	5. The Legend Of Wooley Swamp	Epic 50921
4/17/82	22	8	6. Still In Saigon	Epic 02828
			DANLEERS, The	
			R&B quintet from Brooklyn. Jimmy Weston, lead singer. Group was named after their manager, Danny Webb, who wrote "One Summer Night." Weston died on 6/10/93.	
6/30/58	7	10	1. **One Summer Night** Jockey #7 / Best Seller #14 / Top 100 #16; originally released on AMP-3 2115 as by The Dandleers	Mercury 71322
			DANNY & THE JUNIORS	
			Formed as the Juvenairs while at high school in Philadelphia in 1955. Consisted of Danny Rapp (born 5/10/41; lead), David White (first tenor), Frank Maffei (second tenor) and Joe Terranova (baritone). White later joined The Spokesmen. Appeared in the 1958 movie *Let's Rock*. Danny Rapp committed suicide on 4/5/83.	
12/9/57+	1 (7)	18	● 1. **At The Hop** Top 100 #1(7) / Best Seller #1(5) / Jockey #1(3); #1 R&B hit (5 weeks); song originally written as "Do The Bop"; first released on Singular 711 in 1957	ABC-Para. 9871
3/10/58	19	7	2. Rock And Roll Is Here To Stay Best Seller #19 / Top 100 #19	ABC-Para. 9888
7/21/58	39	1	3. Dottie Best Seller #39 / Top 100 #41	ABC-Para. 9926
10/10/60	27	3	4. Twistin' U.S.A. Frank Slay (orch.)	Swan 4060
			DANNY WILSON	
			Trio from Dundee, Scotland: brothers Gary (lead vocals, guitar) and Kit Clark (keyboards, percussion), with Ged Grimes (bass). Group named after a 1952 Frank Sinatra movie *Meet Danny Wilson*.	
8/1/87	23	8	1. Mary's Prayer Sales #22 / Airplay #22	Virgin 99465

DATE	POS	WKS	ARTIST–RECORD TITLE	LABEL & NO.

DANTE and the EVERGREENS

Dante was born Donald Drowty on 9/8/41, lead singer of pop quartet from Los Angeles. Included Bill Young, future record producer Tony Moon and future Beverly Hills lawyer Frank D. Rosenthal.

DATE	POS	WKS	ARTIST–RECORD TITLE	LABEL & NO.
6/13/60	**15**	8	1. Alley-Oop [N]	Madison 130

D'ARBY, Terence Trent

Born on 3/15/62 in New York City. England-based, soul-pop singer. Last name originally spelled Darby. Was a member of the U.S. Army boxing team.

DATE	POS	WKS	ARTIST–RECORD TITLE	LABEL & NO.
2/27/88	**1** (1)	15	● 1. **Wishing Well** Sales #1(1) / Airplay #2; #1 R&B hit (1 week)	Columbia 07675
6/18/88	**4**	13	2. **Sign Your Name** Sales #4 / Airplay #5	Columbia 07911
10/8/88	**30**	5	3. Dance Little Sister (Part One) Sales #26 / Airplay #30	Columbia 08023

DARIN, Bobby

Born Walden Robert Cassotto on 5/14/36 in the Bronx. Died of heart failure on 12/20/73 in Los Angeles. Vocalist/pianist/guitarist/drummer. First recorded in 1956 with The Jaybirds (Decca). First appeared on TV in March 1956 on "The Tommy Dorsey Show." Won the 1959 Best New Artist Grammy Award. Married to actress Sandra Dee, 1960–67. Nominated for an Oscar for his performance in the 1963 movie *Captain Newman, MD.* Formed own record company, Direction. Inducted into the Rock and Roll Hall of Fame in 1990.

DATE	POS	WKS	ARTIST–RECORD TITLE	LABEL & NO.
6/30/58	**3**	13	● 1. **Splish Splash** Hot 100 #3 / Best Seller #4 / Jockey #5 end; #1 R&B hit (2 weeks)	Atco 6117
8/11/58	**24**	5	2. Early In The Morning **THE RINKY-DINKS** Hot 100 #24 / Best Seller #24; originally issued on Brunswick 55073 as by the Ding Dongs (to conceal Darin's identity; he was under contract at Atco)	Atco 6121
10/27/58	**9**	14	● 3. **Queen Of The Hop**	Atco 6127
2/23/59	**38**	2	4. Plain Jane adapted from the 1844 song "Buffalo Gals"	Atco 6133
5/4/59	**2** (1)	13	● 5. **Dream Lover**	Atco 6140
9/7/59	**1** (9)	22	● 6. **Mack The Knife** written in 1928 as "Moritat" or "Theme From The Threepenny Opera"	Atco 6147
1/25/60	**6**	11	7. **Beyond The Sea** introduced by Benny Goodman in 1948 (from the 1945 French song "La Mer")	Atco 6158
4/4/60	**21**	6	8. Clementine written in 1884 as "Oh, My Darling Clementine"	Atco 6161
6/20/60	**19**	5	9. Won't You Come Home Bill Bailey #1 hit for Arthur Collins in 1902	Atco 6167
10/17/60	**20**	8	10. Artificial Flowers from the musical *Tenderloin* starring Eileen Rodgers	Atco 6179
2/20/61	**14**	7	11. Lazy River #19 hit for Hoagy Carmichael in 1932	Atco 6188
7/10/61	**40**	1	12. Nature Boy #1 hit for Nat King Cole in 1948	Atco 6196
9/11/61	**5**	9	13. **You Must Have Been A Beautiful Baby** #1 hit for Bing Crosby in 1938	Atco 6206

DATE	POS	WKS	ARTIST—RECORD TITLE	LABEL & NO.
1/13/62	**15**	8	14. Irresistible You/	
1/20/62	**30**	5	15. Multiplication	Atco 6214
			from the movie *Come September* starring Bobby Darin and Sandra Dee	
4/14/62	**24**	5	16. What'd I Say (Part 1)	Atco 6221
7/21/62	**3**	9	17. **Things**	Atco 6229
10/27/62	**32**	3	18. If A Man Answers	Capitol 4837
			title song from the movie (again with Darin and Dee)	
2/2/63	**3**	12	19. **You're The Reason I'm Living**	Capitol 4897
5/25/63	**10**	7	20. **18 Yellow Roses**	Capitol 4970
10/8/66	**8**	9	21. **If I Were A Carpenter**	Atlantic 2350
2/11/67	**32**	3	22. Lovin' You	Atlantic 2376

DARREN, James

Born James William Ercolani on 10/3/36 in Philadelphia. Singer/actor, studied acting in New York City. Moved to Hollywood in 1955. Appeared in the movies *Rumble On The Docks, The Brothers Rico, Operation Mad Ball, Gunman's Walk, The Guns Of Navarone, Because They're Young* and *Let No Man Write My Epitaph.* Played Moondoggie, Gidget's boyfriend, in *Gidget, Gidget Goes Hawaiian* and *Gidget Goes To Rome.* Appeared in the TV series "The Time Tunnel," 1966–67, and "T.J. Hooker," 1983–86.

DATE	POS	WKS	ARTIST—RECORD TITLE	LABEL & NO.
11/6/61	**3**	12	1. **Goodbye Cruel World**	Colpix 609
			originally released on Colpix 181 in 1961	
2/17/62	**6**	8	2. **Her Royal Majesty**	Colpix 622
5/5/62	**11**	7	3. Conscience	Colpix 630
8/4/62	**39**	1	4. Mary's Little Lamb	Colpix 644
2/18/67	**35**	2	5. All	Warner 5874
			from the movie *Run for Your Wife* starring Frankie Randall	

DARTELLS, The

Rock band from Oxnard, California. Consisted of Doug Phillips (vocals, bass), Dick Burns, Corky Wilkie, Rich Peil, Randy Ray and Gary Peeler. Phillips died on 5/5/95 (age 50).

DATE	POS	WKS	ARTIST—RECORD TITLE	LABEL & NO.
4/27/63	**11**	9	1. Hot Pastrami	Dot 16453
			first released on Arlen 509 in 1962; revision of Nat Kendricks's "(Do The) Mashed Potatoes"	

DAS EFX

Rap duo of Andre "Dray" Weston (born 9/9/70) and Willie "Skoob" Hines (born 11/27/70) formed at Virginia State. DAS is an acronym for Dray And Skoob (which is "books" spelled backward).

DATE	POS	WKS	ARTIST—RECORD TITLE	LABEL & NO.
6/6/92	**25**	12	● 1. They Want EFX	EastWest 98600
			Sales #12 / Airplay #35	
8/7/93	**20**	10	▲ 2. Check Yo Self	Priority 53830
			ICE CUBE Featuring DAS EFX	
			Sales #9 / Airplay #47; samples "The Message" by Grandmaster Flash & The Furious Five; #1 R&B hit (1 week); cassette maxi-single	

DAVID & DAVID

Los Angeles duo: David Baerwald and David Ricketts.

DATE	POS	WKS	ARTIST—RECORD TITLE	LABEL & NO.
11/15/86	**37**	3	1. Welcome To The Boomtown	A&M 2857
			Sales #31	

DATE	POS	WKS	ARTIST–RECORD TITLE	LABEL & NO.
			DAVID & JONATHAN	
			Songwriting/producing/vocal duo from Bristol, England: Roger Greenaway (David) and Roger Cook (Jonathan). Both later were production team for White Plains. Cook founded Blue Mink.	
1/29/66	18	5	1. Michelle written by John Lennon and Paul McCartney; produced by George Martin	Capitol 5563
			DAVIS, Mac	
			Born on 1/21/42 in Lubbock, Texas. Vocalist/guitarist/composer. Worked as a regional rep for Vee-Jay and Liberty Records. Wrote "In The Ghetto," "Don't Cry Daddy," hits for Elvis Presley. Hosted own musical variety TV series, 1974–76. Appeared in several movies, including *North Dallas Forty* in 1979.	
8/5/72	1 (3)	13	● 1. **Baby Don't Get Hooked On Me** #1 Adult Contemporary hit (3 weeks)	Columbia 45618
5/25/74	11	14	2. One Hell Of A Woman	Columbia 46004
9/7/74	9	10	3. **Stop And Smell The Roses** #1 Adult Contemporary hit (1 week)	Columbia 10018
12/21/74+	15	8	4. Rock N' Roll (I Gave You The Best Years Of My Life)	Columbia 10070
			DAVIS, Paul	
			Born on 4/21/48 in Meridian, Mississippi. Singer/songwriter/producer. Pursued country music in the '80s. Survived a shooting in Nashville on 7/30/86.	
12/7/74+	23	8	1. Ride 'Em Cowboy	Bang 712
9/11/76	35	3	2. Superstar tribute to Elton John, Stevie Wonder, Linda Ronstadt, Joni Mitchell	Bang 726
10/29/77+	7	25	3. **I Go Crazy**	Bang 733
10/7/78	17	13	4. Sweet Life	Bang 738
4/12/80	23	6	5. Do Right	Bang 4808
11/28/81+	11	13	6. Cool Night	Arista 0645
3/20/82	6	13	7. **'65 Love Affair**	Arista 0661
8/28/82	40	2	8. Love Or Let Me Be Lonely	Arista 0697
			DAVIS, Sammy, Jr.	
			Born on 12/8/25 in New York City. Died of throat cancer on 5/16/90. Vocalist/dancer/actor of Broadway, movies and TV. With family dance act, the Will Mastin Trio, in the early 1940s. One of the first black entertainers to gain widespread acclaim from white audiences.	
6/4/55	9	11	1. **Something's Gotta Give/** Best Seller #9 / Juke Box #16 / Jockey #20; from the movie *Daddy Long Legs* starring Fred Astaire	
5/28/55	12	12	2. Love Me Or Leave Me Best Seller #12 / Jockey #20; #2 hit in 1929 for Ruth Etting and title song of her 1955 biopic starring Doris Day; Sy Oliver (orch., above 2)	Decca 29484
7/2/55	13	6	3. That Old Black Magic Jockey #13 / Best Seller #16 / Juke Box #18; Morty Stevens (orch.); #1 hit for Glenn Miller in 1943 (from the movie *Star-Spangled Rhythm* starring Bing Crosby)	Decca 29541
10/6/62	17	10	4. What Kind Of Fool Am I Marty Paich (orch.); from the musical *Stop the World–I Want to Get Off* starring Anthony Newley	Reprise 20048
2/1/64	17	9	5. The Shelter Of Your Arms	Reprise 20216

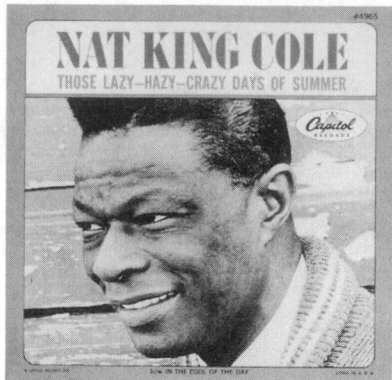

Cassette Single

Joe Cocker's No. 22 hit "High Time We Went" was backed with the soulful "Black Eyed Blues" in 1971. The singer's prolific output was admirably detailed and annotated on a boxed set released by A&M in 1995.

Nat King Cole's final Top 10 hit was 1963's "Those Lazy-Hazy-Crazy Days Of Summer"—though, had his daughter's "posthumous duet" version of "Unforgettable" climbed higher, that 1991 track would hold the distinction.

Phil Collins's "A Groovy Kind Of Love" took the former Mindbenders hit—which reached No. 2 in 1966—up a notch, and scored his fifth No. 1 hit with it in 1988. Its source? The soundtrack of *Buster*, a Hemdale film starring Collins and actress Julie Walters.

Color Me Badd's 1991 debut album *C.M.C.* was an instant winner, featuring two No. 1 hits ("I Ador Mi Amor" and "All 4 Love") and the oft-quoted "I Wanna Sex You Up."

Perry Como spent 18 years as a Top 40 hitmaker during the rock era, though he reached No. 1 only three times: with 1956's "Hot Diggity (Dog Ziggity Boom)," 1957's "Round And Round," and 1958's "Catch A Falling Star."

Sam Cooke's merciless domination of pop radio brought him a nonstop streak of 11 Top 20 hits between 1961 and 1964, of which "Nothing Can Change This Love" climbed to No. 12. Overall, the legendary performer took 29 songs to the Top 40, including three posthumously.

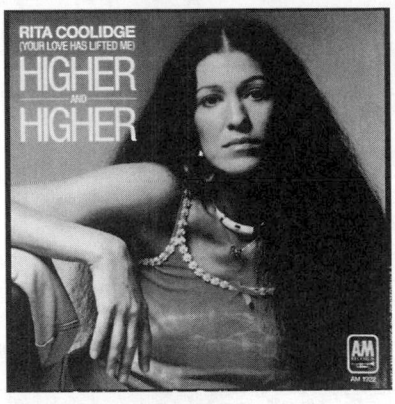

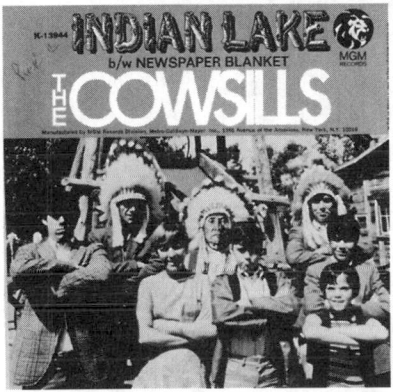

Rita Coolidge's biggest record was her 1977 cover of Jackie Wilson's 1966 No. 6 hit "Your Love Keeps Lifting Me (Higher And Higher). " Interestingly, Coolidge changed the lyric to "has lifted"—and the hit was "lifted higher" to No. 2.

Coolio's combination of rhythm, rap and rhyme—mixed with an obvious sense of humor and a distinctive hairstyle—made him one of the biggest rap artists of the mid-'90s. "Fantastic Voyage," from his 1994 album *It Takes A Thief*, swiftly ascended to No. 3.

Corina's single "Temptation"—the cover of which featured the Manhattan-born singer wearing handcuffs—quickly shot to No. 6 on the Hot 100. Feminists who'd vigorously protested the Rolling Stones' 1976 album *Black And Blue* apparently never noticed.

The Cowsills were a "family rock group" upon whom many suspect the '60s TV show "The Partridge Family" was based. "Indian Lake," which reached No. 10 in 1968, was one of the group's three Top 10 hits.

Johnny Crawford's starring role in TV's "The Rifleman" helped push the young teen singer into the Top 40 four times during 1962-63. But his early single "Daydreams" only peaked at No. 70 in 1961.

Creedence Clearwater Revival's 1970 version of "I Heard It Through The Grapevine" was found on the group's all-time bestselling album, *Cosmo's Factory*. Unlike previous hit versions by Gladys Knight And The Pips and Marvin Gaye, the track failed to even dent the Top 40.

DATE	POS	WKS	ARTIST–RECORD TITLE	LABEL & NO.
6/24/67	37	4	6. Don't Blame The Children [S]	Reprise 0566
1/18/69	11	11	7. I've Gotta Be Me from the Broadway musical *Golden Rainbow* starring Steve Lawrence and Eydie Gorme; #1 Adult Contemporary hit (7 weeks)	Reprise 0779
4/15/72	1 (3)	16	● 8. **The Candy Man** from the movie *Willy Wonka And The Chocolate Factory* starring Gene Wilder; originally recorded as by The Mike Curb Congregation; Davis's vocals dubbed in later; #1 Adult Contemporary hit (2 weeks)	MGM 14320

DAVIS, Skeeter

Born Mary Penick on 12/30/31 in Dry Ridge, Kentucky. Country singer. Recorded with friend Betty Davis as the Davis Sisters, until Betty was killed in a car accident on 8/2/53. Formerly married to Ralph Emery, host of TV's "Nashville Now." Later married Joey Spampinato, the bassist of jazz-rock band NRBQ.

DATE	POS	WKS	ARTIST–RECORD TITLE	LABEL & NO.
9/5/60	39	1	1. (I Can't Help You) I'm Falling Too answer song to Hank Locklin's "Please Help Me, I'm Falling"	RCA 7767
1/16/61	26	2	2. My Last Date (With You) answer song to Floyd Cramer's "Last Date"	RCA 7825
2/16/63	2 (1)	13	3. **The End Of The World** #1 Adult Contemporary hit (4 weeks)	RCA 8098
9/21/63	7	11	4. **I Can't Stay Mad At You**	RCA 8219

DAVIS, Spencer, Group

Davis was born on 7/14/41. Vocalist/rhythm guitarist. Formed his R&B-styled rock group in Birmingham, England, in 1963. Featured Steve Winwood (lead vocals, lead guitar, keyboards), his brother Muff Winwood (bass) and Pete York (drums). Steve Winwood left in 1967 to form the group Traffic; later became a successful solo artist. Muff became senior director of A&R at CBS Records, U.K.

DATE	POS	WKS	ARTIST–RECORD TITLE	LABEL & NO.
1/28/67	7	9	1. **Gimme Some Lovin'**	United Art. 50108
4/8/67	10	7	2. **I'm A Man**	United Art. 50144

DAVIS, Tyrone

Born on 5/4/38 in Greenville, Mississippi, and raised in Saginaw, Michigan. Soul singer. To Chicago in 1959. Worked as valet/chauffeur for Freddy King until 1962. Working local clubs when discovered by Harold Burrage. First recorded for Four Brothers in 1965 as Tyrone The Wonder Boy. His younger sister, Jean Davis, was a member of the group Facts Of Life.

DATE	POS	WKS	ARTIST–RECORD TITLE	LABEL & NO.
1/4/69	5	11	● 1. **Can I Change My Mind** #1 R&B hit (3 weeks)	Dakar 602
4/12/69	34	2	2. Is It Something You've Got	Dakar 605
4/4/70	3	11	● 3. **Turn Back The Hands Of Time** #1 R&B hit (2 weeks)	Dakar 616
8/25/73	32	3	4. There It Is	Dakar 4523
10/30/76	38	4	5. Give It Up (Turn It Loose)	Columbia 10388

DAWN

Pop vocal trio formed in New York City: Tony Orlando (born 4/3/44, New York City), Telma Hopkins (born 10/28/48, Louisville) and Joyce Vincent (born 12/14/46, Detroit). Orlando had recorded solo, 1961–63; Hopkins and Vincent had been backup singers. Orlando was manager for April-Blackwood Music at the time of trio's first hit. Own TV show, 1974–76. All of its hits produced by Hank Medress (The Tokens) and Dave Appell (The Applejacks). Hopkins appeared on TV's "Bosom Buddies," "Gimme A Break" and "Family Matters."

DATE	POS	WKS	ARTIST–RECORD TITLE	LABEL & NO.
8/29/70	3	13	● 1. **Candida**	Bell 903
12/5/70+	1 (3)	16	● 2. **Knock Three Times**	Bell 938
			Tony Orlando with Toni Wine and Ellie Greenwich (vocals, above 2)	
4/10/71	25	5	3. I Play And Sing	Bell 970
7/10/71	33	6	4. Summer Sand	Bell 45107
			DAWN FEATURING TONY ORLANDO:	
11/13/71	39	1	5. What Are You Doing Sunday	Bell 45141
3/17/73	1 (4)	17	● 6. **Tie A Yellow Ribbon Round The Ole Oak Tree**	Bell 45318
			#1 Adult Contemporary hit (2 weeks)	
7/28/73	3	13	● 7. **Say, Has Anybody Seen My Sweet Gypsy Rose**	Bell 45374
			#1 Adult Contemporary hit (3 weeks)	
			TONY ORLANDO & DAWN:	
12/1/73	27	7	8. Who's In The Strawberry Patch With Sally	Bell 45424
9/7/74	7	9	9. **Steppin' Out (Gonna Boogie Tonight)**	Bell 45601
1/11/75	11	8	10. Look In My Eyes Pretty Woman	Bell 45620
3/29/75	1 (3)	10	● 11. **He Don't Love You (Like I Love You)**	Elektra 45240
			#1 Adult Contemporary hit (1 week)	
7/12/75	14	6	12. Mornin' Beautiful	Elektra 45260
9/20/75	34	3	13. You're All I Need To Get By	Elektra 45275
2/21/76	22	6	14. Cupid	Elektra 45302

DAY, Bobby

Born Robert Byrd on 7/1/30 in Ft. Worth, Texas. Died on 7/15/90 of cancer. R&B singer. To Watts, Los Angeles, in 1948. Formed the Hollywood Flames in 1950. Group also recorded as The Flames in 1950. Wrote "Little Bitty Pretty One."

DATE	POS	WKS	ARTIST–RECORD TITLE	LABEL & NO.
8/4/58	2 (2)	19	● 1. **Rock-in Robin**	Class 229
			Hot 100 #2 / Best Seller #4 end; #1 R&B hit (3 weeks)	

DAY, Doris

Born Doris Kappelhoff on 4/3/22 in Cincinnati. Sang briefly with Bob Crosby in 1940 and shortly thereafter became a major star with the Les Brown band (she had 12 charted hits with Brown). Her great solo recording success was soon transcended by Hollywood as Day became the #1 box office star of the late '50s and early '60s. Star of own popular TV series, 1968–73. Her son, Terry Melcher, was a member of The Rip Chords and Bruce And Terry, and a prolific producer (The Beach Boys).

DATE	POS	WKS	ARTIST–RECORD TITLE	LABEL & NO.
7/23/55	13	9	1. I'll Never Stop Loving You	Columbia 40505
			Jockey #13 / Best Seller #15 / Top 100 #93 pre; from the movie *Love Me Or Leave Me* starring Day; Percy Faith (orch.)	
7/7/56	2 (3)	22	● 2. **Whatever Will Be, Will Be (Que Sera, Sera)**	Columbia 40704
			Top 100 #2 / Jockey #2 / Best Seller #3 / Juke Box #3; from the movie *The Man Who Knew Too Much* starring Day and James Stewart; Frank DeVol (orch.)	
7/21/58	6	12	3. **Everybody Loves A Lover**	Columbia 41195
			Jockey #6 end / Hot 100 #14 / Best Seller #17	

DATE	POS	WKS	ARTIST–RECORD TITLE	LABEL & NO.
			DAY, Morris	
			Born in Springfield, Illinois; raised in Minneapolis (in local band Grand Central with schoolmate Prince). Leader of Minneapolis funk group The Time (formerly Prince's backing band). Appeared in the movies *Purple Rain*, *The Adventures Of Ford Fairlane* and *Graffiti Bridge*.	
3/26/88	**23**	6	1. Fishnet Sales #15 / Airplay #24; #1 R&B hit (2 weeks)	Warner 28201
			DAYNE, Taylor	
			Born Leslie Wundermann on 7/3/62 in Long Island, New York. Female singer.	
11/14/87+	**7**	15	● 1. **Tell It To My Heart** Sales #5 / Airplay #10	Arista 9612
3/12/88	**7**	11	2. **Prove Your Love** Sales #7 / Airplay #9	Arista 9676
7/23/88	**3**	16	● 3. **I'll Always Love You** Sales #2 / Airplay #5	Arista 9700
11/26/88+	**2 (1)**	13	4. **Don't Rush Me** Sales #2 / Airplay #2; above 4 from the album *Tell It To My Heart*	Arista 9722
11/4/89	**5**	13	5. **With Every Beat Of My Heart** Airplay #3 / Sales #6	Arista 9895
2/3/90	**1 (1)**	15	● 6. **Love Will Lead You Back** Airplay #1(2) / Sales #1(1); #1 Adult Contemporary hit (4 weeks)	Arista 9938
5/19/90	**4**	12	7. **I'll Be Your Shelter** Airplay #3 / Sales #9	Arista 2005
8/18/90	**12**	10	8. Heart Of Stone Airplay #11 / Sales #18; above 4 from the album *Can't Fight Fate*	Arista 2057
6/19/93	**20**	9	9. Can't Get Enough Of Your Love Airplay #17 / Sales #27; produced by Clivilles & Cole	Arista 12582
			DAZZ BAND	
			Cleveland ultrafunk band, formerly Kinsman Dazz. "Dazz" means "danceable jazz."	
5/15/82	**5**	16	1. **Let It Whip** #1 R&B hit (5 weeks)	Motown 1609
			DEADEYE DICK	
			Pop-rock trio from New Orleans: Caleb Guillotte (guitar), Mark Miller (bass) and Billy Landry (drums). All share vocals. Group name taken from a Kurt Vonnegut novel.	
11/5/94+	**27**	11	● 1. New Age Girl Sales #18 / Airplay #48; later included in the movie *Dumb And Dumber* starring Jim Carrey	Ichiban 232
			DEAD OR ALIVE	
			Dance outfit formed in Liverpool, England, by lead singer Pete Burns (born 8/5/59). Wayne Hussey (later a member of Sisters Of Mercy and Mission) was an early member.	
6/29/85	**11**	11	1. You Spin Me Round (Like A Record) Airplay #11 / Sales #12	Epic 04894
1/31/87	**15**	9	2. Brand New Lover Sales #15 / Airplay #15	Epic 06374

DATE	POS	WKS	ARTIST–RECORD TITLE	LABEL & NO.

DEAL, Bill, & The Rhondels

Eight-man, brassy-rock band from Virginia Beach, Virginia.

DATE	POS	WKS	ARTIST–RECORD TITLE	LABEL & NO.
3/15/69	39	1	1. May I	Heritage 803
			first recorded in 1965 by Maurice Williams	
5/31/69	35	3	2. I've Been Hurt	Heritage 812
9/13/69	23	5	3. What Kind Of Fool Do You Think I Am	Heritage 817

DEAN, Jimmy

Born on 8/10/28 in Plainview, Texas. Country vocalist/pianist/guitarist/composer. With Tennessee Haymakers in Washington, D.C., in 1948. Own Texas Wildcats in 1952. Recorded for Four Star in 1952. Own CBS-TV series, 1957–58; ABC-TV series, 1963–66. Business interests include a restaurant chain and a line of pork sausage. Married country singer Donna Meade on 10/27/91.

DATE	POS	WKS	ARTIST–RECORD TITLE	LABEL & NO.
1/6/58+	32	1	1. Little Sandy Sleighfoot [X-N]	Columbia 41025
			Top 100 #32 / Best Seller #37; Ray Ellis (orch.)	
10/9/61	1 (5)	13	● 2. **Big Bad John** [S]	Columbia 42175
			#1 Adult Contemporary hit (10 weeks); #1 Country hit (2 weeks)	
2/10/62	22	5	3. The Cajun Queen [S]	Columbia 42282
1/20/62	24	3	4. Dear Ivan [S]	Columbia 42259
			background music: "Battle Hymn Of The Republic"	
2/10/62	26	5	5. To A Sleeping Beauty [S]	Columbia 42282
			background music: "Memories"; soliloquy first recorded by Jackie Gleason in 1957	
4/14/62	8	9	6. P.T. 109	Columbia 42338
			based on the sinking of John F. Kennedy's torpedo boat in 1943	
10/6/62	29	5	7. Little Black Book	Columbia 42529
5/22/76	35	2	● 8. I.O.U. [S]	Casino 052
			Jimmy Dean's ode of thanks to his mother	

DEAN AND JEAN

Welton Young and Brenda Lee Jones from Dayton, Ohio.

DATE	POS	WKS	ARTIST–RECORD TITLE	LABEL & NO.
12/14/63+	35	2	1. Tra La La La Suzy	Rust 5067
3/21/64	32	3	2. Hey Jean, Hey Dean	Rust 5075

DeBARGE/El DeBarge

Family group from Grand Rapids, Michigan. Consisted of lead vocalist El (born 6/4/61; keyboards), Mark (trumpet, saxophone), James (keyboards), Randy (bass) and Bunny DeBarge (vocals). Brothers Bobby and Tommy were in Switch. James was briefly married to Janet Jackson in 1984.

DEBARGE:

DATE	POS	WKS	ARTIST–RECORD TITLE	LABEL & NO.
3/26/83	31	6	1. I Like It	Gordy 1645
5/28/83	17	10	2. All This Love	Gordy 1660
			#1 Adult Contemporary hit (3 weeks)	
11/26/83+	18	11	3. Time Will Reveal	Gordy 1705
			#1 R&B hit (5 weeks)	
3/9/85	3	14	4. **Rhythm Of The Night**	Gordy 1770
			Airplay #3 / Sales #3; from the Berry Gordy movie *The Last Dragon* starring Vanity; #1 R&B hit (1 week); #1 Adult Contemporary hit (1 week)	
6/22/85	6	12	5. **Who's Holding Donna Now**	Gordy 1793
			Airplay #6 / Sales #7; #1 Adult Contemporary hit (3 weeks); #1 R&B hit (1 week)	

DATE	POS	WKS	ARTIST–RECORD TITLE	LABEL & NO.
			EL DEBARGE:	

5/17/86	3	13	6. **Who's Johnny**
			     Airplay #3 / Sales #4; theme from the movie *Short Circuit* starring
			     Ally Sheedy
				Gordy 1842

4/7/90	31	4	● 7. The Secret Garden (Sweet Seduction Suite)
			     **QUINCY JONES/Al B. Sure!/James Ingram/El
			     DeBarge/Barry White**
			     Sales #20; #1 R&B hit (1 week)
				Qwest 19992

			DeBARGE, Chico	
			DeBarge sibling, but not a member of the group DeBarge.	
12/27/86+	21	11	1. Talk To Me Airplay #17 / Sales #22	Motown 1858
			DeBURGH, Chris	
			Born Christopher John Davidson on 10/15/48 in Argentina of Irish parentage. British pop-rock singer.	
6/11/83	34	4	1. Don't Pay The Ferryman	A&M 2511
4/4/87	3	14	2. **The Lady In Red** Sales #1(1) / Airplay #4	A&M 2848
			DeCASTRO SISTERS, The	
			Peggy, Babette and Cherie DeCastro; raised on their father's sugar plantation in Cuba.	
5/7/55	17	4	1. Boom Boom Boomerang Juke Box #17 / Best Seller #24; Thurl Ravenscroft (bass voice)	Abbott 3003
			DEE, Joey, & the Starliters	
			Dee was born Joseph DiNicola on 6/11/40 in Passaic, New Jersey. In September 1960, Joey & The Starlighters became the house band at the Peppermint Lounge, New York City. After 1964, group included three members who later formed The Young Rascals, plus guitarist Jimi Hendrix. Appeared in the movies *Hey, Let's Twist* and *Two Tickets To Paris*.	
12/4/61+	1 (3)	14	● 1. **Peppermint Twist - Part I** inspired by New York City's Peppermint Lounge club	Roulette 4401
3/3/62	20	4	2. Hey, Let's Twist	Roulette 4408
3/31/62	6	9	3. **Shout - Part I** above 2 from the movie *Hey, Let's Twist!* starring Dee	Roulette 4416
9/15/62	18	6	4. What Kind Of Love Is This from the movie *Two Tickets to Paris*; written by Johnny Nash	Roulette 4438
6/1/63	36	1	5. Hot Pastrami With Mashed Potatoes - Part I all of above produced by Henry Glover	Roulette 4488
			DEE, Johnny—see LOUDERMILK, John D.	
			DEE, Kiki	
			Born Pauline Matthews on 3/6/47 in Yorkshire, England.	
10/19/74	12	10	1. I've Got The Music In Me **THE KIKI DEE BAND**	Rocket 40293

7/17/76	1 (4)	15	● 2. **Don't Go Breaking My Heart**
			     ELTON JOHN AND KIKI DEE
			     #1 Adult Contemporary hit (1 week)
				Rocket 40585

DATE	POS	WKS	ARTIST–RECORD TITLE	LABEL & NO.
			DEE, Lenny	
2/12/55	**19**	15	Born in the 1920s in Illinois and raised in Florida. Organist. Discovered by Red Foley. 1. Plantation Boogie [I] Juke Box #19 / Best Seller #23	Decca 29360
			DEE, Tommy	
4/13/59	**11**	8	Born Thomas Donaldson on 7/15/36 in Vicker, Virginia. DJ at KFXM-San Bernadino at time of only hit; first recorded by Eddie Cochran. Currently a producer/promoter/record company executive in Nashville. 1. Three Stars [S] a tribute to Buddy Holly, Ritchie Valens and the Big Bopper; Tommy Dee (narration); Carol Kay and the Teen-Aires (vocals)	Crest 1057
			DEEE-LITE	
10/20/90	**4**	13	New York-based dance trio: Super DJ Dmitry Brill (from Kiev, Russia), Jungle DJ Towa "Towa" Tei (from Tokyo, Japan) and vocalist Lady Miss Kier (Kier Kirby from Youngstown, Ohio). Group's name inspired by the tune "It's De-lovely" from the 1936 Cole Porter musical *Red, Hot & Blue*. Brill and Kier are married. Tei left by 1994, replaced by Ani. ● 1. **Groove Is In The Heart** Sales #1(2) / Airplay #6; Bootsy Collins (backing vocal); Q-Tip (of A Tribe Called Quest; rap)	Elektra 64934
			DEELE, The	
4/2/88	**10**	12	R&B funk sextet from Cincinnati, led by Darnell "Dee" Bristol. Included the songwriting/production team of Mark "L.A. Reid" Rooney and Kenneth "Babyface" Edmonds. Reid (cousin of Keith Mitchell of After 7 and son of The Exciters' Herb Rooney and Brenda Reid) married Pebbles in 1989. Former member of Manchild, Edmonds (brother of After 7's Kevon and Melvin Edmonds) began solo career as Babyface in 1989. 1. **Two Occasions** Airplay #8 / Sales #13	Solar 70015
			DEEP BLUE SOMETHING	
10/14/95+	**5**	26	Pop-rock quartet from Dallas: brothers Todd (vocals, bass) and Toby (guitar) Pipes, Kirk Tatom (guitar) and John Kirtland (drums). 1. **Breakfast At Tiffany's** Airplay #4 / Sales #15	Rainmaker 98138
			DEEP PURPLE	
8/24/68 12/7/68	**4** **38**	9 3	British pioneer heavy-metal band formed in 1968: Ritchie Blackmore (guitar), Rod Evans (vocals), Jon Lord (keyboards), Ian Paice (drums) and Nicky Simper (bass). Evans and Simper left in 1969, replaced by Ian Gillan (vocals) and Roger Glover (bass). Evans formed Captain Beyond. Gillan and Glover left in late 1973, replaced by David Coverdale (vocals) and Glenn Hughes (bass). Blackmore left in early 1975 to form Rainbow (which Glover later joined); replaced by American Tommy Bolin (ex-James Gang guitarist; died 12/4/76). Band split in July 1976. Coverdale formed Whitesnake. Blackmore, Lord, Paice, Gillan and Glover reunited in 1984. Hughes joined Black Sabbath as vocalist in 1986. Gillan (who was with Black Sabbath for 1983 *Born Again* album) left in 1989 to form Garth Rockett & The Moonshiners; replaced by Joe Lynn Turner (ex-Rainbow), then returned in 1992 to take Turner's place. 1. **Hush** 2. Kentucky Woman	Tetragramm. 1503 Tetragramm. 1508

DATE	POS	WKS	ARTIST–RECORD TITLE	LABEL & NO.
6/16/73	4	12	● 3. **Smoke On The Water** inspired by the burning of the Montreux Casino on 12/3/71 during a Frank Zappa show for which Deep Purple opened	Warner 7710

DEES, Rick, And His Cast Of Idiots

Dees was born Rigdon Osmond Dees III in Memphis in 1950. DJ working at WMPS-Memphis when he conceived idea for "Disco Duck." Currently one of America's top radio DJs. Host of TV's "Solid Gold" (1984) and his own late-night talk show "Into The Night."

DATE	POS	WKS	ARTIST–RECORD TITLE	LABEL & NO.
9/4/76	1 (1)	16	▲ 1. **Disco Duck (Part 1)** [N]	RSO 857

DEF LEPPARD

Hard-rock quintet formed in Sheffield, England, in 1977: Joe Elliott (vocals), Steve Clark and Pete Willis (guitars), Rick Savage (bass) and Rick Allen (drums; lost his left arm in an auto accident on 12/31/84). Phil Collen replaced Willis in late 1982. Clark died on 1/8/91 of alcohol-related respiratory failure. Guitarist Vivian Campbell (Whitesnake, Dio, Riverdogs, Shadow King) joined in April 1992.

DATE	POS	WKS	ARTIST–RECORD TITLE	LABEL & NO.
4/16/83	12	9	1. Photograph	Mercury 811215
7/9/83	16	9	2. Rock Of Ages	Mercury 812604
10/8/83	28	5	3. Foolin'	Mercury 814178
11/21/87	19	9	4. Animal Sales #16 / Airplay #24	Mercury 888832
2/13/88	10	10	5. **Hysteria** Sales #10 / Airplay #11	Mercury 870004
5/21/88	2 (1)	15	6. **Pour Some Sugar On Me** Airplay #2 / Sales #3	Mercury 870298
8/20/88	1 (1)	13	7. **Love Bites** Airplay #1(2) / Sales #2	Mercury 870402
12/3/88+	3	12	8. **Armageddon It** Sales #1(1) / Airplay #3	Mercury 870692
3/18/89	12	9	9. Rocket Sales #11 / Airplay #13; above 6 from the album *Hysteria*	Mercury 872614
4/11/92	15	11	10. Let's Get Rocked Sales #10 / Airplay #43; "live" version is on the B-side of #15 below	Mercury 866568
7/18/92	36	3	11. Make Love Like A Man Sales #41 / Airplay #57	Mercury 864038
9/5/92	12	15	12. Have You Ever Needed Someone So Bad Sales #14 / Airplay #21	Mercury 864136
1/23/93	34	3	13. Stand Up (Kick Love Into Motion) Airplay #50; above 4 from the album *Adrenalize*	Mercury 864604
9/25/93	12	12	14. Two Steps Behind Airplay #17 / Sales #18; from the movie *Last Action Hero* starring Arnold Schwarzenegger	Columbia 77116
1/22/94	39	2	15. Miss You In A Heartbeat Airplay #53 / Sales #54	Mercury 858080

DeFRANCO FAMILY featuring TONY DeFRANCO

Family group from Ontario: Tony (age 13 in 1973), Merlina (16), Nino (17), Marisa (18) and Benny (19).

DATE	POS	WKS	ARTIST–RECORD TITLE	LABEL & NO.
9/29/73	3	14	● 1. **Heartbeat - It's A Lovebeat**	20th Century 2030
1/26/74	32	4	2. Abra-Ca-Dabra	20th Century 2070
5/25/74	18	6	3. Save The Last Dance For Me	20th Century 2088

DATE	POS	WKS	ARTIST–RECORD TITLE	LABEL & NO.
			DeJOHN SISTERS	
			Julie (born 3/18/31) and Dux (born 1/21/33) DeGiovanni from Chester, Pennsylvania.	
12/25/54+	6	13	1. **(My Baby Don't Love Me) No More** Jockey #6 / Best Seller #8 / Juke Box #11; O.B. Masingill (orch.)	Epic 9085
			DEKKER, Desmond, & The Aces	
			Dekker was born Desmond Dacres on 7/16/41 in Kingston, Jamaica. Leader of reggae group.	
6/7/69	9	7	1. **Israelites**	Uni 55129
			DEL AMITRI	
			Rock quartet formed in Glasgow, Scotland, in 1983: Justin Currie (vocals, bass), David Cummings and Iain Harvie (guitars), and Brian McDermott (drums).	
6/30/90	35	3	1. Kiss This Thing Goodbye Sales #31 / Airplay #33	A&M 1485
9/26/92	30	7	2. Always The Last To Know Airplay #31 / Sales #71	A&M 1604
8/26/95	10	26	3. **Roll To Me** Airplay #6 / Sales #50	A&M 1114
			DELANEY & BONNIE	
			Delaney Bramlett (born 7/1/39, Pontotoc County, Mississippi) and wife Bonnie Lynn Bramlett (born 11/8/44, Acton, Illinois). Married in 1967. Friends—backing artists included, at various times, Leon Russell, Rita Coolidge, Dave Mason, Eric Clapton, Duane Allman and many others.	
6/26/71	13	10	1. Never Ending Song Of Love **DELANEY & BONNIE & FRIENDS**	Atco 6804
10/9/71	20	7	2. Only You Know And I Know	Atco 6838
			DE LA SOUL	
			Psychedelic-rap trio from Amityville, Long Island, New York: Posdnuos (Kelvin Mercer), Trugoy the Dove (David Jolicoeur) and P.A. Pasemaster Mase (Vincent Mason, Jr.).	
7/22/89	34	3	● 1. Me Myself And I Sales #21; #1 R&B hit (1 week)	Tommy Boy 7926
			DELEGATES, The	
			A Dickie Goodman-type recording, featuring DJ Bob DeCarlo.	
11/4/72	8	6	1. **Convention '72** [N] featuring bits of some of the top Pop hits of 1972	Mainstream 5525
			DELFONICS, The	
			Soul group from Philadelphia. Formed in 1965 as the Four Gents. Consisted of William and Wilbert Hart, Ritchie Daniels and Randy Cain. First recorded for Moon Shot in 1967. Daniels left for the service in 1968, group continued as a trio. Cain was replaced by Major Harris in 1971. Harris went solo in 1974.	
2/24/68	4	12	1. **La - La - Means I Love You**	Philly Groove 150
10/5/68	35	4	2. Break Your Promise	Philly Groove 152
1/25/69	35	1	3. Ready Or Not Here I Come (Can't Hide From Love)	Philly Groove 154

DATE	POS	WKS	ARTIST–RECORD TITLE	LABEL & NO.
10/4/69	40	2	4. You Got Yours And I'll Get Mine	Philly Groove 157
2/7/70	10	10	● 5. **Didn't I (Blow Your Mind This Time)**	Philly Groove 161
7/25/70	40	1	6. Trying To Make A Fool Of Me	Philly Groove 162

DELIVERANCE Soundtrack—see WEISSBERG, Eric

DELLS, The

R&B vocal group formed at Thornton Township High School in Harvey, Illinois: Johnny Funches (lead), Marvin Junior (baritone lead), Verne Allison (tenor), Mickey McGill (baritone) and Chuck Barksdale (bass). First recorded as the El-Rays for Chess in 1953. Signed with Vee-Jay in 1955. Group remained intact into the 1980s, with the exception of Funches, who was replaced by Johnny Carter (ex-Flamingos) in 1960.

DATE	POS	WKS	ARTIST–RECORD TITLE	LABEL & NO.
2/17/68	20	7	1. There Is	Cadet 5590
7/20/68	10	10	2. **Stay In My Corner** #1 R&B hit (3 weeks); original version was a #23 R&B hit on Vee-Jay 674 in 1965	Cadet 5612
11/2/68	18	5	3. Always Together	Cadet 5621
2/8/69	38	2	4. Does Anybody Know I'm Here	Cadet 5631
6/21/69	22	6	5. I Can Sing A Rainbow/Love Is Blue	Cadet 5641
8/23/69	10	10	6. **Oh, What A Night** #1 R&B hit (1 week); original version was a #4 R&B hit on Vee-Jay 204 in 1956	Cadet 5649
9/18/71	30	6	7. The Love We Had (Stays On My Mind)	Cadet 5683
6/23/73	34	2	● 8. Give Your Baby A Standing Ovation	Cadet 5696

DELL-VIKINGS, The

Interracial R&B-rock group formed at the Air Force Serviceman's Club in Pittsburgh in 1955. Consisted of Norman Wright, Corinthian "Krips" Johnson, Donald "Gus" Backus, David Lerchey and Clarence Quick. Backus and Lerchey are white, others black. First recorded for Fee Bee and Luniverse labels, then Dot. After discharge from the Air Force, Johnson formed new Dell-Vikings for the Dot label with Chuck Jackson, who went on to a successful solo career. Backus and the other members formed new Del Vikings group for Mercury in 1957. Johnson died on 6/22/90 (age 57) of prostate cancer.

DATE	POS	WKS	ARTIST–RECORD TITLE	LABEL & NO.
3/2/57	4	22	● 1. **Come Go With Me** Best Seller #4 / Top 100 #5 / Jockey #6 / Juke Box #6; first released on Fee Bee 205 in 1956	Dot 15538
7/15/57	9	13	2. **Whispering Bells** Top 100 #9 / Best Seller #10 / Jockey #19; first released on FeeBee 214 in 1956 (as The Del Vikings Feat. Krips Johnson)	Dot 15592
7/15/57	12	1	3. Cool Shake **DEL VIKINGS** Jockey #12 / Top 100 #46	Mercury 71132

DEMENSIONS, The

Pop vocal group from the Bronx: Lenny Del Giudice (Lenny Dell), Marisa Martelli, Howard Margolin, and Charlie Peterson.

DATE	POS	WKS	ARTIST–RECORD TITLE	LABEL & NO.
8/8/60	16	9	1. Over The Rainbow first sung by Judy Garland in the 1939 movie *The Wizard of Oz*; Irv Spice (orch.)	Mohawk 116

DENNIS, Cathy

Born in 1970 in Norwich, England. Vocalist for producer Dancin' Danny D's D-Mob.

DATE	POS	WKS	ARTIST—RECORD TITLE	LABEL & NO.
1/27/90	**10**	12	1. **C'mon And Get My Love** **D MOB Introducing Cathy Dennis** Airplay #10 / Sales #12; from the movie *She-Devil* starring Meryl Streep and Roseanne Barr	FFRR 886798
12/8/90+	**9**	12	2. **Just Another Dream** Sales #8 / Airplay #8	Polydor 877962
3/23/91	**2** (2)	14	3. **Touch Me (All Night Long)** Airplay #2 / Sales #3; #70 R&B hit for Wish Featuring Fonda Rae in 1985; also on the B-side of #4 below	Polydor 879466
7/27/91	**8**	13	4. **Too Many Walls** Airplay #13 / Sales #35; #1 Adult Contemporary hit (2 weeks)	Polydor 867134
10/3/92	**32**	5	5. **You Lied To Me** Airplay #25 / Sales #65	Polydor 863452
			## DENNY, Martin (The Exotic Sounds of) Born on 4/10/11 in New York City. Composer/arranger/pianist. Originated the "Exotic Sounds" in Hawaii, featuring Julius Wechter (Baja Marimba Band) on vibes and marimba.	
4/27/59	**4**	13	● 1. **Quiet Village** [I] written and first recorded in 1952 by Les Baxter (Capitol 2225)	Liberty 55162
11/16/59	**28**	2	2. **The Enchanted Sea** [I]	Liberty 55212
			## DENVER, John Born John Henry Deutschendorf on 12/31/43 in Roswell, New Mexico. To Los Angeles in 1964. With the Chad Mitchell Trio, 1965–68. Wrote "Leaving On A Jet Plane." Starred in the 1977 movie *Oh, God*. Won an Emmy in 1975 for the TV special "An Evening With John Denver."	
6/26/71	**2** (1)	14	● 1. **Take Me Home, Country Roads** Fat City (Bill Danoff and Taffy Nivert of Starland Vocal Band; backing vocals)	RCA 0445
1/6/73	**9**	12	2. **Rocky Mountain High**	RCA 0829
2/16/74	**1** (1)	13	● 3. **Sunshine On My Shoulders** #1 Adult Contemporary hit (2 weeks)	RCA 0213
6/15/74	**1** (2)	11	● 4. **Annie's Song** written by Denver for his wife, Annie Martell (married 1967-83); #1 Adult Contemporary hit (3 weeks)	RCA 0295
10/5/74	**5**	10	● 5. **Back Home Again** #1 Adult Contemporary hit (2 weeks); #1 Country hit (1 week)	RCA 10065
1/11/75	**13**	8	6. **Sweet Surrender** #1 Adult Contemporary hit (1 week)	RCA 10148
4/5/75	**1** (1)	15	● 7. **Thank God I'm A Country Boy** above 2 recorded "live" at the Universal City Amphitheater, California; both were originally studio cuts from the 1974 album *Back Home Again*; #1 Country hit (1 week)	RCA 10239
8/30/75	**1** (1)	13	● 8. **I'm Sorry/** #1 Adult Contemporary hit (2 weeks); #1 Country hit (1 week)	
10/11/75	**2** (4)	7	9. **Calypso** dedicated to Jacques Cousteau and his ship *Calypso*	RCA 10353
12/13/75+	**13**	9	10. **Fly Away** Olivia Newton-John (backing vocal); #1 Adult Contemporary hit (2 weeks)	RCA 10517
3/20/76	**29**	4	11. **Looking For Space** #1 Adult Contemporary hit (1 week); above 4 from the album *Windsong*	RCA 10586
10/2/76	**36**	2	12. **Like A Sad Song** #1 Adult Contemporary hit (1 week)	RCA 10774

DATE	POS	WKS	ARTIST–RECORD TITLE	LABEL & NO.
4/30/77	32	3	13. My Sweet Lady *also the B-side of "Thank God I'm A Country Boy"; recorded in 1971; all of above produced by Milton Okun*	RCA 10911
9/5/81	36	4	14. Some Days Are Diamonds (Some Days Are Stone)	RCA 12246
4/24/82	31	5	15. Shanghai Breezes *#1 Adult Contemporary hit (1 week)*	RCA 13071

DEODATO

Born Eumir De Almeida Deodato on 6/21/42 in Rio de Janeiro, Brazil. Keyboardist/composer/producer/arranger. Kool & The Gang's producer, 1979–82.

DATE	POS	WKS	ARTIST–RECORD TITLE	LABEL & NO.
2/17/73	2 (1)	10	1. **Also Sprach Zarathustra (2001)** [I] *theme from the movie 2001: A Space Odyssey; written by classical composer Richard Strauss in 1896*	CTI 12

DEPECHE MODE

All-synthesized rock band formed in Basildon, England, in 1980 consisting of vocalist David Gahan and synthesizer players Martin L. Gore, Vince Clarke and Andy Fletcher. Clarke left in 1982 (formed Yaz, then Erasure), replaced by Alan Wilder (left in 1995). Group name is French for fast fashion.

DATE	POS	WKS		ARTIST–RECORD TITLE	LABEL & NO.
6/22/85	13	10		1. People Are People *Airplay #11 / Sales #16*	Sire 29221
2/10/90	28	6	●	2. Personal Jesus *Sales #20*	Sire 19941
5/26/90	8	12	●	3. **Enjoy The Silence** *Airplay #4 / Sales #10*	Sire 19885
9/1/90	15	9		4. Policy Of Truth *Airplay #11 / Sales #22*	Sire 19842
3/13/93	37	1	●	5. I Feel You *Sales #14 / Airplay #59*	Sire 18600

DEREK—see CYMBAL, Johnny

DEREK AND THE DOMINOS—see CLAPTON, Eric

DERRINGER, Rick

Born Richard Zehringer on 8/5/47 in Celina, Ohio. Lead singer/guitarist of The McCoys. Performed on and produced sessions for both Edgar and Johnny Winter's bands; also a producer for "Weird Al" Yankovic.

DATE	POS	WKS	ARTIST–RECORD TITLE	LABEL & NO.
3/2/74	23	6	1. Rock And Roll, Hoochie Koo	Blue Sky 2751

DeSARIO, Teri

Pop singer/songwriter from Miami.

DATE	POS	WKS		ARTIST–RECORD TITLE	LABEL & NO.
12/22/79+	2 (2)	16	●	1. **Yes, I'm Ready** **TERI DeSARIO with K.C.** *#1 Adult Contemporary hit (2 weeks)*	Casablanca 2227

DATE	POS	WKS	ARTIST–RECORD TITLE	LABEL & NO.
			DeSHANNON, Jackie	
			Born Sharon Myers on 8/21/44 in Hazel, Kentucky. Vocalist/composer. On radio at age six. First recorded (as Sherry Lee Myers) for Glenn in 1959. To Los Angeles in 1960. Attained prominence as a prolific songwriter (over 600 to date). Co-writer of mega-pop hit "Bette Davis Eyes." Toured with The Beatles for 26 concerts in 1964. Appeared in the movies *Surf Party*, *C'mon Let's Live A Little* and *Hide And Seek*. Married composer/movie scorer Randy Edelman.	
6/19/65	7	9	1. **What The World Needs Now Is Love**	Imperial 66110
7/26/69	4	10	● 2. **Put A Little Love In Your Heart**	Imperial 66385
12/6/69	40	1	3. Love Will Find A Way	Imperial 66419
			DESMOND, Johnny	
			Born Giovanni Desimons on 11/14/20 in Detroit. Died on 9/6/85. Sang with Bob Crosby, Gene Krupa and Glenn Miller's military band. Featured on the "Breakfast Club" radio show throughout the 1950s. Regular on TV's "Your Hit Parade," 1958–59.	
3/26/55	6	11	1. **Play Me Hearts And Flowers (I Wanna Cry)** Jockey #6 / Juke Box #11 / Best Seller #16; Don Jacoby (orch.); introduced by Desmond on 3/6/55 on TV's drama series "Philco Playhouse"	Coral 61379
8/13/55	3	16	2. **The Yellow Rose Of Texas** Jockey #3 / Juke Box #4 / Best Seller #6 / Top 100 #16 pre; adaptation of a Civil War campfire song	Coral 61476
12/3/55	17	1	3. Sixteen Tons Jockey #17 / Top 100 #50; Dick Jacobs (orch., above 2)	Coral 61529
			DES'REE	
			Born Des'ree Weeks in London to West Indian parents. Female singer. In Barbados age 10–13, then back to London.	
11/19/94+	5	30	1. **You Gotta Be** Airplay #2 / Sales #17	550 Music 77551
			DETERGENTS, The	
			Trio from New York: Ron Dante (of The Archies and The Cuff Links), Tommy Wynn and Danny Jordan.	
12/19/64+	19	6	1. Leader Of The Laundromat [N] parody of The Shangri-Las' "Leader Of The Pack"	Roulette 4590
			DETROIT EMERALDS	
			R&B group formed in Little Rock, Arkansas, by the Tilmon brothers: Abrim (died 1982 of a heart attack), Ivory, Cleophus and Raymond. In 1970, group reduced to trio of Abrim, Ivory and friend James Mitchell.	
2/19/72	36	4	1. You Want It, You Got It	Westbound 192
7/29/72	24	7	2. Baby Let Me Take You (In My Arms)	Westbound 203
			DeVAUGHN, William	
			R&B vocalist/songwriter/guitarist from Washington, D.C. Worked for the federal government.	
5/18/74	4	10	● 1. **Be Thankful For What You Got** #1 R&B hit (1 week)	Roxbury 0236

DATE	POS	WKS	ARTIST–RECORD TITLE	LABEL & NO.
			## DEVICE	
			Los Angeles-based, pop-rock trio: Paul Engemann (lead singer), Holly Knight (keyboards, bass) and Gene Black (guitar). Engemann joined Animotion in 1988. Prolific songwriter Knight was a member of Spider.	
8/2/86	35	4	1. Hanging On A Heart Attack Airplay #26 / Sales #37	Chrysalis 42996
			## DEVO	
			Robotic rock group formed in Akron, Ohio, in 1976: brothers Mark (synthesizers) and Bob (vocals, guitar) Mothersbaugh, brothers Jerry (bass) and Bob (guitar) Casale, and Alan Myers (drums). David Kendrick replaced Myers by 1988. Mark and Jerry met while both were art students at Kent State. Devo is short for the theory of "de-evolution" (the regression of mankind).	
10/4/80	14	15	● 1. Whip It	Warner 49550
			## DeVORZON, Barry, and Perry Botkin, Jr.	
			Songwriting/producing/arranging duo based in California. DeVorzon was born on 7/31/34 in New York City. Founded Valiant Records. Leader of Barry And The Tamerlanes. Began prolific songwriting career in the mid-1950s. Botkin was born on 4/16/33 in New York City. Son of orchestra leader Perry Botkin, Sr.	
10/2/76	8	16	● 1. **Nadia's Theme (The Young And The Restless)** [I] originally written as "Cotton's Dream" for the movie *Bless the Beasts & Children*, then used as the theme song for TV's "The Young and the Restless," and finally as the music for Romanian gymnast Nadia Comaneci in the 1976 summer Olympics	A&M 1856
			## DEVOTIONS, The	
			Vocal quintet formed in New York City in 1960: Ray Sanchez (bass, lead), Bob Weisbrod, Bob Hovorka and Frank and Joe Pardo. Broke up before their first hit in 1964.	
4/4/64	36	1	1. Rip Van Winkle [N] first released on Delta 101 and then on Roulette 4406 in 1962	Roulette 4541
			## DEXYS MIDNIGHT RUNNERS	
			Kevin Rowland (born 8/17/53, Wolverhampton, England), leader of eight-piece Birmingham, England, band.	
2/26/83	1 (1)	14	1. **Come On Eileen**	Mercury 76189
			## DeYOUNG, Cliff	
			Born on 2/12/46 in Los Angeles. Actor in many movies (*Harry & Tonto*, *Protocol*, *F/X*, *Glory* and others) and several made-for-TV movies (including "Sunshine").	
2/16/74	17	8	1. My Sweet Lady written by John Denver; from the TV soundtrack "Sunshine"	MCA 40156
			## DeYOUNG, Dennis	
			Born on 2/18/47 in Chicago. Lead singer/keyboardist of Styx.	
9/22/84	10	12	1. **Desert Moon** Airplay #6 / Sales #12	A&M 2666

DATE	POS	WKS	ARTIST—RECORD TITLE	LABEL & NO.
			DIAMOND, Leo	
			Born on 6/29/15 in New York City. Died in Los Angeles on 9/15/66. Arranger/lead harmonica player for The Borrah Minevitch Harmonica Rascals, 1930–46.	
2/19/55	30	1	1. Melody Of Love [I] Best Seller #30; music written in 1903, lyrics added in 1954 by Tom Glazer	RCA 5973
			DIAMOND, Neil	
			Born on 1/24/41 in Brooklyn. Vocalist/guitarist/prolific composer. Worked as songplugger/staff writer in New York City; also wrote under pseudonym Mark Lewis. Neil Diamond is his real name, but he considered changing it to Noah Kaminsky early in his career. First recorded for Duel in 1961. Wrote for "The Monkees" TV show. Wrote score for the movie *Jonathan Livingston Seagull*. Starred in and composed the music for *The Jazz Singer* in 1980.	
9/10/66	6	9	1. **Cherry, Cherry**	Bang 528
11/26/66	16	6	2. I Got The Feelin' (Oh No No)	Bang 536
2/11/67	18	5	3. You Got To Me	Bang 540
4/29/67	10	8	4. **Girl, You'll Be A Woman Soon**	Bang 542
8/5/67	13	7	5. I Thank The Lord For The Night Time	Bang 547
10/28/67	22	6	6. Kentucky Woman Diamond's Bang recordings produced by Jeff Barry and Ellie Greenwich	Bang 551
3/29/69	22	7	7. Brother Love's Travelling Salvation Show	Uni 55109
7/12/69	4	12	▲ 8. **Sweet Caroline (Good Times Never Seemed So Good)**	Uni 55136
11/15/69	6	12	▲ 9. **Holly Holy**	Uni 55175
3/21/70	24	8	10. Shilo first issued on Bang 561 in 1968	Bang 575
5/16/70	30	4	11. Soolaimon (African Trilogy II)	Uni 55224
8/15/70	21	7	12. Solitary Man [R] originally charted in 1966 at #55; #1, 3, 4, 5, 10, 12 from the 1967 album *Just For You*	Bang 578
8/29/70	1 (1)	14	▲ 13. **Cracklin' Rosie**	Uni 55250
11/21/70	20	9	14. He Ain't Heavy...He's My Brother	Uni 55264
12/5/70	36	5	15. Do It #1, 2, 12, 15 from the album *The Feel Of Neil Diamond*	Bang 580
4/3/71	4	8	16. **I Am...I Said**	Uni 55278
11/27/71	14	7	17. Stones/	
		1	18. Crunchy Granola Suite	Uni 55310
5/13/72	1 (1)	12	● 19. **Song Sung Blue** #1 Adult Contemporary hit (7 weeks)	Uni 55326
9/2/72	11	7	20. Play Me	Uni 55346
11/25/72	17	8	21. Walk On Water	Uni 55352
4/21/73	31	4	22. "Cherry Cherry" from Hot August Night [R] "live" version of Diamond's 1966 hit (from the album *Hot August Night*)	MCA 40017
11/24/73	34	3	23. Be from the movie *Jonathan Livingston Seagull*	Columbia 45942
10/19/74	5	10	24. **Longfellow Serenade** #1 Adult Contemporary hit (1 week)	Columbia 10043
3/1/75	34	2	25. I've Been This Way Before #1 Adult Contemporary hit (1 week); most of above hits (Uni, MCA, Columbia) produced by Tom Catalano	Columbia 10084

DATE	POS	WKS	ARTIST–RECORD TITLE	LABEL & NO.
6/26/76	11	8	26. If You Know What I Mean produced by Robbie Robertson (of The Band); #1 Adult Contemporary hit (2 weeks)	Columbia 10366
12/24/77+	16	9	27. Desiree #1 Adult Contemporary hit (1 week)	Columbia 10657
11/4/78	1 (2)	15	● 28. **You Don't Bring Me Flowers** **BARBRA (Streisand) & NEIL**	Columbia 10840
2/17/79	20	6	29. Forever In Blue Jeans	Columbia 10897
1/19/80	17	10	30. September Morn'	Columbia 11175
11/1/80+	2 (3)	17	31. **Love On The Rocks**	Capitol 4939
1/31/81	6	12	32. **Hello Again**	Capitol 4960
5/2/81	8	13	33. **America** #1 Adult Contemporary hit (3 weeks); above 3 from the movie The Jazz Singer starring Diamond	Capitol 4994
11/14/81+	11	12	34. Yesterday's Songs #1 Adult Contemporary hit (6 weeks)	Columbia 02604
3/6/82	27	5	35. On The Way To The Sky	Columbia 02712
6/19/82	35	4	36. Be Mine Tonight	Columbia 02928
10/2/82	5	11	37. **Heartlight** inspired by the movie E.T. starring Henry Thomas; #1 Adult Contemporary hit (4 weeks)	Columbia 03219
2/19/83	35	4	38. I'm Alive all of above (except #14) composed by Diamond	Columbia 03503

DIAMONDS, The

Vocal group from Toronto formed in 1953. Consisted of Dave Somerville (lead), Ted Kowalski (tenor), Phil Leavitt (baritone) and Bill Reed (bass). Recorded for Coral in 1955. Debuted on Mercury in January 1956. Michael Douglas replaced Leavitt in early 1958. Reed and Kowalski replaced in 1959 by Evan Fisher and John Felten (killed in a plane crash in 1982). Frequent personnel changes. Dave teamed with Four Preps' co-founder Bruce Belland as a duo, 1962–69. Bob Duncan (lead) joined in 1978 and re-formed the group, after Felten's death, with new lineup. Group hit the country charts in 1987.

DATE	POS	WKS	ARTIST–RECORD TITLE	LABEL & NO.
3/17/56	12	11	1. Why Do Fools Fall In Love Jockey #12 / Top 100 #16 / Best Seller #18 / Juke Box #19	Mercury 70790
5/12/56	14	11	2. The Church Bells May Ring Best Seller #14 / Juke Box #15 / Jockey #17 / Top 100 #20	Mercury 70835
7/28/56	30	2	3. Love, Love, Love	Mercury 70889
9/29/56	34	1	4. Soft Summer Breeze/	
9/29/56	35	2	5. Ka-Ding-Dong	Mercury 70934
3/16/57	2 (8)	21	● 6. **Little Darlin'** Best Seller #2 / Top 100 #2 / Jockey #2 / Juke Box #2; original version by Maurice Williams's group, The Gladiolas	Mercury 71060
7/15/57	13	2	7. Words Of Love Jockey #13 / Top 100 #76; written by Buddy Holly	Mercury 71128
9/30/57	16	1	8. Zip Zip Jockey #16 / Top 100 #45; David Carroll (orch., all of above)	Mercury 71165
11/4/57	10	8	9. **Silhouettes** Jockey #10 / Top 100 #60	Mercury 71197
1/6/58	4	14	● 10. **The Stroll** Jockey #4 / Top 100 #5 / Best Seller #7	Mercury 71242
5/19/58	37	1	11. High Sign Best Seller #37 / Top 100 #38	Mercury 71291

DATE	POS	WKS	ARTIST–RECORD TITLE	LABEL & NO.
7/28/58	16	1	12. Kathy-O Jockey #16 end / Best Seller #41 / Hot 100 #45; title song from the movie starring Patty McCormack	Mercury 71330
11/17/58	29	6	13. Walking Along original R&B version by the Solitaires in 1957 (Old Town 1034)	Mercury 71366
2/9/59	18	10	14. She Say (Oom Dooby Doom)	Mercury 71404
8/7/61	22	4	15. One Summer Night	Mercury 71831
			DIBANGO, Manu	
			Born in 1934 in Cameroon, Africa. Jazz-R&B saxophonist/pianist.	
7/21/73	35	3	1. Soul Makossa　　　　　　　　　　　　　　[I]	Atlantic 2971
			DICK AND DEEDEE	
			Dick St. John Gosting and Deedee Sperling. Formed duo while students in high school at Santa Monica.	
8/28/61	2 (2)	10	1. **The Mountain's High** first released on Lama 7778 in 1961	Liberty 55350
5/12/62	22	5	2. Tell Me first released on Lama 7783 in 1961	Liberty 55412
4/6/63	17	6	3. Young And In Love	Warner 5342
12/21/63+	27	4	4. Turn Around folk tune introduced in 1959 by Harry Belafonte	Warner 5396
12/12/64+	13	10	5. Thou Shalt Not Steal all of above produced by Don Ralke and The Wilder Bros.	Warner 5482
			DICKENS, "Little" Jimmy	
			Born on 12/19/20 in Bolt, West Virginia. Country singer who stands only 4'11" tall.	
11/13/65	15	5	1. May The Bird Of Paradise Fly Up Your Nose　　　[N] #1 Country hit (2 weeks)	Columbia 43388
			DICKY DOO AND THE DON'TS	
			Vocal group founded by Gerry Granahan in Brooklyn. Group named after the nickname of Dick Clark's son, Dicky Doo. Group featured Harvey Davis (bass), Ray Gangi (guitar), Al Ways (sax) and Dave Alldred (ex-drummer of Buddy Knox and Jimmy Bowen's Rhythm Orchids).	
2/17/58	28	6	1. Click-Clack Top 100 #28 / Best Seller #29	Swan 4001
5/12/58	40	1	2. Nee Nee Na Na Na Na Nu Nu　　　　　　　[I] Top 100 #40 / Best Seller #42	Swan 4006
			DIDDLEY, Bo	
			Born Otha Ellas Bates McDaniel on 12/30/28 in McComb, Mississippi. Unique and influential R&B-rock & roll guitarist/vocalist. Adopted as an infant by his mother's cousin, Mrs. Gussie McDaniel. Moved to Chicago at age seven. Began recording in 1955 with the Chess/Checker label. A "bo diddley" is a one-stringed African guitar. His first record was a two-sided #1 hit on the R&B charts, "Bo Diddley"/"I'm A Man." Inducted into the Rock and Roll Hall of Fame in 1987.	
10/5/59	20	7	1. Say Man　　　　　　　　　　　　　　　[N] Diddley trades insults with maracas player, Jerome Green	Checker 931

DATE	POS	WKS	ARTIST–RECORD TITLE	LABEL & NO.
			DIESEL	
			Rock quartet from Holland: Rob Vunderink (vocals, guitar), Mark Boon (guitars), Frank Papendrecht (bass) and Pim Koopman (drums).	
10/17/81	25	6	1. Sausalito Summernight first released on Regency 96001 in 1981	Regency 7339
			DIGABLE PLANETS	
			Rap outfit from Washington, D.C.: Ishmael "Butterfly" Butler, Mary Ann "Ladybug" Vierra and Craig "Doodle Bug" Irving.	
1/30/93	15	13	● 1. Rebirth Of Slick (Cool Like Dat) Sales #5 / Airplay #26	Pendulum 64674
			DIGITAL UNDERGROUND	
			Rap-funk crew based in Northern California. Features vocalist Eddie "Humpty-Hump" Humphrey. Appeared in the movie *Nothing But Trouble*. 2 Pac was a member in 1991.	
4/14/90	11	14	▲ 1. The Humpty Dance Sales #5 / Airplay #25	Tommy Boy 7944
1/11/92	40	1	● 2. Kiss You Back Sales #23 / Airplay #50; samples Funkadelic's "(not just) Knee Deep - Part I"; cassette maxi-single	Tommy Boy 993
			DINNING, Mark	
			Born on 8/17/33 in Drury, Oklahoma. Died of a heart attack on 3/22/86. Brother of the Dinning Sisters vocal trio. First recorded for MGM in 1957.	
1/4/60	1 (2)	14	● 1. **Teen Angel** written by Mark's sister, Jeannie	MGM 12845
			DINO	
			Born Dino Esposito on 7/20/63 in Encino, California; raised in Hawaii and Connecticut. Former DJ/music director at KCEP in Las Vegas.	
6/24/89	7	14	● 1. **I Like It** Sales #6 / Airplay #7	4th & B'way 7483
10/14/89	23	6	2. Sunshine Airplay #23 / Sales #25	4th & B'way 7489
9/1/90	6	10	3. **Romeo** Airplay #7 / Sales #8	Island 878012
12/22/90+	31	5	4. Gentle Sales #28 / Airplay #38; Delona Tanner (female vocal)	Island 878472
8/7/93	27	11	5. Ooh Child Airplay #16 / Sales #62	EastWest 98398
			DINO, Kenny	
			Born on 9/12/39 in Hicksville, Long Island, New York.	
12/4/61	24	6	1. Your Ma Said You Cried In Your Sleep Last Night	Musicor 1013
			DINO, Paul	
			Born Paul Dino Bertuccini, Jr., on 3/2/35 in Philadelphia. Married for a time to Justine Correlli, a regular on TV's "American Bandstand."	
4/10/61	38	1	1. Ginnie Bell	Promo 2180

DATE	POS	WKS	ARTIST—RECORD TITLE	LABEL & NO.

DINO, DESI & BILLY

Dino (Dean Martin's son, Dean Martin, Jr.), Desi (Lucille Ball and Desi Arnaz's son, Desiderio Arnaz IV) & Billy (a schoolmate from Beverly Hills, William Hinsche). Dino (formerly married to Olympic skater Dorothy Hamill) was killed on 3/21/87 (age 35) when his Air National Guard jet crashed.

DATE	POS	WKS	ARTIST—RECORD TITLE	LABEL & NO.
7/24/65	17	7	1. I'm A Fool	Reprise 0367
10/16/65	25	5	2. Not The Lovin' Kind	Reprise 0401

DION (DION and THE BELMONTS)

Born Dion DiMucci on 7/18/39 in the Bronx. First recorded as Dion & The Timberlanes on Mohawk in 1957. Formed vocal group, Dion & The Belmonts, in the Bronx in 1958. Consisted of Dion (lead), Angelo D'Aleo (born 2/3/40; first tenor), Fred Milano (born 8/22/39; second tenor) and Carlo Mastrangelo (born 10/5/38; bass). Named for Belmont Avenue in the Bronx. Angelo was in the Navy in 1959 and missed some recording and picture sessions. Dion went solo in 1960 as did The Belmonts. Brief reunion with The Belmonts in 1967 and 1972, periodically since then. Also records contemporary Christian songs. Inducted into the Rock and Roll Hall of Fame in 1989.

DION AND THE BELMONTS:

DATE	POS	WKS	ARTIST—RECORD TITLE	LABEL & NO.
5/26/58	22	10	1. I Wonder Why Top 100 #22 / Best Seller #24	Laurie 3013
9/15/58	19	8	2. No One Knows Best Seller #19 end / Hot 100 #24	Laurie 3015
1/5/59	40	1	3. Don't Pity Me	Laurie 3021
4/27/59	5	13	4. **A Teenager In Love**	Laurie 3027
1/11/60	3	11	5. **Where Or When** #1 hit for Hal Kemp & His Orchestra in 1937 (from the Rodgers & Hart musical *Babes In Arms* starring Mitzi Green)	Laurie 3044
5/16/60	30	2	6. When You Wish Upon A Star from the Disney animated movie *Pinocchio*; #1 hit for Glenn Miller in 1940	Laurie 3052
8/15/60	38	1	7. In The Still Of The Night the Cole Porter classic; #3 hit for Tommy Dorsey in 1937	Laurie 3059

DION:

DATE	POS	WKS	ARTIST—RECORD TITLE	LABEL & NO.
11/14/60	12	11	8. Lonely Teenager	Laurie 3070
10/2/61	1 (2)	12	● 9. **Runaround Sue**	Laurie 3110
12/18/61+	2 (1)	13	10. **The Wanderer/**	
12/18/61	36	1	11. The Majestic	Laurie 3115
5/5/62	3	9	12. **Lovers Who Wander**	Laurie 3123
7/21/62	8	8	13. **Little Diane**	Laurie 3134
11/24/62	10	9	14. **Love Came To Me**	Laurie 3145
1/26/63	2 (3)	11	15. **Ruby Baby** #10 R&B hit for The Drifters in 1956	Columbia 42662
3/30/63	21	6	16. Sandy	Laurie 3153
5/4/63	21	6	17. This Little Girl	Columbia 42776
7/27/63	31	3	18. Be Careful Of Stones That You Throw recorded in 1952 by Hank Williams (as Luke The Drifter) on MGM 11309	Columbia 42810

DION DI MUCI:

DATE	POS	WKS	ARTIST—RECORD TITLE	LABEL & NO.
9/28/63	6	8	19. **Donna The Prima Donna**	Columbia 42852

DATE	POS	WKS	ARTIST–RECORD TITLE	LABEL & NO.
11/23/63	6	9	20. **Drip Drop** Del Satins (backing vocals, above 12 - except #18)	Columbia 42917
			DION:	
11/2/68	4	12	● 21. **Abraham, Martin And John** a tribute to Lincoln, King and John and Robert Kennedy	Laurie 3464

DION, Celine

Born on 3/30/68 in Charlemagne, Quebec. Popular singer in France and Canada since her teen years. Youngest of 14 children. Married her longtime manager, Rene Angelil, late 1994.

DATE	POS	WKS	ARTIST–RECORD TITLE	LABEL & NO.
1/5/91	4	15	1. **Where Does My Heart Beat Now** Airplay #3 / Sales #9	Epic 73536
6/1/91	35	1	2. (If There Was) Any Other Way Airplay #28	Epic 73665
2/22/92	9	14	▲ 3. **Beauty And The Beast** **CELINE DION and PEABO BRYSON** Sales #8 / Airplay #17; title song from the Disney animated movie	Epic 74090
5/9/92	4	19	4. **If You Asked Me To** Airplay #3 / Sales #11; #1 Adult Contemporary hit (3 weeks)	Epic 74277
9/12/92	29	6	5. Nothing Broken But My Heart Airplay #35 / Sales #49; #1 Adult Contemporary hit (1 week)	Epic 74336
1/23/93	36	3	6. Love Can Move Mountains Airplay #35; above 4 from the album Celine Dion	Epic 74337
8/28/93	23	7	7. When I Fall In Love **CELINE DION AND CLIVE GRIFFIN** Airplay #28 / Sales #31; from the movie Sleepless In Seattle starring Tom Hanks; #20 hit for Doris Day in 1952	Epic Sound. 77021
12/25/93+	1 (4)	26	▲ 8. **The Power Of Love** Sales #1(5) / Airplay #2; #1 Adult Contemporary hit (4 weeks)	550 Music 77230
5/21/94	23	9	9. Misled Airplay #22 / Sales #52	550 Music 77344

DIRE STRAITS

Rock group formed in London in 1977 by songwriter/producer Mark Knopfler (lead vocals, lead guitar) and his brother David (guitar), with John Illsley (bass) and Pick Withers (drums). David left in mid-1980, replaced by Hal Lindes (left in 1985). Added keyboardist Alan Clark in 1982. Terry Williams replaced drummer Pick Withers in 1983. Guitarist Guy Fletcher added in 1984. Mark and Guy were also members of The Notting Hillbillies in 1990. Dire Straits' 1991 lineup: Knopfler, Illsley, Fletcher and Clark, with Chris White (sax), Paul Franklin (pedal steel), Danny Cummings (percussion), Phil Palmer (guitar) and Chris Whitten (drums).

DATE	POS	WKS	ARTIST–RECORD TITLE	LABEL & NO.
2/17/79	4	12	1. **Sultans Of Swing**	Warner 8736
8/10/85	1 (3)	13	2. **Money For Nothing** Airplay #1(3) / Sales #1(2); Sting (backing vocal, co-writer)	Warner 28950
11/16/85+	7	15	3. **Walk Of Life** Airplay #6 / Sales #8	Warner 28878
3/22/86	19	7	4. So Far Away Airplay #17 / Sales #26	Warner 28789

DIRKSEN, Senator Everett McKinley

Born on 1/4/1896 in Pekin, Illinois. Died on 9/7/69. U.S. senator from Illinois, 1950–69.

DATE	POS	WKS	ARTIST–RECORD TITLE	LABEL & NO.
1/7/67	29	3	1. Gallant Men [S] John Cacavas (orch.); words written by CBS News commentator Charles Osgood	Capitol 5805
			DIRT BAND, The—see NITTY GRITTY DIRT BAND	
			DISCO-TEX & THE SEX-O-LETTES Disco studio group assembled by producer Bob Crewe. Featuring lead voice Sir Monti Rock III (real name: Joseph Montanez, Jr.), owner of a chain of hairdressing salons.	
12/28/74+	10	9	1. **Get Dancin'**	Chelsea 3004
5/17/75	23	5	2. I Wanna Dance Wit' Choo (Doo Dat Dance), Part I	Chelsea 3015
			DIVINYLS Rock group formed in Australia in 1981: Christina Amphlett (vocals), Mark McEntee (guitar), Bjarne Olin (keyboards), Richard Grossman (bass) and J.J. Harris (drums). Grossman joined the Hoodoo Gurus in 1989. By 1991, group reduced to a duo of Amphlett and McEntee.	
3/30/91	4	12	1. **I Touch Myself** Sales #2 / Airplay #7	Virgin 98873
			DIXIEBELLES, The Black female trio from Memphis: Shirley Thomas, Mary Hunt and Mildred Pratcher. Backed by pianist Jerry Smith (of Cornbread And Jerry).	
10/26/63	9	8	1. **(Down At) Papa Joe's**	Sound Stage 7 2507
2/8/64	15	5	2. Southtown, U.S.A.	Sound Stage 7 2517
			DIXIE CUPS, The Black female trio from New Orleans: Barbara Ann Hawkins (born 10/23/43), her sister Rosa Lee Hawkins (born 9/24/44) and their cousin Joan Marie Johnson. Discovered by singer/producer Joe Jones.	
5/16/64	1 (3)	11	1. **Chapel Of Love**	Red Bird 001
8/1/64	12	7	2. People Say	Red Bird 006
11/21/64	39	1	3. You Should Have Seen The Way He Looked At Me	Red Bird 012
5/1/65	20	5	4. Iko Iko	Red Bird 024
			D.J. JAZZY JEFF & THE FRESH PRINCE Philadelphia rap duo: D.J. Jeff Townes (born 1/22/65) and rapper Will Smith (born 9/25/68). Smith stars in the hit TV sitcom "Fresh Prince of Bel Aire"; appeared in the movies *Made In America* and *Six Degrees Of Separation*.	
6/18/88	12	10	● 1. Parents Just Don't Understand Sales #6 / Airplay #19	Jive 1099
8/20/88	15	9	2. A Nightmare On My Street Sales #10 / Airplay #22	Jive 1124
6/29/91	4	13	▲ 3. **Summertime** Sales #2 / Airplay #10; samples Kool & The Gang's "Summer Madness"; #1 R&B hit (1 week)	Jive 1465
11/2/91	20	6	● 4. Ring My Bell Sales #9 / Airplay #54	Jive 42024

DATE	POS	WKS	ARTIST–RECORD TITLE	LABEL & NO.
8/21/93	13	13	**JAZZY JEFF & FRESH PRINCE:** ● 5. Boom! Shake The Room Sales #3 / Airplay #51; samples "Funky Worm" by the Bar-Kays	Jive 42108
			D MOB—see DENNIS, Cathy	
			D.N.A.—see VEGA, Suzanne	
			DOBKINS, Carl, Jr.	
			Born Carl Edward Dobkins on 1/13/41 in Cincinnati. "Junior" added to last name when Carl started singing at age 16. First recorded for Fraternity in 1958. Left music, mid-1960s.	
6/1/59	3	16	1. **My Heart Is An Open Book**	Decca 30803
1/18/60	25	8	2. Lucky Devil	Decca 31020
			DR. BUZZARD'S ORIGINAL "SAVANNAH" BAND	
			New York City 1930s-styled disco group formed by brothers Stony Browder and August Darnell (real name: Thomas August Darnell Browder), with Cory Daye, lead singer. Darnell left in 1980 to form Kid Creole & The Coconuts.	
12/11/76+	27	8	1. Whispering/Cherchez La Femme/Se Si Bon "Whispering" was a #1 hit for Paul Whiteman in 1920; "Se Si Bon" was a #8 hit for Eartha Kitt in 1953	RCA 10827
			DR. DRE	
			Real name: Andre Young, co-founder of N.W.A. and World Class Wreckin' Cru. Raised in Compton, California. Produced Eazy-E, The D.O.C. and Michel'le. Founded Death Row Records in 1992. Half-brother of Warren G.	
2/13/93	2 (1)	24	▲ 1. **Nuthin' But A "G" Thang** Sales #1(1) / Airplay #10; samples Leon Haywood's "I Want'a Do Something Freaky To You"; #1 R&B hit (2 weeks); "G": Gangsta	Death Row 53819
6/5/93	8	14	● 2. **Dre Day** Sales #4 / Airplay #17; Snoop Doggy Dogg (featured rapper, above 2)	Death Row 53827
10/9/93	34	5	3. Let Me Ride Sales #26 / Airplay #44; George Clinton (special guest); samples Parliament's "Mothership Connection (Star Child)"	Death Row 53839
3/25/95	10	18	● 4. **Keep Their Heads Ringin'** Sales #6 / Airplay #31; from the movie Friday starring Ice Cube	Priority 53188
			DR. HOOK	
			Group formed in New Jersey in 1968. Fronted by vocalists/guitarists Ray Sawyer (born 2/1/37; dubbed "Dr. Hook" because of eye patch) and Dennis Locorriere (born 6/13/49). Appeared in and performed the music for the movie *Who Is Harry Kellerman And Why Is He Saying Those Terrible Things About Me?*.	
			DR. HOOK AND THE MEDICINE SHOW:	
5/6/72	5	10	● 1. **Sylvia's Mother**	Columbia 45562
2/3/73	6	11	● 2. **The Cover Of "Rolling Stone"** [N] group actually featured on the cover of *Rolling Stone* magazine on 3/29/73	Columbia 45732
			DR. HOOK:	
2/7/76	6	14	● 3. **Only Sixteen**	Capitol 4171

DATE	POS	WKS	ARTIST–RECORD TITLE	LABEL & NO.
7/31/76	**11**	14	4. A Little Bit More	Capitol 4280
10/14/78+	**6**	16	● 5. **Sharing The Night Together**	Capitol 4621
6/2/79	**6**	16	● 6. **When You're In Love With A Beautiful Woman**	Capitol 4705
11/3/79+	**12**	14	7. Better Love Next Time	Capitol 4785
3/15/80	**5**	15	● 8. **Sexy Eyes**	Capitol 4831
11/29/80	**34**	6	9. Girls Can Get It	Casablanca 2314
3/27/82	**25**	6	10. Baby Makes Her Blue Jeans Talk	Casablanca 2347

DR. JOHN

Born Malcolm "Mac" Rebennack on 11/21/40 in New Orleans. Pioneer "swamp rock"-styled instrumentalist.

DATE	POS	WKS	ARTIST–RECORD TITLE	LABEL & NO.
5/12/73	**9**	13	1. **Right Place Wrong Time**	Atco 6914

DOGGETT, Bill

Born on 2/16/16 in Philadelphia. Leading jazz-R&B organist/pianist. Formed own band in 1938, recorded with the Jimmy Mundy Band in 1939. With the Ink Spots, Illinois Jacquet, Lucky Millinder, Louis Jordan, Ella Fitzgerald, Louis Armstrong, Coleman Hawkins and many others. Formed own combo in 1952. Still active into the '90s with a touring combo.

DATE	POS	WKS	ARTIST–RECORD TITLE	LABEL & NO.
8/25/56	**2 (3)**	22	● 1. **Honky Tonk (Parts 1 & 2)** [I]	King 4950
			Best Seller #2 / Top 100 #2 / Juke Box #2 / Jockey #6; Clifford Scott (saxophone); #1 R&B hit (13 weeks)	
12/15/56+	**26**	5	2. Slow Walk [I]	King 5000
12/2/57	**35**	1	3. Soft [I]	King 5080
			Best Seller #35 / Top 100 #51; #3 R&B hit for Tiny Bradshaw in 1953	

DOLBY, Thomas

Born Thomas Morgan Dolby Robertson of British parentage on 10/14/58 in Cairo, Egypt. Master of computer-generated rock music and self-directed videos. Keyboardist of Bruce Woolley & The Camera Club, and the Lene Lovich band (1979–80). The movie *Howard The Duck* featured Dolby's music under moniker Dolby's Cube. Married to actress Kathleen Beller (Kirby Colby of TV's "Dynasty").

DATE	POS	WKS	ARTIST–RECORD TITLE	LABEL & NO.
3/19/83	**5**	15	1 **She Blinded Me With Science**	Capitol 5204
			first released on Harvest 5204 in 1982	

DOMINO

St. Louis-born rapper Shawn Ivy. Raised in Long Beach, California.

DATE	POS	WKS	ARTIST–RECORD TITLE	LABEL & NO.
12/18/93+	**7**	13	● 1. **Getto Jam**	Outburst 77298
			Sales #3 / Airplay #27	
5/7/94	**27**	8	2. Sweet Potatoe Pie	Outburst 77350
			Sales #18 / Airplay #40	

DATE	POS	WKS	ARTIST–RECORD TITLE	LABEL & NO.
			DOMINO, Fats	
			Born Antoine Domino on 2/26/28 in New Orleans. Classic New Orleans R&B piano-playing vocalist; heavily influenced by Fats Waller and Albert Ammons. Joined the Dave Bartholomew band, mid-1940s. Signed to Imperial record label in 1949. His first recording, "The Fat Man," reportedly was a million seller. Heard on many sessions cut by other R&B artists, including Lloyd Price and Joe Turner. Appeared in the movies *Shake, Rattle And Roll*, *Jamboree!*, *The Big Beat* and *The Girl Can't Help It*. Teamed with co-writer Dave Bartholomew on majority of his hits. Lives in New Orleans with wife, Rosemary, and eight children. Frequently appears in Las Vegas. Inducted into the Rock and Roll Hall of Fame in 1986. Winner of Grammy's Hall of Fame (1987) and Lifetime Achievement (1987) Awards.	
7/16/55	10	13	● 1. **Ain't It A Shame** Juke Box #10 / Best Seller #16 / Top 100 #86 pre; #1 R&B hit (11 weeks)	Imperial 5348
4/7/56	35	1	● 2. Bo Weevil	Imperial 5375
5/5/56	3	18	● 3. **I'm In Love Again/** Juke Box #3 / Best Seller #4 / Top 100 #5 / Jockey #6; #1 R&B hit (9 weeks)	
5/5/56	19	13	4. My Blue Heaven Juke Box #19 / Top 100 #21; #1 hit for both Gene Austin and Paul Whiteman in 1927	Imperial 5386
7/28/56	14	8	5. When My Dreamboat Comes Home Juke Box #14 / Best Seller #21 / Top 100 #22; #3 hit for Guy Lombardo in 1937	Imperial 5396
10/13/56+	2 (3)	21	● 6. **Blueberry Hill** Juke Box #2 / Best Seller #3 / Top 100 #4 / Jockey #7; Grammy Hall Of Fame Award winner in 1987; #2 hit for Glenn Miller in 1940; #1 R&B hit (11 weeks)	Imperial 5407
1/12/57	5	12	● 7. **Blue Monday** Juke Box #5 / Best Seller #9 / Top 100 #9 / Jockey #9; recorded on 3/30/55; from the movie *The Girl Can't Help It* starring Jayne Mansfield; #1 R&B hit (8 weeks)	Imperial 5417
3/9/57	4	14	● 8. **I'm Walkin'** Jockey #4 / Best Seller #5 / Top 100 #5 / Juke Box #5; #1 R&B hit (6 weeks)	Imperial 5428
6/24/57	6	6	● 9. **It's You I Love/** Best Seller #6 / Top 100 #22	
5/27/57	8	13	10. **Valley Of Tears** Best Seller #8 / Top 100 #13 / Jockey #13	Imperial 5442
8/26/57	29	2	11. When I See You Best Seller #29 / Top 100 #36	Imperial 5454
10/21/57	23	6	● 12. Wait And See Best Seller #23 / Top 100 #27; from the movie *Jamboree!* starring Kay Medford	Imperial 5467
12/23/57+	26	9	13. The Big Beat/ Best Seller #26 / Top 100 #36; title song from the movie starring Gogi Grant	
12/30/57+	32	8	14. I Want You To Know Best Seller #32 / Top 100 #48	Imperial 5477
5/5/58	22	7	15. Sick And Tired Best Seller #22 / Top 100 #30; original version recorded in 1957 by Chris Kenner (Imperial 5448)	Imperial 5515
12/1/58+	6	12	● 16. **Whole Lotta Loving**	Imperial 5553
5/25/59	16	7	17. I'm Ready	Imperial 5585
8/10/59	8	10	18. **I Want To Walk You Home/** #1 R&B hit (1 week)	
8/10/59	17	9	19. I'm Gonna Be A Wheel Some Day original version recorded in 1957 by Bobby Mitchell (Imperial 5475)	Imperial 5606

DATE	POS	WKS	ARTIST—RECORD TITLE	LABEL & NO.
11/9/59	**8**	10	20. **Be My Guest/**	
11/9/59	**33**	2	21. I've Been Around	Imperial 5629
2/15/60	**25**	5	22. Country Boy	Imperial 5645
7/4/60	**6**	11	23. **Walking To New Orleans/**	
7/18/60	**21**	7	24. Don't Come Knockin'	Imperial 5675
9/12/60	**15**	9	25. Three Nights A Week	Imperial 5687
11/14/60	**14**	11	26. My Girl Josephine/	
12/5/60	**38**	3	27. Natural Born Lover	Imperial 5704
2/6/61	**22**	6	28. What A Price/	
2/13/61	**33**	4	29. Ain't That Just Like A Woman	Imperial 5723
			#17 hit for Louis Jordan in 1946	
4/3/61	**32**	2	30. Fell In Love On Monday/	
4/17/61	**32**	2	31. Shu Rah	Imperial 5734
6/19/61	**23**	5	32. It Keeps Rainin'	Imperial 5753
7/31/61	**15**	6	33. Let The Four Winds Blow	Imperial 5764
10/23/61	**22**	4	34. What A Party	Imperial 5779
12/25/61+	**30**	3	35. Jambalaya (On The Bayou)	Imperial 5796
			#1 Country hit (14 weeks) for Hank Williams in 1952	
3/17/62	**22**	5	36. You Win Again	Imperial 5816
			#10 Country hit for Hank Williams in 1952	
10/26/63	**35**	2	37. Red Sails In The Sunset	ABC-Para. 10484
			#1 hit for both Bing Crosby and Guy Lombardo in 1935	

DOMINOES—see WARD, Billy

DONALDS, Andru

R&B/reggae vocalist from Kingston, Jamaica.

DATE	POS	WKS	ARTIST—RECORD TITLE	LABEL & NO.
2/4/95	**38**	2	1. Mishale	Metro Blue 58256
			Airplay #49	

DONALDSON, Bo, And The Heywoods

Cincinnati septet led by keyboardist Bo Donaldson (born 6/13/54). Includes Michael Gibbons (vocals), David Krock, Gary Coveyou (married Bo's sister Vicki on 5/25/74), Rick Joswick, Nicky Brunetti and Scott Baker.

DATE	POS	WKS	ARTIST—RECORD TITLE	LABEL & NO.
5/11/74	**1 (2)**	12	● 1. **Billy, Don't Be A Hero**	ABC 11435
8/24/74	**15**	7	2. Who Do You Think You Are	ABC 12006
12/14/74	**39**	1	3. The Heartbreak Kid	ABC 12039

DON & JUAN

Black vocal duo from New York City: Roland Trone (died 1983) and Claude Johnson of The Genies.

DATE	POS	WKS	ARTIST—RECORD TITLE	LABEL & NO.
2/24/62	**7**	9	1. **What's Your Name**	Big Top 3079

DONEGAN, Lonnie, And His Skiffle Group

Donegan was born Anthony Donegan on 4/29/31 in Glasgow, Scotland. Britain's "King of Skiffle." Member of Chris Chris Barber's Jazz Band in 1954.

DATE	POS	WKS	ARTIST—RECORD TITLE	LABEL & NO.
3/31/56	**8**	11	1. **Rock Island Line**	London 1650
			THE LONNIE DONEGAN Skiffle Group	
			Best Seller #8 / Top 100 #10 / Jockey #10 / Juke Box #13; originated in the mid-1930s as an Arkansas prison song; long associated with folk legend Leadbelly	

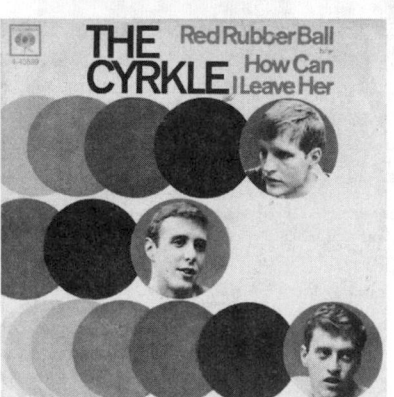

Crosby, Stills & Nash's single "War Games" came from their 1983 live album *Allies*, which—aside from an earlier greatest hits collection—was then the lowest-charting album in the group's once-booming career.

Sheryl Crow's 1994 A&M debut album *Tuesday Night Music Club* boasted such tracks as "All I Wanna Do" and "Strong Enough" and became one of the year's biggest hits. The former backup singer had recorded an earlier album for the label that went unreleased.

The Cyrkle's No. 2 hit "Red Rubber Ball" was well connected in the world of '60s pop. The song itself was co-written by Paul Simon, and the trio's manager was none other than Beatle boss Brian Epstein.

Billy Ray Cyrus's dashing good looks and Top five hit "Achy Breaky Heart" made him one of the most talked-about country artists in years, as well as one very often danced to.

Bobby Darin's remarkably diverse career was celebrated in 1995 by Rhino Records' critically acclaimed 4-CD boxed set *As Long As I'm Singing*. Not included: his 1961 single "Theme From 'Come September.'"

Taylor Dayne's dance-oriented brand of pop brought her seven Top 10 records, but only one—1990's "Love Will Lead You Back"—climbed all the way to No. 1.

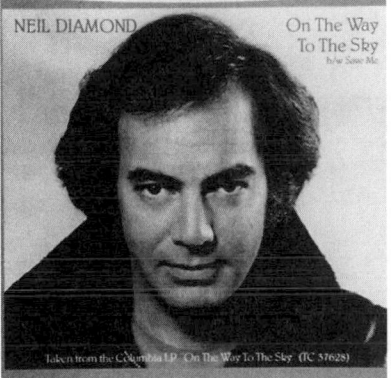

Deadeye Dick's 1994 single "New Age Girl" was noteworthy for bringing the respected R&B-oriented Ichiban label into the pop mainstream, not to mention for cover art that rekindled affection for Pebbles Flintstone.

Jimmy Dean's colorful hit "Big Bad John" held the No. 1 slot for five weeks—longer than any other chart-topper that year except for Bobby Lewis's "Tossin' And Turnin'," which spent seven weeks at the top.

Chico DeBarge's early 1987 single "Talk To Me," which peaked at No. 21, was the singer's only Top 40 achievement. Though his last name was well known, he was never an official member of his siblings' hitmaking group, DeBarge.

Neil Diamond's chart presence—which began in 1966 with his Top 10 hit "Cherry, Cherry"—took an intriguing genre turn in in 1996, when the singer's well-received *Tennessee Moon* set climbed the Country charts.

Dion's first-ever No. 1 single, 1961's "Runaround Sue," was followed by the dual-sided Top 40 hit of "The Wanderer" (which reached No. 2) and its flip, "The Majestic" (which reached No. 36).

Celine Dion's longstanding Canadian success finally took hold in the U.S. with the release of her Top 5 1991 single "Where Does My Heart Beat Now." Her later duet with Peabo Bryson on "Beauty And The Beast" also zoomed into the Top 10 in 1992.

DATE	POS	WKS	ARTIST–RECORD TITLE	LABEL & NO.
8/14/61	5	9	2. Does Your Chewing Gum Lose Its Flavor (On The Bedpost Over Night) [N] #9 hit in 1924 for Ernest Hare & Billy Jones as: "Does The Spearmint Lose Its Flavor On The Bedpost Overnight?"; originally released on Dot 15911 in March 1959	Dot 15911

DONNER, Ral

Born on 2/10/43 in Chicago. Died of cancer on 4/6/84. Narrator for the movie *This Is Elvis*.

DATE	POS	WKS	ARTIST–RECORD TITLE	LABEL & NO.
5/1/61	19	8	1. Girl Of My Best Friend **RAL DONNER & The Starfires** recorded by Elvis Presley in 1960 on his *Elvis Is Back!* album	Gone 5102
7/24/61	4	9	2. **You Don't Know What You've Got (Until You Lose It)**	Gone 5108
11/13/61	39	1	3. Please Don't Go	Gone 5114
2/3/62	18	4	4. She's Everything (I Wanted You To Be)	Gone 5121

DONNIE and THE DREAMERS

Italian-American vocal quartet from New York City. Donnie is Louis Burgio.

DATE	POS	WKS	ARTIST–RECORD TITLE	LABEL & NO.
6/12/61	35	3	1. Count Every Star #4 hit for Ray Anthony's band in 1950	Whale 500

DONOVAN

Born Donovan Phillip Leitch on 5/10/46 near Glasgow, Scotland. Singer/songwriter/guitarist. To London at age 10. Worked Newport Folk Festival in 1965. Wrote score for the movie *If It's Tuesday This Must Be Belgium*. Appeared in the movies *The Pied Piper Of Hamlin* (1972) and *Brother Sun, Sister Moon* (1973). Father of actress Ione Skye (*Say Anything*; married Adam Horovitz [Beastie Boys]) and actor Donovan Leitch, Jr.

DATE	POS	WKS	ARTIST–RECORD TITLE	LABEL & NO.
6/12/65	23	5	1. Catch The Wind	Hickory 1309
8/13/66	1 (1)	10	2. **Sunshine Superman** Jimmy Page (guitar)	Epic 10045
11/19/66	2 (3)	10	● 3. **Mellow Yellow** Paul McCartney (whispering vocals)	Epic 10098
2/25/67	19	5	4. Epistle To Dippy	Epic 10127
8/26/67	11	6	5. There Is A Mountain	Epic 10212
12/9/67	23	5	6. Wear Your Love Like Heaven	Epic 10253
3/30/68	26	5	7. Jennifer Juniper	Epic 10300
6/29/68	5	10	8. **Hurdy Gurdy Man**	Epic 10345
10/19/68	33	4	9. Laleña	Epic 10393
4/26/69	7	10	10. **Atlantis/**	
3/1/69	35	2	11. To Susan On The West Coast Waiting	Epic 10434
8/30/69	36	2	12. Goo Goo Barabajagal (Love Is Hot) **DONOVAN (With The Jeff Beck Group)** all of above written by Donovan; all of above (except #1) produced by Mickie Most	Epic 10510

DATE	POS	WKS	ARTIST–RECORD TITLE	LABEL & NO.
			DOOBIE BROTHERS, The	
			Rock/R&B-styled group formed in San Jose, California, in 1970: Patrick Simmons (vocals, guitar), Tom Johnston (lead vocals, guitar, keyboards), John Hartman (percussion) and Dave Shogren (bass). First recorded for Warner in 1971. Many personnel changes. Michael McDonald (lead vocals, keyboards) joined in 1975. Johnston left in 1978. Johnston wrote majority of hits, 1972–75; McDonald, 1976-83. Disbanded in 1983. Re-formed in early 1988 with Johnston, Simmons, Hartman, Tiran Porter (bass), Mike Hossack (drums) and Bobby LaKind (percussion; died 12/24/92 of cancer).	
9/23/72	11	10	1. Listen To The Music	Warner 7619
2/17/73	35	2	2. Jesus Is Just Alright	Warner 7661
5/26/73	8	11	3. **Long Train Runnin'**	Warner 7698
9/15/73	15	8	4. China Grove	Warner 7728
6/1/74	32	2	5. Another Park, Another Sunday	Warner 7795
1/11/75	1 (1)	12	● 6. **Black Water**	Warner 8062
			originally the B-side of #5 above	
5/17/75	11	9	7. Take Me In Your Arms (Rock Me)	Warner 8092
8/30/75	40	1	8. Sweet Maxine	Warner 8126
5/15/76	13	8	9. Takin' It To The Streets	Warner 8196
1/22/77	37	2	10. It Keeps You Runnin'	Warner 8282
2/10/79	1 (1)	14	● 11. **What A Fool Believes**	Warner 8725
			written by Kenny Loggins and Michael McDonald	
5/19/79	14	9	12. Minute By Minute	Warner 8828
9/15/79	25	6	13. Dependin' On You	Warner 49029
9/6/80	5	11	14. **Real Love**	Warner 49503
12/6/80+	24	7	15. One Step Closer	Warner 49622
			all of above produced by Ted Templeman	
6/3/89	9	9	16. **The Doctor**	Capitol 44376
			Sales #9 / Airplay #11	
			DOORS, The	
			Rock group formed in Los Angeles in 1965. Consisted of Jim Morrison (born 12/8/43, Melbourne, Florida; died 7/3/71, Paris; lead singer), Ray Manzarek (keyboards), Robby Krieger (guitar) and John Densmore (drums). Controversial onstage performances by Morrison caused several arrests and cancellations. Morrison left group on 12/12/70. Appeared in the movie *A Feast Of Friends*. Group disbanded in 1973. 1991 movie *The Doors* was based on group's career; starred Val Kilmer as Morrison. Group inducted into the Rock and Roll Hall of Fame in 1993.	
6/24/67	1 (3)	14	● 1. **Light My Fire**	Elektra 45615
10/7/67	12	7	2. People Are Strange	Elektra 45621
12/30/67+	25	4	3. Love Me Two Times	Elektra 45624
5/4/68	39	3	4. The Unknown Soldier	Elektra 45628
7/13/68	1 (2)	11	● 5. **Hello, I Love You**	Elektra 45635
1/4/69	3	12	● 6. **Touch Me**	Elektra 45646
			last line, "stronger than dirt," sampled from an Ajax commercial	
4/24/71	11	9	7. Love Her Madly	Elektra 45726
7/24/71	14	9	8. Riders On The Storm	Elektra 45738
			DORE, Charlie	
			British female vocalist.	
3/22/80	13	10	1. Pilot Of The Airwaves	Island 49166

DATE	POS	WKS	ARTIST–RECORD TITLE	LABEL & NO.
			DORMAN, Harold	
			Born on 12/23/26 in Drew and raised in Sledge, Mississippi. Died on 10/8/88. To Memphis in 1955; recorded for Sun in 1957. Suffered two strokes in 1984.	
4/18/60	**21**	9	1. Mountain Of Love	Rita 1003
			DORSEY, Jimmy, Orchestra	
			Born on 2/29/04 in Shenandoah, Pennsylvania. Died of cancer on 6/12/57. Esteemed alto sax and clarinet soloist/bandleader. Recorded with his brother Tommy Dorsey in the Dorsey Brothers Orchestra, 1928–35 and 1953–56.	
4/13/57	**2 (4)**	26	● 1. **So Rare** Top 100 #2 / Jockey #2 / Best Seller #3 / Juke Box #6 end; Jimmy (sax); #1 hit for Guy Lombardo in 1937	Fraternity 755
9/9/57	**21**	2	2. June Night Jockey #21 / Best Seller #27 / Top 100 #39; cut 5 days after Jimmy's death, under the direction of Lee Castle (d: 11/16/90); Dick Stabile (sax); Arthur Malvin Singers (vocals, above 2); #2 hit for Ted Lewis in 1924	Fraternity 777
			DORSEY, Lee	
			Born Irving Lee Dorsey on 12/24/24 in New Orleans. Died of emphysema in New Orleans on 12/1/86. Moved to Portland, Oregon, at age 10. Prizefighter in the early '50s as "Kid Chocolate." Major hits produced by Allen Toussaint and Marshall Sehorn.	
9/25/61	**7**	10	1. **Ya Ya** #1 R&B hit (1 week)	Fury 1053
1/20/62	**27**	5	2. Do-Re-Mi	Fury 1056
7/31/65	**28**	4	3. Ride Your Pony	Amy 927
8/13/66	**8**	9	4. **Working In The Coal Mine**	Amy 958
11/19/66	**23**	5	5. Holy Cow	Amy 965
			DORSEY, Tommy, Orchestra	
			Born on 11/19/05 in Mahanoy Plane, Pennsylvania. Choked to death on 11/26/56. Esteemed trombonist/band leader. Tommy and brother Jimmy Dorsey recorded together as the Dorsey Brothers Orchestra, 1928–35 and 1953–56. They hosted a musical variety TV show, "Stage Show," 1954–56. Warren Covington fronted band after Tommy's death.	
9/15/58	**7**	14	● 1. **Tea For Two Cha Cha** [I] **THE TOMMY DORSEY ORCHESTRA STARRING WARREN COVINGTON** Hot 100 #7 / Best Seller #8 end; #1 hit for Marion Harris in 1925	Decca 30704
			DOUBLE	
			Swiss pop duo (pronounced: doo-BLAY) of Kurt Maloo and Felix Haug. Both were in jazz trio Ping Pong.	
8/9/86	**16**	9	1. The Captain Of Her Heart Sales #10 / Airplay #19	A&M 2838
			DOUGLAS, Carl	
			Born in Jamaica; raised in California. Studied engineering in the U.S. and in England.	
11/9/74	**1 (2)**	12	● 1. **Kung Fu Fighting** #1 R&B hit (1 week)	20th Century 2140

DATE	POS	WKS	ARTIST–RECORD TITLE	LABEL & NO.
			DOUGLAS, Carol	
			Born Carol Strickland on 4/7/48 in Brooklyn. Worked on commercials. Member of The Chantels vocal group in the early '70s.	
12/21/74+	**11**	11	1. Doctor's Orders	Midland I. 10113
			DOUGLAS, Mike	
			Born Michael Dowd, Jr., in Chicago on 8/11/25. Longtime syndicated TV talkshow host (1961–80). Singer with Kay Kyser's band, 1945–50 (vocalist on Kyser's #1 hit "Ole Buttermilk Sky" in 1946).	
1/8/66	**6**	7	1. **The Men In My Little Girl's Life**	Epic 9876
			DOVE, Ronnie	
			Born on 9/7/40 in Herndon, Virginia. Discovered while singing in Baltimore. Nearly all of Ronnie's hits were produced by Phil Kahl (vice president of Diamond Records); most were arranged by Bill Justis.	
9/26/64	**40**	1	1. Say You	Diamond 167
11/14/64	**14**	7	2. Right Or Wrong	Diamond 173
4/10/65	**14**	7	3. One Kiss For Old Times' Sake	Diamond 179
6/26/65	**16**	6	4. A Little Bit Of Heaven	Diamond 184
9/18/65	**21**	5	5. I'll Make All Your Dreams Come True	Diamond 188
11/27/65	**25**	4	6. Kiss Away	Diamond 191
			above 4 arranged by Ray Stevens	
2/5/66	**18**	7	7. When Liking Turns To Loving	Diamond 195
5/7/66	**20**	5	8. Let's Start All Over Again	Diamond 198
7/9/66	**27**	4	9. Happy Summer Days	Diamond 205
9/24/66	**22**	5	10. I Really Don't Want To Know	Diamond 208
			#11 hit for Les Paul & Mary Ford in 1954	
12/10/66	**18**	6	11. Cry	Diamond 214
			#1 hit (11 weeks) for Johnnie Ray in 1951	
			DOVELLS, The	
			Vocal group formed at Overbrook High School in Philadelphia. Originally called the Brooktones. Consisted of Leonard Borisoff ("Len Barry"), Arnie Silver, Jerry Gross ("Jerry Summers"), Mike Freda ("Mike Dennis") and Jim Meeley ("Danny Brooks"). Brooks left in 1962. Barry left in late 1963 and recorded solo. Group continued as a trio. Recorded as The Magistrates for MGM in 1968.	
9/18/61	**2 (2)**	14	1. **Bristol Stomp**	Parkway 827
			Bristol: town near Philadelphia	
3/3/62	**37**	2	2. (Do The New) Continental	Parkway 833
6/23/62	**27**	5	3. Bristol Twistin' Annie	Parkway 838
9/15/62	**25**	7	4. Hully Gully Baby	Parkway 845
5/11/63	**3**	11	5. **You Can't Sit Down**	Parkway 867
			DOWELL, Joe	
			Born on 1/23/40 in Bloomington, Indiana. Signed to Mercury's Smash label by Shelby Singleton, Jr.	
7/17/61	**1 (1)**	12	1. **Wooden Heart**	Smash 1708
			based on the German folk song "Muss I Denn"; #1 Adult Contemporary hit (3 weeks); originally sung by Elvis Presley in the 1960 movie G.I. Blues	

DATE	POS	WKS	ARTIST–RECORD TITLE	LABEL & NO.
7/28/62	23	4	2. Little Red Rented Rowboat Stephen Scott Singers (backing vocals); Jerry Kennedy (orch.)	Smash 1759
			DOZIER, Lamont	
			Born on 6/16/41 in Detroit. R&B singer/songwriter/producer. Recorded as Lamont Anthony for Anna in 1961. With the brothers Brian and Eddie Holland in highly successful songwriting/production team for Motown. Trio left Motown in 1968 and formed own Invictus/Hot Wax label. Inducted into the Rock and Roll Hall of Fame in 1990.	
2/16/74	15	9	1. Trying To Hold On To My Woman	ABC 11407
7/6/74	26	6	2. Fish Ain't Bitin'	ABC 11438
			DRAKE, Charlie	
			Born on 6/19/25 in London.	
2/17/62	21	6	1. My Boomerang Won't Come Back　　　　[N]	United Art. 398
			DRAKE, Pete, And His Talking Steel Guitar	
			Drake was born on 10/8/32 in Atlanta. Died on 7/29/88. Was Nashville's top steel guitar sessionman.	
4/11/64	25	5	1. Forever	Smash 1867
			DRAMATICS, The	
			Soul group from Detroit. First recorded for Wingate as the Dynamics, 1966. Members in 1971: Ron Banks (lead singer), William Howard, Larry Demps, Willie Ford and Elbert Wilkins. Howard and Wilkins replaced by L.J. Reynolds and Lenny Mayes in 1973. Reynolds, formerly of Chocolate Syrup, began solo career in 1981. Banks recorded solo in 1983. Drummer Carl Smalls was a member of Undisputed Truth and Sweat Band.	
7/31/71	9	11	1. **Whatcha See Is Whatcha Get**	Volt 4058
3/4/72	5	11	2. **In The Rain** #1 R&B hit (4 weeks)	Volt 4075
			DRAPER, Rusty	
			Born Farrell H. Draper in Kirksville, Missouri. Began career at the age of 12, singing and playing guitar over the radio in Tulsa, Oklahoma.	
8/20/55	18	4	1. Seventeen Best Seller #18 / Top 100 #88 pre	Mercury 70651
10/1/55	3	16	2. **The Shifting, Whispering Sands** Juke Box #3 / Best Seller #6 / Top 100 #7 / Jockey #14; written in 1950	Mercury 70696
12/31/55+	11	12	3. Are You Satisfied? Best Seller #11 / Juke Box #11 / Top 100 #12	Mercury 70757
9/22/56	20	8	4. In The Middle Of The House　　　　[N] Top 100 #20 / Jockey #24; Jack Halloran Singers (backing vocals, above 3); David Carroll (orch., all of above)	Mercury 70921
5/27/57	6	12	5. **Freight Train** Jockey #6 / Top 100 #11 / Best Seller #17; folk song composed in the early 1900s; Dick Noel Singers (backing vocals); Carl Stevens (orch.)	Mercury 71102
			DREAM ACADEMY, The	
			English pop-rock trio: Nick Laird-Clowes (guitar, vocals), Gilbert Gabriel (keyboards) and Kate St. John (vocals).	

DATE	POS	WKS	ARTIST–RECORD TITLE	LABEL & NO.
1/11/86	7	11	1. **Life In A Northern Town** Airplay #4 / Sales #7	Warner 28841
5/31/86	36	3	2. The Love Parade Airplay #32	Reprise 28750

DREAMLOVERS, The

Black vocal quintet formed while in high school in Philadelphia. Backup vocal group for most of Chubby Checker's hits. Named after Bobby Darin's hit record.

DATE	POS	WKS	ARTIST–RECORD TITLE	LABEL & NO.
8/28/61	10	6	1. **When We Get Married**	Heritage 102

DREAM WEAVERS, The

Septet formed at the University of Florida by Gene Adkinson (baritone, ukelele) and Wade Buff (lead vocals). Included Lee Turner, Eddie Newson, Sally Sanborn, Mary Carr and Mary Rude.

DATE	POS	WKS	ARTIST–RECORD TITLE	LABEL & NO.
11/12/55+	7	21	1. **It's Almost Tomorrow** Juke Box #7 / Best Seller #8 / Top 100 #8 / Jockey #10; Jack Pleis (orch.)	Decca 29683
5/19/56	33	1	2. A Little Love Can Go A Long, Long Way **THE DREAM WEAVERS Featuring Wade Buff** from the Goodyear TV Playhouse Production "Joey"; Sy Oliver (orch.)	Decca 29905

DRIFTERS, The

Vocal group formed to showcase lead singer Clyde McPhatter on Atlantic in 1953. Included Gerhart and Andrew Thrasher, Bill Pinkney and McPhatter (who went solo in 1955). Group continued with various lead singers until 1958. In 1958, manager George Treadwell disbanded the group and brought in The Five Crowns and renamed them The Drifters. The majority of The Drifters' pop hits were sung by three different lead singers: Ben E. King (1959–60), Rudy Lewis (1961–63) and Johnny Moore (1957, 1964–66). Rudy died of a heart attack on 5/20/64 (age 27). Many personnel changes throughout career and several groups have used the name in later years. Inducted into the Rock and Roll Hall of Fame in 1988.

DATE	POS	WKS	ARTIST–RECORD TITLE	LABEL & NO.
6/29/59	2 (1)	14	● 1. **There Goes My Baby** #1 R&B hit (1 week)	Atlantic 2025
11/2/59	15	9	● 2. Dance With Me/	
11/23/59	33	5	3. (If You Cry) True Love, True Love Johnny Lee Williams (lead singer)	Atlantic 2040
3/14/60	16	6	4. This Magic Moment	Atlantic 2050
9/19/60	1 (3)	14	● 5. **Save The Last Dance For Me** #1 R&B hit (1 week)	Atlantic 2071
12/31/60+	17	7	6. I Count The Tears Ben E. King (lead singer, all of above - except #3)	Atlantic 2087
4/10/61	32	6	7. Some Kind Of Wonderful	Atlantic 2096
6/26/61	14	8	8. Please Stay	Atlantic 2105
9/25/61	16	9	9. Sweets For My Sweet	Atlantic 2117
3/24/62	28	4	10. When My Little Girl Is Smiling	Atlantic 2134
12/29/62+	5	11	11. **Up On The Roof**	Atlantic 2162
4/6/63	9	8	12. **On Broadway** Phil Spector (guitar solo); Rudy Lewis (lead singer, above 6)	Atlantic 2182
10/5/63	25	5	13. I'll Take You Home	Atlantic 2201
7/11/64	4	12	14. **Under The Boardwalk**	Atlantic 2237
10/10/64	33	5	15. I've Got Sand In My Shoes	Atlantic 2253

DATE	POS	WKS	ARTIST—RECORD TITLE	LABEL & NO.
11/28/64	18	7	16. Saturday Night At The Movies Johnny Moore (lead singer, above 4)	Atlantic 2260
			D.R.S.	
10/30/93	4	15	Male vocal quintet: Endo, Pic, Jail Bait, Deuce Deuce and Blunt. D.R.S. stands for Dirty Rotten Scoundrels. ▲ 1. **Gangsta Lean** Sales #2 / Airplay #13; #1 R&B hit (6 weeks)	Capitol 44958
			DRUSKY, Roy	
6/26/61	35	1	Born on 6/22/30 in Atlanta. Country singer/guitarist; leader of own band, The Loners. Appeared in the movies *The Golden Guitar* and *Forty-Acre Feud.* 1. Three Hearts In A Tangle	Decca 31193
			DUALS	
10/2/61	25	6	Black instrumental duo from Los Angeles: Henry Bellinger and Johnny Lageman. 1. Stick Shift [I] first released on Star Revue 1031 in 1961	Sue 745
			DUBS, The	
11/18/57	23	8	R&B quintet: Richard Blandon (lead; died 12/20/91, age 57), Cleveland Still, Bill Carlisle, Tom Grate and Jim Miller. 1. Could This Be Magic Best Seller #23 / Top 100 #24	Gone 5011
			DUDLEY, Dave	
7/20/63	32	4	Born David Pedruska on 5/3/28 in Spencer, Wisconsin. Country singer/guitarist/songwriter. 1. Six Days On The Road	Golden Wing 3020
			DUICE	
4/10/93	12	26	Male rap duo: Los Angeles-born L.A. Sno and Barbados-born Creo-D. ▲² 1. Dazzey Duks Sales #8 / Airplay #18; title inspired by the short shorts worn by Daisy Duke of TV's "Dukes Of Hazzard"	TMR/Bell. 72501
			DUKE, George—see CLARKE, Stanley	
			DUKE, Patty	
7/17/65 10/30/65	8 22	8 4	Born Anna Marie Duke on 12/14/46 in Elmhurst, New York. Actress. Married actor John Astin. Won an Oscar for her performance in the 1962 movie *The Miracle Worker.* Starred in the TV series "The Patty Duke Show," 1963–65; "It Takes Two," 1982–83; and "Hail To The Chief," 1985. Winner of three Emmys. 1. **Don't Just Stand There** 2. Say Something Funny	United Art. 875 United Art. 915
			DULFER, Candy—see STEWART, David A.	

DATE	POS	WKS	ARTIST—RECORD TITLE	LABEL & NO.
			DUNDAS, David	
			Singer/actor/commercial jingle writer born in Oxford, England.	
11/27/76+	**17**	13	1. Jeans On	Chrysalis 2094
			originally a jingle in England for Brutus Jeans	
			DUPREE, Robbie	
			Born Robert Dupuis in Brooklyn on 12/23/46. Singer/songwriter.	
5/3/80	**6**	15	1. **Steal Away**	Elektra 46621
8/9/80	**15**	12	2. Hot Rod Hearts	Elektra 47005
			DUPREES, The	
			Italian-American vocal quintet from Jersey City: Joseph ("Joey Vann") Canzano (lead singer), Mike Arnone, Tom Bialablow, John Salvato and Joe Santollo. Joey Vann died on 2/28/84 (age 40).	
8/25/62	**7**	9	1. **You Belong To Me**	Coed 569
			#1 hit for Jo Stafford in 1952	
11/10/62	**13**	6	2. My Own True Love	Coed 571
			Tara's Theme from the movie *Gone With The Wind* starring Clark Gable and Vivien Leigh	
9/14/63	**37**	3	3. Why Don't You Believe Me	Coed 584
			#1 hit for Joni James in 1952	
11/30/63	**18**	6	4. Have You Heard	Coed 585
			#4 hit for Joni James in 1953	
			DURAN DURAN	
			Synth-pop-dance band formed in Birmingham, England, in 1978. Consisted of Simon LeBon (vocals), Andy Taylor (guitar), Nick Rhodes (real name: Nicholas James Bates; keyboards), John Taylor (bass) and Roger Taylor (drums). None of the Taylors are related. Group named after a villain in the Jane Fonda movie *Barbarella*. In 1984, Andy and Roger left the group. In 1985, Andy and John recorded with supergroup The Power Station; Simon, Nick and Roger recorded as Arcadia. Duran Duran reduced to a trio in 1986 of Simon, Nick and John. Expanded to a quintet in 1990 with the addition of Warren Cuccurullo (ex-guitarist of Missing Persons) and Sterling Campbell (left by 1993; joined Soul Asylum in 1995).	
1/22/83	**3**	16	● 1. **Hungry Like The Wolf**	Harvest 5195
			first released on Capitol/Harvest 5134 in 1982	
4/9/83	**14**	9	2. Rio	Capitol 5215
			first released on Harvest 5175 in 1982	
6/18/83	**4**	12	3. **Is There Something I Should Know**	Capitol 5233
11/19/83	**3**	12	4. **Union Of The Snake**	Capitol 5290
1/28/84	**10**	10	5. **New Moon On Monday**	Capitol 5309
4/28/84	**1** (2)	15	● 6. **The Reflex**	Capitol 5345
11/3/84	**2** (4)	14	● 7. **The Wild Boys**	Capitol 5417
			Sales #1(2) / Airplay #2	
2/16/85	**16**	8	8. Save A Prayer	Capitol 5438
			Airplay #12 / Sales #21; from the 1982 album *Rio*; "live" version is on the B-side of #14 below	
5/25/85	**1** (2)	13	9. **A View To A Kill**	Capitol 5475
			Sales #1(3) / Airplay #2; title song from the James Bond movie starring Roger Moore	
11/15/86+	**2** (1)	13	10. **Notorious**	Capitol 5648
			Sales #1(1) / Airplay #3	

DATE	POS	WKS	ARTIST–RECORD TITLE	LABEL & NO.
3/14/87	39	1	11. Skin Trade Sales #30	Capitol 5670
			DURANDURAN:	
10/22/88	4	13	12. **I Don't Want Your Love** Sales #3 / Airplay #4	Capitol 44237
1/21/89	22	6	13. All She Wants Is Sales #18 / Airplay #25	Capitol 44287
			DURAN DURAN:	
1/23/93	3	18	● 14. **Ordinary World** Airplay #3 / Sales #6	Capitol 44908
5/8/93	7	16	15. **Come Undone** Airplay #6 / Sales #15	Capitol 44918

DYKE AND THE BLAZERS

Band led by Arlester "Dyke" Christian (born 1943, Brooklyn). With The O'Jays' backing band, the Blazers, in the mid-1960s. Dyke was shot to death on 3/30/71.

DATE	POS	WKS	ARTIST–RECORD TITLE	LABEL & NO.
7/5/69	35	3	1. We Got More Soul	Original Sound 86
11/1/69	36	1	2. Let A Woman Be A Woman - Let A Man Be A Man	Original Sound 89

DYLAN, Bob

Born Robert Allen Zimmerman on 5/24/41 in Duluth, Minnesota. Highly influential singer/songwriter/guitarist/harmonica player. Innovator of folk-rock style. Took stage name from poet Dylan Thomas. To New York City in December 1960. Worked Greenwich Village folk clubs. Signed to Columbia Records in October 1961. Motorcycle crash on 7/29/66 led to short retirement. Appeared in the movies *Don't Look Back* (1965), *Eat The Document* (1969) and *Pat Garrett And Billy The Kid* (1973). Made the 1978 movie *Renaldo And Clara*. New-found Christian faith reflected in his recordings of 1979. Co-starred with Fiona in the 1987 movie *Hearts Of Fire*. Member of the supergroup Traveling Wilburys. Inducted into the Rock and Roll Hall of Fame in 1988. Won Grammy's Lifetime Achievement Award in 1991.

DATE	POS	WKS	ARTIST–RECORD TITLE	LABEL & NO.
5/15/65	39	1	1. Subterranean Homesick Blues B-side "She Belongs To Me" was a hit for Rick Nelson in 1969	Columbia 43242
8/14/65	2 (2)	9	2. **Like A Rolling Stone** features Al Kooper (later of Blood, Sweat & Tears) on organ	Columbia 43346
10/9/65	7	7	3. **Positively 4th Street**	Columbia 43389
4/23/66	2 (1)	9	4. **Rainy Day Women #12 & 35**	Columbia 43592
7/16/66	20	4	5. I Want You	Columbia 43683
10/1/66	33	3	6. Just Like A Woman	Columbia 43792
8/2/69	7	11	7. **Lay Lady Lay** written for his wife, Sarah Lowndes (married 1965–77)	Columbia 44926
12/25/71+	33	4	8. George Jackson Jackson: black militant shot to death in a prison riot	Columbia 45516
9/29/73	12	11	9. Knockin' On Heaven's Door	Columbia 45913
3/29/75	31	3	10. Tangled Up In Blue	Columbia 10106
1/3/76	33	3	11. Hurricane (Part I) dedicated to boxer Rubin "Hurricane" Carter, a convicted murderer	Columbia 10245
10/6/79	24	6	12. Gotta Serve Somebody all of above written by Dylan	Columbia 11072

DATE	POS	WKS	ARTIST–RECORD TITLE	LABEL & NO.
			DYSON, Ronnie	
			Born on 6/5/50 in Washington, D.C.; raised in Brooklyn. Died on 11/10/90 of heart failure complicated by chronic lung disease. Soul singer. Leading role in the Broadway musical *Hair*. Appeared in the movie *Putney Swope*.	
7/25/70	8	9	1. (If You Let Me Make Love To You Then) Why Can't I Touch You? from the off-Broadway musical *Salvation* starring Peter Link	Columbia 45110
4/7/73	28	4	2. One Man Band (Plays All Alone)	Columbia 45776
			E	\
			EAGER, Brenda Lee—see BUTLER, Jerry	
			EAGLES	
			Rock-country group formed in Los Angeles in 1971. Consisted of Glenn Frey (vocals, guitar), Don Henley (drums), Randy Meisner (bass) and Bernie Leadon (guitar). Meisner founded Poco; Leadon had been in the Flying Burrito Brothers; and Frey and Henley were with Linda Ronstadt. Debut album recorded in England in 1972. Don Felder (guitar) added in 1975. Leadon replaced by Joe Walsh in 1975. Meisner replaced by Timothy B. Schmit in 1977. Frey and Henley were the only members to play on all recordings. Disbanded in 1982. Henley, Frey, Felder, Walsh and Schmit reunited in 1994.	
6/24/72	12	8	1. Take It Easy written by Jackson Browne and Glenn Frey	Asylum 11005
9/30/72	9	10	2. **Witchy Woman**	Asylum 11008
2/3/73	22	6	3. Peaceful Easy Feeling above 3 produced by Glyn Johns	Asylum 11013
6/22/74	32	3	4. Already Gone	Asylum 11036
12/28/74+	1 (1)	14	5. **Best Of My Love** #1 Adult Contemporary hit (1 week)	Asylum 45218
6/14/75	1 (1)	14	6. **One Of These Nights**	Asylum 45257
9/27/75	2 (2)	11	7. **Lyin' Eyes**	Asylum 45279
1/17/76	4	14	8. **Take It To The Limit**	Asylum 45293
12/25/76+	1 (1)	13	● 9. **New Kid In Town**	Asylum 45373
3/12/77	1 (1)	15	● 10. **Hotel California**	Asylum 45386
5/28/77	11	8	11. Life In The Fast Lane	Asylum 45403
12/23/78	18	5	12. Please Come Home For Christmas　　　[X]	Asylum 45555
10/13/79	1 (1)	13	● 13. **Heartache Tonight** written by Bob Seger, J.D. Souther, Don Henley and Glenn Frey	Asylum 46545
12/8/79+	8	12	14. **The Long Run** "live" version is on the B-side of #16 below	Asylum 46569
3/1/80	8	12	15. **I Can't Tell You Why**	Asylum 46608
1/10/81	21	7	16. Seven Bridges Road recorded "live" at the Santa Monica Civic Auditorium on 7/28/80; above 13 produced by Bill Szymczyk	Asylum 47100
11/12/94	31	3	17. Get Over It Airplay #40 / Sales #57	Geffen 19376

DATE	POS	WKS	ARTIST–RECORD TITLE	LABEL & NO.
			## EARL, Stacy	
			Born on 12/28/62 in Boston.	
12/21/91+	26	8	1. Love Me All Up Airplay #18	RCA 62116
3/7/92	27	8	2. Romeo & Juliet **STACY EARL (Featuring The Wild Pair)** (Marv Gunn & Bruce Christian); Airplay #22 / Sales #75	RCA 62192
			## EARL-JEAN	
			Ethel "Earl-Jean" McCrea of The Cookies.	
8/8/64	38	1	1. I'm Into Somethin' Good	Colpix 729
			## EARLS, The	
			White doo-wop vocal group from the Bronx: Larry "Chance" Figueiredo, Bob Del Din, Eddie Harder, Jack Wray and Larry Palumbo (died from a blood clot).	
1/12/63	24	4	1. Remember Then	Old Town 1130
			## EARTH, WIND & FIRE	
			Los Angeles-based R&B group formed by Chicago-bred producer/songwriter/vocalist/percussionist/kalimba player Maurice White. In 1969, White, former session drummer for Chess Records and member of The Ramsey Lewis Trio, formed the Salty Peppers; recorded for Capitol. Maurice's brother Verdine White was the group's bassist. Eighteen months later, the brothers hired a new band and recorded as Earth, Wind & Fire, named for the three elements of Maurice's astrological sign. Co-lead singer Philip Bailey joined in 1971. Group generally contained eight to 10 members, with frequent personnel shuffling. Appeared in the movies *That's the Way of the World* (1975) and *Sgt. Pepper's Lonely Hearts Club Band* (1978). Elaborate stage shows featured an array of magic acts and pyrotechnics. Group members Philip Bailey, Wade Flemons, Ronnie Laws and Maurice White had solo hits.	
4/27/74	29	7	1. Mighty Mighty	Columbia 46007
10/12/74	33	2	2. Devotion	Columbia 10026
3/22/75	1 (1)	14	● 3. **Shining Star** #1 R&B hit (2 weeks)	Columbia 10090
7/26/75	12	11	4. That's The Way Of The World	Columbia 10172
12/13/75+	5	12	● 5. **Sing A Song** #1 R&B hit (2 weeks)	Columbia 10251
4/24/76	39	2	6. Can't Hide Love	Columbia 10309
8/14/76	12	12	● 7. **Getaway** #1 R&B hit (2 weeks)	Columbia 10373
12/11/76+	21	10	8. Saturday Nite	Columbia 10439
11/26/77+	13	13	9. Serpentine Fire #1 R&B hit (7 weeks)	Columbia 10625
4/1/78	32	5	10. Fantasy	Columbia 10688
8/5/78	9	9	● 11. **Got To Get You Into My Life** from the movie *Sgt. Pepper's Lonely Hearts Club Band* starring Peter Frampton and The Bee Gees; #1 R&B hit (1 week)	Columbia 10796
12/16/78+	8	11	● 12. **September** #1 R&B hit (1 week)	ARC 10854
5/26/79	6	12	● 13. **Boogie Wonderland** **EARTH, WIND & FIRE with THE EMOTIONS**	ARC 10956
7/28/79	2 (2)	13	● 14. **After The Love Has Gone**	ARC 11033

DATE	POS	WKS	ARTIST–RECORD TITLE	LABEL & NO.
10/31/81	3	16	● 15. **Let's Groove** #1 R&B hit (8 weeks)	ARC 02536
2/12/83	17	10	16. Fall In Love With Me	Columbia 03375

EASTON, Sheena

Born on 4/27/59 in Glasgow, Scotland. Real last name is Orr. Vocalist/actress. Portrayed a singer in the 1980 BBC-TV documentary "The Big Time." Won the 1981 Best New Artist Grammy Award. Portrayed Sonny Crockett's wife in five episodes of TV's "Miami Vice."

DATE	POS	WKS	ARTIST–RECORD TITLE	LABEL & NO.
2/28/81	1 (2)	15	● 1. **Morning Train (Nine To Five)** #1 Adult Contemporary hit (2 weeks); originally titled "Nine To Five," except in U.S. to avoid confusion with Dolly Parton's hit	EMI America 8071
6/6/81	18	9	2. Modern Girl	EMI America 8080
8/22/81	4	14	3. **For Your Eyes Only** title song from the James Bond movie starring Roger Moore	Liberty 1418
12/19/81+	15	12	4. You Could Have Been With Me	EMI America 8101
5/8/82	30	6	5. When He Shines all of above produced by Christopher Neil	EMI America 8113
1/29/83	6	15	6. **We've Got Tonight** **KENNY ROGERS and SHEENA EASTON** #1 Country hit (1 week)	Liberty 1492
9/10/83	9	14	7. **Telefone (Long Distance Love Affair)**	EMI America 8172
2/11/84	25	6	8. Almost Over You	EMI America 8186
9/22/84	7	15	9. **Strut** Sales #4 / Airplay #10	EMI America 8227
1/19/85	9	9	10. **Sugar Walls** Sales #4 / Airplay #12; written and co-produced by Prince (as Alexander Nevermind); above 4 produced by Greg Mathieson	EMI America 8253
11/30/85	29	4	11. Do It For Love Sales #27 / Airplay #29	EMI America 8295
12/24/88+	2 (1)	14	12. **The Lover In Me** Sales #2 / Airplay #4	MCA 53416
12/2/89	36	3	13. The Arms Of Orion **PRINCE with Sheena Easton** Airplay #35 / Sales #37; from the movie *Batman* starring Michael Keaton	Warner 22757
4/20/91	19	9	14. What Comes Naturally Airplay #18 / Sales #19	MCA 53742

EASYBEATS, The

Rock quintet formed in Australia in 1965. To England in 1966. Steven Wright (vocals) and Gordon Fleet (drums) are English. Dick Diamonde (bass) and Harry Vanda (guitar) are Dutch. George Young (guitar; older brother of AC/DC's Angus & Malcolm Young) is Scottish. Young and Vanda formed Flash & The Pan.

DATE	POS	WKS	ARTIST–RECORD TITLE	LABEL & NO.
4/22/67	16	8	1. Friday On My Mind	United Art. 50106

EASY RIDERS, The—see GILKYSON, Terry/ LAINE, Frankie/MARTIN, Dean

ECHOES, The

Brooklyn trio: Tommy Duffy, Harry Doyle and Tom Morrissey.

DATE	POS	WKS	ARTIST–RECORD TITLE	LABEL & NO.
3/27/61	12	9	1. Baby Blue first released on SRG 101 in 1960	Seg-way 103

DATE	POS	WKS	ARTIST–RECORD TITLE	LABEL & NO.

EDDY, Duane

Born on 4/26/38 in Corning, New York. Began playing guitar at age five. At age 13, moved to Tucson, then to Coolidge, Arizona. To Phoenix in 1955, and then began long association with producer/songwriter Lee Hazlewood. Eddy's backing band, The Rebels, included top sessionmen: Larry Knechtel (piano; later with Bread), saxmen Plas Johnson, Jim Horn and Steve Douglas (died of heart failure 4/19/93, age 55), guitarists Al Casey; his wife, Corky Casey; and Donnie Owens; and drummers Jimmy Troxel and Mike Bermani. Billed on most of his records as: "DUANE EDDY His 'Twangy' Guitar And The Rebels." Appeared in the movies *Because They're Young*, *A Thunder Of Drums*, *The Wild Westerners*, *The Savage Seven* and *Kona Coast*. Married to Jessi Colter, 1962–68. Duane originated the "twangy" guitar sound with his '56 red Gretsch 6120 guitar, and is the all-time #1 rock and roll instrumentalist. Inducted into the Rock and Roll Hall of Fame in 1994.

DATE	POS	WKS	ARTIST–RECORD TITLE	LABEL & NO.
7/7/58	6	12	1. **Rebel-'Rouser** [I] Best Seller #6 / Top 100 #6 / Jockey #14 end; The Sharps (later The Rivingtons, rebel yells)	Jamie 1104
9/15/58	27	5	2. Ramrod [I] Best Seller #27 / Hot 100 #28; first released in 1957 on Ford 500 as by Duane Eddy & His Rock-A-Billies	Jamie 1109
11/17/58	15	9	3. Cannonball [I]	Jamie 1111
2/2/59	23	8	4. The Lonely One [I]	Jamie 1117
4/20/59	30	2	5. "Yep!" [I]	Jamie 1122
6/29/59	9	11	6. **Forty Miles Of Bad Road** [I]	Jamie 1126
10/26/59	37	3	7. Some Kind-A Earthquake [I] the shortest record (1:17) ever charted in the Top 40	Jamie 1130
1/11/60	26	5	8. Bonnie Came Back [I] traditional Scottish tune "My Bonnie Lies Over The Ocean"	Jamie 1144
6/6/60	4	12	9. **Because They're Young** [I] title song from the movie starring James Darren and Tuesday Weld	Jamie 1156
10/31/60	27	4	10. Peter Gunn [I] written by Henry Mancini; title theme from the TV series starring Craig Stevens	Jamie 1168
1/16/61	18	7	11. "Pepe" [I] title song from the movie starring Cantinflas	Jamie 1175
4/17/61	39	1	12. Theme From Dixie [I] Anita Kerr Singers & The Jordanaires (vocals); written in 1860	Jamie 1183
8/11/62	33	3	13. The Ballad Of Paladin [I] theme from the TV series "Have Gun-Will Travel" starring Richard Boone	RCA 8047
11/3/62	12	10	14. (Dance With The) Guitar Man	RCA 8087
2/23/63	28	5	15. Boss Guitar Darlene Love & The Blossoms (labeled as The Rebelettes; vocals, above 2)	RCA 8131

EDISON LIGHTHOUSE

British studio group featuring lead singer Tony Burrows (also of The Brotherhood Of Man, First Class, The Pipkins and White Plains).

DATE	POS	WKS	ARTIST–RECORD TITLE	LABEL & NO.
2/28/70	5	12	● 1. **Love Grows (Where My Rosemary Goes)**	Bell 858

EDMUNDS, Dave

Born on 4/15/44 in Cardiff, Wales. Singer/songwriter/guitarist/producer. Formed Love Sculpture in 1967. Formed rockabilly band Rockpile in 1976. Produced for Shakin' Stevens, Brinsley Schwarz and Stray Cats.

DATE	POS	WKS	ARTIST–RECORD TITLE	LABEL & NO.
1/16/71	4	9	1. **I Hear You Knocking** #2 R&B hit for Smiley Lewis in 1955	MAM 3601

DATE	POS	WKS	ARTIST–RECORD TITLE	LABEL & NO.
7/30/83	39	1	2. Slipping Away written and produced by Jeff Lynne (ELO)	Columbia 03877
6/5/61	21	5	**EDSELS, The** R&B quintet from Youngstown, Ohio: George Jones, Jr. (lead; now deceased), Marshall Sewell (bass), Larry Green, Harry Green and James Reynolds. 1. Rama Lama Ding Dong originally released on Dub 2843 in 1958 as "Lama Rama Ding Dong"	Twin 700
1/27/73 5/26/73	3 37	12 2	**EDWARD BEAR** Pop trio from Toronto. Larry Evoy, lead singer. Took name from a character in *Winnie The Pooh*. ● 1. **Last Song** #1 Adult Contemporary hit (2 weeks) 2. Close Your Eyes	Capitol 3452 Capitol 3581
10/16/61	11	9	**EDWARDS, Bobby** Real name: Robert Moncrief. Country singer from Anniston, Alabama. 1. You're The Reason Four Young Men (backing vocals)	Crest 1075
12/4/71+	4	12	**EDWARDS, Jonathan** Born on 7/28/46 in Minnesota. Formed bluegrass band Sugar Creek in 1965. ● 1. **Sunshine**	Capricorn 8021
8/25/58 11/17/58 3/2/59 3/23/59 6/8/59 6/6/60	1 (6) 15 11 27 26 18	19 9 8 4 4 7	**EDWARDS, Tommy** Born on 2/17/22 in Richmond, Virginia. Died on 10/23/69. R&B singer/pianist/songwriter. Began performing at age nine. First recorded for Top in 1949. ● 1. **It's All In The Game**　　　　　　　　　　[R] Hot 100 #1(6) / Best Seller #1(3) end; melody written in 1912 by U.S. Vice President Charles Dawes (under Calvin Coolidge, 1925–29); #1 R&B hit (3 weeks) 2. Love Is All We Need 3. Please Mr. Sun/　　　　　　　　　　　　　[R] 4. The Morning Side Of The Mountain　　　[R] #1, 3, 4: new versions of Edwards's 1951–52 charted hits 5. My Melancholy Baby #9 hit for Walter Van Brunt in 1915 6. I Really Don't Want To Know #11 hit for Les Paul & Mary Ford in 1954; LeRoy Holmes (orch., all of above)	MGM 12688 MGM 12722 MGM 12757 MGM 12794 MGM 12890
7/1/78	8	13	**EGAN, Walter** Born on 7/12/48 in Jamaica, New York. ● 1. **Magnet And Steel** Lindsey Buckingham and Stevie Nicks (backing vocals)	Columbia 10719

DATE	POS	WKS	ARTIST—RECORD TITLE	LABEL & NO.
			8TH DAY, The	
			Five-man, three-woman group of R&B session musicians from Detroit. Assembled by producers Holland-Dozier-Holland in 1966.	
6/5/71	11	10	● 1. She's Not Just Another Woman	Invictus 9087
10/16/71	28	6	2. You've Got To Crawl (Before You Walk)	Invictus 9098
			ELBERT, Donnie	
			Born on 5/25/36 in New Orleans. Died on 1/26/89. Vocalist/multi-instrumentalist. First recorded for DeLuxe in 1957. A&R director for Polygram Records, Canada, in the mid-1980s.	
11/20/71	15	8	1. Where Did Our Love Go	All Platinum 2330
2/12/72	22	6	2. I Can't Help Myself (Sugar Pie, Honey Bunch)	Avco 4587
			EL CHICANO	
			Mexican-American band formed in Los Angeles as the VIP's in 1965, featuring Jerry Salas (lead vocals).	
5/2/70	28	5	1. Viva Tirado - Part I [I] first released on Gordo 703 in 1970	Kapp 2085
12/22/73	40	1	2. Tell Her She's Lovely	MCA 40104
			EL DORADOS, The	
			Chicago R&B quintet featuring Pirkle Lee Moses, Jr., lead singer.	
10/15/55	17	6	1. At My Front Door Best Seller #17 / Top 100 #35; #1 R&B hit (1 week)	Vee-Jay 147
			ELECTRIC INDIAN, The	
			Instrumental group assembled from top Philadelphia studio musicians. Some members later joined MFSB.	
8/23/69	16	8	1. Keem-O-Sabe [I] first released on Marmaduke 4001 in 1969	United Art. 50563
			ELECTRIC LIGHT ORCHESTRA	
			Orchestral rock band formed in Birmingham, England, in 1971, by Roy Wood, Bev Bevan and Jeff Lynne of The Move. Wood left after first album, leaving Lynne as group's leader. Much personnel shuffling from then on. From a group size of eight in 1971, the 1986 ELO consisted of three members: Lynne (vocals, guitar, keyboards), Bevan (drums) and Richard Tandy (keyboards, guitar.) Bevan also recorded with Black Sabbath in 1987. Lynne was a member of the supergroup Traveling Wilburys.	
1/25/75	9	10	**1. Can't Get It Out Of My Head**	United Art. 573
12/13/75+	10	12	**2. Evil Woman**	United Art. 729
4/10/76	14	9	3. Strange Magic	United Art. 770
11/13/76+	13	14	4. Livin' Thing	United Art. 888
3/5/77	24	6	5. Do Ya [R] new version of group's first hit (as The Move, #93 in 1972)	United Art. 939
7/9/77	7	16	● **6. Telephone Line**	United Art. 1000
12/10/77+	13	10	7. Turn To Stone	Jet 1099
3/11/78	17	12	8. Sweet Talkin' Woman	Jet 1145
7/29/78	35	3	9. Mr. Blue Sky	Jet 5050
6/2/79	8	11	**10. Shine A Little Love**	Jet 5057
8/11/79	4	11	● **11. Don't Bring Me Down**	Jet 5060

DATE	POS	WKS	ARTIST–RECORD TITLE	LABEL & NO.
11/17/79	37	2	12. Confusion	Jet 5064
1/26/80	39	2	13. Last Train To London	Jet 5067
			above 4 from the album Discovery	
6/14/80	16	8	● 14. I'm Alive	MCA 41246
8/16/80	13	9	15. All Over The World	MCA 41289
8/30/80	8	10	16. **Xanadu**	MCA 41285
			OLIVIA NEWTON-JOHN/ELECTRIC LIGHT ORCHESTRA	
			above 3 from the movie Xanadu *starring Olivia Newton-John*	
			ELO:	
8/8/81	10	13	17. **Hold On Tight**	Jet 02408
11/28/81	38	2	18. Twilight	Jet 02559
7/9/83	19	9	19. Rock 'N' Roll Is King	Jet 03964
			ELECTRIC LIGHT ORCHESTRA:	
3/1/86	18	7	20. Calling America	CBS Assoc. 05766
			all of above written and produced by Jeff Lynne	
			ELECTRIC PRUNES, The	
			Seattle psychedelic rock quintet. James Lowe, lead singer.	
1/21/67	11	8	1. I Had Too Much To Dream (Last Night)	Reprise 0532
4/22/67	27	5	2. Get Me To The World On Time	Reprise 0564
			ELECTRONIC	
			Collaboration between Manchester, England, natives Bernard Sumner (vocalist of New Order) and Johnny Marr (guitarist of The Smiths, The The and Electrafixion). Outside contributors include Neil Tennant (Pet Shop Boys) on backing vocals, Anne Dudley (The Art Of Noise) on strings and David Palmer on drums.	
5/19/90	38	2	1. Getting Away With It *Airplay #33 / Sales #39*	Warner 19880
			ELEGANTS, The	
			White doo-wop vocal group formed in Staten Island, New York, in 1957: Vito Picone (lead singer), Arthur Venosa, Frank Tardogna, Carmen Romano and James Moschella. All were veterans of other groups.	
7/28/58	1 (1)	16	● 1. **Little Star** *Hot 100 #1 / Best Seller #2; tune adapted from Mozart's (age 5)* *"Twinkle Twinkle Little Star"; #1 R&B hit (4 weeks)*	Apt 25005
			ELGART, Larry, And His Manhattan Swing Orchestra	
			Elgart was born on 3/20/22 in New London, Connecticut. Alto saxman in own band and in brother Les Elgart's band.	
7/3/82	31	5	1. Hooked On Swing [I] *In The Mood/Cherokee/American Patrol/Sing, Sing, Sing/Don't Be* *That Way/Little Brown Jug/Opus #1/Zing Went the Strings of My* *Heart/String of Pearls*	RCA 13219

DATE	POS	WKS	ARTIST—RECORD TITLE	LABEL & NO.
			ELLEDGE, Jimmy	
12/25/61+	22	7	Born on 1/8/43 in Nashville. Discovered by Chet Atkins. 1. Funny How Time Slips Away *written by Willie Nelson; produced by Chet Atkins*	RCA 7946
			ELLIMAN, Yvonne	
			Born on 12/29/51 in Honolulu. Portrayed Mary Magdalene on the concept album and in the rock opera and movie *Jesus Christ Superstar*. Joined with Eric Clapton during his 1974 comeback tour.	
5/22/71	28	6	1. I Don't Know How To Love Him *from the rock opera Jesus Christ Superstar*	Decca 32785
11/6/76	14	12	2. Love Me	RSO 858
4/16/77	15	9	3. Hello Stranger *#1 Adult Contemporary hit (4 weeks)*	RSO 871
2/25/78	1 (1)	16	● 4. **If I Can't Have You** *from the movie Saturday Night Fever starring John Travolta; #2 & 4 written by the Bee Gees*	RSO 884
12/1/79	34	3	5. Love Pains	RSO 1007
			ELLIS, Shirley	
			Born in 1941 in the Bronx. Soul singer/songwriter. Was in the group The Metronomes.	
12/7/63+	8	10	1. **The Nitty Gritty** *promo copies released as "The Real Nitty Gritty" by Shirley Elliston*	Congress 202
1/9/65	3	10	2. **The Name Game**	Congress 230
4/3/65	8	7	3. **The Clapping Song (Clap Pat Clap Slap)** *above 3 written by Shirley's manager and husband, Lincoln Chase*	Congress 234
			EMERSON, LAKE & PALMER	
10/21/72	39	2	English classical-oriented rock trio formed in 1969. Consisted of Keith Emerson (with The Nice; keyboards), Greg Lake (King Crimson; vocals, bass, guitars) and Carl Palmer (Atomic Rooster, Crazy World of Arthur Brown; drums). Group split up in 1979, with Palmer joining supergroup Asia. Emerson and Lake re-grouped in 1986 with new drummer Cozy Powell (Whitesnake). Palmer returned in 1987, replacing Powell who joined Black Sabbath in 1990. 1. From The Beginning	Cotillion 44158
			EMF	
			Techno-funk band from Forest of Dean, England: James Atkin (vocals), Ian Dench (guitar), Derry Brownson (keyboards, percussion), Zac Foley (bass) and Mark Decloedt (drums). EMF stands for the name of New Order groupies called the Epson Mad Funkers.	
5/11/91	1 (1)	16	● 1. **Unbelievable** *Sales #3 / Airplay #4*	EMI 50350
10/26/91	18	5	2. Lies. *Airplay #64 / Sales #69*	EMI 50363
			EMOTIONS, The	
			Black female trio from Chicago, consisting of sisters Wanda (lead), Sheila and Jeanette Hutchinson. First worked as a child gospel group called the Heavenly Sunbeams. Left gospel, became The Emotions in 1968. Jeanette replaced by cousin Theresa Davis in 1970, and later by sister Pamela. Jeanette returned to the group in 1978.	

DATE	POS	WKS	ARTIST–RECORD TITLE	LABEL & NO.
7/19/69	39	1	1. So I Can Love You	Volt 4010
7/2/77	1 (5)	17	● 2. **Best Of My Love** #1 R&B hit (4 weeks)	Columbia 10544
5/26/79	6	12	● 3. **Boogie Wonderland** **EARTH, WIND & FIRE with THE EMOTIONS** above 2 produced by Maurice White (Earth, Wind & Fire)	ARC 10956

ENCHANTMENT

Soul quintet formed in 1966 at Pershing High School in Detroit. Did soundtrack for the movie *Deliver Us From Evil*.

DATE	POS	WKS	ARTIST–RECORD TITLE	LABEL & NO.
3/5/77	25	5	1. Gloria	United Art. 912
3/11/78	33	4	2. It's You That I Need #1 R&B hit (1 week)	Roadshow 1124

ENGLAND DAN & JOHN FORD COLEY

Pop duo from Austin, Texas: Dan Seals (born 2/8/48) and Coley (born 10/13/48). In the late '60s, both were members of Southwest F.O.B. Dan, currently a top country artist, is the brother of Jim Seals of Seals & Crofts and cousin of country singers Johnny Duncan, Troy Seals (Jo Ann & Troy) and Brady Seals (Little Texas). Coley appeared in the 1987 movie *Scenes From The Goldmine*.

DATE	POS	WKS	ARTIST–RECORD TITLE	LABEL & NO.
7/10/76	2 (2)	17	● 1. **I'd Really Love To See You Tonight** #1 Adult Contemporary hit (1 week)	Big Tree 16069
10/30/76	10	12	2. **Nights Are Forever Without You**	Big Tree 16079
6/18/77	21	8	3. It's Sad To Belong #1 Adult Contemporary hit (5 weeks)	Big Tree 16088
11/5/77	23	6	4. Gone Too Far	Big Tree 16102
3/11/78	9	8	5. **We'll Never Have To Say Goodbye Again** #1 Adult Contemporary hit (6 weeks)	Big Tree 16110
4/7/79	10	10	6. Love Is The Answer written by Todd Rundgren; #1 Adult Contemporary hit (2 weeks)	Big Tree 16131

ENGLISH CONGREGATION, The

British group. Brian Keith, lead vocals.

DATE	POS	WKS	ARTIST–RECORD TITLE	LABEL & NO.
2/19/72	29	5	1. Softly Whispering I Love You	Atco 6865

ENIGMA

Enigma is producer Michael Cretu. Born on 5/18/57 in Bucharest, Romania. Moved to Germany in 1975. Worked with Vangelis and The Art Of Noise. Featured vocalist is Cretu's wife, Sandra.

DATE	POS	WKS	ARTIST–RECORD TITLE	LABEL & NO.
3/2/91	5	11	● 1. **Sadeness Part 1** [F] Sales #1(2) / Airplay #6; features traditional Gregorian chants backed by a dance rhythm; sadeness (pronounced: sadness) refers to 18th-century French author/libertine the Marquis de Sade	Charisma 98864
3/26/94	4	21	● 2. **Return To Innocence** Sales #5 / Airplay #7	Charisma 38423

EN VOGUE

Female vocal quartet from the San Francisco Bay area. Formed by the production team of Denzil Foster and Thomas McElroy. Consists of Dawn Robinson, Terry Ellis, Cindy Herron and Maxine Jones. Herron married pro baseball player Glenn Braggs in June of 1993 and acted in the movie *Juice*.

DATE	POS	WKS	ARTIST–RECORD TITLE	LABEL & NO.
5/12/90	2 (1)	17	▲ 1. **Hold On** Sales #1(2) / Airplay #8; #1 R&B hit (2 weeks)	Atlantic 87984

DATE	POS	WKS	ARTIST–RECORD TITLE	LABEL & NO.
10/13/90	38	1	2. Lies Sales #32; #1 R&B hit (1 week)	Atlantic 87893
4/4/92	2 (3)	22	● 3. **My Lovin' (You're Never Gonna Get It)** Airplay #1(4) / Sales #6; #1 R&B hit (2 weeks); remix is on the B-side of #4 below	EastWest 98586
6/27/92	6	17	● 4. **Giving Him Something He Can Feel** Airplay #4 / Sales #10; #1 R&B hit (1 week); #28 hit for Aretha Franklin in 1976 as "Something He Can Feel"	EastWest 98560
9/26/92	8	16	● 5. **Free Your Mind** Sales #13 / Airplay #14	EastWest 98487
12/26/92+	15	12	6. Give It Up, Turn It Loose Airplay #12 / Sales #47	EastWest 98455
5/15/93	36	3	7. Love Don't Love You Airplay #28; above 5 from the album *Funky Divas*	EastWest 98432
1/29/94	3	24	▲ 8. **Whatta Man** **SALT 'N' PEPA with En Vogue** Sales #2 / Airplay #4; samples "What A Man" by Linda Lyndell	Next Plat. 857390
			ENYA	
			Born Eithne Ni Bhraonain (Gaelic spelling of Brennan) on 5/17/61 in County Donegal, Ireland. Member of her siblings' folk-rock group, Clannad, 1980–82.	
3/11/89	24	8	1. Orinoco Flow (Sail Away) Sales #19 / Airplay #28; Orinoco is a river in South America	Geffen 27633
			EPPS, Preston	
			Born in 1931 in Oakland. Bongo player. Discovered by Original Sound owner/Los Angeles DJ, Art Laboe.	
6/1/59	14	9	1. Bongo Rock [I]	Original Sound 4
			EQUALS, The	
			Interracial British-Jamaican quintet led by Eddy Grant (guitar) and Derv Gordon (vocals).	
9/28/68	32	6	1. Baby, Come Back	RCA 9583
			ERASURE	
			British techno-soul duo formed in 1985: composer/producer/multi-instrumentalist Vince Clarke and lyricist/vocalist Andy Bell. Clarke was a member of Depeche Mode and half of the duo Yaz.	
9/10/88	12	11	1. Chains Of Love Sales #10 / Airplay #10	Sire 27844
1/21/89	14	9	2. A Little Respect Sales #13 / Airplay #14	Sire 27738
6/4/94	20	15	3. Always Airplay #17 / Sales #40	Mute/Elek. 64552
			ERIC B. & RAKIM—see WATLEY, Jody	
			ERNIE—see HENSON, Jim	
			ERUPTION	
			London-based, techno-funk quintet of Jamaican natives, featuring lead singers Precious Wilson and Lintel.	
6/10/78	18	6	1. I Can't Stand The Rain	Ariola Am. 7686

DATE	POS	WKS	ARTIST–RECORD TITLE	LABEL & NO.
			ESCAPE CLUB, The	
			London-based rock quartet formed in 1983: Trevor Steel (vocals), John Holliday (guitar), Johnnie Christo (bass) and Milan Zekavica (drums).	
9/17/88	**1** (1)	16	● 1. **Wild, Wild West** Sales #1(1) / Airplay #1(1)	Atlantic 89048
1/21/89	**28**	5	2. Shake For The Sheik Sales #24 / Airplay #28	Atlantic 88983
6/29/91	**8**	14	● 3. **I'll Be There** Sales #6 / Airplay #14	Atlantic 87683
			ESQUIRES, The	
			Soul quintet from Milwaukee formed at North Division High School in 1957 by Gilbert (lead singer), Alvis and Betty Moorer (left in 1965). Joined by Sam Pace in 1961, Shawn Taylor in 1965, and Millard Edwards in 1967.	
9/16/67	**11**	10	1. Get On Up	Bunky 7750
12/16/67	**22**	5	2. And Get Away	Bunky 7752
			ESSEX, David	
			Born David Cook on 7/23/47 in London. Portrayed Christ in the London production of *Godspell*. Star of British movies since 1970.	
1/12/74	**5**	14	● 1. **Rock On**	Columbia 45940
			ESSEX, The	
			R&B quintet formed by members of U.S. Marine Corps at Camp LeJeune, North Carolina in 1962. Consisted of Anita Humes (lead), Walter Vickers, Rodney Taylor, Billie Hill and Rudolph Johnson.	
6/22/63	**1** (2)	10	1. **Easier Said Than Done** #1 R&B hit (2 weeks)	Roulette 4494
9/14/63	**12**	6	2. A Walkin' Miracle	Roulette 4515
			ESTEFAN, Gloria/Miami Sound Machine	
			Latin American-flavored Pop music band based in Miami, led by singer Gloria Estefan with her husband, percussionist Emilio Estefan, Jr. Band formed in 1975. Gloria (born Gloria Fajardo, 12/1/57) came to Miami in 1960 from Cuba, where her father was a bodyguard for President Fulgencio Batista. Emilio emigrated in 1965. On 3/20/90, both were involved in a serious crash involving their tour bus, in which Gloria suffered a broken vertebra but recovered fully within a year.	
			MIAMI SOUND MACHINE:	
11/23/85+	**10**	16	● 1. **Conga** Sales #7 / Airplay #12	Epic 05457
3/29/86	**8**	12	● 2. **Bad Boy** Sales #4 / Airplay #9	Epic 05805

7/26/86	**5**	13	3. **Words Get In The Way**
			        Sales #5 / Airplay #8; #1 Adult contemporary hit (2 weeks); "live"
			        version is on the B-side of #11 below
				Epic 06120

12/13/86+	**25**	8	4. Falling In Love (Uh-Oh) Airplay #23 / Sales #27; above 4 from the album *Primitive Love*	Epic 06352
			GLORIA ESTEFAN AND MIAMI SOUND MACHINE:	
6/13/87	**5**	12	5. **Rhythm Is Gonna Get You** Sales #3 / Airplay #6	Epic 07059

DATE	POS	WKS	ARTIST–RECORD TITLE	LABEL & NO.
10/24/87	36	2	6. Betcha Say That *Sales #33 / Airplay #33*	Epic 07371
1/16/88	6	11	7. **Can't Stay Away From You** *Sales #6 / Airplay #6; #1 Adult Contemporary (1 week)*	Epic 07641
3/26/88	1 (2)	14	● 8. **Anything For You** *Sales #1(2) / Airplay #1(2); #1 Adult Contemporary hit (3 weeks); Spanish version is on the B-side*	Epic 07759
6/25/88	3	13	9. **1-2-3** *Sales #3 / Airplay #5; #1 Adult Contemporary hit (1 week); "live" version is on the B-side of #12 below; above 5 from the album Let It Loose*	Epic 07921
			GLORIA ESTEFAN:	
7/22/89	1 (1)	13	● 10. **Don't Wanna Lose You** *Sales #1(1) / Airplay #1(1); Spanish version is on the B-side*	Epic 68959
10/21/89	11	8	11. Get On Your Feet *Airplay #8 / Sales #13*	Epic 69064
1/13/90	6	11	12. **Here We Are** *Airplay #8 / Sales #8; #1 Adult Contemporary hit (5 weeks)*	Epic 73084
2/2/91	1 (2)	14	13. **Coming Out Of The Dark** *Airplay #1(1) / Sales #3; backing vocalists include Jon Secada and Betty Wright; #1 Adult Contemporary hit (2 weeks); Spanish version is on the B-side*	Epic 73666
11/16/91	22	13	14. Live For Loving You *Airplay #15 / Sales #61*	Epic 73962
10/15/94	13	19	● 15. **Turn The Beat Around** *Airplay #13 / Sales #15; from the movie The Specialist starring Sylvester Stallone*	Crescent M. 77630
2/18/95	27	10	16. Everlasting Love *Airplay #20 / Sales #59*	Epic 77756
			ESTUS, Deon Detroit-born black bassist. Formerly with George Michael, Wham!, Marvin Gaye and Brainstorm.	
3/11/89	5	11	1. **Heaven Help Me** **DEON ESTUS (with George Michael)** *Sales #4 / Airplay #6*	Mika 871538
			ETERNAL London female vocal quartet: sisters Easther and Vernette Bennett, with Louise Nurding and Kelle Bryan.	
2/5/94	19	11	1. Stay *Airplay #16 / Sales #24; #6 R&B hit for Glenn Jones in 1990*	EMI 58113
			ETHERIDGE, Melissa Born on 5/29/61 in Leavenworth, Kansas. Singer/guitarist. Studied guitar at Boston's Berklee College of Music. Discovered in Long Beach, California, by Island Records' founder Chris Blackwell.	
5/7/94	25	26	1. Come To My Window *Airplay #10*	Island 858028
10/1/94+	8	29	2. **I'm The Only One** *Airplay #5 / Sales #36; #1 Adult Contemporary hit (2 weeks)*	Island 854068
2/18/95	16	14	3. If I Wanted To *Airplay #18 / Sales #43*	Island 854238

DATE	POS	WKS	ARTIST–RECORD TITLE	LABEL & NO.
			E.U.	
			E.U.: Experience Unlimited. Ten-member R&B male group from Washington, D.C. Gregory "Sugar Bear" Elliott, lead vocals, bass.	
5/14/88	35	4	1. Da'Butt Sales #26; from the movie *School Daze* starring Spike Lee; #1 R&B hit (1 week)	EMI-Man. 50115
			EUROPE	
			Swedish hard-rock quintet: Joey Tempest (vocals), Kee Marcello (guitar), John Leven (bass), Mic Michaeli (keyboards) and Ian Haugland (drums). Founding guitarist John Norum went solo in 1987.	
2/21/87	8	9	1. **The Final Countdown** Sales #6 / Airplay #8; featured in the movie *Rocky IV* starring Sylvester Stallone	Epic 06416
6/6/87	30	4	2. Rock The Night Sales #30 / Airplay #31	Epic 07091
8/22/87	3	12	3. **Carrie** Airplay #1(1) / Sales #5	Epic 07282
9/24/88	31	4	4. Superstitious Sales #29 / Airplay #31	Epic 07979
			EURYTHMICS	
			Synth/pop duo: Annie Lennox (born 12/25/54, Aberdeen, Scotland; vocals, keyboards, flute, composer) and David Stewart (born 9/9/52, England; keyboards, guitar, synthesizer, composer). Both had been in The Tourists, 1977–80. First album recorded in Cologne, Germany, with drummer Clem Burke (formerly of Blondie). Stewart married Siobhan Fahey of Bananarama on 8/1/87. Lennox appeared in the TV movie *The Room*.	
6/18/83	1 (1)	17	● 1. **Sweet Dreams (Are Made of This)**	RCA 13533
10/15/83	23	6	2. Love Is A Stranger	RCA 13618
2/4/84	4	14	3. **Here Comes The Rain Again**	RCA 13725
5/19/84	21	7	4. Who's That Girl?	RCA 13800
8/11/84	29	5	5. Right By Your Side	RCA 13695
5/11/85	5	13	6. **Would I Lie To You?** Sales #4 / Airplay #6	RCA 14078
8/17/85	22	7	7. There Must Be An Angel (Playing With My Heart) Sales #20 / Airplay #25; Stevie Wonder (harmonica)	RCA 14160
11/2/85	18	8	8. Sisters Are Doin' It For Themselves **EURYTHMICS and ARETHA FRANKLIN** Sales #16 / Airplay #25	RCA 14214
8/30/86	14	9	9. Missionary Man Sales #13 / Airplay #17	RCA 14414
11/4/89	40	1	10. Don't Ask Me Why Sales #31; all of above produced by David Stewart and written by Stewart and Annie Lennox	Arista 9880
			EVANS, Paul	
			Born on 3/5/38 in New York City. First recorded for RCA in 1957. Wrote hits "When" for the Kalin Twins, "Roses Are Red (My Love)" for Bobby Vinton, "I Gotta Know" and "The Next Step Is Love" for Elvis Presley. Wrote the scores for the Broadway show *Loot* and the movie *Live Young*.	
10/5/59	9	11	1. **(Seven Little Girls) Sitting In The Back Seat** [N] with the Curls (female backing duo: Sue Singleton and Sue Terry)	Guaranteed 200
2/15/60	16	7	2. Midnite Special #12 R&B hit for Tiny Grimes in 1948	Guaranteed 205

DATE	POS	WKS	ARTIST–RECORD TITLE	LABEL & NO.
5/30/60	**10**	8	3. **Happy-Go-Lucky-Me**	Guaranteed 208

EVERETT, Betty

Born on 11/23/39 in Greenwood, Mississippi. Vocalist/pianist. Performed in gospel choirs. To Chicago in the late 1950s. First recorded for Cobra in 1958. Toured England in the mid-1960s.

DATE	POS	WKS	ARTIST–RECORD TITLE	LABEL & NO.
3/21/64	**6**	10	1. **The Shoop Shoop Song (It's In His Kiss)**	Vee-Jay 585
9/19/64	**5**	11	2. **Let It Be Me**	Vee-Jay 613
			BETTY EVERETT & JERRY BUTLER	
2/15/69	**26**	6	3. There'll Come A Time	Uni 55100

EVERLY BROTHERS, The

Donald (real name: Isaac Donald) was born on 2/1/37 in Brownie, Kentucky; Philip on 1/19/39 in Chicago. Vocal duo/guitarists/songwriters. Parents were folk and country singers. Don (beginning at age eight) and Phil (age six) sang with parents through high school. Invited to Nashville by Chet Atkins and first recorded there for Columbia in 1955. Signed to Archie Bleyer's Cadence Records in 1957. Phil married for a time to the daughter of Janet Bleyer (Chordettes). Duo split up in July 1973 and reunited in September 1983. Inducted into the Rock and Roll Hall of Fame in 1986. Don's daughter Erin was married for a short time to Axl Rose of Guns N' Roses in 1990.

DATE	POS	WKS	ARTIST–RECORD TITLE	LABEL & NO.
5/27/57	**2** (4)	22	● 1. **Bye Bye Love/** Best Seller #2 / Top 100 #2 / Jockey #2 / Juke Box #9 end; #1 Country hit (7 weeks)	
		1	2. I Wonder If I Care As Much Best Seller flip	Cadence 1315
9/30/57	**1** (4)	20	● 3. **Wake Up Little Susie** Jockey #1(4) / Top 100 #1(2) / Best Seller #1(1); #1 Country hit (8 weeks); #1 R&B hit (1 week)	Cadence 1337
2/17/58	**26**	3	4. This Little Girl Of Mine Best Seller #26 / Top 100 #28; #9 R&B hit for Ray Charles in 1955	Cadence 1342
4/28/58	**1** (5)	16	● 5. **All I Have To Do Is Dream/** Jockey #1(5) / Best Seller #1(4) / Top 100 #1(3); #1 R&B hit (5 weeks); #1 Country hit (3 weeks)	
5/12/58	**30**	2	6. Claudette written by Roy Orbison for his wife	Cadence 1348
8/11/58	**1** (1)	15	● 7. **Bird Dog/** Best Seller #1 / Hot 100 #2; #1 Country hit (6 weeks)	
8/18/58	**10**	11	8. **Devoted To You**	Cadence 1350
11/24/58	**2** (1)	11	9. **Problems/**	
12/15/58	**40**	1	10. Love Of My Life	Cadence 1355
4/20/59	**16**	8	11. Take A Message To Mary/	
4/20/59	**22**	6	12. Poor Jenny above 6 (and #1,3,5,19) written by Boudleaux and Felice Bryant	Cadence 1364
8/24/59	**4**	13	13. **('Til) I Kissed You** The Crickets (backing band)	Cadence 1369
1/25/60	**7**	11	14. **Let It Be Me** Archie Bleyer (orch.)	Cadence 1376
5/2/60	**1** (5)	13	● 15. **Cathy's Clown** #1 R&B hit (1 week)	Warner 5151
6/27/60	**8**	9	16. **When Will I Be Loved**	Cadence 1380
9/12/60	**7**	10	17. **So Sad (To Watch Good Love Go Bad)/**	
9/12/60	**21**	7	18. Lucille	Warner 5163

DATE	POS	WKS	ARTIST–RECORD TITLE	LABEL & NO.
11/28/60	22	4	19. Like Strangers	Cadence 1388
2/13/61	7	10	20. **Walk Right Back/**	
2/13/61	8	9	21. **Ebony Eyes**	Warner 5199
6/12/61	27	3	22. Temptation #3 hit for Bing Crosby in 1934	Warner 5220
10/9/61	20	6	23. Don't Blame Me #6 hit for Ethel Waters in 1933; released as 7" E.P. with "Muskrat", "Walk Right Back" & "Lucille"	Warner 5501 (+2)
2/3/62	6	9	24. **Crying In The Rain**	Warner 5250
6/2/62	9	7	25. **That's Old Fashioned (That's The Way Love** **Should Be)**	Warner 5273
12/5/64	31	2	26. Gone, Gone, Gone	Warner 5478
7/8/67	40	2	27. Bowling Green	Warner 7020

EVERY MOTHERS' SON

Rock quintet formed in Greenwich Village, led by brothers Dennis and Lary Larden.

DATE	POS	WKS	ARTIST–RECORD TITLE	LABEL & NO.
5/27/67	6	12	1. **Come On Down To My Boat**	MGM 13733

EVERYTHING BUT THE GIRL

Pop duo formed in London in 1983: Tracey Thorn (vocals) and Ben Watt (guitar, keyboards, vocals). Group name taken from a furniture store on England's Hull University campus.

DATE	POS	WKS	ARTIST–RECORD TITLE	LABEL & NO.
11/11/95+	2 (1)	23↑	● 1. **Missing** Airplay #1(5) / Sales #12	Atlantic 87124

EXCITERS, The

R&B vocal quartet from Jamaica, New York: Herb Rooney, wife Brenda Reid, Carol Johnson and Lillian Walker.

DATE	POS	WKS	ARTIST–RECORD TITLE	LABEL & NO.
12/15/62+	4	10	1. **Tell Him**	United Art. 544

EXILE

Band formed in Lexington, Kentucky, in 1963 as The Exiles. J.P. Pennington, lead singer. Toured with Dick Clark in 1965. Changed name to Exile in 1973. Pennington left band in early 1989, replaced by Paul Martin. A top country act since 1983.

DATE	POS	WKS	ARTIST–RECORD TITLE	LABEL & NO.
8/5/78	1 (4)	17	● 1. **Kiss You All Over**	Warner/Curb 8589
2/3/79	40	1	2. You Thrill Me	Warner/Curb 8711

EXPOSÉ

Miami-based vocal dance trio assembled by producer/songwriter Lewis Martinee. Consists of Miami native Ann Curless, Los Angeles native Jeanette Jurado and Italian-born, New York-raised Gioia Bruno (replaced by Fairbanks, Alaska native Kelly Moneymaker in 1992).

DATE	POS	WKS	ARTIST–RECORD TITLE	LABEL & NO.
2/14/87	5	12	1. **Come Go With Me** Sales #4 / Airplay #6	Arista 9555
5/30/87	5	11	2. **Point Of No Return** Sales #5 / Airplay #6; new version of group's 1985 Dance/Disco hit on Arista 9326	Arista 9579
9/5/87	7	13	3. **Let Me Be The One** Sales #4 / Airplay #7	Arista 9617

Dr. Dre's massive single "Nuthin' But A 'G' Thang" soared to No. 2 in 1993, making producer Andre "Dr. Dre" Young one of the most influential producers in rap history. The record also helped launch the career of rapper Snoop Doggy Dog.

Donovan's 1966 hit "Sunshine Superman" was the Scottish singer's sole No. 1 hit. In the mid-'90s, while the singer signed with producer Rick Rubin's American Recordings label, his son's group Nancy Boy signed their own deal with Elektra.

The Doors' profound influence on pop music—which has resulted in several compilation albums, videos, and a well-known film by Oliver Stone—was not the result of simple hit singles. The group managed only three Top 10 hits, and 1967's "People Are Strange"— which peaked at No. 12—wasn't one of them.

Duane Eddy's "Theme From Dixie"—a twanged-up version of the Civil War-era perennial—reached No. 39 in 1961; one suspects the track would never have been recorded in the more politically correct '90s.

E.U., short for Experience Unlimited, took a very unlikely song title—namely "Da'Butt"—and placed it in the nether regions of the Top 40 in 1988. The tune, from the soundtrack of Spike Lee's film *School Daze*, climbed to No. 35 before bottoming out.

The Everly Brothers' 1962 hit "That's Old Fashioned (That's The Way Love Should Be)" was the duo's 15th—and last ever—Top 10 single.

Nuthin' But A "G" Thang

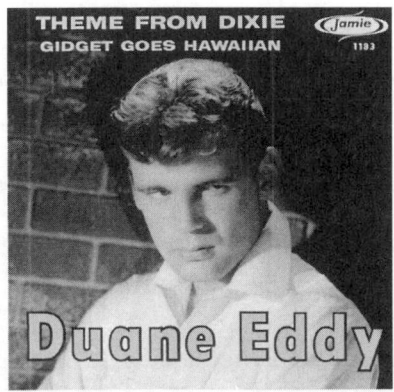

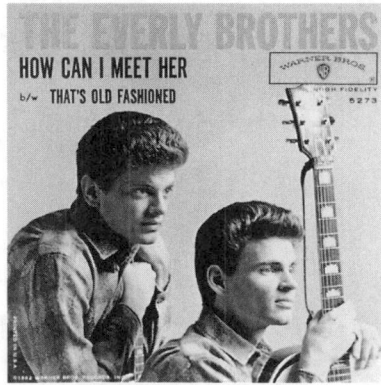

Fabian's pop-star fortunes began to take their tumble in 1960—when after eight Top 40 hits, his "Strollin' In The Springtime" failed to chart entirely.

Percy Faith's instrumental hit "The Theme From 'A Summer Place'" was a nine-week No. 1 hit in 1960. His only other entry into the Top 40, "Theme For Young Lovers," peaked at No. 35 later that year.

Marianne Faithfull's "Go Away From My World" ended her hit single streak by peaking at only No. 89 in late 1965. Beginning with The Rolling Stones-penned "As Tears Go By," the sweet-voiced singer produced four earlier entries into the Top 40.

Ferrante And Teicher's dual-piano approach to MOR music-making produced five Top 40 hits during the '60s, of which only one—1961's "Love Theme From One Eyed Jacks—failed to enter the Top 10.

The Fifth Dimension's late '60s cover versions of Laura Nyro material took "Stoned Soul Picnic," "Sweet Blindness," "Wedding Bell Blues," "Blowing Away" and "Save The Country" into the Top 40. Between the latter two 1970 hits came the non-Nyro track "Puppet Man."

King Floyd's "Baby Let Me Kiss You"—the follow-up to his Top 10 single "Groove Me"—was released on the small Chimneyville label and peaked at No. 29 in 1971. Floyd never had another pop hit again.

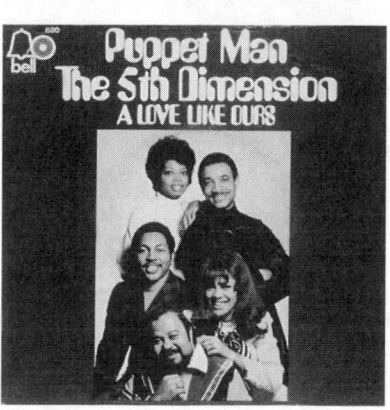

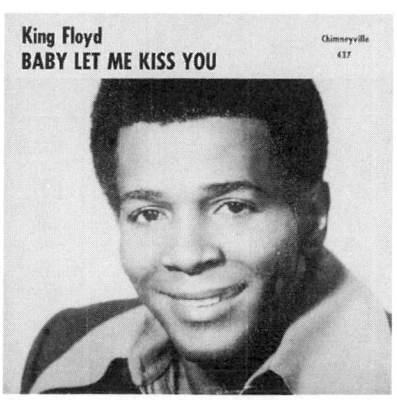

DATE	POS	WKS	ARTIST–RECORD TITLE	LABEL & NO.
12/5/87+	1 (1)	16	4. **Seasons Change** Sales #1(1) / Airplay #2; #1 Adult Contemporary hit (1 week); above 4 from the album *Exposure*	Arista 9640
6/3/89	8	11	● 5. **What You Don't Know** Sales #8 / Airplay #10	Arista 9836
9/2/89	10	12	6. **When I Looked At Him** Airplay #6 / Sales #11	Arista 9868
12/23/89+	9	11	7. **Tell Me Why** Sales #7 / Airplay #13	Arista 9916
4/14/90	17	9	8. Your Baby Never Looked Good In Blue Airplay #11 / Sales #19; above 4 from the album *What You Don't Know*	Arista 2011
11/21/92	28	7	9. I Wish The Phone Would Ring Airplay #21 / Sales #56	Arista 12466
5/15/93	8	21	● 10. **I'll Never Get Over You (Getting Over Me)** Airplay #4 / Sales #14; co-written by Roy Orbison; #1 Adult Contemporary hit (1 week); also on the B-side of #9 above	Arista 12518
			## EXTREME Rock-funk band formed in Boston in 1985: Gary Cherone (vocals), Nuno Bettencourt (guitar; born in Portugal), Pat Badger (bass) and Paul Geary (drums).	
4/13/91	1 (1)	17	● 1. **More Than Words** Sales #1(4) / Airplay #3	A&M 1552
8/24/91	4	17	2. **Hole Hearted** Airplay #6 / Sales #19	A&M 1564
			## EYE TO EYE Pop duo: vocalist Deborah Berg from Seattle and pianist Julian Marshall (of Marshall Hain) from England.	
7/17/82	37	3	1. Nice Girls	Warner 50050

F

DATE	POS	WKS	ARTIST–RECORD TITLE	LABEL & NO.
			## FABARES, Shelley Born Michele Fabares on 1/19/44 in Santa Monica, California. Niece of actress Nanette Fabray. Starred with Elvis Presley in three of his movies. Best known as Mary Stone on "The Donna Reed Show." Married record producer Lou Adler in 1964; later divorced. Cast member of several TV series since 1972, among them "One Day At A Time" (1981–84) and "Coach." Currently married to actor Mike Farrell.	
3/17/62	1 (2)	13	1. **Johnny Angel** The Blossoms (backing vocals)	Colpix 621
6/30/62	21	6	2. Johnny Loves Me	Colpix 636
			## FABIAN Born Fabiano Forte on 2/6/43 in Philadelphia. Discovered at age 14 (because of his good looks and intriguing name) by a chance meeting with Bob Marcucci, owner of Chancellor Records. Began acting career in 1959 with the movie *Hound Dog Man*.	
2/2/59	31	3	1. I'm A Man	Chancellor 1029
4/6/59	9	11	2. **Turn Me Loose**	Chancellor 1033
6/22/59	3	10	3. **Tiger**	Chancellor 1037

DATE	POS	WKS	ARTIST–RECORD TITLE	LABEL & NO.
9/28/59	**29**	3	4. Come On And Get Me	Chancellor 1041
11/30/59	**9**	11	5. **Hound Dog Man/**	
12/7/59	**12**	9	6. This Friendly World	Chancellor 1044
			above 2 from the movie Hound Dog Man *starring Fabian*	
3/14/60	**31**	3	7. About This Thing Called Love/	
3/14/60	**39**	2	8. String Along	Chancellor 1047
			all of above produced by Peter de Angelis	

FABRIC, Bent, and His Piano

Born Bent Fabricius-Bjerre on 12/7/24 in Copenhagen. Head of Metronome Records in Denmark.

DATE	POS	WKS	ARTIST–RECORD TITLE	LABEL & NO.
8/25/62	**7**	12	● 1. **Alley Cat** [I]	Atco 6226
			Danish title: "Omkring et Flygel" ("Around The Piano")	

FABULOUS THUNDERBIRDS, The

Blues-rock band formed in Austin, Texas, in 1977: Kim Wilson (vocals, harmonica), Jimmie Vaughan (guitar; older brother of Stevie Ray Vaughan), Keith Ferguson (bass) and Fran Christina (drums). Preston Hubbard replaced Ferguson in late 1981. Vaughan appeared in the 1989 movie *Great Balls Of Fire* and recorded in The Vaughan Brothers in 1990. Disbanded in June 1990. Reorganized in 1991 with Wilson, Hubbard, Christina and guitarists Duke Robillard and Kid Bangham.

DATE	POS	WKS	ARTIST–RECORD TITLE	LABEL & NO.
5/24/86	**10**	10	1. **Tuff Enuff**	CBS Assoc. 05838
			Sales #11 / Airplay #12	

FACENDA, Tommy

Born on 11/10/39 in Norfolk, Virginia. Backup vocals with Gene Vincent, 1957-58. Nicknamed "Bubba." Discovered by Frank Guida, who wrote Facenda's hit and discovered Gary U.S. Bonds. First recorded for Nasco in 1958. Later became a firefighter in Virginia.

DATE	POS	WKS	ARTIST–RECORD TITLE	LABEL & NO.
11/9/59	**28**	3	1. High School U.S.A. [N]	Atlantic 51 to 78
			first released as "High School U.S.A. Virginia" *on Legrand 1001; Atlantic then released 28 different versions of this record, each mentioning the names of high schools in the following areas: Virginia (Atlantic 51), New York City, North & South Carolina, Washington, D.C., Philadelphia, Detroit, Pittsburgh, Minneapolis & St. Paul, Florida, Newark, Boston, Cleveland, Buffalo, Hartford, Nashville, Indianapolis, Chicago, New Orleans, St. Louis & Kansas City, Georgia & Alabama, Cincinnati, Memphis, Los Angeles, San Francisco, Texas, Seattle & Portland, Denver, Oklahoma (Atlantic 78)*	

FACES

With the departure of lead singer Steve Marriott, who formed Humble Pie, the British rock group Small Faces added, in 1969, former Jeff Beck Group members: Rod Stewart (vocals) and Ron Wood (bass, joined The Rolling Stones in 1976). Other members were Ian McLagen, Kenney Jones (joined The Who in 1978, formed The Law in 1991) and Ronnie Lane (left in 1973, replaced by ex-Free bassist Tetsu Yamauchi). Disbanded in late 1975.

DATE	POS	WKS	ARTIST–RECORD TITLE	LABEL & NO.
11/27/71	**24**	6	1. (I Know) I'm Losing You **ROD STEWART With Faces**	Mercury 73244
1/15/72	**17**	8	2. Stay With Me	Warner 7545

DATE	POS	WKS	ARTIST–RECORD TITLE	LABEL & NO.
			FACE TO FACE	
			Rock group formed in Boston in 1981: Laurie Sargent (vocals), brothers Angelo and Stuart Kimball (guitars), John Ryder (bass) and William Beard (drums). Group appeared as backing band in the movie *Streets Of Fire* for which Sargent recorded actress Diane Lane's vocals.	
7/21/84	38	3	1. 10-9-8	Epic 04430
			FACTS OF LIFE	
			Soul trio formed by Millie Jackson, originally known as The Gospel Truth: Jean Davis (younger sister of Tyrone Davis), Keith William (Imperials, Flamingos) and Chuck Carter.	
4/9/77	31	4	1. Sometimes produced by Millie Jackson; #1 Country hit for Bill Anderson & Mary Lou Turner in 1976	Kayvette 5128
			FAGEN, Donald	
			Born on 1/10/48 in Passaic, New Jersey. Backup keyboardist/vocalist with Jay & The Americans. At New York's Bard College, formed band with Walter Becker and drummer-turned-comic actor Chevy Chase. Fagen and Becker formed Steely Dan in 1972.	
10/30/82	26	7	1. I.G.Y. (What A Beautiful World) I.G.Y.: International Geophysical Year (Jul '57–Dec '58)	Warner 29900
			FAIRCHILD, Barbara	
			Born on 11/12/50 in Lafe, Arkansas; raised in Knobel, Arkansas. Country singer/songwriter.	
5/12/73	32	5	1. Teddy Bear Song #1 Country hit (2 weeks)	Columbia 45743
			FAITH	
			Female R&B singer Faith Evans. Married to rapper The Notorious B.I.G.	
7/15/95	24	12	● 1. You Used To Love Me Sales #13 / Airplay #58	Bad Boy 79025
12/9/95+	21	13	● 2. Soon As I Get Home **FAITH EVANS** Sales #10 / Airplay #64; remix released on Bad Boy 79048	Bad Boy 79040
			FAITH, Adam	
			Born Terence Nelhams on 6/23/40 in London. Actor in movies and on TV. Produced Roger Daltrey's first solo album. Managed Leo Sayer.	
2/20/65	31	2	1. It's Alright **ADAM FAITH With The Roulettes**	Amy 913
			FAITH, Percy	
			Born on 4/7/08 in Toronto. Died of cancer on 2/9/76. Orchestra leader. Moved to the U.S. in 1940. Joined Columbia Records in 1950 as conductor/arranger for company's leading singers (Tony Bennett, Doris Day, Rosemary Clooney, Johnny Mathis and others).	
1/25/60	1 (9)	17	● 1. **The Theme From "A Summer Place"** [I] from the movie *A Summer Place* starring Troy Donahue and Sandra Dee	Columbia 41490
6/27/60	35	1	2. Theme For Young Lovers [I]	Columbia 41655

DATE	POS	WKS	ARTIST–RECORD TITLE	LABEL & NO.
			FAITHFULL, Marianne	
			Born on 12/29/46 in Hampstead, London. Discovered by The Rolling Stones' manager, Andrew Loog Oldham. Involved in a long, tumultuous relationship with Mick Jagger. Acted in several stage and screen productions. Married British art gallery owner John Dunbar, Vibrators bassist Ben Brierly and American playwright Giorgio Dellaterza.	
12/19/64+	22	6	1. As Tears Go By	London 9697
3/27/65	26	5	2. Come And Stay With Me	London 9731
			written by Jackie DeShannon	
6/26/65	32	5	3. This Little Bird	London 9759
9/4/65	24	5	4. Summer Nights	London 9780
			FAITH NO MORE	
			Rock quintet formed in San Francisco in 1980: Michael "Vlad Dracula" Patton (vocals), Jim Martin (guitar), Roddy Bottum (keyboards), Billy Gould (bass) and Mike Bordin (drums). Martin left in 1994, replaced by Dean Menta.	
7/14/90	9	13	● 1. **Epic**	Slash 19813
			Sales #4 / Airplay #19	
			FALCO	
			Born Johann Holzel on 2/19/57 in Vienna, Austria. Male singer/songwriter.	
2/22/86	1 (3)	13	1. **Rock Me Amadeus**	A&M 2821
			Sales #1(3) / Airplay #1(3); tribute to classical composer Wolfgang Amadeus Mozart	
5/17/86	18	8	2. Vienna Calling	A&M 2832
			Airplay #17 / Sales #18	
			FALCON, Billy	
			Born on 7/13/56 in Valley Stream, New York. Rock singer/songwriter/guitarist.	
10/12/91	35	2	1. Power Windows	Jambco 868672
			Sales #73 / Airplay #74; co-produced by Jon Bon Jovi	
			FALCONS, The	
			Detroit R&B group: Eddie Floyd (lead vocals; replaced in 1961 by Wilson Pickett), Bonny "Mack" Rice, Joe Stubbs (brother of the Four Tops' Levi Stubbs), Willie Schofield and Lance Finnie. Backing band, Ohio Untouchables, later became Ohio Players.	
6/8/59	17	10	1. You're So Fine	Unart 2013
			Joe Stubbs (lead singer); originally released on Flick 001 in 1959	
			FALTERMEYER, Harold	
			West German keyboardist/songwriter/arranger/producer. Arranged and played keyboards on the movie scores of *Midnight Express* and *American Gigolo*.	
4/13/85	3	12	1. **Axel F** [I]	MCA 52536
			Sales #2 / Airplay #4; from the movie *Beverly Hills Cop* starring Eddie Murphy (played Axel Foley); #1 Adult Contemporary hit (2 weeks)	

DATE	POS	WKS	ARTIST–RECORD TITLE	LABEL & NO.
			FÄLTSKOG, Agnetha	
			Name pronounced: Ag-nyet-ta Felts-kogue. Born on 4/5/50 in Sweden. Member of Abba.	
10/8/83	29	5	1. Can't Shake Loose	Polydor 815230
			FAME, Georgie, And The Blue Flames	
			Born Clive Powell on 6/26/43 in Lancashire, England. Began as a pianist with Billy Fury's backup group The Blue Flames.	
2/27/65	21	6	1. Yeh, Yeh	Imperial 66086
3/2/68	7	12	2. **The Ballad Of Bonnie And Clyde**	Epic 10283
			GEORGIE FAME	
			inspired by, but not included in, the 1967 movie *Bonnie And Clyde* starring Warren Beatty and Faye Dunaway	
			FANCY	
			English rock quartet. Helen Court, lead singer.	
8/3/74	14	8	1. Wild Thing	Big Tree 15004
11/16/74	19	4	2. Touch Me	Big Tree 16026
			FANNY	
			Female rock quartet from California: vocalists/sisters June and Jean Millington, with Alice DeBuhr and Nickey Barclay. Jean and Alice left in 1974, replaced by Brie Brandt-Howard and Patti Quatro (sister of Suzi Quatro).	
11/6/71	40	1	1. Charity Ball	Reprise 1033
3/15/75	29	4	2. Butter Boy	Casablanca 814
			FANTASTIC JOHNNY C, The	
			Born Johnny Corley on 4/28/43 in Greenwood, South Carolina. Produced and managed by Jesse James.	
11/4/67	7	12	1. **Boogaloo Down Broadway**	Phil-L.A. 305
8/10/68	34	2	2. Hitch It To The Horse	Phil-L.A. 315
			FARDON, Don	
			Born Don Maughn in Coventry, England. Lead singer of English group The Sorrows.	
9/21/68	20	6	1. (The Lament Of The Cherokee) Indian Reservation	GNP Crescendo 405
			FARGO, Donna	
			Born Yvonne Vaughan on 11/10/49 in Mt. Airy, North Carolina. Recorded for Ramco in 1969. Worked as a high school teacher until June 1972. Fargo was stricken with multiple sclerosis in 1979. Has own music publishing company.	
7/8/72	11	10	● 1. The Happiest Girl In The Whole U.S.A.	Dot 17409
11/11/72+	5	14	● 2. **Funny Face**	Dot 17429
			FARRIS, Dionne	
			Female vocalist from Bordentown, New Jersey. Worked with TLC, El DeBarge and Arrested Development.	
2/11/95	4	29	1. **I Know**	Columbia 77750
			Airplay #1(7) / Sales #22	

DATE	POS	WKS	ARTIST–RECORD TITLE	LABEL & NO.
			FASTER PUSSYCAT	
			Hard-rock quintet from Los Angeles: Taime Downe (vocals), Greg Steele and Brent Muscat (guitars), Eric Stacy (bass) and Mark Michals (drums). Michals was replaced by Brett Bradshaw in early 1992. Band name taken from the 1962 action movie *Faster Pussycat! Kill! Kill!*	
4/21/90	28	6	1. House Of Pain Sales #20 / Airplay #39	Elektra 64995
			FAT BOYS	
			Brooklyn-born rap trio: Mark "Prince Markie Dee" Morales, Darren "The Human Beat Box" Robinson and Damon "Kool Rock-ski" Wimbley. Combined weight of over 750 pounds. Appeared in the 1987 movie *Disorderlies*. Robinson died of cardiac arrest on 12/10/95 (age 28).	
8/8/87	12	11	1. Wipeout **FAT BOYS (with The Beach Boys)** Sales #4 / Airplay #20	Tin Pan 885960
7/9/88	16	8	2. The Twist (Yo, Twist!) **FAT BOYS (with Chubby Checker)** Sales #12 / Airplay #17	Tin Pan 887571
			FATHER MC	
			Dancehall reggae singer Timothy Brown. Raised in Brooklyn and Queens. Dropped the M.C. from his name in mid-1993.	
2/16/91	20	8	● 1. I'll Do 4 U **FATHER M.C.** Sales #14 / Airplay #32; samples "Got To Be Real" by Cheryl Lynn	Uptown 53914
2/13/93	37	1	2. Everything's Gonna Be Alright Sales #19 / Airplay #39; samples "Good Times" by Chic	Uptown 54523
			FELICIANO, Jose	
			Born on 9/8/45 in Puerto Rico; raised in New York City. Blind since birth. Virtuoso acoustic guitarist. Composed score for TV's "Chico & The Man." Won the 1968 Best New Artist Grammy Award.	
8/3/68	3	11	1. **Light My Fire**	RCA 9550
10/26/68	25	7	2. Hi-Heel Sneakers	RCA 9641
			FENDER, Freddy	
			Born Baldemar Huerta on 6/4/37 in San Benito, Texas. Mexican-American singer/guitarist. First recorded in Spanish under his real name for Falcon in 1956. Appeared in the movie *The Milagro Beanfield War*. Joined the Texas Tornados in 1990.	
3/8/75	1 (1)	15	● 1. **Before The Next Teardrop Falls** #1 Country hit (2 weeks)	ABC/Dot 17540
7/19/75	8	14	● 2. **Wasted Days And Wasted Nights** originally released on Duncan 1001 in 1959 and Imperial 5670 in 1960; #1 Country hit (2 weeks)	ABC/Dot 17558
11/8/75	20	6	3. Secret Love #1 hit for Doris Day in 1954; #1 Country hit (1 week)	ABC/Dot 17585
3/20/76	32	4	4. You'll Lose A Good Thing #1 Country hit (1 week)	ABC/Dot 17607

DATE	POS	WKS	ARTIST–RECORD TITLE	LABEL & NO.
			FENDERMEN, The	
			Duo of Phil Humphrey (from Stoughton, Wisconsin) and Jim Sundquist (from Niagara, Wisconsin); both were born on 11/26/37. Formed at the University of Wisconsin-Madison.	Soma 1137
6/13/60	5	13	1. **Mule Skinner Blues**	
			written in 1931 by Country great Jimmie Rodgers; originally released on Cuca 1003 in 1959	
			FERGUSON, Jay	
			Born on 5/10/43 in San Fernando Valley, California. Before going solo, formed and led the groups Spirit and Jo Jo Gunne.	
1/28/78	9	12	1. **Thunder Island**	Asylum 45444
6/9/79	31	4	2. Shakedown Cruise	Asylum 46041
			FERGUSON, Johnny	
			Born on 3/22/37 in Nashville. Worked as a DJ in the late 1950s.	MGM 12855
4/18/60	27	3	1. Angela Jones	
			written by John D. Loudermilk	
			FERGUSON, Maynard	
			Born on 5/4/28 in Verdun, Quebec, Canada. Jazz trumpeter. Moved to the U.S. in 1949. Played for Charlie Barnet and then Stan Kenton's Band, 1950–56.	
5/28/77	28	6	1. Gonna Fly Now (Theme From "Rocky") [I]	Columbia 10468
			from the movie *Rocky* starring Sylvester Stallone	
			FERKO STRING BAND	
			Philadelphia string band directed by William Connors. String bands parade annually in Philadelphia's famed New Year's Day Mummers Parade. Also see Nu Tornados.	
6/18/55	14	6	1. Alabama Jubilee [I]	Media 1010
			Juke Box #14 / Best Seller #18; #2 hit for Arthur Collins & Byron Harlan in 1915	
			FERRANTE & TEICHER	
			Piano duo: Arthur Ferrante (born 9/7/21, New York City) and Louis Teicher (born 8/24/24, Wilkes-Barre, Pennsylvania). Met as children while attending Manhattan's performing arts academy Juilliard School. First recorded for Columbia in 1953.	
8/8/60	10	15	1. **Theme From The Apartment** [I]	United Art. 231
			from the Billy Wilder movie *The Apartment* starring Jack Lemmon; 1949 tune originally entitled "Jealous Lover"	
11/28/60+	2 (1)	18	● 2. **Exodus** [I]	United Art. 274
			theme from the Otto Preminger movie starring Paul Newman	
4/17/61	37	1	3. (Love Theme From) One Eyed Jacks [I]	United Art. 300
			from the movie *One Eyed Jacks* starring Marlon Brando	
11/13/61	8	8	4. **Tonight** [I]	United Art. 373
			from the musical *West Side Story*	
11/29/69+	10	11	5. **Midnight Cowboy** [I]	United Art. 50554
			title song from the movie starring Jon Voight and Dustin Hoffman; featuring the "water sound" guitar of Vincent Bell	

DATE	POS	WKS	ARTIST–RECORD TITLE	LABEL & NO.

FERRY, Bryan

Born on 9/26/45 in County Durham, England. Lead singer of Roxy Music. Married socialite Lucy Helmore on 6/26/82.

DATE	POS	WKS		LABEL & NO.
4/16/88	31	3	1. Kiss And Tell Sales #24 / Airplay #34; from the movie *Bright Lights, Big City* starring Michael J. Fox	Reprise 28117

FIELDS, Ernie

Born on 8/26/05 in Nacogdoches, Texas. Trombonist/pianist/bandleader/arranger.

DATE	POS	WKS		LABEL & NO.
10/12/59	4	14	1. **In The Mood** [I] #1 hit for Glenn Miller in 1939	Rendezvous 110

FIESTAS, The

R&B vocal group from Newark, New Jersey: Tommy Bullock (lead), Eddie Morris (tenor), Sam Ingalls (baritone) and Preston Lane (bass).

DATE	POS	WKS		LABEL & NO.
4/27/59	11	11	1. So Fine	Old Town 1062

5TH DIMENSION, The

Los Angeles-based R&B vocal group formed in 1966: Marilyn McCoo, Billy Davis, Jr., Florence LaRue, Lamont McLemore and Ron Townson. McLemore and McCoo had been in the Hi-Fi's; Townson and Davis had been with groups in St. Louis. First called the Versatiles. McCoo and Davis were married in 1969 and have recorded as a duo since 1976.

DATE	POS	WKS			LABEL & NO.
2/4/67	16	7		1. Go Where You Wanna Go	Soul City 753
6/17/67	7	10		2. **Up-Up And Away** above 2 produced by Johnny Rivers (owner of the Soul City label)	Soul City 756
12/9/67	34	1		3. Paper Cup	Soul City 760
2/24/68	29	5		4. Carpet Man above 3 written by Jimmy Webb	Soul City 762
6/22/68	3	12	▲	5. **Stoned Soul Picnic**	Soul City 766
10/26/68	13	6		6. Sweet Blindness	Soul City 768
1/11/69	25	6		7. California Soul written by Ashford & Simpson	Soul City 770
3/15/69	1 (6)	16	▲	8. **Aquarius/Let The Sunshine In (The Flesh Failures)** medley from the Broadway rock musical *Hair* starring Steve Curry; #1 Adult Contemporary hit (2 weeks)	Soul City 772
8/9/69	20	7		9. Workin' On A Groovy Thing written by Neil Sedaka (also #12 below)	Soul City 776
10/4/69	1 (3)	14	▲	10. **Wedding Bell Blues** #1 Adult Contemporary hit (2 weeks)	Soul City 779
1/24/70	21	6		11. Blowing Away above 4 from the album *The Age Of Aquarius*	Soul City 780
5/2/70	24	5		12. Puppet Man	Bell 880
6/27/70	27	5		13. Save The Country #5, 6, 10, 11, 13 written by Laura Nyro	Bell 895
11/21/70	2 (2)	15	▲	14. **One Less Bell To Answer** #1 Adult Contemporary hit (1 week)	Bell 940
3/13/71	19	8		15. Love's Lines, Angles And Rhymes	Bell 965
10/2/71	12	9		16. Never My Love #1 Adult Contemporary hit (1 week)	Bell 45134
1/29/72	37	3		17. Together Let's Find Love above 2 are "live" concert recordings	Bell 45170

DATE	POS	WKS	ARTIST–RECORD TITLE	LABEL & NO.
4/22/72	**8**	13	▲ 18. **(Last Night) I Didn't Get To Sleep At All**	Bell 45195
9/30/72	**10**	12	19. **If I Could Reach You**	Bell 45261
			#1 Adult Contemporary hit (1 week)	
2/10/73	**32**	4	20. **Living Together, Growing Together**	Bell 45310
			from the movie *Lost Horizon* starring Peter Finch; #3–20 produced by Bones Howe	

FIFTH ESTATE, The

Formed in Stamford, Connecticut in 1964 by Wayne Wadhams (composer, keyboards, vocals) and Don Askew (lyricist) as the Demen; recorded on Veep as The "D"-Men. Included Doug Ferrara (bass), Rick Engler (guitar), Bill Shute (guitar) and Ken Evans (drums). Managed by brothers Bill and Steve Jerome.

DATE	POS	WKS	ARTIST–RECORD TITLE	LABEL & NO.
6/10/67	**11**	6	1. **Ding Dong! The Witch Is Dead**	Jubilee 5573
			song originally appeared in the 1939 movie *The Wizard of Oz* starring Judy Garland	

FINE YOUNG CANNIBALS

Pop trio from Birmingham, England: Roland Gift (vocals) and English Beat members David Steele (bass) and Andy Cox (guitar). Band name taken from the 1960 movie *All The Fine Young Cannibals*. Group appeared in the movie *Tin Men*. Gift acted in the movies *Sammy And Rosie Get Laid* and *Scandal*.

DATE	POS	WKS	ARTIST–RECORD TITLE	LABEL & NO.
2/25/89	**1 (1)**	14	● 1. **She Drives Me Crazy**	I.R.S. 53483
			Sales #1(1) / Airplay #2	
5/20/89	**1 (1)**	13	2. **Good Thing**	I.R.S. 53639
			Airplay #1(2) / Sales #2; from the 1987 movie *Tin Men* starring Richard Dreyfuss and Danny DeVito	
8/26/89	**11**	8	3. **Don't Look Back**	I.R.S. 53695
			Sales #8 / Airplay #18	

FINNEGAN, Larry

Born John Lawrence Finneran on 8/10/38 in New York City. Died of a brain tumor on 7/22/73. Moved to Sweden in 1966; headed own record company. To Switzerland in 1967 and back to the U.S. in 1970.

DATE	POS	WKS	ARTIST–RECORD TITLE	LABEL & NO.
3/31/62	**11**	8	1. **Dear One**	Old Town 1113

FIORILLO, Elisa

Los Angeles-based vocalist raised in Philadelphia. Commercial jingle singer as a child. Winner on TV's "Star Search." Signed with Chrysalis in 1985 at age 15.

DATE	POS	WKS	ARTIST–RECORD TITLE	LABEL & NO.
8/15/87	**16**	8	1. **Who Found Who**	Chrysalis 43120
			JELLYBEAN/Elisa Fiorillo	
			Airplay #13 / Sales #14	
12/8/90+	**27**	6	2. **On The Way Up**	Chrysalis 23497
			Sales #23 / Airplay #36	

FIREBALLS, The

Rock and roll band formed while high schoolers in Raton, New Mexico: George Tomsco (born 4/24/40; lead guitar), Dan Trammell (born 7/14/40; rhythm guitar), Eric Budd (born 10/23/38; drums), Stan Lark (born 7/27/40; bass) and Chuck Tharp (born 2/3/41; vocalist). First recorded for Kapp in 1958. Trammell left group in 1959. Doug Roberts (died 11/18/81) replaced Budd in 1962. Tharp quit group in 1960 and was replaced by Jimmy Gilmer (lead vocals, piano). Gilmer was introduced to The Fireballs by their record producer Norman Petty at his famed Clovis, New Mexico, studio.

DATE	POS	WKS	ARTIST–RECORD TITLE	LABEL & NO.
10/26/59	**39**	2	1. Torquay [I]	Top Rank 2008
2/1/60	**24**	6	2. Bulldog [I]	Top Rank 2026

DATE	POS	WKS	ARTIST–RECORD TITLE	LABEL & NO.
8/7/61	27	3	3. Quite A Party [I]	Warwick 644
			JIMMY GILMER AND THE FIREBALLS:	
9/28/63	1 (5)	13	● 4. **Sugar Shack** #1 R&B hit (1 week)	Dot 16487
1/4/64	15	8	5. Daisy Petal Pickin'	Dot 16539
			THE FIREBALLS:	
1/27/68	9	10	6. **Bottle Of Wine**	Atco 6491
			FIREFALL	
			Mellow rock group formed in Boulder, Colorado. Original lineup: Rick Roberts (lead singer), Larry Burnett (guitar), Jack Bartley (lead guitar), Mark Andes (Spirit, Jo Jo Gunne; bass) and Mike Clarke (ex-Byrds; drums). David Muse (keyboards) joined in 1977. Andes joined Heart in 1980. Roberts and Clarke were members of Flying Burrito Brothers. Clarke died on 12/19/93 (age 49) of liver failure.	
9/25/76	9	15	1. **You Are The Woman**	Atlantic 3335
4/30/77	34	3	2. Cinderella	Atlantic 3392
9/17/77	11	12	3. Just Remember I Love You #1 Adult Contemporary hit (2 weeks)	Atlantic 3420
10/28/78	11	10	4. Strange Way	Atlantic 3518
5/10/80	35	3	5. Headed For A Fall all of above (except #3) written by Rick Roberts	Atlantic 3657
2/28/81	37	3	6. Staying With It Lisa Nemzo (female vocal)	Atlantic 3791
			FIREFLIES	
			White doo-wop quartet formed by Gerry Granahan and featuring Ritchie Adams, lead singer (real name: Richard Adam Ziegler).	
9/28/59	21	10	1. You Were Mine	Ribbon 6901
			FIREHOUSE	
			Hard-rock quartet from North Carolina: C.J. Snare (vocals), Bill Leverty (guitar), Perry Richardson (bass) and Michael Foster (drums).	
4/20/91	19	10	1. Don't Treat Me Bad Sales #11 / Airplay #19	Epic 73676
8/3/91	5	16	● 2. **Love Of A Lifetime** Sales #6 / Airplay #10	Epic 73771
9/5/92	8	12	3. **When I Look Into Your Eyes** Sales #11 / Airplay #20	Epic 74440
3/18/95	26	11	4. I Live My Life For You Sales #27 / Airplay #36	Epic 77812
			FIRM, The	
			British supergroup: Jimmy Page (Yardbirds, Led Zeppelin, Honeydrippers; guitar), Paul Rodgers (Free, Bad Company; vocals), Chris Slade (Manfred Mann; drums) and Tony Franklin (keyboards). Disbanded in 1986. Franklin joined Blue Murder in 1989. Slade joined AC/DC in 1990. Rodgers joined The Law in 1991.	
3/16/85	28	6	1. Radioactive Sales #23 / Airplay #28	Atlantic 89586

DATE	POS	WKS	ARTIST–RECORD TITLE	LABEL & NO.
			FIRST CHOICE	
			Female soul trio from Philadelphia, formed as the Debronettes. Consisted of Rochelle Fleming, Annette Guest and Joyce Jones. By 1977, Jones left and Ursula Herring joined. Herring left by 1979 and Debbie Martin joined.	
4/28/73	28	5	1. Armed And Extremely Dangerous	Philly Groove 175
			FIRST CLASS	
			British studio quartet: Tony Burrows (vocals), John Carter, Del John and Chas Mills. Burrows was the vocalist on hits by The Brotherhood Of Man, Edison Lighthouse, The Pipkins and White Plains.	
8/17/74	4	11	1. **Beach Baby**	UK 49022
			FIRST EDITION, The—see ROGERS, Kenny	
			FISCHER, Lisa	
			Native of Fort Greene, Brooklyn, New York. Session singer with Billy Ocean, Melba Moore and others. Touring vocalist with Luther Vandross.	
6/1/91	11	8	1. How Can I Ease The Pain Sales #19 / Airplay #29; #1 R&B hit (2 weeks)	Elektra 64897
			FISHER, Eddie	
			Born Edwin Jack Fisher on 8/10/28 in Philadelphia. At Copacabana night club in New York at age 17. With Buddy Morrow and Charlie Ventura in 1946. On Eddie Cantor's radio show in 1949. In the Armed Forces Special Services, 1952–53. Married to Debbie Reynolds, 1955–59. Other marriages were to Elizabeth Taylor and Connie Stevens. Daughter with Debbie is actress/author Carrie Fisher. Daughter with Connie is singer Tricia Leigh Fisher. Own "Coke Time" 15-minute TV series, 1953–57. Appeared in the movies *All About Eve* (1950), *Bundle Of Joy* (1956) and *Butterfield 8* (1960). Fisher was the #1 idol of bobbysoxers during the early 1950's.	
3/5/55	16	2	1. A Man Chases A Girl (Until She Catches Him)/ Jockey #16 / Juke Box #20 / Best Seller #27; from the movie *There's No Business Like Show Business* starring Ethel Merman	
4/2/55	20	1	2. (I'm Always Hearing) Wedding Bells Juke Box #20	RCA 6015
5/14/55	6	13	3. **Heart** Jockey #6 / Juke Box #13 / Best Seller #15; from the Broadway musical *Damn Yankees* starring Gwen Verdon	RCA 6097
8/27/55	11	8	4. Song Of The Dreamer/ Juke Box #11 / Best Seller #16 / Jockey #16 / Top 100 #43 pre	
		4	5. Don't Stay Away Too Long Best Seller/Juke Box flip	RCA 6196
12/24/55+	7	16	6. **Dungaree Doll/** Top 100 #7 / Juke Box #7 / Best Seller #8 / Jockey #9	
12/31/55	20	1	7. Everybody's Got A Home But Me Jockey #20 / Top 100 #41; from the Broadway musical *Pipe Dream* starring Helen Traubel	RCA 6337
6/30/56	18	7	8. On The Street Where You Live Juke Box #18 / Top 100 #28; from the Broadway musical *My Fair Lady* starring Julie Andrews	RCA 6529
10/20/56	10	17	9. **Cindy, Oh Cindy** Best Seller #10 / Top 100 #10 / Jockey #10 / Juke Box #10; adapted from a sailor's sea chantey; Hugo Winterhalter (orch., all of above)	RCA 6677

DATE	POS	WKS	ARTIST–RECORD TITLE	LABEL & NO.
			FISHER, Miss Toni	
			Born in Los Angeles in 1931.	
11/23/59	3	14	1. **The Big Hurt** first hit recording to feature an electronic "phasing" gimmick	Signet 275
7/14/62	37	1	2. West Of The Wall **TONI FISHER** lyrics inspired by the Berlin Wall crisis (1961)	Big Top 3097
			FITZGERALD, Ella	
5/30/60	27	7	Born on 4/25/18 in Newport News, Virginia. The most-honored jazz singer of all time. Discovered after winning on the "Harlem Amateur Hour" in 1934, she was hired by Chick Webb and in 1938 created a popular sensation with "A-Tisket, A-Tasket." Following Webb's death in 1939, Ella took over the band for three years. Appeared in several movies. Won the Lifetime Achievement Grammy in 1967. Winner of the *Down Beat* poll as top female vocalist more than 20 times and winner of 12 Grammys, she remains among the undisputed royalty of 20th-century popular music. Because of complications from diabetes, had both legs amputated below the knee in 1993. 1. Mack The Knife recorded "live" in concert in West Berlin with the Paul Smith Quartet; written in 1928 as "Moritat" or "Theme From The Threepenny Opera"	Verve 10209
			FIVE AMERICANS, The	
			Dallas-based rock quintet, originally from Oklahoma, led by vocalist Michael Rabon (later with Gladstone). Keyboardist John Durrill wrote Cher's "Dark Lady" and "I Saw A Man And He Danced With His Wife." Member Jimmy Wright married Robin of Jon & Robin & The In Crowd in 1970.	
2/12/66	26	5	1. I See The Light first released on Abnak 109 in 1965	HBR 454
3/18/67	5	9	2. **Western Union**	Abnak 118
6/17/67	36	2	3. Sound Of Love	Abnak 120
9/16/67	36	1	4. Zip Code	Abnak 123
			FIVE BLOBS, The	
			Group is actually the overdubbed vocals of Bernie Nee (since deceased).	
11/3/58	33	3	1. The Blob title song from the movie starring Steve McQueen	Columbia 41250
			FIVE FLIGHTS UP	
			Five-man pop group.	
10/3/70	37	5	1. Do What You Wanna Do	T-A 202
			FIVE KEYS, The	
			R&B quintet originally formed as the Sentimental Four in Newport News, Virginia, late 1940s. Consisted of two sets of brothers: Rudy and Bernie West, and Ripley and Raphael Ingram. In 1949, added Maryland Pierce and changed group name to The Five Keys. Dickie Smith replaced Raphael Ingram. Smith replaced by Ramon Loper in 1953. Rudy West sings lead on the ballads, Maryland Pierce lead on the rhythm tunes.	
12/25/54+	28	2	1. Ling, Ting, Tong Best Seller #28	Capitol 2945
10/6/56	23	6	2. Out Of Sight, Out Of Mind Best Seller #23 / Top 100 #27; Dave Cavanaugh (orch.)	Capitol 3502

DATE	POS	WKS	ARTIST–RECORD TITLE	LABEL & NO.
1/12/57	35	2	3. Wisdom Of A Fool Van Alexander (orch.)	Capitol 3597

FIVE MAN ELECTRICAL BAND

Rock group from Ontario, Canada. Les Emmerson (born 9/17/44), lead singer.

DATE	POS	WKS	ARTIST–RECORD TITLE	LABEL & NO.
7/10/71	3	12	● 1. **Signs**	Lionel 3213
10/30/71	26	6	2. Absolutely Right	Lionel 3220

FIVE SATINS, The

R&B group from New Haven, Connecticut. Consisted of Fred Parris (lead), Al Denby, Jim Freeman, Eddie Martin and Jessie Murphy (piano). Parris was stationed in the Army in Japan when "In The Still Of The Nite" charted, and the group re-formed with Bill Baker (died 8/10/94 of lung cancer, age 58) as lead singer. Parris returned in January 1958, replacing Baker.

DATE	POS	WKS	ARTIST–RECORD TITLE	LABEL & NO.
9/29/56	24	6	1. In The Still Of The Nite Best Seller #24 / Top 100 #29; written by Fred Parris and recorded in a New Haven church basement; originally released on Standord 200; record reportedly has sold multi-millions	Ember 1005
8/12/57	25	8	2. To The Aisle Best Seller #25 / Top 100 #25	Ember 1019

FIVE STAIRSTEPS, The

Soul group from Chicago, consisting of brothers Clarence, Jr., James, Kenneth and Dennis Burke with their sister Alohe. Later joined by their five-year-old brother Cubie. Managed by their father and produced by Curtis Mayfield; later became The Invisible Man's Band.

DATE	POS	WKS	ARTIST–RECORD TITLE	LABEL & NO.
6/20/70	8	11	● 1. **O-o-h Child**	Buddah 165

5000 VOLTS

British disco trio: Tina Charles, Martin Jay and Tony Eyers.

DATE	POS	WKS	ARTIST–RECORD TITLE	LABEL & NO.
11/15/75	26	5	1. I'm On Fire	Philips 40801

FIXX, The

Techno-pop group formed in London in 1979: Cy Curnin (vocals), Jamie West-Oram (guitar), Rupert Greenall (keyboards), Charlie Barrett (bass; left in early 1983) and Adam Woods (drums). Dan K. Brown (bass) joined in 1985.

DATE	POS	WKS	ARTIST–RECORD TITLE	LABEL & NO.
7/9/83	20	8	1. Saved By Zero "live" version is on the B-side of #3 below	MCA 52213
9/10/83	4	13	2. **One Thing Leads To Another**	MCA 52264
12/17/83+	32	7	3. The Sign Of Fire	MCA 52316
9/8/84	15	8	4. Are We Ourselves? Sales #13 / Airplay #21	MCA 52444
6/28/86	19	6	5. Secret Separation Sales #18 / Airplay #29; all of above produced by Rupert Hine	MCA 52832
5/4/91	35	3	6. How Much Is Enough Sales #35 / Airplay #35	Impact 54028

FLACK, Roberta

Born on 2/10/39 in Asheville, North Carolina; raised in Arlington, Virginia. Played piano from an early age. Music scholarship to Howard University at age 15; classmate of Donny Hathaway (soul singer born 10/1/45 in Chicago). Worked as a high school music teacher in North Carolina. Discovered by jazz musician Les McCann. Signed to Atlantic in 1969.

DATE	POS	WKS	ARTIST–RECORD TITLE	LABEL & NO.
7/3/71	29	9	1. You've Got A Friend **ROBERTA FLACK & DONNY HATHAWAY**	Atlantic 2808
3/25/72	**1 (6)**	15	● 2. **The First Time Ever I Saw Your Face** written in 1962; recorded on Flack's 1969 album *First Take*; popularized because of inclusion in the movie *Play Misty For Me* starring Clint Eastwood; #1 Adult Contemporary hit (6 weeks)	Atlantic 2864
6/24/72	5	11	● 3. **Where Is The Love** **ROBERTA FLACK & DONNY HATHAWAY** #1 Adult Contemporary hit (1 week); #1 R&B hit (1 week)	Atlantic 2879
2/3/73	**1 (5)**	13	● 4. **Killing Me Softly With His Song** inspired by the effect of a Don McLean performance upon singer/songwriter Lori Lieberman	Atlantic 2940
10/13/73	30	5	5. Jesse also on the B-side of #9 below; written by Janis Ian; all of above produced by Joel Dorin	Atlantic 2982
7/6/74	**1 (1)**	13	● 6. **Feel Like Makin' Love** #1 R&B hit (5 weeks); #1 Adult Contemporary hit (2 weeks)	Atlantic 3025
3/18/78	**2 (2)**	14	● 7. **The Closer I Get To You** **ROBERTA FLACK & DONNY HATHAWAY** #1 R&B hit (2 weeks)	Atlantic 3463
6/24/78	24	5	8. If Ever I See You Again title song from the movie starring Joe Brooks; #1 Adult Contemporary hit (3 weeks)	Atlantic 3483
4/17/82	13	11	9. Making Love title song from the movie starring Kate Jackson	Atlantic 4005
9/3/83	16	15	10. Tonight, I Celebrate My Love **PEABO BRYSON/ROBERTA FLACK**	Capitol 5242
10/5/91	6	16	11. **Set The Night To Music** **ROBERTA FLACK with Maxi Priest** Airplay #23 / Sales #25	Atlantic 87607
			FLAMING EMBER, The White soul-rock group from Detroit formed as the Flaming Embers: Joe Sladich (guitar), Bill Ellis (piano), Jim Bugnel (bass) and Jerry Plunk (drums).	
11/15/69	26	6	1. Mind, Body and Soul	Hot Wax 6902
6/20/70	24	10	2. Westbound #9	Hot Wax 7003
11/28/70	34	6	3. I'm Not My Brothers Keeper	Hot Wax 7006
			FLAMINGOS, The R&B group formed in Chicago in 1952. Consisted of cousins Zeke and Jake Carey, and cousins Paul Wilson and Johnny Carter, with lead singer Sollie McElroy. First recorded for Chance Records in 1953. In 1954, McElroy departed and was replaced by Nate Nelson. Tommy Hunt and Terry Johnson joined in July 1956, replacing Army-bound Zeke Carey and Johnny Carter. Carey returned in 1958 and group signed with End Records. Nelson joined The Platters in 1966; died of a heart attack on 6/1/84 (age 52). McElroy died on 1/15/95 (age 61).	
6/8/59	11	11	1. I Only Have Eyes For You #2 hit for Ben Selvin in 1934; from the movie musical *Dames* starring Joan Blondell	End 1046
5/23/60	30	3	2. Nobody Loves Me Like You written by Sam Cooke	End 1068

DATE	POS	WKS	ARTIST–RECORD TITLE	LABEL & NO.
			FLARES, The	
			Los Angeles-based R&B quintet, featuring lead singer Aaron Collins of The Cadets/The Jacks.	
10/9/61	25	9	1. Foot Stomping - Part 1	Felsted 8624
			B-side is an instrumental version by The Ramrocks	
			FLASH	
			English rock quartet led by Peter Banks (Yes; guitar) and Colin Carter (vocals).	
7/29/72	29	6	1. Small Beginnings	Capitol 3345
			FLASH CADILLAC & THE CONTINENTAL KIDS	
			Fifties-styled act formed by six students at the University of Colorado. Appeared as the prom band in the movie *American Graffiti*. Flash is lead singer Samuel McFadden (born 3/30/52).	
10/2/76	29	6	1. Did You Boogie (With Your Baby)	Private St. 45079
			with spoken interludes by Wolfman Jack	
			FLEETWOOD MAC	
			Formed as a British blues band in 1967 by ex-John Mayall's Bluesbreakers Peter Green (guitar), Mick Fleetwood (drums) and John McVie (bass), along with guitarist Jeremy Spencer. Many lineup changes followed as group headed toward rock superstardom. Green and Spencer left in 1970. Christine McVie (keyboards) joined in August 1970. Bob Welch (guitar) joined in April 1971, stayed through 1974. Group relocated to California in 1974, whereupon Americans Lindsey Buckingham (guitar) and Stevie Nicks (vocals) joined in January 1975. Buckingham left in summer of 1987. Guitarists/vocalists Billy Burnette (son of Dorsey Burnette) and Rick Vito joined in July 1987. Christine McVie and Nicks quit touring with the band at the end of 1990. Vito left in 1991. In early 1993, Nicks and Burnette left. In late 1993, Bekka Bramlett (leader of The Zoo and daughter of Delaney & Bonnie Bramlett) and Dave Mason joined Mick, John and Christine in band.	
12/13/75+	20	7	1. Over My Head	Reprise 1339
4/10/76	11	11	2. Rhiannon (Will You Ever Win)	Reprise 1345
7/31/76	11	13	3. Say You Love Me	Reprise 1356
1/22/77	10	11	4. **Go Your Own Way**	Warner 8304
4/30/77	1 (1)	13	● 5. **Dreams**	Warner 8371
7/23/77	3	14	6. **Don't Stop**	Warner 8413
10/29/77	9	10	7. **You Make Loving Fun**	Warner 8483
			above 4 from the album *Rumours*	
10/13/79	8	10	8. **Tusk**	Warner 49077
			with U.S.C. Trojan Marching Band, recorded "live" at Dodger Stadium	
12/22/79+	7	11	9. **Sara**	Warner 49150
3/29/80	20	7	10. Think About Me	Warner 49196
6/19/82	4	15	11. **Hold Me**	Warner 29966
9/25/82	12	8	12. Gypsy	Warner 29918
12/11/82+	22	8	13. Love In Store	Warner 29848
4/11/87	5	11	14. **Big Love**	Warner 28398
			Airplay #4 / Sales #6	
7/4/87	19	8	15. Seven Wonders	Warner 28317
			Sales #17 / Airplay #17	
9/12/87	4	13	16. **Little Lies**	Warner 28291
			Sales #3 / Airplay #5; #1 Adult Contemporary hit (4 weeks)	

DATE	POS	WKS	ARTIST–RECORD TITLE	LABEL & NO.
12/26/87+	**14**	10	17. Everywhere Airplay #12 / Sales #13; #1 Adult Contemporary hit (3 weeks); above 4 from the album *Tango In The Night*	Warner 28143
4/28/90	**33**	4	18. Save Me Airplay #28 / Sales #33	Warner 19866
			FLEETWOODS, The	
			Pop trio formed while in high school in Olympia, Washington, in 1958: Gary Troxel (born 11/28/39), Gretchen Christopher (born 2/29/40) and Barbara Ellis (born 2/20/40).	
3/16/59	**1 (4)**	12	● 1. **Come Softly To Me** also released on Dolton 1 and Liberty 55188 in 1959	Dolphin 1
6/22/59	**39**	1	2. Graduation's Here	Dolton 3
9/14/59	**1 (1)**	17	● 3. **Mr. Blue**	Dolton 5
2/29/60	**28**	3	4. Outside My Window	Dolton 15
6/27/60	**23**	4	5. Runaround #20 hit for The Three Chuckles in 1954	Dolton 22
5/8/61	**10**	8	6. **Tragedy**	Dolton 40
10/2/61	**30**	4	7. (He's) The Great Impostor written by Jackie DeShannon and Sharon Sheeley	Dolton 45
11/24/62	**36**	2	8. Lovers By Night, Strangers By Day	Dolton 62
7/13/63	**32**	4	9. Goodnight My Love #7 R&B hit for Jesse Belvin in 1956	Dolton 75
			FLINT, Shelby	
			Born on 9/17/39 in North Hollywood, California. Singer/songwriter.	
2/6/61	**22**	5	1. Angel On My Shoulder	Valiant 6001
			FLIRTATIONS, The	
			Group consisted of Shirley and Earnestine Pearce from South Carolina, and Viola Billups from Alabama. The Pearce sisters had been in the Gypsies, 1962–65.	
5/24/69	**34**	2	1. Nothing But A Heartache	Deram 85038
			FLOATERS, The	
			Detroit soul group: Charles Clarke (lead), Larry Cunningham and brothers Paul & Ralph Mitchell.	
7/30/77	**2 (2)**	11	● 1. **Float On** #1 R&B hit (6 weeks)	ABC 12284
			FLOCK OF SEAGULLS, A	
			New wave quartet formed in Liverpool, England, in 1980: brothers Mike (vocals, keyboards) and Ali (drums) Score, Paul Reynolds (guitar) and Frank Maudsley (bass).	
9/4/82	**9**	10	1. **I Ran (So Far Away)**	Jive 102
1/8/83	**30**	7	2. Space Age Love Song	Jive 2003
6/11/83	**26**	7	3. Wishing (If I Had A Photograph Of You)	Jive 2006

DATE	POS	WKS	ARTIST–RECORD TITLE	LABEL & NO.
			FLOOD, Dick	
			Born on 11/13/32 in Philadelphia. Singer/songwriter.	Monument 408
9/14/59	23	4	1. The Three Bells (The Jimmy Brown Story)	
			French tune written in 1946; #14 hit for Les Compagnons De La Chanson in 1952	
			FLOYD, Eddie	
			Born on 6/25/35 in Montgomery, Alabama; raised in Detroit. Original member of The Falcons, 1955–63. Eddie's uncle, Robert West, founded the Lu Pine record label.	
11/19/66	28	6	● 1. Knock On Wood	Stax 194
			#1 R&B hit (1 week)	
9/7/68	40	2	2. I've Never Found A Girl (To Love Me Like You Do)	Stax 0002
11/16/68	17	9	3. Bring It On Home To Me	Stax 0012
			FLOYD, King	
			Born on 2/13/45 in New Orleans. Soul-funk singer/songwriter. First recorded for Original Sound in 1965.	
12/12/70+	6	13	● 1. **Groove Me**	Chimneyville 435
			#1 R&B hit (4 weeks)	
4/3/71	29	7	2. Baby Let Me Kiss You	Chimneyville 437
			FLYING MACHINE, The	
			Studio project of British songwriters/producers Tony MacAuley and Geoff Stephens. Touring group featured Tony Newman as lead vocalist. Not to be confused with James Taylor's group.	
10/18/69	5	12	● 1. **Smile A Little Smile For Me**	Congress 6000
			FOCUS	
			Dutch progressive-rock quartet led by guitar virtuoso Jan Akkerman and flutist Thijs van Leer.	
4/21/73	9	11	1. **Hocus Pocus** [I]	Sire 704
			FOGELBERG, Dan	
			Born on 8/13/51 in Peoria, Illinois. Vocalist/composer. Worked as a folk singer in Los Angeles. With Van Morrison in the early '70s. Session work in Nashville.	
3/1/75	31	3	1. Part Of The Plan	Epic 50055
			Graham Nash (harmony vocal); Joe Walsh (lead guitar)	
11/4/78	24	7	2. The Power Of Gold	Full Moon 50606
			DAN FOGELBERG/TIM WEISBERG	
			Don Henley (harmony vocal)	
1/19/80	2 (2)	13	3. **Longer**	Full Moon 50824
			#1 Adult Contemporary hit (1 week)	
4/19/80	21	6	4. Heart Hotels	Full Moon 50862
			Tom Scott (sax solo)	
12/27/80+	9	13	5. **Same Old Lang Syne**	Full Moon 50961
9/19/81	7	10	6. **Hard To Say**	Full Moon 02488
			Glenn Frey (harmony vocal)	
12/19/81+	9	16	7. **Leader Of The Band**	Full Moon 02647
			#1 Adult Contemporary hit (2 weeks)	

DATE	POS	WKS	ARTIST–RECORD TITLE	LABEL & NO.
4/24/82	**18**	8	8. Run For The Roses *above 4 from the album* The Innocent Age	Full Moon 02821
11/13/82	**23**	9	9. Missing You	Full Moon 03289
3/5/83	**29**	6	10. Make Love Stay #1 Adult Contemporary hit (1 week)	Full Moon 03525
2/11/84	**13**	10	11. The Language Of Love	Full Moon 04314

FOGERTY, John

Born on 5/28/45 in Berkeley, California. Multi-instrumentalist. With his brother Tom in the Blue Velvets in 1959. Group became the Golliwogs and recorded for Fantasy in 1964. Renamed Creedence Clearwater Revival in 1967. Wrote "Proud Mary," "Have You Ever Seen The Rain," "Bad Moon Rising," "Lookin' Out My Back Door" and many others. Went solo in 1972 and recorded as The Blue Ridge Rangers.

THE BLUE RIDGE RANGERS:

DATE	POS	WKS	ARTIST–RECORD TITLE	LABEL & NO.
1/6/73	**16**	10	1. Jambalaya (On the Bayou) #1 Country hit (14 weeks) for Hank Williams in 1952	Fantasy 689
5/19/73	**37**	2	2. Hearts Of Stone	Fantasy 700

JOHN FOGERTY:

DATE	POS	WKS	ARTIST–RECORD TITLE	LABEL & NO.
10/4/75	**27**	6	3. Rockin' All Over The World	Asylum 45274
1/19/85	**10**	9	4. **The Old Man Down The Road** Airplay #8 / Sales #12	Warner 29100
4/6/85	**20**	6	5. Rock And Roll Girls Airplay #19 / Sales #21	Warner 29053

FOGHAT

British rock quartet: Lonesome Dave Peverett (vocals, guitar; formerly with Savoy Brown), Rod Price (guitar), Tony Stevens (bass) and Roger Earl (drums). Settled in New York City in 1975, many bass player changes since. Price replaced by Erik Cartwright in 1981.

DATE	POS	WKS	ARTIST–RECORD TITLE		LABEL & NO.
1/10/76	**20**	12	1. Slow Ride		Bearsville 0306
12/25/76+	**34**	4	2. Drivin' Wheel		Bearsville 0313
10/15/77	**33**	3	3. I Just Want To Make Love To You "live" version of group's 1972 hit (#83)	[R]	Bearsville 0319
6/24/78	**36**	2	4. Stone Blue		Bearsville 0325
12/8/79+	**23**	10	5. Third Time Lucky (First Time I Was A Fool)		Bearsville 49125

FONTANA, Wayne—see MINDBENDERS, The

FONTANE SISTERS, The

Trio from New Milford, New Jersey: sisters Marge, Bea and Geri, whose family name is Rosse. Backed Perry Como on many of his hits, 1949–52.

DATE	POS	WKS	ARTIST–RECORD TITLE	LABEL & NO.
12/11/54+	**1 (3)**	20	● 1. **Hearts Of Stone** Juke Box #1(3) / Best Seller #1(1) / Jockey #2	Dot 15265
2/26/55	**13**	8	2. Rock Love Juke Box #13 / Best Seller #19	Dot 15333
6/4/55	**13**	6	3. Rollin' Stone/ Juke Box #13	
		2	4. Playmates Juke Box flip; #2 hit for Kay Kyser in 1940	Dot 15370
8/20/55	**3**	15	5. **Seventeen** Juke Box #3 / Best Seller #6 / Jockey #7 / Top 100 #15 pre	Dot 15386

DATE	POS	WKS	ARTIST–RECORD TITLE	LABEL & NO.
11/26/55	**11**	11	6. Daddy-O Top 100 #11 / Juke Box #11 / Best Seller #13 / Jockey #18	Dot 15428
12/31/55	**36**	1	7. Nuttin' For Christmas [X-N]	Dot 15434
3/17/56	**11**	11	8. Eddie My Love Juke Box #11 / Top 100 #12 / Jockey #13 / Best Seller #15	Dot 15450
7/14/56	**38**	1	9. I'm In Love Again	Dot 15462
1/12/57	**13**	10	10. The Banana Boat Song Jockey #13 / Juke Box #14 / Top 100 #22	Dot 15527
4/28/58	**12**	9	11. Chanson d'Amour (Song Of Love) Jockey #12 / Top 100 #68; Billy Vaughn (orch., all of above)	Dot 15736
			FORBERT, Steve	
			Born in 1955 in Meridian, Mississippi. Moved to New York City in 1976.	
1/5/80	**11**	12	1. Romeo's Tune	Nemperor 7525
			FORCE M.D.'S	
			Staten Island-based soul-rap quintet. Originally called Dr. Rock & The M.C.'s. M.D. stands for Musical Diversity. Member Charles "Mercury" Nelson died of a heart attack on 3/10/95 (age 30).	
3/1/86	**10**	11	1. **Tender Love** Airplay #7 / Sales #12; from the all-rap musical movie *Krush Groove* starring Sheila E.	Warner 28818
			FORD, Frankie	
			Born Frank Guzzo on 8/4/39 in Gretna, Louisiana. Appeared with Sophie Tucker, Ted Lewis and Carmen Miranda at local shows at an early age. Appeared in the movie *American Hot Wax*.	
3/9/59	**14**	12	1. Sea Cruise Huey "Piano" Smith (orch.)	Ace 554
			FORD, Lita	
			Born on 9/23/59 in London. Lead guitarist of Los Angeles-based female rock group The Runaways, 1975–79.	
5/14/88	**12**	10	1. Kiss Me Deadly Sales #8 / Airplay #14	RCA 6866
4/22/89	**8**	12	● 2. **Close My Eyes Forever** **LITA FORD (with Ozzy Osbourne)** Sales #4 / Airplay #13	RCA 8899
			FORD, "Tennessee" Ernie	
			Born Ernest Jennings Ford on 2/13/19 in Bristol, Tennessee. Died on 10/17/91 of liver disease. Country singer, revered as America's favorite hymn singer. Began career as a DJ. Host of musical variety TV shows, 1955–65. Favorite expression: "Bless your little pea-pickin' hearts."	
3/19/55	**5**	17	1. **Ballad Of Davy Crockett** Juke Box #5 / Best Seller #6 / Jockey #7; Cliffie Stone (orch.); from the ABC-TV "Disneyland" series, which featured 3 "Davy Crockett" segments	Capitol 3058
11/12/55	**1** (8)	19	● 2. **Sixteen Tons** Juke Box #1(8) / Best Seller #1(7) / Top 100 #1(6) / Jockey #1(6); written in 1947 by Country singer/guitarist Merle Travis; #1 Country hit (10 weeks)	Capitol 3262
3/10/56	**17**	1	3. That's All Jockey #17 / Top 100 #44	Capitol 3343

DATE	POS	WKS	ARTIST–RECORD TITLE	LABEL & NO.
9/23/57	23	1	4. In The Middle Of An Island Jockey #23 / Top 100 #56; Jack Fascinato (orch., above 3)	Capitol 3762

FOREIGNER

British-American rock group formed in New York City in 1976. Consisted of Mick Jones (guitar; not to be confused with Mick Jones of The Clash and Big Audio Dynamite), Lou Gramm (vocals), Ian McDonald (guitar, keyboards), Ed Gagliardi (bass), Al Greenwood (keyboards) and Dennis Elliott (drums). Gagliardi, Gramm and Greenwood are from New York. Most of material written by Jones (Spooky Tooth) and Gramm. Rick Wills (Roxy Music, Small Faces) replaced Gagliardi in 1979. Greenwood and McDonald (King Crimson) left in 1980. Gramm left in 1991 to form Shadow King; replaced by Johnny Edwards. Gramm returned in mid-1992. Wills left in 1992 to join Bad Company; Elliott left to open woodworking business.

DATE	POS	WKS	ARTIST–RECORD TITLE	LABEL & NO.
4/23/77	4	13	1. **Feels Like The First Time**	Atlantic 3394
8/13/77	6	15	2. **Cold As Ice**	Atlantic 3410
1/14/78	20	8	3. Long, Long Way From Home	Atlantic 3439
7/8/78	3	14	● 4. **Hot Blooded**	Atlantic 3488
9/30/78	2 (2)	12	● 5. **Double Vision**	Atlantic 3514
1/20/79	15	8	6. Blue Morning, Blue Day	Atlantic 3543
9/22/79	12	9	7. Dirty White Boy	Atlantic 3618
11/24/79	14	9	8. Head Games "live" version is on the B-side of #12 below	Atlantic 3633
7/11/81	4	17	9. **Urgent** Jr. Walker (sax solo)	Atlantic 3831
10/17/81	2 (10)	19	● 10. **Waiting For A Girl Like You**	Atlantic 3868
3/6/82	26	6	11. Juke Box Hero	Atlantic 4017
6/5/82	26	6	12. Break It Up above 4 from the album 4	Atlantic 4044
12/15/84+	1 (2)	16	● 13. **I Want To Know What Love Is** Airplay #1(2) / Sales #1(1); New Jersey Mass Choir and Jennifer Holliday (backing vocals)	Atlantic 89596
3/23/85	12	10	14. That Was Yesterday Airplay #12 / Sales #17	Atlantic 89571
12/26/87+	6	12	15. **Say You Will** Sales #5 / Airplay #8	Atlantic 89169
4/9/88	5	11	16. **I Don't Want To Live Without You** Airplay #4 / Sales #6; #1 Adult Contemporary hit (1 week); all of above written by Mick Jones and Lou Gramm	Atlantic 89101

FORTUNES, The

English pop quintet led by guitarists/vocalists Glen Dale (Garforth) and Barry Pritchard. Dale left in July 1966, replaced by Scotsman Shel MacRae.

DATE	POS	WKS	ARTIST–RECORD TITLE	LABEL & NO.
9/11/65	7	8	1. **You've Got Your Troubles**	Press 9773
11/27/65	27	4	2. Here It Comes Again	Press 9798
6/19/71	15	9	3. Here Comes That Rainy Day Feeling Again	Capitol 3086

FOSTER, David

Born in Victoria, British Columbia. Keyboardist/composer/arranger. Member of the groups Skylark and Attitudes. Wrote and produced hits for Chicago, Barbra Streisand and others. Married to songwriter/actress Linda Thompson.

DATE	POS	WKS	ARTIST–RECORD TITLE	LABEL & NO.
10/5/85	15	10	1. Love Theme From St. Elmo's Fire　　　[I] Sales #14 / Airplay #15; from the movie St. Elmo's Fire starring Rob Lowe and Demi Moore	Atlantic 89528

DATE	POS	WKS	ARTIST–RECORD TITLE	LABEL & NO.
			FOUNDATIONS, The	
			British interracial R&B-pop group. Lead singer Clem Curtis (from Trinidad) replaced by Colin Young (West Indies) in 1968. Disbanded in 1970.	
1/13/68	11	10	1. Baby, Now That I've Found You	Uni 55038
1/18/69	3	13	● 2. **Build Me Up Buttercup**	Uni 55101
			FOUR ACES Featuring Al Alberts	
			Vocal group from Chester, Pennsylvania: Al Alberts (lead singer), Dave Mahoney (tenor), Sol Vaccaro (baritone) and Lou Silvestri (bass). Worked Ye Olde Mill near Philadelphia, late 1940s. First recorded for Victoria in 1951. Group has undergone several personnel changes over the years.	
1/15/55	3	21	1. **Melody Of Love** Juke Box #3 / Jockey #9 / Best Seller #11; music written in 1903, lyrics added in 1954 by Tom Glazer	Decca 29395
5/28/55	13	6	2. Heart Jockey #13 / Juke Box #20 / Best Seller #23; from the Broadway musical *Damn Yankees* starring Gwen Verdon	Decca 29476
8/27/55	1 (6)	21	● 3. **Love Is A Many-Splendored Thing** Jockey #1(6) / Top 100 #1(3) / Juke Box #1(3) / Best Seller #1(2); title song from the movie starring William Holden and Jennifer Jones	Decca 29625
12/3/55	14	12	4. A Woman In Love Jockey #14 / Top 100 #19 / Best Seller #20; from the movie *Guys and Dolls* starring Marlon Brando	Decca 29725
8/4/56	22	5	5. I Only Know I Love You Jockey #22 / Top 100 #35	Decca 29989
10/20/56	20	2	6. You Can't Run Away From It Jockey #20 / Top 100 #70; title song from the movie starring Jack Lemmon and June Allyson; Jack Pleis (orch., all of above)	Decca 30041
			FOUR COINS, The	
			Vocal group of Greek descent from Canonsburg, Pennsylvania: George Mantalis, Jim Gregorakis, and brothers Michael and George Mahramas. Appeared in the 1957 movie *Jamboree!*	
1/15/55	28	1	1. I Love You Madly Best Seller #28; first recorded by R&B duo Charlie and Ray in 1954 (Herald 438)	Epic 9082
12/10/55	22	8	2. Memories Of You Best Seller #22 / Top 10 #28; from the movie *The Benny Goodman Story* starring Steve Allen; Don Costa (orch., above 2)	Epic 9129
6/17/57	11	13	3. Shangri-La Jockey #11 / Best Seller #22 / Top 100 #23	Epic 9213
10/14/57	28	4	4. My One Sin Best Seller #28 / Top 100 #29	Epic 9229
11/17/58	21	8	5. The World Outside introduced as "Warsaw Concerto" in the 1942 movie *Suicide Squadron* starring Anton Walbrook; Marion Evans (orch., above 3)	Epic 9295
			FOUR ESQUIRES, The	
			Formed group at Boston University: Bill Courtney, Frank Mahoney, Bob Golden and Wally Gold.	
12/16/57	25	1	1. Love Me Forever Jockey #25 / Best Seller #44 / Top 100 #51; Sid Bass (orch.)	Paris 509
11/3/58	21	6	2. Hideaway Richard Hayman (orch.)	Paris 520

DATE	POS	WKS	ARTIST–RECORD TITLE	LABEL & NO.
			FOUR FRESHMEN, The	
			Jazz-styled vocal and instrumental group formed in 1948 while at Arthur Jordan Conservatory of Music in Indianapolis. Consisted of brothers Ross and Don Barbour (now deceased), their cousin Bob Flanigan and Ken Errair.	
6/9/56	**17**	7	1. Graduation Day Jockey #17 / Best Seller #25 / Top 100 #27; Dick Reynolds (orch.)	Capitol 3410
			FOUR JACKS AND A JILL	
			South African quintet; Jill is Glenys Lynne (lead singer).	
5/18/68	**18**	7	1. Master Jack	RCA 9473
			FOUR KNIGHTS, The—see COLE, Nat "King"	
			FOUR LADS, The	
			Vocal group from Toronto: Bernie Toorish (lead tenor), Jimmie Arnold (second tenor), Frankie Busseri (baritone) and Connie Codarini (bass). Sang in choir at St. Michael's Cathedral in Toronto. Worked local hotels and clubs. Worked Le Ruban Bleu in New York City. Signed as backup singers by Columbia in 1950. Backed Johnnie Ray on several of his hits, including his #1 hit "Cry."	
9/3/55	**2 (6)**	25	● 1. **Moments To Remember** Jockey #2 / Best Seller #3 / Top 100 #3 / Juke Box #4	Columbia 40539
1/28/56	**2 (4)**	19	● 2. **No, Not Much!** Jockey #2 / Top 100 #3 / Best Seller #4 / Juke Box #4	Columbia 40629
4/28/56	**3**	18	3. **Standing On The Corner/** Best Seller #3 / Top 100 #3 / Jockey #3 / Juke Box #3; from the Broadway musical *The Most Happy Fella* starring Robert Weede	
4/28/56	**22**	12	4. My Little Angel Best Seller #22 / Jockey #24 / Top 100 #30	Columbia 40674
9/15/56	**16**	6	5. A House With Love In It/ Best Seller #16 / Jockey #20 / Top 100 #23	
9/15/56	**17**	6	6. The Bus Stop Song (A Paper Of Pins) Jockey #17 / Best Seller #22 / Top 100 #23; from the movie *Bus Stop* starring Marilyn Monroe	Columbia 40736
2/2/57	**9**	15	7. **Who Needs You** Jockey #9 / Best Seller #13 / Top 100 #14 / Juke Box #17	Columbia 40811
5/20/57	**17**	4	8. I Just Don't Know Jockey #17 / Top 100 #22	Columbia 40914
12/9/57+	**8**	9	9. **Put A Light In The Window** Jockey #8 / Top 100 #35 / Best Seller #39	Columbia 41058
4/7/58	**10**	7	10. **There's Only One Of You** Jockey #10 / Top 100 #41 / Best Seller #43	Columbia 41136
7/14/58	**12**	6	11. Enchanted Island Jockey #12 / Hot 100 #29 / Best Seller #32; title song from the movie starring Jane Powell Ray Ellis (orch., all of above)	Columbia 41194
11/24/58	**32**	3	12. The Mocking Bird [R] new version of group's 1952 (#23) and 1956 (#67) hits; Joe Mele (orch.)	Columbia 41266
			4 NON BLONDES	
			Rock band formed in San Francisco in 1989: Linda Perry (vocals), Roger Rocha (guitar), Christa Hillhouse (bass) and Dawn Richardson (drums).	
6/5/93	**14**	17	● 1. What's Up Sales #10 / Airplay #30	Interscope 98430

DATE	POS	WKS	ARTIST—RECORD TITLE	LABEL & NO.
			## 4 P.M. (FOR POSITIVE MUSIC)	
			Male vocal quartet formed in Baltimore: brothers Rene and Roberto Pena with Larry McFarland and Marty Ware.	
11/12/94+	8	23	● 1. **Sukiyaki** Sales #10 / Airplay #10	Next Plat. 857736
			## FOUR PREPS, The	
			Vocal group formed while at Hollywood High School: Bruce Belland, Glen Larson, Ed Cobb and Marvin Ingraham. Belland, who was later in duo with Dave Somerville of The Diamonds, is the father of Tracey and Melissa Belland of Voice Of The Beehive. Larson's production company was a creative force behind numerous TV series during the '70s ("BJ & The Bear," "Battlestar Galactica," "McCloud," "Quincy" and others).	
1/20/58	2 (3)	14	● 1. **26 Miles (Santa Catalina)** Jockey #2 / Top 100 #4 / Best Seller #5	Capitol 3845
5/5/58	3	12	2. **Big Man** Jockey #3 / Top 100 #5 / Best Seller #6	Capitol 3960
9/1/58	21	6	3. Lazy Summer Night/ Hot 100 #21 / Best Seller #34; from the movie *Andy Hardy Comes Home* starring Mickey Rooney	
		3	4. Summertime Lies Best Seller flip	Capitol 4023
1/11/60	13	11	5. Down By The Station new version of tune written in 1948	Capitol 4312
5/16/60	24	3	6. Got A Girl [N]	Capitol 4362
9/11/61	17	4	7. More Money For You And Me [N] Mr. Blue/Alley Oop/Smoke Gets In Your Eyes/In This Whole Wide World/A Worried Man/Tom Dooley/A Teenager In Love; Lincoln Mayorga (orch., all of above)	Capitol 4599
			## 4 SEASONS, The	
			Vocal group formed in Newark, New Jersey. In 1955, lead singer Frankie Valli (Francis Castelluccio) formed the Variatones with brothers Nick and Tommy DeVito, and Hank Majewski. Changed name to The Four Lovers in 1956. Bob Gaudio (of The Royal Teens) joined as keyboardist/songwriter in 1959, replacing Nick DeVito. Nick Massi replaced Majewski, and their 1961 lineup was set: Valli, Gaudio, Massi and Tommy DeVito. Group had been doing session work for their producer Bob Crewe and took their new name from a New Jersey bowling alley, The Four Seasons. In 1965, Nick Massi was replaced by the group's arranger Charlie Calello and then by Joe Long. In 1971, Tommy DeVito retired, and Gaudio left (as a performer) the following year. Numerous personnel changes from then on. The songwriting/producing/arranging team of Bob Crewe, Bob Gaudio and Charlie Calello helped rank The 4 Seasons as one of the top American groups of the '60s. Inducted into the Rock and Roll Hall of Fame in 1990. Also recorded as The Wonder Who?	
9/1/62	1 (5)	12	● 1. **Sherry** #1 R&B hit (1 week)	Vee-Jay 456
10/27/62	1 (5)	14	● 2. **Big Girls Don't Cry** #1 R&B hit (3 weeks)	Vee-Jay 465
12/22/62	23	2	3. Santa Claus Is Coming To Town [X] #12 hit for George Hall in 1934	Vee-Jay 478
1/26/63	1 (3)	12	4. **Walk Like A Man**	Vee-Jay 485
5/4/63	22	6	5. Ain't That A Shame!	Vee-Jay 512
7/20/63	3	10	6. **Candy Girl/** written by Larry Santos	
8/10/63	36	3	7. Marlena	Vee-Jay 539

DATE	POS	WKS	ARTIST–RECORD TITLE	LABEL & NO.
11/2/63	36	2	8. New Mexican Rose	Vee-Jay 562
2/8/64	3	11	9. **Dawn (Go Away)**	Philips 40166
3/7/64	16	8	10. Stay	Vee-Jay 582
4/18/64	6	8	11. **Ronnie**	Philips 40185
6/27/64	1 (2)	11	● 12. **Rag Doll**	Philips 40211
6/27/64	28	5	13. Alone	Vee-Jay 597
9/5/64	10	6	14. **Save It For Me**	Philips 40225
11/21/64	20	5	15. Big Man In Town	Philips 40238
1/30/65	12	6	16. Bye, Bye, Baby (Baby Goodbye)	Philips 40260
7/10/65	30	3	17. Girl Come Running	Philips 40305
10/30/65	3	12	18. **Let's Hang On!**	Philips 40317
11/27/65	12	8	19. Don't Think Twice	Philips 40324
			THE WONDER WHO?	
2/12/66	9	6	20. **Working My Way Back To You**	Philips 40350
5/28/66	13	7	21. Opus 17 (Don't You Worry 'Bout Me)	Philips 40370
9/17/66	9	8	22. **I've Got You Under My Skin**	Philips 40393
			#3 hit in 1936 for Ray Noble; from the movie *Born To Dance* starring James Stewart	
12/24/66+	10	8	23. **Tell It To The Rain**	Philips 40412
3/18/67	16	7	24. Beggin'	Philips 40433
6/17/67	9	8	25. **C'mon Marianne**	Philips 40460
11/18/67	30	4	26. Watch The Flowers Grow	Philips 40490
3/9/68	24	5	27. Will You Love Me Tomorrow	Philips 40523
			all of above 4 Seasons' Phillips records (except "Dawn") labeled as: Featuring the "sound" of Frankie Valli	
9/20/75	3	12	28. **Who Loves You**	Warner/Curb 8122
1/31/76	1 (3)	15	● 29. **December, 1963 (Oh, What a Night)**	Warner/Curb 8168
7/4/76	38	2	30. Silver Star	Warner/Curb 8203
			Gerri Polci (drummer; lead vocals, above 2)	
9/17/94	14	20	31. December 1963 (Oh, What A Night) [R]	Curb 76917
			FOUR SEASONS	
			Airplay #8 / Sales #30; dance remix version of #29 above	

FOUR TOPS

Detroit R&B vocal group formed in 1953 as the Four Aims. Consisted of Levi Stubbs (lead singer), Renaldo "Obie" Benson, Lawrence Payton and Abdul "Duke" Fakir. First recorded for Chess in 1956, then Red Top and Columbia, before signing with Motown in 1963. Group has had no personnel changes since its formation. Stubbs was the voice of Audrey II (the voracious vegetation) in the 1986 movie *Little Shop of Horrors*. Group inducted into the Rock and Roll Hall of Fame in 1990. The Supremes, The Temptations, The Miracles and the Four Tops were the "big 4" of the Motown "group sound."

DATE	POS	WKS	ARTIST–RECORD TITLE	LABEL & NO.
8/29/64	11	10	1. **Baby I Need Your Loving**	Motown 1062
2/20/65	24	6	2. Ask The Lonely	Motown 1073
5/22/65	1 (2)	13	3. **I Can't Help Myself**	Motown 1076
			#1 R&B hit (9 weeks)	
8/7/65	5	8	4. **It's The Same Old Song**	Motown 1081
11/20/65	19	6	5. Something About You	Motown 1084
3/12/66	18	6	6. Shake Me, Wake Me (When It's Over)	Motown 1090
9/17/66	1 (2)	12	7. **Reach Out I'll Be There**	Motown 1098
			#1 R&B hit (2 weeks)	
12/24/66+	6	9	8. **Standing In The Shadows Of Love**	Motown 1102

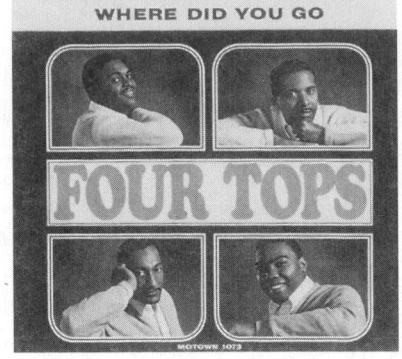

The Four Lads' Top 10 1959 hit "Who Needs You" was the Toronto quartet's seventh major single, and—despite its title—not the major punkfest it might have been.

The 4 Seasons were often viewed as America's hottest vocal group of the early '60s—as Vee Jay Records' 1964 set *The Beatles Vs. The 4 Seasons* attested. "Ronnie" became the group's sixth Top 10 single that same year.

The Four Tops' memorable 1965 tune "Ask The Lonely" was the second of 24 Top 40 records the distinguished vocal group released between 1964 and 1988. In the early '90s the Motown legends teamed with current-day Motown hitmakers Boyz II Men on the "Arsenio Hall" TV show.

Connie Francis released her No. 22 hit "If I Didn't Care" midway between two much larger 1959 hits: the No. 2 "My Happiness" and the No. 5 "Lipstick On Your Collar." The track had been a hit for the Ink Spots 20 years earlier.

Free's "The Stealer"—taken from the influential Brit quartet's 1970 album *Highway*—failed to match the success of its predecessor, the No. 4 hit "All Right Now." By 1974, singer Paul Rodgers and drummer Simon Kirke would leave the band for greater commercial success with hard rockers Bad Company.

Marvin Gaye and Mary Wells's pairing for the Motown single "What's The Matter With You Baby" and "Once Upon A Time" resulted in two separate Top 20 hits in 1964. Gaye would later have hits with duet partners Kim Weston, Diana Ross and Tammi Terrell.

Bobbie Gentry's curious No. 1 smash of 1967, "Ode To Billie Joe," is one of the few chart-toppers actually to have inspired a film. Jeannie C. Riley's 1968 hit "Harper Valley PTA" was another.

The Geto Boys' controversial brand of violent rap, typified by 1991's mesmerizing rap smash "Mind Playing Tricks On Me," drew harsh criticisms in some political circles. Band member Bushwick Bill lost his eye in a 1991 shooting incident.

Debbie Gibson's last gold single, "Electric Youth," followed her all-time chart high, "Lost In Your Eyes," a No. 1 hit for three weeks in 1989. The popular teen singer later pacted with EMI Records in the mid-'90s.

The Gin Blossoms' double-platinum 1993 album *New Miserable Experience* bore several hits, many of which had been penned by already departed songwriter/guitarist Doug Hopkins. Hopkins, who shot himself in late 1993, was the writer of "Hey Jealousy."

Lesley Gore's 1964 hit "Maybe I Know" was one in a series of hits produced by music maestro Quincy Jones. The track, which reached No. 14, summed up '60s teen angst better than most of the era.

Green Jelly knew precisely what was in a name. The New York-based rock collective was originally known as Green Jello, until a well-known food conglomerate asked for a name change in 1993. The group's debut album, *Cereal Killer Soundtrack*, went gold largely due to heavy MTV play.

DATE	POS	WKS	ARTIST–RECORD TITLE	LABEL & NO.
3/18/67	4	8	9. **Bernadette**	Motown 1104
6/3/67	14	6	10. 7 Rooms Of Gloom	Motown 1110
9/30/67	19	5	11. You Keep Running Away	Motown 1113
2/17/68	14	6	12. Walk Away Renee	Motown 1119
5/11/68	20	6	13. If I Were A Carpenter	Motown 1124
			above 7 (except #11) from the album Four Tops Reach Out	
5/30/70	24	8	14. It's All In The Game	Motown 1164
9/26/70	11	10	15. Still Water (Love)	Motown 1170
12/12/70+	14	8	16. River Deep - Mountain High	Motown 1173
			THE SUPREMES & FOUR TOPS	
2/27/71	40	2	17. Just Seven Numbers (Can Straighten Out My Life)	Motown 1175
10/2/71	38	3	18. MacArthur Park (Part II)	Motown 1189
12/2/72+	10	9	19. **Keeper Of The Castle**	Dunhill 4330
2/24/73	4	12	● 20. **Ain't No Woman (Like The One I've Got)**	Dunhill 4339
7/28/73	15	8	21. Are You Man Enough	Dunhill 4354
			from the movie Shaft In Africa *starring Richard Roundtree*	
11/17/73	33	3	22. Sweet Understanding Love	Dunhill 4366
9/19/81	11	11	23. When She Was My Girl	Casablanca 2338
			#1 R&B hit (2 weeks)	
10/1/88	35	2	24. Indestructible	Arista 9706
			Sales #31 / Airplay #38; tune used by NBC-TV for the 1988 Summer Olympics	

FOUR VOICES, The

Male vocal quartet: Allan Chase (tenor), Frank Fosta (bass), Sal Mayo and Bill McBride (baritone). Mitch Miller signed the group to Columbia after seeing them on "Arthur Godfrey's Talent Scouts" TV show. Recorded original version of "Sealed With A Kiss" in 1960 (Columbia 41699).

DATE	POS	WKS	ARTIST–RECORD TITLE	LABEL & NO.
3/17/56	20	4	1. Lovely One	Columbia 40643
			Best Seller #20 / Top 100 #30; Ray Conniff (orch.)	

FOX, Samantha

Born on 4/15/66. British singer. Rose to stardom as a topless model for the U.K. *Daily Sun* newspaper.

DATE	POS	WKS	ARTIST–RECORD TITLE	LABEL & NO.
12/20/86+	4	13	1. **Touch Me (I Want Your Body)**	Jive 1006
			Sales #3 / Airplay #6	
4/2/88	3	14	2. **Naughty Girls (Need Love Too)**	Jive 1089
			Sales #2 / Airplay #5	
12/17/88+	8	12	● 3. **I Wanna Have Some Fun**	Jive 1154
			Sales #4 / Airplay #11; above 2 written, arranged and produced by Full Force	
4/29/89	31	4	4. I Only Wanna Be With You	Jive 1192
			Sales #24 / Airplay #38	

FOXX, Inez

Born on 9/9/42 in Greensboro, North Carolina. Sang with the Gospel Tide Chorus. Accompanied vocally by her brother Charlie Fox (born 10/23/39).

DATE	POS	WKS	ARTIST–RECORD TITLE	LABEL & NO.
8/3/63	7	10	1. **Mockingbird**	Symbol 919
			INEZ FOXX (with Charlie Foxx) *adapted from the same traditional folk lyrics as was the song "Bo Diddley"*	

DATE	POS	WKS	ARTIST–RECORD TITLE	LABEL & NO.
			FOXY	
			Miami-based Latino dance band. Four of group's five members came to Florida with the Cuban emigres of 1959. Lead vocalist/guitarist Ish Ledesma later founded and produced Oxo and Company B. Percussionist Richie Puente is son of luminary Latin bandleader Tito Puente.	
8/26/78	**9**	13	1. **Get Off**	Dash 5046
			Wildflower (background vocals); #1 R&B hit (2 weeks)	
4/28/79	**21**	9	2. Hot Number	Dash 5050
			FRAMPTON, Peter	
			Born on 4/22/50 in Beckenham, England. Vocalist/guitarist/composer. Joined British band The Herd at age 16, before forming Humble Pie in 1969, which he left in 1971 to form Frampton's Camel. Went solo in 1974. Played Billy Shears in the 1978 movie *Sgt. Pepper's Lonely Hearts Club Band*. Near-fatal car crash on 6/29/78 temporarily sidelined his career.	
3/13/76	**6**	14	1. **Show Me The Way**	A&M 1795
7/17/76	**12**	11	2. Baby, I Love Your Way	A&M 1832
			studio versions of above 2 released in 1975 on A&M 1693 and 1738, respectively	
10/9/76	**10**	10	3. **Do You Feel Like We Do**	A&M 1867
			all of above recorded "live" at San Francisco's Winterland	
6/11/77	**2 (3)**	13	4. **I'm In You**	A&M 1941
9/10/77	**18**	10	5. Signed, Sealed, Delivered (I'm Yours)	A&M 1972
6/9/79	**14**	9	6. I Can't Stand It No More	A&M 2148
			FRANCIS, Connie	
			Born Concetta Rosa Maria Franconero on 12/12/38 in Newark, New Jersey. First recorded for MGM in 1955. From 1961 to 1965, appeared in the movies *Where The Boys Are, Follow The Boys, Looking For Love* and *When The Boys Meet The Girls*. Connie stopped performing after she was raped on 11/8/74. Began comeback with a performance on "Dick Clark's Live Wednesday" TV show in 1978. Pop music's #1 female vocalist from the late 1950s to the mid-1960s.	
3/3/58	**4**	13	● 1. **Who's Sorry Now**	MGM 12588
			Top 100 #4 / Best Seller #5 / Jockey #6; there were 5 Top 20 versions of this tune in 1923	
6/9/58	**36**	2	2. I'm Sorry I Made You Cry	MGM 12647
			Top 100 #36 / Best Seller #39; #1 hit for Henry Burr in 1918	
8/4/58	**14**	11	3. Stupid Cupid	MGM 12683
			Best Seller #14 / Hot 100 #17	
11/17/58	**30**	1	4. Fallin'	MGM 12713
			written by Neil Sedaka (also #8 below)	
12/15/58+	**2 (2)**	14	● 5. **My Happiness**	MGM 12738
			David Rose (orch.); there were 5 Top 30 versions of this tune in 1948 (written in 1933)	
3/30/59	**22**	4	6. If I Didn't Care	MGM 12769
			#2 hit for the Ink Spots in 1939	
6/1/59	**5**	12	7. **Lipstick On Your Collar/**	
6/1/59	**9**	11	8. **Frankie**	MGM 12793
9/21/59	**34**	4	9. You're Gonna Miss Me	MGM 12824
12/7/59	**7**	11	● 10. **Among My Souvenirs/**	
			there were 4 Top 20 versions of this song in 1928	
12/21/59	**36**	2	11. God Bless America	MGM 12841
			the Irving Berlin classic, popularized by Kate Smith in 1939; Ray Ellis (orch., above 6)	

DATE	POS	WKS	ARTIST–RECORD TITLE	LABEL & NO.
3/14/60	8	9	● 12. **Mama/** *Italian song written in 1941 (English lyrics added in 1946)*	
3/28/60	17	6	13. Teddy *written by Paul Anka*	MGM 12878
5/16/60	1 (2)	16	● 14. **Everybody's Somebody's Fool/**	
6/6/60	19	8	15. Jealous Of You (Tango Della Gelosia) [F]	MGM 12899
8/22/60	1 (2)	14	16. **My Heart Has A Mind Of Its Own**	MGM 12923
11/21/60	7	10	● 17. **Many Tears Ago**	MGM 12964
1/30/61	4	12	● 18. **Where The Boys Are/** *title song from the movie starring George Hamilton*	
2/20/61	34	2	19. No One	MGM 12971
4/24/61	7	9	20. **Breakin' In A Brand New Broken Heart**	MGM 12995
7/3/61	6	9	● 21. **Together** *#1 Adult Contemporary hit (1 week); #1 hit for Paul Whiteman in 1928*	MGM 13019
10/9/61	14	7	22. (He's My) Dreamboat	MGM 13039
12/4/61+	10	9	23. When The Boy In Your Arms (Is The Boy In Your Heart)/	
1/6/62+	26	1	24. Baby's First Christmas [X]	MGM 13051
2/24/62	1 (1)	10	25. **Don't Break The Heart That Loves You** *#1 Adult Contemporary hit (4 weeks); Don Costa (orch., above 3)*	MGM 13059
5/19/62	7	7	26. **Second Hand Love**	MGM 13074
8/11/62	9	6	27. **Vacation**	MGM 13087
11/3/62	24	4	28. I Was Such A Fool (To Fall In Love With You)	MGM 13096
1/5/63	18	6	29. I'm Gonna' Be Warm This Winter	MGM 13116
3/16/63	17	7	30. Follow The Boys *title song from the movie starring Francis*	MGM 13127
6/8/63	23	5	31. If My Pillow Could Talk	MGM 13143
8/31/63	36	3	32. Drownin' My Sorrows	MGM 13160
11/9/63	28	4	33. Your Other Love	MGM 13176
3/7/64	24	6	34. Blue Winter	MGM 13214
5/30/64	25	5	35. Be Anything (But Be Mine) *#7 hit for Eddy Howard in 1952*	MGM 13237
			FRANKE & THE KNOCKOUTS	
			Soft-rock quintet from New Brunswick, New Jersey: Franke Previte (vocals), Billy Elworthy (guitar), Blake Levinsohn (keyboards), Leigh Foxx (bass) and Claude LeHenaff (drums; left in late 1981). Tommy Ayers (keyboards) joined in early 1982.	
3/28/81	10	14	1. **Sweetheart**	Millennium 11801
8/1/81	27	5	2. You're My Girl	Millennium 11808
5/8/82	24	7	3. Without You (Not Another Lonely Night)	Millennium 13105
			FRANKIE GOES TO HOLLYWOOD	
			Dance-rock quintet from Liverpool, England: William "Holly" Johnson and Paul Rutherford (vocals), Brian Nash (guitar), Mark O'Toole (bass) and Peter Gill (drums). Group's name inspired by publicity recounting Frank Sinatra's move into the movie industry.	
2/2/85	10	10	● 1. **Relax** [R] *Sales #9 / Airplay #10; originally charted in 1984 at #67*	Island 99805

DATE	POS	WKS	ARTIST–RECORD TITLE	LABEL & NO.
			FRANKLIN, Aretha	
			Born on 3/25/42 in Memphis; raised in Buffalo and Detroit. The all-time Queen of Soul Music. Daughter of Rev. Cecil L. Franklin, pastor of New Bethel Church in Detroit. Taught to sing gospel at age 9 by Rev. James Cleveland (died 2/9/91, age 59). First recorded for JVB/Battle in 1956. Signed to Columbia Records in 1960 by John Hammond, then dramatic turn in style and success after signing with Atlantic and working with producer Jerry Wexler. Appeared in the 1980 movie *The Blues Brothers*. Winner of 15 Grammy Awards. In 1987, became the first woman to be inducted into the Rock and Roll Hall of Fame. Won Grammy's Living Legends Award in 1990.	
11/20/61	37	2	1. Rock-A-Bye Your Baby With A Dixie Melody #1 hit for Al Jolson in 1918	Columbia 42157
3/18/67	9	9	● 2. **I Never Loved A Man (The Way I Love You)**	Atlantic 2386
5/6/67	1 (2)	11	● 3. **Respect** written by Otis Redding; King Curtis (sax)	Atlantic 2403
8/5/67	4	8	● 4. **Baby I Love You**	Atlantic 2427
10/7/67	8	8	5. **A Natural Woman (You Make Me Feel Like)**	Atlantic 2441
12/16/67+	2 (2)	11	● 6. **Chain Of Fools** Joe South (blues guitar intro)	Atlantic 2464
3/2/68	5	12	● 7. **(Sweet Sweet Baby) Since You've Been Gone/**	
4/13/68	16	7	8. Ain't No Way written by Aretha's sister, Carolyn Franklin (died 4/25/88, age 43); above 4 from the album *Aretha: Lady Soul*	Atlantic 2486
5/25/68	7	9	● 9. **Think**	Atlantic 2518
8/24/68	6	8	10. **The House That Jack Built/**	
8/24/68	10	10	● 11. **I Say A Little Prayer**	Atlantic 2546
11/23/68	14	8	● 12. See Saw/ above 4 (except #10) from the album *Aretha Now* (also #15 below)	
12/28/68+	31	2	13. My Song	Atlantic 2574
3/1/69	19	6	14. The Weight Duane Allman (slide guitar)	Atlantic 2603
4/26/69	28	6	15. I Can't See Myself Leaving You	Atlantic 2619
8/9/69	13	9	16. Share Your Love With Me	Atlantic 2650
11/15/69	17	7	17. Eleanor Rigby	Atlantic 2683
2/28/70	13	9	18. Call Me	Atlantic 2706
6/13/70	23	5	19. Spirit In The Dark *	Atlantic 2731
8/22/70	11	8	● 20. Don't Play That Song *	Atlantic 2751
12/19/70	37	2	21. Border Song (Holy Moses)/	
		1	22. You And Me * ***ARETHA FRANKLIN With The Dixie Flyers**	Atlantic 2772
3/6/71	19	7	23. You're All I Need To Get By	Atlantic 2787
4/24/71	6	11	● 24. **Bridge Over Troubled Water/**	
		4	25. Brand New Me	Atlantic 2796
8/7/71	2 (2)	11	● 26. **Spanish Harlem** Dr. John (keyboards)	Atlantic 2817
11/6/71	9	8	● 27. **Rock Steady**	Atlantic 2838
3/25/72	5	11	● 28. **Day Dreaming**	Atlantic 2866
6/17/72	26	6	29. All The King's Horses above 3 (and #21 & 25 above) from the album *Young, Gifted & Black*	Atlantic 2883
3/10/73	33	5	30. Master Of Eyes (The Deepness Of Your Eyes)	Atlantic 2941
7/21/73	20	10	31. Angel	Atlantic 2969

DATE	POS	WKS	ARTIST–RECORD TITLE	LABEL & NO.
12/15/73+	**3**	17	● 32. **Until You Come Back To Me (That's What I'm Gonna Do)**	Atlantic 2995
5/4/74	**19**	8	33. I'm In Love *all of above on Atlantic (except #30 & 31) produced by Jerry Wexler*	Atlantic 2999
7/10/76	**28**	6	34. Something He Can Feel *written and produced by Curtis Mayfield*	Atlantic 3326
9/11/82	**24**	6	35. Jump To It *written and produced by Luther Vandross*	Arista 0699
7/6/85	**3**	13	36. **Freeway Of Love** *Sales #2 / Airplay #5*	Arista 9354
10/12/85	**7**	13	37. **Who's Zoomin' Who** *Sales #6 / Airplay #7*	Arista 9410
11/2/85	**18**	8	38. Sisters Are Doin' It For Themselves **EURYTHMICS and ARETHA FRANKLIN** *Sales #16 / Airplay #25*	RCA 14214
2/15/86	**22**	7	39. Another Night *Sales #19 / Airplay #24; above 4 from the album Who's Zoomin' Who?*	Arista 9453
10/11/86	**21**	6	40. Jumpin' Jack Flash *Sales #14 / Airplay #25; produced by Keith Richards; title song from the movie starring Whoopi Goldberg*	Arista 9528
1/24/87	**28**	4	41. Jimmy Lee *Sales #23 / Airplay #34*	Arista 9546
3/7/87	**1** (2)	12	42. **I Knew You Were Waiting (For Me)** **ARETHA FRANKLIN AND GEORGE MICHAEL** *Sales #1(2) / Airplay #1(1)*	Arista 9559
4/29/89	**16**	7	43. Through The Storm **ARETHA FRANKLIN AND ELTON JOHN** *Sales #13 / Airplay #19*	Arista 9809
7/2/94	**26**	8	44. Willing To Forgive *Sales #16 / Airplay #57*	Arista 12680

FREBERG, Stan

Born on 8/7/26 in Pasadena, California. Began career doing impersonations on Cliffie Stone's radio show in 1943. Did cartoon voices for the major movie studios. His first in a long string of brilliant satirical recordings was "John And Marsha" in 1951. Launched highly successful advertising career in early '60s; winner of 21 Clio Awards (outstanding achievement award of the radio and TV ad industry).

DATE	POS	WKS	ARTIST–RECORD TITLE	LABEL & NO.
10/22/55	**16**	2	1. The Yellow Rose Of Texas [C] *Jockey #16 / Top 100 #47 pre; Jud Conlon's Rhythmaires (vocal backing); Alvin Stoller (Yankee Snare Drumming)*	Capitol 3249
4/27/57	**25**	1	2. Banana Boat (Day-O) [C] *Best Seller #25 / Top 100 #43; Peter Leeds (interruptions)*	Capitol 3687
11/18/57	**32**	3	3. Wun'erful, Wun'erful! (Sides uh-one & uh-two) [C] *Best Seller #32 / Top 100 #36; Lawrence Welk parody including a medley of tunes: Bubbles In The Wine/Thank You/Louise/Please/Moonlight and Shadows, and featuring The Lemon Sisters, Peggy Taylor and Daws Butler; Billy May (orch., all of above)*	Capitol 3815

DATE	POS	WKS	ARTIST–RECORD TITLE	LABEL & NO.
			### FRED, John, & His Playboy Band	
			John Fred Gourrier was born on 5/8/41 in Baton Rouge, Louisiana. Formed The Playboys in 1956 as a white band playing R&B music. John played basketball and baseball at LSU and Southeastern Louisiana University; his father, Fred Gourrier, played baseball with the Detroit Tigers.	
12/16/67+	**1** (2)	13	● 1. **Judy In Disguise (With Glasses)** a parody of The Beatles' "Lucy In The Sky With Diamonds"	Paula 282
			### FREDDIE AND THE DREAMERS	
			Lead singer Freddie Garrity was born on 11/14/40 in Manchester, England. Formed The Dreamers in 1961 with Derek Quinn (lead guitar), Roy Crewsdon (guitar), Peter Birrell (bass) and Bernie Dwyer (drums).	
3/27/65	**1** (2)	8	1. **I'm Telling You Now** first released on Capitol 5053 in 1963	Tower 125
4/24/65	36	2	2. I Understand (Just How You Feel)	Mercury 72377
5/15/65	18	5	3. Do The Freddie	Mercury 72428
5/15/65	21	5	4. You Were Made For Me first released on Capitol 5137 in 1964	Tower 127
			### FREE	
			British rock band formed in 1968: Paul Rodgers (vocals), Paul Kossoff (guitar), Simon Kirke (drums) and Andy Fraser (bass). Kossoff and Fraser left in 1972, replaced by Tetsu Yamauchi (bass, later with Faces) and John "Rabbit" Bundrick (keyboards). Kossoff (died 3/19/76 of drug-induced heart failure) formed Back Street Crawler. Rodgers and Kirke formed Bad Company in 1974. Rodgers was lead singer of The Firm (1984–85) and The Law (since 1991).	
9/5/70	**4**	13	1. **All Right Now**	A&M 1206
			### FREEMAN, Bobby	
			Born on 6/13/40 in San Francisco. R&B singer. Formed vocal group the Romancers, at age 14. Later formed R&B group the Vocaleers.	
5/26/58	**5**	12	1. **Do You Want To Dance** Top 100 #5 / Best Seller #6 / Jockey #11	Josie 835
8/18/58	37	1	2. Betty Lou Got A New Pair Of Shoes Hot 100 #37 / Best Seller #40	Josie 841
9/26/60	37	3	3. (I Do The) Shimmy Shimmy	King 5373
7/25/64	**5**	10	4. **C'mon And Swim**	Autumn 2
			### FREEMAN, Ernie	
			Born on 8/16/22 in Cleveland. Died of a heart attack on 5/16/81. Pianist/arranger/producer. Prominent sessionman; on recordings by Frank Sinatra, Dean Martin, Sammy Davis, Jr., and Connie Francis. Recorded as "B. Bumble" on all records under that name except "Nut Rocker." Musical director at Reprise Records for 10 years. Retired in the late '70s.	
11/18/57	**4**	12	1. **Raunchy** [I] Jockey #4 / Best Seller #11 / Top 100 #12; #1 R&B hit (2 weeks)	Imperial 5474
			### FREE MOVEMENT, The	
			Los Angeles-based vocal sextet. Several members formerly with gospel groups.	
9/18/71	**5**	11	1. **I've Found Someone Of My Own**	Decca 32818

DATE	POS	WKS	ARTIST–RECORD TITLE	LABEL & NO.
			FREHLEY, Ace	
			Born on 4/27/51 in the Bronx. Lead guitarist of Kiss until 1983. Formed own band, Frehley's Comet.	
12/2/78+	13	12	1. New York Groove	Casablanca 941
			FRENCH, Nicki	
			Female vocalist. Native of Carlisle, England.	
5/6/95	2 (1)	21	● 1. **Total Eclipse Of The Heart** Airplay #2 / Sales #6	Critique 15539
			FREY, Glenn	
			Born on 11/6/48 in Detroit. Singer/songwriter/guitarist. Founding member of the Eagles. Appeared in episodes of TV's "Miami Vice" and "Wiseguy"; starred in the short-lived CBS series "South of Sunset" in 1993.	
7/17/82	31	5	1. I Found Somebody	Asylum 47466
9/11/82	15	11	2. The One You Love	Asylum 69974
7/14/84	20	9	3. Sexy Girl	MCA 52413
1/19/85	2 (1)	13	4. **The Heat Is On** Sales #1(1) / Airplay #4; from the movie *Beverly Hills Cop* starring Eddie Murphy	MCA 52512
5/4/85	12	11	5. Smuggler's Blues Sales #7 / Airplay #16; also on the B-side of #6 below	MCA 52546
9/28/85	2 (2)	13	6. **You Belong To The City** Sales #1(2) / Airplay #3; above 2 from TV's "Miami Vice" soundtrack	MCA 52651
9/10/88	13	9	7. True Love Sales #12 / Airplay #15	MCA 53363
			FRIDA	
			Born Anni-Frid Lyngstad on 11/15/45 in Narvik, Norway. Member of Abba.	
2/12/83	13	12	1. I Know There's Something Going On produced by Phil Collins	Atlantic 89984
			FRIEDMAN, Dean	
			Singer/songwriter from New Jersey.	
5/21/77	26	10	1. Ariel	Lifesong 45022
			FRIEND AND LOVER	
			Husband-and-wife duo: Jim and Cathy Post.	
6/1/68	10	11	1. **Reach Out Of The Darkness**	Verve F. 5069
			FRIENDS OF DISTINCTION, The	
			Los Angeles-based, soul-MOR group. Original lineup: Floyd Butler, Harry Elston, Jessica Cleaves and Barbara Jean Love. Butler and Elston were in the Hi-Fi's with LaMonte McLemore and Marilyn McCoo (later with The 5th Dimension).	
4/26/69	3	13	● 1. **Grazing In The Grass**	RCA 0107
10/11/69	15	12	● 2. Going In Circles	RCA 0204
3/21/70	6	11	3. **Love Or Let Me Be Lonely**	RCA 0319

DATE	POS	WKS	ARTIST–RECORD TITLE	LABEL & NO.
			FRIJID PINK	
			Rock group formed in Detroit: Kelly Green (lead singer), Gary Thompson (guitar), Tom Beaudry (bass) and Rich Stevens (drums).	
2/21/70	**7**	11	● 1. **House Of The Rising Sun**	Parrot 341
			FROST, Max, And The Troopers	
			Studio group produced by Harley Hatcher and Eddie Beram for Mike Curb Productions. Billy Elder was Max Frost.	
9/28/68	**22**	9	1. Shape Of Things To Come	Tower 419
			from the movie *Wild in the Streets* starring Christopher Jones (as Max Frost); Paul Wibier (vocal)	
			FULLER, Bobby, Four	
			Fuller was born on 10/22/43 in Baytown, Texas. Died mysteriously of asphyxiation in Los Angeles on 7/18/66. Band, formed in El Paso, featured Bobby (lead vocals, guitar) and his brother Randy (bass).	
2/12/66	**9**	8	1. **I Fought The Law**	Mustang 3014
			first released on Exeter 124 in 1965 as by Bobby Fuller (written in 1961)	
5/7/66	**26**	3	2. Love's Made A Fool Of You	Mustang 3016
			written by Buddy Holly	
			FULL FORCE—see LISA LISA AND CULT JAM	
			FUNKADELIC	
			Funk aggregation formed in 1968. Consisted of The Parliaments plus a backing band. While recording for Westbound, group also recorded for Invictus as Parliament in 1971. Formed corporation, "A Parliafunkadelicament Thang," through which they recorded under both names. By 1974, leader/producer George Clinton reorganized the Parliament/Funkadelic corporation to include varying membership. Also see Parliament and The Parliaments.	
11/4/78	**28**	5	● 1. One Nation Under A Groove - Part I	Warner 8618
			#1 R&B hit (6 weeks)	
			FURAY, Richie	
			Born on 5/9/44 in Yello Springs, Ohio. Member of Buffalo Springfield, Poco and The Souther, Hillman, Furay Band.	
12/15/79	**39**	3	1. I Still Have Dreams	Asylum 46534
			FU-SCHNICKENS with Shaquille O'Neal (Shaq-Fu)	
			Brooklyn rap trio: Poc Fu, Chip Fu and Moc Fu. FU stands for "For Unity" and Schnicken is a term invented by group to signify coalition. Shaquille O'Neal (born 3/6/72, Newark, New Jersey) is an all-star center with the NBA's Orlando Magic.	
8/14/93	**39**	1	● 1. What's Up Doc? (Can We Rock?)	Jive 42164
			Sales #21 / Airplay #66	
			FUZZ, The	
			Black female trio from Washington, D.C.: Sheila Young, Barbara Gilliam and Val Williams. Originally called the Passionettes.	
4/17/71	**21**	8	1. I Love You For All Seasons	Calla 174

DATE	POS	WKS	ARTIST–RECORD TITLE	LABEL & NO.

G

DATE	POS	WKS	ARTIST–RECORD TITLE	LABEL & NO.
			GABRIEL, Peter	
			Born on 2/13/50 in London. Lead singer of Genesis, 1966–75. Scored the movies *Birdy* and *The Last Temptation Of Christ*. In 1982, financed the World of Music Arts and Dance (WOMAD) festival.	
12/4/82+	29	10	1. Shock The Monkey	Geffen 29883
5/31/86	1 (1)	14	2. **Sledgehammer**	Geffen 28718
			Sales #1(1) / Airplay #2	
9/27/86	26	7	3. In Your Eyes	Geffen 28622
			Sales #26 / Airplay #27	
1/24/87	8	11	4. **Big Time**	Geffen 28503
			Airplay #4 / Sales #8; Stewart Copeland (of The Police; drums)	
1/23/93	32	5	5. Steam	Geffen 19145
			Airplay #33 / Sales #73	
			GABRIELLE	
			Born Louise Gabrielle Bobb on 4/16/70. Eye-patch-wearing South London-based dance singer.	
12/18/93+	26	17	1. Dreams	Go!/London 857298
			Sales #24 / Airplay #26	
			GADABOUTS, The	
			Illinois quartet: Johnie Barr, Eddie Hayes, Larry Craig and "Wild Bill" Putnam.	
8/4/56	39	1	1. Stranded In The Jungle [N]	Mercury 70898
			GALE, Sunny	
			Born Selma Segal on 2/20/27 in Clayton, New Jersey. Began career with Hal McIntyre's band.	
1/8/55	17	1	1. Let Me Go, Lover!	RCA 5952
			Jockey #17; Hugo Winterhalter (orch.)	
			GALLERY	
			Detroit pop group led by singer/guitarist Jim Gold (born 1/12/47).	
4/29/72	4	13	● 1. **Nice To Be With You**	Sussex 232
10/7/72	22	8	2. I Believe In Music	Sussex 239
			written by Mac Davis	
2/10/73	23	8	3. Big City Miss Ruth Ann	Sussex 248
			GALLOP, Frank	
			Best known as the announcer on Perry Como's TV shows during the 1950s.	
5/7/66	34	5	1. The Ballad Of Irving [C]	Kapp 745
			parody of Lorne Greene's "Ringo"; Irving: "the 142nd fastest gun in the West"	

DATE	POS	WKS	ARTIST–RECORD TITLE	LABEL & NO.
			GAP BAND, The	
			Soul trio from Tulsa, Oklahoma, consisting of brothers Charles, Ronnie and Robert Wilson. Group named for three streets in Tulsa: Greenwood, Archer and Pine. Cousins of Bootsy Collins. Charles is member of the Eurythmics' backing band.	
7/3/82	24	6	1. Early In The Morning #1 R&B hit (3 weeks)	Total Exp. 8201
9/11/82	31	7	2. You Dropped A Bomb On Me	Total Exp. 8203
			GARDNER, Dave	
			Born on 6/11/26 in Jackson, Tennessee. Now deceased. "Brother Dave" had six comedy albums chart in the early 1960s.	
7/22/57	22	4	1. White Silver Sands Best Seller #22 / Top 100 #28	OJ 1002
			GARDNER, Don, and Dee Dee Ford	
			Black vocal duo from Philadelphia. Gardner formed his own group, the Sonotones, in 1953 and recorded for Gotham and Bruce. Ford also plays organ and piano. Also see Jimmy Smith.	
7/7/62	20	7	1. I Need Your Loving	Fire 508
			GARFUNKEL, Art	
			Born on 11/5/41 in Forest Hills, New York. Half of Simon & Garfunkel duo. Appeared in the movies *Catch 22*, *Carnal Knowledge* and *Bad Timing*. Has Master's degree in mathematics from Columbia University.	
			GARFUNKEL:	
10/6/73	9	10	1. **All I Know** #1 Adult Contemporary hit (4 weeks)	Columbia 45926
2/9/74	38	1	2. I Shall Sing written by Van Morrison	Columbia 45983
10/19/74	34	3	3. Second Avenue	Columbia 10020
			ART GARFUNKEL:	
9/27/75	18	12	4. I Only Have Eyes For You from the movie musical *Dames* starring Joan Blondell; #2 hit for Ben Selvin in 1934; #1 Adult Contemporary hit (1 week)	Columbia 10190
1/31/76	39	2	5. Break Away #1 Adult Contemporary hit (1 week)	Columbia 10273
2/11/78	17	7	6. (What A) Wonderful World **ART GARFUNKEL with JAMES TAYLOR & PAUL SIMON** #1 Adult Contemporary hit (5 weeks)	Columbia 10676
			GARI, Frank	
			Born on 4/1/42 in New York City. Appeared in several movies in the late '50s.	
2/13/61	27	5	1. Utopia	Crusade 1020
5/15/61	23	6	2. Lullaby Of Love	Crusade 1021
8/14/61	30	3	3. Princess	Crusade 1022

DATE	POS	WKS	ARTIST–RECORD TITLE	LABEL & NO.
			### GARNETT, Gale	
			Born on 7/17/42 in Auckland, New Zealand. Came to the U.S. in 1951. Worked as an actress from age 15. Appeared on many TV shows.	
9/5/64	4	13	1. **We'll Sing In The Sunshine** #1 Adult Contemporary hit (7 weeks)	RCA 8388
			### GARRETT, Leif	
			Born on 11/8/61 in Hollywood. Began movie career in 1969. Appeared in all three *Walking Tall* movies, as well as *Macon County Line, Bob and Carol and Ted and Alice* and *The Outsiders*.	
9/17/77	20	8	1. Surfin' USA	Atlantic 3423
12/3/77+	13	9	2. Runaround Sue	Atlantic 3440
12/9/78+	10	15	3. **I Was Made For Dancin'**	Scotti Br. 403
			### GATES, David	
			Born on 12/11/40 in Tulsa, Oklahoma. Began career as a session musician, then a songwriter/producer before becoming the lead singer of Bread. Wrote The Murmaids' hit "Popsicles & Icicles."	
2/15/75	29	5	1. Never Let Her Go	Elektra 45223
2/18/78	15	12	2. Goodbye Girl title song from the Neil Simon movie starring Richard Dreyfuss	Elektra 45450
10/7/78	30	5	3. Took The Last Train	Elektra 45500
			### GAYE, Marvin	
			Born Marvin Pentz Gay, Jr. on 4/2/39 in Washington, D.C. Fatally shot by his father after a quarrel on 4/1/84 in Los Angeles. Sang in his father's Apostolic church. In vocal groups the Rainbows and Marquees. Joined Harvey Fuqua in the re-formed Moonglows. To Detroit in 1960. Session work as a drummer at Motown; married to Berry Gordy's sister Anna, 1961–75. First recorded under own name for Tamla in 1961. In seclusion for several months following the death of Tammi Terrell (born 1946, Philadelphia; died 3/16/70). Problems with drugs and the IRS led to his moving to Europe for three years. Inducted into the Rock and Roll Hall of Fame in 1987.	
3/2/63	30	3	1. Hitch Hike	Tamla 54075
6/15/63	10	10	2. **Pride And Joy** Martha & The Vandellas (backing vocals, above 2)	Tamla 54079
11/23/63	22	10	3. Can I Get A Witness The Supremes (backing vocals)	Tamla 54087
3/28/64	15	7	4. You're A Wonderful One	Tamla 54093
6/13/64	17	6	5. What's The Matter With You Baby/	
5/23/64	19	6	6. Once Upon A Time **MARVIN GAYE & MARY WELLS (above 2)**	Motown 1057
6/27/64	15	8	7. Try It Baby The Temptations (backing vocals)	Tamla 54095
10/10/64	27	6	8. Baby Don't You Do It	Tamla 54101
12/12/64+	6	11	9. **How Sweet It Is To Be Loved By You**	Tamla 54107
4/10/65	8	8	10. **I'll Be Doggone** #1 R&B hit (1 week)	Tamla 54112
7/24/65	25	5	11. Pretty Little Baby	Tamla 54117
10/23/65	8	9	12. **Ain't That Peculiar** #1 R&B hit (1 week)	Tamla 54122
3/12/66	29	4	13. One More Heartache above 4 (except #11) produced by Smokey Robinson	Tamla 54129

DATE	POS	WKS	ARTIST–RECORD TITLE	LABEL & NO.
2/4/67	**14**	7	14. It Takes Two **MARVIN GAYE & KIM WESTON**	Tamla 54141
7/22/67	**33**	3	15. Your Unchanging Love above 6 (except #11 & 14) from the album *Moods Of Marvin Gaye*	Tamla 54153
2/3/68	**34**	3	16. You	Tamla 54160
10/19/68	**32**	4	17. Chained	Tamla 54170
11/23/68	**1 (7)**	15	18. **I Heard It Through The Grapevine** #1 R&B hit (7 weeks)	Tamla 54176
5/10/69	**4**	13	19. **Too Busy Thinking About My Baby** #1 R&B hit (6 weeks)	Tamla 54181
9/13/69	**7**	9	20. **That's The Way Love Is**	Tamla 54185
7/11/70	**40**	2	21. The End Of Our Road	Tamla 54195
3/6/71	**2 (3)**	13	22. **What's Going On** #1 R&B hit (5 weeks)	Tamla 54201
7/17/71	**4**	10	23. **Mercy Mercy Me (The Ecology)** #1 R&B hit (2 weeks)	Tamla 54207
10/16/71	**9**	8	24. **Inner City Blues (Make Me Wanna Holler)** #1 R&B hit (2 weeks)	Tamla 54209
12/30/72+	**7**	9	25. **Trouble Man** title song from the movie starring Robert Hooks; "live" version is on the B-side of #30 below	Tamla 54228
7/28/73	**1 (2)**	17	26. **Let's Get It On** #1 R&B hit (6 weeks)	Tamla 54234
10/13/73	**12**	10	27. You're A Special Part Of Me **DIANA ROSS & MARVIN GAYE**	Motown 1280
11/17/73	**21**	8	28. Come Get To This	Tamla 54241
3/30/74	**19**	10	29. My Mistake (Was To Love You) **DIANA ROSS & MARVIN GAYE**	Motown 1269
10/26/74	**28**	3	30. Distant Lover "live" recording; studio version is on the B-side of #28 above	Tamla 54253
5/8/76	**15**	9	31. I Want You #1 R&B hit (1 week)	Tamla 54264
4/23/77	**1 (1)**	15	32. **Got To Give It Up (Pt. I)** recorded "live" at the London Palladium; #1 R&B hit (5 weeks)	Tamla 54280
11/20/82+	**3**	15	● 33. **Sexual Healing** #1 R&B hit (10 weeks)	Columbia 03302
			MARVIN GAYE & TAMMI TERRELL:	
6/3/67	**19**	9	34. Ain't No Mountain High Enough	Tamla 54149
9/30/67	**5**	10	35. **Your Precious Love**	Tamla 54156
12/16/67+	**10**	9	36. **If I Could Build My Whole World Around You**	Tamla 54161
4/27/68	**8**	11	37. **Ain't Nothing Like The Real Thing** #1 R&B hit (1 week)	Tamla 54163
8/10/68	**7**	10	38. **You're All I Need To Get By** #1 R&B hit (5 weeks)	Tamla 54169
10/19/68	**24**	6	39. Keep On Lovin' Me Honey	Tamla 54173
2/15/69	**30**	4	40. Good Lovin' Ain't Easy To Come By Valerie Simpson actually sang female part due to Tammi's poor health; all of above Gaye & Terrell titles written (except #36) and produced (except #34–36) by Ashford & Simpson	Tamla 54179

DATE	POS	WKS	ARTIST–RECORD TITLE	LABEL & NO.
			GAYLE, Crystal	
			Born Brenda Gail Webb on 1/9/51 in Paintsville, Kentucky; raised in Wabash, Indiana. Youngest sister of Loretta Lynn. First country artist to tour China (1979).	
9/24/77	**2** (3)	18	● 1. **Don't It Make My Brown Eyes Blue**	United Art. 1016
			#1 Country hit (4 weeks)	
9/2/78	**18**	11	2. Talking In Your Sleep	United Art. 1214
			#1 Country hit (2 weeks)	
11/3/79	**15**	10	3. Half The Way	Columbia 11087
11/13/82+	**7**	21	4. **You And I**	Elektra 69936
			EDDIE RABBITT with CRYSTAL GAYLE	
			#1 Country hit (1 week)	
			GAYNOR, Gloria	
			Born on 9/7/49 in Newark, New Jersey. Disco singer. With the Soul Satisfiers in 1971.	
12/7/74+	**9**	10	1. **Never Can Say Goodbye**	MGM 14748
1/20/79	**1** (3)	17	▲ 2. **I Will Survive**	Polydor 14508
			G-CLEFS, The	
			Group from Roxbury, Massachusetts: brothers Teddy, Chris, Timmy and Arnold Scott, with Ray Gibson.	
9/15/56	**24**	1	1. Ka-Ding Dong	Pilgrim 715
			Best Seller #24 / Top 100 #53; Freddy Cannon (lead guitar)	
10/16/61	**9**	11	2. **I Understand (Just How You Feel)**	Terrace 7500
			#6 hit for The Four Tunes in 1954; includes the "Auld Lang Syne" tune	
			GEDDES, David	
			Born on 7/1/50. While a teenager, formed the group Rock Garden, which recorded for Capitol.	
8/23/75	**4**	9	1. **Run Joey Run**	Big Tree 16044
11/22/75	**18**	6	2. The Last Game Of The Season (A Blind Man In The Bleachers)	Big Tree 16052
			GEILS, J., Band	
			Formed in Boston in 1967, guitarist Jerome Geils led rock band consisting of Peter "Wolf" Blankfield (vocals), "Magic Dick" Salwitz (harmonica), Seth Justman (keyboards), Danny Klein (bass) and Stephen Jo Bladd (drums). First recorded for Atlantic in 1969. Wolf left for a solo career in the fall of 1983.	
1/15/72	**39**	2	1. Looking For A Love	Atlantic 2844
5/26/73	**30**	6	2. Give It To Me	Atlantic 2953
11/23/74+	**12**	7	3. Must Of Got Lost	Atlantic 3214
1/20/79	**35**	3	4. One Last Kiss	EMI America 8007
3/8/80	**32**	5	5. Come Back	EMI America 8032
5/24/80	**38**	3	6. Love Stinks	EMI America 8039
11/28/81+	**1** (6)	20	● 7. **Centerfold**	EMI America 8102
3/6/82	**4**	12	● 8. **Freeze-Frame**	EMI America 8108
7/3/82	**40**	2	9. Angel In Blue	EMI America 8100
12/11/82+	**24**	7	10. I Do	EMI America 8148
			"live" recording	

DATE	POS	WKS	ARTIST–RECORD TITLE	LABEL & NO.
			GENE & DEBBE	
			Gene Thomas (born 12/4/38, Palestine, Texas) and Debbe Nevills.	
3/9/68	**17**	12	1. Playboy	TRX 5006
			GENERAL PUBLIC	
			British pop band formed in 1984: Dave Wakeling (vocals, guitar), Ranking Roger (vocals, keyboards), Stoker (vocals), Kevin White (guitar), Micky Billingham (keyboards) and Horace Panter (drums). Wakeling and Roger had been in English Beat. General Public disbanded in March 1987. Wakeling and Roger reunited in 1994.	
1/26/85	**27**	5	1. Tenderness Sales #20 / Airplay #26	I.R.S. 9934
4/30/94	**22**	13	2. I'll Take You There Airplay #19 / Sales #46; from the movie *Threesome* starring Lara Flynn Boyle and Stephen Baldwin	Epic Sound. 77452
			GENESIS	
			Formed as a progressive-rock group in England in 1967. Consisted of Peter Gabriel (lead vocals), Anthony Phillips (guitar), Tony Banks (keyboards), Mike Rutherford (guitar, bass) and Chris Stewart (drums; replaced by John Silver in 1968, then John Mayhew in 1969). Phillips and Mayhew left in 1970, replaced by Steve Hackett (guitar) and Phil Collins (drums). Gabriel left in June 1975, with Collins replacing him as new lead singer. Hackett went solo in 1977, leaving group as a trio: Collins, Rutherford and Banks. Added regular members for touring: Americans Chester Thompson (drums), in 1977, and guitarist Daryl Stuermer, In 1978. Collins also recorded in jazz-fusion group Brand X. Rutherford also in own group, Mike + The Mechanics, formed in 1985. Hackett later formed group GTR.	
6/3/78	**23**	5	1. Follow You Follow Me	Atlantic 3474
6/21/80	**14**	11	2. Misunderstanding	Atlantic 3662
11/7/81	**29**	6	3. No Reply At All features the Earth, Wind & Fire horn section	Atlantic 3858
1/23/82	**26**	6	4. Abacab	Atlantic 3891
5/8/82	**40**	2	5. Man On The Corner	Atlantic 4025
7/24/82	**32**	5	6. Paperlate	Atlantic 4053
12/10/83+	**6**	14	7. **That's All!**	Atlantic 89724
6/7/86	**1** (1)	12	8. **Invisible Touch** Airplay #1(3) / Sales #4; "live" version is on the B-side of #17 below	Atlantic 89407
8/23/86	**4**	12	9. **Throwing It All Away** Airplay #2 / Sales #7; #1 Adult Contemporary hit (2 weeks)	Atlantic 89372
11/15/86+	**4**	15	10. **Land Of Confusion** Airplay #3 / Sales #5	Atlantic 89336
2/21/87	**3**	10	11. **Tonight, Tonight, Tonight** Airplay #3 / Sales #3; "live" version is on the B-side of #17 below	Atlantic 89290
5/2/87	**3**	12	12. **In Too Deep** Airplay #3 / Sales #3; #1 Adult Contemporary hit (3 weeks); above 5 from the album *Invisible Touch*	Atlantic 89316
11/9/91+	**12**	16	13. No Son Of Mine Airplay #10 / Sales #31	Atlantic 87571
2/15/92	**7**	14	14. **I Can't Dance** Airplay #11 / Sales #13	Atlantic 87532
5/16/92	**12**	14	15. Hold On My Heart Airplay #9 / Sales #41; #1 Adult Contemporary hit (5 weeks)	Atlantic 87481
8/15/92	**23**	9	16. Jesus He Knows Me Airplay #21 / Sales #72	Atlantic 87454

DATE	POS	WKS	ARTIST–RECORD TITLE	LABEL & NO.
12/12/92+	**21**	9	17. Never A Time Airplay #22; above 5 from the album *We Can't Dance*	Atlantic 87411

GENTRY, Bobbie

Born Roberta Streeter on 7/27/44 in Chickasaw County, Mississippi; raised in Greenwood, Mississippi. Singer/songwriter. Won the 1967 Best New Artist Grammy Award. Married singer Jim Stafford on 10/15/78.

DATE	POS	WKS	ARTIST–RECORD TITLE	LABEL & NO.
8/12/67	**1** (4)	12	● 1. **Ode To Billie Joe**	Capitol 5950
3/8/69	**36**	1	2. Let It Be Me **GLEN CAMPBELL AND BOBBIE GENTRY**	Capitol 2387
1/31/70	**31**	4	3. Fancy	Capitol 2675
3/14/70	**27**	6	4. All I Have To Do Is Dream **BOBBIE GENTRY & GLEN CAMPBELL**	Capitol 2745

GENTRYS, The

Memphis-based rock band formed in 1963. Group featured Larry Raspberry as lead singer.

DATE	POS	WKS	ARTIST–RECORD TITLE	LABEL & NO.
9/25/65	**4**	11	1. **Keep On Dancing** first released on Youngstown 601 in 1965	MGM 13379

GEORGE, Barbara

Born on 8/16/42 in New Orleans. R&B singer/songwriter.

DATE	POS	WKS	ARTIST–RECORD TITLE	LABEL & NO.
12/18/61+	**3**	11	1. **I Know (You Don't Love Me No More)** Melvin Lastie (cornet solo); #1 R&B hit (4 weeks)	A.F.O. 302

GEORGIA SATELLITES

Rock quartet formed in Atlanta in 1980, led by dual guitarists/vocalists Dan Baird and Rick Richards, with bassist Rich Price and drummer Mauro Magellan (born Rio de Janeiro). By 1992, Baird left and Richards joined Izzy Stradlin & The Ju Ju Hounds.

DATE	POS	WKS	ARTIST–RECORD TITLE	LABEL & NO.
12/20/86+	**2** (1)	14	1. **Keep Your Hands To Yourself** Sales #1(1) / Airplay #6	Elektra 69502

GERARDO

Born Gerardo Mejia III on 4/16/65 in Guayaquil, Ecuador. Rapper/actor. To Glendale, California at age 12. Raps in Spanglish (half Spanish, half English). Appeared in the movies *Can't Buy Me Love* and *Colors*.

DATE	POS	WKS	ARTIST–RECORD TITLE	LABEL & NO.
3/2/91	**7**	10	● 1. **Rico Suave** Sales #5 / Airplay #15	Interscope 98871
5/25/91	**16**	6	2. We Want The Funk Sales #22 / Airplay #26; samples Parliament's "Tear The Roof Off The Sucker (Give Up The Funk)"	Interscope 98815

GERRY AND THE PACEMAKERS

Pop-rock group formed in Liverpool, England, in 1959: Gerry Marsden (born 9/24/42; vocals, guitar), Leslie Maguire (piano), Les Chadwick (bass) and Freddie Marsden (drums). The Marsden brothers had been in skiffle bands; Gerry had own rock band Mars-Bars. Signed in 1962 by The Beatles' manager Brian Epstein.

DATE	POS	WKS	ARTIST–RECORD TITLE	LABEL & NO.
6/6/64	**4**	9	1. **Don't Let The Sun Catch You Crying**	Laurie 3251
8/8/64	**9**	7	2. **How Do You Do It?** first released on Laurie 3162 in 1963	Laurie 3261

DATE	POS	WKS	ARTIST–RECORD TITLE	LABEL & NO.
10/17/64	17	6	3. I Like It first released on Laurie 3196 in 1963	Laurie 3271
1/9/65	14	5	4. I'll Be There	Laurie 3279
2/13/65	6	9	5. **Ferry Cross The Mersey** some pressings show title as: "Ferry Across The Mersey"	Laurie 3284
4/24/65	23	5	6. It's Gonna Be Alright above 2 from the movie *Ferry Cross The Mersey* starring Gerry And The Pacemakers	Laurie 3293
10/8/66	28	4	7. Girl On A Swing	Laurie 3354

GETO BOYS, The

Houston-based rap outfit: Richard "Bushwick Bill" Shaw, William "Willie D" Dennis, Brad "Scarface" Jordan and Collins "DJ Ready Red" Lyaseth (left group in early 1991; replaced by Big Mike). Shaw, a Jamaican-born dwarf, lost his right eye in a shooting on 5/10/91.

DATE	POS	WKS	ARTIST–RECORD TITLE	LABEL & NO.
11/2/91+	23	11	● 1. Mind Playing Tricks On Me Sales #6	Rap-A-Lot 7241
6/12/93	40	1	2. Six Feet Deep Sales #20 / Airplay #49; samples "Easy" by the Commodores and "What's Going On" by Marvin Gaye	Rap-A-Lot 53823

GET WET

Pop band featuring Sherri Beachfront as lead singer.

DATE	POS	WKS	ARTIST–RECORD TITLE	LABEL & NO.
5/23/81	39	2	1. Just So Lonely	Boardwalk 02018

GETZ, Stan

Born Stan Gayetzsky on 2/2/27 in Philadelphia. Died of liver cancer on 6/6/91. 17-time winner of *Down Beat* polls as top tenor saxophonist; played with Stan Kenton, 1944–45; Jimmy Dorsey, 1945–46; Benny Goodman, 1946; and Woody Herman, 1947–49. Leader of the Brazilian-born "Bossa Nova" rage of the 1960s.

DATE	POS	WKS	ARTIST–RECORD TITLE	LABEL & NO.
10/27/62	15	10	1. Desafinado [I] **STAN GETZ/CHARLIE BYRD**	Verve 10260
6/20/64	5	10	2. **The Girl From Ipanema** **GETZ/GILBERTO** (Astrud Gilberto, vocal) #1 Adult Contemporary hit (2 weeks); above 2 written by Brazilian composer Antonio Carlos Jobim	Verve 10323

GIANT

Rock quartet formed in Nashville in 1985: brothers Dan (vocals, guitar) and David (drums) Huff, Mike Brignardello (bass) and Alan Pasqua (keyboards).

DATE	POS	WKS	ARTIST–RECORD TITLE	LABEL & NO.
5/5/90	20	8	1. I'll See You In My Dreams Airplay #18 / Sales #22	A&M 1495

GIANT STEPS

English duo: vocalist Campsie and multi-instrumentalist George McFarlane. Both initially worked together as members of the British band Grand Hotel, then as Quick.

DATE	POS	WKS	ARTIST–RECORD TITLE	LABEL & NO.
10/1/88	13	10	1. Another Lover Airplay #12 / Sales #13	A&M 1226

DATE	POS	WKS	ARTIST–RECORD TITLE	LABEL & NO.
			### GIBB, Andy	
			Born Andrew Roy Gibb on 3/5/58 in Manchester, England. Died on 3/10/88 of an inflammatory heart virus in Oxford, England. Moved to Australia when six months old, then back to England at age nine. Youngest brother of Barry, Robin and Maurice Gibb—The Bee Gees. Hosted TV's "Solid Gold," 1981–82.	
5/28/77	**1** (4)	23	● 1. **I Just Want To Be Your Everything**	RSO 872
12/10/77+	**1** (2)	22	● 2. **(Love Is) Thicker Than Water**	RSO 883
4/22/78	**1** (7)	19	▲ 3. **Shadow Dancing**	RSO 893
7/22/78	**5**	13	● 4. **An Everlasting Love**	RSO 904
11/4/78	**9**	13	● 5. **(Our Love) Don't Throw It All Away**	RSO 911
2/2/80	**4**	12	6. **Desire**	RSO 1019
4/19/80	**12**	8	7. I Can't Help It	RSO 1026
			ANDY GIBB AND OLIVIA NEWTON-JOHN	
12/6/80+	**15**	11	8. Time Is Time	RSO 1059
4/11/81	**40**	1	9. Me (Without You)	RSO 1056
			### GIBB, Barry	
			Born on 9/1/46 in Manchester, England. Eldest brother of The Bee Gees. Appeared in the movie *Sgt. Pepper's Lonely Hearts Club Band*. Also see Samantha Sang.	
			BARBRA STREISAND & BARRY GIBB:	
11/15/80+	**3**	15	● 1. **Guilty**	Columbia 11390
2/14/81	**10**	10	2. **What Kind Of Fool**	Columbia 11430
			#1 Adult Contemporary hit (4 weeks)	
			BARRY GIBB:	
9/29/84	**37**	3	3. Shine Shine	MCA 52443
			### GIBB, Robin	
			Born on 12/22/49 in Manchester, England. Twin brother of The Bee Gees' Maurice Gibb.	
8/19/78	**15**	9	1. **Oh! Darling**	RSO 907
			from the movie *Sgt. Pepper's Lonely Hearts Club Band* starring Peter Frampton and The Bee Gees; tune introduced on The Beatles' 1969 album *Abbey Road*	
7/7/84	**37**	4	2. Boys Do Fall In Love	Mirage 99743
			### GIBBS, Georgia	
			Born Fredda Gibbons on 8/17/20 in Worcester, Massachusetts. Sang on the "Lucky Strike" radio show, 1937–38. With Hudson-DeLange band, then with Frankie Trumbauer, 1940, and Artie Shaw, 1942. On the "Garry Moore-Jimmy Durante" radio show in the late '40s, where Moore dubbed her "Her Nibs, Miss Gibbs."	
1/29/55	**2** (1)	19	● 1. **Tweedle Dee**	Mercury 70517
			Jockey #2 / Best Seller #3 / Juke Box #3	
3/26/55	**1** (3)	20	● 2. **Dance With Me Henry (Wallflower)**	Mercury 70572
			Juke Box #1 / Best Seller #2 / Jockey #3; revised version of The Midnighters' #1 1954 R&B hit "Work With Me Annie" and Etta James' #1 1955 R&B hit "The Wallflower"	
7/9/55	**12**	4	3. Sweet And Gentle	Mercury 70647
			Jockey #12; Cuban song ("Me Lo Dijo Adela")	

DATE	POS	WKS	ARTIST–RECORD TITLE	LABEL & NO.
9/17/55	**14**	4	4. I Want You To Be My Baby Jockey #14 / Best Seller #22 / Top 100 #48 pre	Mercury 70685
4/14/56	**36**	1	5. Rock Right	Mercury 70811
5/26/56	**30**	4	6. Kiss Me Another	Mercury 70850
8/25/56	**20**	8	7. Happiness Street Jockey #20 / Top 100 #25	Mercury 70920
12/22/56	**24**	1	8. Tra La La Jockey #24 / Top 100 #39; Glenn Osser (orch.: #1,6-8)	Mercury 70998
10/20/58	**32**	1	9. The Hula Hoop Song Hot 100 #32 / Best Seller #42 end; Hugo Peretti (of Hugo & Luigi; orch.: #2-5,9)	Roulette 4106

GIBBS, Terri

Born on 6/15/54 in Augusta, Georgia. Female country singer/pianist. Blind since birth.

DATE	POS	WKS	ARTIST–RECORD TITLE	LABEL & NO.
2/28/81	**13**	12	1. Somebody's Knockin'	MCA 41309

GIBSON, Debbie

Born on 8/31/70 in Long Island, New York. Singer/songwriter/pianist. Playing piano since age five and songwriting since age six. In 1991, played Eponine in *Les Miserables* on Broadway.

DATE	POS	WKS	ARTIST–RECORD TITLE	LABEL & NO.
6/27/87	**4**	16	● 1. **Only In My Dreams** Sales #3 / Airplay #3	Atlantic 89322
10/24/87	**4**	15	2. **Shake Your Love** Sales #4 / Airplay #4	Atlantic 89187
2/6/88	**3**	13	3. **Out Of The Blue** Sales #3 / Airplay #3	Atlantic 89129
5/7/88	**1** (1)	14	4. **Foolish Beat** Airplay #1(2) / Sales #1(1)	Atlantic 89109
9/3/88	**22**	6	5. Staying Together Sales #19 / Airplay #26; above 5 from the album *Out Of The Blue*	Atlantic 89034
1/28/89	**1** (3)	12	● 6. **Lost In Your Eyes** Airplay #1(3) / Sales #1(2)	Atlantic 88970
4/15/89	**11**	8	● 7. Electric Youth Sales #8 / Airplay #12	Atlantic 88919
7/8/89	**17**	7	8. No More Rhyme Sales #15 / Airplay #17	Atlantic 88885
12/15/90+	**26**	6	9. Anything Is Possible Airplay #26 / Sales #28	Atlantic 87793

GIBSON, Don

Born on 4/3/28 in Shelby, North Carolina. Country singer/songwriter/guitarist. Joined the *Grand Ole Opry* in 1958.

DATE	POS	WKS	ARTIST–RECORD TITLE	LABEL & NO.
3/31/58	**7**	17	1. **Oh Lonesome Me** Best Seller #7 / Top 100 #8 / Jockey #10; #1 Country hit (8 weeks)	RCA 7133
7/14/58	**20**	8	2. Blue Blue Day Jockey #20 / Best Seller #32 / Top 100 #32; originally released in 1957; #1 Country hit (2 weeks)	RCA 7010
3/28/60	**29**	6	3. Just One Time	RCA 7690
7/10/61	**21**	8	4. Sea Of Heartbreak	RCA 7890

GILBERTO, Astrud—see GETZ, Stan

DATE	POS	WKS	ARTIST–RECORD TITLE	LABEL & NO.
			GILDER, Nick	
			Born on 11/7/51 in London. Moved to Vancouver, Canada, at age 10. Founding member of the rock band Sweeney Todd.	
8/5/78	**1** (1)	18	▲ 1. **Hot Child In The City**	Chrysalis 2226
			GILKYSON, Terry, and The Easy Riders	
			Folk trio: Terry Gilkyson, Rick Dehr and Frank Miller. Gilkyson performed with the legendary Weavers folk group in the early 1950s. Gilkyson's son, Tony, is the bass guitarist of the group X.	

2/9/57	**4**	14	1. **Marianne**
			       Juke Box #4 / Top 100 #5 / Jockey #5 / Best Seller #6; adapted
			       from a Bahamian folk song
				Columbia 40817

			GILL, Johnny	
			Born on 5/22/66 in Washington, D.C. Sang in family gospel group, Wings Of Faith, from age five. Joined New Edition in 1988. His brother Randy and cousin Jermaine Mickey are members of II D Extreme.	
5/26/90	**3**	16	● 1. **Rub You The Right Way** Airplay #2 / Sales #4; #1 R&B hit (1 week)	Motown 1982
8/18/90	**10**	10	2. **My, My, My** Sales #9 / Airplay #13; #1 R&B hit (2 weeks)	Motown 2033
11/24/90	**28**	6	3. Fairweather Friend Sales #23 / Airplay #33	Motown 2049

5/16/92	**31**	5	4. Silent Prayer
			       SHANICE featuring Johnny Gill
			       Airplay #29 / Sales #33
				Motown 2165

1/2/93	**33**	2	● 5. Slow And Sexy
			       SHABBA RANKS (featuring Johnny Gill)
			       Sales #14 / Airplay #63
				Epic 74741

			GILL, Vince—see GRANT, Amy	
			GILLEY, Mickey	
			Born on 3/9/36 in Natchez, Louisiana; raised in Ferriday, Louisiana. Country singer/pianist. First cousin to both Jerry Lee Lewis and Reverend Jimmy Swaggart. Owner of Gilleys nightclub in Pasadena, Texas. Gilley and the club were featured in the movie *Urban Cowboy*. The club closed in 1989.	

6/28/80	**22**	9	1. Stand By Me
			       featured in the movie *Urban Cowboy* starring John Travolta and
			       Debra Winger
				Full Moon 46640

			GILMER, Jimmy—see FIREBALLS	
			GILREATH, James	
			Born on 11/14/39 in Prairie, Mississippi. Singer/guitarist/songwriter.	
4/27/63	**21**	6	1. Little Band Of Gold	Joy 274
			GIN BLOSSOMS	
			Pop-rock group formed in Tempe, Arizona, in 1987: Robin Wilson (vocals), Jesse Valenzuela and Scott Johnson (guitars), Bill Leen (bass) and Phillip Rhodes (drums). Early guitarist Doug Hopkins, writer of "Hey Jealousy" and "Found Out About You," died of a self-inflicted bullet wound on 12/5/93 (age 32).	
9/11/93	**25**	11	1. Hey Jealousy Sales #28 / Airplay #31	A&M 0242

DATE	POS	WKS	ARTIST–RECORD TITLE	LABEL & NO.
1/1/94	**25**	17	2. Found Out About You Airplay #14	A&M 0418
6/9/58	**20**	1	**GINO & GINA** Aristedes and Irene Giosasi. Brother-and-sister duo from Brooklyn. Aristedes co-wrote "Sorry (I Ran All The Way Home)." 1. (It's Been A Long Time) Pretty Baby Jockey #20 / Top 100 #34 / Best Seller #39	Mercury 71283
1/5/85	**15**	7	**GIUFFRIA** California-based rock quintet led by Gregg Giuffria (keyboardist with Angel) and David Glen Eisley. Giuffria and member Chuck Wright joined House Of Lords in 1988. 1. Call To The Heart Sales #12 / Airplay #25	MCA 52497
11/25/57	**16**	15	**GLAHE, Will** European accordion player/bandleader. 1. Liechtensteiner Polka　　　　　　　[F] Best Seller #16 / Jockey #18 / Top 100 #19	London 1755
9/18/71	**36**	3	**GLASS BOTTLE, The** Pop group featuring lead singer Gary Criss. 1. I Ain't Got Time Anymore produced by novelty artist Dickie Goodman	Avco Emb. 4575
			GLASS TIGER Canadian rock quintet: Alan Frew (vocals), Sam Reid (keyboards), Al Connelly (guitar), Wayne Parker (bass) and Michael Hanson (drums).	
8/9/86	**2** (1)	14	1. **Don't Forget Me (When I'm Gone)** Sales #1(1) / Airplay #6; Bryan Adams (response vocal)	Manhattan 50037
11/29/86+	**7**	13	2. **Someday** Sales #7 / Airplay #7	Manhattan 50048
3/21/87	**34**	5	3. I Will Be There Airplay #28 / Sales #37	Manhattan 50066
5/7/88	**31**	5	4. I'm Still Searching Sales #26 / Airplay #30	EMI-Man. 50116
6/15/63	**14**	7	**GLAZER, Tom, And The Do-Re-Mi Children's Chorus** Glazer (born 9/3/14 in Philadelphia) is a novelty folk singer. Hosted own ABC radio program, 1945–47. Composed score for the 1957 movie *A Face In The Crowd*. 1. On Top Of Spaghetti　　　　　　[N] parody of the tune "On Top Of Old Smokey"	Kapp 526

DATE	POS	WKS	ARTIST–RECORD TITLE	LABEL & NO.
			GLENCOVES, The	
			Teen folk trio formed at Chaminade High School in Mineola, Long Island, New York, in 1961. Singers/guitarists Don Connors and Bill Byrne with singer Brian Bolger.	
7/27/63	38	2	1. Hootenanny	Select 724
			Hootenanny: an exuberant folk-music gathering and the name of an ABC-TV series, 1963–64	
			GLITTER, Gary	
			Born Paul Gadd on 5/8/44 in Banbury, England. First recorded as Paul Raven in the early '60s, then as Paul Monday; changed name to Gary Glitter in 1971.	
8/5/72	7	9	1. **Rock And Roll Part 2** [I]	Bell 45237
			tune has become "The Sports Anthem" ("The Hey Song") across the U.S.	
12/2/72	35	3	2. I Didn't Know I Loved You (Till I Saw You Rock And Roll)	Bell 45276
			GODLEY & CREME	
			Kevin Godley (born 10/7/45, Manchester, England) and Lol Creme (born 9/19/47, Manchester, England) formed duo after leaving British group 10cc. Prior to 10cc, both were with Hotlegs.	
8/17/85	16	10	1. Cry	Polydor 881786
			Airplay #15 / Sales #16	
			GODSPELL	
			The original cast as featured in the Broadway rock musical *Godspell*.	
6/24/72	13	9	1. Day By Day	Bell 45210
			original cast member Robin Lamont (lead vocal)	
			GO-GO'S	
			Female rock group formed in 1978 in Los Angeles: Belinda Carlisle (vocals), Jane Wiedlin (guitar), Charlotte Caffey (guitar), Kathy Valentine (bass) and Gina Schock (drums). Disbanded in 1984. Reunited briefly in 1990 and again in 1994. Caffey formed The Graces in 1989.	
10/24/81	20	13	1. Our Lips Are Sealed	I.R.S. 9901
2/13/82	2 (3)	15	● 2. **We Got The Beat**	I.R.S. 9903
7/17/82	8	9	3. **Vacation**	I.R.S. 9907
3/31/84	11	10	4. Head Over Heels	I.R.S. 9926
7/14/84	32	5	5. Turn To You	I.R.S. 9928
			GOLD, Andrew	
			Born on 8/2/51 in Burbank, California. Son of soundtrack composer Ernest Gold (*Exodus*) and singer Marni Nixon. Co-founder of the group Bryndle. Session and arranging work for Linda Ronstadt since the early '70s. Member of pop duo Wax in 1986.	
4/16/77	7	13	1. **Lonely Boy**	Asylum 45384
			Linda Ronstadt (backing vocal)	
3/4/78	25	9	2. Thank You For Being A Friend	Asylum 45456
			song later adapted as the theme for the TV series "The Golden Girls" starring Bea Arthur and Betty White	

DATE	POS	WKS	ARTIST–RECORD TITLE	LABEL & NO.
			GOLDEN EARRING	
			Rock band formed in Amsterdam, Holland, in 1967: Barry Hay (vocals), George Kooymans (guitar), Rinus Gerritsen (bass) and Cesar Zuiderwijk (drums).	
6/22/74	**13**	10	1. Radar Love	Track 40202
1/22/83	**10**	15	2. **Twilight Zone**	21 Records 103
			GOLDSBORO, Bobby	
			Born on 1/18/41 in Marianna, Florida. Singer/songwriter/guitarist. To Dothan, Alabama, in 1956. Toured with Roy Orbison, 1962–64. Own syndicated TV show, "The Bobby Goldsboro Show," 1972–75.	
2/15/64	**9**	8	1. **See The Funny Little Clown**	United Art. 672
5/23/64	**39**	2	2. Whenever He Holds You	United Art. 710
2/20/65	**13**	8	3. Little Things	United Art. 810
6/5/65	**27**	6	4. Voodoo Woman	United Art. 862
3/12/66	**23**	5	5. It's Too Late	United Art. 980
1/14/67	**35**	3	6. Blue Autumn	United Art. 50087
3/30/68	**1** (5)	13	● 7. **Honey**	United Art. 50283
			#1 Country hit (3 weeks); #1 Adult Contemporary hit (2 weeks)	
7/13/68	**19**	7	8. Autumn Of My Life	United Art. 50318
11/30/68	**36**	2	9. The Straight Life	United Art. 50461
1/9/71	**11**	11	10. Watching Scotty Grow	United Art. 50727
			written by Mac Davis; #1 Adult Contemporary hit (6 weeks)	
10/6/73	**21**	8	11. Summer (The First Time)	United Art. 251
			GOMM, Ian	
			Born on 3/17/47 in Ealing, England. Member of London band Brinsley Schwarz, 1972–75.	
10/6/79	**18**	5	1. Hold On	Stiff/Epic 50747
			GONE ALL STARS	
			Session band arranged by record company mogul George Goldner.	
3/3/58	**30**	4	1. "7-11" [I]	Gone 5016
			Best Seller #30 / Top 100 #31; rock version of the Perez Prado tune "Mambo No. 5"	
			GONZALEZ	
			British soul-disco band featuring vocals by Linda Taylor and Alan Marshall.	
2/10/79	**26**	5	1. Haven't Stopped Dancing Yet	Capitol 4674
			GOODIE MOB	
			Rap quartet from Atlanta: Cee-Lo, Khujo, T-Mo and Big Gipp. Group name is short for "The Good Die Mostly Over Bullshit."	
11/18/95	**39**	3	1. Cell Therapy	LaFace 24113
			Sales #14	
			GOODMAN, Benny—see CLOONEY, Rosemary	

DATE	POS	WKS	ARTIST–RECORD TITLE	LABEL & NO.
			### GOODMAN, Dickie	
			Born on 4/19/34 in Hewlett, New York. Died on 11/6/89 of a self-inflicted gunshot. Goodman and partner Bill Buchanan originated the novelty "break-in" recordings featuring bits of the original versions of Top 40 hits interwoven throughout the recording. Comedy writer for Jackie Mason and head of music department at 20th Century Fox.	
			BUCHANAN AND GOODMAN:	
8/11/56	**3**	10	● 1. **The Flying Saucer (Parts 1 & 2)** [N] Best Seller #3 / Top 100 #7 / Jockey #9 / Juke Box #9; originally titled "Back To Earth" on Luniverse 101; also released on Radioactive 101 in 1956	Luniverse 101
7/29/57	**18**	8	2. Flying Saucer The 2nd [N] Best Seller #18 / Top 100 #19	Luniverse 105
12/30/57	**32**	2	3. Santa And The Satellite (Parts I & II) [X-N] Top 100 #32 / Best Seller #36; disc jockey Paul Sherman (narration)	Luniverse 107
			DICKIE GOODMAN:	
2/23/74	**33**	4	4. Energy Crisis '74 [N]	Rainy Wed. 206
9/13/75	**4**	7	● 5. **Mr. Jaws** [N]	Cash 451
			### GOO GOO DOLLS	
			Rock trio from Buffalo, New York: Johnny Rzenzik (guitar), Robby Takac (bass) and George Tutuska (drums). All share vocals. Tutuska was replaced by Mike Malinin in 1995.	
10/14/95+	**5**	27↑	1. **Name** Airplay #2 / Sales #31	Warner 17758
			### GORDON, Barry	
			Born on 12/21/48 in Brookline, Massachusetts. Many TV appearances. Appeared in the 1965 Broadway show and movie *A Thousand Clowns*.	
12/17/55	**6**	4	● 1. **Nuttin' For Christmas** [X-N] **ART MOONEY And His ORCHESTRA with Barry Gordon** Best Seller #6 / Top 100 #7 / Juke Box #9 / Jockey #10	MGM 12092
			### GORE, Lesley	
			Born on 5/2/46 in New York City; raised in Tenafly, New Jersey. Discovered by Quincy Jones while singing at a hotel in Manhattan. Appeared in the movies *Girls On The Beach*, *Ski Party* and *The T.A.M.I. Show*.	
5/18/63	**1** (2)	11	1. **It's My Party** #1 R&B hit (3 weeks)	Mercury 72119
7/20/63	**5**	9	2. **Judy's Turn To Cry** sequel to "It's My Party"	Mercury 72143
10/19/63	**5**	11	3. **She's A Fool**	Mercury 72180
1/11/64	**2** (3)	10	4. **You Don't Own Me**	Mercury 72206
4/4/64	**12**	7	5. That's The Way Boys Are	Mercury 72259
6/20/64	**37**	1	6. I Don't Wanna Be A Loser	Mercury 72270
8/15/64	**14**	6	7. Maybe I Know	Mercury 72309
1/23/65	**27**	5	8. Look Of Love	Mercury 72372
7/17/65	**13**	7	9. Sunshine, Lollipops And Rainbows from the movie *Ski Party* starring Frankie Avalon	Mercury 72433
10/9/65	**32**	3	10. My Town, My Guy And Me all of above produced by Quincy Jones	Mercury 72475

DATE	POS	WKS	ARTIST–RECORD TITLE	LABEL & NO.
3/4/67	16	9	11. California Nights co-written by Marvin Hamlisch (also #9 above)	Mercury 72649

GORME, Eydie

Born on 8/16/31 in New York City. Vocalist with the big bands of Tommy Tucker and Tex Beneke in the late 1940s. Featured on Steve Allen's "Tonight Show" from 1953. Married Steve Lawrence on 12/29/57. They recorded as the duo Parker & Penny in 1979.

DATE	POS	WKS	ARTIST–RECORD TITLE	LABEL & NO.
6/16/56	39	1	1. Too Close For Comfort from the Broadway musical *Mr. Wonderful* starring Sammy Davis, Jr.	ABC-Para. 9684
9/1/56	34	3	2. Mama, Teach Me To Dance Sid Feller (orch.)	ABC-Para. 9722
12/30/57	24	1	3. Love Me Forever Jockey #24 / Top 100 #86; Bernie Glow (trumpet solo)	ABC-Para. 9863
5/26/58	11	9	4. You Need Hands Jockey #11 / Best Seller #32 / Top 100 #32; Don Costa (orch., all of above - except #2)	ABC-Para. 9925
2/9/63	7	11	5. **Blame It On The Bossa Nova**	Columbia 42661

STEVE AND EYDIE:

DATE	POS	WKS	ARTIST–RECORD TITLE	LABEL & NO.
8/24/63	28	5	6. I Want To Stay Here	Columbia 42815
1/25/64	35	3	7. I Can't Stop Talking About You Marion Evans (orch., above 3)	Columbia 42932

GOULET, Robert

Born on 11/26/33 in Lawrence, Massachusetts. Began concert career in Edmonton, Canada. Broadway/movie/TV actor. Launched career as Sir Lancelot in the hit Broadway musical *Camelot*. Won the 1962 Best New Artist Grammy Award.

DATE	POS	WKS	ARTIST–RECORD TITLE	LABEL & NO.
11/28/64+	16	9	1. My Love, Forgive Me (Amore, Scusami)	Columbia 43131

GO WEST

British duo of Peter Cox (vocals) and Richard Drummie (guitar, vocals).

DATE	POS	WKS	ARTIST–RECORD TITLE	LABEL & NO.
9/26/87	39	?	1. Don't Look Down - The Sequel Airplay #37; new version of a track from the group's 1985 album *Go West*	Chrysalis 43141
6/23/90	8	13	2. **King Of Wishful Thinking** Airplay #4 / Sales #15; from the movie *Pretty Woman* starring Richard Gere and Julia Roberts; also on the B-side of #3 below	EMI 50307
12/5/92+	14	13	3. Faithful Airplay #13 / Sales #47	EMI 50411

GQ

Bronx soul group: Emmanuel Rahiem LeBlanc (lead singer), Keith Crier, Herb Lane and Paul Service. Group became a trio with the departure of Service in 1980.

DATE	POS	WKS	ARTIST–RECORD TITLE	LABEL & NO.
4/14/79	12	11	● 1. Disco Nights (Rock-Freak) #1 R&B hit (2 weeks)	Arista 0388
8/11/79	20	8	2. I Do Love You	Arista 0426

The **Guess Who**'s early '70s streak of hits did not include "Do You Miss Me Darlin'," pulled from the famed Canadian group's 1970 album *Share The Land*. The set did, however, boast Top 20 hits in the title track and "Hand Me Down World."

Guns N' Roses' swift climb to late '80s notoriety came via their enormously successful Geffen album *Appetite For Destruction*. Bearing such singles as the No. 1 smash "Sweet Child O' Mine" and the No. 5 hit "Paradise City," the album stayed on the charts for 147 weeks.

The Happenings' remake of The Sensations' 1961 hit "Music, Music, Music" was not one of the New Jersey quartet's four Top 20 hits; indeed, the track peaked only at No. 96 in 1968.

Neil Hefti's distinguished career as a jazz arranger and composer might be enough to satiate most musicologists, but most pop fans remember him best as the composer of TV's memorable "Batman Theme"—which reached No. 35 as a bat-single in 1966.

The Hooters' three Top 40 singles—including 1986's No. 18 hit "Day By Day"—were historically overshadowed by their individual involvement with top-selling albums with Cyndi Lauper (1984's *She's So Unusual*) and Joan Osborne (1995's *Relish*).

Whitney Houston's "How Will I Know" was the enormously successful vocalist's second No. 1 single, reaching the top of the charts for two weeks in February 1986. More—and very much of it—was soon to come.

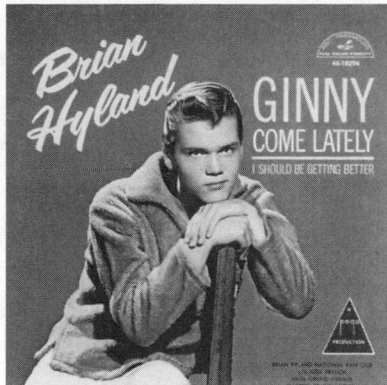

The Human League's second No. 1 single "Human" was a vivid contrast to the synth-pop of 1982's "Don't You Want Me"; instead, master producers Jimmy Jam and Terry Lewis gave the Brit band a warm, urban feel.

Brian Hyland's early '60s career as a teen hitmaker—typified by his third Top 40 hit, 1962's "Ginny Come Lately"—took a notably mature turn in 1970, via his *Uni* album, produced by longtime friend (and fellow '60s idol) Del Shannon.

Billy Idol's solo success during the '80s stood in stark contrast to that of his earlier punk band, Generation X. "To Be A Lover" (1986) was the former William Broad's second Top 10 hit.

Freddie Jackson's first Top 40 hit, 1985's "Rock Me Tonight (For Old Times Sake)," was also the title track of his platinum-selling Top 10 album.

Janet Jackson's 1990 hit "Come Back To Me" was the singer's 10th Top 5 single. Jackson made history twice in the '90s for signing what many believe to be the most lucrative album deals in pop history.

Jermaine Jackson's career took an upward climb at the height of the Jacksonmania of the '80s. Though his track record barely compared to that of his little brother Michael, his 1986 single "I Think It's Love" became his sixth—and last—Top 20 hit.

DATE	POS	WKS	ARTIST–RECORD TITLE	LABEL & NO.
			GRACIE, Charlie	
			Born Charles Graci on 5/14/36 in Philadelphia. Vocalist/guitarist. First recorded for Cadillac in 1951. Regular on "Bandstand" (later "American Bandstand"), 1952–58.	
2/23/57	**1** (2)	14	● 1. **Butterfly**	Cameo 105
			Juke Box #1 / Best Seller #3 / Top 100 #7 / Jockey #13	
5/20/57	**16**	6	2. Fabulous	Cameo 107
			Best Seller #16 / Top 100 #26; Bernie Lowe (orch., above 2)	
			GRAHAM, Larry	
			Born on 8/14/46 in Beaumont, Texas. To Oakland at the age of two. Bass player with Sly & The Family Stone, 1966–72. Formed Graham Central Station in 1973. Went solo in 1980.	
9/13/75	**38**	2	1. Your Love	Warner 8105
			GRAHAM CENTRAL STATION	
			#1 R&B hit (1 week)	
8/9/80	**9**	9	● 2. **One In A Million You**	Warner 49221
			#1 R&B hit (2 weeks)	
			GRAMM, Lou	
			Born on 5/2/50 in Rochester, New York. Lead singer of Foreigner. Member of the rock group Black Sheep, 1970–75. Left Foreigner in 1991 to form Shadow King; returned in 1992.	
2/28/87	**5**	11	1. **Midnight Blue**	Atlantic 89304
			Sales #6 / Airplay #6	
11/18/89+	**6**	14	2. **Just Between You And Me**	Atlantic 88781
			Airplay #3 / Sales #9	
3/31/90	**40**	1	3. True Blue Love	Atlantic 88768
			Airplay #35	
			GRAMMER, Billy	
			Born on 8/28/25 in Benton, Illinois. Country singer/guitarist. Performed regularly on "The Jimmy Dean Show," CBS-TV, 1957–58. Prominent session musician in Nashville.	
12/8/58+	**4**	15	1. **Gotta Travel On**	Monument 400
			based on a 19th-century tune that originated in the British Isles	
			GRANAHAN, Gerry	
			Born on 6/17/39 in Pittston, Pennsylvania. To New York City at age 17. First recorded for Atco as Jerry Grant. Formed Dicky Doo And The Don'ts and The Fireflies. Formed Caprice Records in 1958 and produced many top hits.	
6/16/58	**23**	8	1. No Chemise, Please　　　　　　　　　[N]	Sunbeam 102
			Top 100 #23 / Best Seller #25; Arnie Goland (orch.); tune inspired by the '50s "sack dress" clothing fad	
			GRANATA, Rocco, and the International Quintet	
			Granata was born in Italy in 1938; moved to Belgium at age 10. Singer/songwriter/accordionist.	
11/23/59	**31**	7	1. Marina　　　　　　　　　　　　　　[F]	Laurie 3041

DATE	POS	WKS	ARTIST–RECORD TITLE	LABEL & NO.

GRAND FUNK RAILROAD

Hard-rock band formed in Flint, Michigan, in 1968. Consisted of Mark Farner (guitar), Mel Schacher (bass) and Don Brewer (drums). Band name inspired by Michigan landmark the Grand Trunk Railroad. Brewer and Farner had been in Terry Knight & The Pack; Schacher was bassist with ? & The Mysterians. Knight became producer/manager for Grand Funk, until his firing in March 1972. Craig Frost (keyboards) added in 1973. Disbanded in 1976. Re-formed in 1981, with Farner, Brewer and Dennis Bellinger (bass). Disbanded again shortly thereafter. Farner recorded Contemporary Christian music.

DATE	POS	WKS	ARTIST–RECORD TITLE	LABEL & NO.
9/5/70	**22**	8	1. Closer To Home	Capitol 2877
2/5/72	**29**	5	2. Footstompin' Music	Capitol 3255
11/4/72	**29**	6	3. Rock 'N Roll Soul	Capitol 3363

GRAND FUNK:

DATE	POS	WKS	ARTIST–RECORD TITLE	LABEL & NO.
8/18/73	**1 (1)**	13	● 4. **We're An American Band**	Capitol 3660
12/29/73+	**19**	6	5. Walk Like A Man	Capitol 3760
3/30/74	**1 (2)**	14	● 6. **The Loco-Motion**	Capitol 3840
7/20/74	**11**	8	7. Shinin' On	Capitol 3917
			above 4 produced by Todd Rundgren	
12/21/74+	**3**	12	8. **Some Kind Of Wonderful**	Capitol 4002
4/19/75	**4**	12	9. **Bad Time**	Capitol 4046

GRANT, Amy

Born on 11/25/60 in Augusta, Georgia. The first lady of Contemporary Christian music. Married to singer/songwriter Gary Chapman.

DATE	POS	WKS	ARTIST–RECORD TITLE	LABEL & NO.
7/6/85	**29**	6	1. Find A Way Airplay #28	A&M 2734
10/11/86	**1 (1)**	15	2. **The Next Time I Fall** **PETER CETERA w/AMY GRANT** Airplay #2 / Sales #3; #1 Adult Contemporary hit (2 weeks)	Full Moon 28597
3/9/91	**1 (2)**	16	3. **Baby Baby** Airplay #1(4) / Sales #1(1); song inspired by Grant's 6-week-old daughter, Millie; #1 Adult Contemporary hit (3 weeks)	A&M 1549
6/22/91	**2 (1)**	15	4. **Every Heartbeat** Airplay #2 / Sales #20	A&M 1557
10/12/91	**7**	18	5. **That's What Love Is For** Airplay #9 / Sales #31; #1 Adult Contemporary hit (3 weeks)	A&M 1566
1/25/92	**8**	17	6. **Good For Me** Airplay #6 / Sales #62	A&M 1573
5/16/92	**20**	12	7. **I Will Remember You** Airplay #25 / Sales #37; above 5 from the album *Heart In Motion*	A&M 1600
8/27/94	**18**	11	8. Lucky One Airplay #17 / Sales #30	A&M 0724
2/18/95	**37**	4	9. House Of Love **AMY GRANT with Vince Gill** Sales #38 / Airplay #41	A&M 0802

GRANT, Earl

Born in Oklahoma City in 1931. Died in an automobile accident on 6/10/70. Organist/pianist/vocalist. First recorded for Decca in 1957. Appeared in the movies *Tender Is The Night*, *Imitation Of Life* and *Tokyo Night*.

DATE	POS	WKS	ARTIST–RECORD TITLE	LABEL & NO.
9/29/58	**7**	13	1. **The End** some pressings show title as "(At) The End (Of A Rainbow)"	Decca 30719

DATE	POS	WKS	ARTIST–RECORD TITLE	LABEL & NO.
			GRANT, Eddy	
			Born Edmond Montague Grant on 3/5/48 in Plaisance, Guyana. Moved to London in 1960. Formed group The Equals in London in 1967. Moved to Barbados in 1982.	
5/21/83	**2** (5)	15	▲ 1. **Electric Avenue**	Portrait 03793
6/30/84	**26**	6	2. Romancing The Stone	Portrait 04433
			written for, but not included in, the movie; above 2 recorded in St. Phillip, Barbados	
			GRANT, Gogi	
			Born Audrey Arinsberg on 9/20/24 in Philadelphia. Moved to Los Angeles at age 12. Performed vocals for the movie *The Helen Morgan Story*.	
10/1/55	**9**	10	● 1. **Suddenly There's A Valley**	Era 1003
			Jockey #9 / Best Seller #14 / Top 100 #14 / Juke Box #19	
5/5/56	**1** (8)	22	● 2. **The Wayward Wind**	Era 1013
			Jockey #1(8) / Top 100 #1(7) / Best Seller #1(6) / Juke Box #1(4); Buddy Bregman (orch., above 2)	
			GRANT, Janie	
			Singer/songwriter from Paterson, New Jersey. Real name: Rose Marie Cosili. Discovered by recording artist Gerry Granahan.	
5/15/61	**29**	5	1. Triangle	Caprice 104
			GRASS ROOTS, The	
			Rock group formed in San Francisco in 1964 by drummer Joel Larson and lead singer Bill Fulton. Originally called The Bedouins. New group recruited in 1967 by pop producer Lou Adler and songwriters Steve Barri and P.F. Sloan (known as The Fantastic Baggies). Consisted of Rob Grill (lead singer, bass), Warren Entner and Creed Bratton (guitars), and Rick Coonce (drums). New lineup in 1971 included Entner, Grill, guitarists Reed Kailing and Virgil Webber, and Joel Larson (drums).	
7/16/66	**28**	4	1. Where Were You When I Needed You	Dunhill 4029
6/3/67	**8**	9	2. **Let's Live For Today**	Dunhill 4084
9/2/67	**23**	4	3. Things I Should Have Said	Dunhill 4094
9/21/68	**5**	12	● 4. **Midnight Confessions**	Dunhill 4144
1/11/69	**28**	2	5. Bella Linda	Dunhill 4162
5/17/69	**31**	5	6. The River Is Wide	Dunhill 4187
8/9/69	**15**	10	7. I'd Wait A Million Years	Dunhill 4198
11/22/69	**24**	7	8. Heaven Knows	Dunhill 4217
6/13/70	**35**	3	9. Baby Hold On	Dunhill 4237
2/13/71	**15**	11	10. Temptation Eyes	Dunhill 4263
6/19/71	**9**	9	11. **Sooner Or Later**	Dunhill 4279
10/30/71	**16**	8	12. Two Divided By Love	Dunhill 4289
3/18/72	**34**	3	13. Glory Bound	Dunhill 4302
7/22/72	**39**	2	14. The Runway	Dunhill 4316

DATE	POS	WKS	ARTIST–RECORD TITLE	LABEL & NO.
			GRATEFUL DEAD	
			Legendary psychedelic-rock band formed in San Francisco in 1966. Consisted of Jerry Garcia (lead guitar), Bob Weir (rhythm guitar), Ron "Pigpen" McKernan (organ, harmonica), Phil Lesh (bass) and Bill Kreutzmann (drums). Mickey Hart (2nd drummer) and Tom Constanten (keyboards) added in 1968. Constanten left in 1970; Hart in 1971. Keith Godchaux (piano) and his wife Donna (vocals) joined in 1972. Pigpen died of a liver ailment on 3/8/73. Hart returned in 1975. Brent Mydland (keyboards) added in 1979, replacing Keith and Donna Godchaux. Mydland was a member of Silver. Keith Godchaux died on 7/23/80 from injuries suffered in a motorcycle accident. Weir and Mydland also recorded as Bobby & The Midnites. Mydland died on 7/26/90 (age 37) of a drug overdose; Bruce Hornsby then took over keyboards on tour until Tubes keyboardist Vince Welnick joined band. Garcia died on 8/9/95 (age 53) of natural causes. Incessant touring band with faithful followers known as "Deadheads." Inducted into the Rock and Roll Hall of Fame in 1994.	
8/15/87	9	9	1. **Touch Of Grey** Sales #8 / Airplay #15	Arista 9606
			GRAY, Dobie	
			Born Lawrence Darrow Brown on 7/26/40 in Brookshire/Simonton, Texas. Singer/composer/actor. To Los Angeles in 1960. Recorded under various names—Leonard Victor Ainsworth, Larry Curtis and Larry Dennis. Appeared in the L.A. production of *Hair*. Lead singer of Pollution in 1971.	
1/23/65	13	7	1. The "In" Crowd	Charger 105
3/31/73	5	15	● 2. **Drift Away**	Decca 33057
2/10/79	37	2	3. You Can Do It	Infinity 50003
			GREAN, Charles Randolph, Sounde	
			Grean (born 10/1/13, New York City) is a former A&R director at RCA and Dot Records. Married singer Betty Johnson.	
7/5/69	13	8	1. Quentin's Theme [I] from the cult daytime TV serial "Dark Shadows"	Ranwood 840
			GREAT WHITE	
			Hard-rock group formed in Los Angeles in 1982: Jack Russell (vocals), Mark Kendall (guitar), Lorne Black (bass) and Gary Holland (drums). Audie Desbrow replaced Holland in 1986. Michael Lardie (keyboards) joined in 1987. Tony Montana replaced Black in 1987. Teddy Cook replaced Montana in 1993.	
6/17/89	5	14	● 1. **Once Bitten Twice Shy** Sales #4 / Airplay #6; first released in 1975 on Ian Hunter's self-titled album	Capitol 44366
11/18/89	30	4	2. The Angel Song Sales #27 / Airplay #35	Capitol 44449
			GREAVES, R.B.	
			Born Ronald Bertram Aloysius Greaves on 11/28/44 at the USAF Base in Georgetown, British Guyana. Half American Indian, raised on a Seminole reservation in California. Nephew of Sam Cooke. To England in 1963, as Sonny Childe & The TNT's.	
10/25/69	2 (1)	13	● 1. **Take A Letter Maria**	Atco 6714
2/14/70	27	5	2. Always Something There To Remind Me	Atco 6726

DATE	POS	WKS	ARTIST–RECORD TITLE	LABEL & NO.
			## GRECCO, Cyndi	
			Born on 5/19/52 in New York City.	
6/12/76	25	5	1. Making Our Dreams Come True theme from the TV series "LaVerne & Shirley" starring Penny Marshall and Cindy Williams	Private St. 45086
			## GREEN, Al	
			Born on 4/13/46 in Forest City, Arkansas. Soul singer/songwriter. With gospel group the Greene Brothers. To Grand Rapids, Michigan in 1959. First recorded for Fargo in 1960. In group The Creations, 1964–67. Sang with his brother Robert Green and Lee Virgins in the group Soul Mates, 1967–68. Went solo in 1969. Wrote most of his songs. Returned to gospel music in 1980. Inducted into the Rock and Roll Hall of Fame in 1995.	
8/21/71	11	15	● 1. Tired Of Being Alone	Hi 2194
12/11/71+	1 (1)	15	● 2. Let's Stay Together #1 R&B hit (9 weeks)	Hi 2202
4/8/72	4	11	● 3. Look What You Done For Me	Hi 2211
7/15/72	3	11	● 4. I'm Still In Love With You #1 R&B hit (2 weeks)	Hi 2216
11/4/72	3	12	● 5. You Ought To Be With Me #1 R&B hit (1 week)	Hi 2227
3/3/73	10	9	● 6. Call Me (Come Back Home)	Hi 2235
7/21/73	10	12	● 7. Here I Am (Come And Take Me)	Hi 2247
12/22/73+	19	8	8. Livin' For You #1 R&B hit (1 week)	Hi 2257
5/11/74	32	3	9. Let's Get Married	Hi 2262
11/2/74	7	11	● 10. Sha-La-La (Make Me Happy)	Hi 2274
3/22/75	13	8	11. L-O-V-E (Love) #1 R&B hit (2 weeks)	Hi 2282
11/29/75	28	6	12. Full Of Fire #1 R&B hit (1 week)	Hi 2300
12/18/76+	37	4	13. Keep Me Cryin' all of above produced by Willie Mitchell	Hi 2319
12/3/88+	9	10	14. Put A Little Love In Your Heart **ANNIE LENNOX & AL GREEN** Airplay #8 / Sales #11; from the movie *Scrooged* starring Bill Murray	A&M 1255
			## GREEN, Garland	
			Born Garfield Green, Jr., on 6/24/42 in Leland, Mississippi. Soul singer/pianist.	
10/18/69	20	4	1. Jealous Kind Of Fella	Uni 55143
			## GREENBAUM, Norman	
			Born on 11/20/42 in Malden, Massachusetts. Moved to the West Coast in 1965 and formed the psychedelic jug band Dr. West's Medicine Show & Junk Band.	
3/7/70	3	14	● 1. Spirit In The Sky	Reprise 0885

DATE	POS	WKS	ARTIST–RECORD TITLE	LABEL & NO.
			### GREENE, Lorne Born on 2/12/14 in Ottawa, Canada. Died on 9/11/87 of cardiac arrest. Chief newscaster for CBC radio, 1940–43. Appeared in the movies *The Silver Chalice* and *Tight Spot*; starred in TV's "Bonanza" and "Battlestar Galactica."	
11/7/64	**1** (1)	10	1. **Ringo** [S] #1 Adult Contemporary hit (6 weeks)	RCA 8444
			### GREEN JELLÿ Comical 12-member rock outfit formed in Kenmore, New York, in 1981. Revolving lineup led by Bill Manspeaker (aka Marshall "Duh" Staxx and Moronic Dicktator), has hosted 74 members. Video-only band until its surge in video popularity in 1993 led to release of group's recordings. Originally known as Green Jellö.	
4/24/93	**17**	12	● 1. Three Little Pigs [N] Sales #5	Zoo 14088
			### GREGG, Bobby, and His Friends Gregg's real name is Robert Grego. Jazz drummer from Philadelphia. Performed with Steve Gibson & The Red Caps, 1955–60.	
4/14/62	**29**	5	1. The Jam - Part 1 [I] Roy Buchanan (guitar)	Cotton 1003
			### GRIFFIN, Clive—see DION, Celine	
			### GRIFFITH, Andy Born on 6/1/26 in Mount Airy, North Carolina. Starred in the Broadway, television and movie versions of *No Time For Sergeants*. Best known as Sheriff Andy Taylor on the TV series "The Andy Griffith Show"; also star of TV's "Matlock."	
4/2/55	**26**	1	1. Make Yourself Comfortable [C] Best Seller #26; Jean Wilson (vocal); Burt Massengale (orch.)	Capitol 3057
			### GROCE, Larry Born on 4/22/48 in Dallas. Pop-folk singer/songwriter. Wrote children's songs for Walt Disney Records.	
2/7/76	**9**	9	1. **Junk Food Junkie** [N] recorded "live" at McCabe's nightclub in Santa Monica	Warner/Curb 8165
			### GROOVE THEORY Male-female R&B duo: Bryce Wilson and Amel Larrieux. Wilson, then known as Bryce Luvah, was a member of Mantronix.	
9/23/95	**5**	25	● 1. **Tell Me** Sales #4 / Airplay #11; Trey Lorenz (backing vocal)	Epic 77961
			### GROSS, Henry Born on 4/1/51. Rock singer from Brooklyn. Original lead guitarist of Sha-Na-Na. Toured with The Beach Boys and Aerosmith.	
4/3/76	**6**	13	● 1. **Shannon** song is a tale about the death of a pet dog	Lifesong 45002
8/21/76	**37**	2	2. Springtime Mama above 2 produced by Terry Cashman & Tommy West	Lifesong 45008

DATE	POS	WKS	ARTIST—RECORD TITLE	LABEL & NO.
			GTR	
			British hard-rock quintet: guitarists Steve Hackett (Genesis) and Steve Howe (Yes, Asia), singer Max Bacon, bassist Phil Spalding and drummer Jonathan Mover. Name is short for guitar.	
5/31/86	14	10	1. When The Heart Rules The Mind Sales #9 / Airplay #19	Arista 9470
			GUARALDI, Vince, Trio	
			Guaraldi was born on 7/17/32 in San Francisco. Died of a heart attack on 2/6/76. Pianist/leader of own jazz trio. Formerly with Woody Herman and Cal Tjader. Wrote the music for the "Peanuts" TV specials.	
2/9/63	22	6	1. Cast Your Fate To The Wind [I]	Fantasy 563
			GUESS WHO, The	
			Rock group formed in Winnipeg, Canada, in 1963. Consisted of Allan "Chad Allan" Kobel (guitar, vocals), Randy Bachman (lead guitar), Garry Peterson (drums), Bob Ashley (piano) and Jim Kale (bass). Recorded as The Reflections, and Chad Allan & The Expressions. Ashley replaced by new lead singer Burton Cummings in 1966. Allan left shortly thereafter. Bachman left in 1970 to form Bachman-Turner Overdrive; replaced by Kurt Winter and Greg Leskiw. Leskiw and Kale left in 1972, replaced by Don McDougall and Bill Wallace. Domenic Troiano replaced both Winter and McDougall in 1974. Group disbanded in 1975; several reunions since then.	
6/5/65	22	7	1. Shakin' All Over group is actually Chad Allan & The Expressions	Scepter 1295
4/26/69	6	11	● 2. **These Eyes**	RCA 0102
7/26/69	10	9	● 3. **Laughing/**	
11/8/69	22	6	4. Undun	RCA 0195
1/17/70	5	10	5. **No Time**	RCA 0300
3/28/70	1 (3)	14	● 6. **American Woman/**	
		13	7. No Sugar Tonight all of above include Randy Bachman before his departure	RCA 0325
8/8/70	17	8	8. Hand Me Down World	RCA 0367
11/7/70	10	8	9. **Share The Land**	RCA 0388
6/12/71	29	4	10. Albert Flasher	RCA 0458
9/4/71	19	8	11. Rain Dance	RCA 0522
4/20/74	39	1	12. Star Baby	RCA 0217
8/10/74	6	11	13. **Clap For The Wolfman** featuring bits of dialogue by Wolfman Jack	RCA 0324
12/14/74+	28	4	14. Dancin' Fool all of above (except #1) produced by Jack Richardson	RCA 10075
			GUIDRY, Greg	
			Born on 1/23/50 in St. Louis. Singer/songwriter/pianist.	
3/20/82	17	10	1. Goin' Down	Columbia 02691
			GUITAR, Bonnie	
			Born Bonnie Buckingham on 3/25/23 in Seattle. Own group in the early 1950s. Worked as session guitarist in Los Angeles in the mid-1950s. Owner of Dolphin/Dolton Records.	
4/27/57	6	10	1. **Dark Moon** Jockey #6 / Top 100 #8 / Best Seller #10 / Juke Box #11	Dot 15550

DATE	POS	WKS	ARTIST–RECORD TITLE	LABEL & NO.
			## GUNHILL ROAD	
			Rock trio: Glen Leopold, Gil Roman and Steven Goldrich.	
6/2/73	40	1	1. Back When My Hair Was Short	Kama Sutra 569
			## GUNS N' ROSES	
			Los Angeles-based, hard-rock band: lead singer W. Axl Rose (born 1962, Indiana; real name is William Bailey, natural father's surname is Rose) with bassist Michael "Duff" McKagan, guitarists Izzy Stradlin' (Jeffrey Isbell) and Slash (Saul Hudson), and drummer Steven Adler. Axl Rose married Erin Everly (daughter of Don Everly of The Everly Brothers) on 4/27/90; she filed for divorce three weeks later. Adler left in 1990, replaced by Matt Sorum (who had toured with The Cult). Keyboardist Dizzy Reed joined in 1990. Stradlin' left in late 1991, replaced by Gilby Clarke (of Kill For Thrills). Slash married model Renee Surran in November 1992. Clarke left band in January 1995. Slash, Sorum and Clarke recorded in 1995 in Slash's Snakepit.	
7/23/88	1 (2)	14	● 1. **Sweet Child O' Mine** Sales #1(2) / Airplay #1(2); written by Rose for his then-girlfriend Erin Everly; also on the B-side of #7 below	Geffen 27963
11/5/88	7	12	2. **Welcome To The Jungle** Sales #3 / Airplay #11	Geffen 27759
1/28/89	5	11	3. **Paradise City** Sales #5 / Airplay #5	Geffen 27570
4/22/89	4	10	● 4. **Patience** Sales #3 / Airplay #5	Geffen 22996
7/20/91	29	8	● 5. **You Could Be Mine** Sales #2; from the movie *Terminator 2: Judgment Day* starring Arnold Schwarzenegger	Geffen 19039
2/8/92	33	4	6. **Live And Let Die** Sales #19; title song from the James Bond movie starring Roger Moore	Geffen 19114
6/27/92	3	20	● 7. **November Rain** Sales #4 / Airplay #12	Geffen 19067
9/28/92+	10	17	● 8. **Don't Cry** Sales #5 / Airplay #52	Geffen 19027
			## GUTHRIE, Arlo	
			Born on 7/10/47 in Coney Island, New York. Son of legendary folk singer Woody Guthrie. Starred as himself in the 1969 movie *Alice's Restaurant*, which was based on his 1967 song "Alice's Restaurant Massacree." Often performed in concert with Pete Seeger.	
9/9/72	18	9	1. The City Of New Orleans composed on the train of the same name by folk singer Steve Goodman (his version "Bubbled Under" in 1972 at #113)	Reprise 1103
			## GUY, Jasmine	
			Born on 3/10/64 in Boston and raised in Atlanta. Actress/singer. Whitley Gilbert of TV's "A Different World." Began career with the Alvin Ailey Dance Troupe. Dancer in TV show "Fame." Starred in several off-Broadway shows. Appeared in the movies *School Daze* and *Harlem Nights*.	
10/19/91	34	3	1. Just Want To Hold You Airplay #34 / Sales #52	Warner 19330

DATE	POS	WKS	ARTIST–RECORD TITLE	LABEL & NO.

H

HADDAWAY

Born Nestor Alexander Haddaway in Trinidad. Singer/dancer/choreographer. Moved to Chicago at age nine. Started own company in Cologne, Germany, that organized fashion shows and photo shoots.

DATE	POS	WKS	ARTIST–RECORD TITLE	LABEL & NO.
10/2/93	11	19	● 1. What Is Love Airplay #11 / Sales #13	Arista 12575

HAGAR, Sammy

Born on 10/13/47 in Monterey, California. Rock singer/songwriter/guitarist. Lead singer of Montrose, 1973-75. Replaced David Lee Roth as lead singer of Van Halen in 1985.

DATE	POS	WKS	ARTIST–RECORD TITLE	LABEL & NO.
12/25/82+	13	13	1. Your Love Is Driving Me Crazy	Geffen 29816
8/18/84	38	3	2. Two Sides Of Love	Geffen 29246
10/27/84	26	6	3. I Can't Drive 55 Airplay #26 / Sales #27	Geffen 29173
8/1/87	23	7	4. Give To Live Airplay #23 / Sales #23	Geffen 28314

HAGGARD, Merle

Born on 4/6/37 in Bakersfield, California. Country singer/songwriter/guitarist. Served nearly three years in San Quentin prison on a burglary charge, 1957-60. Signed to Capitol Records in 1965 and then formed backing band, The Strangers. One of the top male vocalists of the country charts with 38 #1 country singles.

DATE	POS	WKS	ARTIST–RECORD TITLE	LABEL & NO.
1/5/74+	28	3	1. If We Make It Through December　　　　[X] #1 Country hit (4 weeks)	Capitol 3746

HAILEY, K-Ci

Born Cedric Hailey on 9/2/69 in Charlotte, North Carolina. Founding member of Jodeci.

DATE	POS	WKS	ARTIST–RECORD TITLE	LABEL & NO.
2/25/95	17	8	1. If You Think You're Lonely Now **K-Ci HAILEY of Jodeci** Sales #7 / Airplay #33; from the movie *Jason's Lyric* starring Forest Whitaker; side 1: "live" version (recorded in Nassau, Bahamas); side 2: studio version	Mercury 856572

HAIRCUT ONE HUNDRED

Pop-rock sextet formed in London in 1980: Nick Heyward (vocals), Graham Jones (guitar), Phil Smith (saxophone), Mark Fox (percussion), Les Nemes (bass) and Blair Cunningham (drums). Disbanded in 1983.

DATE	POS	WKS	ARTIST–RECORD TITLE	LABEL & NO.
7/17/82	37	4	1. Love Plus One	Arista 0672

DATE	POS	WKS	ARTIST–RECORD TITLE	LABEL & NO.
			## HALEY, Bill, And His Comets	
			Haley was born William John Clifton Haley, Jr., on 7/6/25 in Highland Park, Michigan. Died on 2/9/81 of a heart attack in Harlingen, Texas. Began career as a singer with New England country band the Down Homers. Formed the Four Aces of Western Swing in 1948. In 1949 formed the Saddlemen, who recorded on various labels before signing with the Essex label (as Bill Haley and the Saddlemen) in 1952; signed with Decca in 1954. The original Comets band backing Haley on "Rock Around The Clock," recorded on 4/12/54, were Danny Cedrone (lead guitar; died 7/10/54 of a heart attack), Joey D'Ambrose (sax), Billy Williamson (steel guitar), Johnny Grande (piano), Marshall Lytle (bass) and Billy Guesack (session drums; Dick Richards was their live drummer). D'Ambrose, Richards and Lytle left in September 1955 to form the Jodimars. Comets lineup on subsequent recordings included Williamson, Grande, Rudy Pompilli (sax; died 2/5/76, age 47), Al Rex (bass; born Al Piccarelli), Ralph Jones (drums) and Frank Beecher (lead guitar). Inducted into the Rock and Roll Hall of Fame in 1987. Also see The Kingsmen.	
11/20/54+	11	15	1. Dim, Dim The Lights (I Want Some Atmosphere) Best Seller #11 / Jockey #16 / Juke Box #16	Decca 29317
3/19/55	17	2	2. Birth Of The Boogie/ Juke Box #17 / Best Seller #26	
3/5/55	18	8	3. Mambo Rock Best Seller #18	Decca 29418
5/14/55	1 (8)	24	● 4. **(We're Gonna) Rock Around The Clock** Best Seller #1(8)/Juke Box #1(7)/Jockey #1(6)/Top 100 #56 pre; recorded on 4/12/54; Grammy Hall of Fame Award winner in 1982; featured in the movie *Blackboard Jungle* starring Glenn Ford	Decca 29124
7/23/55	15	4	5. Razzle-Dazzle/ Best Seller #15	
		2	6. Two Hound Dogs Best Seller flip	Decca 29552
11/19/55	9	13	7. **Burn That Candle/** Juke Box #9 / Best Seller #16 / Top 100 #20	
11/19/55	23	7	8. Rock-A-Beatin' Boogie Best Seller #23 / Top 100 #41; first recorded by the Esquire Boys in 1953 (Rainbow 200)	Decca 29713
1/14/56	6	15	● 9. **See You Later, Alligator** Best Seller #6 / Top 100 #6 / Jockey #6 / Juke Box #6; first written and recorded in 1955 by Bobby Charles as: "Later Alligator" (#14 R&B hit)	Decca 29791
4/7/56	16	5	10. R-O-C-K/ Juke Box #16 / Best Seller #20 / Top 100 #29; featured in the movie *Rock Around the Clock* starring Alan Freed	
4/7/56	18	5	11. The Saints Rock 'N Roll Best Seller #18 / Top 100 #42; rock version of the spiritual "When The Saints Go Marching In"	Decca 29870
9/1/56	25	4	12. Rip It Up Best Seller #25 / Top 100 #30	Decca 30028
11/24/56	34	3	13. Rudy's Rock [I] named for Haley's saxophonist, Rudy Pompilli	Decca 30085
4/21/58	22	6	14. Skinny Minnie Top 100 #22 / Best Seller #24	Decca 30592
5/25/74	39	1	15. (We're Gonna) Rock Around The Clock [R] re-popularized as the original opening theme of TV's "Happy Days"	MCA 60025

DATE	POS	WKS	ARTIST–RECORD TITLE	LABEL & NO.
			HALL, Aaron	
			Bronx native. Member of the New York City trio Guy, which included his younger brother Damion Hall.	
6/18/94	**14**	15	● 1. I Miss You Sales #8 / Airplay #20	Silas/MCA 54847
			HALL, Daryl	
			Born Daryl Franklin Hohl on 10/11/48 in Philadelphia. Half of Hall & Oates duo.	
8/16/86	**5**	11	1. **Dreamtime** Airplay #4 / Sales #5	RCA 14387
11/15/86	**33**	5	2. Foolish Pride Airplay #30 / Sales #37	RCA 5038
			HALL, Daryl, & John Oates	
			Daryl Hall (see previous entry) and John Oates (born 4/7/49, New York City) met while students at Temple University in 1967. Hall sang backup for many top soul groups before teaming up with Oates in 1972. In the late 1980s, they passed The Everly Brothers as the #1 charting duo of the rock era.	
4/3/76	**4**	17	● 1. **Sara Smile** written for Hall's girlfriend, Sara Allen, sister of songwriter Janna Allen (died 8/25/93 of leukemia, age 37); also on the B-side of #15 below	RCA 10530
8/14/76	**7**	16	2. **She's Gone** [R] originally charted in 1974 at #60	Atlantic 3332
12/25/76	**39**	3	3. Do What You Want, Be What You Are	RCA 10808
2/5/77	**1** (2)	14	● 4. **Rich Girl**	RCA 10860
5/28/77	**28**	4	5. Back Together Again	RCA 10970
9/30/78	**20**	7	6. It's A Laugh	RCA 11371
12/1/79+	**18**	10	7. Wait For Me	RCA 11747
8/30/80	**30**	4	8. How Does It Feel To Be Back	RCA 12048
10/11/80	**12**	14	9. You've Lost That Lovin' Feeling	RCA 12103
2/14/81	**1** (3)	17	● 10. **Kiss On My List** also on the B-side of #19 below	RCA 12142
5/16/81	**5**	14	11. **You Make My Dreams** above 4 from the album Voices	RCA 12217
9/12/81	**1** (2)	17	● 12. **Private Eyes**	RCA 12296
11/21/81+	**1** (1)	17	● 13. **I Can't Go For That (No Can Do)** #1 R&B hit (1 week)	RCA 12357
4/3/82	**9**	11	14. **Did It In A Minute**	RCA 13065
7/24/82	**33**	5	15. Your Imagination above 4 from the album Private Eyes	RCA 13252
11/6/82	**1** (4)	17	● 16. **Maneater** also on the B-side of #20 below	RCA 13354
2/5/83	**7**	15	17. **One On One**	RCA 13421
5/7/83	**6**	12	18. Family Man	RCA 13507
			DARYL HALL JOHN OATES:	
10/29/83	**2** (4)	15	19. **Say It Isn't So**	RCA 13654
2/25/84	**8**	11	20. **Adult Education**	RCA 13714
10/6/84	**1** (2)	16	21. **Out Of Touch** Airplay #1(3) / Sales #3	RCA 13916

DATE	POS	WKS	ARTIST–RECORD TITLE	LABEL & NO.
1/5/85	**5**	11	22. **Method Of Modern Love** Airplay #5 / Sales #7	RCA 13970
3/30/85	**18**	8	23. Some Things Are Better Left Unsaid Airplay #16 / Sales #17	RCA 14035
6/15/85	**30**	6	24. Possession Obsession Airplay #29; above 4 from the album *Big Bam Boom*	RCA 14098
9/15/85	20	7	25. A Nite At The Apollo Live! The Way You Do The Things You Do/My Girl **DARYL HALL JOHN OATES with David Ruffin & Eddie Kendrick** Sales #21 / Airplay #23; recorded at the reopening of New York's Apollo Theatre	RCA 14178
4/23/88	**3**	11	26. **Everything Your Heart Desires** Sales #4 / Airplay #4	Arista 9684
8/6/88	**29**	5	27. Missed Opportunity Sales #29 / Airplay #29	Arista 9727
10/29/88	**31**	3	28. Downtown Life Airplay #32 / Sales #33	Arista 9753
10/20/90	**11**	9	29. So Close Airplay #11 / Sales #14; co-produced by Jon Bon Jovi	Arista 2085
			HALL, Jimmy Born on 4/26/49 in Mobile, Alabama. Leader of the Southern rock bands Wet Willie and Stillwater.	
11/1/80	27	4	1. I'm Happy That Love Has Found You	Epic 50931
			HALL, Larry Born on 6/30/41 in Cincinnati.	
12/7/59+	**15**	11	1. Sandy first released on Hot 1 in 1959	Strand 25007
			HALL, Tom T. Born on 5/25/36 in Olive Hill, Kentucky. Country music storyteller. Wrote "Harper Valley P.T.A." hit for Jeannie C. Riley. Host of "Pop Goes The Country" TV series.	
1/19/74	**12**	9	1. I Love #1 Country hit (2 weeks)	Mercury 73436
			HALOS, The New York City R&B group. Backing group on Curtis Lee's "Pretty Little Angel Eyes."	
8/28/61	25	4	1. "Nag"	7 Arts 709
			HAMILTON, Bobby Real name: Robert Caristo. Native of Locust Valley, Long Island, New York.	
8/4/58	**40**	1	1. Crazy Eyes For You	Apt 25002

DATE	POS	WKS	ARTIST–RECORD TITLE	LABEL & NO.
			### HAMILTON, George, IV	
			Born on 7/19/37 in Winston-Salem, North Carolina. Country-folk-pop singer/songwriter/guitarist. Toured with Buddy Holly, Gene Vincent and The Everly Brothers. Moved to Nashville in 1959 and joined the *Grand Ole Opry*. Own TV series on ABC in 1959, and in Canada in the late 1970s.	
11/17/56	6	14	● 1. **A Rose And A Baby Ruth** Top 100 #6 / Best Seller #7 / Jockey #7 / Juke Box #8; first released on Colonial 420 in 1956 as George Hamilton IV and The Country Gentlemen	ABC-Para. 9765
3/9/57	33	4	2. Only One Love	ABC-Para. 9782
12/9/57+	10	12	3. **Why Don't They Understand** Jockey #10 / Top 100 #17 / Best Seller #19	ABC-Para. 9862
4/7/58	25	1	4. Now And For Always Jockey #25 / Best Seller #37 / Top 100 #37	ABC-Para. 9898
12/15/58+	29	5	5. The Teen Commandments　　　　[S] **PAUL ANKA-GEO. HAMILTON IV-JOHNNY NASH** inspirational talk from the 3 ABC-Paramount artists; Don Costa (orch., all of above)	ABC-Para. 9974
7/20/63	15	7	6. Abilene #1 Country hit (4 weeks)	RCA 8181
			### HAMILTON, Roy	
			Born on 4/16/29 in Leesburg, Georgia. Died of a stroke on 7/20/69. R&B ballad singer. Moved to Jersey City at age 14. Sang with the Searchlight Gospel Singers in 1948.	
4/23/55	6	16	1. **Unchained Melody** Jockey #6 / Juke Box #6 / Best Seller #9; from the movie *Unchained* starring football great Elroy "Crazylegs" Hirsch; #1 R&B hit (3 weeks)	Epic 9102
1/27/58	13	11	2. Don't Let Go Top 100 #13 / Best Seller #14 / Jockey #16; Jesse Stone (orch.)	Epic 9257
2/13/61	12	7	3. You Can Have Her Sammy Lowe (orch.)	Epic 9434
			### HAMILTON, Russ	
			Born Ronald Hulme in 1934 in Liverpool, England. Singer/songwriter.	
8/5/57	4	17	● 1. **Rainbow** Jockey #4 / Best Seller #7 / Top 100 #7; Johnny Gregory (orch.)	Kapp 184
			### HAMILTON, JOE FRANK & REYNOLDS	
			Dan Hamilton, Joe Frank Carollo and Tommy Reynolds. Trio were members of The T-Bones. Reynolds left group in 1972 and was replaced by Alan Dennison. Although Reynolds had left, group still recorded as Hamilton, Joe Frank & Reynolds until July 1976. Hamilton died on 12/23/94 (age 48).	
6/12/71	4	11	● 1. **Don't Pull Your Love**	Dunhill 4276
7/19/75	1 (1)	12	● 2. **Fallin' In Love** #1 Adult Contemporary hit (1 week)	Playboy 6024
12/13/75+	21	8	3. Winners And Losers	Playboy 6054
			### HAMLISCH, Marvin	
			Born on 6/2/44 in New York City. Pianist/composer/conductor for numerous soundtracks. 1973's Best Song Oscar and Grammy winner for "The Way We Were." Won the 1974 Best New Artist Grammy Award.	

DATE	POS	WKS	ARTIST—RECORD TITLE	LABEL & NO.
4/20/74	3	12	● 1. **The Entertainer** [I] written in 1902 by Scott Joplin; featured in the movie *The Sting* starring Paul Newman and Robert Redford; #1 Adult Contemporary hit (1 week)	MCA 40174
			HAMMER—see M.C. HAMMER	
			HAMMER, Jan Born in Prague, Czechoslovakia, on 4/17/48. Jazz-rock keyboard virtuoso. Toured with Sarah Vaughan as conductor/keyboardist. Member of Mahavishnu Orchestra until 1973.	
9/21/85	1 (1)	13	1. **Miami Vice Theme** [I] Sales #1(3) / Airplay #2; from the "Miami Vice" TV series starring Don Johnson	MCA 52666
			HAMMOND, Albert Born on 5/18/42 in London; raised in Gibraltar, Spain. Member of British group Magic Lanterns, 1971.	
11/4/72	5	13	● 1. **It Never Rains In Southern California**	Mums 6011
4/13/74	31	4	2. I'm A Train	Mums 6026
			HAPPENINGS, The Vocal group from Paterson, New Jersey: Bob Miranda (lead), Tom Giuliano (tenor), Ralph DiVito (baritone) and Dave Libert (bass). Bernie LaPorta replaced DiVito in 1968. Originally the Four Graduates, recorded for Rust in 1963.	
7/30/66	3	11	1. **See You In September**	B.T. Puppy 520
10/22/66	12	5	2. Go Away Little Girl	B.T. Puppy 522
4/29/67	3	9	3. **I Got Rhythm** written in 1930 by George & Ira Gershwin for the musical *Girl Crazy* starring Ginger Rogers	B.T. Puppy 527
7/22/67	13	6	4. My Mammy Al Jolson's theme song; written in 1920	B.T. Puppy 530
			HARDCASTLE, Paul Born in London on 12/10/57. Keyboardist/producer. Formed Total Control Records in 1983. Produced Ian Dury & The Blockheads. Formed Fast Forward Records in 1990. Half of the Kiss The Sky duo since 1992.	
6/22/85	15	8	1. 19 Sales #12 / Airplay #19; title refers to the average age of U.S. soldiers in Vietnam	Chrysalis 42860
			HARNELL, Joe Born on 8/2/24 in the Bronx. Conductor/arranger for Frank Sinatra, Peggy Lee and others. Musical director for many TV shows, including "The Mike Douglas Show."	
1/26/63	14	8	1. **Fly Me To The Moon - Bossa Nova** [I] first recorded in 1954 by Kaye Ballard as "In Other Words"	Kapp 497
			HARNEN, Jimmy—see SYNCH	

DATE	POS	WKS	ARTIST–RECORD TITLE	LABEL & NO.
			HARPERS BIZARRE	
			Santa Cruz, California, quintet led by Ted Templeman, who later produced many albums for The Doobie Brothers and Van Halen.	
3/18/67	13	7	1. The 59th Street Bridge Song (Feelin' Groovy) written by Paul Simon; arranged by Leon Russell	Warner 5890
6/17/67	37	3	2. Come To The Sunshine	Warner 7028
			HARPO, Slim	
			Born James Moore on 1/11/24 in Lobdell, Louisiana (aka: Harmonica Slim). Died of a heart attack on 1/31/70. Blues singer/harmonica player.	
7/10/61	34	2	1. Rainin' In My Heart featuring blues guitarist Lightnin' Slim (Otis Hicks)	Excello 2194
3/5/66	16	7	2. Baby Scratch My Back [I] #1 R&B hit (2 weeks)	Excello 2273
			HARRIET	
			Born Harriet Roberts in 1966 in Sheffield, England.	
4/13/91	39	1	1. Temple Of Love Sales #37 / Airplay #38	EastWest 98863
			HARRIS, Betty	
			Born in 1943 in Orlando, Florida. Worked as maid to Big Maybelle, later brought on stage for duets with Maybelle. Worked as road manager for James Carr.	
10/26/63	23	6	1. Cry To Me	Jubilee 5456
			HARRIS, Eddie	
			Born on 10/20/36 in Chicago. Jazz tenor saxophonist/vocalist.	
5/29/61	36	3	1. Exodus [I] jazz version of the main theme from the movie starring Paul Newman	Vee-Jay 378
			HARRIS, Emmylou	
			Born on 4/2/47 in Birmingham, Alabama. Contemporary country vocalist. Sang backup with Gram Parsons until his death in 1973. Own band from 1975.	
4/11/81	37	3	1. Mister Sandman solo version; album version featured harmony vocals by Dolly Parton and Linda Ronstadt; #1 hit for The Chordettes in 1954	Warner 49684
			HARRIS, Major	
			Born on 2/9/47 in Richmond, Virginia. Soul singer. With The Jarmels in the early 1960s. With The Delfonics, 1971–74.	
4/19/75	5	14	● 1. **Love Won't Let Me Wait** #1 R&B hit (1 week)	Atlantic 3248
			HARRIS, Richard	
			Born on 10/1/30 in Limerick, Ireland. Began prolific acting career in 1958. Portrayed King Arthur in the long-running stage production and movie version of *Camelot*.	
5/25/68	2 (1)	10	1. **MacArthur Park**	Dunhill 4134

DATE	POS	WKS	ARTIST–RECORD TITLE	LABEL & NO.
			HARRIS, Rolf	
			Born in Perth, Australia, on 3/30/30. Played piano from age nine. Moved to England in the mid-1950s. Developed his unique "wobble board sound" out of a sheet of Masonite. Had own BBC-TV series from 1970.	
6/22/63	**3**	9	1. **Tie Me Kangaroo Down, Sport** [N] #1 Adult Contemporary hit (3 weeks)	Epic 9596
			HARRIS, Sam	
			Winner of TV's "Star Search" male vocalist category in 1984.	
11/3/84	**36**	3	1. Sugar Don't Bite	Motown 1743
			HARRIS, Thurston	
			Born on 7/11/31 in Indianapolis. Died of a heart attack on 4/14/90. First recorded with the Lamplighters in 1953.	
10/28/57	**6**	13	1. **Little Bitty Pretty One** Best Seller #6 / Top 100 #6 / Jockey #12; The Sharps (later The Rivingtons, backing vocals)	Aladdin 3398
			HARRISON, George	
			Born in Wavertree, Liverpool, England, on 2/24/43. (George believed that his birthdate was 2/25 until finding out in his 40s that he was born at 11:42 p.m. on 2/24.) Formed his first group, the Rebels, at age 13. Joined John Lennon and Paul McCartney in The Quarrymen in 1958; group later evolved into The Beatles, with Harrison as lead guitarist. Organized the Bangladesh benefit concerts at Madison Square Garden in 1971. Member of the 1988 supergroup Traveling Wilburys. In 1992, became the first recipient of The Century Award, *Billboard*'s honor for distinguished creative achievement.	
12/5/70	**1 (4)**	13	● 1. **My Sweet Lord/** a 1976 court ruling found Harrison guilty of "subconscious plagiarism" of The Chiffons' "He's So Fine," when writing "My Sweet Lord"	
		13	2. Isn't It A Pity	Apple 2995
3/6/71	**10**	8	3. **What Is Life**	Apple 1828
8/28/71	**23**	5	4. Bangla-Desh/	
		3	5. Deep Blue all of above produced by Phil Spector and Harrison	Apple 1836
5/26/73	**1 (1)**	11	6. **Give Me Love - (Give Me Peace On Earth)**	Apple 1862
12/14/74+	**15**	6	7. Dark Horse	Apple 1877
2/1/75	**36**	2	8. Ding Dong; Ding Dong	Apple 1879
10/11/75	**20**	6	9. You	Apple 1884
12/11/76+	**25**	7	10. This Song song refers to the plagiarism case involving "My Sweet Lord"	Dark Horse 8294
2/12/77	**19**	7	11. Crackerbox Palace	Dark Horse 8313
3/31/79	**16**	8	12. Blow Away	Dark Horse 8763
5/23/81	**2 (3)**	11	13. **All Those Years Ago** tribute to John Lennon; assisted by Ringo Starr and Paul and Linda McCartney; #1 Adult Contemporary hit (1 week)	Dark Horse 49725
11/14/87+	**1 (1)**	15	14. **Got My Mind Set On You** Sales #1(2) / Airplay #1(1); originally recorded by James Ray in 1962 (Dynamic Sound 503); #1 Adult Contemporary hit (4 weeks)	Dark Horse 28178
2/27/88	**23**	6	15. When We Was Fab Sales #18 / Airplay #31; above 2 produced by Jeff Lynne and Harrison; all of above (except #14) written by Harrison	Dark Horse 28131

DATE	POS	WKS	ARTIST–RECORD TITLE	LABEL & NO.
			HARRISON, Wilbert	
			Born on 1/5/29 in Charlotte, North Carolina. Died on 10/26/94 of a stroke. R&B singer. Joined W.C. Baker band. First recorded for DeLuxe in 1952.	
4/27/59	1 (2)	12	● 1. **Kansas City** an early Leiber-Stoller copyright (1952); originally called "K.C. Lovin'"; #1 R&B hit (7 weeks)	Fury 1023
1/24/70	32	4	2. Let's Work Together (Part 1) first released as "Let's Stick Together" on Fury 1063 in 1961	Sue 11
			HART, Bobby—see BOYCE, Tommy	
			HART, Corey	
			Born in Montreal, Canada; raised in Spain and Mexico. Singer/songwriter/keyboardist.	
6/23/84	7	15	1. **Sunglasses At Night**	EMI America 8203
10/20/84	17	9	2. It Ain't Enough Airplay #17 / Sales #18	EMI America 8236
6/22/85	3	14	3. **Never Surrender** Sales #1(1) / Airplay #3	EMI America 8268
10/5/85	26	6	4. Boy In The Box Sales #26 / Airplay #26	EMI America 8287
12/28/85+	30	7	5. Everything In My Heart Sales #26 / Airplay #30	EMI America 8300
10/11/86	18	7	6. I Am By Your Side Sales #14 / Airplay #22	EMI America 8348
1/31/87	24	5	7. Can't Help Falling In Love Sales #18 / Airplay #34	EMI America 8368
7/23/88	38	2	8. In Your Soul Airplay #39	EMI-Man. 50134
4/21/90	37	2	9. A Little Love Airplay #35 / Sales #39; all of above (except #7) written by Hart	EMI 50239
			HART, Freddie	
			Born Fred Segrest on 12/21/26 in Lochapoka, Alabama. Country singer/songwriter/guitarist.	
9/25/71	17	12	● 1. **Easy Loving** #1 Country hit (3 weeks)	Capitol 3115
			HARTMAN, Dan	
			Born on 12/8/50. Died on 3/22/94 of a brain tumor. Multi-instrumentalist/songwriter/producer from Harrisburg, Pennsylvania. Member of the Edgar Winter Group, 1972–76. Writer/producer of several disco club anthems in the late '70s. Own studio, the Schoolhouse, in Westport, Connecticut.	
12/2/78+	29	7	● 1. Instant Replay	Blue Sky 2772
6/2/84	6	16	2. **I Can Dream About You** from the movie *Streets of Fire* starring Michael Pare	MCA 52378
11/3/84	25	9	3. We Are The Young Sales #21	MCA 52471
3/23/85	39	2	4. Second Nature	MCA 52519
			HARVEY & THE MOONGLOWS—see MOONGLOWS	

DATE	POS	WKS	ARTIST–RECORD TITLE	LABEL & NO.
			## HATHAWAY, Donny	
			Born on 10/1/45 in Chicago; raised in St. Louis. Committed suicide by jumping from the 15th floor of New York City's Essex House hotel on 1/13/79. R&B singer/songwriter/keyboardist/producer/arranger. Gospel singer since age three. Attended Washington, D.C.'s Howard University on a fine arts scholarship; classmate of Roberta Flack. Sang the theme of TV show "Maude." His wife, Eulalah, was a classical singer. Their daughter Lalah Hathaway began her solo recording career in 1990.	
			ROBERTA FLACK & DONNY HATHAWAY:	
7/3/71	29	9	1. You've Got A Friend	Atlantic 2808
6/24/72	5	11	● 2. **Where Is The Love** #1 Adult Contemporary hit (1 week); #1 R&B hit (1 week)	Atlantic 2879
3/18/78	2 (2)	14	● 3. **The Closer I Get To You** #1 R&B hit (2 weeks)	Atlantic 3463
			## HAVENS, Richie	
			Born on 1/21/41 in Brooklyn. Black folk singer/guitarist. Opening act of 1969 Woodstock concert.	
4/24/71	16	9	1. Here Comes The Sun written by George Harrison (on The Beatles' 1969 album *Abbey Road*)	Stormy Forest 656
			## HAWKES, Chesney	
			Male vocalist from England. Son of Len "Chip" Hawkes of The Tremeloes. Starred as Roger Daltrey's son in the movie *Buddy's Song*.	
9/7/91	10	14	1. **The One And Only** Airplay #28 / Sales #53; written by Nik Kershaw	Chrysalis 23730
			## HAWKINS, Dale	
			Born Delmar Allen Hawkins on 8/22/38 in Goldmine, Louisiana. Rockabilly singer/guitarist. Toured with R&B package shows. Record production work since 1965.	
7/1/57	27	5	1. Susie-Q Best Seller #27 / Top 100 #29	Checker 863
10/13/58	32	3	2. La-Do-Dada Hot 100 #32 / Best Seller #44 end	Checker 900
			## HAWKINS, Edwin, Singers	
			Hawkins (born August 1943) formed gospel group with Betty Watson in Oakland in 1967 as the Northern California State Youth Choir. Member Dorothy Morrison went on to a solo career.	
5/3/69	4	9	● 1. **Oh Happy Day** **THE EDWIN HAWKINS' SINGERS Featuring Dorothy Combs Morrison** produced by Paul Anka	Pavilion 20001
5/16/70	6	14	2. **Lay Down (Candles In The Rain)** **MELANIE with The Edwin Hawkins Singers**	Buddah 167
			## HAWKINS, Ronnie	
			Born on 1/10/35 in Huntsville, Arkansas. Formed The Hawks in 1952. To Canada in 1958. Assembled group later known as The Band.	
9/21/59	26	7	1. Mary Lou **RONNIE HAWKINS and The Hawks** original version by Young Jessie in 1955 (Modern 961)	Roulette 4177

DATE	POS	WKS	ARTIST—RECORD TITLE	LABEL & NO.
			HAWKINS, Sophie B.	
			Sophie Ballantine Hawkins, a Manhattan-bred singer. Percussionist in Bryan Ferry's backing band in the early '80s.	
4/25/92	5	17	1. **Damn I Wish I Was Your Lover** Sales #6 / Airplay #6	Columbia 74164
8/12/95	6	30	2. **As I Lay Me Down** Airplay #4 / Sales #25; #1 Adult Contemporary hit (6 weeks)	Columbia 77801
			HAWLEY, Deane	
			Real name: William Dean Hawley. Resides in Pacific Beach, California.	
7/4/60	29	5	1. Look For A Star from the movie *Circus of Horrors* starring Donald Pleasence	Dore 554
			HAYES, Bill	
			Born on 6/5/26 in Harvey, Illinois. Hayes was a regular on Sid Caesar's TV series "Your Show of Shows." Played Doug Williams on the TV soap opera "Days Of Our Lives."	
2/26/55	1 (5)	20	● 1. **The Ballad Of Davy Crockett** Best Seller #1(5) / Jockey #1(3) / Juke Box #1(3); from the ABC-TV "Disneyland" series, which featured 3 "Davy Crockett" segments (Dec. '54-Feb. '55); Archie Bleyer (orch.)	Cadence 1256
2/16/57	33	3	2. Wringle, Wrangle from the movie *Westward Ho, The Wagons* starring Fess Parker; Don Costa (orch.)	ABC-Para. 9785
			HAYES, Isaac	
			Born on 8/20/42 in Covington, Tennessee. Soul singer/songwriter/keyboardist/producer/actor. Session musician for Otis Redding and other artists on the Stax label. Teamed with songwriter David Porter to compose "Soul Man," "Hold On! I'm A Comin'" and many others. Composed movie scores for *Shaft*, *Tough Guys*, *Truck Turner* and *Robin Hood: Men In Tights*.	
9/27/69	37	4	1. By The Time I Get To Phoenix/	
10/18/69	30	5	2. Walk On By	Enterprise 9003
6/12/71	22	5	3. Never Can Say Goodbye	Enterprise 9031
10/23/71	1 (2)	12	4. **Theme From Shaft** from the movie *Shaft* starring Richard Roundtree	Enterprise 9038
3/25/72	30	5	5. Do Your Thing	Enterprise 9042
12/2/72	38	2	6. Theme From The Men [I] from the ABC-TV series "The Men" starring Robert Conrad	Enterprise 9058
1/12/74	30	5	7. Joy - Pt. I	Enterprise 9085
12/8/79+	18	12	8. Don't Let Go	Polydor 2011
			HAYMAN, Richard	
			Born on 3/27/20 in Cambridge, Massachusetts. Conductor/arranger/harmonica soloist.	
2/11/56	11	11	1. (A Theme from) The Three Penny Opera (Moritat) [I] **RICHARD HAYMAN and JAN AUGUST** (August died on 1/17/76) Jockey #11 / Top 100 #12 / Best Seller #13 / Juke Box #13	Mercury 70781

DATE	POS	WKS	ARTIST–RECORD TITLE	LABEL & NO.
			HAYWOOD, Leon	
			Born on 2/11/42 in Houston. Soul singer/keyboardist. With Big Jay McNeely and Sam Cooke in the early '60s.	
11/1/75	**15**	8	1. I Want'a Do Something Freaky To You	20th Century 2228
			HAZLEWOOD, Lee—see SINATRA, Nancy	
			HEAD, Murray	
			British singer/actor. Appeared on the 1970 rock concept album *Jesus Christ Superstar*. Played juvenile lead in the 1971 movie *Sunday, Bloody Sunday*.	
5/8/71	**14**	8	1. Superstar **MURRAY HEAD With The Trinidad Singers** from *Jesus Christ Superstar-A Rock Opera*	Decca 32603
3/23/85	**3**	13	2. **One Night In Bangkok** Sales #2 / Airplay #4; from the Tim Rice, Benny Andersson and Bjorn Ulvaeus musical project *Chess*	RCA 13988
			HEAD, Roy	
			Born on 9/1/41 in Three Rivers, Texas. Rock-country singer/guitarist.	
9/18/65	**2** (2)	9	1. **Treat Her Right** **ROY HEAD And The Traits**	Back Beat 546
12/4/65	**39**	1	2. Just A Little Bit	Scepter 12116
12/18/65	**32**	2	3. Apple Of My Eye **ROY HEAD And The Traits**	Back Beat 555
			HEALEY, Jeff, Band	
			Toronto-based blues-rock trio: vocalist/guitarist Healey with drummer Tom Stephen and bassist Joe Rockman. Healey, blind since age one and guitarist since age three, appeared in the 1989 movie *Road House*.	
7/22/89	**5**	13	1. **Angel Eyes** Sales #4 / Airplay #7	Arista 9808
			HEART	
			Rock band formed in Seattle featuring sisters Nancy (guitar, keyboards) and Ann (vocals) Wilson. Included Michael DeRosier (drums) and founding members Steve Fossen (bass), brothers/guitarists Roger and Mike Fisher. The Fishers left the band in 1979. Howard Leese (guitar) joined in 1980. Fossen and DeRosier left by 1982, replaced by Mark Andes (ex-Spirit, Jo Jo Gunne and Firefall) and Denny Carmassi (ex-Gamma). In 1990, former members Fossen, DeRosier and Roger Fisher joined Alias. Andes left by 1993. Carmassi left in 1994 to join Whitesnake. Nancy married movie director Cameron Crowe.	
5/29/76	**35**	2	1. Crazy On You re-charted in 1978 at #62	Mushroom 7021
9/4/76	**9**	14	2. **Magic Man** "live" recording in Tokyo, Japan is on the B-side of #15 below	Mushroom 7011
7/2/77	**11**	12	3. Barracuda "live" recording in Tokyo, Japan is on the B-side of #14 below	Portrait 70004
5/13/78	**24**	7	4. Heartless	Mushroom 7031
10/28/78	**15**	10	5. Straight On	Portrait 70020
3/17/79	**34**	3	6. Dog & Butterfly	Portrait 70025
3/15/80	**33**	4	7. Even It Up	Epic 50847
11/29/80+	**8**	11	8. **Tell It Like It Is**	Epic 50950
6/19/82	**33**	4	9. This Man Is Mine	Epic 02925

DATE	POS	WKS	ARTIST–RECORD TITLE	LABEL & NO.
6/29/85	**10**	12	10. **What About Love?** Sales #8 / Airplay #14	Capitol 5481
10/5/85	**4**	14	11. **Never** Sales #3 / Airplay #5	Capitol 5512
2/1/86	**1 (1)**	13	12. **These Dreams** Sales #1(1) / Airplay #1(1); #1 Adult Contemporary hit (3 weeks)	Capitol 5541
5/3/86	**10**	10	13. **Nothin' At All** Sales #9 / Airplay #10; above 4 from the album Heart	Capitol 5572
5/23/87	**1 (3)**	15	14. **Alone** Sales #1(2) / Airplay #1(2)	Capitol 44002
8/29/87	**7**	11	15. **Who Will You Run To** Sales #6 / Airplay #6	Capitol 44040
11/28/87+	**12**	11	16. There's The Girl Sales #10 / Airplay #14	Capitol 44089
4/14/90	**2 (2)**	13	● 17. **All I Wanna Do Is Make Love To You** Sales #3 / Airplay #3	Capitol 44507
7/14/90	**23**	7	18. I Didn't Want To Need You Sales #24 / Airplay #25	Capitol 44553
10/20/90	**13**	13	19. Stranded Airplay #8 / Sales #19	Capitol 44621
2/12/94	**39**	2	20. Will You Be There (In The Morning) Airplay #42 / Sales #63	Capitol 58041
			HEATHERTON, Joey	
			Born Johanna Heatherton on 9/14/44 in Rockville Centre, New York. Movie/TV actress.	
7/15/72	**24**	7	1. Gone	MGM 14387
			HEATWAVE	
			Multi-national, interracial group formed in Germany by brothers Johnnie and Keith Wilder of Dayton, Ohio. Johnnie became a paraplegic due to a car accident in 1979.	
8/27/77	**2 (2)**	17	▲ 1. **Boogie Nights**	Epic 50370
2/4/78	**18**	11	● 2. Always And Forever	Epic 50490
6/3/78	**7**	11	● 3. **The Groove Line**	Epic 50524
			HEAVY D. & THE BOYZ	
			Rap group from Mt. Vernon, New York: leader Heavy D. (Dwight Meyers), G. Whiz (Glen Parrish), Trouble T-Roy (Troy Dixon) and DJ Eddie F (Edward Ferrell). Dixon died on 7/15/90 (age 22) from an accidental fall in Indianapolis. Heavy D. appeared in the movie Who's The Man?	
7/20/91	**11**	15	● 1. Now That We Found Love Sales #5 / Airplay #12; Aaron Hall (backing vocal)	Uptown/MCA 54090
1/11/92	**32**	6	2. Is It Good To You Airplay #27 / Sales #28	Uptown/MCA 54200
			HEAVY D & THE BOYZ:	
4/23/94	**20**	13	3. Got Me Waiting Sales #11 / Airplay #28; samples "Don't You Know That" by Luther Vandross	Uptown/MCA 54815
9/3/94	**40**	1	4. Nuttin' But Love Sales #28 / Airplay #40	Uptown/MCA 54865

DATE	POS	WKS	ARTIST–RECORD TITLE	LABEL & NO.
			HEBB, Bobby	
			Born on 7/26/41 in Nashville. Singer/songwriter/multi-instrumentalist. Featured on the *Grand Ole Opry* at age 12. His brother Hal was a member of The Marigolds.	
7/23/66	**2** (2)	11	● 1. **Sunny**	Philips 40365
			written by Hebb after his brother Hal was killed in a mugging	
11/5/66	**39**	1	2. A Satisfied Mind	Philips 40400
			#1 Country hit for Porter Wagoner in 1955	
			HEFTI, Neal	
			Born on 10/29/22 in Hastings, Nebraska. Trumpeter. Gained fame as arranger for Woody Herman (1944–46), Harry James and Count Basie, then as composer of TV themes.	
3/5/66	**35**	4	1. Batman Theme [I]	RCA 8755
			original theme from the "Batman" TV series starring Adam West and Burt Ward	
			HEIGHTS, The	
			Band made up of cast members from the Fox network prime-time TV show of the same name. Show is based on fictional adventures featuring the band. Led by actors/vocalists Shawn Thompson and Jamie Walters.	
10/10/92	**1** (2)	16	● 1. **How Do You Talk To An Angel**	Capitol 44890
			Airplay #3 / Sales #3	
			HELMS, Bobby	
			Born on 8/15/36 in Bloomington, Indiana. Country singer/guitarist. Appeared on father's local TV show.	
10/14/57	**7**	15	● 1. **My Special Angel**	Decca 30423
			Best Seller #7 / Top 100 #7 / Jockey #8; The Anita Kerr Singers (backing vocals); #1 Country hit (4 weeks)	
10/14/57	**36**	2	2. Fraulein	Decca 30194
			Top 100 #36 / Best Seller #46; #1 Country hit (4 weeks)	
12/23/57	**6**	4	● 3. **Jingle Bell Rock** [X]	Decca 30513
			Top 100 #6 / Best Seller #7 / Jockey #11	
12/29/58	**35**	1	4. Jingle Bell Rock [X-R]	Decca 30513
12/26/60	**36**	1	5. Jingle Bell Rock [X-R]	Decca 30513
			HENDERSON, Joe	
			Born in 1938 in Como, Mississippi; raised in Gary, Indiana. Died on 11/7/64. R&B singer. Moved to Nashville in 1958. With the Fairfield Four gospel group.	
6/2/62	**8**	10	1. **Snap Your Fingers**	Todd 1072
			HENDERSON, Michael—see CONNORS, Norman	
			HENDRICKS, Bobby	
			Born on 2/22/38 in Columbus, Ohio. R&B vocalist. With The Swallows in 1956. First recorded with the Flyers for Atco in 1957. With The Drifters in 1958 (sang lead on "Drip Drop").	
9/1/58	**25**	4	1. Itchy Twitchy Feeling	Sue 706
			Hot 100 #25 / Best Seller #35; The Coasters (backing vocals); Jimmy Oliver (orch.)	

DATE	POS	WKS	ARTIST–RECORD TITLE	LABEL & NO.

HENDRIX, Jimi

Born on 11/27/42 in Seattle. Died of a drug overdose in London on 9/18/70. Legendary psychedelic-blues guitarist. Began career as a studio guitarist. In 1965, formed own band, Jimmy James & The Blue Flames. In 1966, discovered by The Animals' bassist Chas Chandler at New York City's Cafe Wha?; Chandler invited Hendrix to London, where he created The Jimi Hendrix Experience with Noel Redding (bass) and Mitch Mitchell (drums). Formed new group in 1969, Band of Gypsys, with Buddy Miles (drums) and Billy Cox (bass). The Jimi Hendrix Experience was inducted into the Rock and Roll Hall of Fame in 1992. Awarded Lifetime Achievement Grammy in 1992.

DATE	POS	WKS	ARTIST–RECORD TITLE	LABEL & NO.
9/28/68	20	8	1. All Along The Watchtower **THE JIMI HENDRIX EXPERIENCE** written by Bob Dylan	Reprise 0767

HENHOUSE FIVE PLUS TOO—see STEVENS, Ray

HENLEY, Don

Born on 7/22/47 in Gilmer, Texas. Singer/songwriter/drummer. Own band, Shiloh, in the early '70s. Worked with Glenn Frey in Linda Ronstadt's backup band, then the two formed the Eagles with Randy Meisner and Bernie Leadon. Went solo in 1982. Married model Sharon Summerall on 5/20/95.

DATE	POS	WKS	ARTIST–RECORD TITLE	LABEL & NO.
11/7/81+	6	15	1. **Leather And Lace** **STEVIE NICKS (with DON HENLEY)** written for Waylon Jennings and Jessi Colter	Modern 7341
11/13/82+	3	14	● 2. **Dirty Laundry** Joe Walsh and Steve Lukather (Toto) (guitar solos)	Asylum 69894
12/8/84+	5	14	3. **The Boys Of Summer** Airplay #5 / Sales #7	Geffen 29141
3/16/85	9	11	4. **All She Wants To Do Is Dance** Airplay #8 / Sales #12; Martha Davis of The Motels and Patty Smyth (harmony vocals)	Geffen 29065
7/6/85	34	5	5. Not Enough Love In The World Airplay #30	Geffen 29012
9/21/85	22	8	6. Sunset Grill Airplay #15 / Sales #27; Patty Smyth (harmony vocal); above 4 from the album *Building The Perfect Beast*	Geffen 28906
7/8/89	8	12	7. **The End Of The Innocence** Airplay #7 / Sales #9; co-written and produced by Bruce Hornsby (also on piano)	Geffen 22925
11/11/89	21	8	8. The Last Worthless Evening Sales #19 / Airplay #22	Geffen 22771
3/24/90	21	8	9. The Heart Of The Matter Airplay #20 / Sales #21	Geffen 19898
8/29/92	2 (6)	20	● 10. **Sometimes Love Just Ain't Enough** **PATTY SMYTH with Don Henley** Sales #3 / Airplay #3; #1 Adult Contemporary hit (4 weeks)	MCA 54403

HENRY, Clarence

Born on 3/19/37 in Algiers, Louisiana. R&B vocalist/pianist/trombonist. With Bobby Mitchell's R&B band, 1953-55. Nicknamed "Frog Man" from his hit "Ain't Got No Home."

DATE	POS	WKS	ARTIST–RECORD TITLE	LABEL & NO.
1/12/57	20	3	1. Ain't Got No Home [N] **CLARENCE HENRY "FROG MAN"** Best Seller #20 / Top 100 #30	Argo 5259
3/20/61	4	11	2. **But I Do** some pressings show title as: "I Don't Know Why"	Argo 5378

DATE	POS	WKS	ARTIST–RECORD TITLE	LABEL & NO.
5/29/61	12	7	3. You Always Hurt The One You Love #1 hit in 1944 for The Mills Brothers	Argo 5388

HENSON, Jim

Born on 9/24/36 in Greenville, Mississippi. Died of a sudden virus on 5/16/90. Creator of The Muppets, that famous crew of puppets starring in TV's "Sesame Street" and "The Muppet Show," also in the movies *The Muppet Movie* and *The Great Muppet Caper.* Henson was the voice for both Ernie and Kermit.

DATE	POS	WKS	ARTIST–RECORD TITLE	LABEL & NO.
8/29/70	16	7	1. Rubber Duckie [N] **ERNIE (JIM HENSON)**	Columbia 45207
10/20/79	25	7	2. Rainbow Connection **KERMIT (JIM HENSON)** from the original soundtrack of *The Muppet Movie*	Atlantic 3610

HERMAN'S HERMITS

Formed in Manchester, England, in 1964. Name derived from cartoon character Sherman of TV's "The Bullwinkle Show." Consisted of Peter "Herman" Noone (born 11/5/47; vocals), Derek Leckenby and Keith Hopwood (guitars), Karl Green (bass) and Barry Whitwam (drums). First called The Heartbeats. Noone left in 1972 for a solo career; formed Los Angeles-based group The Tremblers in late '70s. Hosts own show on music video TV channel VH-1. Leckenby died of non-Hodgkins lymphoma on 6/4/94 (age 48).

DATE	POS	WKS	ARTIST–RECORD TITLE	LABEL & NO.
11/14/64	13	9	1. I'm Into Something Good	MGM 13280
2/20/65	2 (2)	11	2. **Can't You Hear My Heartbeat**	MGM 13310
4/17/65	1 (3)	11	● 3. **Mrs. Brown You've Got A Lovely Daughter**	MGM 13341
4/17/65	5	10	4. **Silhouettes**	MGM 13332
6/5/65	4	8	5. **Wonderful World**	MGM 13354
7/10/65	1 (1)	8	● 6. **I'm Henry VIII, I Am** written in 1911; popularized in England by Harry Champion	MGM 13367
9/25/65	7	8	7. **Just A Little Bit Better**	MGM 13398
1/1/66	8	8	8. **A Must To Avoid**	MGM 13437
2/26/66	3	7	9. **Listen People** from the movie *When the Boys Meet the Girls* starring Connie Francis	MGM 13462
4/16/66	9	7	10. **Leaning On The Lamp Post** #8 & 10 from the movie *Hold On!* starring Herman's Hermits	MGM 13500
7/23/66	12	5	11. This Door Swings Both Ways	MGM 13548
10/15/66	5	8	12. **Dandy** written by Ray Davies of The Kinks	MGM 13603
12/24/66	27	5	13. East West	MGM 13639
3/4/67	4	9	● 14. **There's A Kind Of Hush/**	
3/18/67	35	4	15. No Milk Today	MGM 13681
7/8/67	18	4	16. Don't Go Out Into The Rain (You're Going To Melt)	MGM 13761
9/16/67	39	2	17. Museum written by Donovan	MGM 13787
2/3/68	22	6	18. I Can Take Or Leave Your Loving all of above produced by Mickie Most	MGM 13885

HERNANDEZ, Patrick

Born in 1949 in Paris of a Spanish father and Austrian/Italian mother. Rock-disco singer.

DATE	POS	WKS	ARTIST–RECORD TITLE	LABEL & NO.
8/4/79	16	11	● 1. Born To Be Alive	Columbia 10986

DATE	POS	WKS	ARTIST–RECORD TITLE	LABEL & NO.
			HESITATIONS, The	
			Soul group from Cleveland. Lead singer George "King" Scott was accidentally killed by a bullet from a gun owned by tenor Fred Deal in February 1968.	
2/17/68	**38**	2	1. Born Free	Kapp 878
			title song from the movie starring Virginia McKenna	
			HEYWOOD, Eddie	
			Born on 12/4/15 in Atlanta. Died on 1/2/89. Black jazz pianist/composer/arranger. Played professionally by age 14. Own band in New York City in 1941. Worked with Billie Holiday. To the West Coast in 1947, with own trio. Active into the '70s.	
7/21/56	**11**	18	1. Soft Summer Breeze [I]	Mercury 70863
			Best Seller #11 / Top 100 #12 / Juke Box #13 / Jockey #14	
7/28/56	**2 (2)**	23	● 2. **Canadian Sunset** [I]	RCA 6537
			HUGO WINTERHALTER and his Orchestra with EDDIE HEYWOOD	
			Top 100 #2 / Jockey #2 / Best Seller #3 / Juke Box #3	
			HIBBLER, Al	
			Born on 8/16/15 in Little Rock, Arkansas. Blind since birth, studied voice at Little Rock's Conservatory for the Blind. First recorded with Jay McShann for Decca in 1942. With Duke Ellington, 1943-51. Also recorded with Harry Carney, Tab Smith, Mercer Ellington and Billy Strayhorn.	
4/9/55	**3**	19	1. **Unchained Melody**	Decca 29441
			Jockey #3 / Juke Box #3 / Best Seller #5; from the movie Unchained starring football great Elroy "Crazylegs" Hirsch; #1 R&B hit (1 week)	
10/15/55	**4**	22	2. **He**	Decca 29660
			Best Seller #4 / Top 100 #7 / Jockey #7 / Juke Box #8	
2/25/56	**21**	5	3. 11th Hour Melody	Decca 29789
7/14/56	**22**	2	4. Never Turn Back	Decca 29950
			Jockey #22 / Top 100 #48	
8/25/56	**10**	12	5. **After The Lights Go Down Low**	Decca 29982
			Jockey #10 / Juke Box #14 / Top 100 #15 / Best Seller #20; earlier version released in 1955 on Original 1006; Jack Pleis (orch., all of above)	
			HI-FIVE	
			R&B teen vocal quintet from Waco, Texas, and Oklahoma City: Tony Thompson, Roderick Clark, Russell Neal, Marcus Sanders and Toriano Easley (left after release of first album, replaced by Treston Irby). Clark and Neal left by 1993; Shannon and Terrance joined.	
3/16/91	**1 (1)**	17	● 1. **I Like The Way (The Kissing Game)**	Jive 1424
			Sales #1(2) / Airplay #4; written and produced by Teddy Riley of Guy; #1 R&B hit (2 weeks)	
7/13/91	**8**	13	2. **I Can't Wait Another Minute**	Jive 1445
			Airplay #4 / Sales #15; #1 R&B hit (1 week)	
8/15/92	**5**	16	3. **She's Playing Hard To Get**	Jive 42067
			Airplay #6 / Sales #8	
1/23/93	**38**	2	4. Quality Time	Jive 42109
			Sales #18 / Airplay #54; written, produced and backing vocal by R. Kelly	
11/20/93	**30**	10	5. Never Should've Let You Go	Jive 42178
			Sales #27 / Airplay #40; from the movie Sister Act II: Back In The Habit starring Whoopi Goldberg	

Michael Jackson's 1991 album *Dangerous* stayed at No. 1 for only four weeks and was perceived by many in the industry as a comparative "failure" compared to his 1982 masterwork *Thriller*. Among its singles were "Black Or White," "Remember The Time" and "Who Is It."

Mick Jagger's career as a solo artist contrasted vividly with his longtime success in The Rolling Stones. Though he had four Top 40 hits between 1985 and 1987, his rendition of *Ruthless People*'s title track only reached No. 51.

Sonny James produced two Top 40 pop singles in 1957, including the No. 1 "Young Love." The country singer's 1960 track "Jenny Lou," released on the NRC label, peaked at No. 67.

Jan And Dean scored more than one hit prior to their move to Liberty Records in 1963, though their 1960 Dore single "We Go Together"—which spent seven weeks on the chart and peaked at No. 53—wasn't one of them.

Jay And The Americans' "Livin' Above Your Head" was the group's sole self-penned hit—though it peaked at a disappointing No. 76 in 1966. Soon after, The Walker Brothers scored a hit of their own with it in Britain.

The Jets' 1987 hit "Cross My Broken Heart" was one of three Top 10 singles drawn from MCA's *Beverly Hills Cop II* soundtrack; also on the disk were Bob Seger's "Shakedown" and George Michael's "I Want Your Sex."

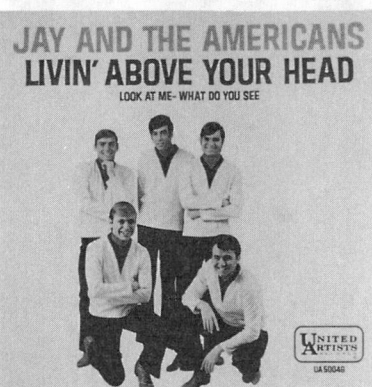

Joan Jett's massive single "I Love Rock 'n' Roll" tied with Paul McCartney's and Stevie Wonder's "Ebony And Ivory" as 1982's longest-running No. 1 hit; both tracks stayed atop the charts for seven full weeks.

Jose Jimenez, a Latino character created by respected writer/actor Bill Dana, achieved two firsts with 1961's comedy single "The Astronaut (Parts 1 & 2)": The so-called "first man in space" scored his first—and last—Top 20 single.

Jive Bunny And The Mastermixers' 1989 hit "Swing The Mood" sampled a host of popular dance tracks—from "In The Mood" to "Tutti Frutti"—and got a gold single in return. Appropriately, noted some critics, the No. 11 single was issued on the Music Factory label.

Billy Joel's power within the music industry was displayed in the early '90s, when EMI Records dropped its plans to reissue an album by his late '60s group The Hassles—reportedly at the singer's direct request.

Elton John's 1978 single "Ego" was his lowest-charting Top 40 hit since 1971's "Friends." Could the absence of his name on the single's picture sleeve—perhaps related to the song's title—have been a factor?

Elton John's astonishing track record of hits grew even larger in 1994 via his participation in the enormously successful soundtrack to Disney's box-office blockbuster *The Lion King*. The album was a No. 1 hit for nine weeks.

DATE	POS	WKS	ARTIST–RECORD TITLE	LABEL & NO.
			HIGGINS, Bertie	
			Born Elbert Higgins on 12/8/44 in Tarpon Springs, Florida. Singer/ songwriter. First recorded for ABC in 1964. Worked as a drummer with the Roemans, 1964–66.	
1/16/82	8	17	● 1. **Key Largo** inspired by the movie starring Humphrey Bogart and Lauren Bacall; #1 Adult Contemporary hit (2 weeks)	Kat Family 02524
			HIGH INERGY	
			Female soul group from Pasadena, California: sisters Barbara and Vernessa Mitchell, Linda Howard and Michelle Rumph. Vernessa left in 1978; group continued as a trio.	
11/19/77	12	11	1. You Can't Turn Me Off (In The Middle Of Turning Me On)	Gordy 7155
			HIGHLIGHTS, The	
			Male vocal quintet formed at DePaul University, Chicago: Frank Pizani (lead), Frank Calzaretta and his brother Tony, Bill Melshimer and Jerry Oleski.	
11/10/56	19	5	1. City Of Angels Best Seller #19 / Top 100 #30	Bally 1016
			HIGHWAYMEN, The	
			Folk quintet formed at Wesleyan University in Middletown, Connecticut: Dave Fisher, Bob Burnett, Steve Trott, Steve Butts and Chan Daniels (died 8/2/75).	
7/31/61	1 (2)	11	● 1. **Michael** 19th-century folk song ("Michael Row The Boat Ashore"); #1 Adult Contemporary hit (5 weeks)	United Art. 258
12/25/61+	13	13	2. Cotton Fields traditional American ballad, copyrighted in 1850	United Art. 370
			HILL, Bunker	
			Born David Walker on 5/5/41 in Washington, D.C. Professional boxer. Ex-lead singer of gospel group Mighty Clouds Of Joy.	
10/13/62	33	3	1. Hide & Go Seek, Part I	Mala 451
			HILL, Dan	
			Born on 6/3/54 in Toronto. Author/singer/songwriter.	
12/24/77+	3	15	● 1. **Sometimes When We Touch**	20th Century 2355
7/25/87	6	13	2. **Can't We Try** **DAN HILL (with Vonda Sheppard)** Sales #4 / Airplay #9	Columbia 07050
			HILL, Jessie	
			Born on 12/9/32 in New Orleans. R&B singer/drummer/pianist. With Huey (Piano) Smith to 1958.	
5/9/60	28	4	1. Ooh Poo Pah Doo - Part II [I]	Minit 607
			HILLSIDE SINGERS, The	
			Nine-member vocal group assembled by producer/arranger Al Ham.	
12/11/71+	13	10	1. I'd Like To Teach The World To Sing (In Perfect Harmony) adapted from a Coca-Cola jingle	Metromedia 231

DATE	POS	WKS	ARTIST–RECORD TITLE	LABEL & NO.
			HILLTOPPERS, The	
			Quartet formed at Western Kentucky College in Bowling Green, Kentucky, in 1952. Group named after the school's nickname. Consisted of Jimmy Sacca (lead singer), Don McGuire, Seymour Spiegelman (died 1987) and Billy Vaughn (died 9/26/91). Vaughn left in 1955 to become Dot's musical director; scored own hits.	
			THE HILLTOPPERS FEATURING JIMMY SACCA:	
7/30/55	**20**	4	1. The Kentuckian Song	Dot 15375
			Best Seller #20; from the movie *The Kentuckian* starring Burt Lancaster	
11/12/55	**8**	13	2. **Only You (And You Alone)**	Dot 15423
			Jockey #8 / Top 100 #9 / Juke Box #10 / Best Seller #16	
1/21/56	**31**	1	3. My Treasure	Dot 15437
10/6/56	**38**	2	4. Ka-Ding-Dong	Dot 15489
			THE HILLTOPPERS Featuring Chuck Schroder	
2/9/57	**3**	13	5. **Marianne**	Dot 15537
			Juke Box #3 / Jockey #6 / Top 100 #8 / Best Seller #12; adapted from a Bahamian folk song	
11/25/57	**22**	4	6. The Joker (That's What They Call Me)	Dot 15662
			Jockey #22 / Best Seller #34 / Top 100 #37	
			HINTON, Joe	
			Born in 1929. Died on 8/13/68 in Boston. Soul singer. With the Chosen Gospel Singers. Lead singer of the Spirits Of Memphis gospel group.	
9/5/64	**13**	9	1. Funny	Back Beat 541
			written by Willie Nelson	
			HIPSWAY	
			Scottish quartet led by vocalist Grahame Skinner. Bassist John McElhone (ex-Altered Images) later joined the group Texas.	
3/14/87	**19**	6	1. The Honeythief	Columbia 06579
			Sales #16 / Airplay #21	
			HIRT, Al	
			Born Alois Maxwell Hirt on 11/7/22 in New Orleans. Trumpet virtuoso. Toured with Jimmy and Tommy Dorsey, Ray McKinley and Horace Heidt. Formed own Dixieland combo (with Pete Fountain) in the late 1950s.	
1/25/64	**4**	13	1. **Java** [I]	RCA 8280
			#1 Adult Contemporary hit (4 weeks)	
5/2/64	**15**	8	2. Cotton Candy [I]	RCA 8346
8/1/64	**30**	4	3. Sugar Lips [I]	RCA 8391
			HODGES, Eddie	
			Born on 3/5/47 in Hattiesburg, Mississippi. Played Frank Sinatra's son in the movie *A Hole In The Head*.	
7/24/61	**12**	8	1. I'm Gonna Knock On Your Door	Cadence 1397
7/7/62	**14**	8	2. (Girls, Girls, Girls) Made To Love	Cadence 1421
			written by Phil Everly (of The Everly Brothers)	

DATE	POS	WKS	ARTIST–RECORD TITLE	LABEL & NO.
			HOFFS, Susanna	
			Born on 1/17/57. Former lead singer of The Bangles. Starred in the 1987 movie *The Allnighter*. Her mother is movie director Tamara Hoffs. Married TV producer M. Jay Roach on 4/17/93.	
3/2/91	30	4	1. My Side Of The Bed Airplay #28 / Sales #32	Columbia 73529
			HOLDEN, Ron	
			Born on 8/7/39 in Seattle. R&B vocalist. In group The Playboys in 1957. Worked as emcee at Art Laboe's "Oldies But Goodies" club, 1972–77.	
4/25/60	7	13	1. **Love You So**	Donna 1315
			HOLLAND, Amy	
			Daughter of country singer Esmereldy and opera singer Harry Boersma. Married to Michael McDonald.	
9/13/80	22	6	1. How Do I Survive produced by Michael McDonald	Capitol 4884
			HOLLAND, Eddie	
			Born on 10/30/39 in Detroit. Singer/songwriter/producer. Member of Motown's hit production trio with brother Brian Holland and Lamont Dozier; wrote many of Motown's greatest hits. Co-founder of the Invictus/Hot Wax label. Holland-Dozier-Holland were inducted into the Rock and Roll Hall of Fame in 1990.	
3/10/62	30	4	1. Jamie	Motown 1021
			HOLLIDAY, Jennifer	
			Born on 10/19/60 in Riverside, Texas. Won 1982 Tony award for best actress in Broadway's *Dreamgirls*. Also appeared in Broadway's *Your Arm's Too Short To Box With God* (1978) and *Sing, Mahalia Sing* (1985).	
7/31/82	22	7	1. And I Am Telling You I'm Not Going from the original Broadway cast *Dreamgirls* starring Holliday; first pressings listed artist as: "Dreamgirls"; #1 R&B hit (4 weeks)	Geffen 29983
			HOLLIES, The	
			Formed in Manchester, England, in 1962. Consisted of Allan Clarke (lead vocals), Graham Nash and Tony Hicks (guitars), Eric Haydock (bass) and Don Rathbone (drums). Clarke and Nash had worked as a duo, the Guytones, added other members, became the Fourtones, Deltas, then The Hollies. First recorded for Parlophone in 1963. Rathbone left in 1963, replaced by Bobby Elliott. Haydock left in 1966, replaced by Bernie Calvert (first heard on "Bus Stop"). Nash left in December 1968 to join David Crosby and Stephen Stills in new trio, replaced by Terry Sylvester, formerly in The Swinging Blue Jeans. Shuffling personnel since then. Clarke, Nash, Hicks and Elliott regrouped briefly in 1983.	
1/8/66	32	4	1. Look Through Any Window	Imperial 66134
8/20/66	5	9	2. **Bus Stop**	Imperial 66186
11/12/66	7	7	3. **Stop Stop Stop**	Imperial 66214
4/15/67	11	9	4. On A Carousel	Imperial 66231
6/24/67	28	3	5. Pay You Back With Interest	Imperial 66240
7/8/67	9	10	6. **Carrie-Anne**	Epic 10180
5/18/68	40	1	7. Jennifer Eccles	Epic 10298
2/7/70	7	11	8. **He Ain't Heavy, He's My Brother**	Epic 10532
7/8/72	2 (2)	13	● 9. **Long Cool Woman (In A Black Dress)**	Epic 10871

DATE	POS	WKS	ARTIST–RECORD TITLE	LABEL & NO.
12/2/72	26	5	10. Long Dark Road	Epic 10920
6/8/74	6	11	● 11. **The Air That I Breathe**	Epic 11100
			all of above produced by Ron Richards	
7/2/83	29	6	12. Stop In The Name Of Love	Atlantic 89819

HOLLOWAY, Brenda

Born on 6/21/46 in Atascadero, California. Soul singer/songwriter. Later a backup singer for Joe Cocker.

DATE	POS	WKS	ARTIST–RECORD TITLE	LABEL & NO.
5/23/64	13	6	1. Every Little Bit Hurts	Tamla 54094
3/27/65	25	5	2. When I'm Gone	Tamla 54111
			written and produced by Smokey Robinson	
11/4/67	39	1	3. You've Made Me So Very Happy	Tamla 54155

HOLLY, Buddy/The Crickets

Born Charles Hardin Holley on 9/7/36 in Lubbock, Texas. One of rock and roll's most original and innovative performers. Began recording western and bop demos with Bob Montgomery in 1954. Signed to Decca label in January 1956 and recorded in Nashville as Buddy Holly & The Three Tunes (Sonny Curtis, lead guitar; Don Guess, bass; and Jerry Ivan Allison, drums). In February 1957, Holly assembled his backing group, The Crickets (Allison; Niki Sullivan, rhythm guitar; and Joe B. Mauldin, bass), for recordings at Norman Petty's studio in Clovis, New Mexico. Signed to Brunswick and Coral labels (subsidiaries of Decca Records). Because of contract arrangements, all Brunswick records were released as The Crickets, and all Coral records were released as Buddy Holly. Holly split from The Crickets in Fall 1958. Holly (age 22), Ritchie Valens and the Big Bopper were killed in a plane crash near Mason City, Iowa, on 2/3/59. Holly was inducted into the Rock and Roll Hall of Fame in 1986.

DATE	POS	WKS	ARTIST–RECORD TITLE	LABEL & NO.
8/19/57	1 (1)	16	● 1. **That'll Be The Day** **THE CRICKETS** Best Seller #1 / Top 100 #3 / Jockey #3; different version released on Decca 30434 in September 1957 as by Buddy Holly And The Three Tunes (recorded July 1956)	Brunswick 55009
11/11/57	3	16	● 2. **Peggy Sue** Best Seller #3 / Top 100 #3 / Jockey #3; first known as "Cindy Lou"; renamed for Allison's girlfriend, Peggy Sue Gerrow, later his wife; B-side is Holly's classic "Everyday"	Coral 61885
12/2/57+	10	13	3. **Oh, Boy!** **THE CRICKETS** Top 100 #10 / Best Seller #11 / Jockey #20; B-side is Holly's original "Not Fade Away"	Brunswick 55035
3/10/58	17	8	4. Maybe Baby **THE CRICKETS** Jockey #17 / Best Seller #18 / Top 100 #18	Brunswick 55053
6/9/58	37	2	5. Rave On Top 100 #37 / Best Seller #41	Coral 61985
8/4/58	27	4	6. Think It Over **THE CRICKETS** Hot 100 #27 / Best Seller #38	Brunswick 55072
8/11/58	32	4	7. Early In The Morning Hot 100 #32 / Best Seller #45; written by Bobby Darin; The Helen Way Singers (backing vocals)	Coral 62006
3/9/59	13	9	8. It Doesn't Matter Anymore written by Paul Anka; Dick Jacobs (orch.)	Coral 62074

DATE	POS	WKS	ARTIST–RECORD TITLE	LABEL & NO.
			HOLLYWOOD ARGYLES	
6/13/60	**1** (1)	12	Gary Paxton recorded "Alley-Oop" as a solo artist; since he was still under contract to Brent Records, where he recorded as Flip of "Skip & Flip," he made up the name Hollywood Argyles. After the song was a hit, Paxton assembled a Hollywood Argyles group. Formed Garpax Records. Paxton is now a gospel artist. ● 1. **Alley-Oop** [N] written by Dallas Frazier; based on the comic strip character	Lute 5905
			HOLLYWOOD FLAMES	
12/2/57+	**11**	12 1	Los Angeles-based R&B group formed in 1950 by Bobby Byrd (aka Bobby Day). Known also as The Flames, Four Flames, Hollywood Four Flames, and The Satellites. Earl Nelson was lead singer in 1957. 1. Buzz-Buzz-Buzz/ Top 100 #11 / Best Seller #12 2. Crazy Best Seller flip	Ebb 119
			HOLMAN, Eddie	
1/10/70	**2** (1)	12	Born on 6/3/46 in Norfolk, Virginia. Soul singer/songwriter. Recorded for Leopard in the early 1960s. ● 1. **Hey There Lonely Girl** recorded in 1963 by Ruby & The Romantics as "Hey There Lonely Boy"	ABC 11240
			HOLMES, Clint	
5/5/73	**2** (2)	15	Born on 5/9/46 in Bournemouth, England. Moved to Buffalo, New York as a child. ● 1. **Playground In My Mind** child's vocal is by producer Paul Vance's son, Philip	Epic 10891
			HOLMES, Rupert	
11/10/79 2/9/80 6/14/80	**1** (3) **6** **32**	16 12 3	Born on 2/24/47 in Cheshire, England. Moved to New York at age six. Member of the studio group Street People. Wrote and arranged for The Drifters, The Platters and Gene Pitney. Arranged/produced for Barbra Streisand. Wrote The Buoys' hit "Timothy" and the Broadway musical Drood. ● 1. **Escape (The Pina Colada Song)** 2. **Him** 3. Answering Machine	Infinity 50035 MCA 41173 MCA 41235
			HOMBRES, The	
10/7/67	**12**	10	Memphis foursome: B.B. Cunningham, Gary Wayne McEwen, Johnny Will Hunter and Jerry Lee Masters. All but Masters were members of Ronny & The Daytonas' touring band. Hunter died in 1976. Cunningham's brother, Bill, was a member of The Box Tops. 1. Let It Out (Let It All Hang Out) first pressings issued as "Let It All Hang Out"; spoken opening copied from Red Ingle's 1948 novelty hit "Cigareetes, Whuskey, And Wild, Wild Women"	Verve F. 5058

DATE	POS	WKS	ARTIST–RECORD TITLE	LABEL & NO.
			HOMER AND JETHRO	
			Henry "Homer" Haynes (born 7/29/17, Knoxville, Tennessee; died 8/7/71; guitar) and Kenneth "Jethro" Burns (born 3/10/23, Knoxville, Tennessee; died 2/4/89; mandolin). Country music's foremost comedy duo from the 1940s until Homer's death. Jethro went on to work with popular folk singer Steve Goodman.	
9/14/59	**14**	7	1. The Battle Of Kookamonga [N] a parody of "The Battle Of New Orleans"; produced by Chet Atkins	RCA 7585
			HONDELLS, The	
			Originally a studio group assembled in Southern California by Gary Usher (died 5/25/90). "Little Honda" featured Usher and Kurt Boetcher (Sagittarius), Brian Wilson (Beach Boys), Glen Campbell, Chuck Girard and Joe Kelly (The Castells), and Ritchie Burns.	
10/3/64	**9**	9	1. **Little Honda** written by Brian Wilson of The Beach Boys	Mercury 72324
			HONEYCOMBS, The	
			English rock quintet featuring Dennis d'Ell (lead singer) and Ann "Honey" Lantree (drums).	
10/10/64	**5**	9	1. **Have I The Right?**	Interphon 7707
			HONEY CONE, The	
			Female soul trio formed in Los Angeles in 1969. Consisted of prominent backup singers: Carolyn Willis (member of The Girlfriends and Bob B. Soxx & The Blue Jeans), Edna Wright (sister of Darlene Love) and Shellie Clark (former Ikette; regular on the TV series "The Jim Nabors Hour," 1969–70). Willis left in 1973; replaced by Denise Mills.	
5/1/71	**1 (1)**	13	● 1. **Want Ads** #1 R&B hit (3 weeks)	Hot Wax 7011
8/21/71	**11**	10	● 2. Stick-Up #1 R&B hit (2 weeks)	Hot Wax 7106
12/11/71+	**15**	8	3. One Monkey Don't Stop No Show Part I	Hot Wax 7110
3/25/72	**23**	6	4. The Day I Found Myself	Hot Wax 7113
			HONEYDRIPPERS, The	
			A rock superstar gathering: vocalist Robert Plant (Led Zeppelin), with guitarists Jimmy Page (The Yardbirds, Led Zeppelin, The Firm), Jeff Beck (The Yardbirds) and Nile Rodgers (Chic).	
10/27/84+	**3**	14	1. **Sea Of Love** Airplay #3 / Sales #4; #1 Adult Contemporary hit (1 week)	Es Paranza 99701
1/26/85	**25**	6	2. Rockin' At Midnight Airplay #25 / Sales #27; #2 R&B hit for Roy Brown in 1949; also available as B-side on early pressings of #1 above	Es Paranza 99686
			HONEYMOON SUITE	
			Rock quintet from Toronto: Johnnie Dee (vocals), Derry Grehan (guitar), Ray Coburn (keyboards), Garry Lalonde (bass) and Dave Betts (drums). Coburn left in 1987, replaced by Rob Preuss.	
4/26/86	**34**	3	1. Feel It Again Airplay #30	Warner 28779

DATE	POS	WKS	ARTIST–RECORD TITLE	LABEL & NO.
			HOOTERS	
			Pop-rock band from Philadelphia: Eric Bazilian (vocals, guitar), Rob Hyman (vocals, keyboards), John Lilley (guitar), Andy King (bass) and David Uosikkinen (drums). Fran Smith, Jr., replaced King in early 1989. Bazilian and Hyman were arrangers/musicians/backing vocalists on Cyndi Lauper's album *She's So Unusual*. Hooter: nickname of Hyman's keyboard-harmonica.	
9/28/85	21	8	1. And We Danced Sales #19 / Airplay #23	Columbia 05568
2/1/86	18	7	2. Day By Day Sales #15 / Airplay #36	Columbia 05730
5/24/86	38	1	3. Where Do The Children Go Airplay #36; Patty Smyth (backing vocal)	Columbia 05854
			HOOTIE & THE BLOWFISH	
			Pop band formed at the University of South Carolina: Darius Rucker (vocals), Mark Bryan (guitar), Dean Felber (bass) and Jim "Soni" Sonefeld (drums).	
12/10/94+	10	34	1. **Hold My Hand** Airplay #2 / Sales #41	Atlantic 87230
4/15/95	9	25	2. **Let Her Cry** Airplay #5 / Sales #32	Atlantic 87231
8/5/95	6	29	3. **Only Wanna Be With You** Airplay #2 / Sales #38	Atlantic 87132
12/2/95+	14	20	4. **Time** Airplay #4	Atlantic 87095
			HOPKIN, Mary	
			Born on 5/3/50 in Pontardawe, Wales. Discovered by the model Twiggy. Married to producer Tony Visconti (who worked with David Bowie), 1971–81.	
10/12/68	2 (3)	12	● 1. **Those Were The Days** melody based on the traditional Russian folk song "Dear For Me"; #1 Adult Contemporary hit (6 weeks)	Apple 1801
5/3/69	13	7	2. Goodbye written by John Lennon and Paul McCartney; above 2 produced by Paul McCartney	Apple 1806
3/28/70	39	2	3. Temma Harbour	Apple 1816
			HORNE, Jimmy "Bo"	
			Born on 9/28/49 in West Palm Beach, Florida. Soul singer/dancer.	
6/24/78	38	1	1. Dance Across The Floor written and produced by H.W. Casey (of KC And The Sunshine Band)	Sunshine S. 1003
			HORNE, Lena	
			Born on 6/30/17 in Brooklyn. Broadway and movie musical star. Long-married to bandleader Lennie Hayton. Her career reached a new peak in early 1980s with her one-woman Broadway show. Won the Lifetime Achievement Grammy in 1989.	
7/9/55	19	1	1. Love Me Or Leave Me Jockey #19; Lennie Hayton (orch.); #2 hit in 1929 for Ruth Etting, and title song of Etting's 1955 biopic starring Doris Day	RCA 6073

DATE	POS	WKS	ARTIST—RECORD TITLE	LABEL & NO.
			HORNSBY, Bruce, And The Range	
			Hornsby was born on 11/23/54 in Williamsburg, Virginia. Singer/pianist/songwriter/leader of jazz-influenced pop quintet The Range. Moved to Los Angeles in 1980. Backing pianist for Sheena Easton's touring band, 1983. Formed The Range in 1984 with Joe Puerta (bass), John Molo (drums), guitarists George Marinelli and David Mansfield (replaced by Peter Harris, who left by 1990). Won 1986 Best New Artist Grammy Award. Hornsby joined Grateful Dead on tour from time to time after Brent Mydland's death.	
10/18/86	1 (1)	15	1. **The Way It Is** Airplay #1(2) / Sales #2; #1 Adult Contemporary hit (2 weeks)	RCA 5023
1/31/87	4	12	2. **Mandolin Rain** Airplay #2 / Sales #5; #1 Adult Contemporary hit (3 weeks); "live" version is on the B-side of #3 below	RCA 5087
5/30/87	14	9	3. Every Little Kiss [R] Airplay #12 / Sales #15; remix of group's 1986 hit (#72)	RCA 5165
5/14/88	5	11	4. **The Valley Road** Sales #5 / Airplay #6; #1 Adult Contemporary hit (1 week)	RCA 7645
8/27/88	35	2	5. Look Out Any Window Sales #34 / Airplay #38	RCA 8678
7/21/90	18	7	6. Across The River Airplay #17 / Sales #23	RCA 2621
			HORTON, Johnny	
			Born on 4/30/25 in Los Angeles; raised in Tyler, Texas. Killed in an auto accident on 11/5/60. Country singer. Married to Billie Jean Jones, widow of country music superstar Hank Williams.	
5/4/59	1 (6)	18	● 1. **The Battle Of New Orleans** original melody written in celebration of the final battle of the War of 1812; #1 Country hit (10 weeks)	Columbia 41339
3/14/60	3	13	2. **Sink The Bismarck** inspired by the movie starring Kenneth More, which is based on the sinking of the German battleship in World War II	Columbia 41568
10/17/60	4	18	3. **North To Alaska** title song from the movie starring John Wayne; #1 Country hit (5 weeks)	Columbia 41782
			HOT	
			Interracial female trio: Gwen Owens, Cathy Carson and Juanita Curiel. First known as Sugar & Spice.	
4/2/77	6	19	● 1. **Angel In Your Arms**	Big Tree 16085
			HOT BUTTER	
			Hot Butter is Moog synthesizer player Stan Free.	
8/19/72	9	12	1. **Popcorn** [I]	Musicor 1458
			HOT CHOCOLATE	
			Interracial rock-soul group formed in London by lead singer Errol Brown in 1970. Included Harvey Hinsley (guitar), Larry Ferguson (keyboards), Tony Wilson (bass), Patrick Olive (congas) and Tony Connor (drums). First recorded for The Beatles' Apple label in 1969. Wilson left in 1975, Olive switched to bass.	
3/8/75	8	9	1. **Emma**	Big Tree 16031
7/5/75	28	4	2. Disco Queen	Big Tree 16038
12/6/75+	3	15	● 3. **You Sexy Thing**	Big Tree 16047

DATE	POS	WKS	ARTIST–RECORD TITLE	LABEL & NO.
8/13/77	**31**	5	4. So You Win Again	Big Tree 16096
12/2/78+	**6**	13	● 5. **Every 1's A Winner** all of above produced by Mickie Most	Infinity 50002
			HOTLEGS	
			British trio: Eric Stewart (formerly of The Mindbenders), Kevin Godley & Lol Creme. Graham Gouldman (The Mindbenders) joined the group later on tour. Quartet evolved into 10cc.	
9/5/70	**22**	6	1. Neanderthal Man	Capitol 2886
			HOUSE OF PAIN	
			Los Angeles-based rap outfit: Erik "Everlast" Schrody, "Danny Boy" O'Connor and Leor "DJ Lethal" DiMant. Met at Taft High School in Woodland Hills, California. Both Schrody and O'Connor were born in the U.S. of Irish parentage. DiMant was born in Latvia.	
7/25/92	**3**	25	▲ 1. **Jump Around** Sales #2 / Airplay #29; samples "Harlem Shuffle" by Bob & Earl and the chorus line from "Jump" by Kris Kross	Tommy Boy 7526
			HOUSTON, David	
			Born on 12/9/38 in Bossier City, Louisiana. Died on 11/30/93 after suffering a ruptured brain aneurysm on 11/25/93. Country singer/songwriter/guitarist. Godson of 1920s pop singer Gene Austin and a descendant of Sam Houston and Robert E. Lee.	
8/27/66	**24**	8	1. Almost Persuaded #1 Country hit (9 weeks)	Epic 10025
			HOUSTON, Thelma	
			Born on 5/7/46 in Leland, Mississippi. Soul singer/actress. Appeared in the movies *Norman...Is That You?*, *Death Scream* and *The Seventh Dwarf*.	
1/29/77	**1** (1)	17	1. **Don't Leave Me This Way** #1 R&B hit (1 week)	Tamla 54278
5/19/79	**34**	3	2. Saturday Night, Sunday Morning	Tamla 54297
			HOUSTON, Whitney	
			Born on 8/9/63 in Newark, New Jersey. Daughter of Cissy Houston and cousin of Dionne Warwick. Began singing career at age 11 with the gospel group New Hope Baptist Junior Choir. As a teen, worked as a backing vocalist for Chaka Khan and Lou Rawls. Pursued modeling career in 1981, appearing in *Glamour* magazine and on the cover of *Seventeen*. Married Bobby Brown on 7/18/92. Starred in the movie *The Bodyguard*.	
6/1/85	**3**	13	● 1. **You Give Good Love** Sales #2 / Airplay #5; #1 R&B hit (1 week)	Arista 9274
8/24/85	**1** (1)	15	● 2. **Saving All My Love For You** Sales #1(2) / Airplay #3; #1 Adult Contemporary hit (3 weeks); #1 R&B hit (1 week)	Arista 9381
12/28/85+	**1** (2)	16	● 3. **How Will I Know** Airplay #1(2) / Sales #1(1); Cissy Houston (Whitney's mother, backing vocal); #1 R&B hit (1 week); #1 Adult Contemporary hit (1 week); also on the B-side of #9 below	Arista 9434
4/5/86	**1** (3)	14	● 4. **Greatest Love Of All** Airplay #1(2) / Sales #1(1); originally released as the B-side of #1 above; #1 Adult Contemporary hit (5 weeks); all of above from the album *Whitney Houston*	Arista 9466
5/16/87	**1** (2)	14	▲ 5. **I Wanna Dance With Somebody (Who Loves Me)** Airplay #1(3) / Sales #1(2); #1 Adult Contemporary hit (3 weeks)	Arista 9598

DATE	POS	WKS	ARTIST–RECORD TITLE	LABEL & NO.
8/8/87	1 (2)	13	6. **Didn't We Almost Have It All** Sales #1(2) / Airplay #1(1); #1 Adult Contemporary hit (3 weeks)	Arista 9616
11/7/87+	1 (1)	14	● 7. **So Emotional** Sales #1(2) / Airplay #2	Arista 9642
3/5/88	1 (2)	13	8. **Where Do Broken Hearts Go** Sales #1(2) / Airplay #1(1); #1 Adult Contemporary hit (3 weeks)	Arista 9674
7/9/88	9	11	9. **Love Will Save The Day** Sales #8 / Airplay #9; above 5 from the album *Whitney*	Arista 9720
9/24/88	5	11	10. **One Moment In Time** Sales #3 / Airplay #7; tune used by NBC-TV for the 1988 Summer Olympics; #1 Adult Contemporary hit (2 weeks)	Arista 9743
10/27/90	1 (1)	14	● 11. **I'm Your Baby Tonight** Airplay #1(1) / Sales #3; #1 R&B hit (2 weeks)	Arista 2108
1/5/91	1 (2)	15	● 12. **All The Man That I Need** Sales #1(1) / Airplay #1(1); Kenny G (sax solo); #1 Adult Contemporary hit (4 weeks); #1 R&B hit (2 weeks); recorded in 1982 by Sister Sledge as "All The Man I Need"	Arista 2156
3/9/91	20	7	● 13. The Star Spangled Banner Sales #3; "live" recording from the National Anthem Ceremony at Super Bowl XXV (1/27/91)	Arista 2207
4/27/91	9	9	14. **Miracle** Sales #8 / Airplay #13	Arista 2222
8/10/91	20	6	15. My Name Is Not Susan Airplay #33 / Sales #44; above 5 (except #13) from the album *I'm Your Baby Tonight*	Arista 12259
11/14/92	1 (14)	24	▲4 16. **I Will Always Love You** Sales #1(14) / Airplay #1(11); written by Dolly Parton in 1974; #1 R&B hit (11 weeks); #1 Adult Contemporary hit (5 weeks)	Arista 12490
1/23/93	4	19	● 17. **I'm Every Woman** Airplay #2 / Sales #11; written by Ashford & Simpson	Arista 12519
3/6/93	4	16	● 18. **I Have Nothing** Airplay #1(6) / Sales #7; #1 Adult Contemporary hit (2 weeks)	Arista 12527
7/17/93	31	6	19. Run To You Airplay #26 / Sales #41; above 4 from the album and movie *The Bodyguard* starring Houston and Kevin Costner	Arista 12570
11/25/95	1 (1)	20	▲ 20. **Exhale (Shoop Shoop)** Sales #1 (1)/Airplay #4; from the movie *Waiting To Exhale* starring Houston; written and produced by Babyface; #1 R&B hit (8 weeks)	Arista 12885
			## HOWARD, Adina	
			Born on 11/14/74 in Grand Rapids, Michigan. Female R&B singer.	
2/25/95	2 (2)	27	▲ 1. **Freak Like Me** Sales #2 / Airplay #9; Michael Speaks (guest vocal); samples "I'd Rather Be With You" by Bootsy Collins	Mecca Don/EW 64484
			## H-TOWN	
			Houston R&B vocal trio: brothers Shazam and John "Dino" Conner with Darryl "GI" Jackson.	
5/1/93	3	20	▲ 1. **Knockin' Da Boots** Sales #1(2) / Airplay #5; #1 R&B hit (4 weeks)	Luke 161
			## HUDSON BROTHERS	
			Bill, Brett and Mark Hudson from Portland, Oregon. Own TV variety show during the summer of 1974; also hosted kiddie TV show "The Hudson Brothers Razzle Dazzle Comedy Show." Bill was married to actress Goldie Hawn.	

DATE	POS	WKS	ARTIST–RECORD TITLE	LABEL & NO.
10/26/74	**21**	5	1. So You Are A Star	Casablanca 0108
8/2/75	**26**	4	2. Rendezvous	Rocket 40417

HUES CORPORATION, The

Black vocal trio formed in Los Angeles in 1969: Bernard Henderson, Fleming Williams and H. Ann Kelley. Williams replaced by Tommy Brown after "Rock The Boat." Brown replaced by Karl Russell in 1975.

DATE	POS	WKS	ARTIST–RECORD TITLE	LABEL & NO.
6/15/74	**1** (1)	10	● 1. **Rock The Boat**	RCA 0232
10/26/74	**18**	5	2. Rockin' Soul	RCA 10066

HUGH, Grayson

Soul-styled white singer/songwriter/pianist from Connecticut.

DATE	POS	WKS	ARTIST–RECORD TITLE	LABEL & NO.
8/5/89	**19**	8	1. Talk It Over Sales #15 / Airplay #24	RCA 8802

HUGHES, Fred

Soul singer from Arkansas. To Los Angeles, formed own band, the Creators.

DATE	POS	WKS	ARTIST–RECORD TITLE	LABEL & NO.
6/19/65	**23**	6	1. Oo Wee Baby, I Love You	Vee-Jay 684

HUGHES, Jimmy

Soul singer from Florence, Alabama. With Singing Clouds gospel group to 1962. Cousin of Percy Sledge.

DATE	POS	WKS	ARTIST–RECORD TITLE	LABEL & NO.
7/11/64	**17**	9	1. Steal Away	Fame 6401

HUGO & LUIGI

Producers/songwriters/label executives Hugo Peretti (born 12/6/16) and Luigi Creatore (born 12/21/20; died 5/1/86). Owned record labels Roulette and Avco/Embassy.

DATE	POS	WKS	ARTIST–RECORD TITLE	LABEL & NO.
1/4/60	**35**	3	1. Just Come Home vocals by a large chorus; written by French songstress Edith Piaf as "C'est l'Amour"	RCA 7639

HUMAN BEINZ, The

Rock band from Youngstown, Ohio: John Richard Belley (lead singer, guitar), Joe "Ting" Markulin (rhythm guitar), John Pachuta (bass) and Mike Tatum (drums).

DATE	POS	WKS	ARTIST–RECORD TITLE	LABEL & NO.
1/6/68	**8**	11	1. **Nobody But Me** originally recorded (and written) by The Isley Brothers in 1962	Capitol 5990

HUMAN LEAGUE, The

Electro-pop band formed in 1977 in Sheffield, England, by synthesists Martyn Ware and Ian Craig Marsh, and lead singer/synthesist Philip Oakey. Vocalists Joanne Catherall and Susanne Sulley joined in October 1980 when Ware and Marsh left to form Heaven 17. Lineup in 1990 included Russell Dennett (guitar) and Neil Sutton (keyboards).

DATE	POS	WKS	ARTIST–RECORD TITLE	LABEL & NO.
4/10/82	**1** (3)	21	● 1. **Don't You Want Me**	A&M 2397
7/2/83	**8**	13	2. **(Keep Feeling) Fascination**	A&M 2547
10/29/83	**30**	5	3. Mirror Man	A&M 2587
9/27/86	**1** (1)	15	4. **Human** Sales #1(1) / Airplay #1(1)	A&M 2861
11/3/90	**32**	3	5. Heart Like A Wheel Airplay #31 / Sales #35	Virgin/A&M 1520

DATE	POS	WKS	ARTIST–RECORD TITLE	LABEL & NO.
4/15/95	31	5	6. Tell Me When Airplay #29 / Sales #75	EastWest 64443

HUMPERDINCK, Engelbert

Born Arnold George Dorsey on 5/2/36 in Madras, India. To Leicester, England, in 1947. First recorded for Decca in 1958. Met Tom Jones's manager, Gordon Mills, in 1965, who suggested his name change to Engelbert Humperdinck (a famous German opera composer). Starred in his own musical variety TV series in 1970.

DATE	POS	WKS	ARTIST–RECORD TITLE	LABEL & NO.
4/29/67	4	10	1. **Release Me (And Let Me Love Again)** #5 Country hit for Jimmy Heap in 1954	Parrot 40011
7/15/67	20	4	2. There Goes My Everything	Parrot 40015
10/14/67	25	5	3. The Last Waltz	Parrot 40019
1/6/68	18	7	4. Am I That Easy To Forget #1 Adult Contemporary hit (1 week); #9 Country hit for Carl Belew in 1959	Parrot 40023
6/1/68	19	5	5. A Man Without Love (Quando M'innamoro) The Sandpipers Italian version "Bubbled Under" in 1968	Parrot 40027
11/23/68	31	3	6. Les Bicyclettes De Belsize	Parrot 40032
9/27/69	38	1	7. I'm A Better Man	Parrot 40040
1/3/70	16	8	8. Winter World Of Love	Parrot 40044
11/20/76+	8	14	● 9. **After The Lovin'** #1 Adult Contemporary hit (2 weeks)	Epic 50270

HUMPHREY, Paul, & His Cool Aid Chemists

Humphrey was born on 10/12/35 in Detroit. Black session drummer. Worked with Wes Montgomery, Les McCann, Kai Winding, Charlie Mingus, Lee Konitz and Gene Ammons in the early '60s. The Cool Aid Chemists were Clarence MacDonald, David T. Walker (Afrique) and Bill Upchurch.

DATE	POS	WKS	ARTIST–RECORD TITLE	LABEL & NO.
5/15/71	29	7	1. Cool Aid [I]	Lizard 21006

HUNTER, Ivory Joe

Born on 10/10/14 in Kirbyville, Texas. Died of lung cancer on 11/8/74. R&B singer/songwriter/pianist. First recorded in 1933 (a cylinder record for the Library Of Congress). Own radio shows, KFDM-Beaumont, Texas, early '40s. Own record labels, Ivory and Pacific, 1944. Signed by King Records, 1947; MGM, 1950. Had 14 Top 10 R&B hits, 1945–50.

DATE	POS	WKS	ARTIST–RECORD TITLE	LABEL & NO.
12/1/56	12	15	● 1. Since I Met You Baby Best Seller #12 / Top 100 #12 / Jockey #14 / Juke Box #14; #1 R&B hit (3 weeks)	Atlantic 1111

HUNTER, John

Rock singer/keyboardist from Chicago.

DATE	POS	WKS	ARTIST–RECORD TITLE	LABEL & NO.
2/16/85	39	2	1. Tragedy	Private I 04643

HUNTER, Tab

Born Arthur Andrew Kelm on 7/11/31 in New York City. Sportsman-turned-movie/TV actor in 1952. Appeared in *Island of Desire, Battle Cry, Damn Yankees, Ride The Wild Surf* and *Lust In The Dust.*

DATE	POS	WKS	ARTIST–RECORD TITLE	LABEL & NO.
1/19/57	1 (6)	17	● 1. **Young Love** Top 100 #1(6) / Jockey #1(6) / Juke Box #1(5) / Best Seller #1(4)	Dot 15533

DATE	POS	WKS	ARTIST–RECORD TITLE	LABEL & NO.
3/30/57	**11**	8	2. Ninety-Nine Ways Top 100 #11 / Jockey #11 / Best Seller #12 / Juke Box #17; written by Charlie Gracie; Billy Vaughn (orch., above 2)	Dot 15548
2/23/59	**31**	4	3. (I'll Be With You In) Apple Blossom Time Don Ralke (orch.); #2 hit for Charles Harrison in 1920	Warner 5032
			HUSKY, Ferlin	
			Born on 12/3/25 in Flat River, Missouri. Country singer/songwriter/guitarist. Recorded as Terry Preston in the early 1950s; also did humorous recordings as Simon Crum.	
3/9/57	**4**	19	1. **Gone** Top 100 #4 / Jockey #4 / Juke Box #4 / Best Seller #5; originally recorded by Husky in 1952 as by Terry Preston; #1 Country hit (10 weeks)	Capitol 3628
12/26/60+	**12**	13	2. Wings Of A Dove #1 Country hit (10 weeks)	Capitol 4406
			HYLAND, Brian	
			Born on 11/12/43 in Queens, New York. Own group, the Delphis, at age 12. In production company with Del Shannon in 1970.	
7/11/60	**1 (1)**	13	● 1. **Itsy Bitsy Teenie Weenie Yellow Polkadot Bikini**[N] first released on Leader 805 in 1960; Hyland was a high school sophomore at the time of this recording; Trudy Packer (female spoken voice)	Kapp 342
9/4/61	**20**	5	2. Let Me Belong To You	ABC-Para. 10236
4/7/62	**21**	6	3. Ginny Come Lately	ABC-Para. 10294
6/30/62	**3**	11	4. **Sealed With A Kiss**	ABC-Para. 10336
10/13/62	**25**	4	5. Warmed Over Kisses (Left Over Love) Stan Applebaum (orch., above 4)	ABC-Para. 10359
8/6/66	**20**	8	6. The Joker Went Wild	Philips 40377
11/26/66	**25**	3	7. Run, Run, Look And See	Philips 40405
10/24/70	**3**	13	● 8. **Gypsy Woman** produced by Del Shannon	Uni 55240
			HYMAN, Dick	
			Born on 3/8/27 in New York City. Piano-playing composer/conductor/ arranger who toured Europe with Benny Goodman in 1950. Staff pianist at WMCA and WNBC-New York, 1951–57. Music director of "Arthur Godfrey And His Friends," 1958–62.	
1/28/56	**8**	15	● 1. **Moritat (A Theme From "The Three Penny Opera")**[I] **THE "UNFORGETTABLE" SOUND OF THE DICK HYMAN TRIO** Jockey #8 / Top 100 #9 / Best Seller #10 / Juke Box #14; written in 1928, known later as "Mack The Knife"	MGM 12149
7/5/69	**38**	2	2. The Minotaur [I] **DICK HYMAN & HIS ELECTRIC ECLECTICS**	Command 4126
			HYNDE, Chrissie—see UB40	

DATE	POS	WKS	ARTIST–RECORD TITLE	LABEL & NO.

I

IAN, Janis

Born Janis Eddy Fink on 4/7/51 in New York City. Singer/songwriter/pianist/guitarist.

DATE	POS	WKS	ARTIST–RECORD TITLE	LABEL & NO.
6/17/67	14	8	1. Society's Child (Baby I've Been Thinking) written in 1965 by Ian (at age 14) about interracial romance	Verve 5027
7/12/75	3	14	2. **At Seventeen** #1 Adult Contemporary hit (2 weeks)	Columbia 10154

ICE CUBE

Real name: O'Shea Jackson. Former lyricist of the Los Angeles rap group N.W.A. Native of Los Angeles. Appeared in the movies *Boyz N The Hood*, *Trespass*, *Higher Learning* and *Friday*. His cousin is Del Tha Funkee Homosapien.

DATE	POS	WKS	ARTIST–RECORD TITLE	LABEL & NO.
3/20/93	15	16	● 1. It Was A Good Day Sales #7 / Airplay #32; samples "Sexy Mama" by The Moments and "Footsteps In The Dark" by The Isley Brothers	Priority 53817
8/7/93	20	10	▲ 2. Check Yo Self **ICE CUBE Featuring DAS EFX** Sales #9 / Airplay #47; cassette maxi-single; samples "The Message" by Grandmaster Flash & The Furious Five; #1 R&B hit (1 week)	Priority 53830
4/2/94	30	8	3. You Know How We Do It Sales #20 / Airplay #46; samples "The Show Is Over" by Evelyn "Champagne" King	Priority 53847
8/27/94	23	11	● 4. Bop Gun (One Nation) **ICE CUBE featuring George Clinton** Sales #12 / Airplay #34; rap version of Funkadelic's "One Nation Under A Groove"	Priority 53155

ICEHOUSE

Rock band formed in Sydney, Australia, in 1978: Iva Davies (vocals, guitar), Anthony Smith (keyboards), Keith Welsh (bass) and John Lloyd (drums). Numerous personnel changes through the '80s, with Davies the only constant. Group name is Australian slang for an insane asylum.

DATE	POS	WKS	ARTIST–RECORD TITLE	LABEL & NO.
12/5/87+	14	11	1. Crazy Sales #11 / Airplay #21	Chrysalis 43156
3/19/88	7	13	2. **Electric Blue** Sales #5 / Airplay #10; co-written by John Oates (of Hall & Oates)	Chrysalis 43201

ICICLE WORKS

Rock trio formed in Liverpool, England, in 1981: Robert Ian McNabb (vocals, guitar), Chris Layhe (bass) and Chris Sharrock (drums).

DATE	POS	WKS	ARTIST–RECORD TITLE	LABEL & NO.
5/26/84	37	4	1. Whisper To A Scream (Birds Fly)	Arista 9155

IDES OF MARCH, The

Rock group formed while classmates at a Chicago high school. Named after a line in Shakespeare's *Julius Caesar*. Lead singer Jim Peterik joined Survivor as keyboardist.

DATE	POS	WKS	ARTIST–RECORD TITLE	LABEL & NO.
4/11/70	2 (1)	10	1. **Vehicle**	Warner 7378

DATE	POS	WKS	ARTIST–RECORD TITLE	LABEL & NO.
			IDOL, Billy	
			Born William Broad on 11/30/55 in Stanmore, Middlesex, England. Leader of the London punk band Generation X, 1977–81. Suffered serious leg injuries in a motorcycle crash on 2/6/90. Appeared in 1991 movie *The Doors*.	
8/7/82	23	9	1. Hot In The City	Chrysalis 2605
6/25/83	36	3	2. White Wedding originally "Bubbled Under" on 11/27/82 on Chrysalis 2648 (#108)	Chrysalis 42697
5/19/84	4	14	3. **Eyes Without A Face**	Chrysalis 42786
9/15/84	29	6	4. Flesh For Fantasy Airplay #29	Chrysalis 42809
10/25/86	6	13	5. **To Be A Lover** Sales #5 / Airplay #9; #45 hit for William Bell in 1969 as "I Forgot To Be Your Lover"	Chrysalis 43024
2/28/87	37	2	6. Don't Need A Gun Sales #32 / Airplay #34	Chrysalis 43087
5/30/87	20	7	7. Sweet Sixteen Sales #16 / Airplay #25	Chrysalis 43114
9/26/87	1 (1)	12	8. **Mony Mony "Live"** Sales #1(1) / Airplay #2; studio version "Bubbled Under" on 9/26/81 on Chrysalis 2543 (#107)	Chrysalis 43161
6/2/90	2 (1)	16	● 9. **Cradle Of Love** Sales #2 / Airplay #5; from the movie *The Adventures of Ford Fairlane* starring Andrew Dice Clay	Chrysalis 23509
			IFIELD, Frank	
			Born on 11/30/37 in Coventry, England. Began career as a teenager in Australia with his own radio and TV shows. Signed to Columbia Records in England in 1959.	
9/22/62	5	8	1. **I Remember You** #1 Adult Contemporary hit (1 week); #9 hit for Jimmy Dorsey in 1942 (from the movie *The Fleet's In* starring Dorothy Lamour)	Vee-Jay 457
			IGLESIAS, Julio	
			Born on 9/23/43 in Madrid. Spanish singer, immensely popular worldwide. Soccer goalie for the pro Real Madrid team until temporary paralysis from a car crash.	
3/31/84	5	12	▲ 1. **To All The Girls I've Loved Before** **JULIO IGLESIAS & WILLIE NELSON** #1 Country hit (2 weeks)	Columbia 04217
8/4/84	19	8	2. All Of You **JULIO IGLESIAS & DIANA ROSS**	Columbia 04507
			IKETTES, The	
			Female R&B trio formed for the Ike & Tina Turner Revue. Atco group consisted of Delores Johnson (lead), Eloise Hester and "Joshie" Jo Armstead. Modern group consisted of Vanetta Fields, Robbie Montgomery and Jessie Smith; later known as The Mirettes.	
2/3/62	19	8	1. I'm Blue (The Gong-Gong Song) Tina Turner (backing vocal)	Atco 6212
4/10/65	36	4	2. Peaches "N" Cream	Modern 1005

DATE	POS	WKS	ARTIST–RECORD TITLE	LABEL & NO.
			ILLUSION, The	
			Long Island-based rock quintet led by vocalist John Vinci and guitarist Richie Cerniglia.	
8/23/69	32	6	1. Did You See Her Eyes	Steed 718
			a slightly different version was issued on Steed 712 in 1969	
			IMMATURE	
			Male R&B trio from Los Angeles of 12-year-olds: Marques Houston, Jerome Jones and Kelton Kessee.	
8/20/94	5	21	● 1. **Never Lie**	MCA 54850
			Sales #2 / Airplay #13	
12/24/94+	16	13	● 2. Constantly	MCA 54948
			Sales #8 / Airplay #40	
			IMPALAS, The	
			Pop vocal quartet from Brooklyn: Joe "Speedo" Frazier, Richard Wagner, Lenny Renda and Tony Carlucci. All members, except black lead singer Frazier, are white.	
4/13/59	2 (2)	11	● 1. **Sorry (I Ran All the Way Home)**	Cub 9022
			some pressings issued only as "I Ran All The Way Home"	
			IMPRESSIONS, The	
			Soul group formed in Chicago in 1957, originally known as The Roosters. Consisted of Jerry Butler, Curtis Mayfield, Sam Gooden and brothers Arthur and Richard Brooks. Butler left for a solo career in 1958, replaced by Fred Cash. The Brooks brothers left in 1962, leaving Mayfield as the trio's leader. Mayfield left in 1970 for a solo career, replaced by Leroy Hutson. In 1973, Hutson was replaced by Reggie Torian and Ralph Johnson. Johnson joined Mystique in 1976. Group did movie soundtrack for *Three The Hard Way* (1974). Butler, Mayfield, Gooden and Cash reunited for a tour in 1983. Group inducted into the Rock and Roll Hall of Fame in 1991.	
6/16/58	11	9	1. For Your Precious Love	Abner 1013
			JERRY BUTLER and The Impressions	
			Best Seller #11 / Top 100 #11 / Jockey #25; released first on Falcon 1013, then on Abner 1013 (also on Vee-Jay 280 in 1958)	
11/20/61	20	8	2. Gypsy Woman	ABC-Para. 10241
10/12/63	4	11	3. **It's All Right**	ABC-Para. 10487
			#1 R&B hit (2 weeks)	
1/25/64	12	7	4. Talking About My Baby	ABC-Para. 10511
4/18/64	14	9	5. I'm So Proud	ABC-Para. 10544
6/27/64	10	10	6. **Keep On Pushing**	ABC-Para. 10554
9/19/64	15	8	7. You Must Believe Me	ABC-Para. 10581
12/12/64+	7	7	8. **Amen**	ABC-Para. 10602
			featured in the movie *Lilies Of The Field* starring Sidney Poitier	
3/6/65	14	5	9. People Get Ready	ABC-Para. 10622
4/24/65	29	4	10. Woman's Got Soul	ABC-Para. 10647
1/1/66	33	2	11. You've Been Cheatin'	ABC-Para. 10750
2/3/68	14	8	12. We're A Winner	ABC 11022
			#1 R&B hit (1 week); Johnny Pate (orch.: #4-12)	
10/5/68	22	7	13. Fool For You	Curtom 1932
12/28/68+	25	6	14. This Is My Country	Curtom 1934
7/12/69	21	9	15. Choice Of Colors	Curtom 1943
			#1 R&B hit (1 week)	

DATE	POS	WKS	ARTIST–RECORD TITLE	LABEL & NO.
6/13/70	**28**	8	16. Check Out Your Mind _all of above (except #1 & 8) written by Curtis Mayfield_	Curtom 1951
6/29/74	**17**	6	17. Finally Got Myself Together (I'm A Changed Man) _#1 R&B hit (2 weeks)_	Curtom 1997

INDECENT OBSESSION

Pop band from Brisbane, Australia: David Dixon (vocals), Michael Szumowski, Andrew Coyne and Darryl Simms. Band's name taken from a Colleen McCullough novel.

9/1/90	**31**	5	1. Tell Me Something _Sales #28 / Airplay #32_	MCA 79029

INDEPENDENTS, The

Soul group consisting of Chuck Jackson, Maurice Jackson, Helen Curry and Eric Thomas. Chuck (no relation to Maurice) and Marvin Yancey, Jr., were producers/writers for the group; later teamed in production work, especially for Natalie Cole, to whom Yancey was once married. Chuck Jackson, not to be confused with the same-named solo singer, is the brother of civil rights leader Rev. Jesse Jackson.

4/28/73	**21**	9	● 1. Leaving Me _#1 R&B hit (1 week)_	Wand 11252

INFORMATION SOCIETY

Techno-dance outfit formed in Minneapolis in 1985: songwriter Paul Robb, vocalist Kurt Valaquen, keyboardist Amanda Kramer and bassist James Cassidy. Reduced to a trio in 1990 with departure of Kramer.

8/27/88	**3**	14	● 1. **What's On Your Mind (Pure Energy)** _Sales #4 / Airplay #4_	Tommy Boy 27826
1/7/89	**9**	10	2. **Walking Away** _Airplay #7 / Sales #10_	Tommy Boy 27736
11/10/90	**28**	5	3. Think _Sales #24 / Airplay #30_	Tommy Boy 19591

INGMANN, Jorgen, & His Guitar

Born Jorgen Ingmann-Pedersen on 4/26/25 in Copenhagen, Denmark.

2/20/61	**2** (2)	13	1. **Apache** [I]	Atco 6184

INGRAM, James

Born on 2/16/56 in Akron, Ohio. R&B vocalist/multi-instrumentalist/composer. Former member of the band Revelation Funk.

9/19/81	**17**	10	1. Just Once **QUINCY JONES Featuring JAMES INGRAM**	A&M 2357
2/13/82	**14**	11	2. One Hundred Ways **QUINCY JONES Featuring JAMES INGRAM**	A&M 2387
12/4/82+	**1** (2)	18	● 3. **Baby, Come To Me** **PATTI AUSTIN with James Ingram** _#1 Adult Contemporary hit (3 weeks)_	Qwest 50036
1/14/84	**19**	9	4. Yah Mo B There **JAMES INGRAM (with Michael McDonald)**	Qwest 29394
10/13/84	**15**	9	5. What About Me? **KENNY ROGERS with KIM CARNES and JAMES INGRAM** _Airplay #14 / Sales #16; #1 Adult Contemporary hit (2 weeks)_	RCA 13899

DATE	POS	WKS	ARTIST–RECORD TITLE	LABEL & NO.
1/24/87	**2** (1)	12	● 6. **Somewhere Out There** **LINDA RONSTADT AND JAMES INGRAM** Sales #1(2) / Airplay #7; from the animated movie *An American Tail*	MCA 52973
4/7/90	**31**	4	● 7. The Secret Garden (Sweet Seduction Suite) **QUINCY JONES/Al B. Sure!/James Ingram/El DeBarge/Barry White** Sales #20; #1 R&B hit (1 week)	Qwest 19992
9/8/90	**1** (1)	15	8. **I Don't Have The Heart** Airplay #1(2) / Sales #2	Warner 19911

INGRAM, Luther

Born on 11/30/44 in Jackson, Tennessee. Soul singer/songwriter. Sang in gospel group with his brothers. First recorded for Smash in 1965. Appeared in the movie *Wattstax*.

DATE	POS	WKS	ARTIST–RECORD TITLE	LABEL & NO.
6/24/72	**3**	13	1. **(If Loving You Is Wrong) I Don't Want To Be Right** #1 R&B hit (4 weeks)	KoKo 2111
1/20/73	**40**	2	2. I'll Be Your Shelter (In Time Of Storm)	KoKo 2113

INNER CIRCLE

Reggae band formed in Kingston, Jamaica, in 1975: Calton Coffie (vocals), Touter Harvey, Lancelot Hall, brothers Ian and Roger Lewis, and Lester Adderly (left by mid-1994).

DATE	POS	WKS	ARTIST–RECORD TITLE	LABEL & NO.
5/15/93	**8**	12	● 1. **Bad Boys** Sales #6 / Airplay #15; theme from the Fox TV series *Cops*	Big Beat 98426
9/11/93	**16**	16	2. Sweat (A La La La La La Long) Sales #16 / Airplay #17	Big Beat 98429

INNOCENCE, The

Group is actually the singing/songwriting/producing duo of Pete Anders and Vinnie Poncia. Also recorded as The Trade Winds.

DATE	POS	WKS	ARTIST–RECORD TITLE	LABEL & NO.
1/7/67	**34**	3	1. There's Got To Be A Word!	Kama Sutra 214

INNOCENTS, The

Pop trio from Sun Valley, California: James West (lead singer), Al Candelaria (bass) and Darron Stankey (guitar, tenor). Backup vocal group for Kathy Young. First recorded as The Echoes for Andex in 1959.

DATE	POS	WKS	ARTIST–RECORD TITLE	LABEL & NO.
9/19/60	**28**	3	1. Honest I Do	Indigo 105
1/9/61	**28**	3	2. Gee Whiz	Indigo 111

INSTANT FUNK

Large funk ensemble formed in Philadelphia in 1977. Led by singer/percussionist James Carmichael. Former backup band for Bunny Sigler.

DATE	POS	WKS	ARTIST–RECORD TITLE	LABEL & NO.
3/31/79	**20**	8	● 1. I Got My Mind Made Up (You Can Get It Girl) #1 R&B hit (3 weeks)	Salsoul 2078

INTRIGUES, The

Soul trio from Philadelphia.

DATE	POS	WKS	ARTIST–RECORD TITLE	LABEL & NO.
10/4/69	**31**	4	1. In A Moment	Yew 1001

DATE	POS	WKS	ARTIST–RECORD TITLE	LABEL & NO.

INTRO

Vocal trio of New Yorkers Kenny Greene (lead) and Clinton Wike with Detroit native Jeff Sanders. Greene wrote Mary J. Blige's "Reminisce" and Father M.C.'s "Close To You" (which featured Intro). Intro stands for Innovative New Talent Reaching Out.

DATE	POS	WKS	ARTIST–RECORD TITLE	LABEL & NO.
10/23/93	33	5	1. **Come Inside** *Sales #21 / Airplay #38; Sebrina Morrison (female voice)*	Atlantic 87317

INTRUDERS, The

Soul group formed in Philadelphia in 1960. Consisted of Sam "Little Sonny" Brown, Eugene "Bird" Daughtry (died 12/25/94, age 55), Phil Terry and Robert "Big Sonny" Edwards. First recorded for Gowen in 1961. Not to be confused with the white rock trio of the same name.

DATE	POS	WKS	ARTIST–RECORD TITLE	LABEL & NO.
4/6/68	6	11	● 1. **Cowboys To Girls** *#1 R&B hit (1 week)*	Gamble 214
8/10/68	26	4	2. (Love Is Like A) Baseball Game	Gamble 217
6/30/73	36	6	3. I'll Always Love My Mama (Part 1)	Gamble 2506

INXS

Rock sextet formed in Sydney, Australia, as The Farris Brothers. Members since group's formation in 1977: Michael Hutchence (lead singer), Kirk Pengilly (guitar, saxophone), Garry Beers (bass) and brothers Tim (guitar), Andy (keyboards, guitar) and Jon (drums) Farriss. Hutchence, who starred in the movies *Dogs In Space* and *Frankenstein Unbound*, also co-founded the band Max Q. Jon Farriss married actress Leslie Bega (from TV's "Head Of The Class") on 2/14/92.

DATE	POS	WKS	ARTIST–RECORD TITLE	LABEL & NO.
5/14/83	30	5	1. The One Thing	Atco 99905
2/15/86	5	14	2. **What You Need** *Airplay #3 / Sales #7*	Atlantic 89460
11/21/87+	1 (1)	17	3. **Need You Tonight** *Sales #1(1) / Airplay #1(1)*	Atlantic 89188
2/27/88	2 (2)	12	4. **Devil Inside** *Sales #2 / Airplay #2*	Atlantic 89144
5/28/88	3	12	5. **New Sensation** *Sales #2 / Airplay #4*	Atlantic 89080
9/17/88	7	11	6. **Never Tear Us Apart** *Airplay #6 / Sales #8; above 4 from the album Kick*	Atlantic 89038
9/22/90	9	9	● 7. **Suicide Blonde** *Airplay #9 / Sales #12*	Atlantic 87860
12/22/90+	8	12	8. **Disappear** *Airplay #9 / Sales #11*	Atlantic 87784
9/12/92	28	7	9. Not Enough Time *Airplay #34 / Sales #52*	Atlantic 87437

IRIS, Donnie

Born Dominic Ierace in Beaver Falls, Pennsylvania. Singer/songwriter/guitarist of the Pittsburgh rock group The Jaggerz. Toured briefly with the funk group Wild Cherry.

DATE	POS	WKS	ARTIST–RECORD TITLE	LABEL & NO.
2/7/81	29	6	1. Ah! Leah!	MCA 51025
2/13/82	37	2	2. Love Is Like A Rock	MCA 51223
5/1/82	25	6	3. My Girl	MCA 52031

DATE	POS	WKS	ARTIST–RECORD TITLE	LABEL & NO.
			IRISH ROVERS, The	
			Irish-born folk quintet formed in Alberta, Canada, in 1964. Brothers Will (vocals) and George Millar, their cousin Joe Millar, Jimmy Ferguson and Wilcil McDowell.	
4/6/68	7	9	1. **The Unicorn**	Decca 32254
4/18/81	37	4	2. Wasn't That A Party **THE ROVERS**	Epic 51007
			IRON BUTTERFLY	
			San Diego heavy-metal band: Doug Ingle (vocals, keyboards), Erik Braunn (guitar), Lee Dorman (bass) and Ron Bushy (drums). Braunn left in late 1969, replaced by Mike Pinera (leader of Blues Image) and Larry Reinhardt. Split in mid-1971. Braunn and Bushy regrouped in early 1975 with Phil Kramer and Howard Reitzes.	
9/28/68	30	7	1. In-A-Gadda-Da-Vida 7" version edited down from original 17-minute album cut	Atco 6606
			IRONHORSE	
			Rock band formed by Bachman-Turner Overdrive founder Randy Bachman.	
4/21/79	36	3	1. Sweet Lui-Louise	Scotti Br. 406
			IRWIN, Big Dee	
			Real name: Difosco Erwin. R&B vocalist; former lead singer of The Pastels. Died on 8/27/95 (age 63).	
7/13/63	38	2	1. Swinging On A Star **BIG DEE IRWIN (with Little Eva)** #1 hit for Bing Crosby in 1944 (from the movie *Going My Way* starring Crosby)	Dimension 1010
			IRWIN, Russ	
			Born in 1968 in Huntington Hills, Long Island, New York. Singer/songwriter.	
10/19/91	28	5	1. My Heart Belongs To You Sales #74	SBK 07363
			ISAAK, Chris	
			Born on 6/26/56 in Stockton, California. San Francisco-based rockabilly singer/songwriter/guitarist. Attended college in Japan. Cameo appearances in the movies *Married To The Mob*, *Silence Of The Lambs* and others, and starred in *Little Buddha*.	
1/19/91	6	11	● 1. **Wicked Game** Sales #3 / Airplay #17; featured in the movie *Wild at Heart* starring Laura Dern and Nicolas Cage	Reprise 19704
			ISLANDERS, The	
			Instrumental duo of Randy Starr (guitar) and Frank Metis (accordion).	
10/19/59	15	8	1. The Enchanted Sea [I]	Mayflower 16

DATE	POS	WKS	ARTIST—RECORD TITLE	LABEL & NO.
			ISLEY BROTHERS, The	
			R&B trio of brothers from Cincinnati. Formed in early 1950s as a gospel group. Consisted of O'Kelly, Ronald and Rudolph Isley. Moved to New York in 1957 and first recorded for Teenage Records. Trio added their younger brothers Ernie (guitar, drums) and Marvin (bass, percussion) Isley and brother-in-law Chris Jasper (keyboards) in September 1969. Formed own T-Neck label the same year. Ernie, Marvin and Chris began recording as the trio Isley, Jasper, Isley in 1984. O'Kelly died of a heart attack on 3/31/86 (age 48); Ronald and Rudolph continued on as The Isley Brothers through 1990. Ernie, Marvin and Ronald reunited as The Isley Brothers in 1991. Ronald married Angela Winbush on 6/26/93.	
6/30/62	**17**	11	1. Twist And Shout	Wand 124
			song first recorded by the Top Notes in 1961 (Atlantic 2115)	
3/19/66	**12**	8	2. This Old Heart Of Mine (Is Weak For You)	Tamla 54128
			Ronald Isley charted a new version with Rod Stewart in 1990	
3/29/69	**2** (1)	12	● 3. **It's Your Thing**	T-Neck 901
			#1 R&B hit (4 weeks)	
6/21/69	**23**	7	4. I Turned You On	T-Neck 902
7/3/71	**18**	9	5. Love The One You're With	T-Neck 930
8/19/72	**24**	7	6. Pop That Thang	T-Neck 935
8/18/73	**6**	15	● 7. **That Lady (Part 1)**	T-Neck 2251
7/12/75	**4**	13	● 8. **Fight The Power Part 1**	T-Neck 2256
			#1 R&B hit (3 weeks)	
11/22/75	**22**	9	9. For The Love Of You (Part 1&2)	T-Neck 2259
8/6/77	**40**	1	10. Livin' In The Life	T-Neck 2264
5/24/80	**39**	2	11. Don't Say Goodnight (It's Time For Love)	
			(Parts 1 & 2)	T-Neck 2290
			#1 R&B hit (4 weeks)	
			IVES, Burl	
			Born on 6/14/09 in Huntington Township, Illinois. Died on 4/14/95. Actor/author/singer. Played semi-pro football. Began Broadway career in the late 1930s. Worked in "This Is The Army" service show during World War II. Own CBS radio show "The Wayfaring Stranger" in 1944. Appeared in many movies, including *Our Man In Havana*, *East Of Eden*, *Cat On A Hot Tin Roof* and *The Big Country*. Narrated the kids' TV classic "Rudolph The Red-Nosed Reindeer." Worked on the TV series "The Bold Ones" in the early 1970s.	
1/6/62	**9**	11	1. **A Little Bitty Tear**	Decca 31330
			#1 Adult Contemporary hit (1 week)	
4/21/62	**10**	8	2. **Funny Way Of Laughin'**	Decca 31371
8/11/62	**19**	4	3. Call Me Mr. In-Between	Decca 31405
12/8/62	**39**	1	4. Mary Ann Regrets	Decca 31433
			IVY THREE, The	
			Formed in 1959 at Adelphi College in New York. Consisted of Charles Koppelman (lead), Art Berkowitz and Don Rubin. Koppelman and Rubin did production work for The Turtles and The Lovin' Spoonful. Label executive Koppelman founded SBK Records in 1989, with Rubin as senior vice president. Koppelman became CEO of EMI Records Group North America in 1991.	
8/29/60	**8**	7	1. **Yogi** [N]	Shell 720
			inspired by the Yogi Bear character from TV's animated "Huckleberry Hound" show	

DATE	POS	WKS	ARTIST–RECORD TITLE	LABEL & NO.

J

DATE	POS	WKS	ARTIST–RECORD TITLE	LABEL & NO.
			JACKS, Terry	
			Native of Winnipeg, Canada. Recorded with wife Susan Jacks as The Poppy Family.	
2/9/74	**1** (3)	15	● 1. **Seasons In The Sun** recorded by The Kingston Trio in 1963 (Capitol 5166); #1 Adult Contemporary hit (1 week)	Bell 45432
			JACKSON, Chuck	
			Born on 7/22/37 in Latta, South Carolina. R&B singer. Cousin of singer Ann Sexton. Moved to Pittsburgh as a child. Left college in 1957 to work with the Raspberry Singers gospel group. With The Dell-Vikings, 1957–59. First recorded as a solo for Beltone in 1960.	
3/13/61	36	2	1. I Don't Want To Cry arranged by Carole King	Wand 106
6/2/62	23	6	2. Any Day Now (My Wild Beautiful Bird)	Wand 122
			JACKSON, Deon	
			Born on 1/26/46 in Ann Arbor, Michigan. Soul singer/clarinetist/drummer.	
2/19/66	11	9	1. Love Makes The World Go Round	Carla 2526
			JACKSON, Freddie	
			Born on 10/2/56 and raised in Harlem. Soul singer/songwriter. Backup singer for Melba Moore, Evelyn King and others. Member of R&B group Mystic Merlin. Since 1985, Jackson's had 10 #1 R&B hits.	
7/13/85	18	8	1. Rock Me Tonight (For Old Times Sake) Sales #18 / Airplay #20; #1 R&B hit (6 weeks)	Capitol 5459
10/5/85	12	11	2. You Are My Lady Sales #7 / Airplay #12; #1 R&B hit (2 weeks)	Capitol 5495
1/25/86	25	6	3. He'll Never Love You (Like I Do) Sales #23 / Airplay #28	Capitol 5535
8/15/87	32	3	4. Jam Tonight Sales #25 / Airplay #38; #1 R&B hit (1 week)	Capitol 44037
			JACKSON, Janet	
			Born on 5/16/66 in Gary, Indiana. Sister of The Jacksons (youngest of nine children). Debuted at age seven at the MGM Grand in Las Vegas with her brothers. At age 10, she played Penny Gordon Woods in the TV series "Good Times," 1977–79; also in the cast of "Diff'rent Strokes," 1981–82, and later "Fame." Married James DeBarge of DeBarge in August 1984; marriage annulled in March 1985. Signed a $32 million contract with Virgin Records in 1991. Starred in the 1993 movie *Poetic Justice*.	
3/22/86	4	13	● 1. **What Have You Done For Me Lately** Sales #3 / Airplay #8; #1 R&B hit (2 weeks)	A&M 2812
6/7/86	3	11	● 2. **Nasty** Sales #1(1) / Airplay #5; #1 R&B hit (2 weeks)	A&M 2830
8/23/86	**1** (2)	13	● 3. **When I Think Of You** Airplay #1(2) / Sales #2	A&M 2855
11/22/86+	5	13	● 4. **Control** Sales #4 / Airplay #4; #1 R&B hit (1 week)	A&M 2877

DATE	POS	WKS		ARTIST–RECORD TITLE	LABEL & NO.
2/7/87	**2** (1)	11		5. **Let's Wait Awhile** Sales #3 / Airplay #4; #1 R&B hit (1 week)	A&M 2906
6/20/87	**14**	10		6. The Pleasure Principle Airplay #13 / Sales #17; #1 R&B hit (1 week); above 6 from the album *Control*	A&M 2927
9/9/89	**1** (4)	13	▲	7. **Miss You Much** Sales #1(3) / Airplay #1(3); #1 R&B hit (2 weeks)	A&M 1445
11/18/89+	**2** (2)	12	●	8. **Rhythm Nation** Sales #2 / Airplay #2; #1 R&B hit (1 week)	A&M 1455
1/20/90	**1** (3)	14	●	9. **Escapade** Airplay #1(4) / Sales #1(2); #1 R&B hit (1 week)	A&M 1490
4/14/90	**4**	12	●	10. **Alright** Airplay #2 / Sales #8	A&M 1479
7/14/90	**2** (2)	11		11. **Come Back To Me** Airplay #1(2) / Sales #7; #1 Adult Contemporary hit (3 weeks)	A&M 1475
9/15/90	**1** (1)	12	●	12. **Black Cat** Airplay #2 / Sales #2; Vernon Reid (of Living Colour; lead guitar)	A&M 1477
12/1/90+	**1** (1)	15	●	13. **Love Will Never Do (Without You)** Airplay #1(3) / Sales #6; above 7 from the album *Janet Jackson's Rhythm Nation 1814*	A&M 1538
5/30/92	**10**	18		14. **The Best Things In Life Are Free** **LUTHER VANDROSS and JANET JACKSON with BBD and Ralph Tresvant** Airplay #5 / Sales #16; from the movie *Mo' Money* starring Damon and Marlon Wayans; #1 R&B hit (1 week)	Perspective 0010
5/1/93	**1** (8)	20	▲	15. **That's The Way Love Goes** Airplay #1(10) / Sales #1(5); samples "Papa Don't Take No Mess" by James Brown; #1 R&B hit (4 weeks)	Virgin 12650
7/31/93	**4**	21	●	16. **If** Airplay #3 / Sales #5; samples "Someday We'll Be Together" by Diana Ross & The Supremes	Virgin 12676
10/23/93	**1** (2)	22	▲	17. **Again** Airplay #1(4) / Sales #2; from the movie *Poetic Justice* starring Jackson and 2 Pac; all of above (except #6,12,14) written and produced by Jimmy Jam & Terry Lewis	Virgin 38404
1/29/94	**10**	16		18. **Because Of Love** Airplay #6 / Sales #29	Virgin 38422
5/28/94	**2** (1)	19	●	19. **Any Time, Any Place/** Airplay #3 / Sales #5; #1 R&B hit (10 weeks)	Virgin 38435
		19		20. And On And On Airplay #38; samples "Family Affair" by Sly & The Family Stone	
10/29/94	**8**	19		21. **You Want This/** Airplay #9 / Sales #12; MC Lyte (rap); above 7 (except #20) from the album *janet.*	
		17		22. 70's Love Groove Sales flip	Virgin 38455
6/17/95	**5**	9	▲	23. **Scream** **MICHAEL JACKSON & JANET JACKSON** Sales #3 / Airplay #12	Epic 78000
9/16/95	**3**	22	●	24. **Runaway** Sales #3 / Airplay #3	A&M 1194

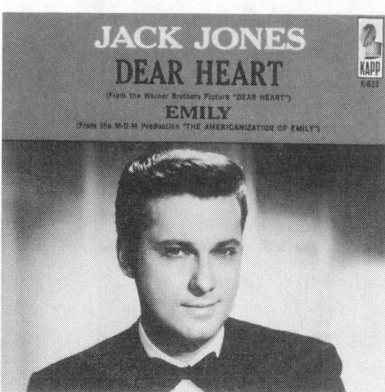

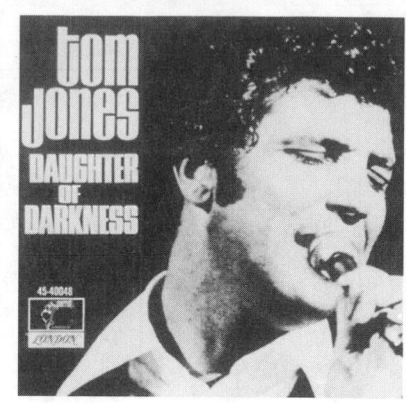

Johnny And The Hurricanes' exhilarating brand of instrumental rock was heard the world over: in the mid-'70s, the group's name would be conspicuously dropped in a song by English rockers The Kinks. Their four Top 40 hits did not include 1960's "Down Yonder," however.

Jack Jones's five appearances in the Top 40 featured three songs drawn from film or theater sources. From the screen came 1963's "Wives And Lovers" and 1964's "Dear Heart"; from Broadway's *Man Of La Mancha*, 1966's "The Impossible Dream (The Quest)."

Tom Jones's "Daughter Of Darkness" was the 12th of 19 Top 40 hits the Welsh singer would release between 1965 and 1988. The track, which reached No. 13, was amply boosted by the exposure Jones received on his 1969-71 television show.

Kenny G's "Forever In Love" single was pulled from his seven-times platinum album *Breathless*. The well-known instrumentalist released an enormously successful Christmas album, *Miracles—The Holiday Album*, two years later.

Claude King's only appearance in the Top 40 came in July 1962 with his No. 6 hit "Wolverton Mountain." A related "answer" song—Jo Ann Campbell's ("I'm The Girl On) Wolverton Mountain"—peaked at No. 38 a few weeks later.

The Knack's "My Sharona" held the No. 1 slot for six weeks in 1979. But composer and group leader Doug Fieger—then perceived as a hot songwriting newcomer—had already surfaced in two earlier bands, RCA's Sky and Ariola-America's Sunset Bombers.

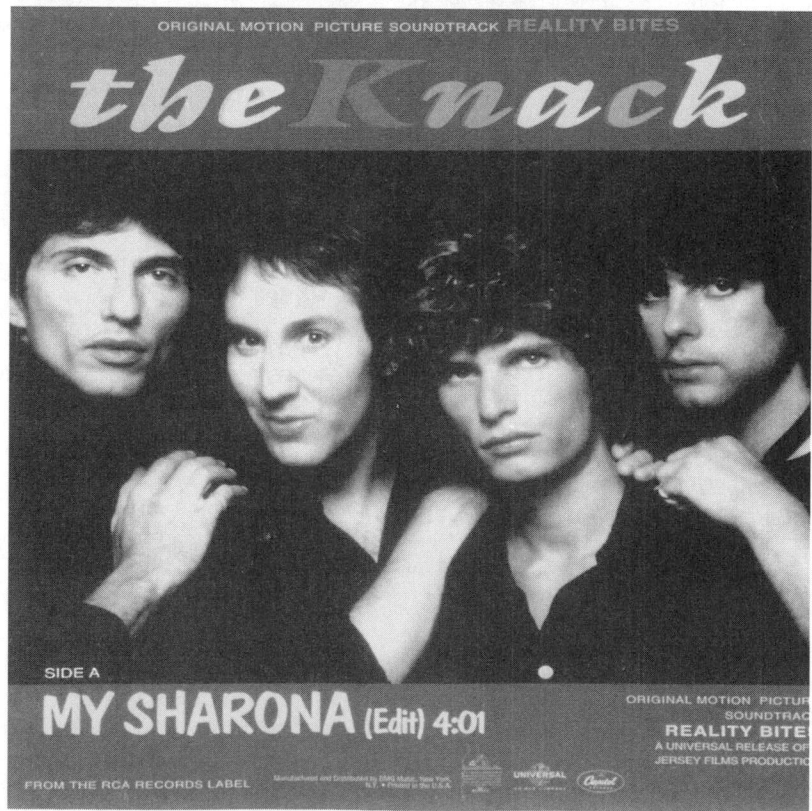

Kriss Kross' youthfulness and propensity for wearing their clothing backward helped catapult their debut album *Totally Krossed Out* to No. 1 in 1992.

Patti LaBelle And Her Blue Bells—as the artist's credit reads on the sleeve to 1964's "You'll Never Walk Alone" from *Carousel*—would later record with singer Laura Nyro, renamed LaBelle. The influential group also released records under the "Blue Belles" spelling.

Cyndi Lauper's momentum as a Grammy winner helped push the peculiarly titled "The Goonies 'R' Good Enough" into the Top 10 in 1985. The film soundtrack containing it also featured tracks by The Bangles, REO Speedwagon, Luther Vandross and Teena Marie.

Brenda Lee's dual-sided 1961 hit single "Fool #1" and "Anybody But Me" hit Nos. 3 and 31 respectively. The so-called "Little Miss Dynamite" had six double-sided Top 40 hits between 1960 and 1963.

John Lennon's first hit to be released under his own name—rather than as the Plastic Ono Band—was 1970's No. 3 smash "Instant Karma (We All Shine On)." A month after it entered the charts, The Beatles were officially defunct.

Huey Lewis And The News had one of the biggest albums of the '80s with 1983's *Sports*. The bestselling set stayed on the Top 200 for 158 weeks and bore five hits, including the No. 6 smash "If This Is It."

DATE	POS	WKS	ARTIST–RECORD TITLE	LABEL & NO.

JACKSON, Jermaine

Born on 12/11/54 in Gary, Indiana. Fourth oldest of The Jacksons. Vocalist/bassist of The Jackson 5 until group left Motown in 1976. Married Hazel Joy Gordy, daughter of Berry Gordy, Jr., on 12/15/73; later divorced. Rejoined The Jacksons in 1984 for their *Victory* album and tour.

DATE	POS	WKS	ARTIST–RECORD TITLE	LABEL & NO.
1/13/73	9	13	1. **Daddy's Home**	Motown 1216
5/3/80	9	14	2. **Let's Get Serious** #1 R&B hit (6 weeks)	Motown 1469
8/30/80	34	4	3. You're Supposed To Keep Your Love For Me above 2 written, produced and arranged by Stevie Wonder	Motown 1490
8/21/82	18	7	4. Let Me Tickle Your Fancy Devo (backing vocals)	Motown 1628
8/4/84	15	10	5. Dynamite	Arista 9190
11/17/84+	13	12	6. Do What You Do Airplay #12 / Sales #14; #1 Adult Contemporary hit (3 weeks)	Arista 9279
3/15/86	16	9	7. I Think It's Love Sales #16 / Airplay #16	Arista 9444

JACKSON, J.J.

Born Jerome Louis Jackson on 4/8/41 in Brooklyn. Soul singer/songwriter. Became permanent resident of England in 1969. Not to be confused with the former MTV VJ of the same name.

DATE	POS	WKS	ARTIST–RECORD TITLE	LABEL & NO.
11/5/66	22	7	1. But It's Alright	Calla 119

JACKSON, Joe

Born on 8/11/55 in Burton-on-Trent, England. Singer/songwriter/pianist, featuring an ever-changing music style. Moved to New York City in 1982.

DATE	POS	WKS	ARTIST–RECORD TITLE	LABEL & NO.
7/7/79	21	8	1. Is She Really Going Out With Him?	A&M 2132
10/16/82	6	15	2. **Steppin' Out**	A&M 2428
2/5/83	18	10	3. Breaking Us In Two	A&M 2510
5/5/84	15	9	4. You Can't Get What You Want (Till You Know What You Want)	A&M 2628

JACKSON, Michael

Born on 8/29/58 in Gary, Indiana. The seventh of nine children. Became lead singer of his brothers' group, The Jackson 5 (later known as The Jacksons), at age five. Played the Scarecrow in the 1978 movie musical *The Wiz*. His 1982 *Thriller* album, with sales of over 40 million copies, is the best-selling album in history. Starred in the 15-minute movie *Captain Eo*, which was shown exclusively at Disneyland and Disneyworld. His 1988 autobiography, *Moonwalker*, became a movie the same year. Winner of 12 Grammy Awards; awarded Grammy's Living Legends Award in 1993. Michael signed a $1 billion multimedia contract with Sony Software on 3/20/91. On 1/25/94, settled out of court after allegations of child sexual molestation were made against Jackson. Michael married Elvis Presley's daughter, Lisa Marie, on 5/26/94.

DATE	POS	WKS	ARTIST–RECORD TITLE	LABEL & NO.
11/6/71	4	13	1. **Got To Be There**	Motown 1191
3/18/72	2 (2)	11	2. **Rockin' Robin**	Motown 1197
6/10/72	16	9	3. I Wanna Be Where You Are	Motown 1202
9/9/72	1 (1)	11	4. **Ben** title song from the movie about a trained rat starring Joseph Campanella	Motown 1207
7/12/75	23	6	5. Just A Little Bit Of You	Motown 1349
9/1/79	1 (1)	12	▲ 6. **Don't Stop 'Til You Get Enough** #1 R&B hit (5 weeks)	Epic 50742

DATE	POS	WKS	ARTIST–RECORD TITLE	LABEL & NO.
11/24/79+	1 (4)	19	▲ 7. **Rock With You** #1 R&B hit (6 weeks); remix is on the B-side of #29 below	Epic 50797
2/23/80	10	11	● 8. **Off The Wall**	Epic 50838
5/10/80	10	11	● 9. **She's Out Of My Life** above 4 from the album *Off The Wall*	Epic 50871
11/13/82+	2 (3)	14	● 10. **The Girl Is Mine** **MICHAEL JACKSON/PAUL McCARTNEY** #1 Adult Contemporary hit (4 weeks); #1 R&B hit (3 weeks)	Epic 03288
1/29/83	1 (7)	17	▲ 11. **Billie Jean** #1 R&B hit (9 weeks)	Epic 03509
3/19/83	1 (3)	18	▲ 12. **Beat It** Eddie Van Halen (lead guitar); #1 R&B hit (1 week)	Epic 03759
6/4/83	5	11	13. **Wanna Be Startin' Somethin'**	Epic 03914
7/30/83	7	11	14. **Human Nature** also see "Right Here/Human Nature" by SWV	Epic 04026
10/15/83	1 (6)	18	▲ 15. **Say Say Say** **PAUL McCARTNEY AND MICHAEL JACKSON**	Columbia 04168
10/22/83	10	9	16. **P.Y.T. (Pretty Young Thing)**	Epic 04165
2/11/84	4	9	▲ 17. **Thriller** above 8 (except #15) from the album *Thriller*	Epic 04364
6/23/84	38	3	18. **Farewell My Summer Love** remix of a recording from 8/31/73	Motown 1739
8/8/87	1 (1)	11	● 19. **I Just Can't Stop Loving You** Sales #1(1) / Airplay #1(1); Siedah Garrett (backing vocal); #1 Adult Contemporary hit (3 weeks); #1 R&B hit (1 week)	Epic 07253
9/19/87	1 (2)	11	20. **Bad** Sales #1(2) / Airplay #1(2); Jimmy Smith (organ solo); #1 R&B hit (3 weeks)	Epic 07418
11/28/87+	1 (1)	13	21. **The Way You Make Me Feel** Sales #2 / Airplay #3; #1 R&B hit (4 weeks)	Epic 07645
2/13/88	1 (2)	13	22. **Man In The Mirror** Airplay #1(3) / Sales #1(2); Siedah Garrett, Winans and Andrae Crouch Choir (backing vocals); #1 R&B hit (1 week)	Epic 07668
5/14/88	1 (1)	11	23. **Dirty Diana** Sales #1(1) / Airplay #3; featuring Steve Stevens (Billy Idol's guitarist)	Epic 07739
8/6/88	11	8	24. **Another Part Of Me** Sales #8 / Airplay #10; #1 R&B hit (1 week)	Epic 07962
11/26/88+	7	11	25. **Smooth Criminal** Sales #5 / Airplay #9; above 7 from the album *Bad*; all of above Epic recordings produced by Quincy Jones	Epic 08044
11/23/91	1 (7)	15	▲ 26. **Black Or White** Sales #1(4) / Airplay #1(4); Bill Bottrell (rap); Slash (of Guns N' Roses; guitar); remix is on the B-side of #27 below	Epic 74100
2/1/92	3	16	● 27. **Remember The Time** Airplay #1(2) / Sales #5; #1 R&B hit (2 weeks)	Epic 74200
5/2/92	6	11	● 28. **In The Closet** Airplay #5 / Sales #15; features the "Mystery Girl," who is Princess Stephanie of Monaco; #1 R&B hit (1 week)	Epic 74266
7/18/92	26	9	29. **Jam** Sales #19 / Airplay #21; Heavy D (rap)	Epic 74333
2/27/93	27	8	30. **Heal The World** Sales #18 / Airplay #24	Epic 74708
4/17/93	14	10	31. **Who Is It** Airplay #14 / Sales #26	Epic 74406

DATE	POS	WKS	ARTIST—RECORD TITLE	LABEL & NO.
7/31/93	7	15	● 32. **Will You Be There** Airplay #6 / Sales #12; from the movie *Free Willy* starring the killer whale Keiko; above 7 from the album *Dangerous*	MJJ/Epic 77060
6/17/95	5	9	▲ 33. **Scream/** **MICHAEL JACKSON & JANET JACKSON** Sales #3 / Airplay #12	
		9	34. Childhood Sales flip; from the movie *Free Willy 2* starring Jason James Richter	Epic 78000
9/2/95	1 (1)	14	▲ 35. **You Are Not Alone** Sales #2 / Airplay #2; written and produced by R. Kelly; #1 R&B hit (4 weeks)	Epic 78002

JACKSON, Millie

Born on 7/15/44 in Thompson, Georgia. Soul singer/songwriter. To Newark, New Jersey, in 1958. Worked as a model in New York City. Professional singing debut at Club Zanzibar in Hoboken, New Jersey, in 1964. First recorded for MGM in 1970.

DATE	POS	WKS	ARTIST—RECORD TITLE	LABEL & NO.
5/13/72	27	6	1. Ask Me What You Want	Spring 123
9/29/73	24	8	2. Hurts So Good from the movie *Cleopatra Jones* starring Tamara Dobson	Spring 139

JACKSON, Rebbie

Born Maureen Jackson on 5/29/50 in Gary, Indiana. Eldest of the nine-sibling Jackson family. Worked with The Jacksons, 1974–77, then went solo.

DATE	POS	WKS	ARTIST—RECORD TITLE	LABEL & NO.
11/17/84	24	8	● 1. Centipede Sales #22; written and produced by Michael Jackson	Columbia 04547

JACKSON, Stonewall

His real name. Born on 11/6/32 in Emerson, North Carolina. Country singer/guitarist/pianist. Descended from General Thomas Jonathan "Stonewall" Jackson.

DATE	POS	WKS	ARTIST—RECORD TITLE	LABEL & NO.
6/8/59	4	12	1. **Waterloo** #1 Country hit (5 weeks)	Columbia 41393

JACKSON, Wanda

Born on 10/20/37 in Maud, Oklahoma. Country-rockabilly singer/songwriter/guitarist. First recorded for Decca in 1954. Toured with Elvis Presley, 1955–56.

DATE	POS	WKS	ARTIST—RECORD TITLE	LABEL & NO.
10/10/60	37	1	1. Let's Have A Party Gene Vincent's Blue Caps (backing); introduced by Elvis Presley as "Party" in his 1957 movie *Loving You*	Capitol 4397
8/14/61	29	3	2. Right Or Wrong	Capitol 4553
11/27/61	27	3	3. In The Middle Of A Heartache	Capitol 4635

JACKSON 5/JACKSONS

Quintet of brothers formed and managed by their father beginning in 1966 in Gary, Indiana. Consisted of Sigmund "Jackie" (born 5/4/51), Toriano "Tito" (born 10/15/53), Jermaine (born 12/11/54), Marlon (born 3/12/57) and lead singer Michael (born 8/29/58). First recorded for Steeltown in 1968. Known as The Jackson 5, 1968–75. Jermaine replaced by Randy (born 10/29/61) in 1976. Jermaine rejoined the group for 1984's highly publicized *Victory* album and tour. Marlon left for a solo career in 1987. Their sisters Rebbie, La Toya and Janet backed the group; each had solo hits. Michael and Janet emerged with superstar solo careers in the '80s. Group lineup since 1989: Jackie, Tito, Jermaine and Randy Jackson.

DATE	POS	WKS	ARTIST–RECORD TITLE	LABEL & NO.
			THE JACKSON 5:	
12/6/69+	1 (1)	16	1. **I Want You Back** #1 R&B hit (4 weeks)	Motown 1157
3/21/70	1 (2)	12	2. **ABC** #1 R&B hit (4 weeks)	Motown 1163
6/6/70	1 (2)	12	3. **The Love You Save/** #1 R&B hit (6 weeks)	
		4	4. I Found That Girl	Motown 1166
9/19/70	1 (5)	16	5. **I'll Be There** #1 R&B hit (6 weeks)	Motown 1171
2/6/71	2 (2)	9	6. **Mama's Pearl**	Motown 1177
4/10/71	2 (3)	11	7. **Never Can Say Goodbye** #1 R&B hit (3 weeks)	Motown 1179
7/31/71	20	6	8. Maybe Tomorrow	Motown 1186
12/25/71+	10	8	9. **Sugar Daddy**	Motown 1194
4/29/72	13	8	10. Little Bitty Pretty One	Motown 1199
7/29/72	16	8	11. Lookin' Through The Windows	Motown 1205
11/18/72	18	8	12. Corner Of The Sky from the Broadway musical *Pippin* starring Ben Vereen	Motown 1214
4/14/73	28	4	13. Hallelujah Day	Motown 1224
9/22/73	28	7	14. Get It Together	Motown 1277
3/30/74	2 (2)	16	15. **Dancing Machine** #1 R&B hit (1 week)	Motown 1286
11/30/74	38	2	16. Whatever You Got, I Want	Motown 1308
2/22/75	15	7	17. I Am Love (Parts I & II)	Motown 1310
			THE JACKSONS:	
12/11/76+	6	15	▲ 18. **Enjoy Yourself**	Epic 50289
5/7/77	28	3	19. Show You The Way To Go	Epic 50350
3/31/79	7	14	▲ 20. **Shake Your Body (Down To The Ground)**	Epic 50656
10/11/80	12	9	21. Lovely One	Epic 50938
1/10/81	22	8	22. Heartbreak Hotel	Epic 50959
6/30/84	3	11	● 23. **State Of Shock** Mick Jagger (guest vocalist)	Epic 04503
8/25/84	17	8	24. Torture	Epic 04575
			JACOBS, Dick, And His Chorus And Orchestra Born on 3/29/18 in New York City. Died in 1988 (age 70) of cancer. Music director of TV's "Your Hit Parade," 1957–58. A&R director for Coral and Brunswick Records. Author of *Who Wrote That Song*.	
4/7/56	22	7	1. "Main Title" And "Molly-O" Jockey #22 / Top 100 #26; from the Otto Preminger movie *The Man With The Golden Arm* starring Frank Sinatra	Coral 61606
11/3/56	16	9	2. Petticoats Of Portugal Jockey #16 / Top 100 #20 / Juke Box #20 / Best Seller #23	Coral 61724
9/16/57	17	4	3. Fascination Jockey #17 / Top 100 #52; from the movie *Love In The Afternoon* starring Gary Cooper and Audrey Hepburn	Coral 61864

DATE	POS	WKS	ARTIST–RECORD TITLE	LABEL & NO.
			JADE	
			Los Angeles-based female vocal trio: Chicagoans Joi Marshall and Tonya Kelly with Houston-born Di Reed.	
8/22/92	**16**	13	1. I Wanna Love You Airplay #10 / Sales #27; from the movie *Class Act* starring Kid 'N Play	Giant 18950
1/30/93	**4**	27	● 2. **Don't Walk Away** Airplay #2 / Sales #10	Giant 18686
7/10/93	**22**	8	3. One Woman Airplay #17 / Sales #37	Giant 18606
12/3/94+	**20**	19	4. Every Day Of The Week Airplay #20 / Sales #30	Giant 17988
			JAGGER, Mick	
			Born Michael Phillip Jagger on 7/26/43 in Dartford, England. Lead singer of The Rolling Stones. Starred in the 1970 movie *Ned Kelly*. Also appeared in the 1992 movie *Freejack*. Married to Nicaraguan model Bianca Peres Morena de Macias, 1971-80. Married actress/model Jerry Hall on 11/24/90. Also see The Jacksons' "State Of Shock" and Carly Simon's "You're So Vain."	
2/16/85	**12**	10	1. Just Another Night Airplay #9 / Sales #12	Columbia 04743
5/25/85	**38**	3	2. Lucky In Love	Columbia 04893
9/7/85	**7**	9	3. **Dancing In The Street** **MICK JAGGER/DAVID BOWIE** Sales #5 / Airplay #8; all proceeds donated to Live-Aid	EMI America 8288
10/24/87	**39**	1	4. Let's Work Sales #37 / Airplay #39	Columbia 07306
			JAGGERZ, The	
			Rock group formed in Pittsburgh in 1965, featuring lead singer Donnie Iris (Dominic Ierace).	
2/14/70	**2 (1)**	11	● 1. **The Rapper**	Kama Sutra 502
			JAMES, Etta	
			Born Jamesetta Hawkins on 1/25/38 in Los Angeles. R&B pioneer. Nicknamed "Miss Peaches." First recorded for Modern in 1954. Recorded duets with Harvey Fuqua of The Moonglows as Etta & Harvey. Frequent bouts with heroin addiction; finally cured in the late '70s. Still active into the '90s. Inducted into the Rock and Roll Hall of Fame in 1993.	
6/6/60	**33**	4	1. All I Could Do Was Cry	Argo 5359
11/21/60	**34**	2	2. My Dearest Darling	Argo 5368
4/3/61	**30**	4	3. Trust In Me #4 hit for Mildred Bailey in 1937	Argo 5385
9/4/61	**39**	2	4. Don't Cry, Baby	Argo 5393
3/31/62	**37**	4	5. Something's Got A Hold On Me	Argo 5409
9/8/62	**34**	2	6. Stop The Wedding	Argo 5418
5/11/63	**25**	6	7. Pushover	Argo 5437
12/30/67+	**23**	7	8. Tell Mama	Cadet 5578
4/6/68	**35**	4	9. Security	Cadet 5594

DATE	POS	WKS	ARTIST—RECORD TITLE	LABEL & NO.
			JAMES, Joni	
			Born Joan Carmello Babbo on 9/22/30 in Chicago. Worked as a dancer from age 12; model during high school. Toured Canada as a dancer in the late 1940s. First recorded for Sharp in 1952. Married to her orchestral arranger/conductor, Tony Acquaviva, 1958–61 (Acquaviva died 9/27/86).	
2/19/55	**2** (1)	16	● 1. **How Important Can It Be?** Jockey #2 / Juke Box #6 / Best Seller #8; Ray Charles Singers (backing vocals)	MGM 11919
10/22/55	**6**	10	2. **You Are My Love** Jockey #6 / Top 100 #15 / Best Seller #18	MGM 12066
8/11/56	**30**	2	3. Give Us This Day David Terry (orch., above 3)	MGM 12288
10/20/58	**19**	8	4. There Goes My Heart #13 hit for Enric Madriguera in 1934	MGM 12706
2/16/59	**33**	4	5. There Must Be A Way #9 hit for both Johnnie Johnston and Charlie Spivak in 1945	MGM 12746
1/25/60	**35**	3	6. Little Things Mean A Lot #1 hit for Kitty Kallen in 1954	MGM 12849
1/23/61	**38**	1	7. My Last Date (With You) lyric version of Floyd Cramer's "Last Date"; Tony Acquaviva (orch., above 4)	MGM 12933
			JAMES, Rick	
			Born James Johnson on 2/1/52 in Buffalo. Funk-rock singer/songwriter/ guitarist. In Mynah Birds band with Neil Young in the late '60s. To London; formed the band Main Line. Returned to the U.S. and formed Stone City Band; produced Teena Marie, Mary Jane Girls, Eddie Murphy and others. In mid-1994, sentenced to five years in prison for assaults on two women.	
8/5/78	**13**	10	1. You And I #1 R&B hit (2 weeks)	Gordy 7156
7/18/81	**40**	2	2. Give It To Me Baby #1 R&B hit (5 weeks)	Gordy 7197
9/5/81	**16**	10	3. Super Freak (Part 1) music used for M.C. Hammer's 1990 hit "U Can't Touch This"	Gordy 7205
9/24/83	**40**	1	4. Cold Blooded #1 R&B hit (6 weeks)	Gordy 1687
8/18/84	**36**	3	5. 17	Gordy 1730
			JAMES, Sonny	
			Born James Loden on 5/1/29 in Hackleburg, Alabama. Country singer/songwriter/guitarist. Nicknamed "The Southern Gentleman." Brought to Capitol Records in Nashville by Chet Atkins. Appeared in the movies *Second Fiddle To A Steel Guitar*, *Nashville Rebel*, *Las Vegas Hillbillies* and *Hillbillys In A Haunted House*.	
1/5/57	**1** (1)	17	● 1. **Young Love** Jockey #1 / Best Seller #2 / Top 100 #2 / Juke Box #4; #1 Country hit (9 weeks)	Capitol 3602
4/20/57	**25**	1	2. First Date, First Kiss, First Love Jockey #25 / Top 100 #39	Capitol 3674

DATE	POS	WKS	ARTIST–RECORD TITLE	LABEL & NO.

JAMES, Tommy, And The Shondells

Born Thomas Jackson on 4/29/47 in Dayton, Ohio. To Niles, Michigan at age 11. Formed pop group The Shondells at age 12. Recorded "Hanky Panky" on the Snap label in 1963. James relocated to Pittsburgh in 1965 after a DJ there popularized "Hanky Panky." Original master was sold to Roulette, whereupon James recruited Pittsburgh group The Raconteurs to become the official Shondells. Consisted of Mike Vale (bass), Pete Lucia (drums), Eddie Gray (guitar) and Ronnie Rosman (organ). Began recording as a solo artist in 1970.

DATE	POS	WKS	ARTIST–RECORD TITLE	LABEL & NO.
6/18/66	**1** (2)	10	● 1. **Hanky Panky** first released on Snap 102 in 1963 as by The Shondells; then on Red Fox 110 in 1965 (The Shondells)	Roulette 4686
8/20/66	21	5	2. Say I Am (What I Am)	Roulette 4695
12/10/66	31	4	3. It's Only Love	Roulette 4710
3/11/67	**4**	12	4. **I Think We're Alone Now**	Roulette 4720
5/6/67	**10**	8	5. **Mirage**	Roulette 4736
7/15/67	25	5	6. I Like The Way	Roulette 4756
9/2/67	18	6	7. Gettin' Together	Roulette 4762
5/4/68	**3**	13	8. **Mony Mony** above 6 produced by Bo Gentry and Ritchie Cordell	Roulette 7008
11/23/68	38	2	9. Do Something To Me	Roulette 7024
12/21/68+	**1** (2)	15	10. **Crimson And Clover**	Roulette 7028
4/5/69	**7**	8	11. **Sweet Cherry Wine**	Roulette 7039
6/28/69	**2** (3)	12	12. **Crystal Blue Persuasion**	Roulette 7050
10/25/69	19	5	13. Ball Of Fire	Roulette 7060
12/20/69+	23	7	14. She	Roulette 7066

TOMMY JAMES:

DATE	POS	WKS	ARTIST–RECORD TITLE	LABEL & NO.
6/26/71	**4**	11	15. **Draggin' The Line**	Roulette 7103
10/23/71	40	1	16. I'm Comin' Home The Stephentown Singers (backing vocals)	Roulette 7110
2/23/80	19	9	17. Three Times In Love #1 Adult Contemporary hit (1 week)	Millennium 11785

JAMIES, The

Pop vocal quartet from Dorchester, Massachusetts, led by Tom Jamison and his sister Serena.

DATE	POS	WKS	ARTIST–RECORD TITLE	LABEL & NO.
9/15/58	26	4	1. Summertime, Summertime Hot 100 #26 / Best Seller #28	Epic 9281
8/4/62	38	1	2. Summertime, Summertime　　　　[R]	Epic 9281

JAN & DEAN

Jan Berry (born 4/3/41) and Dean Torrence (born 3/10/40) formed group called the Barons while attending high school in Los Angeles. Jan & Dean and Barons' member Arnie Ginsburg recorded "Jennie Lee" in Jan's garage. Dean left for a six-month Army Reserve stint, whereupon Jan signed with Doris Day's label, Arwin, and the record was released as by Jan & Arnie. Upon Dean's return from the service, Arnie (not to be confused with the famed DJ of the same name) joined the Navy, and Jan & Dean signed with Herb Alpert's Dore label. Jan was critically injured in an auto accident on 4/19/66. Duo made a comeback in 1978, after their biographical movie *Dead Man's Curve* aired on TV.

DATE	POS	WKS	ARTIST–RECORD TITLE	LABEL & NO.
5/26/58	8	11	1. **Jennie Lee** **JAN & ARNIE** Best Seller #8 / Top 100 #8 / Jockey #17; Don Ralke (orch.)	Arwin 108

DATE	POS	WKS	ARTIST—RECORD TITLE	LABEL & NO.
8/10/59	10	9	2. **Baby Talk**	Dore 522
			originally issued as by Jan & Arnie on Dore 522	
7/10/61	25	4	3. Heart And Soul	Challenge 9111
			Larry Clinton hit #1 in 1938 with this Hoagy Carmichael tune	
4/20/63	28	5	4. Linda	Liberty 55531
			#1 hit in 1947 for Buddy Clark with Ray Noble's orch.	
6/22/63	1 (2)	11	5. **Surf City**	Liberty 55580
			Brian Wilson (backing vocal)	
9/21/63	11	8	6. Honolulu Lulu	Liberty 55613
12/21/63+	10	9	7. **Drag City**	Liberty 55641
3/28/64	8	11	8. **Dead Man's Curve/**	
4/4/64	37	4	9. The New Girl In School	Liberty 55672
7/4/64	3	10	10. **The Little Old Lady (From Pasadena)**	Liberty 55704
10/10/64	16	5	11. Ride The Wild Surf	Liberty 55724
			title song from the movie starring Tab Hunter and Fabian	
11/21/64	25	5	12. Sidewalk Surfin'	Liberty 55727
			new lyrics to the Beach Boys' 1963 recording "Catch A Wave"; above 8 (except #6 & 10) co-written by Brian Wilson (Beach Boys)	
6/26/65	27	4	13. You Really Know How To Hurt A Guy	Liberty 55792
11/13/65	30	2	14. I Found A Girl	Liberty 55833
6/18/66	21	6	15. Popsicle	Liberty 55886
			remix of track from the 1963 album *Drag City* ("Popsicle Truck")	

JANKOWSKI, Horst

Born on 1/30/36 in Berlin. Jazz pianist.

DATE	POS	WKS	ARTIST—RECORD TITLE	LABEL & NO.
6/5/65	12	9	1. A Walk In The Black Forest [I]	Mercury 72425
			#1 Adult Contemporary hit (2 weeks)	

JARMELS, The

R&B vocal group from Richmond, Virginia: Nathaniel Ruff, Ray Smith, Paul Burnett, Earl Christian and Tom Eldridge. Named for a street in Harlem. Major Harris was later a member.

DATE	POS	WKS	ARTIST—RECORD TITLE	LABEL & NO.
8/28/61	12	6	1. A Little Bit Of Soap	Laurie 3098

JARREAU, Al

Born on 3/12/40 in Milwaukee. Soul-jazz vocalist. Has Master's degree in psychology from the University of Iowa. Worked clubs in San Francisco with George Duke.

DATE	POS	WKS	ARTIST—RECORD TITLE	LABEL & NO.
9/12/81	15	11	1. We're In This Love Together	Warner 49746
4/23/83	21	6	2. Mornin'	Warner 29720
			JARREAU	
7/4/87	23	5	3. Moonlighting (Theme)	MCA 53124
			Sales #13 / Airplay #37; theme from the TV series starring Bruce Willis and Cybill Shepherd; #1 Adult Contemporary hit (1 week)	

JAY & THE AMERICANS

Group formed in late 1959 by New York University students as the Harbor-Lites: John "Jay" Traynor (an early member of The Mystics), Sandy Yaguda, Kenny Vance (later a Hollywood musical director) and Howie Kane. Guitarist Marty Sanders joined during production of their first album in 1961. Traynor left after their first hit and was replaced by lead singer Jay Black (real name: David Blatt; born 11/2/38) in 1962.

DATE	POS	WKS	ARTIST—RECORD TITLE	LABEL & NO.
4/7/62	5	11	1. **She Cried**	United Art. 415

DATE	POS	WKS	ARTIST—RECORD TITLE	LABEL & NO.
9/21/63	25	4	2. Only In America	United Art. 626
10/3/64	3	11	3. **Come A Little Bit Closer**	United Art. 759
1/16/65	11	7	4. Let's Lock The Door (And Throw Away The Key)	United Art. 805
6/19/65	4	11	5. **Cara, Mia**	United Art. 881
			#10 hit for David Whitfield (with Mantovani) in 1954	
9/25/65	13	6	6. Some Enchanted Evening	United Art. 919
			there were 6 Top 10 versions of this *South Pacific* song in 1949	
12/4/65	18	6	7. Sunday And Me	United Art. 948
			Neil Diamond's first major hit as a songwriter	
6/11/66	25	4	8. Crying	United Art. 50016
1/25/69	6	10	● 9. **This Magic Moment**	United Art. 50475
1/17/70	19	7	10. Walkin' In The Rain	United Art. 50605

JAY AND THE TECHNIQUES

Interracial R&B-rock group from Allentown, Pennsylvania: Jay Proctor (lead singer; born 10/28/40), Karl Landis, Ronnie Goosly, John Walsh, George Lloyd, Chuck Crowl and Dante Dancho.

DATE	POS	WKS	ARTIST—RECORD TITLE	LABEL & NO.
8/19/67	6	11	1. **Apples, Peaches, Pumpkin Pie**	Smash 2086
11/11/67	14	9	2. Keep The Ball Rollin'	Smash 2124
2/10/68	39	2	3. Strawberry Shortcake	Smash 2142

JAYE, Jerry

Born Gerald Jaye Hatley on 10/19/37 in Manila, Arkansas.

DATE	POS	WKS	ARTIST—RECORD TITLE	LABEL & NO.
5/6/67	29	6	1. My Girl Josephine	Hi 2120
			originally released as "Hello Josephine" on Connie Records	

JAYHAWKS, The

Los Angeles R&B group formed in 1955: James Johnson, Carlton Fisher, Dave Govan and Carver Bunkum. Also see The Vibrations and The Marathons.

DATE	POS	WKS	ARTIST—RECORD TITLE	LABEL & NO.
7/28/56	18	2	1. Stranded In The Jungle [N]	Flash 109
			Best Seller #18 / Top 100 #29	

JAYNETTS, The

R&B female group from the Bronx, formed by producer/composer/owner of J&S Records Zelma "Zell" Sanders. Her daughter, Johnnie Louise Richardson, was part of Johnnie & Joe duo and a touring member of The Jaynetts. Johnnie died from a stroke on 10/25/88.

DATE	POS	WKS	ARTIST—RECORD TITLE	LABEL & NO.
9/7/63	2 (2)	9	1. **Sally, Go 'Round The Roses**	Tuff 369

JAZZY JEFF—see D.J. JAZZY JEFF

JB's, The

James Brown's super-funk backup band led by Fred Wesley.

DATE	POS	WKS	ARTIST—RECORD TITLE	LABEL & NO.
6/23/73	22	6	● 1. Doing It To Death	People 621
			FRED WESLEY & THE J.B's	
			#1 R&B hit (2 weeks); written, produced and arranged by James Brown	

JEFFERSON

British vocalist Geoff Turton. Former lead singer of The Rockin' Berries.

DATE	POS	WKS	ARTIST—RECORD TITLE	LABEL & NO.
1/24/70	23	6	1. Baby Take Me In Your Arms	Janus 106

DATE	POS	WKS	ARTIST–RECORD TITLE	LABEL & NO.

JEFFERSON AIRPLANE/STARSHIP

Formed as Jefferson Airplane (slang for a split paper match used as a marijuana cigarette holder) in San Francisco, 1965. Consisted of Marty Balin and Signe Anderson (vocals), Paul Kantner (vocals, guitar), Jorma Kaukonen (guitar), Jack Casady (bass) and Alexander "Skip" Spence (drums). Grace Slick and Spencer Dryden joined in 1966, replacing Anderson and Spence. Slick had been in the Great Society. Spence then formed Moby Grape. Dryden replaced by Joey Covington in 1970. Casady and Kaukonen left by 1974 to go full time with Hot Tuna. Balin left in 1971, rejoined in 1975, by which time group was renamed Jefferson Starship and consisted of Slick, Kantner, Papa John Creach (Hot Tuna; violin; died 2/22/94), David Freiberg (bass), Craig Chaquico (pronounced: chuck-ee-so; guitar), Pete Sears (bass) and John Barbata (drums). Slick left group from June 1978 to January 1981. In 1979, singer Mickey Thomas joined (replaced Balin), along with Aynsley Dunbar (John Mayall's Bluesbreakers, Mothers Of Invention, Journey) who replaced Barbata. Don Baldwin (formerly with Snail) replaced Dunbar (later with Whitesnake) in 1982. Kantner left in 1984, and, due to legal difficulties, band's name was shortened to Starship; lineup was Slick, Thomas, Sears, Chaquico and Baldwin. Slick left in early 1988. In 1989, the original 1966 lineup—Balin, Slick, Kantner, Kaukonen and Casady—reunited as Jefferson Airplane with Kenny Aronoff (from John Cougar Mellencamp's band) replacing Dryden. Continuing as Starship were Thomas, Chaquico, Baldwin, Brett Bloomfield (bass) and Mark Morgan (keyboards). Starship disbanded in 1990. Group inducted into the Rock and Roll Hall of Fame in 1996.

JEFFERSON AIRPLANE:

DATE	POS	WKS	ARTIST–RECORD TITLE	LABEL & NO.
5/6/67	5	9	1. **Somebody To Love** originally released by the Great Society on North Beach 1001 in 1966, entitled "Someone To Love"	RCA 9140
7/1/67	8	9	2. **White Rabbit**	RCA 9248

JEFFERSON STARSHIP:

DATE	POS	WKS	ARTIST–RECORD TITLE	LABEL & NO.
9/13/75	3	13	3. **Miracles**	Grunt 10367
8/14/76	12	11	4. With Your Love	Grunt 10746
3/25/78	8	11	5. **Count On Me**	Grunt 11196
6/24/78	12	8	6. Runaway	Grunt 11274
11/24/79+	14	10	7. Jane	Grunt 11750
5/2/81	29	6	8. Find Your Way Back	Grunt 12211
11/13/82	28	6	9. Be My Lady	Grunt 13350
3/19/83	38	2	10. Winds Of Change	Grunt 13439
6/9/84	23	8	11. No Way Out	Grunt 13811

STARSHIP:

DATE	POS	WKS	ARTIST–RECORD TITLE	LABEL & NO.
9/28/85	1 (2)	15	● 12. **We Built This City** Airplay #1(2) / Sales #2; veteran DJ Les Garland (DJ voice)	Grunt 14170
1/18/86	1 (1)	13	13. **Sara** Sales #1(1) / Airplay #1(1); #1 Adult Contemporary hit (3 weeks)	Grunt 14253
4/26/86	26	6	14. Tomorrow Doesn't Matter Tonight Airplay #25 / Sales #27	Grunt 14332
2/14/87	1 (2)	15	● 15. **Nothing's Gonna Stop Us Now** Airplay #1(3) / Sales #1(2); from the movie *Mannequin* starring Andrew McCarthy; #1 Adult Contemporary hit (2 weeks)	Grunt 5109
7/18/87	9	10	16. **It's Not Over ('Til It's Over)** Sales #9 / Airplay #13	RCA/Grunt 5225
8/26/89	12	9	17. It's Not Enough Airplay #11 / Sales #15	RCA 9032

DATE	POS	WKS	ARTIST–RECORD TITLE	LABEL & NO.
			### JEFFREY, Joe, Group	
			Jeffrey is an R&B singer/guitarist.	
7/5/69	14	8	1. My Pledge Of Love	Wand 11200
			### JELLYBEAN	
			Born John Benitez on 11/7/57 in New York City. Renowned club DJ/remixer/producer. Remixing career took off with his "Flashdance" and "Maniac" remixes, and was later to include many of Madonna's hits.	
12/21/85+	18	9	1. Sidewalk Talk	EMI America 8297
			Sales #15 / Airplay #19; written by Madonna; Katherine "Katt" Buchanan (vocal)	
8/15/87	16	8	2. Who Found Who	Chrysalis 43120
			JELLYBEAN/Elisa Fiorillo	
			Airplay #13 / Sales #14	
			### JELLY BEANS, The	
			Quintet from Jersey City: sisters Elyse & Maxine Herbert, Alma Brewer, Diane Taylor and Charles Thomas.	
7/18/64	9	7	1. **I Wanna Love Him So Bad**	Red Bird 10003
			### JENKINS, Gordon—see ARMSTRONG, Louis	
			### JENNINGS, Waylon	
			Born on 6/15/37 in Littlefield, Texas. While working as a DJ in Lubbock, Texas, Jennings befriended Buddy Holly. Holly produced Jennings's first record "Jole Blon" in 1958. Jennings then joined with Holly's backing band as bass guitarist on the fateful "Winter Dance Party" tour in 1959. Established himself in the mid-1970s as a leader of the "outlaw" movement in country music. Married to Jessi Colter since 1969. Appeared in the movies *Nashville Rebel* and *MacKintosh And T.J.* Narrator for TV's "The Dukes Of Hazzard."	
3/6/76	25	5	1. Good Hearted Woman	RCA 10529
			WAYLON & WILLIE	
6/11/77	25	7	2. Luckenbach, Texas (Back to the Basics of Love)	RCA 10924
			Willie Nelson (ending vocal)	
11/1/80	21	10	● 3. Theme From The Dukes Of Hazzard (Good Ol' Boys)	RCA 12067
			WAYLON	
			from "The Dukes Of Hazzard" TV series starring John Schneider and Tom Wopat	
			### JENSEN, Kris	
			Born Peter Jensen on 4/4/42 in New Haven, Connecticut. Pop-country singer/guitarist.	
10/6/62	20	6	1. Torture	Hickory 1173
			written by John D. Loudermilk	
			### JESUS JONES	
			Pop-rock quintet formed in London in 1988: Mike Edwards (vocals, guitar), Jerry De Borg (guitar), Iain "Barry D" Baker (keyboards), Al Jaworski (bass) and Simon "Gen" Matthews (drums).	
5/25/91	2 (1)	15	1. **Right Here, Right Now**	SBK 07345
			Airplay #3 / Sales #9	
9/14/91	4	10	2. **Real, Real, Real**	SBK 07364
			Airplay #30 / Sales #67	

DATE	POS	WKS	ARTIST–RECORD TITLE	LABEL & NO.
			JETHRO TULL	
			Progressive-rock group formed in 1968 in Blackpool, England. Led by Ian Anderson (vocals, flute) and Martin Barre (guitar). Band named after 18th-century agriculturist/inventor of seed drill. Lineups from 1971 through 1977 included Anderson, Barre, John Evan (piano), Clive Bunker (drums; replaced by Barriemore Barlow by 1972) and Jeffrey Hammond-Hammond (bass; replaced by 1976 by John Glascock [died 1979]).	
11/25/72+	**11**	10	1. Living In The Past	Chrysalis 2006
11/30/74+	**12**	10	2. Bungle In The Jungle	Chrysalis 2101
			JETS, The	
			Minneapolis-based family band consisting of eight brothers and sisters: Leroy, Eddie, Eugene, Haini, Rudy, Kathi, Elizabeth and Moana Wolfgramm. Their parents are from the South Pacific country of Tonga. All members play at least two instruments. Eugene left group and formed duo Boys Club in 1988.	
5/3/86	**3**	13	1. **Crush On You** Sales #3 / Airplay #4	MCA 52774
1/17/87	**3**	12	2. **You Got It All** Sales #3 / Airplay #3; #1 Adult Contemporary hit (2 weeks)	MCA 52968
6/27/87	**7**	11	3. **Cross My Broken Heart** Sales #7 / Airplay #8; from the movie *Beverly Hills Cop II* starring Eddie Murphy	MCA 53123
11/14/87	**20**	6	4. I Do You Sales #15 / Airplay #21	MCA 53193
2/13/88	**6**	13	5. **Rocket 2 U** Sales #4 / Airplay #7	MCA 53254
5/7/88	**4**	13	6. **Make It Real** Sales #2 / Airplay #4; #1 Adult Contemporary hit (3 weeks); above 4 from the album *Magic*	MCA 53311
			JETT, Joan, & The Blackhearts	
			Born on 9/22/60 in Philadelphia. Played guitar with the Los Angeles female rock band The Runaways, 1975–78. Formed her backing band, The Blackhearts, in 1980. Starred in the 1987 movie *Light Of Day* as the leader of a rock band called The Barbusters.	
2/13/82	**1 (7)**	16	▲ 1. I Love Rock 'N Roll	Boardwalk 135
5/15/82	**7**	10	2. **Crimson And Clover**	Boardwalk 144
8/28/82	**20**	7	3. Do You Wanna Touch Me (Oh Yeah)	Boardwalk 150
7/30/83	**35**	4	4. Fake Friends also released on Blackheart 52256 in 1983	Blackheart 52240
10/15/83	**37**	2	5. Everyday People	Blackheart 52272
3/21/87	**33**	5	6. Light Of Day **THE BARBUSTERS (JOAN JETT AND THE BLACKHEARTS)** Sales #25; title song from the movie starring Michael J. Fox and Michael McKean; written by Bruce Springsteen	Blackheart 06692
8/13/88	**8**	12	7. **I Hate Myself For Loving You** Sales #4 / Airplay #11	Blackheart 07919
12/10/88+	**19**	10	8. Little Liar Sales #15 / Airplay #17	Blackheart 08095
3/3/90	**36**	2	9. Dirty Deeds **JOAN JETT** Airplay #37 / Sales #39	Blackheart 73267

DATE	POS	WKS	ARTIST–RECORD TITLE	LABEL & NO.
			JIGSAW	
			Pop-rock quartet from England: Des Dyer (lead vocals), Clive Scott, Tony Campbell and Barrie Bernard.	
10/11/75	3	14	1. **Sky High**	Chelsea 3022
			from the movie *The Dragon Flies* starring George Lazenby	
3/13/76	30	5	2. Love Fire	Chelsea 3037
			JIMENEZ, Jose	
			Born William Szarthmary on 10/5/24 in Quincy, Massachusetts. Stage name: Bill Dana. Head writer for TV's "Steve Allen Show." Star of own TV series, 1963–65. Created the Latin American comic character Jose Jimenez for Steve Allen's TV series.	
9/18/61	19	4	1. The Astronaut (Parts 1 & 2) [C]	Kapp 409
			interviewed by Don Hinckley	
			JIVE BOMBERS, The	
			New York City R&B quartet: Clarence Palmer, Earl Johnson, Al Tinney and William "Pee Wee" Tinney.	
3/16/57	36	1	1. Bad Boy	Savoy 1508
			JIVE BUNNY and the Mastermixers	
			British dance outfit: DJ Les Hemstock and mixers John Pickles, Andy Pickles and Ian Morgan.	
11/25/89+	11	11	● 1. Swing The Mood	Music Fac. 99140
			Sales #2 / Airplay #27; includes samplings of these tunes: Let's Twist Again (Chubby Checker)/In The Mood (Glenn Miller)/Rock Around The Clock (Bill Haley)/Rock-A-Beatin' Boogie (Bill Haley)/Tutti-Frutti (Little Richard)/Wake Up Little Susie (Everly Brothers)/C'mon Everybody (Eddie Cochran)/Hound Dog (Elvis)/Shake, Rattle And Roll (Bill Haley)/All Shook Up (Elvis)/Jailhouse Rock (Elvis)/At The Hop (Danny & The Juniors); Elvis samplings are by impersonator Pete Willcox	
			JIVE FIVE, The	
			R&B group formed in Brooklyn in 1959: Eugene Pitt (born 11/6/37; lead singer; formerly with The Genies), Jerome Hanna and Billy Prophet (tenors), Richard Harris (baritone) and Norman Johnson (bass). After Johnson's death in 1970, group name changed to Jyve Fyve.	
8/14/61	3	12	1. **My True Story**	Beltone 1006
			#1 R&B hit (3 weeks)	
9/11/65	36	3	2. I'm A Happy Man	United Art. 853
			J.J. FAD	
			Los Angeles female rap trio: M.C.J.B. (Juana Burns), Baby-D (Dania Birks) and Sassy C (Michelle Franklin). J.J. Fad stands for Just Jammin' Fresh And Def.	
6/11/88	30	4	● 1. Supersonic	Ruthless 99328
			Sales #20	
			JO, Damita	
			Born Damita Jo DuBlanc in Austin, Texas. Featured singer with Steve Gibson & The Red Caps (married to Gibson), 1951–53 and 1959–60. Regular on Redd Foxx's TV variety series in 1977.	
11/7/60	22	8	1. I'll Save The Last Dance For You	Mercury 71690
			answer song to The Drifters' "Save The Last Dance For Me"	

DATE	POS	WKS	ARTIST–RECORD TITLE	LABEL & NO.
7/17/61	**12**	7	2. I'll Be There answer song to Ben E. King's "Stand By Me"	Mercury 71840

JO, Sami

Sami Jo Cole. Female country-pop singer from Batesville, Arkansas.			

DATE	POS	WKS	ARTIST–RECORD TITLE	LABEL & NO.
3/23/74	**21**	7	1. Tell Me A Lie	MGM South 7029

JoBOXERS

London-based pop quintet led by American expatriate Dig Wayne (vocals). Includes Bristol, England natives Rob Marche, Dave Collard, Chris Bostock and Sean McLusky.

DATE	POS	WKS	ARTIST–RECORD TITLE	LABEL & NO.
11/5/83	**36**	4	1. Just Got Lucky	RCA 13601

JODECI

Two pairs of brothers/vocalists from Tiny Grove, North Carolina: Joel "JoJo" and Gedric "K-Ci" Hailey, with Dalvin and Donald "DeVante Swing" DeGrate Jr. Group name pronounced: joe-deh-see. The Haileys are cousins of David Hollister (BLACKstreet).

DATE	POS	WKS	ARTIST–RECORD TITLE	LABEL & NO.
11/16/91	**25**	12	1. Forever My Lady Sales #12 / Airplay #29; #1 R&B hit (2 weeks)	Uptown/MCA 54197
5/23/92	**11**	21	● 2. Come & Talk To Me Sales #9 / Airplay #10; #1 R&B hit (2 weeks)	Uptown/MCA 54175
6/19/93	**4**	22	● 3. **Lately** Sales #4 / Airplay #9; "live" recording from MTV's "Unplugged"; #1 R&B hit (4 weeks)	Uptown/MCA 54652
12/11/93+	**15**	17	● 4. Cry For You Sales #9 / Airplay #23; #1 R&B hit (4 weeks)	Uptown/MCA 54723
4/2/94	**25**	8	5. Feenin' Sales #19 / Airplay #37; contains elements of EPMD's "Get Off My Bandwagon"	Uptown/MCA 54798
6/17/95	**14**	15	● 6. Freek'n You Sales #5 / Airplay #56	Uptown/MCA 55023
11/18/95+	**31**	8	7. Love U 4 Life Sales #17 / Airplay #59	Uptown/MCA 55133

JOEL, Billy

Born William Martin Joel on 5/9/49 in Hicksville, Long Island, New York. Formed his first band, The Echoes, in 1964, which later became The Lost Souls. Member of Long Island group The Hassles in the late 1960s. Later formed rock duo Attila with The Hassles' drummer, Jon Small. Signed solo to Columbia Records in 1973. Involved in a serious motorcycle accident in Long Island in 1982. Married supermodel Christie Brinkley on 3/23/85; divorced in 1994. Toured and recorded in Russia in 1987. Recipient of Grammy's Living Legends Award in 1990, and *Billboard's* Century Award in 1994.

DATE	POS	WKS	ARTIST–RECORD TITLE	LABEL & NO.
4/6/74	**25**	4	1. Piano Man	Columbia 45963
12/28/74+	**34**	5	2. The Entertainer above 2 produced by Michael Stewart	Columbia 10064
12/10/77+	**3**	18	● 3. **Just The Way You Are** #1 Adult Contemporary hit (4 weeks)	Columbia 10646
4/15/78	**17**	8	4. Movin' Out (Anthony's Song)	Columbia 10708
6/17/78	**24**	5	5. Only The Good Die Young	Columbia 10750
9/9/78	**17**	9	6. She's Always A Woman above 4 from the album *The Stranger*	Columbia 10788
11/11/78+	**3**	16	● 7. **My Life** Peter Cetera (backing vocal)	Columbia 10853

DATE	POS	WKS	ARTIST–RECORD TITLE	LABEL & NO.
3/3/79	**14**	6	8. Big Shot	Columbia 10913
5/12/79	**24**	4	9. Honesty	Columbia 10959
3/22/80	**7**	11	10. **You May Be Right**	Columbia 11231
5/24/80	**1** (2)	19	● 11. **It's Still Rock And Roll To Me**	Columbia 11276
8/16/80	**19**	9	12. Don't Ask Me Why #1 Adult Contemporary hit (2 weeks)	Columbia 11331
11/1/80	**36**	3	13. Sometimes A Fantasy above 4 from the album *Glass Houses*	Columbia 11379
9/26/81	**17**	8	14. Say Goodbye To Hollywood written for Ronnie Spector (The Ronettes); recorded "live" at the Milwaukee Arena; studio version released on the 1976 album *Turnstiles*	Columbia 02518
12/12/81+	**23**	9	15. She's Got A Way recorded "live" at the Paradise Club in Boston; studio version released on Family 0900 in 1973	Columbia 02628
10/16/82	**20**	8	16. Pressure	Columbia 03244
12/18/82+	**17**	16	17. Allentown	Columbia 03413
7/30/83	**1** (1)	15	18. **Tell Her About It** #1 Adult Contemporary hit (2 weeks)	Columbia 04012
10/8/83	**3**	16	● 19. **Uptown Girl**	Columbia 04149
1/7/84	**10**	11	20. **An Innocent Man** #1 Adult Contemporary hit (1 week)	Columbia 04259
4/7/84	**14**	11	21. The Longest Time #1 Adult Contemporary hit (2 weeks)	Columbia 04400
8/4/84	**27**	7	22. Leave A Tender Moment Alone #1 Adult Contemporary hit (2 weeks)	Columbia 04514
2/9/85	**18**	10	23. Keeping The Faith Airplay #14 / Sales #21; above 6 from the album *An Innocent Man*	Columbia 04681
7/20/85	**9**	11	24. **You're Only Human (Second Wind)** Sales #8 / Airplay #9	Columbia 05417
10/26/85	**34**	3	25. The Night Is Still Young	Columbia 05657
6/21/86	**10**	9	26. **Modern Woman** Sales #10 / Airplay #10; from the movie *Ruthless People* starring Danny DeVito and Bette Midler	Epic 06118
9/6/86	**10**	10	27. **A Matter Of Trust** Sales #9 / Airplay #17	Columbia 06108
12/20/86+	**18**	9	28. This Is The Time Sales #14 / Airplay #23; #1 Adult Contemporary hit (3 weeks); all of above (except #1 & 2) produced by Phil Ramone	Columbia 06526
10/21/89	**1** (2)	15	● 29. **We Didn't Start The Fire** Sales #1(3) / Airplay #1(1)	Columbia 73021
1/27/90	**6**	11	30. **I Go To Extremes** Airplay #6 / Sales #8	Columbia 73091
11/24/90	**37**	3	31. And So It Goes Airplay #32 / Sales #36; above 3 produced by Mick Jones (Foreigner) and Billy Joel	Columbia 73602
8/7/93	**3**	24	32. **The River Of Dreams** Airplay #2 / Sales #7; #1 Adult Contemporary hit (12 weeks)	Columbia 77086
11/27/93	**29**	9	33. All About Soul Airplay #24; Color Me Badd (guest vocals); all of above written by Joel	Columbia 77254

DATE	POS	WKS	ARTIST–RECORD TITLE	LABEL & NO.
			JOE PUBLIC	
			Four-man R&B band from Buffalo, New York: Kevin "Kev" Scott (vocals), Joe "J.R." Carter, Joseph "Jake" Sayles and Dwight "Dew" Wyatt. Band co-wrote Keith Sweat's "Keep It Comin'."	
3/28/92	4	18	1. **Live And Learn** Airplay #3 / Sales #9	Columbia 74012
			JOHN, Elton	
			Born Reginald Kenneth Dwight on 3/25/47 in Pinner, Middlesex, England. Formed his first group Bluesology in 1966. Group backed visiting U.S. soul artists and later became Long John Baldry's backing band. Took the name of Elton John from the first names of Bluesology members Elton Dean and John Baldry. Teamed up with lyricist Bernie Taupin beginning in 1969. Formed Rocket Records in 1973. Played the Pinball Wizard in the movie version of *Tommy*. Elton was the #1 pop artist of the '70s. Inducted into the Rock and Roll Hall of Fame in 1994.	
12/19/70+	8	11	1. **Your Song**	Uni 55265
4/10/71	34	4	2. Friends *title song from the British movie starring Sean Bury*	Uni 55277
1/1/72	24	7	3. Levon	Uni 55314
5/27/72	6	12	4. **Rocket Man**	Uni 55328
8/26/72	8	7	5. **Honky Cat**	Uni 55343
12/23/72+	1 (3)	14	▲ 6. **Crocodile Rock**	MCA 40000
4/21/73	2 (1)	12	● 7. **Daniel** *#1 Adult Contemporary hit (2 weeks)*	MCA 40046
8/11/73	12	9	8. Saturday Night's Alright For Fighting	MCA 40105
11/3/73	2 (3)	14	▲ 9. **Goodbye Yellow Brick Road**	MCA 40148
3/2/74	1 (1)	16	▲ 10. **Bennie And The Jets**	MCA 40198
7/6/74	2 (2)	9	● 11. **Don't Let The Sun Go Down On Me** *Carl Wilson and Bruce Johnston of The Beach Boys and Toni Tennille of Captain & Tennille (backing vocals); also see #49 below*	MCA 40259
9/21/74	4	9	● 12. **The Bitch Is Back** *Dusty Springfield (backing vocal)*	MCA 40297
12/7/74+	1 (2)	10	● 13. **Lucy In The Sky With Diamonds** *with the Reggae guitars of Dr. Winston O'Boogie (John Lennon); song introduced by The Beatles on the group's 1967 album Sgt. Pepper's Lonely Hearts Club Band*	MCA 40344
3/15/75	1 (2)	17	▲ 14. Philadelphia Freedom **THE ELTON JOHN BAND** *tribute to tennis star Billie Jean King and her team, the Philadelphia Freedoms*	MCA 40364
7/12/75	4	10	● 15. **Someone Saved My Life Tonight**	MCA 40421
10/18/75	1 (3)	12	▲ 16. **Island Girl**	MCA 40461
1/31/76	14	5	17. Grow Some Funk Of Your Own/	
		5	18. I Feel Like A Bullet (In The Gun Of Robert Ford) *Ford: the man who shot the outlaw Jesse James*	MCA 40505
7/17/76	1 (4)	15	● 19. **Don't Go Breaking My Heart** **ELTON JOHN and KIKI DEE** *#1 Adult Contemporary hit (1 week)*	Rocket 40585
11/20/76	6	11	● 20. **Sorry Seems To Be The Hardest Word** *#1 Adult Contemporary hit (1 week); "live" version is on the B-side of #42 below*	MCA/Rocket 40645
2/26/77	28	3	21. Bite Your Lip (Get up and dance!) *all of above produced by Gus Dudgeon, and written by Elton John (music) and Bernie Taupin (lyrics); John & Taupin reunited as a team in 1982*	MCA/Rocket 40677

DATE	POS	WKS	ARTIST–RECORD TITLE	LABEL & NO.
4/29/78	34	4	22. Ego	MCA 40892
11/18/78	22	7	23. Part-Time Love	MCA 40973
6/23/79	9	14	● 24. **Mama Can't Buy You Love** #1 Adult Contemporary hit (1 week)	MCA 41042
10/27/79	31	4	25. Victim Of Love	MCA 41126
5/10/80	3	17	● 26. **Little Jeannie** #1 Adult Contemporary hit (2 weeks)	MCA 41236
9/20/80	39	2	27. (Sartorial Eloquence) Don't Ya Wanna Play This Game No More?	MCA 41293
5/30/81	21	6	28. Nobody Wins	Geffen 49722
9/5/81	34	3	29. Chloe	Geffen 49788
4/17/82	13	10	30. Empty Garden (Hey Hey Johnny) tribute to John Lennon	Geffen 50049
8/14/82	12	10	31. Blue Eyes #1 Adult Contemporary hit (2 weeks)	Geffen 29954
5/14/83	12	12	32. I'm Still Standing	Geffen 29639
8/20/83	25	8	33. Kiss The Bride	Geffen 29568
11/19/83+	4	15	34. **I Guess That's Why They Call It The Blues** Stevie Wonder (harmonica solo)	Geffen 29460
6/16/84	5	13	35. **Sad Songs (Say So Much)**	Geffen 29292
9/15/84	16	10	36. Who Wears These Shoes? Airplay #10 / Sales #27	Geffen 29189
1/12/85	38	3	37. In Neon	Geffen 29111
11/2/85	20	10	38. Wrap Her Up Airplay #16 / Sales #27; George Michael (backing vocal)	Geffen 28873
11/23/85+	1 (4)	17	● 39. **That's What Friends Are For** **DIONNE & FRIENDS: Elton John, Gladys Knight and** **Stevie Wonder** Sales #1(5) / Airplay #1(3); song introduced by Rod Stewart on the 1982 movie soundtrack of *Night Shift*; #1 R&B hit (3 weeks); #1 Adult Contemporary hit (2 weeks)	Arista 9422
2/8/86	7	11	40. **Nikita** Airplay #6 / Sales #8; George Michael (backing vocal)	Geffen 28800
7/4/87	36	3	41. Flames Of Paradise **JENNIFER RUSH (with Elton John)** Sales #32 / Airplay #34	Epic 07119
11/28/87+	6	12	42. **Candle In The Wind** Sales #6 / Airplay #7; with The Melbourne Symphony Orchestra; tribute to Marilyn Monroe; recorded "live" in Australia; first recorded for Elton's *Goodbye Yellow Brick Road* album in 1973	MCA 53196
7/2/88	2 (1)	13	43. **I Don't Wanna Go On With You Like That** Sales #2 / Airplay #3; #1 Adult Contemporary hit (1 week)	MCA 53345
10/15/88	19	6	44. A Word In Spanish Sales #15 / Airplay #27	MCA 53408
4/29/89	16	7	45. Through The Storm **ARETHA FRANKLIN AND ELTON JOHN** Sales #13 / Airplay #19	Arista 9809
9/16/89	13	9	46. Healing Hands Sales #8 / Airplay #20; #1 Adult Contemporary hit (1 week)	MCA 53692
2/10/90	18	9	47. Sacrifice Sales #14 / Airplay #25	MCA 53750
6/9/90	28	5	48. Club At The End Of The Street Sales #26 / Airplay #34	MCA 79026

DATE	POS	WKS	ARTIST—RECORD TITLE	LABEL & NO.
12/14/91 +	1 (1)	16	● 49. **Don't Let The Sun Go Down On Me** [R] **GEORGE MICHAEL/ELTON JOHN** Sales #4 / Airplay #4; recorded "live" in London, March 1991; #1 Adult Contemporary hit (2 weeks)	Columbia 74086
7/11/92	9	18	50. **The One** Airplay #8 / Sales #17; #1 Adult Contemporary hit (6 weeks)	MCA 54423
11/28/92	23	9	51. The Last Song Airplay #27 / Sales #30	MCA 54510
4/3/93	30	7	52. Simple Life Airplay #26 / Sales #69; #1 Adult Contemporary hit (3 weeks); #28–52 (except #38–42, 45, 49) produced by Chris Thomas	MCA 54581
6/4/94	4	23	● 53. **Can You Feel The Love Tonight** Airplay #2 / Sales #6; Kiki Dee and Rick Astley (backing vocals); #1 Adult Contemporary hit (8 weeks)	Hollywood 64543
9/17/94	18	11	54. Circle Of Life Airplay #15 / Sales #34; above 2 from the Disney animated movie The Lion King	Hollywood 64516
3/18/95	13	16	55. Believe Airplay #14 / Sales #19; #1 Adult Contemporary hit (2 weeks)	Rocket 856014
12/2/95	34	7	56. Blessed Airplay #31 / Sales #46	Rocket 852394
			JOHN, Little Willie	
			Born William Edgar John on 11/15/37 in Cullendale, Arkansas; raised in Detroit. Died of a heart attack in Washington State Prison on 5/26/68 (convicted of manslaughter in 1966). R&B singer. Brother of Mable John (of The Raeletts). Inducted into the Rock and Roll Hall of Fame in 1996.	
7/14/56	24	9	1. Fever Best Seller #24 / Top 100 #27; #1 R&B hit (5 weeks)	King 4935
4/21/58	20	7	2. Talk To Me, Talk To Me Top 100 #20 / Best Seller #22	King 5108
7/25/60	38	1	3. Heartbreak (It's Hurtin' Me)	King 5356
10/10/60	13	10	4. Sleep #1 hit for Fred Waring's Pennsylvanians in 1924	King 5394
			JOHN, Robert	
			Born Robert John Pedrick, Jr., in Brooklyn in 1946. First recorded at age 12 for Big Top Records. In 1963, recorded as lead singer with Bobby & The Consoles.	
1/29/72	3	13	● 1. **The Lion Sleeps Tonight** #14 hit for The Weavers in 1952 (as "Wimoweh," a South African Zulu song)	Atlantic 2846
6/30/79	1 (1)	19	● 2. **Sad Eyes**	EMI America 8015
8/23/80	31	4	3. Hey There Lonely Girl	EMI America 8049
			JOHN & ERNEST	
			Duo of John Free and Ernest Smith.	
5/12/73	31	4	1. Super Fly Meets Shaft [N] break-in song written and produced by Dickie Goodman	Rainy Wed. 201

DATE	POS	WKS	ARTIST–RECORD TITLE	LABEL & NO.
			JOHNNIE & JOE	
			R&B duo from the Bronx: Johnnie Louise Richardson (died 10/25/88 from a stroke) and Joe Rivers. Johnnie was the daughter of the late J&S Records owner Zelma "Zell" Sanders and a touring member of The Jaynetts.	
5/27/57	8	15	1. **Over The Mountain; Across The Sea** Top 100 #8 / Best Seller #9 / Juke Box #17 end; first released on J&S 1664 in 1957	Chess 1654
			JOHNNY AND THE HURRICANES	
			Rock and roll instrumental band formed as the Orbits in Toledo in 1958: leader Johnny Pocisk "Paris" (saxophone), Paul Tesluk (organ), Dave Yorko (guitar), Lionel "Butch" Mattice (bass) and Tony Kaye (drums; replaced in late 1959 by Bo Savich). First recorded for Twirl in 1958. Paris had own Attila label, 1965–70.	
6/1/59	23	6	1. Crossfire [I] first released on Twirl 1001 in 1958	Warwick 502
8/17/59	5	13	2. **Red River Rock** [I] rock version of "Red River Valley"	Warwick 509
11/16/59	25	6	3. Reveille Rock [I] rock version of the Army bugle call "Reveille"	Warwick 513
2/22/60	15	10	4. Beatnik Fly [I] rock version of "Blue Tail Fly"	Warwick 520
			JOHNNY HATES JAZZ	
			Englishmen Clark Datchler (vocals) and Calvin Hayes (son of producer Mickie Most) with American Mike Nocito. Datchler left in late 1988, replaced by producer/ex-Cure member Phil Thornalley.	
4/2/88	2 (3)	13	1. **Shattered Dreams** Airplay #2 / Sales #3; #1 Adult Contemporary hit (1 week)	Virgin 99383
8/13/88	31	5	2. I Don't Want To Be A Hero Airplay #28 / Sales #33	Virgin 99304
			JOHNS, Sammy	
			Born on 2/7/46 in Charlotte, North Carolina. Own band, the Devilles, 1963–73.	
3/1/75	5	12	● 1. **Chevy Van**	GRC 2046
			JOHNSON—see BROTHERS JOHNSON	
			JOHNSON, Betty	
			Born on 3/16/32 in Charlotte, North Carolina. Married to musical conductor Charles Randolph Green. Regular on Don McNeill's daily "Breakfast Club" radio show, and on NBC-TV's "Tonight Show" starring Jack Parr.	
12/15/56+	9	18	1. **I Dreamed** Jockey #9 / Top 100 #12 / Juke Box #15 / Best Seller #22; Lew Douglas (orch.); featured on an episode of NBC-TV's "Modern Romance"	Bally 1020
6/24/57	25	1	2. Little White Lies Jockey #25 / Top 100 #40; #1 hit for Fred Waring's Pennsylvanians in 1930	Bally 1033
2/24/58	17	11	3. The Little Blue Man [N] Jockey #17 / Top 100 #19 / Best Seller #20; voice of the Little Blue Man: Hugh Downs (host of TV's "20/20")	Atlantic 1169
6/30/58	19	1	4. Dream Jockey #19 / Top 100 #58; #1 hit for the Pied Pipers in 1945; Charles Randolph Green (orch., above 3)	Atlantic 1186

DATE	POS	WKS	ARTIST–RECORD TITLE	LABEL & NO.
			JOHNSON, Don	
			Born on 12/15/49 in Flatt Creek, Missouri. Actor/singer. Played Sonny Crockett on TV's "Miami Vice." Starred in several movies. Married twice to actress Melanie Griffith.	
9/6/86	**5**	10	1. **Heartbeat**	Epic 06285
			Sales #3 / Airplay #6	
11/12/88	**25**	5	2. Till I Loved You	Columbia 08062
			BARBRA STREISAND AND DON JOHNSON	
			Sales #22 / Airplay #32; the love theme from the Broadway musical *Goya*	
			JOHNSON, Marv	
			Born on 10/15/38 in Detroit. Died on 5/16/93 after collapsing at a concert in South Carolina. R&B singer/songwriter/pianist. With the Serenaders vocal group, mid-1950s. First recorded for Kudo in 1958. Worked in sales and promotion for Motown in the early '70s. Recognized as a co-creator of the Motown sound with Berry Gordy.	
4/20/59	**30**	6	1. Come To Me	United Art. 160
			released regionally on Tamla 101; Berry Gordy's first release	
11/16/59+	**10**	16	2. **You Got What It Takes**	United Art. 185
3/21/60	**9**	10	3. **I Love The Way You Love**	United Art. 208
10/10/60	**20**	4	4. (You've Got To) Move Two Mountains	United Art. 241
			The Rayber Voices (female backing singers, all of above)	
			JOHNSON, Michael	
			Born on 8/8/44 in Alamosa, Colorado; raised in Denver. Studied classical guitar in 1966 in Spain. In the Chad Mitchell Trio with John Denver in 1968.	
5/27/78	**12**	10	1. Bluer Than Blue	EMI America 8001
			#1 Adult Contemporary hit (3 weeks)	
9/23/78	**32**	5	2. Almost Like Being In Love	EMI America 8004
			introduced by Frank Sinatra in 1947 (from the musical *Brigadoon*)	
9/29/79	**19**	9	3. This Night Won't Last Forever	EMI America 8019
			JOHNSTON, Tom	
			Native of Visalia, California. Lead singer/guitarist of The Doobie Brothers, 1970–78 and since 1988.	
1/12/80	**34**	2	1. Savannah Nights	Warner 49096
			JO JO GUNNE	
			Los Angeles-based rock quartet formed by Jay Ferguson and Mark Andes (former members of Spirit). Named group after the 1958 Chuck Berry hit. Andes was later with Firefall and Heart.	
4/15/72	**27**	6	1. Run Run Run	Asylum 11003
			JOLI, France	
			Born in 1963 in Montreal. French Canadian singer.	
9/29/79	**15**	8	1. Come To Me	Prelude 8001
			JOMANDA	
			Female R&B vocal trio from New Jersey: Joanne Thomas, Cheri Williams and Renee Washington.	
8/31/91	**40**	1	1. Got A Love For You	Big Beat 5031
			Airplay #26 / Sales #54	

DATE	POS	WKS	ARTIST–RECORD TITLE	LABEL & NO.
			JON & ROBIN and The In Crowd	
			Jon Abnor and Javonne "Robin" Braga (who married Jimmy Wright of The Five Americans in 1970).	
5/27/67	18	6	1. Do It Again A Little Bit Slower	Abnak 119
			JON B.	
			Jon Buck. Born in Rhode Island and based in Altadena, California.	
5/27/95	10	22	● 1. **Someone To Love**	Yab Yum 77895
			JON B. featuring BABYFACE	
			Sales #9 / Airplay #16; from the movie *Bad Boys* starring Martin Lawrence and Will Smith; remix version is on the B-side of #2 below	
10/14/95	25	10	2. Pretty Girl	Yab Yum 77813
			Sales #27 / Airplay #39	
			JONES, Etta	
			Born on 11/25/28 in Aiken, South Carolina. Jazz singer with Earl Hines's orchestra, 1949–52.	
12/12/60	36	1	1. Don't Go To Strangers	Prestige 180
			written in 1954 and introduced by Al Martino (Capitol 2899)	
			JONES, Howard	
			Born on 2/23/55 in Southampton, England. Pop singer/songwriter/synth wizard.	
2/25/84	27	6	1. New Song	Elektra 69766
6/2/84	33	4	2. What Is Love?	Elektra 69737
4/20/85	5	14	3. **Things Can Only Get Better**	Elektra 69651
			Airplay #4 / Sales #8	
8/3/85	19	8	4. Life In One Day	Elektra 69631
			Airplay #16 / Sales #20	
5/3/86	4	14	5. **No One Is To Blame**	Elektra 69549
			Airplay #2 / Sales #6; Phil Collins (drums, backing vocal); #1 Adult Contemporary hit (1 week)	
11/8/86	17	10	6. You Know I Love You...Don't You?	Elektra 69512
			Airplay #12 / Sales #20	
4/8/89	12	11	7. Everlasting Love	Elektra 69308
			Airplay #10 / Sales #12; #1 Adult Contemporary hit (2 weeks)	
8/12/89	30	4	8. The Prisoner	Elektra 69288
			Airplay #28 / Sales #34	
5/23/92	32	5	9. Lift Me Up	Elektra 64779
			Airplay #26	
			JONES, Jack	
			Born on 1/14/38 in Los Angeles. One of the top adult contemporary singers of the '60s. Son of actress Irene Hervey and actor/singer Allan Jones, who had the #8 pop hit "The Donkey Serenade" the year Jack was born. First recorded for Capitol in 1959. Performed the theme for the "Love Boat" TV series. Once married to actress Jill St. John.	
11/30/63+	14	10	1. Wives And Lovers	Kapp 551
			inspired by the movie starring Janet Leigh	
12/26/64+	30	5	2. Dear Heart	Kapp 635
			title song from the movie starring Glenn Ford	

DATE	POS	WKS	ARTIST–RECORD TITLE	LABEL & NO.
3/20/65	**15**	7	3. The Race Is On #1 Adult Contemporary hit (1 week)	Kapp 651

7/16/66	**35**	4	4. The Impossible Dream (The Quest)
			    from the musical *Man of La Mancha* starring Richard Kiley; #1
			    Adult Contemporary hit (1 week)
				Kapp 755

3/25/67	**39**	2	5. Lady #1 Adult Contemporary hit (4 weeks)	Kapp 800
			JONES, Jimmy	
			Born on 6/2/37 in Birmingham, Alabama. Joined the R&B group Sparks Of Rhythm in New York in 1955. Formed own group, the Savoys (later: Pretenders), in 1956.	
1/18/60	**2 (1)**	14	● 1. **Handy Man**	Cub 9049
5/9/60	**3**	10	● 2. **Good Timin'**	Cub 9067
			JONES, Joe	
			Born on 8/12/26 in New Orleans. Pianist/valet for B.B. King in the early 1950s. First recorded for Capitol in 1954. Produced The Dixie Cups and Alvin Robinson.	
10/10/60	**3**	9	1. **You Talk Too Much** first 3 weeks charted on RIC 972	Roulette 4304
			JONES, Linda	
			Born on 1/14/44 in Newark, New Jersey. Died of diabetes on 3/14/72. R&B singer. First recorded for MGM/Cub as Linda Lane in 1963.	
7/22/67	**21**	7	1. Hypnotized	Loma 2070
			JONES, Oran "Juice"	
			Born in Houston in 1959; raised in Harlem. Soul balladeer.	
10/11/86	**9**	9	● 1. **The Rain** Sales #8 / Airplay #10; #1 R&B hit (2 weeks)	Def Jam 06209
			JONES, Quincy	
			Born Quincy Delight Jones, Jr., on 3/14/33 in Chicago; raised in Seattle. Composer/producer/conductor/arranger. Began as a jazz trumpeter with Lionel Hampton, 1950–53. Music director for Mercury Records in 1961, then vice president in 1964. Wrote scores for many movies, 1965–73. Scored TV series "Roots" in 1977. Arranger/producer for hundreds of successful singers and orchestras. Produced Michael Jackson's mega-albums *Off The Wall, Thriller* and *Bad*. Established own Qwest label in 1981. Line producer for the movie *The Color Purple*. Married to actress Peggy Lipton (TV's "Mod Squad"), 1974–89. Most nominated artist in Grammy history with 76 nominations and 25 wins. Won the Grammy's Trustees Award in 1989. Won Grammy's Living Legends Award in 1990. His biographical movie *Listen Up: The Lives Of Quincy Jones* was released in 1990.	
7/22/78	**21**	7	1. Stuff Like That Ashford & Simpson and Chaka Khan (vocals); #1 R&B hit (1 week)	A&M 2043
5/9/81	**28**	5	2. Ai No Corrida (I-No-Ko-ree-da) Dune (vocals)	A&M 2309
9/19/81	**17**	10	3. Just Once **QUINCY JONES Featuring JAMES INGRAM**	A&M 2357
2/13/82	**14**	11	4. One Hundred Ways **QUINCY JONES Featuring JAMES INGRAM**	A&M 2387

DATE	POS	WKS	ARTIST—RECORD TITLE	LABEL & NO.
12/16/89+	18	8	5. I'll Be Good To You **QUINCY JONES Featuring Ray Charles and Chaka Khan** Sales #13 / Airplay #26; #1 R&B hit (2 weeks)	Qwest 22697
4/7/90	31	4	● 6. The Secret Garden (Sweet Seduction Suite) **QUINCY JONES/Al B. Sure!/James Ingram/El DeBarge/Barry White** Sales #20; #1 R&B hit (1 week)	Qwest 19992

JONES, Rickie Lee

Born on 11/8/54 in Chicago. Pop jazz-styled singer/songwriter. Moved to Los Angeles in 1977. Won the 1979 Best New Artist Grammy Award.

DATE	POS	WKS	ARTIST—RECORD TITLE	LABEL & NO.
5/12/79	4	12	1. **Chuck E.'s In Love** Chuck E. is Chuck E. Weiss, a friend that Jones met in L.A.	Warner 8825
9/1/79	40	1	2. Young Blood	Warner 49018

JONES, Shirley—see PARTRIDGE FAMILY, The

JONES, Tom

Born Thomas Jones Woodward on 6/7/40 in Pontypridd, South Wales. Worked local clubs as Tommy Scott; formed own trio The Senators in 1963. Began solo career in London in 1964. Won the 1965 Best New Artist Grammy Award. Host of own TV musical variety series, 1969–71.

DATE	POS	WKS	ARTIST—RECORD TITLE	LABEL & NO.
5/1/65	10	9	1. **It's Not Unusual**	Parrot 9737
7/3/65	3	10	2. **What's New Pussycat?** title song from the movie starring Peter Sellers and Woody Allen	Parrot 9765
9/18/65	27	5	3. With These Hands #7 hit for Eddie Fisher in 1953	Parrot 9787
1/1/66	25	6	4. Thunderball title song from the James Bond movie starring Sean Connery	Parrot 9801
1/21/67	11	7	5. Green, Green Grass Of Home	Parrot 40009
4/1/67	27	4	6. Detroit City	Parrot 40012
4/13/68	15	11	7. Delilah	Parrot 40025
10/5/68	35	2	8. Help Yourself	Parrot 40029
6/7/69	13	9	9. Love Me Tonight	Parrot 40038
8/9/69	6	14	● 10. **I'll Never Fall In Love Again**　　　[R] originally charted in 1967 at #49; same melody as Sammy Kaye's #11 1950 hit "Wanderin'"; #1 Adult Contemporary hit (1 week)	Parrot 40018
1/3/70	5	10	● 11. **Without Love (There Is Nothing)** #1 Adult Contemporary hit (1 week)	Parrot 40045
5/9/70	13	7	12. Daughter Of Darkness #1 Adult Contemporary hit (1 week)	Parrot 40048
8/29/70	14	7	13. I (Who Have Nothing)	Parrot 40051
11/28/70	25	7	14. Can't Stop Loving You all of above produced by Peter Sullivan	Parrot 40056
2/20/71	2 (1)	12	● 15. **She's A Lady** written by Paul Anka	Parrot 40058
6/12/71	26	6	16. Puppet Man/ co-written by Neil Sedaka	
7/3/71	38	3	17. Resurrection Shuffle	Parrot 40064
2/12/77	15	10	18. Say You'll Stay Until Tomorrow #1 Country hit (1 week); #15-18 produced by Gordon Mills	Epic 50308
12/24/88+	31	6	19. Kiss **THE ART OF NOISE Featuring Tom Jones** Sales #23 / Airplay #35	China 871038

DATE	POS	WKS	ARTIST–RECORD TITLE	LABEL & NO.
			JONES GIRLS, The	
			Detroit soul sister trio: Shirley, Brenda and Valorie Jones. Backup singers for Lou Rawls, Teddy Pendergrass and Aretha Franklin. With Diana Ross from 1975–78. Sang with Le Pamplemousse.	
8/18/79	**38**	1	● 1. You Gonna Make Me Love Somebody Else	Phil. Int. 3680
			JOPLIN, Janis	
			Born on 1/19/43 in Port Arthur, Texas. Died of a heroin overdose in Hollywood on 10/4/70. White blues-rock singer. Nicknamed "Pearl." To San Francisco in 1966, joined Big Brother & The Holding Company. Left band to go solo in 1968. The Bette Midler movie *The Rose* was inspired by Joplin's life. Inducted into the Rock and Roll Hall of Fame in 1995.	
2/20/71	**1** (2)	12	1. **Me And Bobby McGee**	Columbia 45314
			first popularized by Roger Miller in 1969 (#12 Country hit)	
			JORDAN, Jeremy	
			Born Don Henson on 9/19/73 in Hammond, Indiana; raised in Calumet City, Illinois. Relative of Tobin Mathews.	
2/20/93	**14**	12	1. The Right Kind Of Love	Giant 18718
			Airplay #11 / Sales #20; co-written and co-produced by Robbie Nevil; from the album *Beverly Hills 90210 (The Soundtrack)*	
6/5/93	**28**	6	2. Wannagirl	Giant 18548
			Airplay #20	
			JORDAN, Montell	
			R&B singer from Los Angeles. Stands 6'8" tall.	
3/11/95	**1** (7)	24	▲ 1. **This Is How We Do It**	PMP/RAL 851468
			Sales #1(8) / Airplay #5; samples "Children's Story" by Slick Rick; #1 R&B hit (7 weeks)	
8/19/95	**21**	6	● 2. Somethin' 4 Da Honeyz	PMP/RAL 856962
			Sales #12 / Airplay #63; contains a replayed sample from "Summer Madness" by Kool & The Gang	
			JOURNEY	
			Rock group formed in San Francisco in 1973. Consisted of Neal Schon, George Tickner (guitars), Gregg Rolie (keyboards, vocals), Ross Valory (bass) and Aynsley Dunbar (John Mayall, Mothers Of Invention; drums). Schon and Rolie had been in Santana. Tickner left in 1975. Steve Perry (lead vocals) added by 1978. In 1979, Steve Smith replaced Dunbar, who later joined Jefferson Starship, then Whitesnake. Jonathan Cain (ex-keyboardist of The Babys) added in 1981, replacing Rolie. In 1986 group pared down to a three-man core: Perry, Schon and Cain. The latter two hooked up with Bad English in 1989. Smith, Valory and Rolie joined The Storm in 1991. Schon with Hardline in 1992.	
8/25/79	**16**	12	1. Lovin', Touchin', Squeezin'	Columbia 11036
3/29/80	**23**	6	2. Any Way You Want It	Columbia 11213
7/5/80	**32**	4	3. Walks Like A Lady	Columbia 11275
4/4/81	**34**	4	4. The Party's Over (Hopelessly In Love)	Columbia 60505
8/1/81	**4**	14	5. **Who's Crying Now**	Columbia 02241
11/7/81	**9**	13	6. **Don't Stop Believin'**	Columbia 02567
1/23/82	**2** (6)	14	7. **Open Arms**	Columbia 02687
6/12/82	**19**	9	8. Still They Ride	Columbia 02883
			above 4 from the album *Escape*	
2/5/83	**8**	16	9. **Separate Ways (Worlds Apart)**	Columbia 03513

Limahl's 1985 Top 20 hit "The Never Ending Story" bore an ironic title; the former Kajagoogoo singer, a teen idol in his Brit homeland, never had a Top 40 hit again.

Lisa Lisa And Cult Jam's second and last No. 1 hit "Lost In Emotion" was a highlight of the group's Top 10 Columbia album *Spanish Fly*. Following diminishing success, the singer signed a solo deal with EMI Records in the mid-'90s.

Kenny Loggins's chart transformation from '70s album rocker to '80s pop soundtrack king was typified by "Meet Me Half Way," from the Sylvester Stallone film *Over The Top*. The track, which peaked at No. 11, was Loggins' second-to-last single to attain Top 40 status.

Los Lobos' remake of Richie Valens's classic '50s hit "La Bamba," featured in Taylor Hackford's 1987 film of the same name, sat at No. 1 for three weeks—considerably beating out the original, which peaked at No. 22 in 1959.

The Lovin' Spoonful's bouncy music of the '60s included two Top 10 hits—"Do You Believe In Magic" and "Did You Ever Have To Make Up Your Mind?"—that resurfaced in the '90s in TV commercials for, respectively, the McDonalds and Dennys restaurant chains.

L.T.D. —short for Love, Togetherness and Devotion—had two major claims to fame: a Top 5 single via 1977's "(Every Time I Turn Around) Back In Love Again," and a lead singer (and later solo star) named Jeffrey Osborne.

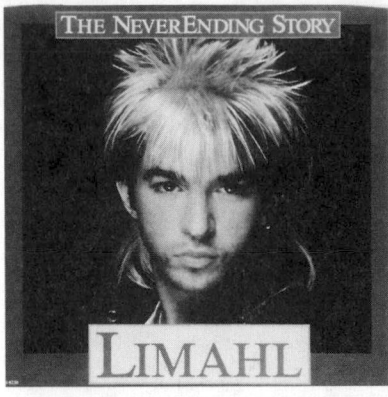

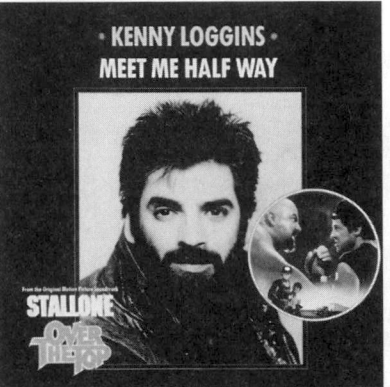

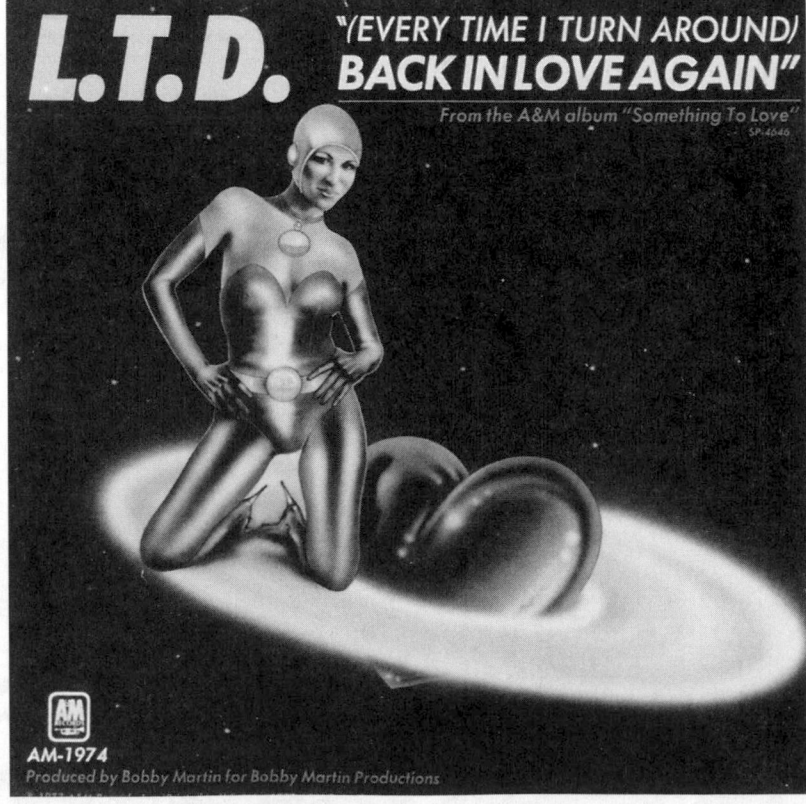

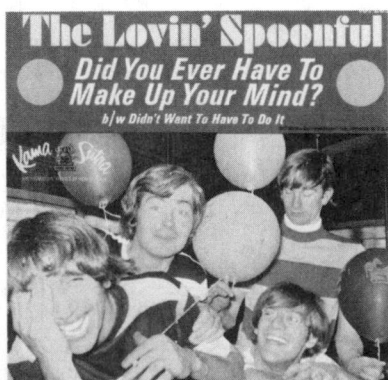

Gloria Lynne's "Be Anything (But Be Mine)" spent a grand total of four weeks on the charts in 1964, peaking at No. 88. Two weeks after it dropped off, Connie Francis's version entered at No. 84 and soon reached No. 25.

Mad Cobra's unique blend of reggae and rap struck a powerful chord among urban audiences of the early '90s. The Jamaican-born Cobra—real name Ewart Everton Brown—had a No. 13 hit with his unique single "Flex."

Madonna's "Rain" came from her controversial 1992 album *Erotica*, which came in two versions, stickered and "clean," and was separately accompanied by a revealing (and bestselling) picture book of the same name.

The Mamas And The Papas—much to the chagrin of copy editors the world over—initially used errant apostrophes in early spellings of their name. Not that it hampered the success of the No. 4 hit "California Dreamin'" in 1966.

Henry Mancini's "Theme From The Great Impostor" spent its sole week on the chart at No. 90 in 1961; six months later, his "Moon River" would zoom to No. 11 and spend 16 weeks in the Top 40. RCA released a much-praised Mancini boxed set in 1995.

Barry Manilow's long streak of Top 40 hits had ended well before the release of his *Swing Street* album in 1987. Indeed, "Hey Mambo," which paired the tunesmith with Kid Creole & The Coconuts, spent its brief chartlife at a peak position of No. 90.

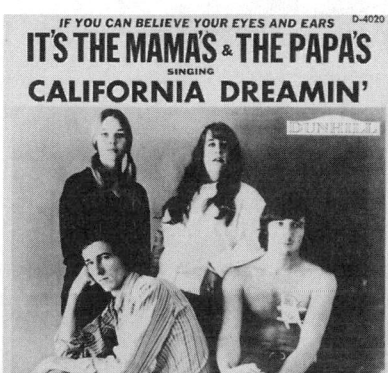

DATE	POS	WKS	ARTIST–RECORD TITLE	LABEL & NO.
4/30/83	12	11	10. Faithfully	Columbia 03840
7/23/83	23	8	11. After The Fall	Columbia 04004
10/22/83	23	7	12. Send Her My Love *above 4 from the album* Frontiers	Columbia 04151
2/2/85	9	11	13. **Only The Young** *Airplay #6 / Sales #20; from the movie* Vision Quest *starring Matthew Modine; also released as the B-side of #14 below; #5–13 produced by Mike Stone*	Geffen 29090
4/19/86	9	10	14. **Be Good To Yourself** *Sales #7 / Airplay #10*	Columbia 05869
7/12/86	17	7	15. Suzanne *Sales #16 / Airplay #19*	Columbia 06134
9/20/86	17	8	16. Girl Can't Help It *Sales #17 / Airplay #17*	Columbia 06302
1/24/87	14	9	17. I'll Be Alright Without You *Airplay #11 / Sales #12; above 4 from the album* Raised On Radio	Columbia 06301
			JUMP 'N THE SADDLE *Chicago-based band. Peter Quinn, lead singer.*	
12/24/83+	15	7	1. The Curly Shuffle　　　　　　　　　　[N] *a Three Stooges parody; first released on Acme 416 in 1983*	Atlantic 89718
			JUNIOR *Full name: Junior Giscombe. R&B-funk singer/songwriter from England.*	
4/10/82	30	3	1. Mama Used To Say	Mercury 76132
			JUNIOR M.A.F.I.A. *Gathering of four rap acts: Klepto, Little Kim, Snakes (Trife & Larceny) and The Sixes (Little Caesar, Chico & Nino Brown). Proteges of The Notorious B.I.G. M.A.F.I.A.: Masters At Finding Intelligent Attitudes.*	
7/29/95	13	11	● 1. Player's Anthem *Sales #7 / Airplay #47; samples "Lodi Dodi" by Doug E. Fresh*	Undeas/Big Beat 98149
			JUSTIS, Bill *Born on 10/14/26 in Birmingham, Alabama. Died on 7/15/82 in Nashville. Session saxophonist/arranger/producer. Led house band for Sun Records.*	
11/18/57	2 (1)	14	● 1. **Raunchy**　　　　　　　　　　　　[I] *Best Seller #2 / Top 100 #3 / Jockey #5; Bill Justis (sax); Sid Manker (guitar); #1 R&B hit (1 week)*	Phillips 3519
			JUST US *Consists of New York City producers Chip Taylor and Al Gorgoni.*	
5/7/66	34	2	1. I Can't Grow Peaches On A Cherry Tree *first released on Minuteman 203 in 1966*	Colpix 803

DATE	POS	WKS	ARTIST–RECORD TITLE	LABEL & NO.

K

KADISON, Joshua

Born on 2/8/65 in Los Angeles. Singer/songwriter/pianist.

DATE	POS	WKS	ARTIST–RECORD TITLE	LABEL & NO.
12/25/93+	26	8	1. Jessie Airplay #21 / Sales #30; produced by Peter Van Hooke (Mike + The Mechanics) and Rod Argent (Zombies/Argent)	SBK 50429
5/14/94	19	15	2. Beautiful In My Eyes Airplay #22 / Sales #26	SBK 58099

KAEMPFERT, Bert

Born on 10/16/23 in Hamburg, Germany. Died on 6/21/80 in Switzerland. Multi-instrumentalist/bandleader/producer/arranger for Polydor Records in Germany. Composed "Strangers In The Night" and "Spanish Eyes" among others. Produced first Beatles recording session.

DATE	POS	WKS	ARTIST–RECORD TITLE	LABEL & NO.
11/21/60+	1 (3)	15	● 1. **Wonderland By Night** [I]	Decca 31141
4/10/61	31	4	2. Tenderly [I] #17 hit for Rosemary Clooney in 1952; Charly Tabor (trumpet, above 2)	Decca 31236
2/13/65	11	10	3. Red Roses For A Blue Lady [I] #3 hit for Vaughn Monroe in 1949	Decca 31722
5/29/65	33	3	4. Three O'Clock In The Morning [I] there were 6 Top 10 versions of this tune from 1921 to 1930; Fred Moch (trumpet, above 2)	Decca 31778

KAJAGOOGOO

Pop-synth quintet formed in London in 1980: Chris "Limahl" Hamill (vocals; left in late 1983), Steve Askew (guitar), Stuart Neale (keyboards), Nick Beggs (bass) and Jez Strode (drums).

DATE	POS	WKS	ARTIST–RECORD TITLE	LABEL & NO.
5/21/83	5	12	1. **Too Shy**	EMI America 8161

KALIN TWINS

Herbert and Harold Kalin, born on 2/16/34 in Port Jervis, New York.

DATE	POS	WKS	ARTIST–RECORD TITLE	LABEL & NO.
6/30/58	5	13	● 1. **When** Hot 100 #5 / Best Seller #7 / Jockey #8; #1 R&B hit (1 week)	Decca 30642
10/20/58	12	9	2. Forget Me Not	Decca 30745

KALLEN, Kitty

Born on 5/25/22 in Philadelphia. Big band singer with Jack Teagarden, Jimmy Dorsey, Harry James and Artie Shaw.

DATE	POS	WKS	ARTIST–RECORD TITLE	LABEL & NO.
2/11/56	39	1	1. Go On With The Wedding **KITTY KALLEN and GEORGIE SHAW** Jack Pleis (orch.)	Decca 29776
11/9/59	34	3	2. If I Give My Heart To You Milton De Lugg (orch.); there were 3 Top 10 versions of this tune in 1954	Columbia 41473
1/12/63	18	6	3. My Coloring Book Ray Ellis (orch.)	RCA 8124

DATE	POS	WKS	ARTIST–RECORD TITLE	LABEL & NO.
			KAMOZE, Ini	
			Male dancehall reggae singer/author/playwright from Kingston, Jamaica. First name pronounced: I-knee. Name means "mountain of the true God."	
10/15/94	**1** (2)	23	● 1. **Here Comes The Hotstepper** Sales #1(8) / Airplay #3; incorporates the 60's song "Land Of 1000 Dances"; originally recorded in early 1992; later included in the movie *Ready To Wear (Pret-A-Porter)* starring Julia Roberts	Columbia 77614
			KANE, Big Daddy	
			Antonio M. Hardy from Brooklyn, New York. Rap lyricist for Cold Chillin' Records. Wrote songs for Roxanne Shante and Biz Markie. Toured as Shante's DJ in 1985. Kane is an acronym for King Asiatic Nobody's Equal. Appeared in the movies *The Meteor Man* and *Posse*.	
9/4/93	**31**	8	1. Very Special Sales #30 / Airplay #31; Spinderella, Laree Williams and Karen Anderson (vocals and rap)	Cold Chillin' 18437
			KANE GANG, The	
			English soul-styled pop trio: vocalists Martin Brammer and Paul Woods with guitarist David Brewis. Band's name derived from the movie *Citizen Kane*.	
12/19/87	**36**	3	1. Motortown Sales #32 / Airplay #40	Capitol 44062
			KANSAS	
			Progressive-rock group formed in Topeka in 1970. Consisted of Steve Walsh (lead vocals, keyboards), Kerry Livgren (guitar, keyboards), Rich Williams (guitar), Robby Steinhardt (violin), Dave Hope (bass) and Phil Ehart (drums). Walsh left in 1981 and was replaced by John Elefante (later a prolific Christian rock producer). Livgren became a popular Contemporary Christian artist in the '80s. Revised lineup in 1986: Walsh, Ehart, Williams, Steve Morse (guitarist from The Dregs) and Billy Greer (bass).	
2/5/77	**11**	13	● 1. Carry On Wayward Son	Kirshner 4267
12/17/77+	**28**	6	2. Point Of Know Return	Kirshner 4273
2/18/78	**6**	15	● 3. **Dust In The Wind**	Kirshner 4274
6/23/79	**23**	8	4. People Of The South Wind	Kirshner 4284
11/8/80	**40**	1	5. Hold On	Kirshner 4291
5/29/82	**17**	9	6. Play The Game Tonight	Kirshner 02903
11/29/86+	**19**	10	7. All I Wanted Sales #18 / Airplay #21	MCA 52958
			KASENETZ-KATZ SINGING ORCHESTRAL CIRCUS	
			Bubblegum rock group assembled by producers Jerry Kasenetz and Jeff Katz. Features members from The 1910 Fruitgum Co./The Ohio Express/The Music Explosion.	
11/9/68	**25**	6	1. Quick Joey Small (Run Joey Run) Joey Levine (lead singer; Ohio Express, Reunion)	Buddah 64
			KATRINA And The WAVES	
			Pop-rock quartet formed in London in 1981: Kansas-born Katrina Leskanich (vocals), Kimberley Rew (guitar; ex-Soft Boys), Vince de la Cruz (bass) and Alex Cooper (drums).	
4/20/85	**9**	13	1. **Walking On Sunshine** Sales #4 / Airplay #10	Capitol 5466

DATE	POS	WKS	ARTIST–RECORD TITLE	LABEL & NO.
9/7/85	37	2	2. Do You Want Crying	Capitol 5450
8/19/89	16	6	3. That's The Way Sales #14 / Airplay #26	SBK 07303

KAYE, Sammy

Born on 3/13/10 in Rocky River, Ohio. Died on 6/2/87 of cancer. Durable leader of popular "sweet" dance band with the slogan "Swing and Sway with Sammy Kaye." Also played clarinet and alto sax. Charted over 100 songs from 1937 to 1953.

DATE	POS	WKS	ARTIST–RECORD TITLE	LABEL & NO.
5/2/64	36	2	1. Charade [I] title song from the movie starring Gary Cooper and Audrey Hepburn	Decca 31589

KC And The SUNSHINE BAND

Disco-R&B band formed in Florida in 1973 by lead singer/keyboardist Harry "KC" Casey (born 1/31/51, Hialeah, Florida) and bassist Richard Finch (born 1/25/54, Indianapolis). Interracial band contained from seven to 11 members.

DATE	POS	WKS	ARTIST–RECORD TITLE	LABEL & NO.
8/2/75	1 (1)	9	1. **Get Down Tonight** #1 R&B hit (1 week)	T.K. 1009
11/1/75	1 (2)	13	2. **That's The Way (I Like It)** #1 R&B hit (1 week)	T.K. 1015
7/31/76	1 (1)	16	3. **(Shake, Shake, Shake) Shake Your Booty** #1 R&B hit (4 weeks)	T.K. 1019
1/29/77	37	2	4. I Like To Do It	T.K. 1020
4/2/77	1 (1)	16	5. **I'm Your Boogie Man**	T.K. 1022
8/13/77	2 (3)	14	6. **Keep It Comin' Love** #1 R&B hit (1 week); above 4 from the album *Part 3*	T.K. 1023
3/25/78	35	3	7. Boogie Shoes originally released as the B-side of #3 above; re-released due to inclusion on the *Saturday Night Fever* soundtrack	T.K. 1025
6/24/78	35	2	8. It's The Same Old Song	T.K. 1028
9/29/79+	1 (1)	18	9. **Please Don't Go**	T.K. 1035
12/22/79+	2 (2)	16	● 10. **Yes, I'm Ready** **TERI DeSARIO with K.C.** #1 Adult Contemporary hit (2 weeks)	Casablanca 2227
2/4/84	18	10	11. Give It Up **KC**	Meca 1001

K-DOE, Ernie

Born Ernest Kador, Jr., on 2/22/36 in New Orleans. R&B singer/songwriter. Recorded with the Blue Diamonds on Savoy in 1954. First solo recording for Specialty in 1955.

DATE	POS	WKS	ARTIST–RECORD TITLE	LABEL & NO.
4/3/61	1 (1)	12	1. **Mother-In-Law** Benny Spellman (bass vocal); #1 R&B hit (5 weeks)	Minit 623

KEEDY

Born Kelly Keedy on 7/26/65 in Abilene, Texas. Female dance singer based in Milwaukee. Married to her songwriting partner Greg Gerard, leader of the group Gerard.

DATE	POS	WKS	ARTIST–RECORD TITLE	LABEL & NO.
4/6/91	15	8	1. Save Some Love Sales #13 / Airplay #15	Arista 2153

DATE	POS	WKS	ARTIST–RECORD TITLE	LABEL & NO.
			KEITH	
			Born James Barry Keefer on 5/7/49 in Philadelphia. First recorded as Keith & The Admirations on Columbia in 1965.	
11/12/66	39	1	1. Ain't Gonna Lie	Mercury 72596
1/7/67	7	9	2. **98.6**	Mercury 72639
			The Tokens (backing vocals, above 2)	
4/8/67	37	2	3. Tell Me To My Face	Mercury 72652
			written by The Hollies	
			KEITH, Lisa	
			Prominent singer/songwriter from Minneapolis. Vocalist on Herb Alpert's "Keep Your Eye On Me," "Diamonds" and "Making Love In The Rain."	
10/30/93	36	3	1. Better Than You	Perspective 7430
			Airplay #33	
			KELLER, Jerry	
			Born on 6/20/37 in Fort Smith, Arkansas. To Tulsa, Oklahoma, at age seven.	
7/20/59	14	8	1. Here Comes Summer	Kapp 277
			KELLY, Grace—see CROSBY, Bing	
			KELLY, Monty, And His Orchestra	
			Born on 6/8/10 in Modesto, California. Died on 3/15/71. Conductor/arranger. Trumpeter with Paul Whiteman in the early 1940s.	
4/4/60	30	3	1. Summer Set [I]	Carlton 527
			KELLY, R., and Public Announcement	
			Robert Kelly is a singer/multi-instrumentalist from Chicago. Public Announcement is his assembly of backing dancers and singers. Married singer Aaliyah on 8/31/94.	
7/18/92	39	1	1. Honey Love	Jive 42031
			Sales #30 / Airplay #42; #1 R&B hit (2 weeks)	
4/24/93	31	7	2. Dedicated	Jive 42115
			Airplay #18 / Sales #55	
			R. KELLY:	
11/13/93	20	10	● 3. Sex Me (Parts I & II)	Jive 42161
			Sales #9 / Airplay #55	
2/19/94	1 (4)	23	▲ 4. **Bump N' Grind**	Jive 42207
			Sales #1(10) / Airplay #7; #1 R&B hit (12 weeks)	
5/28/94	13	15	● 5. Your Body's Callin'	Jive 42220
			Sales #6 / Airplay #17	
11/18/95	4	11	● 6. **You Remind Me Of Something**	Jive 42344
			Sales #2 / Airplay #47; #1 R&B hit (1 week)	
			KEMP, Johnny	
			Singer/dancer/actor/songwriter. Began performing in nightclubs in his native Nassau, Bahamas, at the age of 13. Moved to Harlem in 1979.	
6/25/88	10	11	● 1. **Just Got Paid**	Columbia 07744
			Sales #9 / Airplay #12; #1 R&B hit (2 weeks)	

DATE	POS	WKS	ARTIST–RECORD TITLE	LABEL & NO.
4/15/89	**36**	3	2. Birthday Suit Airplay #33 / Sales #36; from the movie *Sing* starring Lorraine Bracco	Columbia 68569
			KEMP, Tara	
			Singer/songwriter/classically trained pianist from the San Francisco Bay area.	
2/9/91	**3**	15	● 1. **Hold You Tight** Airplay #3 / Sales #7	Giant 19458
6/8/91	**7**	11	2. **Piece Of My Heart** Airplay #9 / Sales #48	Giant 19364
			KENDRICKS, Eddie	
			Born on 12/17/39 in Union Springs, Alabama; raised in Birmingham. Died of lung cancer on 10/5/92. Joined R&B group the Primes in Detroit in the late '50s. Group later evolved into The Temptations; Kendricks sang lead from 1960 to 1971. He later dropped the "s" from his last name.	
9/15/73	**1** (2)	16	1. **Keep On Truckin' (Part 1)** #1 R&B hit (2 weeks)	Tamla 54238
1/26/74	**2** (2)	13	2. **Boogie Down** #1 R&B hit (3 weeks)	Tamla 54243
6/1/74	**28**	4	3. Son Of Sagittarius	Tamla 54247
4/5/75	**18**	10	4. Shoeshine Boy #1 R&B hit (1 week)	Tamla 54257
3/20/76	**36**	3	5. He's A Friend	Tamla 54266
9/14/85	20	7	6. A Nite At The Apollo Live! The Way You Do The Thing You Do/My Girl **DARYL HALL JOHN OATES with David Ruffin & Eddie Kendrick** Sales #21 / Airplay #23; recorded at the reopening of New York's Apollo Theatre	RCA 14178
			KENNEDY, Joyce—see OSBORNE, Jeffrey	
			KENNER, Chris	
			Born on 12/25/29 in Kenner, Louisiana. Died of a heart attack on 1/28/76. R&B singer/songwriter. First recorded for Baton in 1956.	
7/3/61	**2** (3)	10	1. **I Like It Like That, Part 1** first released on Valiant 3229 in 1961	Instant 3229
			KENNY G	
			Born Kenny Gorelick on 7/6/56 in Seattle. Fusion saxophonist. Joined Barry White's Love Unlimited Orchestra at age 17. Graduated Phi Beta Kappa and Magna Cum Laude from the University of Washington with an accounting degree. #1 instrumentalist of the '90s.	
5/16/87	**4**	12	1. **Songbird** [I] Sales #4 / Airplay #5	Arista 9588
9/26/87	**15**	9	2. Don't Make Me Wait For Love Sales #14 / Airplay #18; Lenny Williams (Tower Of Power; vocal)	Arista 9625
11/19/88+	**13**	10	3. Silhouette [I] Sales #10 / Airplay #17	Arista 9751
2/8/92	**12**	12	4. Missing You Now **MICHAEL BOLTON Featuring Kenny G** Airplay #10 / Sales #33; #1 Adult Contemporary hit (3 weeks)	Columbia 74184

DATE	POS	WKS	ARTIST–RECORD TITLE	LABEL & NO.
2/13/93	**18**	13	5. Forever In Love [I] Airplay #13 / Sales #21; #1 Adult Contemporary hit (2 weeks)	Arista 12482
6/19/93	**25**	7	6. By The Time This Night Is Over **KENNY G (with Peabo Bryson)** Airplay #24 / Sales #57; #1 Adult Contemporary hit (2 weeks)	Arista 12565

KENTON, Stan

Born on 2/19/12 in Wichita, Kansas. Died in Los Angeles on 8/25/79. Progressive-jazz bandleader/pianist/composer. Organized his first jazz band in 1941. Third person named to the Jazz Hall of Fame.

DATE	POS	WKS	ARTIST–RECORD TITLE	LABEL & NO.
11/17/62	**32**	4	1. Mama Sang A Song [S]	Capitol 4847

KERMIT—see HENSON, Jim

KHAN, Chaka/Rufus

Khan was born Yvette Marie Stevens on 3/23/53 in Great Lakes, Illinois. Became lead singer of Rufus in 1972. Rufus members Andre Fischer and Kevin Murphy were with The American Breed. Recorded solo and with Rufus since 1978. Sister of vocalists Taka Boom and Mark Stevens (Jamaica Boys). Chaka's daughter Milini is a member of Pretty In Pink.

RUFUS:

DATE	POS	WKS	ARTIST–RECORD TITLE	LABEL & NO.
7/13/74	**3**	12	● 1. **Tell Me Something Good** written by Stevie Wonder	ABC 11427

RUFUS FEATURING CHAKA KHAN:

DATE	POS	WKS	ARTIST–RECORD TITLE	LABEL & NO.
11/2/74	**11**	11	2. You Got The Love #1 R&B hit (1 week)	ABC 12032
3/8/75	**10**	7	3. **Once You Get Started**	ABC 12066
2/14/76	**5**	12	● 4. **Sweet Thing** #1 R&B hit (2 weeks)	ABC 12149
6/12/76	**39**	1	5. Dance Wit Me	ABC 12179
3/12/77	**30**	6	6. At Midnight (My Love Will Lift You Up) #1 R&B hit (2 weeks)	ABC 12239
6/4/77	**32**	3	7. Hollywood	ABC 12269
5/27/78	**38**	3	8. Stay **RUFUS/CHAKA KHAN**	ABC 12349
11/18/78	**21**	8	9. I'm Every Woman **CHAKA KHAN** written by Ashford & Simpson; #1 R&B hit (3 weeks)	Warner 8683
1/19/80	**30**	4	10. Do You Love What You Feel **RUFUS AND CHAKA** #1 R&B hit (3 weeks)	MCA 41131
11/12/83	**22**	8	11. Ain't Nobody **RUFUS AND CHAKA KHAN** #1 R&B hit (1 week)	Warner 29555
9/29/84	**3**	17	● 12. **I Feel For You** **CHAKA KHAN** Sales #2 / Airplay #2; written by Prince; with Grandmaster Melle Mel (rap) and Stevie Wonder (harmonica); #1 R&B hit (3 weeks)	Warner 29195
12/16/89+	**18**	8	13. I'll Be Good To You **QUINCY JONES Featuring Ray Charles and Chaka Khan** Sales #13 / Airplay #26; #1 R&B hit (2 weeks)	Qwest 22697

DATE	POS	WKS	ARTIST–RECORD TITLE	LABEL & NO.
			KIHN, Greg, Band	
			Kihn was born in Baltimore in 1952. Formed band in Berkeley, California, in 1975: Kihn (vocals, guitar), Dave Carpender (guitar), Gary Phillips (keyboards), Steve Wright (bass) and Larry Lynch (drums). Carpender was replaced by Greg Douglass in late 1982. Kihn went solo in late 1984.	
7/11/81	15	13	1. The Breakup Song (They Don't Write 'Em)	Beserkley 47149
3/5/83	2 (1)	14	2. **Jeopardy**	Beserkley 69847
			GREG KIHN:	
3/23/85	30	4	3. Lucky	EMI America 8255
			Sales #25	
			KILGORE, Theola	
			Gospel-blues singer from Shreveport, Louisiana; raised in Oakland.	
5/11/63	21	8	1. The Love Of My Man	Serock 2004
			KIM, Andy	
			Born Andrew Joachim on 12/5/46 in Montreal. His parents were from Lebanon. Pop singer/songwriter. Teamed with Jeff Barry to write "Sugar, Sugar."	
6/1/68	21	8	1. How'd We Ever Get This Way	Steed 707
10/19/68	31	3	2. Shoot'em Up, Baby	Steed 710
6/21/69	9	12	● 3. **Baby, I Love You**	Steed 716
11/8/69	36	1	4. So Good Together	Steed 720
11/28/70	17	8	5. Be My Baby	Steed 729
7/20/74	1 (1)	13	● 6. **Rock Me Gently**	Capitol 3895
11/23/74	28	4	7. Fire, Baby I'm On Fire	Capitol 3962
			KIMBERLY, Adrian	
			Artist is actually a Don Everly (Everly Brothers) production, recorded on Don's own label.	
7/10/61	34	1	1. (The Graduation Song...) Pomp And Circumstance [I]	Calliope 6501
			written in 1902 for the coronation of King Edward VII; song also known as "Land Of Hope And Glory"	
			KING, B.B.	
			Born Riley B. King on 9/16/25 in Itta Bena, Mississippi. The most famous blues singer/guitarist in the world today. Moved to Memphis in 1946. Own radio show on WDIA-Memphis, 1949-50, where he was dubbed "The Beale Street Blues Boy," later shortened to "Blues Boy," then simply "B.B." First recorded for Bullet in 1949. Inducted into the Rock and Roll Hall of Fame in 1987. Won the Lifetime Achievement Grammy award in 1987. Appeared in the movies *Into The Night* (1985) and *Amazon Women On The Moon* (1987).	
6/13/64	34	3	1. Rock Me Baby	Kent 393
5/25/68	39	1	2. Paying The Cost To Be The Boss	BluesWay 61015
1/31/70	15	8	3. The Thrill Is Gone	BluesWay 61032
4/3/71	40	1	4. Ask Me No Questions	ABC 11290
9/22/73	38	2	5. To Know You Is To Love You	ABC 11373
			co-written by Stevie Wonder	
2/9/74	28	6	6. I Like To Live The Love	ABC 11406

DATE	POS	WKS	ARTIST–RECORD TITLE	LABEL & NO.
			KING, Ben E.	
			Born Benjamin Earl Nelson on 9/23/38 in Henderson, North Carolina. To New York in 1947. Worked with The Moonglows for six months while still in high school. Joined the Five Crowns in 1957, who became the new Drifters in 1959. Wrote lyrics to "There Goes My Baby," his first lead performance with The Drifters. Went solo in May 1960.	
1/30/61	10	10	1. **Spanish Harlem**	Atco 6185
5/22/61	4	11	2. **Stand By Me**	Atco 6194
			based on the spiritual "Lord Stand By Me"; #1 R&B hit (4 weeks)	
8/21/61	18	5	3. Amor	Atco 6203
			there were 3 Top 10 versions of this Mexican song in 1944	
5/19/62	11	7	4. Don't Play That Song (You Lied)	Atco 6222
8/3/63	29	6	5. I (Who Have Nothing)	Atco 6267
3/8/75	5	9	6. **Supernatural Thing—Part I**	Atlantic 3241
			#1 R&B hit (1 week)	
11/1/86	9	13	7. **Stand By Me** [R]	Atlantic 89361
			Sales #7 / Airplay #12; featured song from the movie starring Wil Wheaton and River Phoenix; also see #2 above; B-side is The Coasters' "Yakety Yak"	
			KING, Carole	
			Born Carole Klein on 2/9/42 in Brooklyn. Singer/songwriter/pianist. Neil Sedaka wrote his 1959 hit "Oh! Carol" about her. Married lyricist Gerry Goffin in 1958; team wrote four #1 hits: "Will You Love Me Tomorrow," "Go Away Little Girl," "Take Good Care Of My Baby" and "The Loco-Motion." Divorced Goffin in 1968. First solo album in 1970. In 1971, won four Grammys. King and Goffin's daughter, Louise Goffin, began a solo career in 1979. King is one of the most successful female songwriters of the rock era. She and Goffin were inducted as a songwriting team into the Rock and Roll Hall of Fame in 1990.	
9/22/62	22	4	1. It Might As Well Rain Until September	Dimension 2000
			first released on Companion 2000 in 1962	
5/22/71	1 (5)	15	● 2. **It's Too Late/**	
			#1 Adult Contemporary hit (5 weeks)	
		12	3. I Feel The Earth Move	Ode 66015
9/4/71	14	9	4. So Far Away/	
			James Taylor (acoustic guitar)	
		9	5. Smackwater Jack	Ode 66019
			above 4 from the album Tapestry	
2/5/72	9	8	6. **Sweet Seasons**	Ode 66022
12/9/72+	24	7	7. Been To Canaan	Ode 66031
			#1 Adult Contemporary hit (1 week)	
8/11/73	28	5	8. Believe In Humanity	Ode 66035
12/8/73	37	2	9. Corazon [F]	Ode 66039
9/14/74	2 (1)	12	10. **Jazzman**	Ode 66101
1/18/75	9	8	11. **Nightingale**	Ode 66106
			#1 Adult Contemporary hit (1 week)	
3/6/76	28	6	12. Only Love Is Real	Ode 66119
			#1 Adult Contemporary hit (1 week); all of above (except #1) produced by Lou Adler	
8/20/77	30	5	13. Hard Rock Cafe	Capitol 4455
6/14/80	12	10	14. One Fine Day	Capitol 4864

DATE	POS	WKS	ARTIST–RECORD TITLE	LABEL & NO.
6/16/62	6	11	**KING, Claude** Born on 2/5/33 in Shreveport, Louisiana. Country singer/songwriter/ guitarist. Acted in the TV mini-series "The Blue And The Gray" in 1982. ● 1. **Wolverton Mountain** title is an actual place in Arkansas where Clifton Clowers lived (died 8/15/94, age 102); #1 Country hit (9 weeks)	Columbia 42352
5/27/95	13	20	**KING, Diana** Born in Spanish Town, Jamaica. Reggae singer. ● 1. Shy Guy Sales #10 / Airplay #22; from the movie *Bad Boys* starring Martin Lawrence and Will Smith	Work 77678
7/22/78 3/3/79 9/12/81 10/2/82	9 23 40 17	10 8 2 8	**KING, Evelyn "Champagne"** Born on 6/29/60 in the Bronx. To Philadelphia in 1970. Employed as a cleaning woman at Sigma Studios when discovered. ● 1. **Shame** ● 2. I Don't Know If It's Right **EVELYN KING:** 3. I'm In Love #1 R&B hit (1 week) 4. Love Come Down #1 R&B hit (5 weeks)	RCA 11122 RCA 11386 RCA 12243 RCA 13273
4/3/61	29	4	**KING, Freddy** Born Freddie Christian on 9/3/34 in Gilmer, Texas. Died on 12/28/76 of a hepatitis-related heart attack. Blues vocalist/guitarist. Moved to Chicago in 1950. Released albums as Freddie King. 1. Hide Away [I] titled after Mel's Hide Away Lounge in Chicago	Federal 12401
10/23/65	17	7	**KING, Jonathan** Born Kenneth King on 12/6/44 in London. Successful singer/songwriter/ producer. Formed U.K. Records in 1972. Produced Hedgehoppers Anonymous. 1. Everyone's Gone To The Moon	Parrot 9774
2/5/55	30	1	**KING, Peggy** Born on 2/16/30 in Greensburg, Pennsylvania. Regular on TV's "The George Gobel Show," 1954–56. Appeared in the 1957 movie *Zero Hour*. 1. Make Yourself Comfortable Best Seller #30; Percy Faith (orch.)	Columbia 40363
3/3/56	18	2	**KING, Teddi** Born on 9/18/29 in Boston. Died on 11/18/77. Jazz-styled female vocalist. 1. Mr. Wonderful Jockey #18 / Top 100 #32; from the Broadway musical starring Sammy Davis, Jr.	RCA 6392

DATE	POS	WKS	ARTIST—RECORD TITLE	LABEL & NO.
			KING CURTIS	
			Born Curtis Ousley on 2/7/34 in Fort Worth, Texas. Stabbed to death on 8/13/71 in New York City. R&B saxophonist. With Lionel Hampton in 1950. Moved to New York City, did session work. First own recording on Gem in 1953. Played on sessions for Bobby Darin, Aretha Franklin, Brook Benton, Nat King Cole, McGuire Sisters, Andy Williams, The Coasters, The Shirelles and hundreds of others.	
4/7/62	**17**	8	1. Soul Twist [I] **KING CURTIS and THE NOBLE KNIGHTS** #1 R&B hit (2 weeks)	Enjoy 1000
9/23/67	**33**	4	2. Memphis Soul Stew [I]	Atco 6511
10/7/67	**28**	4	3. Ode To Billie Joe [I] **THE KINGPINS**	Atco 6516
			KING HARVEST	
			Six-man, pop-rock group based in Olcott, New York. Formed by Ronny Altback (piano), Rod Novak (sax), Eddie Tulya (guitar) and Doc Robinson (bass).	
1/6/73	**13**	11	1. Dancing In The Moonlight	Perception 515
			KINGPINS, The—see KING CURTIS	
			KINGSMEN, The	
			Group is Bill Haley's band, the Comets (minus Haley).	
9/22/58	**35**	2	1. Week End [I] Best Seller #35 / Hot 100 #84; written by 3 of Bill Haley's Comets: Rudy Pompilli, Frannie Beecher and Billy Williamson	East West 115
			KINGSMEN, The	
			Rock band formed in Portland, Oregon, in 1957. Consisted of Jack Ely (lead singer, guitar), Lynn Easton (drums), Mike Mitchell (guitar), Bob Nordby (bass) and Don Gallucci (keyboards). After release of "Louie Louie" (featuring lead vocal by Ely), Easton took over leadership of band and replaced Ely as lead singer. One of America's premier '60s garage rock bands.	
11/30/63	**2** (6)	13	1. **Louie Louie** originally released on Jerden 712 in 1963	Wand 143
4/4/64	**16**	8	2. Money	Wand 150
1/30/65	**4**	9	3. **The Jolly Green Giant** same tune (different lyrics) as The Olympics' "Big Boy Pete"; lyrics inspired by the "Green Giant" commercials	Wand 172
			KINGSTON TRIO, The	
			Folk trio formed in San Francisco in 1957: Dave Guard (banjo), Bob Shane and Nick Reynolds (guitars). Five of the trio's first six albums hit #1 for a total of 46 weeks. Big break came at San Francisco's Purple Onion, where the group stayed for eight months. Guard left in 1961 to form the Whiskeyhill Singers; John Stewart replaced him. Disbanded in 1968; Shane formed New Kingston Trio. Guard died of lymphoma on 3/22/91 (age 56). Current trio consists of Shane, Reynolds and George Grove (joined group in 1972). Originators of the folk music craze of the 1960s.	
10/6/58	**1** (1)	18	● 1. **Tom Dooley** traditional American folk song written in 1868 as "Tom Dula"	Capitol 4049
3/30/59	**12**	9	2. The Tijuana Jail	Capitol 4167
6/29/59	**15**	6	3. M.T.A. M.T.A.: Metropolitan Transit Authority; protest song written in 1948; melody based on the traditional folk song "The Wreck Of The Old 97"	Capitol 4221

DATE	POS	WKS	ARTIST–RECORD TITLE	LABEL & NO.
9/21/59	20	8	4. A Worried Man *adapted from the traditional American folk song "Worried Man* *Blues" (#14 hit for the Carter Family in 1930)*	Capitol 4271
3/14/60	32	5	5. El Matador	Capitol 4338
8/8/60	37	2	6. Bad Man Blunder [N]	Capitol 4379
3/3/62	21	7	7. Where Have All The Flowers Gone *written by folk legend Pete Seeger*	Capitol 4671
2/23/63	21	5	8. Greenback Dollar	Capitol 4898
4/20/63	8	8	9. **Reverend Mr. Black** *chorus is from the traditional folk song "Lonesome Valley" (#15 hit* *for the Carter Family in 1931)*	Capitol 4951
8/31/63	33	4	10. Desert Pete	Capitol 5005

KINKS, The

Rock group formed in London in 1963 by Ray Davies (lead singer, guitar) and his brother Dave Davies (lead guitar, vocals). Original lineup also included Peter Quaife (bass) and Mike Avory (drums). Numerous personnel changes during the '70s. Ray appeared in the 1986 movie Absolute Beginners. Lineup 1981–95: Ray and Dave Davies, Ian Gibbons (keyboards, left by 1989), Bob Henrit (drums) and Jim Rodford (bass). Henrit and Rodford were members of Argent. Group inducted into the Rock and Roll Hall of Fame in 1990.

DATE	POS	WKS	ARTIST–RECORD TITLE	LABEL & NO.
10/24/64	7	10	1. **You Really Got Me**	Reprise 0306
1/16/65	7	9	2. **All Day And All Of The Night**	Reprise 0334
3/27/65	6	8	3. **Tired Of Waiting For You**	Reprise 0347
7/10/65	23	4	4. Set Me Free	Reprise 0379
9/4/65	34	3	5. Who'll Be The Next In Line	Reprise 0366
1/8/66	13	9	6. A Well Respected Man	Reprise 0420
6/18/66	36	1	7. Dedicated Follower Of Fashion	Reprise 0471
8/27/66	14	7	8. Sunny Afternoon	Reprise 0497
9/12/70	9	12	9. **Lola** *"live" version charted in 1980 at #81*	Reprise 0930
8/19/78	30	5	10. A Rock 'N' Roll Fantasy	Arista 0342
5/28/83	6	12	11. **Come Dancing**	Arista 1054
9/17/83	29	4	12. Don't Forget To Dance	Arista 9075

KISS

Hard-rock band formed in New York City in 1973: Gene Simmons (bass), Paul Stanley (guitar), Ace Frehley (lead guitar) and Peter Criss (drums). Noted for elaborate makeup and highly theatrical stage shows; Simmons was made up as "The Bat Lizard," Stanley as "Star Child," Frehley as "Space Man" and Criss as "The Cat." Criss replaced by Eric Carr in 1981. Frehley replaced by Vinnie Vincent in 1982. Group appeared without makeup for the first time in 1983 on cover of the album Lick It Up. Mark St. John replaced Vincent in 1984. Bruce Kulick, brother of Bob Kulick of Balance, replaced St. John in 1985. Carr died of cancer on 11/25/91 (age 41). Drummer Eric Singer joined in 1991.

DATE	POS	WKS	ARTIST–RECORD TITLE	LABEL & NO.
11/29/75+	12	10	1. Rock And Roll All Nite [R] *"live" version; studio version hit #68 in 1975*	Casablanca 850
4/17/76	31	4	2. Shout It Out Loud *"live" version charted in 1978 at #54*	Casablanca 854
9/25/76	7	13	● 3. **Beth**	Casablanca 863
1/15/77	15	8	4. Hard Luck Woman	Casablanca 873
4/9/77	16	8	5. Calling Dr. Love	Casablanca 880
7/30/77	25	7	6. Christine Sixteen	Casablanca 889

DATE	POS	WKS	ARTIST–RECORD TITLE	LABEL & NO.
4/15/78	39	2	7. Rocket Ride	Casablanca 915
6/16/79	11	11	● 8. I Was Made For Lovin' You	Casablanca 983
2/24/90	8	11	9. **Forever** Sales #5 / Airplay #9	Mercury 876716

KISSOON, Mac And Katie

Brother and sister from Port-of-Spain, Trinidad. Moved to England in the late '50s.

9/4/71	20	9	1. Chirpy Chirpy Cheep Cheep	ABC 11306

KIX

Hard-rock quintet formed in Hagerstown, Maryland, in 1981: Steve Whiteman (vocals), Ronnie Younkins and Brian Forsythe (guitars), Donnie Purnell (bass) and Jimmy Chalfant (drums).

10/21/89	11	13	● 1. Don't Close Your Eyes Sales #8 / Airplay #14	Atlantic 88902

KLF, The

British duo previously known as The Timelords: Bill Drummond (founding member of Big In Japan/former manager of Echo & The Bunnymen and Teardrop Explodes) and Jimmy Cauty (formerly with Zodiac Mindwarp). KLF stands for Kopyright Liberation Front.

7/13/91	5	12	● 1. **3 A.M. Eternal** Sales #5 / Airplay #28	Arista 2230
2/15/92	11	12	2. Justified & Ancient **THE KLF (Featuring Tammy Wynette)** Sales #10 / Airplay #12	Arista 12401

KLYMAXX

Black female band founded by drummer/producer Bernadette Cooper in Los Angeles in 1979. Lead vocals by Lorena Porter Shelby and Joyce "Fenderella" Irby. Pared down to a trio of Shelby, Cheryl Cooley (guitar) and Robbin Grider (keyboards) in 1990.

10/26/85	5	17	1. **I Miss You** Sales #3 / Airplay #6	Constellation 52606
8/2/86	15	8	2. Man Size Love Sales #12 / Airplay #19; from the movie *Running Scared* starring Gregory Hines and Billy Crystal	MCA 52841
6/20/87	18	9	3. I'd Still Say Yes Sales #14 / Airplay #19	Constellation 53028

KNACK, The

Rock group formed in Los Angeles in 1978: Doug Fieger (lead singer, guitar), Berton Averre (lead guitar), Bruce Gary (drums) and Prescott Niles (bass). Disbanded in 1982. Reunited in 1986, except for Gary, who was replaced by drummer Billy Ward. Fieger was a member of the Detroit rock trio Sky.

7/21/79	1 (6)	16	● 1. **My Sharona**	Capitol 4731
9/22/79	11	11	2. Good Girls Don't	Capitol 4771
3/8/80	38	2	3. Baby Talks Dirty	Capitol 4822

DATE	POS	WKS	ARTIST–RECORD TITLE	LABEL & NO.
			KNICKERBOCKERS, The	
			Rock band formed in Bergenfield, New Jersey, in 1964 as the Castle Kings. Lead singer, Buddy Randell, was with The Royal Teens. Member Jimmy Walker replaced Bill Medley, for a time, in The Righteous Brothers. Band named after Knickerbocker Avenue in their hometown.	
1/1/66	20	9	1. Lies	Challenge 59321
			KNIGHT, Frederick	
			Born on 8/15/44 in Alabama. Soul singer/producer.	
5/27/72	27	9	1. I've Been Lonely For So Long	Stax 0117
			KNIGHT, Gladys, & The Pips	
			R&B family group from Atlanta, formed in 1952 when lead singer Gladys was eight years old. Consisted of Gladys (born 5/28/44, Atlanta), her brother Merald "Bubba" Knight and sister Brenda, and cousins William and Eleanor Guest. Named "Pips" for their manager, cousin James "Pip" Woods. First recorded for Brunswick in 1958. Brenda and Eleanor replaced by cousins Edward Patten and Langston George in 1959. Langston left group in 1962 and group has remained a quartet with the same members ever since. Due to legal problems, Gladys could not record with the Pips from 1977 to 1980. Gladys was a cast member of the 1985 TV series "Charlie & Co." Group inducted into the Rock and Roll Hall of Fame in 1996.	
6/5/61	6	10	1. **Every Beat Of My Heart** **PIPS** #1 R&B hit (1 week)	Vee-Jay 386
1/20/62	19	6	2. Letter Full Of Tears	Fury 1054
7/4/64	38	1	3. Giving Up	Maxx 326
8/19/67	39	2	4. Everybody Needs Love	Soul 35034
11/4/67	2 (3)	14	5. **I Heard It Through The Grapevine** #1 R&B hit (6 weeks)	Soul 35039
2/17/68	15	8	6. The End Of Our Road	Soul 35042
7/6/68	40	1	7. It Should Have Been Me	Soul 35045
8/9/69	19	8	8. The Nitty Gritty	Soul 35063
11/15/69	17	10	9. Friendship Train	Soul 35068
4/4/70	25	5	10. You Need Love Like I Do (Don't You) above 7 produced by Norman Whitfield	Soul 35071
12/19/70+	9	12	11. **If I Were Your Woman** #1 R&B hit (1 week)	Soul 35078
6/19/71	17	9	12. I Don't Want To Do Wrong	Soul 35083
1/8/72	27	5	13. Make Me The Woman That You Go Home To	Soul 35091
4/8/72	33	6	14. Help Me Make It Through The Night	Soul 35094
2/17/73	2 (2)	12	15. Neither One Of Us (Wants To Be The First To Say Goodbye) #1 R&B hit (4 weeks)	Soul 35098
6/2/73	19	8	16. Daddy Could Swear, I Declare	Soul 35105
7/7/73	28	7	17. Where Peaceful Waters Flow	Buddah 363
9/15/73	1 (2)	16	● 18. **Midnight Train To Georgia** #1 R&B hit (4 weeks)	Buddah 383
12/8/73+	4	13	● 19. **I've Got To Use My Imagination** #1 R&B hit (1 week)	Buddah 393
3/9/74	3	13	● 20. **Best Thing That Ever Happened To Me** #1 R&B hit (2 weeks); #15, 17, 18, 20 written by Jim Weatherly; above 4 from the album *Imagination*	Buddah 403

DATE	POS	WKS	ARTIST–RECORD TITLE	LABEL & NO.
6/1/74	5	11	● 21. **On And On** written and produced by Curtis Mayfield; from the movie *Claudine* starring Diahann Carroll	Buddah 423
11/16/74	21	9	22. I Feel A Song (In My Heart) #1 R&B hit (2 weeks)	Buddah 433
5/24/75	11	12	23. The Way We Were/Try To Remember	Buddah 463
11/29/75	22	7	24. Part Time Love	Buddah 513
11/23/85+	1 (4)	17	● 25. **That's What Friends Are For** **DIONNE & FRIENDS: Elton John, Gladys Knight and Stevie Wonder** Sales #1(5) / Airplay #1(3); song introduced by Rod Stewart on the 1982 movie soundtrack of *Night Shift*; #1 R&B hit (3 weeks); #1 Adult Contemporary hit (2 weeks)	Arista 9422
1/30/88	13	9	26. Love Overboard Sales #11 / Airplay #20; #1 R&B hit (1 week)	MCA 53210
			KNIGHT, Jean Born on 1/26/43 in New Orleans. Soul songstress.	
6/19/71	2 (2)	13	1. **Mr. Big Stuff** #1 R&B hit (5 weeks)	Stax 0088
			KNIGHT, Robert Born on 4/21/45 in Franklin, Tennessee. Soul singer. Recorded for Dot in 1960.	
10/28/67	13	8	1. Everlasting Love	Rising Sons 705
			KNIGHT, Sonny Born Joseph C. Smith in 1934 in Maywood, Illinois. R&B singer/songwriter/pianist. Wrote book *The Day The Music Died* in 1981 under real name.	
11/24/56	17	9	1. Confidential Juke Box #17 / Best Seller #19 / Top 100 #20; first released on Vita 137 in 1956; Jack Collier (orch.)	Dot 15507
			KNOBLOCK, Fred Born in Jackson, Mississippi. With the rock band Let's Eat in the late 1970s. Member of the country trios Schuyler, Knobloch & Overstreet (SKO) and Schuyler, Knobloch & Bickhardt (SKB).	
7/26/80	18	7	1. Why Not Me also released on Scotti Brothers 600 in 1980; #1 Adult Contemporary hit (2 weeks)	Scotti Br. 518
12/27/80+	28	9	2. Killin' Time **FRED KNOBLOCK AND SUSAN ANTON (Anton is an actress/model)**	Scotti Br. 609
			KNOX, Buddy, with the Rhythm Orchids Born Buddy Wayne Knox on 7/20/33 in Happy, Texas. Formed The Rhythm Orchids at West Texas State University: Knox (guitar), Jimmy Bowen (bass), Don Lanier (guitar) and Dave "Dicky Doo" Alldred (drums). Formed own record label, Triple-D, named after KDDD radio in Dumas, Texas.	
3/2/57	1 (1)	15	● 1. **Party Doll** Best Seller #1 / Top 100 #2 / Juke Box #2 / Jockey #5; originally released on Triple-D 797 in 1956 (B-side "I'm Stickin' With You" by Jimmy Bowen)	Roulette 4002

DATE	POS	WKS	ARTIST–RECORD TITLE	LABEL & NO.
6/3/57	**17**	7	2. Rock Your Little Baby To Sleep **Lieutenant BUDDY KNOX with the Rhythm Orchids** Jockey #17 / Best Seller #23 / Top 100 #23	Roulette 4009
9/9/57	**9**	15	3. **Hula Love** Jockey #9 / Top 100 #12 / Best Seller #13; featured in the movie *Jamboree!* starring Kay Medford	Roulette 4018
8/4/58	**22**	11	4. Somebody Touched Me Hot 100 #22 / Best Seller #32; first recorded in 1954 by Ruth Brown (Atlantic 1044)	Roulette 4082
1/9/61	**25**	4	5. Lovey Dovey **BUDDY KNOX** #2 R&B hit for The Clovers in 1954	Liberty 55290
			KOFFMAN, Moe, Quartette	
			Koffman was born on 12/28/28 in Toronto. Saxophonist with several U.S. big bands, 1950–55.	
2/10/58	**23**	5	1. The Swingin' Shepherd Blues [I] Jockey #23 / Best Seller #36 / Top 100 #36	Jubilee 5311
			KOKOMO	
			Pianist Jimmy Wisner (born 12/8/31, Philadelphia).	
3/6/61	**8**	11	1. **Asia Minor** [I] adapted from the Grieg *Piano Concerto in A minor*	Felsted 8612
			KON KAN	
			Toronto duo: Barry Harris (piano, guitar) and Kevin Wynne (vocals). Became a one-man band when Wynne left in 1989. Name derived from the opposite of Can Con, as in Canadian Content.	
2/4/89	**15**	9	1. I Beg Your Pardon Sales #12 / Airplay #16; includes several lines from Lynn Anderson's "Rose Garden"	Atlantic 88969
			KOOL & THE GANG	
			R&B group formed in Jersey City, New Jersey, in 1964 by bass player Robert "Kool" Bell as the Jazziacs. Session work in New York City, 1964–68. First recorded for De-Lite in 1969. Added lead singer James "J.T." Taylor in 1979. Current lineup consists of brothers Robert and Ronald Bell (sax, keyboards), George Brown (drums), Curtis "Fitz" Williams (keyboards) and Charles Smith (guitar). Taylor left in 1988; replaced by lead singers Gary Brown, Odeen Mays and former Dazz Band lead vocalist Skip Martin. Brown left by 1990.	
10/6/73	**29**	6	1. Funky Stuff	De-Lite 557
1/5/74	**4**	16	● 2. **Jungle Boogie**	De-Lite 559
5/18/74	**6**	11	● 3. **Hollywood Swinging** #1 R&B hit (1 week)	De-Lite 561
10/12/74	**37**	2	4. Higher Plane #1 R&B hit (1 week)	De-Lite 1562
6/28/75	**35**	3	5. Spirit Of The Boogie/ #1 R&B hit (1 week)	
		3	6. Summer Madness [I]	De-Lite 1567
11/10/79+	**8**	14	● 7. **Ladies Night** #1 R&B hit (3 weeks)	De-Lite 801
2/9/80	**5**	13	● 8. **Too Hot** also released as the B-side of "Ladies Night" (on some pressings)	De-Lite 802
11/22/80+	**1 (2)**	21	▲ 9. **Celebration** #1 R&B hit (6 weeks)	De-Lite 807

DATE	POS	WKS	ARTIST–RECORD TITLE	LABEL & NO.
6/27/81	39	2	10. Jones Vs. Jones	De-Lite 813
11/7/81	17	12	11. Take My Heart (You Can Have It If You Want It) *some pressings show title only as: "Take My Heart"; #1 R&B hit (1 week)*	De-Lite 815
4/3/82	10	9	● 12. **Get Down On It**	De-Lite 818
9/11/82	21	7	13. Big Fun	De-Lite 822
12/4/82+	30	7	14. Let's Go Dancin' (Ooh La, La, La) *above 8 produced by Eumir Deodato*	De-Lite 824
12/3/83+	2 (1)	16	● 15. **Joanna** *#1 R&B hit (2 weeks)*	De-Lite 829
3/17/84	13	10	16. Tonight	De-Lite 830
1/5/85	10	13	17. **Misled** *Sales #8 / Airplay #10*	De-Lite 880431
4/20/85	9	11	18. **Fresh** *Sales #6 / Airplay #12; #1 R&B hit (1 week)*	De-Lite 880623
7/27/85	2 (3)	15	● 19. **Cherish** *Sales #1(1) / Airplay #2; #1 Adult Contemporary hit (6 weeks); #1 R&B hit (1 week)*	De-Lite 880869
11/23/85	18	8	20. Emergency *Sales #17 / Airplay #19; above 4 from the album Emergency*	De-Lite 884199
11/22/86+	10	12	21. **Victory** *Sales #6 / Airplay #13*	Mercury 888074
3/14/87	10	10	22. **Stone Love** *Sales #8 / Airplay #16*	Mercury 888292

KORGIS, The

British pop duo: James Warren and Andy Davis (both formerly with Stackridge).

DATE	POS	WKS	ARTIST–RECORD TITLE	LABEL & NO.
11/8/80	18	11	1. Everybody's Got To Learn Sometime	Asylum 47055

KRAFTWERK

Synthesizer band formed in 1970 in Dusseldorf, Germany, by Ralf Hutter and Florian Schneider. Kraftwerk is German for power station.

DATE	POS	WKS	ARTIST–RECORD TITLE	LABEL & NO.
4/12/75	25	5	1. Autobahn　　　　　　　　　　　[I]	Vertigo 203

KRAMER, Billy J., With The Dakotas

Kramer was born William Ashton on 8/19/43 near Liverpool, England. Discovered by The Beatles' manager, Brian Epstein, who teamed him with the group The Dakotas.

DATE	POS	WKS	ARTIST–RECORD TITLE	LABEL & NO.
5/2/64	7	12	1. **Little Children/**	
6/13/64	9	8	2. **Bad To Me** *first released on Liberty 55626 and then Liberty 55667*	Imperial 66027
8/15/64	30	3	3. I'll Keep You Satisfied *first released on Liberty 55643 in 1964*	Imperial 66048
9/19/64	23	5	4. From A Window *above 3 written by John Lennon and Paul McCartney*	Imperial 66051

KRAVITZ, Lenny

Born on 5/26/64 in New York City. Singer/songwriter/multi-instrumentalist. Three-year member of the California Boys Choir. Married to actress Lisa Bonet, 1989–91. Son of actress Roxie Roker (played Helen Willis on TV's "The Jeffersons"; died 12/2/95, age 66).

DATE	POS	WKS	ARTIST–RECORD TITLE	LABEL & NO.
6/22/91	2 (1)	14	1. **It Ain't Over 'Til It's Over** *Airplay #8 / Sales #16*	Virgin 98795

DATE	POS	WKS	ARTIST–RECORD TITLE	LABEL & NO.
			KRIS KROSS	
			Rap duo of Atlanta junior high students: Chris "Mack Daddy" Kelly (born 5/1/78) and Chris "Daddy Mack" Smith (born 1/10/79). Appeared in the movie *Who's The Man?*	
4/11/92	**1** (8)	18	▲² 1. **Jump** Sales #1(9) / Airplay #4	Ruffhouse 74197
6/27/92	**13**	13	● 2. Warm It Up Sales #4 / Airplay #28	Ruffhouse 74376
7/31/93	**19**	10	● 3. Alright **KRIS KROSS featuring Supercat** Sales #9 / Airplay #36; samples "Just A Touch Of Love" by Slave	Ruffhouse 77103
12/16/95+	**12**	15	● 4. Tonite's Tha Night Sales #4 / Airplay #50; Trey Lorenz (backing vocal); contains a portion of "Riding High"	Ruffhouse 78092
			KRISTOFFERSON, Kris	
			Born on 6/22/36 in Brownsville, Texas. Singer/songwriter/actor. Attended England's Oxford University on a Rhodes scholarship. Married to Rita Coolidge, 1973–80. Wrote "Me And Bobby McGee," "For The Good Times" and "Help Me Make It Through The Night." Has starred in many movies since 1972.	
10/2/71	26	6	1. Loving Her Was Easier (Than Anything I'll Ever Do Again)	Monument 8525
7/7/73	**16**	19	● 2. Why Me #1 Country hit (1 week)	Monument 8571
			K7	
			Louis "Kayel" Sharpe, former member of TKA. Rapper from New York City.	
10/16/93	**18**	14	● 1. Come Baby Come Sales #17 / Airplay #30	Tommy Boy 7572
			KUBAN, Bob, And The In-Men	
			Eight-man St. Louis pop-rock band formed by drummer Kuban. Lead singer Walter Scott (real name: Walter Notheis, Jr.), disappeared on 12/27/83; his ex-wife and her husband were charged with Scott's murder after his body was found, three years later, with a gunshot wound to the back.	
2/19/66	**12**	7	1. The Cheater	Musicland 20001
			KUT KLOSE	
			Female vocal trio: Tabitha Duncan, Athena Cage and LaVonn Battle.	
6/10/95	**34**	3	1. I Like Sales #18 / Airplay #60	Keia/Elektra 64486
			K.W.S.	
			Dance trio from Nottingham, England: Chris King, Winnie Williams and "Mystic Meg" St. Joseph.	
8/8/92	**6**	16	● 1. **Please Don't Go** Airplay #4 / Sales #15	Next Plat. 339
			KYPER	
			Born Randall Kyper in Baton Rouge, Louisiana. Rapper.	
8/4/90	**14**	12	● 1. Tic-Tac-Toe Sales #7 / Airplay #31; borrows guitar riffs from "Owner Of A Lonely Heart" by Yes	Atlantic 87910

DATE	POS	WKS	ARTIST–RECORD TITLE	LABEL & NO.

L

LaBELLE, Patti

Born Patricia Holt on 5/24/44 in Philadelphia. Began singing career as leader of the Ordettes, which evolved into The Blue Belles. The quartet, formed in Philadelphia in 1962, included Nona Hendryx, Sarah Dash and Cindy Birdsong. Cindy left in 1967 to join The Supremes. Group continued as a trio. In 1971, the group shortened its name to LaBelle. In 1977, group disbanded and Patti recorded solo. The Blue-Belles were credited on the label as the artists of "I Sold My Heart To The Junkman," a 1962 hit which was actually recorded by The Starlets.

PATTI LABELLE & THE BLUE BELLES:

DATE	POS	WKS	ARTIST–RECORD TITLE	LABEL & NO.
11/2/63	37	3	1. Down The Aisle (Wedding Song)	Newtown 5777
2/8/64	34	1	2. You'll Never Walk Alone first released on Nicetown 5020 in 1963; from the Rodgers & Hammerstein musical *Carousel*	Parkway 896

LABELLE:

DATE	POS	WKS	ARTIST–RECORD TITLE	LABEL & NO.
2/1/75	1 (1)	13	● 3. **Lady Marmalade** #1 R&B hit (1 week)	Epic 50048

PATTI LABELLE:

DATE	POS	WKS	ARTIST–RECORD TITLE	LABEL & NO.
4/6/85	17	9	4. New Attitude Sales #13 / Airplay #24; from the movie *Beverly Hills Cop* starring Eddie Murphy	MCA 52517
4/19/86	1 (3)	15	● 5. **On My Own** **PATTI LaBELLE AND MICHAEL McDONALD** Sales #1(5) / Airplay #1(2); #1 R&B hit (4 weeks)	MCA 52770
8/23/86	29	3	6. Oh, People Sales #26	MCA 52877

LA BOUCHE

Male/female dance duo: Melanie Thornton and Lane McCray.

DATE	POS	WKS	ARTIST–RECORD TITLE	LABEL & NO.
12/16/95+	6	18↑	● 1. **Be My Lover** Sales #6 / Airplay #9	RCA 64446

LADD, Cheryl

Born Cheryl Stoppelmoor on 7/2/51 in Huron, South Dakota. Played Kris Monroe on the TV series "Charlie's Angels." Voice on the cartoon series "Josie & The Pussycats." Married to David Ladd (son of actor Alan Ladd), 1973–79. Married producer/songwriter Brian Russell (Brian & Brenda) in 1981.

DATE	POS	WKS	ARTIST–RECORD TITLE	LABEL & NO.
8/26/78	34	3	1. Think It Over	Capitol 4599

LADY FLASH

Barry Manilow's backup singers: Lorraine Mazzola (lead vocals), Monica Burruss and Debra Byrd. Mazzola was in Reparata & The Delrons, 1966–73.

DATE	POS	WKS	ARTIST–RECORD TITLE	LABEL & NO.
8/14/76	27	6	1. Street Singin' written, produced and arranged by Barry Manilow	RSO 852

DATE	POS	WKS	ARTIST–RECORD TITLE	LABEL & NO.
			L.A. GUNS	
			Hard-rock male band from Hollywood: Philip Lewis (vocals), Tracii Guns and Mick Cripps (guitar), Kelly Nickels (bass), and Steve Riley (drums). Guns was also a member of Contraband in 1991.	
6/16/90	**33**	4	1. The Ballad of Jayne Sales #22	Vertigo 876984
			LAI, Francis	
			French composer/conductor.	
2/27/71	**31**	4	1. Theme From Love Story [I] from the movie *Love Story* starring Ali MacGraw and Ryan O'Neal; Georges Pludermacher (piano solo)	Paramount 0064
			LAID BACK	
			Danish synth-pop duo: Tim Stahl (keyboards) and John Guldberg (guitar). Highly successful in Europe for three years before their U.S. debut.	
4/28/84	**26**	4	1. White Horse	Sire 29346
			LAINE, Frankie	
			Born Frank Paul LoVecchio on 3/30/13 in Chicago. To Los Angeles in the early 1940s. First recorded for Exclusive in 1945. With Johnny Moore's Three Blazers. Signed to the Mercury label in 1947. Dynamic singer whose popularity lasted well into the rock era.	
9/3/55	**17**	3	1. Humming Bird Juke Box #17; Jimmy Carroll (orch.)	Columbia 40526
12/17/55	**19**	10	2. A Woman In Love Best Seller #19 / Top 100 #24; from the movie *Guys And Dolls* starring Marlon Brando; Percy Faith (orch.)	Columbia 40583
12/8/56+	**3**	18	● 3. **Moonlight Gambler** Top 100 #3 / Juke Box #3 / Jockey #4 / Best Seller #5; Ray Conniff (orch.)	Columbia 40780
4/20/57	**10**	8	4. **Love Is A Golden Ring** **FRANKIE LAINE with THE EASY RIDERS** Jockey #10 / Best Seller #22 / Top 100 #23	Columbia 40856
3/4/67	**39**	2	5. I'll Take Care Of Your Cares song first recorded in 1927 by Franklyn Baur (Victor 20504)	ABC 10891
5/6/67	**35**	3	6. Making Memories Peter DeAngelis (orch., above 2)	ABC 10924
3/1/69	**24**	7	7. You Gave Me A Mountain written by Marty Robbins; Jimmy Bowen (orch. and chorus); #1 Adult Contemporary hit (2 weeks)	ABC 11174
			LaMOND, George	
			Born George Garcia on 2/25/67 in Washington, D.C.; raised in the Bronx. With his cousin Joey Kid, formed New York City club band Loose Touch.	
6/23/90	**25**	6	1. Bad Of The Heart Airplay #23 / Sales #25	Columbia 73339
			LANCE, Major	
			Born on 4/4/42 in Chicago. Died on 9/3/94 of heart disease. Soul singer. First recorded for Mercury in 1959. Lived in Britain, 1972–74. Had own Osiris label with Al Jackson of Booker T. & The MG's in 1975. In prison for selling cocaine, 1978–81.	
8/10/63	**8**	10	1. **The Monkey Time**	Okeh 7175

DATE	POS	WKS	ARTIST–RECORD TITLE	LABEL & NO.
11/2/63	13	8	2. Hey Little Girl	Okeh 7181
1/11/64	5	10	3. **Um, Um, Um, Um, Um, Um**	Okeh 7187
4/11/64	20	6	4. The Matador	Okeh 7191
9/19/64	24	5	5. Rhythm	Okeh 7203
4/3/65	40	1	6. Come See	Okeh 7216
			all of above (except #4) written by Curtis Mayfield	

LANE, Mickey Lee

Born Mickey Lee Schreiber in 1945 in Rochester, New York.

11/28/64	38	1	1. Shaggy Dog	Swan 4183

LANG, k.d.

Born Kathryn Dawn Lang on 11/2/61 in Consort, Alberta, Canada.

10/3/92	38	3	1. Constant Craving *Airplay #33 / Sales #65*	Sire 18942

LANSON, Snooky

Born Roy Landman on 3/27/14 in Memphis. Died on 7/2/90. Star of TV's "Your Hit Parade," 1950–57.

12/3/55	20	6	1. It's Almost Tomorrow *Top 100 #20 / Jockey #20 / Juke Box #20*	Dot 15424

LARKS, The

Los Angeles R&B group originally named Don Julian & The Meadowlarks: Don Julian (lead singer), Ted Walters and Charles Morrison.

11/28/64+	7	11	1. **The Jerk**	Money 106

LaROSA, Julius

Born on 1/2/30 in Brooklyn. Regular singer on "Arthur Godfrey And His Friends" TV show until he was fired on the air on 10/19/53. Popular DJ in New York (WNEW) for many years.

7/23/55	13	7	1. Domani (Tomorrow) *Best Seller #13 / Juke Box #13 / Jockey #15*	Cadence 1265
10/8/55	20	5	2. Suddenly There's A Valley *Jockey #20 / Best Seller #22 / Top 100 #29; Archie Bleyer (orch., above 2)*	Cadence 1270
2/18/56	15	7	3. Lipstick And Candy And Rubbersole Shoes *Jockey #15 / Top 100 #21; Joe Reisman (orch.)*	RCA 6416
6/16/58	21	1	4. Torero *Jockey #21; Nick Perito (orch. and chorus)*	RCA 7227

LARSEN-FEITEN BAND

Top session musicians Neil Larsen (keyboards) and Buzz Feiten (guitar). Feiten, a former member of the Paul Butterfield Blues Band, The Rascals and Stevie Wonder's band, joined Mr. Mister in 1989.

9/13/80	29	6	1. Who'll Be The Fool Tonight	Warner 49282

LARSON, Nicolette

Born on 7/17/52 in Helena, Montana; raised in Kansas City. To San Francisco in 1974. Session vocalist with Neil Young, Linda Ronstadt, Van Halen and many others. Also see Nitty Gritty Dirt Band and Christopher Cross.

DATE	POS	WKS	ARTIST—RECORD TITLE	LABEL & NO.
12/23/78+	8	14	1. **Lotta Love** written by Neil Young; #1 Adult Contemporary hit (1 week)	Warner 8664
2/16/80	35	3	2. Let Me Go, Love duet with Michael McDonald	Warner 49130
			LaSALLE, Denise	
			Born Denise Craig on 7/16/39 in LeFlore County, Mississippi. Soul singer.	
9/25/71	13	9	● 1. Trapped By A Thing Called Love #1 R&B hit (1 week)	Westbound 182
			LASLEY, David	
			Born on 8/20/47 in Sault St. Marie, Michigan. Backup singer for James Taylor and others. Member of the studio group Roundtree.	
4/24/82	36	3	1. If I Had My Wish Tonight	EMI America 8111
			LAST, James, Band	
			Last was born on 4/17/29 in Bremen, Germany. Producer/arranger/conductor of big cabaret band.	
4/26/80	28	6	1. The Seduction (Love Theme) [I] from the movie *American Gigolo* starring Richard Gere	Polydor 2071
			LATIMORE	
			Born Benjamin Latimore on 9/7/39 in Charleston, Tennessee. Soul singer. With Steve Alaimo in the '60s.	
11/23/74	31	3	1. Let's Straighten It Out #1 R&B hit (2 weeks)	Glades 1722
3/26/77	37	2	2. Somethin' 'Bout 'Cha above 2 produced by Steve Alaimo	Glades 1739
			LaTOUR	
			William LaTour. Solo artist from Chicago.	
5/4/91	35	4	1. People Are Still Having Sex Sales #25 / Airplay #38	Smash 879666
			LATTISAW, Stacy	
			Born on 11/25/66 in Washington, D.C. Soul singer. Recorded her first album at age 12. Childhood friend of Johnny Gill. Her younger brother Jerry is a member of Me-2-U.	
10/4/80	21	10	1. Let Me Be Your Angel	Cotillion 46001
8/1/81	26	7	2. Love On A Two Way Street	Cotillion 46015
10/22/83	40	1	3. Miracles	Cotillion 99855
			LAUPER, Cyndi	
			Born on 6/20/53 in Queens, New York. Recorded an album for Polydor Records in 1980 with the group Blue Angel. Supported by the Hooters, 1983–84. Won the 1984 Best New Artist Grammy Award. Appeared in the movies *Vibes* and *Life With Mikey*. Married actor David Thornton on 11/24/91.	
1/28/84	2 (2)	14	▲ 1. **Girls Just Want To Have Fun**	Portrait 04120
4/21/84	1 (2)	14	● 2. **Time After Time** #1 Adult Contemporary hit (3 weeks)	Portrait 04432

DATE	POS	WKS	ARTIST–RECORD TITLE	LABEL & NO.
7/28/84	3	14	● 3. **She Bop** Sales #16 pre / Airplay #24 pre	Portrait 04516
10/13/84	5	14	4. **All Through The Night** Airplay #4 / Sales #9; written by Jules Shear (backing vocal)	Portrait 04639
1/12/85	27	6	5. Money Changes Everything Airplay #23 / Sales #28; above 5 from the album *She's So Unusual*	Portrait 04737
6/1/85	10	9	6. **The Goonies 'R' Good Enough** Airplay #10 / Sales #10; from the movie *The Goonies* starring Sean Astin	Portrait 04918
9/13/86	1 (2)	12	7. **True Colors** Airplay #1(2) / Sales #2	Portrait 06247
12/13/86+	3	13	8. **Change Of Heart** Sales #2 / Airplay #5; The Bangles (guest vocals)	Portrait 06431
3/21/87	12	10	9. **What's Going On** Sales #10 / Airplay #12	Portrait 06970
5/20/89	6	10	10. **I Drove All Night** Sales #5 / Airplay #7	Epic 68759
			LAUREN, Rod	
			Born on 3/26/40. Lauren was groomed by RCA in 1960 to be a hot new teen idol.	
1/11/60	31	5	1. If I Had A Girl Shorty Rogers (orch. and chorus)	RCA 7645
			LAURIE SISTERS, The	
4/16/55	30	1	1. Dixie Danny Best Seller #30; Hugo Peretti (of Hugo & Luigi; orch.)	Mercury 70548
			LAWRENCE, Eddie	
			Born Lawrence Eisler on 3/2/19 in New York City. Comedian/actor/author/playwright.	
9/1/56	34	1	1. The Old Philosopher [C] The Sentimental Four (musical accompaniment)	Coral 61671
			LAWRENCE, Joey	
			Born on 4/20/76. Actor/singer from Philadelphia. Acted on TV's "Gimme A Break," 1983–87. Star of the NBC-TV series "Blossom," 1991–94. Acting since age three.	
3/20/93	19	13	1. Nothin' My Love Can't Fix Sales #20 / Airplay #22	Impact 54562
			LAWRENCE, Steve	
			Born Sidney Leibowitz on 7/8/35 in Brooklyn. Regular performer on Steve Allen's "Tonight Show" for five years. First recorded for King in 1952. Married singer Eydie Gorme on 12/29/57; they recorded as Parker & Penny in 1979. Steve and Eydie remain a durable nightclub act.	
1/19/57	18	8	1. The Banana Boat Song Jockey #18 / Top 100 #30	Coral 61761
3/9/57	5	12	2. **Party Doll** Jockey #5 / Top 100 #10 / Juke Box #11 / Best Seller #12; Dick Jacobs (orch., above 2)	Coral 61792
12/14/59+	9	13	3. **Pretty Blue Eyes**	ABC-Para. 10058

DATE	POS	WKS	ARTIST–RECORD TITLE	LABEL & NO.
3/28/60	7	9	4. **Footsteps**	ABC-Para. 10085
4/3/61	9	10	5. **Portrait Of My Love**	United Art. 291
			Don Costa (orch., above 3)	
12/8/62+	1 (2)	12	● 6. **Go Away Little Girl**	Columbia 42601
			#1 Adult Contemporary hit (6 weeks)	
3/30/63	26	6	7. Don't Be Afraid, Little Darlin'	Columbia 42699
6/15/63	27	3	8. Poor Little Rich Girl	Columbia 42795
8/24/63	28	5	9. I Want To Stay Here	Columbia 42815
			STEVE And EYDIE	
11/9/63	26	4	10. Walking Proud	Columbia 42865
1/25/64	35	3	11. I Can't Stop Talking About You	Columbia 42932
			STEVE And EYDIE	
			Marion Evans (orch., above 6)	

LAWRENCE, Vicki

Born on 5/26/49 in Inglewood, California. Regular on Carol Burnett's CBS-TV series, 1967–78. Also starred in TV's "Mama's Family," 1982–87. Married songwriter/singer Bobby Russell in 1972.

DATE	POS	WKS	ARTIST–RECORD TITLE	LABEL & NO.
3/17/73	1 (2)	14	● 1. **The Night The Lights Went Out In Georgia**	Bell 45303
			written by Vicki's husband, Bobby Russell	

LAYNE, Joy

Born in Chicago in the late 1930s.

DATE	POS	WKS	ARTIST–RECORD TITLE	LABEL & NO.
2/16/57	20	5	1. Your Wild Heart	Mercury 71038
			Juke Box #20 / Top 100 #30; Carl Stevens (orch.)	

LEAPY LEE

Born Lee Graham on 7/2/42 in Eastbourne, England. Acted on stage and TV in England.

DATE	POS	WKS	ARTIST–RECORD TITLE	LABEL & NO.
11/9/68	16	8	1. Little Arrows	Decca 32380

LEAVES, The

Los Angeles garage rock quintet: John Beck (lead singer), Robert Lee Reiner, Jim Pons, Tom "Ambrose" Ray and Bobby Arlin.

DATE	POS	WKS	ARTIST–RECORD TITLE	LABEL & NO.
6/18/66	31	4	1. Hey Joe	Mira 222
			released in 1965 as: "Hey Joe, Where You Gonna Go?" on Mira 207	

LeBLANC & CARR

Lenny LeBlanc (born 6/17/51; bass) and Pete Carr (born 4/22/50; lead guitar). Both were session musicians at Muscle Shoals, Alabama. LeBlanc later recorded Contemporary Christian music.

DATE	POS	WKS	ARTIST–RECORD TITLE	LABEL & NO.
2/4/78	13	10	1. Falling	Big Tree 16100

Manfred Mann's "Come Tomorrow" tried mightily to follow up past Top 20 hits "Do Wah Diddy Diddy" and "Sha La La," but—perhaps hampered by its comparatively more meaningful title—peaked only at No. 50 in 1965.

The Marcels' major claim to rock and roll immortality came via their remarkable version of Rodgers and Hart's "Blue Moon." The track, which was perched at No. 1 for three weeks in 1961, has come to define an entire musical era for many and has since been used in numerous film soundtracks.

The Marvelettes' first Top 40 entry—1961's No. 1 hit "Please Mr. Postman"—was superbly covered by The Beatles on the group's second Capitol album. British singer Morrissey would later call Gladys Horton one of his very favorite singers.

Richard Marx's 1988 single "Hold On To The Nights" became his first of three No. 1 hits. While with EMI, the singer's many records separately appeared on the Manhattan, EMI-Manhattan, EMI and Capitol imprints.

The Mary Jane Girls, sidekicks of prolific R&B performer/producer Rick James, scored only one crossover pop hit—1985's "In My House"—despite other notable efforts. Mary Jane Girl Yvette Marine later sued singer Paula Abdul regarding her work on Abdul's 1988 debut album.

Johnny Mathis's "Wild Is The Wind" climbed to No. 22 to in late 1957, then was surpasssed by its flip, "No Love (But Your Love)," which peaked just one notch higher. They were the fifth and sixth of 20 Top 40 career hits for the smooth-voiced singer.

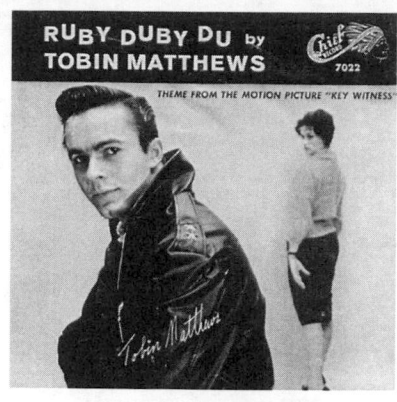

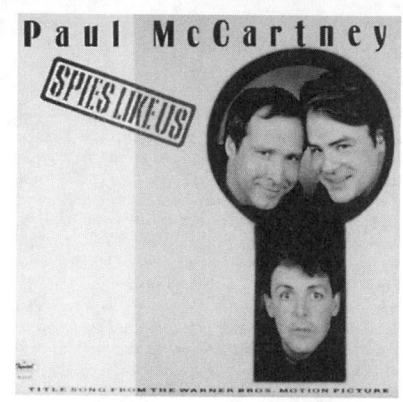

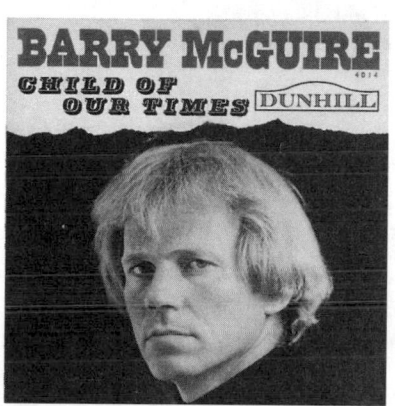

Tobin Matthews staked his claim to Top 40 immortality with the No. 30 hit "Ruby Duby Du" in 1960. Was Frank Sinatra listening when he recorded "Strangers In The Night"?

Paul McCartney's last Top 10 record as a solo artist came via the title track to the 1985 film *Spies Like Us*. He'd return to the top of the charts when the Beatles reunited on 1995's "Free As A Bird."

Bob McFadden and Dor's hit "The Mummy"—which sinisterly crept to No. 39 in 1959—featured none other than poet Rod McKuen, recording pseudonomously as "Dor."

Barry McGuire embraced topicality in 1965 first with his No. 1 hit "Eve Of Destruction," then with "Child Of Our Times," which only climbed to No. 72. For him, the times were indeed rapidly a-changin'.

M.C. Hammer's rapid rise to fame—and subsequent fall from it—was one of the most memorable pop events of the early '90s. His 1990 single "Pray," his third Top 10 hit, actually ranked higher on the chart than did his landmark debut single "U Can't Touch This."

Clyde McPhatter's "Deep In The Heart Of Harlem" came well after the singer had left the Drifters—and two years after the singer had produced "Little Bitty Pretty One," his final Top 40 hit. "Harlem" spent three weeks on the chart and peaked at No. 90.

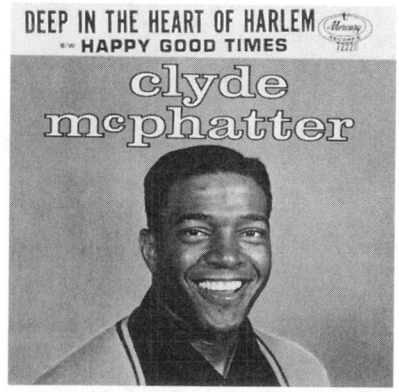

DATE	POS	WKS	ARTIST–RECORD TITLE	LABEL & NO.

LED ZEPPELIN

British heavy-metal rock supergroup formed in October 1968. Consisted of Robert Plant (lead singer), Jimmy Page (guitar), John Paul Jones (bass, keyboards) and John Bonham (drums). First known as the New Yardbirds. Page had been in The Yardbirds, 1966–68. Plant and Bonham had been in a group called Band Of Joy. Led Zeppelin's U.S. tour in 1973 broke many box office records. Formed own Swan Song label in 1974. Appeared in the concert movie *The Song Remains The Same* in 1976. Bonham died on 9/25/80 (age 33) of asphyxiation. Group disbanded in December 1980. Plant and Page formed The Honeydrippers in 1984. Page also with The Firm, 1984–86. "Bonham" is the name of group formed by Jason Bonham, John's son, in 1989. Led Zeppelin's most famous recording, "Stairway To Heaven" (on the album *Led Zeppelin IV*), was never released as a commercial single. Group inducted into the Rock and Roll Hall of Fame in 1995.

DATE	POS	WKS	ARTIST–RECORD TITLE	LABEL & NO.
12/6/69+	4	13	● 1. **Whole Lotta Love**	Atlantic 2690
12/12/70+	16	10	2. Immigrant Song	Atlantic 2777
1/15/72	15	8	3. Black Dog	Atlantic 2849
11/24/73	20	8	4. D'yer Mak'er	Atlantic 2986
5/17/75	38	2	5. Trampled Under Foot	Swan Song 70102
1/12/80	21	8	6. Fool In The Rain	Swan Song 71003

LEE, Brenda

Born Brenda Mae Tarpley on 12/11/44 in Lithonia, Georgia. Professional singer since age six. Signed to Decca Records in 1956. Became known as "Little Miss Dynamite." Successful country singer, 1971–85. Lee ranks as the #1 female singer of the '60s (as designated in *Joel Whitburn's Pop Singles Annual 1955–1994*).

DATE	POS	WKS	ARTIST–RECORD TITLE	LABEL & NO.
2/15/60	4	15	1. **Sweet Nothin's**	Decca 30967
6/6/60	1 (3)	18	● 2. **I'm Sorry/** above 2 written by Ronnie Self (also #12 & 14 below)	
6/20/60	6	9	3. **That's All You Gotta Do** written by Jerry Reed	Decca 31093
9/19/60	1 (1)	13	4. **I Want To Be Wanted/** Italian song: "Per Tutta La Vita"	
10/31/60	40	1	5. Just A Little	Decca 31149
12/19/60	14	3	● 6. Rockin' Around The Christmas Tree [X] recorded in 1958	Decca 30776
1/16/61	7	9	7. **Emotions/**	
2/6/61	33	2	8. I'm Learning About Love	Decca 31195
4/3/61	6	10	9. **You Can Depend On Me** #4 hit for Louis Armstrong in 1932	Decca 31231
6/26/61	4	10	10. **Dum Dum** written by Jackie DeShannon (also #15 below)	Decca 31272
10/9/61	3	12	11. **Fool #1/**	
10/16/61	31	3	12. Anybody But Me	Decca 31309
1/20/62	4	11	13. **Break It To Me Gently**	Decca 31348
4/28/62	6	8	14. **Everybody Loves Me But You**	Decca 31379
7/21/62	15	7	15. Heart In Hand/	
7/21/62	29	4	16. It Started All Over Again	Decca 31407
10/6/62	3	12	17. **All Alone Am I** #1 Adult Contemporary hit (5 weeks)	Decca 31424
2/16/63	32	3	18. Your Used To Be	Decca 31454
4/20/63	6	10	19. **Losing You**	Decca 31478
7/27/63	24	6	20. My Whole World Is Falling Down/	

DATE	POS	WKS	ARTIST–RECORD TITLE	LABEL & NO.
7/27/63	25	5	21. I Wonder	Decca 31510
10/12/63	17	5	22. The Grass Is Greener	Decca 31539
12/28/63+	12	8	23. As Usual	Decca 31570
3/28/64	25	5	24. Think	Decca 31599
10/31/64	17	7	25. Is It True	Decca 31690
6/26/65	13	8	26. Too Many Rivers	Decca 31792
11/13/65	33	3	27. Rusty Bells	Decca 31849
10/29/66	11	8	28. Coming On Strong	Decca 32018
2/11/67	37	2	29. Ride, Ride, Ride	Decca 32079

LEE, Curtis

Born on 10/28/41 in Yuma, Arizona. Pop singer/songwriter.

DATE	POS	WKS	ARTIST–RECORD TITLE	LABEL & NO.
7/17/61	7	8	1. **Pretty Little Angel Eyes** The Halos (backing vocals); produced by Phil Spector	Dunes 2007

LEE, Dickey

Born Dickey Lipscomb on 9/21/36 in Memphis. Pop-country singer/songwriter. First recorded for Sun Records in 1957.

DATE	POS	WKS	ARTIST–RECORD TITLE	LABEL & NO.
9/8/62	6	11	1. **Patches**	Smash 1758
12/29/62+	14	8	2. I Saw Linda Yesterday	Smash 1791
6/19/65	14	7	3. Laurie (Strange Things Happen)	TCF Hall 102

LEE, Jackie

Born on 9/8/28 in Lake Charles, Louisiana. Earl Nelson, of Bob & Earl. Took name from his wife's middle name, Jackie, and his middle name, Lee. Sang lead on Hollywood Flames' "Buzz-Buzz-Buzz."

DATE	POS	WKS	ARTIST–RECORD TITLE	LABEL & NO.
12/18/65+	14	9	1. The Duck	Mirwood 5502

LEE, Johnny

Born John Lee Ham on 7/3/46 in Texas City; raised in Alta Loma, Texas. Country singer/songwriter. Married to actress Charlene Tilton, 1982–84.

DATE	POS	WKS	ARTIST–RECORD TITLE	LABEL & NO.
8/2/80	5	13	● 1. **Lookin' For Love** from the movie *Urban Cowboy* starring John Travolta; #1 Country hit (3 weeks); b-side is "Lyin' Eyes" by the Eagles	Full Moon/Asy. 47004

LEE, Laura

Born Laura Lee Rundless in 1945 in Chicago. Soul singer.

DATE	POS	WKS	ARTIST–RECORD TITLE	LABEL & NO.
10/16/71	36	4	1. Women's Love Rights	Hot Wax 7105

LEE, Leapy—see LEAPY LEE

LEE, Peggy

Born Norma Jean Egstrom on 5/26/20 in Jamestown, North Dakota. Jazz singer with Jack Wardlow band, 1936–40; Will Osborne, 1940–41; and Benny Goodman, 1941–43. Went solo in March 1943. Appeared in the movies *Mister Music* (1950), *The Jazz Singer* (1953) and *Pete Kelly's Blues* (1955). Co-wrote many songs with husband Dave Barbour (married 1943–52). Awarded nearly $4 million in court for her singing in the animated movie *Lady And The Tramp*.

DATE	POS	WKS	ARTIST–RECORD TITLE	LABEL & NO.
3/24/56	14	10	1. Mr. Wonderful Jockey #14 / Top 100 #23 / Best Seller #25; Sy Oliver (orch.); from the Broadway musical starring Sammy Davis, Jr.	Decca 29834

DATE	POS	WKS	ARTIST–RECORD TITLE	LABEL & NO.
7/21/58	8	13	2. **Fever** *Hot 100 #8 / Best Seller #9 / Jockey #10 end; Jack Marshall (orch.)*	Capitol 3998
10/11/69	11	8	3. Is That All There Is *#1 Adult Contemporary hit (2 weeks)*	Capitol 2602
			LEFEVRE, Raymond Conductor/pianist/flutist from Paris.	
11/3/58	30	5	1. The Day The Rains Came [I]	Kapp 231
4/6/68	37	5	2. Ame Caline (Soul Coaxing) [I] *some pressings show title as: "Soul Coaxing (Ame Caline)"*	4 Corners 147
			LEFT BANKE, The Classical-styled New York rock quintet led by Steve Martin (lead singer) and Michael Brown (of Stories; keyboards).	
9/24/66	5	10	1. **Walk Away Renee**	Smash 2041
2/4/67	15	6	2. Pretty Ballerina	Smash 2074
			LEMON PIPERS, The Psychedelic/bubblegum rock quintet from Oxford, Ohio. Ivan Browne, lead singer. Member Bill Bartlett was leader of Ram Jam.	
12/23/67+	1 (1)	12	● 1. **Green Tambourine**	Buddah 23
			LENNON, John/Plastic Ono Band Born on 10/9/40 in Woolton, Liverpool, England. Shot to death on 12/8/80 in New York City. Founding member of The Beatles. Married Cynthia Powell on 8/23/62, had son Julian Lennon. Divorced Cynthia on 11/8/68. Met Yoko Ono in 1966; married her on 3/20/69. Formed Plastic Ono Band in 1969. To New York City in 1971. Fought deportation from the U.S., 1972–76, until he was granted a permanent visa. Won Grammy's Lifetime Achievement Award in 1991. Inducted into the Rock and Roll Hall of Fame in 1994. **PLASTIC ONO BAND:**	
8/9/69	14	6	1. Give Peace A Chance *recorded in a hotel suite in Montreal; Tom Smothers (The Smothers Brothers), Timothy Leary and the Canadian Chapter of Hare Krishna (backing vocals)*	Apple 1809
12/13/69+	30	7	2. Cold Turkey *Eric Clapton (guitar)*	Apple 1813
3/7/70	3	12	● 3. **Instant Karma (We All Shine On)** **JOHN ONO LENNON** *George Harrison (guitar) and Billy Preston (keyboards)*	Apple 1818
4/10/71	11	8	4. Power To The People **JOHN LENNON/PLASTIC ONO BAND; YOKO ONO/PLASTIC ONO BAND**	Apple 1830
10/23/71	3	9	5. Imagine **JOHN LENNON PLASTIC ONO BAND** *above 3 co-produced by Phil Spector*	Apple 1840
12/1/73	18	8	6. Mind Games **JOHN LENNON**	Apple 1868
10/5/74	1 (1)	11	7. **Whatever Gets You Thru The Night** **JOHN LENNON with THE PLASTIC ONO NUCLEAR BAND** *Elton John (backing vocal)*	Apple 1874

DATE	POS	WKS	ARTIST–RECORD TITLE	LABEL & NO.
			JOHN LENNON:	
1/11/75	9	8	8. **#9 Dream**	Apple 1878
4/5/75	20	5	9. Stand By Me	Apple 1881
11/1/80	1 (5)	19	● 10. **(Just Like) Starting Over**	Geffen 49604
1/17/81	2 (3)	17	● 11. **Woman**	Geffen 49644
4/11/81	10	10	12. **Watching The Wheels**	Geffen 49695
1/21/84	5	11	13. **Nobody Told Me**	Polydor 817254
			above 4 recorded in 1980	
			LENNON, Julian	
			Born John Charles Julian Lennon on 4/8/63. Son of Cynthia and John Lennon. First child to be born to any of The Beatles.	
11/10/84+	9	12	1. **Valotte**	Atlantic 89609
			Airplay #7 / Sales #7	
2/2/85	5	12	2. **Too Late For Goodbyes**	Atlantic 89589
			Airplay #4 / Sales #7; #1 Adult Contemporary hit (2 weeks)	
4/27/85	21	8	3. Say You're Wrong	Atlantic 89567
			Airplay #18 / Sales #27	
4/26/86	32	4	4. Stick Around	Atlantic 89437
			LENNON SISTERS, The—see WELK, Lawrence	
			LENNOX, Annie	
			Born on 12/25/54 in Aberdeen, Scotland. Lead singer of the Eurythmics. Studied violin at London's Royal Academy of Music from age 17 to 20. Appeared in the movie *Edward II* and TV movie *The Room*. Married moviemaker Uri Fruchtman.	
12/3/88+	9	10	1. **Put A Little Love In Your Heart**	A&M 1255
			ANNIE LENNOX & AL GREEN	
			Airplay #8 / Sales #11; from the movie *Scrooged* starring Bill Murray	
7/11/92	34	3	2. Why	Arista 12419
			Airplay #38 / Sales #52	
10/3/92	14	19	3. Walking On Broken Glass	Arista 12452
			Airplay #12 / Sales #24	
4/15/95	23	13	4. No More "I Love You's"	Arista 12804
			Sales #22 / Airplay #25; originally recorded by The Lover Speaks	
			LEONETTI, Tommy	
			Born on 9/10/29 in Bergen, New Jersey. Died on 9/15/79. Vocalist with Charlie Spivak and other bands. Featured singer on TV's "Your Hit Parade," 1957–58.	
7/7/56	23	2	1. Free	Capitol 3442
			Jockey #23 / Top 100 #40; Neal Hefti (orch. and chorus)	
			LE ROUX	
			Six-man Louisiana rock band. Jeff Pollard, lead singer. Also known as Louisiana's Le Roux.	
3/20/82	18	6	1. Nobody Said It Was Easy (Lookin' For The Lights)	RCA 13059

DATE	POS	WKS	ARTIST–RECORD TITLE	LABEL & NO.
			LESTER, Ketty	
			Born Revoyda Frierson on 8/16/34 in Hope, Arkansas. To Los Angeles in 1955. Acted in several movies and TV shows (formerly a cast member of "Days Of Our Lives," "Rituals" and "Little House On The Prairie").	
3/10/62	5	11	1. **Love Letters**	Era 3068
			#11 hit for Dick Haymes in 1945 (title song from the movie starring Jennifer Jones)	
			LETTERMEN, The	
			Harmonic vocal group formed in Los Angeles in 1960. Consisted of Tony Butala (born 11/20/40), Jim Pike (born 11/6/38) and Bob Engemann (born 2/19/36). First recorded for Warner Bros. Engemann replaced by Gary Pike (Jim's brother) in 1968. The #1 adult contemporary vocal group of the '60s.	
9/25/61	13	9	1. The Way You Look Tonight	Capitol 4586
			#1 hit for Fred Astaire in 1936 (from the movie *Swing Time*)	
12/4/61+	7	11	2. **When I Fall In Love**	Capitol 4658
			#20 hit for Doris Day in 1952; #1 Adult Contemporary hit (1 week)	
3/10/62	17	7	3. Come Back Silly Girl	Capitol 4699
			first recorded by Steve Lawrence in 1960 (ABC-Paramount 10146)	
7/17/65	16	5	4. Theme From "A Summer Place"	Capitol 5437
			from the 1959 movie *A Summer Place* starring Sandra Dee and Troy Donahue; Jimmie Haskell (orch., all of above)	
1/6/68	7	11	5. **Goin' Out Of My Head/Can't Take My Eyes Off You**	Capitol 2054
8/16/69	12	10	6. Hurt So Bad	Capitol 2482
			LEVEL 42	
			Pop-rock band formed in Manchester, England, in 1980: Mark King (vocals, bass), brothers Boon (guitar) and Phil (drums) Gould and Mike Lindup (keyboards). The Goulds left in October 1987; replaced by Alan Murphy (guitar) and Gary Husband (drums). Murphy died of AIDS on 10/19/89. Alan Holdsworth (guitar) joined in 1991.	
4/5/86	7	14	1. **Something About You**	Polydor 883362
			Sales #4 / Airplay #8	
5/16/87	12	10	2. Lessons In Love	Polydor 883956
			Sales #7 / Airplay #13	
			LEVERT	
			Soul trio from Ohio: Sean and Gerald Levert (sons of The O'Jays' Eddie Levert), and Marc Gordon.	
9/5/87	5	12	● 1. **Casanova**	Atlantic 89217
			Sales #5 / Airplay #6; #1 R&B hit (2 weeks)	
			LEVERT, Gerald	
			Lead singer of the Ohio trio Levert. Son of The O'Jays' Eddie Levert. Also discovered Troop.	
3/21/92	37	1	1. Baby Hold On To Me	EastWest 98639
			GERALD LEVERT (with Eddie Levert)	
			Sales #20 / Airplay #60; #1 R&B hit (1 week)	
8/20/94	28	8	2. I'd Give Anything	EastWest 98244
			Sales #16 / Airplay #42; #4 Country hit for Boy Howdy in 1994 ("She'd Give Anything")	

DATE	POS	WKS	ARTIST–RECORD TITLE	LABEL & NO.

LEWIS, Barbara

Born on 2/9/43 in South Lyon, Michigan. R&B singer/multi-instrumentalist/songwriter (since age nine). First recorded in Chicago in 1961.

DATE	POS	WKS	ARTIST–RECORD TITLE	LABEL & NO.
5/25/63	3	10	1. **Hello Stranger** The Dells (backing vocals); #1 R&B hit (2 weeks)	Atlantic 2184
3/14/64	38	1	2. Puppy Love	Atlantic 2214
7/17/65	11	9	3. Baby, I'm Yours	Atlantic 2283
10/9/65	11	8	4. Make Me Your Baby	Atlantic 2300
8/13/66	28	4	5. Make Me Belong To You	Atlantic 2346

LEWIS, Bobby

Born on 2/17/33 in Indianapolis. R&B singer. Grew up in an orphanage adopted by a Detroit family at age 12. First recorded for the Parrot label in 1952.

DATE	POS	WKS	ARTIST–RECORD TITLE	LABEL & NO.
5/29/61	1 (7)	17	1. **Tossin' And Turnin'** #1 R&B hit (10 weeks)	Beltone 1002
9/11/61	9	7	2. **One Track Mind** Joe Rene (orch., above 2)	Beltone 1012

LEWIS, Gary, And The Playboys

Pop group formed in Los Angeles in 1964. Consisted of Gary (vocals, drums), Al Ramsey, John West (guitars), David Walker (keyboards) and David Costell (bass). Lewis (born Cary Levitch on 7/31/45, name changed at age two) is the son of comedian Jerry Lewis. Group worked regularly at Disneyland in 1964. Lewis inducted into the Army on New Year's Day in 1967, resumed career after discharge in 1968.

DATE	POS	WKS	ARTIST–RECORD TITLE	LABEL & NO.
1/23/65	1 (2)	11	● 1. **This Diamond Ring**	Liberty 55756
4/17/65	2 (2)	9	2. **Count Me In**	Liberty 55778
7/17/65	2 (1)	9	3. **Save Your Heart For Me** #1 Adult Contemporary hit (3 weeks)	Liberty 55809
10/9/65	4	8	4. **Everybody Loves A Clown**	Liberty 55818
12/18/65+	3	11	5. **She's Just My Style**	Liberty 55846
3/19/66	9	7	6. **Sure Gonna Miss Her**	Liberty 55865
5/21/66	8	7*	7. **Green Grass**	Liberty 55880
8/13/66	13	5	8. My Heart's Symphony	Liberty 55898
10/22/66	15	6	9. (You Don't Have To) Paint Me A Picture	Liberty 55914
1/7/67	21	6	10. Where Will The Words Come From	Liberty 55933
6/10/67	39	2	11. Girls In Love	Liberty 55971
7/27/68	19	9	12. Sealed With A Kiss	Liberty 56037

LEWIS, Huey, and the News

Lewis was born Hugh Cregg III on 7/5/50 in New York City. Joined the country-rock band Clover in the late '70s. Formed his six-man pop-rock band, the News, in San Francisco in 1980: Lewis (lead singer), Chris Hayes (lead guitar), Mario Cipollina (bass; brother of Quicksilver Messenger Service guitarist John Cipollina), Bill Gibson (drums), Sean Hopper (keyboards) and Johnny Colla (sax, guitar). Lewis acted in the movie *Short Cuts*.

DATE	POS	WKS	ARTIST–RECORD TITLE	LABEL & NO.
2/20/82	7	13	1. **Do You Believe In Love**	Chrysalis 2589
6/12/82	36	4	2. Hope You Love Me Like You Say You Do	Chrysalis 2604
10/8/83	8	13	3. **Heart And Soul**	Chrysalis 42726
1/28/84	6	13	● 4. **I Want A New Drug**	Chrysalis 42766

DATE	POS	WKS	ARTIST–RECORD TITLE	LABEL & NO.
4/28/84	6	14	5. **The Heart Of Rock & Roll** "live" version is on the B-side of #11 below	Chrysalis 42782
7/28/84	6	13	6. **If This Is It** Sales #20 pre	Chrysalis 42803
10/27/84	18	10	7. **Walking On A Thin Line** Airplay #12 / Sales #28; above 5 from the album *Sports*	Chrysalis 42825
7/6/85	1 (2)	15	● 8. **The Power Of Love** Airplay #1(3) / Sales #1(1); from the movie *Back to the Future* starring Michael J. Fox	Chrysalis 42876
8/9/86	1 (3)	13	9. **Stuck With You** Airplay #1(3) / Sales #1(2); #1 Adult Contemporary hit (3 weeks)	Chrysalis 43019
10/25/86	3	12	10. **Hip To Be Square** Sales #1(1) / Airplay #3	Chrysalis 43065
1/17/87	1 (1)	12	11. **Jacob's Ladder** Airplay #1(1) / Sales #2; written by Bruce Hornsby	Chrysalis 43097
4/11/87	9	10	12. **I Know What I Like** Airplay #10 / Sales #10; Joe Montana, Dwight Clark, Riki Ellison and Ronnie Lott of the 1985 San Francisco 49'ers football team (backing vocals: #10 & 12)	Chrysalis 43108
8/1/87	6	11	13. **Doing It All For My Baby** Airplay #5 / Sales #9; above 5 from the album *Fore!*	Chrysalis 43143
7/23/88	3	12	14. **Perfect World** Airplay #1(1) / Sales #3	Chrysalis 43265
10/29/88	25	6	15. **Small World** Sales #25 / Airplay #26	Chrysalis 43306
5/11/91	11	9	16. **Couple Days Off** Airplay #16 / Sales #25	EMI 50346
8/17/91	21	6	17. **It Hit Me Like A Hammer** Airplay #37	EMI 50364

LEWIS, Jerry

Born Joseph Levitch on 3/16/25 in Newark, New Jersey. Comedian/actor. Formed comedy duo with Dean Martin in 1946, in Atlantic City, that lasted 10 years and 16 movies. Movie debut in 1949 in *My Friend Irma*. His son Gary Lewis was a '60s pop star. National chairman in campaign against muscular dystrophy.

DATE	POS	WKS	ARTIST–RECORD TITLE	LABEL & NO.
11/24/56	10	15	● 1. **Rock-A-Bye Your Baby With A Dixie Melody** Best Seller #10 / Top 100 #12 / Juke Box #13 / Jockey #17; Buddy Bregman (orch.); #1 hit for Al Jolson in 1918	Decca 30124

LEWIS, Jerry Lee

Born on 9/29/35 in Ferriday, Louisiana. Played piano since age nine, professionally since age 15. First recorded for Sun in 1956. Appeared in the movie *Jamboree!* in 1957. Career waned in 1958 after marriage to 13-year-old cousin, Myra Gale Brown, daughter of his bass player. Made comeback in country music beginning in 1968. Nicknamed "The Killer," Lewis has been surrounded by personal tragedies in the past two decades and survived several serious illnesses. Cousin to country singer Mickey Gilley and TV evangelist Jimmy Swaggart. Inducted into the Rock and Roll Hall of Fame in 1986. Jerry's early career is documented in the 1989 movie *Great Balls Of Fire* starring Dennis Quaid.

DATE	POS	WKS	ARTIST–RECORD TITLE	LABEL & NO.
7/15/57	3	20	● 1. **Whole Lot Of Shakin' Going On** Best Seller #3 / Top 100 #3 / Jockey #9; #1 Country hit (2 weeks); #1 R&B hit (2 weeks)	Sun 267

JERRY LEE LEWIS AND HIS PUMPING PIANO:

DATE	POS	WKS	ARTIST–RECORD TITLE	LABEL & NO.
12/2/57+	2 (4)	13	● 2. **Great Balls Of Fire** Best Seller #2 / Top 100 #2 / Jockey #9; #1 Country hit (2 weeks)	Sun 281

DATE	POS	WKS	ARTIST–RECORD TITLE		LABEL & NO.
3/10/58	**7**	9	3. **Breathless** Top 100 #7 / Best Seller #9 / Jockey #23		Sun 288
6/2/58	**21**	8	4. High School Confidential Top 100 #21 / Best Seller #22; title song from the movie starring Russ Tamblyn (song introduced by Lewis in movie)		Sun 296
4/24/61	**30**	4	5. What'd I Say		Sun 356
			JERRY LEE LEWIS:		
1/15/72	**40**	1	6. Me And Bobby McGee		Mercury 73248

LEWIS, Ramsey

Lewis (born 5/27/35, Chicago; piano) formed the Gentlemen Of Swing, a jazz-oriented trio, in 1956 in Chicago. Consisted of Ramsey, Eldee Young (bass) and Isaac "Red" Holt (drums). All had been in The Clefs in the early '50s. First recorded for Chess/Argo in 1956. Disbanded in 1965. Young and Holt then re-formed The Young-Holt Trio. Lewis re-formed his trio with Cleveland Eaton (bass) and Maurice White (later with Earth, Wind & Fire; drums). Reunited with Young and Holt in 1983.

DATE	POS	WKS	ARTIST–RECORD TITLE		LABEL & NO.
			RAMSEY LEWIS TRIO:		
8/21/65	**5**	12	1. **The "In" Crowd**	[I]	Argo 5506
11/27/65	**11**	6	2. Hang On Sloopy	[I]	Cadet 5522
2/5/66	**29**	4	3. A Hard Day's Night	[I]	Cadet 5525
			RAMSEY LEWIS:		
8/20/66	**19**	6	4. Wade In The Water	[I]	Cadet 5541

LIGHTER SHADE OF BROWN, A

Hispanic rap duo of ODM ("One Dope Mexican," Robert Guitterez) and DTTX ("Don't Try To Xerox," Bobby Ramirez), from Riverside, California.

DATE	POS	WKS	ARTIST–RECORD TITLE	LABEL & NO.
2/8/92	**39**	1	1. On A Sunday Afternoon Sales #24 / Airplay #39; featuring Shiro and Huggy Boy; basslines and samples from "Groovin'," "Crystal Blue Persuasion" and "Just My Imagination"	Pump 15186

LIGHTFOOT, Gordon

Born on 11/17/38 in Orillia, Ontario, Canada. Folk-pop-country singer/songwriter/guitarist. Worked on "Country Hoedown," CBC-TV series. Teamed with Jim Whalen as the Two Tones in the mid-1960s. Wrote hit "Early Mornin' Rain" for Peter, Paul and Mary. First recorded for Chateau in 1965.

DATE	POS	WKS	ARTIST–RECORD TITLE	LABEL & NO.
1/23/71	**5**	11	1. **If You Could Read My Mind** #1 Adult Contemporary hit (1 week)	Reprise 0974
5/11/74	**1** (1)	11	● 2. **Sundown** #1 Adult Contemporary hit (2 weeks)	Reprise 1194
10/5/74	**10**	7	3. **Carefree Highway** #1 Adult Contemporary hit (1 week)	Reprise 1309
5/3/75	**26**	4	4. Rainy Day People #1 Adult Contemporary hit (1 week)	Reprise 1328
9/25/76	**2** (2)	13	5. **The Wreck Of The Edmund Fitzgerald** true story of an ore vessel, named after a Milwaukee civic leader, that sank in Lake Superior on 11/10/75	Reprise 1369
3/25/78	**33**	3	6. The Circle Is Small (I Can See It In Your Eyes)	Warner 8518

DATE	POS	WKS	ARTIST–RECORD TITLE	LABEL & NO.
			LIGHTHOUSE	
			Rock band from Toronto. Bob McBride, lead singer.	
10/9/71	24	8	1. One Fine Morning	Evolution 1048
11/25/72	34	5	2. Sunny Days	Evolution 1069
			LIGHTNING SEEDS, The	
			Band with fluctuating lineup spearheaded by U.K. producer/vocalist Ian Broudie (former member of Big In Japan who produced Echo & The Bunnymen, Icicle Works and others).	
7/7/90	31	6	1. Pure Sales #24 / Airplay #38	MCA 53816
			LIMAHL	
			Real name: Chris Hamill (Limahl is an anagram of his last name). Ex-lead singer of Kajagoogoo.	
5/4/85	17	9	1. Never Ending Story Sales #14 / Airplay #19; from the movie *The Never Ending Story* starring Noah Hathaway	EMI America 8230
			LIND, Bob	
			Born on 11/25/44 in Baltimore. Folk-rock singer/songwriter.	
2/12/66	5	9	1. **Elusive Butterfly**	World Pac. 77808
			LINDEN, Kathy	
			Songstress from Moorestown, New Jersey.	
3/31/58	7	11	1. **Billy** Jockey #7 / Top 100 #12 / Best Seller #14; introduced by the American Quartet in 1911 (Victor 16965); #10 hit for Wee Bonnie Baker (of Orrin Tucker's Band) in 1939	Felsted 8510
4/27/59	11	10	2. Goodbye Jimmy, Goodbye Joe Leahy (orch., above 2)	Felsted 8571
			LINDISFARNE	
			Folk-rock quintet from England. Alan Hull, lead singer. Group's name is an island off of Northumberland, U.K. Hull died of a heart attack on 11/18/95 (age 50).	
11/25/78	33	4	1. Run For Home	Atco 7093
			LINDSAY, Mark	
			Born on 3/9/42 in Cambridge, Idaho. Lead singer/saxophonist of Paul Revere & The Raiders. Also recorded with Raider, Keith Allison, and Steve Alaimo as The Unknowns.	
1/10/70	10	11	● 1. **Arizona**	Columbia 45037
7/11/70	25	5	2. Silver Bird	Columbia 45180
			LINEAR	
			Pronounced: lin-EAR. Miami-based male trio: New Yorkers Charlie "Steele" Pennachio (vocals) and Joey Restivo (percussion) with Ecuadoran Wyatt Pauley (guitar).	
3/31/90	5	16	● 1. **Sending All My Love** Sales #6 / Airplay #7	Atlantic 87961

DATE	POS	WKS	ARTIST–RECORD TITLE	LABEL & NO.
5/30/92	**30**	6	2. T.L.C. Airplay #20 / Sales #65	Atlantic 87484

LIPPS, INC.

Pronounced: lip-synch. Funk project from Minneapolis formed by producer/songwriter/multi-instrumentalist Steven Greenberg. Vocals by Cynthia Johnson, Miss Black Minnesota U.S.A. of 1976.

DATE	POS	WKS	ARTIST–RECORD TITLE	LABEL & NO.
4/19/80	**1 (4)**	15	▲ 1. **Funkytown**	Casablanca 2233

LISA LISA AND CULT JAM

Harlem trio: Lisa Velez (born 1/15/67; lead vocals), Mike Hughes and Alex "Spanador" Moseley. Assembled and produced by Full Force.

DATE	POS	WKS	ARTIST–RECORD TITLE	LABEL & NO.
8/3/85	**34**	6	● 1. **I Wonder If I Take You Home** **LISA LISA AND CULT JAM With FULL FORCE** Sales #27	Columbia 04886
8/30/86	**8**	13	● 2. **All Cried Out** **LISA LISA AND CULT JAM WITH FULL FORCE FEATURING PAUL ANTHONY & BOW LEGGED LOU** Sales #8 / Airplay #8	Columbia 05844
			LISA LISA AND CULT JAM:	
5/2/87	**1 (1)**	14	● 3. **Head To Toe** Sales #1(1) / Airplay #1(1); #1 R&B hit (2 weeks)	Columbia 07008
8/22/87	**1 (1)**	13	● 4. **Lost In Emotion** Sales #1(1) / Airplay #1(1); #1 R&B hit (1 week)	Columbia 07267
5/13/89	**29**	4	5. **Little Jackie Wants To Be A Star** Sales #25 / Airplay #36	Columbia 68674
8/3/91	**37**	1	● 6. **Let The Beat Hit 'Em** Sales #19 / Airplay #38; #1 R&B hit (1 week)	Columbia 73847

LITTLE ANTHONY AND THE IMPERIALS

R&B group formed in 1957 in Brooklyn. Consisted of Anthony Gourdine (born 1/8/40), Ernest Wright, Jr., Tracy Lord, Glouster Rogers and Clarence Collins. Anthony first recorded on Winley in 1955 with The DuPonts. Formed The Chesters in 1957; changed name to The Imperials in 1958. Sammy Strain, who joined group in 1964, left in 1975 to join The O'Jays. Gourdine became an Inspirational artist in 1980.

DATE	POS	WKS	ARTIST–RECORD TITLE	LABEL & NO.
8/18/58	**4**	14	1. **Tears On My Pillow** Hot 100 #4 / Best Seller #5 end; also released on End 1027 as by The Imperials	End 1027
1/18/60	**24**	7	2. Shimmy, Shimmy, Ko-Ko-Bop	End 1060
9/5/64	**15**	8	3. I'm On The Outside (Looking In)	DCP 1104
11/21/64	**6**	12	4. **Goin' Out Of My Head**	DCP 1119
2/13/65	**10**	8	5. **Hurt So Bad**	DCP 1128
7/17/65	**16**	7	6. Take Me Back	DCP 1136
11/6/65	**34**	1	7. I Miss You So The 101 Strings (orchestral backing); #20 hit for The Cats and the Fiddle in 1940	DCP 1149

LITTLE CAESAR and The Romans

Los Angeles R&B quintet led by David "Little Caesar" Johnson (born 6/16/34, Chicago).

DATE	POS	WKS	ARTIST–RECORD TITLE	LABEL & NO.
5/29/61	**9**	9	1. **Those Oldies But Goodies (Remind Me Of You)**	Del-Fi 4158

DATE	POS	WKS	ARTIST–RECORD TITLE	LABEL & NO.
			LITTLE DIPPERS, The	
			Pop quartet organized by producer Buddy Killen: Delores Dinning, Emily Gilmore, Darrell McCall and Hurshel Wigintin.	
2/8/60	9	10	1. **Forever**	University 210
			LITTLE EVA	
			Born Eva Narcissus Boyd on 6/29/45 in Bellhaven, North Carolina. Discovered by songwriters Carole King and Gerry Goffin while she was babysitting their daughter Louise Goffin.	
7/21/62	1 (1)	12	● 1. **The Loco-Motion** #1 R&B hit (3 weeks); Carole King (backing vocal)	Dimension 1000
11/24/62	12	8	2. Keep Your Hands Off My Baby	Dimension 1003
2/23/63	20	6	3. Let's Turkey Trot same melody as The Cleftones' 1956 hit "Little Girl Of Mine"	Dimension 1006
7/13/63	38	2	4. Swinging On A Star **BIG DEE IRWIN (with Little Eva)** #1 hit for Bing Crosby in 1944 (from the movie *Going My Way*)	Dimension 1010
			LITTLE JOE & THE THRILLERS	
			R&B vocal group formed in New York City in 1956: Joe Cook (lead), Farris Hill and Richard Frazier (tenors), Donald Burnett (baritone) and Harry Pascle (bass).	
10/7/57	22	9	1. Peanuts Best Seller #22 / Top 100 #23	Okeh 7088
			LITTLE JOEY And The Flips	
			R&B quintet from Philadelphia: Joey Hall (lead; died 1972), James Meagher, John Smith, Jeff Leonard and Fred Gerace.	
7/14/62	33	3	1. Bongo Stomp	Joy 262
			LITTLE MILTON	
			Born Milton Campbell, Jr. on 9/7/34 in Inverness, Mississippi. Blues singer/guitarist. Recorded with Ike Turner at Sun Records, 1953–54. Appeared in the concert movie *Wattstax*, 1972.	
4/24/65	25	7	1. We're Gonna Make It #1 R&B hit (3 weeks)	Checker 1105
			LITTLE RICHARD	
			Born Richard Wayne Penniman on 12/5/32 in Macon, Georgia. R&B-rock and roll singer/pianist. Talent contest win led to first recordings for RCA Victor in 1951. Worked with the Tempo Toppers, 1953–55. Appeared in three early rock and roll movies: *Don't Knock The Rock*, *The Girl Can't Help It* and *Mister Rock 'n' Roll* and the 1986 comedy *Down And Out In Beverly Hills*. Earned theology degree in 1961 and was ordained a minister. Left R&B for gospel music, 1959–62, and again in the mid-1970s. One of the key figures in the transition from R&B to rock and roll. Inducted into the Rock and Roll Hall of Fame in 1986. Won Grammy's Lifetime Achievement Award in 1993.	
1/28/56	17	5	1. Tutti-Frutti Juke Box #17 / Best Seller #18 / Top 100 #21	Specialty 561
4/7/56	6	12	● 2. **Long Tall Sally**/ Best Seller #6 / Top 100 #13 / Juke Box #14 / Jockey #16; #1 R&B hit (8 weeks)	
6/30/56	33	1	3. Slippin' And Slidin' (Peepin' And Hidin')	Specialty 572

DATE	POS	WKS	ARTIST–RECORD TITLE	LABEL & NO.
7/14/56	**17**	7	4. Rip It Up Best Seller #17 / Top 100 #27; #1 R&B hit (2 weeks)	Specialty 579
4/6/57	**21**	7	5. Lucille Best Seller #21 / Top 100 #27; #1 R&B hit (2 weeks)	Specialty 598
6/24/57	**10**	13	6. **Jenny, Jenny** Best Seller #10 / Top 100 #14	Specialty 606
10/7/57	**8**	12	7. **Keep A Knockin'** Top 100 #8 / Best Seller #9 / Jockey #24; from the movie *Mister Rock 'n' Roll* starring Alan Freed	Specialty 611
2/24/58	**10**	10	8. **Good Golly, Miss Molly** Top 100 #10 / Best Seller #13; piano intro inspired by Jackie Brenston's #1 early rock & roll classic from 1951 "Rocket '88'"	Specialty 624
6/23/58	**31**	3	9. Ooh! My Soul Best Seller #31 / Top 100 #35	Specialty 633

LITTLE RIVER BAND

Pop-rock group formed in Australia in 1975. Consisted of Glenn Shorrock (lead singer), Rick Formosa, Beeb Birtles and Graham Goble (guitars), Roger McLachlan (bass) and Derek Pellicci (drums). McLachlan replaced by George McArdle in 1977 and Formosa replaced by David Briggs in 1978. American bassist Wayne Nelson replaced McLachlan in 1980. In 1983, Shorrock replaced by John Farnham and Briggs replaced by Steve Housden. By 1985, Pellicci replaced by Steven Prestwich, and Birtles had left and keyboardist David Hirschfelder joined. Pellicci and Shorrock returned in 1987. By 1992, Goble had left and Peter Beckett, ex-leader of Player, had joined. Band named after a resort town near Melbourne.

DATE	POS	WKS	ARTIST–RECORD TITLE	LABEL & NO.
11/6/76	**28**	6	1. It's A Long Way There	Harvest 4318
9/24/77	**14**	11	2. Help Is On Its Way	Harvest 4428
1/21/78	**16**	9	3. Happy Anniversary	Harvest 4524
8/12/78	**3**	14	4. **Reminiscing**	Harvest 4605
1/27/79	**10**	14	5. **Lady**	Harvest 4667
8/4/79	**6**	14	6. **Lonesome Loser**	Capitol 4748
11/10/79+	**10**	13	7. **Cool Change**	Capitol 4789
9/5/81	**6**	14	8. **The Night Owls**	Capitol 5033
12/26/81+	**10**	15	9. **Take It Easy On Me**	Capitol 5057
5/1/82	**14**	8	10. Man On Your Mind	Capitol 5061
12/4/82+	**11**	13	11. The Other Guy	Capitol 5185
5/28/83	**22**	6	12. We Two	Capitol 5231
8/27/83	**35**	3	13. You're Driving Me Out Of My Mind	Capitol 5256

LITTLE SISTER

Female soul trio organized by Sly Stone for his own record label. Consisted of his sister Vanetta Stewart, Mary Rand and Elva Melton.

DATE	POS	WKS	ARTIST–RECORD TITLE	LABEL & NO.
3/28/70	**22**	6	1. You're The One-Part I	Stone Flower 9000
1/30/71	**32**	3	2. Somebody's Watching You	Stone Flower 9001

LIVING COLOUR

Black rock quartet from New York City. London-born, Brooklyn-raised lead guitarist/songwriter Vernon Reid (see Janet Jackson's "Black Cat"), with vocalist Corey Glover (appeared in the movie *Platoon*), bassist Muzz Skillings and drummer William Calhoun. Skillings left in early 1992, replaced by Doug Wimbish (ex-Tackhead; former member of Sugarhill Records band, backed George Clinton and James Brown). Disbanded in 1995.

DATE	POS	WKS	ARTIST–RECORD TITLE	LABEL & NO.
4/1/89	**13**	9	1. Cult Of Personality Sales #7 / Airplay #17; "live" version is on the B-side of #2	Epic 68611

DATE	POS	WKS	ARTIST—RECORD TITLE	LABEL & NO.
10/14/89	31	3	2. Glamour Boys Airplay #28 / Sales #32; Mick Jagger (producer; backing vocal)	Epic 68548
			LIVING IN A BOX Soul-styled pop trio from England: Richard Darbyshire (vocals), Marcus Vere (keyboards) and Anthony "Tich" Critchlow (drums).	
7/25/87	17	7	1. Living In A Box Sales #13 / Airplay #20	Chrysalis 43104
			L.L. COOL J Real name: James Todd Smith. Rapper from Queens, New York. Stage name is abbreviation for Ladies Love Cool James. Appeared in the movies *Krush Groove*, *The Hard Way* and *Toys*. Starred in the TV show "In The House."	
8/15/87	14	8	1. I Need Love Sales #11 / Airplay #13; #1 R&B hit (1 week)	Def Jam 07350
3/26/88	31	5	● 2. Going Back To Cali Sales #26 / Airplay #32; from the movie *Less Than Zero* starring Robert Downey, Jr.	Def Jam 07679
7/8/89	15	8	● 3. I'm That Type Of Guy Sales #9 / Airplay #28	Def Jam 68902
1/5/91	9	15	● 4. **Around The Way Girl** Sales #5 / Airplay #19	Def Jam 73609
5/11/91	17	9	● 5. Mama Said Knock You Out Sales #5 / Airplay #47	Def Jam 73706
11/18/95	3	20	▲ 6. **Hey Lover** Sales #2 / Airplay #17; Boys II Men (backing vocals); based on the song "The Lady In My Life" by Michael Jackson	Def Jam/RAL 577494
			LOBO Born Roland Kent Lavoie on 7/31/43 in Tallahassee, Florida. Pop singer/songwriter/guitarist. Played with the Legends in Tampa in 1961. The Legends included Jim Stafford, Gerald Chambers, Gram Parsons and Jon Corneal. Lobo is Spanish for wolf. Lavoie formed own publishing company, Boo Publishing, in 1974.	
4/24/71	5	10	1. **Me And You And A Dog Named Boo** #1 Adult Contemporary hit (2 weeks)	Big Tree 112
10/14/72	2 (2)	10	● 2. **I'd Love You To Want Me** #1 Adult Contemporary hit (1 week)	Big Tree 147
1/13/73	8	10	3. **Don't Expect Me To Be Your Friend** #1 Adult Contemporary hit (2 weeks)	Big Tree 158
5/5/73	27	5	4. It Sure Took A Long, Long Time	Big Tree 16001
7/21/73	22	8	5. How Can I Tell Her	Big Tree 16004
5/11/74	37	2	6. Standing At The End Of The Line	Big Tree 15001
4/26/75	27	4	7. Don't Tell Me Goodnight	Big Tree 16033
9/8/79	23	8	8. Where Were You When I Was Falling In Love #1 Adult Contemporary hit (2 weeks)	MCA 41065
			LOCKLIN, Hank Born Lawrence Hankins Locklin on 2/15/18 in McLellan, Florida. Country singer/songwriter/guitarist. Elected mayor of McLellan in the early '60s. Own TV series in Houston and Dallas in the '70s.	
6/13/60	8	15	1. **Please Help Me, I'm Falling** #1 Country hit (14 weeks)	RCA 7692

DATE	POS	WKS	ARTIST–RECORD TITLE	LABEL & NO.
			LOEB, Lisa, & Nine Stories	
			New York-based band. Dallas native Loeb with Tim Bright (guitar), Joe Quigley (bass) and Jonathan Feinberg (drums; left after release of "Stay"). Discovered by actor Ethan Hawke.	
5/28/94	**1** (3)	25	● 1. **Stay (I Missed You)** Airplay #1(4) / Sales #2; from the movie *Reality Bites* starring Winona Ryder	RCA 62870
9/30/95	**18**	12	2. Do You Sleep? Airplay #23 / Sales #24	Geffen 19388
			LOGGINS, Dave	
			Born on 11/10/47 in Mountain City, Tennessee. Pop-country singer/songwriter. Cousin of Kenny Loggins.	
7/13/74	**5**	10	1. **Please Come To Boston** #1 Adult Contemporary hit (1 week)	Epic 11115
			LOGGINS, Kenny	
			Born on 1/7/47 in Everett, Washington; raised in Alhambra, California. Pop-rock singer/songwriter/guitarist. Cousin of Dave Loggins. In band Gator Creek with producer Michael Omartian (later with Rhythm Heritage), later in Second Helping. Worked as a songwriter for Wingate Music; wrote Nitty Gritty Dirt Band's "House At Pooh Corner." Signed in 1971 as a solo artist with Columbia, where he met Jim Messina; they recorded together as Loggins & Messina, 1972–76.	
8/19/78	**5**	15	1. **Whenever I Call You "Friend"** Stevie Nicks (harmony vocal)	Columbia 10794
11/24/79+	**11**	16	2. This Is It Michael McDonald (backing vocal)	Columbia 11109
4/5/80	**36**	2	3. Keep The Fire	Columbia 11215
8/23/80	**7**	12	4. **I'm Alright** theme from the movie *Caddyshack* starring Ted Knight and Rodney Dangerfield	Columbia 11317
9/25/82	**17**	6	5. Don't Fight It **KENNY LOGGINS with Steve Perry**	Columbia 03192
12/11/82+	**15**	13	6. Heart To Heart Michael McDonald (backing vocal)	Columbia 03377
4/2/83	**24**	7	7. Welcome To Heartlight inspired by the writings of children from Heartlight School; also on the B-side of #9 below	Columbia 03555
2/11/84	**1** (3)	16	▲ 8. **Footloose**	Columbia 04310
6/23/84	**22**	8	9. I'm Free (Heaven Helps The Man) above 2 from the movie *Footloose* starring Kevin Bacon	Columbia 04452
4/13/85	**29**	4	10. Vox Humana Airplay #25	Columbia 04849
7/20/85	**40**	1	11. Forever	Columbia 04931
6/7/86	**2** (1)	13	12. **Danger Zone** Sales #1(1) / Airplay #3; from the movie *Top Gun* starring Tom Cruise	Columbia 05893
4/25/87	**11**	12	13. Meet Me Half Way Airplay #10 / Sales #11; from the movie *Over the Top* starring Sylvester Stallone	Columbia 06690
7/30/88	**8**	11	14. **Nobody's Fool** Airplay #6 / Sales #10; theme from the movie *Caddyshack II* starring Jackie Mason and Chevy Chase	Columbia 07971

DATE	POS	WKS	ARTIST–RECORD TITLE	LABEL & NO.
			LOGGINS & MESSINA	
			Duo of Kenneth Clarke Loggins (born 1/7/47, Everett, Washington) and James Messina (born 12/5/47, Maywood, California). Loggins was raised in Alhambra, California; played guitar from age 13. Worked with Second Helping and Gator Creek and recorded in the late '60s. Messina was raised in Harlingen, Texas; played in bands from age 13. Worked as a recording engineer and producer from 1965. Member of Buffalo Springfield and Poco. Duo formed in 1970.	
12/2/72+	4	13	● 1. **Your Mama Don't Dance** **KENNY LOGGINS AND JIM MESSINA**	Columbia 45719
4/28/73	18	8	2. Thinking Of You	Columbia 45815
11/24/73	16	8	3. My Music	Columbia 45952
			LŌ-KEY?	
			Midwest funk fivesome: prof t., Dre, Lance Alexander, "D" and T-Bone.	
12/26/92+	27	9	1. I Got A Thang 4 Ya! Sales #20 / Airplay #31; #1 R&B hit (1 week)	Perspective 0008
			LOLITA	
			Lolita Ditta from Vienna, Austria.	
11/14/60	5	14	1. **Sailor (Your Home Is The Sea)** [F]	Kapp 349
			LONDON, Julie	
			Born on 9/26/26 in Santa Rosa, California. Singer/actress. Played Dixie McCall on the TV series "Emergency." Married to Jack Webb, 1945–53.	
12/3/55	9	13	● 1. **Cry Me A River** Jockey #9 / Top 100 #13 / Juke Box #14 / Best Seller #23; Barney Kessel (guitar); Ray Leatherwood (bass)	Liberty 55006
			LONDON, Laurie	
			Born on 1/19/44 in London. Male vocalist. Recorded only hit record at age 13.	
3/24/58	1 (4)	14	● 1. **He's Got The Whole World (In His Hands)** Jockey #1 / Best Seller #2 / Top 100 #2; traditional Afro-American gospel song; Geoff Love (orch.)	Capitol 3891
			LONDONBEAT	
			Britain-based soul outfit. Vocal trio of Americans Jimmy Helms and George Chandler, with Trinidad native Jimmy Chambers. Backed by British producer/multi-instrumentalist Willy M.	
2/16/91	1 (1)	14	● 1. **I've Been Thinking About You** Airplay #1(2) / Sales #1(1)	Radioactive 54005
6/8/91	18	7	2. A Better Love Airplay #31	Radioactive 54101
			LONDON SYMPHONY ORCHESTRA—see WILLIAMS, John	
			LONG, Shorty	
			Born Frederick Earl Long on 5/20/40 in Birmingham, Alabama. Drowned on 6/29/69 in Ontario, Canada. Soul singer/songwriter. Moved to Detroit in 1959. First recorded for Tri-Phi in 1962.	

DATE	POS	WKS	ARTIST–RECORD TITLE	LABEL & NO.
6/15/68	8	8	1. **Here Comes The Judge** [N] title inspired by a recurrent gag line on TV's "Rowan & Martin's Laugh-In"	Soul 35044
			LOOKING GLASS Rock quartet formed by singer/guitarist Elliot Lurie while at Rutgers University in New Jersey.	
7/1/72	1 (1)	14	● 1. **Brandy (You're A Fine Girl)**	Epic 10874
9/29/73	33	3	2. Jimmy Loves Mary-Anne	Epic 11001
			LOPEZ, Denise Dance singer born in Queens, New York. Recorded under the name "Neecy Dee" in 1984.	
8/6/88	31	5	1. **Sayin' Sorry (Don't Make It Right)** Sales #22	Vendetta 7200
			LOPEZ, Trini Born Trinidad Lopez III on 5/15/37 in Dallas. Pop-folk singer/guitarist. Discovered by Don Costa while performing at PJs nightclub in Los Angeles. Portrayed Pedro Jiminez in the movie *The Dirty Dozen*.	
8/10/63	3	11	1. **If I Had A Hammer** written as "The Hammer Song" by Pete Seeger & Lee Hays of The Weavers in 1958	Reprise 20198
12/14/63+	23	6	2. Kansas City above 2 recorded "live"	Reprise 20236
2/6/65	20	5	3. Lemon Tree	Reprise 0336
5/7/66	39	3	4. I'm Comin' Home, Cindy all of above produced by Don Costa	Reprise 0455
			LORAIN, A'Me Female singer from Simi Valley, California.	
2/24/90	9	12	1. **Whole Wide World** Sales #9 / Airplay #11; from the movie *True Love* starring Annabella Sciorra	RCA 9098
			LORBER, Jeff Jazz fusion keyboardist.	
2/7/87	27	5	1. Facts Of Love **JEFF LORBER Featuring Karyn White** Airplay #27 / Sales #29	Warner 28588
			LORENZ, Trey Born on 1/19/69 in Florence, South Carolina. Attended New York's Fairleigh Dickinson University; earned advertising degree. Sang backup on Mariah Carey's first two albums; male vocal on Carey's hit "I'll Be There."	
10/17/92	19	10	1. Someone To Hold Sales #21 / Airplay #27; co-written and co-produced by Mariah Carey	Epic 74482

DATE	POS	WKS	ARTIST–RECORD TITLE	LABEL & NO.
			LORING, Gloria	
			Born on 12/10/46. Played Liz Curtis on the TV soap "Days Of Our Lives." Married to actor Alan Thicke for 14 years.	

8/2/86	**2** (2)	14	1. **Friends And Lovers**
			    GLORIA LORING & CARL ANDERSON
			    Sales #1(1) / Airplay #2; popularized due to exposure on TV's
			    "Days Of Our Lives"; #1 Adult Contemporary hit (2 weeks)
				USA Carrere 06122

			LOS BRAVOS	
			Rock quintet consisting of four members from Spain and one from Germany. Mike Kennedy, leader.	
9/10/66	**4**	8	1. **Black Is Black**	Press 60002
			LOS INDIOS TABAJARAS	
			Brazilian Indian brothers: Natalicio and Antenor Lima.	

10/12/63	**6**	10	1. **Maria Elena** [I]
			    recorded in 1958; #1 hit in 1941 for Jimmy Dorsey & His
			    Orchestra
				RCA 8216

			LOS LOBOS	
			Hispanic-American rock quintet formed in East Los Angeles in 1973: David Hildago (vocals), Cesar Rosas (guitar), Steve Berlin (saxophone), Conrad Lozano (bass) and Louie Perez (drums).	
7/18/87	**1** (3)	14	1. **La Bamba** [F] Sales #1(3) / Airplay #1(3)	Slash 28336

10/17/87	**21**	7	2. **Come On, Let's Go**
			    Airplay #18 / Sales #24; above 2 from the movie La Bamba
			    starring Lou Diamond Phillips
				Slash 28186

			LOST GENERATION, The	
			Chicago soul quartet: Lowrell Simon (lead), his brother Fred Simon, Larry Brownlee (of The C.O.D.'s; died 1978) and Jesse Dean. Disbanded in 1974. Lowrell began recording solo (as Lowrell) in 1978.	
8/1/70	**30**	5	1. **The Sly, Slick, And The Wicked**	Brunswick 55436
			LOU, Bonnie—see BONNIE	
			LOUDERMILK, John D.	
			Born on 3/31/34 in Durham, North Carolina. Pop-country singer/songwriter/multi-instrumentalist. Wrote "Waterloo," "Tobacco Road," "Indian Reservation" and many others. Recorded as Johnny Dee and Ebe Sneezer in 1957.	

4/6/57	**38**	1	1. **Sittin' In The Balcony**
			    JOHNNY DEE
			    Joe Tanner (guitar)
				Colonial 430

12/4/61	**32**	3	2. **Language Of Love**	RCA 7938
			LOUIE LOUIE	
			Singer/dancer/songwriter Louie Cordero from Southern California. Played Madonna's boyfriend in her "Borderline" video.	
5/26/90	**19**	8	1. **Sittin' In The Lap Of Luxury** Airplay #15 / Sales #18	WTG 73266

DATE	POS	WKS	ARTIST–RECORD TITLE	LABEL & NO.
			LOVE	
			Los Angeles-based rock group led by singer/guitarist Arthur Lee (from Memphis).	
9/10/66	**33**	3	1. 7 And 7 Is	Elektra 45605
			LOVE, Darlene	
			Lead singer of backing group The Blossoms. Sang lead on two songs by The Crystals and with Bob B. Soxx & The Blue Jeans. Born Darlene Wright, Phil Spector suggested that she change her name to Darlene Love. Her sister, Edna Wright, was a member of The Honey Cone. Starred in the off-Broadway show *Leader of The Pack*. Appeared in the 1987 movie *Lethal Weapon*.	
5/11/63	**39**	1	1. (Today I Met) The Boy I'm Gonna Marry	Philles 111
8/24/63	**26**	4	2. Wait Til' My Bobby Gets Home	Philles 114
			above 2 produced by Phil Spector	
			LOVE, Mike—see CELEBRATION	
			LOVE, Monie	
			Born Simone Johnson on 7/2/70 in London. Raised in London and Brooklyn. Female rapper.	
4/20/91	**26**	6	1. It's A Shame (My Sister)	Warner 19515
			Sales #21 / Airplay #31; rap version of the Spinners' 1970 hit "It's A Shame"	
			LOVE AND KISSES	
			Studio group assembled by European disco producer Alec Costandinos. Consisted of vocalists Don Daniels, Elaine Hill, Dianne Brooks and Jean Graham.	
6/24/78	**22**	6	1. Thank God It's Friday	Casablanca 925
			title song from the movie starring Jeff Goldblum	
			LOVE AND ROCKETS	
			British trio: Daniel Ash (guitar, vocals), Kevin Haskins (drums) and David J (bass). All three were members of Bauhaus, 1979–83. Band name taken from the title of an underground comic book.	
6/17/89	**3**	12	1. **So Alive**	RCA 8956
			Sales #3 / Airplay #5	
			LOVERBOY	
			Rock quintet formed in Vancouver, Canada, in 1978: Mike Reno (lead singer), Paul Dean (lead guitar), Scott Smith (bass), Matt Frenette (drums) and Doug Johnson (keyboards; left by 1989).	
3/21/81	**35**	6	1. Turn Me Loose	Columbia 11421
1/9/82	**29**	8	2. Working For The Weekend	Columbia 02589
5/15/82	**26**	6	3. When It's Over	Columbia 02814
			Nancy Nash (backing vocal)	
7/2/83	**11**	11	4. Hot Girls In Love	Columbia 03941
10/29/83	**34**	3	5. Queen Of The Broken Hearts	Columbia 04096
9/14/85	**9**	11	6. **Lovin' Every Minute Of It**	Columbia 05569
			Sales #8 / Airplay #11	
2/15/86	**10**	10	7. **This Could Be The Night**	Columbia 05765
			Airplay #9 / Sales #13	

DATE	POS	WKS	ARTIST–RECORD TITLE	LABEL & NO.
8/23/86	**12**	11	8. Heaven In Your Eyes Airplay #10 / Sales #13; from the movie *Top Gun* starring Tom Cruise	Columbia 06178
10/10/87	**38**	3	9. Notorious Airplay #33	Columbia 07324

LOVE UNLIMITED

Female soul trio from San Pedro, California: sisters Glodean and Linda James, and Diane Taylor. Barry White, who married Glodean on 7/4/74, was their manager and producer.

DATE	POS	WKS	ARTIST–RECORD TITLE	LABEL & NO.
5/6/72	**14**	9	● 1. Walkin' In The Rain With The One I Love featuring Barry White's voice on the telephone	Uni 55319
1/4/75	**27**	7	2. I Belong To You #1 R&B hit (1 week); above 2 written and produced by Barry White	20th Century 2141

LOVE UNLIMITED ORCHESTRA

Forty-piece studio orchestra conducted and arranged by Barry White. Formed to back Love Unlimited, also heard on some of White's solo hits. Kenny G was a member at age 17.

DATE	POS	WKS	ARTIST–RECORD TITLE	LABEL & NO.
12/22/73+	**1** (1)	16	● 1. **Love's Theme** [I] #1 Adult Contemporary hit (2 weeks)	20th Century 2069
3/15/75	**22**	5	2. Satin Soul [I]	20th Century 2162

LOVIN' SPOONFUL, The

Jug-band rock group formed in New York City in 1965. Consisted of John Sebastian (lead vocals, songwriter, guitarist, harmonica), Zal Yanovsky (lead guitar), Steve Boone (bass) and Joe Butler (drums). Sebastian had been with the Even Dozen Jug Band; did session work at Elektra. Yanovsky and Sebastian were members of the Mugwumps with Mama Cass Elliot and Denny Doherty (later with The Mamas & The Papas). Yanovsky replaced by Jerry Yester (keyboards) in 1967. Disbanded in 1968.

DATE	POS	WKS	ARTIST–RECORD TITLE	LABEL & NO.
9/18/65	**9**	8	1. **Do You Believe In Magic**	Kama Sutra 201
12/11/65+	**10**	9	2. **You Didn't Have To Be So Nice**	Kama Sutra 205
3/12/66	**2** (2)	10	3. **Daydream**	Kama Sutra 208
5/14/66	**2** (2)	9	4. **Did You Ever Have To Make Up Your Mind?**	Kama Sutra 209
7/23/66	**1** (3)	10	● 5. **Summer In The City**	Kama Sutra 211
10/22/66	**10**	8	6. **Rain On The Roof**	Kama Sutra 216
12/31/66+	**8**	8	7. **Nashville Cats**	Kama Sutra 219
2/25/67	**15**	5	8. Darling Be Home Soon from the Francis Ford Coppola movie *You're a Big Boy Now* starring Peter Kastner	Kama Sutra 220
5/20/67	**18**	5	9. Six O'Clock all of above produced by Erik Jacobsen	Kama Sutra 225
11/11/67	**27**	3	10. She Is Still A Mystery	Kama Sutra 239

LOWE, Jim

Born on 5/7/27 in Springfield, Missouri. DJ/vocalist/pianist/composer. DJ in New York City when he recorded the pop hit "The Green Door" in 1956.

DATE	POS	WKS	ARTIST–RECORD TITLE	LABEL & NO.
9/29/56	**1** (3)	22	● 1. **The Green Door** Top 100 #1(3) / Juke Box #1(3) / Best Seller #2 / Jockey #2; High Fives (backing vocals); Bob Davie (piano)	Dot 15486
5/13/57	**15**	6	2. Four Walls / Juke Box #15 / Jockey #16 / Best Seller #19 / Top 100 #20	

DATE	POS	WKS	ARTIST–RECORD TITLE	LABEL & NO.
5/13/57	**15**	5	3. Talkin' To The Blues Juke Box #15 / Jockey #20 / Top 100 #21; from the TV production "Modern Romances"; Bob Davie (orch., above 3)	Dot 15569
			LOWE, Nick Born on 3/25/49 in Woodbridge, Suffolk, England. With Brinsley Schwarz, 1970–75, and Rockpile. Married Carlene Carter on 8/18/79; later divorced. Produced albums for Elvis Costello, Graham Parker and others. Co-founder of Little Village.	
8/18/79	**12**	10	1. Cruel To Be Kind	Columbia 11018
			L.T.D. Ten-man, R&B-funk band from Greensboro, North Carolina. Jeffrey Osborne, lead singer. Osborne left in 1980, replaced by Leslie Wilson and Andre Ray. L.T.D. stands for Love, Togetherness and Devotion.	
11/6/76	**20**	9	1. Love Ballad #1 R&B hit (2 weeks)	A&M 1847
11/12/77	**4**	12	● 2. **(Every Time I Turn Around) Back In Love Again** #1 R&B hit (2 weeks)	A&M 1974
1/31/81	**40**	1	3. Shine On	A&M 2283
			LUCAS Danish-born rapper/producer. Son of Danish artist Berta Moltke and American songwriter Paul Secon.	
10/22/94	**29**	7	1. Lucas With The Lid Off Sales #22 / Airplay #46; Junior Dangerous (ragga vocal)	Big Beat 98219
			LUKE—see 2 LIVE CREW	
			LUKE, Robin Born on 3/19/42 in Los Angeles. Recorded "Susie Darlin'" in Hawaii, inspired by his sister, Susie.	
8/18/58	**5**	15	● 1. **Susie Darlin'** Hot 100 #5 / Best Seller #6 end; first released on Bertram International 206 in 1958	Dot 15781
			LULU Born Marie Lawrie on 11/3/48 near Glasgow, Scotland. Married to Maurice Gibb (Bee Gees), 1969–73. Appeared in the 1967 movie *To Sir With Love*. Hosted own U.K. TV show in 1968.	
9/23/67	**1** (5)	15	● 1. **To Sir With Love** title song from the movie starring Sidney Poitier	Epic 10187
1/6/68	**32**	3	2. Best Of Both Worlds	Epic 10260
2/7/70	**22**	8	3. Oh Me Oh My (I'm A Fool For You Baby)	Atco 6722
8/22/81	**18**	10	4. I Could Never Miss You (More Than I Do)	Alfa 7006
			LUMAN, Bob Born on 4/15/37 in Nacogdoches, Texas. Died on 12/27/78. Country-rockabilly singer/songwriter/guitarist. First recorded for Imperial in 1957.	
9/26/60	**7**	9	1. **Let's Think About Living** [N] a jibe at the "death-song" fad of 1960	Warner 5172

DATE	POS	WKS	ARTIST–RECORD TITLE	LABEL & NO.
			LUNDBERG, Victor	
			Born on 9/2/23 in Grand Rapids, Michigan. Died on 2/14/90. News reader at WMAX in Grand Rapids.	
11/25/67	10	4	1. **An Open Letter To My Teenage Son** [S]	Liberty 55996
			LUNIZ	
			Rap duo from Oakland: Yukmouth and Knumskull.	
7/8/95	8	20	▲ 1. **I Got 5 On It** Sales #4 / Airplay #36; samples material by Kool & The Gang	Noo Trybe 38474
			L.V.	
			Male singer/rapper from Los Angeles. L.V. stands for Large Variety.	
8/19/95	1 (3)	35	▲² 1. **Gangsta's Paradise** **COOLIO FEATURING L.V.** Sales #1(7) / Airplay #7; rap version of "Pastime Paradise" by Stevie Wonder (from his 1976 album *Songs In The Key Of Life*); from the movie *Dangerous Minds* starring Michelle Pfeiffer	MCA 55104
			LYMAN, Arthur, Group	
			Lyman was born on the island of Kauai, Hawaii, on 2/2/32. Plays vibraphone, guitar, piano and drums. Formerly with the Martin Denny Trio.	
6/12/61	4	10	1. **Yellow Bird** [I] adapted from a West Indian folk song	Hi Fi 5024
			LYMON, Frankie, and The Teenagers	
			R&B group formed as The Premiers in the Bronx in 1955. Lead singer Lymon was born on 9/30/42 in New York City; died of a drug overdose on 2/28/68. Other members included Herman Santiago and Jimmy Merchant (tenors), Joe Negroni (baritone; died 9/5/78) and Sherman Garnes (bass; died 2/26/77). Group appeared in the movies *Rock, Rock, Rock* and *Mister Rock 'n' Roll*. Inducted into the Rock and Roll Hall of Fame in 1993.	
2/18/56	6	16	● 1. **Why Do Fools Fall In Love** **THE TEENAGERS Featuring FRANKIE LYMON** Best Seller #6 / Top 100 #7 / Juke Box #8 / Jockey #9; #1 R&B hit (5 weeks)	Gee 1002
5/12/56	13	11	2. I Want You To Be My Girl Best Seller #13 / Top 100 #17 / Juke Box #20 / Jockey #25	Gee 1012
8/26/57	20	7	3. Goody Goody Best Seller #20 / Jockey #21 / Top 100 #22; #1 hit for Benny Goodman in 1936; Jimmy Wright (orch., all of above)	Gee 1039
			LYNN, Barbara	
			Born Barbara Lynn Ozen on 1/16/42 in Beaumont, Texas. R&B singer/songwriter/guitarist.	
7/14/62	8	8	1. **You'll Lose A Good Thing** #1 R&B hit (3 weeks)	Jamie 1220
			LYNN, Cheryl	
			Born on 3/11/57 in Los Angeles. Soul singer. Discovered on TV's "Gong Show." Cousin of soul singer D'La Vance.	
1/6/79	12	12	● 1. Got To Be Real #1 R&B hit (1 week)	Columbia 10808

DATE	POS	WKS	ARTIST–RECORD TITLE	LABEL & NO.
			LYNNE, Gloria	
2/29/64	**28**	4	Born on 11/23/31 in New York City. Jazz-styled vocalist. 1. I Wish You Love French song written in 1946 (English lyrics added in 1955)	Everest 2036
			LYNYRD SKYNYRD	
			Southern-rock band formed by Ronnie Van Zant (born 1/15/49; lead singer), Gary Rossington (guitar) and Allen Collins (guitar) while they were in junior high in Jacksonville, Florida, in 1965. Named after their gym teacher Leonard Skinner. Changing lineup featured drummers Bob Burns, Rick Medlocke (later of Blackfoot) and Artimus Pyle; bassists Larry Junstrom (later of 38 Special), Greg Walker (later of Blackfoot), Leon Wilkeson and Ed King (ex-Strawberry Alarm Clock); pianist Billy Powell; and guitarist Steve Gaines. Plane crash on 10/20/77 in Gillsburg, Mississippi, killed Van Zant and members Steve and his sister Cassie Gaines (vocals). Gary and Allen formed the Rossington Collins Band in 1980; split in 1982. Rossington and vocalist Johnny Van Zant (the younger brother of Ronnie and Donnie [lead singer of 38 Special] Van Zant) regrouped with old and new band members for the 1987 Lynyrd Skynyrd Tribute Tour. Collins (paralyzed in a car accident in 1986) died of pneumonia on 1/23/90 (age 37). Rossington, Van Zant, Pyle, Wilkeson, King, Powell regrouped in 1991 with Randall Hall (guitar) and Custer (drums). Pyle left by 1993; replaced by Mike Estes. Custer left by 1994 and Owen Hale joined.	
8/24/74	**8**	11	1. **Sweet Home Alabama** answer song to Neil Young's "Alabama" and "Southern Man"	MCA 40258
1/4/75	**19**	5	2. Free Bird tribute to Duane Allman of The Allman Brothers Band	MCA 40328
7/19/75	**27**	3	3. Saturday Night Special	MCA 40416
1/8/77	**38**	2	4. Free Bird [R] "live" version of #2 above	MCA 40665
1/7/78	**13**	11	5. What's Your Name	MCA 40819

M

DATE	POS	WKS	ARTIST–RECORD TITLE	LABEL & NO.
			M	
8/25/79	**1** (1)	20	M is British pop musician Robin Scott (born 4/1/47). ● 1. **Pop Muzik**	Sire 49033
			MABLEY, Moms	
7/19/69	**35**	2	Born Loretta Mary Aiken on 3/19/1894 in Brevard, North Carolina. Died on 5/23/75. Bawdy comedienne/actress. Charted 13 comedy albums on *Billboard*'s Top Pop Albums charts. Appeared in the movies *Boarding House Blues*, *Emperor Jones* and *Amazing Grace*. 1. Abraham, Martin And John a tribute to Lincoln, King and John and Robert Kennedy	Mercury 72935
			MacGREGOR, Byron	
1/12/74	**4**	9	Born Gary Mack in 1948 in Calgary, Alberta, Canada. Died on 1/3/95 (age 46). News director at CKLW-Detroit when he did the narration for "Americans." Narration was originally written and delivered as an editorial by Gordon Sinclair for CFRB-Toronto on 6/5/73. ● 1. **Americans** [S] backed by an instrumental version of "America The Beautiful"	Westbound 222

DATE	POS	WKS	ARTIST–RECORD TITLE	LABEL & NO.
			MacGREGOR, Mary	
			Born on 5/6/48 in St. Paul, Minnesota. Pop singer.	Ariola Am. 7638
12/25/76+	1 (2)	16	● 1. **Torn Between Two Lovers** written and produced by Peter Yarrow (Peter, Paul & Mary); #1 Adult Contemporary hit (2 weeks)	
10/6/79	39	2	2. Good Friend from the movie *Meatballs* starring Bill Murray	RSO 938
			MACK, Craig	
			Rapper from Long Island, New York. Was a roadie for EPMD. Discovered by producer Sean "Puffy" Combs.	
9/3/94	9	20	▲ 1. **Flava In Ya Ear** Sales #3 / Airplay #44; remix version available on Bad Boy 79010	Bad Boy 79001
3/18/95	38	2	● 2. Get Down Sales #15; remix version available on Bad Boy 79021	Bad Boy 79012
			MACK, Lonnie	
			Born Lonnie McIntosh on 7/18/41 in Aurora, Indiana. Singer/guitarist (since age five). Own country band in 1954. With country singer Troy Seals (cousin of Jim [Seals & Crofts] and Dan Seals and uncle of Brady Seals of Little Texas) in the early '60s. Rediscovered in 1968. Retired from music, 1971–85.	
6/22/63	5	10	1. **Memphis** [I] first recorded by Chuck Berry in 1959 as "Memphis, Tennessee" on Chess 1729	Fraternity 906
9/21/63	24	4	2. Wham! [I]	Fraternity 912
			MacKENZIE, Gisele	
			Born Gisele LeFleche on 1/10/27 in Winnipeg, Canada. Popular singing star of TV's "Your Hit Parade," 1953-57. Own TV variety show, 1957–58. Regular on *The Sid Caesar Show*, 1963–64.	
6/4/55	4	19	1. **Hard To Get** Jockey #4 / Best Seller #5 / Juke Box #5; introduced by MacKenzie on 5/12/55 episode of the NBC-TV series "Justice"	X 0137
			MacRAE, Gordon	
			Born on 3/12/21 in East Orange, New Jersey. Died on 1/24/86 of cancer. Sang with Horace Heidt, 1942–43, and recorded numerous duets with Jo Stafford, late '40s. Starred in the movie musicals *Oklahoma!* and *Carousel*. Actresses Sheila and Meredith were his wife and daughter.	
10/6/58	18	6	1. The Secret Van Alexander (orch.)	Capitol 4033
			MAD COBRA	
			Born Ewart Everton Brown on 3/31/68 in Kingston; raised in St. Mary's, Jamaica. Reggae rapper.	
11/14/92+	13	10	● 1. Flex Sales #9 / Airplay #38	Columbia 74373

DATE	POS	WKS	ARTIST–RECORD TITLE	LABEL & NO.
			MADDOX, Johnny, and The Rhythmasters	
			Born in 1929 in Gallatin, Tennessee. Honky-tonk pianist/band leader.	
2/5/55	**2** (7)	20	● 1. **The Crazy Otto** [I] Best Seller #2 / Juke Box #2 / Jockey #7; medley of tunes inspired by German honky-tonk pianist Crazy Otto: "In der alten Hafenbar"/"In der nacht ist der mensch nicht gern alteine"/"Das machen nur die Beine von Dolores"/"Was macht der alte Seemann"/"Play A Simple Melody"	Dot 15325
			MADIGAN, Betty	
			Singer from Washington, D.C.	
9/8/58	**31**	3	1. Dance Everyone Dance Best Seller #31 / Hot 100 #34; based on the Israeli harvest song "Hava Nagila"; Dick Jacobs (orch.)	Coral 62007
			MADNESS	
			Septet from North London, England. Graham "Suggs" McPherson, vocals. Formed as a ska-pop band in 1978, split up in 1986.	
5/28/83	**7**	13	1. **Our House**	Geffen 29668
9/17/83	**33**	5	2. It Must Be Love	Geffen 29562
			MADONNA	
			Born Madonna Louise Ciccone on 8/16/58 in Bay City, Michigan. To New York in the late '70s; performed with the Alvin Ailey dance troupe. Short-lived member of Breakfast Club, early '80s. Married to actor Sean Penn, 1985–89. Acted in the movies *Desperately Seeking Susan, Dick Tracy, A League Of Their Own* and *Body Of Evidence,* among others. Appeared in Broadway's *Speed-The-Plow.* Released concert tour documentary movie *Truth Or Dare* in 1991. Released adults-only picture book *Sex* in 1992. The top female performer of the past decade.	
12/10/83+	**16**	11	1. Holiday	Sire 29478
4/14/84	**10**	15	2. **Borderline**	Sire 29354
9/1/84	**4**	12	3. **Lucky Star** Airplay #3 / Sales #6	Sire 29177
11/24/84	**1** (6)	14	● 4. **Like A Virgin** Airplay #1(5) / Sales #1(4)	Sire 29210
2/16/85	**2** (2)	12	5. **Material Girl** Airplay #2 / Sales #3	Sire 29083
3/16/85	**1** (1)	14	● 6. **Crazy For You** Airplay #1(1) / Sales #2; from the movie *Vision Quest* starring Matthew Modine	Geffen 29051
5/11/85	**5**	12	● 7. **Angel** Airplay #4 / Sales #9; gold certification is for the 12" single	Sire 29008
8/17/85	**5**	11	8. **Dress You Up** Airplay #3 / Sales #12; above 5 (except #6) from the album *Like A Virgin*	Sire 28919
4/19/86	**1** (1)	13	9. **Live To Tell** Airplay #1(3) / Sales #2; from the movie *At Close Range* starring Sean Penn; #1 Adult Contemporary hit (3 weeks)	Sire 28717
7/5/86	**1** (2)	13	10. **Papa Don't Preach** Sales #1(3) / Airplay #1(2)	Sire 28660
10/4/86	**3**	12	11. **True Blue** Airplay #3 / Sales #4	Sire 28591
12/13/86+	**1** (1)	14	12. **Open Your Heart** Airplay #1(2) / Sales #2	Sire 28508

Christine McVie, like other Fleetwood Mac members, enjoyed considerable success as a solo artist. Her eponymous 1984 solo album yielded two Top 30 hits, including the No. 10 single "Got A Hold On Me."

John Cougar Mellencamp initially made records under the name Johnny Cougar, then added his real surname beginning with his 1983 album *Uh-Huh*. After scoring a multitude of hits, such as 1988's "Check It Out," he'd drop the "Cougar" name for good by 1991.

Sergio Mendes and Brasil 66 produced three Top 20 singles in 1968, all of which were remakes of well-known songs. The hits? Dusty Springfield's "The Look Of Love," the Beatles' "The Fool On The Hill," and Simon & Garfunkel's "Scarborough Fair."

Metallica's characteristically loud brand of thrash metal has never exactly been deemed prime Top 40 material, yet in 1989 the speed-metal group did manage a No. 35 single. The song's name, and the band's overall Top 40 score: "One."

George Michael's huge 1984 smash "Careless Whisper" held the unique distinction of being released by "Wham featuring George Michael"; other releases were either credited to Wham! U.K. or directly to Michael himself.

Lee Michaels' 1971 hit "Do You Know What I Mean" boasted such simplistic lyrics that some critics deemed them, perhaps wryly, existential. After a long stint with A&M, keyboardist Michaels signed with Columbia in 1973.

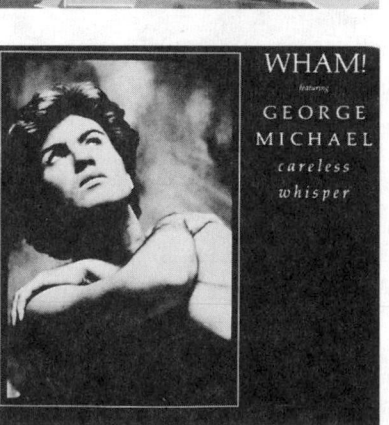

Bette Midler's platinum-selling 1990 hit "From A Distance" outsold its predecessor "Wind Beneath My Wings" (from the film *Beaches*), even though the latter reached No. 1 and "Distance" peaked at No. 2.

Garry Miles had a No. 16 hit in 1960 with "Look For A Star," rather uniquely drawn from the American-International film *Circus Of Horrors*. Miles later made records under the name Buzz Cason.

Mitch Miller's 1961 single "Tunes Of Glory" struggled against another version by the Cambridge Strings, on the charts the same weeks as his. Miller lost; his version peaked No. 88, the Cambridge Strings's at No. 60.

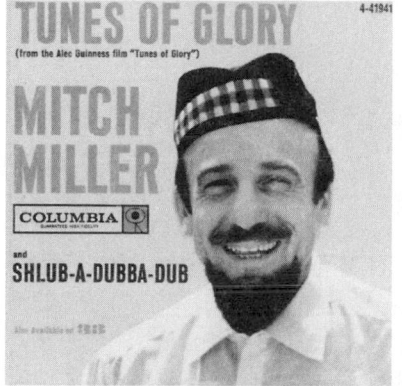

Roger Miller's phonetically challenging batch of early hits included 1964's "Dang Me" and "Chug-A-Lug," and 1965's "Do-Wacka-Do." When he "went straight" with 1965's "King Of The Road," he got the highest-charting single of his career.

Milli Vanilli's late-'80s raft of hit singles—such as 1989's chart-topping "Girl I'm Gonna Miss You"—now stand as historical curios, as it has since been revealed that the pair—Rob Pilatus and Fabrice Morvan—never sang on their own albums.

Hayley Mills's "Let's Get Together," taken from the 1961 film *The Parent Trap*, was the London-born actress's first and only Top 10 hit. Mills's name would later be strategically dropped on Prefab Sprout's critically praised 1985 album *Two Wheels Good*.

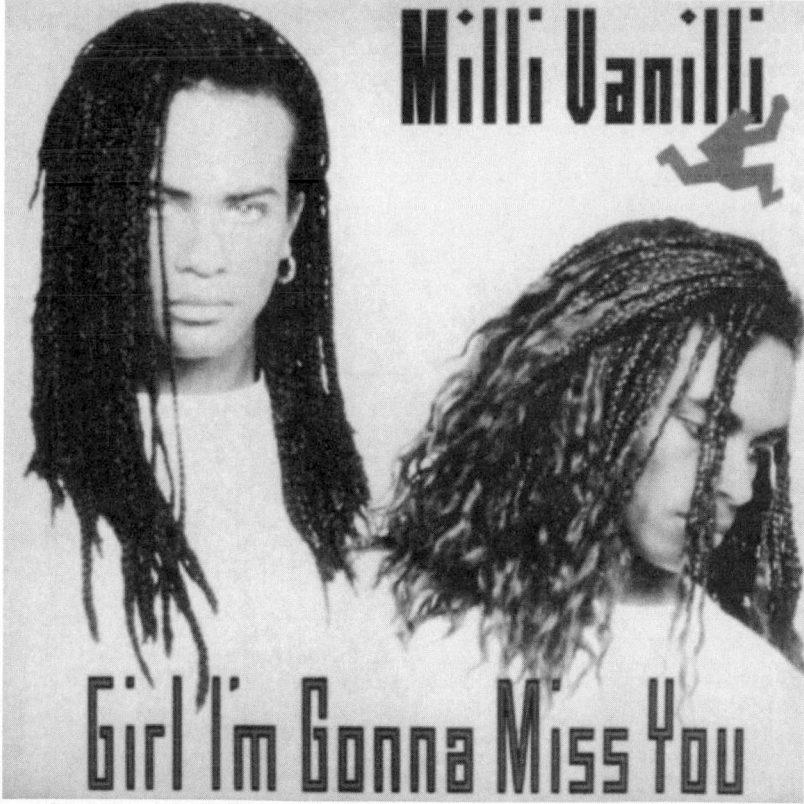

DATE	POS	WKS	ARTIST–RECORD TITLE	LABEL & NO.
3/28/87	4	12	13. **La Isla Bonita** Airplay #3 / Sales #3; #1 Adult Contemporary hit (1 week); above 5 from the album *True Blue*	Sire 28425
7/18/87	1 (1)	11	14. **Who's That Girl** Airplay #1(2) / Sales #1(1)	Sire 28341
9/19/87	2 (3)	11	15. **Causing A Commotion** Airplay #2 / Sales #2; above 2 from the album and movie *Who's That Girl* starring Madonna	Sire 28224
3/18/89	1 (3)	12	▲ 16. **Like A Prayer** Sales #1(3) / Airplay #1(3)	Sire 27539
6/10/89	2 (2)	11	● 17. **Express Yourself** Sales #2 / Airplay #3; also on the B-side of #23 below	Sire 22948
8/19/89	2 (2)	12	18. **Cherish** Airplay #2 / Sales #2; #1 Adult Contemporary hit (2 weeks)	Sire 22883
11/25/89+	20	8	19. Oh Father Sales #16 / Airplay #22	Sire 22723
2/17/90	8	9	● 20. **Keep It Together** Airplay #7 / Sales #7; above 5 from the album *Like A Prayer*	Sire 19986
4/14/90	1 (3)	16	▲² 21. **Vogue** Airplay #1(3) / Sales #1(2)	Sire 19863
6/30/90	10	7	● 22. **Hanky Panky** Airplay #11 / Sales #13; above 2 from the album *I'm Breathless*; inspired by the movie *Dick Tracy* starring Madonna and Warren Beatty	Sire 19789
11/24/90+	1 (2)	13	▲ 23. **Justify My Love** Sales #1(5) / Airplay #2	Sire 19485
3/2/91	9	6	● 24. **Rescue Me** Airplay #5 / Sales #11	Sire 19490
7/4/92	1 (1)	14	● 25. **This Used To Be My Playground** Airplay #2 / Sales #3; from the movie *A League Of Their Own* starring Madonna, Tom Hanks and Geena Davis (not on soundtrack album)	Sire 18822
10/17/92	3	9	● 26. **Erotica** Airplay #2 / Sales #4; contains a sample of "Jungle Boogie" by Kool & The Gang	Maverick 18782
12/5/92+	7	13	27. **Deeper And Deeper** Airplay #8 / Sales #15	Maverick 18639
3/20/93	36	3	28. Bad Girl Sales #36 / Airplay #44	Maverick 18650
7/31/93	14	14	29. Rain Airplay #11 / Sales #31; above 4 from the album *Erotica*	Maverick 18505
4/2/94	2 (4)	24	● 30. **I'll Remember** Airplay #2 / Sales #2; theme from the movie *With Honors* starring Joe Pesci; #1 Adult Contemporary hit (4 weeks)	Maverick/Sire 18247
10/8/94	3	20	● 31. **Secret** Airplay #3 / Sales #11	Maverick/Sire 18035
12/24/94+	1 (7)	27	● 32. **Take A Bow** Airplay #1(9) / Sales #4; Babyface (backing vocal); #1 Adult Contemporary hit (9 weeks)	Maverick/Sire 18000
12/9/95	6	14	33. **You'll See** Sales #6 / Airplay #10	Maverick 17719
			MAESTRO, Johnny	
			Born Johnny Mastrangelo on 5/7/39 in New York City. Lead singer of The Crests and Brooklyn Bridge.	
3/20/61	20	5	1. Model Girl **JOHNNY MASTRO The Voice Of The Crests**	Coed 545

DATE	POS	WKS	ARTIST—RECORD TITLE	LABEL & NO.
5/22/61	33	4	2. What A Surprise **JOHNNY MAESTRO The Voice Of The Crests**	Coed 549
			MAGGARD, Cledus, And The Citizen's Band	
1/24/76	19	9	Born Jay Huguely in Quick Sand, Kentucky. Worked at Leslie Advertising in Greenville, South Carolina when he recorded "The White Knight." 1. The White Knight [N] #1 Country hit (1 week); jargon-laced CB radio conversation	Mercury 73751
			MAGIC LANTERNS	
11/30/68	29	5	Rock quintet from Lancashire, England. Albert Hammond was a member in 1971. 1. Shame, Shame	Atlantic 2560
			MAHARIS, George	
5/26/62	25	5	Born on 9/1/28 in New York City. Movie/TV actor. Played Buz Murdock on TV's "Route 66." 1. Teach Me Tonight #2 hit for The DeCastro Sisters in 1954	Epic 9504
			MAIN INGREDIENT, The	
9/2/72 3/16/74 8/10/74	3 10 35	10 14 2	New York soul trio formed as the Poets in 1964. Consisted of Donald McPherson (died 7/4/71), Luther Simmons, Jr., and Tony Silvester. First recorded as the Poets for Red Bird in 1965. McPherson replaced by Cuba Gooding in 1971; Gooding's son, Cuba Jr., acted in the movies *Boyz N The Hood, Gladiator, A Few Good Men* and *Outbreak*. ● 1. **Everybody Plays The Fool** ● 2. **Just Don't Want To Be Lonely** 3. Happiness Is Just Around The Bend	RCA 0731 RCA 0205 RCA 0305
			MAJORS, The	
9/8/62	22	5	Philadelphia R&B group: Ricky Cordo (lead), Eugene Glass, Frank Troutt, Ronald Gathers and Idella Morris. Produced by Jerry Ragavoy. 1. A Wonderful Dream	Imperial 5855
			MAKEBA, Miriam	
10/28/67	12	8	Born Zensi Miriam Makeba on 3/4/32 in Johannesburg, South Africa. Folk singer. Her five husbands included Hugh Masekela (1964–66) and black-power activist Stokeley Carmichael (married in 1968). 1. Pata Pata [F]	Reprise 0606
			MALO	
4/1/72	18	8	Latin-rock band formed by Jorge Santana (brother of Carlos Santana). Malo is Spanish for Bad. 1. Suavecito	Warner 7559

DATE	POS	WKS	ARTIST–RECORD TITLE	LABEL & NO.

MALTBY, Richard, and his Orchestra

Born on 6/26/14 in Chicago. Died on 8/19/91. Trumpeter/composer/band leader. Attended Northwestern University. Worked with Ethel Merman, Peggy Lee, Dean Martin, Jerry Lewis, Vic Damone and Sarah Vaughan. His son, Richard Maltby, Jr., is a Broadway director/lyricist (*Ain't Misbehavin'*, *Miss Saigon*).

DATE	POS	WKS	ARTIST–RECORD TITLE	LABEL & NO.
3/31/56	14	8	1. (Themes From) "The Man With The Golden Arm" [I] Top 100 #14 / Best Seller #15 / Juke Box #19 / Jockey #20; from the movie *The Man With The Golden Arm* starring Frank Sinatra	Vik 0196

MAMA CASS

Born Ellen Naomi Cohen on 9/19/41 in Baltimore. Died of a heart attack on 7/29/74 in London. Cass Elliot of The Mamas & The Papas.

DATE	POS	WKS	ARTIST–RECORD TITLE	LABEL & NO.
7/27/68	12	8	1. Dream A Little Dream Of Me **MAMA CASS with The Mamas & The Papas** #1 hit for Wayne King in 1931	Dunhill 4145
8/2/69	30	7	2. It's Getting Better	Dunhill 4195
11/15/69	36	3	3. Make Your Own Kind Of Music **MAMA CASS ELLIOT**	Dunhill 4214

MAMAS & THE PAPAS, The

Quartet formed in New York City in 1963. Consisted of John Phillips (born 8/30/35, Paris Island, South Carolina); Holly Michelle Gilliam Phillips (born 6/4/45, Long Beach, California); Dennis Doherty (born 11/29/41, Halifax, Nova Scotia, Canada) and Cass Elliot (see Mama Cass above). John Phillips had been in the Journeymen, married Michelle Gilliam in 1962. Elliot had been in the Mugwumps with Doherty and future Lovin' Spoonful member Zal Yanovsky. Group moved to Los Angeles in 1964. Disbanded in 1968, reunited briefly in 1971. Michelle Phillips acted in the movies *Dillinger* and *Valentino*, and was a cast member of TV's "Knots Landing"; married for eight days to actor Dennis Hopper in 1970. New Mamas & Papas group formed in 1982: John and daughter, actress MacKenzie Phillips, Dennis Doherty and Spanky McFarlane of Spanky & Our Gang. Michelle and John's daughter, Chynna, is a member of the trio Wilson Phillips.

DATE	POS	WKS	ARTIST–RECORD TITLE	LABEL & NO.
2/5/66	4	13	● 1. **California Dreamin'**	Dunhill 4020
4/16/66	1 (3)	10	● 2. **Monday, Monday**	Dunhill 4026
7/9/66	5	8	3. **I Saw Her Again**	Dunhill 4031
11/5/66	24	4	4. Look Through My Window	Dunhill 4050
12/17/66+	5	9	5. **Words Of Love**	Dunhill 4057
3/4/67	2 (3)	9	6. **Dedicated To The One I Love**	Dunhill 4077
5/13/67	5	7	7. **Creeque Alley** name of the street group lived on in the Virgin Islands; a musical biography of the group members	Dunhill 4083
9/2/67	20	5	8. Twelve Thirty (Young Girls Are Coming To The Canyon)	Dunhill 4099
11/4/67	26	5	9. Glad To Be Unhappy from the 1936 Rodgers & Hart musical *On Your Toes*; all of above produced by Lou Adler	Dunhill 4107
7/27/68	12	8	10. Dream A Little Dream Of Me **MAMA CASS with The Mamas & The Papas** #1 hit for Wayne King in 1931	Dunhill 4145

MANCHESTER, Melissa

Born on 2/15/51 in the Bronx. Vocalist/pianist/composer. Father is a bassoon player with the New York Metropolitan Opera Orchestra. She studied songwriting under Paul Simon at the University School of the Arts in the early '70s. Former backup singer for Bette Midler.

DATE	POS	WKS	ARTIST–RECORD TITLE	LABEL & NO.
6/14/75	6	11	1. **Midnight Blue** *#1 Adult Contemporary hit (2 weeks)*	Arista 0116
10/18/75	30	5	2. Just Too Many People	Arista 0146
2/28/76	27	4	3. Just You And I	Arista 0168
1/6/79	10	14	4. **Don't Cry Out Loud**	Arista 0373
11/24/79	39	2	5. Pretty Girls	Arista 0456
4/5/80	32	5	6. Fire In The Morning	Arista 0485
7/10/82	5	15	7. **You Should Hear How She Talks About You**	Arista 0676

MANCINI, Henry

Born on 4/16/24 in Cleveland; raised in Aliquippa, Pennsylvania. Died of cancer on 6/14/94. Leading movie and TV composer/arranger/conductor. Staff composer for Universal Pictures, 1952–58. Winner of four Oscars and 20 Grammys. Married Ginny O'Connor, an original member of Mel Tormé's Mel-Tones.

DATE	POS	WKS	ARTIST–RECORD TITLE	LABEL & NO.
4/18/60	21	8	1. Mr. Lucky　[I] *title song from the TV series starring John Vivyan*	RCA 7705
11/13/61	11	16	2. Moon River *from the movie Breakfast at Tiffany's starring Audrey Hepburn; originally charted for 14 weeks; re-entered on 5/19/62 (#32)*	RCA 7916
3/2/63	33	10	3. Days Of Wine And Roses *title song from the movie starring Jack Lemmon*	RCA 8120
1/25/64	36	4	4. Charade *title song from the movie starring Cary Grant and Audrey Hepburn*	RCA 8256
5/9/64	31	2	5. The Pink Panther Theme　[I] *from the first of the Pink Panther movies starring Peter Sellers*	RCA 8286
5/24/69	1 (2)	12	● 6. **Love Theme From Romeo & Juliet**　[I] *from the movie Romeo & Juliet starring Leonard Whiting and Olivia Hussey; #1 Adult Contemporary hit (8 weeks)*	RCA 0131
2/6/71	13	8	7. (Theme From) Love Story　[I] *from the movie Love Story starring Ryan O'Neal and Ali McGraw*	RCA 9927

MANDELL, Steve—see WEISSBERG, Eric

MANDRELL, Barbara

Born on 12/25/48 in Houston; raised in Oceanside, California. Country singer. Moved to Nashville in 1971. Host of own TV variety series "Barbara Mandrell & The Mandrell Sisters," 1980–82. Suffered severe injuries in an auto accident in 1984, from which she recovered fully.

DATE	POS	WKS	ARTIST–RECORD TITLE	LABEL & NO.
5/12/79	31	5	1. (If Loving You Is Wrong) I Don't Want To Be Right *#1 Country hit (1 week)*	ABC 12451

MANFRED MANN—see MANN, Manfred

MANGIONE, Chuck

Born on 11/29/40 in Rochester, New York. Flugelhorn player/bandleader/composer. Recorded with older brother Gaspare ("Gap") as The Jazz Brothers for Riverside in 1960. To New York City in 1965; played with Maynard Ferguson, Kai Winding, and Art Blakey's Jazz Messengers.

DATE	POS	WKS	ARTIST–RECORD TITLE	LABEL & NO.
3/18/78	4	16	1. **Feels So Good**　[I] *#1 Adult Contemporary hit (1 week)*	A&M 2001
2/16/80	18	9	2. Give It All You Got　[I] *featured song by ABC Sports for the 1980 Winter Olympics; #1 Adult Contemporary hit (3 weeks)*	A&M 2211

DATE	POS	WKS	ARTIST—RECORD TITLE	LABEL & NO.
			MANHATTANS, The	
			Soul vocal group from Jersey City, New Jersey. Consisted of George "Smitty" Smith (died 1970 of spinal meningitis; lead vocals), Winfred "Blue" Lovett (bass), Edward "Sonny" Bivins and Kenneth "Wally" Kelly (tenors) and Richard Taylor (baritone). Smith replaced by Gerald Alston in 1971. First recorded for Piney in 1962. Taylor (aka Abdul Rashid Talhah) left in 1976; died on 12/7/87 (age 47) following lengthy illness. Featured female vocalist Regina Belle began solo career in 1987. Alston went solo in 1988.	
2/15/75	37	2	1. Don't Take Your Love	Columbia 10045
5/29/76	1 (2)	17	▲ 2. **Kiss And Say Goodbye**	Columbia 10310
			#1 R&B hit (1 week)	
5/31/80	5	14	● 3. **Shining Star**	Columbia 11222
			MANHATTAN TRANSFER, The	
			Versatile vocal harmony quartet formed in New York City in 1972: Tim Hauser, Alan Paul, Janis Siegel and Cheryl Bentyne (replaced Laurel Masse in 1979).	
11/1/75	22	5	1. Operator	Atlantic 3292
5/31/80	30	4	2. Twilight Zone/Twilight Tone	Atlantic 3649
			"Twilight Zone" is the theme from the Rod Serling TV series	
6/13/81	7	13	3. **Boy From New York City**	Atlantic 3816
11/5/83	40	2	4. Spice Of Life	Atlantic 89786
			MANILOW, Barry	
			Born Barry Alan Pincus on 6/17/46 in Brooklyn. Vocalist/pianist/composer. Studied at New York's Juilliard School. Music director for the WCBS-TV series "Callback." Worked at New York's Continental Baths bathhouse/nightclub in New York as Bette Midler's accompanist in 1972; later produced her first two albums. First recorded solo as Featherbed. Wrote jingles for Dr. Pepper, Pepsi, State Farm Insurance, Band-Aids and McDonald's ("You Deserve A Break Today", which he also sang).	
12/7/74+	1 (1)	12	● 1. **Mandy**	Bell 45613
			written and charted by Scott English in 1972 as "Brandy"; #1 Adult Contemporary hit (2 weeks)	
3/29/75	12	8	2. It's A Miracle	Arista 0108
			#1 Adult Contemporary hit (1 week)	
7/26/75	6	13	3. **Could It Be Magic**	Arista 0126
			new version of song first released on Bell 45133 in 1971 as by Featherbed Featuring Barry Manilow, and then on Bell 45422 in 1973; inspired by Chopin's Prelude in C Minor	
11/22/75+	1 (1)	16	● 4. **I Write The Songs**	Arista 0157
			written by The Beach Boys' Bruce Johnston (Bruce & Terry); #1 Adult Contemporary hit (2 weeks)	
4/10/76	10	10	5. **Tryin' To Get The Feeling Again**	Arista 0172
			#1 Adult Contemporary hit (1 week)	
10/9/76	29	5	6. This One's For You	Arista 0206
			#1 Adult Contemporary hit (1 week)	
12/25/76+	10	13	7. **Weekend In New England**	Arista 0212
			#1 Adult Contemporary hit (1 week)	
5/28/77	1 (1)	13	● 8. **Looks Like We Made It**	Arista 0244
			#1 Adult Contemporary hit (3 weeks)	
10/22/77	23	5	9. Daybreak	Arista 0273
			"live" recording of tune from the 1976 This One's For You album	
2/18/78	3	16	● 10. **Can't Smile Without You**	Arista 0305
			#1 Adult Contemporary hit (2 weeks)	

DATE	POS	WKS	ARTIST–RECORD TITLE	LABEL & NO.
6/10/78	19	4	11. Even Now 　　　#1 Adult Contemporary hit (3 weeks)	Arista 0330
7/8/78	8	9	● 12. **Copacabana (At The Copa)**	Arista 0339
10/7/78	11	10	13. Ready To Take A Chance Again 　　　above 2 from the movie *Foul Play* starring Goldie Hawn and Chevy Chase	Arista 0357
1/6/79	9	10	14. **Somewhere In The Night** 　　　above 5 (except #13) from the album *Even Now*	Arista 0382
10/20/79	9	11	15. **Ships**	Arista 0464
2/2/80	20	7	16. When I Wanted You 　　　#1 Adult Contemporary hit (1 week)	Arista 0481
5/17/80	36	4	17. I Don't Want To Walk Without You 　　　#2 hit for Harry James in 1942 (from the movie *Sweater Girl* starring Eddie Bracken)	Arista 0501
12/6/80+	10	11	18. **I Made It Through The Rain** 　　　all of above produced by Manilow and Ron Dante (The Archies, The Cuff Links)	Arista 0566
10/17/81	15	10	19. The Old Songs 　　　#1 Adult Contemporary hit (3 weeks)	Arista 0633
1/23/82	21	7	20. Somewhere Down The Road 　　　#1 Adult Contemporary hit (2 weeks)	Arista 0658
4/24/82	32	3	21. Let's Hang On	Arista 0675
9/18/82	38	2	22. Oh Julie	Arista 0698
1/15/83	39	2	23. Memory 　　　theme from the musical *Cats* starring Betty Buckley	Arista 1025
4/9/83	26	7	24. Some Kind Of Friend 　　　also released on Arista 1046 in 1983	Arista 9003
11/26/83+	18	10	25. Read 'Em And Weep	Arista 9101
			MANN, Barry	
			Born Barry Iberman on 2/9/39 in Brooklyn. One of pop music's most prolific songwriters. Wrote with wife, Cynthia Weil, "You've Lost That Lovin' Feelin'," "(You're My) Soul & Inspiration," "Kicks," "Hungry," "We Gotta Get Out Of This Place," and many others. Established own publishing company, Dyad Music.	
8/21/61	7	9	1. **Who Put The Bomp (In The Bomp, Bomp, Bomp)** [N]	ABC-Para. 10237
			MANN, Carl	
			Born on 8/24/42 in Huntingdon, Tennessee. Rockabilly singer/pianist. Toured with Carl Perkins, 1962–64. Left music from 1967 to 1974.	
7/27/59	25	6	1. Mona Lisa 　　　#1 hit for Nat King Cole in 1950	Phillips 3539
			MANN, Gloria	
			Her son, Bob Rosenberg, is the leader of Will To Power.	
2/12/55	18	2	1. Earth Angel (Will You Be Mine) 　　　Juke Box #18 / Best Seller #24	Sound 109
12/24/55+	19	8	2. Teen Age Prayer 　　　Best Seller #19 / Top 100 #21; Sid Bass (orch.)	Sound 126

DATE	POS	WKS	ARTIST–RECORD TITLE	LABEL & NO.

MANN, Herbie

Born Herbert Jay Solomon on 4/16/30 in Brooklyn. Renowned jazz flutist. First recorded with Mat Mathews Quintet for Brunswick in 1953. First recorded as a solo for Bethlehem in 1954.

DATE	POS	WKS	ARTIST–RECORD TITLE	LABEL & NO.
4/26/75	14	6	1. Hijack	Atlantic 3246
3/17/79	26	6	2. Superman	Atlantic 3547

MANN, Manfred

Rock group formed in England in 1964: Manfred Mann (born Michael Lubowitz, 10/21/40, Johannesburg, South Africa; keyboards), Paul Jones (vocals), Mike Hugg (drums), Michael Vickers (guitar) and Tom McGuinness (bass). McGuinness left to form McGuinness Flint in 1970. Manfred Mann formed his new Earth Band in 1971: Mann, Mick Rogers (vocals), Colin Pattenden (bass) and Chris Slade (drums). Rogers replaced by Chris Thompson (vocals, guitar) in 1976. Pattenden replaced by Pat King in June 1977. Thompson also recorded with own group Night in 1979. Lineup in 1979: Mann, Thompson, King, Steve Waller (guitar, vocals) and Geoff Britton (drums). King replaced by Matt Irving in 1981. Earth Band dissolved in 1986.

DATE	POS	WKS	ARTIST–RECORD TITLE	LABEL & NO.
9/12/64	1 (2)	12	1. **Do Wah Diddy Diddy**	Ascot 2157
11/28/64+	12	9	2. Sha La La	Ascot 2165
7/23/66	29	5	3. Pretty Flamingo	United Art. 50040
3/9/68	10	10	4. **Mighty Quinn (Quinn The Eskimo)** written by Bob Dylan	Mercury 72770

MANFRED MANN'S EARTH BAND:

DATE	POS	WKS	ARTIST–RECORD TITLE	LABEL & NO.
12/18/76+	1 (1)	15	● 5. **Blinded By The Light**	Warner 8252
6/4/77	40	1	6. Spirit In The Night [R] remix of the group's 1976 hit (#97); above 2 written by Bruce Springsteen	Warner 8355
2/18/84	22	8	7. Runner	Arista 9143

MANTOVANI And His Orchestra

Born Annunzio Paolo Mantovani on 11/15/05 in Venice, Italy. Died on 3/29/80. Played classical violin in England before forming his own orchestra in the early 1930s. Had first U.S. chart hit in 1935, "Red Sails In The Sunset." Achieved international fame 20 years later with his 40-piece orchestra and distinctive "cascading strings" sound. Charted 45 albums on *Billboard*'s Top Pop Albums charts.

DATE	POS	WKS	ARTIST–RECORD TITLE	LABEL & NO.
7/22/57	12	14	1. Around The World [I] Jockey #12 / Best Seller #23 / Top 100 #25; from the movie *Around The World In 80 Days* starring David Niven; Stan Newsome (trumpet solo)	London 1746
1/23/61	31	2	2. Main Theme from Exodus (Ari's Theme) [I] from the movie *Exodus* starring Paul Newman and Eva Marie Saint	London 1953

MARATHONS, The

The Olympics' Arvee label needed a new single, but since The Olympics were on tour, they brought in The Vibrations, who were under contract with the Chess/Checker label. The Vibrations recorded "Peanut Butter" and Arvee released it as by The Marathons. Chess discovered the fraud, and stopped the Arvee release, and then released a re-recorded version on their subsidiary label, Argo. Arvee followed up with a new song by The Marathons, recorded by an unknown non-Vibrations group.

DATE	POS	WKS	ARTIST–RECORD TITLE	LABEL & NO.
5/22/61	20	7	1. Peanut Butter same tune as The Olympics' 1960 hit "(Baby) Hully Gully"; re-recorded on Argo 5389 in 1961 and labeled as: "Vibrations Named by Others As MARATHONS" or "Vibrations Recorded as MARATHONS"	Arvee 5027

DATE	POS	WKS	ARTIST–RECORD TITLE	LABEL & NO.
			MARCELS, The	
			R&B doo-wop group from Pittsburgh. Consisted of Cornelius "Nini" Harp (lead singer), Ronald "Bingo" Mundy and Gene Bricker (tenors), Richard Knauss (baritone) and Fred Johnson (bass). Knauss replaced by Fred's brother, Allen Johnson, and Bricker replaced by Walt Maddox, mid-1961. Mundy left in late 1961. Allen Johnson died on 9/28/95.	
3/20/61	**1** (3)	11	1. **Blue Moon** there were 3 Top 10 versions of this Rodgers & Hart tune in 1935; #1 R&B hit (2 weeks)	Colpix 186
10/30/61	7	8	2. **Heartaches** #12 hit for Guy Lombardo in 1931; #1 hit for Ted Weems in 1947	Colpix 612
			MARCH, Little Peggy	
			Born Margaret Battavio on 3/7/48 in Lansdale, Pennsylvania. Lived in Germany, 1969–81. Youngest female singer to have a #1 single on the pop charts.	
4/6/63	**1** (3)	11	1. **I Will Follow Him** adapted from the French song "Chariot"; #1 R&B hit (1 week)	RCA 8139
6/29/63	32	3	2. I Wish I Were A Princess	RCA 8189
9/28/63	26	4	3. Hello Heartache, Goodbye Love	RCA 8221
			MARCHAN, Bobby	
			Born on 4/30/30 in Youngstown, Ohio. Vocalist with Huey "Piano" Smith & The Clowns.	
7/11/60	31	4	1. There's Something On Your Mind (Part 2) [N] #1 R&B hit (1 week)	Fire 1022
			MARDONES, Benny	
			Savage, Maryland native.	
7/12/80	**11**	12	1. Into The Night	Polydor 2091
6/3/89	20	7	2. Into The Night [R] Sales #17 / Airplay #25; above 2 are the same version; new version released on Curb 10549 in 1989	Polydor 889368
			MARESCA, Ernie	
			Born on 4/21/39 in the Bronx. Songwriter/vocalist. Wrote "Runaround Sue" and "The Wanderer" for Dion.	
4/21/62	6	9	1. **Shout! Shout! (Knock Yourself Out)**	Seville 117
			MARIE, Teena	
			Born Mary Christine Brockert in Santa Monica in 1957; raised in Venice, California. White funk singer/composer/keyboardist/guitarist/producer/ actress. Produced the group Ozone.	
1/17/81	37	3	1. I Need Your Lovin'	Gordy 7189
2/2/85	4	13	2. **Lovergirl** Airplay #4 / Sales #5	Epic 04619
			MARKETTS, The	
			Hollywood instrumental surf quintet led by Tommy Tedesco.	
2/17/62	31	3	1. Surfer's Stomp [I] **THE MAR-KETS** first released on Union 501 in 1961	Liberty 55401

DATE	POS	WKS	ARTIST—RECORD TITLE	LABEL & NO.
12/28/63+	3	11	2. **Out Of Limits** [I] "surf-ized" version of the "Outer Limits" TV series theme; first pressings issued as "Outer Limits"	Warner 5391
2/26/66	17	5	3. Batman Theme [I] from the hit TV series starring Adam West and Burt Ward	Warner 5696

MAR-KEYS

Instrumental group formed in Memphis in 1958. Consisted of Charles Axton (tenor sax), Wayne Jackson (trumpet), Don Nix (baritone sax), Jerry Lee "Smoochie" Smith (keyboards), Steve Cropper (guitar), Donald "Duck" Dunn (bass) and Terry Johnson (drums). Staff musicians at Stax/Volt. Cropper and Dunn later joined Booker T. & The MG's; also backing work for the Blues Brothers.

7/17/61	3	12	1. **Last Night** [I]	Satellite 107

MARK IV, The

Chicago-based pop-rock quartet.

2/9/59	24	7	1. I Got A Wife [N]	Mercury 71403

MARKHAM, Pigmeat

Born Dewey Markham on 4/18/06 in Durham, North Carolina. Died on 12/13/81. Stage and TV comedian.

7/6/68	19	4	1. Here Comes The Judge [N] title inspired by a recurrent gag line originated by Markham on TV's "Rowan & Martin's Laugh-In"	Chess 2049

MARKY MARK And The Funky Bunch

Marky Mark (born 6/5/71, Boston) is Mark Wahlberg, the younger brother of Donnie Wahlberg of New Kids On The Block. The Funky Bunch is DJ Terry Yancey and three male and two female dancers.

8/10/91	1 (1)	15	● 1. **Good Vibrations** Sales #2 / Airplay #6; samples Loleatta Holloway's 1980 disco hit "Love Sensation"	Interscope 98764
11/23/91	10	12	● 2. **Wildside** Sales #5 / Airplay #30; samples Lou Reed's "Walk On The Wild Side"	Interscope 98673

MARLEY, Ziggy, And The Melody Makers

Kingston, Jamaica, family reggae group. Children of the late reggae master Bob Marley: David "Ziggy" (vocals, guitar), Stephen, Sharon and Cedella Marley.

7/9/88	39	1	1. Tomorrow People Sales #37 / Airplay #40; Jerry Harrison (of Talking Heads; organ)	Virgin 99347

MARLOWE, Marion

Born on 3/7/29 in St. Louis. Featured singer on "Arthur Godfrey And His Friends," 1950–55.

7/16/55	14	2	1. The Man In The Raincoat Jockey #14 / Juke Box #18; Archie Bleyer (orch.)	Cadence 1266

MARMALADE, The

Scottish pop quintet led by vocalist Dean Ford (real name: Thomas McAleese).

4/4/70	10	11	1. **Reflections Of My Life**	London 20058

DATE	POS	WKS	ARTIST–RECORD TITLE	LABEL & NO.
			## M/A/R/R/S	
			U.K.-based, electro-funk group featuring two pairs of brothers: Martyn & Steve Young, with Alex & Rudi Kane. Includes mixers: Chris "CJ" Mackintosh and DJ Dave Dorrell.	
1/16/88	**13**	11	● 1. Pump Up The Volume Sales #11 / Airplay #13	4th & B'way 7452
			## MARSHALL TUCKER BAND, The	
			Southern-rock band formed in South Carolina in 1971: Doug Gray (lead singer), brothers Toy (lead guitarist; died 2/25/93 of respiratory failure, age 45) and Tommy Caldwell, (bass; died 4/28/80 in auto accident, age 30; replaced by Franklin Wilkie), George McCorkle (rhythm guitar), Paul Riddle (drums) and Jerry Eubanks (sax, flute). Caldwell left band in 1984. Marshall Tucker was the owner of the band's rehearsal hall.	
12/20/75	**38**	2	1. Fire On The Mountain Charlie Daniels (fiddle)	Capricorn 0244
4/16/77	**14**	13	2. Heard It In A Love Song	Capricorn 0270
			## MARTERIE, Ralph, And His Orchestra	
			Born on 12/24/14 in Naples, Italy; raised in Chicago. Died on 10/8/78. Very popular early '50s band leader, played trumpet in the '40s for Enric Madriguera, and other bands.	
3/30/57	**25**	3	1. Tricky [I] Jockey #25 / Top 100 #37	Mercury 71050
5/13/57	**10**	6	2. **Shish-Kebab** [I] Jockey #10 / Top 100 #29; same tune as Armenian Jazz Sextet's "Harem Dance"	Mercury 71092
			## MARTHA & THE VANDELLAS	
			Soul group from Detroit, organized by Martha Reeves (born 7/18/41, Alabama) in 1962 with Annette Beard and Rosalind Ashford. Reeves had been in The Del-Phis, recorded for Checkmate. Worked at Motown as A&R secretary, sang backup. Vandellas did backup on several of Marvin Gaye's hits. Beard left group in 1964, replaced by Betty Kelly (formerly with The Velvelettes). Group disbanded 1969–71, re-formed with Martha and sister Lois Reeves, and Sandra Tilley in 1971. Martha Reeves went solo in late 1972. Group inducted into the Rock and Roll Hall of Fame in 1995	
5/18/63	**29**	8	1. Come And Get These Memories	Gordy 7014
8/17/63	**4**	11	2. **Heat Wave** #1 R&B hit (4 weeks)	Gordy 7022
12/7/63+	**8**	9	3. **Quicksand**	Gordy 7025
9/5/64	**2 (2)**	11	● 4. **Dancing In The Street**	Gordy 7033
12/26/64+	**34**	4	5. Wild One	Gordy 7036
3/13/65	**8**	8	6. **Nowhere To Run**	Gordy 7039
9/11/65	**36**	2	7. You've Been In Love Too Long	Gordy 7045
2/19/66	**22**	7	8. My Baby Loves Me	Gordy 7048
11/12/66	**9**	7	9. **I'm Ready For Love**	Gordy 7056
3/18/67	**10**	10	10. **Jimmy Mack** #1 R&B hit (1 week)	Gordy 7058
9/9/67	**25**	6	11. Love Bug Leave My Heart Alone	Gordy 7062
12/2/67	**11**	9	12. Honey Chile **MARTHA REEVES & THE VANDELLAS**	Gordy 7067

DATE	POS	WKS	ARTIST–RECORD TITLE	LABEL & NO.

MARTIKA

Born Marta Marrera on 5/18/69. Los Angeles-based Cuban-American singer/writer/actress/dancer. Starred in the TV program "Kids, Incorporated." Appeared in the 1982 movie musical *Annie*.

DATE	POS	WKS	ARTIST–RECORD TITLE	LABEL & NO.
2/18/89	18	8	1. More Than You Know Sales #17 / Airplay #18	Columbia 08103
6/10/89	1 (2)	13	● 2. **Toy Soldiers** Airplay #1(1) / Sales #2	Columbia 68747
9/30/89	25	5	3. I Feel The Earth Move Sales #27 / Airplay #27	Columbia 68996
9/7/91	10	9	4. **Love...Thy Will Be Done** Sales #24 / Airplay #31; written by Prince	Columbia 73853

MARTIN, Bobbi

Born Barbara Anne Martin on 11/29/43 in Brooklyn; raised in Baltimore. Toured the Far East with Bob Hope's Christmas shows.

DATE	POS	WKS	ARTIST–RECORD TITLE	LABEL & NO.
1/2/65	19	7	1. Don't Forget I Still Love You	Coral 62426
4/11/70	13	10	2. For The Love Of Him #1 Adult Contemporary hit (2 weeks)	United Art. 50602

MARTIN, Dean

Born Dino Crocetti on 6/7/17 in Steubenville, Ohio. Died on 12/25/95. Vocalist/actor. To California in 1937, worked local clubs. Teamed with comedian Jerry Lewis in Atlantic City in 1946. First movie, *My Friend Irma* in 1949. Team broke up after 16th movie *Hollywood Or Bust* in 1956. Appeared in many movies since then; own TV series, 1965–74.

DATE	POS	WKS	ARTIST–RECORD TITLE	LABEL & NO.
12/3/55+	1 (6)	19	● 1. **Memories Are Made Of This** Jockey #1(6) / Best Seller #1(5) / Top 100 #1(5) / Juke Box #1(4); The Easy Riders (backing vocals)	Capitol 3295
4/7/56	27	4	2. Innamorata from the movie *Artists and Models* starring Martin and Jerry Lewis	Capitol 3352
5/26/56	22	6	3. Standing On The Corner Jockey #22 / Top 100 #29; from the musical *The Most Happy Fella* starring Robert Weede; Dick Stabile (orch., above 2)	Capitol 3414
4/7/58	4	18	4. **Return To Me** Best Seller #4 / Top 100 #4 / Jockey #4	Capitol 3894
8/4/58	30	3	5. Angel Baby Hot 100 #30 / Best Seller #43	Capitol 3988
8/11/58	12	10	6. Volare (Nel Blu Dipinto Di Blu) Best Seller #12 / Hot 100 #15; Gus Levene (orch., above 3)	Capitol 4028
7/11/64	1 (1)	13	● 7. **Everybody Loves Somebody** first recorded by Frank Sinatra in 1947 (Columbia 38225); #1 Adult Contemporary hit (8 weeks)	Reprise 0281
10/17/64	6	8	8. **The Door Is Still Open To My Heart** #1 Adult Contemporary hit (1 week); #4 R&B hit for The Cardinals in 1955	Reprise 0307
1/9/65	25	5	9. You're Nobody Till Somebody Loves You #1 Adult Contemporary hit (1 week); #14 Pop hit for Russ Morgan in 1946	Reprise 0333
3/13/65	22	5	10. Send Me The Pillow You Dream On	Reprise 0344
6/12/65	32	3	11. (Remember Me) I'm The One Who Loves You #2 Country hit for Stuart Hamblen in 1950	Reprise 0369
8/21/65	21	7	12. Houston	Reprise 0393
11/13/65	10	8	13. **I Will**	Reprise 0415
3/5/66	32	4	14. Somewhere There's A Someone	Reprise 0443

DATE	POS	WKS	ARTIST–RECORD TITLE	LABEL & NO.
6/11/66	35	1	15. Come Running Back	Reprise 0466
7/22/67	25	4	16. In The Chapel In The Moonlight #1 hit for Shep Fields in 1936; #1 Adult Contemporary hit (3 weeks)	Reprise 0601
9/9/67	38	2	17. Little Ole Wine Drinker, Me #7-17 produced by Jimmy Bowen	Reprise 0608

MARTIN, Marilyn

Raised in Louisville. Background vocalist for Stevie Nicks, Tom Petty, Kenny Loggins and Joe Walsh.

DATE	POS	WKS	ARTIST–RECORD TITLE	LABEL & NO.
10/12/85	1 (1)	16	1. **Separate Lives** **PHIL COLLINS and MARILYN MARTIN** Airplay #1(2) / Sales #2; love theme from the movie *White Nights* starring Mikhail Baryshnikov; #1 Adult Contemporary hit (3 weeks)	Atlantic 89498
2/22/86	28	6	2. Night Moves Airplay #21	Atlantic 89465

MARTIN, Moon

Real name: John Martin. Pop-rock singer/songwriter/guitarist from Oklahoma. Wrote Robert Palmer's hit "Bad Case Of Loving You." Moved to Los Angeles in 1968. Lead guitarist of group Southwind.

DATE	POS	WKS	ARTIST–RECORD TITLE	LABEL & NO.
9/22/79	30	4	1. Rolene	Capitol 4765

MARTIN, Steve

Born on 6/8/45 in Waco, Texas; raised in California. Popular TV and movie comedian. Comedy writer for the "Smothers Brothers Comedy Hour" TV show and others; frequent appearances on "Saturday Night Live," 1970s and '80s. Movies include *The Jerk, All Of Me, Roxanne, Planes, Trains And Automobiles, L.A. Story* and *Leap Of Faith* among many others. Married actress Victoria Tennant; divorced in 1992.

DATE	POS	WKS	ARTIST–RECORD TITLE	LABEL & NO.
7/8/78	17	7	● 1. King Tut [N] **STEVE MARTIN and the Toot Uncommons**	Warner 8577

MARTIN, Tony

Born Alvin Morris, Jr., on 12/25/12 in Oakland. Vocalist/actor. Appeared in such movies as *Music In My Heart, Casbah, Easy To Love* and *Hit The Deck*. Married to actress/dancer Cyd Charisse.

DATE	POS	WKS	ARTIST–RECORD TITLE	LABEL & NO.
5/26/56	10	11	1. **Walk Hand In Hand** Top 100 #10 / Jockey #13 / Juke Box #16 / Best Seller #21	RCA 6493

MARTIN, Trade

Born on 11/19/43 in Union City, New Jersey.

DATE	POS	WKS	ARTIST–RECORD TITLE	LABEL & NO.
11/17/62	28	4	1. That Stranger Used To Be My Girl	Coed 570

MARTIN, Vince

New York group featuring Martin as lead singer. Also see The Tarriers.

DATE	POS	WKS	ARTIST–RECORD TITLE	LABEL & NO.
10/13/56	9	15	1. **Cindy, Oh Cindy** **VINCE MARTIN With The Tarriers** Juke Box #9 / Best Seller #12 / Top 100 #12 / Jockey #12; adapted from a sailor's sea chantey	Glory 247

DATE	POS	WKS	ARTIST–RECORD TITLE	LABEL & NO.
			MARTINDALE, Wink	
			Born Winston Martindale on 12/4/33 in Jackson, Tennessee. DJ since 1950. Own TV shows starting with "Teenage Dance Party." Host of "Tic Tac Dough," "Gambit" and other TV game shows.	
9/28/59	7	12	● 1. **Deck Of Cards** [S] #2 Country hit for T. Texas Tyler in 1948	Dot 15968
			MARTINEZ, Nancy	
			Dance singer/actress born in Quebec.	
12/6/86	32	7	1. For Tonight Sales #29	Atlantic 89371
			MARTINO, Al	
			Born Alfred Cini on 10/7/27 in Philadelphia. Encouraged by success of boyhood friend Mario Lanza. Winner on "Arthur Godfrey's Talent Scouts" in 1952. Portrayed singer Johnny Fontane in the 1972 movie *The Godfather*.	
5/4/63	3	11	1. **I Love You Because** #1 Adult Contemporary hit (2 weeks); #1 Country hit for Leon Payne in 1950	Capitol 4930
8/17/63	15	8	2. Painted, Tainted Rose	Capitol 5000
11/16/63	22	6	3. Living A Lie	Capitol 5060
2/15/64	9	8	4. **I Love You More And More Every Day**	Capitol 5108
5/30/64	20	6	5. Tears And Roses	Capitol 5183
9/12/64	33	4	6. Always Together	Capitol 5239
12/18/65+	15	9	7. Spanish Eyes #1 Adult Contemporary hit (4 weeks)	Capitol 5542
4/2/66	30	4	8. Think I'll Go Somewhere And Cry Myself To Sleep	Capitol 5598
6/17/67	27	5	9. Mary In The Morning #1 Adult Contemporary hit (2 weeks)	Capitol 5904
2/8/75	17	8	10. To The Door Of The Sun (Alle Porte Del Sole) Peter DeAngelis (orch.: #2-4,6-10)	Capitol 3987
12/6/75	33	4	11. Volare	Capitol 4134
			MARVELETTES, The	
			R&B group from Inkster High School, Inkster, Michigan. Formed in 1960 by Gladys Horton, with Georgeanna Marie Tillman Gordon (married Billy Gordon of The Contours), Wanda Young (married Bobby Rogers of The Miracles), Katherine Anderson and Juanita Cowart. Young and Horton both sang lead. Cowart left in 1962. Gordon left in 1965; died on 1/6/80 of lupus. Horton left in 1967, replaced by Anne Bogan (later a member of Love, Peace & Happiness and New Birth). Disbanded in 1969. Also recorded as The Darnells.	
10/16/61	1 (1)	15	● 1. **Please Mr. Postman** #1 R&B hit (7 weeks)	Tamla 54046
3/3/62	34	1	2. Twistin' Postman	Tamla 54054
5/26/62	7	11	3. **Playboy**	Tamla 54060
9/1/62	17	7	4. Beechwood 4-5789	Tamla 54065
12/5/64+	25	8	5. Too Many Fish In The Sea	Tamla 54105
7/3/65	34	1	6. I'll Keep Holding On	Tamla 54116
1/29/66	7	8	7. **Don't Mess With Bill**	Tamla 54126
2/18/67	13	7	8. The Hunter Gets Captured By The Game	Tamla 54143
5/20/67	23	5	9. When You're Young And In Love	Tamla 54150

DATE	POS	WKS	ARTIST–RECORD TITLE	LABEL & NO.
1/6/68	**17**	8	10. My Baby Must Be A Magician #7,8,10: written and produced by Smokey Robinson	Tamla 54158

MARVELOWS, The

R&B group from Chicago Heights, Illinois. First known as the Mystics. Included Melvin Mason (lead), Willie "Sonny" Stevenson, Frank Paden and Johnny Paden. Added Jesse Smith in 1964, became The Marvelows.

DATE	POS	WKS	ARTIST–RECORD TITLE	LABEL & NO.
7/3/65	**37**	1	1. I Do	ABC-Para. 10629

MARX, Richard

Born on 9/16/63 in Chicago. Pop-rock singer/songwriter. Professional jingle singer since age five. Backing singer for Lionel Richie. Married Cynthia Rhodes (lead singer of Animotion) on 1/8/89.

DATE	POS	WKS	ARTIST–RECORD TITLE	LABEL & NO.
7/11/87	**3**	12	1. **Don't Mean Nothing** Sales #4 / Airplay #4	Manhattan 50079
10/17/87	**3**	13	2. **Should've Known Better** Sales #3 / Airplay #4; Fee Waybill (of the Tubes) and Timothy B. Schmit (backing vocals); "live" version is on the B-side of #5 below	Manhattan 50083
1/30/88	**2** (2)	15	3. **Endless Summer Nights** Airplay #2 / Sales #2; "live" version is on the B-side of #7 below	EMI-Man. 50113
6/11/88	**1** (1)	14	4. **Hold On To The Nights** Sales #1(1) / Airplay #1(1), above 4 from the album *Richard Marx*	EMI-Man. 50106
5/6/89	**1** (1)	13	5. **Satisfied** Airplay #1(2) / Sales #3	EMI 50189
7/15/89	**1** (3)	13	▲ 6. **Right Here Waiting** Airplay #1(5) / Sales #1(1); #1 Adult Contemporary hit (6 weeks)	EMI 50219
10/21/89	**4**	11	7. **Angelia** Airplay #4 / Sales #4	EMI 50218
1/27/90	**12**	9	8. Too Late To Say Goodbye Airplay #10 / Sales #14	EMI 50234
5/12/90	**13**	10	9. Children Of The Night Airplay #8 / Sales #17; tribute to the Los Angeles organization helping child prostitutes, above 5 from the album *Repeat Offender*	EMI 50288
11/9/91	**12**	13	10. Keep Coming Back Airplay #10 / Sales #43; #1 Adult Contemporary hit (4 weeks)	Capitol 44753
3/7/92	**9**	16	11. **Hazard** Sales #10 / Airplay #11; #1 Adult Contemporary hit (1 week); "live" version is on the B-side of #13 below	Capitol 44796
6/27/92	**20**	13	12. Take This Heart Airplay #14 / Sales #42	Capitol 44782
1/29/94	**7**	23	13. **Now and Forever** Airplay #5 / Sales #10; #1 Adult Contemporary hit (11 weeks); "live" version is on the B-side of #14 below	Capitol 58005
7/23/94	**20**	11	14. The Way She Loves Me Airplay #20 / Sales #30; includes bonus cassette of "Hold On To The Nights" and "Take It To The Limit" (Capitol 4XPRO-79378)	Capitol 58167

MARY JANE GIRLS

Female "funk & roll" quartet: Joanne McDuffie, Candice Ghant, Kim Wuletich and Yvette Marina. Formed and produced by Rick James. Marina is the daughter of disco singer Pattie Brooks.

DATE	POS	WKS	ARTIST–RECORD TITLE	LABEL & NO.
4/27/85	**7**	12	1. **In My House** Sales #5 / Airplay #9	Gordy 1741

DATE	POS	WKS	ARTIST–RECORD TITLE	LABEL & NO.
			MASEKELA, Hugh	
			Born Hugh Ramapolo Masekela on 4/4/39 in Wilbank, South Africa. Trumpeter/bandleader/arranger. Played trumpet since age 14. To England in 1959; to New York City in 1960. Formed own band in 1964. Married to Miriam Makeba, 1964–66.	
6/22/68	1 (2)	10	● 1. **Grazing In The Grass** [I] #1 R&B hit (4 weeks)	Uni 55066
			MASHMAKHAN	
			Montreal rock quartet led by Pierre Senecal, with Brian Edwards, Jerry Mercer (later with April Wine) and Rayburn Blake.	
11/7/70	31	4	1. As The Years Go By	Epic 10634
			MASON, Barbara	
			Born on 8/9/47 in Philadelphia. First recorded for Crusader in 1964. Wrote all of her Arctic hits.	
6/12/65	5	10	1. **Yes, I'm Ready**	Arctic 105
9/4/65	27	5	2. Sad, Sad Girl	Arctic 108
2/24/73	31	5	3. Give Me Your Love written and produced by Curtis Mayfield	Buddah 331
12/28/74+	28	4	4. From His Woman To You	Buddah 441
			MASON, Dave	
			Born on 5/10/46 in Worcester, England. Vocalist/composer/guitarist. Original member of Traffic from March through December 1967 and from June 1968 on. Joined Delaney & Bonnie for a short time in 1970. Joined Fleetwood Mac in 1993.	
10/8/77	12	10	1. We Just Disagree	Columbia 10575
7/8/78	39	2	2. Will You Still Love Me Tomorrow	Columbia 10749
			MASTA ACE INCORPORATED	
			Masta Ace is a rapper from Brownsville, New York. His posse includes Lord Digga and rap trio Eyceurokk (Master Eyce, Uneek and Diesalrokk). Member of the trio The Crooklyn Dodgers.	
4/2/94	23	9	1. Born To Roll Sales #21 / Airplay #35	Delicious V. 98315
			MATHEWS, Tobin, & Co.	
			Guitarist from Calumet City, Illinois. Relative of Jeremy Jordan.	
11/14/60	30	4	1. Ruby Duby Du [I] from the movie *Key Witness* starring Jeffrey Hunter	Chief 7022
			MATHIS, Johnny	
			Born on 9/30/35 in San Francisco. Studied opera from age 13. Track scholarship at the San Francisco State College. Invited to Olympic tryouts; chose singing career instead. Discovered by George Avakian of Columbia Records. To New York City in 1956. Initially recorded as jazz-styled singer. Columbia A&R executive Mitch Miller switched him to singing pop ballads. One of the top album artists of the rock era, Mathis has charted over 60 entries on *Billboard*'s Top Pop Albums charts.	
5/6/57	14	20	1. Wonderful! Wonderful! Jockey #14 / Top 100 #17 / Best Seller #18	Columbia 40784

DATE	POS	WKS	ARTIST–RECORD TITLE	LABEL & NO.
5/20/57	5	23	● 2. **It's Not For Me To Say** Top 100 #5 / Jockey #5 / Best Seller #6; performed by Mathis in the movie *Lizzie*	Columbia 40851
9/16/57	1 (1)	22	● 3. **Chances Are/** Jockey #1 / Best Seller #4 / Top 100 #5	
10/14/57	9	14	4. **The Twelfth Of Never** Jockey #9 / Top 100 #51; adapted from a folk song known as both "The Riddle Song" and "I Gave My Love A Cherry"	Columbia 40993
12/16/57	22	7	5. Wild Is The Wind/ Jockey #22 / Best Seller #30 / Top 100 #37; title song from the movie starring Anthony Quinn	
1/6/58	21	1	6. No Love (But Your Love) Jockey #21 / Best Seller #37 / Top 100 #48; Ray Conniff (orch., all of above - except #5)	Columbia 41060
2/10/58	22	1	7. Come To Me Jockey #22 / Best Seller #40 / Top 100 #43; from the 12/4/57 Kraft TV Theater production of "Come To Me"	Columbia 41082
5/5/58	21	7	8. All The Time/ Jockey #21 / Best Seller #30 / Top 100 #42; from the Broadway musical *Oh Captain!* starring Tony Randall	
5/19/58	21	7	9. Teacher, Teacher Jockey #21 / Best Seller #30 / Top 100 #43	Columbia 41152
7/14/58	14	11	10. A Certain Smile Jockey #14 / Top 100 #19 / Best Seller #21; title song from the movie starring Joan Fontaine	Columbia 41193
10/20/58	21	8	11. Call Me	Columbia 41253
5/4/59	35	3	12. Someone #5,7-12: Ray Ellis (orch.)	Columbia 41355
7/20/59	20	8	13. Small World from the Broadway musical *Gypsy* starring Ethel Merman	Columbia 41410
10/19/59	12	12	14. Misty introduced by the Erroll Garner Trio in 1954	Columbia 41483
3/28/60	25	5	15. Starbright Glenn Osser (orch., above 3)	Columbia 41583
10/13/62	6	9	16. **Gina**	Columbia 42582
2/9/63	9	10	17. **What Will Mary Say**	Columbia 42666
6/8/63	30	4	18. Every Step Of The Way	Columbia 42799
4/22/78	1 (1)	11	● 19. **Too Much, Too Little, Too Late** **JOHNNY MATHIS/DENIECE WILLIAMS** #1 R&B hit (4 weeks); #1 Adult Contemporary hit (1 week)	Columbia 10693
5/29/82	38	3	20. Friends In Love **DIONNE WARWICK AND JOHNNY MATHIS**	Arista 0673
			MATTHEWS, Ian Born Ian Matthew MacDonald in Lincolnshire, England, in June 1946. Founder of Fairport Convention and Matthews' Southern Comfort. In A&R for Island and Windham Hill record labels, 1984–87.	
4/24/71	23	9	1. Woodstock **MATTHEWS' SOUTHERN COMFORT** written by Joni Mitchell about the legendary 1969 rock festival	Decca 32774
12/16/78+	13	12	2. Shake It	Mushroom 7039

DATE	POS	WKS	ARTIST–RECORD TITLE	LABEL & NO.
			MAURIAT, Paul	
			Born in France in 1925. Moved to Paris at age 10. Formed own touring orchestra at age 17.	
1/27/68	**1** (5)	15	● 1. **Love Is Blue** [I] French song "L'Amour Est Bleu"; #1 Adult Contemporary hit (11 weeks)	Philips 40495
			MAXWELL, Robert, His Harp And Orchestra	
			Born on 4/19/21 in New York City. Jazz harpist/composer. With NBC Symphony under Toscanini at age 17. Also recorded as Mickey Mozart.	
6/8/59	**30**	6	1. Little Dipper [I] **THE MICKEY MOZART QUINTET**	Roulette 4148
4/18/64	**15**	7	2. Shangri-La [I] co-written by Maxwell in 1946	Decca 25622
			MAYER, Nathaniel, And The Fabulous Twilights	
			Born on 2/10/44 in Detroit. R&B vocalist.	
5/26/62	**22**	6	1. Village Of Love	Fortune 449
			MAYFIELD, Curtis	
			Born on 6/3/42 in Chicago. Soul singer/songwriter/producer. With Jerry Butler in the gospel group Northern Jubilee Singers. Joined The Impressions in 1957. Wrote most of the hits for The Impressions, Jerry Butler and himself. Own labels: Windy C, Mayfield and Curtom. Went solo in 1970. Scored the movies *Superfly*, *Claudine*, *A Piece Of The Action* and *Short Eyes*. Appeared in *Short Eyes*. Paralyzed from the chest down when a stage lighting tower fell on him before a concert on 8/13/90.	
1/2/71	29	4	1. (Don't Worry) If There's A Hell Below We're All Going To Go	Curtom 1955
9/23/72	4	11	● 2. **Freddie's Dead (Theme From "Superfly")**	Curtom 1975
11/25/72+	8	13	● 3. **Superfly**	Curtom 1978
			above 2 from the movie *Superfly* starring Ron O'Neal	
8/25/73	39	2	4. Future Shock	Curtom 1987
8/3/74	40	1	5. Kung Fu	Curtom 1999
			M.C. BRAINS	
			Born James De Shannon Davis in Cleveland. Rapper discovered by Michael Bivins (New Edition, Bell Biv DeVoe).	
2/22/92	**21**	10	● 1. Oochie Coochie Sales #6 / Airplay #66	Motown 2146
			M.C. HAMMER	
			Born Stanley Kirk Burrell on 3/30/63 in Oakland. Rapper/producer/founder/leader of The Posse, an eight-member group of dancers, DJs and singers. Burrell was an Oakland A's batboy in the 1970s; his nickname "The Little Hammer" stemmed from his resemblance to baseball great "Hammerin'" Hank Aaron. Oaktown's 3-5-7 and Ace Juice are members of The Posse. Dropped the M.C. from his name in mid-1991; re-added it in 1995.	
4/28/90	**8**	13	1. **U Can't Touch This** Airplay #2 / Sales #18; music is from Rick James's "Super Freak"; available only as a 12" single; #1 R&B hit (1 week)	Capitol 15571

DATE	POS	WKS	ARTIST–RECORD TITLE	LABEL & NO.
7/21/90	4	12	● 2. **Have You Seen Her** Airplay #4 / Sales #5	Capitol 44573
10/6/90	2 (2)	11	● 3. **Pray** Sales #3 / Airplay #5; rhythm track is from Prince's "When Doves Cry"	Capitol 44609
			HAMMER:	
11/23/91+	5	17	▲ 4. **2 Legit 2 Quit** Sales #1(3) / Airplay #37; Sonja "Saja" Moore (female vocal)	Capitol 44785
12/14/91+	7	12	● 5. **Addams Groove** Sales #3 / Airplay #36; from the movie The Addams Family starring Anjelica Huston; incorporates "The Addams Family Theme"	Capitol 44794
5/7/94	26	7	● 6. Pumps And A Bump Sales #11 / Airplay #74; samples "Atomic Dog" by George Clinton	Giant 18218
			MC LYTE	
			Born Lana Moorer on 10/11/71 in Queens; raised in Brooklyn. Female rapper.	
9/18/93	35	4	● 1. RuffNeck Sales #24 / Airplay #45	First Pri. 98401
			McANALLY, Mac	
			Born Lyman McAnally, Jr., on 7/15/57 in Red Bay, Alabama. Session singer/songwriter/guitarist.	
8/13/77	37	2	1. It's A Crazy World	Ariola Am. 7665
			McCALL, C.W.	
			Born William Fries on 11/15/28 in Audubon, Iowa. The character "C.W. McCall" was created for the Mertz Bread Company. Fries was its advertising man. Elected mayor of Ouray, Colorado, in the early '80s.	
3/22/75	40	1	1. Wolf Creek Pass [N]	MGM 14764
12/13/75+	1 (1)	11	● 2. **Convoy** [N] #1 Country hit (6 weeks), jargon-laced CB radio conversation	MGM 14839
			McCANN, Peter	
			Connecticut native. Staff writer with ABC Music. Wrote Jennifer Warnes's hit "Right Time Of The Night."	
5/21/77	5	16	● 1. **Do You Wanna Make Love**	20th Century 2335
			McCARTNEY, Paul/Wings	
			Born James Paul McCartney on 6/18/42 in Allerton, Liverpool, England. Writer of over 50 Top 10 singles. Founding member/bass guitarist of The Beatles. Married Linda Eastman on 3/12/69. First solo album in 1970. Formed group Wings in 1971 with Linda (keyboards, backing vocals), Denny Laine (ex-Moody Blues; guitar) and Denny Seiwell (drums). Henry McCullough (guitar) joined in 1972. Seiwell and McCullough left in 1973. In 1975, Joe English (drums) and ex-Thunderclap Newman guitarist Jimmy McCulloch (died 9/27/79 of heart failure, age 26) joined; both left in 1977. Wings officially disbanded in April 1981. McCartney starred in own movie Give My Regards To Broad Street (1984). Won Lifetime Achievement Grammy in 1990.	
			PAUL MCCARTNEY:	
3/13/71	5	11	1. **Another Day/**	
		9	2. Oh Woman Oh Why	Apple 1829

DATE	POS	WKS	ARTIST–RECORD TITLE	LABEL & NO.
			PAUL & LINDA McCARTNEY:	
8/21/71	**1** (1)	12	● 3. **Uncle Albert/Admiral Halsey**	Apple 1837
			WINGS:	
3/25/72	**21**	6	4. Give Ireland Back To The Irish	Apple 1847
7/8/72	**28**	4	5. Mary Had A Little Lamb/	
		4	6. Little Woman Love	Apple 1851
12/30/72+	**10**	9	7. **Hi, Hi, Hi**	Apple 1857
4/28/73	**1** (4)	15	● 8. **My Love**	Apple 1861
			PAUL McCARTNEY & WINGS	
			#1 Adult Contemporary hit (3 weeks)	
7/21/73	**2** (3)	12	● 9. **Live And Let Die**	Apple 1863
			title song from the James Bond movie starring Roger Moore	
			PAUL McCARTNEY & WINGS:	
12/8/73+	**10**	10	10. **Helen Wheels**	Apple 1869
2/23/74	**7**	10	11. **Jet**	Apple 1871
5/4/74	**1** (1)	13	● 12. **Band On The Run**	Apple 1873
11/23/74+	**3**	10	13. **Junior's Farm/**	
12/14/74+	**17**	8	14. Sally G	Apple 1875
			WINGS:	
6/7/75	**1** (1)	11	● 15. **Listen To What The Man Said**	Capitol 4091
10/25/75	**39**	2	16. Letting Go	Capitol 4145
11/15/75	**12**	6	17. Venus And Mars Rock Show	Capitol 4175
4/17/76	**1** (5)	15	● 18. **Silly Love Songs**	Capitol 4256
			#1 Adult Contemporary hit (1 week)	
7/17/76	**3**	11	● 19. **Let 'Em In**	Capitol 4293
			#1 Adult Contemporary hit (1 week)	
2/19/77	**10**	11	20. **Maybe I'm Amazed**	Capitol 4385
			"live" version of song from McCartney's first solo album in 1970	
12/24/77+	**33**	5	21. Girls' School	Capitol 4504
4/8/78	**1** (2)	12	22. **With A Little Luck**	Capitol 4559
7/15/78	**25**	5	23. I've Had Enough	Capitol 4594
10/14/78	**39**	2	24. London Town	Capitol 4625
3/31/79	**5**	13	● 25. **Goodnight Tonight**	Columbia 10939
6/30/79	**20**	6	26. Getting Closer	Columbia 11020
9/22/79	**29**	4	27. Arrow Through Me	Columbia 11070
5/10/80	**1** (3)	16	● 28. **Coming Up (Live at Glasgow)**	Columbia 11263
			PAUL McCARTNEY & WINGS	
			"live" version (studio version is on the B-side)	
4/10/82	**1** (7)	15	● 29. **Ebony And Ivory**	Columbia 02860
			PAUL McCARTNEY (with Stevie Wonder)	
			#1 Adult Contemporary hit (5 weeks)	
7/17/82	**10**	11	30. **Take It Away**	Columbia 03018
			PAUL McCARTNEY	
11/13/82+	**2** (3)	14	● 31. **The Girl Is Mine**	Epic 03288
			MICHAEL JACKSON/PAUL McCARTNEY	
			#1 Adult Contemporary hit (4 weeks); #1 R&B hit (3 weeks)	
10/15/83	**1** (6)	18	▲ 32. **Say Say Say**	Columbia 04168
			PAUL McCARTNEY AND MICHAEL JACKSON	

DATE	POS	WKS	ARTIST—RECORD TITLE	LABEL & NO.
			PAUL MCCARTNEY:	
1/7/84	**23**	8	33. So Bad	Columbia 04296
10/20/84	**6**	14	34. **No More Lonely Nights**	Columbia 04581
			Airplay #5 / Sales #9; from the movie *Give My Regards to Broad Street* starring McCartney	
12/14/85+	**7**	11	35. **Spies Like Us**	Capitol 5537
			Sales #6 / Airplay #8; title song from the movie starring Chevy Chase and Dan Aykroyd	
8/23/86	**21**	6	36. Press	Capitol 5597
			Sales #17 / Airplay #32	
6/17/89	**25**	5	37. My Brave Face	Capitol 44367
			Sales #20 / Airplay #33; co-written by Elvis Costello	
			McCLAIN, Alton, & Destiny	
			Black female trio: Alton McClain, Delores Warren and Robyrda Stiger. Warren died in a car crash on 2/22/85 (age 32).	
5/19/79	**32**	4	1. It Must Be Love	Polydor 14532
			McCLINTON, Delbert	
			Born on 11/4/40 in Lubbock, Texas. Played harmonica on Bruce Channel's hit "Hey Baby." Leader of The Ron-Dels.	
12/20/80+	**8**	14	1. **Giving It Up For Your Love**	Capitol 4948
			McCLURE, Bobby—see BASS, Fontella	
			McCOO, Marilyn, & Billy Davis, Jr.	
			McCoo (born 9/30/43, Jersey City, New Jersey) and husband Davis (born 6/26/39, St. Louis) were members of The 5th Dimension. Duo hosted own summer variety TV series in 1977. McCoo co-hosted TV's "Solid Gold," 1981–84.	
10/23/76+	**1 (1)**	18	● 1. **You Don't Have To Be A Star (To Be In My Show)**	ABC 12208
			#1 R&B hit (1 week)	
4/2/77	**15**	8	2. Your Love	ABC 12262
			McCOY, Van	
			Born on 1/6/44 in Washington, D.C. Died on 7/6/79 of a heart attack. Pianist/producer/songwriter/singer. Formed own Rock'n label in 1960. A&R man at Scepter/Wand, 1961–64. Own MAXX label, mid-1960s. Produced The Shirelles, Gladys Knight, The Stylistics and Brenda & The Tabulations.	
5/31/75	**1 (1)**	12	● 1. **The Hustle** [I]	Avco 4653
			VAN McCOY & The Soul City Symphony	
			#1 R&B hit (1 week)	
			McCOYS, The	
			Rock band formed in Union City, Indiana. Rick Derringer (real name: Zehringer; vocals, guitar), brother Randy Zehringer (drums), Randy Hobbs (bass; died 8/5/93, age 45) and Ronnie Brandon (keyboards). Rick went solo in 1974.	
9/4/65	**1 (1)**	11	1. **Hang On Sloopy**	Bang 506
11/27/65	**7**	8	2. **Fever**	Bang 511
5/14/66	**22**	6	3. Come On Let's Go	Bang 522

DATE	POS	WKS	ARTIST–RECORD TITLE	LABEL & NO.
			McCRACKLIN, Jimmy	
			Born on 8/13/21 in St. Louis. Singer/harmonica player. Settled in Los Angeles. Professional boxer in the mid-1940s. First recorded for Globe in 1945. Own band, the Blues Blasters, in 1949.	
3/3/58	7	10	1. **The Walk** **JIMMY McCRACKLIN And His Band** Top 100 #7 / Best Seller #11 / Jockey #23	Checker 885
			McCRAE, George	
			Born on 10/19/44 in West Palm Beach, Florida. Duets with wife Gwen McCrae; became her manager.	
6/15/74	1 (2)	10	1. **Rock Your Baby** #1 R&B hit (2 weeks)	T.K. 1004
3/1/75	37	2	2. I Get Lifted	T.K. 1007
			McCRAE, Gwen	
			Born on 12/21/43 in Pensacola, Florida. Married George McCrae, who later became her manager. First recorded with George for Alston in 1969.	
6/21/75	9	8	1. **Rockin' Chair** George McCrae (backing vocal); #1 R&B hit (1 week)	Cat 1996
			McDANIELS, Gene	
			Born Eugene B. McDaniels on 2/12/35 in Kansas City. To Omaha, early 1940s, sang in choirs, attended Omaha Conservatory of Music. Own band, early '50s. Appeared in the movie *It's Trad, Dad* in 1962. Recorded as Universal Jones in 1972.	
4/3/61	3	12	1. **A Hundred Pounds Of Clay**	Liberty 55308
8/7/61	31	2	2. A Tear	Liberty 55344
10/16/61	5	10	3. **Tower Of Strength**	Liberty 55371
2/10/62	10	7	4. **Chip Chip**	Liberty 55405
9/1/62	21	5	5. Point Of No Return	Liberty 55480
12/15/62	31	2	6. Spanish Lace The Johnny Mann Singers (backing vocals, all of above)	Liberty 55510
			McDEVITT, Chas., Skiffle Group	
			British vocal/instrumental group.	
6/10/57	40	1	1. Freight Train folk song composed in the early 1900s; Nancy Wiskey (vocal)	Chic 1008
			McDONALD, Michael	
			Born on 12/2/52 in St. Louis. Vocalist/keyboardist. First recorded for RCA in 1972. Formerly with Steely Dan and The Doobie Brothers. Married to singer Amy Holland. Also see Nicolette Larson, Christopher Cross and Lauren Wood.	
8/28/82	4	13	1. **I Keep Forgettin' (Every Time You're Near)** early pressings show title only as: "I Keep Forgettin'"	Warner 29933
1/14/84	19	9	2. Yah Mo B There **JAMES INGRAM (with Michael McDonald)**	Qwest 29394
8/31/85	34	4	3. No Lookin' Back Airplay #30; co-written by Kenny Loggins	Warner 28960
4/19/86	1 (3)	15	● 4. **On My Own** **PATTI LaBELLE AND MICHAEL McDONALD** Sales #1(5) / Airplay #1(2); #1 R&B hit (4 weeks)	MCA 52770

DATE	POS	WKS	ARTIST–RECORD TITLE	LABEL & NO.
7/12/86	7	13	5. **Sweet Freedom** Sales #6 / Airplay #7; theme from the movie *Running Scared* starring Billy Crystal and Gregory Hines	MCA 52857
			McDOWELL, Ronnie Born on 3/26/50 in Portland, Tennessee. Country singer/songwriter. Sang on the soundtrack for the TV movie "Elvis" in 1979.	
9/17/77	13	9	● 1. The King Is Gone a tribute to Elvis Presley	Scorpion 135
			McFADDEN, Bob, And Dor McFadden is from East Liverpool, Ohio. Began career in 1950 as a singing emcee for a special Navy show called "The Bob McFadden Show." Appeared on the comedy albums *The First Family* and *You Don't Have To Be Jewish*. Dor is poet/singer/songwriter/actor Rod McKuen.	
9/14/59	39	1	1. The Mummy [N] narration, with Jack Hansen (orch.)	Brunswick 55140
			McFADDEN & WHITEHEAD R&B duo of Gene McFadden and John Whitehead from Philadelphia. Wrote songs for many Philadelphia soul acts; defined "The Sound Of Philadelphia." Whitehead recorded solo in 1988. John's sons, Kenny & Johnny, charted as The Whitehead Brothers.	
6/2/79	13	11	▲ 1. Ain't No Stoppin' Us Now #1 R&B hit (1 week)	Phil. Int. 3681
			McFERRIN, Bobby Born on 3/11/50 in New York City. Unaccompanied, jazz-styled improvisation vocalist. Sang the 1987 "Cosby Show" theme and the Levi's 501 Blues jingle. Father was a baritone with the New York Metropolitan Opera.	
8/13/88	1 (2)	13	● 1. **Don't Worry Be Happy** Sales #1(3) / Airplay #2; featured in the movie *Cocktail* starring Tom Cruise	EMI-Man. 50146
			McGOVERN, Maureen Born on 7/27/49 in Youngstown, Ohio. Sang theme of TV show "Angie." Cameo roles in *The Towering Inferno* and *Airplane* (as Sister Angelina). Starred in Broadway's *Pirates Of Penzance* for 14 months.	
7/14/73	1 (2)	11	● 1. **The Morning After** love theme from the movie *The Poseidon Adventure* starring Gene Hackman	20th Century 2010
8/11/79	18	9	2. Different Worlds theme from the TV series "Angie" starring Donna Pescow; #1 Adult Contemporary hit (2 weeks)	Warner/Curb 8835
			McGRAW, Tim Born on 5/1/67 in Delhi, Louisiana. Country singer. Son of ex-professional baseball player Tug McGraw. Tim attended Northeast Louisiana University on several sports scholarships.	
3/19/94	15	10	● 1. Indian Outlaw Sales #4; includes a verse from the #1 1971 hit "Indian Reservation"	Curb 76920
5/28/94	17	13	● 2. Don't Take The Girl Sales #3; #1 Country hit (2 weeks)	Curb 76925

DATE	POS	WKS	ARTIST—RECORD TITLE	LABEL & NO.
9/9/95	25	6	3. I Like It, I Love It Sales #8; #1 Country hit (5 weeks)	Curb 76961
			McGRIFF, Jimmy	
10/27/62	20	7	Born on 4/3/36 in Philadelphia. Jazz-R&B organist/multi-instrumentalist. 1. I've Got A Woman (Part I) [I]	Sue 770
			McGUINN, CLARK & HILLMAN	
4/28/79	33	4	Roger McGuinn (born 7/13/42; vocals, guitar), Gene Clark (born 11/17/44; died 5/24/91; guitar) and Chris Hillman (born 6/4/42; bass). All were founding members of The Byrds. 1. Don't You Write Her Off	Capitol 4693
			McGUIRE, Barry	
8/28/65	1 (1)	10	Born on 10/15/37 in Oklahoma City. Member of The New Christy Minstrels, 1962–65. Currently records Contemporary Christian music. 1. **Eve Of Destruction** backing by the original members of The Grass Roots	Dunhill 4009
			McGUIRE SISTERS, The	
1/8/55	1 (10)	21	Sisters Phyllis (born 2/14/31), Christine (born 7/30/29) and Dorothy (born 2/13/30) from Middletown, Ohio. Replaced The Chordettes on "Arthur Godfrey And His Friends" show in 1953. Phyllis went solo in 1964. Reunited in 1986. ● 1. **Sincerely/** Jockey #1(10) / Juke Box #1(7) / Best Seller #1(6); legendary DJ Alan Freed listed as co-writer	
1/29/55	17	6	2. No More Jockey #17 / Juke Box #17 / Best Seller #23	Coral 61323
3/26/55	11	7	3. It May Sound Silly/ Jockey #11 / Juke Box #14 / Best Seller #23; #14 R&B hit for Ivory Joe Hunter in 1955	
		2	4. Doesn't Anybody Love Me? Juke Box flip	Coral 61369
6/4/55	5	14	5. **Something's Gotta Give/** Jockey #5 / Best Seller #6 / Juke Box #6; from the movie Daddy Long Legs starring Fred Astaire	
		2	6. Rhythm 'N' Blues (Mama's Got The Rhythm - Papa's Got The Blues) Best Seller/Juke Box flip	Coral 61423
10/29/55	10	13	7. **He** Juke Box #10 / Best Seller #12 / Top 100 #12 / Jockey #16	Coral 61501
5/19/56	13	12	8. Picnic/ Top 100 #13 / Jockey #14 / Best Seller #15 / Juke Box #18; based on the theme from the movie starring William Holden	
6/2/56	37	1	9. Delilah Jones based on the "Main Title" theme from the movie The Man with the Golden Arm starring Frank Sinatra	Coral 61627
8/11/56	32	3	10. Weary Blues **THE McGUIRE SISTERS and LAWRENCE WELK And His Champagne Music** traditional tune first recorded in 1923 by The New Orleans Rhythm Kings	Coral 61670
10/27/56	37	3	11. Ev'ry Day Of My Life	Coral 61703

DATE	POS	WKS	ARTIST–RECORD TITLE	LABEL & NO.
12/22/56+	32	3	12. Goodnight My Love, Pleasant Dreams #7 R&B hit for Jesse Belvin in 1956	Coral 61748
1/6/58	1 (4)	19	● 13. **Sugartime** Jockey #1 / Top 100 #5 / Best Seller #7	Coral 61924
6/9/58	25	1	14. Ding Dong Jockey #25 / Top 100 #43 / Best Seller #44; Neal Hefti (orch.: #4, 13, 14)	Coral 61991
1/19/59	11	12	15. May You Always	Coral 62059
4/17/61	20	7	16. Just For Old Time's Sake Dick Jacobs (orch.: #1-3, 5-9, 11-12, 15-16)	Coral 62249

McKENZIE, Bob & Doug

Canadian comedians Rick Moranis and Dave Thomas of "SCTV." Both featured in the movie *Strange Brew*. Moranis later starred in the movies *Ghostbusters*, *Spaceballs*, *Honey, I Shrunk The Kids* and many others. Thomas, the brother of singer Ian Thomas, hosted own CBS-TV series in 1990 and is a cast member of TV's "Grace Under Fire."

DATE	POS	WKS	ARTIST–RECORD TITLE	LABEL & NO.
2/20/82	16	9	1. Take Off [N] Geddy Lee (of Rush; vocal)	Mercury 76134

McKENZIE, Scott

Born Philip Blondheim on 1/10/39 in Jacksonville, Florida; raised in Virginia. Sang with John Phillips (The Mamas & The Papas) in The Journeymen. Co-wrote The Beach Boys' 1988 #1 hit "Kokomo."

DATE	POS	WKS	ARTIST–RECORD TITLE	LABEL & NO.
6/10/67	4	10	1. **San Francisco (Be Sure To Wear Flowers In Your Hair)**	Ode 103
11/11/67	24	3	2. Like An Old Time Movie above 2 written and produced by John Phillips	Ode 105

McKNIGHT, Brian

Born on 6/5/69 in Buffalo, New York. R&B singer/composer. His older brother is Claude McKnight of Take 6.

DATE	POS	WKS	ARTIST–RECORD TITLE	LABEL & NO.
3/6/93	3	20	1. **Love Is** **VANESSA WILLIAMS and BRIAN McKNIGHT** Airplay #2 / Sales #13; from the album *Beverly Hills 90210 (The Soundtrack)*; #1 Adult Contemporary hit (3 weeks)	Giant 18630
7/3/93	13	18	2. One Last Cry Airplay #12 / Sales #18	Mercury 862404

McLAIN, Tommy

Born on 3/15/40 in Jonesville, Louisiana.

DATE	POS	WKS	ARTIST–RECORD TITLE	LABEL & NO.
7/23/66	15	7	1. Sweet Dreams first released on Jin 197 in 1966	MSL 197

McLEAN, Don

Born on 10/2/45 in New Rochelle, New York. Singer/songwriter/poet. The hit "Killing Me Softly" was inspired by Don.

DATE	POS	WKS	ARTIST–RECORD TITLE	LABEL & NO.
12/4/71+	1 (4)	17	● 1. **American Pie - Parts I & II** inspired by the death of Buddy Holly; #1 Adult Contemporary hit (3 weeks)	United Art. 50856
4/1/72	12	10	2. Vincent/ a tribute to artist Vincent Van Gogh	
		7	3. Castles In The Air	United Art. 50887
1/20/73	21	8	4. Dreidel	United Art. 51100

Garnet Mimms & the Enchanters' remake of Jerry Butler & the Impressions' 1958 hit "For Your Precious Love" reached No. 26 in 1963; oddly, Butler's own 1966 solo remake only hit No. 99.

Kylie Minogue never duplicated her overseas success in the U.S., though her biggest hit—a remake of Little Eva's 1962 "The Loco-Motion"—climbed to No. 3 in 1988. Still, Grand Funk's earlier cover went all the way to the top in 1974.

The Miracles' second hit—after 1960's classic No. 2 smash "Shop Around"—came in early 1962 with "What's So Good About Good-by," which peaked at No. 35. With Smokey or without, the Miracles produced 29 Top 40 hits between 1960 and 1975.

Eddie Money's respectable blend of melodic pop and hard rock regularly appeared on the charts between 1978 and 1990. The former New York cop's "I Wanna Go Back" reached No. 14 in 1987.

The Monkees' first No. 1 hit "Last Train To Clarksville" bore the equally melodic "Take A Giant Step" on its flipside. The song had been recorded earlier by the Rising Sons—featuring Taj Mahal and Ry Cooder—but went unreleased until 1992.

The Moody Blues' 1971 single "The Story In Your Eyes" helped push the Brit group's album *Every Good Boy Deserves Favor* to a then-high mark of No. 2 on the album charts. Surprisingly, the band's biggest single, "Nights In White Satin"—which climbed to No. 2 in 1972—came four years after its first release.

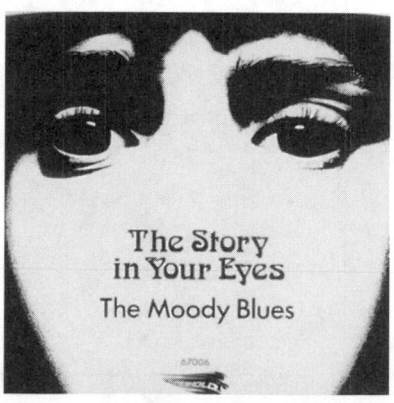

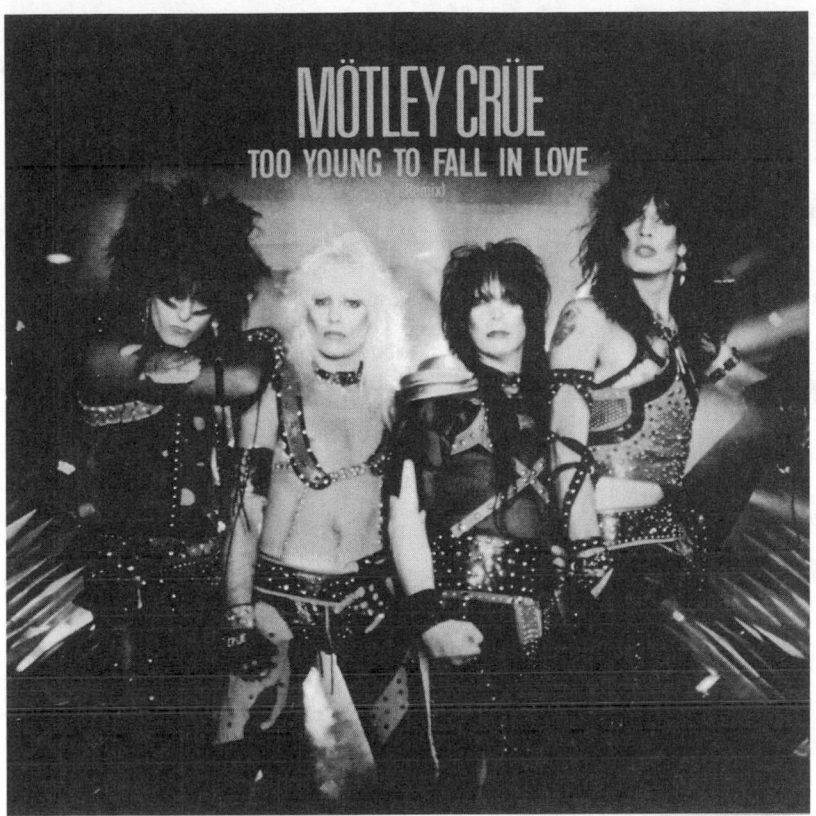

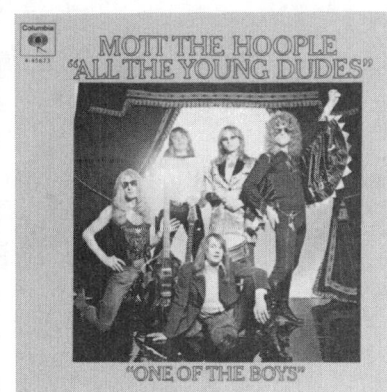

Motley Crue's glam-metal mix initially appealed more to album buyers than singles buyers. The group's triple-platinum 1983 set, *Shout At The Devil,* produced only two charting singles: "Looks That Kill," which reached No. 54, and "Too Young To Fall In Love," which only rose to No. 90.

Mott The Hoople's 1972 hit "All The Young Dudes" peaked at No. 37 and was the well-loved Brit rock group's only entry into the Top 40. Months later, the song's composer/producer David Bowie would score his own Top 40 hit with the re-released version of 1969's "Space Oddity."

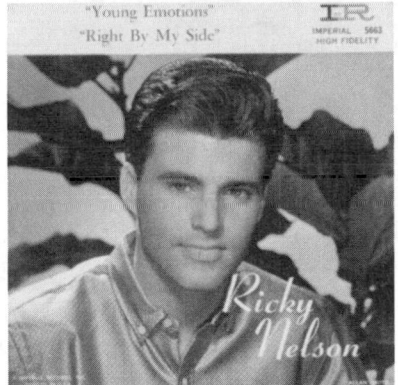

Ricky Nelson's 1960 single "Young Emotions" was the much-loved teen idol's 19th of 35 Top 40 hits. Thirty years later, the singer's two sons, Gunnar and Matthew, scored their first—and only—No. 1 record, "(Can't Live Without Your) Love And Affection."

New Edition's 1985 hit "Mr. Telephone Man" reached No. 12 and was written and produced by Ray Parker, Jr., whose own final Top 20 single "Jamie" rose to No. 14 during the same period.

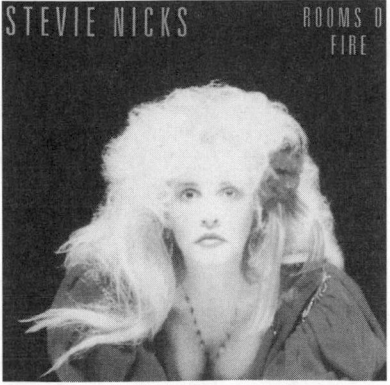

Juice Newton began a four-song Top 10 streak with 1981's "Angel Of The Morning"—a remake of Merilee Rush's 1968 hit—that drew to a close with the next year's appropriately titled "Break It To Me Gently," which peaked at No. 11.

Stevie Nicks was a ubiquitous pop figure during the '80s, both as a solo artist and as part of the enormously successful Fleetwood Mac. "Rooms Of Fire," her last Top 40 single, reached No. 16 in 1989.

DATE	POS	WKS	ARTIST–RECORD TITLE	LABEL & NO.
1/24/81	**5**	15	5. **Crying**	Millennium 11799
5/2/81	23	6	6. Since I Don't Have You	Millennium 11804
12/12/81	36	5	7. Castles In The Air [R] new version of #3 above	Millennium 11819
			McLEAN, Phil	
			Born in Detroit. Veteran DJ on Cleveland's WERE radio station.	
12/18/61+	**21**	6	1. Small Sad Sam [N-S] a parody of "Big Bad John"	Versatile 107
			McNAMARA, Robin	
			Male singer. One of the original cast members of *Hair*.	
7/18/70	**11**	8	1. Lay A Little Lovin' On Me cast of *Hair* (backing vocals)	Steed 724
			McPHATTER, Clyde	
			Born Clyde Lensley McPhatter on 11/15/32 in Durham, North Carolina. Died of a heart attack on 6/13/72 in New York City. Signed by Billy Ward for The Dominoes in 1950. Left The Dominoes in June 1953 to form own group, The Drifters. Drafted in 1954, returned to sing solo. One of the most influential and distinctive male voices of the R&B era. Inducted into the Rock and Roll Hall of Fame in 1987.	
6/9/56	**16**	12	1. Treasure Of Love Best Seller #16 / Juke Box #18 / Top 100 #22; #1 R&B hit (1 week)	Atlantic 1092
2/23/57	**19**	2	2. Without Love (There Is Nothing) Jockey #19 / Top 100 #38	Atlantic 1117
7/8/57	**26**	3	3. Just To Hold My Hand Best Seller #26 / Top 100 #30	Atlantic 1133
10/20/58+	**6**	20	● 4. **A Lover's Question** #1 R&B hit (1 week)	Atlantic 1199
8/3/59	**38**	2	5. Since You've Been Gone written by Neil Sedaka	Atlantic 2028
8/22/60	**23**	5	6. Ta Ta	Mercury 71660
3/24/62	**7**	10	7. **Lover Please**	Mercury 71941
6/30/62	**25**	5	8. Little Bitty Pretty One	Mercury 71987
			McVIE, Christine	
			Born Christine Perfect on 7/12/43 in Birmingham, England. Vocalist/keyboardist with Fleetwood Mac since 1970. Married to Fleetwood Mac bassist John McVie, 1968–77. Stopped touring with group after 1990.	
2/4/84	**10**	11	1. **Got A Hold On Me** #1 Adult Contemporary hit (4 weeks); Steve Winwood (synthesizer)	Warner 29372
5/12/84	**30**	6	2. Love Will Show Us How	Warner 29313
			MEAD, Sister Janet	
			Born in 1938. Australian nun. Gained prominence through her weekly cathedral rock masses and weekly radio programs.	
3/9/74	**4**	11	● 1. **The Lord's Prayer** Biblical text with new music by Arnold Strals	A&M 1491

DATE	POS	WKS	ARTIST–RECORD TITLE		LABEL & NO.

MEAT LOAF

Born Marvin Lee Aday on 9/27/51 in Dallas. Rock singer. Sang lead vocals on Ted Nugent's 1976 *Free-For-All* album. Played Eddie in the Los Angeles production and the movie *The Rocky Horror Picture Show*. Appeared in the movies *Americathon, Roadie, Out Of Bounds, The Squeeze* and *Leap Of Faith*.

DATE	POS	WKS	ARTIST–RECORD TITLE		LABEL & NO.
4/29/78	**11**	13	● 1. Two Out Of Three Ain't Bad		Epic 50513
9/16/78	**39**	2	2. Paradise By The Dashboard Light [N]		Epic 50588
			Ellen Foley (female vocal); Phil Rizzuto (baseball announcer)		
1/20/79	**39**	1	3. You Took The Words Right Out Of My Mouth		Epic 50634
			first released on Epic 50467 in 1977; above 3 produced by Todd Rundgren		
10/2/93	**1** (5)	18	▲ 4. **I'd Do Anything For Love (But I Won't Do That)**		MCA 54626
			Sales #1(7) / Airplay #4; Mrs. Loud (female vocal)		
2/5/94	**13**	13	5. Rock And Roll Dreams Come Through		MCA 54757
			Sales #11 / Airplay #24		
5/28/94	38	3	6. Objects In The Rear View Mirror May Appear Closer Than They Are		MCA 54848
			Sales #31 / Airplay #67; all of above written by Jim Steinman		
10/21/95	**13**	11	● 7. I'd Lie For You (And That's The Truth)		MCA 55134
			Sales #6 / Airplay #43		

MECO

Disco producer Meco Monardo. Born on 11/29/39 in Johnsonburg, Pennsylvania. Played trombone in Cadet Band at West Point. Later moved to New York and became a session musician and arranger. Co-produced Gloria Gaynor's hit "Never Can Say Goodbye."

DATE	POS	WKS	ARTIST–RECORD TITLE		LABEL & NO.
8/27/77	**1** (2)	13	▲ 1. **Star Wars Theme/Cantina Band** [I]		Millennium 604
1/21/78	25	6	2. Theme From Close Encounters [I]		Millennium 608
10/21/78	35	3	3. Themes From The Wizard Of Oz [N]		Millennium 620
7/5/80	18	8	4. Empire Strikes Back (Medley) [I]		RSO 1038
			Darth Vader/Yoda's Theme; all of above inspired by movie themes		
4/3/82	35	3	5. Pop Goes The Movies (Part I) [I]		Arista 0660
			20th Century Fox Trademark/Tara's Theme/The Magnificent Seven/The James Bond Theme/Goldfinger/The Good, The Bad And The Ugly/Theme From The Apartment/Theme From The High & The Mighty		

MEDEIROS, Glenn

Born on 6/24/70 and raised in Hawaii. Discovered through a local radio station talent search.

DATE	POS	WKS	ARTIST–RECORD TITLE		LABEL & NO.
4/4/87	**12**	13	1. Nothing's Gonna Change My Love For You		Amherst 311
			Sales #6 / Airplay #17		
5/26/90	**1** (2)	14	● 2. **She Ain't Worth It**		MCA 79047
			GLENN MEDEIROS Featuring Bobby Brown		
			Airplay #1(3) / Sales #4		
9/22/90	32	4	3. All I'm Missing Is You		MCA 53886
			GLENN MEDEIROS Featuring Ray Parker Jr.		
			Sales #29 / Airplay #29		

DATE	POS	WKS	ARTIST–RECORD TITLE	LABEL & NO.
			MEDLEY, Bill	
			Born on 9/19/40 in Santa Ana, California. Baritone of The Righteous Brothers duo. Co-owner, with Paul Revere of The Raiders, of a Las Vegas nightclub named Kicks.	

10/10/87	**1** (1)	15	● 1. **(I've Had) The Time Of My Life**
			    BILL MEDLEY AND JENNIFER WARNES
			    Airplay #1(2) / Sales #1(1); love theme from the movie *Dirty Dancing* starring Patrick Swayze; #1 Adult Contemporary hit (4 weeks); B-side is Mickey & Sylvia's 1957 hit "Love Is Strange"
				RCA 5224

			MEISNER, Randy	
			Born on 3/8/46 in Scottsbluff, Nebraska. Bassist/vocalist of Poco, 1968–69; Rick Nelson's Stone Canyon Band, 1969–71; and the Eagles, 1971–77.	
11/8/80	**22**	7	1. Deep Inside My Heart Kim Carnes (backing vocal)	Epic 50939
2/7/81	**19**	9	2. Hearts On Fire	Epic 50964
8/28/82	**28**	6	3. Never Been In Love	Epic 03032
			MEL AND TIM	
			Cousins Mel Hardin and Tim McPherson, from Holly Springs, Mississippi.	
11/8/69	**10**	11	● 1. **Backfield In Motion** produced by Gene Chandler	Bamboo 107
9/16/72	**19**	9	2. Starting All Over Again	Stax 0127
			MELANIE	
			Born Melanie Safka on 2/3/47 in Queens, New York. Neighborhood Records formed by Melanie and her husband/producer Peter Schekeryk. Wrote The New Seekers' hit "Look What They've Done To My Song Ma."	
5/16/70	**6**	14	1. **Lay Down (Candles In The Rain)** **MELANIE with The Edwin Hawkins Singers**	Buddah 167
9/5/70	**32**	4	2. Peace Will Come (According To Plan)	Buddah 186
11/27/71	**1** (3)	14	● 3. **Brand New Key**	Neighborhood 4201
2/19/72	**31**	5	4. Ring The Living Bell	Neighborhood 4202
2/26/72	**35**	3	5. The Nickel Song	Buddah 268
4/7/73	**36**	2	6. Bitter Bad	Neighborhood 4210
			MELENDEZ, Lisette	
			Dance singer from East Harlem, New York.	
3/16/91	**35**	4	1. Together Forever Airplay #21 / Sales #33	Fever 73629
			MELLENCAMP, John Cougar	
			Born on 10/7/51 in Seymour, Indiana. Rock singer/songwriter/producer. Worked outside of music until 1975. Given name Johnny Cougar by David Bowie's manager, Tony DeFries. First recorded for MCA in 1976. Directed and starred in the 1992 movie *Falling from Grace*; leader of the Buzzin' Cousins group that appeared in the movie. Married model Elaine Irwin on 9/5/92. **JOHN COUGAR:**	
11/10/79	**28**	8	1. I Need A Lover	Riva 202
11/8/80	**27**	7	2. This Time	Riva 205

DATE	POS	WKS	ARTIST–RECORD TITLE	LABEL & NO.
3/14/81	**17**	12	3. Ain't Even Done With The Night	Riva 207
5/22/82	**2** (4)	22	● 4. **Hurts So Good**	Riva 209
8/7/82	**1** (4)	17	● 5. **Jack & Diane**	Riva 210
11/27/82+	**19**	11	6. Hand To Hold On To	Riva 211
			JOHN COUGAR MELLENCAMP:	
10/22/83	**9**	11	7. **Crumblin' Down**	Riva 214
12/17/83+	**8**	11	8. **Pink Houses**	Riva 215
			acoustic version is on the B-side of #9 below	
3/31/84	**15**	9	9. Authority Song	Riva 216
8/24/85	**6**	13	10. **Lonely Ol' Night**	Riva 880984
			Airplay #5 / Sales #5	
11/16/85	**6**	13	11. **Small Town**	Riva 884202
			Airplay #4 / Sales #6	
2/15/86	**2** (1)	11	12. **R.O.C.K. In The U.S.A.**	Riva 884455
			Airplay #2 / Sales #3; a salute to '60s rock	
5/17/86	**21**	6	13. Rain On The Scarecrow	Riva 884635
			Sales #18 / Airplay #26	
8/2/86	**28**	4	14. Rumbleseat	Riva 884856
			Sales #23 / Airplay #36; above 5 from the album *Scarecrow*	
8/29/87	**9**	10	15. **Paper In Fire**	Mercury 888763
			Sales #9 / Airplay #9	
11/14/87+	**8**	12	16. **Cherry Bomb**	Mercury 888934
			Sales #6 / Airplay #13	
2/27/88	**14**	9	17. Check It Out	Mercury 870126
			Sales #14 / Airplay #14	
5/13/89	**15**	7	18. Pop Singer	Mercury 874012
			Sales #12 / Airplay #22	
			JOHN MELLENCAMP:	
10/19/91	**14**	7	19. Get A Leg Up	Mercury 867890
			Airplay #58 / Sales #75; "live" version is on the B-side of #20 below	
2/29/92	**36**	4	20. Again Tonight	Mercury 866414
			Airplay #40	
6/18/94	**3**	33	21. **Wild Night**	Mercury 858738
			JOHN MELLENCAMP AND ME'SHELL NDEGÉOCELLO	
			Airplay #3 / Sales #6; #1 Adult Contemporary hit (8 weeks)	
			MELLO-TONES, The	
5/13/57	**24**	1	1. Rosie Lee	Gee 1037
			Best Seller #24 / Top 100 #60; Hank Ivory (orch.)	
			MELLOW MAN ACE	
			Born Ulpiano Sergio Reyez in Cuba on 4/12/67. Black Hispanic rapper. Moved to the U.S. at age four. Raised in Southgate, California. His brother "Sen Dog" is a member of Cypress Hill.	
6/9/90	**14**	13	● 1. Mentirosa	Capitol 44533
			Sales #5 / Airplay #28; tune samples Santana's "Evil Ways" and "No One To Depend On"	

DATE	POS	WKS	ARTIST–RECORD TITLE	LABEL & NO.

MELVIN, Harold, And The Blue Notes

Philadelphia soul group, The Blue Notes, formed in 1954: Harold Melvin, Bernard Williams, Jesse Gillis, Jr., Franklin Peaker and Roosevelt Brodie. First recorded for Josie in 1956. Numerous personnel changes until 1970, when Teddy Pendergrass joined as drummer and lead singer. Pendergrass went solo in 1976, replaced by David Ebo.

DATE	POS	WKS	ARTIST–RECORD TITLE	LABEL & NO.
10/28/72	3	11	● 1. **If You Don't Know Me By Now** #1 R&B hit (2 weeks)	Phil. Int. 3520
10/20/73	7	12	● 2. **The Love I Lost (Part 1)** #1 R&B hit (2 weeks)	Phil. Int. 3533
5/3/75	15	10	3. Bad Luck (Part 1)	Phil. Int. 3562
12/20/75+	12	12	4. Wake Up Everybody (Part 1) #1 R&B hit (2 weeks)	Phil. Int. 3579

MEN AT LARGE

Cleveland R&B duo: David Tolliver and Jason Champion. Each weighs over 300 pounds. Discovered by Gerald Levert.

DATE	POS	WKS	ARTIST–RECORD TITLE	LABEL & NO.
4/10/93	31	4	1. So Alone Sales #25 / Airplay #37; co-written and co-produced by Gerald Levert	EastWest 98459

MEN AT WORK

Rock quintet from Melbourne, Australia, formed in 1979. Colin James Hay (lead singer, guitar), Ron Strykert (lead guitar), Greg Ham (sax, keyboards), Jerry Speiser (drums) and John Rees (bass). Won the 1982 Best New Artist Grammy Award. Speiser and Rees left in 1984.

DATE	POS	WKS	ARTIST–RECORD TITLE	LABEL & NO.
8/7/82	1 (1)	17	1. **Who Can It Be Now?**	Columbia 02888
11/27/82+	1 (4)	19	● 2. **Down Under**	Columbia 03303
4/9/83	3	13	3. **Overkill**	Columbia 03795
7/9/83	6	12	4. **It's A Mistake**	Columbia 03959
10/8/83	28	5	5. Dr. Heckyll & Mr. Jive	Columbia 04111

MENDES, Sergio, & Brasil '66

Mendes was born on 2/11/41 in Niteroi, Brazil. Pianist/leader of Latin-styled group originating from Brazil. Member Lani Hall (vocals) married Herb Alpert.

DATE	POS	WKS	ARTIST–RECORD TITLE	LABEL & NO.
6/1/68	4	11	1. **The Look Of Love** from the movie *Casino Royale* starring David Niven and Peter Sellers	A&M 924
8/24/68	6	10	2. **The Fool On The Hill** written by John Lennon and Paul McCartney (from The Beatles' 1967 album *Magical Mystery Tour*); #1 Adult Contemporary hit (6 weeks)	A&M 961
12/7/68	16	6	3. Scarborough Fair	A&M 986

SERGIO MENDES:

DATE	POS	WKS	ARTIST–RECORD TITLE	LABEL & NO.
5/14/83	4	16	4. **Never Gonna Let You Go** Joe Pizzulo and Leza Miller (vocals); #1 Adult Contemporary hit (4 weeks)	A&M 2540
7/7/84	29	7	5. Alibis	A&M 2639

DATE	POS	WKS	ARTIST–RECORD TITLE	LABEL & NO.
			MEN WITHOUT HATS	
			Nucleus of techno-rock band from Montreal consists of Ivan Doroschuk (singer/songwriter) with his brother Stefan (guitar). Fluctuating personnel included their brother Colin, 1983–84.	
7/30/83	3	16	1. **The Safety Dance**	Backstreet 52232
12/19/87+	20	10	2. Pop Goes The World Sales #16 / Airplay #25	Mercury 888859
			MERCHANT, Natalie	
			Born on 10/26/63 in Jamestown, New York. Lead singer of 10,000 Maniacs, 1981–93.	
8/26/95	10	26	1. **Carnival** Airplay #6 / Sales #54	Elektra 64413
			MERCY	
			Florida group led by Jack Sigler, Jr.	
5/3/69	2 (2)	10	● 1. **Love (Can Make You Happy)**	Sundi 6811
			MESSINA, Jim—see LOGGINS & MESSINA	
			METALLICA	
			Heavy-metal quartet formed by Lars Ulrich (drums) and James Hetfield (vocals) in Los Angeles in 1981. Early rhythm guitarist Dave Mustaine (now the leader of Megadeth) was replaced by Kirk Hammett in 1982. Bassist Cliff Burton was killed in a bus crash in Sweden on 9/27/86 (age 24); replaced by Jason Newsted.	
3/25/89	35	4	● 1. One Sales #18	Elektra 69329
8/31/91	16	16	● 2. Enter Sandman Sales #3; "live" version is on the B-side of #4 below	Elektra 64857
1/11/92	35	1	3. The Unforgiven Sales #16	Elektra 64814
4/25/92	34	3	4. Nothing Else Matters Sales #18	Elektra 64770
			METERS, The	
			R&B instrumental group formed in New Orleans in 1966 featuring keyboardist Arthur Neville (brother of Aaron Neville). Group disbanded in 1977, when Art, Aaron, and brothers Charles and Cyril formed The Neville Brothers.	
3/22/69	34	1	1. Sophisticated Cissy [I]	Josie 1001
5/24/69	23	3	2. Cissy Strut [I]	Josie 1005
			METHENY, Pat, Group—see BOWIE, David	
			METHOD MAN	
			Born Clifford Smith in Staten Island, New York. Male rapper. Member of Wu-Tang Clan. Also see The Notorious B.I.G.	
5/13/95	3	13	▲ 1. **I'll Be There For You/You're All I Need To Get By** **METHOD MAN featuring Mary J. Blige** Sales #1(1) / Airplay #33; medley of songs written by Ashford & Simpson; Method Man raps to "I'll Be There For You" (#2 R&B hit for Ashford & Simpson in 1989) and Blige sings chorus of "You're All I Need To Get By"; #1 R&B hit (3 weeks)	Def Jam/RAL 1878

DATE	POS	WKS	ARTIST–RECORD TITLE	LABEL & NO.
9/2/95	13	8	● 2. How High **REDMAN & METHOD MAN** Sales #7 / Airplay #64; from the rap concert movie *The Show*; contains an interpolation of "Fly Robin Fly" and samples "I Am Woman" by The Cover Girls	Def Jam/RAL 9924
10/28/95	37	2	3. Ice Cream **Chef RAEKWON featuring Tony Starks (Ghost Face Killer) and Method Man** Sales #19 / Airplay #74	Loud/RCA 64426
			MFSB Group of studio musicians based at Philadelphia Sigma Sound Studios. Produced by Kenny Gamble and Leon Huff for their own label, Philadelphia International. Also recorded as The James Boys and Family. Name stands for "Mother, Father, Sister, Brother."	
3/16/74	1 (2)	14	● 1. TSOP (The Sound Of Philadelphia) [I] **MFSB featuring The Three Degrees** theme from the TV show "Soul Train"; #1 Adult Contemporary hit (2 weeks); #1 R&B hit (1 week)	Phil. Int. 3540
			MIAMI SOUND MACHINE—see ESTEFAN, Gloria	
			MICHAEL, George/Wham! Born Georgios Kyriacos Panayiotou on 6/25/63 in Bushey, England. Wham!, formed in early '80s, centered around Michael's vocals and songwriting, and included Andrew Ridgeley (born 1/26/63, Bushey, England) on guitar. Their association ended in 1986. Ridgeley pursued race car driving, then solo career in 1990. **WHAM!:**	
10/6/84	1 (3)	14	▲ 1. Wake Me Up Before You Go-Go Sales #1(3) / Airplay #1(3)	Columbia 04552
12/22/84+	1 (3)	17	▲ 2. Careless Whisper **WHAM! Featuring George Michael** Sales #1(3) / Airplay #1(3); #1 Adult Contemporary hit (5 weeks); originally released as a solo single by George Michael	Columbia 04691
4/6/85	1 (2)	14	● 3. Everything She Wants Sales #1(2) / Airplay #1(2)	Columbia 04840
8/3/85	3	12	4. Freedom Sales #3 / Airplay #5; above 4 from the album *Make It Big*	Columbia 05409
12/14/85+	3	12	5. I'm Your Man Sales #3 / Airplay #3	Columbia 05721
5/10/86	7	10	6. A Different Corner **GEORGE MICHAEL** Sales #5 / Airplay #8	Columbia 05888
7/19/86	10	8	7. The Edge Of Heaven Sales #8 / Airplay #10	Columbia 06182
3/7/87	1 (2)	12	8. I Knew You Were Waiting (For Me) **ARETHA FRANKLIN AND GEORGE MICHAEL** Sales #1(2) / Airplay #1(1)	Arista 9559
			GEORGE MICHAEL:	
6/20/87	2 (1)	14	▲ 9. I Want Your Sex Sales #1(2) / Airplay #5; from the movie *Beverly Hills Cop II* starring Eddie Murphy	Columbia 07164

DATE	POS	WKS	ARTIST–RECORD TITLE	LABEL & NO.
10/31/87	**1 (4)**	15	● 10. **Faith** Airplay #1(5) / Sales #1(1)	Columbia 07623
1/23/88	**1 (2)**	13	11. **Father Figure** Airplay #1(4) / Sales #1(1); also see PM Dawn's "Looking Through Patient Eyes"	Columbia 07682
4/16/88	**1 (3)**	14	● 12. **One More Try** Airplay #1(4) / Sales #1(3); #1 Adult Contemporary hit (3 weeks); #1 R&B hit (1 week)	Columbia 07773
7/16/88	**1 (2)**	12	13. **Monkey** Sales #1(2) / Airplay #1(2)	Columbia 07941
10/15/88	**5**	10	14. **Kissing A Fool** Sales #3 / Airplay #6; #1 Adult Contemporary hit (1 week); above 6 from the album *Faith*	Columbia 08050
3/11/89	**5**	11	15. **Heaven Help Me** **DEON ESTUS (with George Michael)** Sales #4 / Airplay #6	Mika 871538
9/8/90	**1 (1)**	10	16. **Praying For Time** Airplay #1(2) / Sales #3	Columbia 73512
11/3/90	**8**	12	● 17. **Freedom** Sales #7 / Airplay #9; different tune from Michael's 1985 Wham! hit	Columbia 73559
2/9/91	**27**	5	18. **Waiting For That Day** Airplay #24 / Sales #28; includes the title line from The Rolling Stones' "You Can't Always Get What You Want"	Columbia 73663
12/14/91+	**1 (1)**	16	● 19. **Don't Let The Sun Go Down On Me** **GEORGE MICHAEL/ELTON JOHN** Sales #4 / Airplay #4; recorded "live" in London, March 1991; #1 Adult Contemporary hit (2 weeks)	Columbia 74086
6/20/92	**10**	12	● 20. **Too Funky** Airplay #6 / Sales #17; from the AIDS benefit album *Red, Hot & Dance*	Columbia 74353
5/22/93	**30**	4	21. **Somebody To Love** **GEORGE MICHAEL and QUEEN** Airplay #25 / Sales #72; recorded "live" at Wembly Stadium for the Freddie Mercury Tribute Concert	Hollywood 64647
			MICHAELS, Lee	
			Born on 11/24/45 in Los Angeles. Rock organist/vocalist.	
9/4/71	**6**	12	1. **Do You Know What I Mean**	A&M 1262
12/25/71	**39**	1	2. Can I Get A Witness	A&M 1303
			MICHEL'Le	
			Michel'le (pronounced: mee-shell-LAY) Toussant is a singer from Los Angeles (18 years old in 1990). Former backing singer of the World Class Wreckin Cru.	
1/20/90	**7**	14	● 1. **No More Lies** Sales #4 / Airplay #14	Ruthless 99149
5/26/90	**29**	5	2. Nicety Sales #21 / Airplay #35	Ruthless 98980
3/2/91	**31**	5	3. Something In My Heart Sales #23 / Airplay #61; above 3 produced by Dr. Dre and Eazy-E	Ruthless 98885

DATE	POS	WKS	ARTIST–RECORD TITLE	LABEL & NO.
			MICKEY and SYLVIA	
			McHouston "Mickey" Baker and Sylvia Vanderpool. Mickey (born 10/15/25, Louisville) was a prolific session guitarist. Sylvia (born 3/6/36, New York City) began solo career in 1973, recorded as Sylvia.	
1/12/57	11	14	1. Love Is Strange Best Seller #11 / Jockey #11 / Top 100 #13 / Juke Box #17; #1 R&B hit (2 weeks)	Groove 0175
			MIDLER, Bette	
			Born on 12/1/45 in Paterson, New Jersey; raised in Hawaii. Vocalist/actress. Appeared in the Broadway show *Fiddler On The Roof* for three years. Won the 1973 Best New Artist Grammy Award. Barry Manilow was her arranger/accompanist in early years. Nominated for an Oscar for performance in *The Rose* (1979). Also appeared in the movies *Down And Out In Beverly Hills, Ruthless People, Beaches, For The Boys* and others.	
1/20/73	17	11	1. Do You Want To Dance?	Atlantic 2928
6/9/73	8	11	2. **Boogie Woogie Bugle Boy** #15 hit for The Andrews Sisters in 1941 (introduced in the movie *Buck Privates* starring Abbott & Costello); #1 Adult Contemporary hit (2 weeks)	Atlantic 2964
11/10/73	40	1	3. Friends above 2 produced by Barry Manilow	Atlantic 2980
7/7/79	40	2	4. Married Men	Atlantic 3582
3/1/80	35	3	5. When A Man Loves A Woman	Atlantic 3643
4/26/80	3	16	● 6. **The Rose** #1 Adult Contemporary hit (5 weeks); above 2 from the movie *The Rose* starring Midler	Atlantic 3656
1/17/81	39	2	7. My Mother's Eyes from the Bette Midler concert movie *Divine Madness*; #8 hit for George Jessel in 1929	Atlantic 3771
4/15/89	1 (1)	15	▲ 8. **Wind Beneath My Wings** Sales #1(1) / Airplay #2; from the movie *Beaches* starring Midler; song also known as "Hero"	Atlantic 88972
10/20/90	2 (1)	19	▲ 9. **From A Distance** Sales #1(1) / Airplay #3; #1 Adult Contemporary hit (6 weeks)	Atlantic 87820
			MIDNIGHTERS, The—see BALLARD, Hank	
			MIDNIGHT OIL	
			Rock group formed in Sydney, Australia, in 1976: Peter Garrett (vocals), Martin Rotsey (guitar), James Moginie (keyboards), Peter Gifford (bass) and Rob Hirst (drums). Gifford was replaced by Dwayne "Bones" Hillman in 1987. Garrett ran for the Australian Senate in 1984.	
5/21/88	17	9	1. Beds Are Burning Sales #11 / Airplay #22	Columbia 07433
			MIDNIGHT STAR	
			R&B-funk group formed in 1976 at Kentucky State University. Lead vocals by Belinda Lipscomb. Until 1988, band led by brothers Reggie (trumpet) and Vincent (trombone) Calloway. Reggie and Vincent produced many artists in the mid-1980s; formed own duo Calloway in 1988.	
1/12/85	18	8	1. Operator Airplay #17 / Sales #18; #1 R&B hit (5 weeks)	Solar 69684

DATE	POS	WKS	ARTIST—RECORD TITLE	LABEL & NO.
			MIKE + THE MECHANICS	
			Rock quintet consisting of bassist Mike Rutherford (Genesis), vocalists Paul Carrack (Ace, Squeeze) and Paul Young (Sad Cafe), drummer Peter Van Hooke (Van Morrison) and keyboardist Adrian Lee.	
1/18/86	6	11	1. **Silent Running (On Dangerous Ground)** Airplay #5 / Sales #7; title track from the movie *On Dangerous Ground*	Atlantic 89488
4/12/86	5	12	2. **All I Need Is A Miracle** Airplay #5 / Sales #8	Atlantic 89450
8/2/86	32	5	3. Taken In Airplay #24 / Sales #37	Atlantic 89404
1/21/89	1 (1)	14	4. **The Living Years** Sales #1(2) / Airplay #1(1); #1 Adult Contemporary hit (4 weeks)	Atlantic 88964
			MILES, Garry	
			Born James Cason on 11/27/39 in Nashville. Lead singer of The Statues and Brenda Lee's backing group, The Casuals. Also recorded as Buzz Cason. Also see Garry Mills, who is a different artist with the original version of "Look For A Star."	
7/18/60	16	9	1. Look For A Star from the British movie *Circus Of Horrors* starring Donald Pleasence	Liberty 55261
			MILES, John	
			Born on 4/23/49 in Jarrow, England. Rock vocalist/guitarist/keyboardist. Guest vocalist with the Alan Parsons Project.	
5/14/77	34	5	1. Slowdown	London 20092
			MILLER, Chuck	
			Boogie pianist from California.	
6/18/55	9	14	1. **The House Of Blue Lights** Best Seller #9 / Jockey #18 / Juke Box #19; #8 hit for Freddie Slack in 1946	Mercury 70627
			MILLER, Jody	
			Born on 11/29/41 in Phoenix; raised in Blanchard, Oklahoma. Pop-country singer.	
5/15/65	12	5	1. Queen Of The House answer song to Roger Miller's "King Of The Road"	Capitol 5402
9/25/65	25	5	2. Home Of The Brave	Capitol 5483
			MILLER, Mitch, & his Orch. and Chorus	
			Born on 7/4/11 in Rochester, New York. Producer/conductor/arranger. Oboe soloist with the CBS Symphony, 1936–47. A&R executive for both Columbia and Mercury Records. Best known for his sing-along albums and 1961–64 TV show.	
8/6/55	1 (6)	19	● 1. **The Yellow Rose Of Texas** Best Seller #1(6) / Jockey #1(6) / Juke Box #1(6) / Top 100 #4 pre; adaptation of a Civil War campfire song	Columbia 40540
2/18/56	19	3	2. Lisbon Antigua (In Old Lisbon) [I] Jockey #19 / Top 100 #30	Columbia 40635
8/11/56	8	12	3. **Theme Song (from "Song For A Summer Night")** [I] Jockey #8 / Best Seller #9 / Top 100 #10 / Juke Box #10; from the 7/8/56 "Studio One" TV production "A Song for a Summer Night"; B-side is a vocal version	Columbia 40730

DATE	POS	WKS	ARTIST–RECORD TITLE	LABEL & NO.
1/27/58	20	11	4. March From The River Kwai and Colonel Bogey [I] Jockey #20 / Best Seller #21 / Top 100 #21; from the movie *The Bridge on the River Kwai* starring Alec Guinness and William Holden; "March" written for the movie; "Bogey" is a traditional march	Columbia 41066
1/26/59	16	10	5. The Children's Marching Song (Nick Nack Paddy Whack) from the movie *The Inn of the Sixth Happiness* starring Ingrid Bergman	Columbia 41317

MILLER, Ned

Born Henry Ned Miller on 4/12/25 in Rains, Utah. Country singer/songwriter. To California in 1956. Signed with Fabor in 1956. Wrote the Gale Storm and Bonnie Guitar hit "Dark Moon."

DATE	POS	WKS	ARTIST–RECORD TITLE	LABEL & NO.
1/26/63	6	8	1. **From A Jack To A King** original version released on Dot 15601 in 1957	Fabor 114

MILLER, Roger

Born on 1/2/36 in Fort Worth, Texas; raised in Erick, Oklahoma. Died of cancer on 10/25/92. Country vocalist/humorist/guitarist/composer. To Nashville in the mid-1950s, began songwriting career. Debuted on the country charts in 1960 on RCA. With Faron Young as writer/drummer in 1962. Won six Grammys in 1965. Own TV show in 1966. Songwriter of 1985's Tony Award-winning Broadway musical *Big River*.

DATE	POS	WKS	ARTIST–RECORD TITLE	LABEL & NO.
7/4/64	7	8	1. **Dang Me** [N] #1 Country hit (6 weeks)	Smash 1881
10/3/64	9	8	2. **Chug-A-Lug** [N]	Smash 1926
1/2/65	31	3	3. Do-Wacka-Do [N]	Smash 1947
2/6/65	4	12	● 4. **King Of The Road** #1 Adult Contemporary hit (10 weeks); #1 Country hit (5 weeks)	Smash 1965
5/22/65	7	7	5. **Engine Engine #9**	Smash 1983
8/7/65	34	2	6. One Dyin' And A Buryin'	Smash 1994
10/2/65	31	3	7. Kansas City Star [N]	Smash 1998
11/27/65	8	8	8. **England Swings** #1 Adult Contemporary hit (1 week)	Smash 2010
3/5/66	26	5	9. Husbands And Wives	Smash 2024
7/23/66	40	1	10. You Can't Roller Skate In A Buffalo Herd [N]	Smash 2043
5/6/67	37	1	11. Walkin' In The Sunshine	Smash 2081
3/16/68	39	6	12. Little Green Apples all of above produced by Jerry Kennedy	Smash 2148

MILLER, Steve, Band

Miller was born on 10/5/43 in Milwaukee; moved to Dallas at age six. Blues-rock singer/songwriter/guitarist. Formed band in high school, The Marksmen, which included Boz Scaggs. While at the University of Wisconsin-Madison, Miller led the blues-rock band the Ardells, later known as the Fabulous Night Trains, featuring Scaggs. After graduating, studied literature at the University of Copenhagen. To San Francisco in 1966; formed the Steve Miller Band, which featured a fluctuating lineup.

DATE	POS	WKS	ARTIST–RECORD TITLE	LABEL & NO.
11/17/73+	1 (1)	16	● 1. **The Joker**	Capitol 3732
			STEVE MILLER:	
6/5/76	11	9	2. Take The Money And Run	Capitol 4260
9/4/76	1 (1)	14	3. **Rock'n Me**	Capitol 4323
1/8/77	2 (2)	15	● 4. **Fly Like An Eagle**	Capitol 4372

DATE	POS	WKS	ARTIST–RECORD TITLE	LABEL & NO.
			STEVE MILLER BAND:	
5/14/77	8	13	5. **Jet Airliner**	Capitol 4424
9/3/77	23	7	6. Jungle Love	Capitol 4466
11/12/77	17	9	7. Swingtown	Capitol 4496
11/14/81	24	9	8. Heart Like A Wheel	Capitol 5068
6/19/82	1 (2)	19	● 9. **Abracadabra**	Capitol 5126
			all of above produced by Steve Miller	

MILLI VANILLI

Europop act formed in Germany by producer Frank Farian (creator of Boney M and Far Corporation). Milli Vanilli is Turkish for positive energy. Originally thought to be Rob Pilatus (from Germany) and Fabrice Morvan (from France). Duo was stripped of its 1989 Best New Artist Grammy Award when it was revealed that they didn't sing on their debut album. Actual vocalists are Charles Shaw, John Davis and Brad Howe.

DATE	POS	WKS	ARTIST–RECORD TITLE	LABEL & NO.
2/4/89	2 (1)	15	▲ 1. **Girl You Know It's True**	Arista 9781
			Sales #1(2) / Airplay #4	
5/20/89	1 (1)	14	● 2. **Baby Don't Forget My Number**	Arista 9832
			Sales #1(1) / Airplay #2	
8/12/89	1 (2)	14	● 3. **Girl I'm Gonna Miss You**	Arista 9870
			Airplay #1(3) / Sales #1(1)	
10/21/89	1 (2)	14	▲ 4. **Blame It On The Rain**	Arista 9904
			Airplay #1(2) / Sales #1(1)	
1/13/90	4	10	5. **All Or Nothing**	Arista 9923
			Airplay #4 / Sales #6; also on the B-side of #3 above; all of above from the album Girl You Know It's True	

MILLS, Frank

Born in Toronto in 1943. Pianist/composer/producer/arranger.

DATE	POS	WKS	ARTIST–RECORD TITLE	LABEL & NO.
3/3/79	3	12	● 1. **Music Box Dancer** [I]	Polydor 14517

MILLS, Garry

British singer. Also see Garry Miles.

DATE	POS	WKS	ARTIST–RECORD TITLE	LABEL & NO.
7/4/60	26	6	1. **Look For A Star - Part I**	Imperial 5674
			original version of song from the British movie Circus Of Horrors starring Donald Pleasence	

MILLS, Hayley

Born on 4/18/46 in London. Daughter of English actor John Mills. Disney teen movie star of *Pollyanna, The Parent Trap, In Search Of The Castaways* and others.

DATE	POS	WKS	ARTIST–RECORD TITLE	LABEL & NO.
9/18/61	8	11	1. **Let's Get Together**	Buena Vista 385
			HAYLEY MILLS and HAYLEY MILLS	
			from the movie The Parent Trap starring Mills	
4/14/62	21	6	2. Johnny Jingo	Buena Vista 395

MILLS, Stephanie

Born on 3/26/56 in Brooklyn. In 1967, appeared for four weeks at the Apollo Theater with The Isley Brothers. At age 15, won starring role of Dorothy in the hit Broadway musical *The Wiz*. Played role for four years. Briefly married to Jeffrey Daniels of Shalamar in 1980.

DATE	POS	WKS	ARTIST–RECORD TITLE	LABEL & NO.
9/1/79	22	6	1. What Cha Gonna Do With My Lovin'	20th Century 2403
8/30/80	6	16	● 2. **Never Knew Love Like This Before**	20th Century 2460

DATE	POS	WKS	ARTIST—RECORD TITLE	LABEL & NO.
7/4/81	40	2	3. Two Hearts **STEPHANIE MILLS Featuring Teddy Pendergrass**	20th Century 2492

MILLS BROTHERS, The

Legendary family vocal group from Piqua, Ohio. Consisted of John, Jr. (born 1911; died 1936), Herbert (born 1912; died 4/12/89), Harry (born 1913; died 6/28/82) and Donald (born 1915). Originally featured unusual vocal style of imitating instruments. Achieved national fame via radio broadcasts and appearances in movies. Father, John, Sr., joined group in 1936, replacing John, Jr.; remained in group until 1956 (died 12/8/67). Group continued as a trio until 1982. Donald and his son John III continued singing as a duo.

DATE	POS	WKS	ARTIST—RECORD TITLE	LABEL & NO.
6/17/57	39	1	1. Queen Of The Senior Prom	Decca 30299
3/3/58	21	2	2. Get A Job Jockey #21	Dot 15695
3/2/68	23	10	3. Cab Driver	Dot 17041

MILSAP, Ronnie

Born on 1/16/46 in Robbinsville, North Carolina. Country singer/pianist/guitarist. Blind since birth; multi-instrumentalist by age 12. With J.J. Cale band; own band from 1965. First charted (Bubbling Under) in 1965 on Scepter Records.

DATE	POS	WKS	ARTIST—RECORD TITLE	LABEL & NO.
8/27/77	16	10	1. It Was Almost Like A Song #1 Country hit (3 weeks)	RCA 10976
1/24/81	24	9	2. Smoky Mountain Rain #1 Country hit (1 week); #1 Adult Contemporary hit (1 week)	RCA 12084
7/11/81	5	15	3. **(There's) No Gettin' Over Me** #1 Country hit (2 weeks)	RCA 12264
11/28/81+	20	11	4. I Wouldn't Have Missed It For The World #1 Country hit (1 week)	RCA 12342
5/29/82	14	9	5. Any Day Now #1 Adult Contemporary hit (5 weeks); #1 Country hit (1 week)	RCA 13216
4/23/83	23	8	6. Stranger In My House	RCA 13470

MIMMS, Garnet, & The Enchanters

Born Garrett Mimms on 11/16/33 in Ashland, West Virginia. Sang in gospel groups the Evening Stars, Norfolk Four, Harmonizing Four. Formed group The Gainors in 1958. The Enchanters (Zola Pearnell, Sam Bell and Charles Boyer) were formed in 1961.

DATE	POS	WKS	ARTIST—RECORD TITLE	LABEL & NO.
9/7/63	4	11	1. **Cry Baby** #1 R&B hit (3 weeks)	United Art. 629
12/21/63+	26	5	2. For Your Precious Love/	
12/7/63	30	4	3. Baby Don't You Weep	United Art. 658
5/7/66	30	3	4. I'll Take Good Care Of You **GARNET MIMMS**	United Art. 995

MINDBENDERS, The

Rock group from Manchester, England: Wayne Fontana (born Glyn Geoffrey Ellis on 10/28/45; lead singer), Eric Stewart (lead guitar, vocals), Bob Lang (bass) and Ric Rothwell (drums). Fontana left in October 1965. Graham Gouldman joined in 1968. Stewart and Gouldman were later members of Hotlegs and 10cc.

DATE	POS	WKS	ARTIST—RECORD TITLE	LABEL & NO.
3/27/65	1 (1)	10	1. **Game Of Love** **WAYNE FONTANA & THE MINDBENDERS** first released on Fontana 1503 in 1964	Fontana 1509

DATE	POS	WKS	ARTIST–RECORD TITLE	LABEL & NO.
4/30/66	**2** (2)	10	2. **A Groovy Kind Of Love**	Fontana 1541

MINEO, Sal

Born on 1/10/39 in New York. Stabbed to death on 2/12/76 in Los Angeles. Broadway/Hollywood actor. Broadway credits include *The Rose Tattoo*, *The King & I* and others. Appeared in the movies *Rebel Without A Cause*, *Rock Pretty Baby* and others.

DATE	POS	WKS	ARTIST–RECORD TITLE	LABEL & NO.
5/20/57	9	13	1. **Start Movin' (In My Direction)/** Best Seller #9 / Top 100 #10 / Jockey #16 / Juke Box #18 end; introduced by Mineo on the 5/1/57 Kraft TV Theater production of "Drummer Man"	Epic 9216
	5		2. Love Affair Best Seller flip	
9/23/57	27	3	3. Lasting Love/ Best Seller #27 / Top 100 #35	Epic 9227
	1		4. You Shouldn't Do That Best Seller flip	

MINOGUE, Kylie

Born on 5/28/68 in Melbourne, Australia. Singer/actress. Began TV acting career at age 11. Was a longtime cast member of the popular Australian soap "Neighbours."

DATE	POS	WKS	ARTIST–RECORD TITLE	LABEL & NO.
7/2/88	28	4	1. I Should Be So Lucky Sales #27 / Airplay #32	Geffen 27922
9/17/88	3	13	● 2. **The Loco-Motion** Sales #1(1) / Airplay #4	Geffen 27752
2/4/89	37	2	3. It's No Secret Sales #35 / Airplay #37	Geffen 27651

MINT CONDITION

Funk sextet from Minneapolis: Stokley Williams (vocals), Homer O'Dell, Larry Waddell, Jeffrey Allen, Keri Lewis and Ricky Kinchen.

DATE	POS	WKS	ARTIST–RECORD TITLE	LABEL & NO.
2/8/92	6	16	● 1. **Breakin' My Heart (Pretty Brown Eyes)** Airplay #6 / Sales #9	Perspective 0004
3/19/94	33	2	2. U Send Me Swingin' Sales #26 / Airplay #47	Perspective 7439

MIRACLES, The

R&B group formed at Northern High School in Detroit in 1955. Consisted of William "Smokey" Robinson (lead), Emerson and Bobby Rogers (tenors), Ronnie White (baritone; died 8/26/95 of leukemia, age 57) and Warren "Pete" Moore (bass). Emerson left in 1956 for U.S. Army, replaced by Claudette Rogers, Smokey's future wife. First recorded for End in 1958. Claudette retired in 1964. Bobby married Wanda Young of The Marvelettes. Smokey wrote many hit songs for the group and other Motown artists. Smokey went solo in 1972, replaced by Billy Griffin.

DATE	POS	WKS	ARTIST–RECORD TITLE	LABEL & NO.
12/31/60+	**2** (1)	13	1. **Shop Around** THE MIRACLES (featuring Bill "Smokey" Robinson) #1 R&B hit (8 weeks)	Tamla 54034
2/17/62	35	2	2. What's So Good About Good-by	Tamla 54053
6/30/62	39	1	3. I'll Try Something New	Tamla 54059
1/12/63	8	10	4. **You've Really Got A Hold On Me** #1 R&B hit (1 week)	Tamla 54073
5/4/63	31	3	5. A Love She Can Count On	Tamla 54078
8/31/63	8	9	6. **Mickey's Monkey**	Tamla 54083

DATE	POS	WKS	ARTIST–RECORD TITLE	LABEL & NO.
1/4/64	35	3	7. I Gotta Dance To Keep From Crying	Tamla 54089
7/25/64	27	4	8. I Like It Like That	Tamla 54098
10/10/64	35	1	9. That's What Love Is Made Of	Tamla 54102
4/17/65	16	7	10. Ooo Baby Baby	Tamla 54113
8/7/65	16	8	11. The Tracks Of My Tears	Tamla 54118
11/6/65	14	6	12. My Girl Has Gone	Tamla 54123
1/22/66	11	7	13. Going To A Go-Go	Tamla 54127
			above 4 from the album Going To A Go-Go	
11/26/66	17	6	14. (Come 'Round Here) I'm The One You Need	Tamla 54140
			SMOKEY ROBINSON & THE MIRACLES:	
3/11/67	20	7	15. The Love I Saw In You Was Just A Mirage	Tamla 54145
7/8/67	23	8	16. More Love	Tamla 54152
11/25/67	4	12	17. **I Second That Emotion**	Tamla 54159
			#1 R&B hit (1 week)	
3/9/68	11	10	18. If You Can Want	Tamla 54162
6/29/68	31	3	19. Yester Love	Tamla 54167
8/31/68	26	6	20. Special Occasion	Tamla 54172
1/25/69	8	11	21. **Baby, Baby Don't Cry**	Tamla 54178
7/19/69	32	4	22. Doggone Right	Tamla 54183
7/19/69	33	2	23. Abraham, Martin And John	Tamla 54184
			a tribute to Lincoln, King and John and Robert Kennedy; above 4 from the album Time Out for Smokey Robinson & The Miracles	
10/4/69	37	3	24. Here I Go Again	Tamla 54183
12/27/69+	37	4	25. Point It Out	Tamla 54189
10/31/70	1 (2)	14	26. **The Tears Of A Clown**	Tamla 54199
			originally released on The Miracles' 1967 album Make It Happen; #1 R&B hit (3 weeks)	
4/17/71	18	8	27. I Don't Blame You At All	Tamla 54205
			THE MIRACLES:	
9/14/74	13	9	28. Do It Baby	Tamla 54248
12/13/75+	1 (1)	19	29. **Love Machine (Part 1)**	Tamla 54262
			MR. BIG	
			Rock quartet: Eric Martin (vocals), Paul Gilbert (guitar), Billy Sheehan (bass) and Pat Torpey (drums). Group took its name from the title of a song by Free.	
1/25/92	1 (3)	17	● 1. **To Be With You**	Atlantic 87580
			Sales #2 / Airplay #3	
5/9/92	16	11	2. Just Take My Heart	Atlantic 87509
			Airplay #25 / Sales #26	
11/6/93	27	7	3. Wild World	Atlantic 87308
			Sales #35 / Airplay #36	
			MR. MISTER	
			Pop-rock quartet formed in Los Angeles in 1983: Richard Page (vocals, bass), Steve Farris (guitar), Steve George (keyboards) and Pat Mastelotto (drums).	
10/19/85	1 (2)	15	1. **Broken Wings**	RCA 14136
			Sales #1(2) / Airplay #1(1)	
1/11/86	1 (2)	13	2. **Kyrie**	RCA 14258
			Sales #1(2) / Airplay #1(2)	

DATE	POS	WKS	ARTIST–RECORD TITLE	LABEL & NO.
4/12/86	**8**	11	3. **Is It Love** Airplay #7 / Sales #14	RCA 14313
9/19/87	**29**	5	4. Something Real (Inside Me/Inside You) Sales #25 / Airplay #30	RCA 5273

MITCHELL, Guy

Born Al Cernik on 2/27/27 in Detroit. Sang briefly with Carmen Cavallaro's orchestra in the late '40s. Appeared in several TV series and in the movies *Those Redheads From Seattle* (1953) and *Red Garters* (1954). Married Playboy Playmate Elsa Sorenson (aka Dane Arden).

DATE	POS	WKS	ARTIST–RECORD TITLE	LABEL & NO.
2/25/56	**23**	4	1. Ninety Nine Years (Dead Or Alive) Jimmy Carroll (orch.)	Columbia 40631
11/3/56	**1** (10)	22	● 2. **Singing The Blues** Juke Box #1(10) / Best Seller #1(9) / Top 100 #1(9) / Jockey #1(9)	Columbia 40769
2/2/57	**16**	8	3. Knee Deep In The Blues Top 100 #16 / Juke Box #16 / Jockey #17 / Best Seller #21; Ray Conniff (orch., above 2)	Columbia 40820
4/13/57	**10**	12	4. **Rock-A-Billy** Best Seller #10 / Top 100 #13 / Juke Box #14 / Jockey #15; Jimmy Carroll (orch.)	Columbia 40877
10/19/59	**1** (2)	16	5. **Heartaches By The Number** Joe Sherman (orch.)	Columbia 41476

MITCHELL, Joni

Born Roberta Joan Anderson on 11/7/43 in Fort McLeod, Alberta, Canada; raised in Saskatoon, Saskatchewan. Singer/songwriter/guitarist/pianist. Moved to New York in 1966. Wrote the hits "Both Sides Now" and "Woodstock." Married her producer/bassist, Larry Klein, in 1982. Recipient of *Billboard*'s Century Award in 1995. Also see James Taylor.

DATE	POS	WKS	ARTIST–RECORD TITLE	LABEL & NO.
12/30/72+	**25**	8	1. You Turn Me On, I'm A Radio Graham Nash (harmonica)	Asylum 11010
4/20/74	**7**	11	2. **Help Me** #1 Adult Contemporary hit (1 week)	Asylum 11034
8/24/74	**22**	7	3. Free Man In Paris David Crosby and Graham Nash (backing vocals); Larry Carlton and Jose Feliciano (guitars)	Asylum 11041
1/25/75	**24**	4	4. Big Yellow Taxi [R] "live" version of Mitchell's 1970 studio hit (#67)	Asylum 45221

MITCHELL, Willie

Born in Ashland, Mississippi, in 1928. Trumpeter/keyboardist/composer/arranger/producer. To Memphis at an early age. With Tuff Green and Al Jackson in the early '50s. Formed own band in 1954, became house band at Home Of The Blues and Hi Records. Eventually became president of Hi Records.

DATE	POS	WKS	ARTIST–RECORD TITLE	LABEL & NO.
10/3/64	**31**	5	1. 20-75 [I] title refers to the record's label number	Hi 2075
4/13/68	**23**	10	2. Soul Serenade [I]	Hi 2140

MOCEDADES

Sextet from Bilbao, Spain, featuring the Amezaga sisters, Amaya and Izaskum.

DATE	POS	WKS	ARTIST–RECORD TITLE	LABEL & NO.
2/16/74	**9**	11	1. **Eres Tu (Touch The Wind)** [F] B-side is the same song sung in English	Tara 100

DATE	POS	WKS	ARTIST–RECORD TITLE	LABEL & NO.
			MODELS	
			Pop-rock quintet formed in Melbourne, Australia, in 1979: Sean Kelly (vocals, guitar), Roger Mason (keyboards), James Valentine (saxophone), James Freud (bass) and Barton Price (drums).	
6/7/86	**37**	4	1. Out Of Mind Out Of Sight Airplay #34 / Sales #36	Geffen 28762
			MODUGNO, Domenico	
			Born on 1/9/28 in Polignano a Mare, Italy. Died of a heart attack on 8/6/94. Singer/actor.	
8/4/58	**1 (5)**	13	● 1. **Nel Blu Dipinto Di Blu (Volare)** [F] Hot 100 #1(5) / Best Seller #1(5); title is Italian for In The Blue Sky Painted Blue (To Fly)	Decca 30677
			MOJO MEN, The	
			San Francisco-based rock quartet: Jimmy Alaimo, Paul Curcio, Don Metchick and Dennis DeCarr. Originally known as Sly and the Mojo Men, led by Sylvester "Sly Stone" Stewart (not on any of their recordings). Jimmy, the cousin of Steve Alaimo, died of heart surgery complications on 6/30/92 (age 53).	
3/18/67	**36**	3	1. Sit Down, I Think I Love You written by Stephen Stills	Reprise 0539
			MOKENSTEF	
			Female vocal trio from Los Angeles: Monifa, Kenya and Stephanie. All three were cheerleaders at Morningside High School in Inglewood, California.	
7/15/95	**7**	18	● 1. **He's Mine** Sales #5 / Airplay #19; contains interpolations of "Be Alright" by Zapp and "Do Me Baby" by Prince	OutBurst 851704
			MOMENTS, The	
			Soul trio from Hackensack, New Jersey, featuring Mark Greene (falsetto lead). Greene left after first record, replaced by William Brown (lead) and Al Goodman. Harry Ray joined after "Love On A Two-Way Street" in 1970. Became Ray, Goodman & Brown in 1978. Ray died of a stroke on 10/1/92 (age 45).	
4/18/70	**3**	14	● 1. **Love On A Two-Way Street** produced by Sylvia (Robinson); #1 R&B hit (5 weeks)	Stang 5012
2/2/74	**17**	9	2. Sexy Mama	Stang 5052
8/2/75	**39**	3	3. Look At Me (I'm In Love) #1 R&B hit (1 week)	Stang 5060
2/16/80	**5**	14	● 4. **Special Lady** **RAY, GOODMAN & BROWN** #1 R&B hit (1 week)	Polydor 2033
			MONEY, Eddie	
			Born Edward Mahoney on 3/2/49 in Brooklyn, New York. Rock singer discovered and subsequently managed by the late West Coast promoter Bill Graham. Formerly an officer with the New York Police Department.	
4/8/78	**11**	11	1. Baby Hold On	Columbia 10663
7/29/78	**22**	8	2. Two Tickets To Paradise	Columbia 10765
2/24/79	**22**	8	3. Maybe I'm A Fool	Columbia 10900
7/24/82	**16**	12	4. Think I'm In Love	Columbia 02964

DATE	POS	WKS	ARTIST–RECORD TITLE	LABEL & NO.
9/27/86	4	12	5. **Take Me Home Tonight** Airplay #4 / Sales #5; Ronnie Spector (The Ronettes) sings the lead line from "Be My Baby"	Columbia 06231
1/24/87	14	10	6. I Wanna Go Back Airplay #10 / Sales #17	Columbia 06569
5/30/87	21	7	7. Endless Nights Sales #19 / Airplay #20	Columbia 07035
10/22/88	9	13	8. **Walk On Water** Airplay #8 / Sales #10	Columbia 08060
2/11/89	24	7	9. The Love In Your Eyes Airplay #20 / Sales #27	Columbia 68532
12/23/89+	11	9	10. Peace In Our Time Sales #9 / Airplay #9	Columbia 73047
1/25/92	21	10	11. I'll Get By Airplay #23 / Sales #39	Columbia 74109

MONICA

Born Monica Arnold on 10/24/80 in Atlanta.

DATE	POS	WKS	ARTIST–RECORD TITLE	LABEL & NO.
5/13/95	2 (3)	27	▲ 1. **Don't Take It Personal (just one of dem days)** Sales #1(1) / Airplay #9; samples "Back Seat (Of My Jeep)" by L.L. Cool J; #1 R&B hit (2 weeks)	Rowdy 35040
10/28/95	7	24	▲ 2. **Before You Walk Out Of My Life/** Sales #6 / Airplay #28; #1 R&B hit (2 weeks)	
		24	3. Like This And Like That Sales flip; samples "Spoonin' Rap" by Sugarhill Gang; Mr. Malik (rap)	Rowdy 35052

MONKEES, The

Formed in Los Angeles in 1965. Chosen from over 400 applicants for new Columbia TV series. Consisted of Davy Jones (born 12/30/45, Manchester, England; vocals), Michael Nesmith (born 12/30/42, Houston; guitar, vocals), Peter Tork (born 2/13/44, Washington, D.C.; bass, vocals) and Micky Dolenz (born 3/8/45, Tarzana, California; drums, vocals). Dolenz had appeared in the TV series "Circus Boy," using the name Mickey Braddock, in 1956. Jones had been a racehorse jockey, and appeared in London musicals *Oliver* and *Pickwick*. Tork had been in the Phoenix Singers; Nesmith had done session work for Stax/Volt. Group starred in the movie *Head* (1968). TV show, 1966–68, dropped after 58 episodes. Tork left in 1968. Group disbanded in 1969; re-formed (minus Nesmith) in 1986.

DATE	POS	WKS	ARTIST–RECORD TITLE	LABEL & NO.
9/24/66	1 (1)	12	● 1. **Last Train To Clarksville**	Colgems 1001
12/17/66	1 (7)	13	● 2. **I'm A Believer/** written by Neil Diamond	
12/31/66+	20	6	3. (I'm Not Your) Steppin' Stone first recorded by Paul Revere & The Raiders on the 1966 album *Midnight Ride*	Colgems 1002
3/25/67	2 (1)	10	● 4. **A Little Bit Me, A Little Bit You/** written by Neil Diamond	
4/15/67	39	1	5. The Girl I Knew Somewhere	Colgems 1004
7/29/67	3	9	● 6. **Pleasant Valley Sunday/**	
8/5/67	11	7	7. Words	Colgems 1007
11/18/67	1 (4)	12	● 8. **Daydream Believer**	Colgems 1012
3/9/68	3	7	● 9. **Valleri/**	
3/30/68	34	1	10. Tapioca Tundra	Colgems 1019
6/22/68	19	6	11. D. W. Washburn	Colgems 1023

DATE	POS	WKS	ARTIST–RECORD TITLE	LABEL & NO.
8/2/86	**20**	7	12.　That Was Then, This Is Now **MICKY DOLENZ AND PETER TORK (OF THE MONKEES)** Sales #16 / Airplay #28	Arista 9505
			MONOTONES, The	
			Doo-wop group from Newark, New Jersey. Charles Patrick, lead singer.	
4/7/58	**5**	12	1.　**Book Of Love** Top 100 #5 / Best Seller #6 / Jockey #9; first released on Mascot 124 in 1957	Argo 5290
			MONRO, Matt	
			Born Terrence Parsons on 12/1/32 in London. Died of liver cancer on 2/7/85. Sang with Cyril Stapleton's Orchestra before going solo.	
6/26/61	**18**	9	1.　My Kind Of Girl	Warwick 636
12/26/64+	**23**	5	2.　Walk Away	Liberty 55745
			MONROE, Vaughn	
			Born on 10/7/11 in Akron, Ohio. Died on 5/21/73. Big-voiced baritone/trumpeter/band leader. Very popular on radio, and featured in several movies.	
11/12/55	**38**	1	1.　Black Denim Trousers And Motorcycle Boots	RCA 6260
2/18/56	**38**	1	2.　Don't Go To Strangers written in 1954 and introduced by Al Martino (Capitol 2899)	RCA 6358
9/8/56	**11**	8	3.　In The Middle Of The House　　　　　　　[N] Jockey #11 / Top 100 #21; Joe Reisman (orch.)	RCA 6619
			MONTE, Lou	
			Born on 4/2/17 in Lyndhurst, New Jersey. Vocalist/guitarist.	
3/17/58	**12**	11	1.　Lazy Mary　　　　　　　　　　　　　　[F] Best Seller #12 / Top 100 #12 / Jockey #22; adapted from the Italian song "Luna Mezzo Mare (The Butcher Boy)"; #5 hit for Rudy Vallee in 1938	RCA 7160
12/15/62+	**5**	9	● 2.　**Pepino The Italian Mouse**　　　　　　[N] Joe Reisman (orch., above 2)	Reprise 20106
			MONTENEGRO, Hugo	
			Born in 1925; raised in New York City. Died on 2/6/81. Conductor/composer. Composed and conducted the movie soundtrack of *Hurry Sundown*.	
4/6/68	**2 (1)**	14	1.　**The Good, The Bad And The Ugly**　　　[I] title song from the movie starring Clint Eastwood; #1 Adult Contemporary hit (3 weeks)	RCA 9423
			MONTEZ, Chris	
			Born Ezekiel Christopher Montanez on 1/17/43 in Los Angeles. Protege of Ritchie Valens.	
9/8/62	**4**	9	1.　**Let's Dance**	Monogram 505
2/12/66	**22**	5	2.　Call Me	A&M 780
5/28/66	**16**	7	3.　The More I See You #7 hit for Dick Haymes in 1945 (from the movie *Billy Rose's Diamond Horseshoe* starring Betty Grable)	A&M 796
9/10/66	**33**	2	4.　There Will Never Be Another You #19 hit for Sammy Kaye in 1943 (from the movie *Iceland* starring Sonja Henie)	A&M 810

DATE	POS	WKS	ARTIST–RECORD TITLE	LABEL & NO.
12/3/66	**36**	2	5. Time After Time #16 hit for Frank Sinatra in 1947 (from the movie *It Happened In Brooklyn*); #2, 3, 5: produced by Herb Alpert	A&M 822

MONTGOMERY, Melba

Born on 10/14/38 in Iron City, Tennessee; raised in Florence, Alabama. Country singer/guitarist/fiddler.

6/8/74	**39**	1	1. No Charge #1 Country hit (1 week)	Elektra 45883

MOODY BLUES, The

Formed in Birmingham, England, in 1964. Consisted of Denny Laine (guitar, vocals), Ray Thomas (flute, vocals), Mike Pinder (keyboards, vocals), Clint Warwick (bass) and Graeme Edge (drums). Laine and Warwick left in the summer of 1966, replaced by Justin Hayward (lead vocals, lead guitar) and John Lodge (vocals, bass). Laine joined Wings in 1971. Switzerland-born Patrick Moraz (former keyboardist of Yes) replaced Pinder in 1978; left group in early 1992.

3/27/65	**10**	8	1. **Go Now!** Denny Laine (Wings), lead singer; song introduced in 1964 by Bessie Banks (Tiger 102)	London 9726
8/24/68	**24**	6	2. Tuesday Afternoon (Forever Afternoon)	Deram 85028
5/30/70	**21**	8	3. Question	Threshold 67004
9/4/71	**23**	7	4. The Story In Your Eyes	Threshold 67006
5/13/72	**29**	7	5. Isn't Life Strange	Threshold 67009
9/2/72	**2** (2)	14	● 6. **Nights In White Satin** released from group's 1968 album *Days of Future Passed*; London Festival Orchestra (orch.)	Deram 85023
2/17/73	**12**	8	7. I'm Just A Singer (In A Rock And Roll Band)	Threshold 67012
9/2/78	**39**	2	8. Steppin' In A Slide Zone	London 270
6/13/81	**12**	9	9. Gemini Dream	Threshold 601
8/15/81	**15**	11	10. The Voice	Threshold 602
9/17/83	**27**	6	11. Sitting At The Wheel	Threshold 604
5/24/86	**9**	12	12. **Your Wildest Dreams** Sales #8 / Airplay #13; #1 Adult Contemporary hit (2 weeks)	Polydor 883906
7/23/88	**30**	4	13. I Know You're Out There Somewhere Sales #27 / Airplay #36	Polydor 887600

MOONEY, Art

Born in Lowell, Massachusetts. Leader of a Detroit-based dance band from the mid-1930s to 1940s. To New York following WWII service. Biggest hit: "I'm Looking Over A Four Leaf Clover" (#1) in 1948.

4/23/55	**6**	17	● 1. **Honey-Babe** Best Seller #6 / Juke Box #6 / Jockey #10; adaptation of a traditional army marching chant, as featured in the movie *Battle Cry* starring Aldo Ray and Tab Hunter	MGM 11900
12/17/55	**6**	4	● 2. **Nuttin' For Christmas** [X-N] **ART MOONEY And His ORCHESTRA with Barry Gordon** Best Seller #6 / Top 100 #7 / Juke Box #9 / Jockey #10	MGM 12092

DATE	POS	WKS	ARTIST–RECORD TITLE	LABEL & NO.
			MOONGLOWS, The	
			R&B group from Louisville. Consisted of lead singers Bobby Lester (died of cancer 10/15/80, age 50) and Harvey Fuqua, with Alexander "Pete" Graves, Prentiss Barnes and Billy Johnson.	
3/26/55	20	1	1. Sincerely	Chess 1581
			Juke Box #20; legendary DJ Alan Freed listed as co-writer; #1 R&B hit (2 weeks)	
10/13/56	25	1	2. See Saw	Chess 1629
			Best Seller #25 / Top 100 #28	
10/20/58	22	4	3. Ten Commandments Of Love	Chess 1705
			HARVEY and The Moonglows	
			MOORE, Bob, and His Orch.	
			Born on 11/30/32 in Nashville. Top session bass player. Led the band on Roy Orbison's sessions for Monument Records. Also worked as sideman for Elvis Presley, Brenda Lee, Pat Boone and others.	
9/11/61	7	10	1. **Mexico** [I]	Monument 446
			#1 Adult Contemporary hit (1 week)	
			MOORE, Bobby, & The Rhythm Aces	
			Formed in Montgomery, Alabama, in 1961. Fronted by Bobby Moore (tenor sax) and Chico Jenkins (vocals).	
7/30/66	27	4	1. Searching For My Love	Checker 1129
			MOORE, Dorothy	
			Born in Jackson, Mississippi, in 1946. Lead singer of The Poppies. Also a popular gospel artist.	
4/10/76	3	16	1. **Misty Blue**	Malaco 1029
9/10/77	27	7	2. I Believe You	Malaco 1042
			written by the Addrisi Brothers	
			MOORE, Jackie	
			R&B singer from Jacksonville, Florida.	
1/23/71	30	7	● 1. Precious, Precious	Atlantic 2681
			MORALES, Michael	
			Born on 4/25/63. Native of San Antonio, Texas.	
6/10/89	15	10	1. Who Do You Give Your Love To?	Wing 887743
			Airplay #14 / Sales #16	
9/9/89	28	6	2. What I Like About You	Wing 889678
			Airplay #21 / Sales #30	
			MORGAN, Jane	
			Born Jane Currier in Boston; raised in Florida. Popular singer in France before achieving U.S. fame via TV and nightclub entertaining.	
9/9/57	7	21	● 1. **Fascination**	Kapp 191
			JANE MORGAN and The Troubadors	
			Jockey #7 / Top 100 #11 / Best Seller #12; from the movie *Love In The Afternoon* starring Gary Cooper and Audrey Hepburn; French melody composed in 1904 as "Valse Tzigane"	
10/13/58	21	10	2. The Day The Rains Came	Kapp 235
			Vic Schoen (orch.)	

DATE	POS	WKS	ARTIST–RECORD TITLE	LABEL & NO.
8/31/59	39	1	3. With Open Arms	Kapp 284

MORGAN, Jaye P.

Born Mary Margaret Morgan in Mancos, Colorado, on 12/3/31. Sang with Frank DeVol's band, 1950–53. Featured on many TV game shows, 1950s–'70s. Sister of recording group The Morgan Brothers.

DATE	POS	WKS	ARTIST–RECORD TITLE	LABEL & NO.
11/27/54+	3	21	1. **That's All I Want From You** Jockey #3 / Best Seller #5 / Juke Box #5	RCA 5896
3/12/55	12	8	2. Danger! Heartbreak Ahead/ Jockey #12 / Juke Box #13 / Best Seller #18	
		1	3. Softly, Softly Best Seller flip	RCA 6016

PERRY COMO AND JAYE P. MORGAN:

DATE	POS	WKS	ARTIST–RECORD TITLE	LABEL & NO.
6/11/55	12	5	4. Chee Chee-oo Chee (Sang the Little Bird)/ Jockey #12 / Juke Box #14 / Best Seller #24	
6/25/55	18	1	5. Two Lost Souls Jockey #18; from the Broadway musical *Damn Yankees* starring Gwen Verdon; Mitchell Ayres (orch., above 2)	RCA 6137

JAYE P. MORGAN:

DATE	POS	WKS	ARTIST–RECORD TITLE	LABEL & NO.
8/20/55	6	14	6. **The Longest Walk/** Jockey #6 / Juke Box #7 / Best Seller #13 / Top 100 #19 pre	
		1	7. Swanee Juke Box flip; #1 hit for Al Jolson in 1920	RCA 6182
11/12/55	14	8	8. Pepper-Hot Baby/ Juke Box #14 / Top 100 #21; Joe Thomas (orch.)	
12/3/55	12	3	9. If You Don't Want My Love Juke Box #12 / Top 100 #40; Hugo Winterhalter (orch., all of above - except #4, 5, 8)	RCA 6282

MORGAN, Russ

Born on 4/29/04 in Scranton, Pennsylvania. Died on 8/8/69. Trombonist/pianist/vocalist/bandleader. Big #1 hit "Cruising Down The River" in 1949. His trademark: "Music In The Morgan Manner."

DATE	POS	WKS	ARTIST–RECORD TITLE	LABEL & NO.
11/12/55	30	4	1. Dogface Soldier from the movie *To Hell and Back* starring Audie Murphy; tune originally written in 1942	Decca 29703
3/17/56	19	3	2. The Poor People Of Paris　　　　　[I] Juke Box #19 / Jockey #23 / Top 100 #26	Decca 29835

MORMON TABERNACLE CHOIR, The

Three-hundred-seventy-five-voice choir directed by Richard P. Condie (died 12/22/85).

DATE	POS	WKS	ARTIST–RECORD TITLE	LABEL & NO.
9/21/59	13	11	1. Battle Hymn Of The Republic with the Philadelphia Orchestra, Eugene Ormandy, conductor; written in 1862; #1 hit for The Columbia Stellar Quartet in 1918	Columbia 41459

MORODER, Giorgio

Born on 4/26/40 in Ortisel, Italy. Electronic composer/conductor/producer for numerous soundtracks. Produced seven of Donna Summer's albums.

DATE	POS	WKS	ARTIST–RECORD TITLE	LABEL & NO.
3/10/79	33	4	1. Chase　　　　　[I] from the movie *Midnight Express* starring Brad Davis	Casablanca 956

DATE	POS	WKS	ARTIST–RECORD TITLE	LABEL & NO.
			MORRISON, Van	
			Born George Ivan on 8/31/45 in Belfast, Ireland. Blue-eyed soul singer/songwriter. Leader of Them. Wrote the classic hit "Gloria." Inducted into the Rock and Roll Hall of Fame in 1993.	
8/19/67	**10**	10	1. **Brown Eyed Girl**	Bang 545
4/25/70	**39**	2	2. Come Running	Warner 7383
12/5/70+	**9**	9	3. **Domino**	Warner 7434
3/6/71	**23**	8	4. Blue Money	Warner 7462
11/20/71	**28**	4	5. Wild Night	Warner 7518
			all of above written by Morrison	
			MOTELS, The	
			Pop-rock group formed in Los Angeles in 1978: Martha Davis (vocals), Guy Perry (guitar), Marty Jourard (keyboards), Michael Goodroe (bass) and Brian Glascock (drums). Guitarist Scott Thurston joined in 1983. Group disbanded in 1987.	
5/29/82	**9**	15	1. **Only The Lonely**	Capitol 5114
9/17/83	**9**	13	2. **Suddenly Last Summer**	Capitol 5271
1/14/84	**36**	3	3. Remember The Nights	Capitol 5246
8/10/85	**21**	7	4. Shame	Capitol 5497
			Airplay #22 / Sales #22	
			MOTHERLODE	
			Canadian pop quartet led by keyboardist William "Smitty" Smith.	
9/13/69	**18**	7	1. When I Die	Buddah 131
			MÖTLEY CRÜE	
			Los Angeles-based hard-rock band: "Vince Neil" Wharton (lead vocals; married mud wrestler Sharisse Rudell), Mick Mars (real name: Bob Deal; guitar), Nikki Sixx (real name: Frank Ferranno; bass; married *Playboy* playmate Brandi Brandt) and "Tommy Lee" Bass (drums; married to actress Heather Locklear until 1993; married actress Pamela Anderson on 2/19/95). Neil left band in February 1992; replaced by John Corabi (ex-Scream).	
8/3/85	**16**	9	1. Smokin' In The Boys Room	Elektra 69625
			Sales #15 / Airplay #15	
6/13/87	**12**	9	2. Girls, Girls, Girls	Elektra 69465
			Sales #9 / Airplay #14	
9/23/89	**6**	9	● 3. **Dr. Feelgood**	Elektra 69271
			Sales #5 / Airplay #12	
1/6/90	**27**	6	4. Kickstart My Heart	Elektra 69248
			Sales #19 / Airplay #31	
3/17/90	**8**	10	5. **Without You**	Elektra 64985
			Sales #6 / Airplay #9	
6/30/90	**19**	7	6. Don't Go Away Mad (Just Go Away)	Elektra 64962
			Airplay #16 / Sales #18; above 4 from the album *Dr. Feelgood*	
1/4/92	**37**	3	7. Home Sweet Home '91 [R]	Elektra 64818
			Sales #42 / Airplay #61; remix of group's 1985 hit (#89)	

DATE	POS	WKS	ARTIST–RECORD TITLE	LABEL & NO.
			MOTT THE HOOPLE	
			British glitter-rock group led by vocalist Ian Hunter. Group name taken from a Willard Manus novel. Various personnel included guitarist Mick Ralphs (left in 1973 to form Bad Company). Hunter left in 1976; members Pete "Overend" Watts, Morgan Fisher and Dale "Buffin" Griffin formed the British Lions.	
11/4/72	37	3	1. All The Young Dudes David Bowie (producer, rhythm guitar, backing vocal, handclaps)	Columbia 45673
			MOUNTAIN	
			New York power-rock group led by Leslie West (born Leslie Weinstein, 10/22/45, New York City) and Felix Pappalardi (born 1939, the Bronx; fatally shot in New York City on 4/17/83, age 44).	
6/13/70	21	9	1. Mississippi Queen	Windfall 532
			MOUTH & MACNEAL	
			Dutch duo: Willem Duyn and Maggie Macneal (real name: Sjoukje Van't Spijker).	
6/17/72	8	12	● 1. **How Do You Do?**	Philips 40715
			MOVING PICTURES	
			Australian six-man pop group led by Alex Smith (vocals). Member Garry Frost later formed the group 1927.	
11/27/82+	29	13	1. What About Me re-charted in 1989 at #46	Network 69952
			MOYET, Alison	
			Born Genevieve Alison-Jane "Alf" Moyet on 6/18/61 in Basildon, Essex, England. Female vocalist of Yaz.	
5/4/85	31	6	1. Invisible Airplay #28	Columbia 04781
			MOZART, Mickey—see MAXWELL, Robert	
			M PEOPLE	
			Dance trio of Michael Pickering (from Manchester, England), Heather Small and Paul Heard (both from London).	
6/18/94	34	3	1. Moving On Up Airplay #30 / Sales #75	Epic 77392
			MULDAUR, Maria	
			Born Maria D'Amato on 9/12/43 in New York City. Member of Jim Kweskin's Jug Band with former husband Geoff Muldaur (divorced in 1972). Maria later became an Inspirational recording artist.	
4/13/74	6	14	1. **Midnight At The Oasis**	Reprise 1183
1/25/75	12	8	2. I'm A Woman	Reprise 1319
			MUNGO JERRY	
			British skiffle quartet: Ray Dorset (lead vocals), Colin Earl, Paul King and Mike Cole.	
7/25/70	3	11	● 1. **In The Summertime**	Janus 125

Night Ranger's hard-rocking brand of pop produced five Top 20 singles between 1984 and 1985. Group bassist Jack Blades later would score platinum as part of '90s group Damn Yankees, a quartet also featuring guitarists Ted Nugent and Tommy Shaw of Styx.

Nilsson's all-time bestselling single "Without You" held the No. 1 slot for four weeks in 1971. The late singer was the subject of both an RCA two-CD retrospective and a MusicMasters tribute album in 1995.

Jack Nitzsche's musical versatility brought him his own Top 40 single with 1963's "The Lonely Surfer"—a commercial tune starkly contrasting with his rare 1972 album *St. Giles Cripplegate*, an instrumental work performed by no less than the London Symphony Orchestra. Both were on Reprise.

The Nutty Squirrels may have felt some mammalian rivalry with the Chipmunks in 1959—particularly since their No. 14 novelty disc "Uh! Oh! Part 2" was the only hit record in their bright-eyed-and-bushy-tailed career.

The Nylons' 1987 remake of Steam's "Na Na Hey Hey Kiss Him Goodbye" didn't quite match the original, chart-wise. While Steam's 1969 version stayed at No. 1 for two weeks, the Canadian quartet's disc climbed only to No. 12.

Billy Ocean's demandingly titled "Get Outta My Dreams, Get Into My Car" was the Trinidad-born singer's final No. 1 hit, climbing to the top slot in early 1988.

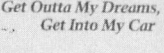

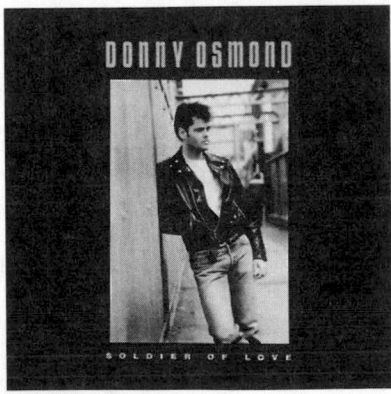

Alexander O'Neal's soulful vocals received their launching via Flyte Tyme, the Minneapolis R&B group that would eventually become The Time. His 1987 hit "Fake" was his only solo Top 40 hit; two other similar chart-toppers shared a vocal credit with singer Cherrelle.

Roy Orbison's "Too Soon To Know" peaked at No. 68 in 1966, scant months after "Twinkle Toes"—the singer's last big hit for a 23-year stretch—cracked the Top 40. In 1989, the legendary vocalist hit again with the Top 10 smash "You Got It."

Orchestral Manoeuvres In The Dark, known to DJs worldwide as OMD, rose from their arty new wave beginnings to produce the Top 5 pop hit "If You Leave," from the talent-filled 1986 soundtrack to *Pretty In Pink*.

The Orlons' energetic telephone plea, "Don't Hang Up," was one of three Top 5 smashes the Philly-based quartet released in 1962-63.

Donny Osmond's surprising career comeback—after he spent the 1970s in teen idolhood—surprised many in 1989. Sixteen years after after his last Top 10 hit, "The Twelfth Of Never," his "Soldier Of Love" shot skyward to No. 2.

Patti Page's long recording career began in 1947 and took her to the top of the charts throughout the '50s and '60s. Her 1962 single "Most People Get Married," which peaked at No. 27, was her second-to-last Top 40 hit.

DATE	POS	WKS	ARTIST–RECORD TITLE	LABEL & NO.
			### MURDOCK, Shirley	
			Former gospel singer from Toledo. Discovered by Roger Troutman (aka Roger), who hired her as a backup singer for his family funk group, Zapp.	
2/28/87	**23**	7	1. As We Lay Sales #17 / Airplay #34	Elektra 69518
			### MURMAIDS, The	
			Los Angeles teenage trio: sisters Carol and Terry Fischer, with Sally Gordon.	
12/7/63+	**3**	11	1. **Popsicles And Icicles** written by David Gates of Bread	Chattahoochee 628
			### MURPHEY, Michael	
			Born Michael Martin Murphey on 5/5/38 in Dallas. Progressive-country singer/songwriter. Toured as Travis Lewis of The Lewis & Clarke Expedition in 1967. Worked as a staff writer for Screen Gems. Appeared in the movies *Take This Job And Shove It* and *Hard Country*. In 1984, changed his artist billing on his singles releases to Michael Martin Murphey.	
10/7/72	**37**	2	1. Geronimo's Cadillac	A&M 1368
5/3/75	**3**	13	● 2. **Wildfire** #1 Adult Contemporary hit (1 week)	Epic 50084
9/13/75	**21**	7	3. Carolina In The Pines	Epic 50131
2/21/76	**39**	2	4. Renegade	Epic 50184
8/28/82	**19**	11	5. What's Forever For #1 Country hit (1 week)	Liberty 1466
			### MURPHY, Eddie	
			Born on 4/3/61 in Hempstead, New York. Comedian/actor. Former cast member of TV's "Saturday Night Live." Starred in the movies *Beverly Hills Cop (I, II & III)*, *Trading Places*, *48 Hrs.*, *Coming To America*, *Boomerang* and many others. Married model Nicole Mitchell on 3/18/93.	
11/9/85	**2 (3)**	14	▲ 1. **Party All The Time** Airplay #2 / Sales #2; written, produced and arranged by Rick James	Columbia 05609
8/19/89	**27**	4	2. Put Your Mouth On Me Sales #23 / Airplay #40	Columbia 68897
			### MURPHY, Walter	
			Born in 1952 in New York City. Studied classical and jazz piano at Manhattan School of Music. Former arranger for Doc Severinsen and "The Tonight Show" orchestra.	
7/4/76	**1 (1)**	22	● 1. **A Fifth Of Beethoven** [I] **WALTER MURPHY & THE BIG APPLE BAND** based on Beethoven's *Fifth Symphony*	Private St. 45073
			### MURRAY, Anne	
			Born Morna Anne Murray on 6/20/45 in Springhill, Nova Scotia. High school teacher for one year after college. With CBC-TV show "Sing Along Jubilee." First recorded for ARC in 1969. Regular on Glen Campbell's "Goodtime Hour" TV series. Currently resides in Toronto.	
8/22/70	**8**	11	● 1. **Snowbird** #1 Adult Contemporary hit (6 weeks)	Capitol 2738
2/10/73	**7**	13	2. **Danny's Song** written by Kenny Loggins for his nephew (also wrote #3 below); #1 Adult Contemporary hit (2 weeks)	Capitol 3481

DATE	POS	WKS	ARTIST—RECORD TITLE	LABEL & NO.
1/19/74	**12**	10	3. Love Song	Capitol 3776
5/25/74	**8**	10	4. **You Won't See Me**	Capitol 3867
			written by John Lennon and Paul McCartney	
8/19/78	**1** (1)	17	● 5. **You Needed Me**	Capitol 4574
2/10/79	**12**	12	6. I Just Fall In Love Again	Capitol 4675
			#1 Adult Contemporary hit (4 weeks); #1 Country hit (3 weeks)	
6/23/79	**25**	7	7. Shadows In The Moonlight	Capitol 4716
			#1 Adult Contemporary hit (3 weeks); #1 Country hit (1 week)	
10/20/79	**12**	11	8. Broken Hearted Me	Capitol 4773
			#1 Adult Contemporary hit (5 weeks); #1 Country hit (1 week)	
1/19/80	**12**	11	9. Daydream Believer	Capitol 4813
			#1 Adult Contemporary hit (1 week)	
10/18/80	**33**	4	10. Could I Have This Dance	Capitol 4920
			from the movie *Urban Cowboy* starring John Travolta and Debra Winger; #1 Country hit (1 week)	
5/2/81	**34**	4	11. Blessed Are The Believers	Capitol 4987
			#1 Country hit (1 week)	
			MUSICAL YOUTH	
			Five schoolboys (ages 11 to 16 in 1983) from Birmingham, England: Dennis Seaton (lead), with brothers Kelvin (guitar) and Michael (keyboards) Grant, and Patrick (bass) and Junior Waite (drums).	
1/15/83	**10**	10	1. **Pass The Dutchie**	MCA 52149
			clean version of the Jamaican hit "Pass The Kouchie" which means "pass the joint"; a dutchie is a Jamaican cooking pot	
			MUSIC EXPLOSION, The	
			Jamie Lyons, lead singer of quintet from Mansfield, Ohio. Produced by Jerry Kasenetz and Jeff Katz.	
5/27/67	**2** (2)	13	● 1. **Little Bit O'Soul**	Laurie 3380
			MUSIC MACHINE, The	
			Los Angeles rock quintet. Sean Bonniwell, lead singer/songwriter. Bassist Keith Olsen became a top record producer in the 1980s.	
12/10/66+	**15**	8	1. Talk Talk	Original Sound 61
			MYLES, Alannah	
			Born in Toronto; raised in Buckhorn, Canada. Rock singer.	
2/3/90	**1** (2)	15	● 1. **Black Velvet**	Atlantic 88742
			Sales #1(3) / Airplay #2	
6/16/90	**36**	4	2. Love Is	Atlantic 87945
			Airplay #28	
			MYLES, Billy	
			New York singer/songwriter. Wrote the Mello-Kings' pop hit "Tonite, Tonite."	
11/25/57	**25**	6	1. The Joker (That's What They Call Me)	Ember 1026
			Best Seller #25 / Top 100 #30	
			MYSTICS, The	
			Quintet from Brooklyn: Phil Cracolici (lead), Bob Ferrante & George Galfo (tenors), Albee Cracolici (baritone) and Allie Contrera (bass). John Trayner of Jay & The Americans was an early member.	
6/15/59	**20**	9	1. Hushabye	Laurie 3028

DATE	POS	WKS	ARTIST–RECORD TITLE	LABEL & NO.

N

NAKED EYES

English duo: Pete Byrne (vocals) and Rob Fisher (keyboards, synthesizer). Split in 1984. Fisher later in duo Climie Fisher.

DATE	POS	WKS	ARTIST–RECORD TITLE	LABEL & NO.
4/23/83	8	13	1. **Always Something There To Remind Me**	EMI America 8155
8/13/83	11	12	2. Promises, Promises	EMI America 8170
12/17/83	37	3	3. When The Lights Go Out	EMI America 8183
9/29/84	39	2	4. (What) In The Name Of Love	EMI America 8219

NAPOLEON XIV

Napoleon is Jerry Samuels, a recording engineer/composer from New York.

7/30/66	3	5	1. **They're Coming To Take Me Away, Ha-Haaa!** [N]	Warner 5831

NASH, Graham

Born on 2/2/42 in Blackpool, England. Co-founding member/guitarist of The Hollies. Formed Crosby, Stills & Nash in 1970.

7/10/71	35	4	1. Chicago	Atlantic 2804
			about Black Panther leader Bobby Seale and the Chicago Seven, who were on trial for conspiracy to riot at the 1968 Democratic convention	
6/10/72	36	4	2. Immigration Man	Atlantic 2873
			GRAHAM NASH & DAVID CROSBY	

NASH, Johnny

Born on 8/19/40 in Houston. Vocalist/guitarist/actor. Appeared on local TV from age 13. With Arthur Godfrey's TV and radio shows, 1956–63. Appeared in the movie *Take A Giant Step* in 1959. Own JoDa label in 1965. Began recording in Jamaica in the late '60s.

2/3/58	23	1	1. A Very Special Love	ABC-Para. 9874
			Jockey #23 / Best Seller #45 / Top 100 #46	
12/15/58+	29	5	2. The Teen Commandments [S]	ABC-Para. 9974
			PAUL ANKA-GEO. HAMILTON IV-JOHNNY NASH	
			inspirational talk from the 3 ABC-Paramount artists	
10/5/68	5	12	3. **Hold Me Tight**	JAD 207
1/24/70	39	1	4. Cupid	JAD 220
			originally released as the B-side of #3 above	
10/7/72	1 (4)	14	● 5. **I Can See Clearly Now**	Epic 10902
			#1 Adult Contemporary hit (4 weeks); Bob Marley's Wailers (backing band)	
3/3/73	12	10	6. Stir It Up	Epic 10949
			written by Bob Marley	

NASHVILLE TEENS, The

British rock sextet. Arthur Sharp, lead singer. Drummer Barry Jenkins joined The Animals in 1966.

10/10/64	14	6	1. Tobacco Road	London 9689

NATE DOGG—see WARREN G.

DATE	POS	WKS	ARTIST–RECORD TITLE	LABEL & NO.
			NATURAL FOUR	
			Soul group led by Chris James, formed in 1967 in San Francisco.	
2/9/74	31	4	1. Can This Be Real	Curtom 1990
			NATURAL SELECTION	
			Funk duo from Minneapolis: Elliott Erickson (vocals) and Frederick Thomas (keyboards).	
8/24/91	2 (2)	19	1. **Do Anything**	EastWest 98724
			NATURAL SELECTION featuring Niki Haris	
			Airplay #3 / Sales #5	
1/25/92	28	4	2. Hearts Don't Think (They Feel)!	EastWest 98652
			Airplay #32	
			NAUGHTON, David	
			Born on 2/13/52. Singer/dancer/actor. Starred in the 1981 movie *An American Werewolf In London* and TV shows "Makin' It" and "My Sister Sam."	
5/12/79	5	16	● 1. **Makin' It**	RSO 916
			from the movie *Meatballs* starring Bill Murray	
			NAUGHTY BY NATURE	
			Rap trio from East Orange, New Jersey: Anthony "Treach" Criss, Vincent Brown and Kier "dj KG" Gist. Appeared in the movies *The Meteor Man* and *Who's The Man?*	
9/28/91	6	18	▲² 1. **O.P.P.**	Tommy Boy 988
			Sales #1(1) / Airplay #24; O.P.P.: Other People's Property; samples "ABC" by The Jackson 5	
2/6/93	8	20	▲ 2. **Hip Hop Hooray**	Tommy Boy 554
			Sales #2 / Airplay #11; #1 R&B hit (1 week); above 2 are cassette maxi-singles	
6/24/95	17	11	● 3. Feel Me Flow	Tommy Boy 7682
			Sales #8 / Airplay #40; samples "Find Yourself" by The Meters	
			NAZARETH	
			Hard-rock group formed in Scotland in 1969: Dan McCafferty (lead singer), Manny Charlton (lead guitar), Pete Agnew (bass) and Darrell Sweet (drums). Billy Rankin (lead guitar) and John Locke (keyboards) added in 1981.	
1/3/76	8	14	● 1. **Love Hurts**	A&M 1671
			song first released in 1961 by Roy Orbison (B-side of "Running Scared")	
			NDEGÉOCELLO, Me'Shell—see MELLENCAMP, John	
			NEELY, Sam	
			Born on 8/22/48 in Cuero, Texas. Performing since age 11. Played clubs in Corpus Christi, especially at The Rogue, in the late '60s. Long residency at the Electric Eel in Corpus Christi in the late '70s.	
10/7/72	29	6	1. Loving You Just Crossed My Mind	Capitol 3381
11/9/74	34	2	2. You Can Have Her	A&M 1612

DATE	POS	WKS	ARTIST–RECORD TITLE	LABEL & NO.
			NEIGHBORHOOD, The	
			Seven-man, two-woman vocal group.	
8/8/70	29	4	1. Big Yellow Taxi	Big Tree 102
			NELSON	
			Gunnar (vocals, bass) and Matthew Nelson (vocals, rhythm guitar), the identical twin sons (born 9/20/67) of the late Ricky Nelson. Their sister is actress Tracy Nelson of TV's "Father Dowling Mysteries."	
8/11/90	1 (1)	14	● 1. **(Can't Live Without Your) Love And Affection** Sales #1(1) / Airplay #4; acoustic version is on the B-side of #4 below	DGC 19689
12/1/90+	6	14	2. **After The Rain** Sales #4 / Airplay #6	DGC 19667
4/6/91	14	9	3. More Than Ever Airplay #12 / Sales #14	DGC 19002
7/27/91	28	5	4. Only Time Will Tell Airplay #42 / Sales #51; all of above from the album *After The Rain*	DGC 19014
			NELSON, Ricky	
			Born Eric Hilliard Nelson on 5/8/40 in Teaneck, New Jersey. Died on 12/31/85 in a plane crash in DeKalb, Texas. Son of bandleader Ozzie Nelson and vocalist Harriet Hilliard. Rick and brother David appeared on Nelson's radio show from March 1949, later on TV, 1952–66. Formed own Stone Canyon Band in 1969. Appeared in the movies *Rio Bravo*, *The Wackiest Ship In The Army* and *Love And Kisses*. Married Kristin Harmon (sister of actor Mark Harmon) in 1963; divorced in 1982. Their daughter Tracy is a movie/TV actress. Their twin sons began recording as Nelson in 1990. Ricky was one of the first teen idols of the rock era. Inducted into the Rock and Roll Hall of Fame in 1987.	
5/13/57	2 (1)	15	● 1. **A Teenager's Romance/** Best Seller #2 / Top 100 #8 / Jockey #8 / Juke Box #12	
5/6/57	4	15	● 2. **I'm Walking** Best Seller #4 / Juke Box #16 / Top 100 #17	Verve 10047
9/16/57	14	7	3. You're My One And Only Love/ Best Seller #14 / Top 100 #16; Gloria Wood (female vocal)	
		5	4. Honey Rock [I] **BARNEY KESSEL** (Ricky not credited on label) Best Seller flip; Barney Kessel (orch., all of above)	Verve 10070
10/7/57	3	18	● 5. **Be-Bop Baby/** Best Seller #3 / Top 100 #5 / Jockey #10	
10/28/57	29	3	6. Have I Told You Lately That I Love You? #24 hit for Bing Crosby & The Andrews Sisters in 1950	Imperial 5463
12/30/57+	2 (3)	14	● 7. **Stood Up/** Best Seller #2 / Top 100 #5 / Jockey #5	
12/30/57+	18	9	8. Waitin' In School Top 100 #18 / Jockey #24	Imperial 5483
4/7/58	4	10	● 9. **Believe What You Say/** Best Seller #4 / Top 100 #8 / Jockey #20	
4/7/58	12	10	10. My Bucket's Got A Hole In It Best Seller #12 / Top 100 #18 / Jockey #25; #2 Country hit for Hank Williams in 1949	Imperial 5503
7/7/58	1 (2)	15	● 11. **Poor Little Fool** Hot 100 #1(2) / Best Seller #1(2) / Jockey #2 end; the first #1 *Hot 100* hit	Imperial 5528

DATE	POS	WKS	ARTIST–RECORD TITLE	LABEL & NO.
10/20/58	7	16	● 12. **Lonesome Town/**	
10/20/58	10	13	13. **I Got A Feeling**	Imperial 5545
3/9/59	6	12	● 14. **Never Be Anyone Else But You/**	
3/16/59	9	10	15. **It's Late**	Imperial 5565
7/13/59	9	9	16. **Just A Little Too Much/**	
			#8–9, 15–16 written by Johnny and/or Dorsey Burnette	
7/13/59	9	8	17. **Sweeter Than You**	Imperial 5595
12/7/59	20	8	18. I Wanna Be Loved/	
12/21/59	38	1	19. Mighty Good	Imperial 5614
5/9/60	12	9	20. Young Emotions	Imperial 5663
9/19/60	27	4	21. I'm Not Afraid/	
9/26/60	34	2	22. Yes Sir, That's My Baby	Imperial 5685
			#1 hit for Gene Austin in 1925	
1/9/61	25	4	23. You Are The Only One	Imperial 5707
5/1/61	1 (2)	15	● 24. **Travelin' Man/**	
5/8/61	9	13	25. **Hello Mary Lou**	Imperial 5741
			written by Gene Pitney	

RICK NELSON:

DATE	POS	WKS	ARTIST–RECORD TITLE	LABEL & NO.
10/9/61	11	9	26. A Wonder Like You/	
10/9/61	16	8	27. Everlovin'	Imperial 5770
3/17/62	5	10	28. **Young World**	Imperial 5805
8/25/62	5	9	29. **Teen Age Idol**	Imperial 5864
12/29/62+	6	9	30. **It's Up To You**	Imperial 5901
			#24, 26, 28, 30 written by Jerry Fuller	
6/15/63	25	5	31. String Along	Decca 31495
10/5/63	12	9	32. Fools Rush In	Decca 31533
			#3 hit for Glenn Miller in 1940	
1/11/64	6	9	33. **For You**	Decca 31574
			first popularized by Glen Gray in 1933 (Brunswick 6606); #1 Adult Contemporary hit (2 weeks)	
5/9/64	26	5	34. The Very Thought Of You	Decca 31612
			#1 hit for Ray Noble in 1934	

RICK NELSON & THE STONE CANYON BAND:

DATE	POS	WKS	ARTIST–RECORD TITLE	LABEL & NO.
1/3/70	33	6	35. She Belongs To Me	Decca 32550
			written by Bob Dylan	
9/16/72	6	12	● 36. **Garden Party**	Decca 32980
			inspired by Nelson's experience in a Madison Square Garden concert; #1 Adult Contemporary hit (2 weeks)	

NELSON, Sandy

Born Sander Nelson on 12/1/38 in Santa Monica, California. Rock and roll drummer. Became prominent studio musician. Heard on "Alley Oop," "To Know Him Is To Love Him," "A Thousand Stars" and many others. Lost portion of right leg in a motorcycle accident in 1963. Returned to performing in 1964.

DATE	POS	WKS	ARTIST–RECORD TITLE		LABEL & NO.
9/14/59	4	12	1. **Teen Beat**	[I]	Original Sound 5
11/20/61	7	12	2. **Let There Be Drums**	[I]	Imperial 5775
3/3/62	29	4	3. Drums Are My Beat	[I]	Imperial 5809

DATE	POS	WKS	ARTIST–RECORD TITLE	LABEL & NO.

NELSON, Willie

Born on 4/30/33 in Ft. Worth; raised in Abbott, Texas. Prolific country singer/songwriter (writer of Patsy Cline's "Crazy" and Faron Young's "Hello Walls"). Played bass for Ray Price. Moved to Nashville in 1960. Moved back to Texas in 1970. Pioneered the "outlaw" country movement. Appeared in several movies including *The Electric Horseman* (1979), *Honeysuckle Rose* (1980) and *Barbarosa* (1982). Won Grammy's Living Legends Award in 1989. Elected to the Country Music Hall of Fame in 1993.

DATE	POS	WKS	ARTIST–RECORD TITLE	LABEL & NO.
10/11/75	21	9	1. Blue Eyes Crying In The Rain written in 1945 by Fred Rose; #1 Country hit (2 weeks)	Columbia 10176
3/6/76	25	5	2. Good Hearted Woman **WAYLON & WILLIE** #1 Country hit (3 weeks)	RCA 10529
9/27/80	20	10	3. On The Road Again from the movie *Honeysuckle Rose* starring Nelson; #1 Country hit (1 week)	Columbia 11351
4/10/82	5	15	▲ 4. Always On My Mind #1 Country hit (2 weeks); #45 Country hit for Brenda Lee in 1972	Columbia 02741
9/18/82	40	3	5. Let It Be Me	Columbia 03073
3/31/84	5	12	▲ 6. To All The Girls I've Loved Before **JULIO IGLESIAS & WILLIE NELSON**	Columbia 04217

NENA

Gabriele "Nena" Kerner (born 3/26/60) with four-member backup group from Hagen, Germany.

DATE	POS	WKS	ARTIST–RECORD TITLE	LABEL & NO.
1/21/84	2 (1)	13	● 1. 99 Luftballons [F] nuclear protest song; English version "99 Red Balloons" is on the B-side	Epic 04108

NEON PHILHARMONIC, The

Chamber-sized orchestra of Nashville Symphony Orchestra musicians. Project headed by Tupper Saussy (composer) and Don Gant (vocals; died 3/6/87, age 44).

DATE	POS	WKS	ARTIST–RECORD TITLE	LABEL & NO.
5/10/69	17	7	1. Morning Girl	Warner 7261

NERO, Peter

Born on 5/22/34 in Brooklyn. Pop-jazz-classical pianist. Won the 1961 Best New Artist Grammy Award.

DATE	POS	WKS	ARTIST–RECORD TITLE	LABEL & NO.
11/20/71	21	8	1. Theme From "Summer Of '42" [I] title song from the movie starring Jennifer O'Neill	Columbia 45399

NERVOUS NORVUS

Born Jimmy Drake in 1912; died in 1968 (age 56). Prior to recording, worked as a truck driver in Oakland, California.

DATE	POS	WKS	ARTIST–RECORD TITLE	LABEL & NO.
6/9/56	8	9	1. Transfusion [N] Best Seller #8 / Top 100 #13 / Jockey #14 / Juke Box #18	Dot 15470
8/11/56	24	4	2. Ape Call [N] Best Seller #24 / Top 100 #28; Red Blanchard (ape calls)	Dot 15485

DATE	POS	WKS	ARTIST–RECORD TITLE	LABEL & NO.
			NESMITH, Michael, & The First National Band	
			Nesmith was born on 12/30/43 in Houston. Professional musician before joining The Monkees. Wrote Linda Ronstadt's hit "Different Drum." Formed own video production company, Pacific Arts, in 1977; produced the movies *Elephant Parts*, *Repo Man* and others.	
9/5/70	**21**	7	1. Joanne	RCA 0368
			NEVIL, Robbie	
			Pop singer/songwriter/guitarist from Los Angeles.	
11/15/86+	**2** (2)	16	1. **C'est La Vie** Sales #1(1) / Airplay #3	Manhattan 50047
3/14/87	**14**	9	2. Dominoes Airplay #13 / Sales #14	Manhattan 50053
6/27/87	**10**	9	3. **Wot's It To Ya** Sales #8 / Airplay #16	Manhattan 50075
1/7/89	**34**	3	4. Back On Holiday Sales #31 / Airplay #32	EMI 50152
8/3/91	**25**	6	5. Just Like You Airplay #43	EMI 50356
			NEVILLE, Aaron	
			Born on 1/24/41 in New Orleans. Member of the New Orleans family group The Neville Brothers. Brother Art was keyboardist of The Meters. Bassist/singer Ivan Neville is his son.	
12/17/66+	**2** (1)	11	1. **Tell It Like It Is** #1 R&B hit (5 weeks)	Par-Lo 101
			LINDA RONSTADT (FEATURING AARON NEVILLE):	
10/28/89	**2** (2)	16	● 2. **Don't Know Much** Sales #1(2) / Airplay #4; #1 Adult Contemporary hit (5 weeks)	Elektra 69261
2/24/90	**11**	9	3. All My Life Sales #10 / Airplay #14; #1 Adult Contemporary hit (3 weeks)	Elektra 64987
			AARON NEVILLE:	
8/24/91	**8**	12	4. **Everybody Plays The Fool** Airplay #19 / Sales #47; #1 Adult Contemporary hit (1 week)	A&M 1563
			NEVILLE, Ivan	
			New Orleans bassist. Son of singer Aaron Neville (of The Neville Brothers). Formerly with Bonnie Raitt's band. Played on The Rolling Stones' *Dirty Work* album.	
11/12/88	**26**	6	1. Not Just Another Girl Sales #27 / Airplay #28	Polydor 887814
			NEWBEATS, The	
			Pop trio: Larry Henley (born 6/30/41, Arp, Texas; lead singer) with brothers Dean and Marc Mathis (born Hahira, Georgia, 3/17/39 and 2/9/42, respectively). Henley co-wrote "Wind Beneath My Wings."	
8/22/64	**2** (2)	11	1. **Bread And Butter**	Hickory 1269
11/7/64	**16**	7	2. Everything's Alright	Hickory 1282
2/20/65	**40**	1	3. Break Away (From That Boy)	Hickory 1290
10/30/65	**12**	9	4. Run, Baby Run (Back Into My Arms)	Hickory 1332

DATE	POS	WKS	ARTIST—RECORD TITLE	LABEL & NO.
			NEW BIRTH, The	
			R&B vocal group portion of New Birth, Inc. (see Nite-Liters). Original group consisted of vocalists Londee Loren, Bobby Downs, Melvin Wilson, Leslie Wilson, Ann Bogan and soloist Alan Frye, with instrumental backing by The Nite-Liters. Melvin, Leslie and Ann recorded as Love, Peace & Happiness in 1972. Ann was also a member of The Marvelettes and in duo Harvey & Ann with Harvey Fuqua.	
5/5/73	35	4	1. I Can Understand It	RCA 0912
8/23/75	36	2	2. Dream Merchant	Buddah 470
			#1 R&B hit (1 week)	
			NEWBURY, Mickey	
			Born Milton S. Newbury, Jr., on 5/19/40 in Houston. Moved to Nashville in 1963; worked as staff writer for Acuff-Rose. Wrote "Just Dropped In (To See What Condition My Condition Was In)."	
12/4/71+	26	7	1. An American Trilogy	Elektra 45750
			Dixie/Battle Hymn Of The Republic/All My Trials	
			NEW CHRISTY MINSTRELS, The	
			Folk/balladeer troupe named after the Christy Minstrels (formed in 1842 by Edwin "Pop" Christy). Group founded and led by Randy Sparks, and featured Barry McGuire, Kenny Rogers (1966) and Kim Carnes (late '60s).	
7/27/63	14	7	1. Green, Green	Columbia 42805
11/16/63	29	3	2. Saturday Night	Columbia 42887
5/16/64	17	9	3. Today	Columbia 43000
			from the movie *Advance to the Rear* starring Glenn Ford	
			NEW COLONY SIX, The	
			Soft-rock group from Chicago: Patrick McBride, Ronnie Rice, Gerry Van Kollenburg, Les Kummel, Chuck Jobes and William Herman. Ray Graffia joined in 1969. Kummel died on 12/18/78 (age 33).	
5/11/68	22	6	1. I Will Always Think About You	Mercury 72775
2/15/69	16	9	2. Things I'd Like To Say	Mercury 72858
			NEW EDITION	
			Boston R&B teen vocal quintet (ages 13 to 15 in 1983): Ralph Tresvant, Ronald DeVoe, Michael Bivins, Ricky Bell and Bobby Brown. Formed in 1982 by future New Kids On The Block and Perfect Gentlemen producer, Maurice Starr. Brown left for solo career in 1986; replaced by Johnny Gill in 1988. Bell, Bivins and DeVoe recorded as Bell Biv DeVoe in 1990. Tresvant and Gill recorded solo in the '90s.	
10/27/84+	4	14	● 1. **Cool It Now**	MCA 52455
			Sales #1(1) / Airplay #9; #1 R&B hit (1 week)	
1/26/85	12	8	2. Mr. Telephone Man	MCA 52484
			Sales #7 / Airplay #13; written and produced by Ray Parker, Jr.; #1 R&B hit (3 weeks)	
4/27/85	35	4	3. Lost In Love	MCA 52553
			Sales #26	
4/12/86	38	2	4. A Little Bit Of Love (Is All It Takes)	MCA 52768
			Sales #26	
9/20/86	21	6	5. Earth Angel	MCA 52905
			Sales #18 / Airplay #32; featured in the movie *The Karate Kid Part II* starring Ralph Macchio	
7/30/88	7	13	6. **If It Isn't Love**	MCA 53264
			Sales #5 / Airplay #8	

DATE	POS	WKS	ARTIST–RECORD TITLE	LABEL & NO.
			NEW ENGLAND	
			East Coast melodic-rock quartet: John Fannon, Jimmy Waldo, Hirsh Gardner and Gary Shea.	
6/16/79	**40**	1	1. Don't Ever Wanna Lose Ya	Infinity 50013
			NEW KIDS ON THE BLOCK	
			Boston teen vocal quintet: Joe McIntyre (born 12/31/72), Donnie Wahlberg (born 8/17/69), Danny Wood (born 5/14/69) and brothers Jordan (born 5/17/70) and Jon (born 11/29/68) Knight. Formed in the summer of 1984 by New Edition founder/producer, Maurice Starr. Shortened group name to NKOTB in 1992.	
8/13/88	**10**	12	1. **Please Don't Go Girl** Sales #9 / Airplay #13	Columbia 07700
1/14/89	**3**	13	● 2. **You Got It (The Right Stuff)** Sales #2 / Airplay #5	Columbia 08092
4/22/89	**1** (1)	14	● 3. **I'll Be Loving You (Forever)** Airplay #1(2) / Sales #1(1)	Columbia 68671
7/22/89	**1** (1)	12	▲ 4. **Hangin' Tough/** Sales #1(1) / Airplay #3	
9/30/89	**8**	10	5. **Didn't I (Blow Your Mind)** Airplay #8 / Sales #8; from the group's 1987 debut album *New Kids On The Block*	Columbia 68960
9/23/89	**2** (1)	10	● 6. **Cover Girl** Sales #2 / Airplay #3; all of above (except #5) from the album *Hangin' Tough*	Columbia 69088
11/25/89	**7**	10	● 7. **This One's For The Children** [X] Sales #6 / Airplay #12	Columbia 73064
5/26/90	**1** (3)	11	▲ 8. **Step By Step** Sales #1(3) / Airplay #1(1)	Columbia 73343
8/4/90	**7**	8	9. **Tonight** Sales #6 / Airplay #8	Columbia 73461
3/7/92	**16**	6	10. If You Go Away **NKOTB** Sales #8 / Airplay #22	Columbia 74255
			NEWMAN, Jimmy	
			Born on 8/27/27 in Big Mamou, Louisiana. Cajun-country singer/guitarist.	
7/22/57	**23**	1	1. Λ Fallen Star Jockey #23 / Top 100 #42	Dot 15574
			NEWMAN, Randy	
			Born on 11/28/43 in New Orleans. Singer/composer/pianist. Nephew of composers Alfred, Emil and Lionel Newman. Scored the movies *Ragtime*, *The Natural* and *Avalon*.	
12/10/77+	**2** (3)	13	● 1. **Short People** [N] Glenn Frey, J.D. Souther and Timothy B. Schmit (backing vocals)	Warner 8492
			NEWMAN, Thunderclap—see **THUNDERCLAP NEWMAN**	

DATE	POS	WKS	ARTIST–RECORD TITLE	LABEL & NO.
			NEW ORDER	
			Techno-dance group formed in 1980 in Manchester, England: Bernard Sumner (guitar, vocals), Stephen Morris, Peter Hook and Gillian Gilbert. Sumner also recorded with Electronic.	
12/5/87	32	8	1. True Faith	Qwest 28271
			Airplay #28 / Sales #35	
6/5/93	28	8	2. Regret	Qwest 18586
			Airplay #21 / Sales #73	
			NEW SEEKERS, The	
			British-Australian group formed by former Seekers' member Keith Potger after disbandment of The Seekers in 1969. Consisted of Eve Graham, Lyn Paul, Peter Doyle, Marty Kristian and Paul Layton.	
9/19/70	14	9	1. Look What They've Done To My Song Ma	Elektra 45699
			THE NEW SEEKERS featuring Eve Graham	
			written by Melanie	
12/18/71+	7	9	1 2. I'd Like To Teach The World To Sing (In Perfect Harmony)	Elektra 45762
			adapted from a Coca-Cola jingle	
4/14/73	29	4	3. Pinball Wizard/See Me, Feel Me	Verve 10709
			from the rock opera *Tommy*	
			NEWTON, Juice	
			Born Judy Kay Newton on 2/18/52 in New Jersey; raised in Virginia Beach. Pop-country singer. Performed folk music from age 13. Moved to Los Angeles with own Silver Spur band in 1974; recorded for RCA in 1975. Group disbanded in 1978. Newton is an accomplished equestrienne.	
3/7/81	4	16	● 1. **Angel Of The Morning**	Capitol 4976
			#1 Adult Contemporary hit (3 weeks)	
6/20/81	2 (2)	19	● 2. **Queen Of Hearts**	Capitol 4997
11/7/81+	7	18	3. **The Sweetest Thing (I've Ever Known)**	Capitol 5046
			#1 Adult Contemporary hit (1 week); #1 Country hit (1 week)	
5/22/82	7	13	4. **Love's Been A Little Bit Hard On Me**	Capitol 5120
			Andrew Gold (guitar)	
9/11/82	11	10	5. **Break It To Me Gently**	Capitol 5148
			#1 Adult Contemporary hit (2 weeks)	
12/18/82+	25	10	6. Heart Of The Night	Capitol 5192
9/3/83	27	5	7. Tell Her No	Capitol 5265
			NEWTON, Wayne	
			Born on 4/3/42 in Roanoke, Virginia. Singer/multi-instrumentalist. Top Las Vegas entertainer. Began singing career with regular appearances on Jackie Gleason's variety TV show in 1962. Appeared in the 1989 James Bond movie *Licence To Kill* and the 1990 movie *The Adventures Of Ford Fairlane*.	
8/3/63	13	8	1. Danke Schoen	Capitol 4989
			written by Bert Kaempfert	
3/27/65	23	5	2. Red Roses For A Blue Lady	Capitol 5366
			#3 hit for Vaughn Monroe in 1949	
6/10/72	4	13	● 3. **Daddy Don't You Walk So Fast**	Chelsea 0100
3/22/80	35	3	4. Years	Aries II 108

DATE	POS	WKS	ARTIST–RECORD TITLE	LABEL & NO.
			NEWTON-JOHN, Olivia	
			Born on 9/26/48 in Cambridge, England. To Australia in 1953. At age 16, won talent contest trip to England; sang with Pat Carroll as Pat & Olivia. With the group Toomorrow, in a British movie of the same name. Grand-daughter of Nobel Prize-winning German physicist Max Born. Appeared in the movies *Grease*, *Xanadu* and *Two Of A Kind*. Married actor Matt Lattanzi in 1984. Opened own chain of clothing boutiques (Koala Blue) in 1984. Battled breast cancer in 1992.	
7/17/71	25	10	1. If Not For You written by Bob Dylan; #1 Adult Contemporary hit (3 weeks)	Uni 55281
12/15/73+	6	14	● 2. **Let Me Be There**	MCA 40101
5/11/74	5	12	● 3. **If You Love Me (Let Me Know)**	MCA 40209
8/24/74	1 (2)	10	● 4. **I Honestly Love You** #1 Adult Contemporary hit (3 weeks)	MCA 40280
2/8/75	1 (1)	11	● 5. **Have You Never Been Mellow** #1 Adult Contemporary hit (1 week)	MCA 40349
6/21/75	3	12	● 6. **Please Mr. Please** #1 Adult Contemporary hit (3 weeks)	MCA 40418
10/11/75	13	7	7. Something Better To Do #1 Adult Contemporary hit (3 weeks)	MCA 40459
1/3/76	30	4	8. Let It Shine/ #1 Adult Contemporary hit (2 weeks)	
		4	9. He Ain't Heavy...He's My Brother	MCA 40495
4/17/76	23	6	10. Come On Over written by Barry and Robin Gibb; #1 Adult Contemporary hit (1 week)	MCA 40525
9/4/76	33	4	11. Don't Stop Believin' #1 Adult Contemporary hit (1 week)	MCA 40600
2/19/77	20	9	12. Sam #1 Adult Contemporary hit (2 weeks)	MCA 40670
4/8/78	1 (1)	16	▲ 13. **You're The One That I Want** **JOHN TRAVOLTA AND OLIVIA NEWTON-JOHN**	RSO 891
7/22/78	3	15	● 14. **Hopelessly Devoted To You**	RSO 903
8/19/78	5	12	● 15. **Summer Nights** **JOHN TRAVOLTA, OLIVIA NEWTON-JOHN & CAST** above 3 from the movie *Grease* starring Newton-John and Travolta	RSO 906
12/9/78+	3	17	● 16. **A Little More Love**	MCA 40975
5/5/79	11	8	17. Deeper Than The Night	MCA 41009
4/19/80	12	8	18. I Can't Help It **ANDY GIBB AND OLIVIA NEWTON-JOHN**	RSO 1026
6/14/80	1 (4)	16	● 19. **Magic** #1 Adult Contemporary hit (5 weeks)	MCA 41247
8/30/80	8	10	20. **Xanadu** **OLIVIA NEWTON-JOHN/ELECTRIC LIGHT ORCHESTRA**	MCA 41285
11/22/80+	20	11	21. Suddenly **OLIVIA NEWTON-JOHN AND CLIFF RICHARD** above 3 from the movie *Xanadu* starring Newton-John	MCA 51007
10/17/81	1 (10)	21	▲ 22. **Physical**	MCA 51182
2/27/82	5	10	● 23. **Make A Move On Me**	MCA 52000
9/25/82	3	13	24. **Heart Attack**	MCA 52100
2/19/83	38	3	25. Tied Up	MCA 52155
11/12/83+	5	14	26. **Twist Of Fate**	MCA 52284
2/25/84	31	5	27. Livin' In Desperate Times above 2 from the movie *Two Of A Kind* starring Newton-John and Travolta	MCA 52341

DATE	POS	WKS	ARTIST–RECORD TITLE	LABEL & NO.
10/26/85	**20**	7	28. Soul Kiss Sales #12 / Airplay #25; all of above (except #15, 18, 20, 26, 27) produced by John Farrar	MCA 52686
			NEW VAUDEVILLE BAND, The	
			Creation of British composer/record producer Geoff Stephens (born 10/1/34, London).	
11/5/66	**1** (3)	13	● 1. **Winchester Cathedral** #1 Adult Contemporary hit (4 weeks)	Fontana 1562
			NEW YORK CITY	
			New York City R&B quartet: Tim McQueen, John Brown, Ed Shell and Claude Johnston. First recorded for Buddah as Triboro Exchange. Name changed in 1972.	
4/28/73	**17**	12	1. I'm Doin' Fine Now	Chelsea 0113
			NICHOLAS, Paul	
			Born Paul Beuselinck on 12/3/45 in Peterborough, England. British theater/movie actor. Played Billy Shears's brother in the 1978 movie *Sgt. Pepper's Lonely Hearts Club Band*.	
9/17/77	**6**	16	● 1. **Heaven On The 7th Floor**	RSO 878
			NICKS, Stevie	
			Born Stephanie Nicks on 5/26/48 in Phoenix; raised in California. Became vocalist of Bay-area group Fritz and subsequently met guitarist Lindsey Buckingham. Teamed up and recorded album *Buckingham-Nicks* in 1973. Joined Fleetwood Mac in January 1975 as vocalist. Quit touring with band after 1990; left in January 1993.	
8/1/81	**3**	15	1. **Stop Draggin' My Heart Around** **STEVIE NICKS (with Tom Petty and The Heartbreakers)**	Modern 7336
11/7/81+	**6**	15	2. **Leather And Lace** **STEVIE NICKS (with DON HENLEY)** written for Waylon Jennings and Jessi Colter	Modern 7341
3/6/82	**11**	10	3. Edge Of Seventeen (Just Like The White Winged Dove)	Modern 7401
6/12/82	**32**	4	4. After The Glitter Fades above 4 from the album *Bella Donna*	Modern 7405
6/18/83	**5**	14	5. **Stand Back**	Modern 99863
9/24/83	**14**	9	6. If Anyone Falls	Modern 99832
1/21/84	**33**	4	7. Nightbird **STEVIE NICKS (with Sandy Stewart)**	Modern 99799
11/30/85+	**4**	13	8. **Talk To Me** Airplay #4 / Sales #5	Modern 99582
3/1/86	**37**	2	9. Needles And Pins **TOM PETTY and the HEARTBREAKERS with STEVIE NICKS** recorded "live" at LA's Wiltern Theater; written by Sonny Bono	MCA 52772
3/8/86	**16**	8	10. I Can't Wait Airplay #14 / Sales #21; all of above produced by Jimmy Iovine	Modern 99565
6/3/89	**16**	7	11. Rooms On Fire Sales #14 / Airplay #18	Modern 99216
			NIELSEN/PEARSON	
			Sacramento pop quartet fronted by lead vocalists/guitarists Reed Nielsen and Mark Pearson.	
11/15/80	**38**	2	1. If You Should Sail	Capitol 4910

DATE	POS	WKS	ARTIST—RECORD TITLE	LABEL & NO.
			NIGHT	
			Sextet led by female vocalist Stevie Lange and Chris Thompson, lead singer/guitarist of Manfred Mann's Earth Band.	
8/4/79	**18**	8	1. Hot Summer Nights	Planet 45903
			written by Walter Egan	
10/20/79	**17**	8	2. If You Remember Me	Planet 45904
			CHRIS THOMPSON & NIGHT	
			first released as only by Chris Thompson; released later on Planet 45909	
			NIGHTINGALE, Maxine	
			Born on 11/2/52 in Wembly, England. First recorded in 1968. Appeared in productions of *Hair, Jesus Christ Superstar, Godspell* and *Savages* in the early '70s.	
3/13/76	**2** (2)	15	● 1. **Right Back Where We Started From**	United Art. 752
7/7/79	**5**	14	● 2. **Lead Me On**	Windsong 11530
			#1 Adult Contemporary hit (7 weeks)	
			NIGHT RANGER	
			Rock group from California: lead singers Kelly Keagy (drums) and Jack Blades (bass), with guitarists Jeff Watson and Brad Gillis, and keyboardist Alan "Fitz" Gerald. Blades and Gillis were members of Rubicon. Gerald left in 1988; band split up in early 1989. Blades joined supergroup Damn Yankees and formed duo with Tommy Shaw.	
2/26/83	**40**	3	1. Don't Tell Me You Love Me	Boardwalk 171
4/21/84	**5**	12	2. **Sister Christian**	MCA/Camel 52350
8/4/84	**14**	11	3. When You Close Your Eyes	MCA/Camel 52420
			Sales #26 pre	
6/8/85	**8**	11	4. **Sentimental Street**	MCA/Camel 52591
			Sales #5 / Airplay #9	
9/21/85	**19**	6	5. Four In The Morning (I Can't Take Any More)	MCA/Camel 52661
			Sales #20 / Airplay #23	
12/7/85+	**17**	10	6. Goodbye	MCA/Camel 52729
			Sales #14 / Airplay #23; all of above (except #2) written by Jack Blades	
			NIKKI	
			Born in Okinawa, Japan; raised in Dayton, Ohio. American male singer/multi-instrumentalist. Backing member of the soul-funk group Sun. Jingle writer for TV commercials.	
6/9/90	**21**	6	1. Notice Me	Geffen 19946
			Airplay #19 / Sales #23	
			NILSSON	
			Born Harry Edward Nelson III on 6/15/41 in Brooklyn. Died on 1/15/94 of a heart attack. Wrote Three Dog Night's hit "One"; scored the movie *Skidoo*, the animated TV movie "The Point" and TV's "The Courtship Of Eddie's Father." Close friend of John Lennon and Ringo Starr.	
9/6/69	**6**	9	1. **Everybody's Talkin'**	RCA 0161
			theme song from the movie *Midnight Cowboy* starring Dustin Hoffman and Jon Voight	
11/29/69	**34**	2	2. I Guess The Lord Must Be In New York City	RCA 0261
5/8/71	**34**	4	3. Me And My Arrow	RCA 0443

DATE	POS	WKS	ARTIST–RECORD TITLE	LABEL & NO.
1/15/72	1 (4)	14	● 4. **Without You** written by Badfinger's Pete Ham and Tom Evans; Gary Wright (piano); #1 Adult Contemporary hit (5 weeks)	RCA 0604
4/8/72	27	6	5. Jump Into The Fire	RCA 0673
7/8/72	8	10	6. **Coconut**	RCA 0718
10/14/72	23	6	7. Spaceman Peter Frampton (guitar)	RCA 0788
5/25/74	39	2	8. Daybreak from the movie *Son Of Dracula* starring Nilsson and Ringo Starr (drums); Peter Frampton (guitar); George Harrison (cowbell)	RCA 0246
			1910 FRUITGUM CO. New Jersey bubblegum quintet: Mark Gutkowski, Floyd Marcus, Pat Karwan, Steve Mortkowitz and Frank Jeckell. Produced by The Music Explosion and Ohio Express producers Jerry Kasenetz and Jeff Katz.	
2/10/68	4	11	● 1. **Simon Says**	Buddah 24
8/10/68	5	11	● 2. **1, 2, 3, Red Light**	Buddah 54
12/7/68	37	3	3. Goody Goody Gumdrops	Buddah 71
2/8/69	5	11	● 4. **Indian Giver**	Buddah 91
6/14/69	38	2	5. Special Delivery	Buddah 114
			95 SOUTH Hip-hop outfit based in Miami: Church's, Black, Lemonhead, Bootyman and K-Knock. Group named after the interstate highway.	
6/19/93	11	16	▲ 1. Whoot, There It Is Sales #5 / Airplay #44; samples Afrika Bambaataa's "Looking For The Perfect Beat"	Wrap 162
			NIRVANA Grunge-rock trio from Aberdeen, Washington: Kurt Cobain (vocals), Chris Novoselic (bass) and Dave Grohl (drums). Early lineup: Cobain, Novoselic, Jason Everman (guitar) and Chad Channing (drums). Everman left in mid-1989. In 1990, Dan Peters (later of Mudhoney) briefly replaced Channing, then Grohl joined. Cobain married Courtney Love, lead singer of rock group Hole, on 2/24/92. Cobain was found dead of a self-inflicted gunshot wound on 4/8/94. Grohl formed Foo Fighters in 1995.	
12/7/91+	6	19	▲ 1. **Smells Like Teen Spirit** Sales #1(2) / Airplay #41	DGC 19050
4/18/92	32	5	2. Come As You Are Sales #27 / Airplay #62	DGC 19120
			NITEFLYTE Disco group led by Howard Johnson and Sandy Torano.	
11/24/79	37	2	1. If You Want It	Ariola Am. 7747
			NITE-LITERS, The R&B band formed in Louisville in 1963 by Harvey Fuqua and Tony Churchill. Expanded to 17 members with two vocal groups and band. Renamed New Birth, Inc., with The Nite-Liters making up the instrumental section. Also see New Birth.	
9/11/71	39	1	1. K-Jee [I]	RCA 0461

DATE	POS	WKS	ARTIST–RECORD TITLE	LABEL & NO.
			NITTY GRITTY DIRT BAND	
			Country-folk-rock group from Long Beach, California. Led by Jeff Hanna (born 7/11/47; vocals, guitar) and John McEuen (born 12/19/45; banjo, mandolin). Changed name to Dirt Band in 1976. Resumed using Nitty Gritty Dirt Band name in 1982. Various members included ex-Eagle Bernie Leadon, who replaced McEuen briefly in early 1987. Revamped quartet since late 1987: Hanna, Jimmy Ibbotson, Bob Carpenter and Jimmie Fadden. Appeared in the movies *For Singles Only* and *Paint Your Wagon*.	
1/2/71	9	13	1. **Mr. Bojangles** prologue: Uncle Charlie And His Dog Teddy	Liberty 56197
			THE DIRT BAND:	
1/12/80	13	11	2. An American Dream Linda Ronstadt (harmony vocal)	United Art. 1330
7/12/80	25	9	3. Make A Little Magic Nicolette Larson (backing vocal)	United Art. 1356
			NITZSCHE, Jack	
			Born Bernard Nitzsche on 4/22/37 in Chicago. Arranger/producer/composer/keyboardist. Arranger for many of Phil Spector's productions. Co-wrote "Needles And Pins" and scored the movies *One Flew Over The Cuckoo's Nest* and *An Officer And A Gentleman*. His wife, Grazia, sang on several of The Blossoms' recordings.	
9/7/63	39	2	1. The Lonely Surfer [I]	Reprise 20202
			NKOTB—see NEW KIDS ON THE BLOCK	
			NOBLE, Nick	
			Born Nicholas Valkan on 6/21/36 in Chicago. Attended Loyola University.	
8/20/55	22	3	1. The Bible Tells Me So Best Seller #22 / Top 100 #61 pre; written by Roy Rogers's wife, Dale Evans; Lew Douglas (orch.)	Wing 90003
3/24/56	27	6	2. To You, My Love first released on Wing 90045 in 1955; French song "Je Ne Sais Pas"; Jack Halloran Choir (backing vocals, above 2)	Mercury 70821
7/15/57	20	1	3. A Fallen Star Jockey #20; first released on Mercury 71117 in 1957; Dick Noel Singers (backing vocals)	Mercury 71124
9/30/57	37	1	4. Moonlight Swim Carl Stevens (orch., above 3)	Mercury 71169
			NOBLES, Cliff, & Co.	
			Nobles was born in Mobile, Alabama, in 1944. Soul bandleader/singer. Moved to Philadelphia in 1965.	
6/8/68	2 (3)	12	● 1. **The Horse** [I]	Phil-L.A. 313
			NOGUEZ, Jacky	
			Popular European society bandleader from Paris.	
7/27/59	24	5	1. Ciao, Ciao Bambina original Italian title: "Piove" [I]	Jamie 1127

DATE	POS	WKS	ARTIST–RECORD TITLE	LABEL & NO.
			NOLAN, Kenny	
			Los Angeles-based singer/songwriter. Wrote "My Eyes Adored You," "Lady Marmalade" and "Get Dancin'." Fronted studio group The Eleventh Hour.	
12/11/76+	**3**	20	● 1. **I Like Dreamin'**	20th Century 2287
5/7/77	**20**	11	2. Love's Grown Deep	20th Century 2331
			NORMAN, Chris—see QUATRO, Suzi	
			NORTH, Freddie	
			Black vocalist from Nashville. Worked in sales and promotion for Nashboro Records. DJ on "Night Train," WLAC-Nashville.	
11/27/71	**39**	1	1. She's All I Got	Mankind 12004
			NOTORIOUS B.I.G., The	
			Brooklyn-born rapper Christopher Wallace. Also known as Biggy Smallz. Arrested on 6/18/95 on robbery and assault charges. Married to singer Faith Evans.	
9/17/94	**27**	10	● 1. Juicy/ Sales #13 / Airplay #50	
		10	2. Unbelievable	Bad Boy 79004
1/28/95	**6**	20	▲ 3. **Big Poppa/** Sales #2 / Airplay #37; samples "Between The Sheets" by The Isley Brothers; remix released with a different B-side on Bad Boy 79019; also released on Bad Boy 79024	
		20	4. Warning Sales flip; samples "Walk On By"	Bad Boy 79015
4/22/95	**13**	14	● 5. Can't You See **TOTAL featuring The Notorious B.I.G.** Sales #9 / Airplay #28; from the movie *New Jersey Drive* starring Sharron Corley; samples "The Payback" by James Brown	Tommy Boy 7676
6/24/95	**2 (3)**	17	▲ 6. **One More Chance/Stay With Me/** Sales #1(5) / Airplay #24; Faith (backing vocal); contains an interpolation of "Stay With Me" by DeBarge; #1 R&B hit (9 weeks)	
		3	7. The What **THE NOTORIOUS B.I.G. and METHOD MAN** Sales flip	Bad Boy 79031
			NOVA, Aldo	
			Born Aldo Scarporuscio in Montreal. Rock singer/songwriter/guitarist/keyboardist.	
5/1/82	**23**	7	1. Fantasy	Portrait 02799
			N2DEEP	
			White rap outfit from Vallejo, California, put together by producer "Johnny Z." Zunino with rappers "Jay Tee" Trujillo and "TL." Lyon.	
8/22/92+	**14**	22	● 1. Back To The Hotel Sales #5 / Airplay #44	Profile 5367
			NIIU	
			Male R&B vocal quartet from New Jersey: Chuckie Howard, Chris Herbert, Don Carlis and Craig Hill.	
1/21/95	**22**	11	1. I Miss You Sales #16 / Airplay #44	Arista 12768

DATE	POS	WKS	ARTIST–RECORD TITLE	LABEL & NO.
			NUGENT, Ted	
			Born on 12/13/48 in Detroit. Heavy-metal rock guitarist; leader of The Amboy Dukes. Joined the supergroup Damn Yankees in 1989.	
9/10/77	30	6	1. Cat Scratch Fever	Epic 50425
			NUMAN, Gary	
			Born Gary Webb on 3/8/58 in Hammersmith, England. Synthesized techno-rock artist.	
3/29/80	9	17	1. **Cars**	Atco 7211
			NU SHOOZ	
			R&B group from Portland, Oregon, centered around husband-and-wife team of guitarist/songwriter John Smith and lead singer Valerie Day.	
4/5/86	3	15	● 1. **I Can't Wait** Sales #3 / Airplay #3	Atlantic 89446
9/6/86	28	8	2. Point Of No Return Sales #21 / Airplay #39	Atlantic 89392
			NU TORNADOS, The	
			Philadelphia string band: Eddie Dono (leader), Phil Dale, Tom Dell, Mike Perna and Louie Mann.	
12/15/58	26	6	1. Philadelphia U.S.A.	Carlton 492
			NUTTY SQUIRRELS, The	
			Creators and voices: Don Elliot (from Sommerville, New Jersey) and Sascha Burland (from New York City)	
11/30/59	14	7	1. Uh! Oh! Part 2 [N]	Hanover 4540
			NYLONS, The	
			Canadian a cappella quartet formed in 1979: Marc Connors, Paul Cooper, Claude Morrison and Arnold Robinson. Connors died on 3/25/91 (age 41).	
6/13/87	12	10	1. Kiss Him Goodbye Sales #10 / Airplay #12	Open Air 0022
			O	
			OAK	
			Northeastern pop group. Rick Pinette, lead singer.	
7/12/80	36	3	1. King Of The Hill **RICK PINETTE AND OAK**	Mercury 76049
			OAK RIDGE BOYS	
			Country-pop vocal group's roots go back to early 1940s when they were formed as a gospel quartet in Oak Ridge, Tennessee. Fluctuating lineup of 40+ members has survived two disbandments in 1946 and 1956. Consistent lineup, 1973–87: Duane Allen (lead), Joe Bonsall (tenor), Richard Sterban (bass) and Bill Golden (baritone). Steve Sanders, group's guitarist, replaced Golden in 1987.	
6/6/81	5	14	▲ 1. **Elvira** #1 Country hit (1 week)	MCA 51084

DATE	POS	WKS	ARTIST–RECORD TITLE	LABEL & NO.
2/13/82	12	9	2. Bobbie Sue #1 Country hit (1 week)	MCA 51231
			O'BANION, John Pop singer from Kokomo, Indiana.	
4/18/81	24	7	1. Love You Like I Never Loved Before	Elektra 47125
			OCASEK, Ric Born Richard Otcasek on 3/23/49 in Baltimore. Lead singer/guitarist/songwriter of The Cars. Appeared in the 1987 movie *Made In Heaven*. Married supermodel/actress Paulina Porizkova on 8/23/89. His son Christopher Otcasek is leader of Glamour Camp.	
10/11/86	15	8	1. Emotion In Motion Sales #16 / Airplay #17	Geffen 28617
			OCEAN Canadian pop quintet: Janice Morgan (vocals), David Tamblyn, Greg Brown, Jeff Jones and Charles Slater.	
3/27/71	● 2 (1)	12	1. **Put Your Hand In The Hand**	Kama Sutra 519
			OCEAN, Billy Born Leslie Sebastian Charles on 1/21/50 in Trinidad. Raised in England, worked as a tailor. Did session work in London. Moved to the U.S. in the late '70s.	
5/1/76	22	6	1. Love Really Hurts Without You	Ariola Am. 7621
9/8/84	● 1 (2)	15	2. **Caribbean Queen (No More Love On The Run)** Sales #1(2) / Airplay #2; #1 R&B hit (4 weeks); same song "African Queen" is on the B-side of #5 below	Jive 9199
12/8/84+	2 (1)	15	3. Loverboy Sales #2 / Airplay #4	Jive 9284
4/13/85	4	13	4. Suddenly Sales #3 / Airplay #3; #1 Adult Contemporary hit (2 weeks)	Jive 9323
7/27/85	24	8	5. Mystery Lady Sales #19 / Airplay #21; above 4 from the album *Suddenly*	Jive 9374
12/21/85+	2 (1)	14	6. **When The Going Gets Tough, The Tough Get Going** Sales #2 / Airplay #2; from the movie *The Jewel of the Nile* starring Michael Douglas and Kathleen Turner	Jive 9432
5/3/86	1 (1)	14	7. **There'll Be Sad Songs (To Make You Cry)** Sales #1(1) / Airplay #1(1); #1 R&B hit (2 weeks); #1 Adult Contemporary hit (1 week)	Jive 9465
8/9/86	10	11	8. **Love Zone** Sales #9 / Airplay #11; #1 R&B hit (1 week)	Jive 9510
11/15/86	16	11	9. Love Is Forever Sales #13 / Airplay #18; #1 Adult Contemporary hit (3 weeks); above 4 from the album *Love Zone*	Jive 9540
2/20/88	1 (2)	14	10. **Get Outta My Dreams, Get Into My Car** Sales #1(2) / Airplay #1(2); #1 R&B hit (1 week)	Jive 9678
6/25/88	17	8	11. The Colour Of Love Sales #13 / Airplay #17	Jive 9707
11/11/89	32	2	12. Licence To Chill Sales #26 / Airplay #38	Jive 1283

DATE	POS	WKS	ARTIST—RECORD TITLE	LABEL & NO.
			O'CONNOR, Sinéad	
			Pronounced: shin-NAYD. Born on 12/12/66 in Glenageary, Ireland. Female singer/songwriter. Gained notoriety for her various protests.	
3/24/90	1 (4)	15	▲ 1. **Nothing Compares 2 U** Airplay #1(4) / Sales #1(3); written by Prince; first recorded by the Minneapolis group The Family	Ensign 23488
			O'DAY, Alan	
			Born on 10/3/40 in Hollywood. Singer/songwriter/pianist. Wrote Helen Reddy's #1 hit "Angie Baby" and The Righteous Brothers' "Rock And Roll Heaven."	
5/7/77	1 (1)	17	● 1. **Undercover Angel**	Pacific 001
			O'DELL, Kenny	
			Born Kenneth Gist, Jr., in Oklahoma (early 1940s). Singer/songwriter/guitarist. Worked with Duane Eddy and own band, Guys And Dolls. Moved to Nashville in 1969. Wrote Charlie Rich's "Behind Closed Doors."	
12/16/67	38	2	1. Beautiful People	Vegas 718
			ODYSSEY	
			New York soul-disco trio: Manila-born Tony Reynolds, and sisters Lillian and Louise Lopez, originally from the Virgin Islands.	
12/17/77+	21	12	1. Native New Yorker	RCA 11129
			OHIO EXPRESS	
			Bubblegum group from Mansfield, Ohio. Produced by Jerry Kasenetz and Jeff Katz (worked with The Music Explosion and 1910 Fruitgum Co.). Joey Levine (born 5/2947; later with Reunion and several Kasenetz-Katz productions) was lead singer on most of the hits.	
11/18/67	29	5	1. Beg, Borrow And Steal originally released as by The Rare Breed on Attack 1401 in 1966	Cameo 483
5/18/68	4	11	● 2. **Yummy Yummy Yummy**	Buddah 38
8/31/68	33	5	3. Down At Lulu's	Buddah 56
11/2/68	15	10	● 4. Chewy Chewy	Buddah 70
4/26/69	30	4	5. Mercy above 4 sung and written by Joey Levine	Buddah 102
			OHIO PLAYERS	
			Originally an R&B instrumental group called the Ohio Untouchables, formed in Dayton in 1959. Backup on The Falcons' records. First recorded for LuPine in 1962. Members during prime, 1973–79: Marshall Jones, Clarence "Satch" Satchell, Jimmy "Diamond" Williams, Marvin "Merv" Pierce, Billy Beck, Ralph "Pee Wee" Middlebrook and Leroy "Sugarfoot" Bonner.	
4/14/73	15	9	● 1. Funky Worm [N] #1 R&B hit (1 week)	Westbound 214
9/22/73	31	6	2. Ecstasy	Westbound 216
9/14/74	13	7	● 3. Skin Tight	Mercury 73609
12/28/74+	1 (1)	12	● 4. **Fire** #1 R&B hit (2 weeks)	Mercury 73643
10/11/75	33	. 3	5. Sweet Sticky Thing #1 R&B hit (1 week)	Mercury 73713
11/22/75+	1 (1)	14	● 6. **Love Rollercoaster** #1 R&B hit (1 week)	Mercury 73734

DATE	POS	WKS	ARTIST–RECORD TITLE	LABEL & NO.
3/27/76	30	5	7. Fopp	Mercury 73775
7/31/76	18	10	8. Who'd She Coo? #1 R&B hit (1 week)	Mercury 73814

O'JAYS, The

R&B group from Canton, Ohio, formed in 1958 as the Triumphs. Consisted of Eddie Levert, Walter Williams, William Powell, Bobby Massey and Bill Isles. Recorded as the Mascots for the King label in 1961. Renamed by Cleveland DJ, Eddie O'Jay. Isles left in 1965. Massey left to become a record producer in 1971; Levert, Williams and Powell continued as a trio. Powell retired from touring due to illness in late 1975 (died 5/26/77); replaced by Sammy Strain, formerly with Little Anthony & The Imperials. Strain returned to his former group by 1993; replaced by Nathaniel Best. Levert's sons Gerald and Sean are members of the trio Levert. Gerald also charted a duet with Eddie.

DATE	POS	WKS	ARTIST–RECORD TITLE	LABEL & NO.
8/12/72	3	12	● 1. **Back Stabbers** #1 R&B hit (1 week)	Phil. Int. 3517
1/27/73	1 (1)	13	● 2. **Love Train** #1 R&B hit (4 weeks)	Phil. Int. 3524
6/30/73	33	2	3. Time To Get Down	Phil. Int. 3531
1/12/74	10	11	4. **Put Your Hands Together**	Phil. Int. 3535
5/4/74	9	10	● 5. **For The Love Of Money**	Phil. Int. 3544
11/15/75+	5	14	● 6. **I Love Music (Part 1)** #1 R&B hit (1 week)	Phil. Int. 3577
3/27/76	20	6	7. Livin' For The Weekend #1 R&B hit (2 weeks)	Phil. Int. 3587
6/3/78	4	11	● 8. **Use Ta Be My Girl** #1 R&B hit (5 weeks)	Phil. Int. 3642
1/5/80	28	5	9. Forever Mine all of above written & produced by Kenneth Gamble and Leon Huff	Phil. Int. 3727

O'KAYSIONS, The

R&B sextet from Wilson, North Carolina: Donny Weaver (lead singer), Ron Turner, Jim Spidel, Wayne Pittman, Jimmy Hennant and Bruce Joyner. Originally called The Kays.

DATE	POS	WKS	ARTIST–RECORD TITLE	LABEL & NO.
9/7/68	5	11	● 1. **Girl Watcher** first released on North State 1001 in 1968	ABC 11094

O'KEEFE, Danny

Born in Spokane, Washington. Singer/songwriter.

DATE	POS	WKS	ARTIST–RECORD TITLE	LABEL & NO.
9/23/72	9	10	1. **Good Time Charlie's Got The Blues**	Signpost 70006

OLDFIELD, Mike

Born on 5/15/53 in Reading, England. Classical-rock, multi-instrumentalist/composer.

DATE	POS	WKS	ARTIST–RECORD TITLE	LABEL & NO.
3/30/74	7	10	1. **Tubular Bells** [I] theme from the movie *The Exorcist* starring Linda Blair; edited version of the 49-minute album version	Virgin 55100

OLIVER

Born William Oliver Swofford on 2/22/45 in North Wilkesboro, North Carolina.

DATE	POS	WKS	ARTIST–RECORD TITLE	LABEL & NO.
6/7/69	3	11	1. **Good Morning Starshine** from the Broadway musical *Hair* starring Steve Curry	Jubilee 5659

DATE	POS	WKS	ARTIST–RECORD TITLE	LABEL & NO.
8/30/69	**2** (2)	12	● 2. **Jean** written by Rod McKuen; from the movie *The Prime of Miss Jean* *Brodie* starring Maggie Smith; #1 Adult Contemporary hit (4 weeks)	Crewe 334
12/20/69	35	2	3. Sunday Mornin' above 3 produced by Bob Crewe	Crewe 337
			## OLLIE & JERRY Duo of Ollie Brown and Jerry Knight (former member of Raydio).	
6/16/84	9	11	1. **Breakin'...There's No Stopping Us** from the movie *Breakin'* starring break-dancers Adolfo Quinones and Michael Chambers	Polydor 821708
			## OLSSON, Nigel Born on 2/10/49 in Merseyside, England. Drummer for Elton John's band, 1971–76.	
1/27/79	18	9	1. Dancin' Shoes	Bang 740
5/19/79	34	4	2. Little Bit Of Soap	Bang 4800
			## OLYMPICS, The R&B group formed at Centennial High School in Compton, California, in 1954 as the Challengers. Consisted of Walter Ward (lead), Eddie Lewis (tenor), Charles Fizer (baritone) and Walter Hammond (baritone). Melvin King replaced Fizer in 1958, remained in group as replacement for Hammond when Fizer returned in 1959. Fizer was was killed in Watts rioting.	
8/4/58	8	11	1. **Western Movies** [N] Hot 100 #8 / Best Seller #11	Demon 1508
6/8/63	40	2	2. The Bounce	Tri Disc 106
			## O'NEAL, Alexander Born on 11/15/53 in Natchez, Mississippi. Minneapolis-based R&B vocalist. Own band, Alexander, in the late 1970s. Lead singer of Flyte Tyme, which included Jimmy "Jam" Harris, Terry Lewis and Monte Moir and later evolved into The Time. Went solo in 1980. Co-producer of Janet Jackson's hit "Control."	
3/29/86	26	6	1. Saturday Love **CHERELLE with ALEXANDER O'NEAL** Sales #19	Tabu 05767
9/5/87	25	6	2. Fake Sales #24 / Airplay #27; #1 R&B hit (2 weeks)	Tabu 07100
3/5/88	28	6	3. Never Knew Love Like This **ALEXANDER O'NEAL featuring Cherrelle** Airplay #26 / Sales #28	Tabu 07646
			## O'NEAL, Shaquille Born on 3/6/72 in Newark, New Jersey. All-star center with the NBA's Orlando Magic. Stands 7'1". Starred in the 1994 movie *Blue Chips*.	
8/14/93	39	1	● 1. What's Up Doc? (Can We Rock?) **FU-SCHNICKENS with Shaquille O'Neal (Shaq-Fu)** Sales #21 / Airplay #66	Jive 42164
11/13/93	35	10	● 2. (I Know I Got) Skillz Sales #15; samples "Snake Eyes" by Main Source	Jive 42177

DATE	POS	WKS	ARTIST–RECORD TITLE	LABEL & NO.
			## 100 PROOF Aged in Soul	
			Soul group from Detroit: Clyde Wilson ("Steve Mancha"), lead; Joe Stubbs and Eddie Anderson ("Eddie Holiday"). Stubbs, brother of Levi Stubbs of the Four Tops, had been in The Contours and The Falcons.	
10/3/70	8	10	● 1. **Somebody's Been Sleeping**	Hot Wax 7004
			## ONE 2 MANY	
			Norwegian trio: keyboardist Dag Kolsrud, guitarist Jan Gisle Ytterdal and female vocalist Camilla Griehsel. Kolsrud was A-ha's world tour musical director.	
5/6/89	37	4	1. Downtown *Airplay #31*	A&M 1272
			## ONYX	
			Rap foursome based in Jamaica, New York: Sticky Fingaz, Big D.S., Fredro Star and Suave Sonny Caesar. Big D.S. left in 1995.	
6/26/93	4	14	▲ 1. **Slam** *Sales #3 / Airplay #23*	JMJ/RAL 77053
			## OPUS	
			Pop-rock quintet from Austria led by vocalist Herwig Rudisser.	
3/15/86	32	5	1. Live Is Life *Sales #23*	Polydor 883730
			## ORBISON, Roy	
			Born on 4/23/36 in Vernon, Texas. Died of a heart attack on 12/6/88 in Madison, Tennessee. Had own band, the Wink Westerners, in 1952. Attended North Texas State University with Pat Boone. First recorded for Je-Wel in early 1956 as leader of The Teen Kings. Toured with Sun Records shows to 1958. Toured with The Beatles in 1963. Wife Claudette killed in a motorcycle accident on 6/7/66; two sons died in a fire in 1968. Resurgence in career beginning in 1985. Inducted into the Rock and Roll Hall of Fame in 1987. Member of the supergroup Traveling Wilburys in 1988.	
6/20/60	2 (1)	15	● 1. **Only The Lonely (Know How I Feel)**	Monument 421
10/17/60	9	8	2. **Blue Angel**	Monument 425
12/31/60+	27	3	3. I'm Hurtin'	Monument 433
4/24/61	1 (1)	15	4. **Running Scared**	Monument 438
8/28/61	2 (1)	14	5. **Crying/**	
10/9/61	25	5	6. Candy Man	Monument 447
3/3/62	4	9	7. **Dream Baby (How Long Must I Dream)**	Monument 456
6/23/62	26	6	8. The Crowd	Monument 461
10/27/62	25	5	9. Leah/	
10/27/62	33	4	10. Workin' For The Man *Bob Moore (orch., all of above)*	Monument 467
2/23/63	7	10	11. **In Dreams**	Monument 806
6/22/63	22	5	12. Falling *B-side is the original version of Jim Reeves' 1966 #1 Country hit "Distant Drums"*	Monument 815
9/28/63	5	10	13. **Mean Woman Blues/** *#11 R&B and Country hit for Elvis Presley in 1957 (from the movie Loving You)*	
10/12/63	29	5	14. Blue Bayou	Monument 824

DATE	POS	WKS	ARTIST–RECORD TITLE	LABEL & NO.
12/21/63	15	5	15. Pretty Paper [X] written by Willie Nelson	Monument 830
4/25/64	9	9	16. **It's Over**	Monument 837
9/5/64	**1 (3)**	14	● 17. **Oh, Pretty Woman** **ROY ORBISON And The Candy Men**	Monument 851
2/20/65	21	6	18. Goodnight	Monument 873
8/7/65	39	2	19. (Say) You're My Girl	Monument 891
9/18/65	25	5	20. Ride Away	MGM 13386
2/12/66	31	4	21. Breakin' Up Is Breakin' My Heart	MGM 13446
5/21/66	39	2	22. Twinkle Toes	MGM 13498
2/18/89	9	11	23. **You Got It** Sales #6 / Airplay #15; written by Roy Orbison, Jeff Lynne and Tom Petty; #1 Adult Contemporary hit (2 weeks)	Virgin 99245

ORCHESTRAL MANOEUVRES IN THE DARK

English electro-pop outfit formed in 1978 and fronted by keyboardists/vocalists Andrew McCluskey and Paul Humphreys. From 1980 to 1989, included drummer Malcolm Holmes and multi-instrumentalist Martin Cooper. Humphreys left band in 1989.

DATE	POS	WKS	ARTIST–RECORD TITLE	LABEL & NO.
10/12/85	26	7	1. So In Love Sales #23 / Airplay #23	A&M 2746
4/5/86	4	13	2. **If You Leave** Airplay #3 / Sales #5; from the movie *Pretty In Pink* starring Molly Ringwald	A&M 2811
11/1/86	19	7	3. (Forever) Live And Die Sales #18 / Airplay #23	A&M 2872
4/16/88	16	9	4. Dreaming Sales #15 / Airplay #15	A&M 3002

ORIGINAL CASTE, The

Canadian quintet. Dixie Lee Innes, lead singer.

DATE	POS	WKS	ARTIST–RECORD TITLE	LABEL & NO.
2/7/70	34	2	1. One Tin Soldier version by Coven became the theme for the 1971 movie *Billy Jack* starring Tom Laughlin	T-A 186

ORIGINALS, The

Soul group formed in Detroit in 1966. Consisted of Freddie Gorman (bass), Crathman Spencer and Henry Dixon (tenors) and Walter Gaines (baritone). Spencer replaced by Ty Hunter (of The Glass House) in 1971.

DATE	POS	WKS	ARTIST–RECORD TITLE	LABEL & NO.
10/18/69	14	13	1. Baby, I'm For Real #1 R&B hit (5 weeks)	Soul 35066
3/7/70	12	9	2. The Bells above 2 written and produced by Marvin Gaye	Soul 35069

ORLANDO, Tony

Born Michael Anthony Orlando Cassavitis on 4/3/44 in New York City of Greek/Puerto Rican parents. Discovered by producer Don Kirshner. Lead singer of Dawn, 1970–77. Hosted weekly TV variety show "Tony Orlando & Dawn," 1974–76. Also see Wind.

DATE	POS	WKS	ARTIST–RECORD TITLE	LABEL & NO.
5/29/61	39	2	1. Halfway To Paradise	Epic 9441
9/4/61	15	7	2. Bless You above 2 arranged by Carole King	Epic 9452

"I Will Always Love You"

RCA
PB 13260

from the movie
"The Best Little Whorehouse in Texas"

Robert Palmer's clean-cut image, combined with his blue-eyed, soulful vocal style, made him a natural in the MTV era. The British singer, who'd earlier recorded with such artists as Alan Bown and Vinegar Joe, had a No. 28 hit with his 1990 single "You're Amazing."

Dolly Parton's 1982 single "I Will Always Love You" climbed to a respectable position of No. 53. Redone by Whitney Houston on 1992's soundtrack to *The Bodyguard*, it became one of the biggest No. 1 hits of the '90s.

The Party's unique claim to fame? They were cast members of 1988's revival of The Mickey Mouse Club. The quintet's 1991 single "In My Dreams" scampered to No. 34; none dared call it cheesy.

Paul & Paula—not to be confused with similar '60s pair Dick & DeeDee—declared their love on the 1963 No. 1 smash "Hey Paula." Six months later appeared its unavoidable followup, "First Quarrel."

Nia Peeples's successful stint as an actress—she starred on the TV series adaptation of *Fame* and hosted her own syndicated dance show—did not preclude having a simultaneous singing career. "Trouble" reached No. 35 in 1988.

Peter And Gordon's second Top 10 hit, "I Go To Pieces," entered the charts in early 1965 and climbed to No. 9. Its writer was none other than American rocker Del Shannon, a much-admired star in the U.K.

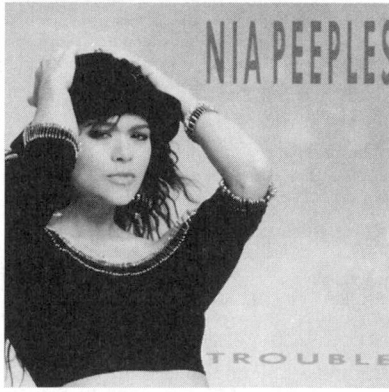

First Quarrel
PAUL & PAULA
b/w
School Is Thru

PHILIPS
40114

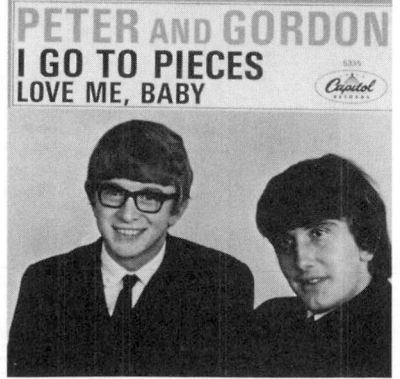

PETER AND GORDON
I GO TO PIECES
LOVE ME, BABY
Capitol

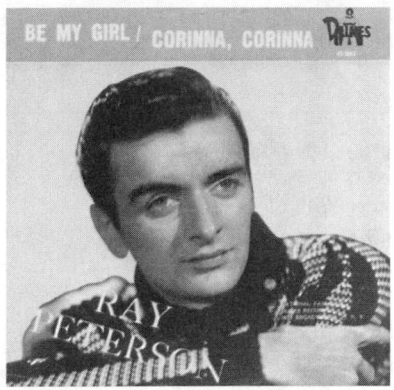

Paul Petersen's "My Dad" single was released in 1962, scant months after Shelley Fabares—his co-star on TV's "The Donna Reed Show"—released her own "Johnny Angel," which reached No. 1. Petersen's song came close, but peaked at No. 6.

Ray Peterson saw his Phil Spector-produced "Corinna, Corinna" rise to No. 9 in early 1961. The singer, who'd previously recorded for RCA, released the disc on his own Dunes label.

Tom Petty & the Heartbreakers' 1991 single "Learning To Fly" was co-produced by former ELO leader Jeff Lynne and climbed to No. 28. The singer's lengthy career was superbly documented in late 1995 on a highly praised 6-CD set issued by MCA Records.

Bobby (Boris) Pickett tied together the concept of monsters and holidays with 1962's dual hits "Monster Mash" and "Monsters' Holiday," the latter a No. 30 seasonal hit. Apparently Easter was not as approachable a target as Halloween and Christmas.

Gene Pitney was one of the '60s most memorable interpreters of the songs of Burt Bacharach and Hal David. Among his hits penned by the pair: 1963's "Twenty Four Hours From Tulsa," "True Love Never Runs Smooth," and the previous year's "(The Man Who Shot) Liberty Valance" and "Only Love Can Break A Heart."

The Platters accumulated 22 Top 40 hits between 1955 and 1967, with four No. 1 hits among them. Though their 1961 hit "To Each His Own" only rose to No. 21, in 1946 it had been a No. 1 hit for three different artists.

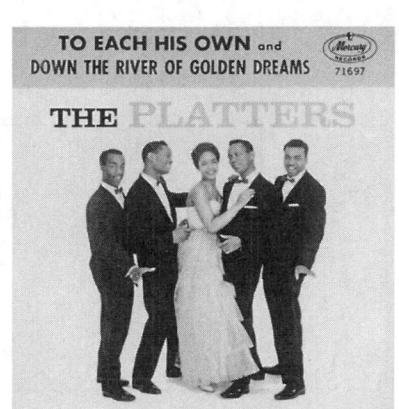

DATE	POS	WKS	ARTIST–RECORD TITLE	LABEL & NO.
			ORLEANS	
			Rock group founded in New York City by John Hall with the Hoppen brothers (Lawrence and Lance), Wells Kelly and Jerry Marotta. Hall and Marotta left in 1977, replaced by Bob Leinbach and R.A. Martin.	
8/30/75	6	11	1. **Dance With Me**	Asylum 45261
8/14/76	5	12	2. **Still The One**	Asylum 45336
4/7/79	11	9	3. Love Takes Time	Infinity 50006
			ORLONS, The	
			R&B group from Philadelphia. Consisted of lead Rosetta Hightower (born 6/23/44), Marlena Davis (born 10/4/44), Steve Caldwell (born 11/22/42) and Shirley Brickley (born 12/9/44; died of a gunshot 10/13/77). Davis and Caldwell left in 1964 and were replaced by Audrey Brickley. Disbanded in 1968.	
6/23/62	2 (2)	11	1. **The Wah Watusi**	Cameo 218
11/3/62	4	11	2. **Don't Hang Up**	Cameo 231
3/2/63	3	10	3. **South Street**	Cameo 243
7/6/63	12	7	4. Not Me	Cameo 257
10/19/63	19	5	5. Cross Fire!	Cameo 273
			ORR, Benjamin	
			Born Benjamin Orzechowski on 8/9/55 in Cleveland. Bassist/vocalist of The Cars.	
1/17/87	24	6	1. Stay The Night Airplay #18 / Sales #26	Elektra 69506
			ORRALL, Robert Ellis, with Carlene Carter	
			Singer/songwriter/pianist Orrall is a native of Lynnfield, Massachusetts (born 5/4/55). Carter (born 9/26/55 to country singers June Carter Cash and Carl Smith) was married to Nick Lowe.	
5/7/83	32	3	1. I Couldn't Say No	RCA 13431
			OSBORNE, Jeffrey	
			Born on 3/9/48 in Providence, Rhode Island. Soul singer/songwriter/drummer. Lead singer of L.T.D. until 1980.	
8/14/82	39	2	1. I Really Don't Need No Light	A&M 2410
11/20/82	29	7	2. On The Wings Of Love	A&M 2434
8/20/83	25	6	3. Don't You Get So Mad	A&M 2561
12/17/83+	30	8	4. Stay With Me Tonight	A&M 2591
10/6/84	40	2	5. The Last Time I Made Love **JOYCE KENNEDY & JEFFREY OSBORNE**	A&M 2656
3/2/85	38	2	6. The Borderlines all of above (except #5) produced by George Duke	A&M 2695
6/28/86	13	11	7. You Should Be Mine (The Woo Woo Song) Sales #13 / Airplay #16	A&M 2814
7/25/87	12	9	8. Love Power **DIONNE WARWICK & JEFFREY OSBORNE** Sales #7 / Airplay #14; #1 Adult Contemporary hit (1 week)	Arista 9567

DATE	POS	WKS	ARTIST–RECORD TITLE	LABEL & NO.
			OSBORNE, Joan	
			Born on 7/8/62 in Anchorage, Kentucky. Singer/songwriter/guitarist. Based in New York City.	Blue Gor./Mer. 852368

12/9/95+	4	19↑	● 1. **One Of Us**
			       Sales #5 / Airplay #5; written by Eric Bazilian (Hooters); contains
			       an introduction of "The Airplane Ride" by Nell Hampton	

			OSBOURNE, Ozzy	
			Born John Michael Osbourne on 12/3/48 in Birmingham, England. Heavy-metal artist; former lead singer of Black Sabbath. Appeared in the 1986 movie *Trick Or Treat*.	

4/22/89	8	12	● 1. **Close My Eyes Forever**
			      LITA FORD (with Ozzy Osbourne)
			      Sales #4 / Airplay #13
				RCA 8899

3/21/92	28	7	2. Mama, I'm Coming Home Sales #17 / Airplay #75	Epic/Assc. 74093
			OSMOND, Donny	
			Born on 12/9/57 in Ogden, Utah. Seventh son of George and Olive Osmond. Donny became a member of The Osmonds in 1963. Owner of production company Night Star.	

5/1/71	7	11	● 1. **Sweet And Innocent**
			      DONNY OSMOND of The Osmonds
			      recorded in 1958 by Roy Orbison on RCA 7381
				MGM 14227

8/21/71	1 (3)	13	● 2. **Go Away Little Girl**	MGM 14285
12/4/71+	9	9	● 3. **Hey Girl/**	
		9	4. I Knew You When	MGM 14322
3/4/72	3	10	● 5. **Puppy Love**	MGM 14367
6/17/72	13	8	6. Too Young #1 hit for Nat "King" Cole in 1951	MGM 14407
9/16/72	13	9	7. Why/	
		9	8. Lonely Boy	MGM/Kolob 14424
3/24/73	8	9	● 9. **The Twelfth Of Never**	MGM/Kolob 14503
8/4/73	23	7	10. A Million To One/	
8/4/73	25	7	11. Young Love	MGM/Kolob 14583

12/15/73+	14	8	12. Are You Lonesome Tonight
			      #4 hit for Vaughn Deleath in 1927; above 8 produced by Mike
			      Curb and Don Costa
				MGM/Kolob 14677

7/24/76	38	3	13. C'mon Marianne	Polydor/Kolob 14320
4/15/89	2 (1)	11	14. **Soldier Of Love** Sales #1(1) / Airplay #4	Capitol 44369
7/15/89	13	9	15. Sacred Emotion Airplay #11 / Sales #15	Capitol 44379
11/3/90	21	9	16. My Love Is A Fire Airplay #18 / Sales #28	Capitol 44634
			OSMOND, Donny And Marie	
			Brother-and-sister co-hosts of own musical/variety TV series, 1976–78. Starred in the movie *Goin' Coconuts*.	

7/27/74	4	10	● 1. **I'm Leaving It (All) Up To You**
			      first recorded by Don & Dewey in 1957; #1 Adult Contemporary hit
			      (1 week)
				MGM/Kolob 14735

DATE	POS	WKS	ARTIST–RECORD TITLE	LABEL & NO.
12/14/74+	8	10	2. **Morning Side Of The Mountain** #1 Adult Contemporary hit (1 week); #16 hit for Paul Weston in 1951	MGM/Kolob 14765
1/24/76	14	13	3. Deep Purple #1 hit for Larry Clinton in 1939	MGM/Kolob 14840
			DONNY & MARIE:	
12/25/76+	21	8	4. Ain't Nothing Like The Real Thing	Polydor/Kolob 14363
1/7/78	38	3	5. (You're My) Soul And Inspiration	Polydor/Kolob 14439
11/18/78	38	2	6. On The Shelf all of above produced by Mike Curb	Polydor/Kolob 14510

DATE	POS	WKS	ARTIST–RECORD TITLE	LABEL & NO.
			OSMOND, Little Jimmy	
			Born on 4/16/63 in Canoga Park, California. Youngest member of the Osmond family.	MGM 14376
6/3/72	38	3	1. Long Haired Lover From Liverpool with The Mike Curb Congregation	

DATE	POS	WKS	ARTIST–RECORD TITLE	LABEL & NO.
			OSMOND, Marie	
			Born Olive Marie Osmond on 10/13/59 in Ogden, Utah. Began performing in concert with her brothers at age 14. Co-hosted the TV series "Ripley's Believe It Or Not," 1985–86. Emerged as a top country artist in the '80s.	
10/6/73	5	12	● 1. **Paper Roses** #1 Country hit (2 weeks)	MGM/Kolob 14609
4/5/75	40	2	2. Who's Sorry Now #3 hit for Isham Jones in 1923; above 2 produced by Sonny James	MGM/Kolob 14786
6/4/77	39	1	3. This Is The Way That I Feel	Polydor/Kolob 14385

DATE	POS	WKS	ARTIST–RECORD TITLE	LABEL & NO.
			OSMONDS, The	
			Family group from Ogden, Utah. Alan (born 6/22/49), Wayne (born 8/28/51), Merrill (born 4/30/53), Jay (born 3/2/55) and Donny Osmond (born 12/9/57). Began as a quartet in 1959, singing religious and barbershop-quartet songs. Regulars on Andy Williams's TV show, 1962–67. Alan, Wayne, Merrill and Jay turned to country music as The Osmond Brothers in the early '80s.	
1/23/71	1 (5)	12	● 1. **One Bad Apple**	MGM 14193
5/29/71	14	7	2. Double Lovin'	MGM 14259
9/18/71	3	12	● 3. **Yo-Yo** written by Joe South	MGM 14295
1/29/72	4	12	● 4. **Down By The Lazy River**	MGM 14324
7/8/72	14	7	5. Hold Her Tight	MGM 14405
11/11/72	14	8	6. Crazy Horses	MGM/Kolob 14450
7/7/73	36	2	7. Goin' Home	MGM/Kolob 14562
10/6/73	36	3	8. Let Me In	MGM/Kolob 14617
9/21/74	10	7	9. **Love Me For A Reason**	MGM/Kolob 14746
8/23/75	22	6	10. The Proud One #1 Adult Contemporary hit (1 week)	MGM/Kolob 14791

DATE	POS	WKS	ARTIST–RECORD TITLE	LABEL & NO.
			O'SULLIVAN, Gilbert	
			Born Raymond O'Sullivan on 12/1/46 in Waterford, Ireland.	
7/1/72	1 (6)	15	● 1. **Alone Again (Naturally)** #1 Adult Contemporary hit (6 weeks)	MAM 3619

DATE	POS	WKS	ARTIST–RECORD TITLE	LABEL & NO.
11/11/72	2 (2)	14	● 2. **Clair** #1 Adult Contemporary hit (3 weeks)	MAM 3626
4/7/73	17	8	3. Out Of The Question	MAM 3628
7/14/73	7	11	● 4. **Get Down**	MAM 3629
11/10/73	25	4	5. Ooh Baby	MAM 3633
			all of above written by O'Sullivan and produced by Gordon Mills	

OTHER ONES, The

Rock sextet consisting of Australian siblings Jayney (vocals), Alf (vocals) and Johnny (bass) Klimek, and Germans Andreas Schwarz-Ruszczynski (guitar), Stephen Gottwald (keyboards) and Uwe Hoffmann (drums).

DATE	POS	WKS	ARTIST–RECORD TITLE	LABEL & NO.
10/10/87	29	4	1. Holiday Airplay #28 / Sales #32	Virgin 99428

OTIS, Johnny, Show

Born John Veliotes of Greek parentage on 12/8/21 in Vallejo, California. R&B bandleader/composer. Johnny's R&B Caravan featured the top R&B artists of the 1950s. Inducted into the Rock and Roll Hall of Fame in 1994.

DATE	POS	WKS	ARTIST–RECORD TITLE	LABEL & NO.
6/30/58	9	15	1. **Willie And The Hand Jive** Hot 100 #9 / Best Seller #14 / Jockey #17	Capitol 3966

OTIS & CARLA—see REDDING, Otis, and/or THOMAS, Carla

OUTFIELD, The

Pop-rock trio formed in London in 1984: Tony Lewis (vocals, bass), John Spinks (guitar) and Alan Jackman (drums). Jackman left by 1990; Lewis and Spinks continued as a duo.

DATE	POS	WKS	ARTIST–RECORD TITLE	LABEL & NO.
3/22/86	6	12	1. **Your Love** Sales #6 / Airplay #6	Columbia 05796
7/12/86	19	7	2. All The Love In The World Airplay #17 / Sales #21	Columbia 05894
7/25/87	31	5	3. Since You've Been Gone Airplay #31 / Sales #32	Columbia 07170
4/29/89	25	6	4. Voices Of Babylon Sales #23 / Airplay #25	Columbia 68601
12/1/90+	21	9	5. For You Sales #21 / Airplay #22	MCA 53935

OUTKAST

Atlanta-based male rap duo: Andre "Dre" Benjamin and Antoine "Big Boi" Patton.

DATE	POS	WKS	ARTIST–RECORD TITLE	LABEL & NO.
4/9/94	37	5	● 1. Player's Ball Sales #15	LaFace 24060

OUTLAWS

Southern-rock band formed in Tampa in 1974. Consisted of guitarists Hughie Thomasson, Billy Jones and Henry Paul, with drummer Monte Yoho and bassist Frank O'Keefe (replaced by Harvey Arnold in 1977). Paul, Yoho and Arnold left by 1980. Paul was a member of the country trio BlackHawk by 1993. Jones died on 2/7/95 (age 45).

DATE	POS	WKS	ARTIST–RECORD TITLE	LABEL & NO.
10/11/75	34	3	1. There Goes Another Love Song	Arista 0150
2/14/81	31	4	2. (Ghost) Riders In The Sky #1 hit (12 weeks) for Vaughn Monroe in 1949	Arista 0582

DATE	POS	WKS	ARTIST–RECORD TITLE	LABEL & NO.
			OUTSIDERS, The	
			Cleveland rock quintet: Sonny Geraci (lead singer), Tom King (guitar), Bill Bruno (lead guitar), Mert Madsen (bass) and Rick Baker (drums). Geraci later led band Climax.	
3/26/66	5	10	1. **Time Won't Let Me**	Capitol 5573
6/4/66	21	5	2. Girl In Love	Capitol 5646
8/20/66	15	6	3. Respectable	Capitol 5701
			written by The Isley Brothers	
12/10/66	37	2	4. Help Me Girl	Capitol 5759
			OWEN, Reg, And His Orchestra	
			Born in February 1928. British bandleader.	
12/22/58+	10	13	1. **Manhattan Spiritual** [I]	Palette 5005
			OWENS, Buck	
			Born Alvis Edgar Owens on 8/12/29 in Sherman, Texas; raised in Mesa, Arizona. Country singer/guitarist/songwriter. Has charted 21 #1 country hits. Moved to Bakersfield, California in 1951. Co-host of TV's "Hee Haw," 1969-86. Backing group: The Buckaroos.	
2/13/65	25	5	1. I've Got A Tiger By The Tail	Capitol 5336
			#1 Country hit (5 weeks)	
			OWENS, Donnie	
			Born on 10/30/38 in Pennsylvania. Accidentally shot to death on 10/27/94. Pop singer. Moved to Phoenix in the early '50s.	
11/3/58	25	8	1. Need You	Guyden 2001
			Duane Eddy (acoustic guitar); The Ben Denton Singers (backing vocals)	
			OXO	
			West Coast pop-rock quartet led by former Foxy member Ish "Angel" Ledesma.	
4/2/83	28	6	1. Whirly Girl	Geffen 29765
			OZARK MOUNTAIN DAREDEVILS	
			Country-rock group from Springfield, Missouri. Nucleus: Larry Lee (keyboards, guitar), Steve Cash (harp), John Dillon (guitar) and Michael Granda (bass).	
6/8/74	25	5	1. If You Wanna Get To Heaven	A&M 1515
3/22/75	3	12	2. **Jackie Blue**	A&M 1654

DATE	POS	WKS	ARTIST–RECORD TITLE	LABEL & NO.

P

PABLO CRUISE

San Francisco pop-rock quartet formed in 1973: Dave Jenkins (vocals, guitar), Bud Cockrell (member of It's A Beautiful Day; bass; vocals), Cory Lerios (keyboards, vocals) and Stephen Price (drums). Cockrell replaced by Bruce Day in 1977. John Pierce replaced Day, and guitarist Angelo Rossi joined in 1980.

DATE	POS	WKS	ARTIST–RECORD TITLE	LABEL & NO.
6/11/77	**6**	14	1. **Whatcha Gonna Do?**	A&M 1920
7/1/78	**6**	12	2. **Love Will Find A Way**	A&M 2048
10/21/78	**21**	8	3. Don't Want To Live Without It	A&M 2076
11/10/79	**19**	10	4. I Want You Tonight	A&M 2195
7/25/81	**13**	11	5. Cool Love	A&M 2349

PACIFIC GAS & ELECTRIC

West Coast blues-rock quintet. Charles Allen, lead singer (died 5/7/90, age 48, Los Angeles). Through 1970 included guitarists Glenn Schwartz and Tom Marshall, bassist Brent Block and drummer Frank Cook. Allen spearheaded a new lineup in 1971, group name shortened to PG&E.

DATE	POS	WKS	ARTIST–RECORD TITLE	LABEL & NO.
6/20/70	**14**	9	1. Are You Ready? The Blackberries (backing vocals)	Columbia 45158

PAGE, Martin

Born on 9/23/59 in Southampton, England. Singer/songwriter. Wrote the hits "We Built This City," "These Dreams" and "King Of Wishful Thinking."

DATE	POS	WKS	ARTIST–RECORD TITLE	LABEL & NO.
2/4/95	**14**	26	1. In The House Of Stone And Light Airplay #4 / Sales #55; #1 Adult Contemporary hit (4 weeks)	Mercury 858940

PAGE, Patti

Born Clara Ann Fowler on 11/8/27 in Muskogee, Oklahoma. One of 11 children. Raised in Tulsa. On radio KTUL with Al Klauser & His Oklahomans, as Ann Fowler, late 1940s. Another singer was billed as "Patti Page" for the Page Milk Company show on KTUL. When she left, Fowler took her place and name. With the Jimmy Joy band in 1947. On "Breakfast Club," Chicago radio in 1947; signed by Mercury Records. Used multi-voice effect on records from 1947. Own TV series "The Patti Page Show," 1955–58, and "The Big Record," 1957–58. Appeared in the 1960 movie *Elmer Gantry*.

DATE	POS	WKS	ARTIST–RECORD TITLE	LABEL & NO.
12/18/54+	**8**	7	1. **Let Me Go, Lover!** Jockey #8 / Juke Box #12 / Best Seller #24	Mercury 70511
11/12/55	**16**	8	2. Croce Di Oro (Cross Of Gold) Top 100 #16 / Juke Box #16 / Jockey #17 / Best Seller #20	Mercury 70713
1/14/56	**11**	8	3. Go On With The Wedding Top 100 #11 / Juke Box #12 / Jockey #16 / Best Seller #17; Jack Rael (orch., all of above)	Mercury 70766
6/16/56	● **2 (2)**	22	4. **Allegheny Moon** Top 100 #2 / Jockey #2 / Juke Box #2 / Best Seller #5	Mercury 70878
11/3/56	**11**	12	5. Mama From The Train Top 100 #11 / Jockey #12 / Juke Box #12 / Best Seller #17	Mercury 70971
3/23/57	**14**	6	6. A Poor Man's Roses (Or A Rich Man's Gold) Jockey #14 / Top 100 #27	Mercury 71059
6/3/57	**3**	17	7. Old Cape Cod/ Jockey #3 / Top 100 #7 / Best Seller #8	
6/3/57	**12**	5	8. Wondering Jockey #12 / Top 100 #35	Mercury 71101

DATE	POS	WKS	ARTIST–RECORD TITLE	LABEL & NO.
11/11/57	23	3	9. I'll Remember Today Jockey #23 / Best Seller #31 / Top 100 #32	Mercury 71189
2/10/58	13	8	10. Belonging To Someone Jockey #13 / Best Seller #32 / Top 100 #34	Mercury 71247
5/5/58	20	1	11. Another Time, Another Place Jockey #20 / Top 100 #81; title song from the movie starring Lana Turner	Mercury 71294
6/30/58	9	10	12. Left Right Out Of Your Heart (Hi Lee Hi Lo Hi Lup Up, Up) Jockey #9 / Hot 100 #13 / Best Seller #14	Mercury 71331
10/20/58	39	1	13. Fibbin' Vic Schoen (orch., above 10)	Mercury 71355
7/4/60	31	5	14. One Of Us (Will Weep Tonight)	Mercury 71639
5/12/62	27	4	15. Most People Get Married	Mercury 71950
5/22/65	8	9	16. **Hush, Hush, Sweet Charlotte** title song from the movie starring Bette Davis	Columbia 43251

PAGE, Tommy

Born on 5/24/69 in West Caldwell, New Jersey.

DATE	POS	WKS	ARTIST–RECORD TITLE	LABEL & NO.
4/15/89	29	6	1. A Shoulder To Cry On Airplay #27 / Sales #30	Sire 27645
2/24/90	1 (1)	13	● 2. **I'll Be Your Everything** Sales #1(1) / Airplay #2; backing vocals by 3 members of New Kids On The Block	Sire 19959

PAIGE, Kevin

White soul-pop singer from Memphis.

DATE	POS	WKS	ARTIST–RECORD TITLE	LABEL & NO.
10/14/89	18	10	1. Don't Shut Me Out Sales #15 / Airplay #20; also on the B-side of #2 below	Chrysalis 23389
2/24/90	29	5	2. Anything I Want Airplay #28 / Sales #31	Chrysalis 23444

PALMER, Robert

Born Alan Palmer on 1/19/49 in Batley, England; raised on the Mediterranean island of Malta. Formed first band, Mandrake Paddle Steamer, in 1969. Lead singer of short-lived supergroup The Power Station.

DATE	POS	WKS	ARTIST–RECORD TITLE	LABEL & NO.
5/6/78	16	9	1. Every Kinda People	Island 100
8/11/79	14	10	2. Bad Case Of Loving You (Doctor, Doctor)	Island 49016
3/8/86	1 (1)	14	● 3. **Addicted To Love** Sales #1(2) / Airplay #2	Island 99570
6/28/86	33	5	4. Hyperactive Sales #29 / Airplay #36	Island 99545
9/13/86	2 (1)	13	5. **I Didn't Mean To Turn You On** Sales #2 / Airplay #2; above 3 produced by Bernard Edwards (Chic)	Island 99537
7/16/88	2 (2)	14	6. **Simply Irresistible** Sales #2 / Airplay #2	EMI-Man. 50133
11/12/88	19	9	7. Early In The Morning Airplay #18 / Sales #19	EMI-Man. 50157
12/22/90+	28	5	8. You're Amazing Sales #21 / Airplay #36	EMI 50338
3/2/91	16	10	9. Mercy Mercy Me (The Ecology)/I Want You Airplay #10 / Sales #21; medley of 2 Marvin Gaye hits	EMI 50344

DATE	POS	WKS	ARTIST–RECORD TITLE	LABEL & NO.
1/9/93	**10**	25	**PAPERBOY** Male rapper from Los Angeles. ▲ 1. **Ditty** Sales #4 / Airplay #21	Next Plat. 357012
7/13/74	**1** (1)	11	**PAPER LACE** English quintet formed in 1969: Phil Wright (born 4/9/48; lead singer, drums), Cliff Fish (bass), Michael Vaughan (lead guitar) and Chris Morris (guitar). Morris later replaced by Carlo Santanna. ● 1. **The Night Chicago Died**	Mercury 73492
5/6/67	**20**	5	**PARADE, The** Los Angeles pop-rock trio led by Jerry Riopelle, and including Murray MacLeod and Smokey Roberds. 1. Sunshine Girl	A&M 841
9/26/60	**18**	7	**PARADONS, The** R&B vocal group from Bakersfield, California: West Tyler, Chuck Weldon, Billy Myers and William Powers. 1. Diamonds And Pearls	Milestone 2003
10/2/61 3/3/62	**5** **34**	11 3	**PARIS SISTERS, The** Albeth, Priscilla and Sherrell Paris from San Francisco. First recorded for Decca in 1954. 1. **I Love How You Love Me** 2. He Knows I Love Him Too Much *above 2 produced by Phil Spector*	Gregmark 6 Gregmark 10
3/12/55 2/9/57	**5** **12**	17 6	**PARKER, Fess** Born on 8/16/27 in Fort Worth, Texas. Actor; starred in the movie *Davy Crockett* and TV's "Daniel Boone," 1964–70. 1. **Ballad Of Davy Crockett** Best Seller #5 / Jockey #10; introduced by Parker in the 12/15/54 "Disneyland" TV episode "Davy Crockett Indian Fighter" 2. Wringle Wrangle Best Seller #12 / Top 100 #21; from the movie *Westward Ho The Wagons* starring Parker	Columbia 40449 Disneyland 43
6/15/85	**39**	3	**PARKER, Graham** Born on 11/18/50 in East London. Pub-rock vocalist/guitarist/songwriter. 1. Wake Up (Next To You) **GRAHAM PARKER AND THE SHOT**	Elektra 69654
2/11/78	**8**	16	**PARKER, Ray, Jr./Raydio** Born on 5/1/54 in Detroit. Prominent session guitarist in California; worked with Stevie Wonder, Barry White and others. Formed band Raydio in 1977 with Arnell Carmichael, Jerry Knight, Larry Tolbert, Darren Carmichael and Charles Fearing. Parker went solo in 1982. Knight later recorded in duo Ollie & Jerry. **RAYDIO:** ● 1. **Jack And Jill**	Arista 0283

DATE	POS	WKS	ARTIST–RECORD TITLE	LABEL & NO.
6/9/79	9	14	2. **You Can't Change That**	Arista 0399
			RAY PARKER JR. & RAYDIO:	
6/7/80	30	5	3. Two Places At The Same Time	Arista 0494
4/25/81	4	15	4. **A Woman Needs Love (Just Like You Do)** #1 R&B hit (2 weeks)	Arista 0592
8/8/81	21	6	5. That Old Song	Arista 0616
			RAY PARKER JR.:	
4/10/82	4	14	6. **The Other Woman**	Arista 0669
8/21/82	38	3	7. Let Me Go	Arista 0695
1/15/83	35	4	8. Bad Boy	Arista 1030
12/10/83+	12	11	9. I Still Can't Get Over Loving You	Arista 9116
6/30/84	1 (3)	14	● 10. **Ghostbusters** from 1984's #1 box-office movie *Ghostbusters* starring Bill Murray; #1 R&B hit (2 weeks)	Arista 9212
12/1/84+	14	11	11. Jamie Airplay #11 / Sales #18	Arista 9293
10/26/85	34	4	12. Girls Are More Fun	Arista 9352
9/22/90	32	4	13. All I'm Missing Is You **GLENN MEDEIROS Featuring Ray Parker Jr.** Sales #29 / Airplay #29	MCA 53886
			PARKER, Robert	
			Born on 10/14/30 in Crescent City, Louisiana. Saxophonist/vocalist/ bandleader. In Professor Longhair's (Roy Byrd) band from 1949. Led house band at Club Tijuana, New Orleans. Prolific session work.	
5/21/66	7	9	1. **Barefootin'**	Nola 721
			PARKS, Michael	
			Born on 4/4/38 in Corona, California. Movie and TV actor/singer. Appeared in the movies *The Man Who Came To Dinner*, *Night Must Fall*, *The Wild Seed* and *Back In Town*. Starred in the 1963 TV series "Channing"; portrayed Jim Bronson in the 1969 TV series "Then Came Bronson."	
3/28/70	20	8	1. Long Lonesome Highway introduced by Parks on 10/29/69 on his TV series "Then Came Bronson"	MGM 14104
			PARLIAMENT	
			Funk aggregation that evolved from The Parliaments. Spearheaded by George Clinton, part of his "A Parliafunkadelicament Thang" corporation. The group's nearly 40 members also recorded under the names Funkadelic, P. Funk All Stars and Parlet, among others.	
6/12/76	15	10	● 1. Tear The Roof Off The Sucker (Give Up The Funk)	Casablanca 856
2/25/78	16	12	● 2. Flash Light #1 R&B hit (3 weeks)	Casablanca 909
			PARLIAMENTS, The	
			Soul group consisting of George Clinton (lead), Raymond Davis, Calvin Simon, Clarence "Fuzzy" Haskins and Grady Thomas. Later evolved into Parliament/Funkadelic aggregation. In 1977, Haskins, Simon and Thomas split from the aggregation; in 1981 they recorded as Funkadelic for LAX Records.	
8/5/67	20	7	1. (I Wanna) Testify	Revilot 207

DATE	POS	WKS	ARTIST–RECORD TITLE	LABEL & NO.
			PARR, John	
			Born in Nottingham, England. Singer/songwriter.	
2/2/85	**23**	8	1. Naughty Naughty	Atlantic 89612
			Airplay #22 / Sales #25	
7/20/85	**1** (2)	14	2. **St. Elmo's Fire (Man In Motion)**	Atlantic 89541
			Sales #1(2) / Airplay #1(1); title song from the movie starring Emilio Estevez and Rob Lowe	
			PARSONS, Alan, Project	
			Duo formed in London in 1975. Consisted of producer Alan Parsons (guitar, keyboards) and lyricist Eric Woolfson (vocals, keyboards). Both had worked at the Abbey Road Studios; Parsons was an engineer, Woolfson a songwriter. Parsons engineered Pink Floyd's *Dark Side Of The Moon* and The Beatles' *Abbey Road* albums. Project features varying musicians and vocalists.	
9/11/76	**37**	2	1. (The System Of) Doctor Tarr And Professor Fether	20th Century 2297
9/24/77	**36**	3	2. I Wouldn't Want To Be Like You	Arista 0260
			ALAN PARSONS	
11/17/79	**27**	8	3. Damned If I Do	Arista 0454
1/24/81	**16**	10	4. Games People Play	Arista 0573
			Lenny Zakatek (vocal, above 2)	
6/6/81	**15**	12	5. Time	Arista 0598
7/31/82	**3**	17	6. **Eye In The Sky**	Arista 0696
3/24/84	**15**	8	7. Don't Answer Me	Arista 9160
6/23/84	**34**	3	8. Prime Time	Arista 9208
			all of above written by Parsons and Woolfson	
			PARSONS, Bill—see BARE, Bobby	
			PARTLAND BROTHERS	
			Canadian duo: Chris (vocals, guitars) and G.P. (vocals, percussion) Partland.	
6/6/87	**27**	5	1. Soul City	Manhattan 50065
			Sales #26 / Airplay #27	
			PARTNERS IN KRYME	
			Rap duo from New York: DJ James Alpern and rapper Richard Usher. Met while speech communications majors at Syracuse University. Kryme stands for Keeping Rhythm Your Motivating Energy.	
5/12/90	**13**	8	● 1. Turtle Power!	SBK 07325
			Sales #12 / Airplay #17; from the movie *Teenage Mutant Ninja Turtles* starring Elias Koteas	
			PARTON, Dolly	
			Born on 1/19/46 in Sevier County, Tennessee. Leading female artist of the country charts. Worked on Knoxville radio show at age 11. First recorded for Gold Band in 1957. To Nashville in 1964. Replaced Norma Jean on the Porter Wagoner TV show, 1967–74. Joined the *Grand Ole Opry* in 1969. Starred in the movies *9 To 5*, *The Best Little Whorehouse In Texas*, *Steel Magnolias* and *Straight Talk*. Hosted own TV variety show in 1987.	
11/12/77+	**3**	13	● 1. **Here You Come Again**	RCA 11123
			#1 Country hit (5 weeks)	
4/8/78	**19**	8	2. Two Doors Down	RCA 11240
9/23/78	**37**	4	3. Heartbreaker	RCA 11296
			#1 Country hit (3 weeks)	
1/13/79	**25**	7	4. Baby I'm Burnin'	RCA 11420

DATE	POS	WKS	ARTIST–RECORD TITLE	LABEL & NO.
5/3/80	36	3	5. Starting Over Again written by Donna Summer and her husband Bruce Sudano; #1 Country hit (1 week)	RCA 11926
12/20/80+	1 (2)	18	● 6. 9 To 5 title song from the movie starring Parton; #1 Adult Contemporary hit (2 weeks); #1 Country hit (1 week)	RCA 12133
9/10/83	1 (2)	18	▲ 7. Islands In The Stream **KENNY ROGERS with Dolly Parton** written by the Bee Gees; #1 Adult Contemporary hit (4 weeks); #1 Country hit (2 weeks)	RCA 13615

PARTRIDGE FAMILY, The

Popularized through "The Partridge Family" TV series, broadcast 1970–74. Recordings by series stars David Cassidy (lead singer) and real-life stepmother Shirley Jones (backing vocals). David, son of actor Jack Cassidy, was born on 4/12/50 in New York City; raised in California. Shirley, born on 3/31/34 in Smithton, Pennsylvania, starred in the movie musicals *Oklahoma* and *The Music Man*; married David's father in 1956.

THE PARTRIDGE FAMILY STARRING SHIRLEY JONES FEATURING DAVID CASSIDY:

DATE	POS	WKS	ARTIST–RECORD TITLE	LABEL & NO.
10/31/70	1 (3)	16	● 1. **I Think I Love You**	Bell 910
2/20/71	6	11	● 2. **Doesn't Somebody Want To Be Wanted**	Bell 963
5/15/71	9	8	3. **I'll Meet You Halfway**	Bell 996
8/21/71	13	10	4. I Woke Up In Love This Morning	Bell 45130
1/1/72	20	6	5. It's One Of Those Nights (Yes Love)	Bell 45160
7/29/72	28	4	6. Breaking Up Is Hard To Do	Bell 45235
1/27/73	39	2	7. Looking Through The Eyes Of Love	Bell 45301

PARTY, The

Dance quintet from Central Florida: Albert Fields, Chase Hampton, Damon Pampolina, Deedee Magno and Tiffini Hale (lead singer). All were cast members of TV's "The Mickey Mouse Club" in 1988.

DATE	POS	WKS	ARTIST–RECORD TITLE	LABEL & NO.
1/25/92	34	2	1. In My Dreams Airplay #30 / Sales #54	Hollywood 64832

PASTELS, The

R&B vocal quartet: Big Dee Irwin (lead singer; died 8/27/95, age 63), Richard Travis, Tony Thomas and Jimmy Willingham. Formed at Air Force base in Narsarssuak, Greenland, in 1954.

DATE	POS	WKS	ARTIST–RECORD TITLE	LABEL & NO.
3/3/58	24	3	1. Been So Long Top 100 #24 / Best Seller #25	Argo 5287

PASTEL SIX, The

Seven-man band from California led by Bob Toten. Ages 18–21 in 1962. Headlined at the Cinnamon Cinder club in North Hollywood.

DATE	POS	WKS	ARTIST–RECORD TITLE	LABEL & NO.
1/19/63	25	5	1. The Cinnamon Cinder (It's A Very Nice Dance)	Zen 102

PATIENCE & PRUDENCE

Los Angeles sister duo: Patience & Prudence McIntyre (ages 11 and 14 in 1956).

DATE	POS	WKS	ARTIST–RECORD TITLE	LABEL & NO.
8/25/56	4	17	● 1. **Tonight You Belong To Me** Best Seller #4 / Juke Box #4 / Jockey #5 / Top 100 #6; #1 hit for Gene Austin in 1927	Liberty 55022

DATE	POS	WKS	ARTIST–RECORD TITLE	LABEL & NO.
12/1/56	**11**	12	2. Gonna Get Along Without Ya Now Jockey #11 / Best Seller #12 / Top 100 #12 / Juke Box #16; #25 hit for Teresa Brewer in 1952; above 2 with duo's father Mack McIntyre's orchestra	Liberty 55040
			### PATTON, Robbie	
8/1/81	**26**	6	English singer/songwriter. Toured with Fleetwood Mac as a guest in 1979. 1. Don't Give It Up co-produced by Fleetwood Mac's Christine McVie	Liberty 1420
			### PATTY & THE EMBLEMS	
8/15/64	**37**	3	Soul group from Camden, New Jersey. Pat Russell, lead singer. 1. Mixed-Up, Shook-Up, Girl	Herald 590
			### PAUL, Billy	
11/18/72	**1** (3)	14	Born Paul Williams on 12/1/34 in Philadelphia. Soul singer; sang on Philadelphia radio broadcasts at age 11. First recorded for Jubilee in 1952. ● 1. **Me And Mrs. Jones** #1 R&B hit (4 weeks)	Phil. Int. 3521
4/20/74	**37**	3	2. Thanks For Saving My Life above 2 written and produced by Kenny Gamble and Leon Huff	Phil. Int. 3538
			### PAUL, Les, and Mary Ford	
			Paul was born Lester Polsfuss on 6/9/16 in Waukesha, Wisconsin. Ford was born Colleen Summer on 7/7/28 in Pasadena; died on 9/30/77. Paul is a self-taught guitarist. Worked local radio stations, then to Chicago, 1932–37. Own trio in 1936. With Fred Waring, 1938–41. Innovator in electric guitar and multi-track recordings. Paul and vocalist Ford married on 12/29/49; divorced in 1963. Paul won the Grammy's Trustees Award in 1983 and was inducted into the Rock and Roll Hall of Fame in 1988.	
7/9/55	**7**	13	1. **Hummingbird** Juke Box #7 / Best Seller #8 / Jockey #8	Capitol 3165
11/12/55	**38**	2	2. Amukiriki (The Lord Willing) Top 100 #38	Capitol 3248
2/23/57	**35**	2	3. Cinco Robles (Five Oaks)	Capitol 3612
9/8/58	**32**	4	4. Put A Ring On My Finger Hot 100 #32 / Best Seller #44	Columbia 41222
7/3/61	**37**	1	5. Jura (I Swear I Love You)	Columbia 41994
			### PAUL & PAULA	
1/12/63	**1** (3)	12	Real names: Ray Hildebrand (born 12/21/40, Joshua, Texas) and Jill Jackson (born 5/20/42, McCaney, Texas). Formed duo at Howard Payne College, Brownwood, Texas. ● 1. **Hey Paula** first released on Le Cam 979 as by Jill & Ray in 1962; #1 R&B hit (2 weeks)	Philips 40084
3/23/63	**6**	8	2. **Young Lovers**	Philips 40096
6/22/63	**27**	4	3. First Quarrel	Philips 40114
			### PAVONE, Rita	
7/4/64	**26**	4	Born in Torino, Italy. Pop singer. 1. Remember Me	RCA 8365

DATE	POS	WKS	ARTIST—RECORD TITLE	LABEL & NO.
			PAYNE, Freda	
			Born on 9/19/45 in Detroit. Sister of The Supremes' Scherrie Payne. Attended the Institute of Musical Arts. To New York in 1963. Performed with Pearl Bailey, Duke Ellington and Quincy Jones. First recorded for Impulse in 1965. Hosted the syndicated TV talk show "For You, Black Woman" in the early '80s.	
5/30/70	3	15	● 1. **Band Of Gold**	Invictus 9075
10/10/70	24	8	2. Deeper & Deeper	Invictus 9080
6/26/71	12	10	● 3. Bring The Boys Home	Invictus 9092
			PEACHES & HERB	
			Soul duo from Washington, D.C.: Herb Fame (born Herbert Feemster, 1942) and Francine Barker (born Francine Hurd, 1947). Fame had been recording solo, Francine sang in vocal group Sweet Things. Marlene Mack filled in for Francine, 1968—69. Re-formed with Fame and Linda Green in 1977.	
2/25/67	21	6	1. Let's Fall In Love #1 hit for Eddy Duchin in 1934	Date 1523
4/15/67	8	9	2. **Close Your Eyes** written by Chuck Willis; #5 R&B hit for The Five Keys in 1955	Date 1549
7/8/67	20	5	3. For Your Love	Date 1563
10/14/67	13	7	4. Love Is Strange	Date 1574
1/13/68	31	3	5. Two Little Kids co-written by Barbara Acklin	Date 1586
1/27/79	5	13	● 6. **Shake Your Groove Thing**	Polydor 14514
3/31/79	1 (4)	15	▲ 7. **Reunited** #1 R&B hit (4 weeks)	Polydor 14547
3/15/80	19	8	8. I Pledge My Love	Polydor 2053
			PEARL, Leslie	
			Pop singer/songwriter/producer from Pennsylvania. Wrote jingles for Pepsi, Ford, Gillette and others. Recorded with sister Debbie in the duo Pearl.	
7/10/82	28	7	1. If The Love Fits Wear It	RCA 13235
			PEARL JAM	
			Seattle-based rock band: vocalist Eddie Vedder (born Eddie Mueller), guitarists Stone Gossard and Mike McCready, bassist Jeff Ament and drummer Dave Abbruzzese (replaced Dave Krusen who played on the album *Ten*). Gossard and Ament were members of Mother Love Bone. All except Krusen recorded with Temple Of The Dog. Band acted in the movie *Singles* as Matt Dillon's band, Citizen Dick. Abbruzzese left band in August 1994. Drummer Jack Irons (ex-Red Hot Chili Peppers) joined in late 1994. McCready also put together Mad Season in 1994.	
11/26/94	18	2	1. Tremor Christ Airplay #69	Epic 77771
12/23/95	7	9	● 2. **I Got Id/** Sales #5 / Airplay #34	
		9	3. Long Road Sales flip; Neil Young (guitar/pump organ/vocal, above 2); both songs accompany Young's *Mirror Ball* album; above 2 only available as CD singles	Epic 78199

DATE	POS	WKS	ARTIST–RECORD TITLE	LABEL & NO.
			PEBBLES	
			Born Perri Alette McKissack. Native of Oakland. Nicknamed "Pebbles" by her family for her resemblance to cartoon character Pebbles Flintstone. Worked with Con Funk Shun in the early '80s while still a teenager. Married to singer/songwriter/producer L.A. Reid of The Deele. Her cousin is vocalist Cherrelle. Put together and managed the female rap group TLC.	
2/27/88	5	12	1. **Girlfriend** Sales #4 / Airplay #6; #1 R&B hit (2 weeks)	MCA 53185
5/28/88	2 (2)	11	2. **Mercedes Boy** Sales #1(1) / Airplay #3; #1 R&B hit (1 week)	MCA 53279
9/8/90	4	13	3. **Giving You The Benefit** Sales #5 / Airplay #5; #1 R&B hit (3 weeks)	MCA 53891
1/12/91	13	9	4. Love Makes Things Happen Sales #7 / Airplay #26; Babyface (backing vocal); #1 R&B hit (2 weeks)	MCA 53973
			PEEBLES, Ann	
			Born on 4/27/47 in East St. Louis. Sang in family gospel group, the Peebles Choir, from age eight.	
12/22/73	38	1	1. I Can't Stand The Rain produced by Willie Mitchell	Hi 2248
			PEEPLES, Nia	
			Born on 12/10/61. Singer/actress. Played Nicole Chapman for three seasons on the TV series "Fame." Hosted "Top Of The Pops" TV show and own syndicated music video dance TV program, "Party Machine." Married to Howard Hewett, 1989-93.	
7/2/88	35	3	1. Trouble Sales #29	Mercury 870154
10/26/91	12	10	2. Street Of Dreams Airplay #11 / Sales #65	Charisma 98690
			PENDERGRASS, Teddy	
			Born on 3/26/50 in Philadelphia. Worked local clubs, became drummer for Harold Melvin's Blue Notes in 1969; lead singer with same group in 1970. Went solo in 1976. In the 1982 movie *Soup For One*. Auto accident on 3/18/82 left him partially paralyzed.	
8/12/78	25	6	● 1. Close The Door #1 R&B hit (2 weeks)	Phil. Int. 3648
7/4/81	40	2	2. Two Hearts **STEPHANIE MILLS Featuring Teddy Pendergrass**	20th Century 2492
			PENGUINS, The	
			R&B vocal group formed in Los Angeles in 1954: Cleveland Duncan (lead), Dexter Tisby (tenor), Bruce Tate (baritone) and Curtis Williams (bass). Group named for trademark on Kool cigarettes.	
12/25/54+	8	15	● 1. **Earth Angel (Will You Be Mine)** Best Seller #8 / Juke Box #10 / Jockey #13; considered to be the top R&B record of all-time in terms of continuous popularity; written by Jesse Belvin and Curtis Williams; #1 R&B hit (3 weeks)	DooTone 348

DATE	POS	WKS	ARTIST–RECORD TITLE	LABEL & NO.
			PENISTON, Ce Ce	
			Born on 9/6/69 in Dayton, Ohio. Moved to Phoenix in 1977. Crowned Miss Black Arizona in 1989.	
11/9/91+	5	22	● 1. **Finally** Airplay #4 / Sales #9; MC Lethal (rap)	A&M 1586
2/29/92	20	11	2. We Got A Love Thang Airplay #11 / Sales #37; Kym Sims (backing vocal)	A&M 1594
6/20/92	15	15	3. Keep On Walkin' Airplay #9 / Sales #18	A&M 1598
2/26/94	32	4	4. I'm In The Mood Airplay #27 / Sales #44	A&M 0460
			PENN, Michael	
			Los Angeles-based singer/songwriter. Older brother of actors Sean and Christopher Penn. Son of actor/director Leo Penn and actress Eileen Ryan.	
2/3/90	13	10	1. No Myth Sales #10 / Airplay #18	RCA 9111
			PEOPLE	
			San Jose, California pop-rock sextet founded by lead guitarist Geoff Levin.	
5/25/68	14	10	1. I Love You	Capitol 2078
			PEOPLE'S CHOICE	
			Philadelphia soul group formed in 1971: Frankie Brunson (vocals), Guy Fiske, Roger Andrews, Dave Thompson and Leon Lee. Lee left in 1973, replaced by Darnell Jordan and Donald Ford.	
9/4/71	38	2	1. I Likes To Do It [I]	Phil-L.A. 349
9/13/75	11	11	● 2. Do It Any Way You Wanna [I] #1 R&B hit (1 week)	TSOP 4769
			PEPPERMINT RAINBOW, The	
			Baltimore group: Doug Lewis (guitar), Skip Harris (bass), Tony Corey (drums), and sisters/vocalists Bonnie and Pat Lamdin. Discovered by producer Paul Leka (Steam).	
4/12/69	32	5	1. Will You Be Staying After Sunday	Decca 32410
			PERFECT GENTLEMEN	
			Boston pre-teen trio produced by New Edition and New Kids On The Block producer, Maurice Starr: Corey Blakely, Maurice Starr, Jr. (Starr's son), and Tyrone Sutton. All were ages 11–12 in 1990.	
4/28/90	10	9	1. **Ooh La La (I Can't Get Over You)** Sales #11 / Airplay #11	Columbia 73379
			PERICOLI, Emilio	
			Born in 1928 in Cesenatico, Italy. Singer/actor.	
6/9/62	6	10	1. **Al Di La'** [F] from the movie *Rome Adventure* starring Troy Donahue; Giampiero Boneschi (orch.)	Warner 5259

DATE	POS	WKS	ARTIST–RECORD TITLE	LABEL & NO.
			PERKINS, Carl	
			Born on 4/9/32 near Tiptonville, Tennessee. Rockabilly singer/guitarist/songwriter. Formed family band consisting of Carl (guitar), brothers Jay B. (guitar) and Clayton (bass), and W.B. Holland (drums). Signed with Flip Records in 1954, recorded "Movie Magg" (Flip 501). Member of Johnny Cash's touring troupe, 1965–75. Appeared in the movie *Into The Night* (1985). Inducted into the Rock and Roll Hall of Fame in 1987.	
3/10/56	**2** (4)	17	1. **Blue Suede Shoes** Juke Box #2 / Best Seller #3 / Top 100 #4 / Jockey #5; Grammy Hall of Fame Award winner in 1986; #1 Country hit (3 weeks)	Sun 234
			PERKINS, Tony	
			Born on 4/14/32 in New York City. Died on 9/12/92 of AIDS. Movie actor. Best Supporting Oscar nominee for *Friendly Persuasion* in 1956. Most famous for his portrayal of deranged killer Norman Bates in the 1960 movie *Psycho*.	
10/7/57	**24**	1	1. Moon-Light Swim Jockey #24 / Top 100 #43; re-issued in 1958 on RCA 7295; Frank DeVol (orch.)	RCA 7020
			PERRY, Steve	
			Born on 1/22/49 in Hanford, California. Lead singer of Journey since 1978.	
9/25/82	**17**	6	1. Don't Fight It **KENNY LOGGINS with Steve Perry**	Columbia 03192
4/14/84	**3**	13	2. **Oh Sherrie**	Columbia 04391
7/7/84	**21**	8	3. She's Mine	Columbia 04496
10/27/84	**40**	1	4. Strung Out	Columbia 04598
12/22/84+	**18**	11	5. Foolish Heart Airplay #12 / Sales #16; above 4 from the album *Street Talk*	Columbia 04693
7/30/94	**29**	7	6. You Better Wait Airplay #25	Columbia 77580
			PERSUADERS, The	
			Soul group formed in New York City in 1969. Consisted of lead Douglas "Smokey" Scott, Willie Holland, James "B.J." Barnes and Charles Stodghill.	
9/18/71	**15**	9	● 1. Thin Line Between Love & Hate #1 R&B hit (2 weeks)	Atco 6822
12/8/73	**39**	3	2. Some Guys Have All The Luck	Atco 6943
			PETER AND GORDON	
			Pop duo formed in London in 1963: Peter Asher (born 6/22/44, London) and Gordon Waller (born 6/4/45, Braemar, Scotland). Peter's sister Jane was Paul McCartney's girlfriend, and Paul wrote their first three chart hits. Toured the U.S. in 1964, appeared on "Shindig," "Hullabaloo" and Ed Sullivan TV shows. Disbanded in 1967. Asher went into production and management, including work with Linda Ronstadt, James Taylor and 10,000 Maniacs.	
5/16/64	**1** (1)	11	1. **A World Without Love** written by Paul McCartney (also #7 below)	Capitol 5175
7/11/64	**12**	6	2. Nobody I Know	Capitol 5211
10/24/64	**16**	6	3. I Don't Want To See You Again above 2 written by John Lennon and Paul McCartney	Capitol 5272
1/23/65	**9**	9	4. **I Go To Pieces** written by Del Shannon	Capitol 5335

DATE	POS	WKS	ARTIST–RECORD TITLE	LABEL & NO.
5/8/65	14	8	5. True Love Ways *written by Buddy Holly and Norman Petty*	Capitol 5406
7/24/65	24	5	6. To Know You Is To Love You *same song as The Teddy Bears' "To Know Him, Is To Love Him"*	Capitol 5461
3/12/66	14	8	7. Woman	Capitol 5579
11/5/66	6	10	**8. Lady Godiva**	Capitol 5740
1/14/67	15	5	9. Knight In Rusty Armour	Capitol 5808
4/15/67	31	3	10. Sunday For Tea	Capitol 5864

PETER, PAUL & MARY

Folk group formed in New York City in 1961. Consisted of Mary Travers (born 11/7/37, Louisville), Peter Yarrow (born 5/31/38, New York City) and Paul Stookey (born 12/30/37, Baltimore). Yarrow had worked the Newport Folk Festival in 1960. Stookey had done TV work, and Travers had been in the Broadway musical *The Next President*. Disbanded in 1971, reunited in 1978.

DATE	POS	WKS	ARTIST–RECORD TITLE	LABEL & NO.
6/9/62	35	2	1. Lemon Tree	Warner 5274
9/8/62	10	8	**2. If I Had A Hammer (The Hammer Song)** *written as "The Hammer Song" by Pete Seeger & Lee Hays of The Weavers in 1958*	Warner 5296
3/30/63	2 (1)	11	**3. Puff (The Magic Dragon)** *#1 Adult Contemporary hit (2 weeks)*	Warner 5348
7/13/63	2 (1)	12	**4. Blowin' In The Wind** *#1 Adult Contemporary hit (5 weeks)*	Warner 5368
9/28/63	9	8	**5. Don't Think Twice, It's All Right** *above 2 written by Bob Dylan*	Warner 5385
12/28/63	35	2	6. Stewball *based on the 1822 ballad "Skewbald"*	Warner 5399
4/4/64	33	3	7. Tell It On The Mountain *adapted from the Christmas spiritual "Go Tell It On The Mountain"; above 4 from the album In The Wind*	Warner 5418
2/13/65	30	4	8. For Lovin' Me *written by Gordon Lightfoot*	Warner 5496
9/2/67	9	8	**9. I Dig Rock And Roll Music**	Warner 7067
12/23/67	35	2	10. Too Much Of Nothing *written by Bob Dylan*	Warner 7092
5/17/69	21	7	11. Day Is Done	Warner 7279
11/8/69	1 (1)	15	● **12. Leaving On A Jet Plane** *written by John Denver; from trio's 1967 album Album 1700; #1 Adult Contemporary hit (3 weeks)*	Warner 7340

PETERS, Bernadette

Born Bernadette Lazzara on 2/28/44 in Queens, New York. Broadway/TV/movie star. Appeared in the movies *The Jerk* and *Annie* among others, and in the TV series "All's Fair," 1976–77.

DATE	POS	WKS	ARTIST–RECORD TITLE	LABEL & NO.
5/10/80	31	5	1. Gee Whiz	MCA 41210

PETERSEN, Paul

Born on 9/23/45 in Glendale, California. Member of Disney's "Mouseketeers"; played Jeff Stone on TV's "Donna Reed Show," 1958–66. Became a paperback novelist in the '70s.

DATE	POS	WKS	ARTIST–RECORD TITLE	LABEL & NO.
3/31/62	19	7	1. She Can't Find Her Keys	Colpix 620
12/15/62+	6	10	**2. My Dad**	Colpix 663

DATE	POS	WKS	ARTIST–RECORD TITLE	LABEL & NO.

PETERSON, Ray

Born on 4/23/39 in Denton, Texas. Started singing in his early teens, while being treated for polio at a Texas hospital. Formed own Dunes label in 1960.

DATE	POS	WKS	ARTIST–RECORD TITLE	LABEL & NO.
6/15/59	25	7	1. The Wonder Of You	RCA 7513
6/27/60	7	11	2. **Tell Laura I Love Her**	RCA 7745
12/19/60+	9	9	3. **Corinna, Corinna** produced by Phil Spector; #18 hit for Red Nichols jazz band (as "Corrine Corrina")	Dunes 2002
9/25/61	29	3	4. Missing You #7 Country hit for Webb Pierce in 1957	Dunes 2006

PETS, The

Member Richard Podolor (Richie Allen) became a top producer; worked with Three Dog Night and Steppenwolf, among others.

DATE	POS	WKS	ARTIST–RECORD TITLE	LABEL & NO.
6/9/58	34	1	1. Cha-Hua-Hua [I] Top 100 #34 / Best Seller #38	Arwin 109

PET SHOP BOYS

British duo formed in 1981: Neil Tennant (vocals) and Chris Lowe (keyboards). Tennant was a writer for the British fan magazine *Smash Hits*. In 1989, Tennant also recorded with the group Electronic.

DATE	POS	WKS	ARTIST–RECORD TITLE	LABEL & NO.
3/15/86	1 (1)	14	1. **West End Girls** Sales #1(2) / Airplay #1(2)	EMI America 8307
6/21/86	10	9	2. **Opportunities (Let's Make Lots Of Money)** Sales #10 / Airplay #11	EMI America 8330
9/26/87	9	10	3. **It's A Sin** Sales #5 / Airplay #10	EMI America 43027
12/26/87+	2 (2)	13	4. **What Have I Done To Deserve This?** **PET SHOP BOYS (and Dusty Springfield)** Sales #1(1) / Airplay #4; also released on EMI America 50107	EMI-Man. 50107
4/9/88	4	10	5. **Always On My Mind** Sales #2 / Airplay #6	EMI-Man. 50123
11/5/88	18	6	6. Domino Dancing Sales #15 / Airplay #23; The Voice In Fashion (backing vocals)	EMI-Man. 50161

PETTY, Tom, And The Heartbreakers

Rock group formed in Los Angeles in 1975. Consisted of Petty (born 10/20/53, Gainesville, Florida; guitar, vocals), Mike Campbell (guitar), Benmont Tench (keyboards), Ron Blair (bass) and Stan Lynch (drums). Petty, Campbell and Tench had been in Florida group Mudcrutch, early '70s. Backed Stevie Nicks on solo album *Bella Donna*. Blair left in 1982, replaced by Howard Epstein (married to Carlene Carter). Toured with Bob Dylan in 1986. Petty appeared in the 1987 movie *Made In Heaven* and was a member of the supergroup Traveling Wilburys.

DATE	POS	WKS	ARTIST–RECORD TITLE	LABEL & NO.
2/18/78	40	1	1. Breakdown originally released on Shelter 62006 in 1977	Shelter 62008
12/8/79+	10	13	2. **Don't Do Me Like That**	Backstreet 41138
2/9/80	15	10	3. Refugee	Backstreet 41169
5/16/81	19	7	4. The Waiting also on the B-side of #15 below	Backstreet 51100
8/1/81	3	15	5. **Stop Draggin' My Heart Around** **STEVIE NICKS (with Tom Petty and The Heartbreakers)**	Modern 7336
12/4/82+	20	11	6. You Got Lucky	Backstreet 52144
3/12/83	21	7	7. Change Of Heart	Backstreet 52181

DATE	POS	WKS	ARTIST–RECORD TITLE	LABEL & NO.
4/6/85	**13**	9	8. Don't Come Around Here No More Sales #8 / Airplay #21	MCA 52496
3/1/86	**37**	2	9. Needles And Pins **TOM PETTY and the HEARTBREAKERS with STEVIE NICKS** recorded "live" at LA's Wiltern Theater; written by Sonny Bono	MCA 52772
5/23/87	**18**	6	10. Jammin' Me Sales #16 / Airplay #23; co-written by Bob Dylan	MCA 53065
			TOM PETTY:	
5/27/89	**12**	9	11. I Won't Back Down Sales #8 / Airplay #19; George Harrison (guitar, backing vocal)	MCA 53369
8/26/89	**23**	7	12. Runnin' Down A Dream Sales #11 / Airplay #31	MCA 53682
12/2/89+	**7**	12	13. **Free Fallin'** Sales #3 / Airplay #9	MCA 53748
			TOM PETTY AND THE HEARTBREAKERS:	
8/3/91	**28**	5	14. Learning To Fly Airplay #63	MCA 54124
2/26/94	**14**	10	15. Mary Jane's Last Dance Sales #15 / Airplay #31	MCA 54732
12/17/94+	**13**	17	16. You Don't Know How It Feels **TOM PETTY** Sales #12 / Airplay #19	Warner 18030
			PHILLIPS, Esther	
			Born Esther Mae Jones on 12/23/35 in Galveston, Texas. One of the first female superstars of R&B. Vocalist/multi-instrumentalist. Moved to Los Angeles in 1940. Recorded and toured with The Johnny Otis Orchestra as "Little Esther," 1948–54; scored seven Top 10 hits on the R&B charts in 1950. Bouts with drug addiction interrupted her career and led to her death on 8/7/84 (liver and kidney failure).	
11/17/62	**8**	10	1. **Release Me** #1 R&B hit (3 weeks); #5 Country hit for Jimmy Heap in 1954; re-charted in 1967 at #93	Lenox 5555
9/20/75	**20**	9	2. What A Diff'rence A Day Makes #5 hit for the Dorsey Brothers Orchestra in 1934	Kudu 925
			PHILLIPS, John	
			Born on 8/30/35 in Paris Island, South Carolina. Co-founder of The Mamas & The Papas. Father of actress MacKenzie Phillips and singer Chynna Phillips (of Wilson Phillips). Co-wrote The Beach Boys' 1988 #1 hit "Kokomo."	
6/20/70	**32**	7	1. Mississippi	Dunhill 4236
			PHILLIPS, Phil, With The Twilights	
			Born John Phillip Baptiste on 3/14/31. Black vocalist from Lake Charles, Louisiana.	
7/20/59	**2** (2)	14	● 1. **Sea Of Love** first released on Khoury's 711 in 1959; #1 R&B hit (1 week)	Mercury 71465
			PHOTOGLO, Jim	
			Pop vocalist from the South Bay area of Los Angeles.	
5/31/80	**31**	4	1. We Were Meant To Be Lovers **PHOTOGLO**	20th Century 2446

DATE	POS	WKS	ARTIST–RECORD TITLE	LABEL & NO.
5/30/81	25	7	2. Fool In Love With You	20th Century 2487

PICKETT, Bobby "Boris", And The Crypt-Kickers

Pickett was born on 2/11/40 in Somerville, Massachusetts. Began recording career in Hollywood while aspiring to be an actor. A member of The Stompers in early 1962. The Crypt-Kickers were Leon Russell, Johnny MacCrae (Ronny & The Daytonas), Rickie Page (The Bermudas) and Gary Paxton (Hollywood Argyles).

DATE	POS	WKS	ARTIST–RECORD TITLE	LABEL & NO.
9/15/62	1 (2)	12	● 1. **Monster Mash** [N]	Garpax 44167
12/22/62	30	4	2. Monsters' Holiday [X-N]	Garpax 44171
6/30/73	10	12	● 3. **Monster Mash** [N-R]	Parrot 348

#1 & 3 are the same version; all of above produced by Gary Paxton

PICKETT, Wilson

Born on 3/18/41 in Prattville, Alabama. Soul singer/songwriter. Sang in local gospel groups. To Detroit in 1955. With The Falcons, 1961–63. Career took off after recording in Memphis with guitarist/producer Steve Cropper. Inducted into the Rock and Roll Hall of Fame in 1991. Sentenced to one year in jail for striking and injuring a pedestrian in New Jersey while driving drunk in 1992.

DATE	POS	WKS	ARTIST–RECORD TITLE	LABEL & NO.
8/14/65	21	6	1. In The Midnight Hour #1 R&B hit (1 week)	Atlantic 2289
3/5/66	13	8	2. 634-5789 (Soulsville, U.S.A.) #1 R&B hit (7 weeks)	Atlantic 2320
8/13/66	6	8	3. **Land Of 1000 Dances** #1 R&B hit (1 week)	Atlantic 2348
12/10/66	23	6	4. Mustang Sally	Atlantic 2365
2/25/67	29	3	5. Everybody Needs Somebody To Love	Atlantic 2381
4/22/67	32	2	6. I Found A Love - Part 1	Atlantic 2394
8/26/67	8	9	7. **Funky Broadway** #1 R&B hit (1 week)	Atlantic 2430
11/11/67	22	5	8. Stag-O-Lee adapted from the traditional folk song "Stack-O-Lee"	Atlantic 2448
5/11/68	15	6	9. She's Lookin' Good	Atlantic 2504
7/6/68	24	4	10. I'm A Midnight Mover written by Bobby Womack	Atlantic 2528
1/4/69	23	6	11. Hey Jude Duane Allman (guitar solo)	Atlantic 2591
5/23/70	25	9	12. Sugar Sugar	Atlantic 2722
10/24/70	14	9	13. Engine Number 9	Atlantic 2765
2/6/71	17	8	● 14. Don't Let The Green Grass Fool You	Atlantic 2781
5/15/71	13	9	● 15. Don't Knock My Love - Pt. 1 #1 R&B hit (1 week)	Atlantic 2797
1/15/72	24	8	16. Fire And Water	Atlantic 2852

PIERCE, Webb

Born on 8/8/21 in West Monroe, Louisiana. Died on 2/24/91 of heart failure. A leading country singer, 1952–58, had 37 consecutive Top 10 hits on *Billboard*'s country charts. Appeared in the movies *Buffalo Guns, Music City USA* and *Road To Nashville*.

DATE	POS	WKS	ARTIST–RECORD TITLE	LABEL & NO.
8/31/59	24	7	1. I Ain't Never written by Mel Tillis	Decca 30923

DATE	POS	WKS	ARTIST–RECORD TITLE	LABEL & NO.
			PILOT	
			Scottish trio: David Paton (lead singer, guitar), Bill Lyall (keyboards; died of AIDS in 1989) and Stuart Tosh (drums).	EMI 3992
5/10/75	5	12	● 1. **Magic**	
			produced by Alan Parsons	
			PINETTE, Rick—see OAK	
			PINK FLOYD	
			English progressive-rock band formed in 1965: David Gilmour (guitar; replaced Syd Barrett in 1968), Roger Waters (bass), Nick Mason (drums) and Rick Wright (keyboards). Wright left in early 1982. Waters went solo in 1984. Band inactive, 1984–86. Gilmour, Mason and Wright regrouped in 1987. Inducted into the Rock and Roll Hall of Fame in 1996. Group name taken from Georgia bluesmen Pink Anderson and Floyd Council.	
6/23/73	13	9	1. Money	Harvest 3609
			from the album *The Dark Side Of The Moon*, which charted for a record-breaking 741 weeks	
2/9/80	1 (4)	19	● 2. **Another Brick In The Wall (Part II)**	Columbia 11187
			PINK LADY	
			Female disco duo from Japan: Mie Nemoto and Kei Masuda. Hosted own summer TV variety show in U.S., 1979.	Elektra 46040
7/21/79	37	3	1. Kiss In The Dark	
			PIPKINS, The	
			British vocal duo: Roger Greenaway and Tony Burrows (low voice). Worked together in studio group White Plains.	Capitol 2819
6/6/70	9	10	1. **Gimme Dat Ding** [N]	
			background tune used on TV's "Benny Hill Show"	
			PIPS—see KNIGHT, Gladys	
			PITNEY, Gene	
			Born on 2/17/41 in Hartford, Connecticut; raised in Rockville, Connecticut. Own band at Rockville High School. Recorded for Decca in 1959 with Ginny Arnell as: Jamie & Jane. Recorded for Blaze in 1960 as Billy Bryan. First recorded under own name for Festival in 1960. Wrote "Hello Mary Lou," "He's A Rebel" and "Rubber Ball."	
2/27/61	39	1	1. (I Wanna) Love My Life Away	Musicor 1002
12/18/61+	13	10	2. Town Without Pity	Musicor 1009
			title song from the movie starring Kirk Douglas	
5/19/62	4	8	3. **(The Man Who Shot) Liberty Valance**	Musicor 1020
			inspired by the movie starring John Wayne and Jimmy Stewart	
9/29/62	2 (1)	11	4. **Only Love Can Break A Heart**	Musicor 1022
			#1 Adult Contemporary hit (2 weeks)	
1/5/63	12	8	5. Half Heaven - Half Heartache	Musicor 1026
4/13/63	12	7	6. Mecca	Musicor 1028
8/3/63	21	6	7. True Love Never Runs Smooth	Musicor 1032
			above 5 from the album *Only Love Can Break A Heart*	
11/16/63	17	6	8. Twenty Four Hours From Tulsa	Musicor 1034
			#3, 4, 7, 8: written by Burt Bacharach and Hal David	
8/29/64	7	10	9. **It Hurts To Be In Love**	Musicor 1040
11/7/64	9	9	10. **I'm Gonna Be Strong**	Musicor 1045

DATE	POS	WKS	ARTIST–RECORD TITLE	LABEL & NO.
3/20/65	31	4	11. I Must Be Seeing Things	Musicor 1070
5/22/65	13	7	12. Last Chance To Turn Around	Musicor 1093
8/21/65	28	4	13. Looking Through The Eyes Of Love	Musicor 1103
12/18/65	37	2	14. Princess In Rags	Musicor 1130
5/14/66	25	5	15. Backstage	Musicor 1171
6/15/68	16	8	16. She's A Heartbreaker	Musicor 1306

PIXIES THREE, The

White teenage female trio (ages 14–16 in 1963) from Hanover, Pennsylvania: Midge Bollinger (lead), Debbie Swisher and Kaye McColl. Bonnie Lony replaced Bollinger in 1964. Swisher replaced Peggy Santiglia as lead singer of The Angels, 1967–68.

DATE	POS	WKS	ARTIST–RECORD TITLE	LABEL & NO.
10/5/63	40	1	1. Birthday Party	Mercury 72130

PLANET SOUL

Miami-based dance duo of producer George Costa and singer Nadine Renee. Brenda Lee replaced Renee in early 1966.

DATE	POS	WKS	ARTIST–RECORD TITLE	LABEL & NO.
11/18/95+	26	18	1. Set U Free Sales #25 / Airplay #25	Strictly R. 12362

PLANT, Robert

Born on 8/20/48 in West Bromwich, England. Lead singer of Led Zeppelin and The Honeydrippers. Studied accounting before becoming lead singer of such British blues groups as Black Snake Moan, The Banned and The Crawling King Snakes. Also with the groups Listen and Band Of Joy. Fully recovered from a serious auto accident in Greece on 8/4/75.

DATE	POS	WKS	ARTIST–RECORD TITLE	LABEL & NO.
9/3/83	20	9	1. Big Log	Es Paranza 99844
12/24/83+	39	5	2. In The Mood	Es Paranza 99820
6/15/85	36	4	3. Little By Little	Es Paranza 99644
6/4/88	25	7	4. Tall Cool One Sales #18 / Airplay #27; Jimmy Page (guitar solo); features brief guitar riffs from Led Zeppelin's "Whole Lotta Love," "Dazed And Confused," "Custard Pie," "Black Dog" and "The Ocean"	Es Paranza 99348

PLASTIC ONO BAND—see LENNON, John

PLATT, Eddie

Saxophonist/bandleader from Cleveland.

DATE	POS	WKS	ARTIST–RECORD TITLE	LABEL & NO.
3/10/58	20	4	1. Tequila [I] Jockey #20 / Best Seller #35 / Top 100 #35	ABC-Para. 9899

DATE	POS	WKS	ARTIST–RECORD TITLE	LABEL & NO.
			PLATTERS, The	
			R&B group formed in Los Angeles in 1953. Consisted of Tony Williams (lead), David Lynch (tenor), Paul Robi (baritone), Herb Reed (bass) and Zola Taylor. Group first recorded for Federal in 1954, with Alex Hodge instead of Robi, and without Zola Taylor. Hit "Only You" was written by manager Buck Ram (died 1/1/91, age 83) and first recorded for Federal. To Mercury in 1955, re-recorded "Only You." Williams left to go solo, replaced by Sonny Turner in 1961. Taylor replaced by Sandra Dawn; Robi replaced by Nate Nelson (formerly in The Flamingos) in 1966. Lynch died of cancer on 1/2/81 (age 61). Nelson died of heart disease on 6/1/84 (age 52). Robi died of cancer on 2/1/89. Williams died of diabetes and emphysema on 8/14/92. Group inducted into the Rock and Roll Hall of Fame in 1990. Several unrelated groups use The Platters' famous name today.	
10/1/55	**5**	20	● 1. **Only You (And You Alone)** Best Seller #5 / Top 100 #5 / Jockey #5 / Juke Box #5; #1 R&B hit (7 weeks); different version released on Federal 12244 in 1954	Mercury 70633
12/24/55+	**1 (2)**	19	● 2. **The Great Pretender** Top 100 #1(2) / Jockey #1(2) / Juke Box #1(1) / Best Seller #2; #1 R&B hit (11 weeks)	Mercury 70753
3/31/56	**4**	16	3. **(You've Got) The Magic Touch** Top 100 #4 / Juke Box #4 / Best Seller #5 / Jockey #5	Mercury 70819
7/7/56	**1 (5)**	20	● 4. **My Prayer/** Top 100 #1(5) / Jockey #1(3) / Best Seller #1(2) / Juke Box #1(1); #1 R&B hit (2 weeks); #2 hit for Glenn Miller in 1939	
8/11/56	**39**	1	5. Heaven On Earth	Mercury 70893
10/6/56	**11**	12	6. You'll Never Never Know/ Juke Box #11 / Top 100 #14 / Best Seller #15 / Jockey #18	
10/6/56	**13**	9	7. It Isn't Right Best Seller #13 / Juke Box #13 / Top 100 #23	Mercury 70948
1/12/57	**20**	6	8. On My Word Of Honor/ Juke Box #20 / Best Seller #23 / Top 100 #27	
1/26/57	**20**	2	9. One In A Million Best Seller #20 / Top 100 #31	Mercury 71011
3/23/57	**11**	11	10. I'm Sorry/ Juke Box #11 / Best Seller #14 / Top 100 #19	
4/13/57	**16**	9	11. He's Mine Best Seller #16 / Juke Box #18 / Top 100 #23 / Jockey #24	Mercury 71032
6/10/57	**24**	7	12. My Dream/ Best Seller #24 / Top 100 #26	
		2	13. I Wanna Best Seller flip	Mercury 71093
4/7/58	**1 (1)**	14	● 14. **Twilight Time** Best Seller #1(1) / Top 100 #1(1) / Jockey #1(1); #1 R&B hit (3 weeks); #8 hit for the Three Suns in 1944	Mercury 71289
12/1/58+	**1 (3)**	16	● 15. **Smoke Gets In Your Eyes** #1 hit for Paul Whiteman's Orchestra in 1934 (from the 1933 musical *Roberta* starring Bob Hope)	Mercury 71383
4/6/59	**12**	11	16. Enchanted	Mercury 71427
2/15/60	**8**	11	17. **Harbor Lights** there were 5 Top 10 versions of this tune in 1950	Mercury 71563
8/22/60	**36**	1	18. Red Sails In The Sunset **THE PLATTERS Featuring TONY WILLIAMS** #1 hit for both Bing Crosby and Guy Lombardo in 1935	Mercury 71656
10/24/60	**21**	8	19. To Each His Own there were 3 #1 versions of this tune in 1946	Mercury 71697
1/30/61	**30**	2	20. If I Didn't Care #2 hit for the Ink Spots in 1939	Mercury 71749

DATE	POS	WKS	ARTIST–RECORD TITLE	LABEL & NO.
8/21/61	**25**	4	21. I'll Never Smile Again *#1 hit for Tommy Dorsey in 1940; David Carroll (orch., above 5)*	Mercury 71847
6/4/66	**31**	5	22. I Love You 1000 Times	Musicor 1166
3/25/67	**14**	7	23. With This Ring	Musicor 1229

PLAYER

Pop-rock group formed in Los Angeles: Peter Beckett (vocals, guitar), John Crowley (vocals, guitar), Ronn Moss (bass), John Friesen (drums) and Wayne Cooke (keyboards). Moss plays Ridge Forrester on the TV soap "The Bold & The Beautiful." Crowley began solo country career in 1988. Beckett joined Little River Band by 1992.

DATE	POS	WKS	ARTIST–RECORD TITLE	LABEL & NO.
11/19/77+	**1 (3)**	16	● 1. **Baby Come Back**	RSO 879
4/1/78	**10**	12	2. **This Time I'm In It For Love**	RSO 890
10/21/78	**27**	3	3. Prisoner Of Your Love	RSO 908

PLAYMATES, The

Donny Conn (born 3/29/30), Morey Carr (born 7/31/32) and Chic Hetti (born 2/26/30) from Waterbury, Connecticut. Solidified act at the University of Connecticut, with more emphasis on comedy than singing.

DATE	POS	WKS	ARTIST–RECORD TITLE	LABEL & NO.
1/27/58	**19**	7	1. Jo-Ann *Best Seller #19 / Top 100 #20*	Roulette 4037
6/9/58	**22**	2	2. Don't Go Home *Jockey #22 / Top 100 #36 / Best Seller #38*	Roulette 4072
11/10/58	**4**	12	● 3. **Beep Beep** [N]	Roulette 4115
7/27/59	**15**	9	4. What Is Love?	Roulette 4160
11/21/60	**37**	2	5. Wait For Me	Roulette 4276

PM DAWN

Jersey City, New Jersey, rap duo of brothers Attrell (born 5/15/70; nicknamed "Prince Be") and Jarrett (born 7/17/71; nicknamed "DJ Minutemix") Cordes. PM Dawn means "from the darkest hour comes the light."

DATE	POS	WKS	ARTIST–RECORD TITLE	LABEL & NO.
10/26/91	**1 (1)**	18	● 1. **Set Adrift On Memory Bliss** *Sales #1(3) / Airplay #2; samples Spandau Ballet's "True"*	Gee St. 866094
2/8/92	**28**	6	2. Paper Doll *Airplay #20 / Sales #46*	Gee St. 866374
9/26/92	**3**	24	● 3. **I'd Die Without You** *Airplay #1(2) / Sales #5; from the movie Boomerang starring Eddie Murphy*	Gee St./LaF. 24034
3/27/93	**6**	19	4. **Looking Through Patient Eyes** *Airplay #4 / Sales #20; samples George Michael's "Father Figure"; Cathy Dennis (backing vocal)*	Gee St. 862024

POCO

Country-rock band formed in Los Angeles by Rusty Young and Buffalo Springfield members Richie Furay and Jim Messina. Changing personnel included future Eagles members Randy Meisner and Timothy B. Schmit. 1979 lineup: Paul Cotton, Charlie Harrison, Kim Bullard and Steve Chapman. Disbanded in late 1984. In 1989, Young, Furay, Messina, Meisner and George Grantham reunited as Poco.

DATE	POS	WKS	ARTIST–RECORD TITLE	LABEL & NO.
2/10/79	**17**	9	1. Crazy Love *#1 Adult Contemporary hit (7 weeks)*	ABC 12439
6/16/79	**20**	7	2. Heart Of The Night	MCA 41023
9/30/89	**18**	8	3. Call It Love *Sales #16 / Airplay #21*	RCA 9038

Poison's brand of melodic hard rock was a crowd pleaser, as demonstrated by the group's No. 1 hit "Every Rose Has Its Thorn." The track's follow-up, curiously, was a cover of Loggins & Messina's "Your Mama Don't Dance."

Sandy Posey's initial 1966 hit, "Born A Woman," carried with it a lyrically passive message that might have upset current-day feminists. Would the title of her last hit—1967's "I Take It Back"— have made things any better?

Elvis Presley's 1957 double-sided hit single contained both his No. 1 smash "(Let Me Be Your) Teddy Bear" and its Top 20 flip, "Loving You." Both tunes came from the Hal Wallis film bearing the latter name.

Elvis Presley's well-documented transition to film star resulted in numerous hits from movies that featured few highlights other than his actual appearance. His 1964 single "Kissin' Cousins," from the like-named MGM film, climbed to No. 12 in 1964.

Johnny Preston, a discovery of the legendary Big Bopper, followed up his 1959 No. 1 hit "Running Bear" with "Cradle Of Love." Another smash, it climbed to No. 7.

Lloyd Price's "Billie Baby," released on his own Double-L label in 1964, spent three weeks on the chart and crested at No. 84. After scoring 10 previous Top 40 hits, he'd never manage another.

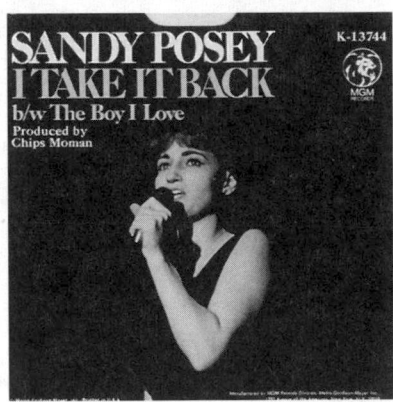

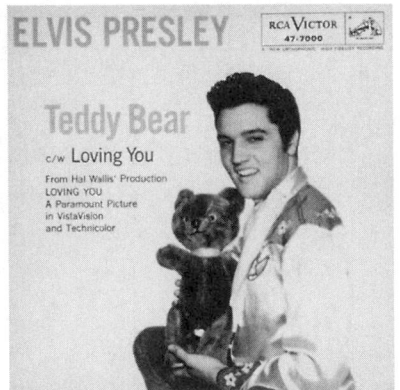

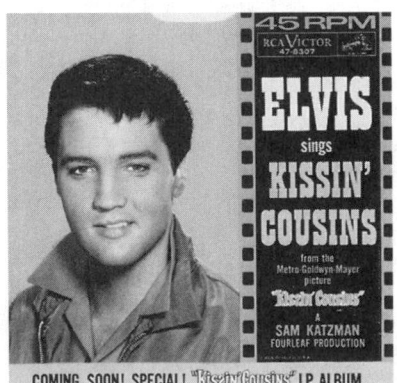

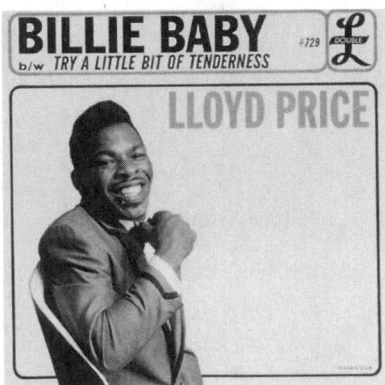

Prince's 1987 track "U Got The Look"—his third hit to spell "you" with one letter—featured the Minneapolis hitmaker backed by none other than Sheena Easton. Prince wrote and produced Easton's Top 10 1985 hit, "Sugar Walls."

Gary Puckett And The Union Gap's initial four Top 10 hits—including 1968's No. 2 smash "Young Girl"—shared one interesting lyrical aspect in common: all were addressed to a woman.

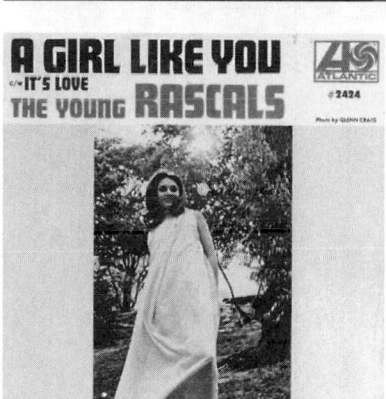

The Rascals still billed themselves as "The Young Rascals" on the 1967 Top 10 hit "A Girl Like You." WIthin a year, they'd drop the adjective and carry on hit-making.

Paul Revere And The Raiders gave a special "featuring Mark Lindsay" credit on their latter-day '60s singles, such as 1969's Top 20 hit "Mr. Sun, Mr. Moon." Two years later, their name shortened to The Raiders, they'd score their last No. 1 covering Don Fardon's "Indian Reservation."

Debbie Reynolds's brief career as a pop hitmaker drew to a close with 1960's No. 25 hit "Am I That Easy To Forget." Radio programmers apparently thought so: it was her third and last Top 40 hit.

Lionel Richie's "Say You, Say Me," drawn from the film *White Knights*, became the former Commodores vocalist's fifth No. 1 smash in 1985. Richie's return to action during 1995's American Music Awards Show was one of the year's musical highlights.

DATE	POS	WKS	ARTIST–RECORD TITLE	LABEL & NO.
1/20/90	39	1	4. Nothin' To Hide Sales #32; co-written and produced by Richard Marx	RCA 9131

POINT BLANK

Six-man rock band from Texas. Bubba Keith, lead singer.

DATE	POS	WKS	ARTIST–RECORD TITLE	LABEL & NO.
8/29/81	39	2	1. Nicole	MCA 51132

POINTER, Bonnie

Born on 7/11/51 in East Oakland, California. Member of the Pointer Sisters, 1971-78.

DATE	POS	WKS	ARTIST–RECORD TITLE	LABEL & NO.
7/28/79	11	15	1. Heaven Must Have Sent You	Motown 1459
2/16/80	40	2	2. I Can't Help Myself (Sugar Pie, Honey Bunch)	Motown 1478

POINTER SISTERS

Soul group formed in Oakland in 1971, consisting of sisters Ruth, Anita, June and Bonnie Pointer. Parents were ministers. Group was originally a trio, joined by youngest sister June in the early '70s. First recorded for Atlantic in 1971. Backup work for Cold Blood, Elvin Bishop, Boz Scaggs, Grace Slick and many others. Sang in nostalgic 1940s style, 1973–77. In the 1976 movie *Car Wash*. Bonnie went solo in 1978, group continued as a trio in new musical style.

DATE	POS	WKS	ARTIST–RECORD TITLE	LABEL & NO.
9/8/73	11	12	1. Yes We Can Can	Blue Thumb 229
11/9/74	13	8	2. Fairytale	ABC/Blue Thumb 254
8/23/75	20	8	3. How Long (Betcha' Got A Chick On The Side) #1 R&B hit (2 weeks); above 3 produced by David Rubinson	ABC/Blue Thumb 265
12/16/78+	2 (2)	16	● 4. **Fire** written by Bruce Springsteen	Planet 45901
4/14/79	30	4	5. Happiness	Planet 45902
8/30/80	3	17	● 6. **He's So Shy**	Planet 47916
6/27/81	2 (3)	16	● 7. **Slow Hand**	Planet 47929
2/13/82	13	10	8. Should I Do It	Planet 47960
7/24/82	16	8	9. American Music	Planet 13254
10/30/82	30	6	10. I'm So Excited	Planet 13327
2/11/84	5	14	11. **Automatic**	Planet 13730
5/12/84	3	15	12. **Jump (For My Love)**	Planet 13780
9/8/84	9	12	13. **I'm So Excited** [R] Sales #7 / Airplay #12; slightly different mix than #10 above	Planet 13857
12/22/84+	6	14	14. **Neutron Dance** Sales #5 / Airplay #5; from the movie *Beverly Hills Cop* starring Eddie Murphy	Planet 13951
7/27/85	11	13	15. Dare Me Sales #8 / Airplay #13	RCA 14126
12/6/86	33	3	16. Goldmine Sales #33 / Airplay #34; #4-16 produced by Richard Perry	RCA 5062

POISON

Hard-rock quartet formed in Harrisburg, Pennsylvania: Bret Michaels (vocals), Bobby Dall (bass), Rikki Rockett (drums) and C.C. DeVille (guitar; left band in early 1992; replaced by Richie Kotzen).

DATE	POS	WKS	ARTIST–RECORD TITLE	LABEL & NO.
4/11/87	9	9	1. **Talk Dirty To Me** Sales #6 / Airplay #11	Capitol 5686
10/17/87	13	9	2. I Won't Forget You Sales #12 / Airplay #12	Enigma 44038

DATE	POS	WKS	ARTIST–RECORD TITLE	LABEL & NO.
5/21/88	6	11	3. **Nothin' But A Good Time** Sales #3 / Airplay #11	Enigma 44145
8/27/88	12	9	4. Fallen Angel Sales #10 / Airplay #15	Enigma 44191
11/12/88	1 (3)	14	● 5. **Every Rose Has Its Thorn** Sales #1(3) / Airplay #1(3)	Enigma 44203
3/4/89	10	10	6. **Your Mama Don't Dance** Sales #9 / Airplay #11; above 4 from the album *Open Up And Say...Ahh!*	Enigma 44293
7/14/90	3	14	● 7. **Unskinny Bop** Sales #3 / Airplay #3	Enigma 44584
10/20/90	4	15	● 8. **Something To Believe In** Sales #4 / Airplay #5; acoustic version is on the B-side of #10 below	Enigma 44617
3/23/91	38	1	9. Ride The Wind Sales #38 / Airplay #39	Enigma 44616
6/29/91	35	2	10. Life Goes On Sales #47 / Airplay #73; above 4 from the album *Flesh & Blood*	Capitol 44705

POLICE, The

Rock trio formed in England in 1977: Gordon "Sting" Sumner (vocals, bass), Andy Summers (guitar) and Stewart Copeland (drums). First guitarist was Henri Padovani, replaced by Summers in 1977. Copeland had been with Curved Air. Inactive as a group since appearance at "Amnesty '86." Sting began recording solo in 1985. Copeland formed group Animal Logic in 1989.

DATE	POS	WKS	ARTIST–RECORD TITLE	LABEL & NO.
4/7/79	32	5	1. Roxanne	A&M 2096
11/22/80+	10	13	2. **De Do Do Do, De Da Da Da**	A&M 2275
2/21/81	10	13	3. **Don't Stand So Close To Me**	A&M 2301
10/10/81	3	15	4. **Every Little Thing She Does Is Magic**	A&M 2371
1/30/82	11	10	5. Spirits In The Material World	A&M 2390
6/4/83	1 (8)	20	● 6. **Every Breath You Take**	A&M 2542
8/27/83	3	13	7. **King Of Pain**	A&M 2569
11/19/83	16	9	8. Synchronicity II	A&M 2571
1/21/84	8	10	9. **Wrapped Around Your Finger** above 4 from the album *Synchronicity*; all of above written by Sting	A&M 2614

PONI-TAILS

Pop female trio from Brush High School in Lyndhurst, Ohio. Consisted of Toni Cistone (lead), LaVerne Novak (high harmony) and Patti McCabe (died 1/17/89). First recorded for Point in 1957.

DATE	POS	WKS	ARTIST–RECORD TITLE	LABEL & NO.
7/28/58	7	12	1. **Born Too Late** Hot 100 #7 / Best Seller #11	ABC-Para. 9934

POP, Iggy

Born James Jewel Osterberg on 4/21/47 in Muskegan, Michigan. Punk-rock pioneer. Leader of The Stooges, 1969–74. Acted in the movies *Cry Baby* and *Hardware*. Adopted nickname "Iggy" from his first band, The Iguanas.

DATE	POS	WKS	ARTIST–RECORD TITLE	LABEL & NO.
1/26/91	28	3	1. Candy Sales #23 / Airplay #38; Kate Pierson (of The B-52's, female vocal)	Virgin 98900

DATE	POS	WKS	ARTIST–RECORD TITLE	LABEL & NO.
			POPPY FAMILY (Featuring Susan Jacks)	
			Canadian pop quartet: Susan (vocals) and husband Terry Jacks (guitar, composer), Craig MacCaw (guitar) and Satwan Singh (percussion). Group and marriage broke up in 1973; Susan and Terry began solo careers.	
4/25/70	2 (2)	13	● 1. **Which Way You Goin' Billy?**	London 129
9/19/70	29	6	2. That's Where I Went Wrong	London 139
			PORTRAIT	
			Male vocal quartet: Eric Kirkland and Michael Angelo Saulsberry (both from Los Angeles), Irving Washington III (from Providence, Rhode Island) and Phillip Johnson (from Tulsa, Oklahoma). In 1995 Johnson was replaced by Kurt Jackson (from Aurora, Colorado).	
12/19/92+	11	18	1. Here We Go Again! Airplay #8 / Sales #17	Capitol 44865
			POSEY, Sandy	
			Born on 6/18/44 in Jasper, Alabama; raised in West Memphis, Arkansas. Worked as a session singer in Nashville and Memphis in the early '60s. Left music, 1968–70.	
8/6/66	12	12	1. Born A Woman	MGM 13501
12/10/66	12	8	2. Single Girl	MGM 13612
4/8/67	31	2	3. What A Woman In Love Won't Do	MGM 13702
7/1/67	12	8	4. I Take It Back	MGM 13744
			POSITIVE K	
			Bronx rapper Darryl Gibson. Became a Muslim in 1982, adopted the name Positive Knowledge Allah.	
2/6/93	14	14	● 1. I Got A Man Sales #5 / Airplay #19	Island 864305
			POST, Mike	
			Born on 9/29/44 in Los Angeles. Record producer/composer of numerous TV and movie scores. Orchestra leader for two TV variety shows: "The Andy Williams Show," 1969–71, and "The Mac Davis Show," 1974–76.	
6/21/75	10	10	1. **The Rockford Files** [I]	MGM 14772
10/3/81	10	10	2. **The Theme From Hill Street Blues** [I] Larry Carlton (guitar)	Elektra 47186
4/3/82	25	7	3. (Theme From) Magnum P.I. [I] all of above are TV series theme songs	Elektra 47400
			POURCEL('S), Franck, French Fiddles	
			Pourcel was born on 1/1/15 in Marseilles, France. String orchestra leader/composer/arranger/violinist.	
4/27/59	9	11	1. **Only You** [I]	Capitol 4165
			POWELL, Jane	
			Born Suzanne Burce on 4/1/29 in Portland, Oregon. Star of many movie musicals, mid-1940s through 1950s.	
10/6/56	15	9	1. True Love Best Seller #15 / Top 100 #24; Buddy Bregman (orch.); Cole Porter song from the movie *High Scoiety* starring Bing Crosby and Frank Sinatra	Verve 2018

DATE	POS	WKS	ARTIST–RECORD TITLE	LABEL & NO.
			POWERS, Joey	
			Born in 1939 in Canonsburg, Pennsylvania. Produced "The John Hills Exercise Show" for NBC-TV. Wrestling instructor at Ohio State University.	
12/7/63+	10	9	1. **Midnight Mary**	Amy 892
			POWER STATION, The	
			Superstar quartet: Robert Palmer (lead singer), Chic's Tony Thompson (drums) and Duran Duran's John Taylor (bass) and Andy Taylor (guitar). Formed as a one-album studio project. Michael Des Barres (Chequered Post) replaced Palmer for the group's 1985 concert tour.	
3/30/85	6	12	1. **Some Like It Hot** Sales #6 / Airplay #8	Capitol 5444
6/22/85	9	10	2. **Get It On** Sales #8 / Airplay #10; revival of 1972's "Bang A Gong" by T. Rex (Marc Bolan)	Capitol 5479
10/5/85	34	3	3. Communication	Capitol 5511
			POZO-SECO SINGERS	
			Native Texan trio: Susan Taylor, Lofton Kline and country star Don Williams (lead singer).	
10/8/66	32	6	1. I Can Make It With You	Columbia 43784
1/14/67	32	4	2. Look What You've Done	Columbia 43927
			PRADO, Perez	
			Born Damaso Perez Prado on 12/11/16 in Mantanzas, Cuba. Died on 9/14/89. Bandleader/organist. Known as "The King Of Mambo." Appeared in the movie *Underwater!*	
3/5/55	1 (10)	26	● 1. **Cherry Pink And Apple Blossom White** [I] Best Seller #1(10) / Juke Box #1(8) / Jockey #1(6); Billy Regis (trumpet solo); from the movie *Underwater!* starring Jane Russell; French song written in 1950	RCA 5965
6/23/58	1 (1)	17	● 2. **Patricia** [I] Top 100 #1(1) / Jockey #1(1) / Best Seller #2; #1 R&B hit (2 weeks)	RCA 7245
			PRATT & McCLAIN	
			Truett Pratt and Jerry McClain, with backing group Brother Love.	
4/24/76	5	10	1. **Happy Days** theme from the TV series starring Ron Howard and Henry Winkler	Reprise 1351
			PRELUDE	
			English folk-based trio: Ian Vardy with Brian and Irene Hume (husband and wife).	
11/2/74	22	5	1. After The Goldrush written by Neil Young (sung acapella)	Island 002
			PREMIERS, The	
			Latin-rock band from San Gabriel, California.	
7/4/64	19	6	1. Farmer John first released on Faro 615 in 1964; recorded "live" at The Rhythm Room in Fullerton, California	Warner 5443

DATE	POS	WKS	ARTIST–RECORD TITLE	LABEL & NO.
			PRESIDENTS, The	
			East Coast soul group consisting of Archie Powell, Bill Shorter and Tony Boyd.	
11/14/70	**11**	9	1. 5-10-15-20 (25-30 Years Of Love)	Sussex 207
			PRESLEY, Elvis	
			"The King of Rock & Roll." Born on 1/8/35 in Tupelo, Mississippi. Died at his Graceland mansion in Memphis on 8/16/77 (age 42) of heart failure caused by prescription drug abuse. Won talent contest at age eight, singing "Old Shep." Moved to Memphis in 1948. First recorded for Sun in 1954. Signed to RCA Records on 11/22/55. With his good looks, a passionate bluesy voice, a great band (Bill Black, bass; Scotty Moore, guitar; D.J. Fontana, drums), a smooth vocal quartet (The Jordanaires), and managed by Tom Parker, Presley blazed his way to the #1 star of rock and roll—a position he has not yet relinquished. Made his nationwide TV debut on "Stage Show" on 1/28/56. Starred in 31 feature movies (beginning with *Love Me Tender* in 1956). In U.S. Army from 3/24/58 to 3/5/60. Married Priscilla Beaulieu on 5/1/67; divorced on 10/11/73. Priscilla pursued acting in the 1980s, beginning with a role on TV's "Dallas." Their only child, Lisa Marie, was born on 2/1/68; married Michael Jackson on 5/26/94. Elvis's last "live" performance was in Indianapolis on 6/26/77. Won the Lifetime Achievement Grammy in 1971. Inducted into the Rock and Roll Hall of Fame in 1986. The first rock and roll artist to be honored by the U.S. Postal Service, with an Elvis Presley commemorative stamp on 1/8/93.	
3/10/56	**1 (8)**	22	▲ 1. **Heartbreak Hotel/** Best Seller #1(8) / Juke Box #1(8) / Top 100 #1(7) / Jockey #1(3); #1 Country hit (17 weeks)	
3/17/56	**19**	10	2. I Was The One Jockey #19 / Top 100 #23	RCA 47-6420
4/28/56	**20**	5	3. Blue Suede Shoes Best Seller #20 / Top 100 #24 / Jockey #24; from the E.P. *Elvis Presley*	RCA EPA-747
6/2/56	**1 (1)**	19	▲ 4. **I Want You, I Need You, I Love You/** Best Seller #1 / Top 100 #3 / Juke Box #3 / Jockey #6; #1 Country hit (2 weeks)	
6/9/56	**31**	3	5. My Baby Left Me written and recorded on RCA by Arthur "Big Boy" Crudup in 1950	RCA 47-6540
8/4/56	**1 (11)**	23	▲³ 6. **Don't Be Cruel/** Best Seller #1(11)/Juke Box #1(11)/Jockey #1(8)/Top 100 #1(7); the Best Sellers and Juke Box charts combined "Don't Be Cruel" and "Hound Dog" as one listing; "Don't Be Cruel" had more #1 weeks as the top side on both the Best Sellers (6 weeks A-side/5 weeks B-side) and Juke Box charts (7 weeks A-side/4 weeks B-side); #1 Country hit (10 weeks); #1 R&B hit (1 week)	● ●
8/4/56	**1 (11)**	23	▲³ 7. **Hound Dog** Best Seller #1(11)/Juke Box #1(11)/Top 100 #2/Jockey #4; Grammy Hall of Fame winner (1988); #1 Country hit (10 weeks); #1 R&B hit (6 weeks); #1 R&B hit for Big Mama Thornton in 1953	RCA 47-6604
10/20/56	**1 (5)**	19	▲² 8. **Love Me Tender/** Best Seller #1(5) / Jockey #1(5) / Top 100 #1(4) / Juke Box #1(1); adapted from the 1861 tune "Aura Lee"; title song from Presley's first movie	
11/10/56	**20**	4	9. Anyway You Want Me (That's How I Will Be) Jockey #20 / Top 100 #27	RCA 47-6643
11/24/56+	**2 (2)**	14	10. **Love Me/** Jockey #2 / Top 100 #6 / Best Seller #7 / Juke Box #8	
12/29/56	**19**	4	11. When My Blue Moon Turns To Gold Again Jockey #19 / Top 100 #27; country song introduced in 1941 by Wiley Walker and Gene Sullivan (Okeh 6374); above 2 from the E.P. *Elvis*	RCA EPA-992

DATE	POS	WKS		ARTIST–RECORD TITLE	LABEL & NO.
1/5/57	24	3		12. Poor Boy Jockey #24 / Top 100 #35; from the Presley movie and the E.P. *Love Me Tender*	RCA EPA-4006
1/26/57	1 (3)	14	▲	**13. Too Much/** Best Seller #1(3) / Juke Box #1(1) / Top 100 #2 / Jockey #2	
2/9/57	21	4		14. Playing For Keeps Jockey #21 / Top 100 #34; #2, 5, 12, 14: on the album *For LP Fans Only*	RCA 47-6800
4/6/57	1 (9)	22	▲²	**15. All Shook Up** Juke Box #1(9) end/Best Seller #1(8)/Top 100 #1(8)/Jockey #1(7); #1 R&B hit (4 weeks); #1 Country hit (1 week)	RCA 47-6870
4/29/57	25	1		16. (There'll Be) Peace In The Valley (For Me) Best Seller #25 / Top 100 #39; from the E.P. *Peace in the Valley*; #5 Country hit for Red Foley in 1951	RCA EPA-4054
6/24/57	1 (7)	18	▲	**17. (Let Me Be Your) Teddy Bear/** Best Seller #1(7) / Top 100 #1(7) / Jockey #1(3); #1 Country hit (1 week); #1 R&B hit (1 week)	
7/8/57	20	13		18. Loving You Jockey #20 / Top 100 #28; above 2 are from the Presley movie *Loving You*	RCA 47-7000
10/14/57	1 (7)	19	▲²	**19. Jailhouse Rock/** Best Seller #1(7) / Top 100 #1(6) / Jockey #1(2); #1 R&B hit (5 weeks); #1 Country hit (1 week)	
10/21/57	18	6		20. Treat Me Nice Jockey #18 / Top 100 #27; above 2 are from the Presley movie *Jailhouse Rock*; #1, 4, 6, 7, 8, 9, 13, 15, 19, 20: on the album *Elvis' Golden Records*	RCA 47-7035
1/27/58	1 (5)	16	▲	**21. Don't/** Best Seller #1(5) / Top 100 #1(1) / Jockey #1(1)	
2/3/58	8	7		**22. I Beg Of You** Top 100 #8 / Jockey #11	RCA 47-7150
4/21/58	2 (1)	13	▲	**23. Wear My Ring Around Your Neck/** Best Seller #2 / Top 100 #3 / Jockey #3; #1 R&B hit (3 weeks)	
5/5/58	15	2		24. Doncha' Think It's Time Jockey #15 / Top 100 #21	RCA 47-7240
6/30/58	1 (2)	14	▲	**25. Hard Headed Woman/** Best Seller #1(2) / Jockey #1(1) / Top 100 #2	
7/14/58	25	4		26. Don't Ask Me Why Jockey #25 / Top 100 #28; above 2 are from the Presley movie *King Creole*	RCA 47-7280
11/10/58	4	14		**27. One Night/** #11 R&B hit for Smiley Lewis in 1956 (originally written as "One Night (Of Sin)")	
11/10/58	8	12	▲	**28. I Got Stung**	RCA 47-7410
3/30/59	2 (1)	11	▲	**29. (Now and Then There's) A Fool Such As I/** #4 Country hit for Hank Snow in 1953	
3/30/59	4	10		**30. I Need Your Love Tonight**	RCA 47-7506
7/13/59	1 (2)	10	●	**31. A Big Hunk O' Love/** above 4 are Presley's only new recordings during his Army hitch	
7/13/59	12	10		32. My Wish Came True written by Ivory Joe Hunter; above 12 (except #25 & 26) are on the album *Elvis' Gold Records-Volume 2*	RCA 47-7600
4/11/60	1 (4)	13	▲	**33. Stuck On You/**	
4/25/60	17	7		34. Fame And Fortune above 2 were recorded 15 days after Presley's Army discharge	RCA 47-7740
7/25/60	1 (5)	16	▲	**35. It's Now Or Never/** adapted from the Italian song "O Sole Mio" of 1899	

DATE	POS	WKS		ARTIST–RECORD TITLE	LABEL & NO.
8/1/60	**32**	2		36. A Mess Of Blues	RCA 47-7777
11/14/60	**1** (6)	14	▲²	**37. Are You Lonesome To-night?/**	
				#4 hit for Vaughn Deleath in 1927	
11/28/60	**20**	8		38. I Gotta Know	RCA 47-7810
2/20/61	**1** (2)	11	▲	**39. Surrender/**	
				adapted from the Italian song "Come Back To Sorrento"	
3/13/61	**32**	2		40. Lonely Man	RCA 47-7850
				from the Presley movie Wild in the Country	
4/24/61	**14**	5		41. Flaming Star	RCA LPC-128
				title song from the movie starring Presley; from the "Compact Double 33" E.P. Elvis By Request	
5/22/61	**5**	7	●	**42. I Feel So Bad/**	
				#8 R&B hit for Chuck Willis in 1954	
6/19/61	**26**	2		43. Wild In The Country	RCA 47-7880
				title song from the movie starring Presley	
9/4/61	**4**	7	●	**44. (Marie's The Name) His Latest Flame/**	
8/28/61	**5**	10		**45. Little Sister**	RCA 47-7908
12/18/61+	**2** (1)	12	▲	**46. Can't Help Falling In Love/**	
				inspired by the French melody "Plasir D'Amour"; #1 Adult Contemporary hit (6 weeks)	
12/18/61+	**23**	5		47. Rock-A-Hula Baby ("Twist" Special)	RCA 47-7968
				above 2 are from the Presley movie Blue Hawaii	
3/24/62	**1** (2)	11	▲	**48. Good Luck Charm/**	
4/7/62	**31**	5		49. Anything That's Part Of You	RCA 47-7992
5/19/62	**15**	7	▲	50. Follow That Dream	RCA EPA-4368
				from the Presley movie and E.P.	
8/11/62	**5**	9	●	**51. She's Not You**	RCA 47-8041
				#33–35, 37–39, 42, 44, 45, 48, 49, 51: on the album Elvis' Golden Records, Volume 3	
10/6/62	**30**	4		52. King Of The Whole Wide World	RCA EPA-4371
				from the Presley movie and E.P. Kid Galahad	
10/27/62	**2** (5)	14	▲	**53. Return To Sender**	RCA 47-8100
				from the Presley movie Girls! Girls! Girls!	
2/23/63	**11**	7	●	54. One Broken Heart For Sale	RCA 47-8134
				from the Presley movie It Happened at the World's Fair	
7/13/63	**3**	8	●	**55. (You're the) Devil In Disguise**	RCA 47-8188
11/2/63	**8**	7	●	**56. Bossa Nova Baby/**	
				from the Presley movie Fun in Acapulco	
11/9/63	**32**	3		57. Witchcraft	RCA 47-8243
				#5 R&B hit for The Spiders in 1956	
3/7/64	**12**	7	●	58. Kissin' Cousins/	
				title song from the Presley movie	
3/14/64	**29**	4		59. It Hurts Me	RCA 47-8307
5/23/64	**34**	2		60. Kiss Me Quick	RCA 447-0639
				recorded on 6/25/61	
5/30/64	**21**	5		61. What'd I Say/	
5/30/64	**29**	4		62. Viva Las Vegas	RCA 47-8360
				above 2 are from the Presley movie Viva Las Vegas	
8/8/64	**16**	6		63. Such A Night	RCA 47-8400
				recorded on 4/4/60	
10/24/64	**16**	8	●	64. Ain't That Loving You Baby/	
				recorded on 6/10/58	
10/31/64	**12**	8		65. Ask Me	RCA 47-8440

DATE	POS	WKS	ARTIST–RECORD TITLE	LABEL & NO.
3/13/65	**21**	6	66. Do The Clam from the Presley movie *Girl Happy*	RCA 47-8500
5/8/65	**3**	11	▲ 67. **Crying In The Chapel** recorded on 10/31/60; #1 Adult Contemporary hit (7 weeks)	RCA 447-0643
7/3/65	**11**	6	68. (Such An) Easy Question recorded on 3/18/62; from the Presley movie *Tickle Me*; #1 Adult Contemporary hit (2 weeks)	RCA 47-8585
9/18/65	**11**	7	● 69. I'm Yours recorded on 6/26/61; #1 Adult Contemporary hit (3 weeks)	RCA 47-8657
12/4/65	**14**	6	● 70. Puppet On A String from the Presley movie *Girl Happy*	RCA 447-0650
1/22/66	**33**	3	● 71. Tell Me Why recorded on 1/12/57	RCA 47-8740
4/9/66	**25**	5	● 72. Frankie And Johnny version of mid-19th century traditional folk song; title song from the Presley movie	RCA 47-8780
7/9/66	**19**	5	73. Love Letters #11 hit for Dick Haymes in 1945	RCA 47-8870
11/5/66	**40**	2	74. Spinout title song from the Presley movie	RCA 47-8941
2/18/67	**33**	4	75. Indescribably Blue #36, 40, 55, 57, 59, 61, 64, 65, 73, 75: on the album *Elvis' Golden Records, Volume 4*	RCA 47-9056
11/4/67	**38**	2	76. Big Boss Man	RCA 47-9341
4/20/68	**28**	4	77. U.S. Male written and originally recorded by Jerry Reed; vocal group on nearly all of above titles: The Jordanaires	RCA 47-9465
12/14/68+	**12**	11	● 78. If I Can Dream	RCA 47-9670
4/12/69	**35**	2	79. Memories from the NBC-TV special "Elvis"	RCA 47-9731
5/17/69	**3**	11	▲ 80. **In The Ghetto** written by Mac Davis	RCA 47-9741
8/2/69	**35**	4	● 81. Clean Up Your Own Back Yard from the Presley movie *The Trouble with Girls (and how to get into it)*	RCA 47-9747
9/20/69	**1** (1)	13	▲ 82. **Suspicious Minds**	RCA 47-9764
12/13/69+	**6**	11	▲ 83. **Don't Cry Daddy/** written by Mac Davis	
		11	84. Rubberneckin' from Presley's last feature movie *Change Of Habit*	RCA 47-9768
2/21/70	**16**	8	● 85. Kentucky Rain written by Eddie Rabbitt	RCA 47-9791
5/23/70	**9**	11	● 86. **The Wonder Of You/** recorded "live" at Las Vegas; #1 Adult Contemporary hit (1 week)	
		11	87. Mama Liked The Roses	RCA 47-9835
8/22/70	**32**	3	● 88. I've Lost You/	
		3	89. The Next Step Is Love	RCA 47-9873
11/7/70	**11**	8	● 90. You Don't Have To Say You Love Me/ #1 Adult Contemporary hit (1 week)	
		8	91. Patch It Up written by Eddie Rabbitt; above 4 are on the soundtrack album *Elvis-That's The Way It Is*	RCA 47-9916
1/2/71	**21**	8	● 92. I Really Don't Want To Know/ #11 hit for Les Paul & Mary Ford in 1954	
		8	93. There Goes My Everything	RCA 47-9960

DATE	POS	WKS	ARTIST–RECORD TITLE	LABEL & NO.
3/27/71	33	4	94. Where Did They Go, Lord/	
		4	95. Rags To Riches	RCA 47-9980
			#1 hit (8 weeks) for Tony Bennett in 1953	
8/14/71	36	2	96. I'm Leavin'	RCA 47-9998
3/11/72	40	1	97. Until It's Time For You To Go	RCA 74-0619
			written by Buffy Sainte-Marie	
9/9/72	2 (1)	12	▲ 98. **Burning Love**	RCA 74-0769
12/23/72+	20	8	● 99. Separate Ways	RCA 74-0815
			featured in the movie *Elvis on Tour*	
5/5/73	17	7	100. Steamroller Blues/	
			written by James Taylor in 1970; from the TV special and album "Aloha from Hawaii via Satellite"	
		7	101. Fool	RCA 74-0910
3/23/74	39	2	102. I've Got A Thing About You Baby/	
			written by Tony Joe White	
		2	103. Take Good Care Of Her	RCA APBO-0196
6/29/74	17	7	104. If You Talk In Your Sleep	RCA APBO-0280
11/9/74	14	9	105. Promised Land	RCA PB-10074
			written by Chuck Berry	
2/15/75	20	6	106. My Boy	RCA PB-10191
			#1 Adult Contemporary hit (1 week)	
6/7/75	35	3	107. T-R-O-U-B-L-E	RCA PB-10278
5/1/76	28	5	108. Hurt/	
			#8 R&B hit for Roy Hamilton in 1955	
		5	109. For The Heart	RCA PB-10601
2/5/77	31	5	110. Moody Blue/	
			#1 Country hit (1 week)	
		5	111. She Thinks I Still Care	RCA PB-10857
			#1 Country hit in 1962 for George Jones; written by Dickey Lee	
7/16/77	18	12	● 112. Way Down	RCA PB-10998
			#1 Country hit (1 week)	
12/3/77	22	7	● 113. My Way	RCA PB-11165
			from the CBS-TV special "Elvis In Concert"; co-written in 1969 by Paul Anka; based on the French standard "Comme D'Habitude"	
2/28/81	28	5	114. Guitar Man [R]	RCA PB-12158
			remix by Felton Jarvis (died 1/3/81) of Presley's 1968 hit (#43); Jerry Reed (guitar); #1 Country hit (1 week)	

PRESTON, Billy

Born on 9/9/46 in Houston. R&B vocalist/keyboardist. To Los Angeles at an early age. With Mahalia Jackson in 1956. Played piano in movie *St. Louis Blues*, 1958. Regular on "Shindig" TV show. Recorded with The Beatles on "Get Back" and "Let It Be"; worked Concert For Bangladesh in 1969. Prominent session man, played on Sly & The Family Stone hits. With The Rolling Stones U.S. tour in 1975.

DATE	POS	WKS	ARTIST–RECORD TITLE	LABEL & NO.
5/13/72	2 (1)	14	● 1. **Outa-Space** [I]	A&M 1320
			#1 R&B hit (1 week)	
5/19/73	1 (2)	14	● 2. **Will It Go Round In Circles**	A&M 1411
10/13/73	4	13	● 3. **Space Race** [I]	A&M 1463
			#1 R&B hit (1 week)	
8/3/74	1 (1)	14	● 4. **Nothing From Nothing**	A&M 1544
1/4/75	22	6	5. Struttin' [I]	A&M 1644
			B-side is the hit song Preston wrote, "You Are So Beautiful"	

DATE	POS	WKS	ARTIST–RECORD TITLE	LABEL & NO.
3/1/80	4	15	6. **With You I'm Born Again** **BILLY PRESTON & SYREETA** Syreeta (Wright) was married to Stevie Wonder; from the movie *Fast Break* starring Gabe Kaplan	Motown 1477

PRESTON, Johnny

Born John Preston Courville on 8/18/39 in Port Arthur, Texas. Discovered by J.P. "Big Bopper" Richardson at the Twilight Club in Port Neches, Texas.

DATE	POS	WKS	ARTIST–RECORD TITLE	LABEL & NO.
12/21/59+	1 (3)	14	● 1. **Running Bear** Indian sounds by the Big Bopper and George Jones; written and backing vocal by the Big Bopper (J.P. Richardson)	Mercury 71474
4/4/60	7	12	2. **Cradle Of Love**	Mercury 71598
7/25/60	14	7	3. Feel So Fine	Mercury 71651

PRETENDERS, The

Rock quartet featuring lead singer/songwriter/guitarist Chrissie Hynde (born 9/7/51, Akron, Ohio). Formed in 1978, early British lineup included guitarist James Honeyman-Scott (died 6/16/82; replaced by Robbie MacIntosh), bassist Pete Farndon (died 4/14/83; replaced in 1982 by Malcolm Foster) and drummer Martin Chambers. Hynde was married to Jim Kerr of Simple Minds. With the exception of Hynde, numerous personnel changes since 1985. Chambers returned to lineup in 1994. Also see UB40.

DATE	POS	WKS	ARTIST–RECORD TITLE	LABEL & NO.
4/12/80	14	12	1. Brass In Pocket (I'm Special)	Sire 49181
1/29/83	5	14	2. **Back On The Chain Gang** from the movie *The King of Comedy* starring Robert DeNiro and Jerry Lewis	Sire 29840
1/7/84	19	9	3. Middle Of The Road	Sire 29444
4/7/84	28	6	4. Show Me	Sire 29317
11/1/86	10	12	5. **Don't Get Me Wrong** Airplay #7 / Sales #11	Sire 28630
9/24/94	16	23	6. I'll Stand By You Airplay #11 / Sales #39	Sire/Warner 18160

PRETTY POISON

Philadelphia dance band founded by Camden, New Jersey, natives Jade Starling (vocals) and Whey Cooler.

DATE	POS	WKS	ARTIST–RECORD TITLE	LABEL & NO.
10/31/87	8	14	● 1. **Catch Me (I'm Falling)** Sales #8 / Airplay #9; from the movie *Hiding Out* starring Jon Cryer	Virgin 99416
5/7/88	36	4	2. Nightime Airplay #33 / Sales #35	Virgin 99350

PRICE, Lloyd

Born on 3/9/33 in Kenner, Louisiana. R&B vocalist/pianist/composer. First recording was the #1 R&B hit "Lawdy Miss Clawdy" on Specialty in 1952. In U.S. Army, 1953-56. Formed own record company, KRC, in 1957; leased "Just Because" to ABC Records. Signed to ABC in 1958. Formed Double-L label in 1963 and Turntable Records in 1969. In later years has continued in music, production, and booking agency work.

DATE	POS	WKS	ARTIST–RECORD TITLE	LABEL & NO.
4/6/57	29	6	1. Just Because melody adapted from "Caro Nome" from Verdi's opera *Rigoletto*	ABC-Para. 9792
1/5/59	1 (4)	15	● 2. **Stagger Lee** adapted from the traditional folk song "Stack-O-Lee"; #1 R&B hit (4 weeks)	ABC-Para. 9972
3/30/59	23	4	3. Where Were You (On Our Wedding Day)?	ABC-Para. 9997

DATE	POS	WKS	ARTIST–RECORD TITLE	LABEL & NO.
5/11/59	2 (3)	14	● 4. **Personality** #1 R&B hit (4 weeks)	ABC-Para. 10018
8/17/59	3	12	5. **I'm Gonna Get Married** #1 R&B hit (3 weeks); Don Costa (orch., above 4)	ABC-Para. 10032
11/23/59	20	9	6. Come Into My Heart	ABC-Para. 10062
2/15/60	14	9	7. Lady Luck	ABC-Para. 10075
5/30/60	40	1	8. No If's - No And's	ABC-Para. 10102
7/18/60	19	7	9. Question	ABC-Para. 10123
10/26/63	21	6	10. Misty introduced by the Erroll Garner Trio in 1954	Double-L 722

PRICE, Ray

Born on 1/12/26 in Perryville, Texas; raised in Dallas. Country singer. Price charted over 80 Top 40 singles on *Billboard*'s country charts. Known as "The Cherokee Cowboy."

DATE	POS	WKS	ARTIST–RECORD TITLE	LABEL & NO.
11/7/70+	11	14	1. For The Good Times written by Kris Kristofferson; #1 Country hit (1 week)	Columbia 45178

PRIDE, Charley

Born on 3/18/38 in Sledge, Mississippi. The most successful black country performer. Discovered by Red Sovine in 1963. Pride has charted 29 #1 singles on *Billboard*'s country charts.

DATE	POS	WKS	ARTIST–RECORD TITLE	LABEL & NO.
12/18/71+	21	11	● 1. Kiss An Angel Good Mornin' #1 Country hit (5 weeks)	RCA 0550

PRIEST, Maxi

Born Max Elliott in London to Jamaican parents. Dancehall reggae singer.

DATE	POS	WKS	ARTIST–RECORD TITLE	LABEL & NO.
12/10/88+	25	7	1. Wild World Airplay #24 / Sales #24	Virgin 99269
8/11/90	1 (1)	17	● 2. **Close To You** Sales #1(1) / Airplay #3	Charisma 98951
10/5/91	6	16	3. **Set The Night To Music** **ROBERTA FLACK with Maxi Priest** Airplay #23 / Sales #25	Atlantic 87607
12/7/91	37	1	4. Housecall (Your Body Can't Lie To Me) **SHABBA RANKS (Featuring Maxi Priest)** Sales #32 / Airplay #39	Epic 73928

PRIMA, Louis, And Keely Smith

Prima was born on 12/7/11 in New Orleans. Died on 8/24/78. Jazz trumpeter/singer/composer/bandleader. Married jazz-styled vocalist Dorothy Keely Smith (born 3/9/32, Norfolk, Virginia) in 1952; divorced in 1961. First appeared with Prima in 1948.

DATE	POS	WKS	ARTIST–RECORD TITLE	LABEL & NO.
11/24/58	18	7	1. That Old Black Magic Sam Butera and The Witnesses (backing combo); performed by Prima & Smith in the movie *Senior Prom*; #1 hit for Glenn Miller in 1943	Capitol 4063
12/12/60+	15	8	2. Wonderland By Night [I] **LOUIS PRIMA**	Dot 16151

DATE	POS	WKS	ARTIST–RECORD TITLE	LABEL & NO.
			PRINCE	
			Born Prince Roger Nelson on 6/7/58 in Minneapolis. Vocalist/multi-instrumentalist/composer/producer. Named for the Prince Roger Trio, led by his father. Self-taught musician; own band, Grand Central, in junior high school. Self-produced first album in 1978. Starred in the movies *Purple Rain*, *Under The Cherry Moon*, *Sign 'O' The Times* and *Graffiti Bridge*. Founded own label, Paisley Park. The Revolution featured Lisa Coleman (keyboards), Wendy Melvoin (guitar), Bobby Z (percussion), Matt "Dr." Fink (keyboards), Eric Leeds (saxophone) and Andre Cymone (bass; replaced by Brownmark in 1981). Coleman and Melvoin formed duo Wendy & Lisa in 1987. Sheila E. (drums) joined Prince's band in 1986. Prince formed new band, New Power Generation (named for the oldest Prince fan club in Britain), in 1990, featuring Levi Seacer, Jr. (guitar), Sonny T. (bass), Tommy Barbarella (keyboard), dancer/percussionists Kirk Johnson and Damon Dickson, Michael Bland (drums), rapper Tony M. and Rosie Gaines (keyboards, vocals; replaced by Mayte [pronounced: my-tie] by 1992). Prince announced that he would no longer record on 4/27/93. Changed his name on 6/7/93 to a combination male/female symbol and announced his separation from New Power Generation. Revealed in September 1993 that he would be called "Victor." His music is featured in The Joffrey's 1993 rock ballet titled *Billboards*. By 1994 referred to as "The Artist Formerly Known As Prince." Married Mayte on 2/14/96.	
12/8/79+	**11**	12	● 1. **I Wanna Be Your Lover** #1 R&B hit (2 weeks)	Warner 49050
3/19/83	**6**	15	2. **Little Red Corvette**	Warner 29746
6/18/83	**12**	10	3. ****1999****	Warner 29896
9/17/83	**8**	11	4. **Delirious**	Warner 29503
6/9/84	**1 (5)**	16	▲ 5. **When Doves Cry** #1 R&B hit (8 weeks)	Warner 29286
			PRINCE AND THE REVOLUTION:	
8/11/84	**1 (2)**	14	● 6. **Let's Go Crazy** Sales #4 pre / Airplay #5 pre; #1 R&B hit (1 week)	Warner 29216
10/6/84	**2 (2)**	11	● 7. **Purple Rain** Sales #2 / Airplay #2	Warner 29174
12/22/84+	**8**	10	8. **I Would Die 4 U** Airplay #8 / Sales #14; above 2 recorded "live" at First Avenue Nightclub in Minneapolis	Warner 29121
3/2/85	**25**	6	9. **Take Me With U** **PRINCE and the REVOLUTION (with Apollonia)** Airplay #20; above 5 from the Prince movie and album *Purple Rain*	Warner 29079
5/18/85	**2 (1)**	14	10. **Raspberry Beret** Airplay #1(1) / Sales #2	Paisley P. 28972
8/3/85	**7**	10	11. **Pop Life** Airplay #7 / Sales #11	Paisley P. 28998
3/8/86	**1 (2)**	13	● 12. **Kiss** Airplay #1(2) / Sales #1(1); #1 R&B hit (4 weeks)	Paisley P. 28751
6/14/86	**23**	6	13. **Mountains** Sales #21 / Airplay #23; above 2 from the movie *Under the Cherry Moon* starring Prince	Paisley P. 28711
			PRINCE:	
3/14/87	**3**	11	14. **Sign 'O' The Times** Sales #3 / Airplay #5; #1 R&B hit (3 weeks)	Paisley P. 28399
8/29/87	**2 (1)**	13	15. **U Got The Look** Sales #2 / Airplay #3; Sheena Easton (backing vocal)	Paisley P. 28289
12/5/87+	**10**	12	16. **I Could Never Take The Place Of Your Man** Sales #9 / Airplay #10	Paisley P. 28288

DATE	POS	WKS	ARTIST–RECORD TITLE	LABEL & NO.
5/14/88	8	9	17. **Alphabet St.** Sales #7 / Airplay #11	Paisley P. 27900
7/1/89	1 (1)	11	▲ 18. **Batdance** Sales #1(3) / Airplay #2; #1 R&B hit (1 week)	Warner 22924
9/2/89	18	7	● 19. Partyman Sales #14 / Airplay #19	Warner 22814
12/2/89	36	3	20. The Arms Of Orion **PRINCE with Sheena Easton** Airplay #35 / Sales #37; above 3 from the Prince soundtrack album *Batman*, from the movie starring Michael Keaton	Warner 22757
8/11/90	6	9	● 21. **Thieves In The Temple** Airplay #5 / Sales #6; from the movie *Graffiti Bridge* starring Prince; #1 R&B hit (1 week)	Paisley P. 19751
			PRINCE And The NEW POWER GENERATION:	
9/28/91	21	5	● 22. Gett Off Sales #8 / Airplay #56	Paisley P. 19225
10/5/91	1 (2)	16	● 23. **Cream** Airplay #5 / Sales #10	Paisley P. 19175
12/21/91+	3	17	24. **Diamonds And Pearls** Airplay #2 / Sales #10; #1 R&B hit (1 week)	Paisley P. 19083
4/18/92	23	7	25. Money Don't Matter 2 Night Airplay #24 / Sales #69; above 4 from the album *Diamonds And* *Pearls*	Paisley P. 19020
10/24/92	36	1	26. My Name Is Prince Sales #22 / Airplay #37	Paisley P. 18707
12/19/92+	7	19	● 27. 7 Airplay #12 / Sales #13; samples "Tramp" by Jimmy McCracklin & Lowell Fulsom	Paisley P. 18824
3/12/94	3	22	● 28. **The Most Beautiful Girl In The World** ♀ Airplay #3 / Sales #5	NPG/Bell. 72514
8/27/94	31	7	29. Letitgo **PRINCE** Sales #32 / Airplay #36	Warner 18074
9/30/95	12	5	30. I Hate U ♀ **with The New Power Generation** Sales #6 / Airplay #46	NPG/Warner 17811
			PRISM Canadian rock group. Ron Tabak, lead singer (replaced by Henry Small in 1981).	
3/13/82	39	2	1. Don't Let Him Know co-written by Bryan Adams	Capitol 5082
			PROBY, P.J. Born James Marcus Smith on 11/6/38 in Houston. To Los Angeles in 1957; performed as Jet Powers. Achieved greater popularity in England than U.S.	
2/25/67	23	5	1. Niki Hoeky a different song, "Neki-Hokey," recorded by The Cleftones in 1956 (Gee 1016)	Liberty 55936

DATE	POS	WKS	ARTIST–RECORD TITLE	LABEL & NO.
			PROCLAIMERS, The	
			Pop duo of twin brothers Craig and Charlie Reid (born 3/5/62) from Edinburgh, Scotland.	
6/26/93	3	16	● 1. **I'm Gonna Be (500 Miles)** Sales #4 / Airplay #11; featured in the movie *Benny & Joon* starring Johnny Depp and Mary Stuart Masterson; originally from duo's 1989 album *Sunshine On Leith*; #21 hit on the Modern Rock Tracks chart in 1989; produced by Pete Wingfield	Chrysalis 24846
			PROCOL HARUM	
			British rock group formed in 1967 by Gary Brooker (vocals, piano) and lyricist Keith Reid. Many personnel changes. Robin Trower was lead guitarist, 1968–71. Band reunited in 1991. Procol is Latin for *beyond these things*.	
7/1/67	5	10	1. **A Whiter Shade Of Pale** melody based on the Bach cantata *Sleepers Awake*	Deram 7507
11/11/67	34	2	2. Homburg	A&M 885
6/24/72	16	8	3. Conquistador "live" recording; featuring the Edmonton Symphony Orchestra	A&M 1347
			PRUETT, Jeanne	
			Born Norma Jean Bowman on 1/30/37 in Pell City, Alabama. Country singer/songwriter. Moved to Nashville in 1956 with her husband, Jack Pruett (guitarist for Marty Robbins). Songwriter for Marty Robbins since 1963.	
6/23/73	28	5	1. Satin Sheets #1 Country hit (3 weeks)	MCA 40015
			PSEUDO ECHO	
			Pop-rock quartet formed in Melbourne, Australia in 1982: Brian Canham (vocals, guitar), James Leigh (keyboards), Pierre Gigliotti (bass) and Vince Leigh (drums).	
6/6/87	6	10	1. **Funky Town** Sales #6 / Airplay #8	RCA 5217
			PSYCHEDELIC FURS	
			British techno-rock band formed in New York in 1978: brothers Richard (vocals) and Tim (bass) Butler, John Ashton (guitar), and Vince Ely (drums). Ely left in 1983; returned briefly in 1989. Richard Butler formed Love Spit Love in 1994.	
5/2/87	26	5	1. Heartbreak Beat Sales #23 / Airplay #28	Columbia 06420
			PUBLIC ENEMY	
			Rap group led by Chuck D. (Carlton Ridenhauer). Includes Flavor Flav (William Drayton), DJ Terminator X (Norman Rogers) and Professor Griff (Richard Griffin). Disbanded briefly in June 1989 due to controversy over anti-Semitic remarks made by Griffin. Griffin left band at the end of 1989. Flavor Flav was sentenced to 90 days in jail on 5/26/95 for a 1993 shooting incident.	
7/30/94	33	5	1. Give It Up Sales #14 / Airplay #70; contains an interpolation of "Opus De Soul" written by Alvertis Isbell and Marvell Thomas	Def Jam 853316

DATE	POS	WKS	ARTIST–RECORD TITLE	LABEL & NO.
			PUCKETT, Gary, And The Union Gap	
			Singer/guitarist Puckett (born 10/17/42, Hibbing, Minnesota) formed The Union Gap in San Diego in 1967; named after the town of Union Gap, Washington. Included Kerry Chater (bass), Paul Whitebread (drums), Dwight Bement (sax) and Gary Withem (keyboards).	
			THE UNION GAP FEATURING GARY PUCKETT:	
12/2/67+	4	15	● 1. Woman, Woman	Columbia 44297
3/16/68	2 (3)	13	● 2. Young Girl	Columbia 44450
			GARY PUCKETT AND THE UNION GAP:	
6/22/68	2 (2)	11	● 3. Lady Willpower	Columbia 44547
9/28/68	7	10	● 4. Over You	Columbia 44644
3/22/69	15	8	5. Don't Give In To Him	Columbia 44788
9/6/69	9	9	6. This Girl Is A Woman Now	Columbia 44967
			PUPPIES, The	
			Brother/sister rap duo from Miami: Calvin Mills III (age nine in 1994) and Tamara Dee Mills (age 13 in 1994). Produced by their father, Calvin Mills II.	
8/13/94	40	1	1. Funky Y-2-C Sales #22	Chaos/Col. 77461
			PURE PRAIRIE LEAGUE	
			Country-rock group formed in Cincinnati in 1971. Numerous personnel changes. Craig Fuller (guitarist/vocalist, 1971–75), joined Little Feat by 1988. Country singer Vince Gill was lead singer from late 1979 to 1983.	
4/12/75	27	3	1. Amie	RCA 10184
5/24/80	10	11	2. Let Me Love You Tonight #1 Adult Contemporary hit (3 weeks)	Casablanca 2266
10/4/80	34	4	3. I'm Almost Ready	Casablanca 2294
5/23/81	28	7	4. Still Right Here In My Heart	Casablanca 2332
			PURIFY, James & Bobby	
			R&B duo: cousins James Purify (born 5/12/44, Pensacola, Florida) and Robert Lee Dickey (born 9/2/39, Tallahassee, Florida). Dickey left in the late '60s. Purify worked solo until 1974, when Ben Moore became Bobby Purify.	
10/22/66	6	10	1. I'm Your Puppet	Bell 648
2/25/67	38	1	2. Wish You Didn't Have To Go	Bell 660
5/13/67	25	5	3. Shake A Tail Feather	Bell 669
10/7/67	23	5	4. Let Love Come Between Us	Bell 685
			PURSELL, Bill	
			Pianist from Tulare, California. Appeared with the Nashville Symphony Orchestra. Taught musical composition at Vanderbilt University.	
2/16/63	9	10	1. Our Winter Love [I]	Columbia 42619
			PYRAMIDS, The	
			Surf band from Long Beach, California: Skip Mercer, Willie Glover, Steve Leonard, Ron McMullen and Tom Pittman. Performed with shaved heads. Appeared in the movie *Bikini Beach*.	
2/22/64	18	6	1. Penetration [I] first released on Best 102 in 1963	Best 13002

DATE	POS	WKS	ARTIST–RECORD TITLE	LABEL & NO.

Q

			Q	
			Pop quartet from Beaver Falls, Pennsylvania. Led by ex-Jaggerz members Robert Peckman and Don Garvin.	
4/9/77	23	7	1. Dancin' Man	Epic 50335
			QUAKER CITY BOYS	
			Philadelphia string band. Tommy Reilly, leader.	
1/26/59	39	1	1. Teasin'	Swan 4023
			QUARTERFLASH	
			Rock group from Portland, Oregon, led by the husband-and-wife team of Marv (guitar) and Rindy (vocals, saxophone) Ross. Originally known as Seafood Mama.	
11/7/81+	3	19	● 1. **Harden My Heart** *originally released as by: Seafood Mama on Whitefire in 1980*	Geffen 49824
3/13/82	16	7	2. Find Another Fool	Geffen 50006
7/2/83	14	11	3. Take Me To Heart	Geffen 29603
			QUATRO, Suzi	
			Born on 6/3/50 in Detroit. Rock singer. Moved to England in 1970, signed with Mickie Most's RAK label. Played Leather Tuscadero on TV's "Happy Days" in 1977. Her older sister Patti was a bassist with Fanny.	
2/24/79	4	15	● 1. **Stumblin' In** **SUZI QUATRO AND CHRIS NORMAN (lead singer of Smokie)**	RSO 917
			QUEEN	
			Rock group formed in England in 1972: Freddie Mercury (born Fred Bulsara on 9/5/46 in Zanzibar; died of AIDS 11/24/91; vocals), Brian May (guitar), John Deacon (bass) and Roger Taylor (drums). May and Taylor had been in the group Smile. Mercury had recorded as Larry Lurex. Wrote soundtrack for the movie *Flash Gordon* in 1980.	
3/29/75	12	10	1. Killer Queen	Elektra 45226
2/7/76	9	17	● 2. **Bohemian Rhapsody** *also see #13 below*	Elektra 45297
6/12/76	16	11	3. You're My Best Friend	Elektra 45318
12/4/76+	13	12	4. Somebody To Love *also see new "live" version (#14 below)*	Elektra 45362
11/26/77+	4	17	▲ 5. **We Are The Champions** B-side "We Will Rock You" did not chart, however, it received extensive airplay because both sides were segued together on the album *News Of The World*	Elektra 45441
12/9/78+	24	6	6. Bicycle Race/	
		6	7. Fat Bottomed Girls	Elektra 45541
1/12/80	1 (4)	17	● 8. **Crazy Little Thing Called Love**	Elektra 46579
8/30/80	1 (3)	21	▲ 9. **Another One Bites The Dust**	Elektra 47031
12/5/81+	29	8	10. Under Pressure **QUEEN & DAVID BOWIE** *also see Vanilla Ice's "Ice Ice Baby"*	Elektra 47235

DATE	POS	WKS	ARTIST–RECORD TITLE	LABEL & NO.
5/15/82	**11**	8	11. Body Language	Elektra 47452
3/3/84	**16**	8	12. Radio Ga-Ga	Capitol 5317
4/4/92	**2** (1)	13	13. **Bohemian Rhapsody** [R]	Hollywood 64794
			Sales #2 / Airplay #9; featured in the movie *Wayne's World* starring Mike Myers and Dana Carvey; proceeds donated to the Magic Johnson Foundation	
5/22/93	**30**	4	14. Somebody To Love [R]	Hollywood 64647
			GEORGE MICHAEL and QUEEN	
			Airplay #25 / Sales #72; recorded "live" at Wembley Stadium for the Freddie Mercury Tribute Concert	

QUEEN LATIFAH

Born Dana Owens in Newark, New Jersey; raised in nearby East Orange. Female rapper. Appeared in the movies *Jungle Fever*, *House Party 2* and *Who's The Man?*; cast member of 1993 Fox TV series "Living Single." CEO of Flavor Unit Records. Latifah is Arabic for delicate and sensitive.

DATE	POS	WKS	ARTIST–RECORD TITLE	LABEL & NO.
12/18/93+	**23**	11	1. U.N.I.T.Y.	Motown 2225
			Sales #16 / Airplay #24; samples "Message From The Inner City" by The Crusaders	

QUEENSRŸCHE

Heavy-metal quintet formed in 1981, in Bellevue, Washington, by high school classmates: Geoff Tate (vocals), Chris DeGarmo and Michael WIlton (guitars), Eddie Jackson (bass), and Scott Rockenfield (drums).

DATE	POS	WKS	ARTIST–RECORD TITLE	LABEL & NO.
4/13/91	**9**	11	1. **Silent Lucidity**	EMI 50345
			Sales #4 / Airplay #15	

? (QUESTION MARK) & THE MYSTERIANS

Early punk-rock quintet. Lead singer Rudy Martinez was born in Mexico and raised in Saginaw, Michigan.

DATE	POS	WKS	ARTIST–RECORD TITLE	LABEL & NO.
9/17/66	**1** (1)	12	● 1. **96 Tears**	Cameo 428
			first released on Pa-Go-Go 102 in 1966	
12/10/66	**22**	6	2. I Need Somebody	Cameo 441
			? & THE MYSTERIANS	

QUIET RIOT

Heavy-metal rock quartet from Los Angeles: Kevin DuBrow (lead singer), Carlos Cavazo (guitar), Frankie Banali (drums) and Rudy Sarzo (bass); replaced by Chuck Wright in 1985). DuBrow and Wright left group in 1987; replaced by Paul Shortino (vocals) and Sean McNabb (bass).

DATE	POS	WKS	ARTIST–RECORD TITLE	LABEL & NO.
10/15/83	**5**	14	● 1. **Cum On Feel The Noize**	Pasha 04005
1/28/84	**31**	4	2. Bang Your Head (Metal Health)	Pasha 04267

QUIN-TONES, The

York, Pennsylvania, group consisting of Roberta Haymon (lead singer), Phyllis Carr, Carolyn Holmes, Kenny Sexton, Jeannie Crist and Ronnie Scott (pianist).

DATE	POS	WKS	ARTIST–RECORD TITLE	LABEL & NO.
9/8/58	**18**	6	1. Down The Aisle Of Love	Hunt 321
			Best Seller #18 / Hot 100 #20; first released on Red Top 108 in 1958	

DATE	POS	WKS	ARTIST–RECORD TITLE	LABEL & NO.

R

RABBITT, Eddie

Born Edward Thomas Rabbitt on 11/27/44 in Brooklyn; raised in East Orange, New Jersey. Country singer/songwriter/guitarist. First recorded for 20th Century in 1964. Moved to Nashville in 1968. Became established after Elvis Presley recorded his song "Kentucky Rain."

DATE	POS	WKS	ARTIST–RECORD TITLE	LABEL & NO.
3/3/79	30	4	1. Every Which Way But Loose title song from the movie starring Clint Eastwood; #1 Country hit (3 weeks)	Elektra 45554
7/14/79	13	10	2. Suspicions #1 Country hit (1 week)	Elektra 46053
7/26/80	5	15	● 3. **Drivin' My Life Away** from the movie *Roadie* starring Meat Loaf; #1 Country hit (1 week)	Elektra 46656
12/6/80+	1 (2)	18	● 4. **I Love A Rainy Night** #1 Adult Contemporary hit (3 weeks); #1 Country hit (1 week)	Elektra 47066
8/8/81	5	15	5. **Step By Step** #1 Country hit (1 week)	Elektra 47174
12/5/81+	15	10	6. Someone Could Lose A Heart Tonight #1 Country hit (1 week)	Elektra 47239
5/22/82	35	4	7. I Don't Know Where To Start	Elektra 47435
11/13/82+	7	21	8. **You And I** **EDDIE RABBITT with CRYSTAL GAYLE** #1 Country hit (1 week)	Elektra 69936

RADIOHEAD

Rock quintet from Oxford, England: Thom E. Yorke (vocals), brothers Jonny (guitar) and Colin (bass) Greenwood, Ed O'Brien (guitar) and Phil Selway (drums).

DATE	POS	WKS	ARTIST–RECORD TITLE	LABEL & NO.
8/7/93	34	5	1. Creep Sales #23	Capitol 44932

RAEKWON

Shallah Raekwon. Member of Wu-Tang Clan. Also known as Chef Raekwon a.k.a. Lou Diamonds.

DATE	POS	WKS	ARTIST–RECORD TITLE	LABEL & NO.
10/28/95	37	2	1. Ice Cream **Chef RAEKWON featuring Tony Starks (Ghost Face Killer) and** Method Man Sales #19 / Airplay #74	Loud/RCA 64426

RAFFERTY, Gerry

Born on 4/16/47 in Paisley, Scotland. Singer/songwriter/guitarist. Co-leader of Stealers Wheel.

DATE	POS	WKS	ARTIST–RECORD TITLE	LABEL & NO.
5/13/78	2 (6)	15	● 1. **Baker Street** Raphael Ravenscroft (sax solo)	United Art. 1192
8/26/78	12	10	2. Right Down The Line #1 Adult Contemporary hit (4 weeks)	United Art. 1233
1/6/79	28	6	3. Home And Dry	United Art. 1266
6/16/79	17	7	4. Days Gone Down (Still Got The Light In Your Eyes)	United Art. 1298
9/8/79	21	8	5. Get It Right Next Time	United Art. 1316

RAIDERS—see REVERE, Paul

DATE	POS	WKS	ARTIST–RECORD TITLE	LABEL & NO.
			## RAINBOW	
			Hard-rock band led by British guitarist Ritchie Blackmore and bassist Roger Glover, both members of Deep Purple. Fluctuating lineup included vocalists Ronnie James Dio and Joe Lynn Turner, keyboardist Tony Carey and drummer Cozy Powell (Emerson, Lake & Powell). Group split up upon re-formation of Deep Purple in 1984. In 1990, Turner joined Deep Purple and Powell joined Black Sabbath.	
6/19/82	40	1	1. Stone Cold	Mercury 76146
			## RAINDROPS, The	
			Songwriting team of Ellie Greenwich (born 10/23/40) and husband Jeff Barry (born 4/3/38). Divorced in 1965, but continued to work together. Barry wrote "Tell Laura I Love Her"; team wrote "Be My Baby," "Da Doo Ron Ron," "Chapel Of Love," "River Deep-Mountain High," "Hanky Panky," "Leader of The Pack" and many more. Barry produced such mega-hits as "Sugar Sugar" (Archies) and "I'm A Believer" (Monkees).	
8/31/63	17	7	1. The Kind Of Boy You Can't Forget	Jubilee 5455
			## RAINWATER, Marvin	
			Born Marvin Karlton Percy on 7/2/25 in Wichita, Kansas. Rockabilly singer of Cherokee Indian heritage. Worked on Arthur Godfrey's TV show in 1955.	
6/10/57	18	12	● 1. Gonna Find Me A Bluebird Juke Box #18 end / Best Seller #19 / Top 100 #22	MGM 12412
			## RAITT, Bonnie	
			Born on 11/8/49 in Burbank, California. Veteran blues-rock singer/guitarist. Daughter of Broadway actor/singer John Raitt. Winner of four Grammys for her 1989 album *Nick Of Time*. Married actor Michael O'Keefe on 4/28/91.	
8/17/91	5	15	1. **Something To Talk About** Sales #14 / Airplay #19	Capitol 44724
1/18/92	18	10	2. I Can't Make You Love Me Sales #23 / Airplay #25	Capitol 44729
5/23/92	34	4	3. Not The Only One Airplay #35	Capitol 44764
4/9/94	19	10	4. Love Sneakin' Up On You Airplay #14	Capitol 58125
3/4/95	33	6	5. You Got It Airplay #36 / Sales #42; from the movie *Boys On The Side* starring Whoopi Goldberg	Arista 12795
			## RAMBEAU, Eddie	
			Born Edward Flurie on 6/30/43 in Hazleton, Pennsylvania. Pop singer/songwriter.	
6/5/65	35	2	1. Concrete And Clay	DynoVoice 204
			## RAM JAM	
			East Coast rock quartet led by Bill Bartlett (lead guitarist of The Lemon Pipers). Member Howie Blauvelt played bass in Billy Joel's group, The Hassles; died of a heart attack on 10/25/93 (age 44).	
7/23/77	18	8	1. Black Betty written by legendary black folksinger Hudie Ledbetter (Leadbelly)	Epic 50357

DATE	POS	WKS	ARTIST–RECORD TITLE	LABEL & NO.
			RAMRODS	
			Instrumental rock quartet from Connecticut: Vincent Bell Lee (lead guitar; not to be confused with Vincent Bell [Gambella]), his cousin Eugene Moore (since deceased), Richard Lane and his sister Claire.	
2/20/61	30	1	1. (Ghost) Riders In The Sky [I] #1 hit for Vaughn Monroe in 1949	Amy 813
			RAN-DELLS, The	
			Brothers Steve and Robert Rappaport, and cousin John Spirt from Villas, New Jersey.	
8/31/63	16	8	1. Martian Hop [N]	Chairman 4403
			RANDOLPH, Boots	
			Born Homer Louis Randolph III on 6/3/27 in Paducah, Kentucky. Premier Nashville session saxophonist.	
3/30/63	35	3	1. Yakety Sax [I] inspired by the sax solo by King Curtis in The Coasters' 1957 hit "Yakety Yak"; original version released in 1958 as by: Randy Randolph on RCA 7395	Monument 804
			RANDY & THE RAINBOWS	
			White doo-wop group from Queens, New York, originally called Jr. And The Counts. Consisted of Dominick "Randy" Safuto (lead) and brother Frank Safuto, brothers Mike and Sal Zero, and Ken Arcipowski.	
7/27/63	10	10	1. **Denise**	Rust 5059
			RANKS, Shabba	
			Born Rawlston Fernando Gordon on 1/17/66 in Sturgetown, Jamaica. Dancehall reggae singer. Formerly known as Jamaican DJ Don.	

12/7/91	37	1	1. Housecall (Your Body Can't Lie To Me)
			   SHABBA RANKS (Featuring Maxi Priest)
			   Sales #32 / Airplay #39
				Epic 73928

8/1/92	40	1	2. Mr. Loverman Sales #23 / Airplay #55; from the movie *Deep Cover* starring Larry Fishburne; Chevelle Franklin (female vocal)	Epic 74257

1/2/93	33	2	● 3. Slow And Sexy
			   SHABBA RANKS (featuring Johnny Gill)
			   Sales #14 / Airplay #63
				Epic 74741

			RAPPIN' 4-TAY	
			Born Anthony Forte in San Francisco in 1969. Male rapper.	
11/12/94	36	9	1. Playaz Club Sales #26 / Airplay #49	Chrysalis 58267

4/29/95	39	2	2. I'll Be Around
			   RAPPIN' 4-TAY FEATURING THE SPINNERS
			   Sales #26 / Airplay #63; Rappin' 4-Tay raps new verse over the Spinners hit (#3 in 1972) with its original music and chorus
				Rag Top 58331

DATE	POS	WKS	ARTIST–RECORD TITLE	LABEL & NO.

RARE EARTH

Nucleus of Detroit rock group: Gil Bridges (saxophone, flute), John Persh (trombone, bass) and Pete Rivera (drums; born Pete Hoorelbeke). Worked as the Sunliners in the '60s. In 1970, added Ed Guzman (percussion) and Ray Monette (replaced guitarist Rob Richards). Mark Olson replaced Kenneth James (keyboards) in 1971. Many changes thereafter. Persh died in 1979 of a staph virus. Olson died of alcohol-related complications in 1982. Guzman died on 7/29/93 (age 49).

DATE	POS	WKS	ARTIST–RECORD TITLE	LABEL & NO.
4/4/70	4	17	1. **Get Ready**	Rare Earth 5012
8/22/70	7	11	2. **(I Know) I'm Losing You**	Rare Earth 5017
1/2/71	17	8	3. Born To Wander	Rare Earth 5021
8/7/71	7	10	4. **I Just Want To Celebrate**	Rare Earth 5031
12/18/71+	19	7	5. Hey Big Brother	Rare Earth 5038
6/17/78	39	2	6. Warm Ride	Prodigal 0640
			written by the Bee Gees	

RASCALS, The

Blue-eyed, soul-pop quartet formed in New York City in 1964. Consisted of Felix Cavaliere, Dino Danelli, Eddie Brigati and Gene Cornish. All except Danelli had been in Joey Dee's Starliters. Brigati and Cornish left in 1971, replaced by Robert Popwell, Buzzy Feiten and Ann Sutton. Group disbanded in 1972. Cavaliere, Cornish and Danelli reunited in June 1988.

THE YOUNG RASCALS:

DATE	POS	WKS	ARTIST–RECORD TITLE	LABEL & NO.
3/26/66	1 (1)	12	1. **Good Lovin'**	Atlantic 2321
7/9/66	20	4	2. You Better Run	Atlantic 2338
2/25/67	16	9	3. I've Been Lonely Too Long	Atlantic 2377
5/6/67	1 (4)	11	● 4. **Groovin'**	Atlantic 2401
7/22/67	10	8	5. **A Girl Like You**	Atlantic 2424
9/23/67	4	9	6. **How Can I Be Sure**	Atlantic 2438
12/23/67+	20	5	7. It's Wonderful	Atlantic 2463

THE RASCALS:

DATE	POS	WKS	ARTIST–RECORD TITLE	LABEL & NO.
4/20/68	3	11	● 8. **A Beautiful Morning**	Atlantic 2493
7/27/68	1 (5)	13	● 9. **People Got To Be Free**	Atlantic 2537
12/14/68+	24	6	10. A Ray Of Hope	Atlantic 2584
3/1/69	39	2	11. Heaven	Atlantic 2599
6/7/69	27	5	12. See	Atlantic 2634
9/20/69	26	5	13. Carry Me Back	Atlantic 2664

RASPBERRIES

Pop-rock band formed in Mentor, Ohio, in 1971: Eric Carmen (lead singer, guitar), Wally Bryson (lead guitar), David Smalley (bass) and Jim Bonfanti (drums). Smalley and Bonfanti replaced by Scott McCarl and Michael McBride in 1974. Carmen went solo in 1975.

DATE	POS	WKS	ARTIST–RECORD TITLE	LABEL & NO.
8/19/72	5	11	● 1. **Go All The Way**	Capitol 3348
12/9/72+	16	9	2. I Wanna Be With You	Capitol 3473
5/12/73	35	7	3. Let's Pretend	Capitol 3546
10/12/74	18	6	4. Overnight Sensation (Hit Record)	Capitol 3946

DATE	POS	WKS	ARTIST–RECORD TITLE	LABEL & NO.
			RATT	
			Hard-rock quintet formed in Los Angeles in 1981: Stephen Pearcy (vocals), Warren DeMartini and Robbin Crosby (guitars), Juan Croucier (bass) and Bobby Blotzer (drums; member of Contraband in 1991). Pearcy left band in early 1992 and formed Arcade.	
7/14/84	12	10	1. Round And Round	Atlantic 89693
8/17/85	40	1	2. Lay It Down	Atlantic 89546
			RAWLS, Lou	
			Born on 12/1/35 in Chicago. With the Pilgrim Travelers gospel group, 1957–59. Summer replacement TV show "Lou Rawls & The Golddiggers" in 1969. Appeared in the movies *Angel Angel, Down We Go* and *Believe In Me*. Voice of many Budweiser beer ads and featured singer in the "Garfield" TV specials.	
10/15/66	13	8	1. Love Is A Hurtin' Thing #1 R&B hit (1 week)	Capitol 5709
5/6/67	29	4	2. Dead End Street the first 1:27 of this tune is a monologue by Rawls	Capitol 5869
8/30/69	18	8	3. Your Good Thing (Is About To End)	Capitol 2550
10/16/71	17	11	4. A Natural Man	MGM 14262
7/10/76	2 (2)	13	● 5. **You'll Never Find Another Love Like Mine** #1 R&B hit (2 weeks); #1 Adult Contemporary hit (1 week)	Phil. Int. 3592
2/25/78	24	8	6. Lady Love	Phil. Int. 3634
			RAY, Diane	
			Born on 9/1/42 in Gastonia, North Carolina.	
9/7/63	31	3	1. Please Don't Talk To The Lifeguard first recorded by Andrea Carroll in 1961 (Epic 9450)	Mercury 72117
			RAY, James	
			Born James Ray Raymond in 1941, in Washington, D.C. Was living on the street when discovered by Gerry Granahan's label. He died soon after his success as a singer.	
12/25/61+	22	7	1. If You Gotta Make A Fool Of Somebody Hutch Davie (orch.)	Caprice 110
			RAY, Johnnie	
			Born on 1/10/27 in Dallas, Oregon. Died on 2/25/90 of liver failure. Wore hearing aid since age 14. First recorded for Okeh in 1951. Famous for emotion-packed delivery, with R&B influences. Appeared in three movies.	
9/8/56	2 (1)	23	● 1. **Just Walking In The Rain** Top 100 #2 / Juke Box #2 / Best Seller #3 / Jockey #3; first recorded by The Prisonaires in 1953 (Sun 186)	Columbia 40729
1/19/57	10	10	2. **You Don't Owe Me A Thing/** Best Seller #10 / Top 100 #10 / Jockey #10 / Juke Box #12; written by Marty Robbins	
2/2/57	36	2	3. Look Homeward, Angel	Columbia 40803
5/6/57	12	5	4. Yes Tonight, Josephine Jockey #12 / Top 100 #18; Ray Conniff (orch. and chorus, all of above)	Columbia 40893

DATE	POS	WKS	ARTIST–RECORD TITLE	LABEL & NO.
			RAYBURN, Margie	
			Born in Madera, California. Member of The Sunnysiders; also sang with Ray Anthony's orchestra. Married Norman Milkin of The Sunnysiders.	
11/11/57	9	13	1. **I'm Available**	Liberty 55102
			Jockey #9 / Best Seller #15 / Top 100 #16; written by Dave Burgess (The Champs)	
			RAYDIO—see PARKER, Ray, Jr.	
			RAY, GOODMAN & BROWN—see MOMENTS, The	
			RAYS, The	
			R&B group formed in New York City in 1955: Harold Miller (lead), Walter Ford and David Jones (tenors) and Harry James (baritone). First recorded for Chess in 1955.	
10/21/57	3	17	● 1. **Silhouettes/**	
			Top 100 #3 / Best Seller #4 / Jockey #5; first released on XYZ 102 in 1957	
		4	2. Daddy Cool	Cameo 117
			Best Seller flip	
			REA, Chris	
			Born on 3/4/51 in Middlesborough, England. Pop-rock singer/songwriter. Hugely popular in Europe.	
7/29/78	12	10	1. Fool (If You Think It's Over)	United Art. 1198
			#1 Adult Contemporary hit (3 weeks)	
			READY FOR THE WORLD	
			Black sextet from Flint, Michigan, formed in 1982: Melvin Riley, Jr. (lead singer), Gordon Strozier, Gregory Potts, Willie Triplett, John Eaton and Gerald Valentine.	
8/24/85	1 (1)	13	1. **Oh Sheila**	MCA 52636
			Sales #1(1) / Airplay #3; #1 R&B hit (2 weeks)	
1/25/86	21	6	2. Digital Display	MCA 52734
			Sales #14	
12/27/86+	9	12	3. **Love You Down**	MCA 52947
			Sales #9 / Airplay #12; #1 R&B hit (2 weeks)	
			REAL LIFE	
			Rock band formed in Melbourne, Australia, in 1982: David Sterry (vocals, guitar), Richard Zatorski (keyboards), Allan Johnson (bass) and Danny Simcic (drums). By 1990, Steve Williams had replaced Zatorski.	
1/14/84	29	6	1. Send Me An Angel	Curb 52287
5/5/84	40	1	2. Catch Me I'm Falling	Curb 52362
6/10/89	26	8	3. Send Me An Angel '89 [R]	Curb 10531
			Airplay #22 / Sales #28; new recording of #1 above	
			REAL McCOY	
			Trio based in Berlin, Germany: Olaf "OJ" Jeglitza, Patricia Petersen and Vanessa Mason.	
9/17/94	3	40	▲ 1. **Another Night**	Arista 12724
			Airplay #2 / Sales #2	

DATE	POS	WKS	ARTIST–RECORD TITLE	LABEL & NO.
3/11/95	3	17	● 2. **Run Away** Airplay #4 / Sales #6	Arista 12808
6/24/95	19	13	3. Come And Get Your Love Sales #21 / Airplay #29	Arista 12834

REBELS, The

Buffalo DJ Tom Shannon and producer Phil Todaro (Shan-Todd label) recruited the Buffalo group The Rebels (aka: The Rockin' Rebels) to record Shannon's theme song "Wild Weekend." Consisted of twins Mickey and Jim Kipler, Paul Balon and Tom Gorman. Later Swan recordings that were billed as The Rockin' Rebels were by a different group that recorded as the Hot-Toddys in 1959.

DATE	POS	WKS	ARTIST–RECORD TITLE	LABEL & NO.
1/26/63	8	12	1. **Wild Weekend** [I] first released on Mar-Lee 0094 in 1960	Swan 4125

REDBONE

American Indian "swamp-rock" group formed in Los Angeles in 1968. Consisted of brothers Lolly (lead vocals, guitar) and Pat Vegas (lead vocals, bass), Anthony Bellamy (guitar) and Peter De Poe (drums). The Vegas brothers had been session musicians and worked the "Shindig" TV show.

DATE	POS	WKS	ARTIST–RECORD TITLE	LABEL & NO.
1/8/72	21	7	1. The Witch Queen Of New Orleans	Epic 10749
2/9/74	5	18	● 2. **Come And Get Your Love**	Epic 11035

REDDING, Gene

Born in Anderson, Indiana, in 1945. Discovered by Etta James at a USO Club in Anchorage, Alaska.

DATE	POS	WKS	ARTIST–RECORD TITLE	LABEL & NO.
7/6/74	24	5	1. This Heart	Haven 7000

REDDING, Otis

Born on 9/9/41 in Dawson, Georgia. Killed in a plane crash in Lake Monona in Madison, Wisconsin, on 12/10/67 (crash also killed four members of the Bar-Kays). Soul singer/songwriter/producer/pianist. First recorded with Johnny Jenkins & The Pinetoppers on Confederate in 1960. Own label, Jotis. Inducted into the Rock and Roll Hall of Fame in 1989.

DATE	POS	WKS	ARTIST–RECORD TITLE	LABEL & NO.
6/19/65	21	6	1. I've Been Loving You Too Long (To Stop Now)	Volt 126
10/23/65	35	3	2. Respect	Volt 128
4/2/66	31	3	3. Satisfaction	Volt 132
10/29/66	29	4	4. Fa-Fa-Fa-Fa-Fa (Sad Song)	Volt 138
12/31/66+	25	6	5. Try A Little Tenderness #6 hit for Ted Lewis in 1933	Volt 141
6/3/67	26	4	6. Tramp **OTIS & CARLA**	Stax 216
9/23/67	30	2	7. Knock On Wood **OTIS & CARLA**	Stax 228
2/10/68	1 (4)	14	● 8. **(Sittin' On) The Dock Of The Bay** recorded 3 days before Redding's death; #1 R&B hit (3 weeks)	Volt 157
5/11/68	25	5	9. The Happy Song (Dum-Dum)	Volt 163
7/27/68	36	1	10. Amen	Atco 6592
12/14/68+	21	5	11. Papa's Got A Brand New Bag recorded "live" at the Whisky A Go-Go	Atco 6636

The **Righteous Brothers**' memorable streak of blue-eyed soul hits drew to a temporary close with 1966's "Go Ahead And Cry." Following its rise to No. 30, the group went without a Top 40 hit until 1974's "Rock And Roll Heaven" single on Haven Records.

Miguel Rios's 1970 hit "A Song Of Joy" was based on Beethoven's *Ninth Symphony* and reached No. 14—not good enough to beat Walter Murphy & The Big Apple Band's 1976 No. 1 smash "A Fifth Of Beethoven," based on the composer's *Fifth Symphony*.

Marty Robbins's 1960 single "Big Iron" peaked at No. 26 on the chart; the song was his first hit to follow his all-time biggest smash, "El Paso."

The **Rolling Stones**' spectacular career as "England's newest hitmakers" officially began Stateside with their first Top 40 hit, 1964's "Tell Me (You're Coming Back)."

Diana Ross And The Supremes and **The Temptations**' joint 1968 single "I'm Gonna Make You Love Me" reached No. 2, thus becoming The Supremes' 16th Top 5 hit and The Tempts' eighth.

Roxette's stunning record of hitmaking was one of the '90s biggest surprises. Between 1989 and 1992, the Swedish duo released four No. 1 and two No. 2 smashes; 1990's "Dangerous" spent two weeks at No. 2.

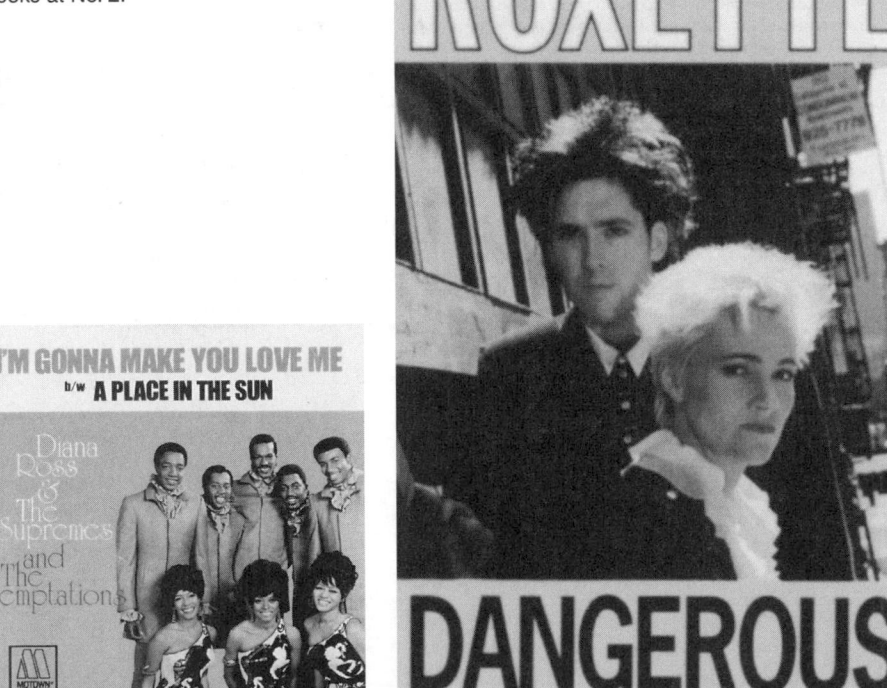

Run-D.M.C.'s reputation as early rap stars was cemented with the crossover success of 1986's "Walk This Way," which teamed the trio with Aerosmith, and its follow-up "You Be Illin'," which reached No. 29 and endlessly delighted grammar teachers.

Bobby Rydell's No. 5 1960 smash "Swingin' School" was backed by "Ding-A-Ling," which ascended to No. 18 and bore absolutely no lyrical similarities to Chuck Berry's 1972 chart-topper of nearly the same name.

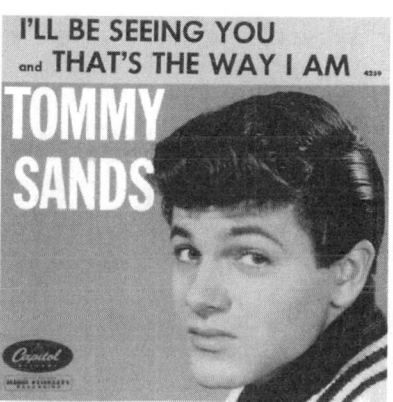

Salt-N-Pepa's massive status as single-sellers was well illustrated by their first two Top 40 hits, 1987's "Push It" and 1990's "Expression." Though neither track entered the Top 10, both went platinum.

Tommy Sands's version of "I'll Be Seeing You" never shared the sucess of his three Top 40 hits in 1957-58—nor did the 1961 version of it, sung by his then-father-in-law, Frank Sinatra, which peaked at No. 58.

Santana's 30-year career of Latin Rock music-making has so far resulted in only one hit with a full Spanish lyric—1971's Top 20 hit "Oye Como Va."

Scorpions were one of very few metal bands to navigate a smooth course into the pop charts. The German hard rockers went gold with their Top 5 single "Wind Of Change" in 1991.

DATE	POS	WKS	ARTIST–RECORD TITLE	LABEL & NO.
			REDDY, Helen	
			Born on 10/25/41 in Melbourne, Australia. Family was in show business; Helen made stage debut at age four. Own TV series in the early '60s. Migrated to New York in 1966. To Los Angeles in 1968. Acted in the movies *Airport 1975* (1974), *Pete's Dragon* (1977) and *Sgt. Pepper's Lonely Hearts Club Band* (1978).	
5/8/71	13	9	1. I Don't Know How To Love Him from the rock opera *Jesus Christ Superstar*	Capitol 3027
10/14/72	1 (1)	14	● 2. **I Am Woman** from the movie *Stand Up and Be Counted* starring Stella Stevens	Capitol 3350
3/10/73	12	10	3. Peaceful	Capitol 3527
7/28/73	1 (1)	14	● 4. **Delta Dawn** #1 Adult Contemporary hit (2 weeks)	Capitol 3645
11/17/73	3	13	● 5. **Leave Me Alone (Ruby Red Dress)** #1 Adult Contemporary hit (4 weeks)	Capitol 3768
3/30/74	15	9	6. Keep On Singing #1 Adult Contemporary hit (2 weeks)	Capitol 3845
7/20/74	9	12	7. **You And Me Against The World** includes a brief spoken dialogue with Helen's daughter, Tracy; #1 Adult Contemporary hit (1 week)	Capitol 3897
11/2/74	1 (1)	13	● 8. **Angie Baby** #1 Adult Contemporary hit (1 week)	Capitol 3972
3/1/75	22	5	9. Emotion #1 Adult Contemporary hit (1 week)	Capitol 4021
7/26/75	35	2	10. Bluebird written by Leon Russell	Capitol 4108
8/30/75	8	9	11. **Ain't No Way To Treat A Lady** #1 Adult Contemporary hit (1 week)	Capitol 4128
12/27/75+	19	9	12. Somewhere In The Night	Capitol 4192
8/21/76	29	5	13. I Can't Hear You No More/ #1 Adult Contemporary hit (1 week)	
		4	14. Music Is My Life	Capitol 4312
6/11/77	18	12	15. You're My World	Capitol 4418
			REDEYE	
			Rock quartet led by Dave Hodgkins and Douglas "Red" Mark.	
12/26/70+	27	7	1. Games	Pentagram 204
			RED HOT CHILI PEPPERS	
			Los Angeles-based rap-styled rock foursome: Anthony Kiedis (vocals), Michael "Flea" Balzary (bass), Hillel Slovak (guitar) and Jack Irons (drums). Slovak died of a heroin overdose on 6/25/88 (age 26); replaced by John Frusciante. Irons left in 1988 and later joined Eleven, then Pearl Jam; replaced by Chad Smith. Frusciante left in May 1992; replaced by Zander Schloss (Thelonious Monster, The Magnificent Bastards), then by Arik Marshall, then by Jesse Tobias and finally by Dave Navarro (Jane's Addiction) in September 1993. Kiedis appeared in the movie *Point Break*. Flea and Kiedis appeared in the movie *The Chase*.	
4/18/92	2 (1)	23	● 1. **Under The Bridge** Sales #2 / Airplay #3	Warner 18978
9/11/93	22	11	2. Soul To Squeeze Sales #10 / Airplay #43; from the movie *Coneheads* starring Dan Aykroyd and Jane Curtin	Warner 18401

DATE	POS	WKS	ARTIST–RECORD TITLE	LABEL & NO.
			REDMAN	
			Rapper from Newark, New Jersey. Discovered by Erick Sermon of EPMD.	
9/2/95	**13**	8	● 1. How High	Def Jam/RAL 9924
			REDMAN & METHOD MAN	
			Sales #7 / Airplay #64; from the rap concert movie *The Show*; contains an interpolation of "Fly Robin Fly" and samples "I Am Woman" by The Cover Girls	
			REDNEX	
			Studio group from Sweden.	
4/1/95	**25**	11	● 1. Cotton Eye Joe	Battery 46501
			Sales #8 / Airplay #75; dance version of traditional hillbilly song	
			REED, Dan, Network	
			Funk-rock quintet based in Portland, Oregon; led by singer/composer Dan Reed.	
4/30/88	**38**	2	1. Ritual	Mercury 870183
			Sales #27	
			REED, Jerry	
			Born Jerry Reed Hubbard on 3/20/37 in Atlanta. Country singer/guitarist/songwriter/actor. Among his many movies, co-starred in *Gator* and *Smokey & The Bandit I & II*. Own TV series "Concrete Cowboys." Elvis Presley recorded two of Reed's songs: "U.S. Male" and "Guitar Man."	
1/9/71	**8**	14	● 1. **Amos Moses** [N]	RCA 9904
5/29/71	**9**	9	2. **When You're Hot, You're Hot** [N]	RCA 9976
			#1 Country hit (5 weeks)	
			REED, Jimmy	
			Born Mathis James Reed on 9/6/25 in Dunleith, Mississippi. Died from an epileptic seizure on 8/29/76. Distinctive, influential blues singer/guitarist/harmonica player/songwriter, active until his death. Afflicted with epilepsy since 1957. Inducted into the Rock and Roll Hall of Fame in 1991.	
11/4/57	**32**	3	1. Honest I Do	Vee-Jay 253
			Top 100 #32 / Best Seller #36	
2/29/60	**37**	2	2. Baby What You Want Me To Do	Vee-Jay 333
			REED, Lou	
			Born Louis Firbank on 3/2/42 in Freeport, Long Island, New York. Lead singer/songwriter of the New York seminal rock band Velvet Underground. Appeared in the movie *One Trick Pony*.	
3/31/73	**16**	8	1. Walk On The Wild Side	RCA 0887
			produced by David Bowie and Mick Ronson	
			REESE, Della	
			Born Delloreese Patricia Early on 7/6/31 in Detroit. With Mahalia Jackson gospel troupe, 1945–49; with Erskine Hawkins in the early '50s. Solo since 1957. Actress/singer on many TV shows. Appeared in the movies *Let's Rock* (1958) and *Harlem Nights* (1989). Own TV series "Della" in 1970. Played Della Rogers on the TV series "Chico & The Man," 1976–78. Also on TV's "The Royal Family."	
9/9/57	**12**	13	1. And That Reminds Me	Jubilee 5292
			Jockey #12 / Best Seller #23 / Top 100 #29; lyric version of the Italian instrumental "Autumn Concerto"; Honey Dreamers (backing vocals); Billy Rock (orch.)	

DATE	POS	WKS	ARTIST–RECORD TITLE	LABEL & NO.
10/5/59	2 (1)	15	2. **Don't You Know** same melody as Sammy Kaye's 1952 hit "You"; adapted from "Musetta's Waltz" from the Puccini opera *La Boheme*; #1 R&B hit (2 weeks)	RCA 7591
12/28/59+	16	8	3. Not One Minute More Glenn Osser (orch., above 2)	RCA 7644
			REEVES, Jim	
			Born James Travis Reeves on 8/20/24 in Panola County, Texas. Killed in a plane crash on 7/31/64 in Nashville. Aspirations of a professional baseball career cut short by an ankle injury. DJ at KWKH-Shreveport, Louisiana, home of the "Louisiana Hayride," early '50s. First recorded for Macy's in 1950. Joined "Hayride" cast in 1953. Joined the *Grand Ole Opry* in 1955. Own ABN-Radio series in 1957. Appeared in the 1963 movie *Kimberley Jim*. Elected to the Country Music Hall of Fame in 1967.	
5/6/57	11	14	1. Four Walls Jockey #11 / Top 100 #12 / Juke Box #13 / Best Seller #14; #1 Country hit (8 weeks)	RCA 6874
1/11/60	2 (3)	20	● 2. **He'll Have To Go** #1 Country hit (14 weeks)	RCA 7643
7/11/60	37	1	3. I'm Gettin' Better	RCA 7756
11/28/60	31	4	4. Am I Losing You	RCA 7800
			REEVES, Martha—see MARTHA & THE VANDELLAS	
			REFLECTIONS, The	
			Detroit pop-rock quartet: Tony Micale (lead vocals), Dan Bennie, Phil Castrodale and John Dean.	
5/2/64	6	9	1. **(Just Like) Romeo & Juliet**	Golden World 9
			RE-FLEX	
			Techno-rock quartet formed in London in 1982: Baxter (vocals, guitar), Paul Fishman (keyboards), Nigel Ross-Scott (bass) and Roland Vaughan Kerridge (drums).	
2/18/84	24	5	1. The Politics Of Dancing	Capitol 5301
			REGENTS, The	
			Bronx vocal group formed as the Desires in 1958: Guy Villari (lead), Sal Cuomo, Chuck Fassert, Don Jacabucci and Tony "Hot Rod" Gravagna. "Barbara-Ann," written for Fassert's sister, was first recorded as a demo in 1958. Group had disbanded by the time "Barbara-Ann" was released.	
5/22/61	13	7	1. Barbara-Ann first released on Cousins 1002 in 1961	Gee 1065
7/31/61	28	4	2. Runaround	Gee 1071
			REGINA	
			New York native Regina Richards.	
7/19/86	10	12	1. **Baby Love** Sales #10 / Airplay #11	Atlantic 89417

DATE	POS	WKS	ARTIST—RECORD TITLE	LABEL & NO.
			REID, Clarence	
			Born on 2/14/45 in Cochran, Georgia. Soul singer/composer/arranger/producer. With the Miami vocal group The Delmiros in the early '60s. Also recorded as Blowfly.	
9/13/69	40	2	1. Nobody But You Babe answer song to The Isley Brothers' "It's Your Thing"	Alston 4574
			R.E.M.	
			Athens, Georgia, rock quartet formed in 1980: Michael Stipe (vocals), Peter Buck (guitar), Mike Mills (bass) and Bill Berry (drums). Developed huge following with college audiences in the early 1980s as one of the first "alternative rock" bands. Buck, Mills and Berry also recorded with Warren Zevon as the Hindu Love Gods in 1990. Berry fully recovered from a brain aneurysm suffered on stage in Lausanne, Switzerland, on 3/1/95. R.E.M. is abbreviation for Rapid Eye Movement, the dream stage of sleep.	
10/17/87	9	10	1. **The One I Love** Sales #5 / Airplay #13	I.R.S. 53171
2/25/89	6	11	2. **Stand** Sales #4 / Airplay #5; became the theme for TV's "Get A Life" starring Chris Elliott	Warner 27688
4/20/91	4	14	● 3. **Losing My Religion** Sales #5 / Airplay #8	Warner 19392
8/10/91	10	11	4. **Shiny Happy People** Airplay #25 / Sales #38; Kate Pierson of The B 52's (backing vocals)	Warner 19242
11/28/92	28	8	5. Drive Sales #32 / Airplay #34	Warner 18729
3/13/93	30	6	6. Man On The Moon Airplay #26 / Sales #56; tribute to the late comedian Andy Kaufman	Warner 18642
10/16/93	29	7	7. Everybody Hurts Sales #34 / Airplay #38	Warner 18638
10/1/94	21	18	8. What's The Frequency, Kenneth? Airplay #14 / Sales #31	Warner 18050
1/21/95	19	7	9. Bang And Blame Airplay #17 / Sales #52	Warner 17994
			REMBRANDTS, The	
			Duo of Danny Wilde and Phil Solem. Both were members of the Los Angeles pop band Great Buildings.	
3/16/91	14	9	1. Just The Way It Is, Baby Airplay #15 / Sales #18	Atco 98874
9/30/95	17	10	2. I'll Be There For You/ Airplay #1(8) / Sales #35; debuted on the Hot 100 Airplay chart on 5/20/95; theme from the TV series "Friends" starring Courteney Cox; #1 Adult Contemporary hit (7 weeks)	
		10	3. This House Is Not A Home Sales flip	EastWest 64384
			RENAY, Diane	
			Born Renee Diane Kushner in Philadelphia.	
2/15/64	6	8	1. **Navy Blue** #1 Adult Contemporary hit (1 week)	20th Century 456
4/25/64	29	4	2. Kiss Me Sailor	20th Century 477

DATE	POS	WKS	ARTIST–RECORD TITLE	LABEL & NO.
			RENE & RENE	
			Mexican-American duo from Laredo, Texas: Rene Ornelas (born 8/26/36) and Rene Herrera (born 10/2/35).	
12/14/68+	14	9	1. Lo Mucho Que Te Quiero (The More I Love You)	White Whale 287
			RENO, Mike, and Ann Wilson	
			Lead singers of Loverboy and Heart, respectively.	
5/19/84	7	13	1. **Almost Paradise...Love Theme From Footloose** from the movie *Footloose* starring Kevin Bacon and Lori Singer; #1 Adult Contemporary hit (1 week)	Columbia 04418
			REO SPEEDWAGON	
			Rock quintet formed in 1968 in Champaign, Illinois. By 1976, consisted of Kevin Cronin (lead vocals, rhythm guitar), Gary Richrath (lead guitar), Neal Doughty (keyboards), Bruce Hall (bass) and Alan Gratzer (drums). Gratzer left in 1988, replaced by former Santana drummer Graham Lear. Lineup in 1990: Cronin, Doughty and Hall, joined by new members Bryan Hitt, Dave Amato and Jesse Harms (left by 1991). Group named after a 1911 fire truck.	
12/27/80+	1 (1)	20	▲ 1. **Keep On Loving You**	Epic 50953
3/28/81	5	15	● 2. **Take It On The Run**	Epic 01054
7/4/81	24	6	3. Don't Let Him Go	Epic 02127
8/29/81	20	7	4. In Your Letter above 4 from the album *Hi Infidelity*	Epic 02457
6/19/82	7	13	5. **Keep The Fire Burnin'**	Epic 02967
10/2/82	26	6	6. Sweet Time	Epic 03175
11/17/84	29	5	7. I Do'wAnna Know Airplay #27	Epic 04659
1/26/85	1 (3)	14	● 8. **Can't Fight This Feeling** Airplay #1(3) / Sales #1(2)	Epic 04713
4/20/85	19	9	9. One Lonely Night Airplay #19 / Sales #21	Epic 04848
8/17/85	34	3	10. Live Every Moment above 4 from the album *Wheels Are Turnin'*	Epic 05412
2/28/87	16	7	11. That Ain't Love Sales #16 / Airplay #17	Epic 06656
9/19/87	19	8	12. In My Dreams Airplay #17 / Sales #18	Epic 07255
7/30/88	20	9	13. Here With Me Airplay #19 / Sales #23	Epic 07901
			RESTLESS HEART	
			Nashville country-rock quintet consisting of former session musicians Larry Stewart (vocals), David Innis, Greg Jennings, Paul Gregg and John Dittrich. Stewart went solo in early 1992. Keyboardist Innis left in early 1993. Remaining three continued on with two backing musicians.	
5/30/87	33	5	1. I'll Still Be Loving You Sales #29 / Airplay #40; #1 Country hit (1 week)	RCA 5065
12/5/92+	11	13	2. When She Cries Airplay #12 / Sales #22	RCA 62412
			REUNION	
			RCA studio group. Joey Levine (Ohio Express), lead singer.	
9/28/74	8	10	1. **Life Is A Rock (But The Radio Rolled Me)** [N]	RCA 10056

DATE	POS	WKS	ARTIST–RECORD TITLE	LABEL & NO.

REVELS, The

Philadelphia group formed in high school, led by John Kelly.

DATE	POS	WKS	ARTIST–RECORD TITLE	LABEL & NO.
11/23/59	35	2	1. Midnight Stroll originally released as: "Dead Man's Stroll"; Harold Karr (orch.)	Norgolde 103

REVERE, Paul, And The Raiders

Pop-rock group formed in Portland, Oregon, in 1960. Group featured Paul Revere (born 1/7/42, Boise, Idaho; keyboards) and Mark Lindsay (lead singer). To Los Angeles in 1965. Appeared on daily ABC-TV show "Where The Action Is" in 1965. Own TV show "Happening" in 1968. Lindsay and Raider member Keith Allison recorded with Steve Alaimo as The Unknowns in 1966. Country star Freddy Weller with group, 1967–71. Group had many personnel changes.

DATE	POS	WKS	ARTIST–RECORD TITLE	LABEL & NO.
4/17/61	38	1	1. Like, Long Hair [I] based on Rachmaninoff's "Prelude In C-Sharp Minor"	Gardena 116
12/25/65+	11	11	2. Just Like Me	Columbia 43461
3/26/66	4	12	3. Kicks the first major hit with an anti-drug message	Columbia 43556
7/9/66	6	7	4. Hungry	Columbia 43678
10/15/66	20	5	5. The Great Airplane Strike	Columbia 43810
12/17/66+	4	10	6. Good Thing	Columbia 43907
3/4/67	22	6	7. Ups And Downs	Columbia 44018
5/6/67	5	8	8. Him Or Me - What's It Gonna Be?	Columbia 44094
9/2/67	17	5	9. I Had A Dream	Columbia 44227
2/24/68	19	6	10. Too Much Talk	Columbia 44444
7/13/68	27	6	11. Don't Take It So Hard	Columbia 44553
3/8/69	18	9	12. Mr. Sun, Mr. Moon	Columbia 44744
6/14/69	20	8	13. Let Me	Columbia 44854
			RAIDERS:	
5/29/71	1 (1)	15	● 14. Indian Reservation (The Lament Of The Cherokee Reservation Indian)	Columbia 45332
10/2/71	23	6	15. Birds Of A Feather	Columbia 45453

REYNOLDS, Debbie

Born Mary Reynolds on 4/1/32 in El Paso, Texas. Leading lady of '50s musicals and later in comedies. Married Eddie Fisher on 9/26/55; divorced in 1959. Mother of actress/author Carrie Fisher.

DATE	POS	WKS	ARTIST–RECORD TITLE	LABEL & NO.
7/22/57	1 (5)	23	● 1. Tammy Top 100 #1(5) / Jockey #1(5) / Best Seller #1(3); from the movie *Tammy and the Bachelor* starring Reynolds; Joseph Gershenson (orch.)	Coral 61851
1/20/58	20	1	2. A Very Special Love Jockey #20 / Top 100 #83; George Cates (orch.)	Coral 61897
2/22/60	25	8	3. Am I That Easy To Forget Billy Vaughn (orch.); #9 Country hit for Carl Belew in 1959	Dot 15985

REYNOLDS, Jody

Born on 12/3/38 in Denver. Male rockabilly singer/guitarist.

DATE	POS	WKS	ARTIST–RECORD TITLE	LABEL & NO.
5/26/58	5	14	1. Endless Sleep Best Seller #5 / Top 100 #5 / Jockey #7; Al Casey (guitar)	Demon 1507

DATE	POS	WKS	ARTIST—RECORD TITLE	LABEL & NO.

REYNOLDS, Lawrence

Singer from Mobile, Alabama.

DATE	POS	WKS	ARTIST—RECORD TITLE	LABEL & NO.
10/11/69	28	6	1. Jesus Is A Soul Man	Warner 7322

RHYTHM HERITAGE

Los Angeles studio group assembled by prolific producers Steve Barri and Michael Omartian (keyboards). Vocals by Oren and Luther Waters. Omartian was in band Gator Creek with Kenny Loggins.

DATE	POS	WKS	ARTIST—RECORD TITLE	LABEL & NO.
1/10/76	1 (1)	12	● 1. **Theme From S.W.A.T.** [I] from the ABC-TV series "S.W.A.T." starring Steve Forrest	ABC 12135
5/8/76	20	8	2. Baretta's Theme ("Keep Your Eye On The Sparrow") from the TV series "Baretta" starring Robert Blake	ABC 12177

RHYTHM SYNDICATE—see RYTHM SYNDICATE

RICH, Charlie

Born on 12/14/32 in Colt, Arkansas. Died of an acute blood clot on 7/25/95. Rockabilly-country singer/pianist/songwriter. First played jazz and blues. Own jazz group, the Velvetones, mid-1950s, while in U.S. Air Force. Session work with Sun Records in 1958. Known as "The Silver Fox."

DATE	POS	WKS	ARTIST—RECORD TITLE	LABEL & NO.
5/2/60	22	9	1. Lonely Weekends The Gene Lowery Chorus (backing vocals)	Phillips 3552
9/25/65	21	7	2. Mohair Sam	Smash 1993
6/9/73	15	12	● 3. Behind Closed Doors #1 Country hit (2 weeks)	Epic 10950
10/27/73	1 (2)	17	● 4. **The Most Beautiful Girl** #1 Country hit (3 weeks); #1 Adult Contemporary hit (3 weeks)	Epic 11040
2/23/74	18	8	5. There Won't Be Anymore originally released on RCA 8336 in 1964; #1 Country hit (2 weeks)	RCA 0195
3/9/74	11	9	6. A Very Special Love Song #1 Country hit (3 weeks); #1 Adult Contemporary hit (1 week)	Epic 11091
8/24/74	24	7	7. I Love My Friend #1 Country hit (1 week); #1 Adult Contemporary hit (1 week)	Epic 20006
6/28/75	19	6	8. Every Time You Touch Me (I Get High) #1 Adult Contemporary hit (1 week)	Epic 50103

RICHARD, Cliff

Born Harry Rodger Webb on 10/14/40 in Lucknow, India, of British parentage. Vocalist/actor/guitarist. To England in 1948. Worked in skiffle groups, mid-1950s. Backing band: The Drifters (later: The Shadows). Richard also recorded Inspirational music since 1967. The Shadows disbanded in 1969. Superstar in England, with over 80 charted hits, including 10 #1 singles. Appeared in the British movies *Expresso Bongo*, *The Young Ones*, *Summer Holiday* and *Wonderful Life*.

DATE	POS	WKS	ARTIST—RECORD TITLE	LABEL & NO.
11/2/59	30	4	1. Living Doll **CLIFF RICHARD and The Drifters** from the movie *Serious Charge* starring Anthony Quayle	ABC-Para. 10042
1/18/64	25	7	2. It's All In The Game	Epic 9633
8/14/76	6	12	● 3. **Devil Woman**	Rocket 40574
11/17/79+	7	14	4. **We Don't Talk Anymore**	EMI America 8025
4/5/80	34	3	5. Carrie	EMI America 8035
9/27/80	10	13	6. **Dreaming**	EMI America 8057

DATE	POS	WKS	ARTIST–RECORD TITLE	LABEL & NO.
11/22/80+	**20**	11	7. Suddenly **OLIVIA NEWTON-JOHN AND CLIFF RICHARD** from the movie *Xanadu* starring Newton-John	MCA 51007
1/24/81	**17**	11	8. A Little In Love	EMI America 8068
2/6/82	**23**	8	9. Daddy's Home "live" recording	EMI America 8103

RICHIE, Lionel

Born on 6/20/49 in Tuskegee, Alabama. Grew up on the campus of Tuskegee Institute where his grandfather worked. Former lead singer of the Commodores. Appeared in the movie *Thank God It's Friday* (1978).

DATE	POS	WKS	ARTIST–RECORD TITLE	LABEL & NO.
7/18/81	**1 (9)**	19	▲ 1. **Endless Love** **DIANA ROSS & LIONEL RICHIE** title song from the movie starring Brooke Shields; #1 R&B hit (7 weeks); #1 Adult Contemporary hit (3 weeks)	Motown 1519
10/23/82	**1 (2)**	13	● 2. **Truly** #1 Adult Contemporary hit (4 weeks)	Motown 1644
1/22/83	**4**	16	3. **You Are** #1 Adult Contemporary hit (6 weeks)	Motown 1657
4/16/83	**5**	12	4. **My Love** #1 Adult Contemporary hit (4 weeks)	Motown 1677
10/1/83	**1 (4)**	17	● 5. **All Night Long (All Night)** #1 R&B hit (7 weeks); #1 Adult Contemporary hit (4 weeks)	Motown 1698
12/3/83+	**7**	14	6. **Running With The Night**	Motown 1710
3/10/84	**1 (2)**	17	● 7. **Hello** #1 Adult Contemporary hit (6 weeks); #1 R&B hit (3 weeks)	Motown 1722
7/7/84	**3**	14	8. **Stuck On You** #1 Adult Contemporary hit (5 weeks)	Motown 1746
10/13/84	**8**	13	9. **Penny Lover** Airplay #5 / Sales #13; #1 Adult Contemporary hit (4 weeks); above 5 from the album *Can't Slow Down*	Motown 1762
11/9/85	**1 (4)**	16	● 10. **Say You, Say Me** Airplay #1(5) / Sales #1(3); from the movie *White Nights* starring Mikhail Baryshnikov; #1 Adult Contemporary hit (5 weeks), #1 R&B hit (2 weeks)	Motown 1819
7/19/86	**2 (2)**	14	11. **Dancing On The Ceiling** Airplay #1(1) / Sales #3	Motown 1843
10/18/86	**9**	10	12. **Love Will Conquer All** Airplay #8 / Sales #8; #1 Adult Contemporary hit (2 weeks)	Motown 1866
1/10/87	**7**	10	13. **Ballerina Girl** Sales #5 / Airplay #8; #1 Adult Contemporary hit (4 weeks)	Motown 1873
4/18/87	**20**	7	14. Se La Sales #17 / Airplay #23; above 5 from the album *Dancing On The Ceiling*	Motown 1883
5/23/92	**21**	9	15. Do It To Me Sales #23 / Airplay #31; #1 R&B hit (1 week)	Motown 2160

RIDDLE, Nelson

Born on 6/1/21 in Oradell, New Jersey. Died on 10/6/85. Trombonist/arranger with Charlie Spivak and Tommy Dorsey in the '40s. One of the most in-demand of all arranger/conductors for many top artists, including Frank Sinatra (several classic '50s albums), Nat King Cole, Ella Mae Morse, and more recently, Linda Ronstadt; also arranger/musical director for many movies.

DATE	POS	WKS	ARTIST–RECORD TITLE	LABEL & NO.
12/31/55+	**1 (4)**	24	● 1. **Lisbon Antigua** [I] Best Seller #1(4) / Jockey #1(2) / Top 100 #2 / Juke Box #2; from a 1937 Portuguese song "Lisboa Antigua"	Capitol 3287

DATE	POS	WKS	ARTIST–RECORD TITLE	LABEL & NO.
3/31/56	20	4	2. Port Au Prince [I] Jockey #20 / Top 100 #32	Capitol 3374
8/4/56	39	2	3. Theme From "The Proud Ones" [I] title song from the movie starring Robert Ryan	Capitol 3472
8/4/62	30	3	4. Route 66 Theme [I] from the CBS-TV series starring George Maharis and Martin Milner	Capitol 4741

RIFF

Male vocal quintet from Paterson, New Jersey, formed at Eastside High School: Kenny Kelly, Steven Capers, Jr., Anthony Fuller, Dwayne Jones and Michael Best. Appeared as themselves (singing the alma mater) in the 1989 movie *Lean On Me*, which was based on their school.

DATE	POS	WKS	ARTIST–RECORD TITLE	LABEL & NO.
4/27/91	25	6	1. My Heart Is Failing Me Sales #24 / Airplay #29	SBK 07342

RIGHTEOUS BROTHERS, The

Blue-eyed soul duo: Bill Medley (born 9/19/40, Santa Ana, California; baritone) and Bobby Hatfield (born 8/10/40, Beaver Dam, Wisconsin; tenor). Formed duo in 1962. First recorded as the Paramours for Smash in 1962. On "Hullabaloo" and "Shindig" TV shows. Split up, 1968–74. Medley went solo, replaced by Jimmy Walker (The Knickerbockers); rejoined Hatfield in 1974.

DATE	POS	WKS	ARTIST–RECORD TITLE	LABEL & NO.
12/26/64+	1 (2)	13	1. **You've Lost That Lovin' Feelin'**	Philles 124
4/17/65	9	10	2. **Just Once In My Life**	Philles 127
7/31/65	4	11	3. **Unchained Melody** also see #11 & 12 below	Philles 129
12/11/65+	5	8	4. **Ebb Tide** #2 hit for Frank Chacksfield in 1953; all of above produced by Phil Spector	Philles 130
3/19/66	1 (3)	11	● 5. **(You're My) Soul And Inspiration**	Verve 10383
6/18/66	18	5	6. He	Verve 10406
8/27/66	30	3	7. Go Ahead And Cry	Verve 10430
6/15/74	3	10	8. **Rock And Roll Heaven**	Haven 7002
10/5/74	20	4	9. Give It To The People	Haven 7004
12/7/74	32	3	10. Dream On	Haven 7006
9/8/90	13	11	11. Unchained Melody [R] Airplay #3; featured in the movie *Ghost* starring Patrick Swayze and Demi Moore; #1 Adult Contemporary hit (2 weeks); available only on vinyl	Verve F. 871882
10/13/90	19	12	▲ 12. Unchained Melody [R] Sales #4; newly recorded 1990 version; available only on cassette	Curb 76842

RIGHT SAID FRED—see R*S*F (RIGHT SAID FRED)

RILEY, Cheryl Pepsii

Native of Brooklyn. R&B singer. Discovered by the group Full Force.

DATE	POS	WKS	ARTIST–RECORD TITLE	LABEL & NO.
12/10/88	32	5	1. Thanks For My Child Sales #31 / Airplay #31; written, produced and arranged by Full Force; #1 R&B hit (1 week)	Columbia 07996

DATE	POS	WKS	ARTIST–RECORD TITLE	LABEL & NO.
			RILEY, Jeannie C.	
			Born Jeanne Carolyn Stephenson on 10/19/45 in Anson, Texas. Country singer.	
8/31/68	**1** (1)	12	● 1. **Harper Valley P.T.A.** written by Tom T. Hall; #1 Country hit (3 weeks)	Plantation 3
			RINKY-DINKS, The—see DARIN, Bobby	
			RIOS, Miguel	
			Born in Granada, Spain, in 1944.	
6/20/70	**14**	8	1. A Song Of Joy (Himno A La Alegria) based on the last movement of Beethoven's Ninth Symphony; Waldo de los Rios, conductor; #1 Adult Contemporary hit (2 weeks)	A&M 1193
			RIP CHORDS, The	
			California group featuring the duo of Terry Melcher (Doris Day's son; produced The Byrds, Paul Revere & The Raiders) and Bruce Johnston (Beach Boys). Touring group featured a different foursome.	
1/4/64	**4**	11	1. **Hey Little Cobra**	Columbia 42921
5/23/64	**28**	5	2. Three Window Coupe co-written by Jan Berry (Jan & Dean)	Columbia 43035
			RIPERTON, Minnie	
			Born on 11/8/47 in Chicago. Died of cancer on 7/12/79 in Los Angeles. Recorded as Andrea Davis on Chess in 1966. Lead singer of the rock-R&B sextet Rotary Connection, 1967–70. In Stevie Wonder's backup group Wonderlove in 1973.	
2/15/75	**1** (1)	13	● 1. **Lovin' You**	Epic 50057
			RITCHIE FAMILY, The	
			Philadelphia disco group named for arranger/producer Ritchie Rome. Group featured various session singers and musicians.	
9/6/75	**11**	12	1. Brazil [I] #2 hit for Xavier Cugat in 1943	20th Century 2218
10/2/76	**17**	11	2. The Best Disco In Town	Marlin 3306
			RITENOUR, Lee	
			Born on 1/11/52 in Los Angeles. Guitarist/composer/arranger. Top session guitarist. Has appeared on more than 200 albums. Nicknamed "Captain Fingers." Member of jazz outfits Brass Fever and Fourplay.	
5/23/81	**15**	9	1. Is It You Eric Tagg (vocal)	Elektra 47124
			RITTER, Tex	
			Born Maurice Woodward Ritter on 1/12/05 near Murvaul, Texas. Died of a heart attack on 1/3/74. Country singer/actor. Starred in over 80 Hollywood Westerns, 1935–45. Elected to the Country Music Hall of Fame in 1964. His son, John Ritter, starred in the TV series "Three's Company," "Hearts Afire" and others, plus many movies.	
7/7/56	**28**	6	1. The Wayward Wind Harry Geller (orch.)	Capitol 3430
8/14/61	**20**	4	2. I Dreamed Of A Hill-Billy Heaven [S] Ralph Carmichael (orch.); #10 Country hit for Eddie Dean in 1955	Capitol 4567

DATE	POS	WKS	ARTIST–RECORD TITLE	LABEL & NO.
			RIVERS, Johnny	
			Born John Ramistella on 11/7/42 in New York City; raised in Baton Rouge. Rock and roll singer/guitarist/songwriter/producer. Recorded with the Spades for Suede in 1957. Named Johnny Rivers by DJ Alan Freed in 1958. To Los Angeles in 1961. Recorded for 12 different labels (1958–64) before his smash debut on Imperial. Began own Soul City label in 1966. Recorded Christian music in the early '80s.	
6/13/64	**2 (2)**	10	1. **Memphis** first recorded by Chuck Berry in 1959 as "Memphis, Tennessee" on Chess 1729	Imperial 66032
8/22/64	**12**	7	2. Maybelline *above 2 written by Chuck Berry*	Imperial 66056
11/14/64	**9**	9	3. **Mountain Of Love**	Imperial 66075
2/27/65	**20**	4	4. Midnight Special *written by Leadbelly, whose first recorded version was released in 1941 (Victor 27266)*	Imperial 66087
6/19/65	**7**	8	5. **Seventh Son** *written by blues great, Willie Dixon*	Imperial 66112
10/30/65	**26**	4	6. Where Have All The Flowers Gone	Imperial 66133
1/15/66	**35**	3	7. Under Your Spell Again *#4 Country hit for Buck Owens in 1959*	Imperial 66144
3/26/66	**3**	10	8. **Secret Agent Man** *from the TV series "Secret Agent" starring Patrick McGoohan*	Imperial 66159
6/25/66	**19**	6	9. (I Washed My Hands In) Muddy Water *#8 hit for Stonewall Jackson in 1965; #1, 2, 4, 5, 9 recorded "live" at the Whisky A Go-Go*	Imperial 66175
10/8/66	**1 (1)**	12	10. **Poor Side Of Town**	Imperial 66205
2/18/67	**3**	8	11. **Baby I Need Your Lovin'**	Imperial 66227
6/17/67	**10**	6	12. **The Tracks Of My Tears** *all of above produced by Lou Adler*	Imperial 66244
12/2/67+	**14**	8	13. Summer Rain	Imperial 66267
11/11/72+	**6**	14	● 14. **Rockin' Pneumonia - Boogie Woogie Flu**	United Art. 50960
5/5/73	**38**	2	15. Blue Suede Shoes	United Art. 198
8/9/75	**22**	5	16. Help Me Rhonda *Brian Wilson of The Beach Boys (backing vocal)*	Epic/Soul City 50121
7/30/77	**10**	15	● 17. **Swayin' To The Music (Slow Dancin')** *also released on Soul City 008 as "Slow Dancin'"*	Big Tree 16094
			RIVIERAS, The	
			Teenage rock and roll band. Evolved from a South Bend, Indiana high school group known as The Playmates. Lead singer, Marty Fortson, left for the Marines after recording "California Sun." Band's manager, Bill Dobslaw, was the lead singer on recordings of subsequent hits.	
2/1/64	**5**	9	1. **California Sun**	Riviera 1401
			ROACHFORD	
			British-based, soul-rock band: Andrew Roachford (vocals, keyboards), Hawi Gondwe (guitar), Derrick Taylor (bass) and Chris Taylor (drums).	
5/27/89	**25**	5	1. Cuddly Toy (Feel For Me) *Sales #25 / Airplay #26*	Epic 68549
			ROAD APPLES, The	
			Boston-based pop group led by singer/guitarist David Finnerty.	
12/27/75+	**35**	4	1. Let's Live Together	Polydor 14285

DATE	POS	WKS	ARTIST–RECORD TITLE	LABEL & NO.
			ROB BASE & D.J. E-Z ROCK	
			Harlem rap duo: Robert Ginyard with DJ Rodney "Skip" Bryce.	
10/15/88	36	3	▲ 1. It Takes Two Sales #23; includes sampling of Lyn Collins' 1972 hit "Think (About It)"	Profile 5186
			ROBBINS, Marty	
			Born Martin David Robinson on 9/26/25 in Glendale, Arizona. Died of a heart attack on 12/8/82. Country singer/guitarist/songwriter. Own radio show with K-Bar Cowboys, late 1940s. Own TV show, "Western Caravan," KPHO-Phoenix, 1951. First recorded for Columbia in 1952. Regular on the *Grand Ole Opry* since 1953. Own Robbins label in 1958. Raced stock cars. Movies: *Road To Nashville* and *Guns Of A Stranger*. Robbins, Eddy Arnold, Jim Reeves and Johnny Cash were the first major country stars to have a big impact on the pop charts.	
11/24/56	17	7	1. Singing The Blues Juke Box #17 / Top 100 #26; #1 Country hit (13 weeks)	Columbia 21545
4/27/57	2 (1)	21	● 2. **A White Sport Coat (And A Pink Carnation)** Best Seller #2 / Top 100 #3 / Jockey #4 / Juke Box #4 end; #1 Country hit (5 weeks)	Columbia 40864
12/9/57+	15	9	3. The Story Of My Life Jockey #15 / Top 100 #30 / Best Seller #31; #1 Country hit (4 weeks)	Columbia 41013
5/5/58	26	5	4. Just Married Best Seller #26 / Top 100 #35; #1 Country hit (2 weeks)	Columbia 41143
8/25/58	27	5	5. She Was Only Seventeen (He Was One Year More)	Columbia 41208
3/16/59	38	3	6. The Hanging Tree title song from the movie starring Gary Cooper; Ray Conniff (orch., above 5)	Columbia 41325
11/30/59+	1 (2)	16	7. **El Paso** #1 Country hit (/ weeks)	Columbia 41511
4/11/60	26	4	8. Big Iron	Columbia 41589
8/1/60	31	3	9. Is There Any Chance	Columbia 41686
12/5/60	34	5	10. Ballad Of The Alamo from the movie *The Alamo* starring John Wayne	Columbia 41809
2/13/61	3	12	11. **Don't Worry** song is famous for its "fuzz-bass" guitar break; #1 Country hit (10 weeks)	Columbia 41922
8/18/62	16	7	12. Devil Woman #1 Country hit (8 weeks)	Columbia 42486
12/8/62	18	5	13. Ruby Ann #1 Country hit (1 week)	Columbia 42614
			ROBERT & JOHNNY	
			Bronx R&B duo: Robert Carr (died 5/18/93) and Johnny Mitchell.	
3/3/58	32	6	1. We Belong Together Best Seller #32 / Top 100 #33	Old Town 1047
			ROBERTS, Austin	
			Born on 9/19/45 in Newport News, Virginia. Writer of several country songs. Collaborator on the cartoon series "Scooby Doo" and "Josie & The Pussycats." Replaced Gene Pistilli in Buchanan Brothers/Cashman, Pistilli & West trio in 1972.	
11/11/72	12	10	1. Something's Wrong With Me	Chelsea 0101
8/30/75	9	9	2. **Rocky**	Private St. 45020

DATE	POS	WKS	ARTIST–RECORD TITLE	LABEL & NO.
			ROBERTS, Kane	
			Boston rock singer/guitarist. Guitar work with Alice Cooper, Rod Stewart and Berlin.	
6/22/91	38	2	1. Does Anybody Really Fall In Love Anymore? songwriters include Jon Bon Jovi and Richie Sambora	DGC 19009
			ROBERTSON, Don	
			Born on 12/5/22 in Peking, China; moved to Chicago at age four. Pianist/composer. Created the Nashville piano style. Wrote "Born To Be With You," "Hummingbird," "Please Help Me I'm Falling" and "Ringo." Also wrote several of Elvis Presley's hits.	
5/5/56	6	14	1. **The Happy Whistler** [I] Jockey #6 / Best Seller #9 / Top 100 #9 / Juke Box #12	Capitol 3391
			ROBIC, Ivo	
			Pronounced: eevo robish. Born near Zagreb, Yugoslavia, on 1/29/27.	
8/31/59	13	11	1. Morgen [F] **IVO ROBIC and The Song-Masters** German song also known as: "One More Sunrise"	Laurie 3033
			ROBIN S	
			Robin Stone, female singer from Jamaica, New York.	
5/1/93	5	22	● 1. **Show Me Love** Airplay #3 / Sales #10	Big Beat 10118
			ROBINSON, Floyd	
			Born in 1937 in Nashville. Singer/guitarist/composer. Worked on local radio with his high school band, the Eagle Rangers, at age 12. Own programs on WLAC and WSM-Nashville.	
8/3/59	20	12	1. Makin' Love produced by Chet Atkins	RCA 7529
			ROBINSON, Smokey	
			Born William Robinson on 2/19/40 in Detroit. Formed The Miracles (then called the Matadors) at Northern High School in 1955. First recorded for End in 1958. Married Miracles' member Claudette Rogers in 1963; later divorced. Left The Miracles on 1/29/72. Wrote dozens of hit songs for Motown artists. Vice President of Motown Records, 1985–1988. Inducted into the Rock and Roll Hall of Fame in 1987. Won Grammy's Living Legends Award in 1989.	
1/19/74	27	6	1. Baby Come Close	Tamla 54239
5/31/75	26	6	2. Baby That's Backatcha #1 R&B hit (1 week)	Tamla 54258
10/18/75	36	3	3. The Agony And The Ecstasy	Tamla 54261
11/17/79+	4	17	4. **Cruisin'**	Tamla 54306
5/3/80	31	4	5. Let Me Be The Clock	Tamla 54311
3/21/81	2 (3)	16	● 6. **Being With You** #1 R&B hit (5 weeks)	Tamla 54321
2/27/82	33	5	7. Tell Me Tomorrow - Part I	Tamla 1601
5/9/87	8	12	8. **Just To See Her** Sales #8 / Airplay #8; #1 Adult Contemporary hit (1 week)	Motown 1877
8/15/87	10	11	9. **One Heartbeat** Airplay #10 / Sales #11	Motown 1897

DATE	POS	WKS	ARTIST–RECORD TITLE	LABEL & NO.
			### ROBINSON, Vicki Sue	
			Born in Philadelphia in 1955. Disco vocalist. Appeared in the original Broadway productions of *Hair* and *Jesus Christ Superstar*.	
6/19/76	**10**	13	1. **Turn The Beat Around**	RCA 10562
			### ROCHELL AND THE CANDLES with Johnny Wyatt	
			Los Angeles R&B group consisting of lead Johnny Wyatt (born 1938; died 1983), Rochell Henderson, Melvin Sasso and T.C. Henderson.	
3/27/61	**26**	4	1. Once Upon A Time	Swingin' 623
			### ROCK-A-TEENS	
			Rock and roll teen sextet from Richmond, Virginia: Vic Mizelle (leader), Boo Walke, Billy Cook, Paul Dixon, Eddie Robertson and Billy Smith.	
10/12/59	**16**	9	1. Woo-Hoo [I] first released on Doran 3515 in 1959	Roulette 4192
			### ROCKETS	
			Detroit rock band led by David Gilbert (vocals), Jim McCarty (guitar) and John Badanjek (drums).	
8/11/79	**30**	6	1. Oh Well	RSO 935
			### ROCKWELL	
			Born Kennedy Gordy on 3/15/64 in Detroit. Son of Motown chairman, Berry Gordy, Jr.	
2/11/84	**2** (3)	14	● 1. **Somebody's Watching Me** Michael Jackson (backing vocal); #1 R&B hit (5 weeks)	Motown 1702
6/23/84	**35**	2	2. Obscene Phone Caller	Motown 1731
			### ROCKY FELLERS, The	
			Consists of a father and his four sons (Eddie, Albert, Tony and Junior Feller) from Manila, Philippines.	
4/27/63	**16**	8	1. Killer Joe	Scepter 1246
			### RODGERS, Eileen	
			Born in Pittsburgh in 1933. Featured vocalist in Charlie Spivak's band, 1954-56.	
9/8/56	**18**	10	1. Miracle Of Love Jockey #18 / Top 100 #19 / Best Seller #23	Columbia 40708
9/29/58	**26**	4	2. Treasure Of Your Love Ray Conniff (orch., above 2)	Columbia 41214
			### RODGERS, Jimmie	
			Born James Frederick Rodgers on 9/18/33 in Camas, Washington. Vocalist/guitarist/pianist. Formed first group while in the Air Force. Own NBC-TV variety series in 1959. Career hampered following mysterious assault on the San Diego Freeway on 12/1/67, which left him with a fractured skull. Returned to performing a year later. Starred in the movies *The Little Shepherd Of Kingdom Come* and *Back Door To Hell*.	
8/19/57	**1** (4)	23	● 1. **Honeycomb** Jockey #1(4) / Best Seller #1(2) / Top 100 #1(2); #1 R&B hit (2 weeks); introduced by Georgie Shaw in 1954 on Decca 28937	Roulette 4015

DATE	POS	WKS	ARTIST–RECORD TITLE	LABEL & NO.
11/18/57	3	14	● 2. **Kisses Sweeter Than Wine** Jockey #3 / Top 100 #7 / Best Seller #8; adapted from an Irish folk song; #19 hit for The Weavers in 1951	Roulette 4031
2/24/58	7	9	● 3. **Oh-Oh, I'm Falling In Love Again** Jockey #7 / Top 100 #22 / Best Seller #23	Roulette 4045
5/19/58	3	15	● 4. **Secretly/** Best Seller #3 / Jockey #3 / Top 100 #4	
5/26/58	16	1	5. Make Me A Miracle Jockey #16 / Top 100 #54	Roulette 4070
8/11/58	10	10	6. **Are You Really Mine** Hot 100 #10 / Best Seller #10	Roulette 4090
12/1/58	11	10	7. Bimbombey	Roulette 4116
3/30/59	36	3	8. I'm Never Gonna Tell Hugo Peretti (of Hugo & Luigi; orch., all of above)	Roulette 4129
6/15/59	32	4	9. Ring-A-Ling-A-Lario/	
7/6/59	40	1	10. Wonderful You	Roulette 4158
10/12/59	32	3	11. Tucumcari	Roulette 4191
2/1/60	24	5	12. T.L.C. Tender Love And Care Joe Reisman (orch., above 4)	Roulette 4218
6/18/66	37	2	13. It's Over	Dot 16861
10/14/67	31	4	14. Child Of Clay	A&M 871

ROE, Tommy

Born on 5/9/42 in Atlanta. Pop-rock singer/guitarist/composer. Formed band The Satins at Brown High School, worked local dances in the late 1950s. Group recorded for Judd in 1960. Moved to Britain in the mid-1960s, returned in 1969.

DATE	POS	WKS	ARTIST–RECORD TITLE	LABEL & NO.
8/11/62	1 (2)	11	● 1. **Sheila** first released on Judd 1022 in 1962	ABC-Para. 10329
11/3/62	35	2	2. Susie Darlin'	ABC-Para. 10362
10/26/63	3	11	3. **Everybody**	ABC-Para. 10478
2/8/64	36	4	4. Come On above 4 produced by Felton Jarvis	ABC-Para. 10515
7/2/66	8	10	● 5. **Sweet Pea**	ABC 10762
10/1/66	6	11	6. **Hooray For Hazel**	ABC 10852
1/28/67	23	5	7. It's Now Winters Day	ABC 10888
2/15/69	1 (4)	13	● 8. **Dizzy**	ABC 11164
5/17/69	29	3	9. Heather Honey	ABC 11211
12/6/69+	8	11	● 10. **Jam Up Jelly Tight**	ABC 11247
9/25/71	25	7	11. Stagger Lee adapted from the traditional folk song "Stack-O-Lee"; above 4 produced by Steve Barri	ABC 11307

ROGER

Born Roger Troutman in Hamilton, Ohio. Leader of the family electro-funk group Zapp (Roger, Lester, Larry and Tony). Worked with Sly Stone and George Clinton. Father of male singer Lynch.

DATE	POS	WKS	ARTIST–RECORD TITLE	LABEL & NO.
12/12/87+	3	13	1. **I Want To Be Your Man** Sales #3 / Airplay #5; #1 R&B hit (1 week)	Reprise 28229

DATE	POS	WKS	ARTIST–RECORD TITLE	LABEL & NO.

ROGERS, Julie

Born Julie Rolls on 4/6/43 in London.

DATE	POS	WKS	ARTIST–RECORD TITLE	LABEL & NO.
12/5/64+	10	9	1. **The Wedding** Argentinian hit "La Novia" introduced in the U.S. in 1961 by Anita Bryant (Columbia 42148); #1 Adult Contemporary hit (3 weeks)	Mercury 72332

ROGERS, Kenny/First Edition

Born Kenneth Donald Rogers on 8/21/38 in Houston. With high school band the Scholars in 1958. Bass player of jazz group the Bobby Doyle Trio, recorded for Columbia. First recorded for Carlton in 1958. In Kirby Stone Four and The New Christy Minstrels, mid-1960s. Formed and fronted The First Edition in 1967. Original lineup included Thelma Camacho, Mike Settle, Terry Williams and Mickey Jones. All but Jones were members of The New Christy Minstrels. Group hosted own syndicated TV variety show "Rollin" in 1972. Rogers split from group in 1973. Starred in movies *The Gambler I, II & III*, *Coward Of The County* and *Six Pack*. Married Marianne Gordon of TV's "Hee Haw" in 1977.

THE FIRST EDITION:

DATE	POS	WKS	ARTIST–RECORD TITLE	LABEL & NO.
2/24/68	5	8	1. Just Dropped In (To See What Condition My Condition Was In)	Reprise 0655
2/8/69	19	8	2. But You Know I Love You	Reprise 0799

KENNY ROGERS AND THE FIRST EDITION:

DATE	POS	WKS	ARTIST–RECORD TITLE	LABEL & NO.
7/5/69	6	9	3. **Ruby, Don't Take Your Love To Town** written by Mel Tillis	Reprise 0829
10/25/69	26	6	4. Ruben James some pressings show title as: "Reuben James"	Reprise 0854
3/14/70	11	12	5. Something's Burning written by Mac Davis	Reprise 0888
7/25/70	17	8	6. Tell It All Brother	Reprise 0923
11/14/70	33	5	7. Heed The Call	Reprise 0953

KENNY ROGERS:

DATE	POS	WKS	ARTIST–RECORD TITLE	LABEL & NO.
4/23/77	5	13	● 8. **Lucille** #1 Country hit (2 weeks)	United Art. 929
9/10/77	28	4	9. Daytime Friends #1 Country hit (1 week)	United Art. 1027
7/15/78	32	3	10. Love Or Something Like It #1 Country hit (1 week)	United Art. 1210
12/23/78+	16	13	11. The Gambler #1 Country hit (3 weeks)	United Art. 1250
5/12/79	5	13	● 12. **She Believes In Me** #1 Country hit (2 weeks); #1 Adult Contemporary hit (2 weeks)	United Art. 1273
9/22/79	7	12	13. **You Decorated My Life** #1 Country hit (2 weeks)	United Art. 1315
12/1/79+	3	15	● 14. **Coward Of The County** #1 Country hit (3 weeks)	United Art. 1327
4/12/80	4	14	15. **Don't Fall In Love With A Dreamer** **KENNY ROGERS with Kim Carnes**	United Art. 1345
6/28/80	14	8	16. Love The World Away from the movie *Urban Cowboy* starring John Travolta and Debra Winger; above 9 produced by Larry Butler	United Art. 1359

DATE	POS	WKS	ARTIST–RECORD TITLE	LABEL & NO.
10/4/80	1 (6)	19	● 17. **Lady** written by Lionel Richie; #1 Adult Contemporary hit (4 weeks); #1 Country hit (1 week)	Liberty 1380
4/25/81	14	12	18. What Are We Doin' In Love **DOTTIE WEST (with Kenny Rogers)** #1 Country hit (1 week)	Liberty 1404
6/13/81	3	14	19. **I Don't Need You** #1 Adult Contemporary hit (6 weeks); #1 Country hit (2 weeks)	Liberty 1415
9/12/81	14	10	20. Share Your Love With Me Gladys Knight & The Pips and Lionel Richie (backing vocals); #1 Adult Contemporary hit (2 weeks)	Liberty 1430
1/16/82	13	11	21. Through The Years #1 Adult Contemporary hit (2 weeks); above 5 (except #18) produced by Lionel Richie	Liberty 1444
7/24/82	13	10	22. Love Will Turn You Around from the movie *Six Pack* starring Rogers; #1 Adult Contemporary hit (2 weeks); #1 Country hit (1 week)	Liberty 1471
1/29/83	6	15	23. **We've Got Tonight** **KENNY ROGERS and SHEENA EASTON** #1 Country hit (1 week)	Liberty 1492
5/28/83	37	3	24. All My Life	Liberty 1495
9/10/83	1 (2)	18	▲ 25. **Islands In The Stream** **KENNY ROGERS with Dolly Parton** #1 Adult Contemporary hit (4 weeks); #1 Country hit (2 weeks)	RCA 13615
2/4/84	23	6	26. This Woman above 2 feature writing and production work by the Bee Gees	RCA 13710
10/13/84	15	9	27. What About Me? **KENNY ROGERS with KIM CARNES and JAMES INGRAM** Airplay #14 / Sales #16; #1 Adult Contemporary hit (2 weeks)	RCA 13899

ROGERS, Timmie "Oh Yeah!"

Born on 7/4/15 in Detroit. Black vaudeville and nightclub comedian.

DATE	POS	WKS	ARTIST–RECORD TITLE	LABEL & NO.
11/4/57	36	4	1. Back To School Again Top 100 #36 / Best Seller #37; Bernie Lowe (orch.)	Cameo 116

ROLLING STONES, The

British R&B-influenced rock group formed in London in January 1963. Consisted of Mick Jagger (born 7/26/43; vocals), Keith Richards (born 12/18/43; lead guitar), Brian Jones (born 2/28/42; died 7/3/69; guitar), Bill Wyman (born 10/24/36; bass) and Charlie Watts (born 6/2/41; drums). Jagger was the lead singer of Blues, Inc. The Stones took their name from a Muddy Waters song. Promoted as the bad boys in contrast to The Beatles. First U.K. tour, with The Ronettes, in 1964. Jones left group shortly before drowning; replaced by Mick Taylor (born 1/17/48). In 1975, Ron Wood (ex-Jeff Beck Group, ex-Faces) replaced Taylor. Movie *Gimme Shelter* is a documentary of the Stones's controversial Altamont concert on 12/6/69 at which a concertgoer was murdered by a member of the Hell's Angels. Won Lifetime Achievement Grammy in 1986. Inducted into the Rock and Roll Hall of Fame in 1989. Wyman left band in late 1992. Bassist Darryl Jones (billed as a "side musician") played on the 1994 *Voodoo Lounge* album and tour. Considered by many to be the world's all-time greatest rock and roll band.

DATE	POS	WKS	ARTIST–RECORD TITLE	LABEL & NO.
8/1/64	24	5	1. Tell Me (You're Coming Back)	London 9682
8/22/64	26	6	2. It's All Over Now	London 9687
11/7/64	6	9	3. **Time Is On My Side**	London 9708
1/30/65	19	5	4. Heart Of Stone	London 9725
4/10/65	9	8	5. **The Last Time**	London 9741
6/19/65	1 (4)	12	● 6. **(I Can't Get No) Satisfaction**	London 9766

DATE	POS	WKS	ARTIST–RECORD TITLE	LABEL & NO.
10/16/65	1 (2)	11	7. **Get Off Of My Cloud**	London 9792
1/8/66	6	6	8. **As Tears Go By**	London 9808
3/5/66	2 (3)	9	9. 19th Nervous Breakdown	London 9823
5/21/66	1 (2)	10	10. **Paint It, Black**	London 901
7/16/66	8	8	11. **Mothers Little Helper/**	
8/6/66	24	4	12. Lady Jane	London 902
10/8/66	9	6	13. Have You Seen Your Mother, Baby, Standing In	
			The Shadow?	London 903
2/4/67	1 (1)	9	● 14. **Ruby Tuesday**	London 904
9/23/67	14	6	15. Dandelion	London 905
			all of above produced by Andrew Loog Oldham	
1/13/68	25	4	16. She's A Rainbow	London 906
6/15/68	3	11	17. **Jumpin' Jack Flash**	London 908
7/26/69	1 (4)	14	● 18. **Honky Tonk Women**	London 910
5/1/71	1 (2)	12	19. **Brown Sugar**	Rolling St. 19100
7/3/71	28	5	20. Wild Horses	Rolling St. 19101
5/6/72	7	9	21. **Tumbling Dice**	Rolling St. 19103
7/29/72	22	4	22. Happy	Rolling St. 19104
9/22/73	1 (1)	13	● 23. **Angie**	Rolling St. 19105
			Angie is Angie Barnet, David Bowie's wife, 1970–80	
2/2/74	15	6	24. Doo Doo Doo Doo Doo (Heartbreaker)	Rolling St. 19109
			above 8 produced by Jimmy Miller	
8/17/74	16	7	25. It's Only Rock 'N Roll (But I Like It)	Rolling St. 19301
11/16/74	17	7	26. Ain't Too Proud To Beg	Rolling St. 19302
5/8/76	10	7	27. **Fool To Cry**	Rolling St. 19304
6/10/78	1 (1)	16	● 28. **Miss You**	Rolling St. 19307
9/23/78	8	9	29. **Beast Of Burden**	Rolling St. 19309
			"live" version is on the B-side of #36 below	
1/13/79	31	4	30. Shattered	Rolling St. 19310
7/5/80	3	14	31. **Emotional Rescue**	Rolling St. 20001
10/18/80	26	5	32. She's So Cold	Rolling St. 21001
8/29/81	2 (3)	19	33. **Start Me Up**	Rolling St. 21003
12/12/81+	13	12	34. Waiting On A Friend	Rolling St. 21004
4/10/82	20	6	35. Hang Fire	Rolling St. 21300
7/3/82	25	5	36. Going To A Go-Go	Rolling St. 21301
			"live" recording	
11/19/83	9	10	37. **Undercover Of The Night**	Rolling St. 99813
3/22/86	5	10	38. **Harlem Shuffle**	Rolling St. 05802
			Sales #5 / Airplay #7	
6/14/86	28	4	39. One Hit (To The Body)	Rolling St. 05906
			Sales #23 / Airplay #36	
9/9/89	5	9	40. **Mixed Emotions**	Rolling St. 69008
			Sales #4 / Airplay #11	
11/25/89	23	8	41. Rock And A Hard Place	Rolling St. 73057
			Sales #19 / Airplay #23; above 17 produced by The Glimmer Twins (Jagger & Richards)	

DATE	POS	WKS	ARTIST–RECORD TITLE	LABEL & NO.
			ROMANTICS, The	
			Pop-rock quartet formed in Detroit in 1977: Wally Palmar (vocals, guitar), Coz Canler (guitar), Mike Skill (bass) and Jimmy Marinos (drums; replaced by David Petratos in 1985).	
12/3/83+	**3**	15	1. **Talking In Your Sleep**	Nemperor 04135
3/31/84	**37**	3	2. One In A Million	Nemperor 04373
			ROMEO VOID	
			San Francisco new wave quintet formed in 1979. Debora Iyall, lead singer.	
10/20/84	**35**	2	1. A Girl In Trouble (Is A Temporary Thing)	Columbia 04534
			RONALD AND RUBY	
			Ronald Gumby and Beverly "Ruby" Ross (born 1939). The New Jersey-born Ross wrote "Dim, Dim The Lights," "Lollipop," "Judy's Turn To Cry" and "Candy Man."	
3/24/58	**20**	3	1. Lollipop Jockey #20 / Top 100 #39 / Best Seller #40	RCA 7174
			RONDO, Don	
			Baritone singer from New York City. Sang on TV/radio commercials.	
11/3/56	**11**	12	1. Two Different Worlds Jockey #11 / Top 100 #19 / Best Seller #23; Dave Terry (orch.)	Jubilee 5256
7/29/57	**7**	15	2. **White Silver Sands** Jockey #7 / Best Seller #9 / Top 100 #10; Billy Rock (orch.)	Jubilee 5288
			RONETTES, The	
			Formed in New York City as the Darling Sisters in 1958. Consisted of Veronica Bennett (Ronnie Spector, born 8/10/45), sister Estelle Bennett Vann (born 7/22/44) and cousin Nedra Talley Ross (born 1/27/46). Sang professionally since junior high school. Backup work for Phil Spector in 1962. Group disbanded in 1966. Veronica married to Phil Spector, 1968–74.	
9/14/63	**2 (3)**	10	1. **Be My Baby** also see Eddie Money's "Take Me Home Tonight"	Philles 116
1/11/64	**24**	6	2. Baby, I Love You	Philles 118
5/16/64	**39**	1	3. (The Best Part Of) Breakin' Up	Philles 120
7/18/64	**34**	4	4. Do I Love You?	Philles 121
11/21/64	**23**	7	5. Walking In The Rain all of above produced by Phil Spector	Philles 123
			RONNIE and THE HI-LITES	
			R&B vocal quintet from Jersey City. Male lead singer Ronnie Goodson (13 years old in 1962) died of a brain tumor on 11/4/80.	
4/21/62	**16**	8	1. I Wish That We Were Married	Joy 260
			RONNY & THE DAYTONAS	
			Nashville group specializing in hot-rod music. Ronny is John "Bucky" Wilkin (born 4/26/46, Tulsa; vocals; son of country songwriter Marijohn Wilkin). Backed on recordings by well-known sessionmen Bobby Russell (wrote "Little Green Apples"), Chips Moman (prolific producer) and Johnny MacRae (member of Bobby "Boris" Pickett's Crypt-Kickers), among others. The touring group, which featured an entirely different lineup, later charted as The Hombres.	

DATE	POS	WKS	ARTIST—RECORD TITLE	LABEL & NO.
8/22/64	4	10	1. **G.T.O.**	Mala 481
1/8/66	27	5	2. Sandy	Mala 513
			above 2 produced by Bill Justis	

RONSTADT, Linda

Born on 7/15/46 in Tucson, Arizona. While in high school formed folk trio The Three Ronstadts (with sister and brother). To Los Angeles in 1964. Formed the Stone Poneys with Bobby Kimmel (guitar) and Ken Edwards (keyboards); recorded for Sidewalk in 1966. Went solo in 1968. In 1971 formed backing band with Glenn Frey, Don Henley, Randy Meisner and Bernie Leadon (later became the Eagles). In *Pirates Of Penzance* operetta in New York City in 1980, also in the movie version in 1983. Also see Nitty Gritty Dirt Band.

DATE	POS	WKS	ARTIST—RECORD TITLE	LABEL & NO.
12/9/67+	13	13	1. Different Drum **STONE PONEYS Featuring Linda Ronstadt** written by Mike Nesmith	Capitol 2004
9/12/70	25	7	2. Long Long Time	Capitol 2846
1/4/75	1 (1)	10	3. **You're No Good** Andrew Gold (guitar solo)	Capitol 3990
4/26/75	2 (2)	13	4. **When Will I Be Loved** #1 Country hit (1 week)	Capitol 4050
10/4/75	5	10	5. **Heat Wave**	Asylum 45282
1/24/76	25	6	6. Tracks Of My Tears	Asylum 45295
9/4/76	11	11	7. That'll Be The Day	Asylum 45340
10/8/77	3	16	▲ 8. **Blue Bayou**	Asylum 45431
10/29/77	5	12	9. **It's So Easy** Buddy Holly song first recorded by The Crickets in 1958 (Brunswick 55094)	Asylum 45438
2/25/78	31	3	10. Poor Poor Pitiful Me written by Warren Zevon	Asylum 45462
5/20/78	32	3	11. Tumbling Dice	Asylum 45479
9/9/78	16	8	12. Back In The U.S.A.	Asylum 45519
11/18/78+	7	13	13. **Ooh Baby Baby** David Sanborn (sax solo)	Asylum 45546
2/9/80	10	12	14. **How Do I Make You**	Asylum 46602
4/19/80	8	11	15. **Hurt So Bad**	Asylum 46624
7/19/80	31	4	16. I Can't Let Go	Asylum 46654
10/23/82	29	5	17. Get Closer	Asylum 69948
1/29/83	37	3	18. I Knew You When	Asylum 69853
1/24/87	2 (1)	12	● 19. **Somewhere Out There** **LINDA RONSTADT AND JAMES INGRAM** Sales #1(2) / Airplay #7; from the animated movie *An American Tail*	MCA 52973

LINDA RONSTADT (FEATURING AARON NEVILLE):

DATE	POS	WKS	ARTIST—RECORD TITLE	LABEL & NO.
10/28/89	2 (2)	16	● 20. **Don't Know Much** Sales #1(2) / Airplay #4; song also known as "All I Need To Know"; #1 Adult Contemporary hit (5 weeks)	Elektra 69261
2/24/90	11	9	21. All My Life Sales #10 / Airplay #14; written by Karla Bonoff; #1 Adult Contemporary hit (3 weeks); all of above (except #1 & 2) produced by Peter Asher	Elektra 64987

DATE	POS	WKS	ARTIST-RECORD TITLE	LABEL & NO.
			ROOFTOP SINGERS, The	
			Folk trio from New York City: Erik Darling, Willard Svanoe and Lynne Taylor (died 1982). Disbanded in 1967. Darling was a member of The Tarriers in 1956 and The Weavers, 1958–62. Taylor was a vocalist with Benny Goodman and Buddy Rich.	
1/12/63	**1** (2)	11	● 1. **Walk Right In**	Vanguard 35017
			originally recorded in 1929 by Gus Cannon's Jug Stompers; #1 Adult Contemporary hit (5 weeks)	
4/20/63	**20**	5	2. Tom Cat	Vanguard 35019
			ROSE, David	
			Born on 6/15/10 in London. Died on 8/23/90 of heart disease. Moved to Chicago at an early age. Conductor/composer/arranger for numerous movies. Scored many TV series, such as "The Red Skelton Show," "Bonanza" and "Little House On The Prairie." Married to Martha Raye, 1938–41, and Judy Garland, 1941–43.	
6/2/62	**1** (1)	13	● 1. **The Stripper** [I]	MGM 13064
			#1 Adult Contemporary hit (2 weeks)	
			ROSE GARDEN, The	
			West Virginia quintet: Diana Di Rose (lead singer), Johnny Noreen (lead guitar), James Groshong (guitar), William Fleming (bass, piano) and Bruce Boudin (drums).	
12/9/67	**17**	7	1. Next Plane To London	Atco 6510
			ROSE ROYCE	
			Eight-member backing band formed in Los Angeles in the early '70s. Backed Edwin Starr as Total Concept Unlimited in 1973. Backed The Temptations, became regular band for Undisputed Truth. Lead vocalist Gwen Dickey added, name changed to Rose Royce in 1976. Did soundtrack for the movie Car Wash.	
12/11/76+	**1** (1)	14	▲ 1. **Car Wash**	MCA 40615
			#1 R&B hit (2 weeks)	
3/19/77	**10**	10	2. **I Wanna Get Next To You**	MCA 40662
			above 2 from the movie Car Wash starring Richard Pryor and Franklin Ajaye	
10/22/77	**39**	2	3. Do Your Dance - Part 1	Whitfield 8440
1/13/79	**32**	4	4. Love Don't Live Here Anymore	Whitfield 8712
			all of above produced and arranged by Norman Whitfield	
			ROSIE And The Originals	
			San Diego group—Rosalie Hamlin, lead singer.	
12/12/60+	**5**	12	1. **Angel Baby**	Highland 1011
			ROSS, Diana	
			Born Diane Earle on 3/26/44 in Detroit. In vocal group The Primettes, first recorded for LuPine in 1960. Lead singer of The Supremes, 1961–69. Went solo in late 1969. Oscar nominee for the 1972 movie Lady Sings The Blues. Also appeared in the movies Mahogany and The Wiz. Own Broadway show An Evening With Diana Ross, 1976. Married Norwegian shipping magnate Arne Naess in 1986. Ross would rank among the Top 5 artists of the rock era if her solo and Supremes' hits were combined.	
5/2/70	**20**	8	1. Reach Out And Touch (Somebody's Hand)	Motown 1165
8/15/70	**1** (3)	13	2. **Ain't No Mountain High Enough**	Motown 1169
			#1 R&B hit (1 week)	

DATE	POS	WKS	ARTIST–RECORD TITLE	LABEL & NO.
1/9/71	**16**	8	3. Remember Me	Motown 1176
5/15/71	**29**	5	4. Reach Out I'll Be There	Motown 1184
9/11/71	**38**	3	5. Surrender	Motown 1188
			all of above written (except #4) and produced by Ashford & Simpson	
3/3/73	**34**	4	6. Good Morning Heartache	Motown 1211
			from the movie *Lady Sings The Blues*, starring Diana Ross (inspired by Billie Holiday's 1946 recording on Decca 23676)	
7/7/73	**1** (1)	16	7. **Touch Me In The Morning**	Motown 1239
			#1 Adult Contemporary hit (1 week)	
10/13/73	**12**	10	8. You're A Special Part Of Me	Motown 1280
			DIANA ROSS & MARVIN GAYE	
1/26/74	**14**	8	9. Last Time I Saw Him	Motown 1278
			#1 Adult Contemporary hit (3 weeks)	
3/30/74	**19**	10	10. My Mistake (Was To Love You)	Motown 1269
			DIANA ROSS & MARVIN GAYE	
11/22/75+	**1** (1)	13	11. Theme From Mahogany (Do You Know Where You're Going To)	Motown 1377
			from the movie *Mahogany* starring Ross; #1 Adult Contemporary hit (1 week)	
4/24/76	**1** (2)	13	12. **Love Hangover**	Motown 1392
			#1 R&B hit (1 week)	
8/21/76	**25**	8	13. One Love In My Lifetime	Motown 1398
12/3/77+	**27**	7	14. Gettin' Ready For Love	Motown 1427
8/18/79	**19**	9	15. The Boss	Motown 1462
8/9/80	**1** (4)	17	● 16. **Upside Down**	Motown 1494
			#1 R&B hit (4 weeks)	
10/4/80	**5**	14	17. **I'm Coming Out**	Motown 1491
11/15/80+	**9**	15	18. **It's My Turn**	Motown 1496
			title song from the movie starring Jill Clayburgh and Michael Douglas	
7/18/81	**1** (9)	19	▲ 19. **Endless Love**	Motown 1519
			DIANA ROSS & LIONEL RICHIE	
			title song from the movie starring Brooke Shields; #1 R&B hit (7 weeks); #1 Adult Contemporary hit (3 weeks)	
10/24/81	**7**	14	20. **Why Do Fools Fall In Love**	RCA 12349
1/30/82	**8**	10	21. **Mirror, Mirror**	RCA 13021
10/16/82	**10**	10	22. **Muscles**	RCA 13348
			written and produced by Michael Jackson	
3/19/83	**40**	2	23. So Close	RCA 13424
7/23/83	**31**	3	24. Pieces Of Ice	RCA 13549
8/4/84	**19**	8	25. All Of You	Columbia 04507
			JULIO IGLESIAS & DIANA ROSS	
9/22/84	**19**	8	26. Swept Away	RCA 13864
			Sales #17 / Airplay #18; written and produced by Daryl Hall	
3/9/85	**10**	9	27. **Missing You**	RCA 13966
			Sales #5 / Airplay #13; dedicated to Marvin Gaye; written and produced by Lionel Richie; #1 R&B hit (3 weeks)	
			ROSS, Jack	
			West Coast nightclub entertainer/trumpet player. Died on 12/16/82 (age 66).	
4/7/62	**16**	6	1. Cinderella [C]	Dot 16333

DATE	POS	WKS	ARTIST–RECORD TITLE	LABEL & NO.
			ROSS, Jackie	
			Born on 1/30/46 in St. Louis. Sang gospel on her parents' radio show at age three. Moved to Chicago in 1954. First recorded for Sar in 1962.	
8/15/64	**11**	8	1. Selfish One	Chess 1903
			ROSS, Spencer	
			Ross is actually conductor/arranger Robert Mersey. Composed arrangements for Gordon Jenkins's orchestra. Arranging work for Big Top and Columbia Records.	
1/18/60	**13**	10	1. Tracy's Theme [I] from the 12/7/59 TV drama special "Philadelphia Story"; Jimmy Abato (sax)	Columbia 41532
			ROTH, David Lee	
			Born on 10/10/55 in Bloomington, Indiana. Lead singer of Van Halen, 1973–85.	
1/26/85	**3**	11	1. **California Girls** Airplay #3 / Sales #4; Carl Wilson (backing vocal)	Warner 29102
4/20/85	**12**	10	2. Just A Gigolo/I Ain't Got Nobody Airplay #11 / Sales #16; "Just A Gigolo": #1 hit for Ted Lewis in 1931; "I Ain't Got Nobody": #3 hit for Marion Harris in 1921; arrangement copied from a Louis Prima recording (V-Disc in 1944)	Warner 29040
7/26/86	**16**	8	3. Yankee Rose Sales #15 / Airplay #22	Warner 28656
1/30/88	**6**	11	4. **Just Like Paradise** Sales #4 / Airplay #8	Warner 28119
			ROUTERS, The	
			Rock and roll instrumental quintet led by Mike Gordon. Member Scott Engel joined The Walker Bros.	
11/24/62	**19**	7	1. Let's Go (pony) [I]	Warner 5283
			ROVER BOYS, The	
			Vocal quartet: Brooklyn-born Billy Alberts (lead singer), British-born Doug Wells and Canadian natives Larry Amato and Al Osten. Named after a series of children's books written by Arthur Winfield.	
5/19/56	**16**	7	1. Graduation Day Jockey #16 / Best Seller #19 / Top 100 #20; Don Costa (orch.)	ABC-Para. 9700
			ROVERS—see IRISH ROVERS	
			ROXETTE	
			Male/female Swedish pop-rock duo: Marie Fredriksson (born 5/30/58; vocals) and Per Gessle (born 6/12/59; songwriter).	
2/25/89	**1** (1)	13	● 1. **The Look** Airplay #1(2) / Sales #2; also on the B-side of #2 below	EMI 50190
6/24/89	**14**	9	2. Dressed For Success Sales #12 / Airplay #18	EMI 50204
9/9/89	**1** (1)	14	3. **Listen To Your Heart** Airplay #1(1) / Sales #3	EMI 50223
1/6/90	**2** (2)	14	4. **Dangerous** Sales #2 / Airplay #3; above 4 from the album *Look Sharp!*	EMI 50233

DATE	POS	WKS	ARTIST–RECORD TITLE	LABEL & NO.
4/21/90	**1** (2)	17	● 5. **It Must Have Been Love** Airplay #1(3) / Sales #2; from the movie *Pretty Woman* starring Richard Gere and Julia Roberts	EMI 50283
3/16/91	**1** (1)	14	6. **Joyride** Sales #1(1) / Airplay #2	EMI 50342
6/29/91	**2** (1)	13	7. **Fading Like A Flower (Every Time You Leave)** Airplay #11 / Sales #23	EMI 50355
11/23/91+	**32**	8	8. Spending My Time Airplay #32 / Sales #49	EMI 50366
3/28/92	**36**	4	9. Church Of Your Heart Airplay #34; above 4 from the album *Joyride*	EMI 50380

ROXY MUSIC

English art-rock band. Nucleus consisted of Bryan Ferry (vocals, keyboards), Phil Manzanera (guitar) and Andy MacKay (horns).

DATE	POS	WKS	ARTIST–RECORD TITLE	LABEL & NO.
2/21/76	30	5	1. Love Is The Drug	Atco 7042

ROYAL, Billy Joe

Born on 4/3/42 in Valdosta, Georgia; raised in Marietta, Georgia. Guitarist/pianist/drummer. Own band, the Corvettes, while in high school. First recorded for Fairlane in 1961. Moved to Cincinnati in 1963.

DATE	POS	WKS	ARTIST–RECORD TITLE	LABEL & NO.
7/31/65	9	8	1. **Down In The Boondocks**	Columbia 43305
10/9/65	14	8	2. I Knew You When	Columbia 43390
1/15/66	38	1	3. I've Got To Be Somebody above 3 written and produced by Joe South	Columbia 43465
11/1/69	15	10	4. Cherry Hill Park	Columbia 44902

ROYAL GUARDSMEN, The

Novelty-pop sextet from Ocala, Florida. Consisted of Barry Winslow (vocals, guitar), Chris Nunley (vocals), Tom Richards (lead guitar), Bill Balough (bass) and Billy Taylor (organ). "Snoopy" songs inspired by Snoopy the Beagle in the "Peanuts" comic strip.

DATE	POS	WKS	ARTIST–RECORD TITLE	LABEL & NO.
12/17/66	**2** (4)	11	● 1. **Snoopy Vs. The Red Baron** [N]	Laurie 3366
3/11/67	15	5	2. The Return Of The Red Baron [N]	Laurie 3379
1/4/69	35	5	3. Baby Let's Wait first released on Laurie 3359 in 1966; all of above produced by Phil Gernhard	Laurie 3461

ROYAL PHILHARMONIC ORCHESTRA, The

British – Louis Clark, conductor (born in Birmingham, England; arranger for ELO).

DATE	POS	WKS	ARTIST–RECORD TITLE	LABEL & NO.
11/28/81+	10	12	1. **Hooked On Classics** [I] **LOUIS CLARK CONDUCTING THE ROYAL PHILHARMONIC** **ORCHESTRA** Tchaikovsky Piano Concerto No. 1/Flight of the Bumble Bee/Mozart Symphony No. 40 in G Minor/Rhapsody In Blue/Karelia Suite/The Marriage of Figaro/Romeo & Juliet/Trumpet Voluntary/Hallelujah Chorus/Grieg Piano Concerto in A Minor/March of the Toreadors/1812 Overture	RCA 12304

Jon Secada's multi-platinum success in the early '90s came as the direct result of friendship with Gloria Estefan. The Cuban-born Secada co-wrote six songs on Estefan's double-platinum 1991 album *Into The Light*.

Bob Seger's 1979 hit "Old Time Rock & Roll" was memorably lip-synched by actor Tom Cruise—wearing only his underwear—in the film *Risky Business*.

The Shadows Of Knight were Chicago-area punks of the highest order in the mid-'60s. The group cracked the Top 40 twice in 1966 with "Gloria" and "Oh Yeah," then saw follow-up single "Bad Little Woman" stumble, peaking at No. 91.

Bunny Sigler's follow-up to his No. 22 hit "Let The Good Times Roll & Feel So Good" arrived via 1967's "Lovey Dovey & (You're So Fine)," which scraped the chart's bottom at No. 86. The singer later enjoyed a renewed R&B career as a producer and performer at Philadelphia International.

Carly Simon's 1986 hit "Coming Around Again," from Nora Ephron's film *Heartburn*, was the singer's first Top 20 hit released by Arista Records. Since pairing with her sister Lucy in the mid-'60s, the singer had been signed to the Columbia, Elektra and Warner Bros. labels.

Frank Sinatra's much-loved Reprise recordings—including "Pocketful Of Miracles," from the 1962 film of the same name—were collected in full and reissued in a gargantuan boxed set in 1995. Cost? A mere $499.

Dusty Springfield's reputation as one of Great Britain's finest-ever vocalists stems first from her string of terrific Philips singles of the '60s—including 1967's "I'll Try Anything"—and her classic Atlantic album of 1969, *Dusty In Memphis.*

Rick Springfield's "Love Is Alright Tonite" single bore the same canine countenance that graced the cover of the singer's 1981 breakout album, *Working Class Dog.* Ten years earlier, Springfield had scored his first Top 20 hit with "Speak To The Sky."

Bruce Springsteen's 1988 single "One Step Up" topped out at No. 13, thus breaking a nonstop string of Top 10 singles that began with 1984's "Dancing In The Dark."

Stacey Q personified the one-hit wonder "dance diva" that was often the norm in the mid-'80s—except the Los Angeles-based singer had roots in new wave rock (Enigma Records band SSQ) and actually had two hits, including 1987's "We Connect," which peaked at No. 35.

Ringo Starr's 1972 single "Back Off Boogaloo" was one of three Top 40 hits by the former Beatle that had been produced by ex-partner George Harrison. Starr's touring All Star Band would later become a significant concert moneymaker in the early '90s.

Cat Stevens's 1974 hit "Oh Very Young" was one of several Stevens songs to impress a generation of fans during that decade. Controversy brewed in 1987 when one-time fans 10,000 Maniacs recorded Stevens's 1971 hit "Peace Train"—and then pulled it off their album in protest of Stevens's politics.

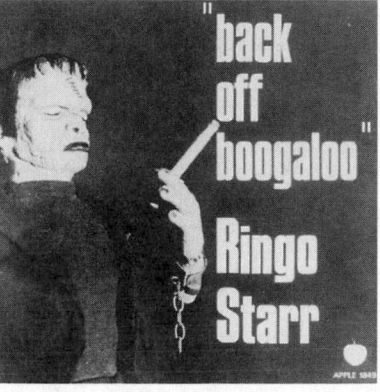

DATE	POS	WKS	ARTIST–RECORD TITLE	LABEL & NO.
			ROYAL SCOTS DRAGOON GUARDS, The	
			The military band of Scotland's armored regiment. Led by bagpipe soloist Major Tony Crease.	
5/27/72	**11**	8	1. Amazing Grace [I] **THE PIPES AND DRUMS AND THE MILITARY BAND OF THE ROYAL SCOTS DRAGOON GUARDS** Pipe Major Tony Crease (bagpipes solo); Rev. John Newton wrote the words in 1779; William Walker composed the melody in 1844	RCA 0709
			ROYAL TEENS	
			Quartet from Fort Lee, New Jersey. Consisted of Bob Gaudio, Bill Crandall, Billy Dalton and Tom Austin. Crandall was replaced by Larry Qualiano, and Joseph "Joe Villa" Francavilla joined as vocalist in late 1958. In 1960, Gaudio joined The 4 Seasons. Al Kooper joined the group for a short time in 1959.	
2/3/58	**3**	12	1. **Short Shorts** Top 100 #3 / Best Seller #4 / Jockey #6; first released on Power 215 in 1957	ABC-Para. 9882
11/16/59	**26**	6	2. Believe Me	Capitol 4261
			ROYALTONES, The	
			Rock and roll instrumental group from Dearborn, Michigan. Formed in 1957 as the Paragons. Featuring tenor saxophonist George Katsakis.	
11/10/58	**17**	10	1. Poor Boy [I]	Jubilee 5338
			ROZALLA	
			Born Rozalla Miller on 3/18/64 in Ndola, Zambia. Lives in Zimbabwe and London.	
7/25/92	**37**	4	1. Everybody's Free (To Feel Good) Airplay #26 / Sales #50	Epic 74388
			R*S*F (Right Said Fred)	
			British trio: brothers Fred (guitar) and Richard Fairbrass (vocals) with Rob Manzoli (lead guitar). The brothers run a fitness gym in South London. Group name was the title of a song by Bernard Cribbins popular in Britain in 1962.	
1/18/92	**1 (3)**	17	▲ 1. **I'm Too Sexy** [N] Sales #1(7) / Airplay #8	Charisma 98671
			RTZ	
			Rock quintet formed in Boston in 1989: Brad Delp (vocals), Barry Goudreau (guitar), Brian Maes (keyboards), Tim Archibald (bass) and David Stefanelli (drums). Delp and Goudreau were members of Boston. Goudreau was also with Orion The Hunter. RTZ stands for Return To Zero.	
2/15/92	**26**	8	1. Until Your Love Comes Back Around Airplay #30 / Sales #71	Giant 19051
			RUBETTES, The	
			British pop-rock quintet featuring Paul DaVinci, lead singer.	
8/31/74	**37**	2	1. Sugar Baby Love	Polydor 15089

DATE	POS	WKS	ARTIST–RECORD TITLE	LABEL & NO.
			RUBICON	
			Bay area septet led by horn player Jerry Martini (member of Sly & The Family Stone, 1966–76). Group included Jack Blades and Brad Gillis of Night Ranger.	
4/8/78	**28**	3	1. I'm Gonna Take Care Of Everything	20th Century 2362
			RUBY AND THE ROMANTICS	
			Akron, Ohio, R&B quintet: Ruby Nash Curtis (born 11/12/39, New York City; lead), Ed Roberts (died of cancer 8/10/93, age 57) and George Lee (tenors), Ronald Mosley (baritone) and Leroy Fann (bass; died 1973).	
2/23/63	**1** (1)	10	1. **Our Day Will Come** #1 R&B hit (2 weeks)	Kapp 501
6/15/63	**16**	6	2. My Summer Love	Kapp 525
8/31/63	**27**	5	3. Hey There Lonely Boy	Kapp 544
			RUDE BOYS	
			Cleveland R&B vocal quartet: Larry Marcus, Melvin Sephus, and brothers Edward Lee "Buddy" Banks and J. Little. Marcus is the cousin of B.B. King. Group discovered by Levert.	
3/30/91	**16**	12	1. Written All Over Your Face Sales #11 / Airplay #22; #1 R&B hit (1 week)	Atlantic 87805
			RUFFIN, David	
			Born Davis Eli Ruffin on 1/18/41 in Meridian, Mississippi. Died of a drug overdose on 6/1/91. Brother of Jimmy Ruffin. With the Dixie Nightingales gospel group. Recorded for Anna in 1960. Co lead singer of The Temptations, 1963–68.	
2/22/69	**9**	9	1. **My Whole World Ended (The Moment You Left Me)**	Motown 1140
11/29/75+	**9**	11	2. **Walk Away From Love** #1 R&B hit (1 week)	Motown 1376
9/14/85	20	7	3. A Nite At The Apollo Live! The Way You Do The Things You Do/My Girl **DARYL HALL JOHN OATES with David Ruffin & Eddie Kendrick** Sales #21 / Airplay #23; recorded at the reopening of New York's Apollo Theatre	RCA 14178
			RUFFIN, Jimmy	
			Born on 5/7/39 in Collinsville, Mississippi. Brother of David Ruffin. Backup work at Motown in the early '60s. First recorded for Miracle in 1961.	
9/10/66	**7**	14	1. **What Becomes Of The Brokenhearted**	Soul 35022
12/24/66+	**17**	8	2. I've Passed This Way Before	Soul 35027
4/8/67	**29**	3	3. Gonna Give Her All The Love I've Got	Soul 35032
3/22/80	**10**	9	4. **Hold On To My Love** co-written and produced by Robin Gibb	RSO 1021
			RUFUS—see KHAN, Chaka	
			RUGBYS, The	
			Steve McNicol (guitar), Mike Mornei (bass), Ed Vernon (keyboards) and Glenn Howerton (drums).	
9/27/69	**24**	6	1. You, I	Amazon 1

DATE	POS	WKS	ARTIST–RECORD TITLE	LABEL & NO.
			RUNDGREN, Todd	
			Born on 6/22/48 in Upper Darby, Pennsylvania. Virtuoso musician/songwriter/producer/engineer. Leader of groups Nazz and Utopia. Produced Meat Loaf's *Bat Out Of Hell* album and produced albums for Badfinger, Grand Funk Railroad, The Tubes, XTC, Patti Smith and many others.	
12/26/70+	20	9	1. We Gotta Get You A Woman **RUNT**	Ampex 31001
5/6/72	16	9	2. I Saw The Light *most pressings available on blue vinyl*	Bearsville 0003
11/10/73	5	12	3. **Hello It's Me**	Bearsville 0009
6/26/76	34	3	4. Good Vibrations	Bearsville 0309
7/8/78	29	5	5. Can We Still Be Friends *all of above written (except #4) and produced by Rundgren*	Bearsville 0324
			RUN-D.M.C.	
			Rap trio from Queens, New York: rappers Joseph Simmons (Run), Darryl McDaniels (DMC), with DJ Jason Mizell (Jam Master Jay). Appeared in the movies *Krush Groove* and *Tougher Than Leather*.	
8/16/86	4	10	● 1. **Walk This Way** *Sales #2 / Airplay #7; with Aerosmith's Steve Tyler (vocals) and Joe Perry (guitar)*	Profile 5112
11/29/86	29	7	2. You Be Illin' *Sales #26 / Airplay #36*	Profile 5119
4/3/93	21	10	● 3. Down With The King *Sales #7 / Airplay #46; samples "Where Do I Go" by the original Broadway cast of Hair*	Profile 5391
			RUNT—see RUNDGREN, Todd	
			RUSH	
			Canadian power-rock trio formed in Toronto in 1969: Geddy Lee (vocals, bass; real name: Gary Lee Weinrib), Alex Lifeson (guitar; real name: Alex Zivojinovich) and John Rutsey (drums). Neil Peart replaced Rutsey in July 1974. Also see Bob & Doug McKenzie.	
10/9/82	21	6	1. New World Man	Mercury 76179
			RUSH, Jennifer	
			Native of Queens, New York.	
7/4/87	36	3	1. Flames Of Paradise **JENNIFER RUSH (with Elton John)** *Sales #32 / Airplay #34*	Epic 07119
			RUSH, Merrillee, & The Turnabouts	
			From Seattle, Washington. Discovered by fellow Northwesterners Paul Revere & The Raiders.	
6/1/68	7	12	1. **Angel Of The Morning**	Bell 705
			RUSHEN, Patrice	
			Born on 9/30/54 in Los Angeles. Jazz-soul vocalist/pianist/songwriter. Much session work with Jean Luc-Ponty, Lee Ritenour and Stanley Turrentine.	
6/5/82	23	7	1. Forget Me Nots	Elektra 47427

DATE	POS	WKS	ARTIST–RECORD TITLE	LABEL & NO.
			RUSSELL, Bobby	
			Born on 4/19/41 in Nashville. Died of a heart attack on 11/19/92. Wrote "The Night The Lights Went Out In Georgia," "Honey," "Little Green Apples" and "The Joker Went Wild." First husband of Vicki Lawrence.	
11/23/68	**36**	2	1. 1432 Franklin Pike Circle Hero	Elf 90020
8/28/71	**28**	7	2. Saturday Morning Confusion [N]	United Art. 50788
			RUSSELL, Brenda	
			Born Brenda Gordon in Brooklyn. Soul singer/keyboardist/composer. To Toronto at age 12. Recorded as duo Brian & Brenda with former husband Brian Russell in 1978; co-hosted the Canadian TV series "Music Machine." Session work for Barbra Streisand, Elton John, Bette Midler and many others.	
10/13/79	**30**	6	1. So Good, So Right	Horizon 123
4/2/88	**6**	13	2. **Piano In The Dark**	A&M 3003
			Sales #6 / Airplay #11; Joe Esposito (of Brooklyn Dreams, backing vocal)	
			RUSSELL, Leon	
			Born on 4/2/41 in Lawton, Oklahoma. Rock singer/songwriter/multi-instrumentalist sessionman. Early in session career known as Russell Bridges. Regular with Phil Spector's "Wall of Sound" session group. Formed Shelter Records with British producer Denny Cordell in 1970. Recorded as Hank Wilson in 1973. Married Mary McCreary (vocalist with Little Sister, part of Sly Stone's "family") in 1976. Formed Paradise label in 1976. Wrote "Superstar" and "This Masquerade." Also see Joe Cocker.	
9/23/72	**11**	7	1. Tight Rope	Shelter 7325
			B-side is Russell's original recording of George Benson's 1976 hit "This Masquerade"	
9/13/75	**14**	10	2. Lady Blue	Shelter 40378
			written for Russell's daughter, Blue	
			RYAN, Charlie, and the Timberline Riders	
			Born in Graceville, Minnesota; raised in Montana. Country singer.	
8/8/60	**33**	4	1. Hot Rod Lincoln [N-S]	4 Star 1733
			originally released on Souvenir 101 in 1955; original version by Tiny Hill charted in 1951	
			RYDELL, Bobby	
			Born Robert Ridarelli on 4/26/42 in Philadelphia. Regular on Paul Whiteman's amateur TV show, 1951–54. Drummer with Rocco & His Saints, which included Frankie Avalon on trumpet in 1956. First recorded for Veko in 1957. Appeared in the movies *Bye Bye Birdie* and *That Lady From Peking*.	
8/10/59	**11**	9	1. Kissin' Time	Cameo 167
			Georgie Young And The Rockin' Bocs (backing group)	
10/26/59	**6**	14	2. **We Got Love**	Cameo 169
2/8/60	**2 (1)**	13	● 3. **Wild One/**	
2/22/60	**19**	10	4. Little Bitty Girl	Cameo 171
5/16/60	**5**	8	5. **Swingin' School/**	
			from the movie *Because They're Young* starring James Darren and Tuesday Weld	
5/16/60	**18**	8	6. Ding-A-Ling	Cameo 175
8/1/60	**4**	11	7. **Volare**	Cameo 179
11/14/60	**14**	10	8. Sway	Cameo 182
			#15 hit for Dean Martin in 1954	

DATE	POS	WKS	ARTIST–RECORD TITLE	LABEL & NO.
2/6/61	11	8	9. Good Time Baby	Cameo 186
5/8/61	21	5	10. That Old Black Magic	Cameo 190
			#1 hit for Glenn Miller in 1943 (from the movie *Star-Spangled Rhythm* starring Bing Crosby)	
7/10/61	25	5	11. The Fish	Cameo 192
			melody is similar to The Shirelles' "Mama Said"	
11/6/61	21	6	12. I Wanna Thank You	Cameo 201
12/25/61	21	3	13. Jingle Bell Rock [X]	Cameo 205
			BOBBY RYDELL CHUBBY CHECKER	
3/10/62	18	7	14. (I've Got) Bonnie	Cameo 209
6/23/62	14	7	15. I'll Never Dance Again	Cameo 217
10/27/62	10	8	16. **The Cha-Cha-Cha**	Cameo 228
			melody and arrangement are similar to "Rinky Dink" by Dave "Baby" Cortez	
2/23/63	23	6	17. Butterfly Baby	Cameo 242
6/1/63	17	5	18. Wildwood Days	Cameo 252
			#1–3, 5, 6, 9, 12, 15–18 written by Kal Mann, Bernie Lowe and Dave Appell	
12/7/63+	4	12	19. **Forget Him**	Cameo 280

RYDER, Mitch, And The Detroit Wheels

Born William Levise, Jr., on 2/26/45 in Detroit. Leader of white soul-rock group The Detroit Wheels. Group was originally known as Billy Lee & The Rivieras. Renamed by its producer Bob Crewe. Ryder went solo in 1967. Formed new rock group, Detroit, in 1971. Band members Jim McCarty (guitar) and John Badanjek (drums) joined The Rockets in 1972.

DATE	POS	WKS	ARTIST–RECORD TITLE	LABEL & NO.
1/8/66	10	8	1. **Jenny Take A Ride!**	New Voice 806
			medley: Little Richard's "Jenny, Jenny" and Chuck Willis's "C.C. Rider"	
3/26/66	17	6	2. Little Latin Lupe Lu	New Voice 808
10/22/66	4	14	3. **Devil With A Blue Dress On & Good Golly Miss Molly**	New Voice 817
2/18/67	6	9	4. **Sock It To Me-Baby!**	New Voice 820
5/13/67	24	4	5. Too Many Fish In The Sea & Three Little Fishes	New Voice 822
			"Three Little Fishes" was a #1 hit for Kay Kyser in 1939	
			MITCH RYDER:	
9/30/67	30	4	6. What Now My Love	DynoVoice 901
			written in France in 1962 by Gilbert Becaud as: "Et Maintenant"; all of above produced by Bob Crewe	

RYTHM SYNDICATE

R&B band from Connecticut: Evan Rogers (vocals), Carl Sturken (guitar), John Nevin, Rob Mingrino and Kevin Cloud. Rogers and Sturken produced Donny Osmond's "Soldier Of Love" and "Sacred Emotion." Changed Rythm Syndicate to Rhythm Syndicate after the first album.

DATE	POS	WKS	ARTIST–RECORD TITLE	LABEL & NO.
6/15/91	2 (2)	13	1. **P.A.S.S.I.O.N.**	Impact 54046
			Airplay #5 / Sales #19	
9/28/91	13	8	2. Hey Donna	Impact 54208
			Airplay #29	

DATE	POS	WKS	ARTIST–RECORD TITLE	LABEL & NO.
			# S	
			SAADIQ, Raphael	
4/8/95	**19**	12	Member of Tony! Toni! Toné! Formerly known as Raphael Wiggins. 1. Ask Of You **RAPHAEL SAADIQ (of Tony! Toni! Toné!)** Sales #10 / Airplay #30; contains the melody of "Sukiyaki"; from the movie *Higher Learning* starring Laurence Fishburne	550 Music 77862
			SADE	
			Name pronounced: SHAH-day. Born Helen Folasade Adu on 1/16/59 in Ibadan, Nigeria; moved to London at age four. Appeared in the 1986 movie *Absolute Beginners*. Former designer of menswear. Won the 1985 Best New Artist Grammy Award.	
3/30/85	**5**	13	1. **Smooth Operator** Airplay #4 / Sales #6; #1 Adult Contemporary hit (2 weeks)	Portrait 04807
12/28/85+	**5**	13	2. **The Sweetest Taboo** Sales #6 / Airplay #6; #1 Adult Contemporary hit (1 week)	Portrait 05713
4/19/86	**20**	7	3. Never As Good As The First Time Sales #20 / Airplay #20	Portrait 05846
6/11/88	**16**	8	4. Paradise Sales #15 / Airplay #21; #1 R&B hit (1 week); remix version is on the B-side of #5 below	Epic 07904
1/23/93	**28**	4	5. No Ordinary Love Sales #32 / Airplay #33	Epic 74734
			SADLER, SSgt. Barry (U.S. Army Special Forces)	
			Born on 11/1/40 in Carlsbad, New Mexico. Died of heart failure on 11/5/89 in Tennessee. Staff Sergeant of U.S. Army Special Forces (aka Green Berets). Served in Vietnam until injuring leg in booby trap. Shot in the head during a 1988 robbery attempt at his Guatemala home; suffered brain damage.	
2/19/66	**1 (5)**	11	● 1. **The Ballad Of The Green Berets** #1 Adult Contemporary hit (5 weeks)	RCA 8739
5/14/66	**28**	4	2. The "A" Team	RCA 8804
			SAFARIS	
			Los Angeles-based pop quartet formed in 1959: Jim Stephens (lead singer), Richard Clasky, Marvin Rosenberg and Shelly Briar.	
7/11/60	**6**	11	1. **Image Of A Girl** with The Phantom's Band	Eldo 101
			SA-FIRE	
			Real name: Wilma Cosme. Latin American dance singer from New York City.	
3/18/89	**12**	12	1. Thinking Of You Airplay #9 / Sales #14	Cutting 872502

DATE	POS	WKS	ARTIST–RECORD TITLE	LABEL & NO.
			SAGA Rock group formed in Toronto in 1976: Michael Sadler (vocals), brothers Ian (guitar) and Jim (bass) Crichton, Jim Gilmour (keyboards) and Steve Negus (drums).	
1/29/83	26	8	1. On The Loose	Portrait 03359
			SAGER, Carole Bayer Born on 3/8/46 in New York City. Prolific pop lyricist. Married to Burt Bacharach, 1982–91. Collaborated in writing "A Groovy Kind Of Love," "Midnight Blue," "Nobody Does It Better," "When I Need You" and many others. Wrote lyrics for many movie scores.	
6/13/81	30	7	1. Stronger Than Before	Boardwalk 02054
			SAIGON KICK Hard-rock quartet formed in Miami in 1988: Matt Kramer (vocals), Jason Bieler (guitar), Tom DeFile (bass) and Phil Varone (drums). DeFile was replaced by Chris McLernon in 1993.	
10/17/92	12	15	● 1. Love Is On The Way Sales #12 / Airplay #20	Third Stone 98530
			SAILCAT Country-rock duo: Court Pickett and John Wyker.	
7/15/72	12	10	1. Motorcycle Mama	Elektra 45782
			SAINTE-MARIE, Buffy Born on 2/20/41 of Cree Indian parents on Piapot Reserve, Saskatchewan, Canada. Folk singer/songwriter. Raised in Maine. Co-writer of "Up Where We Belong." Semi-regular of TV's "Sesame Street" cast, 1976–91.	
4/29/72	38	2	1. Mister Can't You See	Vanguard 35151
			ST. PETERS, Crispian Born Peter Smith on 4/5/44 in Swanley, Kent, England. Pop singer/guitarist.	
7/9/66	4	8	1. **The Pied Piper**	Jamie 1320
7/22/67	36	2	2. You Were On My Mind	Jamie 1310
			SAKAMOTO, Kyu Native of Kawasaki, Japan. Kyu (pronounced: cue) was one of 520 people killed in the crash of the Japan Airlines 747 near Tokyo on 8/12/85 (age 43).	
5/25/63	1 (3)	12	● 1. **Sukiyaki** [F] #1 Adult Contemporary hit (5 weeks); released in Japan as "Ue O Muite Aruko" (I Look Up When I Walk)	Capitol 4945
			SALSOUL ORCHESTRA Disco orchestra conducted by Philadelphia producer/arranger Vincent Montana, Jr. Vocalists included Phyllis Rhodes, Ronni Tyson, Carl Helm, Philip Hurt and Jocelyn Brown.	
2/14/76	18	9	1. Tangerine [I] #1 hit for Jimmy Dorsey in 1942 (from the movie *The Fleet's In* starring Dorothy Lamour)	Salsoul 2004
10/30/76	30	5	2. Nice 'N' Naasty	Salsoul 2011

DATE	POS	WKS	ARTIST–RECORD TITLE	LABEL & NO.
			SALT-N-PEPA	
			Queens-based female rap trio: Cheryl "Salt" James, Sandra "Pepa" Denton (from Kingston, Jamaica) and Dee Dee "DJ Spinderella LaToya" Roper. Appeared in the movie *Who's The Man?*.	
12/26/87+	**19**	13	▲ 1. Push It Sales #18 / Airplay #21	Next Plat. 315
4/21/90	**26**	8	▲ 2. Expression Sales #17	Next Plat. 329
5/11/91	**21**	14	● 3. Do You Want Me Sales #8 / Airplay #10	Next Plat. 331
10/12/91	**13**	13	● 4. Let's Talk About Sex Sales #9 / Airplay #17	Next Plat. 333
10/23/93	**4**	23	● 5. **Shoop** Airplay #2 / Sales #2; samples "I'm Blue" by The Sweet Inspirations and "Super Sporm" by Captain Sky	Next Plat. 857314
1/29/94	**3**	24	▲ 6. **Whatta Man** **SALT 'N' PEPA with En Vogue** Sales #2 / Airplay #4; samples "What A Man" by Linda Lyndell	Next Plat. 857390
10/15/94	**32**	5	7. None Of Your Business Sales #19 / Airplay #74; originally released on Next Plateau 857578 with "Heaven 'N Hell" as the A-side	Next Plat. 857776
10/28/95	**38**	3	8. Ain't Nuthin' But A She Thing Sales #17	London 850346
			SALVO, Sammy	
			Pop vocalist from Birmingham, Alabama.	
3/3/58	**23**	1	1. Oh Julie Jockey #23 / Top 100 #78	RCA 7097
			SAM & DAVE	
			Samuel Moore (born 10/12/35, Miami) and David Prater (born 5/9/37, Ocilla, Georgia). Moore had been with the Melionaires gospel group, and Prater was a solo artist prior to their meeting in Miami in 1961. First recorded for Alston in 1962. Duo produced by Isaac Hayes and David Porter. Prater was killed in a car crash on 4/9/88.	
6/4/66	**21**	7	● 1. Hold On! I'm A Comin' #1 R&B hit (1 week)	Stax 189
9/30/67	**2 (3)**	11	● 2. **Soul Man** #1 R&B hit (7 weeks)	Stax 231
2/17/68	**9**	9	3. **I Thank You**	Stax 242
			SAM THE SHAM and The PHARAOHS	
			Dallas rock & roll group formed in the early 1960s, featuring lead singer Domingo "Sam" Samudio (born 1940, Dallas). Included Ray Stinnet, David Martin, Jerry Patterson and Butch Gibson. First recorded for Tupelo in 1963. Samudio went solo in 1970. Formed new band in 1974. On the 1982 movie soundtrack *The Border*. Sam later became a street preacher in Memphis. Martin died on 8/2/87 (age 50).	
5/1/65	**2 (2)**	14	● 1. **Wooly Bully** originally released on XL 906 in 1964	MGM 13322
8/21/65	**26**	4	2. Ju Ju Hand	MGM 13364
11/13/65	**33**	3	3. Ring Dang Doo	MGM 13397
7/2/66	**2 (2)**	11	● 4. **Lil' Red Riding Hood**	MGM 13506
10/15/66	**22**	5	5. The Hair On My Chinny Chin Chin	MGM 13581

DATE	POS	WKS	ARTIST—RECORD TITLE	LABEL & NO.
1/21/67	27	4	6. How Do You Catch A Girl all of above produced by Stan Kesler	MGM 13649
			SANDERS, Felicia	
5/28/55	29	3	Born in New York City; raised in California. Died on 2/7/75. Vocalist on Percy Faith's 1953 #1 hit "Song From Moulin Rouge." 1. Blue Star (The "Medic" Theme) Best Seller #29; Norman Leyden (orch.); from the TV series starring Richard Boone	Columbia 40508
			SANDPEBBLES, The	
1/6/68	22	6	Consisted of Calvin White, Andrea Bolden and Lonzine Wright. White had been lead singer of the Gospel Wonders. Group name changed to C & The Shells in 1969. 1. Love Power	Calla 141
			SANDPIPERS, The	
			Los Angeles-based trio: Jim Brady (born 8/24/44), Michael Piano (born 10/26/44) and Richard Shoff (born 4/30/44); met while in the Mitchell Boys Choir.	
8/13/66	9	9	1. **Guantanamera** [F] Pete Seeger adapted this song from a poem by Cuban writer Jose Marti	A&M 806
11/12/66	30	4	2. Louie, Louie [F]	A&M 819
5/2/70	17	8	3. Come Saturday Morning from the movie *The Sterile Cuckoo* starring Liza Minnelli	A&M 1134
			SANDS, Jodie	
6/10/57	15	9	Pop singer from Philadelphia. 1. With All My Heart Jockey #15 / Top 100 #20 / Best Seller #21; Peter DeAngelis (orch.)	Chancellor 1003
			SANDS, Tommy	
			Born on 8/27/37 in Chicago. Pop singer/actor. Mother was a vocalist with Art Kassel's band. Married Nancy Sinatra in 1960; divorced in 1965. In the movies *Sing Boy Sing, Mardi Gras, Babes In Toyland* and *The Longest Day*.	
2/23/57	2 (2)	12	● 1. **Teen-Age Crush** Best Seller #2 / Top 100 #3 / Jockey #4 / Juke Box #7; introduced by Sands on the 1/30/57 Kraft TV production of "The Singing Idol"	Capitol 3639
5/27/57	16	8	2. Goin' Steady/ Jockey #16 / Best Seller #18 / Top 100 #19; #2 Country hit for Faron Young in 1953	
		2	3. Ring My Phone Best Seller flip; from the Kraft NBC-TV show "Flesh and Blood"	Capitol 3723
2/24/58	24	2	4. Sing Boy Sing Jockey #24 / Best Seller #46 / Top 100 #46; title song from the movie starring Sands; Bob Bain (orch., all of above)	Capitol 3867
			SANFORD/TOWNSEND BAND, The	
7/16/77	9	12	Los Angeles-based rock band led by Ed Sanford and John Townsend. 1. **Smoke From A Distant Fire**	Warner 8370

DATE	POS	WKS	ARTIST–RECORD TITLE	LABEL & NO.
1/7/78	3	17	**SANG, Samantha** Born Cheryl Gray on 8/5/53 in Melbourne, Australia. Began career on Melbourne radio at age eight. ▲ 1. **Emotion** Barry Gibb (backing vocal); written by Barry and Robin Gibb	Private St. 45178
10/9/65	27	5	**SAN REMO GOLDEN STRINGS** 1. Hungry For Love [I]	Ric-Tic 104

12/10/77+	15	12	**SANTA ESMERALDA**
			Spanish-flavored disco studio project produced by Nicolas Skorsky and Jean-Manuel de Scarano.
			   1. Don't Let Me Be Misunderstood
			    SANTA ESMERALDA Starring Leroy Gomez
				Casablanca 902

4/13/63
 	
3/8/69
	10
	
	32
		6
		
		2
			SANTAMARIA, Mongo
			Born Ramon Santamaria on 4/7/22 in Havana, Cuba. Bandleader/conga, bongo and percussion player. Member of bands led by Perez Prado, Tito Puente and Cal Tjader. Own group from 1961. Appeared in the the movie *Made In Paris* in 1966.
			   1. **Watermelon Man** [I]
			    written by Herbie Hancock
			   2. Cloud Nine [I]
				Battle 45909
				
				Columbia 44740

2/7/70
11/21/70+
3/6/71
10/30/71
3/11/72
11/19/77
2/17/79
1/19/80
5/16/81
8/28/82
	9
	4
	13
	12
	36
	27
	32
	35
	17
	15
		11
		12
		8
		8
		4
		5
		3
		3
		11
		10
			SANTANA
			Latin-rock group formed in San Francisco in 1966. Consisted of Devadip Carlos Santana (born 7/20/47, Autlan de Navarro, Mexico; vocals, guitar), Gregg Rolie (keyboards) and David Brown (bass). Added percussionists Michael Carabello, Jose Chepitos Areas and Michael Shrieve in 1969. Worked Fillmore West and Woodstock in 1969. Neal Schon (guitar) added in 1971. Santana began solo work in 1972. Schon and Rolie formed Journey in 1973. Shrieve left in 1975 to form Automatic Man.
			   1. **Evil Ways**
			   2. **Black Magic Woman**
			   3. Oye Como Va [F]
			   4. Everybody's Everything
			   5. No One To Depend On
			   6. She's Not There
			   7. Stormy
			   8. You Know That I Love You
			   9. Winning
			   10. Hold On
				Columbia 45069
				Columbia 45270
				Columbia 45330
				Columbia 45472
				Columbia 45552
				Columbia 10616
				Columbia 10873
				Columbia 11144
				Columbia 01050
				Columbia 03160

8/17/59 12/14/59	1 (2) 23	13 7	**SANTO & JOHNNY** Brooklyn-born guitar duo: Santo Farina (born 10/24/37; steel guitar) and his brother Johnny (born 4/30/41; rhythm guitar). Sister Ann Farina helped with songwriting. ● 1. **Sleep Walk** [I] 2. Tear Drop [I]	Canadian A. 103 Canadian A. 107

DATE	POS	WKS	ARTIST–RECORD TITLE	LABEL & NO.
			SANTOS, Larry	
			Born on 6/2/41 in Oneonta, New York. Wrote "Candy Girl" by The 4 Seasons. Worked as a jingle singer. First recorded with The Tones in 1959 on Baton.	
4/3/76	36	2	1. We Can't Hide It Anymore	Casablanca 844
			SAPPHIRES, The	
			Philadelphia R&B trio: Carol Jackson (lead singer), George Garner and Joe Livingston.	
2/22/64	25	5	1. Who Do You Love	Swan 4162
			SAYER, Leo	
			Born Gerard Sayer on 5/21/48 in Shoreham, England. With Patches in the early '70s. Songwriting team with David Courtney, 1972–75. Own British TV show in 1978 and again in 1983.	
3/22/75	9	9	1. **Long Tall Glasses (I Can Dance)**	Warner 8043
11/6/76+	1 (1)	17	● 2. **You Make Me Feel Like Dancing**	Warner 8283
3/26/77	1 (1)	14	● 3. **When I Need You**	Warner 8332
			#1 Adult Contemporary hit (1 week)	
7/23/77	17	10	4. How Much Love	Warner 8319
11/5/77	38	2	5. Thunder In My Heart	Warner 8465
1/28/78	36	2	6. Easy To Love	Warner 8502
10/18/80	2 (5)	15	● 7. **More Than I Can Say**	Warner 49565
			#1 Adult Contemporary hit (3 weeks)	
2/14/81	23	6	8. Living In A Fantasy	Warner 49657
			SCAGGS, Boz	
			Born William Royce Scaggs on 6/8/44 in Ohio; raised in Texas. Joined Steve Miller's band, The Marksmen, in 1959 in Dallas. Hooked up with Miller at University of Wisconsin in The Ardells, later known as The Fabulous Night Trains. Joined R&B band The Wigs in 1963. To Europe in 1964; toured as a folk singer. Re-joined Miller in 1967, solo since 1969. Retired from music and opened a restaurant in San Francisco, 1983–87. Made a comeback in 1988.	
5/22/76	38	3	1. It's Over	Columbia 10319
8/7/76	3	15	● 2. **Lowdown**	Columbia 10367
3/19/77	11	12	3. Lido Shuffle	Columbia 10491
			B-side is Scaggs's original version of Rita Coolidge's hit "We're All Alone"	
4/19/80	15	9	4. Breakdown Dead Ahead	Columbia 11241
7/12/80	17	9	5. JoJo	Columbia 11281
			Ray Parker, Jr. (guitar, above 2)	
9/6/80	14	10	6. Look What You've Done To Me	Columbia 11349
			from the movie *Urban Cowboy* starring John Travolta and Debra Winger; Glenn Frey, Don Henley and Timothy B. Schmit (backing vocals)	
12/27/80+	14	9	7. Miss Sun	Columbia 11406
			Lisa Dal Bello (backing vocal)	
6/11/88	35	4	8. Heart Of Mine	Columbia 07780
			Airplay #33 / Sales #34	

DATE	POS	WKS	ARTIST–RECORD TITLE	LABEL & NO.

7/21/84	7	15	**SCANDAL FEATURING PATTY SMYTH**
			Rock band from New York City: Patty Smyth (vocals), Zack Smith and Keith Mack (guitars), Ivan Elias (bass), and Thommy Price (drums).
			    1. **The Warrior**
			        Sales #19 pre / Airplay #26 pre
				Columbia 04424

6/13/81	2 (2)	18	**SCARBURY, Joey** Born on 6/7/55 in Ontario, California. Session singer for producer Mike Post. 1 1. Theme From "Greatest American Hero" (Believe It or Not) from the "Greatest American Hero" TV series starring William Katt	Elektra 47147

12/31/94+	37	3	**SCARFACE**
			Born Brad Jordan on 11/9/69 in Houston. Member of The Geto Boys.
			    1. I Never Seen A Man Cry (aka I Seen A Man Die)
			        Sales #19
				Rap-A-Lot 38461

3/12/88	20	8	**SCARLETT & BLACK**
			Keyboardist/singer/songwriter Robin Hild and songwriter Sue West (former backing vocalist for Doctor And The Medics).
			    1. You Don't Know
			        Sales #19 / Airplay #21
				Virgin 99405

11/12/83	14	10	**SCHILLING, Peter**
			Born on 1/28/56 in Stuttgart, Germany. Pop singer/songwriter.
			    1. Major Tom (Coming Home)
			        inspired by David Bowie's 1973 hit "Space Oddity"
				Elektra 69811

10/24/87	25	5	**SCHMIT, Timothy B.**
			Born on 10/30/47 in Sacramento. Member of Poco, 1970–77, and the Eagles, 1977–82.
			    1. Boys Night Out
			        Sales #21 / Airplay #30
				MCA 53137

6/27/81	14	11	**SCHNEIDER, John** Born on 4/8/59 in Mount Kisco, New York. Moved to Atlanta at age 14. Country singer/actor. Played Bo Duke on TV's "The Dukes Of Hazzard." Appeared in many TV movies. Scriptwriter/director. 1. It's Now Or Never	Scotti Br. 02105

4/9/55	14	6	**SCHUMANN, Walter, The Voices of**
			Born in New York City. Died in August 1958 (age 44). Leader of own choral group. Composer of the theme for TV's "Dragnet."
			    1. The Ballad Of Davy Crockett
			        Jockey #14 / Best Seller #29; from the ABC-TV "Disneyland" series which featured 3 "Davy Crockett" segments (Dec. '54–Feb. '55)
				RCA 6041

DATE	POS	WKS	ARTIST–RECORD TITLE	LABEL & NO.
			SCHWARTZ, Eddie	
			Canadian singer/songwriter. Wrote Pat Benatar's "Hit Me With Your Best Shot."	
1/16/82	28	7	1. All Our Tomorrows	Atco 7342
			SCORPIONS	
			German heavy-metal rock quintet: Rudolf Schenker (Michael Schenker's brother, lead guitar), Klaus Meine (lead singer), Matthias Jabs (guitar), Francis Buchholz (bass) and Herman Rarebell (drums). Buchholz left band in 1992; replaced by Ralph Rieckermann.	
4/28/84	25	7	1. Rock You Like A Hurricane	Mercury 818440
6/29/91	4	16	● 2. **Wind Of Change**	Mercury 868180
			Sales #5 / Airplay #9	
			SCOTT, Bobby	
			Born on 1/29/37 in Mount Pleasant, New York. Died on 11/5/90 of lung cancer. Jazz pianist/vocalist/composer/arranger. Wrote "Taste Of Honey" and "He Ain't Heavy, He's My Brother." Production work for Aretha Franklin and Johnny Mathis.	
1/21/56	13	10	1. Chain Gang	ABC-Para. 9658
			Jockey #13 / Juke Box #13 / Top 100 #15 / Best Seller #17; Don Costa (orch.)	
			SCOTT, Freddie	
			Born on 4/24/33 in Providence, Rhode Island. Recorded first hit while working as a songwriter for Columbia Music.	
8/10/63	10	9	1. **Hey, Girl**	Colpix 692
2/18/67	39	2	2. Are You Lonely For Me	Shout 207
			#1 R&B hit (4 weeks)	
			SCOTT, Jack	
			Born Jack Scafone, Jr., on 1/28/36 in Windsor, Ontario, Canada. Rock and roll-ballad singer/songwriter/guitarist. Moved to Hazel Park, Michigan, in 1946. First recorded for ABC-Paramount in 1957.	
7/7/58	3	16	● 1. **My True Love/**	
			Hot 100 #3 / Best Seller #7 / Jockey #13 end	
6/16/58	11	18	2. Leroy	Carlton 462
			Best Seller #11 / Top 100 #25	
10/20/58	28	4	3. With Your Love	Carlton 483
12/28/58+	8	13	4. **Goodbye Baby**	Carlton 493
8/3/59	35	4	5. The Way I Walk	Carlton 514
1/18/60	5	13	● 6. **What In The World's Come Over You**	Top Rank 2028
5/9/60	3	12	7. **Burning Bridges/**	
5/30/60	34	2	8. Oh, Little One	Top Rank 2041
9/5/60	38	2	9. It Only Happened Yesterday	Top Rank 2055
			The Chantones (backing vocals, all of above)	
			SCOTT, Linda	
			Born Linda Joy Sampson on 6/1/45 in Queens, New York. Moved to Teaneck, New Jersey, at age 11. Vocalist on Arthur Godfrey's CBS radio show, late 1950s. Co-host of TV's "Where The Action Is." Joined Army, 1970–72. Later earned a degree in theology and is currently a music teacher/director at the Christian Academy in New York.	

DATE	POS	WKS	ARTIST–RECORD TITLE	LABEL & NO.
4/3/61	3	10	1. **I've Told Every Little Star** #10 hit for Jack Denny in 1933 (from the Broadway musical *Music in the Air* starring Walter Slezak)	Canadian A. 123
7/24/61	9	10	2. **Don't Bet Money Honey**	Canadian A. 127
11/27/61	12	8	3. I Don't Know Why #2 hit for Wayne King in 1931	Canadian A. 129

SCOTT, Peggy, & Jo Jo Benson

Soul duo; Benson formerly sang with Chuck Willis and The Blue Notes.

DATE	POS	WKS	ARTIST–RECORD TITLE	LABEL & NO.
7/6/68	31	7	1. Lover's Holiday	SSS Int'l. 736
11/30/68	27	4	2. Pickin' Wild Mountain Berries	SSS Int'l. 748
2/15/69	37	3	3. Soulshake	SSS Int'l. 761

SCRITTI POLITTI

British trio: Green Gartside (vocals), Fred Maher (drums) and David Gamson (keyboards). Italian name means Political Writing.

DATE	POS	WKS	ARTIST–RECORD TITLE	LABEL & NO.
10/26/85	11	13	1. Perfect Way Airplay #10 / Sales #11	Warner 28949

SEA, Johnny

Born on 7/15/40 in Gulfport, Mississippi. Joined the "Louisiana Hayride" while still in high school. Real last name: Seay.

DATE	POS	WKS	ARTIST–RECORD TITLE	LABEL & NO.
6/25/66	35	2	1. Day For Decision [S] answer song to Barry McGuire's "Eve Of Destruction"	Warner 5820

SEAL

Born Sealhenry Samuel on 2/19/63 in Paddington, England, of Nigerian/Brazilian descent. Male singer.

DATE	POS	WKS	ARTIST–RECORD TITLE	LABEL & NO.
7/13/91	7	13	1. **Crazy** Sales #17 / Airplay #19	ZTT/Sire 19298
7/9/94	21	14	2. Prayer For The Dying Airplay #16 / Sales #56	ZTT/Sire 18138
7/8/95	1 (1)	32	● 3. **Kiss From A Rose** Airplay #1(1) / Sales #5; from the movie *Batman Forever* starring Val Kilmer; #1 Adult Contemporary hit (12 weeks)	ZTT/Sire 17896

SEALS & CROFTS

Pop duo: Jim Seals (born 10/17/41, Sidney, Texas; guitar, fiddle, saxophone) and Dash Crofts (born 8/14/40, Cisco, Texas; drums, mandolin, keyboards, guitar). With Dean Beard, recorded for Edmoral and Atlantic in 1957. To Los Angeles in 1958. With The Champs, 1958–65. Own group, the Dawnbreakers, in the late '60s; entire band converted to Baha'i faith in 1969. Jim is the brother of "England" Dan Seals and the cousin of country singers Troy Seals (Jo Ann & Troy), Brady Seals (Little Texas) and Johnny Duncan.

DATE	POS	WKS	ARTIST–RECORD TITLE	LABEL & NO.
10/21/72	6	11	1. **Summer Breeze**	Warner 7606
2/17/73	20	9	2. Hummingbird	Warner 7671
6/16/73	6	12	3. **Diamond Girl**	Warner 7708
10/13/73	21	8	4. We May Never Pass This Way (Again)	Warner 7740
5/17/75	18	8	5. I'll Play For You	Warner 8075
6/5/76	6	15	6. **Get Closer** **SEALS & CROFTS (Featuring Carolyn Willis)**	Warner 8190

DATE	POS	WKS	ARTIST–RECORD TITLE	LABEL & NO.
10/22/77	28	5	7. My Fair Share love theme from the movie *One on One* starring Robby Benson	Warner 8405
5/27/78	18	7	8. You're The Love all of above produced by Louie Shelton	Warner 8551

SEARCHERS, The

Rock quartet from Liverpool, England, formed in 1960: Mike Pender and John McNally (vocals, guitars), Tony Jackson (vocals, bass) and Chris Curtis (drums). Worked as backup band for Johnny Sandon; toured England and worked Star Club in Hamburg, Germany. Left Sandon in 1962. Jackson replaced by Frank Allen in 1965. Curtis replaced by John Blunt in 1966. Blunt replaced by Billy Adamson in 1969. Pender left in 1985 and formed own Searchers group; replaced by Spencer James.

DATE	POS	WKS	ARTIST–RECORD TITLE	LABEL & NO.
3/21/64	13	8	1. Needles And Pins written by Sonny Bono and Jack Nitzsche	Kapp 577
6/20/64	16	8	2. Don't Throw Your Love Away	Kapp 593
9/12/64	34	3	3. Some Day We're Gonna Love Again	Kapp 609
11/14/64	35	2	4. When You Walk In The Room written by Jackie DeShannon	Kapp 618
12/19/64+	3	11	5. **Love Potion Number Nine**	Kapp 27
2/20/65	29	3	6. What Have They Done To The Rain	Kapp 644
4/10/65	21	4	7. Bumble Bee #5 & 7 released on Kapp's "Winners Circle Series" label	Kapp 49

SEBASTIAN, John

Born on 3/17/44 in New York City. Played with the Even Dozen Jug Band as "John Benson" in 1964. Did session work for Elektra Records and toured with Mississippi John Hurt. Formed The Lovin' Spoonful in 1965. Went solo in 1968. Continues to write and perform into the '90s.

DATE	POS	WKS	ARTIST–RECORD TITLE	LABEL & NO.
4/10/76	1 (1)	11	● 1. **Welcome Back** from the ABC-TV series "Welcome Back Kotter" starring Gabriel Kaplan	Reprise 1349

SECADA, Jon

Cuban-born, Miami-raised singer/songwriter. Left Cuba in 1971 at age eight. Earned a Master's degree in jazz at the University of Miami. Co-wrote six songs on Gloria Estefan's album *Into The Light* and was a backing vocalist for that tour. Legally changed first name from Juan to Jon in 1990.

DATE	POS	WKS	ARTIST–RECORD TITLE	LABEL & NO.
5/23/92	5	30	● 1. **Just Another Day** Airplay #3 / Sales #8; Gloria Estefan (backing vocal); Spanish version on B-side "Otro Dia Mas Sin Verte" hit #1 on *Billboard*'s Hot Latin Tracks charts	SBK 07383
10/24/92	13	21	2. Do You Believe In Us Airplay #12 / Sales #29	SBK 50408
3/6/93	18	17	3. Angel Airplay #10 / Sales #33	SBK 50406
7/17/93	27	8	4. I'm Free Airplay #15; all of above from the album *Jon Secada*	SBK 50434
5/14/94	10	27	5. **If You Go** Airplay #6 / Sales #15	SBK 58156
1/21/95	29	6	6. Mental Picture Airplay #28	SBK 58272

DATE	POS	WKS	ARTIST–RECORD TITLE	LABEL & NO.
			SECRETS, The	
			Cleveland white female quartet: Kragen Gray, Josie Allen, Carole Raymont and Pat Miller.	
12/7/63	18	6	1. The Boy Next Door	Philips 40146
			SEDAKA, Neil	
			Born on 3/13/39 in Brooklyn. Pop singer/songwriter/pianist. Studied piano since elementary school. Formed songwriting team with lyricist Howard Greenfield while attending Lincoln High School (partnership lasted over 20 years). Recorded with The Tokens on Melba in 1956. Attended Juilliard School for classical piano. Prolific hit songwriter. Career revived in 1974 after signing with Elton John's new Rocket label.	
12/28/58+	14	9	1. The Diary	RCA 7408
10/26/59	9	13	2. **Oh! Carol**	RCA 7595
			written for singer/songwriter Carole King	
4/18/60	9	9	3. **Stairway To Heaven**	RCA 7709
8/29/60	17	9	4. You Mean Everything To Me/	
10/3/60	28	3	5. Run Samson Run	RCA 7781
12/31/60+	4	12	6. **Calendar Girl**	RCA 7829
5/8/61	11	7	7. Little Devil	RCA 7874
11/27/61+	6	11	8. **Happy Birthday, Sweet Sixteen**	RCA 7957
7/7/62	1 (2)	12	9. **Breaking Up Is Hard To Do**	RCA 8046
			also see #18 below	
10/20/62	5	9	10. **Next Door To An Angel**	RCA 8086
2/16/63	17	7	11. Alice In Wonderland	RCA 8137
5/18/63	26	5	12. Let's Go Steady Again	RCA 8169
12/7/63	33	4	13. Bad Girl	RCA 8254
			all of above produced by Al Nevins and Don Kirshner	
11/16/74+	1 (1)	15	14. **Laughter In The Rain**	Rocket 40313
			#1 Adult Contemporary hit (2 weeks)	
4/26/75	22	5	15. The Immigrant	Rocket 40370
			dedicated to John Lennon (because of his immigration difficulties); #1 Adult Contemporary hit (1 week)	
8/2/75	27	4	16. That's When The Music Takes Me	Rocket 40426
9/20/75	1 (3)	12	● 17. **Bad Blood**	Rocket 40460
			Elton John (backing vocal)	
12/27/75+	8	11	18. **Breaking Up Is Hard To Do** [R]	Rocket 40500
			slow version of Sedaka's 1962 hit; #1 Adult Contemporary hit (1 week)	
5/1/76	16	7	19. Love In The Shadows	Rocket 40543
7/24/76	36	2	20. Steppin' Out	Rocket 40582
5/10/80	19	10	21. Should've Never Let You Go	Elektra 46615
			NEIL SEDAKA and DARA SEDAKA (Neil's daughter)	
			SEDUCTION	
			Female vocal trio from New York: Idalis Leon (born 6/15/66), April Harris (born 3/25/67) and Michelle Visage (born 9/20/68). Leon left in 1990, replaced by Sinoa Loren (born 12/6/66). Leon is now a VJ for MTV.	
9/2/89	23	8	1. You're My One And Only (True Love)	Vendetta 1433
			Sales #21 / Airplay #24; Martha Wash (of The Weather Girls; uncredited lead vocal)	
12/9/89+	2 (2)	14	● 2. **Two To Make It Right**	Vendetta 1464
			Sales #2 / Airplay #2; samples The Art Of Noise/Tom Jones's version of "Kiss"	

DATE	POS	WKS	ARTIST–RECORD TITLE	LABEL & NO.
3/17/90	**13**	10	3. Heartbeat Sales #12 / Airplay #15	Vendetta 1473

7/7/90	**11**	10	4. Could This Be Love
			        Airplay #7 / Sales #15; all of above from the album *Nothing*
			        Matters Without Love
				Vendetta 1509

SEEDS, The

Los Angeles garage-rock quartet: Sky Saxon (born Richard Marsh; lead singer, bass), Jan Savage (guitar), Rick Aldridge (drums) and Daryl Hooper (keyboards).

DATE	POS	WKS	ARTIST–RECORD TITLE	LABEL & NO.
2/11/67	**36**	3	1. Pushin' Too Hard	GNP Crescendo 372

SEEKERS, The

Australian-born pop-folk quartet: Judith Durham (born 7/3/43; lead singer), Keith Potger (guitar), Bruce Woodley (Spanish guitar) and Athol Guy (standup bass). Potger formed The New Seekers in 1970.

DATE	POS	WKS	ARTIST–RECORD TITLE	LABEL & NO.
4/10/65	**4**	10	1. **I'll Never Find Another You**	Capitol 5383
6/26/65	**19**	6	2. A World Of Our Own	Capitol 5430
12/31/66+	**2** (2)	12	● 3. **Georgy Girl** title song from the movie starring Lynn Redgrave and James Mason	Capitol 5756

SEGER, Bob

Born on 5/6/45 in Dearborn, Michigan; raised in Detroit. Rock singer/songwriter/guitarist. First recorded in 1966, formed the System in 1968. Left music to attend college in 1969, returned in 1970. Formed own backing group The Silver Bullet Band in 1976: Alto Reed (horns), Robyn Robbins (keyboards), Drew Abbott (guitar), Chris Campbell (bass) and Charlie Allen Martin (drums). Various personnel changes since then.

DATE	POS	WKS	ARTIST–RECORD TITLE	LABEL & NO.
1/25/69	**17**	9	1. Ramblin' Gamblin' Man **BOB SEGER SYSTEM**	Capitol 2297
1/15/77	**4**	13	2. **Night Moves**	Capitol 4369
5/14/77	**24**	4	3. Mainstreet	Capitol 4422
			BOB SEGER & THE SILVER BULLET BAND:	
6/3/78	**4**	11	4. **Still The Same**	Capitol 4581
8/19/78	**12**	10	5. Hollywood Nights	Capitol 4618
11/25/78+	**13**	11	6. We've Got Tonite	Capitol 4653
5/5/79	**28**	5	7. Old Time Rock & Roll above 4 from the album *Stranger In Town*	Capitol 4702
			BOB SEGER:	
3/1/80	**6**	12	8. **Fire Lake** Glenn Frey, Don Henley and Timothy B. Schmit (backing vocals)	Capitol 4836
5/10/80	**5**	11	9. **Against The Wind**	Capitol 4863
8/16/80	**14**	9	10. You'll Accomp'ny Me	Capitol 4904
9/26/81	**5**	12	11. **Tryin' To Live My Life Without You** recorded "live" at Boston Garden on 10/6/80	Capitol 5042
			BOB SEGER & THE SILVER BULLET BAND:	
12/18/82+	**2** (4)	19	12. **Shame On The Moon** #1 Adult Contemporary hit (2 weeks); Glenn Frey (backing vocal)	Capitol 5187
3/26/83	**12**	9	13. Even Now	Capitol 5213
6/11/83	**27**	6	14. Roll Me Away	Capitol 5235

DATE	POS	WKS	ARTIST–RECORD TITLE	LABEL & NO.
12/1/84+	**17**	8	15. Understanding Sales #16 / Airplay #19; from the movie *Teachers* starring Nick Nolte and JoBeth Williams	Capitol 5413
3/29/86	**13**	9	16. American Storm Sales #9 / Airplay #18	Capitol 5532
5/31/86	**12**	9	17. Like A Rock Sales #9 / Airplay #19	Capitol 5592
5/30/87	**1** (1)	14	18. **Shakedown** **BOB SEGER** Sales #1(2) / Airplay #1(1); from the movie *Beverly Hills Cop II* starring Eddie Murphy	MCA 53094
9/14/91	**24**	5	19. The Real Love Sales #54 / Airplay #62; Patty Smyth and J.D. Souther (backing vocals); Craig Frost of Grand Funk Railroad (organ)	Capitol 44743

SELENA

Born Selena Quintanilla Perez on 4/16/71 in Corpus Christi, Texas. Shot to death by Yolanda Saldivar (founder of Selena's fan club) on 3/31/95.

DATE	POS	WKS	ARTIST–RECORD TITLE	LABEL & NO.
10/28/95	**22**	13	1. Dreaming Of You Sales #16 / Airplay #25	EMI Latin 58490

SELLARS, Marilyn

Country singer from Northfield, Minnesota. Worked as an airline stewardess.

DATE	POS	WKS	ARTIST–RECORD TITLE	LABEL & NO.
9/28/74	**37**	2	1. One Day At A Time also released on Mega 205	Mega 1205

SEMBELLO, Michael

Born on 4/17/54 in Philadelphia. Session guitarist/producer/composer/arranger/vocalist. Guitarist on Stevie Wonder's albums, 1974–79.

DATE	POS	WKS	ARTIST–RECORD TITLE	LABEL & NO.
7/2/83	**1** (2)	16	1. **Maniac** from the movie *Flashdance* starring Jennifer Beals	Casablanca 812516
10/29/83	**34**	2	2. Automatic Man	Warner 29485

SENATOR BOBBY

Senator Bobby is Bill Minkin of a comedy troupe called The Hardly-Worthit Players. Another of the members is talk-show host Dennis Wholey. Records feature voice impressions of Senator Robert Kennedy and Senator Everett McKinley Dirksen.

DATE	POS	WKS	ARTIST–RECORD TITLE	LABEL & NO.
1/21/67	**20**	4	1. Wild Thing [C]	Parkway 127

SENSATIONS, The

Philadelphia R&B vocal quartet: Yvonne Mills Baker (lead), Sam Armstrong (baritone), Richard Curtain (tenor) and Alphonso Howell (bass). First recorded for Atco in 1955 (made the R&B charts in 1956).

DATE	POS	WKS	ARTIST–RECORD TITLE	LABEL & NO.
2/10/62	**4**	12	1. **Let Me In**	Argo 5405

SERENDIPITY SINGERS, The

Nine-member, pop-folk group organized at the University of Colorado.

DATE	POS	WKS	ARTIST–RECORD TITLE	LABEL & NO.
3/21/64	**6**	11	1. **Don't Let The Rain Come Down (Crooked Little Man)** some pressing show title only as: "Crooked Little Man"	Philips 40175
6/13/64	**30**	5	2. Beans In My Ears [N]	Philips 40198

DATE	POS	WKS	ARTIST–RECORD TITLE	LABEL & NO.
			SEVILLE, David, (The Music of)	
			Born Ross Bagdasarian on 1/27/19 in Fresno, California. Died on 1/16/72. To Los Angeles in 1950. Appeared in the movies *Viva Zapata*, *Stalag 17* and *Rear Window*. Wrote "Come On-a My House." Creator of The Chipmunks.	
4/14/58	**1** (3)	18	● 1. **Witch Doctor** [N] Top 100 #1(3) / Best Seller #1(2) / Jockey #2; #1 R&B hit (1 week)	Liberty 55132
7/14/58	**34**	2	2. The Bird On My Head [N] Best Seller #34 / Top 100 #36	Liberty 55140
			SEXTON, Charlie	
			Born on 8/11/68 in Austin, Texas. Rock singer/guitarist. Lead guitarist for Joe Ely's band. Co-founder of the Arc Angels. Appeared in the movie *Thelma & Louise*.	
2/8/86	**17**	10	1. Beat's So Lonely Sales #9 / Airplay #30	MCA 52715
			SEYMOUR, Phil	
			Born on 5/15/52 in Tulsa, Oklahoma. Died of lymphoma on 8/17/93. Vocalist/drummer/bassist. Formerly with the Dwight Twilley Band.	
2/21/81	**22**	7	1. Precious To Me	Boardwalk 5703
			SHADES OF BLUE	
			Detroit group discovered by Edwin Starr: Linda Kerr, Robert Kerr, Ernest Dernai and Nick Marinelli.	
5/28/66	**12**	8	1. Oh How Happy	Impact 1007
			SHADOWS OF KNIGHT, The	
			Chicago-area garage band: Jim Sohns (lead singer), Joe Kelley (lead guitarist), Warren Rogers (bass), Jerry McGeorge (rhythm guitar) and Tom Schiffour (drums).	
4/16/66	**10**	8	1. **Gloria** written by Van Morrison	Dunwich 116
7/2/66	**39**	1	2. Oh Yeah	Dunwich 122
			SHAGGY	
			Born Orville Richard Burrell on 10/22/68 in Kingston, Jamaica. Reggae singer. Moved to Brooklyn at age 18. During his four years as a marine, served in Kuwait for Operation Desert Storm.	
6/17/95	**3**	23	▲ 1. **Boombastic/** Sales #1(2) / Airplay #27; samples "Baby Let Me Kiss You" by King Floyd; #1 R&B hit (1 week)	
		17	2. Summer Time **SHAGGY (featuring Rayvon)** Sales flip; #3 hit for Mungo Jerry in 1970 as "In The Summertime"	Virgin 38482
			SHAI	
			Vocal quartet formed at Howard University in Washington, D.C. Consists of Garfield A. Bright, Marc Gay, Carl "Groove" Martin and Darnell Van Rensalier. Group name pronounced: shy.	
10/24/92	**2** (8)	24	▲ 1. **If I Ever Fall In Love** Sales #2 / Airplay #2	Gasoline A. 54518

DATE	POS	WKS	ARTIST–RECORD TITLE	LABEL & NO.
2/13/93	**10**	20	● 2. **Comforter** Airplay #8 / Sales #15	Gasoline A. 54596
7/3/93	**10**	20	3. **Baby I'm Yours** Airplay #5 / Sales #24	Gasoline A. 54574
7/2/94	**34**	6	4. The Place Where You Belong Sales #25 / Airplay #52; from the movie *Beverly Hills Cop III* starring Eddie Murphy	MCA 54807

SHAKESPEAR'S SISTER

Female duo of British native Siobhan Fahey and Detroit native Marcella Detroit. Fahey, wife of Dave Stewart (Eurythmics), was a member of Bananarama. Detroit is Marcy Levy who recorded with Robin Gibb, sang backup for Eric Clapton and co-wrote "Lay Down Sally." Disbanded in 1993.

DATE	POS	WKS	ARTIST–RECORD TITLE	LABEL & NO.
7/25/92	**4**	14	● 1. **Stay** Sales #4 / Airplay #17	London 869730

SHALAMAR

Black vocal trio formed in 1978 by Don Cornelius, the producer/host of TV's "Soul Train." Consisted of vocalists/dancers Jody Watley and Jeffrey Daniels with Gerald Brown. Howard Hewett replaced Brown in early 1979. Watley and Daniels (former husband of Stephanie Mills) pursued solo careers in 1984; replaced by Delisa Davis (former Miss Teenage Georgia and Miss Tennessee State) and Micki Free. Hewett left in 1985, replaced by Sydney Justin (former football defensive back with the Los Angeles Rams).

DATE	POS	WKS	ARTIST–RECORD TITLE	LABEL & NO.
4/16/77	**25**	8	1. Uptown Festival (Part 1) Going To A Go-Go/I Can't Help Myself (Sugar Pie, Honey Bunch)/Uptight (Everything's Alright)/Stop! In The Name Of Love/It's The Same Old Song; recorded by anonymous session singers prior to formation of actual group	Soul Train 10885
2/2/80	**8**	13	● 2. **The Second Time Around** #1 R&B hit (1 week)	Solar 11709
8/6/83	**22**	10	3. Dead Giveaway	Solar 69819
4/14/84	**17**	10	4. Dancing In The Sheets from the movie *Footloose* starring Kevin Bacon and Lori Singer	Columbia 04372

SHAMEN, The

Techno-rave dance group from Aberdeen, Scotland, formed by Colin "Shamen" Angus and Will "Sin" Sinnott (drowned on 5/23/90, age 31). Features rapper Mr. C.

DATE	POS	WKS	ARTIST–RECORD TITLE	LABEL & NO.
2/22/92	**38**	2	1. Move Any Mountain (Progen 91) Airplay #36 / Sales #41	Epic 74044

SHANA

Born Shana Petrone on 5/8/72 in Parkridge, Illinois; raised in Ft. Lauderdale, Florida.

DATE	POS	WKS	ARTIST–RECORD TITLE	LABEL & NO.
1/13/90	**40**	1	1. I Want You Sales #35 / Airplay #40	Vision 4511

SHANGRI-LAS, The

"Girl group" formed at Andrew Jackson High School in Queens, New York. Consisted of two sets of sisters: Mary (lead singer) and Betty Weiss, and twins Mary Ann and Marge Ganser. Mary Ann died of encephalitis in 1971; Marge died of a drug overdose.

DATE	POS	WKS	ARTIST–RECORD TITLE	LABEL & NO.
9/5/64	**5**	9	1. **Remember (Walkin' in the Sand)**	Red Bird 008
10/24/64	**1** (1)	10	2. **Leader Of The Pack**	Red Bird 014

DATE	POS	WKS	ARTIST–RECORD TITLE	LABEL & NO.
1/16/65	**18**	5	3. Give Him A Great Big Kiss	Red Bird 018
6/19/65	**29**	4	4. Give Us Your Blessings	Red Bird 030
11/20/65	**6**	8	5. **I Can Never Go Home Anymore**	Red Bird 043
2/26/66	**33**	2	6. Long Live Our Love	Red Bird 048
			above 5 produced by George "Shadow" Morton	

SHANICE

Born Shanice Wilson on 5/14/73 in Pittsburgh. To Los Angeles at age seven. Began singing commercial jingles at age eight (appeared in a Kentucky Fried Chicken commercial with Ella Fitzgerald).

DATE	POS	WKS	ARTIST–RECORD TITLE	LABEL & NO.
12/14/91+	**2 (3)**	21	1. **I Love Your Smile**	Motown 2093
			Airplay #1(5) / Sales #6; #1 R&B hit (4 weeks)	
5/16/92	**31**	5	2. Silent Prayer	Motown 2165
			SHANICE featuring Johnny Gill	
			Airplay #29 / Sales #33	
11/14/92+	**4**	20	3. **Saving Forever For You**	Giant 18719
			Airplay #4 / Sales #6; from the album Beverly Hills 90210 (The Soundtrack)	

SHANNON

Brenda Shannon Greene from Washington, D.C. Began singing career at York University.

DATE	POS	WKS	ARTIST–RECORD TITLE	LABEL & NO.
1/7/84	**8**	12	● 1. **Let The Music Play**	Mirage 99810

SHANNON, Del

Born Charles Westover on 12/30/34 in Coopersville, Michigan. Died on 2/8/90 of a self-inflicted gunshot wound. With U.S. Army "Get Up And Go" radio show in Germany. Discovered by Ann Arbor DJ/producer Ollie McLaughlin. Formed own Berlee label in 1963. Wrote "I Go To Pieces" for Peter & Gordon. To Los Angeles in 1966; production work.

DATE	POS	WKS	ARTIST–RECORD TITLE	LABEL & NO.
3/27/61	**1 (4)**	12	● 1. **Runaway**	Big Top 3067
			electric organ (musitron) solo by co-writer Max Crook	
6/19/61	**5**	11	2. **Hats Off To Larry**	Big Top 3075
10/9/61	**28**	5	3. So Long Baby	Big Top 3083
1/6/62	**38**	2	4. Hey! Little Girl	Big Top 3091
1/26/63	**12**	7	5. Little Town Flirt	Big Top 3131
7/25/64	**22**	7	6. Handy Man	Amy 905
12/19/64+	**9**	10	7. **Keep Searchin' (We'll Follow The Sun)**	Amy 915
3/13/65	**30**	4	8. Stranger In Town	Amy 919
1/23/82	**33**	4	9. Sea Of Love	Network 47951
			produced by Tom Petty	

SHARP, Dee Dee

Born Dione LaRue on 9/9/45 in Philadelphia. Backing vocalist at Cameo Records in 1961. Married record producer Kenny Gamble in 1967, recorded as Dee Dee Sharp Gamble.

DATE	POS	WKS	ARTIST–RECORD TITLE	LABEL & NO.
3/10/62	**3**	12	1. **Slow Twistin'**	Parkway 835
			CHUBBY CHECKER (with Dee Dee Sharp)	
3/17/62	**2 (2)**	15	● 2. **Mashed Potato Time**	Cameo 212
			#1 R&B hit (4 weeks)	
6/23/62	**9**	9	3. **Gravy (For My Mashed Potatoes)**	Cameo 219
11/10/62	**5**	9	4. **Ride!**	Cameo 230

DATE	POS	WKS	ARTIST–RECORD TITLE	LABEL & NO.
3/9/63	10	9	5. **Do The Bird**	Cameo 244
11/2/63	33	5	6. Wild!	Cameo 274

SHAW, Georgie

DATE	POS	WKS	ARTIST–RECORD TITLE	LABEL & NO.
11/12/55	23	6	1. No Arms Can Ever Hold You (Like These Arms Of Mine) Top 100 #23 / Best Seller #25	Decca 29679
2/11/56	39	1	2. Go On With The Wedding **KITTY KALLEN and GEORGIE SHAW** Jack Pleis (orch., above 2)	Decca 29776

SHAW, Tommy

Born in Montgomery, Alabama. Lead guitarist of Styx, 1976–84. Joined superstar rock group, Damn Yankees, in 1990. Recorded in Shaw/Blades duo with Jack Blades, bassist of Night Ranger and Damn Yankees; both share vocals.

DATE	POS	WKS	ARTIST–RECORD TITLE	LABEL & NO.
11/3/84	33	3	1. Girls With Guns	A&M 2676

SHEILA E.

Born Sheila Escovedo on 12/12/59 in San Francisco. Singer/percussionist. With father Pete Escovedo in the band Azteca in the mid-1970s. Toured with Lionel Richie; since 1986, toured and recorded with Prince. Brother Peto was in Con Funk Shun. Uncle Coke Escovedo is a noted percussionist.

DATE	POS	WKS	ARTIST–RECORD TITLE	LABEL & NO.
7/21/84	7	16	1. **The Glamorous Life** Sales #7 / Airplay #14	Warner 29285
12/8/84	34	5	2. The Belle Of St. Mark Airplay #26 / Sales #30	Warner 29180
12/28/85+	11	12	3. A Love Bizarre Airplay #10 / Sales #12; from the movie *Krush Groove* starring Sheila E.; Prince (backing vocal)	Paisley P. 28890

SHELLS, The

Brooklyn R&B vocal quintet: Nathaniel "Little Nate" Bouknight (lead), Gus Geter (baritone), Bobby Nurse and Randy Alston (tenors) and Danny Small (bass).

DATE	POS	WKS	ARTIST–RECORD TITLE	LABEL & NO.
12/31/60+	21	5	1. Baby Oh Baby record originally released in 1957	Johnson 104

SHEP AND THE LIMELITES

R&B vocal trio from New York City: James "Shep" Sheppard, lead (formerly with The Heartbeats) and tenors Clarence Bassett and Charles Baskerville (formerly in The Videos). Group disbanded after Sheppard's death on 1/24/70.

DATE	POS	WKS	ARTIST–RECORD TITLE	LABEL & NO.
4/10/61	2 (1)	11	1. **Daddy's Home** answer song to The Heartbeats' "A Thousand Miles Away"	Hull 740

SHEPHERD SISTERS

New York-based family quartet from Middletown, Ohio: Martha, Mary Lou, Gayle and Judy.

DATE	POS	WKS	ARTIST–RECORD TITLE	LABEL & NO.
11/4/57	18	7	1. Alone (Why Must I Be Alone) Best Seller #18 / Top 100 #20 / Jockey #22	Lance 125

DATE	POS	WKS	ARTIST–RECORD TITLE	LABEL & NO.
			SHEPPARD, T.G.	
			Born William Browder on 7/20/42 in Alamo, Tennessee. Country singer. Moved to Memphis in 1960. Worked as backup singer with Travis Wammack's band.	
5/16/81	37	2	1. I Loved 'Em Every One #1 Country hit (1 week)	Warner/Curb 49690
			SHEPPARD, Vonda—see HILL, Dan	
			SHERIFF	
			Canadian rock quintet. Freddy Curci, lead singer. Disbanded in 1983. Members Wolf Hassel and Arnold Lanni formed the duo Frozen Ghost in 1987. Bandmates Curci and Steve DeMarchi formed Alias in 1990.	
12/17/88+	1 (1)	13	● 1. When I'm With You [R] Sales #1(1) / Airplay #1(1); originally charted in 1983 at #61; #1 Adult Contemporary hit (1 week)	Capitol 44302
			SHERMAN, Allan	
			Born Allan Copelon on 11/30/24 in Chicago. Died on 11/21/73. Began as a professional comedy writer for Jackie Gleason, Joe E. Lewis and others. Creator/producer of TV's "I've Got A Secret." Began recording career in 1962 with 3 consecutive #1 comedy albums.	
8/10/63	2 (3)	8	1. Hello Mudduh, Hello Fadduh! (A Letter From Camp) [C] adaptation of Ponchielli's *Dance of the Hours*; Lou Busch (orch.)	Warner 5378
5/8/65	40	1	2. Crazy Downtown [C] parody of Petula Clark's "Downtown"	Warner 5614
			SHERMAN, Bobby	
			Born on 7/22/43 in Santa Monica, California. Regular on TV's "Shindig"; played Jeremy Bolt on TV's "Here Come The Brides." First recorded for Starcrest in 1962. Currently involved in TV production.	
9/6/69	3	11	● 1. Little Woman	Metromedia 121
12/6/69+	9	9	● 2. La La La (If I Had You)	Metromedia 150
2/28/70	9	11	● 3. Easy Come, Easy Go	Metromedia 177
6/6/70	24	5	4. Hey, Mister Sun	Metromedia 188
8/15/70	5	13	● 5. Julie, Do Ya Love Me	Metromedia 194
2/27/71	16	7	6. Cried Like A Baby	Metromedia 206
5/15/71	29	5	7. The Drum	Metromedia 217
			SHERRYS, The	
			Female R&B group from Philadelphia. Formed by Joe Cook, included his daughters Dinell (lead) and Delphine. Cook had own hit in 1957, "Peanuts," as Little Joe & The Thrillers.	
11/10/62	35	2	1. Pop Pop Pop-Pie	Guyden 2068
			SHIELDS, The	
			R&B group formed by Los Angeles producer George Motola solely to record "You Cheated." Frankie Ervin (lead), Jesse Belvin (falsetto), Johnny "Guitar" Watson, Mel Williams and Buster Williams.	
9/15/58	12	9	1. You Cheated Best Seller #12 end / Hot 100 #15; first released on Tender 513 in 1958	Dot 15805

DATE	POS	WKS	ARTIST–RECORD TITLE	LABEL & NO.

SHIRELLES, The

R&B "girl group" from Passaic, New Jersey. Consisted of Shirley Owens Alston (born 6/10/41), Beverly Lee (born 8/3/41), Doris Kenner (born 8/2/41) and Addie "Micki" Harris (born 1/22/40; died 6/10/82). Formed in junior high school as the Poquellos. First recorded for Tiara in 1958. Kenner left group in 1968; returned in 1975. Alston left for solo career in 1975, recorded as Lady Rose. Group inducted into the Rock and Roll Hall of Fame in 1996.

DATE	POS	WKS	ARTIST–RECORD TITLE	LABEL & NO.
10/17/60	39	3	1. Tonights The Night	Scepter 1208
12/12/60+	**1 (2)**	15	2. **Will You Love Me Tomorrow**	Scepter 1211
			first released on Scepter 1211 as simply "Tomorrow"	
2/6/61	3	14	3. **Dedicated To The One I Love** [R]	Scepter 1203
			originally charted in 1959 at #83	
5/1/61	4	8	4. **Mama Said**	Scepter 1217
10/23/61	21	5	5. Big John	Scepter 1223
1/6/62	8	11	6. **Baby It's You**	Scepter 1227
3/31/62	**1 (3)**	13	● 7. **Soldier Boy**	Scepter 1228
7/7/62	22	6	8. Welcome Home Baby	Scepter 1234
10/6/62	36	3	9. Stop The Music	Scepter 1237
12/15/62+	19	9	10. Everybody Loves A Lover	Scepter 1243
4/20/63	4	9	11. **Foolish Little Girl**	Scepter 1248
7/13/63	26	4	12. Don't Say Goodnight And Mean Goodbye	Scepter 1255

SHIRLEY, Don

Born on 1/27/27 in Kingston, Jamaica. Pianist/organist.

DATE	POS	WKS	ARTIST–RECORD TITLE	LABEL & NO.
10/9/61	40	1	1. Water Boy [I]	Cadence 1392
			DON SHIRLEY TRIO	
			late 19th-century prison work song	

SHIRLEY (AND COMPANY)

Shirley Goodman (formerly of Shirley & Lee), and a group of studio musicians. Included Kenny Jeremiah of the Soul Survivors.

DATE	POS	WKS	ARTIST–RECORD TITLE	LABEL & NO.
2/22/75	12	8	1. Shame, Shame, Shame	Vibration 532
			Jesus Alvarez (male vocal); written and produced by Sylvia Robinson (Mickey & Sylvia); #1 R&B hit (1 week)	

SHIRLEY & LEE

New Orleans R&B duo formed in the early '50s. Shirley Goodman (born 6/19/36) and Leonard Lee (born 6/29/36; died 10/23/76). First recorded for Aladdin in 1952. Billed as The Sweethearts Of The Blues; recorded together until 1963. Also see Shirley (And Company).

DATE	POS	WKS	ARTIST–RECORD TITLE	LABEL & NO.
9/8/56	20	9	1. Let The Good Times Roll	Aladdin 3325
			Best Seller #20 / Top 100 #27; #1 R&B hit (3 weeks)	
1/5/57	38	1	2. I Feel Good	Aladdin 3338
			different song than their 1955 R&B hit "Feel So Good"	

SHOCKING BLUE, The

Dutch rock quartet: Mariska Veres (lead singer), Robbie van Leeuwen (guitar), Cor van Beek (drums) and Klaasje van der Wal (bass). Disbanded in 1974.

DATE	POS	WKS	ARTIST–RECORD TITLE	LABEL & NO.
12/20/69+	**1 (1)**	13	● 1. **Venus**	Colossus 108

Ray Stevens' mid-'60s cast of musical characters included Ahab The Arab, Gitarzan, the Jones of "Along Came Jones" and Harry The Hairy Ape, whose like-named single reached No. 17 in 1963.

Rod Stewart's "Broken Arrow" hit the Top 20 in 1991, 20 years after the raspy-voiced British singer first scored his very first American hit, the No. 1 smash "Maggie May."

Sandy Stewart's TV career—she was a regular on Perry Como's show—doubtlessly helped "My Coloring Book" rise to the Top 20 in 1963. Another Sandy Stewart—an associate of singer Stevie Nicks—recorded for Modern Records in the mid-'80s.

Sting's rise to fame in Brit new wave trio The Police was eventually overshadowed by his equally impressive career as a solo artist, launched via 1985's *The Dream Of The Blue Turtles*. Included on that album was the No. 8 hit "Fortress Around Your Heart."

Donna Summer was disco's reigning diva in the mid '70s, one of Casablanca Records' major stars since 1975's "Love To Love You Baby." After scoring 11 Top 10 hits for the label, she moved to Geffen—who released the No. 21 hit "There Goes My Baby" on 1984—and her career slowed considerably.

The Supremes' first Top 40 hit, "When The Lovelight Starts Shining Through His Eyes," entered the charts in late 1963, but the Diana Ross-led trio's "Your Heart Belongs To Me" had hit the charts—and peaked at No. 95—in August 1962.

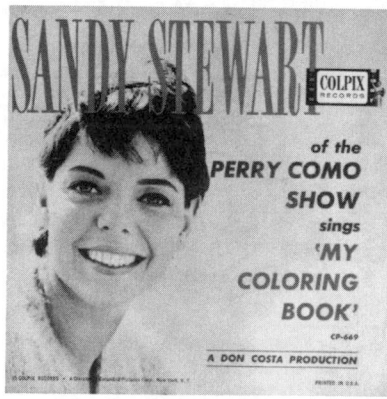

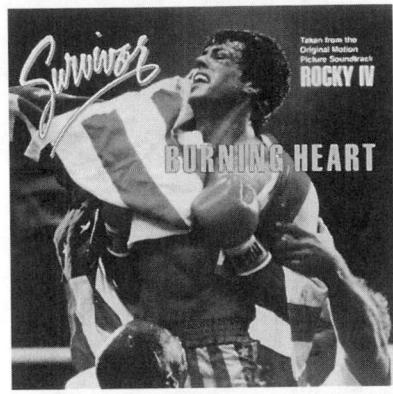

Survivor was accurately named, as the '80s group's founder was keyboardist Jim Peterick, whose previous group The Ides Of March had a No. 2 hit with "Vehicle" in 1970. Survivor's "Burning Heart," taken from 1985's *Rocky IV* soundtrack, likewise reached No. 2

Swing Out Sister brought a sophisticated blend of British pop and R&B to the Top 40 in the late '80s via such hits as "Twilight World," which reached No. 31 in 1988. The group later covered The Delfonics' "La La (Means I Love You)" in 1994.

Bobby Taylor And The Vancouvers cracked the Top 40 in 1968 with "Does Your Mama Know About Me." The Canadian band featured guitarist Tommy Chong, later of famous comedy duo Cheech & Chong.

Tears For Fears' 1989 album *The Seeds Of Love* bore the No. 2 "Sowing The Seeds Of Love" and was the last to include group co-founder and bassist/vocalist Curt Smith, who departed for a solo career. The album also introduced singer Oleta Adams to the masses.

Tiffany's five Top 40 hits featured four that reached the Top 10—including dual remakes of Tommy James & The Shondells' "I Think We're Alone Now" and The Beatles' (renamed) "I Saw Him Standing There"—and "Radio Romance," her last hit, which reached No. 35 in 1989.

Johnny Tillotson's five-year stretch of Top 40 hitdom drew to a gradual close by 1965, concluding with his No. 35 MGM Records hit "Heartaches By The Number."

DATE	POS	WKS	ARTIST–RECORD TITLE	LABEL & NO.
			SHONDELL, Troy	
			Born on 5/14/44 in Fort Wayne, Indiana. Pop-country singer/songwriter.	
9/25/61	6	12	1. **This Time**	Liberty 55353
			first released on Gaye 2010 (as Troy Shundell) and then on Goldcrest 161 in 1961	
			SHORE, Dinah	
			Born Frances Rose Shore on 3/1/17 in Winchester, Tennessee. Died of cancer on 2/24/94. One of the most popular female vocalists of the 1940 to mid-1950s era. Sang with Xavier Cugat 1939–40. Hostess of the 15-minute, award-winning early evening TV variety "The Dinah Shore Show," 1951–57; then hosted the very popular "Dinah Shore Chevy Show," 1956–63. Own morning talk show "Dinah's Place," 1970–80. Married to actor George Montgomery, 1943–62.	
5/21/55	12	3	1. **Whatever Lola Wants (Lola Gets)**	RCA 6077
			Jockey #12 / Best Seller #28; from the Broadway musical *Damn Yankees* starring Gwen Verdon	
12/10/55	20	1	2. **Love And Marriage**	RCA 6266
			Jockey #20 / Top 100 #42; from the TV production "Our Town" starring Frank Sinatra	
2/23/57	19	10	3. **Chantez-Chantez (Shan-Tay, "Sing")**	RCA 6792
			Jockey #19 / Top 100 #27	
9/9/57	15	7	4. **Fascination**	RCA 6980
			Jockey #15 / Top 100 #98; from the movie *Love in the Afternoon* starring Gary Cooper and Audrey Hepburn	
12/2/57	24	1	5. **I'll Never Say "Never Again" Again**	RCA 7056
			Jockey #24; #4 hit for Ozzie Nelson in 1935; Harry Zimmerman (orch., all of above)	
			SIGLER, Bunny	
			Born Walter Sigler on 3/27/41 in Philadelphia. R&B vocalist/multi-instrumentalist/composer/producer. First recorded for V-Tone in 1959.	
7/22/67	22	7	1. **Let The Good Times Roll & Feel So Good**	Parkway 153
			medley of 2 Shirley & Lee top R&B hits	
			SILHOUETTES, The	
			Philadelphia R&B doo-wop group formed as the Tornadoes by William Horton (lead), Richard Lewis (tenor), Earl Beal (baritone) and Raymond Edwards (bass). Horton died in January 1995 (age 65).	
1/20/58	1 (2)	13	● 1. **Get A Job**	Ember 1029
			Top 100 #1 / Best Seller #2 / Jockey #3; first released on Junior 391 in 1957; #1 R&B hit (6 weeks)	
			SILK	
			Atlanta R&B male vocal quintet: Timothy Cameron, Jimmy Gates, Jr., Jonathan Rasboro, Gary Jenkins and Gary Glenn. Discovered by Keith Sweat. Not to be confused with the Philadelphia R&B band from 1977.	
2/27/93	1 (2)	22	▲ 1. **Freak Me**	Keia/Elektra 64654
			Airplay #1(3) / Sales #1(2); #1 R&B hit (8 weeks)	
7/10/93	26	6	2. **Girl U For Me/**	
			Sales #30 / Airplay #38	
		6	3. **Lose Control**	Keia/Elektra 64643
			Airplay #48; above 3 co-written and co-produced by Keith Sweat	

DATE	POS	WKS	ARTIST–RECORD TITLE	LABEL & NO.
			SILKIE, The	
			Folk quartet formed in 1963 at Hull University in Hull, England. Silvia Tatler, lead singer.	
11/6/65	**10**	7	1. **You've Got To Hide Your Love Away** The Beatles contributed musical accompaniment & production assistance; song is from The Beatles' movie *Help!*	Fontana 1525
			SILVER	
			Country-rock quintet led by John Batdorf (of Batdorf & Rodney). Included organist Brent Mydland, who later joined the Grateful Dead (died 7/26/90 of a drug overdose, age 37).	
8/7/76	**16**	12	1. **Wham Bam** first pressings listed title as: "Wham Bam Shang-A-Lang"	Arista 0189
			SILVER CONDOR	
			Rock quintet: Joe Cerisano (vocals), Earl Slick (guitar), John Corey (keyboards), Jay Davis (bass) and Claude Pepper (drums). Slick joined Phantom, Rocker & Slick in 1985.	
8/29/81	**32**	4	1. You Could Take My Heart Away	Columbia 02268
			SILVER CONVENTION	
			German studio disco act assembled by producer Michael Kunze and writer/arranger Silvester Levay. Female vocal trio formed in 1976 consisting of Penny McLean, Ramona Wolf and Linda Thompson.	
10/25/75	**1** (3)	13	● 1. **Fly, Robin, Fly** [I] #1 R&B hit (1 week)	Midland I. 10339
4/17/76	**2** (3)	15	● 2. **Get Up And Boogie (That's Right)**	Midland I. 10571
			SILVETTI	
			Argentinian Bebu Silvetti.	
3/19/77	**39**	3	1. Spring Rain [I]	Salsoul 2014
			SIMEONE, Harry, Chorale	
			Simeone was born on 5/9/11 in Newark, New Jersey. Arranger/conductor for movies and TV shows. Began career as staff music arranger for CBS radio, followed by 14 years as an arranger for Fred Waring.	
12/28/58	**13**	6	● 1. The Little Drummer Boy [X]	20th Fox 121
12/28/59	**15**	3	2. The Little Drummer Boy [X-R]	20th Fox 121
12/19/60	**24**	3	3. The Little Drummer Boy [X-R]	20th Fox 121
12/25/61	**22**	2	4. The Little Drummer Boy [X-R]	20th Fox 121
12/15/62	**28**	3	5. The Little Drummer Boy [X-R]	20th Fox 121
			SIMMONS, Gene	
			Born in Tupelo, Mississippi, in 1933. Nicknamed "Jumpin' Gene."	
8/29/64	**11**	8	1. Haunted House [N]	Hi 2076
			SIMMONS, Patrick	
			Born on 1/23/50 in Aberdeen, Washington; raised in San Jose, California. Vocalist/guitarist. Original member of The Doobie Brothers; wrote their hit "Black Water."	
4/16/83	**30**	5	1. So Wrong	Elektra 69839

DATE	POS	WKS	ARTIST–RECORD TITLE	LABEL & NO.
			SIMON, Carly	
			Born on 6/25/45 in New York City. Pop vocalist/songwriter. Father is co-founder of Simon & Schuster publishing house. Folk duo with sister Lucy (The Simon Sisters), mid-1960s. Won the 1971 Best New Artist Grammy Award. Married James Taylor on 11/3/72; divorced in 1983.	
6/5/71	10	10	1. **That's The Way I've Always Heard It Should Be**	Elektra 45724
1/1/72	13	10	2. Anticipation	Elektra 45759
12/16/72+	1 (3)	14	● 3. **You're So Vain** Mick Jagger (backing vocal); #1 Adult Contemporary hit (2 weeks)	Elektra 45824
4/21/73	17	9	4. The Right Thing To Do	Elektra 45843
2/16/74	5	13	● 5. **Mockingbird** **CARLY SIMON & JAMES TAYLOR** adapted from the same traditional folk lyrics as was the song "Bo Diddley"	Elektra 45880
6/1/74	14	6	6. Haven't Got Time For The Pain James Taylor (acoustic guitar)	Elektra 45887
5/24/75	21	5	7. Attitude Dancing Carole King (backing vocal)	Elektra 45246
8/27/77	2 (3)	15	● 8. **Nobody Does It Better** from the James Bond movie *The Spy Who Loved Me* starring Roger Moore; #1 Adult Contemporary hit (7 weeks)	Elektra 45413
5/6/78	6	11	9. **You Belong To Me** James Taylor (backing vocal)	Elektra 45477
9/23/78	36	3	10. Devoted To You **CARLY SIMON and JAMES TAYLOR**	Elektra 45506
8/23/80	11	13	● 11. Jesse	Warner 49518
12/6/86+	18	9	12. Coming Around Again Sales #15 / Airplay #30; from the movie *Heartburn* starring Meryl Streep and Jack Nicholson	Arista 9525
			SIMON, Joe	
			Born on 9/2/43 in Simmesport, Louisiana. Moved to Oakland in 1959. First recorded with vocal group the Golden Tones for Hush in 1960.	
6/8/68	25	7	1. (You Keep Me) Hangin' On	Sound Stage 7 2608
3/29/69	13	11	● 2. The Chokin' Kind #1 R&B hit (3 weeks)	Sound Stage 7 2628
2/6/71	40	3	3. Your Time To Cry	Spring 108
12/11/71+	11	11	● 4. Drowning In The Sea Of Love	Spring 120
8/19/72	11	8	● 5. Power Of Love #1 R&B hit (2 weeks)	Spring 128
4/14/73	37	2	6. Step By Step	Spring 133
8/25/73	18	8	7. Theme From Cleopatra Jones **JOE SIMON featuring The Mainstreeters** title song from the movie starring Tamara Dobson	Spring 138
5/10/75	8	11	8. **Get Down, Get Down (Get On The Floor)** #1 R&B hit (2 weeks)	Spring 156

DATE	POS	WKS	ARTIST—RECORD TITLE	LABEL & NO.

SIMON, Paul

Born on 10/13/41 in Newark, New Jersey; raised in Queens, New York. Vocalist/composer/guitarist. Met Art Garfunkel in high school, recorded together as Tom & Jerry in 1957. Worked as Jerry Landis, Tico And The Triumphs, Paul Kane, Harrison Gregory and True Taylor in the early '60s. To England, 1963–64. Returned to the U.S. and recorded first album with Garfunkel in 1965. Went solo in 1971. Married to actress/author Carrie Fisher, 1983–85. Married singer Edie Brickell on 5/30/92. Appeared in the movies *Annie Hall* and *One-Trick Pony*. Winner of 12 Grammy Awards.

DATE	POS	WKS	ARTIST—RECORD TITLE	LABEL & NO.
2/19/72	4	11	1. **Mother And Child Reunion**	Columbia 45547
4/22/72	22	8	2. Me And Julio Down By The Schoolyard	Columbia 45585
			a "live" version is on the B-side of "Wake Up Little Susie" by Simon & Garfunkel	
6/2/73	2 (2)	11	3. **Kodachrome**	Columbia 45859
8/18/73	2 (1)	14	● 4. **Loves Me Like A Rock**	Columbia 45907
			PAUL SIMON (with The Dixie Hummingbirds)	
			#1 Adult Contemporary hit (2 weeks)	
1/5/74	35	3	5. American Tune	Columbia 45900
			based on the classical piece "O Sacred Heart" by Johann Sebastian Bach	
9/6/75	23	6	6. Gone At Last	Columbia 10197
			PAUL SIMON/PHOEBE SNOW and The Jessy Dixon Singers	
1/3/76	1 (3)	13	● 7. **50 Ways To Leave Your Lover**	Columbia 10270
			#1 Adult Contemporary hit (2 weeks); Patti Austin, Phoebe Snow and Valerie Simpson (backing vocals)	
5/29/76	40	2	8. Still Crazy After All These Years	Columbia 10332
11/5/77+	5	14	9. **Slip Slidin' Away**	Columbia 10630
			Oak Ridge Boys (backing vocals)	
2/11/78	17	7	10. (What A) Wonderful World	Columbia 10676
			ART GARFUNKEL with JAMES TAYLOR & PAUL SIMON	
			#1 Adult Contemporary hit (5 weeks)	
8/16/80	6	12	11. **Late In The Evening**	Warner 49511
11/22/80	40	2	12. One-Trick Pony	Warner 49601
			above 2 from the movie *One-Trick Pony* starring Simon	
4/25/87	23	7	13. You Can Call Me Al	Warner 28667
			Airplay #20 / Sales #27	

SIMON & GARFUNKEL

Folk-rock duo from New York City: Paul Simon and Art Garfunkel. Recorded as Tom & Jerry in 1957. Duo split in 1964; Simon was working solo in England; Garfunkel was in graduate school. They re-formed in 1965 and stayed together until 1971. Reunited briefly in 1981 for national tour. Inducted into the Rock and Roll Hall of Fame in 1990.

DATE	POS	WKS	ARTIST—RECORD TITLE	LABEL & NO.
12/4/65+	1 (2)	12	● 1. **The Sounds Of Silence**	Columbia 43396
2/26/66	5	10	2. **Homeward Bound**	Columbia 43511
5/14/66	3	10	3. **I Am A Rock**	Columbia 43617
8/27/66	25	4	4. The Dangling Conversation	Columbia 43728
11/19/66	13	6	5. A Hazy Shade Of Winter	Columbia 43873
4/1/67	16	7	6. At The Zoo	Columbia 44046
			B-side is Simon & Garfunkel's original version of "The 59th Street Bridge Song (Feelin' Groovy)"	
8/12/67	23	5	7. Fakin' It	Columbia 44232
3/16/68	11	9	8. Scarborough Fair (/Canticle)	Columbia 44465
			a medieval folk ballad first published in 1673; song also known as "Parsley, Sage, Rosemary And Thyme"	

DATE	POS	WKS	ARTIST–RECORD TITLE	LABEL & NO.
5/4/68	1 (3)	12	● 9. **Mrs. Robinson** from the movie *The Graduate* starring Dustin Hoffman and Anne Bancroft (soundtrack versions are different)	Columbia 44511
4/19/69	7	9	10. **The Boxer**	Columbia 44785
2/14/70	1 (6)	13	● 11. **Bridge Over Troubled Water** Larry Knechtel (piano); #1 Adult Contemporary hit (6 weeks)	Columbia 45079
4/18/70	4	12	● 12. **Cecilia**	Columbia 45133
9/26/70	18	8	13. El Condor Pasa Simon wrote the lyrics to this 18th Century Peruvian folk melody; above 4 from the album *Bridge Over Troubled Water*	Columbia 45237
11/1/75	9	9	14. **My Little Town** #1 Adult Contemporary hit (2 weeks); all of above written by Paul Simon	Columbia 10230
2/11/78	17	7	15. (What A) Wonderful World **ART GARFUNKEL with JAMES TAYLOR & PAUL SIMON** #1 Adult Contemporary hit (5 weeks)	Columbia 10676
5/1/82	27	6	16. Wake Up Little Susie recorded "live" in New York's Central Park on 9/19/81	Warner 50053

SIMONE, Nina

Born Eunice Waymon on 2/21/33 in Tryon, South Carolina. Jazz-influenced vocalist/pianist/composer. Attended Juilliard School of Music in New York City. Devoted more time to political activism in the 1970s, infrequent recording.

DATE	POS	WKS	ARTIST–RECORD TITLE	LABEL & NO.
8/24/59	18	11	1. I Loves You, Porgy from George Gershwin's 1935 folk opera *Porgy And Bess*	Bethlehem 11021

SIMPLE MINDS

Scottish pop-rock group. Nucleus of band: Jim Kerr (lead singer; formerly married to Chrissie Hynde of The Pretenders; later married Patsy Kensit of Eighth Wonder), Michael MacNeil (keyboards), Charles Burchill (guitar, keyboards), John Giblin (bass) and Mel Gaynor (drums). MacNeil and Giblin left in '89.

DATE	POS	WKS	ARTIST–RECORD TITLE	LABEL & NO.
3/23/85	1 (1)	14	1. **Don't You (Forget About Me)** Sales #1(2) / Airplay #1(1); from the movie *The Breakfast Club* starring Molly Ringwald and Emilio Estevez	A&M 2703
10/26/85	3	16	2. **Alive & Kicking** Airplay #3 / Sales #5	A&M 2783
2/8/86	14	9	3. Sanctify Yourself Airplay #14 / Sales #16	A&M 2810
5/3/86	28	6	4. All The Things She Said Airplay #26 / Sales #27	A&M 2828
6/29/91	40	1	5. See The Lights Airplay #72	A&M 1553

SIMPLY RED

Manchester, England, group: vocalist Mick "Red" Hucknall (born 6/8/60), keyboardists Fritz McIntyre and Tim Kellett, Tony Bowers (bass), Chris Joyce (drums) and Sylvan Richardson (guitar). 1991 lineup: Hucknall, McIntyre, Kellett, saxophonist Ian Kirkham, Brazilian guitarist Heitor T.P. and Japanese drummer Gota.

DATE	POS	WKS	ARTIST–RECORD TITLE	LABEL & NO.
5/10/86	1 (1)	14	1. **Holding Back The Years** Sales #1(1) / Airplay #3	Elektra 69564
8/30/86	28	6	2. Money$ Too Tight (To Mention) Airplay #27 / Sales #29; originally released in 1985 on Elektra 69607	Elektra 69528

DATE	POS	WKS	ARTIST–RECORD TITLE	LABEL & NO.
4/18/87	27	6	3. The Right Thing Sales #26 / Airplay #26	Elektra 69487
5/27/89	1 (1)	15	● 4. **If You Don't Know Me By Now** Sales #1(1) / Airplay #1(1); #1 Adult Contemporary hit (6 weeks)	Elektra 69297
11/2/91	23	4	5. Something Got Me Started Airplay #43	EastWest 98711

SIMS, Kym

Born on 12/28/66 in Chicago. Former commercial jingle singer (Shasta soft drinks). Also see CeCe Peniston.

DATE	POS	WKS	ARTIST–RECORD TITLE	LABEL & NO.
2/1/92	38	1	1. Too Blind To See It Airplay #22	Atco 98667

SINATRA, Frank

Born Francis Albert Sinatra on 12/12/15 in Hoboken, New Jersey. With Harry James, 1939–40; first recorded for Brunswick in 1939; with Tommy Dorsey, 1940–42. Went solo in late 1942 and charted 40 Top 10 hits through 1954. Appeared in many movies from 1941 on. Won an Oscar for the movie *From Here To Eternity* in 1953. Own TV show in 1957. Own Reprise record company in 1961, sold to Warner Bros. in 1963. Won the Lifetime Achievement Grammy in 1965. Married to actress Ava Gardner, 1951–57. Married to actress Mia Farrow, 1966 to 1968. Announced his retirement in 1970, but made comeback in 1973. Regarded by many as the greatest popular singer of the 20th century.

DATE	POS	WKS	ARTIST–RECORD TITLE	LABEL & NO.
1/22/55	19	4	1. Melody Of Love **FRANK SINATRA and RAY ANTHONY And His Orchestra** Jockey #19; music written in 1903, lyrics added in 1954 by Tom Glazer	Capitol 3018
5/7/55	1 (2)	21	2. **Learnin' The Blues** Jockey #1 / Best Seller #2 / Juke Box #2	Capitol 3102
9/24/55	13	5	3. Same Old Saturday Night Jockey #13 / Top 100 #65 pre	Capitol 3218
11/5/55	5	15	4. **Love And Marriage** Top 100 #5 / Jockey #5 / Best Seller #6 / Juke Box #7; introduced by Sinatra on TV's "Producer's Showcase" production of "Our Town" (9/19/55); song currently used as the theme for TV's "Married With Children" starring Ed O'Neill and Katey Sagal	Capitol 3260
12/17/55+	7	9	5. **(Love Is) The Tender Trap** Jockey #7 / Top 100 #23 / Best Seller #24; from the movie *The Tender Trap* starring Sinatra	Capitol 3290
3/24/56	21	3	6. Flowers Mean Forgiveness Jockey #21 / Top 100 #35	Capitol 3350
6/2/56	13	6	7. (How Little It Matters) How Little We Know Jockey #13 / Top 100 #30	Capitol 3423
11/3/56+	3	17	8. **Hey! Jealous Lover** Jockey #3 / Top 100 #6 / Juke Box #7 / Best Seller #8	Capitol 3552
2/9/57	15	6	9. Can I Steal A Little Love Jockey #15 / Top 100 #20; from the movie *Rock Pretty Baby* starring Sal Mineo	Capitol 3608
7/22/57	25	1	10. You're Cheatin' Yourself (If You're Cheatin' On Me) Jockey #25	Capitol 3744
10/28/57+	2 (1)	17	11. **All The Way** Jockey #2 / Best Seller #15 / Top 100 #15; from the movie *The Joker Is Wild* starring Sinatra	Capitol 3793
1/20/58	6	14	12. Witchcraft Jockey #6 / Best Seller #20 / Top 100 #20	Capitol 3859

DATE	POS	WKS	ARTIST–RECORD TITLE	LABEL & NO.
5/12/58	22	1	13. How Are Ya' Fixed For Love? **FRANK SINATRA and KEELY SMITH** Jockey #22 / Top 100 #97, Billy May (orch.)	Capitol 3952
9/7/59	30	1	14. High Hopes **FRANK SINATRA "and a bunch of kids"** from the movie *A Hole in the Head* starring Sinatra	Capitol 4214
11/16/59	38	3	15. Talk To Me	Capitol 4284
11/28/60	25	2	16. Ol' MacDonald adaptation of children's song originating in the early 1700's; Nelson Riddle (orch., all of above - except #1 & 13)	Capitol 4466
1/20/62	34	3	17. Pocketful Of Miracles title song from the movie starring Bette Davis	Reprise 20040
10/10/64	27	6	18. Softly, As I Leave You	Reprise 0301
1/30/65	32	3	19. Somewhere In Your Heart	Reprise 0332
1/15/66	28	4	20. It Was A Very Good Year #1 Adult Contemporary hit (1 week)	Reprise 0429
5/28/66	1 (1)	11	● 21. **Strangers In The Night** from the movie *A Man Could Get Killed* starring James Garner; #1 Adult Contemporary hit (7 weeks)	Reprise 0470
9/17/66	25	5	22. Summer Wind #1 Adult Contemporary hit (1 week)	Reprise 0509
12/3/66	4	9	23. **That's Life** #1 Adult Contemporary hit (3 weeks)	Reprise 0531
3/25/67	1 (4)	11	● 24. **Somethin' Stupid** **NANCY SINATRA & FRANK SINATRA** #1 Adult Contemporary hit (9 weeks)	Reprise 0561
8/26/67	30	4	25. The World We Knew (Over And Over) #1 Adult Contemporary hit (5 weeks); Ernie Freeman (orch., above 8 - except #20,22,24)	Reprise 0610
11/16/68	23	5	26. Cycles	Reprise 0764
4/12/69	27	6	27. My Way co-written by Paul Anka	Reprise 0817
5/31/80	32	6	28. Theme From New York, New York introduced in the movie musical *New York, New York* by Liza Minnelli (her version "Bubbled Under" in 1977 at #104)	Reprise 49233

SINATRA, Nancy

Born on 6/8/40 in Jersey City, New Jersey. First child of Nancy and Frank Sinatra. Moved to Los Angeles while a child. Made national TV debut with father and Elvis Presley in 1959. Married to Tommy Sands, 1960–65. Appeared on "Hullabaloo," "American Bandstand" and own specials in the mid-1960s. Appeared in the movies *For Those Who Think Young, Get Yourself A College Girl, The Oscar* and *Speedway* (with Elvis Presley).

DATE	POS	WKS	ARTIST–RECORD TITLE	LABEL & NO.
2/5/66	1 (1)	12	● 1. **These Boots Are Made For Walkin'**	Reprise 0432
4/30/66	7	7	2. **How Does That Grab You, Darlin'?**	Reprise 0461
7/30/66	36	2	3. Friday's Child	Reprise 0491
12/10/66	5	9	● 4. **Sugar Town** #1 Adult Contemporary hit (2 weeks)	Reprise 0527
3/25/67	1 (4)	11	● 5. **Somethin' Stupid** **NANCY SINATRA & FRANK SINATRA** #1 Adult Contemporary hit (9 weeks)	Reprise 0561
4/8/67	15	5	6. Love Eyes	Reprise 0559
7/8/67	14	7	7. Jackson **NANCY SINATRA & LEE HAZLEWOOD**	Reprise 0595
10/7/67	24	4	8. Lightning's Girl	Reprise 0620

DATE	POS	WKS	ARTIST–RECORD TITLE	LABEL & NO.
			NANCY SINATRA & LEE HAZLEWOOD:	
11/4/67	**20**	4	9. Lady Bird	Reprise 0629
			B-side "Sand" Bubbled Under (POS 107)	
1/27/68	**26**	5	10. Some Velvet Morning	Reprise 0651
			all of above produced and written (except #5 & 7) by Lee Hazlewood	
			SINCLAIR, Gordon	
			Born on 6/3/1900 in Toronto. Died on 5/17/84. Canadian broadcaster/author.	
1/26/74	**24**	4	1. The Americans (A Canadian's Opinion) [S]	Avco 4628
			originally broadcast as an editorial on 6/5/73 on CFRB-Toronto	
			SINGING DOGS, The (Don Charles Presents)	
			An actual recording of dogs barking, produced by Don Charles in Copenhagen.	
12/17/55	**22**	1	1. Oh! Susanna [N]	RCA 6344
			Best Seller #22 / Top 100 #37; written in 1848 by Stephen Foster; DJ copies labeled as: "Dolly's Oh! Susanna" (Dogs: Dolly, Pearl, Caesar & King)	
			SINGING NUN, The	
			Sister Luc-Gabrielle (real name: Jeanine Deckers) from the Fichermont, Belgium, convent. Recorded under the name Soeur Sourire ("Sister Smile"). Committed suicide on 3/31/85 (age 52).	
11/16/63	**1 (4)**	12	1. **Dominique** [F]	Philips 40152
			#1 Adult Contemporary hit (4 weeks)	
			SIOUXSIE AND THE BANSHEES	
			Avant-punk band formed in 1976 by vocalist Siouxsie Sioux (Susan Dallion) and bassist Steve Severin (Steve Havoc). Fluctuating personnel around group's nucleus: Sioux, Severin and Budgie (drums; joined in 1979). Husband and wife Sioux and Budgie also recorded as The Creatures.	
9/21/91	**23**	6	1. Kiss Them For Me	Geffen 19031
			Airplay #50 / Sales #58	
			SIR DOUGLAS QUINTET	
			Tex-Mex rock band led by Doug Sahm (born 11/6/41) from San Antonio. Co-founded by country singer Augie Meyers.	
4/17/65	**13**	9	1. She's About A Mover	Tribe 8308
3/5/66	**31**	5	2. The Rains Came	Tribe 8314
3/15/69	**27**	6	3. Mendocino	Smash 2191
			SIR MIX-A-LOT	
			Seattle rapper Anthony Ray. Appeared as the host of the anthology TV series "The Watcher."	
5/2/92	**1 (5)**	24	▲² 1. **Baby Got Back**	Def Amer. 18947
			Sales #1(9) / Airplay #16	

DATE	POS	WKS	ARTIST–RECORD TITLE	LABEL & NO.
			SISTER SLEDGE	
			Sisters Debra, Joni, Kim and Kathy Sledge from North Philadelphia. First recorded as Sisters Sledge for Money Back label in 1971. Worked as backup vocalists.	
3/10/79	9	13	1. **He's The Greatest Dancer** #1 R&B hit (1 week)	Cotillion 44245
5/12/79	2 (2)	11	● 2. **We Are Family** #1 R&B hit (1 week)	Cotillion 44251
3/6/82	23	6	3. My Guy	Cotillion 47000
			SIX TEENS, The	
			Los Angeles R&B sextet: Trudy Williams and Ed Wells (leads), Richard Owens, Darryl Lewis, Beverly Pecot and Louise Williams. In 1956, members ranged in age from 14 to 19.	
9/1/56	25	1	1. A Casual Look Best Seller #25 / Top 100 #48	Flip 315
			69 BOYZ	
			Hip-hop quartet from Jacksonville, Florida: Thrill "Van" (lead rapper), Fast, Slow and Rottweiler "Mike Mike." All members were born in 1969.	
8/6/94+	8	31	▲ 1. **Tootsee Roll** Sales #3 / Airplay #38; produced by 95 South; remix version released on Rip-It 6912	Rip-It 6911
			SKEE-LO	
			Male rapper from Riverside, California.	
7/29/95	13	13	● 1. **I Wish** Sales #7 / Airplay #58	Sunshine 78032
			SKID ROW	
			New York hard-rock quintet: Toronto native Sebastian "Bach" Bierk (vocals), Dave Sabo and Scott Hill (guitars), Rachel Bolan (bass) and Rob Affuso (drums).	
7/29/89	4	13	● 1. **18 And Life** Sales #4 / Airplay #6	Atlantic 88883
12/9/89+	6	13	2. **I Remember You** Sales #3 / Airplay #13	Atlantic 88886
			SKIP & FLIP	
			Gary "Flip" Paxton and Clyde "Skip" Battin. Met at the University of Arizona, and appeared on "Arizona Jubilee" in 1958 as the Rockabillies. Paxton formed the Hollywood Argyles, and later started own Garpax record label.	
7/27/59	11	9	1. It Was I	Brent 7002
4/25/60	11	10	2. Cherry Pie originally popularized in 1954 by the R&B duo Marvin & Johnny	Brent 7010
			SKYLARK	
			Pop group from Vancouver. Lead singers Donny Gerrard and B.J. (Bonnie Jean) Cook with keyboardist David Foster and drummer Duris Maxwell. Foster was later with Attitudes, then a hit producer/songwriter/solo artist.	
3/31/73	9	14	1. **Wildflower**	Capitol 3511

DATE	POS	WKS	ARTIST–RECORD TITLE	LABEL & NO.
			SKYLINERS, The	
			Pittsburgh white vocal quintet: Jimmy Beaumont (born 10/21/40; lead), Janet Vogel (died 2/21/80, suicide) and Wally Lester (tenors), Joe VerScharen (baritone) and Jackie Taylor (bass voice, guitarist).	
3/23/59	**12**	10	1. Since I Don't Have You	Calico 103
6/15/59	**26**	7	2. This I Swear	Calico 106
6/20/60	**24**	6	3. Pennies From Heaven	Calico 117
			#1 hit for Bing Crosby in 1936	
			SKYY	
			Brooklyn R&B-pop-funk octet. Vocals by sisters Denise, Delores and Bonnie Dunning. Organized by Randy Muller, former leader of Brass Construction.	
2/20/82	**26**	4	1. Call Me	Salsoul 2152
			#1 R&B hit (2 weeks)	
			SLADE	
			Hard-rock quartet formed in Wolverhampton, England in 1966: Noddy Holder (vocals), David Hill (guitar), Jim Lea (bass, keyboards) and Don Powell (drums).	
5/5/84	**20**	8	1. Run Runaway	CBS Assoc. 04398
8/11/84	**37**	3	2. My Oh My	CBS Assoc. 04528
			SLAUGHTER	
			Las Vegas hard-rock quartet led by vocalist Mark Slaughter, who, with bandmate Dana Strum (bass), was a member of the Vinnie Vincent Invasion. Includes guitarist Tim Kelly and drummer Blas Elias.	
6/2/90	**27**	6	1. Up All Night	Chrysalis 23486
			Sales #15	
9/22/90	**19**	8	2. Fly To The Angels	Chrysalis 23527
			Sales #9 / Airplay #35	
2/16/91	**39**	1	3. Spend My Life	Chrysalis 23605
			Sales #27	
			SLAVE	
			Funk band from Dayton, Ohio, formed by Steve Washington (trumpet) in 1975; left by 1981. Longtime members of group included Mark "The Hansolor" Adams (bass), Floyd Miller (vocals, horns) and Danny Webster (vocals, guitar). Studio vocalist Steve Arrington was a member from 1979–82.	
7/23/77	**32**	6	1. Slide [I]	Cotillion 44218
			#1 R&B hit (1 week)	
			SLEDGE, Percy	
			Born in 1941 in Leighton, Alabama. Worked local clubs with Esquires Combo until going solo. Pleaded guilty to tax evasion on 4/7/94.	
4/30/66	**1** (2)	10	● 1. **When A Man Loves A Woman**	Atlantic 2326
			#1 R&B hit (4 weeks)	
8/6/66	**17**	6	2. Warm And Tender Love	Atlantic 2342
11/19/66	**20**	7	3. It Tears Me Up	Atlantic 2358
7/22/67	**40**	1	4. Love Me Tender	Atlantic 2414
			adapted from the 1861 tune "Aura Lee"	
4/6/68	**11**	11	5. Take Time To Know Her	Atlantic 2490
			all of above produced by Quin Ivy and Marlin Greene	

DATE	POS	WKS	ARTIST–RECORD TITLE	LABEL & NO.
			SLY & THE FAMILY STONE	
			San Francisco interracial "psychedelic soul" group formed by Sylvester "Sly Stone" Stewart (born 3/15/44, Dallas; lead singer, keyboards), Sly's brother Freddie Stone (guitar), Cynthia Robinson (trumpet), Jerry Martini (saxophone), Sly's sister Rosie Stone (piano, vocals), Sly's cousin Larry Graham (bass) and Gregg Errico (drums). Sly recorded gospel at age four. Producer and writer for Bobby Freeman, The Mojo Men, The Beau Brummels. Formed own groups, The Stoners in 1966 and the Family Stone in 1967. Played Woodstock Festival in 1969. Career waned in the mid-1970s. Worked with George Clinton in 1982. Graham formed Graham Central Station in 1973. Group inducted into the Rock and Roll Hall of Fame in 1993. Also see Rubicon and Little Sister.	
3/2/68	8	12	1. **Dance To The Music**	Epic 10256
1/4/69	1 (4)	14	● 2. **Everyday People**	Epic 10407
			#1 R&B hit (2 weeks)	
4/26/69	22	6	3. Stand!	Epic 10450
8/30/69	2 (2)	13	4. **Hot Fun In The Summertime**	Epic 10497
1/10/70	1 (2)	12	● 5. **Thank You (Falettinme Be Mice Elf Agin)/**	
			#1 R&B hit (5 weeks)	
		12	6. Everybody Is A Star	Epic 10555
6/20/70	38	3	7. I Want To Take You Higher [R]	Epic 10450
			originally charted in 1969 at #60	
11/13/71	1 (3)	13	● 8. **Family Affair**	Epic 10805
			#1 R&B hit (5 weeks)	
2/26/72	23	6	9. Runnin' Away	Epic 10829
7/14/73	12	13	● 10. If You Want Me To Stay	Epic 11017
8/17/74	32	3	11. Time For Livin'	Epic 11140
			all of above written and produced by Sly Stone	
			SLY FOX	
			Black-and-white duo: Gary "Mudbone" Cooper (P-Funk) and Michael Camacho.	
2/15/86	7	14	1. **Let's Go All The Way**	Capitol 5552
			Sales #6 / Airplay #7; originally released on Capitol 5463	
			SMALL, Millie	
			Born Millicent Smith on 10/6/46 in Jamaica. Nicknamed "The Blue Beat Girl."	
6/6/64	2 (1)	9	1. **My Boy Lollipop**	Smash 1893
9/5/64	40	2	2. Sweet William	Smash 1920
			SMALL FACES	
			British rock quartet: Steve Marriott (guitar), Ronnie Lane (bass), Ian McLagen (organ) and Kenney Jones (drums). In 1968, Marriott formed Humble Pie. Remaining members evolved into Faces in 1969; disbanded in 1975. Jones joined The Who in 1978, formed The Law in 1991. Marriott died in a fire on 4/20/91 (age 44).	
1/13/68	16	8	1. Itchycoo Park	Immediate 501
			SMASHING PUMPKINS, The	
			Rock quartet formed in Chicago in 1989: Billy Corgan (vocals, guitar), James Iha (guitar), D'Arcy Wretzky (bass) and Jimmy Chamberlin (drums). Wretzky married Kerry Brown (drummer of Catherine) on 6/7/94.	
11/11/95+	22	12	● 1. Bullet With Butterfly Wings	Virgin 38522
			Sales #20 / Airplay #26	

DATE	POS	WKS	ARTIST–RECORD TITLE	LABEL & NO.
			SMITH	
			Los Angeles-based rock quintet fronted by St. Louis blues rocker Gayle McCormick.	
10/4/69	5	11	1. **Baby It's You**	Dunhill 4206
			SMITH, Frankie	
			Philadelphia native. Wrote and produced for Philadelphia International in the late 1970s, and later for WMOT.	
7/11/81	30	7	● 1. Double Dutch Bus based on the double-dutch jump rope game; certified gold for both 7" and 12" singles; #1 R&B hit (4 weeks)	WMOT 5356
			SMITH, Huey (Piano), And The Clowns	
			Smith was born on 1/26/34 in New Orleans. With Earl King in the early 1950s. Recorded with Eddie "Guitar Slim" Jones' band, 1951–54. Much session work in New Orleans. Own band, The Clowns, in 1957 with Bobby Marchan (vocals). Marchan left in 1960, replaced by Curly Smith. Also see Frankie Ford.	
3/31/58	9	9	1. **Don't You Just Know It** Top 100 #9 / Best Seller #13	Ace 545
			SMITH, Hurricane	
			Born Norman Smith in northern England in 1923. Vocalist/producer/engineer/session musician. Produced early Pink Floyd albums and did some engineering for The Beatles.	
12/23/72+	3	12	1. **Oh, Babe, What Would You Say?**	Capitol 3383
			SMITH, Jimmy	
			Born on 12/8/25 in Norristown, Pennsylvania. Pioneer jazz organist. Won Major Bowes Amateur Show in 1934. With father (James, Sr.) in song-and-dance team, 1942. With Don Gardner & The Sonotones, recorded for Bruce in 1953. Smith first recorded with own trio for Blue Note in 1956.	
6/9/62	21	7	1. Walk On The Wild Side [I] **JIMMY SMITH AND THE BIG BAND** title song from the movie starring Laurence Harvey and Jane Fonda	Verve 10255
			SMITH, Keely—see PRIMA, Louis, and SINATRA, Frank	
			SMITH, Michael W.	
			Contemporary Christian singer/keyboardist/songwriter from Kenova, West Virginia. To Nashville in 1978. Touring keyboardist for Amy Grant in 1982. Wrote Amy Grant's hits "Find A Way" and "Stay For Awhile."	
6/8/91	6	11	1. **Place In This World** Airplay #17 / Sales #21; co-written by Amy Grant	Reunion 19019
10/31/92	27	5	2. I Will Be Here For You Airplay #36 / Sales #37; #1 Adult Contemporary hit (2 weeks)	Reunion 19139
			SMITH, O.C.	
			Born Ocie Lee Smith on 6/21/36 in Mansfield, Louisiana. To Los Angeles in 1939. Sang while in U.S. Air Force, 1953–57. First recorded for Cadence in 1956. With Count Basie, 1961–63.	
4/20/68	40	2	1. The Son Of Hickory Holler's Tramp	Columbia 44425

DATE	POS	WKS	ARTIST–RECORD TITLE	LABEL & NO.
9/21/68	**2** (1)	12	● 2. **Little Green Apples**	Columbia 44616
9/20/69	34	2	3. Daddy's Little Man	Columbia 44948

SMITH, Patti, Group

Smith was born on 12/31/46 in Chicago; raised in New Jersey. Poet-turned-punk rocker. As a freelance rock journalist, wrote articles for *Rolling Stone*, *Crawdaddy* and *Creem*. Has published several books of poetry. Married to Fred "Sonic" Smith of the MC5 from 1980 until his death in 1994. Left music industry from September 1979 to 1988 to raise a family. Band included Lenny Kaye, Richard Sohl, Jay Dee Daughtery and Ivan Kral. Not to be confused with Patty Smyth of Scandal.

DATE	POS	WKS	ARTIST–RECORD TITLE	LABEL & NO.
5/13/78	13	9	1. Because The Night written by Smith and Bruce Springsteen	Arista 0318

SMITH, Ray

Born on 10/31/34 in Melber, Kentucky; committed suicide on 11/29/79. Recorded for Sun Records, 1958–62.

DATE	POS	WKS	ARTIST–RECORD TITLE	LABEL & NO.
2/1/60	22	8	1. Rockin' Little Angel	Judd 1016

SMITH, Rex

Born on 9/19/56 in Jacksonville, Florida. Vocalist/Actor. Starred in several Broadway musicals and in TV movie "Sooner Or Later." Appeared in the movies *The Pirates Of Penzance* and *Streethawk*. Recorded duet with rock singer Rachel Sweet (born 1963, Akron, Ohio).

DATE	POS	WKS	ARTIST–RECORD TITLE	LABEL & NO.
5/12/79	10	10	● 1. **You Take My Breath Away** introduced by Smith on 3/25/79 in the TV movie "Sooner or Later"; released with 3 different B-sides	Columbia 10908
8/8/81	32	4	2. Everlasting Love **REX SMITH/RACHEL SWEET**	Columbia 02169

SMITH, Sammi

Born on 8/5/43 in Orange, California; raised in Oklahoma. Female country singer. Moved to Nashville in 1967.

DATE	POS	WKS	ARTIST–RECORD TITLE	LABEL & NO.
2/20/71	8	11	● 1. **Help Me Make It Through The Night** written by Kris Kristofferson; #1 Country hit (3 weeks)	Mega 0015

SMITH, Somethin', & The Redheads

Trio from UCLA: Smith (vocals, guitar), Saul Striks (piano) and Major Short (violin).

DATE	POS	WKS	ARTIST–RECORD TITLE	LABEL & NO.
4/2/55	7	23	1. **It's A Sin To Tell A Lie** Best Seller #7 / Juke Box #8 / Jockey #9; #1 hit for Fats Waller in 1936	Epic 9093
7/14/56	27	3	2. In A Shanty In Old Shanty Town #1 hit for Ted Lewis in 1932	Epic 9168

SMITH, Verdelle

Black songstress from St. Petersburg, Florida.

DATE	POS	WKS	ARTIST–RECORD TITLE	LABEL & NO.
8/13/66	38	2	1. Tar And Cement	Capitol 5632

SMITH, Whistling Jack

Studio session production featuring the Mike Sammes Singers. Billy Moeller (born 2/2/46, Liverpool, England) was later hired to tour as Whistling Jack Smith.

DATE	POS	WKS	ARTIST–RECORD TITLE	LABEL & NO.
5/13/67	20	5	1. I Was Kaiser Bill's Batman [I]	Deram 85005

DATE	POS	WKS	ARTIST–RECORD TITLE	LABEL & NO.
			SMITHEREENS, The	
			Power-pop quartet formed in New Jersey in 1980: Pat DiNizio (vocals, guitar), Jim Babjak (guitar), Mike Mesaros (bass) and Dennis Diken (drums).	
3/10/90	38	2	1. A Girl Like You Sales #34 / Airplay #40	Enigma 44480
3/14/92	37	5	2. Too Much Passion Airplay #36	Capitol 44784
			SMOKIE	
			British pop-rock quartet: Chris Norman (lead singer), Alan Silson (guitar), Terry Utley (bass) and Pete Spencer (drums). Also see Suzi Quatro.	
1/22/77	25	8	1. Living Next Door To Alice	RSO 860
			SMYTH, Patty	
			Born on 6/26/57 in New York City. Lead singer of Scandal. In the 1980s, was married to punk rocker Richard Hell Television.	
8/29/92	2 (6)	20	● 1. **Sometimes Love Just Ain't Enough** **PATTY SMYTH with Don Henley** Sales #3 / Airplay #3; #1 Adult Contemporary hit (4 weeks)	MCA 54403
2/13/93	33	4	2. No Mistakes Airplay #33	MCA 54554
			SNAP!	
			German studio group assembled by producers Michael Muenzing and Luca Anzilotti. Group includes a revolving lineup of lead singers including Turbo B, Jackie Harris, Penny Ford, Thea Austin, Niki Harris and Summer (real name: Paula Brown).	
6/2/90	2 (1)	16	▲ 1. **The Power** Sales #1(3) / Airplay #11	Arista 2013
10/13/90	35	2	● 2. Ooops Up Sales #25	Arista 2060
9/19/92+	5	30	● 3. **Rhythm Is A Dancer** Airplay #4 / Sales #5	Arista 12437
			SNEAKER	
			Los Angeles-based pop-rock sextet. Mitch Crane, lead singer.	
12/19/81+	34	6	1. More Than Just The Two Of Us	Handshake 02557
			SNIFF 'n' the TEARS	
			British rock group led by Paul Roberts (vocals) and Loz Netto (guitar). Roberts joined The Stranglers in 1991.	
8/18/79	15	9	1. Driver's Seat	Atlantic 3604
			SNOOP DOGGY DOGG	
			Born Calvin Broadus in 1971 in Long Beach, California. Childhood friend of Dr. Dre and Warren G. & Nate Dogg. Arrested in connection with a drive-by shooting in Los Angeles on 8/25/93.	
12/4/93+	8	10	● 1. **What's My Name?** Sales #6 / Airplay #17	Death Row 98340
2/19/94	8	15	● 2. **Gin & Juice** Sales #5 / Airplay #22; samples "Watching You" by Slave; above 2 produced by Dr. Dre	Death Row 98318

DATE	POS	WKS	ARTIST–RECORD TITLE	LABEL & NO.
			SNOW	
			Born Darren O'Brien on 10/30/69. White male reggae singer from Toronto.	
2/6/93	**1** (7)	19	▲ 1. **Informer** Sales #1(6) / Airplay #4	EastWest 98471
6/5/93	19	9	2. **Girl, I've Been Hurt** Airplay #16 / Sales #22	EastWest 98438
			SNOW, Phoebe	
			Born Phoebe Laub on 7/17/52 in New York City; raised in New Jersey. Vocalist/guitarist/songwriter. Began performing in Greenwich Village in the early '70s.	
2/8/75	5	11	1. **Poetry Man** #1 Adult Contemporary hit (1 week)	Shelter 40353
9/6/75	23	6	2. Gone At Last **PAUL SIMON/PHOEBE SNOW and The Jessy Dixon Singers**	Columbia 10197
			SOFT CELL	
			British electro-rock duo: Marc Almond (vocals) and David Ball (synthesizer). Almond began solo career in late 1988.	
5/22/82	8	15	1. **Tainted Love** first recorded in 1964 by Gloria Jones on Champion Records; promo copies (Sire 1028) issued as a medley: "Tainted Love/Where Did Our Love Go"	Sire 49855
			SOHO	
			London-based trio of guitarist Timothy Brinkhurst (born 11/20/60) and vocalists/twin sisters Jacqueline and Pauline Cuff (born 11/25/62; both are psychiatric nurses).	
10/20/90	14	9	● 1. Hippychick Sales #8 / Airplay #22; samples a riff from The Smiths' "How Soon Is Now"	Savage/Atco 98908
			SOMMERS, Joanie	
			Born on 2/24/41 in Buffalo; moved to California in 1954. Sang Pepsi-Cola jingles in the early and mid-1960s.	
6/16/62	7	11	1. **Johnny Get Angry**	Warner 5275
			SONNY & CHER	
			Husband-and-wife duo: Cher (born 5/20/46) and Sonny Bono (born 2/16/35). Began career as session singers for Phil Spector. First recorded as Caesar & Cleo for Vault in 1963. Married in 1963; divorced in 1974. Appeared in the movies *Good Times* (1966) and *Chastity* (1968). Own CBS-TV variety series, 1971-74. Brief TV reunion in 1975. Sonny was mayor of Palm Springs, California, 1988-92; elected to Congress in 1994.	
7/31/65	**1** (3)	10	● 1. **I Got You Babe** a "live" version is on the B-side of #9 below	Atco 6359
9/4/65	10	8	2. **Laugh At Me** **SONNY**	Atco 6369
9/11/65	8	9	3. **Baby Don't Go** originally released in 1964 on Reprise 0309; 0392 released with 2 different B-sides: "Walkin' The Quetzal" and "Love Is Strange"	Reprise 0392
9/25/65	20	4	4. Just You	Atco 6345
10/23/65	15	6	5. But You're Mine	Atco 6381

DATE	POS	WKS	ARTIST–RECORD TITLE	LABEL & NO.
2/12/66	**14**	6	6. What Now My Love *written in France in 1962 by Gilbert Becaud as "Et Maintenant"*	Atco 6395
10/15/66	**21**	4	7. Little Man	Atco 6440
1/28/67	**6**	8	8. **The Beat Goes On**	Atco 6461
11/13/71	**7**	11	9. **All I Ever Need Is You** *#1 Adult Contemporary hit (5 weeks)*	Kapp 2151
3/11/72	**8**	11	10. **A Cowboys Work Is Never Done**	Kapp 2163
8/5/72	**32**	5	11. When You Say Love *adapted from a Budweiser jingle*	Kapp 2176
			SOPWITH "CAMEL", The San Francisco quintet. Peter Kraemer, lead singer.	
1/28/67	**26**	4	1. Hello Hello	Kama Sutra 217
			S.O.S. BAND, The Funk-R&B band from Atlanta. Lead singer/keyboardist Mary Davis went solo in 1986, various personnel changes since. Name means "Sounds Of Success."	
6/28/80	**3**	14	▲ 1. **Take Your Time (Do It Right) Part 1** *#1 R&B hit (5 weeks)*	Tabu 5522
			SOUL, David Born David Solberg on 8/28/43 in Chicago. Played Ken Hutchinson on TV's "Starsky & Hutch," 1975–79. Began career as a folk singer and appeared several times on "The Merv Griffin Show" as "The Covered Man" (wore a ski mask).	
2/19/77	**1 (1)**	13	● 1. **Don't Give Up On Us** *#1 Adult Contemporary hit (1 week)*	Private St. 45129
			SOUL, Jimmy Born James McCleese in New York City in 1942; raised in North Carolina and Portsmouth, Virginia. Died of a heart attack on 6/25/88. Worked with gospel groups, including the Nightingales, billed as: The Wonder Boy.	
5/5/62	**22**	8	1. Twistin' Matilda *twist version of the calypso song "Matilda" (popularized by Harry Belafonte)*	S.P.Q.R. 3300
4/20/63	**1 (2)**	11	2. **If You Wanna Be Happy** *#1 R&B hit (1 week)*	S.P.Q.R. 3305
			SOUL ASYLUM Rock band formed in Minneapolis in 1983: Dave Pirner (vocals, guitar), Daniel Murphy (guitar), Karl Mueller (bass) and Grant Young (drums). Pirner appeared in the movie *Reality Bites*. Young replaced by Sterling Campbell (ex-Duran Duran) in 1995.	
7/10/93	**5**	19	● 1. **Runaway Train** *Sales #5 / Airplay #9*	Columbia 74966
7/1/95	**20**	8	2. Misery *Airplay #16 / Sales #30*	Columbia 77959

DATE	POS	WKS	ARTIST–RECORD TITLE	LABEL & NO.
			SOUL CHILDREN, The	
			Group formed by songwriters Isaac Hayes and David Porter. Consisted of Anita Louis, Shelbra Bennett, John Colbert and Norman West. Colbert later recorded as J. Blackfoot.	
3/23/74	36	2	1. I'll Be The Other Woman	Stax 0182
			SOUL FOR REAL	
			Vocal quartet of the Dalyrimple brothers from Long Island: Choc, Dre, Bri and Jason. In 1995, all were between the ages of 14 and 20.	
1/28/95	2 (4)	21	● 1. **Candy Rain**	Uptown 54906
			Sales #1(3) / Airplay #11; #1 R&B hit (3 weeks)	
5/13/95	17	24	● 2. Every Little Thing I Do	Uptown 55032
			Sales #12 / Airplay #20; samples "Outstanding" by The Gap Band; above 2 co-written/co-produced by Heavy D.	
			SOUL SURVIVORS	
			White-soul band from New York City and Philadelphia. Formed by the Ingui brothers, Charles & Richard, and Kenny Jeremiah. Re-formed by the Inguis in 1972. Jeremiah was later in Shirley (And Company).	
9/23/67	4	12	1. **Expressway (To Your Heart)**	Crimson 1010
1/20/68	33	3	2. Explosion (In Your Soul)	Crimson 1012
			actual title: "Explosion (In My Soul)"	
			S.O.U.L. S.Y.S.T.E.M. Introducing Michelle Visage	
			Dance outfit produced by Robert Clivilles and David Cole (C & C Music Factory), featuring vocalist Michelle Visage (Seduction).	
1/23/93	34	2	1. It's Gonna Be A Lovely Day	Arista 12486
			Airplay #21 / Sales #43; from the movie The Bodyguard starring starring Kevin Costner and Whitney Houston; rap version of Bill Withers's 1978 hit "Lovely Day"	
			SOUL II SOUL	
			South London soul outfit led by the duo of Beresford "Jazzie B." Romeo and Nellee Hooper. Features female vocalists Caron Wheeler, Do'Reen and Rose Windross and musical backing by the Reggae Philharmonic Orchestra. Wheeler left in 1990.	
7/29/89	11	10	▲ 1. Keep On Movin'	Virgin 99205
			Sales #8 / Airplay #12; #1 R&B hit (2 weeks)	
10/14/89	4	18	▲ 2. **Back To Life (However Do You Want Me)**	Virgin 99171
			Sales #3 / Airplay #5; #1 R&B hit (1 week)	
			SOUNDS OF SUNSHINE	
			Brothers Walt, Warner and George Wilder from Los Angeles. Also recorded as the Wilder Brothers.	
7/24/71	39	2	1. Love Means (You Never Have To Say You're Sorry)	Ranwood 896
			song title taken from a line of dialogue in the movie Love Story starring Ali MacGraw and Ryan O'Neal	
			SOUNDS ORCHESTRAL	
			British studio project produced by John Schroeder. Included arranger/producer Johnny Pearson on piano.	
4/10/65	10	11	1. **Cast Your Fate To The Wind** [I]	Parkway 942
			#1 Adult Contemporary hit (3 weeks)	

DATE	POS	WKS	ARTIST–RECORD TITLE	LABEL & NO.
			SOUP DRAGONS, The	
			Pop-rock quartet from Glasgow, Scotland: Sean Dickinson (vocals), Jim McCulloch (guitar), Sushil Dade (bass) and Paul Quinn (drums).	
9/19/92	35	4	1. Divine Thing Sales #39 / Airplay #41	Big Life 865764
			SOUTH, Joe	
			Born Joe Souter on 2/28/40 in Atlanta. Successful Nashville session guitarist/songwriter in the mid-1960s. Wrote "Down In The Boondocks," "Hush" and "Rose Garden."	
2/1/69	12	9	1. Games People Play	Capitol 2248
1/17/70	12	9	2. Walk A Mile In My Shoes **JOE SOUTH and The Believers**	Capitol 2704
			SOUTHER, J.D.	
			Born John David Souther in Detroit; raised in Amarillo, Texas. Formed Longbranch Pennywhistle with Glenn Frey. Teamed with Chris Hillman and Richie Furay as The Souther, Hillman, Furay Band in 1974.	
10/20/79	7	13	1. **You're Only Lonely** #1 Adult Contemporary hit (5 weeks)	Columbia 11079
3/14/81	11	10	2. Her Town Too **JAMES TAYLOR AND J.D. SOUTHER**	Columbia 60514
			SOUTHER, HILLMAN, FURAY BAND, The	
			Country-rock sextet formed as a supergroup featuring J.D. Souther, Chris Hillman and Richie Furay.	
9/21/74	27	4	1. Fallin' In Love	Asylum 45201
			SOVINE, Red	
			Born Woodrow Wilson Sovine on 7/17/18 in Charleston, West Virginia. Died of a heart attack on 4/14/80. Country singer/songwriter/guitarist.	
8/28/76	40	1	● 1. Teddy Bear [S] classic "truck-drivin'" song; #1 Country hit (3 weeks)	Starday 142
			SPANDAU BALLET	
			Pop-rock quintet formed in London in 1979: Tony Hadley (vocals), brothers Gary (guitar) and Martin (bass) Kemp, Steve Norman (saxophone) and John Keeble (drums). The Kemps starred in the 1990 movie *The Krays*. Gary Kemp, later in *The Bodyguard*, married actress Sadie Frost (of the 1992 movie *Bram Stoker's Dracula*).	
8/27/83	4	13	1. **True** #1 Adult Contemporary hit (1 week); also see PM Dawn's "Set Adrift On Memory Bliss"	Chrysalis 42720
12/17/83+	29	6	2. Gold	Chrysalis 42743
9/1/84	34	4	3. Only When You Leave	Chrysalis 42792
			SPANKY AND OUR GANG	
			Folk-pop group formed in Chicago in 1966 featuring lead singer Elaine "Spanky" McFarlane (born 6/19/42, Peoria, Illinois). Included Malcolm Hale, Kenny Hodges, Lefty Baker, Nigel Pickering and John Seiter. Spanky became lead singer of the new Mamas & The Papas, early '80s.	
6/3/67	9	5	1. **Sunday Will Never Be The Same**	Mercury 72679
9/16/67	31	3	2. Making Every Minute Count	Mercury 72714

DATE	POS	WKS	ARTIST–RECORD TITLE	LABEL & NO.
10/28/67	14	9	3. Lazy Day	Mercury 72732
2/3/68	30	4	4. Sunday Mornin'	Mercury 72765
5/18/68	17	7	5. Like To Get To Know You	Mercury 72795

SPENCE, Judson

Born in Pascagoula, Mississippi. Singer/songwriter/multi-instrumentalist.

DATE	POS	WKS	ARTIST–RECORD TITLE	LABEL & NO.
11/26/88	32	4	1. Yeah, Yeah, Yeah Airplay #29 / Sales #34	Atlantic 88999

SPENCER, Tracie

Born on 7/12/76 in Waterloo, Iowa. Won the singing competition on TV's "Star Search" in 1986.

DATE	POS	WKS	ARTIST–RECORD TITLE	LABEL & NO.
11/19/88	38	3	1. Symptoms Of True Love Airplay #39	Capitol 44140
1/26/91	3	14	2. **This House** Sales #4 / Airplay #8	Capitol 44652

SPIDER

New York-based rock quintet: South African native Amanda Blue (vocals), Holly Knight, Anton Fig, Keith Lentin and Jimmy Lowell. Keyboardist Knight, a prolific songwriter, later joined Device and then went solo. Drummer Fig joined house band of TV's "Late Night With David Letterman."

DATE	POS	WKS	ARTIST–RECORD TITLE	LABEL & NO.
6/7/80	39	2	1. New Romance (It's A Mystery)	Dreamland 100

SPIN DOCTORS

Rock quartet formed at New York's New School of Jazz: Christopher Barron (vocals), Eric Schenkman (guitar), Mark White (bass) and Aaron Comess (drums).

DATE	POS	WKS	ARTIST–RECORD TITLE	LABEL & NO.
11/14/92	17	12	1. Little Miss Can't Be Wrong Sales #23 / Airplay #24	Epic/Assc. 74473
2/20/93	7	22	2. **Two Princes** Airplay #6 / Sales #14	Epic/Assc. 74804

SPINNERS

R&B vocal group from Ferndale High School near Detroit. Originally known as the Domingoes. Discovered by producer/lead singer of The Moonglows, Harvey Fuqua, and became the Spinners in 1961. First recorded on Fuqua's Tri-Phi label. Many personnel changes. G.C. Cameron was lead singer, 1968-72. 1972 hit lineup included Phillippe Wynne (tenor; died 7/14/84), Bobbie Smith (tenor), Billy Henderson (tenor), Henry Fambrough (baritone) and Pervis Jackson (bass). Wynne left group in 1977 and toured with Parliament/Funkadelic; replaced by John Edwards.

DATE	POS	WKS	●	ARTIST–RECORD TITLE	LABEL & NO.
7/17/61	27	5		1. That's What Girls Are Made For Harvey Fuqua (of The Moonglows; lead vocal)	Tri-Phi 1001
8/14/65	35	2		2. I'll Always Love You	Motown 1078
8/22/70	14	10		3. It's A Shame written and produced by Stevie Wonder	V.I.P. 25057
10/7/72	3	11	●	4. **I'll Be Around** #1 R&B hit (5 weeks)	Atlantic 2904
1/20/73	4	12	●	5. **Could It Be I'm Falling In Love** #1 R&B hit (1 week)	Atlantic 2927
5/19/73	11	11	●	6. One Of A Kind (Love Affair) #1 R&B hit (4 weeks)	Atlantic 2962

DATE	POS	WKS	ARTIST–RECORD TITLE	LABEL & NO.
9/8/73	29	3	7. Ghetto Child *above 4 from the album* Spinners *(Atlantic 7256)*	Atlantic 2973
2/23/74	20	8	8. Mighty Love—Pt. 1 *#1 R&B hit (2 weeks)*	Atlantic 3006
6/8/74	18	6	9. I'm Coming Home	Atlantic 3027
8/3/74	1 (1)	15	● 10. **Then Came You** **DIONNE WARWICKE AND SPINNERS** *originally released on Atlantic 3029 earlier in 1974*	Atlantic 3202
10/26/74	15	5	11. Love Don't Love Nobody—Pt. I	Atlantic 3206
4/5/75	37	2	12. Living A Little, Laughing A Little	Atlantic 3252
8/30/75	5	13	● 13. **"They Just Can't Stop It" the (Games People Play)** *first pressings issued only as: "Games People Play"; #1 R&B hit (1 week)*	Atlantic 3284
1/24/76	36	3	14. Love Or Leave	Atlantic 3309
10/2/76	2 (3)	17	● 15. **The Rubberband Man** *#1 R&B hit (1 week); #4-15 produced and arranged by Thom Bell*	Atlantic 3355
1/26/80	2 (2)	16	● 16. **Working My Way Back To You/Forgive Me, Girl** *although a medley, first pressings issued only as: "Working My Way Back To You"*	Atlantic 3637
5/24/80	4	14	17. Cupid/I've Loved You For A Long Time	Atlantic 3664
4/29/95	39	2	18. I'll Be Around [R] **RAPPIN' 4-TAY FEATURING THE SPINNERS** *Sales #26 / Airplay #63; Rappin' 4-Tay raps new verse over the Spinners hit (#3 in 1972) with its original music and chorus*	Rag Top 58331

SPIRAL STARECASE

Sacramento pop-rock quintet: Pat Upton (lead), Harvey Kaplan, Dick Lopes, Bobby Raymond and Vinny Parello.

DATE	POS	WKS	ARTIST–RECORD TITLE	LABEL & NO.
5/3/69	12	11	1. More Today Than Yesterday	Columbia 44741

SPIRIT

Los Angeles eclectic rock group: Jay Ferguson (lead singer), Mark Andes (bass), Ed Cassidy (drums), Randy California (guitar) and John Locke (keyboards). Ferguson and Andes left to form Jo Jo Gunne in mid-1971. Andes became an original member of Firefall in 1975; joined Heart in 1983.

DATE	POS	WKS	ARTIST–RECORD TITLE	LABEL & NO.
3/8/69	25	5	1. I Got A Line On You	Ode 115

SPOKESMEN, The

Johnny Madara, David White and Roy Gilmore. White was with Danny & The Juniors.

DATE	POS	WKS	ARTIST–RECORD TITLE	LABEL & NO.
10/9/65	36	3	1. The Dawn Of Correction *answer song to Barry McGuire's "Eve Of Destruction"; also see Johnny Sea's "Day For Decision"*	Decca 31844

SPRINGFIELD, Dusty

Born Mary O'Brien on 4/16/39 in London, England. Vocalist/guitarist. In The Lana Sisters vocal group. With brother Tom Springfield and Tim Feild in folk trio The Springfields, 1960–63.

DATE	POS	WKS	ARTIST–RECORD TITLE	LABEL & NO.
2/15/64	12	7	1. I Only Want To Be With You	Philips 40162
5/2/64	38	2	2. Stay Awhile	Philips 40180
7/11/64	6	10	3. **Wishin' And Hopin'**	Philips 40207
6/4/66	4	10	4. **You Don't Have To Say You Love Me**	Philips 40371
10/1/66	20	5	5. All I See Is You	Philips 40396

DATE	POS	WKS	ARTIST–RECORD TITLE	LABEL & NO.
4/22/67	40	2	6. I'll Try Anything	Philips 40439
10/14/67	22	5	7. The Look Of Love from the James Bond movie spoof *Casino Royale* starring David Niven and Peter Sellers	Philips 40465
12/14/68+	10	10	8. **Son-Of-A Preacher Man**	Atlantic 2580
5/24/69	31	4	9. The Windmills Of Your Mind from the movie *The Thomas Crown Affair* starring Steve McQueen and Faye Dunaway	Atlantic 2623
11/29/69	24	9	10. A Brand New Me	Atlantic 2685
12/26/87+	2 (2)	13	11. **What Have I Done To Deserve This?** **PET SHOP BOYS (and Dusty Springfield)** Sales #1(1) / Airplay #4; also released on EMI America 50107	EMI-Man. 50107

SPRINGFIELD, Rick

Born on 8/23/49 in Sydney, Australia. Singer/actor/songwriter. With top Australian teen-idol band Zoot before going solo in 1972. Turned to acting in the late '70s; played Noah Drake on the TV soap opera "General Hospital" in the early '80s. Starred in the movie *Hard To Hold* in 1984.

DATE	POS	WKS	ARTIST–RECORD TITLE	LABEL & NO.
9/2/72	14	9	1. Speak To The Sky	Capitol 3340
5/9/81	1 (2)	22	● 2. **Jessie's Girl**	RCA 12201
9/12/81	8	12	3. **I've Done Everything For You** written by Sammy Hagar	RCA 12166
12/26/81+	20	10	4. Love Is Alright Tonite	RCA 13008
3/13/82	2 (4)	16	5. **Don't Talk To Strangers**	RCA 13070
6/19/82	21	9	6. What Kind Of Fool Am I	RCA 13245
10/9/82	32	5	7. I Get Excited	RCA 13303
4/23/83	9	13	8. **Affair Of The Heart**	RCA 13497
7/23/83	18	11	9. Human Touch	RCA 13576
11/12/83	23	6	10. Souls	RCA 13650
3/17/84	5	12	11. **Love Somebody**	RCA 13738
6/9/84	26	6	12. Don't Walk Away	RCA 13813
9/8/84	20	9	13. Bop 'Til You Drop Airplay #16 / Sales #28; above 3 from the movie *Hard to Hold* starring Springfield	RCA 13861
12/15/84+	27	6	14. Bruce [N] Sales #27 / Airplay #27; recorded in 1978; an autobiographical song about Springfield being mistaken for Bruce Springsteen	Mercury 880405
4/20/85	26	6	15. Celebrate Youth Sales #24 / Airplay #26	RCA 14047
7/13/85	22	8	16. State Of The Heart Sales #20 / Airplay #23	RCA 14120
3/5/88	22	6	17. Rock Of Life Sales #20 / Airplay #21; all of above (except #3) written by Springfield	RCA 6853

SPRINGFIELDS, The

English folk trio: Dusty Springfield and brother Tom Springfield and Tim Feild.

DATE	POS	WKS	ARTIST–RECORD TITLE	LABEL & NO.
9/1/62	20	6	1. Silver Threads And Golden Needles	Philips 40038

DATE	POS	WKS	ARTIST–RECORD TITLE	LABEL & NO.
			SPRINGSTEEN, Bruce	
			Born on 9/23/49 in Freehold, New Jersey. Rock singer/songwriter/guitarist. Worked local clubs in New Jersey and Greenwich Village, mid-1960s. Own E-Street Band in 1973, consisted of Clarence Clemons (saxophone), David Sancious and Danny Federici (keyboards), Gary Tallent (bass) and Vini Lopez (drums). Sancious and Lopez replaced by Roy Bittan and Max Weinberg (became musical director for TV's "Late Night With Conan O'Brien" in 1993). Miami Steve Van Zandt (guitar) joined group in 1975. Springsteen wrote Manfred Mann's Earth Band's "Blinded By The Light" and the Pointer Sisters' "Fire." After *Born To Run*, a court injunction prevented the release of any new albums until 1978. Married to model/actress Julianne Phillips, 1985–89. Appeared in the 1987 movie *Hail! Hail! Rock 'N' Roll*. Split from the E-Street Band in November 1989. Married Patti Scialfa, former singer with the E-Street Band, on 6/8/91.	
10/11/75	23	5	1. Born To Run	Columbia 10209
7/15/78	33	2	2. Prove It All Night	Columbia 10763
11/8/80	5	14	3. **Hungry Heart** Mark Volman and Howard Kaylan of The Turtles (backing vocals)	Columbia 11391
2/21/81	20	6	4. Fade Away	Columbia 11431
5/26/84	2 (4)	15	▲ 5. **Dancing In The Dark** B-side "Pink Cadillac" was a hit for Natalie Cole in 1988	Columbia 04463
8/18/84	7	13	6. **Cover Me** Airplay #7 / Sales #9	Columbia 04561
11/24/84+	9	11	7. **Born In The U.S.A.** Sales #9 / Airplay #11	Columbia 04680
3/2/85	6	12	8. **I'm On Fire** Airplay #5 / Sales #7	Columbia 04772
6/8/85	5	13	9. **Glory Days** Airplay #4 / Sales #7	Columbia 04924
9/14/85	9	9	10. **I'm Goin' Down** Sales #8 / Airplay #9	Columbia 05603
12/21/85+	6	9	11. **My Hometown** Sales #5 / Airplay #7; #1 Adult Contemporary hit (1 week); B-side "Santa Claus Is Comin' To Town" was certified Gold in 1992; above 7 from the album *Born In The U.S.A.*	Columbia 05728
11/29/86	8	9	12. **War** **BRUCE SPRINGSTEEN & THE E STREET BAND** Sales #8 / Airplay #12; recorded "live" at the LA Coliseum on 9/30/85	Columbia 06432
10/3/87	5	11	13. **Brilliant Disguise** Sales #5 / Airplay #5	Columbia 07595
12/19/87+	9	11	14. **Tunnel Of Love** Sales #6 / Airplay #15	Columbia 07663
3/19/88	13	8	15. One Step Up Sales #11 / Airplay #18	Columbia 07726
3/21/92	16	9	16. Human Touch/ Airplay #14 / Sales #27	
		9	17. Better Days	Columbia 74273
3/5/94	9	15	● 18. **Streets Of Philadelphia** Airplay #7 / Sales #10; from the movie *Philadelphia* starring Tom Hanks and Denzel Washington	Columbia 77384
			SPYRO GYRA	
			Jazz-pop band formed in 1975 in Buffalo, New York. Led by saxophonist Jay Beckenstein (born 5/14/51).	
7/28/79	24	8	1. Morning Dance [I] #1 Adult Contemporary hit (1 week)	Infinity 50011

DATE	POS	WKS	ARTIST–RECORD TITLE	LABEL & NO.
			SQUEEZE	
			English pop-rock group formed in 1974 and led by vocalists/guitarists Chris Difford and Glenn Tilbrook. Originally known as UK Squeeze due to confusion with American band Tight Squeeze. Paul Carrack (Ace, Mike + The Mechanics) was keyboardist/vocalist in 1981 of fluctuating lineup; re-joined in 1993.	
10/17/87	**15**	10	1. Hourglass Sales #16 / Airplay #16	A&M 2967
1/23/88	**32**	5	2. 853-5937 Sales #30 / Airplay #33	A&M 2994
			SQUIER, Billy	
			Born on 5/12/50 in Wellesley Hills, Massachusetts. Hard-rock singer/songwriter/guitarist.	
6/20/81	**17**	11	1. The Stroke	Capitol 5005
10/17/81	**35**	3	2. In The Dark	Capitol 5040
11/27/82	**32**	6	3. Everybody Wants You	Capitol 5163
7/14/84	**15**	12	4. Rock Me Tonite	Capitol 5370
			STACEY Q	
			Real name: Stacey Swain. Dance singer from Los Angeles.	
8/16/86	**3**	13	1. **Two Of Hearts** Sales #1(1) / Airplay #7	Atlantic 89381
2/21/87	**35**	4	2. We Connect Sales #29	Atlantic 89331
			STAFFORD, Jim	
			Born on 1/16/44 in Eloise, Florida. Singer/songwriter/guitarist. Moved to Nashville after high school graduation. Own summer variety TV show in 1975, and co-host of "Those Amazing Animals," 1980–81. Married Bobbie Gentry in 1978.	
7/14/73	**39**	1	1. Swamp Witch	MGM 14496
12/29/73+	**3**	15	● 2. **Spiders & Snakes**	MGM 14648
5/4/74	**12**	9	3. My Girl Bill [N]	MGM 14718
7/20/74	**7**	11	4. **Wildwood Weed** [N]	MGM 14737
			above 4 from the album *Jim Stafford*	
1/18/75	**24**	5	5. Your Bulldog Drinks Champagne [N]	MGM 14775
9/27/75	**37**	2	6. I Got Stoned And I Missed It [N]	MGM 14819
			all of above produced by Lobo and Phil Gernhard	
			STAFFORD, Jo	
			Born on 11/12/20 in Coalinga, California. Member of Tommy Dorsey's vocal group The Pied Pipers, 1940–43. Married to orchestra leader Paul Weston; recorded together as the novelty duo Jonathan & Darlene Edwards. Stafford also recorded as the hillbilly Cinderella G. Stump in 1947. Jo Stafford and Dinah Shore rank as the top 2 female vocalists of the pre-rock era.	
10/15/55	**13**	7	1. Suddenly There's A Valley Jockey #13 / Top 100 #16 / Juke Box #18 / Best Seller #21; Norman Luboff Choir (backing vocals)	Columbia 40559
12/3/55+	**14**	14	2. It's Almost Tomorrow Juke Box #14 / Top 100 #19 / Jockey #20 / Best Seller #25	Columbia 40595
12/22/56	**38**	1	3. On London Bridge Paul Weston (orch., all of above)	Columbia 40782

DATE	POS	WKS	ARTIST–RECORD TITLE	LABEL & NO.
			STAFFORD, Terry	
			Born in Hollis, Oklahoma; raised in Amarillo, Texas. Died on 3/17/96. Elvis Presley sound-alike. Moved to California in 1960. Appeared in the movie *Wild Wheels*.	
3/21/64	3	10	1. **Suspicion**	Crusader 101
			first recorded in 1962 by Elvis Presley for his *Pot Luck* album	
6/6/64	25	6	2. I'll Touch A Star	Crusader 105
			STALLION	
			Denver-based quintet. Buddy Stephens, lead singer.	
4/23/77	37	2	1. Old Fashioned Boy (You're The One)	Casablanca 877
			STALLONE, Frank	
			Born on 7/30/50 in Philadelphia. Singer/actor. Brother of Sylvester Stallone.	
8/20/83	10	10	1. **Far From Over**	RSO 815023
			from the movie *Staying Alive* starring John Travolta	
			STAMPEDERS	
			Pop-rock trio from Calgary: Rick Dodson, Ronnie King and Kim Berly.	
9/11/71	8	10	1. **Sweet City Woman**	Bell 45120
4/3/76	40	2	2. Hit The Road Jack	Quality 501
			featuring a telephone conversation with Wolfman Jack	
			STAMPLEY, Joe	
			Born on 6/6/43 in Springhill, Louisiana. Country singer. Leader of The Uniques.	
3/3/73	37	3	1. Soul Song	Dot 17442
			#1 Country hit (1 week)	
			STANDELLS, The	
			Los Angeles-area early punk-rock quartet: Dick Dodd (lead singer, drums), Larry Tamblyn and Tony Valentino (guitars) and Gary Lane (bass). Dodd was an original Mouseketeer. Tamblyn is the brother of actor Russ.	
6/11/66	11	9	1. Dirty Water	Tower 185
			written and produced by Ed Cobb (Four Preps)	
			STANLEY, Michael, Band	
			Cleveland rock group: Michael Stanley (born Michael Stanley Gee on 3/25/48; vocals, guitar), Kevin Raleigh (vocals, keyboards), Bob Pelander (keyboards), Tommy Dobeck (drums), Michael Gismondi (bass), Rick Bell (sax) and Gary Markasky (lead guitar; replaced by Danny Powers in 1983). Raleigh recorded solo in 1989.	
1/10/81	33	5	1. He Can't Love You	EMI America 8063
			Clarence Clemmons (sax solo)	
11/12/83	39	1	2. My Town	EMI America 8178
			STANSFIELD, Lisa	
			Born on 4/11/66. Lead singer of Blue Zone U.K. from Roachdale, England. Vocalist on Coldcut's 1989 club hit "People Hold On."	
2/24/90	3	14	▲ 1. **All Around The World**	Arista 9928
			Sales #1(1) / Airplay #3; #1 R&B hit (2 weeks)	

TLC—whose blend of rap and R&B made them one of the mid-'90s biggest-selling acts—scored a No. 6 hit with their "Ain't 2 Proud 2 Beg." Ironically, the similarly named hit sung by both the Temptations and the Rolling Stones never charted as high.

Tony! Toni! Tone!'s 1990 smash "Feels Good" went gold and hit the Top 10; the duo later cracked the Top 40 with a cover of Albert Hammond's Top 5 1972 hit "It Never Rains In Southern California."

Tina Turner's long-lived career received a memorable shot in the arm with her multi-platinum 1984 album *Private Dancer*. Her appearance in the 1985 film *Max Max—Beyond Thunderdome* also produced her No. 2 smash "We Don't Need Another Hero."

Tina Turner's 1990 hit "Steamy Windows" was penned by none other than Tony Joe White, whose memorable self-penned hit "Polk Salad Annie" was a Top 10 hit back in 1969.

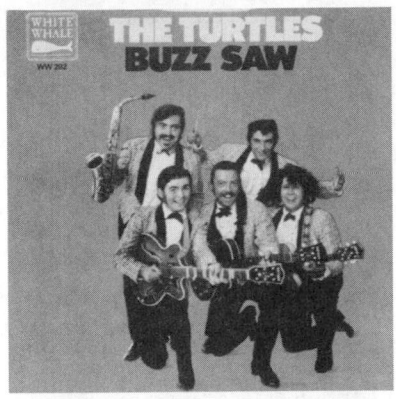

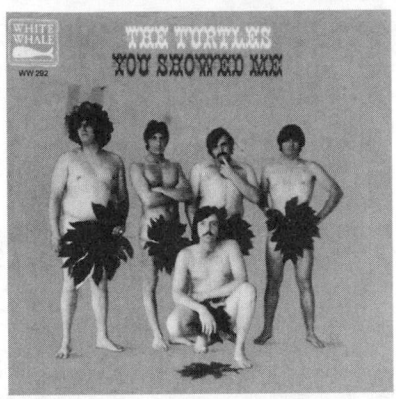

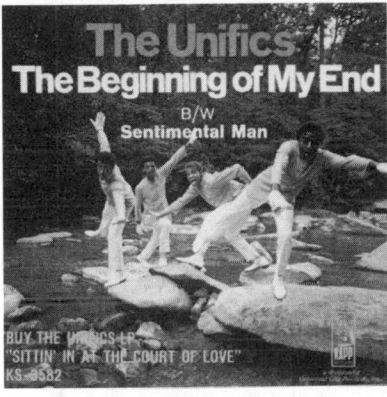

The Turtles' last of five Top 10 hits between 1965 and 1969 was their rendition of Byrds Jim McGuinn & Gene Clark's "You Showed Me." Its flip, "Buzz Saw," was a surf instrumental.

The Unifics faced heady R&B competition in 1969. As "The Beginning Of My End" struggled to reach its No. 36 high, it battled Top 10 tracks like "I Heard It Through The Grapevine" (Marvin Gaye), "Soulful Strut" (Young-Holt Unlimited), and "Everyday People" (Sly & The Family Stone).

Vangelis's lengthy career as an award-winning keyboard instrumentalist reached its peak of popularity with his No. 1 hit "Main Theme" from *Chariots Of Fire*. The keyboardist had previously been a member of both Yes and Aphrodite's Child.

Van Halen's career seemed temporarily in jeopardy in 1985 when original vocalist David Lee Roth departed for a solo career and was replaced by Sammy Hagar. But the hits—such as 1988's No. 3 "When It's Love"—kept on coming.

Bobby Vee's 1962 hit—the rather specifically titled "Please Don't Ask About Barbara"—was the former Robert Velline's sixth of 14 career Top 40 hits.

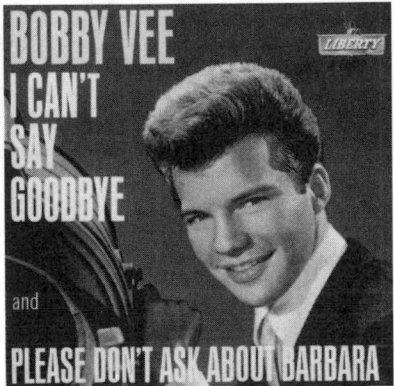

DATE	POS	WKS	ARTIST–RECORD TITLE	LABEL & NO.
6/16/90	**14**	8	2. You Can't Deny It Sales #11 / Airplay #18; #1 R&B hit (1 week)	Arista 2024
9/8/90	**21**	7	3. This Is The Right Time Airplay #20 / Sales #24	Arista 2049
11/23/91+	**27**	9	4. Change Airplay #24 / Sales #40	Arista 12362

STAPLE SINGERS, The

Family soul group consisting of Roebuck "Pop" Staples (born 12/28/15, Winoma, Mississippi), with his son Pervis (who left in 1971) and daughters Cleotha, Yvonne and lead singer Mavis Staples. Roebuck was a blues guitarist in his teens, later with the Golden Trumpets gospel group. Moved to Chicago in 1935. Formed own gospel group in early '50s. First recorded for United in 1953. Mavis recorded solo in 1970.

DATE	POS	WKS	ARTIST–RECORD TITLE	LABEL & NO.
3/20/71	**27**	5	1. Heavy Makes You Happy (Sha-Na-Boom Boom)	Stax 0083
11/13/71	**12**	10	2. Respect Yourself	Stax 0104
4/15/72	**1** (1)	14	3. **I'll Take You There** #1 R&B hit (4 weeks)	Stax 0125
8/26/72	**38**	3	4. This World	Stax 0137
4/14/73	**33**	3	5. Oh La De Da	Stax 0156
11/10/73	**9**	11	● 6. **If You're Ready (Come Go With Me)** #1 R&B hit (3 weeks)	Stax 0179
3/23/74	**23**	7	7. Touch A Hand, Make A Friend all of above produced by Al Bell	Stax 0196
11/1/75	**1** (1)	12	● 8. **Let's Do It Again** written and produced by Curtis Mayfield; title song from the movie starring Sidney Poitier and Bill Cosby; #1 R&B hit (2 weeks)	Curtom 0109

STAPLETON, Cyril, And His Orchestra

Stapleton was born on 12/31/14 in Nottingham, England. Died on 2/25/74. British bandleader.

DATE	POS	WKS	ARTIST–RECORD TITLE	LABEL & NO.
9/29/56	**25**	2	1. The Italian Theme [I]	London 1672
1/19/59	**13**	10	2. The Children's Marching Song (Nick Nack Taddy Whack) with the children from the movie *The Inn of the Sixth Happiness* starring Ingrid Bergman	London 1851

STARBUCK

Atlanta pop-rock septet. Bruce Blackman, lead singer.

DATE	POS	WKS	ARTIST–RECORD TITLE	LABEL & NO.
5/29/76	**3**	14	1. **Moonlight Feels Right**	Private St. 45039
5/21/77	**38**	2	2. Everybody Be Dancin'	Private St. 45144

STARCHER, Buddy

Born Oby Edgar Starcher on 3/16/06 near Ripley, West Virginia. Worked on WFBR-Baltimore in 1928. Worked as a DJ on WCAU, WIBG-Philadelphia. Own band from 1937. Managed KWBA-Bayton, Texas in the early '70s.

DATE	POS	WKS	ARTIST–RECORD TITLE	LABEL & NO.
5/14/66	**39**	1	1. History Repeats Itself [S] an accounting of "coincidental" parallels between the careers and deaths of Presidents Lincoln and Kennedy	Boone 1038

DATE	POS	WKS	ARTIST–RECORD TITLE	LABEL & NO.
			STARGARD	
			Disco trio: Rochelle Runnells, Debra Anderson and Janice Williams. Appeared as The Diamonds in the movie *Sgt. Pepper's Lonely Hearts Club Band*.	
3/4/78	**21**	7	1. Theme Song From "Which Way Is Up" title song from the movie starring Richard Pryor; #1 R&B hit (2 weeks)	MCA 40825
			STARLAND VOCAL BAND	
			Washington, D.C.-based pop quartet: Bill and wife Taffy Danoff, John Carroll and future wife Margot Chapman. Bill and Taffy had fronted the folk quintet Fat City. Bill co-wrote "Take Me Home, Country Roads" with friend John Denver. Denver owned Windsong record label. Won the 1976 Best New Artist Grammy.	
6/5/76	**1 (2)**	14	● 1. **Afternoon Delight**	Windsong 10588
			STARLETS, The	
			Female R&B vocal group from Chicago: Dynetta Boone (aka Liz Walker) (lead), Jane Hall, Maxine Edwards (sister of Earl Edwards of The Dukays), Mickey McKinney, Jeanette Miles and Bernice Williams. While under contract to PAM Records, The Starlets recorded "I Sold My Heart To The Junkman" on the Newtown label. Newtown listed one of their artists, The Blue-Belles (Patti LaBelle's group), on the label.	
6/12/61	**38**	2	1. Better Tell Him No	PAM 1003
5/12/62	**15**	7	2. I Sold My Heart To The Junkman **THE BLUE-BELLES**	Newtown 5000
			STARPOINT	
			Black sextet from Maryland: brothers Ernesto, George, Orlando and Gregory Phillips, with Renee Diggs and Kayode Adeyemo. Formed as Lycindiana, did session work for Motown and All-Platinum Records.	
11/16/85	**25**	9	1. Object Of My Desire Sales #19 / Airplay #30	Elektra 69621
			STARR, Brenda K.	
			Born Brenda Kaplan on 10/15/66 in Manhattan. Singer/movie actress from New York City of Puerto Rican heritage. Daughter of Harvey Kaplan (Spiral Starecase).	
5/7/88	**13**	12	1. I Still Believe Sales #10 / Airplay #14	MCA 53288
9/3/88	**24**	7	2. What You See Is What You Get Sales #16 / Airplay #26	MCA 53367
			STARR, Edwin	
			Born Charles Hatcher on 1/21/42 in Nashville; raised in Cleveland. In vocal group, the Futuretones; recorded for Tress in 1957. With Bill Doggett Combo, 1963–65. Recorded duets with Sandra "Blinky" Williams in 1969.	
9/4/65	**21**	6	1. Agent Double-O-Soul	Ric-Tic 103
3/22/69	**6**	9	2. **Twenty-Five Miles**	Gordy 7083
7/25/70	**1 (3)**	13	3. **War**	Gordy 7101
1/2/71	**26**	4	4. Stop The War Now	Gordy 7104

DATE	POS	WKS	ARTIST–RECORD TITLE	LABEL & NO.
			STARR, Kay	
			Born Katherine Starks on 7/21/22 in Dougherty, Oklahoma; raised in Dallas and Memphis. With Joe Venuti's orchestra at age 15, and sang briefly with Glenn Miller, Charlie Barnet and Bob Crosby before launching solo career in 1945. In the movies *Make Believe Ballroom* and *When You're Smiling*.	
8/6/55	17	1	1. Good And Lonesome	RCA 6146
			Juke Box #17; Hal Mooney (orch. and chorus)	
1/7/56	1 (6)	20	● 2. **Rock And Roll Waltz**	RCA 6359
			Juke Box #1(6) / Top 100 #1(4) / Best Seller #1(1) / Jockey #1(1); Hugo Winterhalter (orch. and chorus)	
6/30/56	40	1	3. Second Fiddle	RCA 6541
			Joe Reisman (orch. and chorus)	
9/16/57	9	10	4. **My Heart Reminds Me**	RCA 6981
			Jockey #9 / Top 100 #53; Pete King (orch.); lyric version of the Italian instrumental "Autumn Concerto"	
			STARR, Randy	
			Born Warren Nadel on 7/2/30 in New York City. Pop singer/songwriter/guitarist. Dentist since 1956. Wrote many tunes for Elvis Presley's soundtracks. Formed instrumental duo, The Islanders, with Frank Metis.	
5/6/57	32	2	1. After School	Dale 100
			"Bugs" Bower (orch.)	
			STARR, Ringo	
			Born Richard Starkey on 7/7/40 in Dingle, Liverpool, England. Played with Rory Storm and the Hurricanes before joining The Beatles following ousting of drummer Pete Best in 1962. First solo album in 1970. Acted in the movies *Candy* (made in 1967, released in 1969), *The Magic Christian, 200 Motels, Born To Boogie, Blindman, That'll Be The Day, Cave Man* and Paul McCartney's *Give My Regards To Broad Street*. Played Mr. Conductor on PBS-TV's "Shining Time Station," 1989–91. Married actress Barbara Bach in 1981.	
5/8/71	4	11	● 1. **It Don't Come Easy**	Apple 1831
			Badfinger (harmony vocals)	
4/15/72	9	7	2. **Back Off Boogaloo**	Apple 1849
			above 2 produced by George Harrison	
10/20/73	1 (1)	12	● 3. **Photograph**	Apple 1865
			George Harrison (harmony vocal, 12-string guitar)	
12/29/73+	1 (1)	12	● 4. **You're Sixteen**	Apple 1870
			Nilsson (backing vocal); Paul McCartney (kazoo)	
3/23/74	5	11	5. **Oh My My**	Apple 1872
			Billy Preston (keyboards); Tom Scott (sax); Martha Reeves and Merry Clayton (backing vocals)	
11/30/74+	6	10	6. **Only You**	Apple 1876
			#1 Adult Contemporary hit (1 week)	
2/22/75	3	10	7. **No No Song**/	
			written by Hoyt Axton	
		10	8. Snookeroo	Apple 1880
			written by Elton John and Bernie Taupin	
7/5/75	31	3	9. **It's All Down To Goodnight Vienna**/	
			written by John Lennon	
		3	10. Oo-Wee	Apple 1882
			above 5 from the album *Goodnight Vienna*	
10/16/76	26	6	11. A Dose Of Rock 'N' Roll	Atlantic 3361
			Peter Frampton (guitar); Melissa Manchester (backing vocal)	

DATE	POS	WKS	ARTIST–RECORD TITLE	LABEL & NO.
12/5/81	38	2	12. Wrack My Brain written and produced by George Harrison (also, guitar and backing vocal)	Boardwalk 130
			STARSHIP—see JEFFERSON STARSHIP	
			STARS on 45	
			Dutch session vocalists and musicians assembled by producer Jaap Eggermont. The John Lennon vocals by Bas Muys.	
5/2/81	1 (1)	14	● 1. **Medley** Intro "Venus"/Sugar Sugar/No Reply/I'll Be Back/Drive My Car/Do You Want To Know A Secret/We Can Work It Out/I Should Have Known Better/Nowhere Man/You're Going To Lose That Girl/Stars on 45	Radio 3810
4/17/82	28	5	2. Stars on 45 III **STARS ON (A Tribute To Stevie Wonder)** Uptight Everything's All Right/My Cherie Amour/Yester Me, Yester You/Master Blaster/You Are The Sunshine Of My Life/Isn't She Lovely/Stars On Jingle/Sir Duke/I Wish/I Was Made To Love Her/Superstition/Fingertips	Radio 4019
			STARZ	
			New York-based rock quintet: Michael Lee Smith (brother of Rex Smith; lead singer), Peter Sweval (bass), Richie Ranno (guitar), Brenden Harkin (guitar) and Joe X. Dube (drums).	
4/30/77	33	2	1. Cherry Baby	Capitol 4399
			STATLER BROTHERS, The	
			Country vocal quartet from Staunton, Virginia. Consisted of brothers Harold and Don Reid, Phil Balsley and Lew DeWitt. In 1983, Jimmy Fortune replaced DeWitt, who died from Crohn's disease on 8/15/90 (age 52). Currently host their own Nashville Network cable TV variety show.	
12/11/65+	4	9	1. **Flowers On The Wall**	Columbia 43315
			STATON, Candi	
			Born in Hanceville, Alabama. Sang with the Jewel Gospel Trio from age 10. Went solo in 1968. Married for a time to Clarence Carter.	
10/3/70	24	9	1. Stand By Your Man	Fame 1472
6/26/76	20	11	2. Young Hearts Run Free #1 R&B hit (1 week)	Warner 8181
			STATUS QUO, The	
			English rock quintet: Francis Michael Rossi, Rick Parfitt, Roy Lynes, John Coghlan and Alan Lancaster. Immensely popular in England, where they've charted over 35 hits, 20 of which went Top 10.	
6/29/68	12	11	1. Pictures Of Matchstick Men	Cadet Con. 7001
			STEALERS WHEEL	
			Scottish group led by Gerry Rafferty (vocals, guitar) and Joe Egan (vocals, keyboards).	
3/31/73	6	13	1. **Stuck In The Middle With You**	A&M 1416
3/9/74	29	3	2. Star	A&M 1483

DATE	POS	WKS	ARTIST–RECORD TITLE	LABEL & NO.
			STEAM	
			New York City studio group assembled by producer Paul Leka.	
11/8/69	**1** (2)	13	● 1. **Na Na Hey Hey Kiss Him Goodbye**	Fontana 1667
			STEEL BREEZE	
			Ric Jacobs, lead singer of six-man pop band from California.	
9/18/82	**16**	11	1. You Don't Want Me Anymore	RCA 13283
2/19/83	**30**	6	2. Dreamin' Is Easy	RCA 13427
			STEELHEART	
			Hard-rock quintet from Norwalk, Connecticut, led by vocalist Michael Matijevic.	
6/1/91	**23**	9	1. I'll Never Let You Go (Angel Eyes)	MCA 53801
			Sales #11 / Airplay #71	
			STEELY DAN	
			Los Angeles-based, pop/jazz-styled group formed by Donald Fagen (born 1/10/48, Passaic, New Jersey; keyboards, vocals) and Walter Becker (born 2/20/50, New York City; bass, vocals). Group, primarily known as a studio unit, featured Fagen and Becker with various studio musicians. Actor/comedian Chevy Chase was the band's drummer in its formative years. Fagen and Becker went their separate ways in 1981. Drummer Jimmy Hodder drowned on 6/5/90 (age 42). Fagen and Becker reunited for a concert tour in 1993.	
12/30/72+	**6**	11	1. **Do It Again**	ABC 11338
4/7/73	**11**	11	2. Reeling In The Years	ABC 11352
6/8/74	**4**	11	3. **Rikki Don't Lose That Number**	ABC 11439
6/21/75	**37**	2	4. Black Friday	ABC 12101
1/7/78	**11**	11	5. Peg	ABC 12320
			Michael McDonald (backing vocal)	
5/6/78	**19**	8	6. Deacon Blues	ABC 12355
7/1/78	**22**	5	7. FM (No Static At All)	MCA 40894
			from the movie *FM* starring Michael Brandon	
9/23/78	**26**	5	8. Josie	ABC 12404
12/13/80+	**10**	13	9. **Hey Nineteen**	MCA 51036
3/28/81	**22**	7	10. Time Out Of Mind	MCA 51082
			Mark Knopfler of Dire Straits (guitar solo); all of above written by Fagen & Becker and produced by Gary Katz	
			STEIN, Lou	
			Born on 4/22/22 in Philadelphia. Pianist with Ray McKinley, 1941–42 and 1946–47. Studio and free-lance musician into the '70s.	
3/30/57	**31**	3	1. Almost Paradise [I]	RKO Unique 385
			Bill Fontaine (orch.)	
			STEINMAN, Jim	
			Born in New York City. Wrote and arranged all cuts on Meat Loaf's *Bat Out Of Hell (I & II)* albums.	
7/18/81	**32**	6	1. Rock And Roll Dreams Come Through	Epic 02111
			Rory Dodd (vocal)	

DATE	POS	WKS	ARTIST–RECORD TITLE	LABEL & NO.
			### STEPHENSON, Van	
			Nashville-based singer/songwriter from Ohio. First songwriting break came with Crystal Gayle's 1979 country hit "Your Kisses Will." Hit pop charts with rock songs. Co-wrote several country hits for Restless Heart. Co-founded country trio BlackHawk in 1993.	
5/12/84	**22**	10	1. Modern Day Delilah	MCA 52376
			### STEPPENWOLF	
			Hard-rock quintet formed in Los Angeles in 1967. Original lineup: John Kay (born Joachim Krauledat on 4/12/44 in Tilsit, East Germany; vocals, guitar) Michael Monarch (guitar), Goldy McJohn (keyboards), Nick St. Nicholas (bass), Mars Bonfire (born Dennis Edmonton; guitar) and brother Jerry Edmonton (drums; died in a car crash 11/28/93). All but Monarch were members of Canadian group Sparrow. Many personnel changes except for Kay. Group named after a Herman Hesse novel.	
7/20/68	**2 (3)**	12	● 1. **Born To Be Wild**	Dunhill 4138
10/26/68	**3**	13	● 2. **Magic Carpet Ride**	Dunhill 4161
3/15/69	**10**	8	3. **Rock Me**	Dunhill 4182
9/6/69	**31**	5	4. Move Over	Dunhill 4205
2/7/70	**39**	1	5. Monster	Dunhill 4221
5/9/70	**35**	3	6. Hey Lawdy Mama	Dunhill 4234
			all of above produced by Gabriel Mekler	
10/5/74	**29**	3	7. Straight Shootin' Woman	Mums 6031
			### STEREO MC'S	
			Trio of remixers from Gee Street Records based in East London: Rob Birch, Nick "The Head" Hallam and Owen "If" Rossiter. Features touring/video vocalist Cath Coffey.	
7/20/91	**39**	1	1. Elevate My Mind	4th & B'way 447519
			Sales #35 / Airplay #41	
4/24/93	**20**	11	2. Connected	Gee St. 864744
			Airplay #24 / Sales #29; samples Jimmy "Bo" Horne's R&B hit "Let Me (Let Me Be Your Lover)"	
			### STEREOS, The	
			R&B quintet from Steubenville, Ohio. Originally called the Buckeyes. Consisted of Bruce Robinson (lead), Nathaniel Hicks, Sam Profit, George Otis and Ronnie Collins.	
10/16/61	**29**	3	1. I Really Love You	Cub 9095
			### STEVE & EYDIE—see LAWRENCE, Steve, and/or GORME, Eydie	
			### STEVENS, April—see TEMPO, Nino	
			### STEVENS, Cat	
			Born Steven Georgiou on 7/21/47 in London. Began career playing folk music at Hammersmith College in 1966. Contracted tuberculosis in 1968 and spent over a year recuperating. Adopted new style when he re-emerged. Lived in Brazil in the mid-1970s. Converted to Muslim religion in 1979, took name Yusef Islam.	
3/6/71	**11**	10	1. Wild World	A&M 1231
7/10/71	**30**	7	2. Moon Shadow	A&M 1265
10/9/71	**7**	10	3. **Peace Train**	A&M 1291
			#1 Adult Contemporary hit (3 weeks)	

DATE	POS	WKS	ARTIST–RECORD TITLE	LABEL & NO.
4/22/72	6	11	4. **Morning Has Broken** *#1 Adult Contemporary hit (1 week)*	A&M 1335
12/2/72+	16	9	5. Sitting *all of above produced by Paul Samwell-Smith*	A&M 1396
8/4/73	31	5	6. The Hurt	A&M 1418
4/20/74	10	11	7. **Oh Very Young**	A&M 1503
8/24/74	6	9	8. **Another Saturday Night**	A&M 1602
1/11/75	26	4	9. Ready	A&M 1645
8/16/75	33	4	10. Two Fine People	A&M 1700
7/23/77	33	3	11. (Remember The Days Of The) Old Schoolyard	A&M 1948

STEVENS, Connie

Born Concetta Ingolia on 8/8/38 in Brooklyn. Played Cricket Blake on TV's "Hawaiian Eye," 1959–63. Appeared in the movies *Eighteen And Anxious, Rockabye Baby, Parrish, Never Too Late, Grease 2, Back To The Beach* and others. Married for a time to Eddie Fisher; singer Tricia Leigh Fisher is their daughter.

DATE	POS	WKS	ARTIST–RECORD TITLE	LABEL & NO.
4/27/59	4	11	● 1. **Kookie, Kookie (Lend Me Your Comb)** [N] **EDWARD BYRNES And CONNIE STEVENS**	Warner 5047
3/14/60	3	17	2. **Sixteen Reasons** *Don Ralke (orch., above 2)*	Warner 5137

STEVENS, Dodie

Born Geraldine Ann Pasquale on 2/17/46 in Chicago; raised in California. Discovered while singing on Art Linkletter's "House Party" TV show at age 8. First recorded as Geri Pace on Gold Star in 1954.

DATE	POS	WKS	ARTIST–RECORD TITLE	LABEL & NO.
3/9/59	3	14	● 1. **Pink Shoe Laces** *Bobby Hammack (orch.)*	Crystalette 724

STEVENS, Ray

Born Ray Ragsdale on 1/24/39 in Clarkdale, Georgia. Attended Georgia State University, studied music theory and composition. First recorded for Prep Records in 1957. Production work in the mid-1960s. Numerous appearances on Andy Williams's TV show in the late '60s. Own TV show in summer of 1970. Featured on "Music Country" TV show, 1973–74. The #1 novelty recording artist of the past 35 years.

DATE	POS	WKS	ARTIST–RECORD TITLE	LABEL & NO.
9/18/61	35	1	1. Jeremiah Peabody's Poly Unsaturated Quick Dissolving Fast Acting *Pleasant Tasting Green And Purple Pills* [N]	Mercury 71843
7/14/62	5	9	2. **Ahab, The Arab** [N]	Mercury 71966
6/29/63	17	6	3. Harry The Hairy Ape [N]	Mercury 72125
8/31/68	28	3	4. Mr. Businessman	Monument 1083
4/26/69	8	10	● 5. **Gitarzan** [N]	Monument 1131
7/26/69	27	4	6. Along Came Jones [N]	Monument 1150
4/18/70	1 (2)	13	● 7. **Everything Is Beautiful** *#1 Adult Contemporary hit (3 weeks)*	Barnaby 2011
4/27/74	1 (3)	12	● 8. **The Streak** [N]	Barnaby 600
5/24/75	14	10	9. Misty *introduced by the Erroll Garner Trio in 1954*	Barnaby 614
2/5/77	40	1	10. In The Mood [N] **HENHOUSE FIVE PLUS TOO** *#1 hit for Glenn Miller in 1939*	Warner 8301

DATE	POS	WKS	ARTIST–RECORD TITLE	LABEL & NO.
			STEVENSON, B.W.	
			Born Louis Stevenson on 10/5/49 in Dallas. Died on 4/28/88 after heart surgery.	
8/25/73	**9**	12	1. **My Maria**	RCA 0030
			#1 Adult Contemporary hit (1 week); Larry Carlton (guitar)	
			STEVIE B	
			Miami-born Steven B. Hill. R&B singer/self-taught musician. In high school band with R&B artist Howard Johnson.	
4/8/89	**32**	5	1. I Wanna Be The One	LMR 74003
			Sales #26 / Airplay #37	
7/29/89	**37**	2	2. In My Eyes	LMR 74004
			Sales #34	
3/10/90	**29**	5	3. Love Me For Life	LMR 84006
			Sales #29 / Airplay #30	
7/28/90	**15**	8	4. Love & Emotion	LMR 2645
			Airplay #14 / Sales #16	
10/27/90	**1 (4)**	16	● 5. **Because I Love You (The Postman Song)**	LMR 2724
			Airplay #1(5) / Sales #1(1); #1 Adult Contemporary hit (2 weeks)	
2/23/91	**12**	9	6. I'll Be By Your Side	LMR 2758
			Airplay #11 / Sales #13	
4/1/95	**29**	12	7. Dream About You/	
			Airplay #24 / Sales #45	
		12	8. Funky Melody	Emporia/Thump 2205
			Sales flip	
			STEVIE V—see ADVENTURES OF	
			STEWART, Al	
			Born on 9/5/45 in Glasgow, Scotland. Pop-rock singer/composer/guitarist.	
1/22/77	**8**	10	1. **Year Of The Cat**	Janus 266
			written about British comedian Tony Hancock	
10/21/78	**7**	13	2. **Time Passages**	Arista 0362
			#1 Adult Contemporary hit (10 weeks)	
2/17/79	**29**	4	3. Song On The Radio	Arista 0389
			above 3 produced by Alan Parsons	
9/27/80	**24**	6	4. Midnight Rocks	Arista 0552
			STEWART, Amii	
			Born in Washington, D.C., in 1956. Disco singer/dancer/actress. Appeared in the Broadway musical *Bubbling Brown Sugar*. Her niece is singer Sinitta.	
2/24/79	**1 (1)**	14	▲ 1. **Knock On Wood**	Ariola Am. 7736
			STEWART, Billy	
			Born on 3/24/37 in Washington, D.C. Died in an auto accident on 1/17/70. R&B vocalist/composer/keyboardist. Discovered by Bo Diddley in 1956. First recorded for Chess/Argo in 1956. Did not record, 1957–62. Nicknamed "Fat Boy." First cousin of Grace Ruffin of The Jewels.	
5/1/65	**26**	4	1. I Do Love You	Chess 1922
7/10/65	**24**	5	2. Sitting In The Park	Chess 1932
8/6/66	**10**	7	3. **Summertime**	Chess 1966
			from George Gershwin's 1935 folk opera *Porgy And Bess*; #12 hit for Billie Holiday in 1936	

DATE	POS	WKS	ARTIST–RECORD TITLE	LABEL & NO.
11/5/66	29	5	4. Secret Love #1 hit for Doris Day in 1954	Chess 1978
			STEWART, David A. Born on 9/9/52 in Sunderland, England. Half of the Eurythmics duo. Multi-instrumentalist/composer/producer. Married Siobhan Fahey (Bananarama, Shakespear's Sister) on 8/1/87.	
6/8/91	11	9	1. Lily Was Here [I] **DAVID A. STEWART Introducing Candy Dulfer** (saxophonist from Amsterdam); Airplay #26 / Sales #55; from the Dutch movie *Lily Was Here* starring Marion Van Thijn	Arista 2187
			STEWART, Jermaine Chicago-bred singer. Dancer on TV's "Soul Train." Worked as backup vocalist for Shalamar and Boy George.	
6/28/86	5	13	1. **We Don't Have To Take Our Clothes Off** Sales #4 / Airplay #5	Arista 9424
4/16/88	27	5	2. Say It Again Airplay #24 / Sales #26	Arista 9636
			STEWART, John Born on 9/5/39 in San Diego. Member of The Kingston Trio, 1961–67. Wrote "Daydream Believer."	
6/2/79	5	13	1. **Gold** Stevie Nicks (backing vocal); Lindsey Buckingham (guitar)	RSO 931
9/29/79	28	5	2. Midnight Wind Stevie Nicks (backing vocal); Lindsey Buckingham (backing vocal; guitar)	RSO 1000
1/26/80	34	4	3. Lost Her In The Sun	RSO 1016
			STEWART, Rod Born Roderick Stewart on 1/10/45 in London. Worked as a folk singer in Europe in the early '60s. Recorded for English Decca, 1964. With the Hoochie Coochie Men, Steampacket and Shotgun Express. Joined Jeff Beck Group, 1967–69. With Faces, 1969–75; also recorded solo during this time. Left Faces in December 1975. Won Grammy's Living Legends Award in 1989. Married to actress Alana Hamilton, 1979–84. Married supermodel Rachel Hunter on 12/15/90. Inducted into the Rock and Roll Hall of Fame in 1994. Into his third decade as one of rock music's leading hit-makers.	
8/28/71	1 (5)	15	● 1. **Maggie May** Pete Sears (of Jefferson Starship; piano); Ron Wood (guitar)	Mercury 73224
11/27/71	24	6	2. (I Know) I'm Losing You **ROD STEWART With Faces**	Mercury 73244
9/16/72	13	7	3. You Wear It Well	Mercury 73330
12/16/72	40	1	4. Angel written by Jimi Hendrix	Mercury 73344
10/23/76	1 (8)	17	● 5. **Tonight's The Night (Gonna Be Alright)** French whispers by Rod's then-love, Swedish actress Britt Ekland	Warner 8262
2/26/77	21	9	6. The First Cut Is The Deepest written by Cat Stevens	Warner 8321
7/2/77	30	4	7. The Killing Of Georgie (Part I And II) also on the B-side of #25 below	Warner 8396
11/26/77+	4	15	● 8. **You're In My Heart (The Final Acclaim)** also on the B-side of #26 below	Warner 8475

DATE	POS	WKS	ARTIST–RECORD TITLE	LABEL & NO.
3/11/78	28	4	9. Hot Legs	Warner 8535
5/27/78	22	6	10. I Was Only Joking also on the B-side of #19 below	Warner 8568
12/23/78+	1 (4)	18	▲ 11. **Da Ya Think I'm Sexy?**	Warner 8724
5/12/79	22	6	12. Ain't Love A Bitch	Warner 8810
11/29/80+	5	17	13. **Passion**	Warner 49617
10/31/81	5	15	14. **Young Turks**	Warner 49843
2/13/82	20	8	15. Tonight I'm Yours (Don't Hurt Me)	Warner 49886
6/11/83	14	9	16. **Baby Jane**	Warner 29608
10/1/83	35	3	17. What Am I Gonna Do (I'm So In Love With You)	Warner 29564
6/2/84	6	13	18. **Infatuation** Jeff Beck (guitar solo)	Warner 29256
9/15/84	10	10	19. **Some Guys Have All The Luck** Airplay #8 / Sales #19	Warner 29215
6/14/86	6	12	20. **Love Touch** Airplay #4 / Sales #7; theme from the movie *Legal Eagles* starring Robert Redford and Debra Winger	Warner 28668
6/4/88	12	9	21. Lost In You Sales #9 / Airplay #17	Warner 27927
9/10/88	12	10	22. **Forever Young** Sales #13 / Airplay #13; Andy Taylor (guitar solo, above 2)	Warner 27796
1/28/89	4	13	23. **My Heart Can't Tell You No** Airplay #3 / Sales #5	Warner 27729
6/10/89	11	10	24. Crazy About Her Sales #10 / Airplay #13; above 4 from the album *Out Of Order*	Warner 27657
12/2/89+	3	14	25. **Downtown Train** Airplay #2 / Sales #3; #1 Adult Contemporary hit (1 week)	Warner 22685
4/7/90	10	10	26. **This Old Heart Of Mine** [R] **ROD STEWART (with Ronald Isley)** Airplay #7 / Sales #15; #1 Adult Contemporary hit (5 weeks); solo version by Stewart charted in 1976 at #83	Warner 19983
3/23/91	5	14	27. **Rhythm Of My Heart** Airplay #3 / Sales #9	Warner 19366
7/27/91	10	11	28. **The Motown Song** **ROD STEWART (with The Temptations)** Airplay #24 / Sales #36	Warner 19322
11/16/91+	20	14	29. Broken Arrow Airplay #19 / Sales #35; written by Robbie Robertson (The Band)	Warner 19274
5/15/93	5	17	● 30. **Have I Told You Lately** Sales #6 / Airplay #7; written by Van Morrison; studio version first made the Adult Contemporary charts on 11/28/92 (# 33); #1 Adult Contemporary hit (5 weeks)	Warner 18511
9/11/93	19	12	31. Reason To Believe [R] **ROD STEWART (with Ronnie Wood)** Airplay #12 / Sales #67; studio version charted in 1971 at #62	Warner 18427
12/4/93+	1 (3)	20	▲ 32. **All For Love** **BRYAN ADAMS ROD STEWART STING** Sales #1(5) / Airplay #3; from the movie *The Three Musketeers* starring Kiefer Sutherland and Charlie Sheen	A&M 0476
2/12/94	36	3	33. Having A Party **ROD STEWART (with Ronnie Wood)** Airplay #31; guitarist Wood with Jeff Beck Group, Faces and Rolling Stones; above 4 (except #32) are "live" versions from Stewart's *Unplugged...And Seated* album	Warner 18424

DATE	POS	WKS	ARTIST–RECORD TITLE	LABEL & NO.
			### STEWART, Sandy	
			Born Sandra Galitz on 7/10/37 in Philadelphia. Regular on the Eddie Fisher and Perry Como TV shows.	
1/12/63	20	5	1. My Coloring Book Don Costa (orch.)	Colpix 669
			### STEWART, Sandy—see NICKS, Stevie	
			### STIGERS, Curtis	
			Born in Boise, Idaho. Vocalist/saxophonist.	
10/5/91	9	11	1. **I Wonder Why** Airplay #28 / Sales #62	Arista 12331
			### STILLS, Stephen	
			Born on 1/3/45 in Dallas. Member of Buffalo Springfield and Crosby, Stills & Nash. Group Manassas included Chris Hillman (The Byrds), Dallas Taylor, Fuzzy Samuels, Paul Harris, Al Perkins and Joe Lala.	
12/19/70+	14	10	1. Love The One You're With Rita Coolidge, David Crosby, Graham Nash & John Sebastian (backing vocals)	Atlantic 2778
3/27/71	37	2	2. Sit Yourself Down Rita Coolidge, David Crosby, Mama Cass, Graham Nash & John Sebastian (backing vocals)	Atlantic 2790
			### STING	
			Born Gordon Sumner on 10/2/51 in Wallsend, England. Lead singer/bass guitarist of The Police. Appeared in the movies *Quadrophenia, Dune, The Bride, Plenty* and others. Married actress/producer Trudie Styler in early 1992. Nicknamed "Sting" because of a yellow and black jersey he liked to wear.	
6/15/85	3	14	1. **If You Love Somebody Set Them Free** Airplay #3 / Sales #3	A&M 2738
9/7/85	8	11	2. **Fortress Around Your Heart** Sales #7 / Airplay #7	A&M 2767
11/23/85	17	9	3. Love Is The Seventh Wave Airplay #17 / Sales #19	A&M 2787
2/1/86	16	8	4. Russians Airplay #15 / Sales #17; samples "Romance" melody from Russian composer Sergei Prokofiev's *Lieutenant Kije Suite*; above 4 from the album *The Dream Of The Blue Turtles*	A&M 2799
10/24/87	7	12	5. **We'll Be Together** Sales #6 / Airplay #8	A&M 2983
2/6/88	15	8	6. Be Still My Beating Heart Sales #14 / Airplay #15	A&M 2992
2/2/91	5	9	7. **All This Time** Sales #8 / Airplay #9; a "live, unplugged" version is on the B-side of #8 below	A&M 1541
3/20/93	17	11	8. If I Ever Lose My Faith In You Airplay #14 / Sales #67	A&M 0111
7/17/93	23	8	9. Fields Of Gold Airplay #12 / Sales #66	A&M 0258
12/4/93+	1 (3)	20	▲ 10. **All For Love** **BRYAN ADAMS ROD STEWART STING** Sales #1(5) / Airplay #3; from the movie *The Three Musketeers* starring Kiefer Sutherland and Charlie Sheen	A&M 0476

DATE	POS	WKS	ARTIST–RECORD TITLE	LABEL & NO.
12/17/94	38	1	11. When We Dance Airplay #40 / Sales #49	A&M 0846

STITES, Gary

			Born on 7/23/40 in Denver. Pop singer/songwriter/guitarist.	
5/18/59	24	5	1. Lonely For You tune arranged similar to Conway Twitty's "It's Only Make Believe"	Carlton 508

STOLOFF, Morris

			Born on 8/1/1898 in Philadelphia. Died on 4/16/80. Composer/conductor/violinist. Became musical director for Columbia Pictures in 1936. Winner of three Academy Awards.	
4/21/56	1 (3)	22	● 1. **Moonglow and Theme From "Picnic"** [I] **MORRIS STOLOFF Conducting The Columbia Pictures Orchestra** Jockey #1 / Best Seller #2 / Top 100 #2/ Juke Box #4; from the movie *Picnic* starring William Holden and Kim Novak; 4 Top 10 versions of "Moonglow" charted in 1934	Decca 29888

STONE, Cliffie, and His Orchestra

			Stone was born Clifford Snyder on 3/1/17 in Burbank, California. Bass player/orchestra/square-dance bandleader. Worked with the Anson Weeks and Freddie Slack bands in the late 1930s. Became a country DJ in the mid-1940s. Wrote many country songs.	
8/13/55	14	4	1. The Popcorn Song [N] Juke Box #14 / Best Seller #25; Bob Roubian (vocal)	Capitol 3131

STONE, Kirby, Four

			Stone was born on 4/27/18 in New York City. His quartet includes Eddie Hall, Larry Foster and Mike Gardner. Stone was musical director for various TV shows.	
7/28/58	25	1	1. Baubles, Bangles And Beads Jockey #25 end / Hot 100 #50; Jimmy Carroll (orch.); from the musical *Kismet* starring Alfred Drake; introduced by Peggy Lee in 1953	Columbia 41183

STONEBOLT

			Pop-rock quintet from Vancouver, Canada. Dave Willis, lead singer.	
9/30/78	29	5	1. I Will Still Love You	Parachute 512

STONE PONEYS—see RONSTADT, Linda

STOOKEY, Paul

			Born on 12/30/37 in Baltimore. Paul of Peter, Paul & Mary.	
9/4/71	24	9	1. Wedding Song (There Is Love)	Warner 7511

STORIES

			New York rock quartet: Ian Lloyd (lead singer, bass), Michael Brown (founding member of Left Banke; keyboards), Steve Love (guitar) and Bryan Madey (drums). Brown left group in 1973, replaced by Ken Aaronson (bass; later with Hagar, Schon, Aaronson, Shrieve) and Ken Bichel (keyboards).	
7/14/73	1 (2)	15	● 1. **Brother Louie**	Kama Sutra 577

DATE	POS	WKS	ARTIST–RECORD TITLE	LABEL & NO.
			STORM, Billy	
			Born on 6/29/38 in Dayton, Ohio. Lead singer of The Valiants.	
5/18/59	28	6	1. I've Come Of Age	Columbia 41356
			Frank DeVol (orch.); melody is from "Tchaikowsky's 5th Symphony (2nd movement)"	
			STORM, Gale	
			Born Josephine Cottle on 4/5/22 in Bloomington, Texas. Moved to Hollywood in 1939; leading lady in movies during the '40s and early '50s. Own TV series "My Little Margie," 1952–55, also "The Gale Storm Show," 1956–62.	
10/22/55	2 (3)	17	● 1. **I Hear You Knocking**	Dot 15412
			Top 100 #2 / Juke Box #2 / Best Seller #3 / Jockey #4; #2 R&B hit for Smiley Lewis in 1955	
12/24/55+	6	12	2. **Teen Age Prayer/**	
			Jockey #6 / Juke Box #6 / Top 100 #9 / Best Seller #13	
12/31/55+	5	9	3. **Memories Are Made Of This**	Dot 15436
			Jockey #5 / Top 100 #16	
3/3/56	9	14	4. **Why Do Fools Fall In Love**	Dot 15448
			Jockey #9 / Juke Box #14 / Best Seller #15 / Top 100 #15	
5/5/56	6	14	5. **Ivory Tower**	Dot 15458
			Jockey #6 / Juke Box #6 / Top 100 #10 / Best Seller #15	
4/29/57	4	18	6. **Dark Moon**	Dot 15558
			Juke Box #4 end / Top 100 #5 / Best Seller #6 / Jockey #6; Billy Vaughn (orch.)	
			STORM, The	
			Co-lead vocalists Gregg Rolie (formerly with Santana and Journey; keyboards) and Kevin Chalfant (notable songwriter), with Josh Ramos (guitar), and Journey's rhythm section of Ross Valory and Steve Smith (also with jazz fusion group Steps Ahead). Chalfant was the lead singer of 707.	
1/4/92	26	6	1. I've Got A Lot To Learn About Love	Interscope 98726
			Airplay #26	
			STRANGELOVES, The	
			Writers/producers Bob Feldman, Jerry Goldstein and Richard Gottehrer. Team wrote/produced The Angels' "My Boyfriend's Back," produced The McCoys' "Hang On Sloopy" and charted as The Sheep. Gottehrer became a partner in Sire Records and produced the Go-Go's' first two albums and Blondie's debut album.	
7/10/65	11	8	1. I Want Candy	Bang 501
10/23/65	39	1	2. Cara-Lin	Bang 508
2/5/66	30	4	3. Night Time	Bang 514
			STRAWBERRY ALARM CLOCK	
			West Coast psychedelic-rock sextet: Ed King (lead guitar), Mark Weitz (keyboards), Lee Freeman (guitar), Gary Lovetro (bass), George Bunnel (bass) and Randy Seol (drums). King joined Lynyrd Skynyrd, 1973–75. Originally known as Thee Sixpence.	
10/14/67	1 (1)	14	● 1. **Incense And Peppermints**	Uni 55018
			Greg Munford (16-year-old leader of L.A. band, the Shapes; lead vocal); originally released on All-American 373 in 1967	
1/27/68	23	6	2. Tomorrow	Uni 55046

DATE	POS	WKS	ARTIST–RECORD TITLE	LABEL & NO.
			STRAY CATS	
			Long Island, New York, rockabilly trio: Brian Setzer (born 4/10/60; lead singer, guitar), Lee Rocker (born Leon Drucher; string bass) and Slim Jim Phantom (born Jim McDonell; drums). Recorded two albums in Britain in 1981 and 1982. Group disbanded in 1984; reunited in 1988. Phantom and Rocker formed trio Phantom, Rocker & Slick in 1985. Setzer portrayed Eddie Cochran in the movie *La Bamba*. Phantom portrayed Charlie Parker's drummer in the movie *Bird*. Phantom married to actress Britt Ekland, 1984–93.	
10/23/82	9	13	1. **Rock This Town**	EMI America 8132
1/8/83	3	14	2. **Stray Cat Strut**	EMI America 8122
			originally "Bubbled Under" for 6 weeks beginning 7/17/82	
8/20/83	5	12	3. **(She's) Sexy + 17**	EMI America 8168
12/3/83	35	3	4. I Won't Stand In Your Way	EMI America 8185
			all of above written by Brian Setzer and produced by Dave Edmunds	
			STREET PEOPLE	
			Two-man, two-woman studio group, including Rupert Holmes.	
2/21/70	36	5	1. Jennifer Tomkins	Musicor 1365
			STREISAND, Barbra	
			Born Barbara Joan Streisand on 4/24/42 in Brooklyn. Made Broadway debut in *I Can Get It For You Wholesale*, 1962. Lead role in Broadway's *Funny Girl*, 1964. Movie debut in *Funny Girl* in 1968 (tied with Katharine Hepburn for Best Actress Oscar); also starred in *A Star Is Born*, *Hello Dolly*, *Funny Lady*, *The Way We Were* and many others. Produced/directed/starred in the movies *Yentl* and *Prince Of Tides*. Married to actor Elliott Gould, 1963–71.	
5/23/64	5	12	1. **People**	Columbia 42965
			from the Broadway musical *Funny Girl* starring Streisand; #1 Adult Contemporary hit (3 weeks)	
1/22/66	32	3	2. Second Hand Rose	Columbia 43469
			#3 hit in 1922 for Fanny Brice (the subject of *Funny Girl*)	
12/12/70+	6	12	3. **Stoney End**	Columbia 45236
8/28/71	40	1	4. Where You Lead	Columbia 45414
			also see #5 below for medley version	
8/12/72	37	4	5. Sweet Inspiration/Where You Lead	Columbia 45626
12/22/73+	1 (3)	17	● 6. **The Way We Were**	Columbia 45944
			title song from the movie starring Streisand and Robert Redford; #1 Adult Contemporary hit (2 weeks)	
1/8/77	1 (3)	18	● 7. **Love Theme From "A Star Is Born" (Evergreen)**	Columbia 10450
			from the movie *A Star Is Born* starring Streisand and Kris Kristofferson; #1 Adult Contemporary hit (6 weeks)	
5/28/77	4	14	8. **My Heart Belongs To Me**	Columbia 10555
			#1 Adult Contemporary hit (4 weeks)	
7/1/78	25	5	9. Songbird	Columbia 10756
			#1 Adult Contemporary hit (2 weeks)	
8/26/78	21	6	10. Love Theme From "Eyes Of Laura Mars" (Prisoner)	Columbia 10777
			from the movie *Eyes of Laura Mars* starring Faye Dunaway	
11/4/78	1 (2)	15	● 11. **You Don't Bring Me Flowers**	Columbia 10840
			BARBRA & NEIL (Diamond)	
7/7/79	3	13	● 12. **The Main Event/Fight**	Columbia 11008
			from the movie *The Main Event* starring Streisand and Ryan O'Neal	
10/27/79	1 (2)	13	● 13. **No More Tears (Enough Is Enough)**	Columbia 11125
			BARBRA STREISAND/DONNA SUMMER 12" single available on Casablanca 20199	

DATE	POS	WKS	ARTIST–RECORD TITLE	LABEL & NO.
2/23/80	37	3	14. Kiss Me In The Rain	Columbia 11179
9/13/80	1 (3)	19	● 15. **Woman In Love** #1 Adult Contemporary hit (5 weeks)	Columbia 11364
11/15/80+	3	15	● 16. **Guilty** **BARBRA STREISAND & BARRY GIBB**	Columbia 11390
2/14/81	10	10	17. **What Kind Of Fool** **BARBRA STREISAND & BARRY GIBB** #1 Adult Contemporary hit (4 weeks); above 3 written and produced by Barry Gibb (Bee Gees)	Columbia 11430
11/28/81+	11	11	18. Comin' In And Out Of Your Life	Columbia 02621
12/10/83	40	2	19. The Way He Makes Me Feel from the movie *Yentl* starring Streisand; #1 Adult Contemporary hit (2 weeks)	Columbia 04177
11/12/88	25	5	20. Till I Loved You **BARBRA STREISAND AND DON JOHNSON** Sales #22 / Airplay #32; love theme from the Broadway musical *Goya*	Columbia 08062

STRING-A-LONGS, The

Instrumental quintet: Keith McCormack, Aubrey Lee de Cordova, Richard Stephens and Jimmy Torres (guitars) and Don Allen (drums).

DATE	POS	WKS	ARTIST–RECORD TITLE	LABEL & NO.
1/23/61	3	13	1. **Wheels** [I]	Warwick 603
4/17/61	35	2	2. Brass Buttons [I]	Warwick 625

STRONG, Barrett

Born on 2/5/41 in Mississippi. R&B singer/songwriter. Wrote many of The Temptations' hits with Norman Whitfield, including "Just My Imagination," "Papa Was A Rollin' Stone" and "Ball Of Confusion."

DATE	POS	WKS	ARTIST–RECORD TITLE	LABEL & NO.
3/21/60	23	8	1. Money (That's what I want) also released on Tamla 54027 and 54029 in 1960	Anna 1111

STRUNK, Jud

Born Justin Strunk, Jr., on 6/11/36 in Jamestown, New York; raised in Farmington, Maine. Killed in a plane crash on 10/15/81. Regular on TV's "Laugh In."

DATE	POS	WKS	ARTIST–RECORD TITLE	LABEL & NO.
3/24/73	14	10	1. Daisy A Day Mike Curb Congregation (backing vocals)	MGM 14463

STRYPER

Christian heavy-metal band from Orange County, California: brothers Michael (vocals) and Robert (drums) Sweet, with Oz Fox (guitar) and Tim Gaines (bass). Michael left in mid-1992.

DATE	POS	WKS	ARTIST–RECORD TITLE	LABEL & NO.
12/26/87+	23	8	1. Honestly Sales #22 / Airplay #23	Enigma 75009

STYLE COUNCIL, The

English duo: Paul Weller (ex-vocalist of The Jam) and Mick Talbot (keyboards). Expanded to a trio in 1988 with the addition of female vocalist Dee C. Lee.

DATE	POS	WKS	ARTIST–RECORD TITLE	LABEL & NO.
5/12/84	29	6	1. My Ever Changing Moods	Geffen 29359

DATE	POS	WKS	ARTIST–RECORD TITLE	LABEL & NO.
			STYLISTICS, The	
			Soul group from Philadelphia formed in 1968. Consisted of Russell Thompkins, Jr. (born 3/21/51; lead), Airrion Love, James Smith, James Dunn and Herbie Murrell. Thompkins, Love and Smith sang with the Percussions; Murrell and Dunn with the Monarchs, 1965–68. First recorded for Sebring in 1969.	
7/17/71	39	1	1. Stop, Look, Listen (To Your Heart)	Avco Emb. 4572
11/27/71+	9	13	● 2. **You Are Everything**	Avco 4581
3/11/72	3	14	● 3. **Betcha By Golly, Wow**	Avco 4591
			THE STYLISTICS featuring RUSSELL THOMPKINS, JR.	
7/1/72	25	6	4. People Make The World Go Round	Avco 4595
			all of above from the album *The Stylistics* (Avco 33023)	
11/11/72	10	8	● 5. **I'm Stone In Love With You**	Avco 4603
3/3/73	5	9	● 6. **Break Up To Make Up**	Avco 4611
6/9/73	23	5	7. You'll Never Get To Heaven (If You Break My Heart)	Avco 4618
11/17/73	14	11	8. Rockin' Roll Baby	Avco 4625
4/13/74	2 (2)	14	● 9. **You Make Me Feel Brand New**	Avco 4634
			all of above produced by Thom Bell	
8/17/74	18	7	10. Let's Put It All Together	Avco 4640
			STYX	
			Chicago-based rock quintet: Dennis DeYoung (vocals, keyboards), Tommy Shaw (lead guitar), James Young (guitar), and twin brothers John (drums) and Chuck (bass) Panozzo. Band earlier known as TW4. Shaw replaced John Curulewski in 1976. Most songs written by Dennis DeYoung and/or Tommy Shaw. Band broke up when DeYoung and Shaw went solo in 1984. Reunited in 1990 with guitarist Glen Burtnick replacing Shaw, who joined Damn Yankees. In Greek mythology, Styx is a river of Hades.	
1/18/75	6	11	1. **Lady**	Wooden N. 10102
3/27/76	27	5	2. Lorelei	A&M 1786
12/18/76	36	3	3. Mademoiselle	A&M 1877
10/29/77+	8	15	4. **Come Sail Away**	A&M 1977
4/1/78	29	4	5. Fooling Yourself (The Angry Young Man)	A&M 2007
10/21/78	21	7	6. Blue Collar Man (Long Nights)	A&M 2087
4/7/79	16	13	7. Renegade	A&M 2110
10/20/79	1 (2)	14	● 8. **Babe**	A&M 2188
1/19/80	26	5	9. Why Me	A&M 2206
1/24/81	3	15	10. **The Best Of Times**	A&M 2300
3/28/81	9	13	11. **Too Much Time On My Hands**	A&M 2323
2/12/83	3	16	● 12. **Mr. Roboto**	A&M 2525
4/30/83	6	13	13. **Don't Let It End**	A&M 2543
6/2/84	40	2	14. Music Time	A&M 2625
1/26/91	3	12	15. **Show Me The Way**	A&M 1536
			Sales #5 / Airplay #6	
5/18/91	25	6	16. Love At First Sight	A&M 1548
			Airplay #25	
			SUAVE	
			Born on 2/22/66 in Los Angeles. Son of Waymond Anderson, Sr. (member of GQ).	
4/23/88	20	7	1. My Girl	Capitol 44124
			Sales #16 / Airplay #25	

DATE	POS	WKS	ARTIST–RECORD TITLE	LABEL & NO.
			SUBWAY	
			Teen vocal quartet from Chicago: Eric McNeal, Roy Jones, Keith Thomas and Trerail Puckett.	
2/18/95	**15**	14	● 1. This Lil' Game We Play **SUBWAY featuring 702** Sales #7 / Airplay #25	Biv 10 0252
			SUGARHILL GANG	
			Harlem, New York, rap trio: Michael "Wonder Mike" Wright, Guy "Master Gee" O'Brien and Henry "Big Bank Hank" Jackson. The first commercially successful rap group.	
1/5/80	**36**	2	1. Rapper's Delight the first "rap" record to make the *Hot 100*; rhythm track taken from Chic's "Good Times"; first issued commercially only as a 12" single	Sugar Hill 542
			SUGARLOAF	
			Rock quartet from Denver: Jerry Corbetta (lead singer, keyboards), Bob Webber (guitar), Bob Raymond (bass) and Bob MacVittie (drums). Robert Yeazel (guitar, vocals) joined in 1971. By 1974, Myron Pollock replaced MacVittie, and Yeazel had left.	
9/19/70	**3**	12	1. **Green-Eyed Lady**	Liberty 56183
2/1/75	**9**	11	2. **Don't Call Us, We'll Call You** **SUGARLOAF/JERRY CORBETTA** features brief snippet of The Beatles' "I Feel Fine"	Claridge 402
			SUMMER, Donna	
			Born Adrian Donna Gaines on 12/31/48 in Boston. With group Crow, played local clubs. Appeared in the German production of *Hair*, European productions of *Godspell*, *The Me Nobody Knows* and *Porgy And Bess*. Settled in Germany, where she recorded "Love To Love You Baby." Appeared in the 1978 movie *Thank God It's Friday*. Married Bruce Sudano (Alive & Kicking and Brooklyn Dreams) in 1980. Dubbed "The Queen of Disco."	
12/20/75+	**2** (2)	14	● 1. **Love To Love You Baby**	Oasis 401
9/3/77	**6**	14	● 2. **I Feel Love**	Casablanca 884
1/28/78	**37**	3	3. **I Love You**	Casablanca 907
6/3/78	**3**	14	● 4. **Last Dance** from the movie *Thank God It's Friday* starring Jeff Goldblum and Debra Winger	Casablanca 926
9/30/78	**1** (3)	15	● 5. **MacArthur Park**	Casablanca 939
1/20/79	**4**	14	● 6. **Heaven Knows** **DONNA SUMMER with Brooklyn Dreams**	Casablanca 959
4/28/79	**1** (3)	17	▲ 7. **Hot Stuff** Jeff "Skunk" Baxter of The Doobie Brothers (guitar solo)	Casablanca 978
6/9/79	**1** (5)	15	▲ 8. **Bad Girls** #1 R&B hit (1 week)	Casablanca 988
9/15/79	**2** (2)	14	● 9. **Dim All The Lights**	Casablanca 2201
10/27/79	**1** (2)	13	● 10. **No More Tears (Enough Is Enough)** **BARBRA STREISAND/DONNA SUMMER** 12" single available on Casablanca 20199	Columbia 11125
1/26/80	**5**	12	● 11. **On The Radio**	Casablanca 2236
9/27/80	**3**	13	● 12. **The Wanderer**	Geffen 49563
10/11/80	**36**	3	13. **Walk Away** above 7 (except #10–12) from the album *Bad Girls*	Casablanca 2300
1/10/81	**33**	3	14. Cold Love	Geffen 49634

DATE	POS	WKS	ARTIST–RECORD TITLE	LABEL & NO.
3/28/81	40	2	15. Who Do You Think You're Foolin' all of above (except #10) produced by Giorgio Moroder and Pete Bellotte	Geffen 49664
7/17/82	10	11	16. **Love Is In Control (Finger On The Trigger)**	Geffen 29982
2/5/83	33	6	17. The Woman In Me	Geffen 29805
6/18/83	3	17	18. **She Works Hard For The Money** #1 R&B hit (3 weeks)	Mercury 812370
9/1/84	21	8	19. There Goes My Baby Airplay #27 pre	Geffen 29291
5/20/89	7	10	● 20. **This Time I Know It's For Real** Sales #4 / Airplay #8	Atlantic 88899

SUMMER, Henry Lee

Rock singer from Brazil, Indiana. Received full college basketball scholarship.

DATE	POS	WKS	ARTIST–RECORD TITLE	LABEL & NO.
4/2/88	20	7	1. I Wish I Had A Girl Sales #17 / Airplay #24	CBS Assoc. 07720
7/1/89	18	8	2. Hey Baby Airplay #15 / Sales #18	CBS Assoc. 68891

SUNNY & THE SUNGLOWS

Group from San Antonio, Texas, formed in 1959 and led by Sunny Ozuna, with Jesse, Oscar and Ray Villanueva, Tony Tostado, Gilbert Fernandez and Alfred Luna.

DATE	POS	WKS	ARTIST–RECORD TITLE	LABEL & NO.
9/28/63	11	9	1. Talk To Me originally released on Sunglow in 1963 as by The Sunglows	Tear Drop 3014

SUNNYSIDERS, The

Vocal/instrumental group: Freddy Morgan (banjo; died 1970), Jad Paul and Margie Rayburn (who later recorded solo). Morgan was a member of Spike Jones & The City Slickers, 1947-58.

DATE	POS	WKS	ARTIST–RECORD TITLE	LABEL & NO.
5/21/55	12	10	1. Hey, Mr. Banjo Juke Box #12 / Jockey #19 / Best Seller #20	Kapp 113

SUNSCREEM

British techno-pop quintet: Lucia Holm (vocals), Darren Woodford (guitar), Paul Carnell (keyboards), Rob Fricker (bass) and Sean Wright (drums).

DATE	POS	WKS	ARTIST–RECORD TITLE	LABEL & NO.
4/10/93	36	5	1. Love U More Airplay #28	Columbia 74769

SUNSHINE COMPANY, The

Southern California pop quintet featuring lead singer Mary Nance.

DATE	POS	WKS	ARTIST–RECORD TITLE	LABEL & NO.
11/18/67	36	3	1. Back On The Street Again	Imperial 66260

SUPERCAT—see KRIS KROSS

SUPERTRAMP

British rock quintet: Roger Hodgson (vocals, guitar), Rick Davies (vocals, keyboards), John Helliwell (sax), Dougie Thomson (bass) and Bob Siebenberg (drums). Hodgson went solo in 1983.

DATE	POS	WKS	ARTIST–RECORD TITLE	LABEL & NO.
5/17/75	35	2	1. Bloody Well Right	A&M 1660
7/2/77	15	11	2. Give A Little Bit	A&M 1938
4/28/79	6	13	3. **The Logical Song**	A&M 2128

DATE	POS	WKS	ARTIST–RECORD TITLE	LABEL & NO.
8/4/79	**15**	8	4. Goodbye Stranger	A&M 2162
11/3/79	**10**	11	5. **Take The Long Way Home**	A&M 2193
10/4/80	**15**	8	6. Dreamer	A&M 2269
			recorded "live" at the Paris Pavillon on 11/29/79; original studio version is on the B-side of #1 above	
10/30/82	**11**	11	7. It's Raining Again	A&M 2502
2/26/83	**31**	5	8. My Kind Of Lady	A&M 2517
6/8/85	**28**	7	9. Cannonball	A&M 2731
			Sales #25	

SUPREMES, The

R&B vocal group from Detroit, formed as the Primettes in 1959. Consisted of lead singer Diana Ross (born 3/26/44), Mary Wilson (born 3/6/44), Florence Ballard (born 6/30/43; died 2/22/76 of cardiac arrest) and Barbara Martin. Recorded for LuPine in 1960. Signed to Motown's Tamla label in 1960. Changed name to The Supremes in 1961; Martin left shortly thereafter. Worked as backing vocalists for Motown until 1964. Backed Marvin Gaye on "Can I Get A Witness." Ballard discharged from group in 1967; replaced by Cindy Birdsong, formerly with Patti LaBelle's Blue Belles. Ross left in 1969 for solo career, replaced by Jean Terrell. Birdsong left in 1972, replaced by Lynda Lawrence. Terrell and Lawrence left in 1973. Mary Wilson re-formed group with Scherrie Payne (sister of Freda Payne) and Cindy Birdsong. Birdsong left again in 1976, replaced by Susaye Greene. In 1978, Wilson toured England with Karen Ragland and Karen Jackson, but lost rights to the name "Supremes" thereafter. Inducted into the Rock and Roll Hall of Fame in 1988.

DATE	POS	WKS	ARTIST–RECORD TITLE	LABEL & NO.
12/28/63+	**23**	7	1. When The Lovelight Starts Shining Through His Eyes	Motown 1051
7/18/64	**1 (2)**	13	2. **Where Did Our Love Go**	Motown 1060
10/10/64	**1 (4)**	12	3. **Baby Love**	Motown 1066
11/21/64	**1 (2)**	13	4. **Come See About Me**	Motown 1068
			above 4 from the album *Where Did Our Love Go*	
3/6/65	**1 (2)**	10	5. **Stop! In The Name Of Love**	Motown 1074
5/8/65	**1 (1)**	10	6. **Back In My Arms Again**	Motown 1075
			#1 R&B hit (1 week)	
8/14/65	**11**	7	7. Nothing But Heartaches	Motown 1080
10/30/65	**1 (2)**	10	8. **I Hear A Symphony**	Motown 1083
1/29/66	**5**	8	9. **My World Is Empty Without You**	Motown 1089
5/7/66	**9**	7	10. **Love Is Like An Itching In My Heart**	Motown 1094
8/20/66	**1 (2)**	11	11. **You Can't Hurry Love**	Motown 1097
			#1 R&B hit (2 weeks)	
11/5/66	**1 (2)**	10	12. **You Keep Me Hangin' On**	Motown 1101
			#1 R&B hit (4 weeks)	
2/4/67	**1 (1)**	10	13. **Love Is Here And Now You're Gone**	Motown 1103
			#1 R&B hit (2 weeks)	
4/15/67	**1 (1)**	10	14. **The Happening**	Motown 1107
			title song from the movie starring Anthony Quinn	

DIANA ROSS AND THE SUPREMES:

DATE	POS	WKS	ARTIST–RECORD TITLE	LABEL & NO.
8/19/67	**2 (2)**	10	15. **Reflections**	Motown 1111
11/25/67	**9**	6	16. **In And Out Of Love**	Motown 1116
4/6/68	**28**	5	17. Forever Came Today	Motown 1122
			all of above written by Eddie Holland, Lamont Dozier and Brian Holland	
7/6/68	**30**	3	18. Some Things You Never Get Used To	Motown 1126
10/26/68	**1 (2)**	15	19. **Love Child**	Motown 1135

DATE	POS	WKS	ARTIST–RECORD TITLE	LABEL & NO.
12/14/68+	2 (2)	12	20. **I'm Gonna Make You Love Me** **DIANA ROSS AND THE SUPREMES & THE TEMPTATIONS**	Motown 1137
2/1/69	10	7	21. **I'm Livin' In Shame** some pressings show title as: "I'm Living In Shame"	Motown 1139
3/22/69	25	6	22. I'll Try Something New **DIANA ROSS AND THE SUPREMES & THE TEMPTATIONS**	Motown 1142
4/26/69	27	5	23. The Composer	Motown 1146
6/14/69	31	4	24. No Matter What Sign You Are	Motown 1148
11/15/69	1 (1)	15	25. **Someday We'll Be Together** #1 R&B hit (4 weeks)	Motown 1156
			THE SUPREMES:	
3/14/70	10	10	26. **Up The Ladder To The Roof**	Motown 1162
8/1/70	21	8	27. Everybody's Got The Right To Love	Motown 1167
11/21/70	7	12	28. **Stoned Love** #1 R&B hit (1 week)	Motown 1172
12/12/70+	14	8	29. River Deep—Mountain High **THE SUPREMES & FOUR TOPS**	Motown 1173
5/22/71	16	8	30. Nathan Jones	Motown 1182
1/29/72	16	9	31. Floy Joy	Motown 1195
6/3/72	37	3	32. Automatically Sunshine	Motown 1200
8/7/76	40	1	33. I'm Gonna Let My Heart Do The Walking	Motown 1391
			SURFACE	
			Soul trio from New Jersey: Bernard Jackson (lead singer), David Townsend (son of producer/songwriter Ed Townsend) and Dave Conley (former horn player with Mandrill).	
6/20/87	20	8	1. Happy Airplay #19 / Sales #21	Columbia 06611
7/29/89	5	11	● 2. **Shower Me With Your Love** Sales #5 / Airplay #6; #1 R&B hit (1 week)	Columbia 68746
11/24/90+	1 (2)	18	● 3. **The First Time** Airplay #1(2) / Sales #2; #1 Adult Contemporary hit (2 weeks); #1 R&B hit (1 week)	Columbia 73502
6/1/91	17	8	4. Never Gonna Let You Down Airplay #28 / Sales #47	Columbia 73643
			SURFARIS, The	
			Teenage surf band from Glendora, California: Ron Wilson (drummer; died of an aneurysm, May 1989), Jim Fuller (lead guitar), Bob Berryhill (rhythm guitar), Pat Connolly (bass) and Jim Pash (sax, clarinet).	
7/6/63	2 (1)	10	1. **Wipe Out** [I] originally released on DFS 12 and then on Princess 50 in 1963	Dot 16479
8/27/66	16	11	2. Wipe Out [I-R] same version as #1 above	Dot 144
			SURVIVOR	
			Rock group formed in Chicago in 1978: Dave Bickler (vocals), Frankie Sullivan (guitar), Jim Peterik (keyboards; former lead singer of Ides Of March), Stephan Ellis (bass) and Marc Droubay (drums). Bickler replaced by Jimi Jamison in early 1984. Droubay and Ellis left in early 1988.	
11/21/81	33	4	1. Poor Man's Son	Scotti Br. 02560

DATE	POS	WKS	ARTIST–RECORD TITLE	LABEL & NO.
6/26/82	1 (6)	18	▲² 2. **Eye Of The Tiger** from the movie *Rocky III* starring Sylvester Stallone	Scotti Br. 02912
10/16/82	17	7	3. American Heartbeat	Scotti Br. 03213
10/20/84	13	13	4. I Can't Hold Back Airplay #11 / Sales #15	Scotti Br. 04603
2/9/85	8	11	5. **High On You** Airplay #8 / Sales #13	Scotti Br. 04685
5/11/85	4	14	6. **The Search Is Over** Airplay #4 / Sales #6; #1 Adult Contemporary hit (4 weeks)	Scotti Br. 04871
11/23/85+	2 (2)	16	7. **Burning Heart** Sales #1(1) / Airplay #2; from the movie *Rocky IV* starring Sylvester Stallone	Scotti Br. 05663
11/15/86+	9	13	8. **Is This Love** Airplay #8 / Sales #8	Scotti Br. 06381
			SWAN, Billy	
			Born on 5/12/42 in Cape Girardeau, Missouri. Singer/songwriter/keyboardist/guitarist. Wrote "Lover Please" for Clyde McPhatter. Produced Tony Joe White's first three albums. Toured with Kris Kristofferson from the early '70s. Formed band Black Tie with Randy Meisner in 1986.	
10/26/74	1 (2)	12	● 1. **I Can Help** #1 Country hit (2 weeks)	Monument 8621
			SWANN, Bettye	
			Born Betty Jean Champion on 10/24/44 in Shreveport, Louisiana. Moved to Los Angeles in the late '50s. In vocal group the Fawns, recorded for Money in 1964.	
7/1/67	21	7	1. Make Me Yours #1 R&B hit (2 weeks)	Money 126
4/19/69	38	2	2. Don't Touch Me	Capitol 2382
			SWAYZE, Patrick (featuring Wendy Fraser)	
			Movie actor Swayze was born on 8/18/52 in Houston, Texas. Starred in *Red Dawn, Dirty Dancing, Road House, Ghost* and others.	
1/16/88	3	13	1. **She's Like The Wind** Airplay #2 / Sales #2; from the movie *Dirty Dancing* starring Swayze; #1 Adult Contemporary hit (2 weeks); B-side is Maurice Williams & The Zodiacs' 1960 #1 hit "Stay"	RCA 5363
			SWEAT, Keith	
			Born and raised in Harlem. Soul singer/songwriter. Worked as a commodities broker on Wall Street.	
2/6/88	5	13	● 1. **I Want Her** Sales #5 / Airplay #5; #1 R&B hit (3 weeks); a different mix is on the B-side of #3 below	Vintertn. 69431
6/30/90	14	12	● 2. Make You Sweat Sales #10 / Airplay #14; #1 R&B hit (1 week)	Vintertn. 64961
12/22/90+	7	12	3. **I'll Give All My Love To You** Sales #4 / Airplay #12; #1 R&B hit (1 week)	Vintertn. 64915
1/4/92	17	10	4. Keep It Comin' Airplay #15 / Sales #45; co-written by the members of Joe Public; #1 R&B hit (2 weeks)	Elektra 64812

DATE	POS	WKS	ARTIST–RECORD TITLE	LABEL & NO.
			SWEATHOG	
			Rock quartet: Lenny Lee Goldsmith (guitar), Robert "B.J." Morris (guitar), Dave Johnson (bass) and Barry Eugene "Frosty" Frost (drums).	
12/11/71	33	4	1. Hallelujah	Columbia 45492
			SWEET	
			English rock band: Brian Connolly (lead singer), Steve Priest (bass, vocals), Andy Scott (guitar, keyboards) and Mick Tucker (drums).	
3/17/73	3	15	● 1. **Little Willy**	Bell 45251
8/2/75	5	14	2. **Ballroom Blitz**	Capitol 4055
11/22/75+	5	11	● 3. **Fox On The Run**	Capitol 4157
3/6/76	20	7	4. Action	Capitol 4220
4/15/78	8	14	5. **Love Is Like Oxygen**	Capitol 4549
			SWEET, Rachel—see SMITH, Rex	
			SWEET INSPIRATIONS, The	
			R&B vocal quartet: Cissy Houston, Estelle Brown, Sylvia Shemwell and Myrna Smith. Spent nearly six years as studio group, primarily for Atlantic. Work included backing Aretha Franklin and Elvis Presley. Cissy, mother of Whitney Houston, recorded solo in 1970.	
3/30/68	18	10	1. Sweet Inspiration	Atlantic 2476
			SWEET SENSATION	
			Eight-member soul group from Manchester, England, led by Marcel King (vocals), with additional vocals by St. Clair Palmer, Vincent James and Junior Daye.	
2/15/75	14	8	1. Sad Sweet Dreamer	Pye 71002
			SWEET SENSATION	
			Female trio from New York City: Betty LeBron, and sisters Margie and Mari Fernandez. Mari replaced in 1989 by Sheila Bega.	
3/25/89	14	8	1. Sincerely Yours Sales #9 / Airplay #21; featuring a short rap break by Romeo J.D.	Atco 99246
7/15/89	23	7	2. Hooked On You [R] Sales #16 / Airplay #25; remix of group's 1987 hit (#64)	Atco 99210
3/31/90	13	10	3. Love Child Airplay #13 / Sales #16	Atco 98983
7/7/90	1 (1)	13	4. **If Wishes Came True** Airplay #2 / Sales #5	Atco 98953
			SWINGING BLUE JEANS, The	
			Rock quartet from Liverpool, England: Ray Ennis and Ralph Ellis (guitars), Norman Kuhlke (drums) and Les Braid (bass).	
3/28/64	24	5	1. Hippy Hippy Shake	Imperial 66021
			SWINGIN' MEDALLIONS	
			Eight-man rock and roll band from Greenwood, South Carolina, led by John McElrath.	
6/4/66	17	6	1. Double Shot (Of My Baby's Love) originally released on 4 Sale 6230 in 1965	Smash 2033

DATE	POS	WKS	ARTIST–RECORD TITLE	LABEL & NO.
			SWING OUT SISTER	
			British jazz-pop trio: Corinne Drewery (vocals), Andy Connell and Martin Jackson. Drewery was a fashion designer. Reduced to a duo in 1989 with departure of Jackson.	
9/26/87	6	11	1. **Breakout** Sales #4 / Airplay #5; #1 Adult Contemporary hit (2 weeks)	Mercury 888016
2/20/88	31	3	2. Twilight World Sales #23	Mercury 888484
			SWITCH	
			Soul-funk sextet from Mansfield, Ohio: Bobby DeBarge, Phillip Ingram (lead vocals), Greg Williams, Tommy DeBarge, Eddie Fluellen and Jody Sims. Discovered by Jermaine Jackson. DeBarge brothers were later in family group DeBarge. Bobby DeBarge died of AIDS on 8/16/95 (age 36).	
12/2/78	36	3	1. There'll Never Be	Gordy 7159
			SWV (Sisters With Voices)	
			New York female vocal trio: Cheryl "Coko" Gamble, Tamara "Taj" Johnson and Leanne "Lelee" Lyons.	
3/6/93	6	21	● 1. **I'm So Into You** Sales #5 / Airplay #6	RCA 62451
5/8/93	1 (2)	22	▲ 2. **Weak** Airplay #2 / Sales #2; #1 R&B hit (2 weeks)	RCA 62521
7/31/93	2 (3)	19	● 3. **Right Here/Human Nature/** [R] Sales #4 / Airplay #5; new mix of "Right Here" (#92 in 1993) with excerpts from Michael Jackson's "Human Nature"; #1 R&B hit (7 weeks)	
		19	4. Downtown Airplay #36	RCA 62614
4/23/94	18	15	5. Anything Airplay #16 / Sales #19; from the movie *Above The Rim* starring Tupac Shakur (2 Pac) and Duane Martin; samples the song "Get Up And Dance"	RCA 62834
			SYBIL	
			Sybil Lynch from Paterson, New Jersey.	
11/4/89	20	9	● 1. Don't Make Me Over Sales #23 / Sales #24	Next Plat. 325
			SYLVERS, Foster	
			Born on 2/25/62 in Memphis. Youngest member of The Sylvers family group. Production work on Janet Jackson's first album.	
6/30/73	22	8	1. Misdemeanor first released on Pride 1031 in 1973	MGM 14580
			SYLVERS, The	
			Memphis family of 10 brothers and sisters: Olympia-Ann, Leon, Charmaine, James, Edmund, Ricky, Angelia, Pat, Jonathon and Foster Sylvers. Leon formed the group Dynasty in 1979.	
3/13/76	1 (1)	15	● 1. **Boogie Fever** #1 R&B hit (1 week)	Capitol 4179
11/13/76+	5	17	● 2. **Hot Line**	Capitol 4336
5/21/77	17	10	3. High School Dance	Capitol 4405

DATE	POS	WKS	ARTIST–RECORD TITLE	LABEL & NO.
			SYLVESTER	
			Born Sylvester James on 9/6/47 in Los Angeles. Died on 12/16/88 of AIDS-related complications. Moved to San Francisco in 1967. With vocal group the Cockettes. Appeared in the movie *The Rose*. Backing vocals by Martha Wash, Izora Rhodes (later known as Two Tons O' Fun and The Weather Girls) and Jeanie Tracy.	
9/30/78	**19**	10	1. Dance (Disco Heat)	Fantasy 827
2/17/79	**36**	3	2. You Make Me Feel (Mighty Real)	Fantasy 846
			above 2 released together on a 12" single (Fantasy 102)	
5/5/79	**40**	2	3. I (Who Have Nothing)	Fantasy 855
			all of above produced by Harvey Fuqua	
			SYLVIA	
			Born Sylvia Vanderpool on 5/6/36 in New York City. Singer/songwriter/producer. First recorded with Hot Lips Page for Columbia in 1950, as Little Sylvia. Half of Mickey & Sylvia duo. Married Joe Robinson, owner of All-Platinum/Vibration Records (later known as Sugar Hill). Their son Joey was leader of West Street Mob.	
4/21/73	**3**	13	● 1. **Pillow Talk**	Vibration 521
			#1 R&B hit (2 weeks)	
			SYLVIA	
			Born Sylvia Kirby on 12/9/56 in Kokomo, Indiana. Country singer. Moved to Nashville in 1975. Worked as a secretary for producer Tom Collins. Solo debut in 1979.	
10/9/82	**15**	9	● 1. Nobody	RCA 13223
			#1 Country hit (1 week)	
			SYMS, Sylvia	
			Born on 12/2/17 in Brooklyn. Collapsed onstage during a Manhattan performance on 5/10/92 and died of a heart attack. Dubbed the "world's greatest saloon singer" by Frank Sinatra. Discovered by actress Mae West in 1948. Star of several musical comedies.	
6/16/56	**20**	2	1. I Could Have Danced All Night	Decca 29903
			Jockey #20 / Top 100 #35; from the Broadway musical My Fair Lady starring Julie Andrews and Rex Harrison	
9/1/56	**21**	3	2. English Muffins And Irish Stew	Decca 29969
			Jockey #21 / Top 100 #51; Jack Pleis (orch., above 2)	
			SYNCH	
			Pop-rock sextet from Wilkes-Barre, Pennsylvania. Jimmy Harnen, lead singer.	
4/22/89	**10**	11	1. **Where Are You Now?** [R]	WTG 68625
			JIMMY HARNEN W/SYNCH	
			Sales #9 / Airplay #12; originally charted on 3/1/86 at #77	
			SYNDICATE OF SOUND	
			San Jose garage-rock quintet: Don Baskin (lead singer), Jim Sawyers (guitar), Bob Gonzalez (bass), John Sharkey (rhythm guitar) and John Duckworth (drums).	
6/25/66	**8**	6	1. **Little Girl**	Bell 640
			first released on Hush 228 in 1966	
			SYREETA—see PRESTON, Billy	

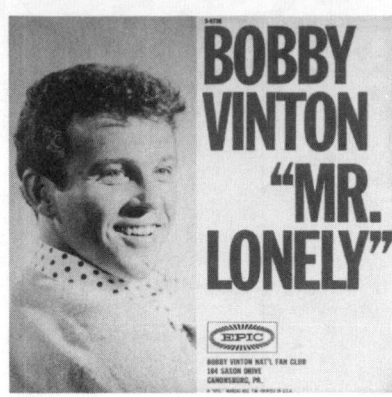

Bobby Vinton's final No. 1 hit was 1964's "Mr. Lonely," his fourth since 1962's "Roses Are Red (My Love)." The hitmaker, who later took a left turn and made a career change to a polka artist, scored his final Top 40 hit with 1975's "Beer Barrel Polka."

Vixen's hard-rocking style led many critics to call them a "female hair band" in the late '80s. The major difference between their No. 22 hit "Cryin'" and Roy Orbison's 1961 classic "Crying" was therefore deemed little more than a simple apostrophe.

Jr. Walker And The All Stars' first Top 10 single took off like a bullet in 1965. What else to expect from a tune called "Shotgun"?

Mary Wells, one of Motown's first and most widely admired signings, was the label's first artist to score a No. 1 single. No, it wasn't 1962's "You Beat Me To The Punch"; it was 1964's "My Guy." Both tracks were penned by Smokey Robinson.

Whitesnake's studied combination of glamour-boy looks and British hard rock sensibility brought the long-lived quintet four Top 40 singles between 1987 and 1990. Their last, "The Deeper The Love," reached No. 28 in 1990.

Roger Williams's all-time biggest record was his 1955 rendition of "Autumn Leaves," which topped the charts for four weeks in 1955. Eleven years later, he reached the Top 10 again with his "Born Free" instrumental.

Vanessa Williams's scandolous appearance in *Penthouse* apparently had little effect upon her singing career; "Save The Best For Last" topped the Hot 100 in 1992.

Wilson Phillips' third No. 1 single, 1991's "You're In Love," gave many the impression that the group would be a recording powerhouse. But within two years the trio "temporarily" disbanded. Singer Carnie Wilson would later begin a brief career as a talk-show host.

Little Stevie Wonder's first-ever single, 1962's "(I Call It Pretty Music, But...) The Old People Call It The Blues," failed to chart at all, but three singles later, his "Fingertips—Pt. 2" soared to No. 1 for three weeks.

"Weird Al" Yankovic's regular parodies of other artist's hits—such as Nirvana's 1991 track "Smells Like Teen Spirit"—were predictable but highly humorous, and always well received. In early '96, Yankovic took on a well-known Coolio hit and produced "Amish Paradise."

Kathy Young's "Happy Birthday Blues," which peaked at No. 30 in 1961, couldn't match her powerful pop hit "A Thousand Stars," an oldie still getting airplay in the '90s.

Zhane realized the implicit peril in taking on a moniker that might be difficult to verbalize, so, to the delight of DJs everywhere, the Philly-based duo named their 1994 gold debut album *Pronounced Jah-Nay*.

DATE	POS	WKS	ARTIST–RECORD TITLE	LABEL & NO.
			SYSTEM, The	
			New York City-based techno-funk duo: Mic Murphy (born Raleigh, North Carolina; vocals, guitar) and David Frank (born Dayton, Ohio; synthesizer).	
5/16/87	4	13	1. **Don't Disturb This Groove**	Atlantic 89320
			Sales #4 / Airplay #4; #1 R&B hit (1 week)	
			T	
			TACO	
			Born Taco Ockerse in 1955 to Dutch parents in Jakarta, Indonesia. German-based singer.	
7/23/83	4	14	● 1. **Puttin' On The Ritz**	RCA 13574
			written in 1929 by Irving Berlin; #1 hit for Harry Richman in 1930	
			TAG TEAM	
			Hip-hop duo based in Atlanta: Cecil Glenn ("D.C. The Brain Supreme") and Steve Gibson ("Steve Rollin"). High school classmates in Denver.	
6/12/93	2 (7)	41	▲⁴ 1. **Whoomp! (There It Is)**	Life 79500
			Sales #1(16) / Airplay #9; samples Kano's "I'm Ready"; #1 R&B hit (1 week)	
			TAKE THAT	
			British Pop vocal group: Gary Barlow (lead), Howard Donald, Jason Orange, Mark Owen and Robbie Williams (left in early 1995).	
9/2/95	7	25	1. **Back For Good**	Arista 12848
			Sales #9 / Airplay #12	
			TALKING HEADS	
			New York City-based new wave quartet: David Byrne (lead singer, guitar), Jerry Harrison (keyboards, guitar), Tina Weymouth (bass) and husband Chris Frantz (drums). Formed as a trio of Byrne, Weymouth and Frantz at the Rhode Island School of Design in 1974. Harrison was a member of The Modern Lovers. Disbanded in late 1991. Also see Tom Tom Club.	
12/23/78+	26	9	1. Take Me To The River	Sire 1032
9/3/83	9	11	2. **Burning Down The House**	Sire 29565
11/8/86	25	7	3. Wild Wild Life	Sire 28629
			Sales #23 / Airplay #25	
			TALK TALK	
			British rock band: Mark Hollis (vocals), Simon Brenner (keyboards), Paul Webb (bass) and Lee Harris (drums). Brenner left in 1983.	
4/21/84	31	6	1. It's My Life	EMI America 8195
			TA MARA & THE SEEN	
			Minneapolis quintet led by Margaret Cox, a veteran Minneapolis night club singer. Group includes guitarist Oliver Leiber, son of songwriter Jerry Leiber (of Leiber & Stoller).	
11/30/85+	24	10	1. Everybody Dance	A&M 2768
			Airplay #22 / Sales #26	

DATE	POS	WKS	ARTIST–RECORD TITLE	LABEL & NO.
			TAMI SHOW	
			Pop sextet formed in late 1985 in Chicago. Fronted by sisters Cathy and Claire Massey. The *T.A.M.I. Show* is a 1964 movie of a superstar concert in Santa Monica, California.	
9/7/91	28	5	1. The Truth	RCA 2694
			TAMS, The	
			Atlanta R&B quintet: brothers Charles and Joseph (lead singer) Pope, with Robert Smith, Floyd Ashton and Horace Key. First recorded for Swan in 1960. Joseph Pope died on 3/16/96 (age 63).	
1/18/64	9	9	1. **What Kind Of Fool (Do You Think I Am)**	ABC-Para. 10502
			TANEGA, Norma	
			Born on 1/30/39 in Vallejo, California. Singer/songwriter/pianist/guitarist.	
3/19/66	22	6	1. Walkin' My Cat Named Dog	New Voice 807
			TARRIERS, The	
			Folk trio: Erik Darling (tenor, banjo), Bob Carey (bass, guitar) and future movie actor Alan Arkin (baritone, guitar). Darling replaced Pete Seeger in The Weavers, 1958-62, then formed The Rooftop Singers.	
10/13/56	9	15	1. Cindy, Oh Cindy **VINCE MARTIN With The Tarriers** Juke Box #9 / Best Seller #12 / Top 100 #12 / Jockey #12; adapted from a sailor's sea chantey	Glory 247
12/22/56+	4	16	2. The Banana Boat Song Juke Box #4 / Best Seller #5 / Top 100 #6 / Jockey #6; based on a Jamaican folk song brought to the U.S. in the late '40s	Glory 249
			TASTE OF HONEY, A	
			Soul-disco quartet, formed in Los Angeles in 1972. Consisted of Janice Marie Johnson (vocals, guitar), Hazel Payne (vocals, bass), Perry Kimble (keyboards) and Donald Johnson (drums). Re-formed in 1980 with Janice Johnson and Hazel Payne. Won the 1978 Best New Artist Grammy Award.	
7/22/78	1 (3)	17	▲ 1. **Boogie Oogie Oogie** #1 R&B hit (1 week)	Capitol 4565
4/11/81	3	16	● 2. **Sukiyaki** #1 Adult Contemporary hit (2 weeks); #1 R&B hit (1 week)	Capitol 4953
			TAVARES	
			Family R&B group from New Bedford, Massachusetts. Consisted of brothers Ralph, Antone "Chubby," Feliciano "Butch," Arthur "Pooch" and Perry Lee "Tiny" Tavares. Worked as Chubby & The Turnpikes, 1964–69. Butch was married to Lola Falana.	
11/3/73	35	3	1. Check It Out	Capitol 3674
5/17/75	25	5	2. Remember What I Told You To Forget/	
		1	3. My Ship	Capitol 4010
8/23/75	10	13	4. **It Only Takes A Minute** #1 R&B hit (1 week)	Capitol 4111
7/10/76	15	11	● 5. Heaven Must Be Missing An Angel (Part 1)	Capitol 4270
12/11/76	34	2	6. Don't Take Away The Music	Capitol 4348
4/23/77	22	7	7. Whodunit #1 R&B hit (1 week)	Capitol 4398

DATE	POS	WKS	ARTIST–RECORD TITLE	LABEL & NO.
4/15/78	32	4	8. More Than A Woman from the movie *Saturday Night Fever* starring John Travolta; written by the Bee Gees	Capitol 4500
11/20/82	33	9	9. A Penny For Your Thoughts	RCA 13292

TAYLOR, Andy

Born on 2/16/61 in Dolver-Hampton, England. Lead guitarist of Duran Duran and The Power Station.

DATE	POS	WKS	ARTIST–RECORD TITLE	LABEL & NO.
7/5/86	24	7	1. Take It Easy Airplay #23 / Sales #24; from the movie *American Anthem* starring Mitch Gaylord	Atlantic 89414

TAYLOR, Bobby, & The Vancouvers

Interracial sextet based in Vancouver, Canada. Included guitarist Tommy Chong (of Cheech & Chong fame), Wes Henderson, Robbie King, Ted Lewis and Eddie Patterson. Bobby Taylor discovered The Jackson 5.

DATE	POS	WKS	ARTIST–RECORD TITLE	LABEL & NO.
5/18/68	29	5	1. Does Your Mama Know About Me	Gordy 7069

TAYLOR, James

Born on 3/12/48 in Boston. Singer/songwriter/guitarist. With older brother Alex in the Fabulous Corsairs in 1964. In New York group The Flying Machine in 1967, with friend Danny Kortchmar. Moved to England in 1968, recorded for Peter Asher. Married Carly Simon on 11/3/72; divorced in 1983. Appeared in the movie *Two Lane Blacktop* with Dennis Wilson in 1973. Sister Kate and brothers Alex (died 3/12/93) and Livingston Taylor also recorded. Their father, Isaac, was the dean of the University of North Carolina medical school until 1971. Also see Carly Simon.

DATE	POS	WKS	ARTIST–RECORD TITLE	LABEL & NO.
9/26/70	3	14	1. **Fire And Rain**	Warner 7423
3/20/71	37	1	2. Country Road	Warner 7460
6/19/71	1 (1)	12	● 3. **You've Got A Friend** #1 Adult Contemporary hit (1 week)	Warner 7498
10/16/71	31	5	4. Long Ago And Far Away Joni Mitchell (backing vocal, above); Carole King (piano: #1,2,4)	Warner 7521
12/16/72+	14	9	5. Don't Let Me Be Lonely Tonight	Warner 7655
2/16/74	5	13	● 6. **Mockingbird** **CARLY SIMON & JAMES TAYLOR** adapted from the same traditional folk lyrics as was the song "Bo Diddley"	Elektra 45880
7/19/75	5	10	7. **How Sweet It Is (To Be Loved By You)** David Sanborn (sax); #1 Adult Contemporary hit (1 week)	Warner 8109
8/7/76	22	8	8. Shower The People #1 Adult Contemporary hit (1 week); Carly Simon (harmony vocal, above 2)	Warner 8222
7/9/77	4	13	9. **Handy Man** #1 Adult Contemporary hit (1 week)	Columbia 10557
11/5/77	20	9	10. Your Smiling Face	Columbia 10602
2/11/78	17	7	11. (What A) Wonderful World **ART GARFUNKEL with JAMES TAYLOR & PAUL SIMON** #1 Adult Contemporary hit (5 weeks)	Columbia 10676
9/23/78	36	3	12. Devoted To You **CARLY SIMON and JAMES TAYLOR**	Elektra 45506
6/30/79	28	5	13. Up On The Roof	Columbia 11005
3/14/81	11	10	14. Her Town Too **JAMES TAYLOR AND J.D. SOUTHER**	Columbia 60514

DATE	POS	WKS	ARTIST–RECORD TITLE	LABEL & NO.
			TAYLOR, John	
			Born on 6/20/60 in Birmingham, England. Bass guitarist of Duran Duran and The Power Station.	
4/5/86	23	6	1. I Do What I Do...(Theme for 9 1/2 Weeks) **John TAYLOR Jonathan ELIAS** Sales #18 / Airplay #26; from the movie *9 1/2 Weeks* starring Mickey Rourke and Kim Basinger	Capitol 5551
			TAYLOR, Johnnie	
			Born on 5/5/38 in Crawfordsville, Arkansas. With gospel group the Highway QC's in Chicago, early 1950s. In vocal group the Five Echoes, recorded for Sabre in 1954. In the Soul Stirrers gospel group before going solo. First solo recording for SAR in 1961. Known as The Soul Philosopher.	
11/2/68	5	13	● 1. **Who's Making Love** #1 R&B hit (3 weeks)	Stax 0009
1/25/69	20	8	2. Take Care Of Your Homework	Stax 0023
5/31/69	36	5	3. Testify (I Wonna)	Stax 0033
7/18/70	37	2	4. Steal Away	Stax 0068
11/14/70	39	2	5. I Am Somebody Part II	Stax 0078
2/13/71	28	5	6. Jody's Got Your Girl And Gone #1 R&B hit (2 weeks)	Stax 0085
7/14/73	11	12	● 7. **I Believe In You (You Believe In Me)** #1 R&B hit (2 weeks)	Stax 0161
10/27/73	15	8	8. Cheaper To Keep Her	Stax 0176
3/16/74	34	2	9. We're Getting Careless With Our Love	Stax 0193
3/6/76	1 (4)	13	▲ 10. **Disco Lady** first single certified platinum by R.I.A.A.; #1 R&B hit (6 weeks)	Columbia 10281
6/26/76	33	3	11. Somebody's Gettin' It all of above produced by Don Davis	Columbia 10334
			TAYLOR, Little Johnny	
			Born Johnny Young on 2/11/43 in Memphis. Blues singer/harmonica player. To Los Angeles in 1950. With Mighty Clouds Of Joy and Stars Of Bethel gospel groups. Duets with Ted Taylor (no relation) in the '70s.	
9/14/63	19	8	1. Part Time Love #1 R&B hit (1 week)	Galaxy 722
			TAYLOR, Livingston	
			Born on 11/21/50 in Boston. James Taylor's younger brother. Hosted TV's "This Week's Music" in 1984.	
12/16/78+	30	5	1. I Will Be In Love With You	Epic 50604
9/13/80	38	2	2. First Time Love	Epic 50894
			TAYLOR, R. Dean	
			Born in Toronto in 1939. First recorded for Parry in 1960. Co-wrote The Supremes' hit "Love Child."	
9/19/70	5	13	1. **Indiana Wants Me**	Rare Earth 5013
			T-BONES, The	
			A Joe Saraceno studio production. Also see Hamilton, Joe Frank & Reynolds.	
12/25/65+	3	11	1. **No Matter What Shape (Your Stomach's In)** [I] tune is from an Alka Seltzer jingle	Liberty 55836

DATE	POS	WKS	ARTIST–RECORD TITLE	LABEL & NO.
			TCHAIKOVSKY, Bram—see BRAM TCHAIKOVSKY	
			TEARS FOR FEARS	
			British duo: Roland Orzabal (born 8/22/61; vocals, guitar, keyboards) and Curt Smith (born 6/24/61; vocals, bass). Adopted name from Arthur Janev's book *Prisoners Of Pain* in 1981. Smith left duo by 1992.	
4/13/85	**1** (2)	14	1. **Everybody Wants To Rule The World**	Mercury 880659
			Sales #1(2) / Airplay #1(2)	
6/29/85	**1** (3)	13	● 2. **Shout**	Mercury 880294
			Airplay #1(3) / Sales #1(2)	
9/21/85	**3**	12	3. **Head Over Heels**	Mercury 880899
			Airplay #2 / Sales #4	
5/3/86	**27**	6	4. Mothers Talk	Mercury 884638
			Sales #26 / Airplay #28; above 4 from the album *Songs From The Big Chair*	
9/9/89	**2** (1)	12	5. **Sowing The Seeds Of Love**	Fontana 874710
			Sales #1(2) / Airplay #4	
1/27/90	**36**	2	6. Woman In Chains	Fontana 876248
			Sales #25; Oleta Adams (female vocal); Phil Collins (drums)	
8/21/93	**25**	9	7. Break It Down Again	Mercury 862330
			Airplay #18 / Sales #61	
			TECHNIQUES	
			White pop vocal group: Jim Tinney, Jim Moore, Jim Falin and Buddy Harold (real name: Beauford Harold Funk). All were students at Georgia Tech University.	
11/25/57	**29**	2	1. Hey! Little Girl	Roulette 4030
			Best Seller #29 / Top 100 #33; first released on Stars 551 in 1957	
			TECHNOTRONIC	
			Dance outfit created by Belgian DJ/producer Thomas DeQuincey (real name: Jo Bogaert) and female rapper Ya Kid K (of Hi Tek 3). Non-vocalist Felly, a model from Zaire, fronted the group for videos.	
11/11/89+	**2** (2)	16	▲ 1. **Pump Up The Jam**	SBK 07311
			TECHNOTRONIC Featuring FELLY	
			Sales #1(4) / Airplay #6	
2/17/90	**7**	12	● 2. **Get Up! (Before The Night Is Over)**	SBK 07315
			Sales #5 / Airplay #11	
7/4/92	**6**	18	3. **Move This**	SBK 50400
			TECHNOTRONIC featuring YA KID K	
			Airplay #5 / Sales #10; featured in a 1992 Revlon TV commercial	
			TEDDY BEARS, The	
			Los Angeles trio: Phil Spector (born 12/26/40, Bronx), Carol Connors (lead singer; real name: Annette Kleinbard) and Marshall Leib. Spector became a well-known writer and producer; owner of Philles Records. He was inducted into the Rock and Roll Hall of Fame in 1989. Connors co-wrote "Gonna Fly Now" (theme from the movie *Rocky*).	
10/13/58	**1** (3)	18	● 1. **To Know Him, Is To Love Him**	Dore 503
			Sandy Nelson (drums)	

DATE	POS	WKS	ARTIST–RECORD TITLE	LABEL & NO.
			TEEGARDEN & VAN WINKLE	
			David Teegarden (drums) and Skip Knape (keyboards). Teegarden later joined Bob Seger's band, 1978–81.	
10/17/70	22	5	1. God, Love And Rock & Roll	Westbound 170
			TEENAGERS, The—see LYMON, Frankie	
			TEEN QUEENS, The	
			R&B duo formed in Los Angeles in 1955 by Betty and Rosie Collins, sisters of Aaron Collins of The Cadets/Jacks.	
3/10/56	14	8	1. Eddie My Love Best Seller #14 / Juke Box #16 / Top 100 #22	RPM 453
			TEE SET, The	
			Dutch quintet: Peter Tetteroo (vocals), Hans Van Eijck, Dill Bennink, Franklin Madjid and Joop Blom.	
2/7/70	5	10	1. **Ma Belle Amie**	Colossus 107
			TEMPO, Nino, & April Stevens	
			Nino (born Antonio Lo Tempio on 1/6/35) and sister April Stevens (born Carol Lo Tempio on 4/29/36) from Niagara Falls, New York. Prior to teaming up, Nino was a session saxophonist and April had recorded solo.	
10/5/63	1 (1)	12	1. **Deep Purple** #1 hit for Larry Clinton & His Orchestra in 1939	Atco 6273
12/28/63+	11	7	2. Whispering #1 hit for Paul Whiteman & His Orchestra in 1920	Atco 6281
3/14/64	32	3	3. Stardust #1 hit for Isham Jones & His Orchestra in 1931	Atco 6286
10/1/66	26	5	4. All Strung Out	White Whale 236
			TEMPOS, The	
			Pittsburgh pop vocal quartet: Mike Lazo, Gene Schachter, Jim Drake and Tom Minoto. First recorded for Kapp in 1957.	
8/10/59	23	6	1. See You In September Billy Mure (orch.)	Climax 102
			TEMPTATIONS, The	
			White quartet from Flushing, New York: Neil Stevens, Larry Curtis, Artie Sands and Artie Marin.	
5/9/60	29	3	1. Barbara	Goldisc 3001

DATE	POS	WKS	ARTIST–RECORD TITLE	LABEL & NO.
			TEMPTATIONS, The	
			Detroit soul group formed in 1960. Consisted of Eddie Kendricks (died of lung cancer 10/5/92, age 52), Paul Williams (died 8/17/73), Melvin Franklin (died 2/23/95, age 52), Otis Williams (not to be confused with the same-named member of the Charms) and Elbridge Bryant, who was replaced by David Ruffin in 1964. Originally called the Primes and Elgins, first recorded for Miracle in 1961. Ruffin (died of a drug overdose 6/1/91, age 50; cousin of Billy Stewart) replaced by Dennis Edwards (ex-Contours) in 1968. Kendricks and Paul Williams left in 1971, replaced by Ricky Owens (ex-Vibrations) and Richard Street. Owens was replaced by Damon Harris. Harris left in 1975, replaced by Glenn Leonard. Edwards left group, 1977-79; replaced by Louis Price. Ali Ollie Woodson replaced Edwards, 1984–87. 1988 lineup: Otis Williams, Franklin, Street, Edwards and Ron Tyson. Recognized as America's all-time favorite soul group. Inducted into the Rock and Roll Hall of Fame in 1989.	
3/21/64	11	8	1. The Way You Do The Things You Do	Gordy 7028
7/4/64	33	4	2. I'll Be In Trouble	Gordy 7032
9/26/64	26	6	3. Girl (Why You Wanna Make Me Blue)	Gordy 7035
1/30/65	1 (1)	11	4. **My Girl** #1 R&B hit (6 weeks)	Gordy 7038
4/17/65	18	7	5. It's Growing	Gordy 7040
8/7/65	17	7	6. Since I Lost My Baby	Gordy 7043
11/6/65	13	6	7. My Baby	Gordy 7047
3/26/66	29	3	8. Get Ready #1 R&B hit (1 week); all of above (except #3) written and produced by Smokey Robinson	Gordy 7049
6/11/66	13	10	9. Ain't Too Proud To Beg #1 R&B hit (8 weeks)	Gordy 7054
9/3/66	3	9	10. **Beauty Is Only Skin Deep** #1 R&B hit (5 weeks)	Gordy 7055
12/3/66	8	8	11. **(I Know) I'm Losing You** #1 R&B hit (2 weeks)	Gordy 7057
5/13/67	8	8	12. **All I Need**	Gordy 7061
8/12/67	6	9	13. **You're My Everything**	Gordy 7063
10/21/67	14	8	14. (Loneliness Made Me Realize) It's You That I Need above 4 from the album With A Lot O' Soul	Gordy 7065
1/27/68	4	11	15. **I Wish It Would Rain** #1 R&B hit (3 weeks)	Gordy 7068
5/18/68	13	8	16. I Could Never Love Another (After Loving You) #1 R&B hit (1 week)	Gordy 7072
8/17/68	26	5	17. Please Return Your Love To Me	Gordy 7074
11/23/68+	6	11	18. **Cloud Nine**	Gordy 7081
12/14/68+	2 (2)	12	19. **I'm Gonna Make You Love Me** **DIANA ROSS AND THE SUPREMES & THE TEMPTATIONS**	Motown 1137
2/22/69	6	11	20. **Run Away Child, Running Wild** #1 R&B hit (2 weeks)	Gordy 7084
3/22/69	25	6	21. I'll Try Something New **DIANA ROSS AND THE SUPREMES & THE TEMPTATIONS**	Motown 1142
5/31/69	20	6	22. Don't Let The Joneses Get You Down	Gordy 7086
8/30/69	1 (2)	15	23. **I Can't Get Next To You** #1 R&B hit (5 weeks)	Gordy 7093
1/24/70	7	10	24. **Psychedelic Shack**	Gordy 7096
6/6/70	3	13	25. **Ball Of Confusion (That's What The World Is Today)**	Gordy 7099
10/17/70	33	4	26. Ungena Za Ulimwengu (Unite The World)	Gordy 7102

DATE	POS	WKS	ARTIST–RECORD TITLE	LABEL & NO.
2/20/71	**1 (2)**	13	27. **Just My Imagination (Running Away With Me)** #1 R&B hit (3 weeks)	Gordy 7105
11/20/71	**18**	8	28. Superstar (Remember How You Got Where You Are)	Gordy 7111
3/18/72	**30**	4	29. Take A Look Around	Gordy 7115
10/28/72	**1 (1)**	12	30. **Papa Was A Rollin' Stone**	Gordy 7121
3/10/73	**7**	11	31. **Masterpiece** #1 R&B hit (2 weeks)	Gordy 7126
7/7/73	**40**	2	32. The Plastic Man	Gordy 7129
9/8/73	**35**	4	33. Hey Girl (I Like Your Style)	Gordy 7131
1/12/74	**27**	4	34. Let Your Hair Down #1 R&B hit (1 week); #9-34 written and produced (except #12) by Norman Whitfield	Gordy 7133
2/1/75	**40**	1	35. Happy People co-written by Lionel Richie; #1 R&B hit (1 week)	Gordy 7138
4/19/75	**26**	9	36. Shakey Ground #1 R&B hit (1 week)	Gordy 7142
8/23/75	**37**	2	37. Glasshouse	Gordy 7144
7/27/91	**10**	11	38. **The Motown Song** **ROD STEWART (with The Temptations)** Airplay #24 / Sales #36	Warner 19322

10cc

English art-rock group that evolved from Hotlegs. Consisted of Eric Stewart (guitar), Graham Gouldman (bass), Lol Creme (guitar, keyboards) and Kevin Godley (drums). Stewart and Gouldman were members of The Mindbenders. Godley & Creme left in 1976, replaced by drummer Paul Burgess. Added members Rick Fenn, Stuart Tosh and Duncan MacKay in 1978. Gouldman later in duo Wax.

DATE	POS	WKS	ARTIST–RECORD TITLE	LABEL & NO.
6/14/75	**2 (3)**	11	1. **I'm Not In Love**	Mercury 73678
1/29/77	**5**	14	● 2. **The Things We Do For Love**	Mercury 73875
6/25/77	**40**	1	3. People In Love	Mercury 73917

10,000 MANIACS

Group from Jamestown, New York, formed in 1981: Natalie Merchant (vocals), Robert Buck (guitar), Dennis Drew (keyboards), Steven Gustafson (bass) and Jerome Augustyniak (drums). Merchant left in August of 1993.

DATE	POS	WKS	ARTIST–RECORD TITLE	LABEL & NO.
11/27/93+	**11**	24	1. Because The Night Airplay #8 / Sales #29; "live" recording from group's MTV Unplugged album	Elektra 64595

TEN YEARS AFTER

British blues-rock quartet formed in 1966: Alvin Lee (born 12/19/44, Nottingham, England; vocals, guitar), Leo Lyons (bass), Chick Churchill (keyboards) and Ric Lee (drums). Inactive as band, 1975–88.

DATE	POS	WKS	ARTIST–RECORD TITLE	LABEL & NO.
11/20/71	**40**	2	1. I'd Love To Change The World	Columbia 45457

TEPPER, Robert

Rock singer from Bayonne, New Jersey. Co-wrote "Into The Night" with Benny Mardones.

DATE	POS	WKS	ARTIST–RECORD TITLE	LABEL & NO.
3/1/86	**22**	7	1. No Easy Way Out Airplay #19 / Sales #23; from the movie Rocky IV starring Sylvester Stallone	Scotti Br. 05750

DATE	POS	WKS	ARTIST—RECORD TITLE	LABEL & NO.

TERRELL, Tammi

Born Tammy Montgomery in 1946 in Philadelphia. Died of a brain tumor on 3/16/70. First recorded for Wand in 1961. Worked with the James Brown Revue. Tumor diagnosed after she collapsed on stage in 1967. Married briefly to boxer Ernie Terrell (brother of Jean Terrell of The Supremes).

MARVIN GAYE & TAMMI TERRELL:

DATE	POS	WKS	ARTIST—RECORD TITLE	LABEL & NO.
6/3/67	19	9	1. Ain't No Mountain High Enough	Tamla 54149
9/30/67	5	10	2. **Your Precious Love**	Tamla 54156
12/16/67+	10	9	3. **If I Could Build My Whole World Around You**	Tamla 54161
4/27/68	8	11	4. **Ain't Nothing Like The Real Thing** #1 R&B hit (1 week)	Tamla 54163
8/10/68	7	10	5. **You're All I Need To Get By** #1 R&B hit (5 weeks)	Tamla 54169
10/19/68	24	6	6. Keep On Lovin' Me Honey	Tamla 54173
2/15/69	30	4	7. Good Lovin' Ain't Easy To Come By Valerie Simpson actually sang female part due to Terrell's poor health; all of above written (except #3) and produced (except #1–3) by Ashford & Simpson	Tamla 54179

TERRY, Tony

Born on 3/12/64 in Pinehurst, North Carolina; raised in Washington, D.C. Soul-funk singer. Former backing vocalist for Sweet Sensation and the Boogie Boys.

DATE	POS	WKS	ARTIST—RECORD TITLE	LABEL & NO.
9/28/91	14	10	1. With You Airplay #16 / Sales #27	Epic 73713

TESLA

Hard-rock quintet formed in Sacramento in 1984: Jeff Keith (vocals), Frank Hannon and Tommy Skeoch (guitars), Brian Wheat (bass) and Troy Luccketta (drums). Band named after the inventor of the alternating current generator, Nikola Tesla.

DATE	POS	WKS	ARTIST—RECORD TITLE	LABEL & NO.
11/11/89+	10	16	● 1. **Love Song** Sales #4 / Airplay #18	Geffen 22856
2/9/91	8	13	2. **Signs** Sales #4 / Airplay #15	Geffen 19653

TEX, Joe

Born Joseph Arrington, Jr., on 8/8/33 in Rogers, Texas. Died of a heart attack on 8/13/82. Sang with local gospel groups. Won recording contract during Apollo Theater talent contest in 1954. First recorded for King in 1955. Converted to the Muslim faith, changed name to Joseph Hazziez in July 1972.

DATE	POS	WKS	ARTIST—RECORD TITLE	LABEL & NO.
1/2/65	5	8	1. **Hold What You've Got**	Dial 4001
10/16/65	23	5	2. I Want To (Do Everything For You) #1 R&B hit (3 weeks)	Dial 4016
1/1/66	29	4	3. A Sweet Woman Like You #1 R&B hit (1 week)	Dial 4022
6/18/66	39	1	4. S.Y.S.L.J.F.M. (The Letter Song) S.Y.S.L.J.F.M.: "Save Your Sweet Love Just For Me"	Dial 4028
4/8/67	35	3	5. Show Me	Dial 4055
11/25/67	10	10	● 6. **Skinny Legs And All** "live" recording	Dial 4063
3/2/68	33	3	7. Men Are Gettin' Scarce	Dial 4069

DATE	POS	WKS	ARTIST–RECORD TITLE	LABEL & NO.
2/26/72	2 (2)	16	● 8. **I Gotcha** #1 R&B hit (1 week); all of above written by Joe Tex	Dial 1010
4/23/77	12	10	● 9. Ain't Gonna Bump No More (With No Big Fat Woman) all of above produced by Buddy Killen	Epic 50313

THEM

Rock quintet from Belfast, Northern Ireland: Van Morrison (lead singer), Billy Harrison, Alan Henderson, John McAuley and Peter Bardens. Disbanded in late 1966. Morrison went on to a highly successful solo career. Bardens formed Camel in 1972; recorded solo in 1987.

DATE	POS	WKS	ARTIST–RECORD TITLE	LABEL & NO.
6/26/65	24	6	1. Here Comes The Night	Parrot 9749
12/4/65	33	2	2. Mystic Eyes	Parrot 9796

THINK

Studio group assembled by producers Lou Stallman and Bobby Susser.

DATE	POS	WKS	ARTIST–RECORD TITLE	LABEL & NO.
1/1/72	23	5	1. Once You Understand featuring dialogue between a teenager and his parents	Laurie 3583

THIN LIZZY

Rock band of Dublin, Ireland, natives Phil Lynott (born 8/20/51; died 1/4/86; vocals, bass) and Brian Downey (drums), with guitarists Brian Robertson (from Glasgow) and Scott Gorham (from California).

DATE	POS	WKS	ARTIST–RECORD TITLE	LABEL & NO.
6/5/76	12	9	1. The Boys Are Back In Town	Mercury 73786

3RD BASS

White rappers from Queens, New York: Prime Minister Pete Nice (Pete Nash) and MC Serch (Michael Berrin). Supported by black DJ Richie Rich (Richard Lawson). Disbanded in early 1992. Nash and Lawson continued as duo: Prime Minister Pete Nice and DJ Daddy Rich; Berrin went solo.

DATE	POS	WKS	ARTIST–RECORD TITLE	LABEL & NO.
8/10/91	29	6	● 1. Pop Goes The Weasel Sales #10 / Airplay #48; samples Peter Gabriel's "Sledgehammer", Stevie Wonder's "You Haven't Done Nothin'" and The Who's "Eminence Front"	Def Jam 73728

38 SPECIAL

Southern-rock band formed in Jacksonville, Florida, in 1975: Donnie Van Zant (younger brother of Lynyrd Skynyrd's Ronnie Van Zant; vocals), Don Barnes and Jeff Carlisi (guitars), Larry Junstrom (bass), and Steve Brookins and Jack Grondin (drums). By 1988, Barnes and Brookins replaced by Danny Chauncey (guitar) and Max Carl (keyboards). Barnes returned in 1992 to replace Carl.

DATE	POS	WKS	ARTIST–RECORD TITLE	LABEL & NO.
4/18/81	27	6	1. Hold On Loosely	A&M 2316
5/22/82	10	12	2. **Caught Up In You**	A&M 2412
10/2/82	38	2	3. You Keep Runnin' Away	A&M 2431
12/3/83+	19	9	4. If I'd Been The One	A&M 2594
2/18/84	20	8	5. Back Where You Belong	A&M 2615
10/27/84	25	5	6. Teacher Teacher Sales #25 / Airplay #27; from the movie *Teachers* starring Nick Nolte and JoBeth Williams	Capitol 5405
5/24/86	14	9	7. Like No Other Night Airplay #11 / Sales #17	A&M 2831
3/11/89	6	14	8. **Second Chance** THIRTY EIGHT SPECIAL Airplay #5 / Sales #9; #1 Adult Contemporary hit (2 weeks)	A&M 1273

DATE	POS	WKS	ARTIST–RECORD TITLE	LABEL & NO.
8/31/91	33	4	9. The Sound Of Your Voice Airplay #59	Charisma 98773

THOMAS, B.J.

Born Billy Joe Thomas on 8/7/42 in Hugo, Oklahoma; raised in Rosenberg, Texas. Sang in church choir as a teenager. Joined band, the Triumphs, while in high school. Thomas has featured gospel music since 1976.

DATE	POS	WKS	ARTIST–RECORD TITLE	LABEL & NO.
3/12/66	8	10	1. **I'm So Lonesome I Could Cry** **B.J. THOMAS AND THE TRIUMPHS** written in 1949 by Hank Williams	Scepter 12129
6/4/66	22	5	2. Mama	Scepter 12139
7/23/66	34	4	3. Billy And Sue **B.J. THOMAS AND THE TRIUMPHS** first released on Bragg 103 and then on Warner 5491 in 1964	Hickory 1395
8/3/68	28	7	4. The Eyes Of A New York Woman	Scepter 12219
12/14/68+	5	12	● 5. **Hooked On A Feeling**	Scepter 12230
11/22/69+	1 (4)	19	● 6. **Raindrops Keep Fallin' On My Head** from the movie *Butch Cassidy and the Sundance Kid* starring Paul Newman and Robert Redford; #1 Adult Contemporary hit (7 weeks)	Scepter 12265
4/11/70	26	6	7. Everybody's Out Of Town	Scepter 12277
7/11/70	9	10	8. **I Just Can't Help Believing** #1 Adult Contemporary hit (1 week)	Scepter 12283
1/9/71	38	3	9. Most Of All	Scepter 12299
3/13/71	16	9	10. No Love At All	Scepter 12307
8/14/71	34	3	11. Mighty Clouds Of Joy	Scepter 12320
2/26/72	15	9	12. Rock And Roll Lullaby Duane Eddy (guitar); The Blossoms and Dave Somerville (of the Diamonds; backing vocals); #1 Adult Contemporary hit (1 week)	Scepter 12344
3/1/75	1 (1)	14	1 13. (Hey Won't You Play) Another Somebody Done Somebody Wrong Song #1 Country hit (1 week); #1 Adult Contemporary hit (1 week)	ABC 12054
8/6/77	17	10	14. Don't Worry Baby	MCA 40735

THOMAS, Carla

Born on 12/21/42 in Memphis. Daughter of Rufus Thomas. Sang with the Teentown Singers at age 10. First recorded with Rufus for Satellite in 1960. Also recorded duets with Otis Redding.

DATE	POS	WKS	ARTIST–RECORD TITLE	LABEL & NO.
2/20/61	10	10	1. **Gee Whiz (Look At His Eyes)** originally released on Satellite 104 in 1960	Atlantic 2086
9/24/66	14	10	2. B-A-B-Y	Stax 195
			OTIS & CARLA:	
6/3/67	26	4	3. Tramp	Stax 216
9/23/67	30	2	4. Knock On Wood	Stax 228

THOMAS, Ian

Canadian singer/songwriter. Brother of SCTV comedian Dave Thomas, aka Doug McKenzie.

DATE	POS	WKS	ARTIST–RECORD TITLE	LABEL & NO.
12/29/73+	34	3	1. Painted Ladies	Janus 224

DATE	POS	WKS	ARTIST—RECORD TITLE	LABEL & NO.
			THOMAS, Irma	
			Born Irma Lee on 2/18/41 in Ponchatoula, Louisiana. The Soul Queen of New Orleans. Discovered by New Orleans bandleader Tommy Ridgley.	
4/25/64	17	7	1. Wish Someone Would Care	Imperial 66013
			THOMAS, Rufus	
			Born on 3/26/17 in Cayce, Mississippi; raised in Memphis. R&B singer/songwriter/choreographer. Father of singers Vaneese and Carla Thomas. First recorded for Talent in 1950. DJ at WDIA-Memphis, 1953–74. Recorded for Alligator Records in the late '80s.	
11/2/63	10	9	1. **Walking The Dog**	Stax 140
2/28/70	28	8	2. Do The Funky Chicken	Stax 0059
1/23/71	25	8	3. (Do The) Push And Pull Part I	Stax 0079
			#1 R&B hit (2 weeks)	
9/18/71	31	4	4. The Breakdown (Part I)	Stax 0098
			THOMAS, Timmy	
			Born on 11/13/44 in Evansville, Indiana. Soul singer/songwriter/keyboardist. Studio musician at Gold Wax Records in Memphis. Moved to Miami in 1970. Session work for Betty Wright and KC & The Sunshine Band.	
12/23/72+	3	11	1. **Why Can't We Live Together**	Glades 1703
			#1 R&B hit (2 weeks)	
			THOMPSON, Chris—see NIGHT	
			THOMPSON, Kay	
			Born on 11/9/13 in St. Louis. Wrote *Eloise* series of children's books. Appeared in the movie musical *Funny Face*, 1957.	
3/17/56	39	2	1. Eloise [N]	Cadence 1286
			Archie Bleyer (orch.)	
			THOMPSON, Sue	
			Born Eva Sue McKee on 7/19/26 in Nevada, Missouri; raised in San Jose, California. Became a popular country singer in the '70s.	
9/25/61	5	11	1. **Sad Movies (Make Me Cry)**	Hickory 1153
			#1 Adult Contemporary hit (1 week)	
1/13/62	3	11	2. **Norman**	Hickory 1159
7/21/62	31	5	3. Have A Good Time	Hickory 1174
10/20/62	17	6	4. James (Hold The Ladder Steady)	Hickory 1183
2/6/65	23	4	5. Paper Tiger	Hickory 1284
			all of above (except #3) written by John D. Loudermilk	
			THOMPSON TWINS	
			British trio: Tom Bailey (lead singer, synthesizer), Alannah Currie (xylophone, percussion; native of New Zealand) and Joe Leeway (conga, synthesizer). Leeway left in 1986. Bailey and Currie recorded in 1993 as Babble.	
3/12/83	30	5	1. Lies	Arista 1024
2/25/84	3	15	2. **Hold Me Now**	Arista 9164
6/9/84	11	9	3. Doctor! Doctor!	Arista 9209
10/5/85	6	14	4. **Lay Your Hands On Me**	Arista 9396
			Airplay #5 / Sales #7	

DATE	POS	WKS	ARTIST–RECORD TITLE	LABEL & NO.
1/25/86	**8**	11	5. **King For A Day** Airplay #7 / Sales #8	Arista 9450
4/25/87	**31**	5	6. Get That Love Sales #27 / Airplay #30	Arista 9577
10/28/89	**28**	4	7. Sugar Daddy Airplay #27 / Sales #31	Warner 22819

THOMSON, Ali

Singer/songwriter from Glasgow, Scotland. Younger brother of Supertramp's Dougie Thomson.

DATE	POS	WKS	ARTIST–RECORD TITLE	LABEL & NO.
7/12/80	**15**	9	1. Take A Little Rhythm	A&M 2243

THREE DEGREES, The

Philadelphia R&B trio discovered by Richard Barrett. Originally consisted of Fayette Pinkney, Linda Turner and Shirley Porter. Turner and Porter replaced by Sheila Ferguson and Valerie Holiday in 1966.

DATE	POS	WKS	ARTIST–RECORD TITLE	LABEL & NO.
7/25/70	**29**	4	1. Maybe	Roulette 7079
3/16/74	**1** (2)	14	● 2. **TSOP (The Sound Of Philadelphia)** [I] **MFSB featuring The Three Degrees** theme from the TV show "Soul Train"; #1 Adult Contemporary hit (2 weeks); #1 R&B hit (1 week)	Phil. Int. 3540
10/19/74	**2** (1)	13	▲ 3. **When Will I See You Again** #1 Adult Contemporary hit (1 week)	Phil. Int. 3550

THREE DOG NIGHT

Los Angeles pop-rock group formed in 1968 featuring lead singers Danny Hutton (born 9/10/42), Cory Wells (born 2/5/42) and Chuck Negron (born 6/8/42). Disbanded in the mid-1970s. Re-formed in the mid-1980s.

DATE	POS	WKS	ARTIST–RECORD TITLE	LABEL & NO.
3/29/69	**29**	4	1. Try A Little Tenderness #6 hit for Ted Lewis in 1933	Dunhill 4177
5/31/69	**5**	12	● 2. **One** written by Nilsson	Dunhill 4191
8/16/69	**4**	12	3. **Easy To Be Hard** from the Broadway rock musical *Hair* starring Steve Curry	Dunhill 4203
11/8/69	**10**	12	4. **Eli's Coming** written by Laura Nyro	Dunhill 4215
3/7/70	**15**	8	5. Celebrate all of above produced by Gabriel Mekler	Dunhill 4229
6/6/70	**1** (2)	13	● 6. **Mama Told Me (Not To Come)** written by Randy Newman	Dunhill 4239
9/12/70	**15**	8	7. Out In The Country	Dunhill 4250
12/5/70+	**19**	9	8. One Man Band	Dunhill 4262
3/27/71	**1** (6)	15	● 9. **Joy To The World** written by Hoyt Axton (also #12 below)	Dunhill 4272
7/17/71	**7**	11	10. **Liar** written by Russ Ballard	Dunhill 4282
11/20/71	**4**	10	● 11. **An Old Fashioned Love Song** #1 Adult Contemporary hit (1 week)	Dunhill 4294
1/8/72	**5**	10	12. **Never Been To Spain**	Dunhill 4299
4/1/72	**12**	8	13. The Family Of Man	Dunhill 4306
8/26/72	**1** (1)	9	● 14. **Black & White** #1 Adult Contemporary hit (1 week)	Dunhill 4317
12/9/72+	**19**	9	15. Pieces Of April	Dunhill 4331

DATE	POS	WKS	ARTIST–RECORD TITLE	LABEL & NO.
6/2/73	**3**	13	● 16. **Shambala**	Dunhill 4352
11/17/73	**17**	6	17. Let Me Serenade You	Dunhill 4370
			above 12 produced by Richard Podolor	
4/13/74	**4**	12	● 18. **The Show Must Go On**	Dunhill 4382
			co-written by Leo Sayer	
7/13/74	**16**	8	19. Sure As I'm Sittin' Here	Dunhill 15001
11/2/74	**33**	3	20. Play Something Sweet (Brickyard Blues)	Dunhill 15013
8/9/75	**32**	3	21. Til The World Ends	ABC 12114
			3T	
			Vocal trio of brothers Taryll, T.J. and Taj Jackson. Sons of Jacksons' member Tito Jackson.	MJJ Music 77913
10/28/95+	**15**	25↑	● 1. Anything	
			Sales #9 / Airplay #22	
			THUNDER, Johnny	
			Born Gil Hamilton on 8/15/41 in Leesburg, Florida. R&B singer discovered by producer Teddy Vann.	Diamond 129
1/5/63	**4**	9	1. **Loop De Loop**	
			THUNDERCLAP NEWMAN	
			British trio: Andy Newman (keyboards), John "Speedy" Keene (vocals) and Jimmy McCulloch (guitarist with Wings, 1975-77; died 9/27/79, age 26). Group put together by Pete Townshend.	Track 2656
10/25/69	**37**	2	1. Something In The Air	
			from the movie *The Magic Christian* starring Peter Sellers and Ringo Starr	
			TIERRA	
			East Los Angeles group formed in 1972. Band led by the Salas brothers: Steve (trombone, timbales) and Rudy (guitar); both formerly with El Chicano.	Boardwalk 5702
12/13/80+	**18**	15	1. Together	
			TIFFANY	
			Born Tiffany Darwisch on 10/2/71. California pop singer, originally from Oklahoma.	
9/26/87	**1** (2)	13	1. **I Think We're Alone Now**	MCA 53167
			Sales #1(2) / Airplay #1(2)	
12/12/87+	**1** (2)	14	2. **Could've Been**	MCA 53231
			Airplay #1(3) / Sales #1(2); #1 Adult Contemporary hit (1 week)	
3/12/88	**7**	9	3. **I Saw Him Standing There**	MCA 53285
			Sales #2 / Airplay #8; female version of The Beatles' "I Saw Her Standing There"	
12/3/88+	**6**	14	4. **All This Time**	MCA 53371
			Sales #7 / Airplay #9	
4/1/89	**35**	1	5. Radio Romance	MCA 53623
			Sales #26; all of above produced by George E. Tobin	
			TIJUANA BRASS, The—see ALPERT, Herb	

DATE	POS	WKS	ARTIST–RECORD TITLE	LABEL & NO.
			TILLOTSON, Johnny	
			Born on 4/20/39 in Jacksonville, Florida; raised in Palatka, Florida. On local radio "Young Folks Revue" from age nine. DJ on WWPF. Appeared on the "Toby Dowdy" TV show in Jacksonville, then own show. Signed by Cadence Records in 1958. Appeared in the movie *Just For Fun*.	
10/24/60	2 (1)	12	1. **Poetry In Motion**	Cadence 1384
2/6/61	25	5	2. Jimmy's Girl	Cadence 1391
8/28/61	7	8	3. **Without You**	Cadence 1404
1/20/62	35	1	4. Dreamy Eyes [R]	Cadence 1409
			originally charted in 1958 at #63	
5/19/62	3	12	5. **It Keeps Right On A-Hurtin'**	Cadence 1418
8/25/62	17	6	6. Send Me The Pillow You Dream On	Cadence 1424
11/17/62	24	5	7. I Can't Help It (If I'm Still In Love With You)	Cadence 1432
			classic Country hit by Hank Williams	
3/23/63	24	6	8. Out Of My Mind	Cadence 1434
8/24/63	18	7	9. You Can Never Stop Me Loving You	Cadence 1437
11/30/63+	7	10	10. **Talk Back Trembling Lips**	MGM 13181
			#1 Country hit for Ernest Ashworth in 1963	
3/14/64	37	2	11. Worried Guy	MGM 13193
6/6/64	36	2	12. I Rise, I Fall	MGM 13232
11/28/64	31	6	13. She Understands Me	MGM 13284
			song charted in 1966 by Bobby Vinton as: "Dum-De-Da"	
10/2/65	35	2	14. Heartaches By The Number	MGM 13376
			#2 Country hit for Ray Price in 1959	
			'TIL TUESDAY	
			Pop quartet formed in Boston in 1983: Aimee Mann (vocals, bass), Robert Holmes (guitar), Joey Pesce (keyboards; replaced by Michael Montes in 1988) and Michael Hausmann (drums).	
5/18/85	8	13	1. **Voices Carry**	Epic 04795
			Airplay #7 / Sales #9	
11/1/86	26	5	2. What About Love	Epic 06289
			Sales #24 / Airplay #30	
			TIMBUK 3	
			Austin-based husband-and-wife duo: Pat and Barbara Kooyman MacDonald, and a tape machine. Met while Barbara was attending the University of Wisconsin in 1978.	
11/22/86	19	9	1. The Future's So Bright, I Gotta Wear Shades	I.R.S. 52940
			Sales #14 / Airplay #24	
			TIME, The	
			Funk group formed in Minneapolis by Prince and Morris Day in 1981. Original lineup: Morris Day (lead singer), Terry Lewis, Jimmy "Jam" Harris, Monte Moir, Jesse Johnson and Jellybean Johnson. Lewis, Harris and Moir left before band's featured role in the movie *Purple Rain*. Paul "St. Paul" Peterson and Lewis's half-brother, Jerome Benton, joined in 1984; group disbanded later that year. Day and Jesse Johnson went solo; Lewis and Harris became highly successful songwriting/producing team. Lewis married Karyn White. Original lineup plus Benton regrouped in 1990.	
1/5/85	20	10	1. Jungle Love	Warner 29181
			Airplay #14 / Sales #23	
4/13/85	36	2	2. The Bird	Warner 29094
			Airplay #28; above 2 from the movie *Purple Rain* starring Prince and Apollonia Kotero	

DATE	POS	WKS	ARTIST–RECORD TITLE	LABEL & NO.
7/14/90	9	11	● 3. **Jerk-Out** Sales #9 / Airplay #9; #1 R&B hit (1 week)	Paisley P. 19750
4/23/88	21	8	**TIMES TWO** Male duo of vocalists/keyboardists from Pt. Reyes, California: Shanti Jones and Johnny Dollar. 1. **Strange But True** Airplay #20 / Sales #21	Reprise 27998
7/12/86	8	12	**TIMEX SOCIAL CLUB** Rap trio from Berkeley, California: Michael Marshall, Marcus Thompson and Alex Hill. Produced by Jay King, who later formed and fronted Club Nouveau. 1. **Rumors** Airplay #6 / Sales #8; #1 R&B hit (2 weeks)	Jay 7001
5/5/90 1/19/91	40 1 (1)	1 16	**TIMMY -T-** Born Timmy Torres on 9/23/67 in Fresno, California. 1. **Time After Time** Sales #30 ▲ 2. **One More Try** Sales #1(5) / Airplay #2; a different version is on the B-side of #1 above	Jam City 5003 Quality 15114
5/8/71	20	6	**TIN TIN** Australian duo: Steve Kipner (keyboards) and Steve Groves (guitar). Disbanded in 1973. Kipner later co-wrote Chicago's "Hard Habit To Break" and Olivia Newton-John's "Physical" and "Twist Of Fate." 1. **Toast And Marmalade For Tea**	Atco 6794
6/8/68	17	6	**TINY TIM** Born Herbert Khaury on 4/12/30 in New York City. Novelty singer/ukulele player. Shot to national attention with appearances on TV's "Rowan & Martin's Laugh-In." Married "Miss Vicki" on Johnny Carson's "Tonight Show" on 12/18/69; divorced in 1977. 1. **Tip-Toe Thru' The Tulips With Me** [N] #1 hit (10 weeks) for Nick Lucas in 1929 (from the movie musical *Gold Diggers of Broadway* starring Nancy Welford)	Reprise 0679
3/21/92 6/27/92 10/3/92	6 2 (6) 7	17 24 21	**TLC** Atlanta-based teenage female rap trio: Tionne "T-Boz" Watkins, Lisa "Left Eye" Lopes and Rozonda "Chilli" Thomas. Founded and managed by Pebbles. Lopes was sentenced to five years probation for setting fire, on 6/9/94, to the house of her boyfriend, Andre Rison, a receiver for the Atlanta Falcons football team. Group filed for Chapter 11 bankruptcy in 1995. ▲ 1. **Ain't 2 Proud 2 Beg** Sales #3 / Airplay #9; samples James Brown's "Escape-ism," Kool & The Gang's "Jungle Boogie," AWB's "School Boy Crush," Silver Convention's "Fly, Robin, Fly" and Bob James's "Take Me To The Mardi Gras" ▲ 2. **Baby-Baby-Baby** Airplay #1(2) / Sales #3; #1 R&B hit (2 weeks) ● 3. **What About Your Friends** Sales #6 / Airplay #7	LaFace 24008 LaFace 24028 LaFace 24025

DATE	POS	WKS	ARTIST–RECORD TITLE	LABEL & NO.
2/27/93	30	5	4. Hat 2 Da Back Sales #24 / Airplay #29; samples "Big Ole Butt" (L.L. Cool J) and "What Makes You Happy" (KC & The Sunshine Band); all of above from the album *Ooooooohhh...On The TLC Tip*	LaFace 24043
11/19/94+	1 (4)	29	▲ 5. **Creep** Sales #1(5) / Airplay #3; samples "Hey Young World" by Slick Rick; #1 R&B hit (9 weeks)	LaFace 24082
3/4/95	2 (3)	19	● 6. **Red Light Special** Sales #2 / Airplay #4	LaFace 24097
6/10/95	1 (7)	28	▲ 7. **Waterfalls** Sales #1(3) / Airplay #2	LaFace 24107
11/18/95	5	16	● 8. **Diggin' On You** Sales #5 / Airplay #10; above 4 from the album *CrazySexyCool*	LaFace 24119
			## TOAD THE WET SPROCKET Pop quartet from Santa Barbara, California: Glen Phillips (vocals), Todd Nichols (guitar), Dean Dinning (bass) and Randy Guss (drums). Name taken from a Monty Python skit.	
7/25/92	15	18	1. All I Want Airplay #8 / Sales #28	Columbia 74355
12/19/92+	18	11	2. Walk On The Ocean Airplay #21 / Sales #57	Columbia 74706
7/16/94	33	4	3. Fall Down Airplay #31	Columbia 77474
			## TOBY BEAU Texas pop quintet: Balde Silva (vocals), Danny McKenna, Rob Young, Steve Zipper and Ron Rose.	
7/1/78	13	12	1. My Angel Baby #1 Adult Contemporary hit (1 week)	RCA 11250
			## TODD, Art And Dotty Pop duo consisting of Arthur W. Todd (born 3/11/20) and Dotty Todd (born 6/22/23), both from Elizabeth, New Jersey. Married in 1941.	
4/21/58	6	11	1. **Chanson d'Amour (Song Of Love)** Jockey #6 / Best Seller #13 / Top 100 #13	Era 1064
			## TODD, Nick Born Nicholas Boone on 6/1/35 in Jacksonville, Florida. Pat Boone's younger brother.	
2/10/58	21	2	1. At The Hop Jockey #21 / Top 100 #70; Billy Vaughn (orch.)	Dot 15675
			## TOKENS, The Vocal group originally formed as the Linc-Tones at Lincoln High School in Brooklyn in 1955. Consisted of Hank Medress, Neil Sedaka, Eddie Rabkin and Cynthia Zolitin. First recorded for Melba in 1956. Rabkin replaced by Jay Siegel in 1956. Zolitin and Sedaka left in 1958. Medress then formed Darrell & The Oxfords, 1958–59, then re-formed The Tokens with brothers Phil and Mitch Margo and recorded for Warwick in 1960. Formed own label, B.T. Puppy, in 1964 and produced The Happenings. Medress produced Tony Orlando & Dawn, and then left The Tokens, who continued as a trio and recorded as Cross Country in 1973.	
4/24/61	15	6	1. Tonight I Fell In Love	Warwick 615

DATE	POS	WKS	ARTIST–RECORD TITLE	LABEL & NO.
11/27/61	**1** (3)	13	● 2. **The Lion Sleeps Tonight** #14 hit for The Weavers in 1952 (as "Wimoweh" - a South African Zulu song)	RCA 7954
4/9/66	30	5	3. I Hear Trumpets Blow	B.T. Puppy 518
5/20/67	36	2	4. Portrait Of My Love	Warner 5900
			TOMMY TUTONE San Francisco rock band led by Tommy Heath (vocals) and Jim Keller (lead guitar).	
6/21/80	38	2	1. Angel Say No	Columbia 11278
3/13/82	4	16	● 2. **867-5309/Jenny**	Columbia 02646
			TOM TOM CLUB Studio funk project formed by Talking Heads members/husband-and-wife Chris Frantz and Tina Weymouth. Production work for Ziggy Marley & The Melody Makers, Happy Mondays and others.	
4/10/82	31	4	1. Genius Of Love lyrics mention funk masters Bootsy Collins, Hamilton Bohannon, Kurtis Blow and James Brown	Sire 49882
			TONE LŌC L.A.-based rapper, Anthony Smith. Stage name (pronounced: tone loke) derived from his Spanish nickname "Antonio Loco." Contributed voice to the animated movie *Bebe's Kids* and appeared in the movies *Surf Ninjas, Posse* and *Ace Ventura: Pet Detective*.	
12/24/88+	**2** (1)	14	▲² 1. **Wild Thing** Sales #1(2) / Airplay #3	Delicious V. 102
3/18/89	3	11	▲ 2. **Funky Cold Medina** Sales #2 / Airplay #5	Delicious V. 104
			TONEY, Oscar, Jr. Born on 5/26/39 in Selma, Alabama; raised in Columbus, Georgia. R&B singer.	
6/17/67	23	5	1. For Your Precious Love	Bell 672
			TONY AND JOE Tony Savonne and Joe Saraceno. Also see The T-Bones.	
8/4/58	33	1	1. The Freeze Hot 100 #33 / Best Seller #39	Era 1075
			TONY! TONI! TONÉ! R&B-funk trio from Oakland, California. Brothers Dwayne and Raphael Wiggins, with cousin Timothy Christian. Appeared in the movie *House Party 2*. Dwayne assembled Simple E.	
9/22/90	9	17	● 1. **Feels Good** Sales #5 / Airplay #15; #1 R&B hit (2 weeks)	Wing 877436
2/2/91	34	4	2. It Never Rains (In Southern California) Sales #19; #1 R&B hit (2 weeks)	Wing 879068
			TONY TONI TONÉ:	
6/26/93	7	17	● 3. **If I Had No Loot** Sales #7 / Airplay #9; samples "The 'P' Is Free" by KRS-1, "The Wrong Nigga To Fuck Wit" by Ice Cube and "Knock On Wood" by Eddie Floyd	Wing 859056

DATE	POS	WKS	ARTIST–RECORD TITLE	LABEL & NO.
10/9/93	10	14	● 4. **Anniversary** *Sales #8 / Airplay #11*	Wing 859566
2/5/94	31	6	5. (Lay Your Head On My) Pillow *Airplay #28 / Sales #28*	Wing 858260
			## TORME, Mel	
			Born Melvin Howard on 9/13/25 in Chicago. Jazz singer/songwriter/ pianist/drummer/actor. Wrote Nat King Cole's "The Christmas Song." Appeared in the movies *Higher And Higher* and *Pardon My Rhythm.* Frequently appeared as himself on TV's "Night Court." Nicknamed "The Velvet Fog."	
12/15/62	36	3	1. Comin' Home Baby *Klaus Ogermann (orch.)*	Atlantic 2165
			## TORNADOES, The	
			English surf-rock instrumental quintet organized by producer Joe Meek in 1962. Original lineup: Alan Caddy (lead guitar), George Bellamy, Roger LaVerne Jackson, Heinz Burt and Clem Cattini. Meek committed suicide on 2/3/67.	
11/17/62	1 (3)	13	1. **Telstar** [I]	London 9561
			## TOROK, Mitchell	
			Born on 10/28/29 in Houston. Singer/songwriter/guitarist. First recorded in 1948.	
4/29/57	25	3	1. Pledge Of Love *Best Seller #25 / Top 100 #26*	Decca 30230
8/31/59	27	6	2. Caribbean *original version by Torok hit #1 on the Country charts in 1953 on Abbott 140*	Guyden 2018
			## TOTAL	
			Female vocal trio from New York City: JaKima Raynor, Keisha Spivey and Pam Long.	
4/22/95	13	14	● 1. Can't You See **TOTAL featuring The Notorious B.I.G.** *Sales #9 / Airplay #28; from the movie New Jersey Drive starring Sharron Corley; samples "The Payback" by James Brown*	Tommy Boy 7676
			## TOTO	
			Pop-rock group formed in Los Angeles in 1978. Consisted of Bobby Kimball (vocals; his real last name is not Toteaux, as widely rumored), Steve Lukather (guitar), David Paich and Steve Porcaro (keyboards), David Hungate (bass) and Jeff Porcaro (drums; died 8/5/92, age 38). Prominent session musicians, most notably behind Boz Scaggs in the late '70s. Hungate was replaced by Mike Porcaro in 1983. (The Porcaros are brothers.) Kimball replaced by Fergie Fredericksen in 1984; Fredericksen replaced by Joseph Williams (conductor John Williams's son) in 1986. Steve Porcaro left in 1988. Paich and his father, Marty, won an Emmy for writing the theme for the TV series "Ironside."	
11/11/78+	5	14	● 1. **Hold The Line**	Columbia 10830
2/9/80	26	8	2. 99	Columbia 11173
5/8/82	2 (5)	18	● 3. **Rosanna** *written about Steve Porcaro's then-girlfriend, actress Rosanna Arquette*	Columbia 02811
9/11/82	30	5	4. Make Believe	Columbia 03143
11/20/82+	1 (1)	16	● 5. **Africa**	Columbia 03335

DATE	POS	WKS	ARTIST–RECORD TITLE	LABEL & NO.
3/26/83	**10**	12	6. **I Won't Hold You Back** #1 Adult Contemporary hit (3 weeks); above 4 from the album *Toto IV*	Columbia 03597
11/24/84	**30**	6	7. Stranger In Town Airplay #22	Columbia 04672
9/27/86	**11**	12	8. I'll Be Over You Sales #10 / Airplay #11; #1 Adult Contemporary hit (2 weeks)	Columbia 06280
2/7/87	**38**	2	9. Without Your Love Airplay #32	Columbia 06570
3/26/88	**22**	8	10. Pamela Sales #17 / Airplay #20	Columbia 07715

TOWER OF POWER

Interracial Oakland-based R&B-funk band formed by sax player Emilio "Mimi" Castillo in the late '60s. Lenny Williams sang lead, 1972–75. Originally known as the Motowns.

DATE	POS	WKS	ARTIST–RECORD TITLE	LABEL & NO.
8/26/72	**29**	5	1. You're Still A Young Man	Warner 7612
6/16/73	**17**	11	2. So Very Hard To Go	Warner 7687
8/24/74	**26**	4	3. Don't Change Horses (In The Middle Of A Stream)	Warner 7828

TOWNSELL, Lidell, & M.T.F.

Townsell is a DJ/mixer from Chicago. M.T.F., which stands for More Than Friends, is made up of singer Martell and rapper Silk E.

DATE	POS	WKS	ARTIST–RECORD TITLE	LABEL & NO.
3/28/92	**26**	12	1. Nu Nu Airplay #20 / Sales #25	Mercury 866780

TOWNSEND, Ed

Born on 4/16/29 in Fayetteville, Tennessee. R&B singer/songwriter. His son David is a member of Surface. Wrote Marvin Gaye's "Let's Get It On."

DATE	POS	WKS	ARTIST–RECORD TITLE	LABEL & NO.
4/28/58	**13**	13	1. For Your Love Jockey #13 / Best Seller #15 / Top 100 #15; Gerald Wilson (orch.)	Capitol 3926

TOWNSHEND, Pete

Born on 5/19/45 in London. Lead guitarist/songwriter of The Who. First solo album *Who Came First*, 1972. Own publishing house, Eel Pie Press, mid-1970s. Currently plagued by a significant hearing loss.

DATE	POS	WKS	ARTIST–RECORD TITLE	LABEL & NO.
7/5/80	**9**	12	1. **Let My Love Open The Door**	Atco 7217
12/21/85+	**26**	7	2. Face The Face Sales #24 / Airplay #27	Atco 99590

TOYS, The

Soul trio from Woodrow Wilson High School, Jamaica, New York: Barbara Harris, June Montiero and Barbara Parritt. Appearances on "Shindig" TV show in 1965. Appeared in the movie *The Girl In Daddy's Bikini*.

DATE	POS	WKS	ARTIST–RECORD TITLE	LABEL & NO.
10/2/65	**2** (3)	11	● 1. **A Lover's Concerto** adapted from Bach's *Minuet From The Anna Magdalena Notebook*	DynoVoice 209
1/1/66	**18**	6	2. Attack	DynoVoice 214

DATE	POS	WKS	ARTIST–RECORD TITLE	LABEL & NO.
			T'PAU	
			Group from Shrewsbury, England. Carol Decker, lead singer. Band named after a Vulcan Princess in an episode of the TV series "Star Trek."	
6/6/87	4	16	1. **Heart And Soul** *Airplay #3 / Sales #5*	Virgin 99466
			TRADE WINDS, The	
			New York City pop singing/songwriting/production duo: Pete Anders (Andreoli) and Vinnie Poncia. First recorded with group The Videls. Also recorded as The Innocence. Poncia produced several albums for Ringo Starr and Melissa Manchester.	
2/27/65	32	4	1. New York's A Lonely Town	Red Bird 020
			TRAMMPS, The	
			Philadelphia disco group. Key members: Jimmy Ellis (lead tenor), Earl Young (lead bass), Harold and Stanley Wade (tenors) and Robert Upchurch (baritone). Own Golden Fleece label in 1973.	
2/21/76	35	4	1. Hold Back The Night	Buddah 507
6/5/76	27	5	2. That's Where The Happy People Go	Atlantic 3306
3/25/78	11	13	3. Disco Inferno *from the movie Saturday Night Fever starring John Travolta; some pressings have #2 above as the B-side*	Atlantic 3389
			TRASHMEN, The	
			Minneapolis/St. Paul surf-rock quartet: Tony Andreason, Dal Winslow, Bob Reed and Steve Wahrer (died of throat cancer 1/21/89, age 47). Both hits taken from tunes by The Rivingtons: "Papa-Oom-Mow-Mow" and "The Bird's The Word."	
12/28/63+	4	10	1. **Surfin' Bird**	Garrett 4002
2/29/64	30	4	2. Bird Dance Beat	Garrett 4003
			TRAVIS & BOB	
			Travis Pritchett and Bob Weaver from Jackson, Alabama.	
4/6/59	8	9	1. **Tell Him No**	Sandy 1017
			TRAVOLTA, John	
			Born on 2/18/54 in Englewood, New Jersey. Actor/singer. Played Vinnie Barbarino on the TV series "Welcome Back Kotter." Starred in the movies *Saturday Night Fever, Grease, Urban Cowboy, Look Who's Talking* and others. Married actress Kelly Preston on 9/5/91.	
6/12/76	10	10	1. **Let Her In**	Midland I. 10623
11/27/76	38	2	2. Whenever I'm Away From You	Midland I. 10780
3/19/77	34	3	3. All Strung Out On You	Midland I. 10907
4/8/78	1 (1)	16	▲ 4. **You're The One That I Want** **JOHN TRAVOLTA AND OLIVIA NEWTON-JOHN**	RSO 891
8/19/78	5	12	● 5. **Summer Nights** **JOHN TRAVOLTA, OLIVIA NEWTON-JOHN & CAST** *above 2 from the movie Grease starring Travolta and Newton-John*	RSO 906

DATE	POS	WKS	ARTIST–RECORD TITLE	LABEL & NO.
			TREMELOES, The	
			British pop-rock quartet: Alan Blakely, Dave Munden, Ricky West and Len "Chip" Hawkes. Group originally formed by Brian Poole (born 11/3/41, England). Alan was the brother of Mike Blakely of Christie. Hawkes is the father of singer Chesney Hawkes.	
5/6/67	13	8	1. Here Comes My Baby written by Cat Stevens	Epic 10139
7/15/67	11	10	2. Silence Is Golden originally recorded by The 4 Seasons in 1964 (B-side of "Rag Doll")	Epic 10184
10/21/67	36	4	3. Even The Bad Times Are Good	Epic 10233
			TRESVANT, Ralph	
			Born on 5/16/68 and raised in Roxbury, Massachusetts. Member of New Edition. Appeared in the movie *House Party 2*.	
11/17/90+	4	16	● 1. **Sensitivity** Airplay #3 / Sales #3; #1 R&B hit (1 week)	MCA 53932
4/6/91	34	3	2. Stone Cold Gentleman Sales #32 / Airplay #34; Bobby Brown (guest rapper)	MCA 54043
5/30/92	10	18	3. **The Best Things In Life Are Free** **LUTHER VANDROSS and JANET JACKSON with BBD and Ralph Tresvant** Airplay #5 / Sales #16; #1 R&B hit (1 week)	Perspective 0010
			T. REX	
			British rock group led by Marc Bolan (born Marc Feld, 7/30/47, London; killed in an auto accident on 9/16/77). Guitarist Jack Green joined in 1973 and left a year later to join Pretty Things.	
1/29/72	10	11	1. **Bang A Gong (Get It On)** Howard Kaylan & Mark Volman of The Turtles (backing vocals)	Reprise 1032
			TRIPLETS, The	
			Triplet sisters Diana, Sylvia and Vicky Villegas. Born on 4/18/65, seven minutes apart. Raised in Mexico by their American mother and Mexican father. Gained recognition after winning an "MTV Basement Tapes" competition in 1986.	
4/6/91	14	10	1. You Don't Have To Go Home Tonight Airplay #12 / Sales #13	Mercury 878864
			TRIUMPH	
			Canadian hard-rock trio formed in Toronto in 1975. Consisted of Rik Emmett (guitar, vocals), Gil Moore (drums, vocals) and Mike Levine (keyboards, bass). Emmett went solo in 1988. Phil X (guitar) joined by 1992.	
8/25/79	38	2	1. Hold On	RCA 11569
10/18/86	27	5	2. Somebody's Out There Sales #20 / Airplay #40	MCA 52898
			TRIUMPHS, The—see THOMAS, B.J.	
			TROCCOLI, Kathy	
			New York City native. Grammy-nominated Contemporary Christian artist. Backing singer with Taylor Dayne.	
3/7/92	14	14	1. Everything Changes Airplay #7 / Sales #50	Reunion 19118

DATE	POS	WKS	ARTIST–RECORD TITLE	LABEL & NO.
			TROGGS, The	
			British rock quartet from Andover, England. Reg Presley (real name: Reg Ball; lead singer), Chris Britton (guitar), Pete Staples (bass) and Ronnie "Bond" Bullis (drums; died 11/13/92, age 51).	
7/9/66	1 (2)	9	1. **Wild Thing/**	
			same version charted simultaneously on Fontana 1548	
9/3/66	29	2	2. With A Girl Like You	Atco 6415
			same version charted simultaneously on Fontana 1552	
3/23/68	7	12	3. **Love Is All Around**	Fontana 1607
			TROY, Doris	
			Born Doris Higginson on 1/6/37 in New York City. R&B vocalist/songwriter. Used Doris Payne as her pen name. The off-Broadway musical *Mama, I Want To Sing* is based on her life. Backing vocalist on Pink Floyd's album *Dark Side Of The Moon*.	
7/6/63	10	8	1. **Just One Look**	Atlantic 2188
			TRUE, Andrea, Connection	
			Disco act led by white Nashville-born vocalist Andrea True. True moved to New York in 1968 and wrote commercials for radio and TV. Her break came while singing at the Riverboat in the Empire State Building in 1974.	
4/24/76	4	16	● 1. **More, More, More (Pt. 1)**	Buddah 515
3/26/77	27	5	2. N.Y., You Got Me Dancing	Buddah 564
			TUBES, The	
			San Francisco theater-rock troupe led by vocalist Fee Waybill (born John Waldo on 9/17/50 in Omaha, Nebraska). Group appeared in the movie musical *Xanadu* with Olivia Newton-John in 1980.	
8/1/81	35	3	1. Don't Want To Wait Anymore	Capitol 5007
5/7/83	10	12	2. **She's A Beauty**	Capitol 5217
			TUCKER, Tanya	
			Born on 10/10/58 in Seminole, Texas; raised in Wilcox, Arizona. Prominent country singer. Played bit part in the movie *Jeremiah Johnson* in 1972.	
6/7/75	37	2	1. Lizzie And The Rainman	MCA 40402
			#1 Country hit (1 week)	
			TUCKER, Tommy	
			Born Robert Higginbotham on 3/5/39 in Springfield, Ohio. Died of poisoning on 1/22/82. R&B vocalist/pianist. First recorded for Hi in 1959.	
2/29/64	11	8	1. Hi-Heel Sneakers	Checker 1067
			TUNE WEAVERS, The	
			Boston R&B quartet consisting of Margo Sylvia (lead), husband John Sylvia (bass), Gilbert Lopez (Margo's brother; tenor) and Charlotte Davis (Margo's cousin). Margo died of a heart attack/stroke on 10/25/91.	
9/23/57	5	14	1. **Happy, Happy Birthday Baby**	Checker 872
			Top 100 #5 / Best Seller #8 / Jockey #12; first released on Casa Grande 4037 in 1957; Frank Paul (orch.)	

DATE	POS	WKS	ARTIST–RECORD TITLE	LABEL & NO.
			TURBANS, The	
			Philadelphia R&B quartet: Al Banks (lead), Matthew Platt (tenor), Charles Williams (baritone) and Andrew "Chet" Jones (bass). Disbanded in 1961.	
1/14/56	33	1	1. When You Dance	Herald 458
			TURNER, Ike & Tina	
			Husband-and-wife duo: guitarist Ike Turner (born 11/5/31 in Clarksdale, Mississippi) and vocalist Tina Turner (born Anna Mae Bullock on 11/26/38 in Brownsville, Tennessee). Married 1958–76. At age 11, Ike was backing pianist for bluesmen Sonny Boy Williamson (Aleck Ford) and Robert Nighthawk (of the Nighthawks). Formed own band, the Kings of Rhythm, while in high school; backed Jackie Brenston's hit "Rocket '88.'" Prolific session, production and guitar work during the 1950s. In 1960, developed a dynamic stage show around Tina; "The Ike & Tina Turner Revue" featuring her backing vocalists, The Ikettes, and Ike's Kings Of Rhythm. Disbanded in 1974. In the mid-1980s, Tina emerged as a successful solo artist. Duet inducted into the Rock and Roll Hall of Fame in 1991.	
10/3/60	27	6	1. A Fool In Love	Sue 730
9/4/61	14	5	2. It's Gonna Work Out Fine	Sue 749
			Mickey & Sylvia (backing vocals)	
1/13/62	38	2	3. Poor Fool	Sue 753
8/8/70	34	6	4. I Want To Take You Higher	Liberty 56177
			IKE & TINA TURNER & THE IKETTES	
2/13/71	4	11	● 5. **Proud Mary**	Liberty 56216
10/27/73	22	6	6. Nutbush City Limits	United Art. 298
			a "live" solo version by Tina is on the B-side of her "Private Dancer"	
			TURNER, Jesse Lee	
			Rockabilly singer from Bowling, Texas.	
1/26/59	20	6	1. The Little Space Girl [N]	Carlton 496
			TURNER, Sammy	
			Born Samuel Black on 6/2/32 in Paterson, New Jersey. Tommy Edwards-styled vocalist.	
7/6/59	3	14	1. **Lavender-Blue**	Big Top 3016
			originally released on Pacific 3016 in 1958; #4 hit for Sammy Kaye in 1949	
11/16/59	19	7	2. Always	Big Top 3029
			originally released on Pacific 3029 in 1959; 4 versions hit the Top 10 in 1926	
			TURNER, Spyder	
			Born Dwight D. Turner in 1947 in Beckley, West Virginia. Soul vocalist.	
1/14/67	12	8	1. Stand By Me [N]	MGM 13617
			vocal impressions of Jackie Wilson, David Ruffin, Billy Stewart, Smokey Robinson and Chuck Jackson	
			TURNER, Tina	
			Born Anna Mae Bullock on 11/26/38 in Brownsville, Tennessee. R&B-rock vocalist/actress. Half of Ike & Tina Turner duo, when married to Ike, 1958–76. Appeared in the movies *Tommy* (1975; cast as the Acid Queen) and *Mad Max-Beyond Thunderdome* (1985). With Ike, inducted into the Rock and Roll Hall of Fame in 1991.	
2/18/84	26	7	1. Let's Stay Together	Capitol 5322

DATE	POS	WKS	ARTIST–RECORD TITLE	LABEL & NO.
6/23/84	**1 (3)**	18	● 2. **What's Love Got To Do With It** Sales #18 pre	Capitol 5354
10/6/84	**5**	13	3. **Better Be Good To Me** Airplay #5 / Sales #6	Capitol 5387
1/26/85	**7**	12	4. **Private Dancer** Sales #7 / Airplay #10; written by Mark Knopfler (of Dire Straits); Jeff Beck (guitar)	Capitol 5433
5/18/85	**37**	3	5. Show Some Respect above 5 from the album *Private Dancer*	Capitol 5461
7/20/85	**2 (1)**	12	6. **We Don't Need Another Hero (Thunderdome)** Sales #3 / Airplay #3	Capitol 5491
10/12/85	**15**	10	7. One Of The Living Sales #13 / Airplay #14; above 2 from the movie *Mad Max- Beyond Thunderdome* starring Mel Gibson and Turner	Capitol 5518
12/7/85+	**15**	9	8. It's Only Love **BRYAN ADAMS/TINA TURNER** Airplay #14 / Sales #16	A&M 2791
9/6/86	**2 (3)**	12	9. **Typical Male** Sales #1(2) / Airplay #2	Capitol 5615
12/20/86+	**30**	5	10. Two People Sales #27 / Airplay #32	Capitol 5644
3/7/87	**13**	7	11. What You Get Is What You See Sales #12 / Airplay #16	Capitol 5668
9/23/89	**15**	8	12. The Best Sales #12 / Airplay #20; Edgar Winter (sax solo); also on the B- side of #13 below	Capitol 44442
1/6/90	**39**	1	13. Steamy Windows Sales #32	Capitol 44473
7/3/93	**9**	17	14. **I Don't Wanna Fight** Airplay #3 / Sales #28; from Tina's autobiographical movie *What's Love Got To Do With It* starring Angela Bassett and Laurence Fishburne; #1 Adult Contemporary hit (7 weeks)	Virgin 12652

TURTLES, The

Pop-folk-rock group formed at Westchester High School in Los Angeles in
1961. Led by Mark Volman (born 4/19/47, Los Angeles) and Howard
Kaylan (born Howard Kaplan on 6/22/47, New York City). First called the
Nightriders; then the Crossfires. Recorded for Capco in 1963. Name
changed to The Turtles in 1965. Many personnel changes except for Volman
and Kaylan. Group disbanded in 1970. Volman and Kaylan joined the
Mothers Of Invention. Went out as a duo in 1972 and recorded as
Phlorescent Leech & Eddie and later as Flo & Eddie. Did soundtrack for the
movie *Strawberry Shortcake*. Toured again as The Turtles in 1985.

8/21/65	**8**	8	1. **It Ain't Me Babe** written by Bob Dylan	White Whale 222
11/20/65	**29**	4	2. Let Me Be	White Whale 224
2/19/66	**20**	9	3. You Baby	White Whale 227
3/4/67	**1 (3)**	12	● 4. **Happy Together**	White Whale 244
5/27/67	**3**	8	5. **She'd Rather Be With Me**	White Whale 249
8/26/67	**12**	7	6. You Know What I Mean	White Whale 254
12/2/67	**14**	7	7. She's My Girl	White Whale 260
10/12/68	**6**	9	8. Elenore	White Whale 276
1/25/69	**6**	9	9. **You Showed Me**	White Whale 292

DATE	POS	WKS	ARTIST–RECORD TITLE	LABEL & NO.
			TUXEDO JUNCTION	
			Female disco studio group assembled by producers W. Michael Lewis and Lauren Rinder.	
7/1/78	32	2	1. Chattanooga Choo Choo	Butterfly 1205
			#1 hit for Glenn Miller in 1941 (from the movie *Sun Valley Serenade* starring Sonja Henie)	
			TWAIN, Shania	
			Shania pronounced: shu-NYE-uh. Born on 8/28/65 in Windsor, Ontario. Country singer. Married to Robert John "Mutt" Lange, producer of Def Leppard, The Cars, Foreigner and many others.	
7/8/95	31	7	1. Any Man Of Mine	Mercury 856448
			Sales #13; #1 Country hit (2 weeks)	
			12 GAUGE	
			Born Isiah Pinkney in Augusta, Georgia. Rapper.	
3/26/94	28	9	● 1. Dunkie Butt (Please Please Please)	Danzalot 75373
			Sales #10	
			20 FINGERS featuring GILLETTE	
			Duo of Chicago-based producers Charles Babie and Manfred Mohr, with female rapper Sandra Gillette.	
11/12/94+	14	18	● 1. Short Dick Man [N]	SOS/Zoo 14194
			Sales #4 / Airplay #55; clean version available on DJW 114 (cassette maxi-single) and on Zoo 14193 as "Short Short Man"	
			TWILLEY, Dwight	
			Born on 6/6/51 in Tulsa, Oklahoma. Rock singer/songwriter/pianist. Formed the Dwight Twilley Band with Phil Seymour (bass, drums; died of lymphoma 8/17/93, age 41) in 1974.	
6/21/75	16	8	1. I'm On Fire	Shelter 40380
			DWIGHT TWILLEY BAND	
3/3/84	16	10	2. Girls	EMI America 8196
			TWISTED SISTER	
			Hard-rock quintet from Long Island, New York, led by Dee Snider (born 3/15/55, Massapequa, Long Island). Included Jay French (guitar), Eddie Ojeda (guitar), Mark Mendosa (bass) and A.J. Pero (drums). Pero replaced by Joey Franco in 1987. Disbanded in late 1987.	
8/18/84	21	7	1. We're Not Gonna Take It	Atlantic 89641
			TWITTY, Conway	
			Born Harold Lloyd Jenkins on 9/1/33 in Friars Point, Mississippi; raised in Helena, Arkansas. Died of an abdominal aneurysm on 6/5/93. Superstar country singer who charted 40 #1 country hits. Formed own group, the Phillips County Ramblers, at age 10. Offered a professional contract with the Philadelphia Phillies when drafted. With service band Cimmarons in Japan, early 1950s. Changed his name in 1957 (borrowed from Conway, Arkansas, and Twitty, Texas) and first recorded for Sun (unissued recordings). Appeared in the the movies *Sexpot Goes To College* and *College Confidential*. Switched from pop to country music in 1965. Moved to Nashville in 1968. Own tourist complex, Twitty City, in Hendersonville, Tennessee.	
9/29/58	1 (2)	17	● 1. It's Only Make Believe	MGM 12677

DATE	POS	WKS	ARTIST—RECORD TITLE	LABEL & NO.
2/16/59	28	7	2. The Story Of My Love	MGM 12748
8/24/59	29	3	3. Mona Lisa *#1 hit for Nat King Cole in 1950 (from the movie Captain Carey, U.S.A. starring Alan Ladd)*	MGM 12804
10/12/59	10	13	4. **Danny Boy** *based on the traditional Irish song "Londonderry Air" of 1855*	MGM 12826
1/18/60	6	10	● 5. **Lonely Blue Boy** *originally recorded (unreleased) by Elvis Presley as "Danny" for the movie King Creole*	MGM 12857
4/25/60	26	5	6. What Am I Living For	MGM 12886
7/11/60	35	5	7. Is A Blue Bird Blue	MGM 12911
1/16/61	22	5	8. C'est Si Bon (It's So Good) *#21 hit for Danny Kaye in 1950*	MGM 12969
9/15/73	22	7	9. You've Never Been This Far Before *#1 Country hit (3 weeks)*	MCA 40094
			2 IN A ROOM Dance duo from Washington Heights, New York: rapper Rafael "Dose" Vargas and remixer Roger "Rog Nice" Pauletta.	
11/10/90	15	12	● 1. Wiggle It *Sales #7 / Airplay #24*	Cutting 98887
			2 LIVE CREW, The Miami-based rap outfit: David "Mr. Mixx" Hobbs, Chris "Kid-Ice" Wong Won, Mark "Brother Marquis" Ross and leader, Luther "Luke Skyywalker" Campbell (owner of Luke Records). Group's obscenity arrests sparked national censorship controversy in 1990. By 1994, group consisted of Campbell, Won and Larry "Verb" Dobson, with special appearances by Rudy Ray "Dolomite" Moore; changed name to The New 2 Live Crew.	
10/21/89	26	9	● 1. Me So Horny *Sales #18*	Skyywalker 130
8/4/90	20	7	● 2. Banned In The U.S.A. **LUKE Featuring 2 LIVE CREW** *Sales #8; tune based on Bruce Springsteen's "Born In The U.S.A."*	Luke 98915
			2 PAC Rapper/actor Tupac Amaru Shakur. Member of Digital Underground in 1991. Appeared in the movies *Nothing But Trouble, Juice* and *Poetic Justice.* Numerous run-ins with the law. Found guilty on 2/10/94 of the 1993 assault and battery of *Menace II Society* co-director Allen Hughes. Shot five times during a robbery in Manhattan on 11/29/94. Sentenced to up to four years in prison on 2/7/95 for a 1993 sexual assault.	
8/21/93	11	15	● 1. I Get Around *Sales #5 / Airplay #24; samples "Computer Land" by Zapp*	Interscope 98372
11/13/93+	12	14	● 2. Keep Ya Head Up *Sales #8 / Airplay #15; samples "O-o-h Child" by The Five Stairsteps and "Be Alright" by Roger*	Interscope 98345
3/11/95	9	17	▲ 3. **Dear Mama/** *Sales #3 / Airplay #39; samples "In My Wildest Dreams" by Joe Sample and "Sadie" by The Spinners*	
		5	4. Old School *Sales flip; samples "We Share" by the Soul Searchers and "Dedication" by Brand Nubian*	Interscope 98273

DATE	POS	WKS	ARTIST–RECORD TITLE	LABEL & NO.
			2 UNLIMITED	
			Techno-house duo from Amsterdam: Ray "Kid Ray" Slijngaard (born 6/28/71) and Anita Dells (born 12/25/71).	
4/1/95	38	2	1. Get Ready For This [R]	Radikal/Crtq. 15535
			Airplay #33; first charted in 1992 at #76	
			TYCOON	
			New York-based pop-rock sextet. Norman Mershon, lead singer.	
4/28/79	26	5	1. Such A Woman	Arista 0398
			TYLER, Bonnie	
			Born Gaynor Hopkins on 6/8/53 in Swansea, Wales. Worked local clubs until the mid-1970s. Distinctive raspy vocals caused by operation to remove throat nodules in 1976.	
4/22/78	3	15	● 1. **It's A Heartache**	RCA 11249
			Mike Gibbins of Badfinger (drums)	
8/13/83	1 (4)	18	● 2. **Total Eclipse Of The Heart**	Columbia 03906
4/7/84	34	4	3. Holding Out For A Hero	Columbia 04370
			from the movie *Footloose* starring Kevin Bacon and Lori Singer	
			TYMES, The	
			Soul group formed in Philadelphia in 1956. Consisted of George Williams (lead), George Hilliard, Donald Banks, Albert Berry and Norman Burnett. First called the Latineers. Berry and Hilliard were replaced by female singers Terri Gonzalez and Melanie Moore in the early '70s.	
6/22/63	1 (1)	12	1. **So Much In Love**	Parkway 871
			originally titled "So In Love"	
8/31/63	7	8	2. **Wonderful! Wonderful!**	Parkway 884
1/4/64	19	6	3. Somewhere	Parkway 891
12/28/68	39	1	4. People	Columbia 44630
			from the movie *Funny Girl* starring Barbra Streisand	
9/7/74	12	8	5. You Little Trustmaker	RCA 10022

U

DATE	POS	WKS	ARTIST–RECORD TITLE	LABEL & NO.
			UB40	
			British interracial reggae octet formed in 1978. Ali Campbell (born 2/15/59, Birmingham, England), lead singer. UB40 stands for Unemployment Benefits, form 40. Other members are Ali's brother Robin Campbell, Earl Falconer, Michael Virtue, Terence "Astro" Wilson, Norman Hassan, Brian Travers and James Brown.	
3/17/84	34	4	1. Red Red Wine	A&M 2600
9/7/85	28	4	2. I Got You Babe	A&M 2758
			UB40 WITH CHRISSIE HYNDE	
			Sales #24	
9/3/88	1 (1)	12	● 3. **Red Red Wine** [R]	A&M 1244
			Sales #1(2) / Airplay #1(1); longer version than #1 above (includes rap by Astro)	
10/27/90	6	15	● 4. **The Way You Do The Things You Do**	Virgin 98978
			Sales #5 / Airplay #10	
5/18/91	7	12	5. **Here I Am (Come And Take Me)**	Virgin 99141
			Airplay #9 / Sales #23	

DATE	POS	WKS	ARTIST–RECORD TITLE	LABEL & NO.
6/5/93	1 (7)	23	▲ 6. **Can't Help Falling In Love** Airplay #1(4) / Sales #2; from the movie *Sliver* starring Sharon Stone and William Baldwin	Virgin 12653
			UGLY KID JOE Rock band from Isla Vista, California: Whitfield Crane (vocals), Klaus Eichstadt and Roger Lahr (guitars), Cordell Crockett (bass), and Mark Davis (drums). By 1992, Dave Fortman had replaced Lahr.	
4/25/92	9	11	1. **Everything About You.** Sales #5 / Airplay #37; from the movie *Wayne's World* starring Mike Myers and Dana Carvey (not on the album soundtrack)	Mercury 866632
3/6/93	6	13	● 2. **Cats In The Cradle** Sales #4 / Airplay #27	Stardog 864888
			U-KREW, The Rap quintet from Portland, Oregon, formed as The Untouchable Krew in October 1984. Led by drum programmer Larry Bell, with lead vocals by Kevin Morse.	
3/24/90	24	7	1. If U Were Mine Sales #17 / Airplay #31	Enigma 75051
			ULLMAN, Tracey Born on 12/30/59 in Buckinghamshire, England. Actress/singer/comedienne. Own variety-style TV show on Fox network, 1987–90. Appeared in the movies *I Love You To Death*, *Plenty* and *Give My Regards To Broad Street*.	
3/17/84	8	11	1. **They Don't Know**	MCA/Stiff 52347
			UNDERGROUND SUNSHINE Rock quartet: Chris Connors and Jane Little (both from Wisconsin), with Frank and Betty Kohl (from Germany).	
8/23/69	26	5	1. Birthday originally recorded by The Beatles on the 1968 *White Album*	Intrepid 75002
			UNDISPUTED TRUTH, The Soul group consisting of Joe Harris, Billie Calvin and Brenda Evans. Many personnel changes thereafter.	
7/31/71	3	13	1. **Smiling Faces Sometimes**	Gordy 7108
			UNIFICS, The Soul vocal group formed at Howard University in Washington, D.C. Al Johnson, lead singer. Member Hal Worthington shot to death on 2/20/90 (age 42).	
10/19/68	25	5	1. Court Of Love	Kapp 935
1/18/69	36	4	2. The Beginning Of My End	Kapp 957
			UNION GAP, The—see PUCKETT, Gary	
			UNIT FOUR plus TWO English pop-rock sextet. Tommy Moeller, lead singer.	
5/29/65	28	4	1. Concrete And Clay	London 9751

DATE	POS	WKS	ARTIST–RECORD TITLE	LABEL & NO.
			UNV	
			Detroit soul vocal quartet: brothers John and Shawn Powe, John Clay and Demetrius Peete. Clay also plays keyboards. UNV stands for Universal Nubian Voices.	
7/10/93	**29**	7	1. Something's Goin' On Sales #17 / Airplay #36	Maverick 18564
			UPCHURCH, Philip, Combo	
			Upchurch was born on 7/19/41 in Chicago. R&B guitarist. Session player for George Benson, Quincy Jones, The Jacksons and many others.	
6/26/61	**29**	3	1. You Can't Sit Down Part 2 [I]	Boyd 3398
			URBAN DANCE SQUAD	
			Amsterdam, Holland-based interracial rap-metal crew. Rapper Patrick "Rude Boy" Remington, backed by the rhythm section of Magic Stick, DNA, Silly Sil and Tres Manos.	
2/2/91	**21**	7	1. Deeper Shade Of Soul Sales #8	Arista 2026
			URIAH HEEP	
			British hard-rock band. Key members: David Byron (lead singer), Mick Box (lead guitar) and Ken Hensley (keyboards; later with Blackfoot). John Lawton replaced Byron in 1977. Peter Goalby replaced Lawton in 1982.	
9/16/72	**39**	3	1. Easy Livin	Mercury 73307
			USA for AFRICA	
			USA: United Support of Artists. A collection of 46 major artists formed to help the suffering people of Africa and the U.S.	
3/23/85	**1 (4)**	12	▲⁴ 1. **We Are The World** Sales #1(5) / Airplay #1(4); soloists (in order): Lionel Richie, Stevie Wonder, Paul Simon, Kenny Rogers, James Ingram, Tina Turner, Billy Joel, Michael Jackson, Diana Ross, Dionne Warwick, Willie Nelson, Al Jarreau, Bruce Springsteen, Kenny Loggins, Steve Perry, Daryl Hall, Huey Lewis, Cyndi Lauper, Kim Carnes, Bob Dylan, and Ray Charles; written by Michael Jackson and Lionel Richie; #1 Adult Contemporary hit (2 weeks); #1 R&B hit (2 weeks)	Columbia 04839
			US3	
			Name pronounced: us three. Jazz/rap collaboration by London producers Mel Simpson (keyboards) and Geoff Wilkinson (samples). Samples of recordings on the Blue Note jazz record label serve as the backdrop for new rap solos and jazz playing by some of Britain's top players.	
1/22/94	**9**	18	● 1. **Cantaloop** Sales #6 / Airplay #20; featuring Rahsaan (rap) and Gerard Presencer (trumpet); samples "Cantaloupe Island" by Herbie Hancock and the introduction from "A Night In Birdland, Vol. 1" by the Art Blakey Quintet	Blue Note 44945
			UTOPIA	
			Pop-rock group formed by Todd Rundgren (guitar, vocals) in 1974. Lineup since 1977 included Kasim Sulton (bass), Roger Powell (keyboards) and John "Willie" Wilcox (drums).	
3/29/80	**27**	5	1. Set Me Free	Bearsville 49180

DATE	POS	WKS	ARTIST–RECORD TITLE	LABEL & NO.
			U2	
			Rock band formed in Dublin, Ireland, in 1976. Consists of Paul "Bono" Hewson (vocals), Dave "The Edge" Evans (guitar), Adam Clayton (bass) and Larry Mullen, Jr. (drums). Met while students at Dublin's Mount Temple High School. Emerged in 1987 as a leading rock act. Released concert tour documentary movie *Rattle And Hum* in 1988.	
12/1/84	33	5	1. Pride (In The Name Of Love) a tribute to Rev. Martin Luther King	Island 99704
4/4/87	**1** (3)	13	2. **With Or Without You** Airplay #1(3) / Sales #1(1)	Island 99469
6/20/87	**1** (2)	13	3. **I Still Haven't Found What I'm Looking For** Airplay #1(1) / Sales #2	Island 99430
10/3/87	13	9	4. Where The Streets Have No Name Sales #11 / Airplay #16	Island 99408
10/8/88	3	13	● 5. **Desire** Sales #1(1) / Airplay #5	Island 99250
1/14/89	14	8	6. Angel Of Harlem Sales #11 / Airplay #14; a tribute to Billie Holiday; above 2 from the U2 concert tour movie *Rattle and Hum*	Island 99254
12/14/91+	9	15	7. **Mysterious Ways** Airplay #11 / Sales #16	Island 866188
3/28/92	10	14	8. **One** Airplay #7 / Sales #17	Island 866533
8/8/92	32	6	9. Even Better Than The Real Thing Airplay #43 / Sales #55	Island 866977
12/5/92	35	5	10. Who's Gonna Ride Your Wild Horses Airplay #42 / Sales #42; above 4 from the album *Achtung Baby*	Island 864521
6/24/95	16	10	11. Hold Me, Thrill Me, Kiss Me, Kill Me Airplay #15 / Sales #19; from the movie *Batman Forever* starring Val Kilmer	Island 87131

V

DATE	POS	WKS	ARTIST–RECORD TITLE	LABEL & NO.
			VALE, Jerry	
			Born Genaro Vitaliano on 7/8/32 in the Bronx. Pop ballad singer.	
3/24/56	30	5	1. Innamorata (Sweetheart) from the movie *Artists & Models* starring Dean Martin and Jerry Lewis	Columbia 40634
7/28/56	14	17	2. You Don't Know Me Best Seller #14 / Top 100 #14 / Juke Box #14 / Jockey #15; Percy Faith (orch., above 2)	Columbia 40710
1/23/65	24	4	3. Have You Looked Into Your Heart #1 Adult Contemporary hit (1 week)	Columbia 43181
			VALENS, Ritchie	
			Born Richard Valenzuela on 5/13/41 in Pacoima, California. Killed in the plane crash that also took the lives of Buddy Holly and the Big Bopper on 2/3/59. Latin rock and roll singer/songwriter/guitarist. Appeared in the movie *Go Johnny Go*. The 1987 movie *La Bamba* was based on his life.	
12/15/58+	**2** (2)	18	● 1. **Donna/**	
1/19/59	22	8	2. La Bamba [F]	Del-Fi 4110

DATE	POS	WKS	ARTIST–RECORD TITLE	LABEL & NO.
			VALENTE, Caterina	
			Born on 1/14/31 in Paris of Italian parentage. Popular European singer/dancer. Sings in six languages.	
4/9/55	8	14	1. **The Breeze And I (Andalucia)**	Decca 29467
			Jockey #8 / Best Seller #13; Werner Muller (orch.); #1 hit for Jimmy Dorsey in 1940	
			VALENTI, John	
			Blue-eyed soul singer from Chicago.	
10/30/76	37	2	1. Anything You Want	Ariola Am. 7625
			VALENTINO, Mark	
			Born Anthony Busillo on 3/12/42 in Philadelphia.	
12/8/62	27	3	1. The Push And Kick	Swan 4121
			Frank Slay (orch.)	
			VALINO, Joe	
			Pop singer from South Philadelphia.	
10/27/56	12	14	1. Garden Of Eden	Vik 0226
			Top 100 #12 / Jockey #12 / Best Seller #13 / Juke Box #13; George Siravo (orch.)	
			VALJEAN	
			Born Valjean Johns on 11/19/34 in Shattuck, Oklahoma. Pianist.	
6/16/62	28	4	1. Theme From Ben Casey [I]	Carlton 573
			from the TV series "Ben Casey" starring Vince Edwards; Jon Neel (orch.)	
			VALLI, Frankie	
			Born Francis Castellucio on 5/3/37 in Newark, New Jersey. Recorded his first solo single in 1953 as Frank Valley on the Corona label. Formed own group, the Variatones, in 1955 and changed its name to The Four Lovers in 1956, which evolved into The 4 Seasons by 1961. Began solo work in 1965. Suffered from a disease that caused hearing loss in the late '70s; corrected by surgery.	
2/12/66	39	1	1. (You're Gonna) Hurt Yourself	Smash 2015
6/3/67	2 (1)	14	● 2. **Can't Take My Eyes Off You**	Philips 40446
9/16/67	18	5	3. I Make A Fool Of Myself	Philips 40484
1/20/68	29	4	4. To Give (The Reason I Live)	Philips 40510
1/18/75	1 (1)	14	● 5. **My Eyes Adored You**	Private St. 45003
6/14/75	6	9	6. **Swearin' To God**	Private St. 45021
			all of above produced by Bob Crewe	
11/8/75	11	8	7. Our Day Will Come	Private St. 45043
5/8/76	36	2	8. Fallen Angel	Private St. 45074
6/17/78	1 (2)	15	▲ 9. **Grease**	RSO 897
			title song from the movie starring John Travolta and Olivia Newton-John	

DATE	POS	WKS	ARTIST–RECORD TITLE	LABEL & NO.
			VALLI, June	
			Born on 6/30/30 in the Bronx. Died on 3/12/93. Co-star of "Lucky Strike Hit Parade" for three years in the 1950s. Voice for Chiquita Banana commercials. Married Chicago DJ Howard Miller.	
5/14/55	29	1	1. Unchained Melody	RCA 6078
			Best Seller #29; from the movie *Unchained* starring Elroy "Crazylegs" Hirsch; Hugh Winterhalter (orch.)	
4/18/60	29	4	2. Apple Green	Mercury 71588
			VANDENBERG	
			Dutch hard-rock band led by Adrian Vandenberg (guitar, keyboards; joined Whitesnake in 1989), Bert Heerink (lead singer), Dick Kemper (bass) and Jos Zoomer (drums).	
3/12/83	39	2	1. Burning Heart	Atco 99947
			VANDROSS, Luther	
			Born on 4/20/51 in New York City. Soul singer/producer/songwriter. Commercial jingle singer, then a top session vocalist/arranger. Sang lead on a few of Change's early albums. Appeared in the movie *The Meteor Man*.	
11/14/81	33	4	1. Never Too Much	Epic 02409
			#1 R&B hit (2 weeks)	
10/29/83	27	5	2. How Many Times Can We Say Goodbye	Arista 9073
			DIONNE WARWICK AND LUTHER VANDROSS	
4/27/85	29	6	3. 'Til My Baby Comes Home	Epic 04760
			Sales #26; Billy Preston (organ solo)	
12/27/86+	15	11	4. Stop To Love	Epic 06523
			Sales #14 / Airplay #14; #1 R&B hit (2 weeks)	
3/4/89	30	4	5. She Won't Talk To Me	Epic 08513
			Airplay #33 / Sales #35	
2/10/90	6	15	● 6. **Here And Now**	Epic 73029
			Sales #6 / Airplay #7; #1 R&B hit (2 weeks)	
5/11/91	4	12	7. **Power Of Love/Love Power**	Epic 73778
			Airplay #14 / Sales #22; Cissy Houston, Darlene Love, Lisa Fischer and others (backing vocals); #1 R&B hit (2 weeks)	
9/14/91	9	11	8. **Don't Want To Be A Fool**	Epic 73879
			Airplay #21	
5/30/92	10	18	9. **The Best Things In Life Are Free**	Perspective 0010
			LUTHER VANDROSS and JANET JACKSON with BBD and Ralph Tresvant	
			Airplay #5 / Sales #16; from the movie *Mo' Money* starring Damon and Marlon Wayans; #1 R&B hit (1 week)	
9/10/94	2 (1)	13	● 10. **Endless Love**	Columbia 77629
			LUTHER VANDROSS & MARIAH CAREY	
			Sales #2 / Airplay #5	
			VAN DYKE, Leroy	
			Born on 10/4/29 in Spring Fork, Missouri. Worked as a newspaper reporter. Served in U.S. Army in the early 1950s. Former livestock auctioneer. Appeared in the movie *What Am I Bid?* in 1967.	
12/8/56+	19	7	1. Auctioneer [N]	Dot 15503
			Juke Box #19 / Best Seller #21 / Top 100 #29; Andy Nelson (guitar)	
11/20/61	5	12	2. **Walk On By**	Mercury 71834
			#1 Country hit (19 weeks)	

DATE	POS	WKS	ARTIST–RECORD TITLE	LABEL & NO.
3/31/62	**35**	2	3. If A Woman Answers (Hang Up The Phone) *The Merry Melody Singers (backing vocals, above 2)*	Mercury 71926

VANGELIS

Born Evangelos Papathanassiou on 3/29/43 in Valos, Greece. Keyboardist/composer. Moved to Paris during the late 1960s, then to London in the mid-1970s. Formed rock band Aphrodite's Child in France with Demis Roussos, 1968—early '70s.

DATE	POS	WKS	ARTIST–RECORD TITLE	LABEL & NO.
2/20/82	**1** (1)	15	1. **Chariots Of Fire - Titles** [I] *from the Academy Award-winning movie Chariots of Fire starring Ian Charleson and Ben Cross; #1 Adult Contemporary hit (5 weeks); first pressings issued only as: "Titles"*	Polydor 2189

VAN HALEN

Hard-rock band formed in Pasadena, California in 1974. Consisted of David Lee Roth (born 10/10/55; vocals), Eddie Van Halen (born 1/26/57; guitar), Michael Anthony (born 6/20/55; bass) and Alex Van Halen (born 5/8/55; drums). The Van Halen brothers were born in Nijmegen, The Netherlands; moved to Pasadena in 1968. Sammy Hagar replaced Roth as lead singer in 1985. Eddie married actress Valerie Bertinelli on 4/11/81.

DATE	POS	WKS	ARTIST–RECORD TITLE	LABEL & NO.
3/11/78	**36**	3	1. You Really Got Me	Warner 8515
5/26/79	**15**	9	2. Dance The Night Away	Warner 8823
3/13/82	**12**	9	3. (Oh) Pretty Woman *first pressings shown as: "Pretty Woman"*	Warner 50003
6/26/82	**38**	3	4. Dancing In The Street	Warner 29986
1/21/84	**1** (5)	15	● 5. **Jump**	Warner 29384
4/21/84	**13**	10	6. I'll Wait	Warner 29307
6/30/84	**13**	10	7. Panama *all of above produced by Ted Templeman*	Warner 29250
3/29/86	**3**	11	8. **Why Can't This Be Love** *Airplay #2 / Sales #7*	Warner 28740
6/14/86	**22**	7	9. Dreams *Airplay #18 / Sales #25*	Warner 28702
8/30/86	**22**	9	10. Love Walks In *Airplay #15 / Sales #24*	Warner 28626
6/18/88	**34**	2	11. Black And Blue *Sales #29*	Warner 27891
7/23/88	**5**	12	12. **When It's Love** *Airplay #4 / Sales #7*	Warner 27827
11/5/88	**13**	10	13. Finish What Ya Started *Sales #14 / Airplay #16*	Warner 27746
3/11/89	**35**	3	14. Feels So Good *Airplay #35; above 4 from the album OU812*	Warner 27565
11/2/91	**27**	5	15. Top Of The World *Airplay #49*	Warner 19151
4/15/95	**30**	9	16. Can't Stop Lovin' You *Airplay #32 / Sales #44*	Warner 17909

VANILLA FUDGE

Psychedelic-rock quartet formed in New York in 1966. Consisted of Mark Stein (lead singer, keyboards), Vinnie Martell (guitar), Tim Bogert (bassist with Cactus, Rod Stewart and Jeff Beck) and Carmine Appice (drummer with Cactus, Jeff Beck, Rod Stewart, KGB and Blue Murder).

DATE	POS	WKS	ARTIST–RECORD TITLE	LABEL & NO.
8/3/68	**6**	9	1. **You Keep Me Hangin' On** [R] *originally charted in 1967 at #67*	Atco 6590

DATE	POS	WKS	ARTIST–RECORD TITLE	LABEL & NO.
10/26/68	38	4	2. Take Me For A Little While	Atco 6616

VANILLA ICE

Born Robert Van Winkle on 10/31/68 in Miami Lakes, Florida. White Dallas-based rapper. Starred in the movie *Cool As Ice*.

DATE	POS	WKS	ARTIST–RECORD TITLE	LABEL & NO.
9/22/90	1 (1)	15	▲ 1. **Ice Ice Baby** Sales #1(4) / Airplay #1(2); bass line sampled from "Under Pressure" by Queen & David Bowie	SBK 07335
12/15/90+	4	12	● 2. **Play That Funky Music** Sales #2 / Airplay #11; a different mix is on the B-side of #1 above	SBK 07339

VANITY FARE

British pop quintet: Trevor Brice (vocals), Dick Allix, Tony Jarrett, Tony Goulden and Barry Landeman.

DATE	POS	WKS	ARTIST–RECORD TITLE	LABEL & NO.
12/20/69+	12	9	1. Early In The Morning	Page One 21027
5/16/70	5	14	● 2. **Hitchin' A Ride**	Page One 21029

VANNELLI, Gino

Born on 6/16/52 in Montreal. Pop singer/songwriter. His brother Ross produced Earth, Wind & Fire, Howard Hewett and The California Raisins.

DATE	POS	WKS	ARTIST–RECORD TITLE	LABEL & NO.
10/26/74	22	5	1. People Gotta Move	A&M 1614
10/14/78	4	13	2. **I Just Wanna Stop**	A&M 2072
4/4/81	6	14	3. **Living Inside Myself**	Arista 0588

VANWARMER, Randy

Born Randall Van Wormer on 3/30/55 in Indian Hills, Colorado. Singer/songwriter/guitarist. Moved to England at age 12; returned to U.S. in 1979. Charted two country hits in 1988.

DATE	POS	WKS	ARTIST–RECORD TITLE	LABEL & NO.
4/21/79	4	14	● 1. **Just When I Needed You Most** #1 Adult Contemporary hit (2 weeks)	Bearsville 0334

VAPORS, The

British pub-rock quartet: David Fenton (vocals), Ed Bazalgette (guitar), Steve Smith (bass) and Howard Smith (drums).

DATE	POS	WKS	ARTIST–RECORD TITLE	LABEL & NO.
11/15/80	36	3	1. Turning Japanese also released on United Artists 1364 in 1980	Liberty 1364

VAUGHAN, Frankie

Born Frank Abelson on 2/3/28 in Liverpool. Popular entertainer in England. Appeared in the movie *Let's Make Love* (1960). In London cast of *42nd Street* in 1985.

DATE	POS	WKS	ARTIST–RECORD TITLE	LABEL & NO.
7/28/58	22	1	1. Judy Jockey #22 / Top 100 #100; Mark Jeffrey (orch.)	Epic 9273

DATE	POS	WKS	ARTIST–RECORD TITLE	LABEL & NO.

VAUGHAN, Sarah

Born on 3/27/24 in Newark, New Jersey. Died of lung cancer on 4/3/90. Jazz singer. Dubbed "The Divine One." Studied piano, 1931–39. Won amateur contest at the Apollo Theater in 1942, which led to her joining Earl Hines's band as vocalist/second pianist. First recorded solo for Continental in 1944. With Billy Eckstine, 1944–45. Married manager/trumpeter George Treadwellin in 1947. Later husbands included pro football player Clyde Atkins and trumpeter Waymon Reed. Performed into the '80s. Won the Lifetime Achievement Grammy in 1989.

DATE	POS	WKS	ARTIST–RECORD TITLE	LABEL & NO.
11/27/54+	6	15	1. **Make Yourself Comfortable** Jockey #6 / Best Seller #8 / Juke Box #8	Mercury 70469
2/26/55	12	9	2. How Important Can It Be? Jockey #12 / Best Seller #18 / Juke Box #20	Mercury 70534
4/23/55	6	11	3. **Whatever Lola Wants** Jockey #6 / Juke Box #9 / Best Seller #12; from the Broadway musical *Damn Yankees* starring Gwen Verdon	Mercury 70595
7/16/55	14	1	4. Experience Unnecessary Jockey #14	Mercury 70646
12/3/55	11	7	5. C'est La Vie Jockey #11 / Top 100 #22	Mercury 70727
3/3/56	13	7	6. Mr. Wonderful Jockey #13 / Top 100 #38; from the Broadway musical starring Sammy Davis Jr.	Mercury 70777
7/21/56	19	7	7. Fabulous Character Jockey #19 / Top 100 #27; Hugo Peretti (of Hugo & Luigi; orch., all of above)	Mercury 70885
1/12/57	19	5	8. The Banana Boat Song Jockey #19 / Top 100 #31; David Carroll (orch.)	Mercury 71020
8/17/59	7	11	● 9. **Broken-Hearted Melody**	Mercury 71477

VAUGHN, Billy, And His Orchestra

Born Richard Vaughn on 4/12/19 in Glasgow, Kentucky. Died of cancer on 9/26/91. Organized The Hilltoppers vocal group in 1952. Music director for Dot Records. Arranger/conductor for Pat Boone, Gale Storm, The Fontane Sisters and many other Dot artists. Vaughn had more pop hits than any other orchestra leader during the rock era.

DATE	POS	WKS	ARTIST–RECORD TITLE	LABEL & NO.
12/11/54+	2 (1)	27	● 1. **Melody Of Love** [I] Best Seller #2 / Jockey #2 / Juke Box #3; music written in 1903, lyrics added in 1954 by Tom Glazer	Dot 15247
9/24/55	5	15	2. **The Shifting Whispering Sands (Parts 1 & 2)** [S] Best Seller #5 / Top 100 #5 pre / Jockey #5 / Juke Box #10; written in 1950; Ken Nordine (narration)	Dot 15409
2/25/56	37	2	3. A Theme From (The Three Penny Opera) "Moritat"[I] written in 1928; later known as: "Mack The Knife"	Dot 15444
9/8/56	18	6	4. When The White Lilacs Bloom Again [I] Juke Box #18 / Jockey #21 / Top 100 #22; written in 1928	Dot 15491
12/16/57	10	7	5. **Raunchy/** [I] Jockey #10 / Best Seller #25 / Top 100 #33	
1/13/58	5	21	● 6. **Sail Along Silvery Moon** [I] Best Seller #5 / Top 100 #5 / Jockey #6; #4 hit for Bing Crosby in 1937	Dot 15661
4/14/58	30	4	7. Tumbling Tumbleweeds [I] Best Seller #30 / Top 100 #35; #13 hit for the Sons of The Pioneers in 1934	Dot 15710
8/25/58	20	8	8. La Paloma [I] Best Seller #20 / Hot 100 #26; Spanish tango written in 1864	Dot 15795

DATE	POS	WKS	ARTIST–RECORD TITLE	LABEL & NO.
2/2/59	37	1	9. Blue Hawaii [I] #5 hit for Bing Crosby in 1937 (from the movie *Waikiki Wedding* starring Crosby)	Dot 15879
7/18/60	19	7	10. Look For A Star [I] from the movie *Circus of Horrors* starring Donald Pleasence	Dot 16106
3/6/61	28	3	11. Wheels [I]	Dot 16174
8/11/62	13	8	12. A Swingin' Safari [I] written by Bert Kaempfert	Dot 16374

VEE, Bobby

Born Robert Velline on 4/30/43 in Fargo, North Dakota. Formed The Shadows with his brother and a friend in 1959. After Buddy Holly's death in a plane crash, The Shadows filled in on Buddy's next scheduled show in Fargo. First recorded for Soma in 1959. Appeared in the movies *Swingin' Along*, *It's Trad, Dad*, *Play It Cool*, *C'mon Let's Live A Little* and *Just For Fun*. Still performing on oldies tours.

DATE	POS	WKS	ARTIST–RECORD TITLE	LABEL & NO.
9/5/60	6	13	1. **Devil Or Angel** originally a #3 R&B hit for The Clovers in 1956	Liberty 55270
12/12/60+	6	11	2. **Rubber Ball**	Liberty 55287
2/27/61	33	3	3. Stayin' In	Liberty 55296
8/21/61	1 (3)	11	● 4. **Take Good Care Of My Baby**	Liberty 55354
11/20/61	2 (1)	13	5. **Run To Him**	Liberty 55388
3/17/62	15	6	6. Please Don't Ask About Barbara	Liberty 55419
6/9/62	15	6	7. Sharing You	Liberty 55451
9/15/62	20	6	8. Punish Her	Liberty 55479
12/22/62+	3	11	9. **The Night Has A Thousand Eyes**	Liberty 55521
4/13/63	13	7	10. Charms	Liberty 55530
7/20/63	34	2	11. Be True To Yourself	Liberty 55581
8/12/67	3	13	● 12. **Come Back When You Grow Up** **BOBBY VEE And The Strangers**	Liberty 55964
12/16/67	37	2	13. Beautiful People **BOBBY VEE And The Strangers**	Liberty 56009
5/18/68	35	4	14. My Girl/Hey Girl	Liberty 56033

VEGA, Suzanne

Born on 8/12/59 in New York City. Singer/songwriter/guitarist. Married record producer Mitchell Froom (ex-Gamma) on 3/17/95.

DATE	POS	WKS	ARTIST–RECORD TITLE	LABEL & NO.
7/4/87	3	12	1. **Luka** Sales #2 / Airplay #3	A&M 2937
11/3/90	5	14	● 2. **Tom's Diner** **D.N.A. Featuring SUZANNE VEGA** Sales #2 / Airplay #9; special mix of Vega's original acapella recording (B-side of "Solitude Standing"); re-mixed by D.N.A. (2 DJs from Bristol, England)	A&M 1529

VELVETS, The

R&B doo-wop quintet from Odessa, Texas: Virgil Johnson (lead), Will Soloman (baritone), Mark Prince (bass), and tenors Bob Thursby and Clarence Rigby (died in a car crash, 1978).

DATE	POS	WKS	ARTIST–RECORD TITLE	LABEL & NO.
6/26/61	26	4	1. Tonight (Could Be The Night)	Monument 441

DATE	POS	WKS	ARTIST–RECORD TITLE	LABEL & NO.

VENTURES, The

Guitar-based instrumental rock and roll band formed in the Seattle/Tacoma, Washington, area. Consisted of guitarists Nokie Edwards (born 5/9/39; bass), Bob Bogle (born 1/16/37; lead) and Don Wilson (born 2/10/37; rhythm), and drummer Howie Johnson (died 1988). First recorded for own Blue Horizon label in 1959. Johnson was injured in an auto accident and was replaced by Mel Taylor in 1961. Taylor formed Mel Taylor & The Dynamics in 1973, returned in 1978. Edwards left in 1967, replaced by Gerry McGee. Edwards returned in 1972 and then left again in 1985. Added keyboardist John Durrill in 1969. Latest recordings feature Bogle, Wilson, Taylor and McGee. Group still active into the '90s; extremely popular in Japan.

DATE	POS	WKS	ARTIST–RECORD TITLE	LABEL & NO.
7/25/60	**2** (1)	14	1. **Walk—Don't Run** [I] first released on Blue Horizon 101 in 1959; written by jazz guitarist Johnny Smith	Dolton 25
11/14/60	**15**	10	2. Perfidia [I] 5 versions hit the Top 15 in 1941	Dolton 28
2/13/61	**29**	5	3. Ram-Bunk-Shush [I]	Dolton 32
8/1/64	**8**	7	4. **Walk-Don't Run '64** [I-R] new version of #1 above	Dolton 96
11/21/64	**35**	3	5. Slaughter On Tenth Avenue [I] written by Richard Rodgers in 1936	Dolton 300
4/12/69	**4**	9	6. **Hawaii Five-O** [I] from the TV series starring Jack Lord	Liberty 56068

VENUS, Vik (Alias: Your Main Moon Man)

Radio personality Jack Spector. Died of a heart attack on the air at WHLI-Long Island, New York, on 3/8/94 (age 66). One of the original "Good Guys" at WMCA-New York, 1961–72. At New York's WHN, 1972–76; hosted "Saturday Night Sock Hop" at WCBS, 1976-86.

DATE	POS	WKS	ARTIST–RECORD TITLE	LABEL & NO.
7/26/69	**38**	3	1. Moonflight [N] a Dickie Goodman-type recording	Buddah 118

VERA, Billy

Born William McCord on 5/28/44 in Riverside, California; raised in Westchester County, New York. Wrote hit songs for many pop, R&B and country artists. Appeared in the movies *Buckaroo Banzai* and *The Doors* and the HBO movie *Baja Oklahoma*. Formed The Beaters (an R&B-based 10-piece band) in Los Angeles in 1979.

DATE	POS	WKS	ARTIST–RECORD TITLE	LABEL & NO.
3/23/68	**36**	1	1. Country Girl - City Man **BILLY VERA & JUDY CLAY**	Atlantic 2480
6/6/81	**39**	2	2. I Can Take Care Of Myself **BILLY & THE BEATERS**	Alfa 7002
12/6/86+	**1** (2)	15	● 3. **At This Moment** [R] **BILLY VERA & THE BEATERS** Sales #1(2) / Airplay #1(1); originally charted in 1981 at #79; re-charted due to play on the TV series "Family Ties" starring Michael J. Fox; #1 Adult Contemporary hit (1 week)	Rhino 74403

VERNE, Larry

Born on 2/8/36 in Minneapolis. Photo studio worker-turned-singer by chance. A trio of California songwriters (Fred Darian, Al DeLory and Joe Van Winkle) who worked in Verne's building selected him to record "Mr. Custer" because of his Southern drawl.

DATE	POS	WKS	ARTIST–RECORD TITLE	LABEL & NO.
9/5/60	**1** (1)	10	1. **Mr. Custer** [N]	Era 3024

DATE	POS	WKS	ARTIST–RECORD TITLE	LABEL & NO.

VIBRATIONS, The

Los Angeles R&B vocal group. Originally recorded as The Jayhawks. Consisted of James Johnson, Carlton Fisher, Richard Owens, Dave Govan and Don Bradley. Also recorded the hit "Peanut Butter" as The Marathons. Owens joined The Temptations for a short time in 1971.

DATE	POS	WKS	ARTIST–RECORD TITLE	LABEL & NO.
3/13/61	25	4	1. The Watusi tune is similar to Hank Ballard & The Midnighters' "Let's Go, Let's Go, Let's Go"	Checker 969
4/25/64	26	5	2. My Girl Sloopy original title of "Hang On Sloopy" by The McCoys	Atlantic 2221

VILLAGE PEOPLE

Campy New York City disco group formed by French producer Jacques Morali (died of AIDS 11/15/91, age 44). Consisted of Victor Willis (lead singer), Randy Jones, David Hodo, Felipe Rose, Glenn Hughes and Alexander Briley. Willis replaced by Ray Simpson (brother of Valerie Simpson of Ashford & Simpson) in late 1979. Group appeared in the 1980 movie *Can't Stop The Music*.

DATE	POS	WKS	ARTIST–RECORD TITLE	LABEL & NO.
7/29/78	25	6	● 1. Macho Man	Casablanca 922
11/11/78+	2 (3)	20	▲ 2. **Y.M.C.A.**	Casablanca 945
3/31/79	3	13	● 3. **In The Navy**	Casablanca 973

VILLAGE STOMPERS, The

Dixieland-styled band from Greenwich Village, New York.

DATE	POS	WKS	ARTIST–RECORD TITLE	LABEL & NO.
10/5/63	2 (1)	12	1. **Washington Square** [I] #1 Adult Contemporary hit (3 weeks)	Epic 9617

VINCENT, Gene, and His Blue Caps

Born Vincent Eugene Craddock on 2/11/35 in Norfolk, Virginia. Died from an ulcer hemorrhage on 10/12/71. Innovative rock and roll singer/songwriter/guitarist. Injured left leg in motorcycle accident in 1953, had to wear steel brace thereafter. Formed the Blue Caps in Norfolk in 1956. Appeared in the movies *The Girl Can't Help It* and *Hot Rod Gang*. To England, 1960–67. Injured in car crash that killed Eddie Cochran in England in 1960.

DATE	POS	WKS	ARTIST–RECORD TITLE	LABEL & NO.
6/23/56	7	15	1. **Be-Bop-A-Lula** Best Seller #7 / Top 100 #9 / Juke Box #10 / Jockey #11	Capitol 3450
9/16/57	13	12	2. Lotta Lovin'/ Best Seller #13 / Top 100 #14 / Jockey #18	
		7	3. Wear My Ring Best Seller flip; co-written by Bobby Darin	Capitol 3763
1/13/58	23	1	4. Dance To The Bop Jockey #23 / Top 100 #43 / Best Seller #44	Capitol 3839

VINTON, Bobby

Born Stanley Robert Vinton on 4/16/35 in Canonsburg, Pennsylvania. Father was a bandleader. Formed own band while in high school; toured as backing band for Dick Clark's "Caravan of Stars" in 1960. Left band for a singing career in 1962. Own musical variety TV series, 1975–78.

DATE	POS	WKS	ARTIST–RECORD TITLE	LABEL & NO.
6/16/62	1 (4)	13	● 1. **Roses Are Red (My Love)** #1 Adult Contemporary hit (4 weeks)	Epic 9509
9/15/62	12	7	2. Rain Rain Go Away	Epic 9532
9/22/62	38	2	3. I Love You The Way You Are	Diamond 121
1/5/63	33	3	4. Trouble Is My Middle Name/	
1/12/63	38	2	5. Let's Kiss And Make Up	Epic 9561

DATE	POS	WKS	ARTIST–RECORD TITLE	LABEL & NO.
3/30/63	**21**	6	6. Over The Mountain (Across The Sea)	Epic 9577
6/1/63	**3**	10	7. **Blue On Blue**	Epic 9593
8/24/63	**1 (3)**	12	8. **Blue Velvet** #1 Adult Contemporary hit (8 weeks); #16 hit for Tony Bennett in 1951	Epic 9614
12/7/63+	**1 (4)**	12	9. **There! I've Said It Again** #1 Adult Contemporary hit (5 weeks); #1 hit for Vaughn Monroe in 1945; song introduced in 1941 by the Benny Carter Orch. (Bluebird 11090)	Epic 9638
3/7/64	**9**	8	10. **My Heart Belongs To Only You** introduced by June Christy in 1953	Epic 9662
5/30/64	**13**	6	11. Tell Me Why #2 hit for The Four Aces in 1952	Epic 9687
8/22/64	**17**	6	12. Clinging Vine	Epic 9705
11/7/64	**1 (1)**	14	13. **Mr. Lonely**	Epic 9730
3/20/65	**17**	5	14. Long Lonely Nights	Epic 9768
5/22/65	**22**	6	15. L-O-N-E-L-Y	Epic 9791
10/16/65	**38**	1	16. What Color (Is A Man)	Epic 9846
12/25/65+	**23**	6	17. Satin Pillows	Epic 9869
5/28/66	**40**	1	18. Dum-De-Da song charted in 1964 by Johnny Tillotson as: "She Understands Me"	Epic 10014
12/17/66+	**11**	8	19. Coming Home Soldier	Epic 10090
10/14/67	**6**	11	20. **Please Love Me Forever**	Epic 10228
1/27/68	**24**	4	21. Just As Much As Ever	Epic 10266
4/13/68	**33**	6	22. Take Good Care Of My Baby	Epic 10305
8/3/68	**23**	5	23. Halfway To Paradise	Epic 10350
11/16/68	**9**	12	● 24. **I Love How You Love Me**	Epic 10397
5/3/69	**34**	2	25. To Know You Is To Love You	Epic 10461
7/12/69	**34**	2	26. The Days Of Sand And Shovels	Epic 10485
3/18/72	**24**	8	27. Every Day Of My Life	Epic 10822
7/8/72	**19**	10	28. Sealed With A Kiss	Epic 10861
10/12/74	**3**	11	● 29. **My Melody Of Love** #1 Adult Contemporary hit (1 week)	ABC 12022
4/19/75	**33**	2	30. Beer Barrel Polka/ #1 hit for Will Glahe in 1939	
		2	31. Dick And Jane	ABC 12056
			VIRTUES, The	
			Philadelphia rock and roll instrumental trio led by Frank ("Virtue") Virtuoso.	
3/23/59	**5**	12	1. **Guitar Boogie Shuffle** [I] first released on Sure 501 in 1958; tune based on "Guitar Boogie" by Arthur Smith on MGM 10293	Hunt 324
			VISAGE, Michelle—see S.O.U.L. S.Y.S.T.E.M.	
			VISCOUNTS, The	
			New Jersey instrumental quintet: Harry Haller (tenor saxophone), brothers Bobby (guitar) and Joe Spievak (bass), Larry Vecchio (organ) and Clark Smith (drums).	
1/1/66	**39**	1	1. Harlem Nocturne [I-R] originally charted in 1959 at #52	Amy 940

DATE	POS	WKS	ARTIST–RECORD TITLE	LABEL & NO.
			VIXEN	
			Female hard-rock quartet formed in Los Angeles: Janet Gardner (vocals, guitar), Jan Kuehnemund (guitar), Share Pedersen (bass) and Roxy Petrucci (drums). Pedersen was part of Contraband in 1991.	
10/29/88	26	5	1. Edge Of A Broken Heart Sales #21 / Airplay #31; written, produced and arranged by Richard Marx	EMI-Man. 50141
2/25/89	22	6	2. Cryin' Sales #16 / Airplay #30	EMI-Man. 50167
			VOGUES, The	
			Vocal group formed in Turtle Creek, Pennsylvania, in 1960. Consisted of Bill Burkette (lead), Hugh Geyer and Chuck Blasko (tenors) and Don Miller (baritone). Met in high school.	
10/9/65	4	9	1. **You're The One** first released on Blue Star 229 in 1965	Co & Ce 229
12/11/65+	4	12	2. **Five O'Clock World**	Co & Ce 232
3/19/66	21	6	3. Magic Town	Co & Ce 234
6/25/66	29	4	4. The Land Of Milk And Honey	Co & Ce 238
7/13/68	7	11	● 5. **Turn Around, Look At Me**	Reprise 0686
9/21/68	7	8	6. **My Special Angel** #1 Adult Contemporary hit (2 weeks)	Reprise 0766
12/7/68	27	4	7. Till	Reprise 0788
3/29/69	34	2	8. No, Not Much	Reprise 0803
			VOICES THAT CARE	
			Benefit spearheaded by David Foster and his fiancée, Linda Thompson Jenner (ex-wife of Olympian Bruce Jenner), supporting the Persian Gulf allied troops and their families. Among superstar choir: Kevin Costner, Meryl Streep, Billy Crystal, Richard Gere, Gloria Estefan, Wayne Gretzky and many others.	
3/30/91	11	11	● 1. Voices That Care Sales #4 / Airplay #19; lead vocals: Ralph Tresvant, Randy Travis, Celine Dion, Peter Cetera, Bobby Brown, Brenda Russell, Luther Vandross, Garth Brooks, Kathy Mattea, Nelson, Michael Bolton, Little Richard, Pointer Sisters, Fresh Prince, Mark Knopfler, Kenny G and Warren Wiebe; co-written by Cetera, Foster and Jenner	Giant 19350
			VOLUME'S, The	
			Detroit R&B quintet featuring lead singer Ed Union.	
6/2/62	22	6	1. I Love You	Chex 1002
			VOUDOURIS, Roger	
			Born on 12/29/54 in Sacramento, California. Pop singer/songwriter/guitarist.	
4/28/79	21	10	1. Get Used To It	Warner 8762
			VOXPOPPERS, The	
			New York City vocal quintet featuring brothers Freddie, Sal and Harry Tamburo.	
5/5/58	18	1	1. Wishing For Your Love Jockey #18 / Best Seller #41 / Top 100 #44; first released on Amp 3 1004 in 1958	Mercury 71282

DATE	POS	WKS	ARTIST–RECORD TITLE	LABEL & NO.

W

WADE, Adam

Born on 3/17/37 in Pittsburgh. Attended Virginia State College and worked as lab assistant with Dr. Jonas Salk team. TV actor/host of the 1975 game show "Musical Chairs." Worked in *Guys & Dolls* musical in Las Vegas in 1978. TV talk-show host in Los Angeles in the '80s.

DATE	POS	WKS	ARTIST–RECORD TITLE	LABEL & NO.
3/27/61	7	10	1. **Take Good Care Of Her**	Coed 546
5/29/61	5	9	2. **The Writing On The Wall**	Coed 550
8/7/61	10	7	3. **As If I Didn't Know**	Coed 553

WADSWORTH MANSION

Rock quartet: Steve Jablecki (lead vocals), Wayne Gagnon, John Poole and Mike Jablecki.

DATE	POS	WKS	ARTIST–RECORD TITLE	LABEL & NO.
2/13/71	7	7	1. **Sweet Mary**	Sussex 209

WAGNER, Jack

Born on 10/3/59 in Washington, Missouri. Played Frisco Jones on the TV soap opera "General Hospital"; joined the cast of "Santa Barbara" in 1991.

DATE	POS	WKS	ARTIST–RECORD TITLE	LABEL & NO.
11/24/84+	2 (2)	12	1. **All I Need**	Qwest 29238
			Sales #2 / Airplay #2; #1 Adult Contemporary hit (2 weeks)	

WAIKIKIS, The

Belgian instrumental group.

DATE	POS	WKS	ARTIST–RECORD TITLE	LABEL & NO.
1/9/65	33	3	1. Hawaii Tattoo [I]	Kapp 30

WAILERS, The

Teenage rock and roll instrumental quintet from Tacoma, Washington, formed in 1958 by rhythm guitarist John Greek. Original lineup also included Rich Dangel, Mark Marush, Kent Morrill and Mike Burk.

DATE	POS	WKS	ARTIST–RECORD TITLE	LABEL & NO.
6/1/59	36	2	1. Tall Cool One [I]	Golden Crest 518
5/30/64	38	1	2. Tall Cool One [I-R]	Golden Crest 518

WAINWRIGHT, Loudon, III

Born on 9/5/46 in Chapel Hill, North Carolina. Satirical folk singer/songwriter. Acted in three episodes of "M*A*S*H" as Capt. Calvin Spaulding. Appeared in the movies *The Slugger's Wife* and *Jacknife*. Married briefly to Kate McGarrigle (McGarrigle Sisters), mid-1970s, and Suzzy Roche (The Roches), the '80s.

DATE	POS	WKS	ARTIST–RECORD TITLE	LABEL & NO.
2/24/73	16	9	1. Dead Skunk [N]	Columbia 45726

WAITE, John

Born on 7/4/55 in Lancashire, England. Lead singer of The Babys and Bad English.

DATE	POS	WKS	ARTIST–RECORD TITLE	LABEL & NO.
7/21/84	1 (1)	16	1. **Missing You**	EMI America 8212
			Sales #8 pre / Airplay #17 pre	
11/10/84	37	4	2. Tears	EMI America 8238
8/31/85	25	6	3. Every Step Of The Way	EMI America 8282
			Sales #21 / Airplay #24	

DATE	POS	WKS	ARTIST–RECORD TITLE	LABEL & NO.
			## WAKELIN, Johnny, & The Kinshasa Band	
			British group led by singer/songwriter Wakelin.	
8/16/75	21	6	1. Black Superman - "Muhammad Ali"　　　[N]	Pye 71012
			## WALKER, Chris	
			Houston-born soul singer/jazz bassist. Played bass with Ornette Coleman for three years. Worked as musical director for Regina Belle.	
4/18/92	29	6	1. Take Time Airplay #28; Shazzy (female rapper)	Pendulum 64813
			## WALKER, Jr., & The All Stars	
			R&B group formed in South Bend, Indiana, by Walker (born Autry DeWalt II in Blythesville, Arkansas, 1931; died 11/23/95, age 64). Included Walker (sax, vocals), Willie Woods (guitar), Vic Thomas (organ) and James Graves (drums). First recorded for Harvey in 1962. Most recent group included son Autry DeWalt, Jr., on drums.	
3/6/65	4	10	1. **Shotgun** #1 R&B hit (4 weeks)	Soul 35008
7/3/65	36	2	2. Do The Boomerang	Soul 35012
8/21/65	29	5	3. Shake And Fingerpop	Soul 35013
5/21/66	20	6	4. (I'm A) Road Runner all of above from the album *Shotgun*	Soul 35015
9/3/66	18	5	5. How Sweet It Is (To Be Loved By You)	Soul 35024
3/11/67	31	4	6. Pucker Up Buttercup	Soul 35030
12/23/67+	24	6	7. Come See About Me	Soul 35041
9/14/68	31	6	8. Hip City - Pt. 2	Soul 35048
6/21/69	4	11	9. **What Does It Take (To Win Your Love)** #1 R&B hit (2 weeks)	Soul 35062
11/22/69	16	9	10. These Eyes	Soul 35067
2/28/70	21	9	11. Gotta Hold On To This Feeling	Soul 35070
8/1/70	32	4	12. Do You See My Love (For You Growing)	Soul 35073
			## WALKER BROS., The	
			Los Angeles pop trio: Scott Engel, Gary Leeds and John Maus. More popular in England than the U.S. (charted 10 hits in the U.K.).	
11/13/65	16	6	1. Make It Easy On Yourself first released on Smash 2000 in 1965	Smash 2009
4/30/66	13	7	2. The Sun Ain't Gonna Shine (Anymore)	Smash 2032
			## WALLACE, Jerry	
			Born on 12/15/28 in Guilford, Missouri; raised in Glendale, Arizona. Pop-country singer/guitarist. First recorded for Allied in 1951. Appeared on the TV shows "Night Gallery" and "Hec Ramsey."	
9/15/58	11	9	1. How The Time Flies Hot 100 #11 / Best Seller #33 end	Challenge 59013
9/7/59	8	15	● 2. **Primrose Lane** **JERRY WALLACE With the Jewels**	Challenge 59047
2/1/60	36	2	3. Little Coco Palm	Challenge 59060
1/9/61	26	4	4. There She Goes #3 Country hit for Carl Smith in 1955	Challenge 59098
12/22/62+	24	7	5. Shutters And Boards co-written by movie star Audie Murphy	Challenge 9171

DATE	POS	WKS	ARTIST–RECORD TITLE	LABEL & NO.
8/22/64	19	7	6. In The Misty Moonlight	Challenge 59246
9/30/72	38	2	7. If You Leave Me Tonight I'll Cry from TV's "Rod Serling's Night Gallery: The Tune In Dan's Cafe"; #1 Country hit (2 weeks)	Decca 32989

WALSH, Joe

Born on 11/20/47 in Wichita, Kansas. Rock singer/songwriter/guitarist. Member of The James Gang, 1969–71, and the Eagles, 1975–82. Own band, Barnstorm, 1972–75, featured drummer Joe Vitale and bassist Kenny Passarelli.

DATE	POS	WKS	ARTIST–RECORD TITLE	LABEL & NO.
9/22/73	23	7	1. Rocky Mountain Way	Dunhill 4361
7/1/78	12	9	2. Life's Been Good	Asylum 45493
6/14/80	19	8	3. All Night Long from the movie Urban Cowboy starring John Travolta and Debra Winger	Full Moon 46639
6/27/81	34	4	4. A Life Of Illusion	Asylum 47144

WALTERS, Jamie

Male singer/actor. Former lead singer of The Heights. Cast member of TV's "Beverly Hills 90210."

DATE	POS	WKS	ARTIST–RECORD TITLE	LABEL & NO.
3/4/95	16	20	1. Hold On Airplay #12 / Sales #34	Atlantic 87240

WAMMACK, Travis

Born in 1946 in Walnut, Mississippi; raised in Memphis. Prolific session guitarist of the FAME studios in Muscle Shoals, Alabama.

DATE	POS	WKS	ARTIST–RECORD TITLE	LABEL & NO.
8/9/75	38	2	1. (Shu-Doo-Pa-Poo-Poop) Love Being Your Fool	Capricorn 0239

WANDERLEY, Walter

Brazilian organist/pianist/composer. Died of cancer on 9/4/86 (age 55).

DATE	POS	WKS	ARTIST–RECORD TITLE	LABEL & NO.
10/1/66	26	4	1. Summer Samba (So Nice)　　　　　　　　　[I]	Verve 10421

WANG CHUNG

British pop-rock group: Jack Hues (lead singer, guitar, keyboards), Nick Feldman (bass, keyboards) and Darren Costin (drums). Costin left in 1985. Originally known as Huang Chung.

DATE	POS	WKS	ARTIST–RECORD TITLE	LABEL & NO.
3/10/84	38	3	1. Don't Let Go	Geffen 29377
5/26/84	16	10	2. Dance Hall Days	Geffen 29310
10/25/86	2 (2)	15	3. **Everybody Have Fun Tonight** Airplay #2 / Sales #2	Geffen 28562
2/14/87	9	11	4. **Let's Go!** Airplay #6 / Sales #10	Geffen 28531
7/25/87	36	2	5. Hypnotize Me Airplay #33; from the movie Innerspace starring Dennis Quaid and Martin Short	Geffen 28359

DATE	POS	WKS	ARTIST–RECORD TITLE	LABEL & NO.
			## WAR	
			Band formed in Long Beach, California, in 1969. Consisted of Lonnie Jordan (keyboards), Howard Scott (guitar), Charles Miller (saxophone; murdered in 1980), Morris "B.B." Dickerson (bass), Harold Brown and Thomas "Papa Dee" Allen (percussion; died of a cerebral hemorrhage 8/30/88) and Lee Oskar (harmonica). Eric Burdon's backup band until 1971. Dickerson was replaced by Luther Rabb. Jordan and Oskar also recorded solo. Alice Tweed Smyth (vocals) added in 1978. Pat Rizzo (horns) and Ron Hammon (former member of Aalon; percussion) added in 1979. Smyth left group in 1982. Lineup by 1994: Jordan, Scott, Brown and Hammon with Rae Valentine, Charles Green, Kerry Campbell, Tetsuya Nakamura and Sal Rodriguez.	
7/11/70	3	13	● 1. **Spill The Wine** **ERIC BURDON AND WAR**	MGM 14118
9/25/71	35	2	2. All Day Music also on the B-side of #11 below	United Art. 50815
4/1/72	16	10	● 3. Slippin' Into Darkness a "live" recording is on the B-side of #8 below	United Art. 50867
12/30/72+	7	9	● 4. **The World Is A Ghetto**	United Art. 50975
3/24/73	2 (2)	12	● 5. **The Cisco Kid**	United Art. 163
8/4/73	8	10	6. **Gypsy Man**	United Art. 281
12/8/73+	15	10	7. Me And Baby Brother	United Art. 350
7/13/74	33	2	8. Ballero [I] "live" recording	United Art. 432
6/14/75	6	13	● 9. **Why Can't We Be Friends?**	United Art. 629
10/11/75	7	11	10. **Low Rider** #1 R&B hit (1 week)	United Art. 706
7/31/76	7	12	● 11. **Summer** #1 Adult Contemporary hit (1 week)	United Art. 834
2/11/78	39	2	12. Galaxy all of above produced by Jerry Goldstein	MCA 40820
			## WARD, Anita	
			Born on 12/20/57 in Memphis. R&B-disco vocalist. Toured in Rust College female quartet.	
5/26/79	1 (2)	15	1. **Ring My Bell** written and produced by Frederick Knight; #1 R&B hit (5 weeks)	Juana 3422
			## WARD, Billy, And His Dominoes	
			R&B group formed as The Dominoes in New York in 1950 by Ward (born in Los Angeles) and talent agent Rose Marks. Consisted of Ward (piano), Clyde McPhatter (lead), Charlie White (tenor), Joe Lamont (baritone) and Bill Brown (bass). Signed by King/Federal in 1950. Lead singers, at various times: Clyde McPhatter, 1950–53; Jackie Wilson, 1953–57; and Eugene Mumford.	
9/15/56	13	6	1. St. Therese Of The Roses Jockey #13 / Best Seller #20 / Top 100 #27; Jackie Wilson (lead singer); Jack Pleis (orch.)	Decca 29933
7/15/57	12	17	● 2. Star Dust Jockey #12 / Top 100 #13 / Best Seller #14; there have been 19 charted versions of this Hoagy Carmichael tune	Liberty 55071
10/7/57	20	8	3. Deep Purple Best Seller #20 / Top 100 #22; 3 versions of this tune hit the Top 10 in 1939; Vic Schoen (orch., above 2)	Liberty 55099

DATE	POS	WKS	ARTIST—RECORD TITLE	LABEL & NO.
			WARD, Dale	
			Pop-country vocalist. Dale was not a member of The Crescendos, as rumored.	
2/1/64	25	5	1. Letter From Sherry	Dot 16520
			Robin Ward (female vocal), not related to Dale Ward	
			WARD, Joe	
			Eight-year-old boy from New York City. Discovered by Steve Allen. On NBC-TV's "Juvenile Jury" from ages five to nine. Prolific commercial songwriter/producer/arranger/singer as an adult.	
12/24/55	20	3	1. Nuttin For Xmas [X-N]	King 4854
			Juke Box #20 / Best Seller #22 / Top 100 #22; Dave Terry (orch.)	
			WARD, Robin	
			Born Jacqueline Eloise McDonnell in Hawaii. Pop singer from Nebraska. Also see Dale Ward.	
11/16/63	14	7	1. Wonderful Summer	Dot 16530
			WARNES, Jennifer	
			Born in Seattle and raised in Orange County, California. Pop/MOR-styled vocalist. Lead actress in the Los Angeles production of *Hair*. Also recorded as Jennifer Warren and simply as Jennifer.	
2/26/77	6	14	1. **Right Time Of The Night**	Arista 0223
			#1 Adult Contemporary hit (1 week)	
9/22/79	19	8	2. I Know A Heartache When I See One	Arista 0430
10/2/82	1 (3)	15	▲ 3. **Up Where We Belong**	Island 99996
			JOE COCKER and JENNIFER WARNES	
			love theme from the movie *An Officer and a Gentleman* starring Richard Gere	
10/10/87	1 (1)	15	● 4. **(I've Had) The Time Of My Life**	RCA 5224
			BILL MEDLEY AND JENNIFER WARNES	
			Airplay #1(2) / Sales #1(1); love theme from the movie *Dirty Dancing* starring Patrick Swayze; #1 Adult Contemporary hit (4 weeks); B-side is Mickey & Sylvia's 1957 hit "Love Is Strange"	
			WARRANT	
			Male hard-rock band from Los Angeles: Jani Lane (vocals), Erik Turner (guitar), Joey Allen (guitar), Jerry Dixon (bass) and Steven Sweet (drums). Lane married Bobbie Brown, spokesmodel champion on TV's "Star Search," on 7/27/91.	
6/10/89	27	6	1. Down Boys	Columbia 68606
			Airplay #26 / Sales #28	
8/5/89	2 (2)	14	● 2. **Heaven**	Columbia 68985
			Sales #1(1) / Airplay #2	
2/3/90	20	9	3. Sometimes She Cries	Columbia 73095
			Airplay #15 / Sales #23	
9/29/90	10	9	4. **Cherry Pie**	Columbia 73510
			Sales #6 / Airplay #18	
1/5/91	10	11	5. **I Saw Red**	Columbia 73597
			Airplay #11 / Sales #12	
			WARREN G	
			Rapper Warren G (born Warren Griffin III in Long Beach, California) is the half-brother of Dr. Dre; also wrote, produced and performed on Mista Grimm's "Indo Smoke" and on Slick Rick's "Behind Bars." Childhood friend of Snoop Doggy Dogg.	

DATE	POS	WKS	ARTIST—RECORD TITLE	LABEL & NO.
5/7/94	2 (3)	18	▲ 1. **Regulate** **WARREN G. & NATE DOGG** *Sales #1(2) / Airplay #15; samples Michael McDonald's "I Keep Forgettin'"; from the movie Above The Rim starring Tupac Shakur (2 Pac) and Duane Martin*	Death Row 98280
7/30/94	9	14	● 2. **This DJ** *Sales #5 / Airplay #20*	Viol./RAL 853236

WARWICK, Dionne

Born Marie Dionne Warwick on 12/12/40 in East Orange, New Jersey. In church choir from age six. With the Drinkard Singers gospel group. Formed trio, the Gospelaires, with sister Dee Dee Warwick and their aunt Cissy Houston. (Dionne is a cousin of Whitney Houston.) Attended Hartt College Of Music, Hartford, Connecticut. Much backup studio work in New York during the late '50s. Added an "e" to her last name for a time in the early '70s. She was Burt Bacharach and Hal David's main "voice" for the songs they composed. Co-hosted TV's "Solid Gold" 1980–81, 1985–86.

DATE	POS	WKS	ARTIST—RECORD TITLE	LABEL & NO.
1/5/63	21	7	1. Don't Make Me Over	Scepter 1239
1/4/64	8	9	2. **Anyone Who Had A Heart**	Scepter 1262
5/9/64	6	11	3. **Walk On By**	Scepter 1274
9/19/64	34	3	4. You'll Never Get To Heaven (If You Break My Heart)	Scepter 1282
11/7/64	20	6	5. Reach Out For Me	Scepter 1285
1/22/66	39	1	6. Are You There (With Another Girl)	Scepter 12122
4/23/66	8	8	7. **Message To Michael**	Scepter 12133
7/16/66	22	5	8. Trains And Boats And Planes	Scepter 12153
10/22/66	26	5	9. I Just Don't Know What To Do With Myself	Scepter 12167
5/27/67	15	9	10. Alfie *title song from the movie starring Michael Caine*	Scepter 12187
8/26/67	32	3	11. The Windows Of The World	Scepter 12196
2/3/68	2 (4)	11	12. **(Theme From) Valley Of The Dolls/** *from the movie starring Sharon Tate and Patty Duke*	
11/4/67	4	10	● 13. **I Say A Little Prayer**	Scepter 12203
4/27/68	10	9	14. **Do You Know The Way To San Jose**	Scepter 12216
9/21/68	33	4	15. Who Is Gonna Love Me?	Scepter 12226
11/23/68	19	6	16. Promises, Promises *from the Broadway musical (also #20 below) starring Jerry Orbach*	Scepter 12231
2/8/69	7	11	17. **This Girl's In Love With You**	Scepter 12241
6/7/69	37	3	18. The April Fools *title song from the movie starring Jack Lemmon*	Scepter 12249
10/11/69	16	7	19. You've Lost That Lovin' Feeling	Scepter 12262
1/3/70	6	10	20. **I'll Never Fall In Love Again** *#1 Adult Contemporary hit (3 weeks)*	Scepter 12273
5/9/70	32	3	21. Let Me Go To Him	Scepter 12276
10/31/70	37	2	22. Make It Easy On Yourself *"live" recording; all of above written (except #12 & 19) and produced by Burt Bacharach and Hal David*	Scepter 12294
8/3/74	1 (1)	15	● 23. **Then Came You** **DIONNE WARWICKE AND SPINNERS** *originally released on Atlantic 3029 earlier in 1974*	Atlantic 3202
7/28/79	5	17	● 24. **I'll Never Love This Way Again**	Arista 0419
12/15/79+	15	11	25. Deja Vu *#1 Adult Contemporary hit (1 week); above 2 produced by Barry Manilow (backing vocals by Manilow and Ron Dante)*	Arista 0459

DATE	POS	WKS	ARTIST–RECORD TITLE	LABEL & NO.
9/6/80	**23**	6	26. No Night So Long *#1 Adult Contemporary hit (3 weeks)*	Arista 0527
5/29/82	**38**	3	27. Friends In Love **DIONNE WARWICK AND JOHNNY MATHIS**	Arista 0673
11/6/82+	**10**	13	28. **Heartbreaker** *Barry Gibb (backing vocal); #1 Adult Contemporary hit (1 week)*	Arista 1015
10/29/83	**27**	5	29. How Many Times Can We Say Goodbye **DIONNE WARWICK AND LUTHER VANDROSS**	Arista 9073
11/23/85+	**1 (4)**	17	● 30. **That's What Friends Are For** **DIONNE & FRIENDS: Elton John, Gladys Knight and Stevie Wonder** *Sales #1(5) / Airplay #1(3); song introduced by Rod Stewart on the 1982 movie soundtrack of Night Shift; #1 R&B hit (3 weeks); #1 Adult Contemporary hit (2 weeks)*	Arista 9422
7/25/87	**12**	9	31. Love Power **DIONNE WARWICK & JEFFREY OSBORNE** *Sales #7 / Airplay #14; #1 Adult Contemporary hit (1 week)*	Arista 9567

WASHINGTON, Baby

Born Justine Washington (aka: Jeanette Washington) on 11/13/40 in Bamberg, South Carolina; raised in Harlem. R&B vocalist/pianist. Sang in '50s vocal group The Hearts. First recorded solo for J&S in 1957.

DATE	POS	WKS	ARTIST–RECORD TITLE	LABEL & NO.
6/1/63	**40**	1	1. That's How Heartaches Are Made	Sue 783

WASHINGTON, Dinah

Born Ruth Lee Jones on 8/29/24 in Tuscaloosa, Alabama. Died on 12/14/63 (overdose of alcohol and pills). Jazz-blues vocalist/pianist. Moved to Chicago in 1927. With Sallie Martin Gospel Singers, 1940–41; local club work in Chicago, 1941-43. With Lionel Hampton, 1943–46. First recorded for Keynote in 1943. Solo touring from 1946. Married seven times, once to singer Eddie Chamblee. Inducted into the Rock and Roll Hall of Fame in 1993 as an early influence.

DATE	POS	WKS	ARTIST–RECORD TITLE	LABEL & NO.
6/22/59	**8**	14	1. **What A Diff'rence A Day Makes** *#5 hit for the Dorsey Brothers in 1934*	Mercury 71435
10/26/59	**17**	8	2. Unforgettable *#12 hit for Nat King Cole in 1952*	Mercury 71508
2/8/60	**5**	12	● 3. **Baby (You've Got What It Takes)** **DINAH WASHINGTON & BROOK BENTON** *#1 R&B hit (10 weeks)*	Mercury 71565
6/6/60	**7**	10	4. **A Rockin' Good Way (To Mess Around And Fall In Love)** **DINAH WASHINGTON & BROOK BENTON** *#1 R&B hit (4 weeks); tune first recorded by The Spaniels in 1958*	Mercury 71629
7/18/60	**24**	6	5. This Bitter Earth *#1 R&B hit (1 week)*	Mercury 71635
11/7/60	**30**	2	6. Love Walked In *3 versions of this Gershwin tune hit the Top 10 in 1938*	Mercury 71696
11/6/61	**23**	6	7. September In The Rain *#1 hit for Guy Lombardo in 1937*	Mercury 71876
6/23/62	**36**	3	8. Where Are You *#5 hit for Mildred Bailey in 1937*	Roulette 4424

DATE	POS	WKS	ARTIST–RECORD TITLE	LABEL & NO.
			WASHINGTON, Grover, Jr.	
			Born on 12/12/43 in Buffalo. Jazz-R&B saxophonist. Prolific session artist In Philadelphia. Bill Withers had several solo hits.	
3/7/81	**2** (3)	16	1. **Just The Two Of Us** **GROVER WASHINGTON, JR. (with Bill Withers)**	Elektra 47103
			WASHINGTON, Keith	
			Detroit native. Supporting vocalist while a teen for The Dramatics. Former backing vocalist for The Jacksons and Miki Howard.	
7/13/91	**40**	1	1. **Kissing You** Sales #41 / Airplay #75; #1 R&B hit (1 week)	Qwest 19414
			WAS (NOT WAS)	
			Detroit R&B ensemble fronted by composer/bassist Don Fagenson ("Don Was") and lyricist/flutist David Weiss ("David Was"). Includes vocalists Sweet Pea Atkinson and Sir Harry Bowens. Group appeared in the movie *The Freshman*.	
11/5/88	**16**	10	1. **Spy In The House Of Love** Sales #9 / Airplay #26	Chrysalis 43266
2/18/89	**7**	9	2. **Walk The Dinosaur** Sales #5 / Airplay #10	Chrysalis 43331
			WATERFRONT	
			Male pop-rock duo of singer Chris Duffy and guitarist Phil Cillia from Cardiff, Wales. Band name derived from the Marlon Brando movie *On The Waterfront*.	
5/6/89	**10**	10	1. **Cry** Saes #8 / Airplay #10	Polydor 871110
			WATERS, Crystal	
			Female R&B-dance singer from South New Jersey. Majored in computer science at Howard University. Her father is jazz musician Jr. Waters; her aunt is Ethel Waters.	
6/1/91	**8**	9	● 1. **Gypsy Woman (She's Homeless)** Sales #8 / Airplay #16	Mercury 868208
7/9/94	**11**	34	● 2. 100% Pure Love Airplay #9 / Sales #13	Mercury 858485
			WATLEY, Jody	
			Born on 1/30/59 in Chicago. Female vocalist of Shalamar, 1977-84, and former dancer on TV's "Soul Train." Her godfather was Jackie Wilson. Won the 1987 Best New Artist Grammy Award.	
3/21/87	**2** (4)	14	1. **Looking For A New Love** Sales #1(3) / Airplay #2; #1 R&B hit (3 weeks)	MCA 52956
10/24/87	**6**	14	2. **Don't You Want Me** Sales #5 / Airplay #6	MCA 53162
2/27/88	**10**	10	3. **Some Kind Of Lover** Airplay #9 / Sales #10	MCA 53235
4/1/89	**2** (2)	12	● 4. **Real Love** Sales #1(2) / Airplay #3; #1 R&B hit (1 week)	MCA 53484
7/8/89	**9**	11	5. **Friends** **JODY WATLEY (With Eric B. & Rakim)** Sales #5 / Airplay #14	MCA 53660

DATE	POS	WKS	ARTIST–RECORD TITLE	LABEL & NO.
11/18/89+	**4**	14	6. **Everything** Airplay #5 / Sales #7	MCA 53714
3/21/92	**19**	11	7. I'm The One You Need Airplay #14	MCA 54276
			WATTS 103rd STREET RHYTHM BAND—see WRIGHT, Charles	
			WA WA NEE	
			Australian-based dance band. Includes Australians Steve Williams and brothers Mark and Paul Gray, plus Chris Sweeney (from the U.S.) and Phil Witchett (from New Zealand).	
10/31/87	**35**	3	1. Sugar Free Airplay #31 / Sales #34	Epic 07283
			WAYLON & WILLIE—see JENNINGS, Waylon, and/or NELSON, Willie	
			WAYNE, Thomas, With The DeLons	
			Born Thomas Wayne Perkins on 7/22/40 in Battsville, Mississippi. Killed in an auto accident on 8/15/71. Brother of guitarist Luther Perkins of Johnny Cash's band.	
2/16/59	**5**	13	1. **Tragedy** produced by Scotty Moore (Elvis Presley's former guitarist)	Fernwood 109
			WEATHERLY, Jim	
			Born on 3/17/43 in Pontotoc, Mississippi. Pop-country singer/songwriter. Wrote Gladys Knight's hits "Neither One Of Us," "Midnight Train To Georgia" and "Best Thing That Ever Happened To Me." Played quarterback for the University of Mississippi.	
10/12/74	**11**	8	1. The Need To Be	Buddah 420
			WEBER, Joan	
			Born in 1936; raised in Paulsboro, New Jersey. Died on 5/13/81 (age 45).	
12/4/54	**1 (4)**	16	● 1. **Let Me Go Lover** Jockey #1(4) / Juke Box #1(4) / Best Seller #1(2); written in 1953 as "Let Me Go Devil" and first recorded by Georgie Shaw; Weber's version was an overnight sensation after being featured 6 times on the 11/15/54 "Studio One" CBS-TV production; Jimmy Carroll (orch.)	Columbia 40366
			WEDNESDAY	
			Canadian pop quartet: Mike O'Neil (vocals), Paul Andrew-Smith, John Dufek and Randy Begg.	
2/16/74	**34**	4	1. Last Kiss	Sussex 507
			WE FIVE	
			California pop quintet: Beverly Bivens (lead singer), Mike Stewart (brother of John Stewart), Pete Fullerton, Bob Jones and Jerry Burgan.	
8/7/65	**3**	13	1. **You Were On My Mind** #1 Adult Contemporary hit (5 weeks)	A&M 770
12/25/65	**31**	2	2. Let's Get Together	A&M 784

DATE	POS	WKS	ARTIST–RECORD TITLE	LABEL & NO.
			WEISBERG, Tim—see FOGELBERG, Dan	
			WEISSBERG, Eric, & Steve Mandell	
			Prominent session musicians. Both had worked with Judy Collins and John Denver. Eric was a member of The Tarriers.	Warner 7659
2/3/73	**2** (4)	11	● 1. **Dueling Banjos** [I] tune written in 1955 as "Feuding Banjos" by Arthur "Guitar Boogie" Smith; from the movie *Deliverance* starring Burt Reynolds; #1 Adult Contemporary hit (2 weeks)	
			WELCH, Bob	
			Born on 7/31/46 in Los Angeles. Guitarist/vocalist with Fleetwood Mac, 1971–74. Formed the British rock group Paris in 1976. His father, Robert L. Welch, was a major movie/TV producer.	
11/19/77+	**8**	11	1. **Sentimental Lady** Christine McVie and Lindsey Buckingham (backing vocals)	Capitol 4479
2/25/78	**14**	10	2. Ebony Eyes	Capitol 4543
7/1/78	**31**	3	3. Hot Love, Cold World originally released as the B-side of #1 above	Capitol 4588
3/17/79	**19**	8	4. Precious Love	Capitol 4685
			WELCH, Lenny	
			Born on 5/15/38 in Asbury Park, New Jersey. Black pop vocalist.	
11/23/63	**4**	12	1. **Since I Fell For You** "Bubbled Under" in 1967 on Columbia 44007 (#134); #20 hit for Paul Gayten in 1947	Cadence 1439
4/11/64	**25**	5	2. Ebb Tide featured in the movie *Sweet Bird Of Youth* starring Paul Newman; both Frank Chacksfield and Vic Damone had Top 10 versions in 1953	Cadence 1422
2/14/70	**34**	4	3. Breaking Up Is Hard To Do	Common. U. 3004
			WELK, Lawrence, And His Orchestra	
			Born on 3/11/03 in Strasburg, North Dakota. Died of pneumonia on 5/17/92. Accordionist and polka/sweet band leader since the mid-1920s. Band's style labeled as "champagne music." Own national TV musical variety show began on 7/2/55 and ran on ABC until 9/4/71. New episodes in syndication, 1971–82. Re-runs are still enjoying immense popularity.	
3/3/56	**17**	2	1. Moritat (A Theme From "The Threepenny Opera") [I] **LAWRENCE WELK And His Sparkling Sextet** Juke Box #17 / Top 100 #31	Coral 61574
4/7/56	**17**	2	2. The Poor People Of Paris [I] Juke Box #17 / Top 100 #45	Coral 61592
8/11/56	**32**	3	3. Weary Blues **THE McGUIRE SISTERS and LAWRENCE WELK And His Champagne Music** traditional tune first recorded in 1923 by The New Orleans Rhythm Kings	Coral 61670
9/29/56	**15**	10	4. Tonight You Belong To Me **LAWRENCE WELK And His Sparkling Strings (with The Lennon Sisters and The Sparklers)** Top 100 #15 / Best Seller #16 / Jockey #16 / Juke Box #17; #1 hit for Gene Austin in 1927	Coral 61701
12/5/60	**21**	3	5. Last Date [I]	Dot 16145

DATE	POS	WKS	ARTIST–RECORD TITLE	LABEL & NO.

12/31/60+	**1** (2)	13	● 6. **Calcutta** [I]
			        written in Germany in 1958; above 2 feature Frank Scott (on piano
			        and harpsichord, respectively)
				Dot 16161

			WELLS, Mary	
			Born on 5/13/43 in Detroit. Diagnosed with throat cancer, August 1990; died on 7/26/92. R&B vocalist. At age 17, presented "Bye Bye Baby," a tune she had written for Jackie Wilson, to Wilson's producer, Berry Gordy, Jr. Gordy signed her to his newly formed label, Motown. Wells was the first to have a Top 10 and #1 single for that label. Married for a time to Cecil Womack (brother of Bobby Womack).	
8/21/61	**33**	3	1. I Don't Want To Take A Chance	Motown 1011
5/5/62	**8**	10	2. **The One Who Really Loves You**	Motown 1024
8/25/62	**9**	9	3. **You Beat Me To The Punch** #1 R&B hit (1 week)	Motown 1032
12/15/62+	**7**	10	4. **Two Lovers** #1 R&B hit (4 weeks)	Motown 1035
3/9/63	**15**	6	5. Laughing Boy	Motown 1039
7/6/63	**40**	1	6. Your Old Stand By	Motown 1042
10/12/63	**22**	7	7. You Lost The Sweetest Boy /	Motown 1048
1/25/64	**29**	6	8. What's Easy For Two Is So Hard For One	

4/11/64	**1** (2)	13	9. **My Guy**
			    #1 R&B hit (2 weeks); above 8 (except #7) written and produced
			    by Smokey Robinson
				Motown 1056

6/13/64	**17**	6	10. What's The Matter With You Baby /	
5/23/64	**19**	6	11. Once Upon A Time **MARVIN GAYE & MARY WELLS (above 2)**	Motown 1057
1/30/65	**34**	2	12. Use Your Head	20th Century 555
			WESLEY, Fred—see JB's	
			WEST, Dottie	
			Born Dorothy Marsh on 10/11/32 in McMinnville, Tennessee. Died on 9/4/91 from injuries suffered in a car accident. Country singer.	

4/25/81	**14**	12	1. What Are We Doin' In Love
			    DOTTIE WEST (with Kenny Rogers)
			    #1 Country hit (1 week)
				Liberty 1404

			WEST COAST RAP ALL-STARS, The	
			Rap benefit for inner city youth: Above The Law, Body & Soul, Def Jef, Digital Underground, Eazy-E, Ice-T, J.J. Fad, King Tee, M.C. Hammer, Michel'le, N.W.A., Oaktown's 3-5-7, Tone Lōc and Young M.C.	
8/11/90	**35**	3	● 1. We're All In The Same Gang Sales #17; produced by Dr. Dre	Warner 19819
			WESTON, Kim—see GAYE, Marvin	
			WET WILLIE	
			Mobile, Alabama, rock band led by brothers Jack (bass) and Jimmy (vocals) Hall.	
7/6/74	**10**	11	1. **Keep On Smilin'**	Capricorn 0043
1/28/78	**30**	4	2. Street Corner Serenade	Epic 50478
6/30/79	**29**	5	3. Weekend	Epic 50714

DATE	POS	WKS	ARTIST–RECORD TITLE	LABEL & NO.
			WHAM!—see MICHAEL, George	
			WHEN IN ROME	
			U.K.-based trio: Clive Farrington (vocals), Michael Floreale (keyboards) and Andrew Mann (vocals).	
10/22/88	**11**	13	1. The Promise Sales #9 / Airplay #12	Virgin 99323
			WHISPERS, The	
			Los Angeles soul group formed in 1964. Consisted of Gordy Harmon, twin brothers Walter and Wallace "Scotty" Scott, Marcus Hutson and Nicholas Caldwell. First recorded for Dore in 1964. Harmon replaced in 1973 by Leaveil Degree, who was briefly a member of Friends Of Distinction. The Scotts also recorded as Walter & Scotty since 1993. Group founded the Black Tie record label.	
3/15/80	**19**	8	● 1. And The Beat Goes On #1 R&B hit (5 weeks)	Solar 11894
5/24/80	**28**	4	2. Lady	Solar 11928
3/28/81	**28**	5	3. It's A Love Thing	Solar 12154
7/11/87	**7**	12	4. **Rock Steady** Airplay #5 / Sales #8; #1 R&B hit (1 week)	Solar 70006
			WHISTLE	
			Formed as a Brooklyn rap trio in 1985 with Garvin Dublin, Brian Faust and Rickford Bennett. By late 1988, Kerry "Kraze" Hodge was added and Dublin left, replaced by Tarek Stevens; group pursued R&B format.	
5/19/90	**35**	4	1. Always And Forever Sales #31 / Airplay #34	Select 2014
			WHITCOMB, Ian	
			Born on 7/10/41 in Woking, England. Pop singer/songwriter/author. Currently resides in California.	
6/19/65	**8**	8	1. **You Turn Me On (Turn On Song)** **IAN WHITCOMB And Bluesville**	Tower 134
			WHITE, Barry	
			Born on 9/12/44 in Galveston, Texas; raised in Los Angeles. Soul singer/songwriter/keyboardist/producer/arranger. With Upfronts vocal group, recorded for Lummtone in 1960. A&R man for Mustang/Bronco, 1966–67. Formed Love Unlimited in 1969, which included future wife Glodean James. Leader of 40-piece Love Unlimited Orchestra.	
5/5/73	**3**	12	● 1. **I'm Gonna Love You Just A Little More Baby** #1 R&B hit (2 weeks)	20th Century 2018
9/1/73	**32**	6	2. I've Got So Much To Give	20th Century 2042
11/17/73+	**7**	15	● 3. **Never, Never Gonna Give Ya Up**	20th Century 2058
8/10/74	**1** (1)	9	● 4. **Can't Get Enough Of Your Love, Babe** #1 R&B hit (3 weeks)	20th Century 2120
11/16/74+	**2** (2)	12	● 5. **You're The First, The Last, My Everything** #1 R&B hit (1 week)	20th Century 2133
3/22/75	**8**	7	6. **What Am I Gonna Do With You** #1 R&B hit (1 week)	20th Century 2177
6/21/75	**40**	2	7. I'll Do For You Anything You Want Me To	20th Century 2208
1/24/76	**32**	4	8. Let The Music Play	20th Century 2265

DATE	POS	WKS	ARTIST–RECORD TITLE	LABEL & NO.
10/1/77	4	12	● 9. **It's Ecstasy When You Lay Down Next To Me** #1 R&B hit (5 weeks)	20th Century 2350
5/27/78	24	5	10. Oh What A Night For Dancing all of above written (except #9) and produced by Barry White	20th Century 2365
4/7/90	31	4	● 11. **The Secret Garden (Sweet Seduction Suite)** **QUINCY JONES/Al B. Sure!/James Ingram/El DeBarge/Barry White** Sales #20; #1 R&B hit (1 week)	Qwest 19992
11/5/94	18	15	12. Practice What You Preach Sales #9; #1 R&B hit (3 weeks)	A&M 0778

WHITE, Karyn

Born on 10/14/65. Prominent session singer from Los Angeles. Touring vocalist with O'Bryan in 1984. Recorded with jazz-fusion keyboardist Jeff Lorber in 1986. Married to superproducer Terry Lewis (member of The Time).

DATE	POS	WKS	ARTIST–RECORD TITLE	LABEL & NO.
2/7/87	27	5	1. Facts Of Love **JEFF LORBER Featuring Karyn White** Airplay #27 / Sales #29	Warner 28588
11/26/88+	7	14	● 2. **The Way You Love Me** Sales #6 / Airplay #7; #1 R&B hit (1 week)	Warner 27773
2/25/89	8	10	● 3. **Superwoman** Airplay #9 / Sales #10; #1 R&B hit (3 weeks)	Warner 27783
7/1/89	6	12	4. **Secret Rendezvous** Sales #6 / Airplay #8	Warner 27863
8/24/91	1 (1)	19	5. **Romantic** #1 R&B hit (1 week)	Warner 19319
12/21/91+	12	13	6. The Way I Feel About You Airplay #7 / Sales #68	Warner 19088

WHITE, Tony Joe

Born on 7/23/43 in Oak Grove, Louisiana. Bayou rock singer/songwriter. Wrote Brook Benton's hit "Rainy Night In Georgia."

DATE	POS	WKS	ARTIST–RECORD TITLE	LABEL & NO.
7/26/69	8	8	1. **Polk Salad Annie** produced by Billy Swan	Monument 1104

WHITE LION

New York-based rock band: Mike Tramp (Denmark native; vocals), James Lomenzo (bass), Vito Bratta (guitar) and Greg D'Angelo (founding member of Anthrax; drums). Lomenzo and D'Angelo left in 1991, replaced by Tommy Caradonna and Jimmy DeGrasso (ex-Y&T).

DATE	POS	WKS	ARTIST–RECORD TITLE	LABEL & NO.
4/9/88	8	11	1. **Wait** Sales #7 / Airplay #7	Atlantic 89126
12/17/88+	3	12	2. **When The Children Cry** Sales #3 / Airplay #3	Atlantic 89015

WHITE PLAINS

English studio group featuring Tony Burrows (vocals), who was also with The Brotherhood Of Man, Edison Lighthouse, First Class and The Pipkins.

DATE	POS	WKS	ARTIST–RECORD TITLE	LABEL & NO.
5/23/70	13	10	1. My Baby Loves Lovin'	Deram 85058

DATE	POS	WKS	ARTIST–RECORD TITLE	LABEL & NO.
			WHITESNAKE	
			Ex-Deep Purple vocalist David Coverdale, who recorded solo as Whitesnake in 1977, formed British heavy-metal band in 1978. Coverdale fronted ever-changing lineup. Early members included his Deep Purple bandmates, keyboardist Jon Lord, 1979–84, and drummer Ian Paice, 1979–81. Players in 1987 included John Sykes (guitar), Neil Murray (bass) and Aynsley Dunbar (former Jefferson Starship drummer). Sykes left in 1988 to form Blue Murder. Ex-Dio guitarist Vivian Campbell was a member, 1987–88, later with Riverdogs, Shadow King and Def Leppard. 1989 lineup included Steve Vai (David Lee Roth's former guitarist), Adrian Vandenberg (former guitarist of Vandenberg), Rudy Sarzo (bass) and Tommy Aldridge (drums). Lineup in 1994: Coverdale, Vandenberg, Sarzo, Warren De Martini (guitar), Paul Mirkovich (keyboards) and Denny Carmassi (former drummer of Heart). Coverdale married actress Tawny Kitaen on 2/17/89; divorced by 1992.	
8/8/87	**1** (1)	14	1. **Here I Go Again** Sales #1(1) / Airplay #1(1)	Geffen 28339
11/7/87	**2** (1)	13	2. **Is This Love** Airplay #2 / Sales #2	Geffen 28233
12/16/89	**37**	3	3. Fool For Your Loving　　　　　　　　[R] Sales #36 / Airplay #39; new version of group's 1980 hit (#53)	Geffen 22715
2/17/90	**28**	6	4. The Deeper The Love Airplay #25 / Sales #27	Geffen 19951
			WHITING, Margaret	
			Born on 7/22/24 in Detroit; raised in Hollywood. Daughter of popular composer Richard Whiting ("Till We Meet Again"). Very popular 1946–54, she had over 40 charted pop hits.	
12/8/56	**20**	5	1. The Money Tree Jockey #20 / Top 100 #49; Billy May (orch.)	Capitol 3586
11/19/66	**26**	5	2. The Wheel Of Hurt #1 Adult Contemporary hit (4 weeks)	London 101
			WHITTAKER, Roger	
			Born on 3/22/36 in Nairobi, Kenya. British adult contemporary singer.	
5/10/75	**19**	9	1. The Last Farewell first released on Whittaker's 1971 album A Special Kind Of Man; #1 Adult Contemporary hit (1 week)	RCA 50030
			WHO, The	
			Rock group formed in London in 1964. Consisted of Roger Daltrey (born 3/1/44; lead singer), Pete Townshend (born 5/19/45; guitar, vocals), John Entwistle (born 10/9/44; bass) and Keith Moon (born 8/23/47; drums). Originally known as the High Numbers in 1964. All but Moon had been in The Detours. Developed stage antics of destroying their instruments. 1969 rock opera album *Tommy* became a movie in 1975. Solo work by members began in 1972. Moon died of a drug overdose on 9/7/78, replaced by Kenney Jones (formerly with Small Faces). 1973 rock opera album *Quadrophenia* became a movie in 1979. The Who's biographical movie *The Kids Are Alright* was released in 1979. Eleven fans trampled to death at group's concert in Cincinnati on 12/3/79. Disbanded in 1982. Regrouped at "Live Aid" in 1986. Daltrey, Townshend and Entwistle reunited with an ensemble of 15 for a U.S. tour in 1989. Jones formed The Law with Paul Rodgers in 1991. Inducted into the Rock and Roll Hall of Fame in 1990.	
5/20/67	**24**	4	1. Happy Jack	Decca 32114
10/28/67	**9**	9	2. **I Can See For Miles**	Decca 32206
5/4/68	**40**	2	3. Call Me Lightning	Decca 32288
8/31/68	**25**	6	4. Magic Bus	Decca 32362
5/3/69	**19**	5	5. Pinball Wizard	Decca 32465

DATE	POS	WKS	ARTIST–RECORD TITLE	LABEL & NO.
8/23/69	37	2	6. I'm Free	Decca 32519
8/1/70	27	6	7. Summertime Blues "live" recording	Decca 32708
10/17/70	12	9	8. See Me, Feel Me excerpt from the *Tommy* album finale "We're Not Gonna Take It" (#5 & 6 above are also from the 1969 rock opera album *Tommy*)	Decca 32729
8/7/71	15	10	9. Won't Get Fooled Again written for the aborted movie project *Lifehouse*	Decca 32846
12/4/71	34	5	10. Behind Blue Eyes	Decca 32888
8/5/72	17	8	11. Join Together	Decca 32983
1/13/73	39	2	12. The Relay	Track 33041
1/3/76	16	10	13. Squeeze Box	MCA 40475
9/16/78	14	9	14. Who Are You	MCA 40948
4/4/81	18	10	15. You Better You Bet	Warner 49698
10/9/82	28	6	16. Athena all of above (except #7) written by Pete Townshend	Warner 29905
			WIEDLIN, Jane	
			Born on 5/20/58 in Oconomowoc, Wisconsin; raised in California. Rhythm guitarist of the Go-Go's.	
6/11/88	9	10	1. **Rush Hour** Sales #8 / Airplay #13	EMI-Man. 50118
			WILCOX, Harlow, and the Oakies	
			Wilcox is a top session guitarist from Norman, Oklahoma.	
11/22/69	30	6	1. Groovy Grubworm [I]	Plantation 28
			WILD CHERRY	
			White funk band formed in Steubenville, Ohio, in the early '70s. Consisted of Robert Parissi (lead vocals, guitar), Bryan Bassett (guitar), Mark Avsec (keyboards), Allen Wentz (bass) and Ron Beitle (drums).	
7/31/76	1 (3)	18	▲ 1. **Play That Funky Music** #1 R&B hit (2 weeks)	Epic 50225
			WILDE, Kim	
			Born Kim Smith on 11/18/60 in Chiswick, England. Pop-rock singer. Daughter of singer Marty Wilde.	
7/17/82	25	8	1. Kids In America	EMI America 8110
4/18/87	1 (1)	13	2. **You Keep Me Hangin' On** Sales #1(2) / Airplay #1(1)	MCA 53024
			WILDER, Matthew	
			Born on 1/24/53 in Manhattan. Singer/songwriter/keyboardist. Session singer for Rickie Lee Jones and Bette Midler.	
11/26/83+	5	14	1. **Break My Stride**	Private I 04113
3/24/84	33	4	2. The Kid's American	Private I 04363

DATE	POS	WKS	ARTIST—RECORD TITLE	LABEL & NO.
			WILLIAMS, Andy	
			Born Howard Andrew Williams on 12/3/28 in Wall Lake, Iowa. Formed quartet with his brothers and eventually moved to Los Angeles. With Bing Crosby on hit "Swingin' On A Star," 1944. With comedienne Kay Thompson in the mid-1940s. Went solo in 1952. On Steve Allen's "Tonight Show," 1952–55. Own NBC-TV variety series, 1962–67, 1969–71. Appeared in the movie *I'd Rather Be Rich* in 1964. Formerly married to singer/actress Claudine Longet. One of America's greatest pop-MOR singers.	
8/18/56	7	17	1. **Canadian Sunset**	Cadence 1297
			Jockey #7 / Top 100 #8 / Juke Box #9 / Best Seller #10	
12/22/56	33	3	2. Baby Doll	Cadence 1303
			title song from the movie starring Carroll Baker	
3/2/57	1 (3)	14	3. **Butterfly**	Cadence 1308
			Top 100 #1(3) / Jockey #1(2) / Juke Box #2 / Best Seller #4	
6/3/57	8	14	4. **I Like Your Kind Of Love**	Cadence 1323
			Jockey #8 / Top 100 #9 / Best Seller #10 / Juke Box #19 end; Peggy Powers (female vocal)	
10/14/57	17	3	5. Lips Of Wine	Cadence 1336
			Jockey #17 / Top 100 #39	
2/24/58	3	14	6. **Are You Sincere**	Cadence 1340
			Jockey #3 / Top 100 #10 / Best Seller #11	
9/22/58	17	6	7. Promise Me, Love	Cadence 1351
1/12/59	11	15	8. The Hawaiian Wedding Song (Ke Kali Nei Au)	Cadence 1358
			song written in 1926, with new lyrics added	
9/28/59	5	11	9. **Lonely Street**	Cadence 1370
12/28/59+	7	9	10. **The Village Of St. Bernadette**	Cadence 1374
6/5/61	37	2	11. The Bilbao Song	Cadence 1398
			new Johnny Mercer lyrics to song from the 1929 German musical *Happy End*; Archie Bleyer (orch., all of above)	
7/14/62	38	1	12. Stranger On The Shore	Columbia 42451
11/3/62	39	1	13. Don't You Believe It	Columbia 42523
3/23/63	2 (4)	12	14. **Can't Get Used To Losing You/**	
			#1 Adult Contemporary hit (4 weeks)	
4/13/63	26	7	15. Days Of Wine And Roses	Columbia 42674
			title song from the movie starring Jack Lemmon and Lee Remick	
7/6/63	13	8	16. Hopeless	Columbia 42784
1/25/64	13	8	17. A Fool Never Learns	Columbia 42950
5/16/64	34	4	18. Wrong For Each Other	Columbia 43015
10/3/64	28	5	19. On The Street Where You Live	Columbia 43128
			from the movie *My Fair Lady* starring Audrey Hepburn and Rex Harrison	
12/19/64+	24	7	20. Dear Heart	Columbia 43180
			title song from the movie starring Glenn Ford	
4/24/65	36	3	21. And Roses And Roses	Columbia 43257
10/16/65	40	1	22. Ain't It True	Columbia 43358
			above 10 produced by Robert Mersey	
4/22/67	34	3	23. Music To Watch Girls By	Columbia 44065
			tune used in a Diet Pepsi commercial	
11/30/68	33	4	24. Battle Hymn Of The Republic	Columbia 44650
			with the St. Charles Borromeo Choir; recorded at St. Patrick's Cathedral on 6/8/68 as a eulogy to Senator Robert F. Kennedy	
5/3/69	22	7	25. Happy Heart	Columbia 44818
			#1 Adult Contemporary hit (2 weeks)	

DATE	POS	WKS	ARTIST–RECORD TITLE	LABEL & NO.
2/27/71	9	10	26. **(Where Do I Begin) Love Story** from the movie *Love Story* starring Ryan O'Neal and Ali McGraw; #1 Adult Contemporary hit (4 weeks)	Columbia 45317
5/20/72	34	4	27. Love Theme From "The Godfather" (Speak Softly Love) from the movie *The Godfather* starring Marlon Brando	Columbia 45579

WILLIAMS, Billy

Born on 12/28/10 in Waco, Texas. Died on 10/17/72 in Chicago. Lead singer of The Charioteers, 1930-50. Formed own Billy Williams Quartet with Eugene Dixon, Claude Riddick and John Ball in 1950. Many appearances on TV, especially "Your Show Of Shows" with Sid Caesar. By the early '60s, had lost voice due to diabetes. Moved to Chicago and worked as a social worker until his death.

DATE	POS	WKS	ARTIST–RECORD TITLE	LABEL & NO.
6/17/57	3	18	● 1. **I'm Gonna Sit Right Down And Write Myself A Letter/** Jockey #3 / Top 100 #6 / Best Seller #7; #5 hit for Fats Waller in 1935	
		5	2. Date With The Blues Best Seller flip	Coral 61830
2/16/59	39	3	3. Nola #3 instrumental hit for bandleader Vincent Lopez in 1922; Dick Jacobs (orch., above 3)	Coral 62069

WILLIAMS, Danny

Born on 1/7/42 in Port Elizabeth, South Africa. Moved to England in 1960.

DATE	POS	WKS	ARTIST–RECORD TITLE	LABEL & NO.
4/4/64	9	10	1. **White On White**	United Art. 685

WILLIAMS, Deniece

Born Deniece Chandler on 6/3/51 in Gary, Indiana. Soul vocalist/ songwriter. Recorded for Toddlin' Town, early 1960s. Member of Wonderlove, Stevie Wonder's backup group, 1972–75. Also a popular Inspirational artist.

DATE	POS	WKS	ARTIST–RECORD TITLE	LABEL & NO.
3/5/77	25	7	1. Free	Columbia 10429
4/22/78	1 (1)	11	● 2. **Too Much, Too Little, Too Late** **JOHNNY MATHIS/DENIECE WILLIAMS** #1 R&B hit (4 weeks); #1 Adult Contemporary hit (1 week)	Columbia 10693
5/1/82	10	9	3. **It's Gonna Take A Miracle** #1 R&B hit (2 weeks)	ARC 02812
4/14/84	1 (2)	14	▲ 4. **Let's Hear It For The Boy** from the movie *Footloose* starring Kevin Bacon and Lori Singer; #1 R&B hit (3 weeks)	Columbia 04417

WILLIAMS, Don

Born on 5/27/39 in Floydada, Texas. Country singer/songwriter/guitarist. Charted 17 #1 country hits. Leader of the Pozo-Seco Singers. Appeared in the movies *W.W. & The Dixie Dancekings* and *Smokey & The Bandit II*.

DATE	POS	WKS	ARTIST–RECORD TITLE	LABEL & NO.
11/15/80	24	9	1. I Believe In You #1 Country hit (2 weeks)	MCA 41304

WILLIAMS, John

Born on 2/8/32 in New York City. Noted composer/conductor of many top box-office movie hits. Succeeded Arthur Fiedler as conductor of the Boston Pops Orchestra in 1980; resigned in 1993 but continued as music adviser. Winner of 15 Grammys. Williams's son, Joseph, became a member of Toto in 1986.

DATE	POS	WKS	ARTIST–RECORD TITLE	LABEL & NO.
9/13/75	32	4	1. Main Title (Theme From "Jaws") [I]	MCA 40439

DATE	POS	WKS	ARTIST—RECORD TITLE		LABEL & NO.
8/13/77	10	7	2. **Star Wars (Main Title)** [I] performed by The London Symphony Orchestra		20th Century 2345
1/21/78	13	8	3. Theme From "Close Encounters Of The Third Kind"[I] all of above from soundtracks composed by Williams		Arista 0300

WILLIAMS, Larry

Born on 5/10/35 in New Orleans. Committed suicide on 1/7/80 in Los Angeles. R&B-rock and roll singer/songwriter/pianist. With Lloyd Price in the early '50s. Convicted of narcotics dealing in 1960; jail term interrupted his career. The Beatles recorded his songs "Slow Down," "Dizzy Miss Lizzie" and "Bad Boy."

DATE	POS	WKS	ARTIST—RECORD TITLE	LABEL & NO.
7/8/57	5	17	1. **Short Fat Fannie/** Best Seller #5 / Top 100 #6 / Jockey #15; #1 R&B hit (1 week)	
		5	2. High School Dance Best Seller flip	Specialty 608
11/11/57	14	14	3. Bony Moronie Best Seller #14 / Top 100 #18	Specialty 615

WILLIAMS, Mason

Born on 8/24/38 in Abilene, Texas. Folk guitarist/songwriter/author/photographer/TV comedy writer ("The Smothers Brothers Comedy Hour," 1967–69; "Saturday Night Live," 1980).

DATE	POS	WKS	ARTIST—RECORD TITLE	LABEL & NO.
7/13/68	2 (2)	11	1. **Classical Gas** [I] #1 Adult Contemporary hit (3 weeks)	Warner 7190

WILLIAMS, Maurice, & The Zodiacs

R&B vocal group from Lancaster, South Carolina, led by pianist/songwriter Maurice Williams. Originally recorded as The Gladiolas; became The Zodiacs in 1959. Williams re-formed group with Wiley Bennett, Henry Gaston, Charles Thomas, Albert Hill and Little Willie Morrow in 1960.

DATE	POS	WKS	ARTIST—RECORD TITLE	LABEL & NO.
10/10/60	1 (1)	14	1. **Stay**	Herald 552

WILLIAMS, Otis—see CHARMS

WILLIAMS, Roger

Born Louis Weertz in 1925 in Omaha. Learned to play the piano by age three. Educated at Drake University, Idaho State University, and Juilliard School of Music. Took lessons from Lenny Tristano and Teddy Wilson. Win on the TV show "Arthur Godfrey's Talent Scouts" led to recording contract.

DATE	POS	WKS	ARTIST—RECORD TITLE		LABEL & NO.
8/20/55	1 (4)	26	●	1. **Autumn Leaves** [I] Best Seller #1 / Top 100 #2 pre / Juke Box #2 / Jockey #3; from the 1947 French song "Les Feuilles Mortes"	Kapp 116
1/14/56	38	1		2. Wanting You [I] from the 1928 musical *The New Moon* starring Evelyn Herbert	Kapp 127
3/24/56	37	1		3. La Mer (Beyond The Sea) [I] introduced by Benny Goodman in 1948; Glenn Osser (orch., above 3)	Kapp 138
3/16/57	15	10		4. Almost Paradise [I] Jockey #15 / Best Seller #22 / Top 100 #26	Kapp 175
11/11/57	22	7	●	5. Till Jockey #22 / Top 100 #27 / Best Seller #28; Marty Gold (orch., above 2)	Kapp 197
9/8/58	10	11		6. **Near You** [I] Hot 100 #10 / Best Seller #16 end; Hal Kanner (orch.); #1 hit (17 weeks) for Francis Craig in 1947	Kapp 233

DATE	POS	WKS	ARTIST—RECORD TITLE	LABEL & NO.
10/15/66	7	14	7. **Born Free** title song from the movie starring Virginia McKenna; Ralph Carmichael (orch.); #1 Adult Contemporary hit (6 weeks)	Kapp 767

WILLIAMS, Vanessa

Born on 3/18/63 in Tarrytown, New York. In 1983, became the first black woman to win the Miss America pageant; relinquished crown after *Penthouse* magazine scandal. Married Ramon Hervey (manager of Babyface) in February 1987. Began hosting "Soul of VH-1" on video music TV channel in 1991. Starred in the Broadway production *Kiss Of The Spider Woman*. Appeared in the movie *Harley Davidson & The Marlboro Man* and the TV mini-series "The Jacksons: An American Dream."

DATE	POS	WKS	ARTIST—RECORD TITLE	LABEL & NO.
2/11/89	8	11	1. **Dreamin'** Sales #8 / Airplay #10; #1 R&B hit (2 weeks)	Wing 871078
9/21/91	18	11	2. Running Back To You Airplay #17 / Sales #33; #1 R&B hit (2 weeks)	Wing 867518
2/15/92	1 (5)	23	● 3. **Save The Best For Last** Airplay #1(8) / Sales #2; #1 R&B hit (3 weeks); #1 Adult Contemporary hit (3 weeks)	Wing 865136
6/13/92	26	9	4. Just For Tonight Airplay #27 / Sales #48	Wing 865888
3/6/93	3	20	5. Love Is **VANESSA WILLIAMS and BRIAN McKNIGHT** Airplay #2 / Sales #13; from the album *Beverly Hills 90210 (The Soundtrack)*; #1 Adult Contemporary hit (3 weeks)	Giant 18630
12/10/94+	18	16	6. The Sweetest Days Airplay #21 / Sales #21	Wing 851110
7/8/95	4	19	● 7. **Colors Of The Wind** Sales #4 / Airplay #11; from the Walt Disney animated movie *Pocahontas*	Hollywood 64001

WILLIS, Bruce

Born on 3/19/55 in Penns Grove, New Jersey. Played David Addison on TV's "Moonlighting." Starred in the *Die Hard* movies and others. Child's voice in the *Look Who's Talking* movies. Married actress Demi Moore on 11/21/87.

DATE	POS	WKS	ARTIST—RECORD TITLE	LABEL & NO.
1/31/87	5	10	1. **Respect Yourself** Sales #5 / Airplay #6	Motown 1876

WILLIS, Chuck

Born on 1/31/28 in Atlanta. Died of peritonitis on 4/10/58. R&B singer/songwriter. Billed as "King of the Stroll."

DATE	POS	WKS	ARTIST—RECORD TITLE	LABEL & NO.
5/13/57	12	8	1. C. C. Rider Top 100 #12 / Best Seller #13; inspired the "Stroll" dance craze; #1 R&B hit (2 weeks); #14 hit for Ma Rainey in 1925 (as "See See Rider Blues")	Atlantic 1130
3/10/58	33	3	2. Betty And Dupree Best Seller #33 / Top 100 #33; Jesse Stone (orch., above 2)	Atlantic 1168
5/12/58	9	17	● 3. **What Am I Living For/** Jockey #9 / Best Seller #15 / Top 100 #15; #1 R&B hit (1 week)	
5/26/58	24	2	4. Hang Up My Rock And Roll Shoes Reggie Obrecht (orch., above 2)	Atlantic 1179

DATE	POS	WKS	ARTIST–RECORD TITLE	LABEL & NO.
			WILL TO POWER	
			Florida-based trio formed and fronted by producer Bob Rosenberg with Dr. J. and Maria Mendez. Rosenberg is the son of singer Gloria Mann. By 1990, reduced to a duo of Rosenberg and Elin Michaels. Group name taken from the work of 19th-century German philosopher Frederich Nietzsche.	
10/15/88	**1** (1)	15	● 1. **Baby, I Love Your Way/Freebird Medley (Free Baby)** Sales #1(1) / Airplay #1(1)	Epic 08034
12/8/90+	**7**	12	2. **I'm Not In Love** Airplay #4 / Sales #7	Epic 73636
			WILSON, Al	
			Born on 6/19/39 in Meridian, Mississippi. Soul singer/drummer. Moved to San Bernadino, California in the late '50s. Member of The Rollers, 1960–62.	
9/21/68	**27**	5	1. The Snake produced by Johnny Rivers (owned Soul City Records)	Soul City 767
11/24/73+	**1** (1)	16	● 2. **Show And Tell**	Rocky Road 30073
11/9/74	**30**	3	3. La La Peace Song	Rocky Road 30200
5/1/76	**29**	4	4. I've Got A Feeling (We'll Be Seeing Each Other Again)	Playboy 6062
			WILSON, Ann	
			Born on 6/19/51 in San Diego. Lead singer of the rock group Heart.	
5/19/84	**7**	13	1. **Almost Paradise...Love Theme From Footloose** **MIKE RENO and ANN WILSON** from the movie *Footloose* starring Kevin Bacon and Lori Singer; #1 Adult Contemporary hit (1 week)	Columbia 04418
1/21/89	**6**	10	2. **Surrender To Me** **ANN WILSON AND ROBIN ZANDER** (lead singer of Cheap Trick) Sales #5 / Airplay #8; from the movie *Tequila Sunrise* starring Mel Gibson and Michelle Pfeiffer	Capitol 44288
			WILSON, Brian—see BEACH BOYS, The	
			WILSON, Danny—see DANNY	
			WILSON, J. Frank, and The Cavaliers	
			Wilson was born on 12/11/41 in Lufkin, Texas. Died on 10/4/91 after a long illness. Band formed in San Angelo, Texas. The Cavaliers: Sid Holmes (guitar), Lewis Elliott (bass) and Ray Smith (drums).	
9/26/64	**2** (1)	12	1. **Last Kiss** first released on Le Cam 722 and then on Tamara 761 in 1964	Josie 923
			WILSON, Jackie	
			Born on 6/9/34 in Detroit. Died on 1/21/84. Sang with local gospel groups; became an amateur boxer. Worked as a solo singer until 1953, then joined Billy Ward's Dominoes as Clyde McPhatter's replacement. Solo since 1957. Godfather of Jody Watley. Cousin of Hubert Johnson of The Contours. Wilson collapsed from a stroke, on stage, at the Latin Casino in Cherry Hill, New Jersey, on 9/25/75; spent rest of his life in hospitals. Inducted into the Rock and Roll Hall of Fame in 1987.	
4/21/58	**22**	10	1. To Be Loved Top 100 #22 / Best Seller #23; Milton DeLugg (orch.)	Brunswick 55052
12/8/58+	**7**	16	2. **Lonely Teardrops** #1 R&B hit (7 weeks)	Brunswick 55105

DATE	POS	WKS	ARTIST–RECORD TITLE	LABEL & NO.
4/13/59	13	9	3. That's Why (I Love You So)	Brunswick 55121
7/6/59	20	6	4. I'll Be Satisfied	Brunswick 55136
			above 4 co-written by Berry Gordy, Jr.	
10/12/59	37	1	5. You Better Know It	Brunswick 55149
			from the movie Go Johnny Go starring Wilson and Alan Freed; #1 R&B hit (1 week)	
1/4/60	34	3	6. Talk That Talk	Brunswick 55165
4/11/60	4	12	● 7. **Night/**	
			based on Saint-Saens Samson & Delilah aria "My Heart At Thy Sweet Voice"	
4/25/60	15	9	8. Doggin' Around	Brunswick 55166
			#1 R&B hit (3 weeks)	
8/1/60	12	9	9. (You Were Made For) All My Love/	
8/1/60	15	8	10. A Woman, A Lover, A Friend	Brunswick 55167
			#1 R&B hit (4 weeks)	
10/24/60	8	12	11. **Alone At Last/**	
			based on Tchaikovsky's "Piano Concerto in B Flat"	
11/28/60	32	2	12. Am I The Man	Brunswick 55170
1/16/61	9	6	13. **My Empty Arms**	Brunswick 55201
			based on "Vesti La Giubba" from the opera I Pagliacci	
3/27/61	20	5	14. Please Tell Me Why/	
3/27/61	40	1	15. Your One And Only Love	Brunswick 55208
6/26/61	19	5	16. I'm Comin' On Back To You	Brunswick 55216
9/11/61	37	2	17. Years From Now	Brunswick 55219
2/3/62	34	4	18. The Greatest Hurt	Brunswick 55221
			Bob Mersey (orch.)	
3/23/63	5	9	19. **Baby Workout**	Brunswick 55239
			#1 R&B hit (3 weeks); Dick Jacobs (orch., all of above - except #1 & 18)	
8/10/63	33	1	20. Shake! Shake! Shake!	Brunswick 55246
11/19/66	11	8	21. Whispers (Gettin' Louder)	Brunswick 55300
9/2/67	6	9	22. **(Your Love Keeps Lifting Me) Higher And Higher**	Brunswick 55336
			#1 R&B hit (1 week)	
12/16/67	32	2	23. Since You Showed Me How To Be Happy	Brunswick 55354
8/31/68	34	2	24. I Get The Sweetest Feeling	Brunswick 55381

WILSON, Meri

Born in Japan; raised in Marietta, Georgia. Currently the director of elementary education for Georgia.

DATE	POS	WKS	ARTIST–RECORD TITLE	LABEL & NO.
7/2/77	18	10	● 1. Telephone Man [N]	GRT 127
			produced by Boomer Castleman and Jim Rutledge (of Bloodrock)	

WILSON, Nancy

Born on 2/20/37 in Chillicothe; raised in Columbus, Ohio. Jazz stylist with Rusty Bryant's Carolyn Club Band in Columbus. First recorded for Dot in 1956. Moved to New York City in 1959.

DATE	POS	WKS	ARTIST–RECORD TITLE	LABEL & NO.
7/18/64	11	7	1. (You Don't Know) How Glad I Am	Capitol 5198
6/15/68	29	9	2. Face It Girl, It's Over	Capitol 2136

DATE	POS	WKS	ARTIST–RECORD TITLE	LABEL & NO.
			WILSON PHILLIPS	
			Vocal/songwriting trio of sisters Carnie and Wendy Wilson, with Chynna Phillips. Carnie and Wendy's father is Brian Wilson (The Beach Boys). Chynna, the daughter of Michelle and John Phillips (The Mamas & The Papas), acted in the movie *Caddyshack II*. Carnie became host of own TV talk show in 1995.	
4/7/90	**1** (1)	18	● 1. **Hold On** Sales #2 / Airplay #2; #1 Adult Contemporary hit (1 week)	SBK 07322
7/21/90	**1** (2)	15	● 2. **Release Me** Airplay #1(3) / Sales #3; #1 Adult Contemporary hit (1 week); "live" versions of above 2 are on the B-side of #4 below	SBK 07327
10/27/90	**4**	15	3. **Impulsive** Airplay #2 / Sales #8; Joe Walsh (rhythm & slide guitar)	SBK 07337
2/23/91	**1** (1)	14	4. **You're In Love** Airplay #1(1) / Sales #2; #1 Adult Contemporary hit (4 weeks)	SBK 07343
6/15/91	**12**	9	5. The Dream Is Still Alive Airplay #29; above 5 from the album *Wilson Phillips*	SBK 07356
5/23/92	**20**	8	6. You Won't See Me Cry Sales #22 / Airplay #27	SBK 07385
9/12/92	**30**	3	7. Give It Up Airplay #40 / Sales #42; all of above produced by Glen Ballard	SBK 50398
			WILTON PLACE STREET BAND	
			Los Angeles studio project produced and arranged by Trevor Lawrence (resided on Wilton Place in L.A.).	
3/12/77	**24**	7	1. Disco Lucy (I Love Lucy Theme) [I] discofied theme from the TV series "I Love Lucy" starring Lucille Ball	Island 078
			WINCHESTER, Jesse	
			Born on 5/17/44 in Shreveport, Louisiana. Pop singer/songwriter/guitarist. Moved to Canada in 1967 to avoid the draft; became a Canadian citizen in 1973.	
5/30/81	**32**	5	1. Say What	Bearsville 49711
			WIND	
			New York studio group featuring Tony Orlando as lead singer.	
10/4/69	**28**	4	1. Make Believe	Life 200
			WINDING, Kai	
			Born on 5/18/22 in Aarhus, Denmark. Died on 5/6/83. Jazz trombonist. Moved to U.S. in 1934. With Benny Goodman and Stan Kenton in the mid-1940s.	
7/27/63	**8**	9	1. **More** [I] theme from the movie *Mondo Cane*	Verve 10295
			WING AND A PRAYER FIFE AND DRUM CORPS., The	
			Studio group from New York City; vocals by Linda November, Vivian Cherry, Arlene Martell and Helen Miles.	
12/20/75+	**14**	12	1. Baby Face 4 versions hit the Top 10 in 1926	Wing & Prayer 103

DATE	POS	WKS	ARTIST–RECORD TITLE	LABEL & NO.
			WINGER	
			Hard-rock quartet formed in New York City in 1986: Kip Winger (vocals, bass), Reb Beach (guitar), Paul Taylor (keyboards; left in 1992) and Rod Morgenstein (drums). Kip was a member of Alice Cooper's band.	
4/8/89	**26**	6	1. Seventeen Sales #24 / Airplay #28	Atlantic 88958
7/8/89	**19**	9	2. Headed For A Heartbreak Airplay #18 / Sales #20	Atlantic 88922
11/17/90+	**12**	12	3. Miles Away Sales #8 / Airplay #14	Atlantic 87824
			WINGFIELD, Pete	
			Born on 5/7/48. Keyboardist from England. Worked with Freddy King, Jimmy Witherspoon and Van Morrison. In Olympic Runners band. Turned to production work in the '80s.	
10/25/75	**15**	8	1. Eighteen With A Bullet hit #18 with a bullet on the 11/22/75 Hot 100 chart	Island 026
			WINGS—see McCARTNEY, Paul	
			WINSTONS, The	
			Washington, D.C., soul septet: Richard Spencer (lead), Ray Maritano, Quincy Mattison, Phil Tolotta, Sonny Peckrol and G.C. Coleman. Toured as backup band for The Impressions.	
6/14/69	**7**	10	● 1. **Color Him Father**	Metromedia 117
			WINTER, Edgar, Group	
			Winter was born on 12/28/46 in Beaumont, Texas. Albino rock singer/keyboardist/saxophonist. Younger brother of rock guitarist Johnny Winter. Edgar Winter Group included Dan Hartman, 1972–76; Ronnie Montrose, 1972–74; and Rick Derringer, 1974–76.	
4/21/73	**1 (1)**	14	● 1. **Frankenstein** [I] Ronnie Montrose (lead guitar)	Epic 10967
9/8/73	**14**	9	2. Free Ride	Epic 11024
8/10/74	**33**	2	3. River's Risin' **EDGAR WINTER** above 3 produced by Rick Derringer	Epic 11143
			WINTERHALTER, Hugo, And His Orchestra	
			Winterhalter was born on 8/15/09 in Wilkes-Barre, Pennsylvania. Died of cancer on 9/17/73. Conductor/arranger for RCA Records, 1950–63.	
12/18/54+	**25**	5	1. Song Of The Barefoot Contessa Best Seller #25; from the movie The Barefoot Contessa starring Humphrey Bogart and Ava Gardner	RCA Victor 5888
7/28/56	**2 (2)**	23	● 2. **Canadian Sunset** [I] **HUGO WINTERHALTER and his Orchestra with EDDIE HEYWOOD** Top 100 #2 / Jockey #2 / Best Seller #3 / Juke Box #3	RCA 6537
			WINWOOD, Steve	
			Born on 5/12/48 in Birmingham, England. Rock singer/keyboardist/guitarist. Lead singer of Spencer Davis Group, Blind Faith and Traffic.	
2/28/81	**7**	12	1. **While You See A Chance**	Island 49656

DATE	POS	WKS	ARTIST—RECORD TITLE	LABEL & NO.
7/5/86	**1** (1)	14	2. **Higher Love** Airplay #1(2) / Sales #2; Chaka Khan (backing vocal)	Island 28710
10/25/86	**20**	7	3. Freedom Overspill Airplay #19 / Sales #21; Joe Walsh (slide guitar)	Island 28595
3/14/87	**8**	12	4. **The Finer Things** Airplay #4 / Sales #9; #1 Adult Contemporary hit (3 weeks)	Island 28498
7/4/87	**13**	10	5. Back In The High Life Again Airplay #10 / Sales #16; James Taylor (backing vocal); #1 Adult Contemporary hit (3 weeks); above 4 from the album *Back In The High Life*	Island 28472
11/7/87	**9**	12	6. **Valerie** [R] Airplay #7 / Sales #14; new version of Winwood's 1982 hit (#70)	Island 28231
6/18/88	**1** (4)	14	7. **Roll With It** Airplay #1(4) / Sales #1(1); #1 Adult Contemporary hit (2 weeks)	Virgin 99326
9/10/88	**6**	11	8. **Don't You Know What The Night Can Do?** Airplay #6 / Sales #8	Virgin 99290
12/10/88+	**11**	11	9. Holding On Airplay #10 / Sales #13; #1 Adult Contemporary hit (2 weeks)	Virgin 99261
11/17/90	**18**	9	10. One And Only Man Airplay #16 / Sales #21	Virgin 98892

WITHERS, Bill

Born on 7/4/38 in Slab Fork, West Virginia. Soul vocalist/guitarist/composer. Moved to California in 1967 and made demo records of his songs. Married to actress Denise Nicholas.

DATE	POS	WKS	ARTIST—RECORD TITLE	LABEL & NO.
8/14/71	**3**	12	● 1. **Ain't No Sunshine** produced by Booker T. Jones	Sussex 219
5/27/72	**1** (3)	14	● 2. **Lean On Me** #1 R&B hit (1 week)	Sussex 235
9/9/72	**2** (2)	10	● 3. **Use Me**	Sussex 241
3/3/73	**31**	5	4. Kissing My Love	Sussex 250
1/21/78	**30**	4	5. Lovely Day all of above written by Withers	Columbia 10627
3/7/81	**2** (3)	16	6. **Just The Two Of Us** **GROVER WASHINGTON, JR. (with Bill Withers)**	Elektra 47103

WOLF, Peter

Born Peter Blankfield on 3/7/46 in the Bronx. Lead singer of the J. Geils Band until 1983. Married actress Faye Dunaway on 8/7/74; divorced in 1979. Not to be confused with the producer of the same name.

DATE	POS	WKS	ARTIST—RECORD TITLE	LABEL & NO.
7/28/84	**12**	10	1. Lights Out	EMI America 8208
11/17/84	**36**	2	2. I Need You Tonight	EMI America 8241
3/21/87	**15**	9	3. Come As You Are Sales #13 / Airplay #15	EMI America 8350

WOLFMAN JACK—see GUESS WHO and STAMPEDERS

DATE	POS	WKS	ARTIST–RECORD TITLE	LABEL & NO.
			WOMACK, Bobby	
			Born on 3/4/44 in Cleveland. Soul vocalist/guitarist/songwriter. Sang in family gospel group, the Womack Brothers. Group recorded for SAR as The Valentinos and The Lovers, 1962–64. Toured as guitarist with Sam Cooke. Backup guitarist on many sessions, including Wilson Pickett, The Box Tops, Joe Tex, Aretha Franklin and Janis Joplin. Married for a time to Sam Cooke's widow, Barbara. Bobby's brother Cecil and Sam Cooke's daughter Linda recorded as Womack & Womack. Nicknamed "The Preacher."	
1/8/72	27	7	1. That's The Way I Feel About Cha	United Art. 50847
1/13/73	31	6	● 2. Harry Hippie	United Art. 50946
			Peace (backing group, above 2)	
8/11/73	29	6	3. Nobody Wants You When You're Down And Out	United Art. 255
3/9/74	10	11	● 4. **Lookin' For A Love**	United Art. 375
			#1 R&B hit (3 weeks)	
			WONDER, Stevie	
			Born Steveland Morris on 5/13/50 in Saginaw, Michigan. Singer/songwriter/multi-instrumentalist/producer. Blind since birth. Signed to Motown in 1960, did backup work. First recorded in 1962, named "Little Stevie Wonder" by Berry Gordy, Jr. Married to Syreeta Wright, 1970–72. Near-fatal auto accident on 8/16/73. Winner of 17 Grammy Awards. Appeared in the movies *Bikini Beach* and *Muscle Beach Party*. Inducted into the Rock and Roll Hall of Fame in 1989.	
7/6/63	1 (3)	12	1. **Fingertips - Pt 2**	Tamla 54080
			LITTLE STEVIE WONDER	
			"live" recording featuring Wonder on harmonica and bongos; #1 R&B hit (6 weeks)	
10/19/63	33	4	2. Workout Stevie, Workout	Tamla 54086
			LITTLE STEVIE WONDER	
7/11/64	29	4	3. Hey Harmonica Man	Tamla 54096
1/22/66	3	9	4. **Uptight (Everything's Alright)**	Tamla 54124
			#1 R&B hit (5 weeks)	
5/7/66	20	4	5. Nothing's Too Good For My Baby	Tamla 54130
7/30/66	9	8	6. **Blowin In The Wind**	Tamla 54136
			written by Bob Dylan; #1 R&B hit (1 week)	
11/26/66	9	8	7. **A Place In The Sun**	Tamla 54139
4/1/67	32	3	8. Travlin' Man	Tamla 54147
6/24/67	2 (2)	12	9. **I Was Made To Love Her**	Tamla 54151
			#1 R&B hit (4 weeks)	
10/21/67	12	5	10. I'm Wondering	Tamla 54157
4/27/68	9	9	11. **Shoo-Be-Doo-Be-Doo-Da-Day**	Tamla 54165
			#1 R&B hit (1 week)	
8/17/68	35	3	12. You Met Your Match	Tamla 54168
11/9/68	2 (2)	11	13. **For Once In My Life**	Tamla 54174
6/21/69	4	11	14. **My Cherie Amour/**	
3/22/69	39	1	15. I Don't Know Why	Tamla 54180
			above 4 from the album *For Once In My Life*	
11/1/69	7	12	16. **Yester-Me, Yester-You, Yesterday**	Tamla 54188
2/21/70	26	5	17. Never Had A Dream Come True	Tamla 54191
7/4/70	3	13	18. **Signed, Sealed, Delivered I'm Yours**	Tamla 54196
			#1 R&B hit (6 weeks)	
10/31/70	9	8	19. **Heaven Help Us All**	Tamla 54200
3/27/71	13	9	20. We Can Work It Out	Tamla 54202
			above 4 from the album *Signed Sealed & Delivered*	

DATE	POS	WKS	ARTIST—RECORD TITLE	LABEL & NO.
9/4/71	8	11	21. **If You Really Love Me**	Tamla 54208
6/24/72	33	5	22. Superwoman (Where Were You When I Needed You)	Tamla 54216
12/9/72+	1 (1)	13	23. **Superstition** #1 R&B hit (3 weeks)	Tamla 54226
3/31/73	1 (1)	13	24. **You Are The Sunshine Of My Life** Jim Gilstrap and Gloria Barley (first verse soloists); #1 Adult Contemporary hit (2 weeks)	Tamla 54232
9/1/73	4	12	25. **Higher Ground** #1 R&B hit (1 week)	Tamla 54235
11/24/73+	8	14	26. **Living For The City** #1 R&B hit (2 weeks)	Tamla 54242
4/27/74	16	9	27. Don't You Worry 'Bout A Thing	Tamla 54245
8/17/74	1 (1)	14	28. **You Haven't Done Nothin** The Jackson 5 (backing vocals); #1 R&B hit (2 weeks)	Tamla 54252
11/30/74+	3	14	29. **Boogie On Reggae Woman** #1 R&B hit (2 weeks)	Tamla 54254
12/4/76+	1 (1)	15	30. **I Wish** #1 R&B hit (5 weeks)	Tamla 54274
4/16/77	1 (3)	13	31. **Sir Duke** a tribute to Duke Ellington; #1 R&B hit (1 week)	Tamla 54281
9/17/77	32	4	32. Another Star	Tamla 54286
12/3/77+	36	5	33. As above 4 from the album *Songs In The Key Of Life* (a classic cut, "Isn't She Lovely," was not released as a single)	Tamla 54291
11/10/79	4	14	34. **Send One Your Love** #1 Adult Contemporary hit (4 weeks)	Tamla 54303
10/4/80	5	16	35. **Master Blaster (Jammin')** inspired by Bob Marley; #1 R&B hit (7 weeks)	Tamla 54317
1/17/81	11	11	36. I Ain't Gonna Stand For It	Tamla 54320
1/30/82	4	13	37. **That Girl** #1 R&B hit (9 weeks)	Tamla 1602
4/10/82	1 (7)	15	● 38. **Ebony And Ivory** **PAUL McCARTNEY (with Stevie Wonder)** #1 Adult Contemporary hit (5 weeks)	Columbia 02860
6/19/82	13	9	39. Do I Do	Tamla 1612
9/1/84	1 (3)	15	● 40. **I Just Called To Say I Love You** Sales #1(3) / Airplay #1(3); #1 R&B hit (3 weeks); #1 Adult Contemporary hit (3 weeks)	Motown 1745
12/15/84+	17	10	41. Love Light In Flight Airplay #15 / Sales #19; above 2 from the movie *The Woman in Red* starring Gene Wilder	Motown 1769
9/14/85	1 (1)	14	42. **Part-Time Lover** Airplay #1(3) / Sales #2; Luther Vandross (backing vocal); #1 R&B hit (6 weeks); #1 Adult Contemporary hit (3 weeks)	Tamla 1808
11/23/85+	1 (4)	17	● 43. **That's What Friends Are For** **DIONNE & FRIENDS: Elton John, Gladys Knight and Stevie Wonder** Sales #1(5) / Airplay #1(3); song introduced by Rod Stewart on the movie soundtrack of *Night Shift*; #1 R&B hit (3 weeks) #1 Adult Contemporary hit (2 weeks)	Arista 9422
12/14/85+	10	11	44. **Go Home** Airplay #11 / Sales #11; #1 Adult Contemporary hit (1 week)	Tamla 1817
3/22/86	24	6	45. Overjoyed Sales #18 / Airplay #26; #1 Adult Contemporary hit (2 weeks)	Tamla 1832
11/7/87	19	7	46. Skeletons Sales #11 / Airplay #32; #1 R&B hit (2 weeks)	Motown 1907

DATE	POS	WKS	ARTIST–RECORD TITLE	LABEL & NO.
			### WONDER WHO?—see 4 SEASONS	
			### WOOD, Brenton	
			Born Alfred Smith on 7/26/41 in Shreveport; raised in San Pedro, California. Soul singer/songwriter/pianist. First recorded with Little Freddy & The Rockets in 1958.	
6/24/67	34	1	1. The Oogum Boogum Song	Double Shot 111
9/9/67	9	10	2. **Gimme Little Sign**	Double Shot 116
12/16/67	34	3	3. Baby You Got It	Double Shot 121
			### WOOD, Lauren	
			Pop singer/songwriter/keyboardist; originally from Pittsburgh.	
10/27/79	24	6	1. Please Don't Leave Michael McDonald (harmony vocal)	Warner 49043
			### WOODS, Stevie	
			R&B vocalist based in Los Angeles. Originally from Columbus, Ohio. Son of jazz great Rusty Bryant.	
11/14/81	25	10	1. Steal The Night	Cotillion 46016
3/20/82	38	3	2. Just Can't Win 'Em All	Cotillion 46030
			### WOOLEY, Sheb	
			Born Shelby F. Wooley on 4/10/21 near Erick, Oklahoma. Singer/songwriter/actor. Played Pete Nolan in the TV series "Rawhide." Also made comical recordings under pseudonym Ben Colder. Appeared in the movies *High Noon, Rocky Mountain, Giant* and *Hoosiers.* Wrote theme song for "Hee Haw."	
6/2/58	1 (6)	14	● 1. **The Purple People Eater** [N] Best Seller #1(6) / Top 100 #1(6) / Jockey #1(4)	MGM 12651
			### WORLD PARTY	
			London-based group featuring keyboardist/vocalist/producer/engineer Karl Wallinger from North Wales (formerly of The Waterboys). Features Wallinger with an ever changing lineup.	
4/4/87	27	5	1. Ship Of Fools (Save Me From Tomorrow) Sales #20 / Airplay #37	Chrysalis 43052
			### WRAY, Link, & His Ray Men	
			Wray was born on 5/2/35 in Dunn, North Carolina. Rock and roll guitarist. Part Native American. Joined family band The Palomino Ranch Gang in the early '50s. First recorded as "Lucky" Wray for Starday in 1956. Recorded with rockabilly singer Robert Gordon in late '70s.	
5/12/58	16	10	1. Rumble [I] Best Seller #16 / Top 100 #16	Cadence 1347
3/16/59	23	3	2. Raw-Hide [I] **LINK WRAY AND THE WRAYMEN**	Epic 9300
			### WRECKX-N-EFFECT	
			Male rap group: Aqil Davidson, Markell Riley and Brandon Mitchell (died in 1990 of gunshot fire). Riley is the brother of Guy member/prolific producer Teddy Riley.	
10/24/92	2 (3)	23	▲² 1. **Rump Shaker** Sales #1(3) / Airplay #8; samples "Back To The Hotel" by N2Deep	MCA 54388

DATE	POS	WKS	ARTIST–RECORD TITLE	LABEL & NO.
			WRIGHT, Betty	
			Born on 12/21/53 in Miami. Soul singer. In family gospel group, Echoes Of Joy, from 1956. First recorded for Deep City in 1966. Hostess of TV talk shows in Miami.	
9/7/68	33	2	1. Girls Can't Do What The Guys Do	Alston 4569
12/11/71+	6	12	● 2. **Clean Up Woman**	Alston 4601
5/6/78	8	14	3. **Dance With Me**	Drive 6269
			PETER BROWN with Betty Wright	
			WRIGHT, Charles, And The Watts 103rd Street Rhythm Band	
			Wright was born in 1942 in Clarksdale, Mississippi. Vocalist/pianist/guitarist/producer/leader of an eight-man soul-funk band from the Watts section of Los Angeles. Evolved from the Soul Runners. Big break came through assistance from comedian Bill Cosby.	
3/22/69	11	10	1. Do Your Thing	Warner 7250
			THE WATTS 103RD STREET RHYTHM BAND	
5/30/70	16	10	2. Love Land	Warner 7365
9/12/70	12	10	3. Express Yourself	Warner 7417
			WRIGHT, Dale	
			Born Harlan Dale Riffe on 2/4/38 in Middletown, Ohio. Pop singer. Worked as a DJ in the Midwest.	
2/24/58	38	2	1. She's Neat	Fraternity 792
			DALE WRIGHT with the Rock-Its	
			Best Seller #38 / Top 100 #39	
			WRIGHT, Gary	
			Born on 4/26/43 in Creskill, New Jersey. Pop-rock singer/songwriter/keyboardist. Appeared in "Captain Video" TV series at age seven. In the Broadway play *Fanny*. Co-leader of the rock group Spooky Tooth.	
1/31/76	2 (3)	14	● 1. **Dream Weaver**	Warner 8167
5/15/76	2 (2)	18	2. **Love Is Alive**	Warner 8143
8/1/81	16	10	3. Really Wanna Know You	Warner 49769
			WRIGHT, Priscilla	
			Fourteen years old in 1955. Her father, Don Wright, was the leader of a choir in London, Ontario.	
6/25/55	16	9	1. The Man In The Raincoat	Unique 303
			PRISCILLA WRIGHT With Don Wright and The Septette	
			Jockey #16 / Best Seller #18 / Juke Box #20	
			WYNETTE, Tammy	
			Born Virginia Wynette Pugh on 5/5/42 in Itawamba County, Mississippi. With 20 #1 country hits, dubbed "The First Lady of Country Music." Discovered by producer Billy Sherrill. Married to country star George Jones, 1969–75.	
12/28/68+	19	9	1. Stand By Your Man	Epic 10398
			#1 Country hit (3 weeks)	
2/15/92	11	12	2. Justified & Ancient	Arista 12401
			THE KLF (Featuring Tammy Wynette)	
			Sales #10 / Airplay #12	

DATE	POS	WKS	ARTIST—RECORD TITLE	LABEL & NO.

X

XSCAPE

Female R&B quartet formed at the Tri-City Performing Arts School in Atlanta: sisters LaTocha and Tamika Scott, with Kandi Burruss and Tameka Cottle.

DATE	POS	WKS	ARTIST—RECORD TITLE	LABEL & NO.
10/2/93	**2** (1)	17	▲ 1. **Just Kickin' It** Sales #1(1) / Airplay #5; #1 R&B hit (4 weeks)	So So Def 77119
1/8/94	**8**	14	● 2. **Understanding** Sales #7 / Airplay #15; #1 R&B hit (2 weeks)	So So Def 77335
7/15/95	**32**	6	● 3. **Feels So Good** Sales #15	So So Def 77921
10/14/95	**8**	14	● 4. **Who Can I Run To?** Sales #5 / Airplay #29; originally recorded by The Jones Girls in 1979; #1 R&B hit (1 week)	So So Def 78056

Y

YA KID K—see TECHNOTRONIC

YANKOVIC, "Weird Al"

Born on 10/24/59 in Lynwood, California. Novelty singer/accordionist. Specializes in song parodies. Starred in the 1989 movie *UHF*.

DATE	POS	WKS	ARTIST—RECORD TITLE	LABEL & NO.
3/17/84	**12**	7	● 1. **Eat It** [N] parody of Michael Jackson's "Beat It"; Rick Derringer (guitar)	Rock 'n' Roll 04374
5/9/92	**35**	2	2. **Smells Like Nirvana** [N] Sales #12; parody of Nirvana's "Smells Like Teen Spirit"	Scotti Br. 75314

YARBROUGH, Glenn

Born on 1/12/30 in Milwaukee. Lead singer of The Limeliters, 1959–63. Folk singer.

DATE	POS	WKS	ARTIST—RECORD TITLE	LABEL & NO.
4/17/65	**12**	9	1. **Baby The Rain Must Fall** title song from the movie starring Lee Remick and Steve McQueen	RCA 8498

YARBROUGH & PEOPLES

Dallas soul duo: Cavin Yarbrough and Alisa Peoples. Discovered by The Gap Band.

DATE	POS	WKS	ARTIST—RECORD TITLE	LABEL & NO.
3/14/81	**19**	7	● 1. **Don't Stop The Music** #1 R&B hit (5 weeks)	Mercury 76085

YARDBIRDS, The

Legendary rock group formed in Surrey, England, in 1963. Consisted of Keith Relf (electrocuted 5/14/76, age 33; vocals, harmonica), Anthony "Top" Topham and Chris Dreja (guitars), Paul "Sam" Samwell-Smith (bass, keyboards) and Jim McCarty (drums). Formed as the Metropolitan Blues Quartet at Kingston Art School. Topham replaced by Eric Clapton in 1963. Clapton replaced by Jeff Beck in 1965. Samwell-Smith left in 1966, Dreja switched to bass and Jimmy Page (guitar) was added. Beck left in December 1966. Group disbanded in July 1968. Page formed the New Yardbirds in October 1968, which evolved into Led Zeppelin. Relf and McCarty formed Renaissance in 1969. Relf later in Armageddon, 1975; McCarty in Illusion, 1977.

DATE	POS	WKS	ARTIST—RECORD TITLE	LABEL & NO.
6/5/65	**6**	9	1. **For Your Love**	Epic 9790

DATE	POS	WKS	ARTIST–RECORD TITLE	LABEL & NO.
8/21/65	9	8	2. **Heart Full Of Soul** *above 2 written by Graham Gouldman (10cc)*	Epic 9823
11/20/65	17	7	3. I'm A Man *revival of Bo Diddley's classic 1955 R&B hit*	Epic 9857
4/9/66	11	8	4. Shapes Of Things *first released on Epic 9891 in 1966*	Epic 10006
7/16/66	13	7	5. Over Under Sideways Down	Epic 10035
12/24/66	30	4	6. Happenings Ten Years Time Ago	Epic 10094
			## YELLOW BALLOON, The	
			Pop quintet from Oregon and Arizona, formed by Don Grady (Robbie Douglas of "My Three Sons"). Alex Valdez, lead singer.	
4/29/67	25	5	1. Yellow Balloon	Canterbury 508
			## YES	
			Progressive-rock group formed in London in 1968. Consisted of Jon Anderson (vocals), Peter Banks (guitar), Tony Kaye (keyboards), Chris Squire (bass) and Bill Bruford (drums). Banks replaced by Steve Howe in 1971. Kaye (joined Badfinger in 1978) replaced by Rick Wakeman in 1971. Bruford left to join King Crimson, replaced by Alan White in late 1972. Wakeman replaced by Patrick Moraz in 1974, re-joined in 1976 when Moraz left. Wakeman and Anderson left in 1980, replaced by The Buggles' Trevor Horne (guitar) and Geoff Downes (keyboards). Group disbanded in 1980. Howe and Downes joined Asia. Re-formed in 1983 with Anderson, Kaye, Squire, White and South African guitarist Trevor Rabin. Anderson left group in 1988. Anderson, Bruford, Wakeman and Howe formed self-named group in early 1989. Yes reunited in 1991 with Anderson, Bruford, Wakeman, Howe, Kaye, Squire, White and Rabin. Bruford, Wakeman and Howe had left group by 1994.	
12/4/71	40	2	1. Your Move	Atlantic 2819
3/4/72	13	10	2. Roundabout	Atlantic 2854
11/19/83+	1 (2)	17	3. **Owner Of A Lonely Heart**	Atco 99817
3/24/84	24	7	4. Leave It	Atco 99787
10/31/87	30	6	5. Love Will Find A Way *Sales #27 / Airplay #30*	Atco 99449
2/6/88	40	1	6. Rhythm Of Love *Sales #40*	Atco 99419
			## YOST, Dennis—see CLASSICS IV	
			## YOUNG, Barry	
			Pop singer patterned after Dean Martin.	
12/4/65+	13	7	1. One Has My Name (The Other Has My Heart) *#1 Country hit for Jimmy Wakely in 1948*	Dot 16756
			## YOUNG, Faron	
			Born on 2/25/32 in Shreveport, Louisiana. Country singer/guitarist. Charted over 30 Top 10 country hits. Appeared in the movies *The Young Sheriff*, *Daniel Boone* and *Hidden Guns*. Founder and one-time publisher of the *Music City News* magazine in Nashville.	
5/1/61	12	11	1. Hello Walls *written by Willie Nelson; #1 Country hit (9 weeks)*	Capitol 4533

DATE	POS	WKS	ARTIST–RECORD TITLE	LABEL & NO.
			YOUNG, John Paul	
			Born in Glasgow, Scotland, in 1953 and raised in Australia. Pop singer/songwriter/pianist.	
8/5/78	7	15	1. **Love Is In The Air** #1 Adult Contemporary hit (2 weeks)	Scotti Br. 402
			YOUNG, Kathy, with The Innocents	
			Young was born on 10/21/45 in Santa Ana, California. Pop singer. Married for a time to a member of The Walker Bros. Also see The Innocents.	
10/31/60	3	15	1. **A Thousand Stars** originally recorded in 1954 by the R&B group, The Rivileers (Baton 200)	Indigo 108
3/6/61	30	6	2. Happy Birthday Blues	Indigo 115
			YOUNG, Neil	
			Born on 11/12/45 in Toronto. Rock singer/songwriter/guitarist. Formed rock band the Mynah Birds, featuring lead singer Rick James, early '60s. Moved to Los Angeles in 1966 and formed Buffalo Springfield. Went solo in 1969 with backing band Crazy Horse. Joined with Crosby, Stills & Nash, 1970–71. Appeared in the 1987 movie *Made In Heaven*. Reunited with Crosby, Stills & Nash in 1988 to record the *American Dream* album. Inducted into the Rock and Roll Hall of Fame in 1995.	
12/5/70	33	3	1. Only Love Can Break Your Heart	Reprise 0958
2/12/72	1 (1)	13	● 2. **Heart Of Gold** Linda Ronstadt and James Taylor (backing vocals)	Reprise 1065
5/20/72	31	4	3. Old Man	Reprise 1084
			YOUNG, Paul	
			Born on 1/17/56 in Bedfordshire, England. Pop rock vocalist/guitarist.	
3/3/84	22	8	1. Come Back And Stay	Columbia 04313
6/1/85	1 (1)	15	● 2. **Everytime You Go Away** Sales #1(2) / Airplay #1(1); written by Daryl Hall (appeared on Hall & Oates's 1980 *Voices* album); #1 Adult Contemporary hit (2 weeks)	Columbia 04867
9/21/85	13	9	3. I'm Gonna Tear Your Playhouse Down Sales #13 / Airplay #13	Columbia 05577
8/18/90	8	11	4. **Oh Girl** Airplay #6 / Sales #14; #1 Adult Contemporary hit (3 weeks)	Columbia 73377
2/22/92	22	6	5. What Becomes Of The Brokenhearted Airplay #26 / Sales #39; from the movie *Fried Green Tomatoes* starring Kathy Bates and Jessica Tandy; #1 Adult Contemporary hit (2 weeks)	MCA 54331
			YOUNG, Victor, And His Singing Strings	
			Born on 8/8/1900 in Chicago. Died on 11/11/56. Conductor/composer/violinist. Wrote "Stella By Starlight," "My Foolish Heart," "Blue Star," and many others. Composed the movie score for *Around The World In 80 Days*.	
7/8/57	13	9	1. (Main Theme) Around The World [I] Jockey #13 / Best Seller #20 / Top 100 #26; from the movie *Around the World in 80 Days* starring David Niven; B-side is Bing Crosby's charted vocal version	Decca 30262

DATE	POS	WKS	ARTIST—RECORD TITLE	LABEL & NO.
			YOUNGBLOODS, The	
			Folk rock group led by vocalist Jesse Colin Young (born Perry Miller on 11/11/44). Band formed in New York City in late 1965, moved to California in late 1967.	
8/2/69	5	12	● 1. **Get Together** [R] re-popularized as theme for National Conference of Christians & Jews; originally charted in 1967 at #62	RCA 9752
			YOUNG-HOLT UNLIMITED	
			Chicago instrumental soul group: Eldee Young (bass), Isaac "Red" Holt (drums; both of the Ramsey Lewis Trio) and Don Walker (piano). Walker left by 1968.	
1/21/67	40	2	1. Wack Wack [I] **THE YOUNG HOLT TRIO**	Brunswick 55305
12/7/68+	3	12	● 2. **Soulful Strut** [I] instrumental track used for Barbara Acklin's "Am I The Same Girl"	Brunswick 55391
			YOUNG MC	
			Born Marvin Young on 5/10/67 in England; raised in Queens, New York. Rapper. Co-writer of Tone Loc's "Wild Thing" and "Funky Cold Medina." Graduated with economics degree from University of Southern California.	
8/26/89	7	20	▲ 1. **Bust A Move** Sales #2 / Airplay #14	Delicious V. 105
1/6/90	33	3	2. Principal's Office Sales #21	Delicious V. 99137
			YOUNG RASCALS—see RASCALS	
			YO-YO	
			Born Yolanda Whitaker on 8/4/71 in Los Angeles. Female rapper. Member of Ice Cube's posse.	
6/29/91	36	3	1. **You Can't Play With My Yo-Yo** Sales #17; Ice Cube (rap); co-written by James Brown	EastWest 98831
			YURO, Timi	
			Born Rosemarie Timothy Aurro Yuro on 8/4/40 in Chicago. Moved to Los Angeles in 1952. First recorded for Liberty in 1959. Lost voice in 1980 and underwent three throat operations.	
7/31/61	4	10	1. **Hurt** #8 R&B hit for Roy Hamilton in 1955	Liberty 55343
8/11/62	12	6	2. What's A Matter Baby (Is It Hurting You)	Liberty 55469
8/10/63	24	7	3. Make The World Go Away	Liberty 55587

Z

DATE	POS	WKS	ARTIST—RECORD TITLE	LABEL & NO.
			ZABACH, Florian	
			Born on 8/15/21 in Chicago. Violinist/composer. Host of his own TV variety series in 1956.	
9/29/56	40	1	1. **When The White Lilacs Bloom Again** [I] written in 1928	Mercury 70936

DATE	POS	WKS	ARTIST–RECORD TITLE	LABEL & NO.
			ZACHARIAS, Helmut, And His Magic Violins	
9/8/56	**12**	7	German violinist. 1. When The White Lilacs Bloom Again [I] <small>Jockey #12 / Top 100 #16 / Best Seller #19 / Juke Box #19</small>	Decca 30039
			ZACHERLE, John, "The Cool Ghoul"	
3/10/58	**6**	7	Born on 9/26/18 in Philadelphia. Hosted horror movies on WCAU-TV in Philadelphia during the late '50s. 1. **Dinner With Drac (Part 1)** [N] <small>Top 100 #6 / Best Seller #8; Part 2 (B-side) is a less "gory" version</small>	Cameo 130
			ZADORA, Pia	
2/12/83	**36**	3	Born Pia Schipani in 1955 in New York City. (Derived Zadora from her mother's maiden name: Zadorowski.) Stage and movie actress/singer. Appeared in the movies *Butterfly*, *The Lonely Lady* and *Hairspray*. 1. The Clapping Song	Elektra/Curb 69889
			ZAGER, Michael, Band	
4/29/78	**36**	4	Disco studio group led by keyboardist/writer/arranger Michael Zager (born 1943, Jersey City, New Jersey). Member of Ten Wheel Drive, 1968–73. 1. Let's All Chant [I]	Private St. 45184
			ZAGER & EVANS	
6/28/69	**1 (6)**	12	Folk-rock duo from Lincoln, Nebraska: Denny Zager and Rick Evans (both sing and play guitar). ● 1. **In The Year 2525 (Exordium & Terminus)** <small>released regionally in 1968 on Truth 8082; #1 Adult Contemporary hit (2 weeks)</small>	RCA 0174
			ZAHND, Ricky, & The Blue Jeaners	
12/24/55	**21**	2	Zahnd was born on 7/22/46 in New York City. Lawyer since 1972. Vice president of the New York Knicks basketball team and the New York Rangers hockey team, 1979–86. 1. (I'm Gettin') Nuttin' For Christmas [X-N] <small>Best Seller #21 / Top 100 #40; Tony Mottola (orch.)</small>	Columbia 40576
			ZANDER, Robin—see WILSON, Ann	
			ZAPPA, Frank	
9/4/82	**32**	3	Born Francis Vincent Zappa, Jr., on 12/21/40 in Baltimore, Maryland, of Sicilian parentage. Died of prostate cancer on 12/4/93. Rock music's leading satirist. Singer/songwriter/guitarist/activist. Raised in California. Formed The Mothers Of Invention in 1965. Appeared in the movies *200 Motels* and *Baby Snakes*. Father of Dweezil and Moon Unit Zappa (both performed in the 1991 Peace Choir, "Give Peace A Chance"). Inducted into the Rock and Roll Hall of Fame in 1995. 1. Valley Girl [N] <small>featuring Frank's daughter, Moon Unit Zappa</small>	Barking P. 02972

DATE	POS	WKS	ARTIST–RECORD TITLE	LABEL & NO.
			ZEVON, Warren	
			Born on 1/24/47 in Chicago. Rock singer/songwriter/pianist. Parents were Russian immigrants. Recorded with female vocalist Tule Livingston as the duo Lyme & Cybelle in 1966. Worked as the keyboardist/bandleader for The Everly Brothers, shortly before their breakup. Wrote Linda Ronstadt's "Poor Poor Pitiful Me." Recorded with three R.E.M. members as the Hindu Love Gods in 1990.	
4/22/78	21	6	1. Werewolves Of London produced by Jackson Browne; Fleetwood Mac's Mick Fleetwood (drums) and John McVie (bass guitar)	Asylum 45472
			ZHANÉ	
			Pronounced: Jah-Nay. Female duo formed at Philadelphia's Temple University: Renee Neufville and Jean Norris.	
9/18/93	6	20	● 1. **Hey Mr. D.J.** Airplay #5 / Sales #6; samples Michael Wycoff's "Looking Up To You"	Flavor Unit 77177
1/29/94	17	14	2. Groove Thang Sales #18 / Airplay #20	Motown 2228
7/30/94	40	1	3. Sending My Love Sales #36 / Airplay #67; above 3 co-written and produced by Naughty By Nature	Illtown/Mot. 2242
12/10/94	28	5	4. Shame Airplay #31 / Sales #37; from the movie *A Low Down Dirty Shame* starring Keenan Ivory Wayans	Hollyw./Jive 42269
			ZODIACS, The—see WILLIAMS, Maurice	
			ZOMBIES, The	
			British rock quintet: Rod Argent (keyboards), Colin Blunstone (vocals), Paul Atkinson (guitar), Chris White (bass) and Hugh Grundy (drums). Group disbanded in late 1967. Rod formed Argent in 1969.	
11/7/64	2 (1)	12	1. **She's Not There**	Parrot 9695
1/30/65	6	8	2. **Tell Her No**	Parrot 9723
2/22/69	3	11	● 3. **Time Of The Season** recorded in 1967	Date 1628
			ZZ TOP	
			Boogie-rock trio formed in Houston in 1969: Billy Gibbons (vocals, guitar), Dusty Hill (vocals, bass) and Frank Beard (drums). All were born in 1949 in Texas. Gibbons had been lead guitarist in Moving Sidewalks, a Houston psychedelic-rock band. Hill and Beard had played in American Blues, based in Dallas. Group appeared in the movie *Back To The Future III*.	
8/16/75	20	4	1. Tush	London 220
3/1/80	34	3	2. I Thank You	Warner 49163
5/7/83	37	3	3. Gimme All Your Lovin	Warner 29693
6/2/84	8	12	4. **Legs**	Warner 29272
10/26/85	8	13	5. **Sleeping Bag** Airplay #7 / Sales #10	Warner 28884
2/8/86	21	7	6. Stages Airplay #16 / Sales #27	Warner 28810
4/19/86	22	7	7. Rough Boy Airplay #17 / Sales #25	Warner 28733
8/30/86	35	3	8. Velcro Fly Airplay #30; above 4 from the album *Afterburner*; all of above produced by Bill Ham	Warner 28650

THE SONGS

Lists, alphabetically, all titles in the artist section. The artist's name is listed next to each title along with the highest position attained and year of peak popularity. Some titles show the letter F as a position, indicating the title was listed as a flip side and did not chart on its own.

A song with more than one charted version is listed once, with the artists' names listed below the title in chronological order. Songs that have the same title but are different tunes are listed separately, with the most popular title listed first. This will make it easy to determine which songs are the same composition, the number of charted versions of a particular song, and which of these are the most popular.

Cross references have been used throughout to aid in finding a title.

Please keep the following in mind when searching for titles:

Titles such a "I.O.U.," "D.O.A.," and "SOS" will be found at the beginning of their respective letters; however, titles such as "T-R-O-U-B-L-E" and "R-O-C-K," which are spellings of words, are listed with their regular spellings.

Two-word titles which have the exact same spelling as one-word titles are listed together alphabetically. ("Dream Lover" is listed directly before "Dreamlover.")

Titles which are identical, except for an apostrophized word in one of the titles, are shown together. ("Lovin' You" appears immediately above "Loving You.")

POS/YR	RECORD TITLE/ARTIST

A

POS/YR	RECORD TITLE/ARTIST
28/66	"A" Team...SSgt. Barry Sadler
1/70	ABC...Jackson 5 (also see: O.P.P.)
26/82	Abacab...Genesis
16/64	Abigail Beecher...Freddy Cannon
15/63	Abilene...George Hamilton IV
31/60	About This Thing Called Love...Fabian
32/74	Abra-Ca-Dabra...DeFranco Family
1/82	Abracadabra...Steve Miller Band
	Abraham, Martin And John
4/68	Dion
33/69	Miracles
35/69	Moms Mabley
8/71	Tom Clay (medley)
26/71	Absolutely Right...Five Man Electrical Band
4/92	Achy Breaky Heart...Billy Ray Cyrus
18/90	Across The River...Bruce Hornsby & The Range
13/65	Action...Freddy Cannon
20/76	Action...Sweet
7/92	Addams Groove...Hammer
1/86	Addicted To Love...Robert Palmer
	Admiral Halsey ..see: Uncle Albert
8/84	Adult Education...Daryl Hall - John Oates
9/83	Affair Of The Heart...Rick Springfield
16/57	Affair To Remember (Our Love Affair)...Vic Damone
1/83	Africa...Toto
6/89	After All...Cher & Peter Cetera
18/70	After Midnight...Eric Clapton
32/57	After School...Randy Starr
23/83	After The Fall...Journey
32/82	After The Glitter Fades...Stevie Nicks
22/74	After The Goldrush...Prelude
10/56	After The Lights Go Down Low...Al Hibbler
2/79	After The Love Has Gone...Earth, Wind & Fire
8/77	After The Lovin'...Engelbert Humperdinck
6/91	After The Rain...Nelson
1/76	Afternoon Delight...Starland Vocal Band
1/93	Again...Janet Jackson
36/92	Again Tonight...John Mellencamp
1/84	Against All Odds (Take A Look At Me Now)...Phil Collins
5/80	Against The Wind...Bob Seger

POS/YR	RECORD TITLE/ARTIST
21/65	Agent Double-O-Soul...Edwin Starr
36/75	Agony And The Ecstasy...Smokey Robinson
29/81	Ah! Leah!...Donnie Iris
5/62	Ahab, The Arab...Ray Stevens
28/81	Ai No Corrida (I-No-Ko-ree-da)...Quincy Jones
17/81	Ain't Even Done With The Night...John Cougar
12/77	Ain't Gonna Bump No More (With No Big Fat Woman)...Joe Tex
39/66	Ain't Gonna Lie...Keith
20/57	Ain't Got No Home...Clarence "Frog man" Henry
24/70	Ain't It Funky Now...James Brown
40/65	Ain't It True...Andy Williams
22/79	Ain't Love A Bitch...Rod Stewart
	Ain't No Mountain High Enough
19/67	Marvin Gaye & Tammi Terrell
1/70	Diana Ross
13/79	Ain't No Stoppin' Us Now...McFadden & Whitehead
3/71	Ain't No Sunshine...Bill Withers
16/68	Ain't No Way...Aretha Franklin
8/75	Ain't No Way To Treat A Lady...Helen Reddy
4/73	Ain't No Woman (Like The One I've Got)...Four Tops
22/83	Ain't Nobody...Rufus & Chaka Khan
	Ain't Nothing Like The Real Thing
8/68	Marvin Gaye & Tammi Terrell
21/77	Donny & Marie Osmond
20/64	Ain't Nothing You Can Do...Bobby Bland
38/95	Ain't Nuthin' But A She Thing...Salt-N-Pepa
19/64	Ain't She Sweet...Beatles
	Ain't That A Shame
1/55	Pat Boone
10/55	Fats Domino
22/63	4 Seasons
35/79	Cheap Trick
33/61	Ain't That Just Like A Woman...Fats Domino
16/64	Ain't That Loving You Baby...Elvis Presley
8/65	Ain't That Peculiar...Marvin Gaye
6/92	Ain't 2 Proud 2 Beg...TLC
	Ain't Too Proud To Beg
13/66	Temptations
17/74	Rolling Stones
21/72	Ain't Understanding Mellow...Jerry Butler & Brenda Lee Eager
6/74	Air That I Breathe...Hollies

POS/YR	RECORD TITLE/ARTIST
31/70	**Airport Love Theme**...Vincent Bell
	Al Di La'
6/62	Emilio Pericoli
29/64	Ray Charles Singers
14/55	**Alabama Jubilee**...Ferko String Band
	(Aladdin's Theme) ..see: Whole New World
	Alamo ..see: Ballad Of The
29/71	**Albert Flasher**...Guess Who
	Alfie
32/66	Cher
15/67	Dionne Warwick
29/84	**Alibis**...Sergio Mendes
17/63	**Alice In Wonderland**...Neil Sedaka
27/68	**Alice Long (You're Still My Favorite Girlfriend)**...Tommy Boyce & Bobby Hart
29/81	**Alien**...Atlanta Rhythm Section
34/72	**Alive**...Bee Gees
14/78	**Alive Again**...Chicago
3/85	**Alive & Kicking**...Simple Minds
35/67	**All**...James Darren
29/93	**All About Soul**...Billy Joel
3/62	**All Alone Am I**...Brenda Lee
20/68	**All Along The Watchtower**...Jimi Hendrix Experience
2/59	**All American Boy**...Bill Parsons
3/90	**All Around The World**...Lisa Stansfield
11/56	**All At Once You Love Her**...Perry Como
2/76	**All By Myself**...Eric Carmen
8/86	**All Cried Out**...Lisa Lisa & Cult Jam With Full Force
7/65	**All Day And All Of The Night**...Kinks
35/71	**All Day Music**...War
19/88	**All Fired Up**...Pat Benatar
1/92	**All 4 Love**...Color Me Badd
1/94	**All For Love**...Bryan Adams/Rod Stewart/Sting
33/60	**All I Could Do Was Cry**...Etta James
7/71	**All I Ever Need Is You**...Sonny & Cher
	All I Have To Do Is Dream
1/58	Everly Brothers
14/63	Richard Chamberlain
27/70	Bobbie Gentry & Glen Campbell
9/73	**All I Know**...Garfunkel
2/85	**All I Need**...Jack Wagner
8/67	**All I Need**...Temptations
5/86	**All I Need Is A Miracle**...Mike + The Mechanics

POS/YR	RECORD TITLE/ARTIST
	All I Really Want To Do
15/65	Cher
40/65	Byrds
20/66	**All I See Is You**...Dusty Springfield
2/94	**All I Wanna Do**...Sheryl Crow
2/90	**All I Wanna Do Is Make Love To You**...Heart
15/92	**All I Want**...Toad The Wet Sprocket
19/87	**All I Wanted**...Kansas
32/90	**All I'm Missing Is You**...Glenn Medeiros (Feat. Ray Parker, Jr.)
19/61	**All In My Mind**...Maxine Brown
11/90	**All My Life**...Linda Ronstadt/Aaron Neville
37/83	**All My Life**...Kenny Rogers
	All My Love ..see: (You Were Made For)
19/80	**All Night Long**...Joe Walsh
1/83	**All Night Long (All Night)**...Lionel Richie
	(All of a Sudden) My Heart Sings
15/59	Paul Anka
38/65	Mel Carter
19/84	**All Of You**...Julio Iglesias & Diana Ross
4/90	**All Or Nothing**...Milli Vanilli
28/82	**All Our Tomorrows**...Eddie Schwartz
2/80	**All Out Of Love**...Air Supply
38/58	**All Over Again**...Johnny Cash
13/80	**All Over The World**...Electric Light Orchestra
12/83	**All Right**...Christopher Cross (also see: Alright)
4/70	**All Right Now**...Free
22/89	**All She Wants Is**...Duranduran
9/85	**All She Wants To Do Is Dance**...Don Henley
1/57	**All Shook Up**...Elvis Presley
	All Strung Out
26/66	Nino Tempo & April Stevens
34/77	John Travolta
2/93	**All That She Wants**...Ace Of Base
26/72	**All The King's Horses**...Aretha Franklin
19/86	**All The Love In The World**...Outfield
1/91	**All The Man That I Need**...Whitney Houston
28/86	**All The Things She Said**...Simple Minds
21/58	**All The Time**...Johnny Mathis
2/58	**All The Way**...Frank Sinatra
37/72	**All The Young Dudes**...Mott The Hoople
17/83	**All This Love**...DeBarge
5/91	**All This Time**...Sting
6/89	**All This Time**...Tiffany

POS/YR	RECORD TITLE/ARTIST
2/81	**All Those Years Ago**...George Harrison
5/84	**All Through The Night**...Cyndi Lauper
36/83	**All Time High**...Rita Coolidge
35/77	**All You Get From Love Is A Love Song**...Carpenters
1/67	**All You Need Is Love**...Beatles
2/56	**Allegheny Moon**...Patti Page
17/83	**Allentown**...Billy Joel
7/62	**Alley Cat**...Bent Fabric
	Alley-Oop
1/60	Hollywood Argyles
15/60	Dante & the Evergreens
32/59	**Almost Grown**...Chuck Berry
32/78	**Almost Like Being In Love**...Michael Johnson
25/84	**Almost Over You**...Sheena Easton
	Almost Paradise
15/57	Roger Williams
31/57	Lou Stein
7/84	**Almost Paradise...Love Theme From Footloose**...Mike Reno & Ann Wilson
24/66	**Almost Persuaded**...David Houston
28/78	**Almost Summer**...Celebration featuring Mike Love
1/87	**Alone**...Heart
1/72	**Alone Again (Naturally)**...Gilbert O'Sullivan
8/60	**Alone At Last**...Jackie Wilson
	Alone (Why Must I Be Alone)
18/57	Shepherd Sisters
28/64	Four Seasons
	Along Came Jones
9/59	Coasters
27/69	Ray Stevens
14/85	**Along Comes A Woman**...Chicago
7/66	**Along Comes Mary**...Association
8/88	**Alphabet St.**...Prince
32/74	**Already Gone**...Eagles
4/90	**Alright**...Janet Jackson
19/93	**Alright**...Kris Kross feat. Supercat **(also see: All Right)**
2/73	**Also Sprach Zarathustra (2001)**...Deodato
40/62	**Alvin Twist**...Chipmunks
3/59	**Alvin's Harmonica**...Chipmunks
33/60	**Alvin's Orchestra**...Chipmunks
1/87	**Always**...Atlantic Starr
4/94	**Always**...Bon Jovi
19/59	**Always**...Sammy Turner
20/94	**Always**...Erasure

POS/YR	RECORD TITLE/ARTIST
	Always And Forever
18/78	Heatwave
35/90	Whistle
20/94	**Always In My Heart**...Tevin Campbell
	Always On My Mind
5/82	Willie Nelson
4/88	Pet Shop Boys
	Always Something There To Remind Me ..see: (There's)
30/92	**Always The Last To Know**...Del Amitri
18/68	**Always Together**...Dells
33/64	**Always Together**...Al Martino
31/60	**Am I Losing You**...Jim Reeves
	Am I That Easy To Forget
25/60	Debbie Reynolds
18/68	Engelbert Humperdinck
32/60	**Am I The Man**...Jackie Wilson
1/86	**Amanda**...Boston
24/94	**Amazing**...Aerosmith
	Amazing Grace
15/71	Judy Collins
11/72	Royal Scots Dragoon Guards
37/68	**Ame Caline (Soul Coaxing)**...Raymond Lefevre
	Amen
7/65	Impressions
36/68	Otis Redding
8/81	**America**...Neil Diamond
27/72	**American City Suite**...Cashman & West
13/80	**American Dream**...Dirt Band
17/82	**American Heartbeat**...Survivor
16/82	**American Music**...Pointer Sisters
1/72	**American Pie**...Don McLean
13/86	**American Storm**...Bob Seger
26/72	**American Trilogy**...Mickey Newbury
35/74	**American Tune**...Paul Simon
1/70	**American Woman**...Guess Who
	Americans
4/74	Byron MacGregor
24/74	Gordon Sinclair
27/75	**Amie**...Pure Prairie League
7/59	**Among My Souvenirs**...Connie Francis
18/61	**Amor**...Ben E. King
	(Amos & Andy Song) ..see: Like A Sunday In Salem
8/71	**Amos Moses**...Jerry Reed
38/55	**Amukiriki (The Lord Willing)**...Les Paul & Mary Ford
37/57	**Anastasia**...Pat Boone
22/67	**And Get Away**...Esquires

POS/YR	RECORD TITLE/ARTIST
22/82	**And I Am Telling You I'm Not Going**...Jennifer Holliday
12/64	**And I Love Her**...Beatles
29/73	**And I Love You So**...Perry Como
F/94	**And On And On**...Janet Jackson
21/94	**And Our Feelings**...Babyface
36/65	**And Roses And Roses**...Andy Williams
37/90	**And So It Goes**...Billy Joel
	And That Reminds Me
9/57	Kay Starr
12/57	Della Reese
19/80	**And The Beat Goes On**...Whispers
21/85	**And We Danced**...Hooters
2/69	**And When I Die**...Blood, Sweat & Tears
3/88	**Angel**...Aerosmith
5/85	**Angel**...Madonna
18/93	**Angel**...Jon Secada
20/73	**Angel**...Aretha Franklin
40/72	**Angel**...Rod Stewart
	Angel Baby
5/61	Rosie & The Originals
29/92	Angelica
30/58	**Angel Baby**...Dean Martin
5/89	**Angel Eyes**...Jeff Healey Band **(also see: I'll Never Let You Go)**
40/82	**Angel In Blue**...J. Geils Band
6/77	**Angel In Your Arms**...Hot
14/89	**Angel Of Harlem**...U2
	Angel Of The Morning
7/68	Merrilee Rush
4/81	Juice Newton
22/61	**Angel On My Shoulder**...Shelby Flint
38/80	**Angel Say No**...Tommy Tutone
33/58	**Angel Smile**...Nat "King" Cole
30/89	**Angel Song**...Great White
27/60	**Angela Jones**...Johnny Ferguson
4/89	**Angelia**...Richard Marx
11/56	**Angels In The Sky**...Crew Cuts
22/59	**Angels Listened In**...Crests
1/73	**Angie**...Rolling Stones **(also see: Different Worlds)**
1/74	**Angie Baby**...Helen Reddy
	(Angry Young Man) ..see: Fooling Yourself
19/87	**Animal**...Def Leppard
1/74	**Annie's Song**...John Denver
10/93	**Anniversary**...Tony Toni Tone
1/80	**Another Brick In The Wall (Part II)**...Pink Floyd
5/71	**Another Day**...Paul McCartney

POS/YR	RECORD TITLE/ARTIST
1/89	**Another Day In Paradise**...Phil Collins
13/88	**Another Lover**...Giant Steps
3/94	**Another Night**...Real McCoy
22/86	**Another Night**...Aretha Franklin
1/80	**Another One Bites The Dust**...Queen
32/74	**Another Park, Another Sunday**...Doobie Brothers
11/88	**Another Part Of Me**...Michael Jackson
32/76	**Another Rainy Day In New York City**...Chicago
7/93	**Another Sad Love Song**...Toni Braxton
	Another Saturday Night
10/63	Sam Cooke
6/74	Cat Stevens
22/60	**Another Sleepless Night**...Jimmy Clanton
	Another Somebody Done Somebody Wrong Song ..see: (Hey Won't You Play)
32/77	**Another Star**...Stevie Wonder
20/58	**Another Time, Another Place**...Patti Page
32/80	**Answering Machine**...Rupert Holmes
	(Anthony's Song) ..see: Movin' Out
13/72	**Anticipation**...Carly Simon
	Any Day Now
23/62	Chuck Jackson
14/82	Ronnie Milsap
31/95	**Any Man Of Mine**...Shania Twain
	Any Other Way ..see: (If There Was)
2/94	**Any Time, Any Place**...Janet Jackson
14/65	**Any Way You Want It**...Dave Clark Five
23/80	**Any Way You Want It**...Journey
31/61	**Anybody But Me**...Brenda Lee
31/60	**Anymore**...Teresa Brewer
8/64	**Anyone Who Had A Heart**...Dionne Warwick
15/96	**Anything**...3T
18/94	**Anything**...SWV (Sisters With Voices)
1/88	**Anything For You**...Gloria Estefan & Miami Sound Machine
29/90	**Anything I Want**...Kevin Paige
26/91	**Anything Is Possible**...Debbie Gibson
31/62	**Anything That's Part Of You**...Elvis Presley
37/76	**Anything You Want**...John Valenti
33/76	**Anytime (I'll Be There)**...Paul Anka
12/94	**Anytime You Need A Friend**...Mariah Carey
20/56	**Anyway You Want Me (That's How I Will Be)**...Elvis Presley
2/61	**Apache**...Jorgen Ingmann
	Apartment ..see: Theme From The
24/56	**Ape Call**...Nervous Norvus

POS/YR	RECORD TITLE/ARTIST	POS/YR	RECORD TITLE/ARTIST
	Apple Blossom Time .. see: (I'll Be With You In)	8/61	**Asia Minor**...Kokomo
29/60	**Apple Green**...June Valli	12/64	**Ask Me**...Elvis Presley
32/65	**Apple Of My Eye**...Roy Head	18/56	**Ask Me**...Nat "King" Cole
6/67	**Apples, Peaches, Pumpkin Pie**...Jay & The Techniques	40/71	**Ask Me No Questions**...B.B. King
		27/72	**Ask Me What You Want**...Millie Jackson
37/69	**April Fools**...Dionne Warwick	19/95	**Ask Of You**...Raphael Saadiq
28/56	**April In Paris**...Count Basie	24/65	**Ask The Lonely**...Four Tops
1/57	**April Love**...Pat Boone	19/61	**Astronaut, The**...Jose Jimenez
1/69	**Aquarius/Let The Sunshine In (The Flesh** **Failures)**...5th Dimension	30/77	**At Midnight (My Love Will Lift You** **Up)**...Rufus, Feat. Chaka Khan
15/84	**Are We Ourselves?**...Fixx		**At My Front Door**
39/69	**Are You Happy**...Jerry Butler	7/55	Pat Boone
39/67	**Are You Lonely For Me**...Freddy Scott	17/55	El Dorados
	Are You Lonesome To-night?	3/75	**At Seventeen**...Janis Ian
1/60	Elvis Presley		**(At The Copa) ..see: Copacabana**
14/74	Donny Osmond		**At The Hop**
15/73	**Are You Man Enough**...Four Tops	1/58	Danny & The Juniors
14/70	**Are You Ready?**...Pacific Gas & Electric	21/58	Nick Todd
10/58	**Are You Really Mine**...Jimmie Rodgers	18/66	**At The Scene**...Dave Clark Five
11/56	**Are You Satisfied?**...Rusty Draper	16/67	**At The Zoo**...Simon & Garfunkel
3/58	**Are You Sincere**...Andy Williams	1/87	**At This Moment**...Billy Vera & The Beaters
39/66	**Are You There (With Another** **Girl)**...Dionne Warwick	6/94	**At Your Best (You Are Love)**...Aaliyah
		28/82	**Athena**...Who
26/77	**Ariel**...Dean Friedman	27/81	**Atlanta Lady (Something About Your** **Love)**...Marty Balin
10/70	**Arizona**...Mark Lindsay		
3/89	**Armageddon It**...Def Leppard	7/69	**Atlantis**...Donovan
28/73	**Armed And Extremely Dangerous**...First Choice	39/80	**Atomic**...Blondie
		18/66	**Attack**...Toys
36/89	**Arms Of Orion**...Prince with Sheena Easton	21/75	**Attitude Dancing**...Carly Simon
9/91	**Around The Way Girl**...L.L. Cool J	15/73	**Aubrey**...Bread
	Around The World In 80 Days	19/57	**Auctioneer**...Leroy VanDyke
12/57	Mantovani		**Auld Lang Syne ..see: I Understand**
13/57	Victor Young	15/84	**Authority Song**...John Cougar Mellencamp
25/57	Bing Crosby	25/75	**Autobahn**...Kraftwerk
29/79	**Arrow Through Me**...Wings	5/84	**Automatic**...Pointer Sisters
1/81	**Arthur's Theme (Best That You Can** **Do)**...Christopher Cross	34/83	**Automatic Man**...Michael Sembello
		37/72	**Automatically Sunshine**...Supremes
20/60	**Artificial Flowers**...Bobby Darin		**Autumn Leaves**
36/78	**As**...Stevie Wonder	1/55	Roger Williams
6/95	**As I Lay Me Down**...Sophie B. Hawkins	35/55	Steve Allen/George Cates
10/61	**As If I Didn't Know**...Adam Wade	19/68	**Autumn Of My Life**...Bobby Goldsboro
	As Tears Go By	18/56	**Autumn Waltz**...Tony Bennett
22/65	Marianne Faithfull	3/85	**Axel F**...Harold Faltermeyer
6/66	Rolling Stones		
31/70	**As The Years Go By**...Mashmakhan		
12/64	**As Usual**...Brenda Lee		
23/87	**As We Lay**...Shirley Murdock		
37/80	**Ashes By Now**...Rodney Crowell		

POS/YR	RECORD TITLE/ARTIST

B

POS/YR	RECORD TITLE/ARTIST
26/90	**B.B.D. (I Thought It Was Me)?**...Bell Biv DeVoe
1/79	**Babe**...Styx
4/95	**Baby**...Brandy
14/66	**B-A-B-Y**...Carla Thomas
1/91	**Baby Baby**...Amy Grant
2/92	**Baby-Baby-Baby**...TLC
8/69	**Baby, Baby Don't Cry**...Miracles
12/61	**Baby Blue**...Echoes
14/72	**Baby Blue**...Badfinger
1/78	**Baby Come Back**...Player
32/68	**Baby, Come Back**...Equals
27/74	**Baby Come Close**...Smokey Robinson
1/83	**Baby, Come To Me**...Patti Austin with James Ingram
33/56	**Baby Doll**...Andy Williams
1/89	**Baby Don't Forget My Number**...Milli Vanilli
1/72	**Baby Don't Get Hooked On Me**...Mac Davis
8/65	**Baby Don't Go**...Sonny & Cher
39/64	**Baby, Don't You Cry (The New Swingova Rhythm)**...Ray Charles
	Baby Don't You Do It
27/64	Marvin Gaye
34/72	Band
30/63	**Baby Don't You Weep**...Garnet Mimms & The Enchanters
14/76	**Baby Face**...Wing & A Prayer Fife & Drum Corps.
1/92	**Baby Got Back**...Sir Mix-A-Lot
11/78	**Baby Hold On**...Eddie Money
35/70	**Baby Hold On**...Grass Roots
26/84	**Baby I Lied**...Deborah Allen
4/67	**Baby I Love You**...Aretha Franklin
	Baby, I Love You
24/64	Ronettes
9/69	Andy Kim
	Baby, I Love Your Way
12/76	Peter Frampton
1/88	Will To Power (medley)
6/94	Big Mountain
	Baby I Need Your Loving
11/64	Four Tops
3/67	Johnny Rivers
3/71	**Baby I'm-A Want You**...Bread
25/79	**Baby I'm Burnin'**...Dolly Parton
14/69	**Baby, I'm For Real**...Originals
10/93	**Baby I'm Yours**...Shai
11/65	**Baby I'm Yours**...Barbara Lewis
16/90	**Baby, It's Tonight**...Jude Cole
	Baby It's You
8/62	Shirelles
5/69	Smith
14/83	**Baby Jane**...Rod Stewart
29/71	**Baby Let Me Kiss You**...King Floyd (also see: Boombastic)
24/72	**Baby Let Me Take You (In My Arms)**...Detroit Emeralds
35/69	**Baby Let's Wait**...Royal Guardsmen
1/64	**Baby Love**...Supremes
10/86	**Baby Love**...Regina
25/82	**Baby Makes Her Blue Jeans Talk**...Dr. Hook
11/68	**Baby, Now That I've Found You**...Foundations
21/61	**Baby Oh Baby**...Shells
16/66	**Baby Scratch My Back**...Slim Harpo
6/61	**Baby Sittin' Boogie**...Buzz Clifford
23/70	**Baby Take Me In Your Arms**...Jefferson
10/59	**Baby Talk**...Jan & Dean
38/80	**Baby Talks Dirty**...Knack
26/75	**Baby That's Backatcha**...Smokey Robinson
12/65	**Baby The Rain Must Fall**...Glenn Yarbrough
4/77	**Baby, What A Big Surprise**...Chicago
37/60	**Baby What You Want Me To Do**...Jimmy Reed
5/63	**Baby Workout**...Jackie Wilson
34/67	**Baby You Got It**...Brenton Wood
34/67	**Baby You're A Rich Man**...Beatles
5/60	**Baby (You've Got What It Takes)**...Dinah Washington & Brook Benton
26/61	**Baby's First Christmas**...Connie Francis
5/94	**Back & Forth**...Aaliyah
7/95	**Back For Good**...Take That
5/74	**Back Home Again**...John Denver
37/81	**Back In Black**...AC/DC
	Back In Love Again see: (Every Time I Turn Around)
1/65	**Back In My Arms Again**...Supremes
26/94	**Back In The Day**...Ahmad
13/87	**Back In The High Life Again**...Steve Winwood
38/77	**Back In The Saddle**...Aerosmith
	Back In The U.S.A.
37/59	Chuck Berry
16/78	Linda Ronstadt

POS/YR	RECORD TITLE/ARTIST
9/72	**Back Off Boogaloo**...Ringo Starr
34/89	**Back On Holiday**...Robbie Nevil
33/80	**Back On My Feet Again**...Babys
5/83	**Back On The Chain Gang**...Pretenders
36/67	**Back On The Street Again**...Sunshine Company
3/72	**Back Stabbers**...O'Jays
4/89	**Back To Life (However Do You Want Me)**...Soul II Soul
36/57	**Back To School Again**...Timmie "Oh Yeah!" Rogers
14/93	**Back To The Hotel**...N2Deep **(also see: Rump Shaker)**
28/77	**Back Together Again**...Daryl Hall & John Oates
40/73	**Back When My Hair Was Short**...Gunhill Road
20/84	**Back Where You Belong**...38 Special
10/69	**Backfield In Motion**...Mel & Tim
25/66	**Backstage**...Gene Pitney
1/87	**Bad**...Michael Jackson
1/73	**Bad, Bad Leroy Brown**...Jim Croce
1/75	**Bad Blood**...Neil Sedaka
8/86	**Bad Boy**...Miami Sound Machine
35/83	**Bad Boy**...Ray Parker, Jr.
36/57	**Bad Boy**...Jive Bombers
8/93	**Bad Boys**...Inner Circle
14/79	**Bad Case Of Loving You (Doctor, Doctor)**...Robert Palmer
33/63	**Bad Girl**...Neil Sedaka
36/93	**Bad Girl**...Madonna
1/79	**Bad Girls**...Donna Summer
15/75	**Bad Luck**...Harold Melvin & The Bluenotes
37/60	**Bad Man Blunder**...Kingston Trio
1/88	**Bad Medicine**...Bon Jovi
2/69	**Bad Moon Rising**...Creedence Clearwater Revival
25/90	**Bad Of The Heart**...George LaMond
4/75	**Bad Time**...Grand Funk
9/64	**Bad To Me**...Billy J. Kramer With The Dakotas
2/78	**Baker Street**...Gerry Rafferty
3/70	**Ball Of Confusion (That's What The World Is Today)**...Temptations
19/69	**Ball Of Fire**...Tommy James & The Shondells
14/58	**Ballad Of A Teenage Queen**...Johnny Cash
7/68	**Ballad Of Bonnie And Clyde**...Georgie Fame

POS/YR	RECORD TITLE/ARTIST
	Ballad Of Davy Crockett
1/55	Bill Hayes
5/55	"Tennessee" Ernie Ford
5/55	Fess Parker
14/55	Voices of Walter Schumann
34/66	**Ballad Of Irving**...Frank Gallop
33/90	**Ballad of Jayne**...L.A. Guns
8/69	**Ballad Of John And Yoko**...Beatles
33/62	**Ballad Of Paladin**...Duane Eddy
34/60	**Ballad Of The Alamo**...Marty Robbins
1/66	**Ballad Of The Green Berets**...SSgt. Barry Sadler
18/57	**Ballerina**...Nat "King" Cole
7/87	**Ballerina Girl**...Lionel Richie
33/74	**Ballero**...War
5/75	**Ballroom Blitz**...Sweet
	Banana Boat (Day-O)/Banana Boat Song
4/57	Tarriers
5/57	Harry Belafonte
13/57	Fontane Sisters
18/57	Steve Lawrence
19/57	Sarah Vaughan
25/57	Stan Freberg
3/70	**Band Of Gold**...Freda Payne
	Band Of Gold
4/56	Don Cherry
11/56	Kit Carson
32/66	Mel Carter
1/74	**Band On The Run**...Paul McCartney & Wings
35/67	**Banda, A**...Herb Alpert
18/55	**Bandit (O'Cangaceiro)**...Eddie Barclay
	Bang A Gong (Get It On)
10/72	T. Rex
9/85	Power Station
19/95	**Bang And Blame**...R.E.M.
2/66	**Bang Bang (My Baby Shot Me Down)** ...Cher
22/68	**Bang-Shang-A-Lang**...Archies
31/84	**Bang Your Head (Metal Health)**...Quiet Riot
23/71	**Bangla-Desh**...George Harrison
15/55	**Banjo's Back In Town**...Teresa Brewer
20/90	**Banned In The U.S.A.**...Luke Feat. 2 Live Crew
29/60	**Barbara**...Temptations
	Barbara-Ann
13/61	Regents
2/66	Beach Boys
7/66	**Barefootin'**...Robert Parker
20/76	**Baretta's Theme ("Keep Your Eye On The Sparrow")**...Rhythm Heritage

POS/YR	RECORD TITLE/ARTIST
11/77	**Barracuda**...Heart
	Baseball Game ..see: (Love Is Like A)
15/73	**Basketball Jones Featuring Tyrone Shoelaces**...Cheech & Chong **(also see: Love Jones)**
1/89	**Batdance**...Prince
	Batman Theme
17/66	Marketts
35/66	Neal Hefti
37/71	**Battle Hymn Of Lt. Calley**...C Company Featuring Terry Nelson
	Battle Hymn Of The Republic
13/59	Mormon Tabernacle Choir
33/68	Andy Williams
14/59	**Battle Of Kookamonga**...Homer & Jethro
1/59	**Battle Of New Orleans**...Johnny Horton
25/58	**Baubles, Bangles And Beads**...Kirby Stone Four
34/73	**Be**...Neil Diamond
25/64	**Be Anything (But Be Mine)**...Connie Francis
7/56	**Be-Bop-A-Lula**...Gene Vincent
3/57	**Be-Bop Baby**...Ricky Nelson
31/63	**Be Careful Of Stones That You Throw**...Dion
9/86	**Be Good To Yourself**...Journey
29/94	**Be Happy**...Mary J. Blige
35/82	**Be Mine Tonight**...Neil Diamond
	Be My Baby
2/63	Ronettes
17/70	Andy Kim
8/59	**Be My Guest**...Fats Domino
28/82	**Be My Lady**...Jefferson Starship
6/96	**Be My Lover**...La Bouche
9/85	**Be Near Me**...ABC
15/88	**Be Still My Beating Heart**...Sting
4/74	**Be Thankful For What You Got**...William DeVaughn
6/63	**Be True To Your School**...Beach Boys
34/63	**Be True To Yourself**...Bobby Vee
30/89	**Be With You**...Bangles
4/74	**Beach Baby**...First Class
12/81	**Beach Boys Medley**...Beach Boys
30/64	**Beans In My Ears**...Serendipity Singers
8/78	**Beast Of Burden**...Rolling Stones
6/67	**Beat Goes On**...Sonny & Cher
1/83	**Beat It**...Michael Jackson **(also see: Eat It)**
17/86	**Beat's So Lonely**...Charlie Sexton
12/82	**Beatles' Movie Medley**...Beatles
15/60	**Beatnik Fly**...Johnny & The Hurricanes

POS/YR	RECORD TITLE/ARTIST
19/94	**Beautiful In My Eyes**...Joshua Kadison
15/95	**Beautiful Life**...Ace Of Base
3/68	**Beautiful Morning**...Rascals
	Beautiful People
37/67	Bobby Vee
38/67	Kenny O'Dell
15/72	**Beautiful Sunday**...Daniel Boone
9/92	**Beauty And The Beast**...Celine Dion & Peabo Bryson
3/66	**Beauty Is Only Skin Deep**...Temptations
3/64	**Because**...Dave Clark Five
1/90	**Because I Love You (The Postman Song)**...Stevie B
10/94	**Because Of Love**...Janet Jackson
27/88	**Because Of You**...Cover Girls
	Because The Night
13/78	Patti Smith Group
11/94	10,000 Maniacs
4/60	**Because They're Young**...Duane Eddy
10/93	**Bed Of Roses**...Bon Jovi
17/88	**Beds Are Burning**...Midnight Oil
17/62	**Beechwood 4-5789**...Marvelettes
24/58	**Been So Long**...Pastels
24/73	**Been To Canaan**...Carole King
4/58	**Beep Beep**...Playmates
33/75	**Beer Barrel Polka**...Bobby Vinton
17/65	**Before And After**...Chad & Jeremy
7/95	**Before I Let You Go**...Blackstreet
23/78	**Before My Heart Finds Out**...Gene Cotton
1/75	**Before The Next Teardrop Falls**...Freddy Fender
7/95	**Before You Walk Out Of My Life**...Monica
29/67	**Beg, Borrow And Steal**...Ohio Express
16/67	**Beggin'**...4 Seasons
36/69	**Beginning Of My End**...Unifics
7/71	**Beginnings**...Chicago
34/71	**Behind Blue Eyes**...Who
15/73	**Behind Closed Doors**...Charlie Rich
2/81	**Being With You**...Smokey Robinson
13/95	**Believe**...Elton John
28/73	**Believe In Humanity**...Carole King
26/59	**Believe Me**...Royal Teens
4/58	**Believe What You Say**...Ricky Nelson
28/69	**Bella Linda**...Grassroots
34/84	**Belle Of St. Mark**...Sheila E.
12/70	**Bells, The**...Originals
13/58	**Belonging To Someone**...Patti Page
1/72	**Ben**...Michael Jackson
	Ben Casey ..see: Theme From

POS/YR	RECORD TITLE/ARTIST
5/68	**Bend Me, Shape Me**...American Breed
1/74	**Bennie And The Jets**...Elton John
4/67	**Bernadette**...Four Tops
14/57	**Bernardine**...Pat Boone
16/75	**Bertha Butt Boogie**...Jimmy Castor Bunch
15/89	**Best, The**...Tina Turner
17/76	**Best Disco In Town**...Ritchie Family
34/95	**Best Friend**...Brandy
32/68	**Best Of Both Worlds**...Lulu
1/77	**Best Of My Love**...Emotions
1/75	**Best Of My Love**...Eagles
3/81	**Best Of Times**...Styx
39/64	**(Best Part Of) Breakin' Up**...Ronettes
3/74	**Best Thing That Ever Happened To Me**...Gladys Knight & The Pips
10/92	**Best Things In Life Are Free**...Luther Vandross & Janet Jackson
3/72	**Betcha By Golly, Wow**...Stylistics
	(Betcha Got A Chick On The Side) ..see: **How Long**
36/87	**Betcha Say That**...Gloria Estefan & Miami Sound Machine
7/76	**Beth**...Kiss
1/81	**Bette Davis Eyes**...Kim Carnes
5/84	**Better Be Good To Me**...Tina Turner
F/92	**Better Days**...Bruce Springsteen
18/91	**Better Love**...Londonbeat
12/80	**Better Love Next Time**...Dr. Hook
38/61	**Better Tell Him No**...Starlets
36/93	**Better Than You**...Lisa Keith
33/58	**Betty And Dupree**...Chuck Willis
37/58	**Betty Lou Got A New Pair Of Shoes**...Bobby Freeman
40/61	**Bewildered**...James Brown
	Beyond The Sea
37/56	Roger Williams
6/60	Bobby Darin
	Bible Tells Me So
7/55	Don Cornell
22/55	Nick Noble
24/79	**Bicycle Race**...Queen
1/61	**Big Bad John**...Jimmy Dean
26/58	**Big Beat**...Fats Domino
38/58	**Big Bopper's Wedding**...Big Bopper
38/67	**Big Boss Man**...Elvis Presley
23/73	**Big City Miss Ruth Ann**...Gallery
19/61	**Big Cold Wind**...Pat Boone
21/82	**Big Fun**...Kool & The Gang
1/62	**Big Girls Don't Cry**...4 Seasons

POS/YR	RECORD TITLE/ARTIST
1/59	**Big Hunk O' Love**...Elvis Presley
3/59	**Big Hurt**...Miss Toni Fisher
26/60	**Big Iron**...Marty Robbins
21/61	**Big John**...Shirelles
20/83	**Big Log**...Robert Plant
5/87	**Big Love**...Fleetwood Mac
3/58	**Big Man**...Four Preps
20/64	**Big Man In Town**...4 Seasons
6/95	**Big Poppa**...Notorious B.I.G.
F/58	**Big River**...Johnny Cash
14/79	**Big Shot**...Billy Joel
8/87	**Big Time**...Peter Gabriel
	Big Yellow Taxi
29/70	Neighborhood
24/75	Joni Mitchell
3/80	**Biggest Part Of Me**...Ambrosia
37/61	**Bilbao Song**...Andy Williams
	Bill Bailey ..see: **Won't You Come Home**
1/83	**Billie Jean**...Michael Jackson
7/58	**Billy**...Kathy Linden
34/66	**Billy And Sue**...B.J. Thomas
1/74	**Billy, Don't Be A Hero**...Bo Donaldson & The Heywoods
	Billy Jack ..see: **One Tin Soldier**
11/58	**Bimbombey**...Jimmie Rodgers
36/85	**Bird, The**...Time (also see: **Do The**)
30/64	**Bird Dance Beat**...Trashmen
1/58	**Bird Dog**...Everly Brothers
34/58	**Bird On My Head**...David Seville
12/63	**Birdland**...Chubby Checker
3/65	**Birds And The Bees**...Jewel Akens
23/71	**Birds Of A Feather**...Raiders
17/55	**Birth Of The Boogie**...Bill Haley
26/69	**Birthday**...Underground Sunshine
40/63	**Birthday Party**...Pixies Three
36/89	**Birthday Suit**...Johnny Kemp
4/74	**Bitch Is Back**...Elton John
28/77	**Bite Your Lip (Get up and dance!)**...Elton John
4/64	**Bits And Pieces**...Dave Clark Five
36/73	**Bitter Bad**...Melanie
34/88	**Black And Blue**...Van Halen
1/72	**Black & White**...Three Dog Night
18/77	**Black Betty**...Ram Jam
1/90	**Black Cat**...Janet Jackson

POS/YR	RECORD TITLE/ARTIST
	Black Denim Trousers
6/55	Cheers
38/55	Vaughn Monroe
15/72	**Black Dog**...Led Zeppelin
F/71	**Black-Eyed Blues**...Joe Cocker
37/75	**Black Friday**...Steely Dan
4/66	**Black Is Black**...Los Bravos
4/71	**Black Magic Woman**...Santana
1/91	**Black Or White**...Michael Jackson
13/69	**Black Pearl**...Checkmates, Ltd.
17/57	**Black Slacks**...Joe Bennett
21/75	**Black Superman - "Muhammad Ali"**...Johnny Wakelin
1/90	**Black Velvet**...Alannah Myles
1/75	**Black Water**...Doobie Brothers
7/63	**Blame It On The Bossa Nova**...Eydie Gorme
1/89	**Blame It On The Rain**...Milli Vanilli
1/90	**Blaze Of Glory**...Jon Bon Jovi
39/64	**Bless Our Love**...Gene Chandler
15/61	**Bless You**...Tony Orlando
34/95	**Blessed**...Elton John
34/81	**Blessed Are The Believers**...Anne Murray
	(Blind Man In The Bleachers) ..see: Last Game Of The Season
1/77	**Blinded By The Light**...Manfred Mann's Earth Band
33/58	**Blob, The**...Five Blobs
35/75	**Bloody Well Right**...Supertramp
2/55	**Blossom Fell**...Nat "King" Cole
16/79	**Blow Away**...George Harrison
	Blowin' In The Wind
2/63	Peter, Paul & Mary
9/66	Stevie Wonder
21/70	**Blowing Away**...5th Dimension
6/91	**Blowing Kisses In The Wind**...Paula Abdul
9/60	**Blue Angel**...Roy Orbison
35/67	**Blue Autumn**...Bobby Goldsboro
	Blue Bayou
29/63	Roy Orbison
3/77	Linda Ronstadt
20/58	**Blue Blue Day**...Don Gibson
21/78	**Blue Collar Man (Long Nights)**...Styx
12/82	**Blue Eyes**...Elton John
21/75	**Blue Eyes Crying In The Rain**...Willie Nelson
37/59	**Blue Hawaii**...Billy Vaughn
8/84	**Blue Jean**...David Bowie
5/57	**Blue Monday**...Fats Domino
23/71	**Blue Money**...Van Morrison

POS/YR	RECORD TITLE/ARTIST
1/61	**Blue Moon**...Marcels
15/79	**Blue Morning, Blue Day**...Foreigner
3/63	**Blue On Blue**...Bobby Vinton
	Blue Star
29/55	Felicia Sanders
F/55	Les Baxter
	Blue Suede Shoes
2/56	Carl Perkins
20/56	Elvis Presley
38/73	Johnny Rivers
16/60	**Blue Tango**...Bill Black's Combo
1/63	**Blue Velvet**...Bobby Vinton
24/64	**Blue Winter**...Connie Francis
	Blueberry Hill
29/56	Louis Armstrong & Gordon Jenkins
2/57	Fats Domino
35/75	**Bluebird**...Helen Reddy
12/78	**Bluer Than Blue**...Michael Johnson
36/62	**Blues (Stay Away From Me)**...Ace Cannon
37/67	**Blues' Theme**...Davie Allan & The Arrows
	Bo Weevil
17/56	Teresa Brewer
35/56	Fats Domino
	(also see: Boll Weevil)
12/82	**Bobbie Sue**...Oak Ridge Boys
8/59	**Bobby Sox To Stockings**...Frankie Avalon
3/62	**Bobby's Girl**...Marcie Blane
36/94	**Body & Soul**...Anita Baker
11/82	**Body Language**...Queen
	Bohemian Rhapsody
9/76	Queen
2/92	Queen
2/61	**Boll Weevil Song**...Brook Benton
19/61	**Bonanza**...Al Caiola
14/59	**Bongo Rock**...Preston Epps
33/62	**Bongo Stomp**...Little Joey & The Flips
	Bonnie And Clyde ..see: Ballad Of
26/60	**Bonnie Came Back**...Duane Eddy
	(also see: My Bonnie)
14/57	**Bony Moronie**...Larry Williams
7/67	**Boogaloo Down Broadway**...Fantastic Johnny C
12/77	**Boogie Child**...Bee Gees
2/74	**Boogie Down**...Eddie Kendricks
1/76	**Boogie Fever**...Sylvers
2/77	**Boogie Nights**...Heatwave
3/75	**Boogie On Reggae Woman**...Stevie Wonder
1/78	**Boogie Oogie Oogie**...Taste Of Honey
35/78	**Boogie Shoes**...KC & The Sunshine Band

POS/YR	RECORD TITLE/ARTIST
6/79	Boogie Wonderland...Earth, Wind & Fire with The Emotions
8/73	Boogie Woogie Bugle Boy...Bette Midler
5/58	Book Of Love...Monotones
17/55	Boom Boom Boomerang...DeCastro Sisters
13/93	Boom! Shake The Room...Jazzy Jeff & Fresh Prince
3/95	Boombastic...Shaggy
	Boomerang ..see: Do The
34/94	Booti Call...Blackstreet
36/71	Booty Butt...Ray Charles
23/94	Bop Gun (One Nation)...Ice Cube Feat. George Clinton
20/84	Bop 'Til You Drop...Rick Springfield
33/83	Border, The...America
37/70	Border Song...Aretha Franklin
10/84	Borderline...Madonna
38/85	Borderlines...Jeffrey Osborne
12/66	Born A Woman...Sandy Posey
	Born Free
7/66	Roger Williams
38/68	Hesitations
9/85	Born In The U.S.A....Bruce Springsteen (also see: Banned In The U.S.A.)
16/79	Born To Be Alive...Patrick Hernandez
3/89	Born To Be My Baby...Bon Jovi
2/68	Born To Be Wild...Steppenwolf
5/56	Born To Be With You...Chordettes
23/94	Born To Roll...Masta Ace Incorporated
23/75	Born To Run...Bruce Springsteen
17/71	Born To Wander...Rare Earth
7/58	Born Too Late...Poni-Tails
19/79	Boss, The...Diana Ross
28/63	Boss Guitar...Duane Eddy
	Bossa Nova ..also see: Fly Me To The Moon
8/63	Bossa Nova Baby...Elvis Presley
8/68	Both Sides Now...Judy Collins
25/93	Both Sides Of The Story...Phil Collins
9/68	Bottle Of Wine...Fireballs
19/80	Boulevard...Jackson Browne
40/63	Bounce, The...Olympics
40/67	Bowling Green...Everly Brothers
7/69	Boxer, The...Simon & Garfunkel
	Boy From New York City
8/65	Ad Libs
7/81	Manhattan Transfer
	Boy I'm Gonna Marry ..see: (Today I Met)
26/85	Boy In The Box...Corey Hart
2/69	Boy Named Sue...Johnny Cash

POS/YR	RECORD TITLE/ARTIST
18/63	Boy Next Door...Secrets
10/59	Boy Without A Girl...Frankie Avalon
12/76	Boys Are Back In Town...Thin Lizzy
37/84	Boys Do Fall In Love...Robin Gibb
25/87	Boys Night Out...Timothy B. Schmit
5/85	Boys Of Summer...Don Henley
1/71	Brand New Key...Melanie
15/87	Brand New Lover...Dead Or Alive
	Brand New Me
24/69	Dusty Springfield
F/71	Aretha Franklin
1/72	Brandy (You're A Fine Girl)...Looking Glass
35/61	Brass Buttons...String-A-Longs
14/80	Brass In Pocket (I'm Special)...Pretenders
11/75	Brazil...Ritchie Family
2/64	Bread And Butter...Newbeats
39/76	Break Away...Art Garfunkel
40/65	Break Away (From That Boy)...Newbeats
25/93	Break It Down Again...Tears For Fears
	Break It To Me Gently
4/62	Brenda Lee
11/82	Juice Newton
26/82	Break It Up...Foreigner
5/84	Break My Stride...Matthew Wilder
6/87	Breakout...Swing Out Sister
5/73	Break Up To Make Up...Stylistics
35/68	Break Your Promise...Delfonics
8/84	Breakdance...Irene Cara
31/71	Breakdown, The...Rufus Thomas
40/78	Breakdown...Tom Petty
15/80	Breakdown Dead Ahead...Boz Scaggs
5/96	Breakfast At Tiffany's...Deep Blue Something
7/61	Breakin' In A Brand New Broken Heart...Connie Francis
6/92	Breakin' My Heart (Pretty Brown Eyes)...Mint Condition
9/84	Breakin'...There's No Stopping Us...Ollie & Jerry
	Breakin' Up ..see: (Best Part Of)
31/66	Breakin' Up Is Breakin' My Heart...Roy Orbison
22/81	Breaking Away...Balance
	Breaking Up Is Hard To Do
1/62	Neil Sedaka
34/70	Lenny Welch
28/72	Partridge Family
8/76	Neil Sedaka
18/83	Breaking Us In Two...Joe Jackson

POS/YR	RECORD TITLE/ARTIST
15/81	**Breakup Song (They Don't Write 'Em)**...Greg Kihn Band
3/94	**Breathe Again**...Toni Braxton
7/58	**Breathless**...Jerry Lee Lewis
8/55	**Breeze And I (Andalucia)**...Caterina Valente
5/77	**Brick House**...Commodores
	Bridge Over Troubled Water
1/70	Simon & Garfunkel
6/71	Aretha Franklin
5/87	**Brilliant Disguise**...Bruce Springsteen
	Bring It On Home To Me
13/62	Sam Cooke
32/65	Animals
17/68	Eddie Floyd
29/67	**Bring It Up**...James Brown
12/71	**Bring The Boys Home**...Freda Payne
2/61	**Bristol Stomp**...Dovells
27/62	**Bristol Twistin' Annie**...Dovells
20/92	**Broken Arrow**...Rod Stewart
12/79	**Broken Hearted Me**...Anne Murray
7/59	**Broken-Hearted Melody**...Sarah Vaughan
1/85	**Broken Wings**...Mr. Mister
9/95	**Brokenhearted**...Brandy
1/73	**Brother Louie**...Stories
22/69	**Brother Love's Travelling Salvation Show**...Neil Diamond
32/70	**Brother Rapp**...James Brown
10/67	**Brown Eyed Girl**...Van Morrison
1/71	**Brown Sugar**...Rolling Stones
27/95	**Brown Sugar**...D'Angelo
27/85	**Bruce**...Rick Springfield
3/89	**Buffalo Stance**...Neneh Cherry
3/69	**Build Me Up Buttercup**...Foundations
24/60	**Bulldog**...Fireballs
22/96	**Bullet With Butterfly Wings**...Smashing Pumpkins
21/65	**Bumble Bee**...Searchers
21/61	**Bumble Boogie**...B. Bumble & The Stingers
1/94	**Bump N' Grind**...R. Kelly
12/75	**Bungle In The Jungle**...Jethro Tull
9/55	**Burn That Candle**...Bill Haley
40/81	**Burnin' For You**...Blue Öyster Cult
3/60	**Burning Bridges**...Jack Scott
34/71	**Burning Bridges**...Mike Curb Congregation
9/83	**Burning Down The House**...Talking Heads
2/86	**Burning Heart**...Survivor
39/83	**Burning Heart**...Vandenberg
2/72	**Burning Love**...Elvis Presley
5/66	**Bus Stop**...Hollies

POS/YR	RECORD TITLE/ARTIST
17/56	**Bus Stop Song (A Paper Of Pins)**...Four Lads
7/89	**Bust A Move**...Young MC
25/63	**Bust Out**...Busters
4/63	**Busted**...Ray Charles
34/79	**Bustin' Loose**...Chuck Brown
4/61	**But I Do**...Clarence Henry
22/66	**But It's Alright**...J.J. Jackson
19/69	**But You Know I Love You**...First Edition
15/65	**But You're Mine**...Sonny & Cher
29/75	**Butter Boy**...Fanny
	Butterfly
1/57	Charlie Gracie
1/57	Andy Williams
23/63	**Butterfly Baby**...Bobby Rydell
11/58	**Buzz-Buzz-Buzz**...Hollywood Flames
	By The Time I Get To Phoenix
26/67	Glen Campbell
37/69	Isaac Hayes
25/93	**By The Time This Night Is Over**...Kenny G (with Peabo Bryson)
12/65	**Bye, Bye, Baby (Baby Goodbye)**...4 Seasons
2/57	**Bye Bye Love**...Everly Brothers

C

POS/YR	RECORD TITLE/ARTIST
	C.C. Rider
12/57	Chuck Willis
34/63	LaVern Baker
10/66	Animals
	(also see: Jenny Take A Ride!)
2/87	**C'est La Vie**...Robbie Nevil
11/55	**C'est La Vie**...Sarah Vaughan
22/61	**C'est Si Bon (It's So Good)**...Conway Twitty
	C'mon ..see: Come On
22/57	**Ca, C'est L'amour**...Tony Bennett
23/68	**Cab Driver**...Mills Brothers
22/62	**Cajun Queen**...Jimmy Dean
1/61	**Calcutta**...Lawrence Welk
4/61	**Calendar Girl**...Neil Sedaka
4/66	**California Dreamin'**...Mama's & The Papa's
	California Girls
3/65	Beach Boys
3/85	David Lee Roth
16/67	**California Nights**...Lesley Gore
25/69	**California Soul**...5th Dimension
5/64	**California Sun**...Rivieras
18/89	**Call It Love**...Poco

POS/YR	RECORD TITLE/ARTIST
1/80	**Call Me**...Blondie
13/70	**Call Me**...Aretha Franklin
21/58	**Call Me**...Johnny Mathis
22/66	**Call Me**...Chris Montez
26/82	**Call Me**...Skyy
10/73	**Call Me (Come Back Home)**...Al Green
40/68	**Call Me Lightning**...Who
19/62	**Call Me Mr. In-Between**...Burl Ives
6/74	**Call On Me**...Chicago
22/63	**Call On Me**...Bobby Bland
15/85	**Call To The Heart**...Giuffria
18/86	**Calling America**...Electric Light Orchestra
16/77	**Calling Dr. Love**...Kiss
32/77	**Calling Occupants Of Interplanetary Craft**...Carpenters
2/75	**Calypso**...John Denver
5/69	**Can I Change My Mind**...Tyrone Davis
	Can I Get A Witness
22/63	Marvin Gaye
39/71	Lee Michaels
15/57	**Can I Steal A Little Love**...Frank Sinatra
27/95	**Can I Touch You...There?**...Michael Bolton
31/74	**Can This Be Real**...Natural Four
	(Can We Rock?) ..see: What's Up Doc?
29/78	**Can We Still Be Friends**...Todd Rundgren
9/94	**Can We Talk**...Tevin Campbell
4/94	**Can You Feel The Love Tonight**...Elton John
16/56	**Can You Find It In Your Heart**...Tony Bennett
38/78	**Can You Fool**...Glen Campbell
1/64	**Can't Buy Me Love**...Beatles
36/95	**Can't Cry Anymore**...Sheryl Crow
1/85	**Can't Fight This Feeling**...REO Speedwagon
5/74	**Can't Get Enough**...Bad Company
	Can't Get Enough Of Your Love, Babe
1/74	Barry White
20/93	Taylor Dayne
9/75	**Can't Get It Out Of My Head**...Electric Light Orchestra
2/63	**Can't Get Used To Losing You**...Andy Williams
	Can't Help Falling In Love
2/62	Elvis Presley
24/87	Corey Hart
1/93	UB40
39/76	**Can't Hide Love**...Earth, Wind & Fire
2/92	**Can't Let Go**...Mariah Carey
1/90	**(Can't Live Without Your) Love And Affection**...Nelson

POS/YR	RECORD TITLE/ARTIST
29/83	**Can't Shake Loose**...Agnetha Faltskog
3/78	**Can't Smile Without You**...Barry Manilow
6/88	**Can't Stay Away From You**...Gloria Estefan & Miami Sound Machine
6/90	**Can't Stop**...After 7
13/77	**Can't Stop Dancin'**...Captain & Tennille
12/90	**Can't Stop Fallin' Into Love**...Cheap Trick
30/95	**Can't Stop Lovin' You**...Van Halen
25/70	**Can't Stop Loving You**...Tom Jones
2/91	**Can't Stop This Thing We Started**...Bryan Adams
	Can't Take My Eyes Off You
2/67	Frankie Valli
7/68	Lettermen (medley)
6/87	**Can't We Try**...Dan Hill/Vonda Sheppard
2/65	**Can't You Hear My Heartbeat**...Herman's Hermits
13/95	**Can't You See**...Total featuring The Notorious B.I.G.
4/64	**Can't You See That She's Mine**...Dave Clark Five
20/87	**Can'tcha Say (You Believe In Me)/Still In Love**...Boston
	Canadian Sunset
2/56	Hugo Winterhalter/Eddie Heywood
7/56	Andy Williams
3/70	**Candida**...Dawn
6/88	**Candle In The Wind**...Elton John
	(Candles In The Rain) ..see: Lay Down
21/87	**Candy**...Cameo
28/91	**Candy**...Iggy Pop
3/63	**Candy Girl**...Four Seasons
1/72	**Candy Man**...Sammy Davis, Jr.
25/61	**Candy Man**...Roy Orbison
2/95	**Candy Rain**...Soul For Real
15/58	**Cannonball**...Duane Eddy
28/85	**Cannonball**...Supertramp
9/94	**Cantaloop**...US3
16/86	**Captain Of Her Heart**...Double
1/77	**Car Wash**...Rose Royce
39/65	**Cara-Lin**...Strangeloves
4/65	**Cara Mia**...Jay & The Americans
10/74	**Carefree Highway**...Gordon Lightfoot
1/85	**Careless Whisper**...Wham!/George Michael
27/59	**Caribbean**...Mitchell Torok
1/84	**Caribbean Queen (No More Love On The Run)**...Billy Ocean
10/95	**Carnival**...Natalie Merchant
18/58	**Carol**...Chuck Berry

POS/YR	RECORD TITLE/ARTIST
21/75	**Carolina In The Pines**...Michael Murphey
32/66	**Caroline, No**...Brian Wilson
29/68	**Carpet Man**...5th Dimension
3/87	**Carrie**...Europe
34/80	**Carrie**...Cliff Richard
9/67	**Carrie-Anne**...Hollies
26/69	**Carry Me Back**...Rascals
11/77	**Carry On Wayward Son**...Kansas
9/80	**Cars**...Gary Numan
5/87	**Casanova**...Levert
27/67	**Casino Royale**...Herb Alpert
	Cast Your Fate To The Wind
22/63	Vince Guaraldi Trio
10/65	Sounds Orchestral
	Castles In The Air
F/72	Don McLean
36/81	Don McLean
25/56	**Casual Look**...Six Teens
26/67	**Cat In The Window (The Bird In The Sky)**...Petula Clark
30/77	**Cat Scratch Fever**...Ted Nugent
	Cat's In The Cradle
1/74	Harry Chapin
6/93	Ugly Kid Joe
1/58	**Catch A Falling Star**...Perry Como
8/87	**Catch Me (I'm Falling)**...Pretty Poison
40/84	**Catch Me I'm Falling**...Real Life
23/65	**Catch The Wind**...Donovan
4/65	**Catch Us If You Can**...Dave Clark Five
23/62	**Caterina**...Perry Como
1/60	**Cathy's Clown**...Everly Brothers
	Cats In The Cradle ..see: Cat's
37/87	**Caught Up In The Rapture**...Anita Baker
10/82	**Caught Up In You**...38 Special
2/87	**Causing A Commotion**...Madonna
	(Cave Man) ..see: Troglodyte
4/70	**Cecilia**...Simon & Garfunkel
15/70	**Celebrate**...Three Dog Night
26/85	**Celebrate Youth**...Rick Springfield
1/81	**Celebration**...Kool & The Gang
39/95	**Cell Therapy**...Goodie Mob
1/82	**Centerfold**...J. Geils Band
24/84	**Centipede**...Rebbie Jackson
14/58	**Certain Smile**...Johnny Mathis
23/58	**Cerveza**...Boots Brown
10/62	**Cha-Cha-Cha**...Bobby Rydell
34/58	**Cha-Hua-Hua**...Pets
2/60	**Chain Gang**...Sam Cooke
13/56	**Chain Gang**...Bobby Scott

POS/YR	RECORD TITLE/ARTIST
2/68	**Chain Of Fools**...Aretha Franklin
32/68	**Chained**...Marvin Gaye
17/62	**Chains**...Cookies
10/56	**Chains Of Love**...Pat Boone
12/88	**Chains Of Love**...Erasure
1/57	**Chances Are**...Johnny Mathis
27/92	**Change**...Lisa Stansfield
31/65	**Change Is Gonna Come**...Sam Cooke
3/87	**Change Of Heart**...Cyndi Lauper
19/78	**Change Of Heart**...Eric Carmen
21/83	**Change Of Heart**...Tom Petty
37/77	**Changes In Latitudes, Changes In Attitudes**...Jimmy Buffett
	Chanson d'Amour (Song Of Love)
6/58	Art & Dotty Todd
12/58	Fontane Sisters
19/57	**Chantez-Chantez**...Dinah Shore
6/58	**Chantilly Lace**...Big Bopper
	Chapel In The Moonlight
32/65	Bachelors
25/67	Dean Martin
1/64	**Chapel Of Love**...Dixie Cups
	Charade
36/64	Sammy Kaye
36/64	Henry Mancini
1/82	**Chariots Of Fire - Titles**...Vangelis
40/71	**Charity Ball**...Fanny
2/59	**Charlie Brown**...Coasters
13/63	**Charms**...Bobby Vee
33/79	**Chase**...Giorgio Moroder
39/91	**Chasin' The Wind**...Chicago
	Chattanooga Choo Choo
36/62	Floyd Cramer
32/78	Tuxedo Junction
34/60	**Chattanooga Shoe Shine Boy**...Freddy Cannon
15/73	**Cheaper To Keep Her**...Johnnie Taylor
12/66	**Cheater, The**...Bob Kuban
14/88	**Check It Out**...John Cougar Mellencamp
35/73	**Check It Out**...Tavares
28/70	**Check Out Your Mind**...Impressions
20/93	**Check Yo Self**...Ice Cube Feat. DAS EFX
12/55	**Chee Chee-oo Chee (Sang the Little Bird)**...Perry Como & Jaye P. Morgan
32/78	**Cheeseburger In Paradise**...Jimmy Buffett
	Cherchez La Femme ..see: Whispering
	Cherish
1/66	Association
9/71	David Cassidy

POS/YR	RECORD TITLE/ARTIST
2/85	**Cherish**...Kool & The Gang
2/89	**Cherish**...Madonna
33/77	**Cherry Baby**...Starz
8/88	**Cherry Bomb**...John Cougar Mellencamp
	Cherry, Cherry
6/66	Neil Diamond
31/73	Neil Diamond (Live)
15/69	**Cherry Hill Park**...Billy Joe Royal
10/90	**Cherry Pie**...Warrant
11/60	**Cherry Pie**...Skip & Flip
	Cherry Pink And Apple Blossom White
1/55	Perez "Prez" Prado
14/55	Alan Dale
5/75	**Chevy Van**...Sammy Johns
15/68	**Chewy Chewy**...Ohio Express
35/71	**Chicago**...Graham Nash
9/71	**Chick-A-Boom (Don't Ya Jes' Love It)**...Daddy Dewdrop
31/67	**Child Of Clay**...Jimmie Rodgers
F/95	**Childhood**...Michael Jackson
13/90	**Children Of The Night**...Richard Marx
	Children's Marching Song
13/59	Cyril Stapleton
16/59	Mitch Miller
38/60	**China Doll**...Ames Brothers
10/83	**China Girl**...David Bowie
15/73	**China Grove**...Doobie Brothers
10/62	**Chip Chip**...Gene McDaniels
	Chipmunk Song
1/58	Chipmunks
39/61	Chipmunks
40/62	Chipmunks
29/80	**Chiquitita**...Abba
20/71	**Chirpy Chirpy Cheep Cheep**...Mac & Katie Kissoon
34/81	**Chloe**...Elton John
21/69	**Choice Of Colors**...Impressions
13/69	**Chokin' Kind**...Joe Simon
26/68	**Choo Choo Train**...Box Tops
23/94	**Choose**...Color Me Badd
F/55	**Chop Chop Boom**...Crew-Cuts
25/77	**Christine Sixteen**...Kiss
4/79	**Chuck E.'s In Love**...Rickie Lee Jones
9/64	**Chug-A-Lug**...Roger Miller
14/56	**Church Bells May Ring**...Diamonds
10/83	**Church Of The Poison Mind**...Culture Club
36/92	**Church Of Your Heart**...Roxette
24/59	**Ciao, Ciao Bambina**...Jacky Noguez

POS/YR	RECORD TITLE/ARTIST
	Cinco Robles (Five Oaks)
22/57	Russell Arms
35/57	Les Paul & Mary Ford
16/62	**Cinderella**...Jack Ross
34/77	**Cinderella**...Firefall
	Cindy, Oh Cindy
9/56	Vince Martin/The Tarriers
10/56	Eddie Fisher
8/62	**Cindy's Birthday**...Johnny Crawford
11/69	**Cinnamon**...Derek
25/63	**Cinnamon Cinder (It's A Very Nice Dance)**...Pastel Six
7/88	**Circle In The Sand**...Belinda Carlisle
33/78	**Circle Is Small (I Can See It In Your Eyes)**...Gordon Lightfoot
18/94	**Circle Of Life**...Elton John
38/82	**Circles**...Atlantic Starr
2/73	**Cisco Kid**...War
23/69	**Cissy Strut**...Meters
18/85	**C-I-T-Y**...John Cafferty
19/56	**City Of Angels**...Highlights
18/72	**City Of New Orleans**...Arlo Guthrie
2/72	**Clair**...Gilbert O'Sullivan
	Clam ..see: Do The
6/74	**Clap For The Wolfman**...Guess Who
	Clapping Song (Clap Pat Clap Slap)
8/65	Shirley Ellis
36/83	Pia Zadora
38/59	**Class, The**...Chubby Checker
2/68	**Classical Gas**...Mason Williams
30/58	**Claudette**...Everly Brothers
6/72	**Clean Up Woman**...Betty Wright
35/69	**Clean Up Your Own Back Yard**...Elvis Presley
21/60	**Clementine**...Bobby Darin
	Cleopatra Jones ..see: Theme From
28/58	**Click-Clack**...Dickey Doo & The Don'ts
17/64	**Clinging Vine**...Bobby Vinton
40/80	**Clones (We're All)**...Alice Cooper
	Close Encounters ..see: Theme From
8/89	**Close My Eyes Forever**...Lita Ford/Ozzy Osbourne
25/78	**Close The Door**...Teddy Pendergrass
12/62	**Close To Cathy**...Mike Clifford
1/90	**Close To You**...Maxi Priest **(also see: They Long To Be)**
8/67	**Close Your Eyes**...Peaches & Herb
37/73	**Close Your Eyes**...Edward Bear

POS/YR	RECORD TITLE/ARTIST
2/78	**Closer I Get To You**...Roberta Flack with Donny Hathaway
22/70	**Closer To Home**...Grand Funk Railroad
38/83	**Closer You Get**...Alabama
	Cloud Nine
6/69	Temptations
32/69	Mongo Santamaria
28/90	**Club At The End Of The Street**...Elton John
F/80	**Cocaine**...Eric Clapton
25/57	**Cocoanut Woman**...Harry Belafonte
8/72	**Coconut**...Nilsson
6/77	**Cold As Ice**...Foreigner
40/83	**Cold Blooded**...Rick James
1/89	**Cold Hearted**...Paula Abdul
33/81	**Cold Love**...Donna Summer
7/67	**Cold Sweat**...James Brown
30/70	**Cold Turkey**...Plastic Ono Band
	Colonel Bogey ..see: March From The River Kwai
7/69	**Color Him Father**...Winstons
16/67	**Color My World**...Petula Clark
4/95	**Colors Of The Wind**...Vanessa Williams
F/71	**Colour My World**...Chicago
17/88	**Colour Of Love**...Billy Ocean
3/64	**Come A Little Bit Closer**...Jay & The Americans
7/70	**Come And Get It**...Badfinger
29/63	**Come And Get These Memories**...Martha & The Vandellas
	Come And Get Your Love
5/74	Redbone
19/95	Real McCoy
26/65	**Come And Stay With Me**...Marianne Faithfull
11/92	**Come & Talk To Me**...Jodeci
15/87	**Come As You Are**...Peter Wolf
32/92	**Come As You Are**...Nirvana
18/93	**Come Baby Come**...K7
32/80	**Come Back**...J. Geils Band
22/84	**Come Back And Stay**...Paul Young
17/62	**Come Back Silly Girl**...Lettermen
2/90	**Come Back To Me**...Janet Jackson
3/67	**Come Back When You Grow Up**...Bobby Vee
38/58	**Come Closer To Me (Acercate Mas)**...Nat "King" Cole
6/83	**Come Dancing**...Kinks
21/73	**Come Get To This**...Marvin Gaye

POS/YR	RECORD TITLE/ARTIST
	Come Go With Me
4/57	Dell-Vikings
18/82	Beach Boys
5/87	**Come Go With Me**...Expose
14/65	**Come Home**...Dave Clark Five
33/93	**Come Inside**...Intro
20/59	**Come Into My Heart**...Lloyd Price
30/74	**Come Monday**...Jimmy Buffett
36/64	**Come On**...Tommy Roe
29/59	**Come On And Get Me**...Fabian
10/90	**C'mon And Get My Love**...D Mob/Cathy Dennis
5/64	**C'mon And Swim**...Bobby Freeman
6/67	**Come On Down To My Boat**...Every Mothers' Son
1/83	**Come On Eileen**...Dexys Midnight Runners
35/59	**C'mon Everybody**...Eddie Cochran
	Come On Let's Go
22/66	McCoys
21/87	Los Lobos
28/62	**Come On Little Angel**...Belmonts
	C'mon Marianne
9/67	4 Seasons
38/76	Donny Osmond
23/76	**Come On Over**...Olivia Newton-John
17/66	**(Come 'Round Here) I'm The One You Need**...Miracles
39/70	**Come Running**...Van Morrison
35/66	**Come Running Back**...Dean Martin
8/78	**Come Sail Away**...Styx
17/70	**Come Saturday Morning**...Sandpipers
40/65	**Come See**...Major Lance
	Come See About Me
1/64	Supremes
24/68	Jr. Walker & The All Stars
1/59	**Come Softly To Me**...Fleetwoods
15/79	**Come To Me**...France Joli
22/58	**Come To Me**...Johnny Mathis
30/59	**Come To Me**...Marv Johnson
25/94	**Come To My Window**...Melissa Etheridge
37/67	**Come To The Sunshine**...Harpers Bizarre
	Come Together
1/69	Beatles
23/78	Aerosmith
7/93	**Come Undone**...Duran Duran
30/95	**Comedown**...Bush
10/93	**Comforter**...Shai
36/62	**Comin' Home Baby**...Mel Torme
11/82	**Comin' In And Out Of Your Life**...Barbra Streisand

POS/YR	RECORD TITLE/ARTIST
18/87	**Coming Around Again**...Carly Simon
20/89	**Coming Home**...Cinderella
11/67	**Coming Home Soldier**...Bobby Vinton
11/66	**Coming On Strong**...Brenda Lee
1/91	**Coming Out Of The Dark**...Gloria Estefan
1/80	**Coming Up**...Paul McCartney
30/69	**Commotion**...Creedence Clearwater Revival
34/85	**Communication**...Power Station
32/94	**Completely**...Michael Bolton
27/69	**Composer, The**...Supremes
	Concrete And Clay
28/65	Unit Four plus Two
35/65	Eddie Rambeau
17/56	**Confidential**...Sonny Knight
37/79	**Confusion**...Electric Light Orchestra
10/86	**Conga**...Miami Sound Machine
20/93	**Connected**...Stereo MC's
16/72	**Conquistador**...Procol Harum
11/62	**Conscience**...James Darren
38/92	**Constant Craving**...k.d. lang
16/95	**Constantly**...Immature
33/61	**Continental Walk**...Hank Ballard (also see: Do The New)
5/87	**Control**...Janet Jackson
8/72	**Convention '72**...Delegates
1/76	**Convoy**...C.W. McCall
32/73	**Cook With Honey**...Judy Collins
29/71	**Cool Aid**...Paul Humphrey
10/80	**Cool Change**...Little River Band
4/85	**Cool It Now**...New Edition
7/66	**Cool Jerk**...Capitols
13/81	**Cool Love**...Pablo Cruise
11/82	**Cool Night**...Paul Davis
12/57	**Cool Shake**...Del Vikings
8/78	**Copacabana (At The Copa)**...Barry Manilow
37/73	**Corazon**...Carole King
9/61	**Corinna, Corinna**...Ray Peterson
18/72	**Corner Of The Sky**...Jackson 5
15/64	**Cotton Candy**...Al Hirt
25/95	**Cotton Eye Joe**...Rednex
13/62	**Cotton Fields**...Highwaymen
33/80	**Could I Have This Dance**...Anne Murray
37/72	**Could It Be Forever**...David Cassidy
4/73	**Could It Be I'm Falling In Love**...Spinners
6/75	**Could It Be Magic**...Barry Manilow
11/90	**Could This Be Love**...Seduction
23/57	**Could This Be Magic**...Dubs
1/88	**Could've Been**...Tiffany

POS/YR	RECORD TITLE/ARTIST
3/77	**Couldn't Get It Right**...Climax Blues Band
35/61	**Count Every Star**...Donnie & The Dreamers
2/65	**Count Me In**...Gary Lewis & The Playboys
8/78	**Count On Me**...Jefferson Starship
25/60	**Country Boy**...Fats Domino
11/76	**Country Boy (You Got Your Feet In L.A.)**...Glen Campbell
36/68	**Country Girl - City Man**...Billy Vera & Judy Clay
37/71	**Country Road**...James Taylor
11/91	**Couple Days Off**...Huey Lewis & The News
25/68	**Court Of Love**...Unifics
31/64	**Cousin Of Mine**...Sam Cooke
2/89	**Cover Girl**...New Kids On The Block
7/84	**Cover Me**...Bruce Springsteen
31/89	**Cover Of Love**...Michael Damian
6/73	**Cover Of "Rolling Stone"**...Dr. Hook
3/80	**Coward Of The County**...Kenny Rogers
6/68	**Cowboys To Girls**...Intruders
8/72	**Cowboys Work Is Never Done**...Sonny & Cher
19/77	**Crackerbox Palace**...George Harrison
1/70	**Cracklin' Rosie**...Neil Diamond
2/90	**Cradle Of Love**...Billy Idol
7/60	**Cradle Of Love**...Johnny Preston
7/91	**Crazy**...Seal
9/61	**Crazy**...Patsy Cline
14/88	**Crazy**...Icehouse
17/94	**Crazy**...Aerosmith
29/90	**Crazy**...Boys
F/58	**Crazy**...Hollywood Flames
11/89	**Crazy About Her**...Rod Stewart
36/60	**Crazy Arms**...Bob Beckham
	Crazy Downtown ..see: Downtown
40/58	**Crazy Eyes For You**...Bobby Hamilton
1/85	**Crazy For You**...Madonna
14/72	**Crazy Horses**...Osmonds
15/85	**Crazy In The Night (Barking At Airplanes)**...Kim Carnes
	Crazy Little Mama ..see: At My Front Door
1/80	**Crazy Little Thing Called Love**...Queen
15/58	**Crazy Love**...Paul Anka
17/79	**Crazy Love**...Poco
29/79	**Crazy Love**...Allman Brothers Band
22/72	**Crazy Mama**...J.J. Cale
35/76	**Crazy On You**...Heart
2/55	**Crazy Otto (medley)**...Johnny Maddox
1/91	**Cream**...Prince & The N.P.G.

POS/YR	RECORD TITLE/ARTIST
1/95	**Creep**...TLC
34/93	**Creep**...Radiohead
5/67	**Creeque Alley**...Mamas & The Papas
16/71	**Cried Like A Baby**...Bobby Sherman
	Crimson And Clover
1/69	Tommy James & The Shondells
7/82	Joan Jett
16/55	**Croce Di Oro (Cross Of Gold)**...Patti Page
1/73	**Crocodile Rock**...Elton John
	(Crooked Little Man) ..see: Don't Let The Rain Come Down
19/63	**Cross Fire!**...Orlons
23/59	**Crossfire**...Johnny & The Hurricanes
7/87	**Cross My Broken Heart**...Jets
	Cross Of Gold ..see: Croce Di Oro
28/69	**Crossroads**...Cream
26/62	**Crowd, The**...Roy Orbison
9/84	**Cruel Summer**...Bananarama
12/79	**Cruel To Be Kind**...Nick Lowe
4/80	**Cruisin'**...Smokey Robinson
29/90	**Cruising For Bruising**...Basia
9/83	**Crumblin' Down**...John Cougar Mellencamp
F/71	**Crunchy Granola Suite**...Neil Diamond
3/86	**Crush On You**...Jets
10/89	**Cry**...Waterfront
16/85	**Cry**...Godley & Creme
18/66	**Cry**...Ronnie Dove
4/63	**Cry Baby**...Garnet Mimms & The Enchanters
18/56	**Cry Baby**...Bonnie Sisters
38/62	**Cry Baby Cry**...Angels
7/91	**Cry For Help**...Rick Astley
15/94	**Cry For You**...Jodeci
2/68	**Cry Like A Baby**...Box Tops
	Cry Me A River
9/55	Julie London
11/70	Joe Cocker
23/63	**Cry To Me**...Betty Harris
12/93	**Cryin'**...Aerosmith
22/89	**Cryin'**...Vixen
	Crying
2/61	Roy Orbison
25/66	Jay & The Americans
5/81	Don McLean
15/93	**Crying Game**...Boy George
3/65	**Crying In The Chapel**...Elvis Presley
6/62	**Crying In The Rain**...Everly Brothers
6/66	**Crying Time**...Ray Charles

POS/YR	RECORD TITLE/ARTIST
2/69	**Crystal Blue Persuasion**...Tommy James & The Shondells
25/89	**Cuddly Toy (Feel For Me)**...Roachford
13/89	**Cult Of Personality**...Living Colour
5/83	**Cum On Feel The Noize**...Quiet Riot
	Cupid
17/61	Sam Cooke
39/70	Johnny Nash
22/76	Dawn
4/80	Spinners (medley)
	Curious Mind ..see: Um, Um, Um, Um, Um, Um
15/84	**Curly Shuffle**...Jump 'N The Saddle
10/75	**Cut The Cake**...AWB
15/83	**Cuts Like A Knife**...Bryan Adams
23/68	**Cycles**...Frank Sinatra

D

POS/YR	RECORD TITLE/ARTIST
36/71	**D.O.A.**...Bloodrock
19/68	**D. W. Washburn**...Monkees
20/73	**D'yer Mak'er**...Led Zeppelin
35/88	**Da'Butt**...E.U.
	Da Doo Ron Ron
3/63	Crystals
1/77	Shaun Cassidy
1/79	**Da Ya Think I'm Sexy?**...Rod Stewart
F/57	**Daddy Cool**...Rays
19/73	**Daddy Could Swear, I Declare**...Gladys Knight & The Pips
4/72	**Daddy Don't You Walk So Fast**...Wayne Newton
	Daddy-O
11/55	Fontane Sisters
14/55	Bonnie Lou
	Daddy's Home
2/61	Shep & The Limelites
9/73	Jermaine Jackson
23/82	Cliff Richard
34/69	**Daddy's Little Man**...O.C. Smith
14/73	**Daisy A Day**...Jud Strunk
20/75	**Daisy Jane**...America
15/64	**Daisy Petal Pickin'**...Jimmy Gilmer/Fireballs
5/92	**Damn I Wish I Was Your Lover**...Sophie B. Hawkins
27/79	**Damned If I Do**...Alan Parsons Project
38/78	**Dance Across The Floor**...Jimmy "Bo" Horne

POS/YR	RECORD TITLE/ARTIST
8/64	**Dance, Dance, Dance**...Beach Boys
6/78	**Dance, Dance, Dance (Yowsah, Yowsah, Yowsah)**...Chic **(also see: How To Dance)**
19/78	**Dance (Disco Heat)**...Sylvester
31/58	**Dance Everyone Dance**...Betty Madigan
16/84	**Dance Hall Days**...Wang Chung
30/88	**Dance Little Sister**...Terence Trent D'Arby
10/61	**Dance On Little Girl**...Paul Anka
19/58	**Dance Only With Me**...Perry Como
24/61	**(Dance The) Mess Around**...Chubby Checker
15/79	**Dance The Night Away**...Van Halen
23/58	**Dance To The Bop**...Gene Vincent
8/68	**Dance To The Music**...Sly & The Family Stone
39/76	**Dance Wit Me**...Rufus Feat. Chaka Khan
6/75	**Dance With Me**...Orleans
8/78	**Dance With Me**...Peter Brown/Betty Wright
15/59	**Dance With Me**...Drifters
1/55	**Dance With Me Henry (Wallflower)**...Georgia Gibbs
12/62	**(Dance With The) Guitar Man**...Duane Eddy
28/75	**Dancin' Fool**...Guess Who
23/77	**Dancin' Man**...Q
12/62	**Dancin' Party**...Chubby Checker
18/79	**Dancin' Shoes**...Nigel Olsson
2/84	**Dancing In The Dark**...Bruce Springsteen
13/73	**Dancing In The Moonlight**...King Harvest
17/84	**Dancing In The Sheets**...Shalamar
	Dancing In The Street
2/64	Martha & The Vandellas
38/82	Van Halen
7/85	Mick Jagger/David Bowie
2/74	**Dancing Machine**...Jackson 5
2/86	**Dancing On The Ceiling**...Lionel Richie
1/77	**Dancing Queen**...Abba
14/67	**Dandelion**...Rolling Stones
5/66	**Dandy**...Herman's Hermits
7/64	**Dang Me**...Roger Miller
12/55	**Danger! Heartbreak Ahead**...Jaye P. Morgan
2/86	**Danger Zone**...Kenny Loggins
2/90	**Dangerous**...Roxette
25/66	**Dangling Conversation**...Simon & Garfunkel
	Dangling On A String ..see: (You've Got Me)
2/73	**Daniel**...Elton John

POS/YR	RECORD TITLE/ARTIST
13/63	**Danke Schoen**...Wayne Newton
10/59	**Danny Boy**...Conway Twitty
7/73	**Danny's Song**...Anne Murray
11/85	**Dare Me**...Pointer Sisters
32/90	**Dare To Fall In Love**...Brent Bourgeois
15/75	**Dark Horse**...George Harrison
1/74	**Dark Lady**...Cher
	Dark Moon
4/57	Gale Storm
6/57	Bonnie Guitar
19/68	**Darlin'**...Beach Boys
15/67	**Darling Be Home Soon**...Lovin' Spoonful
7/55	**Darling Je Vous Aime Beaucoup**...Nat "King" Cole
F/57	**Date With The Blues**...Billy Williams
13/70	**Daughter Of Darkness**...Tom Jones
	Davy Crockett ..see: Ballad Of
3/64	**Dawn (Go Away)**...Four Seasons
36/65	**Dawn Of Correction**...Spokesmen
4/72	**Day After Day**...Badfinger
13/72	**Day By Day**...Godspell
18/86	**Day By Day**...Hooters
5/72	**Day Dreaming**...Aretha Franklin
35/66	**Day For Decision**...Johnny Sea
23/72	**Day I Found Myself**...Honey Cone
21/87	**Day-In Day-Out**...David Bowie
21/69	**Day Is Done**...Peter, Paul & Mary
	Day-O ..see: Banana Boat
	Day The Rains Came
21/58	Jane Morgan
30/58	Raymond Lefevre
5/66	**Day Tripper**...Beatles
23/77	**Daybreak**...Barry Manilow
39/74	**Daybreak**...Nilsson
2/66	**Daydream**...Lovin' Spoonful
	Daydream Believer
1/67	Monkees
12/80	Anne Murray
17/79	**Days Gone Down (Still Got The Light In Your Eyes)**...Gerry Rafferty
34/69	**Days Of Sand And Shovels**...Bobby Vinton
	Days Of Wine And Roses
26/63	Andy Williams
33/63	Henry Mancini
28/77	**Daytime Friends**...Kenny Rogers
3/77	**Dazz**...Brick
12/93	**Dazzey Duks**...Duice
10/81	**De Do Do Do, De Da Da Da**...Police
19/78	**Deacon Blues**...Steely Dan

POS/YR	RECORD TITLE/ARTIST
29/67	**Dead End Street**...Lou Rawls
22/83	**Dead Giveaway**...Shalamar
8/64	**Dead Man's Curve**...Jan & Dean
16/73	**Dead Skunk**...Loudon Wainwright III
30/90	**Deadbeat Club**...B-52's
	Dear Heart
24/65	Andy Williams
30/65	Jack Jones
24/62	**Dear Ivan**...Jimmy Dean
9/62	**Dear Lady Twist**...Gary (U.S.) Bonds
13/62	**Dear Lonely Hearts**...Nat "King" Cole
9/95	**Dear Mama**...2 Pac
11/62	**Dear One**...Larry Finnegan
20/95	**December**...Collective Soul
	December, 1963 (Oh, What a Night)
1/76	Four Seasons
14/94	Four Seasons
7/59	**Deck Of Cards**...Wink Martindale
7/58	**Dede Dinah**...Frankie Avalon
31/93	**Dedicated**...R. Kelly & Public Announcement
36/66	**Dedicated Follower Of Fashion**...Kinks
	Dedicated To The One I Love
3/61	Shirelles
2/67	Mamas & The Papas
F/71	**Deep Blue**...George Harrison
22/80	**Deep Inside My Heart**...Randy Meisner
	Deep Purple
20/57	Billy Ward & His Dominoes
1/63	Nino Tempo & April Stevens
14/76	Donny & Marie Osmond
7/93	**Deeper And Deeper**...Madonna
24/70	**Deeper & Deeper**...Freda Payne
21/91	**Deeper Shade Of Soul**...Urban Dance Squad
11/79	**Deeper Than The Night**...Olivia Newton-John
28/90	**Deeper The Love**...Whitesnake
15/80	**Deja Vu**...Dionne Warwick
22/60	**Delaware**...Perry Como
40/58	**Delicious!**...Jim Backus & Friend
15/68	**Delilah**...Tom Jones
	Delilah Jones ..see: Man With The Golden Arm
8/83	**Delirious**...Prince
1/73	**Delta Dawn**...Helen Reddy
10/63	**Denise**...Randy & The Rainbows
25/79	**Dependin' On You**...Doobie Brothers
5/83	**Der Kommissar**...After The Fire
15/62	**Desafinado**...Stan Getz/Charlie Byrd

POS/YR	RECORD TITLE/ARTIST
10/84	**Desert Moon**...Dennis DeYoung
33/63	**Desert Pete**...Kingston Trio
8/71	**Desiderata**...Les Crane
3/88	**Desire**...U2
4/80	**Desire**...Andy Gibb
16/78	**Desiree**...Neil Diamond
	Detroit City
16/63	Bobby Bare
27/67	Tom Jones
	Devil In Disguise ..see: (You're the)
2/88	**Devil Inside**...INXS
6/60	**Devil Or Angel**...Bobby Vee
3/79	**Devil Went Down To Georgia**...Charlie Daniels Band
4/66	**Devil With A Blue Dress On (medley)**...Mitch Ryder
6/76	**Devil Woman**...Cliff Richard
16/62	**Devil Woman**...Marty Robbins
36/77	**Devil's Gun**...C.J. & Co.
	Devoted To You
10/58	Everly Brothers
36/78	Carly Simon & James Taylor
33/74	**Devotion**...Earth, Wind & Fire
13/89	**Dial My Heart**...Boys
24/72	**Dialogue**...Chicago
6/73	**Diamond Girl**...Seals & Crofts
5/87	**Diamonds**...Herb Alpert
3/92	**Diamonds And Pearls**...Prince & The N.P.G.
18/60	**Diamonds And Pearls**...Paradons
35/75	**Diamonds And Rust**...Joan Baez
1/57	**Diana**...Paul Anka
10/64	**Diane**...Bachelors
14/59	**Diary, The**...Neil Sedaka
15/72	**Diary**...Bread
F/75	**Dick And Jane**...Bobby Vinton
9/82	**Did It In A Minute**...Daryl Hall & John Oates
29/76	**Did You Boogie (With Your Baby)**...Flash Cadillac & The Continental Kids
2/66	**Did You Ever Have To Make Up Your Mind?**...Lovin' Spoonful
32/69	**Did You See Her Eyes**...Illusion
	Didn't I (Blow Your Mind This Time)
10/70	Delfonics
8/89	New Kids On The Block
1/87	**Didn't We Almost Have It All**...Whitney Houston
	Died In Your Arms ..see: (I Just)
7/86	**Different Corner**...George Michael

POS/YR	RECORD TITLE/ARTIST
13/68	**Different Drum**...Stone Poneys/Linda Ronstadt
18/79	**Different Worlds**...Maureen McGovern
5/95	**Diggin' On You**...TLC
14/86	**Digging Your Scene**...Blow Monkeys
21/86	**Digital Display**...Ready For The World
2/79	**Dim All The Lights**...Donna Summer
11/55	**Dim, Dim The Lights (I Want Some Atmosphere)**...Bill Haley
18/60	**Ding-A-Ling**...Bobby Rydell **(also see: My Ding-A-Ling)**
25/58	**Ding Dong**...McGuire Sisters
36/75	**Ding Dong; Ding Dong**...George Harrison
11/67	**Ding Dong! The Witch Is Dead**...Fifth Estate
6/58	**Dinner With Drac**...John Zacherle
25/90	**Dirty Cash (Money Talks)**...Adventures Of Stevie V
36/90	**Dirty Deeds**...Joan Jett
1/88	**Dirty Diana**...Michael Jackson
3/83	**Dirty Laundry**...Don Henley
11/66	**Dirty Water**...Standells
12/79	**Dirty White Boy**...Foreigner
36/67	**Dis-Advantages Of You**...Brass Ring
8/91	**Disappear**...INXS
1/76	**Disco Duck**...Rick Dees
11/78	**Disco Inferno**...Trammps
1/76	**Disco Lady**...Johnnie Taylor
24/77	**Disco Lucy (I Love Lucy Theme)**...Wilton Place Street Band
12/79	**Disco Nights (Rock-Freak)**...G.Q.
28/75	**Disco Queen**...Hot Chocolate
	(Disco 'Round) ..see: I Love The Nightlife
28/74	**Distant Lover**...Marvin Gaye
30/66	**Distant Shores**...Chad & Jeremy
10/93	**Ditty**...Paperboy
35/92	**Divine Thing**...Soup Dragons
	Dixie ..see: Theme From
30/55	**Dixie Danny**...Laurie Sisters
1/69	**Dizzy**...Tommy Roe
	Do ..also see: Doo
2/91	**Do Anything**...Natural Selection
13/82	**Do I Do**...Stevie Wonder
11/92	**Do I Have To Say The Words?**...Bryan Adams
34/64	**Do I Love You?**...Ronettes
36/70	**Do It**...Neil Diamond
6/73	**Do It Again**...Steely Dan

POS/YR	RECORD TITLE/ARTIST
20/68	**Do It Again**...Beach Boys
18/67	**Do It Again A Little Bit Slower**...Jon & Robin & The In Crowd
11/75	**Do It Any Way You Wanna**...Peoples Choice
13/74	**Do It Baby**...Miracles
29/85	**Do It For Love**...Sheena Easton
19/79	**Do It Or Die**...Atlanta Rhythm Section
2/74	**Do It ('Til You're Satisfied)**...B.T. Express
21/92	**Do It To Me**...Lionel Richie
3/90	**Do Me!**...Bell Biv DeVoe
27/62	**Do-Re-Mi**...Lee Dorsey
23/80	**Do Right**...Paul Davis
38/68	**Do Something To Me**...Tommy James & The Shondells
1/80	**Do That To Me One More Time**...Captain & Tennille
10/63	**Do The Bird**...Dee Dee Sharp
36/65	**Do The Boomerang**...Jr. Walker & The All Stars
21/65	**Do The Clam**...Elvis Presley
18/65	**Do The Freddie**...Freddie & The Dreamers **(also see: Letís Do The Freddie)**
28/70	**Do The Funky Chicken**...Rufus Thomas
37/62	**(Do The New) Continental**...Dovells
25/71	**(Do The) Push And Pull**...Rufus Thomas
13/84	**Do They Know It's Christmas?**...Band Aid
31/65	**Do-Wacka-Do**...Roger Miller
1/64	**Do Wah Diddy Diddy**...Manfred Mann
13/85	**Do What You Do**...Jermaine Jackson
37/70	**Do What You Wanna Do**...Five Flights Up
39/76	**Do What You Want, Be What You Are**...Daryl Hall & John Oates
24/77	**Do Ya**...Electric Light Orchestra
	Do Ya Think I'm Sexy? ..see: Da Ya
18/77	**Do Ya Wanna Get Funky With Me**...Peter Brown
7/82	**Do You Believe In Love**...Huey Lewis & the News
	Do You Believe In Magic
9/65	Lovin' Spoonful
31/78	Shaun Cassidy
13/92	**Do You Believe In Us**...Jon Secada
10/76	**Do You Feel Like We Do**...Peter Frampton
10/68	**Do You Know The Way To San Jose**...Dionne Warwick
6/71	**Do You Know What I Mean**...Lee Michaels
	Do You Know Where You're Going To ..see: Theme From Mahogany

POS/YR	RECORD TITLE/ARTIST
	Do You Love Me
3/62	Contours
11/64	Dave Clark Five
11/88	Contours
30/80	**Do You Love What You Feel**...Rufus & Chaka
2/83	**Do You Really Want To Hurt Me**...Culture Club
4/90	**Do You Remember?**...Phil Collins
32/70	**Do You See My Love (For You Growing)**...Jr. Walker & The All Stars
18/95	**Do You Sleep?**...Lisa Loeb & Nine Stories
40/94	**Do You Wanna Get Funky**...C+C Music Factory
5/77	**Do You Wanna Make Love**...Peter McCann
20/82	**Do You Wanna Touch Me (Oh Yeah)**...Joan Jett
37/85	**Do You Want Crying**...Katrina & The Waves
21/91	**Do You Want Me**...Salt-N-Pepa
	Do You Want To Dance
5/58	Bobby Freeman
12/65	Beach Boys
17/73	Bette Midler
2/64	**Do You Want To Know A Secret**...Beatles
39/77	**Do Your Dance**...Rose Royce
11/69	**Do Your Thing**...Watts 103rd Street Rhythm Band
30/72	**Do Your Thing**...Isaac Hayes
	Dock Of The Bay ..see: (Sittin' On)
9/89	**Doctor, The**...Doobie Brothers
11/84	**Doctor! Doctor!**...Thompson Twins (also see: Bad Case Of Loving You)
6/89	**Dr. Feelgood**...Mötley Crüe
28/83	**Dr. Heckyll & Mr. Jive**...Men At Work
	Doctor Kildare ..see: Theme From
8/72	**Doctor My Eyes**...Jackson Browne
	Doctor Tarr ..see: (System Of)
	Dr. Zhivago ..see: Somewhere My Love
11/75	**Doctor's Orders**...Carol Douglas
38/69	**Does Anybody Know I'm Here**...Dells
38/91	**Does Anybody Really Fall In Love Anymore?**...Kane Roberts
7/71	**Does Anybody Really Know What Time It Is?**...Chicago
36/83	**Does It Make You Remember**...Kim Carnes
34/91	**Does She Love That Man?**...Breathe/David Glasper
5/61	**Does Your Chewing Gum Lose Its Flavor (On The Bedpost Over Night)**...Lonnie Donegan

POS/YR	RECORD TITLE/ARTIST
29/68	**Does Your Mama Know About Me**...Bobby Taylor
19/79	**Does Your Mother Know**...Abba
F/55	**Doesn't Anybody Love Me?**...McGuire Sisters
6/71	**Doesn't Somebody Want To Be Wanted**...Partridge Family
34/79	**Dog & Butterfly**...Heart
30/55	**Dogface Soldier**...Russ Morgan
15/60	**Doggin' Around**...Jackie Wilson
32/69	**Doggone Right**...Miracles
6/87	**Doing It All For My Baby**...Huey Lewis & the News
22/73	**Doing It To Death**...JB's
31/60	**Doll House**...Donnie Brooks
13/55	**Domani (Tomorrow)**...Julius LaRosa
1/63	**Dominique**...Singing Nun
9/71	**Domino**...Van Morrison
18/88	**Domino Dancing**...Pet Shop Boys
14/87	**Dominoes**...Robbie Nevil
1/58	**Don't**...Elvis Presley
15/84	**Don't Answer Me**...Alan Parsons Project
19/80	**Don't Ask Me Why**...Billy Joel
25/58	**Don't Ask Me Why**...Elvis Presley
40/89	**Don't Ask Me Why**...Eurythmics
26/63	**Don't Be Afraid, Little Darlin'**...Steve Lawrence
	Don't Be Angry
14/55	Crew-Cuts
25/55	Nappy Brown
	Don't Be Cruel
1/56	Elvis Presley
11/60	Bill Black's Combo
4/88	Cheap Trick
8/88	**Don't Be Cruel**...Bobby Brown
9/61	**Don't Bet Money Honey**...Linda Scott
20/61	**Don't Blame Me**...Everly Brothers
37/67	**Don't Blame The Children**...Sammy Davis, Jr.
1/62	**Don't Break The Heart That Loves You**...Connie Francis
4/79	**Don't Bring Me Down**...Electric Light Orchestra
12/66	**Don't Bring Me Down**...Animals
9/75	**Don't Call Us, We'll Call You**...Sugarloaf
	Don't Cha ..see: Doncha'
26/74	**Don't Change Horses (In The Middle Of A Stream)**...Tower Of Power
36/71	**Don't Change On Me**...Ray Charles
11/89	**Don't Close Your Eyes**...Kix

693

POS/YR	RECORD TITLE/ARTIST
13/85	**Don't Come Around Here No More**...Tom Petty
21/60	**Don't Come Knockin'**...Fats Domino
35/73	**Don't Cross The River**...America
10/83	**Don't Cry**...Asia
10/91	**Don't Cry**...Guns N' Roses
39/61	**Don't Cry, Baby**...Etta James
6/70	**Don't Cry Daddy**...Elvis Presley
10/79	**Don't Cry Out Loud**...Melissa Manchester
4/87	**Don't Disturb This Groove**...System
	Don't Do It ..see: Baby Don't You Do It
10/80	**Don't Do Me Like That**...Tom Petty
2/87	**Don't Dream It's Over**...Crowded House
23/72	**Don't Ever Be Lonely (A Poor Little Fool Like Me)**...Cornelius Brothers & Sister Rose
40/79	**Don't Ever Wanna Lose Ya**...New England
8/73	**Don't Expect Me To Be Your Friend**...Lobo
4/80	**Don't Fall In Love With A Dreamer**...Kenny Rogers with Kim Carnes
12/76	**(Don't Fear) The Reaper**...Blue Öyster Cult
17/82	**Don't Fight It**...Kenny Loggins/Steve Perry
1/57	**Don't Forbid Me**...Pat Boone
19/65	**Don't Forget I Still Love You**...Bobbi Martin
2/86	**Don't Forget Me (When I'm Gone)**...Glass Tiger
29/83	**Don't Forget To Dance**...Kinks
10/86	**Don't Get Me Wrong**...Pretenders
15/69	**Don't Give In To Him**...Gary Puckett & The Union Gap
26/81	**Don't Give It Up**...Robbie Patton
37/68	**Don't Give Up**...Petula Clark
1/77	**Don't Give Up On Us**...David Soul
19/90	**Don't Go Away Mad (Just Go Away)**...Mötley Crüe
1/76	**Don't Go Breaking My Heart**...Elton John & Kiki Dee
22/58	**Don't Go Home**...Playmates
17/62	**Don't Go Near The Indians**...Rex Allen
18/67	**Don't Go Out Into The Rain (You're Going To Melt)**...Herman's Hermits
	Don't Go To Strangers
38/56	Vaughn Monroe
36/60	Etta Jones
4/62	**Don't Hang Up**...Orlons
21/79	**Don't Hold Back**...Chanson
2/77	**Don't It Make My Brown Eyes Blue**...Crystal Gayle
8/65	**Don't Just Stand There**...Patty Duke

POS/YR	RECORD TITLE/ARTIST
13/71	**Don't Knock My Love**...Wilson Pickett
2/89	**Don't Know Much**...Linda Ronstadt/Aaron Neville
12/88	**Don't Know What You Got (Till It's Gone)**...Cinderella
	Don't Leave Me This Way
1/77	Thelma Houston
40/87	Communards
	Don't Let Go
13/58	Roy Hamilton
18/80	Isaac Hayes
38/84	**Don't Let Go**...Wang Chung
24/81	**Don't Let Him Go**...REO Speedwagon
39/82	**Don't Let Him Know**...Prism
6/83	**Don't Let It End**...Styx
14/73	**Don't Let Me Be Lonely Tonight**...James Taylor
	Don't Let Me Be Misunderstood
15/65	Animals
15/78	Santa Esmeralda
35/69	**Don't Let Me Down**...Beatles with Billy Preston
17/71	**Don't Let The Green Grass Fool You**...Wilson Pickett
20/69	**Don't Let The Joneses Get You Down**...Temptations
6/64	**Don't Let The Rain Come Down (Crooked Little Man)**...Serendipity Singers
39/67	**Don't Let The Rain Fall Down On Me**...Critters
4/64	**Don't Let The Sun Catch You Crying**...Gerry & The Pacemakers
	Don't Let The Sun Go Down On Me
2/74	Elton John
1/92	George Michael/Elton John
4/78	**Don't Look Back**...Boston
11/89	**Don't Look Back**...Fine Young Cannibals
39/87	**Don't Look Down - The Sequel**...Go West
4/85	**Don't Lose My Number**...Phil Collins
	Don't Make Me Over
21/63	Dionne Warwick
20/89	Sybil
15/87	**Don't Make Me Wait For Love**...Kenny G
3/87	**Don't Mean Nothing**...Richard Marx
33/65	**Don't Mess Up A Good Thing**...Fontella Bass & Bobby McClure
7/66	**Don't Mess With Bill**...Marvelettes
37/87	**Don't Need A Gun**...Billy Idol
34/83	**Don't Pay The Ferryman**...Chris DeBurgh
40/59	**Don't Pity Me**...Dion & The Belmonts

POS/YR	RECORD TITLE/ARTIST
	Don't Play That Song
11/62	Ben E. King
11/70	Aretha Franklin
	Don't Pull Your Love
4/71	Hamilton, Joe Frank & Reynolds
27/76	Glen Campbell (medley)
2/89	**Don't Rush Me**...Taylor Dayne
26/63	**Don't Say Goodnight And Mean Goodbye**...Shirelles
39/80	**Don't Say Goodnight (It's Time For Love)**...Isley Brothers
7/63	**Don't Say Nothin' Bad (About My Baby)**...Cookies
15/72	**Don't Say You Don't Remember**...Beverly Bremers
20/63	**Don't Set Me Free**...Ray Charles
9/88	**Don't Shed A Tear**...Paul Carrack
18/89	**Don't Shut Me Out**...Kevin Paige
5/67	**Don't Sleep In The Subway**...Petula Clark
10/81	**Don't Stand So Close To Me**...Police
F/55	**Don't Stay Away Too Long**...Eddie Fisher
3/77	**Don't Stop**...Fleetwood Mac
9/81	**Don't Stop Believin'**...Journey
33/76	**Don't Stop Believin'**...Olivia Newton-John
19/81	**Don't Stop The Music**...Yarbrough & Peoples
1/79	**Don't Stop 'Til You Get Enough**...Michael Jackson
34/76	**Don't Take Away The Music**...Tavares
2/95	**Don't Take It Personal (just one of dem days)**...Monica
27/68	**Don't Take It So Hard**...Paul Revere & The Raiders
17/94	**Don't Take The Girl**...Tim McGraw
32/59	**Don't Take Your Guns To Town**...Johnny Cash
37/75	**Don't Take Your Love**...Manhattans
2/82	**Don't Talk To Strangers**...Rick Springfield
27/75	**Don't Tell Me Goodnight**...Lobo
10/89	**Don't Tell Me Lies**...Breathe
40/83	**Don't Tell Me You Love Me**...Night Ranger
	Don't Think Twice, It's All Right
9/63	Peter, Paul & Mary
12/65	Wonder Who?
22/60	**Don't Throw Away All Those Teardrops**...Frankie Avalon
	Don't Throw It All Away ..see: (Our Love)
16/64	**Don't Throw Your Love Away**...Searchers
38/69	**Don't Touch Me**...Bettye Swann
19/91	**Don't Treat Me Bad**...Firehouse

POS/YR	RECORD TITLE/ARTIST
4/94	**Don't Turn Around**...Ace Of Base
4/93	**Don't Walk Away**...Jade
26/84	**Don't Walk Away**...Rick Springfield
2/90	**Don't Wanna Fall In Love**...Jane Child
1/89	**Don't Wanna Lose You**...Gloria Estefan
9/91	**Don't Want To Be A Fool**...Luther Vandross
21/78	**Don't Want To Live Without It**...Pablo Cruise
35/81	**Don't Want To Wait Anymore**...Tubes
3/61	**Don't Worry**...Marty Robbins
	Don't Worry Baby
24/64	Beach Boys
17/77	B.J. Thomas
1/88	**Don't Worry Be Happy**...Bobby McFerrin
29/71	**(Don't Worry) If There's A Hell Below We're All Going To Go**...Curtis Mayfield
	Don't Ya Wanna Play This Game No More ..see: (Sartorial Eloquence)
	Don't You ..also see: Doncha'
39/62	**Don't You Believe It**...Andy Williams
6/67	**Don't You Care**...Buckinghams
1/85	**Don't You (Forget About Me)**...Simple Minds
	Don't You Forget It ..see: (I Love You)
25/83	**Don't You Get So Mad**...Jeffrey Osborne
9/58	**Don't You Just Know It**...Huey (Piano) Smith
2/59	**Don't You Know**...Della Reese
6/88	**Don't You Know What The Night Can Do?**...Steve Winwood
1/82	**Don't You Want Me**...Human League
6/87	**Don't You Want Me**...Jody Watley
16/74	**Don't You Worry 'Bout A Thing**...Stevie Wonder
	(Don't You Worry 'Bout Me) ..see: Opus 17
33/79	**Don't You Write Her Off**...McGuinn, Clark & Hillman
15/58	**Doncha' Think It's Time**...Elvis Presley
2/59	**Donna**...Ritchie Valens
6/63	**Donna The Prima Donna**...Dion
15/74	**Doo Doo Doo Doo Doo (Heartbreaker)**...Rolling Stones
	Door Is Still Open To My Heart
F/55	Don Cornell
6/64	Dean Martin
35/74	**Doraville**...Atlanta Rhythm Section
26/76	**Dose Of Rock 'N' Roll**...Ringo Starr
39/58	**Dottie**...Danny & The Juniors
22/71	**Double Barrel**...Dave & Ansil Collins

POS/YR	RECORD TITLE/ARTIST
30/81	Double Dutch Bus...Frankie Smith
14/71	Double Lovin'...Osmonds
17/66	Double Shot (Of My Baby's Love)...Swingin' Medallions
2/78	Double Vision...Foreigner
33/68	Down At Lulu's...Ohio Express
9/63	(Down At) Papa Joe's...Dixiebelles
27/89	Down Boys...Warrant
4/72	Down By The Lazy River...Osmonds
13/60	Down By The Station...Four Preps
9/65	Down In The Boondocks...Billy Joe Royal
3/69	Down On The Corner...Creedence Clearwater Revival
18/58	Down The Aisle Of Love...Quin-Tones
37/63	Down The Aisle (Wedding Song)...Patti LaBelle & The Blue Belles
1/83	Down Under...Men At Work
21/93	Down With The King...Run-D.M.C.
	Downtown
1/65	Petula Clark
40/65	Allan Sherman (Crazy Downtown)
37/89	Downtown...One 2 Many
F/93	Downtown...SWV-Sisters With Voices
31/88	Downtown Life...Daryl Hall/John Oates
3/90	Downtown Train...Rod Stewart
	Dr. ..see: Doctor
10/64	Drag City...Jan & Dean
4/71	Draggin' The Line...Tommy James
28/81	Draw Of The Cards...Kim Carnes
8/93	Dre Day...Dr. Dre
19/58	Dream...Betty Johnson
12/68	Dream A Little Dream Of Me...Mama Cass
29/95	Dream About You...Stevie B
	Dream Baby (How Long Must I Dream)
4/62	Roy Orbison
31/71	Glen Campbell
37/84	Dream (Hold On To Your Dream)...Irene Cara
12/91	Dream Is Still Alive...Wilson Phillips
2/59	Dream Lover...Bobby Darin
1/93	Dreamlover...Mariah Carey
	Dream Merchant
38/67	Jerry Butler
36/75	New Birth
6/76	Dream On...Aerosmith
32/74	Dream On...Righteous Brothers
25/65	Dream On Little Dreamer...Perry Como
26/79	Dream Police...Cheap Trick
2/76	Dream Weaver...Gary Wright

POS/YR	RECORD TITLE/ARTIST
	Dreamboat ..see: (He's My)
15/80	Dreamer...Supertramp
8/89	Dreamin'...Vanessa Williams
11/60	Dreamin'...Johnny Burnette
10/80	Dreaming...Cliff Richard
16/88	Dreaming...Orchestral Manoeuvres In The Dark
27/79	Dreaming...Blondie
30/83	Dreamin' Is Easy...Steel Breeze
22/95	Dreaming Of You...Selena
1/77	Dreams...Fleetwood Mac
22/86	Dreams...Van Halen
26/94	Dreams...Gabrielle
32/68	Dreams Of The Everyday Housewife...Glen Campbell
5/86	Dreamtime...Daryl Hall
35/62	Dreamy Eyes...Johnny Tillotson
21/73	Dreidel...Don McLean
5/85	Dress You Up...Madonna
14/89	Dressed For Success...Roxette
5/73	Drift Away...Dobie Gray
6/63	Drip Drop...Dion
3/84	Drive...Cars
28/92	Drive...R.E.M.
15/79	Driver's Seat...Sniff 'n' the Tears
5/80	Drivin' My Life Away...Eddie Rabbitt
34/77	Drivin' Wheel...Foghat
36/63	Drownin' My Sorrows...Connie Francis
11/72	Drowning In The Sea Of Love...Joe Simon
29/71	Drum, The...Bobby Sherman
29/62	Drums Are My Beat...Sandy Nelson
20/67	Dry Your Eyes...Brenda & The Tabulations
14/66	Duck, The...Jackie Lee
14/87	Dude (Looks Like A Lady)...Aerosmith
2/73	Dueling Banjos...Eric Weissberg & Steve Mandell
1/62	Duke Of Earl...Gene Chandler
	Dukes Of Hazzard ..see: Theme From The
	Dum-De-Da ..see: She Understands Me
4/61	Dum Dum...Brenda Lee (also see: Happy Song)
7/56	Dungaree Doll...Eddie Fisher
28/94	Dunkie Butt (Please Please Please)...12 Gauge
18/77	Dusic...Brick
6/78	Dust In The Wind...Kansas
30/60	Dutchman's Gold...Walter Brennan/Billy Vaughn

POS/YR	RECORD TITLE/ARTIST
15/84	**Dynamite**...Jermaine Jackson
10/75	**Dynomite**...Bazuka

E

POS/YR	RECORD TITLE/ARTIST
9/74	**Earache My Eye (Featuring Alice Bowie)**...Cheech & Chong
12/70	**Early In The Morning**...Vanity Fare
	Early In The Morning
24/58	Rinky-Dinks
32/58	Buddy Holly
	Early In The Morning
24/82	Gap Band
19/88	Robert Palmer
	Earth Angel
3/55	Crew-Cuts
8/55	Penguins
18/55	Gloria Mann
21/86	New Edition
1/63	**Easier Said Than Done**...Essex
27/66	**East West**...Herman's Hermits
4/77	**Easy**...Commodores
	(also see: Six Feet Deep)
9/70	**Easy Come, Easy Go**...Bobby Sherman
39/72	**Easy Livin**...Uriah Heep
2/85	**Easy Lover**...Philip Bailey/Phil Collins
17/71	**Easy Loving**...Freddie Hart
	Easy Question ..see: (Such An)
4/69	**Easy To Be Hard**...Three Dog Night
36/78	**Easy To Love**...Leo Sayer
12/84	**Eat It**...Weird Al Yankovic
	Ebb Tide
25/64	Lenny Welch
5/66	Righteous Brothers
1/82	**Ebony And Ivory**...Paul McCartney (with Stevie Wonder)
8/61	**Ebony Eyes**...Everly Brothers
14/78	**Ebony Eyes**...Bob Welch
40/69	**Echo Park**...Keith Barbour
31/73	**Ecstasy**...Ohio Players
	Eddie My Love
11/56	Fontane Sisters
14/56	Chordettes
14/56	Teen Queens
26/88	**Edge Of A Broken Heart**...Vixen
10/86	**Edge Of Heaven**...Wham!
11/82	**Edge Of Seventeen (Just Like The White Winged Dove)**...Stevie Nicks
26/77	**Edge Of The Universe**...Bee Gees

POS/YR	RECORD TITLE/ARTIST
34/78	**Ego**...Elton John
1/65	**Eight Days A Week**...Beatles
32/88	**853-5937**...Squeeze
14/66	**Eight Miles High**...Byrds
4/82	**867-5309/Jenny**...Tommy Tutone
21/71	**Eighteen**...Alice Cooper
4/89	**18 And Life**...Skid Row
15/75	**Eighteen With A Bullet**...Pete Wingfield
10/63	**18 Yellow Roses**...Bobby Darin
	Ein Schiff Wird Kommen ..see: Never On Sunday
18/70	**El Condor Pasa**...Simon & Garfunkel
32/60	**El Matador**...Kingston Trio
1/60	**El Paso**...Marty Robbins
30/58	**El Rancho Rock**...Champs
17/63	**El Watusi**...Ray Barretto **(also see: Wah Watusi, & Watusi)**
	Eleanor Rigby
11/66	Beatles
35/68	Ray Charles
17/69	Aretha Franklin
26/72	**Elected**...Alice Cooper
6/85	**Election Day**...Arcadia
2/83	**Electric Avenue**...Eddy Grant
7/88	**Electric Blue**...Icehouse
11/89	**Electric Youth**...Debbie Gibson
6/68	**Elenore**...Turtles
39/91	**Elevate My Mind**...Stereo MC's
	11th Hour Melody
21/56	Al Hibbler
35/56	Lou Busch
10/69	**Eli's Coming**...Three Dog Night
39/56	**Eloise**...Kay Thompson
5/66	**Elusive Butterfly**...Bob Lind
5/81	**Elvira**...Oak Ridge Boys
18/85	**Emergency**...Kool & The Gang
8/75	**Emma**...Hot Chocolate
3/78	**Emotion**...Samantha Sang
22/75	**Emotion**...Helen Reddy
15/86	**Emotion In Motion**...Ric Ocasek
3/80	**Emotional Rescue**...Rolling Stones
1/91	**Emotions**...Mariah Carey
7/61	**Emotions**...Brenda Lee
18/80	**Empire Strikes Back (medley)**...Meco
13/57	**Empty Arms**...Teresa Brewer
13/82	**Empty Garden (Hey Hey Johnny)**...Elton John
12/59	**Enchanted**...Platters
12/58	**Enchanted Island**...Four Lads

POS/YR	RECORD TITLE/ARTIST
	Enchanted Sea
15/59	Islanders
28/59	Martin Denny
7/58	**End, The**...Earl Grant
	End Of Our Road
15/68	Gladys Knight & The Pips
40/70	Marvin Gaye
8/89	**End Of The Innocence**...Don Henley
1/92	**End of the Road**...Boyz II Men
2/63	**End Of The World**...Skeeter Davis
	Endless Love
1/81	Diana Ross & Lionel Richie
2/94	Luther Vandross & Mariah Carey
21/87	**Endless Nights**...Eddie Money
5/58	**Endless Sleep**...Jody Reynolds
2/88	**Endless Summer Nights**...Richard Marx
12/59	**Endlessly**...Brook Benton
33/74	**Energy Crisis '74**...Dickie Goodman
7/65	**Engine Engine #9**...Roger Miller
14/70	**Engine Number 9**...Wilson Pickett
8/65	**England Swings**...Roger Miller
21/56	**English Muffins And Irish Stew**...Sylvia Syms
8/90	**Enjoy The Silence**...Depeche Mode
6/77	**Enjoy Yourself**...Jacksons
	(Enough Is Enough) ..see: No More Tears
16/91	**Enter Sandman**...Metallica
3/74	**Entertainer, The**...Marvin Hamlisch
31/65	**Entertainer, The**...Tony Clarke
34/75	**Entertainer, The**...Billy Joel
9/90	**Epic**...Faith No More
19/67	**Epistle To Dippy**...Donovan
9/74	**Eres Tu (Touch The Wind)**...Mocedades
3/92	**Erotica**...Madonna
1/90	**Escapade**...Janet Jackson
1/79	**Escape (The Pina Colada Song)**...Rupert Holmes
35/71	**Escape-ism**...James Brown **(also see: Ainít 2 Proud 2 Beg)**
19/62	**Eso Beso (That Kiss!)**...Paul Anka
1/89	**Eternal Flame**...Bangles
1/65	**Eve Of Destruction**...Barry McGuire **(also see: Dawn of Correction, & Day For Decision)**
32/92	**Even Better Than The Real Thing**...U2
33/80	**Even It Up**...Heart
12/83	**Even Now**...Bob Seger
19/78	**Even Now**...Barry Manilow
36/67	**Even The Bad Times Are Good**...Tremeloes

POS/YR	RECORD TITLE/ARTIST
5/82	**Even The Nights Are Better**...Air Supply
	Evergreen ..see: Love Theme From A Star Is Born
5/78	**Everlasting Love**...Andy Gibb
	Everlasting Love
13/67	Robert Knight
6/74	Carl Carlton
32/81	Rex Smith/Rachel Sweet
27/95	Gloria Estefan
12/89	**Everlasting Love**...Howard Jones
16/61	**Everlovin'**...Rick Nelson
6/61	**Every Beat Of My Heart**...Pips
1/83	**Every Breath You Take**...Police
	Every Day ..also see: Everyday
	Every Day Of My Life
37/56	McGuire Sisters
24/72	Bobby Vinton
20/95	**Every Day Of The Week**...Jade
2/91	**Every Heartbeat**...Amy Grant
16/78	**Every Kinda People**...Robert Palmer
13/64	**Every Little Bit Hurts**...Brenda Holloway
14/87	**Every Little Kiss**...Bruce Hornsby & The Range
3/89	**Every Little Step**...Bobby Brown
17/95	**Every Little Thing I Do**...Soul For Real
3/81	**Every Little Thing She Does Is Magic**...Police
39/58	**Every Night (I Pray)**...Chantels
	Every 1's A Winner ..see: Everyone's
25/85	**Every Step Of The Way**...John Waite
30/63	**Every Step Of The Way**...Johnny Mathis
	Every Time ..also see: Everytime
13/79	**Every Time I Think Of You**...Babys
4/77	**(Every Time I Turn Around) Back In Love Again**...L.T.D.
19/75	**Every Time You Touch Me (I Get High)**...Charlie Rich
30/79	**Every Which Way But Loose**...Eddie Rabbitt
5/81	**Every Woman In The World**...Air Supply
3/63	**Everybody**...Tommy Roe
38/77	**Everybody Be Dancin'**...Starbuck
24/86	**Everybody Dance**...Ta Mara & The Seen
38/78	**Everybody Dance**...Chic
8/90	**Everybody Everybody**...Black Box
2/86	**Everybody Have Fun Tonight**...Wang Chung
29/93	**Everybody Hurts**...R.E.M.
F/70	**Everybody Is A Star**...Sly & The Family Stone

POS/YR	RECORD TITLE/ARTIST
15/64	**Everybody Knows (I Still Love You)**...Dave Clark Five
31/59	**Everybody Likes To Cha Cha Cha**...Sam Cooke
4/65	**Everybody Loves A Clown**...Gary Lewis & The Playboys
	Everybody Loves A Lover
6/58	Doris Day
19/63	Shirelles
6/62	**Everybody Loves Me But You**...Brenda Lee
1/64	**Everybody Loves Somebody**...Dean Martin
32/78	**Everybody Needs Love**...Stephen Bishop
39/67	**Everybody Needs Love**...Gladys Knight & The Pips
29/67	**Everybody Needs Somebody To Love**...Wilson Pickett
	Everybody Plays The Fool
3/72	Main Ingredient
8/91	Aaron Neville
1/85	**Everybody Wants To Rule The World**...Tears For Fears
32/82	**Everybody Wants You**...Billy Squier
12/71	**Everybody's Everything**...Santana
37/92	**Everybody's Free (To Feel Good)**...Rozalla
20/55	**Everybody's Got A Home But Me**...Eddie Fisher
21/70	**Everybody's Got The Right To Love**...Supremes
18/80	**Everybody's Got To Learn Sometime**...Korgis
26/70	**Everybody's Out Of Town**...B.J. Thomas
1/60	**Everybody's Somebody's Fool**...Connie Francis
6/69	**Everybody's Talkin'**...Nilsson
24/94	**Everyday**...Phil Collins
36/83	**Everyday I Write The Book**...Elvis Costello
	Everyday People
1/69	Sly & The Family Stone
37/83	Joan Jett
	(also see: People Everyday)
19/69	**Everyday With You Girl**...Classics IV
6/79	**Every 1's A Winner**...Hot Chocolate
17/65	**Everyone's Gone To The Moon**...Jonathan King
4/90	**Everything**...Jody Watley
9/92	**Everything About You**....Ugly Kid Joe
14/92	**Everything Changes**...Kathy Troccoli
1/91	**(Everything I Do) I Do It For You**...Bryan Adams
5/72	**Everything I Own**...Bread
30/86	**Everything In My Heart**...Corey Hart

POS/YR	RECORD TITLE/ARTIST
1/70	**Everything Is Beautiful**...Ray Stevens
1/85	**Everything She Wants**...Wham!
10/68	**Everything That Touches You**...Association
3/88	**Everything Your Heart Desires**...Daryl Hall/John Oates
16/64	**Everything's Alright**...Newbeats
37/93	**Everything's Gonna Be Alright**...Father MC
38/70	**Everything's Tuesday**...Chairman Of The Board
1/85	**Everytime You Go Away**...Paul Young
14/88	**Everywhere**...Fleetwood Mac
9/70	**Evil Ways**...Santana **(also see: Mentirosa)**
10/76	**Evil Woman**...Electric Light Orchestra
19/70	**Evil Woman Don't Play Your Games With Me**...Crow
1/95	**Exhale (Shoop Shoop)**...Whitney Houston
	Exodus
2/61	Ferrante & Teicher
31/61	Mantovani
36/61	Eddie Harris
	Exorcist, Theme From ..see: Tubular Bells
14/55	**Experience Unnecessary**...Sarah Vaughan
33/68	**Explosion (In Your Soul)**...Soul Survivors
4/75	**Express**...B.T. Express
2/89	**Express Yourself**...Madonna
12/70	**Express Yourself**...Charles Wright
26/90	**Expression**...Salt-N-Pepa
4/67	**Expressway (To Your Heart)**...Soul Survivors
3/82	**Eye In The Sky**...Alan Parsons Project
1/82	**Eye Of The Tiger**...Survivor
28/68	**Eyes Of A New York Woman**...B.J. Thomas
	Eyes Of Laura Mars ..see: Love Theme From
4/84	**Eyes Without A Face**...Billy Idol

F

POS/YR	RECORD TITLE/ARTIST
22/78	**FM (No Static At All)**...Steely Dan
37/94	**Fa All Y'all**...Da Brat
29/66	**Fa-Fa-Fa-Fa-Fa (Sad Song)**...Otis Redding
16/57	**Fabulous**...Charlie Gracie
19/56	**Fabulous Character**...Sarah Vaughan
29/68	**Face It Girl, It's Over**...Nancy Wilson
26/86	**Face The Face**...Pete Townshend
27/87	**Facts Of Love**...Jeff Lorber Featuring Karyn White

POS/YR	RECORD TITLE/ARTIST
20/81	Fade Away...Bruce Springsteen
2/91	Fading Like A Flower (Every Time You Leave)...Roxette
28/90	Fairweather Friend...Johnny Gill
13/74	Fairytale...Pointer Sisters
1/87	Faith...George Michael
14/93	Faithful...Go West
12/83	Faithfully...Journey
25/87	Fake...Alexander O'Neal
35/83	Fake Friends...Joan Jett
23/67	Fakin' It...Simon & Garfunkel
33/94	Fall Down...Toad The Wet Sprocket
17/83	Fall In Love With Me...Earth, Wind & Fire
12/88	Fallen Angel...Poison
36/76	Fallen Angel...Frankie Valli
	Fallen Star
20/57	Nick Noble
23/57	Jimmy Newman
30/58	Fallin'...Connie Francis
13/78	Falling...LeBlanc & Carr
22/63	Falling...Roy Orbison
1/75	Fallin' In Love...Hamilton, Joe Frank & Reynolds
27/74	Fallin' In Love...Souther, Hillman, Furay Band
25/87	Falling In Love (Uh-Oh)...Miami Sound Machine
1/75	Fame...David Bowie
4/80	Fame...Irene Cara
17/60	Fame And Fortune...Elvis Presley
1/71	Family Affair...Sly & The Family Stone (also see: And On And On)
6/83	Family Man...Daryl Hall & John Oates
12/72	Family Of Man...Three Dog Night
31/70	Fancy...Bobbie Gentry
39/77	Fancy Dancer...Commodores
38/60	Fannie Mae...Buster Brown
12/76	Fanny (Be Tender With My Love)...Bee Gees
3/94	Fantastic Voyage...Coolio
1/95	Fantasy...Mariah Carey
23/82	Fantasy...Aldo Nova
32/78	Fantasy...Earth, Wind & Fire
18/94	Far Behind...Candlebox
10/83	Far From Over...Frank Stallone
38/84	Farewell My Summer Love...Michael Jackson
19/64	Farmer John...Premiers
21/87	Fascinated...Company B

POS/YR	RECORD TITLE/ARTIST
	Fascination
7/57	Jane Morgan
15/57	Dinah Shore
17/57	Dick Jacobs (also see: Keep Feeling)
6/88	Fast Car...Tracy Chapman
F/79	Fat Bottomed Girls...Queen
1/88	Father Figure...George Michael (also see: Looking Through Patient Eyes)
34/86	Feel It Again...Honeymoon Suite
1/74	Feel Like Makin' Love...Roberta Flack
10/75	Feel Like Makin' Love...Bad Company
17/95	Feel Me Flow...Naughty By Nature
	Feel So Fine
14/60	Johnny Preston
22/67	Bunny Sigler (medley)
	Feelin' Groovy ..see: 59th Street Bridge
10/73	Feelin' Stronger Every Day...Chicago
33/72	Feeling Alright...Joe Cocker
6/75	Feelings...Morris Albert
9/90	Feels Good...Tony! Toni! Tone!
4/77	Feels Like The First Time...Foreigner
4/78	Feels So Good...Chuck Mangione
32/95	Feels So Good...Xscape
35/89	Feels So Good...Van Halen
20/81	Feels So Right...Alabama
25/94	Feenin'...Jodeci
32/61	Fell In Love On Monday...Fats Domino
13/76	Fernando...Abba
6/65	Ferry Cross The Mersey...Gerry & The Pacemakers
	Fever
24/56	Little Willie John
8/58	Peggy Lee
7/65	McCoys
23/78	Ffun...Con Funk Shun
39/58	Fibbin'...Patti Page
23/93	Fields Of Gold...Sting
1/76	Fifth Of Beethoven...Walter Murphy
1/76	50 Ways To Leave Your Lover...Paul Simon
13/67	59th Street Bridge Song (Feelin' Groovy)...Harpers Bizarre
	Fight ..see: Main Event
	Fight For Your Right (To Party!) ..see: (You Gotta)
4/75	Fight The Power...Isley Brothers
	(Final Acclaim) ..see: You're In My Heart
8/87	Final Countdown...Europe
5/92	Finally...Ce Ce Peniston

POS/YR	RECORD TITLE/ARTIST
17/74	Finally Got Myself Together (I'm A Changed Man)...Impressions
29/85	Find A Way...Amy Grant
16/82	Find Another Fool...Quarterflash
27/61	Find Another Girl...Jerry Butler
29/81	Find Your Way Back...Jefferson Starship
22/84	Fine Fine Day...Tony Carey
8/87	Finer Things...Steve Winwood
7/60	Finger Poppin' Time...Hank Ballard
1/63	Fingertips...Little Stevie Wonder
13/88	Finish What Ya Started...Van Halen
35/79	Fins...Jimmy Buffett
1/75	Fire...Ohio Players
2/68	Fire...Crazy World Of Arthur Brown
2/79	Fire...Pointer Sisters
17/81	Fire And Ice...Pat Benatar
3/70	Fire And Rain...James Taylor
24/72	Fire And Water...Wilson Pickett
28/74	Fire, Baby I'm On Fire...Andy Kim
32/80	Fire In The Morning...Melissa Manchester
6/80	Fire Lake...Bob Seger
38/75	Fire On The Mountain...Marshall Tucker Band
20/58	Firefly...Tony Bennett
21/77	First Cut Is The Deepest...Rod Stewart
25/57	First Date, First Kiss, First Love...Sonny James
33/84	First Day Of Summer...Tony Carey
20/60	First Name Initial...Annette
37/69	First Of May...Bee Gees
14/95	1st Of Tha Month...Bone thugs-n-harmony
27/63	First Quarrel...Paul & Paula
1/91	First Time...Surface
1/72	First Time Ever I Saw Your Face...Roberta Flack
	(First Time I Was A Fool) ..see: Third Time Lucky
38/80	First Time Love...Livingston Taylor
25/61	Fish, The...Bobby Rydell
26/74	Fish Ain't Bitin'...Lamont Dozier
23/88	Fishnet...Morris Day
	(500 Miles) ..see: I'm Gonna Be
10/63	500 Miles Away From Home...Bobby Bare
4/66	Five O'Clock World...Vogues
	(Five Oaks) ..see: Cinco Robles
27/78	5.7.0.5....City Boy
11/70	5-10-15-20 (25-30 Years Of Love)...Presidents
1/88	Flame, The...Cheap Trick

POS/YR	RECORD TITLE/ARTIST
36/87	Flames Of Paradise...Jennifer Rush (with Elton John)
14/61	Flaming Star...Elvis Presley
28/66	Flamingo...Herb Alpert
16/78	Flash Light...Parliament
1/83	Flashdance...What A Feeling...Irene Cara
9/94	Flava In Ya Ear...Craig Mack
29/84	Flesh For Fantasy...Billy Idol
13/93	Flex...Mad Cobra
2/77	Float On...Floaters
21/56	Flowers Mean Forgiveness...Frank Sinatra
4/66	Flowers On The Wall...Statler Brothers
16/72	Floy Joy...Supremes
7/61	Fly, The...Chubby Checker
13/76	Fly Away...John Denver
2/77	Fly Like An Eagle...Steve Miller
14/63	Fly Me To The Moon-Bossa Nova...Joe Harnell
1/75	Fly, Robin, Fly...Silver Convention (also see: Ain't 2 Proud 2 Beg, & How High)
19/90	Fly To The Angels...Slaughter
38/78	Flying High...Commodores
3/56	Flying Saucer...Buchanan & Goodman
18/57	Flying Saucer The 2nd...Buchanan & Goodman
15/62	Follow That Dream...Elvis Presley
17/63	Follow The Boys...Connie Francis
23/78	Follow You Follow Me...Genesis
32/68	Folsom Prison Blues...Johnny Cash
7/56	Fool, The...Sanford Clark
F/73	Fool...Elvis Presley
22/68	Fool For You...Impressions
37/89	Fool For Your Loving...Whitesnake
12/78	Fool (If You Think It's Over)...Chris Rea
27/60	Fool In Love...Ike & Tina Turner
25/81	Fool In Love With You...Jim Photoglo
21/80	Fool In The Rain...Led Zeppelin
13/64	Fool Never Learns...Andy Williams
3/61	Fool #1...Brenda Lee
6/68	Fool On The Hill...Sergio Mendes & Brasil '66
2/59	Fool Such As I...Elvis Presley
10/76	Fool To Cry...Rolling Stones
20/55	Fooled...Perry Como
3/76	Fooled Around And Fell In Love...Elvin Bishop
28/83	Foolin'...Def Leppard

POS/YR	RECORD TITLE/ARTIST
38/95	Foolin' Around...Changing Faces
29/78	**Fooling Yourself (The Angry Young Man)** ...Styx
1/88	**Foolish Beat**...Debbie Gibson
18/85	**Foolish Heart**...Steve Perry
4/63	**Foolish Little Girl**...Shirelles
33/86	**Foolish Pride**...Daryl Hall
29/59	**Fools Hall Of Fame**...Pat Boone
	Fools Rush In
24/60	Brook Benton
12/63	Rick Nelson
25/61	**Foot Stomping**...Flares
1/84	**Footloose**...Kenny Loggins
7/60	**Footsteps**...Steve Lawrence
29/72	**Footstompin' Music**...Grand Funk Railroad
30/76	**Fopp**...Ohio Players
23/59	**For A Penny**...Pat Boone
3/71	**For All We Know**...Carpenters
30/86	**For America**...Jackson Browne
26/71	**(For God's Sake) Give More Power To The People**...Chi-Lites
30/65	**For Lovin' Me**...Peter, Paul & Mary
28/61	**For My Baby**...Brook Benton
23/58	**For My Good Fortune**...Pat Boone
2/68	**For Once In My Life**...Stevie Wonder
	For Sentimental Reasons ..see: (I Love You)
11/71	**For The Good Times**...Ray Price
F/76	**For The Heart**...Elvis Presley
13/70	**For The Love Of Him**...Bobbi Martin
9/74	**For The Love Of Money**...O'Jays
22/75	**For The Love Of You**...Isley Brothers
32/86	**For Tonight**...Nancy Martinez
7/67	**For What It's Worth**...Buffalo Springfield
6/64	**For You**...Rick Nelson
21/91	**For You**...Outfield
F/70	**For You Blue**...Beatles
4/81	**For Your Eyes Only**...Sheena Easton
6/65	**For Your Love**...Yardbirds
	For Your Love
13/58	Ed Townsend
20/67	Peaches & Herb
	For Your Precious Love
11/58	Jerry Butler & The Impressions
26/64	Garnet Mimms & The Enchanters
23/67	Oscar Toney, Jr.
8/90	**Forever**...Kiss

POS/YR	RECORD TITLE/ARTIST
	Forever
9/60	Little Dippers
25/64	Pete Drake
	(also see: Iíll Be Loving You)
40/85	**Forever**...Kenny Loggins
28/68	**Forever Came Today**...Supremes
35/56	**Forever Darling**...Ames Brothers
20/79	**Forever In Blue Jeans**...Neil Diamond
18/93	**Forever In Love**...Kenny G
19/86	**(Forever) Live And Die**...Orchestral Manoeuvres In The Dark
15/92	**Forever Love**...Color Me Badd
26/85	**Forever Man**...Eric Clapton
28/80	**Forever Mine**...O'Jays
25/91	**Forever My Lady**...Jodeci
12/88	**Forever Young**...Rod Stewart
1/89	**Forever Your Girl**...Paula Abdul
4/64	**Forget Him**...Bobby Rydell
12/58	**Forget Me Not**...Kalin Twins
23/82	**Forget Me Nots**...Patrice Rushen
2/80	**Forgive Me, Girl (medley)**...Spinners
13/55	**Forgive My Heart**...Nat "King" Cole
8/85	**Fortress Around Your Heart**...Sting
14/69	**Fortunate Son**...Creedence Clearwater Revival
9/59	**Forty Miles Of Bad Road**...Duane Eddy
36/79	**Found A Cure**...Ashford & Simpson
25/94	**Found Out About You**...Gin Blossoms
19/85	**Four In The Morning (I Can't Take Any More)**...Night Ranger
	Four Walls
11/57	Jim Reeves
15/57	Jim Lowe
36/68	**1432 Franklin Pike Circle Hero**...Bobby Russell
5/76	**Fox On The Run**...Sweet
1/73	**Frankenstein**...Edgar Winter Group
9/59	**Frankie**...Connie Francis
	Frankie And Johnny
20/61	Brook Benton
14/63	Sam Cooke
25/66	Elvis Presley
36/57	**Fraulein**...Bobby Helms
	Freak ..also see: Freek
2/95	**Freak Like Me**...Adina Howard
1/93	**Freak Me**...Silk
4/72	**Freddie's Dead**...Curtis Mayfield
20/71	**Free**...Chicago
23/56	**Free**...Tommy Leonetti

POS/YR	RECORD TITLE/ARTIST
25/77	**Free**...Deniece Williams
6/96	**Free As A Bird**...Beatles
	Free Bird
19/75	Lynyrd Skynyrd
38/77	Lynyrd Skynyrd (Live)
7/90	**Free Fallin'**...Tom Petty
22/74	**Free Man In Paris**...Joni Mitchell
14/73	**Free Ride**...Edgar Winter Group
F/74	**Free Wheelin'**...Bachman-Turner Overdrive
8/92	**Free Your Mind**...En Vogue
3/85	**Freedom**...Wham!
8/90	**Freedom**...George Michael
20/86	**Freedom Overspill**...Steve Winwood
14/95	**Freek'n You**...Jodeci
3/85	**Freeway Of Love**...Aretha Franklin
33/58	**Freeze, The**...Tony & Joe
4/82	**Freeze-Frame**...J. Geils Band
	Freight Train
6/57	Rusty Draper
40/57	Chas. McDevitt Skiffle Group
9/85	**Fresh**...Kool & The Gang
18/92	**Friday I'm In Love**...Cure
	(Friday Night) ..see: Livin' It Up
16/67	**Friday On My Mind**...Easybeats
36/66	**Friday's Child**...Nancy Sinatra
5/56	**Friendly Persuasion (Thee I Love)**...Pat Boone
9/89	**Friends**...Jody Watley With Eric B. & Rakim
34/71	**Friends**...Elton John
40/73	**Friends**...Bette Midler
2/86	**Friends And Lovers**...Gloria Loring & Carl Anderson
38/82	**Friends In Love**...Dionne Warwick & Johnny Mathis
17/69	**Friendship Train**...Gladys Knight & The Pips
32/61	**Frogg**...Brothers Four
2/90	**From A Distance**...Bette Midler
6/63	**From A Jack To A King**...Ned Miller
23/64	**From A Window**...Billy J. Kramer With The Dakotas
28/75	**From His Woman To You**...Barbara Mason
39/72	**From The Beginning**...Emerson, Lake & Palmer
11/56	**From The Candy Store On The Corner To The Chapel On The Hill**...Tony Bennett
28/75	**Full Of Fire**...Al Green
	Fun ..also see: Ffun
5/64	**Fun, Fun, Fun**...Beach Boys

POS/YR	RECORD TITLE/ARTIST
6/94	**Funkdafied**...Da Brat
8/67	**Funky Broadway**...Wilson Pickett
3/89	**Funky Cold Medina**...Tone Lōc
39/68	**Funky Judge**...Bull & The Matadors
F/95	**Funky Melody**...Stevie B
15/71	**Funky Nassau**...Beginning Of The End
14/68	**Funky Street**...Arthur Conley
29/73	**Funky Stuff**...Kool & The Gang
15/73	**Funky Worm**...Ohio Players
40/94	**Funky Y-2-C**...Puppies
	Funkytown
1/80	Lipps, Inc.
6/87	Pseudo Echo
25/61	**Funny**...Maxine Brown
5/73	**Funny Face**...Donna Fargo
	Funny How Time Slips Away
22/62	Jimmy Elledge
13/64	Joe Hinton
10/62	**Funny Way Of Laughin'**...Burl Ives
39/73	**Future Shock**...Curtis Mayfield
19/86	**Future's So Bright, I Gotta Wear Shades**...Timbuk 3

G

POS/YR	RECORD TITLE/ARTIST
4/64	**G.T.O.**...Ronny & The Daytonas
39/78	**Galaxy**...War
29/67	**Gallant Men**...Senator Everett McKinley Dirksen
4/69	**Galveston**...Glen Campbell
16/79	**Gambler, The**...Kenny Rogers
1/65	**Game Of Love**...Wayne Fontana & The Mindbenders
27/71	**Games**...Redeye
12/69	**Games People Play**...Joe South (also see: They Just Can't Stop It)
16/81	**Games People Play**...Alan Parsons Project
21/93	**Gangsta**...Bell Biv DeVoe
4/93	**Gangsta Lean**...D.R.S.
1/95	**Gangsta's Paradise**...Coolio Featuring L.V.
12/56	**Garden Of Eden**...Joe Valino
6/72	**Garden Party**...Rick Nelson
21/58	**Gee, But It's Lonely**...Pat Boone
19/56	**Gee Whittakers!**...Pat Boone
28/61	**Gee Whiz**...Innocents

POS/YR	RECORD TITLE/ARTIST
	Gee Whiz (Look At His Eyes)
10/61	Carla Thomas
31/80	Bernadette Peters
12/81	**Gemini Dream**...Moody Blues
33/81	**General Hospi-Tale**...Afternoon Delights
31/82	**Genius Of Love**...Tom Tom Club
	(also see: Fantasy)
31/91	**Gentle**...Dino
39/68	**Gentle On My Mind**...Glen Campbell
33/72	**George Jackson**...Bob Dylan
	Georgia On My Mind
1/60	Ray Charles
36/90	Michael Bolton
2/67	**Georgy Girl**...Seekers
37/72	**Geronimo's Cadillac**...Michael Murphey
	Get A Job
1/58	Silhouettes
21/58	Mills Brothers
14/91	**Get A Leg Up**...John Mellencamp
14/93	**Get Away**...Bobby Brown
12/76	**Getaway**...Earth, Wind & Fire
1/69	**Get Back**...Beatles with Billy Preston
6/76	**Get Closer**...Seals & Crofts (Feat. Carolyn Willis)
29/82	**Get Closer**...Linda Ronstadt
10/75	**Get Dancin'**...Disco-Tex & The Sex-O-Lettes
7/73	**Get Down**...Gilbert O'Sullivan
38/95	**Get Down**...Craig Mack
8/75	**Get Down, Get Down (Get On The Floor)**...Joe Simon
10/82	**Get Down On It**...Kool & The Gang
1/75	**Get Down Tonight**...K.C. & The Sunshine Band
5/91	**Get Here**...Oleta Adams
24/71	**Get It On**...Chase
	(also see: Bang A Gong)
21/79	**Get It Right Next Time**...Gerry Rafferty
28/73	**Get It Together**...Jackson 5
40/67	**Get It Together**...James Brown
27/67	**Get Me To The World On Time**...Electric Prunes
9/78	**Get Off**...Foxy
	(also see: Gett Off)
1/65	**Get Off Of My Cloud**...Rolling Stones
18/72	**Get On The Good Foot**...James Brown
11/67	**Get On Up**...Esquires
11/89	**Get On Your Feet**...Gloria Estefan
1/88	**Get Outta My Dreams, Get Into My Car**...Billy Ocean
31/94	**Get Over It**...Eagles

POS/YR	RECORD TITLE/ARTIST
	Get Ready
29/66	Temptations
4/70	Rare Earth
38/95	**Get Ready For This**...2 Unlimited
31/87	**Get That Love**...Thompson Twins
30/76	**Get The Funk Out Ma Face**...Brothers Johnson
	Get Together
31/65	We Five
5/69	Youngbloods
2/76	**Get Up And Boogie (That's Right)**...Silver Convention
	(Get up and dance!) ..see: Bite Your Lip
7/90	**Get Up! (Before The Night Is Over)**...Technotronic
34/71	**Get Up, Get Into It, Get Involved**...James Brown
	Get Up I Feel Like Being A Sex Machine ..see: Sex Machine
21/79	**Get Used To It**...Roger Voudouris
26/85	**Getcha Back**...Beach Boys
21/91	**Gett Off**...Prince & The N.P.G.
27/78	**Gettin' Ready For Love**...Diana Ross
18/67	**Gettin' Together**...Tommy James & The Shondells
38/90	**Getting Away With It**...Electronic
20/79	**Getting Closer**...Wings
7/94	**Getto Jam**...Domino
29/73	**Ghetto Child**...Spinners
	(Ghost) Riders In The Sky
30/61	Ramrods
31/81	Outlaws
22/56	**Ghost Town**...Don Cherry
33/88	**Ghost Town**...Cheap Trick
1/84	**Ghostbusters**...Ray Parker Jr.
37/83	**Gimme All Your Lovin**...ZZ Top
9/70	**Gimme Dat Ding**...Pipkins
12/69	**Gimme Gimme Good Lovin'**...Crazy Elephant
9/67	**Gimme Little Sign**...Brenton Wood
	Gimme Some Lovin'
7/67	Spencer Davis Group
18/80	Blues Brothers
8/94	**Gin & Juice**...Snoop Doggy Dogg
6/62	**Gina**...Johnny Mathis
9/58	**Ginger Bread**...Frankie Avalon
38/61	**Ginnie Bell**...Paul Dino
21/62	**Ginny Come Lately**...Brian Hyland
17/86	**Girl Can't Help It**...Journey
30/65	**Girl Come Running**...4 Seasons

POS/YR	RECORD TITLE/ARTIST
5/64	Girl From Ipanema...Stan Getz/Astrud Gilberto
39/67	Girl I Knew Somewhere...Monkees
27/90	Girl I Used To Know...Brother Beyond
1/89	Girl I'm Gonna Miss You...Milli Vanilli
19/93	Girl, I've Been Hurt...Snow
21/66	Girl In Love...Outsiders
35/84	Girl In Trouble (Is A Temporary Thing)...Romeo Void
2/83	Girl Is Mine...Michael Jackson/Paul McCartney
10/67	Girl Like You...Young Rascals
32/95	Girl Like You...Edwyn Collins
38/90	Girl Like You...Smithereens
19/61	Girl Of My Best Friend...Ral Donner
37/79	Girl Of My Dreams...Bram Tchaikovsky
28/66	Girl On A Swing...Gerry & The Pacemakers
5/68	Girl Watcher...O'Kaysions
26/64	Girl (Why You Wanna Make Me Blue)...Temptations
13/57	Girl With The Golden Braids...Perry Como
26/93	Girl U For Me...Silk
2/89	Girl You Know It's True...Milli Vanilli
10/67	Girl, You'll Be A Woman Soon...Neil Diamond
5/88	Girlfriend...Pebbles
16/84	Girls...Dwight Twilley
34/85	Girls Are More Fun...Ray Parker Jr.
34/80	Girls Can Get It...Dr. Hook
33/68	Girls Can't Do What The Guys Do...Betty Wright
12/87	Girls, Girls, Girls...Mötley Crüe
14/62	(Girls, Girls, Girls) Made To Love...Eddie Hodges
33/64	Girls Grow Up Faster Than Boys...Cookies
39/67	Girls In Love...Gary Lewis & The Playboys
2/84	Girls Just Want To Have Fun...Cyndi Lauper
6/90	Girls Nite Out...Tyler Collins
33/78	Girls' School...Wings
33/84	Girls With Guns...Tommy Shaw
8/69	Gitarzan...Ray Stevens
15/77	Give A Little Bit...Supertramp
18/65	Give Him A Great Big Kiss...Shangri-Las
21/72	Give Ireland Back To The Irish...Wings
18/80	Give It All You Got...Chuck Mangione
30/73	Give It To Me...J. Geils Band
40/81	Give It To Me Baby...Rick James
20/74	Give It To The People...Righteous Brothers

POS/YR	RECORD TITLE/ARTIST
26/95	Give It 2 You...Da Brat
18/84	Give It Up...KC
30/92	Give It Up...Wilson Phillips
33/94	Give It Up...Public Enemy
15/69	Give It Up Or Turnit A Loose...James Brown
15/93	Give It Up, Turn It Loose...En Vogue
38/76	Give It Up (Turn It Loose)...Tyrone Davis
40/75	Give It What You Got...B.T. Express
	Give Me ..also see: Gimme
3/70	Give Me Just A Little More Time...Chairmen Of The Board
1/73	Give Me Love - (Give Me Peace On Earth)...George Harrison
4/80	Give Me The Night...George Benson
31/73	Give Me Your Love...Barbara Mason
	Give More Power To The People ..see: (For God's Sake)
14/69	Give Peace A Chance...Plastic Ono Band
23/87	Give To Live...Sammy Hagar
30/56	Give Us This Day...Joni James
29/65	Give Us Your Blessings...Shangri-Las
29/92	Give U My Heart...Babyface (Featuring Toni Braxton)
34/73	Give Your Baby A Standing Ovation...Dells
	Giving Him Something He Can Feel ..see: Something He Can Feel
8/81	Giving It Up For Your Love...Delbert McClinton
38/64	Giving Up...Gladys Knight & The Pips
38/89	Giving Up On Love...Rick Astley
4/90	Giving You The Benefit...Pebbles
3/88	Giving You The Best That I Got...Anita Baker
6/64	Glad All Over...Dave Clark Five
19/55	Glad Rag Doll...Crazy Otto
26/67	Glad To Be Unhappy...Mamas & The Papas
7/84	Glamorous Life...Sheila E.
31/89	Glamour Boys...Living Colour
37/75	Glasshouse...Temptations
8/56	Glendora...Perry Como
2/82	Gloria...Laura Branigan
10/66	Gloria...Shadows Of Knight
25/77	Gloria...Enchantment
34/72	Glory Bound...Grass Roots
5/85	Glory Days...Bruce Springsteen
1/86	Glory Of Love...Peter Cetera
30/66	Go Ahead And Cry...Righteous Brothers
5/72	Go All The Way...Raspberries

POS/YR	RECORD TITLE/ARTIST
	Go Away Little Girl
1/63	Steve Lawrence
12/66	Happenings
1/71	Donny Osmond
36/70	**Go Back**...Crabby Appleton
32/71	**Go Down Gamblin'**...Blood, Sweat & Tears
10/86	**Go Home**...Stevie Wonder
23/84	**Go Insane**...Lindsey Buckingham
5/60	**Go, Jimmy, Go**...Jimmy Clanton
10/65	**Go Now!**...Moody Blues
	Go On With The Wedding
11/56	Patti Page
39/56	Kitty Kallen/Georgie Shaw
16/67	**Go Where You Wanna Go**...5th Dimension
10/77	**Go Your Own Way**...Fleetwood Mac
36/59	**God Bless America**...Connie Francis
18/61	**God, Country And My Baby**...Johnny Burnette
22/70	**God, Love And Rock & Roll**...Teegarden & Van Winkle
39/66	**God Only Knows**...Beach Boys
	Godfather ..see: Love Theme From The
17/82	**Goin' Down**...Greg Guidry
36/73	**Goin' Home**...Osmonds
	Goin' Out Of My Head
6/64	Little Anthony & The Imperials
7/68	Lettermen (medley)
16/57	**Goin' Steady**...Tommy Sands
31/88	**Going Back To Cali**...L.L. Cool J
35/64	**Going Going Gone**...Brook Benton
15/69	**Going In Circles**...Friends Of Distinction
	Going To A Go-Go
11/66	Miracles
25/82	Rolling Stones
11/69	**Going Up The Country**...Canned Heat
5/79	**Gold**...John Stewart
29/84	**Gold**...Spandau Ballet
10/76	**Golden Years**...David Bowie
8/65	**Goldfinger**...Shirley Bassey
33/86	**Goldmine**...Pointer Sisters
	Gone
4/57	Ferlin Husky
24/72	Joey Heatherton
23/75	**Gone At Last**...Paul Simon/Phoebe Snow
31/64	**Gone, Gone, Gone**...Everly Brothers
23/77	**Gone Too Far**...England Dan & John Ford Coley
	(Gong-Gong Song) ..see: I'm Blue
18/57	**Gonna Find Me A Bluebird**...Marvin Rainwater

POS/YR	RECORD TITLE/ARTIST
	Gonna Fly Now (Theme From 'Rocky')
1/77	Bill Conti
28/77	Maynard Ferguson
11/56	**Gonna Get Along Without Ya Now**...Patience & Prudence
29/67	**Gonna Give Her All The Love I've Got**...Jimmy Ruffin
1/91	**Gonna Make You Sweat (Everybody Dance Now)**...C & C Music Factory
36/69	**Goo Goo Barabajagal (Love Is Hot)**...Donovan/Jeff Beck Group
30/95	**Good**...Better Than Ezra
17/55	**Good And Lonesome**...Kay Starr
7/92	**Good Enough**...Bobby Brown
	Good Foot ..see: Get On The
8/92	**Good For Me**...Amy Grant
39/79	**Good Friend**...Mary MacGregor
11/79	**Good Girls Don't**...Knack
	Good Golly, Miss Molly
10/58	Little Richard
4/76	Mitch Ryder (medley)
25/76	**Good Hearted Woman**...Waylon & Willie
18/63	**Good Life**...Tony Bennett
1/66	**Good Lovin'**...Young Rascals
30/69	**Good Lovin' Ain't Easy To Come By**...Marvin Gaye & Tammi Terrell
36/75	**Good Lovin' Gone Bad**...Bad Company
1/62	**Good Luck Charm**...Elvis Presley
34/73	**Good Morning Heartache**...Diana Ross
3/69	**Good Morning Starshine**...Oliver
11/64	**Good News**...Sam Cooke
21/69	**Good Old Rock 'N Roll (medley)**...Cat Mother & the All Night News Boys
28/92	**Good Stuff**...B-52's
2/68	**Good, The Bad And The Ugly**...Hugo Montenegro
1/89	**Good Thing**...Fine Young Cannibals
4/67	**Good Thing**...Paul Revere & The Raiders
11/61	**Good Time Baby**...Bobby Rydell
9/72	**Good Time Charlie's Got The Blues**...Danny O'Keefe
1/79	**Good Times**...Chic
	(also see: Everything's Gonna Be Alright, & Rapper's Delight)
11/64	**Good Times**...Sam Cooke
3/60	**Good Timin'**...Jimmy Jones
40/79	**Good Timin'**...Beach Boys
	Good Vibrations
1/66	Beach Boys
34/76	Todd Rundgren

POS/YR	RECORD TITLE/ARTIST
1/91	**Good Vibrations**...Marky Mark & The Funky Bunch
13/69	**Goodbye**...Mary Hopkin
17/86	**Goodbye**...Night Ranger
8/59	**Goodbye Baby**...Jack Scott
33/64	**Goodbye Baby (Baby Goodbye)**...Solomon Burke
3/61	**Goodbye Cruel World**...James Darren
15/78	**Goodbye Girl**...David Gates
33/86	**Goodbye Is Forever**...Arcadia
11/59	**Goodbye Jimmy, Goodbye**...Kathy Linden
31/68	**Goodbye My Love**...James Brown
15/79	**Goodbye Stranger**...Supertramp
7/72	**Goodbye To Love**...Carpenters
2/73	**Goodbye Yellow Brick Road**...Elton John
21/65	**Goodnight**...Roy Orbison
	Goodnight My Love
32/57	McGuire Sisters
32/63	Fleetwoods
27/69	Paul Anka
5/79	**Goodnight Tonight**...Wings
20/57	**Goody Goody**...Frankie Lymon/Teenagers
37/68	**Goody Goody Gumdrops**...1910 Fruitgum Co.
12/83	**Goody Two Shoes**...Adam Ant
10/85	**Goonies 'R' Good Enough**...Cyndi Lauper
24/60	**Got A Girl**...Four Preps
10/84	**Got A Hold On Me**...Christine McVie
40/91	**Got A Love For You**...Jomanda
39/58	**Got A Match?**...Daddy-O's
20/94	**Got Me Waiting**...Heavy D & The Boyz
1/88	**Got My Mind Set On You**...George Harrison
12/79	**Got To Be Real**...Cheryl Lynn (also see: I'll Do 4 U)
4/71	**Got To Be There**...Michael Jackson
	Got To Get You Into My Life
7/76	Beatles
9/78	Earth, Wind & Fire
22/65	**Got To Get You Off My Mind**...Solomon Burke
1/77	**Got To Give It Up**...Marvin Gaye
21/70	**Gotta Hold On To This Feeling**...Jr. Walker & The All Stars
24/79	**Gotta Serve Somebody**...Bob Dylan
4/59	**Gotta Travel On**...Billy Grammer
	Graduation Day
16/56	Rover Boys
17/56	Four Freshmen

POS/YR	RECORD TITLE/ARTIST
34/61	**(Graduation Song...) Pomp And Circumstance**...Adrian Kimberly
39/59	**Graduation's Here**...Fleetwoods
17/63	**Grass Is Greener**...Brenda Lee
9/62	**Gravy (For My Mashed Potatoes)**...Dee Dee Sharp
	Grazing In The Grass
1/68	Hugh Masekela
3/69	Friends Of Distinction
1/78	**Grease**...Frankie Valli
20/66	**Great Airplane Strike**...Paul Revere & The Raiders
2/58	**Great Balls Of Fire**...Jerry Lee Lewis
	Great Imposter ..see: (He's) The
1/56	**Great Pretender**...Platters
	Greatest American Hero ..see: Theme From
34/62	**Greatest Hurt**...Jackie Wilson
	Greatest Love Of All
24/77	George Benson
1/86	Whitney Houston
	Green Berets ..see: Ballad Of
1/56	**Green Door**...Jim Lowe
3/70	**Green-Eyed Lady**...Sugarloaf
8/66	**Green Grass**...Gary Lewis & The Playboys
14/63	**Green, Green**...New Christy Minstrels
11/67	**Green, Green Grass Of Home**...Tom Jones
39/68	**Green Light**...American Breed
3/62	**Green Onions**...Booker T. & The MG's
2/69	**Green River**...Creedence Clearwater Revival
1/68	**Green Tambourine**...Lemon Pipers
21/63	**Greenback Dollar**...Kingston Trio
2/60	**Greenfields**...Brothers Four
4/90	**Groove Is In The Heart**...Deee-Lite
7/78	**Groove Line**...Heatwave
6/71	**Groove Me**...King Floyd
17/94	**Groove Thang**...Zhane'
	Groovin'
1/67	Young Rascals
21/67	Booker T. & The M.G.'s
30/69	**Groovy Grubworm**...Harlow Wilcox
	Groovy Kind Of Love
2/66	Mindbenders
1/88	Phil Collins
12/70	**Groovy Situation**...Gene Chandler
14/76	**Grow Some Funk Of Your Own**...Elton John
9/66	**Guantanamera**...Sandpipers
11/58	**Guess Things Happen That Way**...Johnny Cash

POS/YR	RECORD TITLE/ARTIST
31/59	**Guess Who**...Jesse Belvin
3/81	**Guilty**...Barbra Streisand & Barry Gibb
5/59	**Guitar Boogie Shuffle**...Virtues
11/72	**Guitar Man**...Bread
	(also see: Dance With The)
28/81	**Guitar Man**...Elvis Presley
10/55	**Gum Drop**...Crew-Cuts
12/82	**Gypsy**...Fleetwood Mac
24/63	**Gypsy Cried**...Lou Christie
8/73	**Gypsy Man**...War
	Gypsy Woman
20/61	Impressions
3/70	Brian Hyland
8/91	**Gypsy Woman (She's Homeless)**...Crystal Waters
1/71	**Gypsys, Tramps & Thieves**...Cher

H

POS/YR	RECORD TITLE/ARTIST
2/69	**Hair**...Cowsills
22/66	**Hair On My Chinny Chin Chin**...Sam The Sham & The Pharaohs
1/73	**Half-Breed**...Cher
12/63	**Half Heaven - Half Heartache**...Gene Pitney
15/79	**Half The Way**...Crystal Gayle
	Halfway To Paradise
39/61	Tony Orlando
23/68	Bobby Vinton
33/71	**Hallelujah**...Sweathog
28/73	**Hallelujah Day**...Jackson 5
	Hand Jive ..see: Willie And The Hand Jive
17/70	**Hand Me Down World**...Guess Who
19/83	**Hand To Hold On To**...John Cougar
2/88	**Hands To Heaven**...Breathe
	Handy Man
2/60	Jimmy Jones
22/64	Del Shannon
4/77	James Taylor
9/69	**Hang 'Em High**...Booker T. & The MG's
20/82	**Hang Fire**...Rolling Stones
23/91	**Hang In Long Enough**...Phil Collins
8/74	**Hang On In There Baby**...Johnny Bristol
	Hang On Sloopy
26/64	Vibrations (My Girl)
1/65	McCoys
11/65	Ramsey Lewis Trio
24/58	**Hang Up My Rock And Roll Shoes**...Chuck Willis

POS/YR	RECORD TITLE/ARTIST
	Hangin' On ..see: (You Keep Me)
1/89	**Hangin' Tough**...New Kids On The Block
35/86	**Hanging On A Heart Attack**...Device
38/59	**Hanging Tree**...Marty Robbins
1/66	**Hanky Panky**...Tommy James & The Shondells
10/90	**Hanky Panky**...Madonna
	Happening, The
1/67	Supremes
32/67	Herb Alpert
30/66	**Happenings Ten Years Time Ago**...Yardbirds
11/72	**Happiest Girl In The Whole U.S.A.**....Donna Fargo
30/79	**Happiness**...Pointer Sisters
35/74	**Happiness Is Just Around The Bend**...Main Ingredient
	Happiness Street
20/56	Georgia Gibbs
38/56	Tony Bennett
20/87	**Happy**...Surface
22/72	**Happy**...Rolling Stones
16/78	**Happy Anniversary**...Little River Band
30/61	**Happy Birthday Blues**...Kathy Young with The Innocents
6/62	**Happy Birthday, Sweet Sixteen**...Neil Sedaka
5/76	**Happy Days**...Pratt & McClain
10/60	**Happy-Go-Lucky-Me**...Paul Evans
5/57	**Happy, Happy Birthday Baby**...Tune Weavers
22/69	**Happy Heart**...Andy Williams
24/67	**Happy Jack**...Who
19/76	**Happy Music**...Blackbyrds
1/59	**Happy Organ**...Dave 'Baby' Cortez
40/75	**Happy People**...Temptations
34/59	**Happy Reindeer**...Dancer, Prancer & Nervous
25/68	**Happy Song (Dum-Dum)**...Otis Redding
27/66	**Happy Summer Days**...Ronnie Dove
1/67	**Happy Together**...Turtles
6/56	**Happy Whistler**...Don Robertson
8/60	**Harbor Lights**...Platters
	Hard Day's Night
1/64	Beatles
29/66	Ramsey Lewis Trio
3/84	**Hard Habit To Break**...Chicago
1/58	**Hard Headed Woman**...Elvis Presley
15/77	**Hard Luck Woman**...Kiss
30/77	**Hard Rock Cafe**...Carole King

POS/YR	RECORD TITLE/ARTIST
4/55	Hard To Get...Gisele MacKenzie
26/91	Hard To Handle...Black Crowes
7/81	Hard To Say...Dan Fogelberg
1/82	Hard To Say I'm Sorry...Chicago
3/82	Harden My Heart...Quarterflash
39/66	Harlem Nocturne...Viscounts
5/86	Harlem Shuffle...Rolling Stones
1/68	Harper Valley P.T.A....Jeannie C. Riley
31/73	Harry Hippie...Bobby Womack
17/63	Harry The Hairy Ape...Ray Stevens
13/75	Harry Truman...Chicago
30/93	Hat 2 Da Back...TLC
5/61	Hats Off To Larry...Del Shannon
11/64	Haunted House...Gene Simmons
	Hava Nagila ..see: Dance Everyone Dance
31/62	Have A Good Time...Sue Thompson
5/64	Have I The Right?...Honeycombs
5/93	Have I Told You Lately...Rod Stewart
29/57	Have I Told You Lately That I Love You?...Ricky Nelson
12/92	Have You Ever Needed Someone So Bad...Def Leppard
1/95	Have You Ever Really Loved A Woman?...Bryan Adams
8/71	Have You Ever Seen The Rain...Creedence Clearwater Revival
18/63	Have You Heard...Duprees
24/65	Have You Looked Into Your Heart...Jerry Vale
1/75	Have You Never Been Mellow...Olivia Newton-John
	Have You Seen Her
3/71	Chi-Lites
4/90	M.C. Hammer
	(Have You Seen My Wife Mr. Jones) ..see: New York Mining Disaster 1941
9/66	Have You Seen Your Mother, Baby, Standing In The Shadow?...Rolling Stones
14/74	Haven't Got Time For The Pain...Carly Simon
26/79	Haven't Stopped Dancing Yet...Gonzalez
	Having A Party
17/62	Sam Cooke
36/94	Rod Stewart (with Ronnie Wood)
	Having My Baby ..see: (You're)
4/69	Hawaii Five-O...Ventures
33/65	Hawaii Tattoo...Waikikis
11/59	Hawaiian Wedding Song (Ke Kali Nei Au)...Andy Williams

POS/YR	RECORD TITLE/ARTIST
9/92	Hazard...Richard Marx
	Hazy Shade Of Winter
13/66	Simon & Garfunkel
2/88	Bangles
	He
4/55	Al Hibbler
10/55	McGuire Sisters
18/66	Righteous Brothers
	He Ain't Heavy, He's My Brother
7/70	Hollies
20/70	Neil Diamond
F/76	Olivia Newton-John
33/81	He Can't Love You...Michael Stanley Band
	He Don't Love You (Like I Love You)
7/60	Jerry Butler
1/75	Tony Orlando & Dawn
34/62	He Knows I Love Him Too Much...Paris Sisters
	He Will Break Your Heart ..see: He Don't Love You
	He'll Have To Go (Stay)
2/60	Jim Reeves
4/60	Jeanne Black
25/86	He'll Never Love You (Like I Do)...Freddie Jackson
36/76	He's A Friend...Eddie Kendricks
30/81	He's A Liar...Bee Gees
1/62	He's A Rebel...Crystals
1/58	He's Got The Whole World (In His Hands)...Laurie London
7/95	He's Mine...MoKenStef
16/57	He's Mine...Platters
14/61	(He's My) Dreamboat...Connie Francis
1/63	He's So Fine...Chiffons
3/80	He's So Shy...Pointer Sisters
11/63	He's Sure The Boy I Love...Crystals
30/61	(He's) The Great Impostor...Fleetwoods
9/79	He's The Greatest Dancer...Sister Sledge
14/79	Head Games...Foreigner
3/85	Head Over Heels...Tears For Fears
11/84	Head Over Heels...Go-Go's
1/87	Head To Toe...Lisa Lisa & Cult Jam
35/80	Headed For A Fall...Firefall
19/89	Headed For A Heartbreak...Winger
27/93	Heal The World...Michael Jackson
13/89	Healing Hands...Elton John
14/77	Heard It In A Love Song...Marshall Tucker Band
	Heart
6/55	Eddie Fisher
13/55	Four Aces

POS/YR	RECORD TITLE/ARTIST
4/87	**Heart And Soul**...T'Pau
8/83	**Heart And Soul**...Huey Lewis & the News
	Heart And Soul
18/61	Cleftones
25/61	Jan & Dean
3/82	**Heart Attack**...Olivia Newton-John
9/65	**Heart Full Of Soul**...Yardbirds
21/80	**Heart Hotels**...Dan Fogelberg
15/62	**Heart In Hand**...Brenda Lee
24/81	**Heart Like A Wheel**...Steve Miller Band
32/90	**Heart Like A Wheel**...Human League
1/79	**Heart Of Glass**...Blondie
1/72	**Heart Of Gold**...Neil Young
35/88	**Heart Of Mine**...Boz Scaggs
6/84	**Heart Of Rock & Roll**...Huey Lewis & the News
12/90	**Heart Of Stone**...Taylor Dayne
19/65	**Heart Of Stone**...Rolling Stones
20/90	**Heart Of Stone**...Cher
21/90	**Heart Of The Matter**...Don Henley
20/79	**Heart Of The Night**...Poco
25/83	**Heart Of The Night**...Juice Newton
15/83	**Heart To Heart**...Kenny Loggins
1/79	**Heartache Tonight**...Eagles
7/61	**Heartaches**...Marcels
	Heartaches By The Number
1/59	Guy Mitchell
35/65	Johnny Tillotson
5/86	**Heartbeat**...Don Johnson
13/90	**Heartbeat**...Seduction
3/73	**Heartbeat - It's A Lovebeat**...DeFranco Family
26/87	**Heartbreak Beat**...Psychedelic Furs
1/56	**Heartbreak Hotel**...Elvis Presley
22/81	**Heartbreak Hotel**...Jacksons
38/60	**Heartbreak (It's Hurtin' Me)**...Little Willie John
39/74	**Heartbreak Kid**...Bo Donaldson & The Heywoods
10/83	**Heartbreaker**...Dionne Warwick **(also see: Doo Doo Doo Doo Doo)**
23/80	**Heartbreaker**...Pat Benatar
37/78	**Heartbreaker**...Dolly Parton
24/78	**Heartless**...Heart
5/82	**Heartlight**...Neil Diamond
8/81	**Hearts**...Marty Balin
28/92	**Hearts Don't Think (They Feel)!**...Natural Selection

POS/YR	RECORD TITLE/ARTIST
	Hearts Of Stone
1/55	Fontane Sisters
15/55	Charms
20/61	Bill Black's Combo
37/73	Blue Ridge Rangers
19/81	**Hearts On Fire**...Randy Meisner
26/87	**Hearts On Fire**...Bryan Adams
2/85	**Heat Is On**...Glenn Frey
4/82	**Heat Of The Moment**...Asia
19/91	**Heat Of The Moment**...After 7
6/87	**Heat Of The Night**...Bryan Adams
	Heat Wave
4/63	Martha & The Vandellas
5/75	Linda Ronstadt
29/69	**Heather Honey**...Tommy Roe
1/85	**Heaven**...Bryan Adams
2/89	**Heaven**...Warrant
39/69	**Heaven**...Rascals
5/89	**Heaven Help Me**...Deon Estus (with George Michael)
9/70	**Heaven Help Us All**...Stevie Wonder
12/86	**Heaven In Your Eyes**...Loverboy
1/87	**Heaven Is A Place On Earth**...Belinda Carlisle
4/79	**Heaven Knows**...Donna Summer
24/69	**Heaven Knows**...Grass Roots
15/76	**Heaven Must Be Missing An Angel**...Tavares
11/79	**Heaven Must Have Sent You**...Bonnie Pointer
39/56	**Heaven On Earth**...Platters
6/77	**Heaven On The 7th Floor**...Paul Nicholas
40/59	**Heavenly Lover**...Teresa Brewer
27/71	**Heavy Makes You Happy (Sha-Na-Boom Boom)**...Staple Singers
33/70	**Heed The Call**...Kenny Rogers & The First Edition
10/74	**Helen Wheels**...Paul McCartney
1/84	**Hello**...Lionel Richie
6/81	**Hello Again**...Neil Diamond
20/84	**Hello Again**...Cars
1/64	**Hello, Dolly!**...Louis Armstrong
1/67	**Hello Goodbye**...Beatles
26/63	**Hello Heartache, Goodbye Love**...Little Peggy March
26/67	**Hello Hello**...Sopwith "Camel"
35/73	**Hello Hurray**...Alice Cooper
1/68	**Hello, I Love You**...Doors
5/73	**Hello It's Me**...Todd Rundgren

POS/YR	RECORD TITLE/ARTIST
9/61	**Hello Mary Lou**...Ricky Nelson
2/63	**Hello Mudduh, Hello Fadduh! (A Letter From Camp)**...Allan Sherman
24/76	**Hello Old Friend**...Eric Clapton
	Hello Stranger
3/63	Barbara Lewis
15/77	Yvonne Elliman
12/61	**Hello Walls**...Faron Young
23/60	**Hello Young Lovers**...Paul Anka
1/65	**Help!**...Beatles
14/77	**Help Is On Its Way**...Little River Band
7/74	**Help Me**...Joni Mitchell
	Help Me Girl
29/66	Animals
37/66	Outsiders
	Help Me Make It Through The Night
8/71	Sammi Smith
33/72	Gladys Knight & The Pips
	Help Me, Rhonda
1/65	Beach Boys
22/75	Johnny Rivers
35/68	**Help Yourself**...Tom Jones
6/62	**Her Royal Majesty**...James Darren
11/81	**Her Town Too**...James Taylor & J.D. Souther
6/90	**Here And Now**...Luther Vandross
23/77	**Here Come Those Tears Again**...Jackson Browne
13/67	**Here Comes My Baby**...Tremeloes
14/59	**Here Comes Summer**...Jerry Keller
15/71	**Here Comes That Rainy Day Feeling Again**...Fortunes
1/94	**Here Comes The Hotstepper**...Ini Kamoze
8/68	**Here Comes The Judge**...Shorty Long
19/68	**Here Comes The Judge**...Pigmeat Markham
24/65	**Here Comes The Night**...Them
4/84	**Here Comes The Rain Again**...Eurythmics
16/71	**Here Comes The Sun**...Richie Havens
	Here I Am (Come And Take Me)
10/73	Al Green
7/91	UB40
5/81	**Here I Am (Just When I Thought I Was Over You)**...Air Supply
1/87	**Here I Go Again**...Whitesnake
37/69	**Here I Go Again**...Miracles
27/65	**Here It Comes Again**...Fortunes
6/90	**Here We Are**...Gloria Estefan
3/91	**Here We Go**...C + C Music Factory
11/93	**Here We Go Again!**...Portrait
15/67	**Here We Go Again**...Ray Charles
20/88	**Here With Me**...REO Speedwagon

POS/YR	RECORD TITLE/ARTIST
3/78	**Here You Come Again**...Dolly Parton
1/93	**Hero**...Mariah Carey
12/67	**Heroes And Villains**...Beach Boys
1/62	**Hey! Baby**...Bruce Channel
18/89	**Hey Baby**...Henry Lee Summer
12/67	**Hey Baby (They're Playing Our Song)**...Buckinghams
19/72	**Hey Big Brother**...Rare Earth
23/64	**Hey, Bobba Needle**...Chubby Checker
7/78	**Hey Deanie**...Shaun Cassidy
	Hey Donna
13/91	Rythm Syndicate
13/91	Rythm Syndicate
	Hey, Girl
10/63	Freddie Scott
35/68	Bobby Vee (medley)
9/72	Donny Osmond
35/73	**Hey Girl (I Like Your Style)**...Temptations
29/64	**Hey Harmonica Man**...Stevie Wonder
3/57	**Hey! Jealous Lover**...Frank Sinatra
25/93	**Hey Jealousy**...Gin Blossoms
32/64	**Hey Jean, Hey Dean**...Dean & Jean
31/66	**Hey Joe**...Leaves
	Hey Jude
1/68	Beatles
23/69	Wilson Pickett
36/89	**Hey Ladies**...Beastie Boys
35/70	**Hey Lawdy Mama**...Steppenwolf
31/67	**Hey, Leroy, Your Mama's Callin' You**...Jimmy Castor
20/62	**Hey, Let's Twist**...Joey Dee & The Starliters
4/64	**Hey Little Cobra**...Rip Chords
13/63	**Hey Little Girl**...Major Lance
20/59	**Hey Little Girl**...Dee Clark
29/57	**Hey! Little Girl**...Techniques
38/62	**Hey! Little Girl**...Del Shannon
3/95	**Hey Lover**...LL Cool J
12/55	**Hey, Mr. Banjo**...Sunnysiders
6/93	**Hey Mr. D.J.**....Zhane'
24/70	**Hey, Mister Sun**...Bobby Sherman
10/81	**Hey Nineteen**...Steely Dan
1/63	**Hey Paula**...Paul & Paula
	Hey There Lonely Girl (Boy)
27/63	Ruby & The Romantics
2/70	Eddie Holman
31/80	Robert John
F/71	**Hey Tonight**...Creedence Clearwater Revival
16/68	**Hey, Western Union Man**...Jerry Butler

POS/YR	RECORD TITLE/ARTIST
1/75	(Hey Won't You Play) Another Somebody Done Somebody Wrong Song...B.J. Thomas
21/75	Hey You...Bachman-Turner Overdrive
14/70	Hi-De-Ho...Blood, Sweat & Tears
	Hi-Heel Sneakers
11/64	Tommy Tucker
25/68	Jose Feliciano
10/73	Hi, Hi, Hi...Wings
33/62	Hide & Go Seek...Bunker Hill
29/61	Hide Away...Freddy King
21/58	Hideaway...Four Esquires
20/62	Hide 'Nor Hair...Ray Charles
3/91	High Enough...Damn Yankees
	High-Heel ..see: Hi-Heel
30/59	High Hopes...Frank Sinatra
8/85	High On You...Survivor
21/58	High School Confidential...Jerry Lee Lewis
17/77	High School Dance...Sylvers
F/57	High School Dance...Larry Williams
28/59	High School U.S.A....Tommy Facenda
37/58	High Sign...Diamonds
22/71	High Time We Went...Joe Cocker
	Higher & Higher ..see: (Your Love Keeps Lifting Me)
4/73	Higher Ground...Stevie Wonder
1/86	Higher Love...Steve Winwood
37/74	Higher Plane...Kool & The Gang
26/79	Highway Song...Blackfoot
14/75	Hijack...Herbie Mann
	Hill Street Blues ..see: Theme From
6/80	Him...Rupert Holmes
5/67	Him Or Me - What's It Gonna Be?...Paul Revere & The Raiders
31/68	Hip City...Jr. Walker & The All Stars
8/93	Hip Hop Hooray...Naughty By Nature
37/67	Hip Hug-Her...Booker T. & The M.G.'s
3/86	Hip To Be Square...Huey Lewis & the News
24/64	Hippy Hippy Shake...Swinging Blue Jeans
14/90	Hippychick...Soho
	His Latest Flame ..see: (Marie's the Name)
39/66	History Repeats Itself...Buddy Starcher
9/80	Hit Me With Your Best Shot...Pat Benatar
	(Hit Record) ..see: Overnight Sensation
	Hit The Road Jack
1/61	Ray Charles
40/76	Stampeders
30/63	Hitch Hike...Marvin Gaye
34/68	Hitch It To The Horse...Fantastic Johnny C

POS/YR	RECORD TITLE/ARTIST
	(Hitchhiker, The) ..see: Popeye
5/70	Hitchin' A Ride...Vanity Fare
9/73	Hocus Pocus...Focus
35/76	Hold Back The Night...Trammps
14/72	Hold Her Tight...Osmonds
4/82	Hold Me...Fleetwood Mac
3/84	Hold Me Now...Thompson Twins
8/65	Hold Me, Thrill Me, Kiss Me...Mel Carter
16/95	Hold Me, Thrill Me, Kiss Me, Kill Me...U2
5/68	Hold Me Tight...Johnny Nash
40/83	Hold Me 'Til The Mornin' Comes...Paul Anka
10/95	Hold My Hand...Hootie & The Blowfish
1/90	Hold On...Wilson Phillips
2/90	Hold On...En Vogue
15/82	Hold On...Santana
16/95	Hold On...Jamie Walters
18/79	Hold On...Ian Gomm
38/79	Hold On...Triumph
40/80	Hold On...Kansas
21/66	Hold On! I'm A Comin'...Sam & Dave
27/81	Hold On Loosely....38 Special
12/92	Hold On My Heart...Genesis
10/81	Hold On Tight...ELO
10/80	Hold On To My Love...Jimmy Ruffin
1/88	Hold On To The Nights...Richard Marx
5/79	Hold The Line...Toto
5/65	Hold What You've Got...Joe Tex
3/91	Hold You Tight...Tara Kemp
5/72	Hold Your Head Up...Argent
37/82	Holdin' On...Tane Cain
11/89	Holding On...Steve Winwood
17/75	Holdin' On To Yesterday...Ambrosia
1/86	Holding Back The Years...Simply Red
34/84	Holding Out For A Hero...Bonnie Tyler
4/91	Hole Hearted...Extreme
16/67	Holiday...Bee Gees
16/84	Holiday...Madonna
29/87	Holiday...Other Ones
6/69	Holly Holy...Neil Diamond
32/77	Hollywood...Rufus, Feat. Chaka Khan
12/78	Hollywood Nights...Bob Seger
6/74	Hollywood Swinging...Kool & The Gang
23/66	Holy Cow...Lee Dorsey
34/67	Homburg...Procol Harum
28/79	Home And Dry...Gerry Rafferty
25/65	Home Of The Brave...Jody Miller

POS/YR	RECORD TITLE/ARTIST
37/92	**Home Sweet Home '91**...Mötley Crüe
5/66	**Homeward Bound**...Simon & Garfunkel
28/60	**Honest I Do**...Innocents
32/57	**Honest I Do**...Jimmy Reed
23/88	**Honestly**...Stryper
24/79	**Honesty**...Billy Joel
1/68	**Honey**...Bobby Goldsboro
6/55	**Honey-Babe**...Art Mooney
11/67	**Honey Chile**...Martha & The Vandellas
19/70	**Honey Come Back**...Glen Campbell
27/74	**Honey, Honey**...Abba
39/92	**Honey Love**...R. Kelly & Public Announcement
F/57	**Honey Rock**...Ricky Nelson
1/57	**Honeycomb**...Jimmie Rodgers
19/87	**Honeythief, The**...Hipsway
8/72	**Honky Cat**...Elton John
2/56	**Honky Tonk (Parts 1 & 2)**...Bill Doggett
1/69	**Honky Tonk Women**...Rolling Stones
11/63	**Honolulu Lulu**...Jan & Dean
23/61	**Hoochi Coochi Coo**...Hank Ballard
23/96	**Hook**...Blues Traveler
17/64	**Hooka Tooka**...Chubby Checker
	Hooked On A Feeling
5/69	B.J. Thomas
1/74	Blue Swede
10/82	**Hooked On Classics**...Royal Philharmonic Orchestra
31/82	**Hooked On Swing (medley)**...Larry Elgart
23/89	**Hooked On You**...Sweet Sensation
6/66	**Hooray For Hazel**...Tommy Roe
38/63	**Hootenanny**...Glencoves
36/82	**Hope You Love Me Like You Say You Do**...Huey Lewis & the News
13/63	**Hopeless**...Andy Williams
28/93	**Hopelessly**...Rick Astley
3/78	**Hopelessly Devoted To You**...Olivia Newton-John
2/68	**Horse, The**...Cliff Nobles & Co.
1/72	**Horse With No Name**...America
3/78	**Hot Blooded**...Foreigner
1/78	**Hot Child In The City**...Nick Gilder
1/56	**Hot Diggity (Dog Ziggity Boom)**...Perry Como
2/69	**Hot Fun In The Summertime**...Sly & The Family Stone
11/83	**Hot Girls In Love**...Loverboy
23/82	**Hot In The City**...Billy Idol
28/78	**Hot Legs**...Rod Stewart

POS/YR	RECORD TITLE/ARTIST
5/77	**Hot Line**...Sylvers
31/78	**Hot Love, Cold World**...Bob Welch
21/79	**Hot Number**...Foxy
15/71	**Hot Pants**...James Brown
11/63	**Hot Pastrami**...Dartells
36/63	**Hot Pastrami With Mashed Potatoes**...Joey Dee
15/80	**Hot Rod Hearts**...Robbie Dupree
	Hot Rod Lincoln
26/60	Johnny Bond
33/60	Charlie Ryan
9/72	Commander Cody
14/69	**Hot Smoke & Sasafrass**...Bubble Puppy
1/79	**Hot Stuff**...Donna Summer
18/79	**Hot Summer Nights**...Night
1/77	**Hotel California**...Eagles
3/63	**Hotel Happiness**...Brook Benton
1/56	**Hound Dog**...Elvis Presley
9/59	**Hound Dog Man**...Fabian
15/87	**Hourglass**...Squeeze
9/55	**House Of Blue Lights**...Chuck Miller
37/95	**House Of Love**...Amy Grant with Vince Gill
28/90	**House Of Pain**...Faster Pussycat
	House Of The Rising Sun
1/64	Animals
7/70	Frijid Pink
6/68	**House That Jack Built**...Aretha Franklin
16/56	**House With Love In It**...Four Lads
37/91	**Housecall (Your Body Can't Lie To Me)**...Shabba Ranks (Feat. Maxi Priest)
21/65	**Houston**...Dean Martin
33/60	**How About That**...Dee Clark
38/92	**How About That**...Bad Company
	How Am I Supposed To Live Without You
12/83	Laura Branigan
1/90	Michael Bolton
22/58	**How Are Ya' Fixed For Love?**...Frank Sinatra & Keely Smith
12/81	**How 'Bout Us**...Champaign
	How Can I Be Sure
4/67	Young Rascals
25/72	David Cassidy
11/91	**How Can I Ease The Pain**...Lisa Fischer
3/88	**How Can I Fall?**...Breathe
22/73	**How Can I Tell Her**...Lobo
3/90	**How Can We Be Lovers**...Michael Bolton
1/71	**How Can You Mend A Broken Heart**...Bee Gees
1/77	**How Deep Is Your Love**...Bee Gees
10/80	**How Do I Make You**...Linda Ronstadt

POS/YR	RECORD TITLE/ARTIST
22/80	**How Do I Survive**...Amy Holland
27/67	**How Do You Catch A Girl**...Sam The Sham & The Pharaohs
8/72	**How Do You Do?**...Mouth & Macneal
9/64	**How Do You Do It?**...Gerry & The Pacemakers
1/92	**How Do You Talk To An Angel**...Heights
30/80	**How Does It Feel To Be Back**...Daryl Hall & John Oates
7/66	**How Does That Grab You, Darlin'?**...Nancy Sinatra
	How Glad I Am ..see: (You Don't Know)
13/95	**How High**...Redman/Method Man
	How Important Can It Be?
2/55	Joni James
12/55	Sarah Vaughan
F/55	Teresa Brewer
13/56	**(How Little It Matters) How Little We Know**...Frank Sinatra
3/75	**How Long**...Ace
20/75	**How Long (Betcha' Got A Chick On The Side)**...Pointer Sisters
27/83	**How Many Times Can We Say Goodbye**...Dionne Warwick & Luther Vandross
35/94	**How Many Ways**...Toni Braxton
3/78	**How Much I Feel**...Ambrosia
35/91	**How Much Is Enough**...Fixx
17/77	**How Much Love**...Leo Sayer
	How Sweet It Is (To Be Loved By You)
6/65	Marvin Gaye
18/66	Jr. Walker & The All Stars
5/75	James Taylor
11/58	**How The Time Flies**...Jerry Wallace
20/86	**(How To Be A) Millionaire**...ABC
25/91	**How To Dance**...Bingoboys/Princessa
1/86	**How Will I Know**...Whitney Houston
12/78	**How You Gonna See Me Now**...Alice Cooper
21/68	**How'd We Ever Get This Way**...Andy Kim
14/60	**Hucklebuck, The**...Chubby Checker
	Hula Hoop Song
32/58	Georgia Gibbs
38/58	Teresa Brewer
9/57	**Hula Love**...Buddy Knox
25/62	**Hully Gully Baby**...Dovells
1/86	**Human**...Human League
7/83	**Human Nature**...Michael Jackson **(also see: Right Here)**
16/92	**Human Touch**...Bruce Springsteen

POS/YR	RECORD TITLE/ARTIST
18/83	**Human Touch**...Rick Springfield
	Hummingbird
7/55	Les Paul & Mary Ford
17/55	Frankie Laine
20/73	**Hummingbird**...Seals & Crofts
3/92	**Humpin' Around**...Bobby Brown
11/90	**Humpty Dance**...Digital Underground
3/61	**Hundred Pounds Of Clay**...Gene McDaniels
6/66	**Hungry**...Paul Revere & The Raiders
4/88	**Hungry Eyes**...Eric Carmen
27/65	**Hungry For Love**...San Remo Golden Strings
5/80	**Hungry Heart**...Bruce Springsteen
3/83	**Hungry Like The Wolf**...Duran Duran
13/67	**Hunter Gets Captured By The Game**...Marvelettes
5/68	**Hurdy Gurdy Man**...Donovan
33/76	**Hurricane**...Bob Dylan
	Hurt
4/61	Timi Yuro
28/76	Elvis Presley
31/73	**Hurt, The**...Cat Stevens
	Hurt So Bad
10/65	Little Anthony & The Imperials
12/69	Lettermen
8/80	Linda Ronstadt
	Hurt Yourself ..see: (You're Gonna)
2/72	**Hurting Each Other**...Carpenters
2/82	**Hurts So Good**...John Cougar
24/73	**Hurts So Good**...Millie Jackson
26/66	**Husbands And Wives**...Roger Miller
4/68	**Hush**...Deep Purple
8/65	**Hush, Hush, Sweet Charlotte**...Patti Page
20/59	**Hushabye**...Mystics
1/75	**Hustle, The**...Van McCoy
33/86	**Hyperactive**...Robert Palmer
36/87	**Hypnotize Me**...Wang Chung
21/67	**Hypnotized**...Linda Jones
10/88	**Hysteria**...Def Leppard

I

POS/YR	RECORD TITLE/ARTIST
26/82	**I.G.Y. (What A Beautiful World)**...Donald Fagen
35/76	**I.O.U.**...Jimmy Dean
25/63	**I Adore Him**...Angels
1/91	**I Adore Mi Amor**...Color Me Badd
11/81	**I Ain't Gonna Stand For It**...Stevie Wonder

POS/YR	RECORD TITLE/ARTIST
	I Ain't Got Nobody ..see: **Just A Gigolo**
36/71	**I Ain't Got Time Anymore**...Glass Bottle
24/59	**I Ain't Never**...Webb Pierce
1/56	**I Almost Lost My Mind**...Pat Boone
3/66	**I Am A Rock**...Simon & Garfunkel
18/86	**I Am By Your Side**...Corey Hart
4/71	**I Am...I Said**...Neil Diamond
15/75	**I Am Love**...Jackson 5
39/70	**I Am Somebody**...Johnnie Taylor
1/72	**I Am Woman**...Helen Reddy
8/58	**I Beg Of You**...Elvis Presley
15/89	**I Beg Your Pardon**...Kon Kan **(also see: Rose Garden)**
8/95	**I Believe**...Blessid Union Of Souls
33/64	**I Believe**...Bachelors
33/82	**I Believe**...Chilliwack
22/72	**I Believe In Music**...Gallery
24/80	**I Believe In You**...Don Williams
11/73	**I Believe In You (You Believe In Me)**...Johnnie Taylor
15/75	**(I Believe) There's Nothing Stronger Than Our Love**...Paul Anka/Odia Coates
27/77	**I Believe You**...Dorothy Moore
27/75	**I Belong To You**...Love Unlimited
28/95	**I Belong To You**...Toni Braxton
	I Can Dance ..see: **Long Tall Glasses**
6/84	**I Can Dream About You**...Dan Hartman
24/69	**I Can Hear Music**...Beach Boys
1/74	**I Can Help**...Billy Swan
5/95	**I Can Love You Like That**...All-4-One
32/66	**I Can Make It With You**...Pozo-Seco Singers
6/65	**I Can Never Go Home Anymore**...Shangri-Las
	I Can See Clearly Now
1/72	Johnny Nash
18/94	Jimmy Cliff
9/67	**I Can See For Miles**...Who
	(I Can See It In Your Eyes) ..see: **Circle Is Small**
22/69	**I Can Sing A Rainbow (medley)**...Dells
39/81	**I Can Take Care Of Myself**...Billy & The Beaters
22/68	**I Can Take Or Leave Your Loving**...Herman's Hermits
35/73	**I Can Understand It**...New Birth
7/92	**I Can't Dance**...Genesis
26/84	**I Can't Drive 55**...Sammy Hagar
1/69	**I Can't Get Next To You**...Temptations

POS/YR	RECORD TITLE/ARTIST
	(I Can't Get No) Satisfaction
1/65	Rolling Stones
31/66	Otis Redding
1/82	**I Can't Go For That (No Can Do)**...Daryl Hall & John Oates
34/66	**I Can't Grow Peaches On A Cherry Tree**...Just Us
29/76	**I Can't Hear You No More**...Helen Reddy
12/80	**I Can't Help It**...Andy Gibb & Olivia Newton-John
24/62	**I Can't Help It (If I'm Still In Love With You)**...Johnny Tillotson
	I Can't Help Myself
1/65	Four Tops
22/72	Donnie Elbert
40/80	Bonnie Pointer
39/60	**(I Can't Help You) I'm Falling Too**...Skeeter Davis **(also see: Please Help Me, I'm Falling)**
13/84	**I Can't Hold Back**...Survivor
31/80	**I Can't Let Go**...Linda Ronstadt
22/56	**I Can't Love You Enough**...LaVern Baker
18/92	**I Can't Make You Love Me**...Bonnie Raitt
28/69	**I Can't See Myself Leaving You**...Aretha Franklin
10/81	**I Can't Stand It**...Eric Clapton
14/79	**I Can't Stand It No More**...Peter Frampton
28/68	**I Can't Stand Myself (When You Touch Me)**...James Brown
	I Can't Stand The Rain
38/73	Ann Peebles
18/78	Eruption
7/63	**I Can't Stay Mad At You**...Skeeter Davis
9/68	**I Can't Stop Dancing**...Archie Bell
1/62	**I Can't Stop Loving You**...Ray Charles
35/64	**I Can't Stop Talking About You**...Steve & Eydie
8/80	**I Can't Tell You Why**...Eagles
37/68	**I Can't Turn You Loose**...Chambers Brothers
3/86	**I Can't Wait**...Nu Shooz
16/86	**I Can't Wait**...Stevie Nicks
8/91	**I Can't Wait Another Minute**...Hi-Five
32/66	**I Chose To Sing The Blues**...Ray Charles
20/56	**I Could Have Danced All Night**...Sylvia Syms
13/68	**I Could Never Love Another (After Loving You)**...Temptations
18/81	**I Could Never Miss You (More Than I Do)**...Lulu
10/88	**I Could Never Take The Place Of Your Man**...Prince

POS/YR	RECORD TITLE/ARTIST
9/66	I Couldn't Live Without Your Love...Petula Clark
32/83	I Couldn't Say No...Robert Ellis Orrall with Carlene Carter
17/61	I Count The Tears...Drifters
6/59	I Cried A Tear...LaVern Baker
	I Didn't Get To Sleep At All ..see: (Last Night)
35/72	I Didn't Know I Loved You (Till I Saw You Rock And Roll)...Gary Glitter
2/86	I Didn't Mean To Turn You On...Robert Palmer
23/90	I Didn't Want To Need You...Heart
9/67	I Dig Rock And Roll Music...Peter, Paul & Mary
	I Do
37/65	Marvelows
24/83	J. Geils Band
15/76	I Do, I Do, I Do, I Do, I Do...Abba
	I Do It For You ..see: (Everything I Do)
	I Do Love You
26/65	Billy Stewart
20/79	GQ
37/60	(I Do The) Shimmy Shimmy...Bobby Freeman
29/84	I Do'wAnna Know...REO Speedwagon
23/86	I Do What I Do...(Theme for 9 1/2 Weeks)...John Taylor
20/87	I Do You...Jets
18/71	I Don't Blame You At All...Miracles
39/83	I Don't Care Anymore...Phil Collins
1/90	I Don't Have The Heart...James Ingram
23/91	I Don't Know Anybody Else...Black Box
	I Don't Know How To Love Him
13/71	Helen Reddy
28/71	Yvonne Elliman
23/79	I Don't Know If It's Right...Evelyn "Champagne" King
35/82	I Don't Know Where To Start...Eddie Rabbitt
12/61	I Don't Know Why...Linda Scott (also see: But I Do)
39/69	I Don't Know Why...Stevie Wonder
8/75	I Don't Like To Sleep Alone...Paul Anka
38/87	I Don't Mind At All...Bourgeois Tagg
3/81	I Don't Need You...Kenny Rogers
	I Don't Wanna ..also see: I Don't Want To
37/64	I Don't Wanna Be A Loser...Lesley Gore
1/91	I Don't Wanna Cry...Mariah Carey
9/93	I Don't Wanna Fight...Tina Turner

POS/YR	RECORD TITLE/ARTIST
2/88	I Don't Wanna Go On With You Like That...Elton John
3/88	I Don't Wanna Live Without Your Love...Chicago
35/65	I Don't Wanna Lose You Baby...Chad & Jeremy
20/69	I Don't Want Nobody To Give Me Nothing...James Brown
31/88	I Don't Want To Be A Hero...Johnny Hates Jazz
22/64	I Don't Want To Be Hurt Anymore...Nat King Cole
	I Don't Want To Be Right ..see: (If Loving You Is Wrong)
36/61	I Don't Want To Cry...Chuck Jackson
17/71	I Don't Want To Do Wrong...Gladys Knight & The Pips
5/88	I Don't Want To Live Without You...Foreigner
34/64	I Don't Want To See Tomorrow...Nat King Cole
16/64	I Don't Want To See You Again...Peter & Gordon
39/65	I Don't Want To Spoil The Party...Beatles
33/61	I Don't Want To Take A Chance...Mary Wells
36/80	I Don't Want To Walk Without You...Barry Manilow
4/88	I Don't Want Your Love...Duranduran
9/57	I Dreamed...Betty Johnson
20/61	I Dreamed Of A Hill-Billy Heaven...Tex Ritter
6/89	I Drove All Night...Cyndi Lauper
12/61	I Fall To Pieces...Patsy Cline
21/74	I Feel A Song (In My Heart)...Gladys Knight & The Pips
1/64	I Feel Fine...Beatles
3/84	I Feel For You...Chaka Khan
38/57	I Feel Good...Shirley & Lee
F/76	I Feel Like A Bullet (In The Gun Of Robert Ford)...Elton John
6/77	I Feel Love...Donna Summer
5/61	I Feel So Bad...Elvis Presley
	I Feel The Earth Move
F/71	Carole King
25/89	Martika
37/93	I Feel You...Depeche Mode
9/66	I Fought The Law...Bobby Fuller Four
30/65	I Found A Girl...Jan & Dean
32/67	I Found A Love...Wilson Pickett

POS/YR	RECORD TITLE/ARTIST
31/82	**I Found Somebody**...Glenn Frey
10/88	**I Found Someone**...Cher
F/70	**I Found That Girl**...Jacksons
1/64	**I Get Around**...Beach Boys
11/93	**I Get Around**...2 Pac
32/82	**I Get Excited**...Rick Springfield
37/75	**I Get Lifted**...George McCrae
34/68	**I Get The Sweetest Feeling**...Jackie Wilson
2/88	**I Get Weak**...Belinda Carlisle
7/78	**I Go Crazy**...Paul Davis
6/90	**I Go To Extremes**...Billy Joel
9/65	**I Go To Pieces**...Peter & Gordon
10/58	**I Got A Feeling**...Ricky Nelson
25/69	**I Got A Line On You**...Spirit
14/93	**I Got A Man**...Positive K
10/73	**I Got A Name**...Jim Croce
27/93	**I Got A Thang 4 Ya!**...Lo-Key?
24/59	**I Got A Wife**...Mark IV
20/62	**I Got A Woman**...Jimmy McGriff
27/73	**I Got Ants In My Pants**...James Brown
8/95	**I Got 5 On It**...Luniz
7/95	**I Got Id**...Pearl Jam
20/79	**I Got My Mind Made Up (You Can Get It Girl)**...Instant Funk
3/67	**I Got Rhythm**...Happenings
37/75	**I Got Stoned And I Missed It**...Jim Stafford
8/58	**I Got Stung**...Elvis Presley
6/68	**I Got The Feelin'**...James Brown
16/66	**I Got The Feelin' (Oh No No)**...Neil Diamond
28/63	**I Got What I Wanted**...Brook Benton
	I Got You Babe
1/65	Sonny & Cher
28/85	UB40 With Chrissie Hynde
3/65	**I Got You (I Feel Good)**...James Brown
2/72	**I Gotcha**...Joe Tex
35/64	**I Gotta Dance To Keep From Crying**...Miracles
20/60	**I Gotta Know**...Elvis Presley
4/84	**I Guess That's Why They Call It The Blues**...Elton John
34/69	**I Guess The Lord Must Be In New York City**...Nilsson
17/67	**I Had A Dream**...Paul Revere & The Raiders
11/67	**I Had Too Much To Dream (Last Night)**...Electric Prunes
8/88	**I Hate Myself For Loving You**...Joan Jett
12/95	**I Hate U**...Prince with The New Power Generation

POS/YR	RECORD TITLE/ARTIST
36/64	**I Have A Boyfriend**...Chiffons
4/93	**I Have Nothing**...Whitney Houston
1/65	**I Hear A Symphony**...Supremes
30/66	**I Hear Trumpets Blow**...Tokens
	I Hear You Knocking
2/55	Gale Storm
4/71	Dave Edmunds
4/87	**I Heard A Rumour**...Bananarama
	I Heard It Through The Grapevine
2/67	Gladys Knight & The Pips
1/68	Marvin Gaye
1/74	**I Honestly Love You**...Olivia Newton-John
1/84	**I Just Called To Say I Love You**...Stevie Wonder
9/70	**I Just Can't Help Believing**...B.J. Thomas
1/87	**I Just Can't Stop Loving You**...Michael Jackson
1/87	**(I Just) Died In Your Arms**...Cutting Crew
17/57	**I Just Don't Know**...Four Lads
26/66	**I Just Don't Know What To Do With Myself**...Dionne Warwick
17/61	**I Just Don't Understand**...Ann-Margret
12/79	**I Just Fall In Love Again**...Anne Murray
4/78	**I Just Wanna Stop**...Gino Vannelli
1/77	**I Just Want To Be Your Everything**...Andy Gibb
7/71	**I Just Want To Celebrate**...Rare Earth
33/77	**I Just Want To Make Love To You**...Foghat
4/82	**I Keep Forgettin' (Every Time You're Near)**...Michael McDonald **(also see: Regulate)**
	I Kissed You ..see: ('Til)
1/87	**I Knew You Were Waiting (For Me)**...Aretha Franklin & George Michael
	I Knew You When
14/65	Billy Joe Royal
F/72	Donny Osmond
37/83	Linda Ronstadt
4/95	**I Know**...Dionne Farris
19/79	**I Know A Heartache When I See One**...Jennifer Warnes
3/65	**I Know A Place**...Petula Clark
35/93	**(I Know I Got) Skillz**...Shaquille O'Neal
	(I Know) I'm Losing You
8/66	Temptations
7/70	Rare Earth
24/71	Rod Stewart With Faces
13/83	**I Know There's Something Going On**...Frida
9/87	**I Know What I Like**...Huey Lewis & the News

POS/YR	RECORD TITLE/ARTIST
3/62	I Know (You Don't Love Me No More)...Barbara George
30/88	I Know You're Out There Somewhere...Moody Blues
19/62	I Left My Heart In San Francisco...Tony Bennett
34/95	I Like...Kut Klose
3/77	I Like Dreamin'...Kenny Nolan
7/89	I Like It...Dino
17/64	I Like It...Gerry & The Pacemakers
31/83	I Like It...DeBarge
25/95	I Like It, I Love It...Tim McGraw
	I Like It Like That
2/61	Chris Kenner
7/65	Dave Clark Five
27/64	I Like It Like That...Miracles
25/67	I Like The Way...Tommy James & The Shondells
1/91	I Like The Way (The Kissing Game)...Hi-Five
37/77	I Like To Do It...KC & The Sunshine Band
28/74	I Like To Live The Love...B.B. King
8/57	I Like Your Kind Of Love...Andy Williams
38/71	I Likes To Do It...People's Choice
31/89	I Live By The Groove...Paul Carrack
13/88	I Live For Your Love...Natalie Cole
26/95	I Live My Life For You...Firehouse
12/74	I Love...Tom T. Hall
1/81	I Love A Rainy Night...Eddie Rabbitt
	I Love How You Love Me
5/61	Paris Sisters
9/68	Bobby Vinton
	I Love Lucy ..see: Disco Lucy
5/76	I Love Music...O'Jays
21/57	I Love My Baby (My Baby Loves Me)...Jill Corey
24/74	I Love My Friend...Charlie Rich
1/82	I Love Rock 'N Roll...Joan Jett
5/78	I Love The Nightlife (Disco 'Round)...Alicia Bridges
9/60	I Love The Way You Love...Marv Johnson
12/81	I Love You...Climax Blues Band
14/68	I Love You...People
22/62	I Love You...Volume's
37/78	I Love You...Donna Summer
3/63	I Love You Because...Al Martino
39/63	(I Love You) Don't You Forget It...Perry Como
30/66	I Love You Drops...Vic Dana

POS/YR	RECORD TITLE/ARTIST
21/71	I Love You For All Seasons...Fuzz
17/58	(I Love You) For Sentimental Reasons...Sam Cooke
40/60	I Love You In The Same Old Way...Paul Anka
28/55	I Love You Madly...Four Coins
9/64	I Love You More And More Every Day...Al Martino
31/66	I Love You 1000 Times...Platters
26/93	I Love You Period....Dan Baird
38/62	I Love You The Way You Are...Bobby Vinton
2/92	I Love Your Smile...Shanice
37/81	I Loved 'Em Every One...T.G. Sheppard
18/59	I Loves You, Porgy...Nina Simone
10/81	I Made It Through The Rain...Barry Manilow
18/67	I Make A Fool Of Myself...Frankie Valli
37/68	I Met Her In Church...Box Tops
5/85	I Miss You...Klymaxx
14/94	I Miss You...Aaron Hall
22/95	I Miss You...NIIU
	I Miss You So
34/57	Chris Connor
33/59	Paul Anka
34/65	Little Anthony & The Imperials
19/81	I Missed Again...Phil Collins
31/65	I Must Be Seeing Things...Gene Pitney
28/79	I Need A Lover...John Cougar
14/87	I Need Love...L.L. Cool J
22/66	I Need Somebody...? & The Mysterians
25/76	I Need To Be In Love...Carpenters
9/72	I Need You...America
37/82	I Need You...Paul Carrack
36/84	I Need You Tonight...Peter Wolf
4/59	I Need Your Love Tonight...Elvis Presley
37/81	I Need Your Lovin'...Teena Marie
20/62	I Need Your Loving...Don Gardner & Dee Dee Ford
12/77	I Never Cry...Alice Cooper
9/67	I Never Loved A Man (The Way I Love You)...Aretha Franklin
37/95	I Never Seen A Man Cry (aka I Seen A Man Die)...Scarface
	I Only Have Eyes For You
11/59	Flamingos
18/75	Art Garfunkel
22/56	I Only Know I Love You...Four Aces

POS/YR	RECORD TITLE/ARTIST
	I Only Want To Be With You
12/64	Dusty Springfield
12/76	Bay City Rollers
31/89	Samantha Fox
25/71	**I Play And Sing**...Dawn
19/80	**I Pledge My Love**...Peaches & Herb
9/82	**I Ran (So Far Away)**...Flock Of Seagulls
39/82	**I Really Don't Need No Light**...Jeffrey Osborne
	I Really Don't Want To Know
18/60	Tommy Edwards
22/66	Ronnie Dove
21/71	Elvis Presley
29/61	**I Really Love You**...Stereos
8/89	**I Remember Holding You**...Boys Club
5/62	**I Remember You**...Frank Ifield
6/90	**I Remember You**...Skid Row
36/64	**I Rise, I Fall**...Johnny Tillotson
5/66	**I Saw Her Again**...Mamas & The Papas
	I Saw Her (Him) Standing There
14/64	Beatles
7/88	Tiffany
14/63	**I Saw Linda Yesterday**...Dickey Lee
10/91	**I Saw Red**...Warrant
16/72	**I Saw The Light**...Todd Rundgren
	I Say A Little Prayer
4/67	Dionne Warwick
10/68	Aretha Franklin
4/67	**I Second That Emotion**...Miracles
26/66	**I See The Light**...Five Americans
38/74	**I Shall Sing**...Art Garfunkel
1/74	**I Shot The Sheriff**...Eric Clapton
28/88	**I Should Be So Lucky**...Kylie Minogue
15/62	**I Sold My Heart To The Junkman**...Blue-Belles
6/69	**I Started A Joke**...Bee Gees
13/88	**I Still Believe**...Brenda K. Starr
12/84	**I Still Can't Get Over Loving You**...Ray Parker Jr.
39/79	**I Still Have Dreams**...Richie Furay
1/87	**I Still Haven't Found What I'm Looking For**...U2
1/94	**I Swear**...All-4-One
12/67	**I Take It Back**...Sandy Posey
13/67	**I Thank The Lord For The Night Time**...Neil Diamond
	I Thank You
9/68	Sam & Dave
34/80	ZZ Top
1/70	**I Think I Love You**...Partridge Family

POS/YR	RECORD TITLE/ARTIST
16/86	**I Think It's Love**...Jermaine Jackson
	I Think We're Alone Now
4/67	Tommy James & The Shondells
1/87	Tiffany
4/91	**I Touch Myself**...Divinyls
23/69	**I Turned You On**...Isley Brothers
	I Understand (Just How You Feel)
9/61	G-Clefs
36/65	Freddie & The Dreamers
33/59	**I Waited Too Long**...LaVern Baker
17/56	**I Walk The Line**...Johnny Cash
F/57	**I Wanna**...Platters
12/86	**I Wanna Be A Cowboy**...Boys Don't Cry
14/63	**I Wanna Be Around**...Tony Bennett
6/94	**I Wanna Be Down**...Brandy
20/59	**I Wanna Be Loved**...Ricky Nelson
2/90	**I Wanna Be Rich**...Calloway
32/89	**I Wanna Be The One**...Stevie B
16/72	**I Wanna Be Where You Are**...Michael Jackson
16/73	**I Wanna Be With You**...Raspberries
11/80	**I Wanna Be Your Lover**...Prince
23/75	**I Wanna Dance Wit' Choo**...Disco-Tex & The Sex-O-Lettes
1/87	**I Wanna Dance With Somebody (Who Loves Me)**...Whitney Houston
10/77	**I Wanna Get Next To You**...Rose Royce
14/87	**I Wanna Go Back**...Eddie Money
8/89	**I Wanna Have Some Fun**...Samantha Fox
35/85	**I Wanna Hear It From Your Lips**...Eric Carmen
36/68	**I Wanna Live**...Glen Campbell
9/64	**I Wanna Love Him So Bad**...Jelly Beans
39/61	**(I Wanna) Love My Life Away**...Gene Pitney
16/92	**I Wanna Love You**...Jade
2/91	**I Wanna Sex You Up**...Color Me Badd
	(I Wanna) Testify
20/67	Parliaments
36/69	Johnnie Taylor
21/61	**I Wanna Thank You**...Bobby Rydell
6/84	**I Want A New Drug**...Huey Lewis & the News
11/65	**I Want Candy**...Strangeloves
5/88	**I Want Her**...Keith Sweat
	I Want To ..also see: I Wanna, & I Want'a
1/60	**I Want To Be Wanted**...Brenda Lee
3/88	**I Want To Be Your Man**...Roger
23/65	**I Want To (Do Everything For You)**...Joe Tex
36/66	**I Want To Go With You**...Eddy Arnold

POS/YR	RECORD TITLE/ARTIST
1/64	I Want To Hold Your Hand...Beatles
1/85	I Want To Know What Love Is...Foreigner
28/63	I Want To Stay Here...Steve & Eydie
	I Want To Take You Higher
34/70	Ike & Tina Turner
38/70	Sly & The Family Stone
8/59	I Want To Walk You Home...Fats Domino
	I Want You
15/76	Marvin Gaye
16/91	Robert Palmer (medley)
20/66	I Want You...Bob Dylan
40/90	I Want You...Shana
1/70	I Want You Back...Jackson 5
37/81	I Want You, I Need You...Chris Christian
1/56	I Want You, I Need You, I Love You...Elvis Presley
	I Want You To Be My Baby
14/55	Georgia Gibbs
18/55	Lillian Briggs
13/56	I Want You To Be My Girl...Frankie Lymon & The Teenagers
32/58	I Want You To Know...Fats Domino
7/79	I Want You To Want Me...Cheap Trick
19/79	I Want You Tonight...Pablo Cruise
7/79	I Want Your Love...Chic
2/87	I Want Your Sex...George Michael
15/75	I Want'a Do Something Freaky To You...Leon Haywood (also see: Nuthin' But A ìGî Thang)
29/73	I Was Checkin' Out She Was Checkin' In...Don Covay
20/67	I Was Kaiser Bill's Batman...Whistling Jack Smith
10/79	I Was Made For Dancin'...Leif Garrett
11/79	I Was Made For Lovin' You...Kiss
2/67	I Was Made To Love Her...Stevie Wonder
22/78	I Was Only Joking...Rod Stewart
24/62	I Was Such A Fool (To Fall In Love With You)...Connie Francis
19/56	I Was The One...Elvis Presley
19/66	(I Washed My Hands In) Muddy Water...Johnny Rivers
	I (Who Have Nothing)
29/63	Ben E. King
14/70	Tom Jones
40/79	Sylvester
10/65	I Will...Dean Martin
1/92	I Will Always Love You...Whitney Houston
22/68	I Will Always Think About You...New Colony Six

POS/YR	RECORD TITLE/ARTIST
27/92	I Will Be Here For You...Michael W. Smith
30/79	I Will Be In Love With You...Livingston Taylor
34/87	I Will Be There...Glass Tiger
1/63	I Will Follow Him...Little Peggy March
20/92	I Will Remember You...Amy Grant
29/78	I Will Still Love You...Stonebolt
1/79	I Will Survive...Gloria Gaynor
1/77	I Wish...Stevie Wonder
13/95	I Wish...Skee-Lo
20/88	I Wish I Had A Girl...Henry Lee Summer
32/63	I Wish I Were A Princess...Little Peggy March
4/68	I Wish It Would Rain...Temptations
3/90	I Wish It Would Rain Down...Phil Collins
16/62	I Wish That We Were Married...Ronnie & The Hi-Lites
28/92	I Wish The Phone Would Ring...Expose
28/64	I Wish You Love...Gloria Lynne
13/71	I Woke Up In Love This Morning...Partridge Family
12/89	I Won't Back Down...Tom Petty
13/87	I Won't Forget You...Poison
10/83	I Won't Hold You Back...Toto
11/74	I Won't Last A Day Without You...Carpenters
35/83	I Won't Stand In Your Way...Stray Cats
25/63	I Wonder...Brenda Lee
F/57	I Wonder If I Care As Much...Everly Brothers
34/85	I Wonder If I Take You Home...Lisa-Lisa & Cult Jam with Full Force
8/68	I Wonder What She's Doing Tonite...Tommy Boyce & Bobby Hart
21/63	I Wonder What She's Doing Tonight...Barry & The Tamerlanes
9/91	I Wonder Why...Curtis Stigers
22/58	I Wonder Why...Dion & The Belmonts
8/85	I Would Die 4 U...Prince
20/82	I Wouldn't Have Missed It For The World...Ronnie Milsap
22/56	I Wouldn't Know Where To Begin...Eddy Arnold
36/77	I Wouldn't Want To Be Like You...Alan Parsons
1/76	I Write The Songs...Barry Manilow
3/92	I'd Die Without You...PM Dawn
1/93	I'd Do Anything For Love (But I Won't Do That)...Meat Loaf

POS/YR	RECORD TITLE/ARTIST
28/94	**I'd Give Anything**...Gerald Levert
13/95	**I'd Lie For You (And That's The Truth)**...Meat Loaf
	I'd Like To Teach The World To Sing (In Perfect Harmony)
7/72	New Seekers
13/72	Hillside Singers
40/71	**I'd Love To Change The World**...Ten Years After
2/72	**I'd Love You To Want Me**...Lobo
38/80	**I'd Rather Leave While I'm In Love**...Rita Coolidge
2/76	**I'd Really Love To See You Tonight**...England Dan & John Ford Coley
18/87	**I'd Still Say Yes**...Klymaxx
15/69	**I'd Wait A Million Years**...Grass Roots
36/73	**I'll Always Love My Mama**...Intruders
3/88	**I'll Always Love You**...Taylor Dayne
35/65	**I'll Always Love You**...Spinners
14/87	**I'll Be Alright Without You**...Journey
	I'll Be Around
3/72	Spinners
39/95	Rappin' 4-Tay Featuring The Spinners
12/91	**I'll Be By Your Side**...Stevie B
8/65	**I'll Be Doggone**...Marvin Gaye
	I'll Be Good To You
3/76	Brothers Johnson
18/90	Quincy Jones Feat. Ray Charles & Chaka Khan
4/56	**I'll Be Home**...Pat Boone
33/64	**I'll Be In Trouble**...Temptations
1/89	**I'll Be Loving You (Forever)**...New Kids On The Block
11/86	**I'll Be Over You**...Toto
20/59	**I'll Be Satisfied**...Jackie Wilson
36/74	**I'll Be The Other Woman**...Soul Children
	I'll Be There
1/70	Jackson 5
1/92	Mariah Carey
8/91	**I'll Be There**...Escape Club
12/61	**I'll Be There**...Damita Jo **(also see: Stand By Me)**
14/65	**I'll Be There**...Gerry & The Pacemakers
1/89	**I'll Be There For You**...Bon Jovi
3/95	**I'll Be There For You (medley)**...Method Man feat. Mary J. Blige
17/95	**I'll Be There For You**...Rembrandts
31/59	**(I'll Be With You In) Apple Blossom Time**...Tab Hunter
1/90	**I'll Be Your Everything**...Tommy Page

POS/YR	RECORD TITLE/ARTIST
4/90	**I'll Be Your Shelter**...Taylor Dayne
40/73	**I'll Be Your Shelter (In Time Of Storm)**...Luther Ingram
18/58	**I'll Come Running Back To You**...Sam Cooke
25/64	**I'll Cry Instead**...Beatles
20/91	**I'll Do 4 U**...Father M.C.
40/75	**I'll Do For You Anything You Want Me To**...Barry White
21/92	**I'll Get By**...Eddie Money
7/91	**I'll Give All My Love To You**...Keith Sweat
9/74	**I'll Have To Say I Love You In A Song**...Jim Croce
34/65	**I'll Keep Holding On**...Marvelettes
30/64	**I'll Keep You Satisfied**...Billy J. Kramer With The Dakotas
21/65	**I'll Make All Your Dreams Come True**...Ronnie Dove
1/94	**I'll Make Love To You**...Boyz II Men
9/71	**I'll Meet You Halfway**...Partridge Family
14/62	**I'll Never Dance Again**...Bobby Rydell
6/69	**I'll Never Fall In Love Again**...Tom Jones
6/70	**I'll Never Fall In Love Again**...Dionne Warwick
4/65	**I'll Never Find Another You**...Seekers
8/93	**I'll Never Get Over You (Getting Over Me)**...Expose
23/91	**I'll Never Let You Go (Angel Eyes)**...Steelheart
5/79	**I'll Never Love This Way Again**...Dionne Warwick
24/57	**I'll Never Say "Never Again" Again**...Dinah Shore
25/61	**I'll Never Smile Again**...Platters
13/55	**I'll Never Stop Loving You**...Doris Day
18/75	**I'll Play For You**...Seals & Crofts
2/94	**I'll Remember**...Madonna **(also see: In The Still Of The Nite)**
23/57	**I'll Remember Today**...Patti Page
34/58	**I'll Remember Tonight**...Pat Boone
22/60	**I'll Save The Last Dance For You**...Damita Jo **(also see: Save The Last Dance For Me)**
20/90	**I'll See You In My Dreams**...Giant
32/62	**I'll See You In My Dreams**...Pat Boone
16/94	**I'll Stand By You**...Pretenders
33/87	**I'll Still Be Loving You**...Restless Heart
39/67	**I'll Take Care Of Your Cares**...Frankie Laine
30/66	**I'll Take Good Care Of You**...Garnet Mimms

POS/YR	RECORD TITLE/ARTIST
25/63	**I'll Take You Home**...Drifters
	I'll Take You There
1/72	Staple Singers
22/94	General Public
25/64	**I'll Touch A Star**...Terry Stafford
40/67	**I'll Try Anything**...Dusty Springfield
	I'll Try Something New
39/62	Miracles
25/69	Supremes & Temptations
9/83	**I'll Tumble 4 Ya**...Culture Club
13/84	**I'll Wait**...Van Halen
15/58	**I'll Wait For You**...Frankie Avalon
1/66	**I'm A Believer**...Monkees
38/69	**I'm A Better Man**...Engelbert Humperdinck
17/65	**I'm A Fool**...Dino, Desi & Billy
24/61	**I'm A Fool To Care**...Joe Barry
35/71	**I'm A Greedy Man**...James Brown
36/65	**I'm A Happy Man**...Jive Five
38/59	**I'm A Hog For You**...Coasters
10/67	**I'm A Man**...Spencer Davis Group
17/65	**I'm A Man**...Yardbirds
31/59	**I'm A Man**...Fabian
24/68	**I'm A Midnight Mover**...Wilson Pickett
20/66	**(I'm A) Road Runner**...Jr. Walker & The All Stars
25/61	**I'm A Telling You**...Jerry Butler
31/74	**I'm A Train**...Albert Hammond
12/75	**I'm A Woman**...Maria Muldaur
16/80	**I'm Alive**...Electric Light Orchestra
35/83	**I'm Alive**...Neil Diamond
34/80	**I'm Almost Ready**...Pure Prairie League
7/80	**I'm Alright**...Kenny Loggins
20/55	**(I'm Always Hearing) Wedding Bells**...Eddie Fisher
9/57	**I'm Available**...Margie Rayburn
19/62	**I'm Blue (The Gong-Gong Song)**...Ikettes
40/71	**I'm Comin' Home**...Tommy James
18/74	**I'm Coming Home**...Spinners
39/66	**I'm Comin' Home, Cindy**...Trini Lopez
19/61	**I'm Comin' On Back To You**...Jackie Wilson
5/80	**I'm Coming Out**...Diana Ross
19/64	**I'm Crying**...Animals
17/73	**I'm Doin' Fine Now**...New York City
17/76	**I'm Easy**...Keith Carradine
	I'm Every Woman
21/78	Chaka Khan
4/93	Whitney Houston
	I'm Falling Too ..see: (I Can't Help You)
27/93	**I'm Free**...Jon Secada

POS/YR	RECORD TITLE/ARTIST
37/69	**I'm Free**...Who
22/84	**I'm Free (Heaven Helps The Man)**...Kenny Loggins
	(I'm Gettin') ..also see: Nuttin' For Christmas
37/60	**I'm Gettin' Better**...Jim Reeves
9/85	**I'm Goin' Down**...Bruce Springsteen
22/95	**I'm Goin' Down**...Mary J. Blige
17/59	**I'm Gonna Be A Wheel Some Day**...Fats Domino
3/93	**I'm Gonna Be (500 Miles)**...Proclaimers
9/64	**I'm Gonna Be Strong**...Gene Pitney
18/63	**I'm Gonna' Be Warm This Winter**...Connie Francis
3/59	**I'm Gonna Get Married**...Lloyd Price
12/61	**I'm Gonna Knock On Your Door**...Eddie Hodges
40/76	**I'm Gonna Let My Heart Do The Walking**...Supremes
3/73	**I'm Gonna Love You Just A Little More Baby**...Barry White
	I'm Gonna Make You Love Me
26/68	Madeline Bell
2/69	Supremes & Temptations
10/69	**I'm Gonna Make You Mine**...Lou Christie
3/57	**I'm Gonna Sit Right Down And Write Myself A Letter**...Billy Williams
28/78	**I'm Gonna Take Care Of Everything**...Rubicon
13/85	**I'm Gonna Tear Your Playhouse Down**...Paul Young
27/80	**I'm Happy That Love Has Found You**...Jimmy Hall
1/65	**I'm Henry VIII, I Am**...Herman's Hermits
27/61	**I'm Hurtin'**...Roy Orbison
19/74	**I'm In Love**...Aretha Franklin
40/81	**I'm In Love**...Evelyn King
	I'm In Love Again
3/56	Fats Domino
38/56	Fontane Sisters
32/94	**I'm In The Mood**...Ce Ce Peniston
38/61	**I'm In The Mood For Love**...Chimes
2/77	**I'm In You**...Peter Frampton
	I'm Into Something Good
13/64	Herman's Hermits
38/64	Earl-Jean
12/73	**I'm Just A Singer (In A Rock And Roll Band)**...Moody Blues
33/61	**I'm Learning About Love**...Brenda Lee
36/71	**I'm Leavin'**...Elvis Presley

POS/YR	RECORD TITLE/ARTIST
	I'm Leaving It Up To You
1/63	Dale & Grace
4/74	Donny & Marie Osmond
10/69	**I'm Livin' In Shame**...Supremes
	I'm Losing You ..see: (I Know)
40/59	**I'm Movin' On**...Ray Charles
37/73	**I'm Never Gonna Be Alone Anymore**...Cornelius Brothers & Sister Rose
36/59	**I'm Never Gonna Tell**...Jimmie Rodgers
27/60	**I'm Not Afraid**...Ricky Nelson
14/78	**I'm Not Gonna Let It Bother Me Tonight**...Atlanta Rhythm Section
	I'm Not In Love
2/75	10cc
7/91	Will To Power
4/75	**I'm Not Lisa**...Jessi Colter
34/70	**I'm Not My Brothers Keeper**...Flaming Ember
32/86	**I'm Not The One**...Cars
20/67	**(I'm Not Your) Steppin' Stone**...Monkees
6/85	**I'm On Fire**...Bruce Springsteen
16/75	**I'm On Fire**...Dwight Twilley Band
26/75	**I'm On Fire**...5000 Volts
15/64	**I'm On The Outside (Looking In)**...Little Anthony & The Imperials
9/94	**I'm Ready**...Tevin Campbell
16/59	**I'm Ready**...Fats Domino
9/66	**I'm Ready For Love**...Martha & The Vandellas
	I'm So Excited
30/82	Pointer Sisters
9/84	Pointer Sisters
6/93	**I'm So Into You**...SWV
8/66	**I'm So Lonesome I Could Cry**...B.J. Thomas
14/64	**I'm So Proud**...Impressions
1/60	**I'm Sorry**...Brenda Lee
1/75	**I'm Sorry**...John Denver
11/57	**I'm Sorry**...Platters
36/58	**I'm Sorry I Made You Cry**...Connie Francis
14/57	**I'm Stickin' With You**...Jimmy Bowen
3/72	**I'm Still In Love With You**...Al Green
31/88	**I'm Still Searching**...Glass Tiger
12/83	**I'm Still Standing**...Elton John
10/72	**I'm Stone In Love With You**...Stylistics
1/65	**I'm Telling You Now**...Freddie & The Dreamers
15/89	**I'm That Type Of Guy**...L.L. Cool J
38/62	**(I'm The Girl On) Wolverton Mountain**...Jo Ann Campbell

POS/YR	RECORD TITLE/ARTIST
	I'm The One Who Loves You ..see: (Remember Me)
19/92	**I'm The One You Need**...Jody Watley **(also see: Come ëRound Here)**
8/95	**I'm The Only One**...Melissa Etheridge
1/92	**I'm Too Sexy**...R*S*F (Right Said Fred)
27/57	**I'm Waiting Just For You**...Pat Boone
	I'm Walkin'
4/57	Fats Domino
4/57	Ricky Nelson
12/67	**I'm Wondering**...Stevie Wonder
1/90	**I'm Your Baby Tonight**...Whitney Houston
1/77	**I'm Your Boogie Man**...KC & The Sunshine Band
3/86	**I'm Your Man**...Wham!
6/66	**I'm Your Puppet**...James & Bobby Purify
11/65	**I'm Yours**...Elvis Presley
33/59	**I've Been Around**...Fats Domino
35/69	**I've Been Hurt**...Bill Deal
9/87	**I've Been In Love Before**...Cutting Crew
27/72	**I've Been Lonely For So Long**...Frederick Knight
16/67	**I've Been Lonely Too Long**...Young Rascals
21/65	**I've Been Loving You Too Long (To Stop Now)**...Otis Redding
9/74	**(I've Been) Searchin' So Long**...Chicago
1/91	**I've Been Thinking About You**...Londonbeat
34/75	**I've Been This Way Before**...Neil Diamond
28/59	**I've Come Of Age**...Billy Storm
8/81	**I've Done Everything For You**...Rick Springfield
5/71	**I've Found Someone Of My Own**...Free Movement
29/76	**I've Got A Feeling (We'll Be Seeing Each Other Again)**...Al Wilson
26/92	**I've Got A Lot To Learn About Love**...Storm
18/83	**I've Got A Rock N' Roll Heart**...Eric Clapton
39/74	**I've Got A Thing About You Baby**...Elvis Presley
25/65	**I've Got A Tiger By The Tail**...Buck Owens
18/62	**(I've Got) Bonnie**...Bobby Rydell
5/77	**I've Got Love On My Mind**...Natalie Cole
33/64	**I've Got Sand In My Shoes**...Drifters
32/73	**I've Got So Much To Give**...Barry White
12/74	**I've Got The Music In Me**...Kiki Dee Band
	I've Got To ..also see: I've Gotta
38/66	**I've Got To Be Somebody**...Billy Joe Royal

POS/YR	RECORD TITLE/ARTIST
4/74	I've Got To Use My Imagination...Gladys Knight & The Pips
9/66	I've Got You Under My Skin...4 Seasons
11/69	I've Gotta Be Me...Sammy Davis, Jr.
8/68	I've Gotta Get A Message To You...Bee Gees
25/78	I've Had Enough...Wings
6/59	I've Had It...Bell Notes
1/87	(I've Had) The Time Of My Life...Bill Medley & Jennifer Warnes
32/70	I've Lost You...Elvis Presley
4/80	I've Loved You For A Long Time (medley)...Spinners
3/82	I've Never Been To Me...Charlene
40/68	I've Never Found A Girl (To Love Me Like You Do)...Eddie Floyd
17/67	I've Passed This Way Before...Jimmy Ruffin
3/61	I've Told Every Little Star...Linda Scott
37/95	Ice Cream...Chef Raekwon feat. Tony Starks & Method Man
1/90	Ice Ice Baby...Vanilla Ice
9/91	Iesha...Another Bad Creation
4/71	If...Bread
4/93	If...Janet Jackson
32/62	If A Man Answers...Bobby Darin
35/62	If A Woman Answers (Hang Up The Phone)...Leroy Van Dyke
14/83	If Anyone Falls...Stevie Nicks
7/58	If Dreams Came True...Pat Boone
24/78	If Ever I See You Again...Roberta Flack
10/84	If Ever You're In My Arms Again...Peabo Bryson
12/69	If I Can Dream...Elvis Presley
1/78	If I Can't Have You...Yvonne Elliman
10/68	If I Could Build My Whole World Around You...Marvin Gaye & Tammi Terrell
10/72	If I Could Reach You...5th Dimension
3/89	If I Could Turn Back Time...Cher
	If I Didn't Care
22/59	Connie Francis
30/61	Platters
2/92	If I Ever Fall In Love...Shai
17/93	If I Ever Lose My Faith In You...Sting
39/75	If I Ever Lose This Heaven...AWB
34/59	If I Give My Heart To You...Kitty Kallen
31/60	If I Had A Girl...Rod Lauren
	If I Had A Hammer
10/62	Peter, Paul & Mary
3/63	Trini Lopez
36/82	If I Had My Wish Tonight...David Lasley

POS/YR	RECORD TITLE/ARTIST
7/93	If I Had No Loot...Tony Toni Tone
23/65	If I Loved You...Chad & Jeremy
8/55	If I May...Nat "King" Cole/Four Knights
34/65	If I Ruled The World...Tony Bennett
39/79	If I Said You Have A Beautiful Body Would You Hold It Against Me...Bellamy Brothers
16/95	If I Wanted To...Melissa Etheridge
	If I Were A Carpenter
8/66	Bobby Darin
20/68	Four Tops
36/70	Johnny Cash & June Carter
9/71	If I Were Your Woman...Gladys Knight & The Pips
19/84	If I'd Been The One...38 Special
7/88	If It Isn't Love...New Edition
	(If Loving You Is Wrong) I Don't Want To Be Right
3/72	Luther Ingram
31/79	Barbara Mandrell
23/63	If My Pillow Could Talk...Connie Francis
25/71	If Not For You...Olivia Newton-John
29/86	If She Knew What She Wants...Bangles
17/87	If She Would Have Been Faithful......Chicago
28/82	If The Love Fits Wear It...Leslie Pearl
35/91	(If There Was) Any Other Way...Celine Dion
	If There's A Hell Below ..see: (Don't Worry)
6/84	If This Is It...Huey Lewis & the News
28/73	If We Make It Through December...Merle Haggard
1/90	If Wishes Came True...Sweet Sensation
4/92	If You Asked Me To...Celine Dion
11/68	If You Can Want...Miracles
5/71	If You Could Read My Mind...Gordon Lightfoot
33/59	(If You Cry) True Love, True Love...Drifters
	If You Don't Know Me By Now
3/72	Harold Melvin & The Bluenotes
1/89	Simply Red
12/55	If You Don't Want My Love...Jaye P. Morgan
10/94	If You Go...Jon Secada
16/92	If You Go Away...NKOTB
22/62	If You Gotta Make A Fool Of Somebody...James Ray
11/76	If You Know What I Mean...Neil Diamond
4/86	If You Leave...Orchestral Manoeuvres In The Dark

POS/YR	RECORD TITLE/ARTIST
1/76	**If You Leave Me Now**...Chicago
38/72	**If You Leave Me Tonight I'll Cry**...Jerry Wallace
8/70	**(If You Let Me Make Love To You Then) Why Can't I Touch You?**...Ronnie Dyson
8/95	**If You Love Me**...Brownstone
5/74	**If You Love Me (Let Me Know)**...Olivia Newton-John
3/85	**If You Love Somebody Set Them Free**...Sting
37/63	**If You Need Me**...Solomon Burke
16/91	**If You Needed Somebody**...Bad Company
8/71	**If You Really Love Me**...Stevie Wonder
17/79	**If You Remember Me**...Chris Thompson & Night
38/80	**If You Should Sail**...Nielsen/Pearson
17/74	**If You Talk In Your Sleep**...Elvis Presley
17/95	**If You Think You're Lonely Now**...K-Ci Hailey
1/63	**If You Wanna Be Happy**...Jimmy Soul
25/74	**If You Wanna Get To Heaven**...Ozark Mountain Daredevils
37/79	**If You Want It**...Niteflyte
12/73	**If You Want Me To Stay**...Sly & The Family Stone
24/90	**If U Were Mine**...U-Krew
9/73	**If You're Ready (Come Go With Me)**...Staple Singers
	Iko Iko
20/65	Dixie Cups
14/89	Belle Stars
6/60	**Image Of A Girl**...Safaris
7/78	**Imaginary Lover**...Atlanta Rhythm Section
3/71	**Imagine**...John Lennon
22/75	**Immigrant, The**...Neil Sedaka
16/71	**Immigrant Song**...Led Zeppelin
36/72	**Immigration Man**...Graham Nash & David Crosby
35/66	**Impossible Dream**...Jack Jones
4/90	**Impulsive**...Wilson Phillips
17/83	**In A Big Country**...Big Country
30/68	**In-A-Gadda-Da-Vida**...Iron Butterfly
31/69	**In A Moment**...Intrigues
27/56	**In A Shanty In Old Shanty Town**...Somethin' Smith & The Redheads
11/80	**In America**...Charlie Daniels Band
9/67	**In And Out Of Love**...Supremes
	'In' Crowd
5/65	Ramsey Lewis Trio
13/65	Dobie Gray

POS/YR	RECORD TITLE/ARTIST
7/63	**In Dreams**...Roy Orbison
19/87	**In My Dreams**...REO Speedwagon
34/92	**In My Dreams**...Party
37/89	**In My Eyes**...Stevie B
7/85	**In My House**...Mary Jane Girls
10/60	**In My Little Corner Of The World**...Anita Bryant
23/63	**In My Room**...Beach Boys
38/85	**In Neon**...Elton John
19/81	**In The Air Tonight**...Phil Collins
	In The Chapel In The Moonlight ..see: Chapel
6/92	**In The Closet**...Michael Jackson
35/81	**In The Dark**...Billy Squier
3/69	**In The Ghetto**...Elvis Presley
33/67	**In The Heat Of The Night**...Ray Charles
14/95	**In The House Of Stone And Light**...Martin Page
27/61	**In The Middle Of A Heartache**...Wanda Jackson
	In The Middle Of An Island
9/57	Tony Bennett
23/57	Tennessee Ernie Ford
	In The Middle Of The House
11/56	Vaughn Monroe
20/56	Rusty Draper
	In The Midnight Hour
21/65	Wilson Pickett
30/73	Cross Country
19/64	**In The Misty Moonlight**...Jerry Wallace
	In The Mood
4/59	Ernie Fields
40/77	Henhouse Five Plus Too **(also see: Swing The Mood)**
39/84	**In The Mood**...Robert Plant
	In The Name Of Love ..see: (What)
3/79	**In The Navy**...Village People
5/72	**In The Rain**...Dramatics
38/60	**In The Still Of The Night**...Dion & The Belmonts
	In The Still Of The Nite
24/56	Five Satins
3/93	Boyz II Men
	In The Summertime
3/70	Mungo Jerry
F/95	Shaggy (featuring Rayvon)
1/69	**In The Year 2525 (Exordium & Terminus)**...Zager & Evans
27/93	**In These Arms**...Bon Jovi
3/87	**In Too Deep**...Genesis
26/86	**In Your Eyes**...Peter Gabriel

POS/YR	RECORD TITLE/ARTIST
20/81	**In Your Letter**...REO Speedwagon
5/89	**In Your Room**...Bangles
38/88	**In Your Soul**...Corey Hart
1/67	**Incense And Peppermints**...Strawberry Alarm Clock
33/67	**Indescribably Blue**...Elvis Presley
35/88	**Indestructible**...Four Tops
5/69	**Indian Giver**...1910 Fruitgum Co.
10/68	**Indian Lake**...Cowsills
15/94	**Indian Outlaw**...Tim McGraw
	Indian Reservation
20/68	Don Fardon
1/71	Raiders
5/70	**Indiana Wants Me**...R. Dean Taylor
6/84	**Infatuation**...Rod Stewart
1/93	**Informer**...Snow
	Innamorata
27/56	Dean Martin
30/56	Jerry Vale
9/71	**Inner City Blues (Make Me Wanna Holler)**...Marvin Gaye
10/84	**Innocent Man**...Billy Joel
19/93	**Insane In The Brain**...Cypress Hill
32/76	**Inseparable**...Natalie Cole
34/66	**Inside-Looking Out**...Animals
3/70	**Instant Karma**...John Ono Lennon
29/79	**Instant Replay**...Dan Hartman
	Into The Night
11/80	Benny Mardones
20/89	Benny Mardones
10/85	**Invincible**...Pat Benatar
31/85	**Invisible**...Alison Moyet
40/83	**Invisible Hands**...Kim Carnes
1/86	**Invisible Touch**...Genesis
15/62	**Irresistible You**...Bobby Darin
	Irving ..see: Ballad Of
35/60	**Is A Blue Bird Blue**...Conway Twitty
32/92	**Is It Good To You**...Heavy D. & The Boyz
8/86	**Is It Love**...Mr. Mister
34/69	**Is It Something You've Got**...Tyrone Davis
17/64	**Is It True**...Brenda Lee
15/81	**Is It You**...Lee Ritenour
21/79	**Is She Really Going Out With Him?**...Joe Jackson
11/69	**Is That All There Is**...Peggy Lee
31/60	**Is There Any Chance**...Marty Robbins
4/83	**Is There Something I Should Know**...Duran Duran
2/87	**Is This Love**...Whitesnake

POS/YR	RECORD TITLE/ARTIST
9/87	**Is This Love**...Survivor
1/75	**Island Girl**...Elton John
30/57	**Island In The Sun**...Harry Belafonte
37/82	**Island Of Lost Souls**...Blondie
1/83	**Islands In The Stream**...Kenny Rogers with Dolly Parton
F/70	**Isn't It A Pity**...George Harrison
13/77	**Isn't It Time**...Babys
29/72	**Isn't Life Strange**...Moody Blues
9/69	**Israelites**...Desmond Dekker & The Aces
17/84	**It Ain't Enough**...Corey Hart
8/65	**It Ain't Me Babe**...Turtles
2/91	**It Ain't Over 'Til It's Over**...Lenny Kravitz
13/59	**It Doesn't Matter Anymore**...Buddy Holly
4/71	**It Don't Come Easy**...Ringo Starr
10/70	**It Don't Matter To Me**...Bread
21/91	**It Hit Me Like A Hammer**...Huey Lewis & The News
29/64	**It Hurts Me**...Elvis Presley
7/64	**It Hurts To Be In Love**...Gene Pitney
13/56	**It Isn't Right**...Platters
23/61	**It Keeps Rainin'**...Fats Domino
3/62	**It Keeps Right On A-Hurtin'**...Johnny Tillotson
37/77	**It Keeps You Runnin'**...Doobie Brothers
11/55	**It May Sound Silly**...McGuire Sisters
22/62	**It Might As Well Rain Until September**...Carole King
25/83	**It Might Be You**...Stephen Bishop
3/67	**It Must Be Him**...Vikki Carr
32/79	**It Must Be Love**...Alton McClain & Destiny
33/83	**It Must Be Love**...Madness
1/90	**It Must Have Been Love**...Roxette
5/72	**It Never Rains In Southern California**...Albert Hammond
34/91	**It Never Rains (In Southern California)**...Tony! Toni! Tone!
38/60	**It Only Happened Yesterday**...Jack Scott
11/56	**It Only Hurts For A Little While**...Ames Brothers
10/75	**It Only Takes A Minute**...Tavares
40/68	**It Should Have Been Me**...Gladys Knight & The Pips
29/62	**It Started All Over Again**...Brenda Lee
27/73	**It Sure Took A Long, Long Time**...Lobo
14/67	**It Takes Two**...Marvin Gaye & Kim Weston
36/88	**It Takes Two**...Rob Base & D.J. E-Z Rock
20/66	**It Tears Me Up**...Percy Sledge
15/93	**It Was A Good Day**...Ice Cube

POS/YR	RECORD TITLE/ARTIST
28/66	**It Was A Very Good Year**...Frank Sinatra
16/77	**It Was Almost Like A Song**...Ronnie Milsap
11/59	**It Was I**...Skip & Flip
10/88	**It Would Take A Strong Strong Man**...Rick Astley
37/77	**It's A Crazy World**...Mac McAnally
3/78	**It's A Heartache**...Bonnie Tyler
20/78	**It's A Laugh**...Daryl Hall & John Oates
28/76	**It's A Long Way There**...Little River Band
28/81	**It's A Love Thing**...Whispers
8/66	**It's A Man's Man's Man's World**...James Brown
12/75	**It's A Miracle**...Barry Manilow
13/84	**It's A Miracle**...Culture Club
6/83	**It's A Mistake**...Men At Work
32/70	**It's A New Day**...James Brown
14/70	**It's A Shame**...Spinners
26/91	**It's A Shame (My Sister)**...Monie Love
9/87	**It's A Sin**...Pet Shop Boys
7/55	**It's A Sin To Tell A Lie**...Somethin' Smith & The Redheads
31/75	**It's All Down To Goodnight Vienna**...Ringo Starr
	It's All In The Game
1/58	Tommy Edwards
25/64	Cliff Richard
24/70	Four Tops
26/64	**It's All Over Now**...Rolling Stones
4/63	**It's All Right**...Impressions
	It's Almost Tomorrow
20/55	David Carroll
20/55	Snooky Lanson
7/56	Dream Weavers
14/56	Jo Stafford
31/65	**It's Alright**...Adam Faith With The Roulettes
20/58	**(It's Been A Long Time) Pretty Baby**...Gino & Gina
4/77	**It's Ecstasy When You Lay Down Next To Me**...Barry White
30/69	**It's Getting Better**...Mama Cass
12/72	**It's Going To Take Some Time**...Carpenters
34/93	**It's Gonna Be A Lovely Day**...S.O.U.L. S.Y.S.T.E.M. **(also see: Lovely Day)**
23/65	**It's Gonna Be Alright**...Gerry & The Pacemakers
10/82	**It's Gonna Take A Miracle**...Deniece Williams
14/61	**It's Gonna Work Out Fine**...Ike & Tina Turner

POS/YR	RECORD TITLE/ARTIST
18/65	**It's Growing**...Temptations
10/71	**It's Impossible**...Perry Como
	(It's In His Kiss) ..see: Shoop Shoop Song
38/83	**It's Inevitable**...Charlie
3/59	**It's Just A Matter Of Time**...Brook Benton
3/89	**(It's Just) The Way That You Love Me**...Paula Abdul
9/59	**It's Late**...Ricky Nelson
23/66	**It's My Life**...Animals
31/84	**It's My Life**...Talk Talk
1/63	**It's My Party**...Lesley Gore
9/81	**It's My Turn**...Diana Ross
7/89	**It's No Crime**...Babyface
37/89	**It's No Secret**...Kylie Minogue
12/89	**It's Not Enough**...Starship
5/57	**It's Not For Me To Say**...Johnny Mathis
9/87	**It's Not Over ('Til It's Over)**...Starship
10/65	**It's Not Unusual**...Tom Jones
	It's Now Or Never
1/60	Elvis Presley
14/81	John Schneider
23/67	**It's Now Winters Day**...Tommy Roe
29/76	**It's O.K.**...Beach Boys
20/72	**It's One Of Those Nights (Yes Love)**...Partridge Family
15/86	**It's Only Love**...Bryan Adams/Tina Turner
31/66	**It's Only Love**...Tommy James & The Shondells
	It's Only Make Believe
1/58	Conway Twitty
10/70	Glen Campbell
16/74	**It's Only Rock 'N Roll (But I Like It)**...Rolling Stones
9/64	**It's Over**...Roy Orbison
37/66	**It's Over**...Jimmie Rodgers
38/76	**It's Over**...Boz Scaggs
11/82	**It's Raining Again**...Supertramp
21/77	**It's Sad To Belong**...England Dan & John Ford Coley
5/77	**It's So Easy**...Linda Ronstadt
2/91	**It's So Hard To Say Goodbye To Yesterday**...Boyz II Men
1/80	**It's Still Rock And Roll To Me**...Billy Joel
	It's The Same Old Song
5/65	Four Tops
35/78	KC & The Sunshine Band
4/59	**It's Time To Cry**...Paul Anka
1/71	**It's Too Late**...Carole King
23/66	**It's Too Late**...Bobby Goldsboro

POS/YR	RECORD TITLE/ARTIST
4/58	**It's Too Soon To Know**...Pat Boone
6/63	**It's Up To You**...Rick Nelson
20/68	**It's Wonderful**...Young Rascals
6/57	**It's You I Love**...Fats Domino
33/78	**It's You That I Need**...Enchantment
2/69	**It's Your Thing**...Isley Brothers
25/56	**Italian Theme**...Cyril Stapleton
25/58	**Itchy Twitchy Feeling**...Bobby Hendricks
16/68	**Itchycoo Park**...Small Faces
1/60	**Itsy Bitsy Teenie Weenie Yellow Polkadot Bikini**...Brian Hyland
	Ivory Tower
2/56	Cathy Carr
6/56	Gale Storm
11/56	Charms
18/57	**Ivy Rose**...Perry Como

J

POS/YR	RECORD TITLE/ARTIST
1/82	**Jack & Diane**...John Cougar
8/78	**Jack And Jill**...Raydio
3/75	**Jackie Blue**...Ozark Mountain Daredevils
14/67	**Jackson**...Nancy Sinatra & Lee Hazlewood
1/87	**Jacob's Ladder**...Huey Lewis & the News
1/57	**Jailhouse Rock**...Elvis Presley
26/92	**Jam**...Michael Jackson
29/62	**Jam, The**...Bobby Gregg
32/87	**Jam Tonight**...Freddie Jackson
8/70	**Jam Up Jelly Tight**...Tommy Roe
14/57	**Jamaica Farewell**...Harry Belafonte
	Jambalaya (On The Bayou)
30/62	Fats Domino
16/73	Blue Ridge Rangers
17/62	**James (Hold The Ladder Steady)**...Sue Thompson
14/85	**Jamie**...Ray Parker Jr.
30/62	**Jamie**...Eddie Holland
18/87	**Jammin' Me**...Tom Petty
14/80	**Jane**...Jefferson Starship
4/90	**Janie's Got A Gun**...Aerosmith
4/64	**Java**...Al Hirt
	Jaws ..see: Theme From & Mr. Jaws
	Jayne ..see: Ballad of
2/74	**Jazzman**...Carole King
20/69	**Jealous Kind Of Fella**...Garland Green
	Jealous Lover ..see: Theme From The Apartment

POS/YR	RECORD TITLE/ARTIST
19/60	**Jealous Of You**...Connie Francis
2/69	**Jean**...Oliver
17/77	**Jeans On**...David Dundas
8/58	**Jennie Lee**...Jan & Arnie
40/68	**Jennifer Eccles**...Hollies
26/68	**Jennifer Juniper**...Donovan
36/70	**Jennifer Tomkins**...Street People
	Jenny ..see: 867-5309
10/57	**Jenny, Jenny**...Little Richard
10/66	**Jenny Take A Ride!**...Mitch Ryder & The Detroit Wheels
2/83	**Jeopardy**...Greg Kihn Band
35/61	**Jeremiah Peabody's Poly Unsaturated Pills**...Ray Stevens
7/65	**Jerk, The**...Larks
9/90	**Jerk-Out**...Time
11/80	**Jesse**...Carly Simon
30/73	**Jesse**...Roberta Flack
26/94	**Jessie**...Joshua Kadison
1/81	**Jessie's Girl**...Rick Springfield
	Jesus Christ Superstar ..see: Superstar
23/92	**Jesus He Knows Me**...Genesis
28/69	**Jesus Is A Soul Man**...Lawrence Reynolds
35/73	**Jesus Is Just Alright**...Doobie Brothers
7/74	**Jet**...Paul McCartney
8/77	**Jet Airliner**...Steve Miller Band
	Jim Dandy
17/57	LaVern Baker
25/74	Black Oak Arkansas
28/87	**Jimmy Lee**...Aretha Franklin
33/73	**Jimmy Loves Mary-Anne**...Looking Glass
10/67	**Jimmy Mack**...Martha & The Vandellas
25/61	**Jimmy's Girl**...Johnny Tillotson
	Jingle Bell Rock
6/57	Bobby Helms
35/58	Bobby Helms
36/60	Bobby Helms
21/61	Bobby Rydell/Chubby Checker
10/70	**Jingle Jangle**...Archies
1/75	**Jive Talkin'**...Bee Gees
19/58	**Jo-Ann**...Playmates
17/80	**JoJo**...Boz Scaggs
2/84	**Joanna**...Kool & The Gang
21/70	**Joanne**...Michael Nesmith
28/71	**Jody's Got Your Girl And Gone**...Johnnie Taylor
19/90	**Joey**...Concrete Blonde
	John And Yoko ..see: Ballad Of
1/62	**Johnny Angel**...Shelley Fabares

POS/YR	RECORD TITLE/ARTIST
8/58	**Johnny B. Goode**...Chuck Berry
7/62	**Johnny Get Angry**...Joanie Sommers
21/62	**Johnny Jingo**...Hayley Mills
21/62	**Johnny Loves Me**...Shelley Fabares
35/62	**Johnny Will**...Pat Boone
17/72	**Join Together**...Who
1/74	**Joker, The**...Steve Miller Band
	Joker (That's What They Call Me)
22/57	Hilltoppers
25/57	Billy Myles
20/66	**Joker Went Wild**...Brian Hyland
4/65	**Jolly Green Giant**...Kingsmen
39/81	**Jones Vs. Jones**...Kool & The Gang
18/60	**Josephine**...Bill Black's Combo
26/78	**Josie**...Steely Dan
16/68	**Journey To The Center Of The Mind**...Amboy Dukes
6/72	**Joy**...Apollo 100 featuring Tom Parker
30/74	**Joy**...Isaac Hayes
1/71	**Joy To The World**...Three Dog Night
1/91	**Joyride**...Roxette
26/65	**Ju Ju Hand**...Sam The Sham & the Pharaohs
22/58	**Judy**...Frankie Vaughan
	Judy Blue Eyes ..see: Suite
1/68	**Judy In Disguise (With Glasses)**...John Fred
33/75	**Judy Mae**...Boomer Castleman
5/63	**Judy's Turn To Cry**...Lesley Gore
27/94	**Juicy**...Notorious B.I.G.
10/56	**Juke Box Baby**...Perry Como
26/82	**Juke Box Hero**...Foreigner
5/70	**Julie, Do Ya Love Me**...Bobby Sherman
1/84	**Jump**...Van Halen
1/92	**Jump**...Kris Kross
3/92	**Jump Around**...House Of Pain
3/84	**Jump (For My Love)**...Pointer Sisters
27/72	**Jump Into The Fire**...Nilsson
28/60	**Jump Over**...Freddy Cannon
13/87	**Jump Start**...Natalie Cole
24/82	**Jump To It**...Aretha Franklin
	Jumpin' Jack Flash
3/68	Rolling Stones
21/86	Aretha Franklin
21/57	**June Night**...Jimmy Dorsey
4/74	**Jungle Boogie**...Kool & The Gang (also see: Ain't 2 Proud 2 Beg, & Erotica)
8/72	**Jungle Fever**...Chakachas
20/85	**Jungle Love**...Time
23/77	**Jungle Love**...Steve Miller Band

POS/YR	RECORD TITLE/ARTIST
3/75	**Junior's Farm**...Paul McCartney
9/76	**Junk Food Junkie**...Larry Groce
37/61	**Jura (I Swear I Love You)**...Les Paul & Mary Ford
4/58	**Just A Dream**...Jimmy Clanton
9/90	**Just A Friend**...Biz Markie
12/85	**Just A Gigolo/I Ain't Got Nobody**...David Lee Roth
8/65	**Just A Little**...Beau Brummels
40/60	**Just A Little**...Brenda Lee
39/65	**Just A Little Bit**...Roy Head
7/65	**Just A Little Bit Better**...Herman's Hermits
23/75	**Just A Little Bit Of You**...Michael Jackson
9/59	**Just A Little Too Much**...Ricky Nelson
7/77	**Just A Song Before I Go**...Crosby, Stills & Nash
5/92	**Just Another Day**...Jon Secada
9/91	**Just Another Dream**...Cathy Dennis
12/85	**Just Another Night**...Mick Jagger
19/85	**Just As I Am**...Air Supply
	Just As Much As Ever
32/59	Bob Beckham
24/68	Bobby Vinton
7/59	**Just Ask Your Heart**...Frankie Avalon
19/64	**Just Be True**...Gene Chandler
14/89	**Just Because**...Anita Baker
29/57	**Just Because**...Lloyd Price
6/90	**Just Between You And Me**...Lou Gramm
8/57	**Just Between You And Me**...Chordettes
21/81	**Just Between You And Me**...April Wine
12/57	**Just Born (To Be Your Baby)**...Perry Como
38/82	**Just Can't Win 'Em All**...Stevie Woods
35/60	**Just Come Home**...Hugo & Luigi
10/74	**Just Don't Want To Be Lonely**...Main Ingredient
5/68	**Just Dropped In (To See What Condition My Condition Was In)**...First Edition
20/61	**Just For Old Time's Sake**...McGuire Sisters
26/92	**Just For Tonight**...Vanessa Williams
36/83	**Just Got Lucky**...JoBoxers
10/88	**Just Got Paid**...Johnny Kemp
18/59	**Just Keep It Up**...Dee Clark
2/93	**Just Kickin' It**...Xscape
33/66	**Just Like A Woman**...Bob Dylan
40/88	**Just Like Heaven**...Cure
8/89	**Just Like Jesse James**...Cher
11/66	**Just Like Me**...Paul Revere & The Raiders
6/88	**Just Like Paradise**...David Lee Roth
6/64	**(Just Like) Romeo & Juliet**...Reflections

POS/YR	RECORD TITLE/ARTIST
1/80	**(Just Like) Starting Over**...John Lennon
25/91	**Just Like You**...Robbie Nevil
26/58	**Just Married**...Marty Robbins
1/71	**Just My Imagination**...Temptations
17/81	**Just Once**...Quincy Jones Feat. James Ingram
9/65	**Just Once In My Life**...Righteous Brothers
10/63	**Just One Look**...Doris Troy
29/60	**Just One Time**...Don Gibson
24/61	**Just Out Of Reach (Of My Two Open Arms)**...Solomon Burke
11/77	**Just Remember I Love You**...Firefall
40/71	**Just Seven Numbers (Can Straighten Out My Life)**...Four Tops
39/81	**Just So Lonely**...Get Wet
16/92	**Just Take My Heart**...Mr. Big
2/81	**Just The Two Of Us**...Grover Washington, Jr. (with Bill Withers)
14/91	**Just The Way It Is, Baby**...Rembrandts
3/78	**Just The Way You Are**...Billy Joel
7/76	**Just To Be Close To You**...Commodores
26/57	**Just To Hold My Hand**...Clyde McPhatter
8/87	**Just To See Her**...Smokey Robinson
30/75	**Just Too Many People**...Melissa Manchester
2/56	**Just Walking In The Rain**...Johnnie Ray
34/91	**Just Want To Hold You**...Jasmine Guy
27/78	**Just What I Needed**...Cars
4/79	**Just When I Needed You Most**...Randy Vanwarmer
20/65	**Just You**...Sonny & Cher
27/76	**Just You And I**...Melissa Manchester
4/73	**Just You 'N' Me**...Chicago
11/92	**Justified & Ancient**...KLF (Feat. Tammy Wynette)
1/91	**Justify My Love**...Madonna

K

39/71	**K-Jee**...Nite-Liters
	Ka-Ding Dong
24/56	G-Clefs
35/56	Diamonds
38/56	Hilltoppers
	Kansas City
1/59	Wilbert Harrison
23/64	Trini Lopez
31/65	**Kansas City Star**...Roger Miller
1/84	**Karma Chameleon**...Culture Club
16/58	**Kathy-O**...Diamonds

POS/YR	RECORD TITLE/ARTIST
16/69	**Keem-O-Sabe**...Electric Indian
8/57	**Keep A Knockin'**...Little Richard
12/91	**Keep Coming Back**...Richard Marx
8/83	**(Keep Feeling) Fascination**...Human League
17/92	**Keep It Comin'**...Keith Sweat
2/77	**Keep It Comin' Love**...KC & The Sunshine Band
8/90	**Keep It Together**...Madonna
37/77	**Keep Me Cryin'**...Al Green
4/65	**Keep On Dancing**...Gentrys
24/68	**Keep On Lovin' Me Honey**...Marvin Gaye & Tammi Terrell
1/81	**Keep On Loving You**...REO Speedwagon
11/89	**Keep On Movin'**...Soul II Soul
10/64	**Keep On Pushing**...Impressions
15/74	**Keep On Singing**...Helen Reddy
10/74	**Keep On Smilin'**...Wet Willie
1/73	**Keep On Truckin'**...Eddie Kendricks
15/92	**Keep On Walkin'**...Ce Ce Peniston
9/65	**Keep Searchin'**...Del Shannon
14/67	**Keep The Ball Rollin'**...Jay & The Techniques
29/92	**Keep The Faith**...Bon Jovi
36/80	**Keep The Fire**...Kenny Loggins
7/82	**Keep The Fire Burnin'**...REO Speedwagon
10/95	**Keep Their Heads Ringin'**...Dr. Dre
12/94	**Keep Ya Head Up**...2 Pac
	Keep Your Eye On The Sparrow ..see: Baretta's Theme
12/62	**Keep Your Hands Off My Baby**...Little Eva
2/87	**Keep Your Hands To Yourself**...Georgia Satellites
10/73	**Keeper Of The Castle**...Four Tops
18/85	**Keeping The Faith**...Billy Joel
20/55	**Kentuckian Song**...Hilltoppers
16/70	**Kentucky Rain**...Elvis Presley
	Kentucky Woman
22/67	Neil Diamond
38/68	Deep Purple
6/58	**Kewpie Doll**...Perry Como
8/82	**Key Largo**...Bertie Higgins
4/66	**Kicks**...Paul Revere & The Raiders
27/90	**Kickstart My Heart**...Mötley Crüe
33/84	**Kid's American**...Matthew Wilder
7/60	**Kiddio**...Brook Benton
25/82	**Kids In America**...Kim Wilde
16/63	**Killer Joe**...Rocky Fellers
12/75	**Killer Queen**...Queen
28/81	**Killin' Time**...Fred Knoblock & Susan Anton

POS/YR	RECORD TITLE/ARTIST
1/73	**Killing Me Softly With His Song**...Roberta Flack
30/77	**Killing Of Georgie**...Rod Stewart
1/67	**Kind Of A Drag**...Buckinghams
17/63	**Kind Of Boy You Can't Forget**...Raindrops
8/86	**King For A Day**...Thompson Twins
40/72	**King Heroin**...James Brown
13/77	**King Is Gone**...Ronnie McDowell
3/83	**King Of Pain**...Police
36/80	**King Of The Hill**...Rick Pinette & Oak
4/65	**King Of The Road**...Roger Miller **(also see: Queen Of The House)**
30/62	**King Of The Whole Wide World**...Elvis Presley
8/90	**King Of Wishful Thinking**...Go West
17/78	**King Tut**...Steve Martin
31/74	**Kings Of The Party**...Brownsville Station
	Kiss
1/86	Prince
31/89	Art Of Noise/Tom Jones **(also see: How To Dance, & Two To Make It Right)**
21/72	**Kiss An Angel Good Mornin'**...Charley Pride
1/76	**Kiss And Say Goodbye**...Manhattans
31/88	**Kiss And Tell**...Bryan Ferry
25/65	**Kiss Away**...Ronnie Dove
1/95	**Kiss From A Rose**...Seal
	Kiss Him Goodbye ..see: Na Na Hey Hey
37/79	**Kiss In The Dark**...Pink Lady
30/56	**Kiss Me Another**...Georgia Gibbs
12/88	**Kiss Me Deadly**...Lita Ford
15/68	**Kiss Me Goodbye**...Petula Clark
37/80	**Kiss Me In The Rain**...Barbra Streisand
34/64	**Kiss Me Quick**...Elvis Presley
29/64	**Kiss Me Sailor**...Diane Renay
1/81	**Kiss On My List**...Daryl Hall & John Oates
25/83	**Kiss The Bride**...Elton John
23/91	**Kiss Them For Me**...Siouxsie & The Banshees
35/90	**Kiss This Thing Goodbye**...Del Amitri
1/78	**Kiss You All Over**...Exile
40/92	**Kiss You Back**...Digital Underground
8/89	**Kisses On The Wind**...Neneh Cherry
3/57	**Kisses Sweeter Than Wine**...Jimmie Rodgers
12/64	**Kissin' Cousins**...Elvis Presley
35/61	**Kissin' On The Phone**...Paul Anka
11/59	**Kissin' Time**...Bobby Rydell

POS/YR	RECORD TITLE/ARTIST
5/88	**Kissing A Fool**...George Michael **(Kissing Game) ..see: I Like The Way**
31/73	**Kissing My Love**...Bill Withers
40/91	**Kissing You**...Keith Washington
16/57	**Knee Deep In The Blues**...Guy Mitchell
15/67	**Knight In Rusty Armour**...Peter & Gordon
	Knock On Wood
28/66	Eddie Floyd
30/67	Otis & Carla
1/79	Amii Stewart **(also see: If I Had No Loot)**
1/71	**Knock Three Times**...Dawn
9/90	**Knockin' Boots**...Candyman
3/93	**Knockin' Da Boots**...H-Town
12/73	**Knockin' On Heaven's Door**...Bob Dylan
14/77	**Knowing Me, Knowing You**...Abba
	Ko Ko Mo (I Love You So)
2/55	Perry Como
6/55	Crew-Cuts
2/73	**Kodachrome**...Paul Simon
1/88	**Kokomo**...Beach Boys
4/59	**Kookie, Kookie (Lend Me Your Comb)**...Edward Byrnes & Connie Stevens
40/74	**Kung Fu**...Curtis Mayfield
1/74	**Kung Fu Fighting**...Carl Douglas
1/86	**Kyrie**...Mr. Mister

L

	La Bamba
22/59	Ritchie Valens
1/87	Los Lobos
9/58	**La Dee Dah**...Billy & Lillie
32/58	**La-Do-Dada**...Dale Hawkins
4/87	**La Isla Bonita**...Madonna
9/70	**La La La (If I Had You)**...Bobby Sherman
4/68	**La-La Means I Love You**...Delfonics
30/74	**La La Peace Song**...Al Wilson
	La Mer ..see: Beyond The Sea
20/58	**La Paloma**...Billy Vaughn
8/80	**Ladies Night**...Kool & The Gang
1/80	**Lady**...Kenny Rogers
6/75	**Lady**...Styx
10/79	**Lady**...Little River Band
28/80	**Lady**...Whispers
39/67	**Lady**...Jack Jones
20/67	**Lady Bird**...Nancy Sinatra & Lee Hazlewood

POS/YR	RECORD TITLE/ARTIST
14/75	**Lady Blue**...Leon Russell
6/66	**Lady Godiva**...Peter & Gordon
3/87	**Lady In Red**...Chris DeBurgh
24/66	**Lady Jane**...Rolling Stones
24/78	**Lady Love**...Lou Rawls
30/83	**Lady Love Me (One More Time)**...George Benson
14/60	**Lady Luck**...Lloyd Price
4/68	**Lady Madonna**...Beatles
1/75	**Lady Marmalade**...LaBelle
2/68	**Lady Willpower**...Gary Puckett & The Union Gap
8/81	**Lady (You Bring Me Up)**...Commodores
33/68	**Lalena**...Donovan
	(Lament Of Cherokee) ..see: Indian Reservation
4/87	**Land Of Confusion**...Genesis
	Land Of Hope And Glory ..see: (Graduation Song)
29/66	**Land Of Milk And Honey**...Vogues
	Land Of 1000 Dances
30/65	Cannibal & The Headhunters
6/66	Wilson Pickett
13/84	**Language Of Love**...Dan Fogelberg
32/61	**Language Of Love**...John D. Loudermilk
	Lara's Theme ..see: Somewhere My Love
13/65	**Last Chance To Turn Around**...Gene Pitney
21/76	**Last Child**...Aerosmith
3/78	**Last Dance**...Donna Summer
	Last Date
2/60	Floyd Cramer
21/60	Lawrence Welk
	(also see: My Last Date With You)
19/75	**Last Farewell**...Roger Whittaker
18/75	**Last Game Of The Season (A Blind Man In The Bleachers)**...David Geddes
	Last Kiss
2/64	J. Frank Wilson
34/74	Wednesday
36/89	**Last Mile**...Cinderella
3/61	**Last Night**...Mar-Keys
8/72	**(Last Night) I Didn't Get To Sleep At All**...5th Dimension
3/73	**Last Song**...Edward Bear
23/92	**Last Song**...Elton John
9/65	**Last Time**...Rolling Stones
40/84	**Last Time I Made Love**...Joyce Kennedy & Jeffrey Osborne
14/74	**Last Time I Saw Him**...Diana Ross
1/66	**Last Train To Clarksville**...Monkees

POS/YR	RECORD TITLE/ARTIST
39/80	**Last Train To London**...Electric Light Orchestra
25/67	**Last Waltz**...Engelbert Humperdinck
40/66	**Last Word In Lonesome Is Me**...Eddy Arnold
21/89	**Last Worthless Evening**...Don Henley
27/57	**Lasting Love**...Sal Mineo
6/80	**Late In The Evening**...Paul Simon
4/93	**Lately**...Jodeci
10/65	**Laugh At Me**...Sonny
15/65	**Laugh, Laugh**...Beau Brummels
10/69	**Laughing**...Guess Who
15/63	**Laughing Boy**...Mary Wells
1/75	**Laughter In The Rain**...Neil Sedaka
14/65	**Laurie (Strange Things Happen)**...Dickey Lee
3/59	**Lavender-Blue**...Sammy Turner
	LaVerne & Shirley Theme ..see: Making Our Dreams Come True
13/83	**Lawyers In Love**...Jackson Browne
11/70	**Lay A Little Lovin' On Me**...Robin McNamara
6/70	**Lay Down (Candles In The Rain)**...Melanie/Edwin Hawkins Singers
3/78	**Lay Down Sally**...Eric Clapton
16/56	**Lay Down Your Arms**...Chordettes
40/85	**Lay It Down**...Ratt
7/69	**Lay Lady Lay**...Bob Dylan
6/85	**Lay Your Hands On Me**...Thompson Twins
7/89	**Lay Your Hands On Me**...Bon Jovi
31/94	**(Lay Your Head On My) Pillow**...Tony Toni Tone
	Layla
10/72	Derek & The Dominos
12/92	Eric Clapton (Live)
14/67	**Lazy Day**...Spanky & Our Gang
40/64	**Lazy Elsie Molly**...Chubby Checker
12/58	**Lazy Mary**...Lou Monte
14/61	**Lazy River**...Bobby Darin
21/58	**Lazy Summer Night**...Four Preps
1/78	**Le Freak**...Chic
5/79	**Lead Me On**...Maxine Nightingale
9/82	**Leader Of The Band**...Dan Fogelberg
19/65	**Leader Of The Laundromat**...Detergents
1/64	**Leader Of The Pack**...Shangri-Las
25/62	**Leah**...Roy Orbison
	Lean On Me
1/72	Bill Withers
1/87	Club Nouveau

POS/YR	RECORD TITLE/ARTIST
9/66	**Leaning On The Lamp Post**...Herman's Hermits
1/55	**Learnin' The Blues**...Frank Sinatra
28/91	**Learning To Fly**...Tom Petty
6/82	**Leather And Lace**...Stevie Nicks/Don Henley
11/89	**Leave A Light On**...Belinda Carlisle
27/84	**Leave A Tender Moment Alone**...Billy Joel
24/84	**Leave It**...Yes
3/73	**Leave Me Alone (Ruby Red Dress)**...Helen Reddy
21/73	**Leaving Me**...Independents
1/69	**Leaving On A Jet Plane**...Peter, Paul & Mary
9/58	**Left Right Out Of Your Heart**...Patti Page
	(Legend Of Billy Jack) ..see: One Tin Soldier
31/80	**Legend Of Wooley Swamp**...Charlie Daniels Band
8/84	**Legs**...ZZ Top
	Lemon Tree
35/62	Peter, Paul & Mary
20/65	Trini Lopez
11/58	**Leroy**...Jack Scott
31/68	**Les Bicyclettes De Belsize**...Engelbert Humperdinck
34/68	**Lesson, The**...Vikki Carr
12/87	**Lessons In Love**...Level 42
	Let A Man Come In And Do The Popcorn
21/69	James Brown (Part One)
40/70	James Brown (Part Two)
36/69	**Let A Woman Be A Woman - Let A Man Be A Man**...Dyke & The Blazers
3/76	**Let 'Em In**...Wings
34/89	**Let Go**...Sharon Bryant
9/95	**Let Her Cry**...Hootie & The Blowfish
10/76	**Let Her In**...John Travolta
39/85	**Let Him Go**...Animotion
1/70	**Let It Be**...Beatles
	Let It Be Me
7/60	Everly Brothers
5/64	Betty Everett & Jerry Butler
36/69	Glen Campbell & Bobbie Gentry
40/82	Willie Nelson
	Let It Go ..see: Letitgo
12/67	**Let It Out (Let It All Hang Out)**...Hombres
23/74	**Let It Ride**...Bachman-Turner Overdrive
30/76	**Let It Shine**...Olivia Newton-John
32/93	**Let It Snow**...Boyz II Men
5/82	**Let It Whip**...Dazz Band

POS/YR	RECORD TITLE/ARTIST
23/67	**Let Love Come Between Us**...James & Bobby Purify
20/69	**Let Me**...Paul Revere & The Raiders
29/65	**Let Me Be**...Turtles
31/80	**Let Me Be The Clock**...Smokey Robinson
7/87	**Let Me Be The One**...Expose
29/95	**Let Me Be The One**...Blessid Union Of Souls
6/74	**Let Me Be There**...Olivia Newton-John
21/80	**Let Me Be Your Angel**...Stacy Lattisaw
1/57	**(Let Me Be Your) Teddy Bear**...Elvis Presley
20/61	**Let Me Belong To You**...Brian Hyland
38/82	**Let Me Go**...Ray Parker Jr.
35/80	**Let Me Go, Love**...Nicolette Larson
	Let Me Go, Lover!
1/55	Joan Weber
6/55	Teresa Brewer
8/55	Patti Page
17/55	Sunny Gale
32/70	**Let Me Go To Him**...Dionne Warwick
4/62	**Let Me In**...Sensations
36/73	**Let Me In**...Osmonds
10/80	**Let Me Love You Tonight**...Pure Prairie League
34/93	**Let Me Ride**...Dr. Dre
17/73	**Let Me Serenade You**...Three Dog Night
18/82	**Let Me Tickle Your Fancy**...Jermaine Jackson
9/80	**Let My Love Open The Door**...Pete Townshend
37/91	**Let The Beat Hit 'Em**...Lisa Lisa & Cult Jam
16/58	**Let The Bells Keep Ringing**...Paul Anka
	Let The Four Winds Blow
29/57	Roy Brown
15/61	Fats Domino
	Let The Good Times Roll
20/56	Shirley & Lee
22/67	Bunny Sigler (medley)
7/60	**Let The Little Girl Dance**...Billy Bland
8/84	**Let The Music Play**...Shannon
32/76	**Let The Music Play**...Barry White
	Let The Sunshine In ..see: Aquarius
	Let Them ..also see: Let 'Em
7/61	**Let There Be Drums**...Sandy Nelson
27/74	**Let Your Hair Down**...Temptations
1/76	**Let Your Love Flow**...Bellamy Brothers
28/71	**Let Your Love Go**...Bread
36/78	**Let's All Chant**...Michael Zager Band
1/83	**Let's Dance**...David Bowie
4/62	**Let's Dance**...Chris Montez

POS/YR	RECORD TITLE/ARTIST
1/75	Let's Do It Again...Staple Singers
40/65	Let's Do The Freddie...Chubby Checker
	(also see: Do The Freddie)
21/67	Let's Fall In Love...Peaches & Herb
1/73	Let's Get It On...Marvin Gaye
32/74	Let's Get Married...Al Green
15/92	Let's Get Rocked...Def Leppard
9/80	Let's Get Serious...Jermaine Jackson
8/61	Let's Get Together...Hayley Mills
	(also see: Get Together)
9/87	Let's Go!...Wang Chung
14/79	Let's Go...Cars
19/62	Let's Go (pony)...Routers
39/61	Let's Go Again...Hank Ballard
7/86	Let's Go All The Way...Sly Fox
1/84	Let's Go Crazy...Prince
30/83	Let's Go Dancin' (Ooh La, La, La)...Kool & The Gang
31/66	Let's Go Get Stoned...Ray Charles
6/60	Let's Go, Let's Go, Let's Go...Hank Ballard
26/63	Let's Go Steady Again...Neil Sedaka
3/81	Let's Groove...Earth, Wind & Fire
	Let's Hang On!
3/65	4 Seasons
32/82	Barry Manilow
37/60	Let's Have A Party...Wanda Jackson
1/84	Let's Hear It For The Boy...Deniece Williams
38/63	Let's Kiss And Make Up...Bobby Vinton
20/63	Let's Limbo Some More...Chubby Checker
8/67	Let's Live For Today...Grass Roots
35/76	Let's Live Together...Road Apples
11/65	Let's Lock The Door...Jay & The Americans
35/73	Let's Pretend...Raspberries
18/74	Let's Put It All Together...Stylistics
20/66	Let's Start All Over Again...Ronnie Dove
	Let's Stay Together
1/72	Al Green
26/84	Tina Turner
31/74	Let's Straighten It Out...Latimore
13/91	Let's Talk About Sex...Salt-N-Pepa
7/60	Let's Think About Living...Bob Luman
20/63	Let's Turkey Trot...Little Eva
8/61	Let's Twist Again...Chubby Checker
2/87	Let's Wait Awhile...Janet Jackson
39/87	Let's Work...Mick Jagger
	Let's Work Together
26/70	Canned Heat
32/70	Wilbert Harrison
31/94	Letitgo...Prince

POS/YR	RECORD TITLE/ARTIST
	Letter, The
1/67	Box Tops
20/69	Arbors
7/70	Joe Cocker with Leon Russell
25/64	Letter From Sherry...Dale Ward
19/62	Letter Full Of Tears...Gladys Knight & The Pips
	Letter Song ..see: S.Y.S.L.J.F.M.
25/58	Letter To An Angel...Jimmy Clanton
33/73	Letter To Myself...Chi-Lites
39/75	Letting Go...Wings
24/72	Levon...Elton John
7/71	Liar...Three Dog Night
12/65	Liar, Liar...Castaways
	Liberty Valance ..see: (Man Who Shot)
32/89	Licence To Chill...Billy Ocean
14/68	Licking Stick - Licking Stick...James Brown
11/77	Lido Shuffle...Boz Scaggs
13/62	Lie To Me...Brook Benton
16/57	Liechtensteiner Polka...Will Glahe
18/91	Lies....EMF
20/66	Lies...Knickerbockers
27/87	Lies...Jonathan Butler
30/83	Lies...Thompson Twins
38/90	Lies...En Vogue
35/91	Life Goes On...Poison
7/86	Life In A Northern Town...Dream Academy
19/85	Life In One Day...Howard Jones
11/77	Life In The Fast Lane...Eagles
6/92	Life Is A Highway...Tom Cochrane
8/74	Life Is A Rock (But The Radio Rolled Me)...Reunion
34/81	Life Of Illusion...Joe Walsh
12/78	Life's Been Good...Joe Walsh
32/92	Lift Me Up...Howard Jones
	Light My Fire
1/67	Doors
3/68	Jose Feliciano
33/87	Light Of Day...Barbusters (Joan Jett)
1/66	Lightnin' Strikes...Lou Christie
24/67	Lightning's Girl...Nancy Sinatra
12/84	Lights Out...Peter Wolf
11/67	(Lights Went Out In) Massachusetts...Bee Gees
27/66	Like A Baby...Len Barry
1/89	Like A Prayer...Madonna
12/86	Like A Rock...Bob Seger
2/65	Like A Rolling Stone...Bob Dylan
36/76	Like A Sad Song...John Denver

POS/YR	RECORD TITLE/ARTIST
6/83	**Little Red Corvette**...Prince
23/62	**Little Red Rented Rowboat**...Joe Dowell
2/66	**Lil' Red Riding Hood**...Sam The Sham & The Pharaohs
11/63	**Little Red Rooster**...Sam Cooke
14/89	**Little Respect**...Erasure
32/57	**Little Sandy Sleighfoot**...Jimmy Dean
5/61	**Little Sister**...Elvis Presley
20/59	**Little Space Girl**...Jesse Lee Turner
1/58	**Little Star**...Elegants
13/65	**Little Things**...Bobby Goldsboro
35/60	**Little Things Mean A Lot**...Joni James
20/83	**Little Too Late**...Pat Benatar
12/63	**Little Town Flirt**...Del Shannon
25/57	**Little White Lies**...Betty Johnson
3/73	**Little Willy**...Sweet
3/69	**Little Woman**...Bobby Sherman
F/72	**Little Woman Love**...Wings
	Live And Die ..see: (Forever)
4/92	**Live And Learn**...Joe Public
	Live And Let Die
2/73	Wings
33/92	Guns N' Roses
34/85	**Live Every Moment**...REO Speedwagon
22/91	**Live For Loving You**...Gloria Estefan
32/86	**Live Is Life**...Opus
40/88	**Live My Life**...Boy George
1/86	**Live To Tell**...Madonna
20/76	**Livin' For The Weekend**...O'Jays
19/74	**Livin' For You**...Al Green
31/84	**Livin' In Desperate Times**...Olivia Newton-John
40/77	**Livin' In The Life**...Isley Brothers
15/79	**Livin' It Up (Friday Night)**...Bell & James
1/87	**Livin' On A Prayer**...Bon Jovi
18/93	**Livin' On The Edge**...Aerosmith
13/77	**Livin' Thing**...Electric Light Orchestra
22/63	**Living A Lie**...Al Martino
37/75	**Living A Little, Laughing A Little**...Spinners
30/59	**Living Doll**...Cliff Richard
8/74	**Living For The City**...Stevie Wonder
17/87	**Living In A Box**...Living In A Box
23/81	**Living In A Fantasy**...Leo Sayer
22/72	**Living In A House Divided**...Cher
4/86	**Living In America**...James Brown
20/94	**Living In Danger**...Ace Of Base
9/89	**Living In Sin**...Bon Jovi

POS/YR	RECORD TITLE/ARTIST
11/73	**Living In The Past**...Jethro Tull
6/81	**Living Inside Myself**...Gino Vannelli
25/77	**Living Next Door To Alice**...Smokie
32/73	**Living Together, Growing Together**...5th Dimension
1/89	**Living Years**...Mike & The Mechanics
37/75	**Lizzie And The Rainman**...Tanya Tucker
14/69	**Lo Mucho Que Te Quiero**...Rene & Rene
F/78	**Load-Out, The**...Jackson Browne
	Loco-Motion, The
1/62	Little Eva
1/74	Grand Funk
3/88	Kylie Minogue
12/63	**Loddy Lo**...Chubby Checker
6/79	**Logical Song**...Supertramp
9/70	**Lola**...Kinks
	Lollipop
2/58	Chordettes
20/58	Ronald & Ruby
39/78	**London Town**...Wings
14/67	**(Loneliness Made Me Realize) It's You That I Need**...Temptations
22/65	**L-O-N-E-L-Y**...Bobby Vinton
6/60	**Lonely Blue Boy**...Conway Twitty
	Lonely Boy
1/59	Paul Anka
F/72	Donny Osmond
7/77	**Lonely Boy**...Andrew Gold
6/62	**Lonely Bull (El Solo Torro)**...Tijuana Brass feat. Herb Alpert
3/71	**Lonely Days**...Bee Gees
24/59	**Lonely For You**...Gary Stites
26/58	**Lonely Island**...Sam Cooke
32/61	**Lonely Man**...Elvis Presley
3/76	**Lonely Night (Angel Face)**...Captain & Tennille
6/85	**Lonely Ol' Night**...John Cougar Mellencamp
23/59	**Lonely One**...Duane Eddy
5/75	**Lonely People**...America
5/59	**Lonely Street**...Andy Williams
39/63	**Lonely Surfer**...Jack Nitzsche
7/59	**Lonely Teardrops**...Jackie Wilson
12/60	**Lonely Teenager**...Dion
22/60	**Lonely Weekends**...Charlie Rich
6/79	**Lonesome Loser**...Little River Band
7/58	**Lonesome Town**...Ricky Nelson
31/71	**Long Ago And Far Away**...James Taylor
1/70	**Long And Winding Road**...Beatles

POS/YR	RECORD TITLE/ARTIST
F/70	**Long As I Can See The Light**...Creedence Clearwater Revival
2/72	**Long Cool Woman (In A Black Dress)**...Hollies
26/72	**Long Dark Road**...Hollies
38/72	**Long Haired Lover From Liverpool**...Little Jimmy Osmond
33/66	**Long Live Our Love**...Shangri-Las
17/65	**Long Lonely Nights**...Bobby Vinton
20/70	**Long Lonesome Highway**...Michael Parks
25/70	**Long Long Time**...Linda Ronstadt
20/78	**Long, Long Way From Home**...Foreigner
	(Long Nights) ..see: Blue Collar Man
F/95	**Long Road**...Pearl Jam
8/80	**Long Run**...Eagles
9/75	**Long Tall Glasses (I Can Dance)**...Leo Sayer
	Long Tall Sally
6/56	Little Richard
8/56	Pat Boone
22/77	**Long Time**...Boston
8/73	**Long Train Runnin'**...Doobie Brothers
2/80	**Longer**...Dan Fogelberg
14/84	**Longest Time**...Billy Joel
6/55	**Longest Walk**...Jaye P. Morgan
5/74	**Longfellow Serenade**...Neil Diamond
1/89	**Look, The**...Roxette
39/75	**Look At Me (I'm In Love)**...Moments
1/88	**Look Away**...Chicago
	Look For A Star
16/60	Garry Miles
19/60	Billy Vaughn
26/60	Garry Mills
29/60	Deane Hawley
36/57	**Look Homeward, Angel**...Johnnie Ray
14/61	**Look In My Eyes**...Chantels
11/75	**Look In My Eyes Pretty Woman**...Dawn
	Look Of Love
22/67	Dusty Springfield
4/68	Sergio Mendes & Brasil '66
18/83	**Look Of Love**...ABC
27/65	**Look Of Love**...Lesley Gore
35/88	**Look Out Any Window**...Bruce Hornsby & The Range
32/66	**Look Through Any Window**...Hollies
24/66	**Look Through My Window**...Mamas & The Papas
14/70	**Look What They've Done To My Song Ma**...New Seekers
4/72	**Look What You Done For Me**...Al Green
32/67	**Look What You've Done**...Pozo Seco Singers

POS/YR	RECORD TITLE/ARTIST
14/80	**Look What You've Done To Me**...Boz Scaggs
5/58	**Looking Back**...Nat "King" Cole
	Lookin' For A Love
39/72	J. Geils Band
10/74	Bobby Womack
5/80	**Lookin' For Love**...Johnny Lee
2/70	**Lookin' Out My Back Door**...Creedence Clearwater Revival
16/72	**Lookin' Through The Windows**...Jackson 5
2/87	**Looking For A New Love**...Jody Watley
39/83	**Looking For A Stranger**...Pat Benatar
29/76	**Looking For Space**...John Denver
6/93	**Looking Through Patient Eyes**...PM Dawn
	Looking Through The Eyes Of Love
28/65	Gene Pitney
39/73	Partridge Family
1/77	**Looks Like We Made It**...Barry Manilow
4/63	**Loop De Loop**...Johnny Thunder
4/74	**Lord's Prayer**...Sister Janet Mead
27/76	**Lorelei**...Styx
F/93	**Lose Control**...Silk
10/94	**Loser**...Beck
4/91	**Losing My Religion**...R.E.M.
6/63	**Losing You**...Brenda Lee
34/80	**Lost Her In The Sun**...John Stewart
1/87	**Lost In Emotion**...Lisa Lisa & Cult Jam
3/80	**Lost In Love**...Air Supply
35/85	**Lost In Love**...New Edition
12/88	**Lost In You**...Rod Stewart
1/89	**Lost In Your Eyes**...Debbie Gibson
35/61	**Lost Love**...H.B. Barnum
9/77	**Lost Without Your Love**...Bread
8/79	**Lotta Love**...Nicolette Larson
13/57	**Lotta Lovin'**...Gene Vincent
	Louie Louie
2/63	Kingsmen
30/66	Sandpipers
F/57	**Love Affair**...Sal Mineo
	Love And Affection ..see: (Can't Live Without Your)
15/90	**Love & Emotion**...Stevie B
	Love And Marriage
5/55	Frank Sinatra
20/55	Dinah Shore
17/91	**Love And Understanding**...Cher
25/91	**Love At First Sight**...Styx

POS/YR	RECORD TITLE/ARTIST
	Love Ballad
20/76	L.T.D.
18/79	George Benson
	Love Being Your Fool ..see: (Shu-Doo-Pa-Poo-Poop)
1/88	**Love Bites**...Def Leppard
11/86	**Love Bizarre**...Sheila E.
25/67	**Love Bug Leave My Heart Alone**...Martha & The Vandellas
10/62	**Love Came To Me**...Dion
2/69	**Love (Can Make You Happy)**...Mercy
36/93	**Love Can Move Mountains**...Celine Dion
23/88	**Love Changes (Everything)**...Climie Fisher
	Love Child
1/68	Supremes
13/90	Sweet Sensation
17/82	**Love Come Down**...Evelyn King
32/79	**Love Don't Live Here Anymore**...Rose Royce
15/74	**Love Don't Love Nobody**...Spinners
36/93	**Love Don't Love You**...En Vogue
15/67	**Love Eyes**...Nancy Sinatra
30/76	**Love Fire**...Jigsaw
5/70	**Love Grows (Where My Rosemary Goes)**...Edison Lighthouse
1/76	**Love Hangover**...Diana Ross
11/71	**Love Her Madly**...Doors
8/76	**Love Hurts**...Nazareth
7/73	**Love I Lost**...Harold Melvin & The Bluenotes
20/67	**Love I Saw In You Was Just A Mirage**...Miracles
5/89	**Love In An Elevator**...Aerosmith
36/77	**Love In 'C' Minor**...Cerrone
22/83	**Love In Store**...Fleetwood Mac
15/82	**Love In The First Degree**...Alabama
16/76	**Love In The Shadows**...Neil Sedaka
24/89	**Love In Your Eyes**...Eddie Money
3/93	**Love Is**...Vanessa Williams & Brian McKnight
36/90	**Love Is**...Alannah Myles
5/83	**Love Is A Battlefield**...Pat Benatar
10/57	**Love Is A Golden Ring**...Frankie Laine
13/66	**Love Is A Hurtin' Thing**...Lou Rawls
	Love Is A Many-Splendored Thing
1/55	Four Aces
26/55	Don Cornell
23/83	**Love Is A Stranger**...Eurythmics
4/91	**Love Is A Wonderful Thing**...Michael Bolton

POS/YR	RECORD TITLE/ARTIST
2/76	**Love Is Alive**...Gary Wright
7/68	**Love Is All Around**...Troggs
15/58	**Love Is All We Need**...Tommy Edwards
20/82	**Love Is Alright Tonite**...Rick Springfield
1/68	**Love Is Blue**...Paul Mauriat
16/86	**Love Is Forever**...Billy Ocean
1/67	**Love Is Here And Now You're Gone**...Supremes
10/82	**Love Is In Control (Finger On The Trigger)**...Donna Summer
7/78	**Love Is In The Air**...John Paul Young
26/68	**(Love Is Like A) Baseball Game**...Intruders
37/82	**Love Is Like A Rock**...Donnie Iris
9/66	**Love Is Like An Itching In My Heart**...Supremes
8/78	**Love Is Like Oxygen**...Sweet
12/92	**Love Is On The Way**...Saigon Kick
	Love Is Strange
11/57	Mickey & Sylvia
13/67	Peaches & Herb
10/79	**Love Is The Answer**...England Dan & John Ford Coley
30/76	**Love Is The Drug**...Roxy Music
17/85	**Love Is The Seventh Wave**...Sting
7/56	**(Love Is) The Tender Trap**...Frank Sinatra
1/78	**(Love Is) Thicker Than Water**...Andy Gibb
16/73	**Love Jones**...Brighter Side Of Darkness (also see: Basketball Jones)
16/70	**Love Land**...Charles Wright
	Love Letters
5/62	Ketty Lester
19/66	Elvis Presley
1/57	**Love Letters In The Sand**...Pat Boone
17/85	**Love Light In Flight**...Stevie Wonder
13/75	**L-O-V-E (Love)**...Al Green
	Love, Love, Love
30/56	Clovers
30/56	Diamonds
1/76	**Love Machine**...Miracles
15/68	**Love Makes A Woman**...Barbara Acklin
11/66	**Love Makes The World Go Round**...Deon Jackson
26/63	**Love (Makes the World Go 'Round)**...Paul Anka
33/58	**Love Makes The World Go 'Round**...Perry Como
13/91	**Love Makes Things Happen**...Pebbles
2/57	**Love Me**...Elvis Presley
14/76	**Love Me**...Yvonne Elliman
26/92	**Love Me All Up**...Stacy Earl

POS/YR	RECORD TITLE/ARTIST
1/64	**Love Me Do**...Beatles
10/74	**Love Me For A Reason**...Osmonds
29/90	**Love Me For Life**...Stevie B
	Love Me Forever
24/57	Eydie Gorme
25/57	Four Esquires
	Love Me Or Leave Me
12/55	Sammy Davis, Jr.
19/55	Lena Horne
	Love Me Tender
1/56	Elvis Presley
21/62	Richard Chamberlain
40/67	Percy Sledge
11/57	**Love Me To Pieces**...Jill Corey
22/82	**Love Me Tomorrow**...Chicago
13/69	**Love Me Tonight**...Tom Jones
25/68	**Love Me Two Times**...Doors
12/62	**Love Me Warm And Tender**...Paul Anka
	Love Me With All Your Heart
3/64	Ray Charles Singers
38/66	Bachelors
39/71	**Love Means (You Never Have To Say You're Sorry)**...Sounds Of Sunshine
	Love My Life Away ..see: (I Wanna)
5/91	**Love Of A Lifetime**...Firehouse
40/58	**Love Of My Life**...Everly Brothers
21/63	**Love Of My Man**...Theola Kilgore
40/91	**Love On A Rooftop**...Desmond Child
	Love On A Two-Way Street
3/70	Moments
26/81	Stacy Lattisaw
2/81	**Love On The Rocks**...Neil Diamond
36/76	**Love Or Leave**...Spinners
	Love Or Let Me Be Lonely
6/70	Friends Of Distinction
40/82	Paul Davis
32/78	**Love Or Something Like It**...Kenny Rogers
13/88	**Love Overboard**...Gladys Knight & The Pips
34/79	**Love Pains**...Yvonne Elliman
36/86	**Love Parade**...Dream Academy
37/82	**Love Plus One**...Haircut One Hundred
	Love Potion Number Nine
23/59	Clovers
3/65	Searchers
	Love Power
22/68	Sandpebbles
4/91	Luther Vandross (medley)
12/87	**Love Power**...Dionne Warwick & Jeffrey Osborne
22/76	**Love Really Hurts Without You**...Billy Ocean

POS/YR	RECORD TITLE/ARTIST
1/76	**Love Rollercoaster**...Ohio Players
3/89	**Love Shack**...B-52's
31/63	**Love She Can Count On**...Miracles
33/93	**Love Shoulda Brought You Home**...Toni Braxton
19/94	**Love Sneakin' Up On You**...Bonnie Raitt
40/63	**Love So Fine**...Chiffons
3/76	**Love So Right**...Bee Gees
5/84	**Love Somebody**...Rick Springfield
2/89	**Love Song**...Cure
10/90	**Love Song**...Tesla
12/74	**Love Song**...Anne Murray
38/80	**Love Stinks**...J. Geils Band
	Love Story ..see: Theme From
1/90	**Love Takes Time**...Mariah Carey
11/79	**Love Takes Time**...Orleans
	Love The One You're With
14/71	Stephen Stills
18/71	Isley Brothers
14/80	**Love The World Away**...Kenny Rogers
1/77	**Love Theme From A Star Is Born (Evergreen)**...Barbra Streisand
21/78	**Love Theme From Eyes Of Laura Mars (Prisoner)**...Barbra Streisand
37/61	**(Love Theme From) One Eyed Jacks**...Ferrante & Teicher
	Love Theme From One On One ..see: My Fair Share
1/69	**Love Theme From Romeo & Juliet**...Henry Mancini
15/85	**Love Theme From St. Elmo's Fire**...David Foster
34/72	**Love Theme From The Godfather**...Andy Williams
10/91	**Love...Thy Will Be Done**...Martika
2/76	**Love To Love You Baby**...Donna Summer
6/86	**Love Touch**...Rod Stewart
1/73	**Love Train**...O'Jays
30/60	**Love Walked In**...Dinah Washington
22/86	**Love Walks In**...Van Halen
30/71	**Love We Had (Stays On My Mind)**...Dells
9/86	**Love Will Conquer All**...Lionel Richie
6/78	**Love Will Find A Way**...Pablo Cruise
30/87	**Love Will Find A Way**...Yes
40/69	**Love Will Find A Way**...Jackie DeShannon
1/75	**Love Will Keep Us Together**...Captain & Tennille
1/90	**Love Will Lead You Back**...Taylor Dayne

POS/YR	RECORD TITLE/ARTIST
1/91	**Love Will Never Do (Without You)**...Janet Jackson
9/88	**Love Will Save The Day**...Whitney Houston
30/84	**Love Will Show Us How**...Christine McVie
13/82	**Love Will Turn You Around**...Kenny Rogers
5/75	**Love Won't Let Me Wait**...Major Harris
9/87	**Love You Down**...Ready For The World
31/96	**Love U 4 Life**...Jodeci
1/79	**Love You Inside Out**...Bee Gees
24/81	**Love You Like I Never Loved Before**...John O'Banion
36/93	**Love U More**...Sunscreem
26/58	**Love You Most Of All**...Sam Cooke
1/70	**Love You Save**...Jackson 5
7/60	**Love You So**...Ron Holden
10/86	**Love Zone**...Billy Ocean
7/82	**Love's Been A Little Bit Hard On Me**...Juice Newton
20/77	**Love's Grown Deep**...Kenny Nolan
19/71	**Love's Lines, Angles And Rhymes**...5th Dimension
26/66	**Love's Made A Fool Of You**...Bobby Fuller Four
1/74	**Love's Theme**...Love Unlimited Orchestra
30/78	**Lovely Day**...Bill Withers
12/80	**Lovely One**...Jacksons
20/56	**Lovely One**...Four Voices
2/89	**Lover In Me**...Sheena Easton
7/62	**Lover Please**...Clyde McPhatter
2/65	**Lover's Concerto**...Toys
31/68	**Lover's Holiday**...Peggy Scott & Jo Jo Benson
40/80	**Lover's Holiday**...Change
31/61	**Lover's Island**...Blue Jays
6/59	**Lover's Question**...Clyde McPhatter
2/85	**Loverboy**...Billy Ocean
4/85	**Lovergirl**...Teena Marie
36/62	**Lovers By Night, Strangers By Day**...Fleetwoods
3/62	**Lovers Who Wander**...Dion
2/73	**Loves Me Like A Rock**...Paul Simon
25/61	**Lovey Dovey**...Buddy Knox
9/85	**Lovin' Every Minute Of It**...Loverboy
16/79	**Lovin', Touchin', Squeezin'**...Journey
26/71	**Loving Her Was Easier (Than Anything I'll Ever Do Again)**...Kris Kristofferson
1/75	**Lovin' You**...Minnie Riperton
32/67	**Lovin' You**...Bobby Darin
20/57	**Loving You**...Elvis Presley

POS/YR	RECORD TITLE/ARTIST
29/72	**Loving You Just Crossed My Mind**...Sam Neely
7/75	**Low Rider**...War
3/76	**Lowdown**...Boz Scaggs
35/71	**Lowdown**...Chicago
	Lt. Calley ..see: Battle Hymn Of
29/94	**Lucas With The Lid Off**...Lucas
5/77	**Lucille**...Kenny Rogers
	Lucille
21/57	Little Richard
21/60	Everly Brothers
25/77	**Luckenbach, Texas**...Waylon Jennings
30/85	**Lucky**...Greg Kihn
25/60	**Lucky Devil**...Carl Dobkins, Jr.
38/85	**Lucky In Love**...Mick Jagger
14/59	**Lucky Ladybug**...Billy & Lillie
25/57	**Lucky Lips**...Ruth Brown
18/94	**Lucky One**...Amy Grant
20/84	**Lucky One**...Laura Branigan
4/84	**Lucky Star**...Madonna
29/70	**Lucretia Mac Evil**...Blood, Sweat & Tears
1/75	**Lucy In The Sky With Diamonds**...Elton John
3/87	**Luka**...Suzanne Vega
16/56	**Lullaby Of Birdland**...Blue Stars
23/61	**Lullaby Of Love**...Frank Gari
2/75	**Lyin' Eyes**...Eagles
27/90	**Lyin' To Myself**...David Cassidy

M

POS/YR	RECORD TITLE/ARTIST
15/59	**M.T.A.**...Kingston Trio
5/70	**Ma Belle Amie**...Tee Set
	MacArthur Park
2/68	Richard Harris
38/71	Four Tops
1/78	Donna Summer
22/74	**Machine Gun**...Commodores
25/78	**Macho Man**...Village People
	Mack The Knife
8/56	Dick Hyman Trio
11/56	Richard Hayman & Jan August
17/56	Lawrence Welk
20/56	Louis Armstrong
37/56	Billy Vaughn
1/59	Bobby Darin
27/60	Ella Fitzgerald
3/86	**Mad About You**...Belinda Carlisle

POS/YR	RECORD TITLE/ARTIST
	Made To Love ..see: (Girls, Girls, Girls)
36/76	**Mademoiselle**...Styx
23/60	**Madison, The**...Al Brown's Tunetoppers
30/60	**Madison Time**...Ray Bryant Combo
1/71	**Maggie May**...Rod Stewart
1/80	**Magic**...Olivia Newton-John
5/75	**Magic**...Pilot
12/84	**Magic**...Cars
25/68	**Magic Bus**...Who
3/68	**Magic Carpet Ride**...Steppenwolf
9/76	**Magic Man**...Heart
4/58	**Magic Moments**...Perry Como
	Magic Touch ..see: (You've Got)
21/66	**Magic Town**...Vogues
39/77	**Magical Mystery Tour**...Ambrosia
8/78	**Magnet And Steel**...Walter Egan
35/61	**Magnificent Seven**...Al Caiola
	Magnum P.I. ..see: Theme From
	Mahogany ..see: Theme From
3/79	**Main Event/Fight**...Barbra Streisand
	Main Theme From Exodus ..see: Exodus
	Main Title And Molly-O ..see: Man With The Golden Arm
24/77	**Mainstreet**...Bob Seger
36/61	**Majestic, The**...Dion
14/83	**Major Tom (Coming Home)**...Peter Schilling
25/80	**Make A Little Magic**...Dirt Band
5/82	**Make A Move On Me**...Olivia Newton-John
28/69	**Make Believe**...Wind
30/82	**Make Believe**...Toto
	Make It Easy On Yourself
20/62	Jerry Butler
16/65	Walker Bros.
37/70	Dionne Warwick
22/71	**Make It Funky**...James Brown
5/92	**Make It Happen**...Mariah Carey
4/88	**Make It Real**...Jets
1/70	**Make It With You**...Bread
36/92	**Make Love Like A Man**...Def Leppard
29/83	**Make Love Stay**...Dan Fogelberg
16/58	**Make Me A Miracle**...Jimmie Rodgers
28/66	**Make Me Belong To You**...Barbara Lewis
3/88	**Make Me Lose Control**...Eric Carmen
9/70	**Make Me Smile**...Chicago
27/72	**Make Me The Woman That You Go Home To**...Gladys Knight & The Pips
11/65	**Make Me Your Baby**...Barbara Lewis
21/67	**Make Me Yours**...Bettye Swann

POS/YR	RECORD TITLE/ARTIST
	Make The World Go Away
24/63	Timi Yuro
6/65	Eddy Arnold
14/90	**Make You Sweat**...Keith Sweat
36/69	**Make Your Own Kind Of Music**...Mama Cass Elliot
	Make Yourself Comfortable
6/55	Sarah Vaughan
26/55	Andy Griffith
30/55	Peggy King
5/79	**Makin' It**...David Naughton
20/59	**Makin' Love**...Floyd Robinson
13/82	**Making Love**...Roberta Flack
31/67	**Making Every Minute Count**...Spanky & Our Gang
35/87	**Making Love In The Rain**...Herb Alpert
2/83	**Making Love Out Of Nothing At All**...Air Supply
35/67	**Making Memories**...Frankie Laine
25/76	**Making Our Dreams Come True**...Cyndi Grecco
	Mama ..also see: Mamma
8/60	**Mama**...Connie Francis
22/66	**Mama**...B.J. Thomas
9/79	**Mama Can't Buy You Love**...Elton John
14/63	**Mama Didn't Lie**...Jan Bradley
11/56	**Mama From The Train**...Patti Page
28/92	**Mama, I'm Coming Home**...Ozzy Osbourne
F/70	**Mama Liked The Roses**...Elvis Presley
11/57	**Mama Look At Bubu**...Harry Belafonte
4/61	**Mama Said**...Shirelles
17/91	**Mama Said Knock You Out**...L.L. Cool J
	Mama Sang A Song
32/62	Stan Kenton
38/62	Walter Brennan
34/56	**Mama, Teach Me To Dance**...Eydie Gorme
1/70	**Mama Told Me (Not To Come)**...Three Dog Night
30/82	**Mama Used To Say**...Junior
2/71	**Mama's Pearl**...Jackson 5
18/55	**Mambo Rock**...Bill Haley
19/66	**Mame**...Herb Alpert
32/76	**Mamma Mia**...Abba
16/55	**Man Chases A Girl**...Eddie Fisher
31/79	**Man I'll Never Be**...Boston
1/88	**Man In The Mirror**...Michael Jackson
	Man In The Raincoat
14/55	Marion Marlowe
16/55	Priscilla Wright
40/82	**Man On The Corner**...Genesis

POS/YR	RECORD TITLE/ARTIST
30/93	**Man On The Moon**...R.E.M.
14/82	**Man On Your Mind**...Little River Band
15/86	**Man Size Love**...Klymaxx
4/62	**(Man Who Shot) Liberty Valance**...Gene Pitney
	Man With The Golden Arm (Main Title/Molly-O/Delilah Jones)
14/56	Richard Maltby
16/56	Elmer Bernstein
22/56	Dick Jacobs
37/56	McGuire Sisters
19/68	**Man Without Love (Quando M'innamoro)**...Engelbert Humperdinck
4/87	**Mandolin Rain**...Bruce Hornsby & The Range
1/75	**Mandy**...Barry Manilow
1/82	**Maneater**...Daryl Hall & John Oates
10/57	**Mangos**...Rosemary Clooney
10/59	**Manhattan Spiritual**...Reg Owen
1/83	**Maniac**...Michael Sembello
2/86	**Manic Monday**...Bangles
7/60	**Many Tears Ago**...Connie Francis
20/58	**March From The River Kwai and Colonel Bogey**...Mitch Miller
8/77	**Margaritaville**...Jimmy Buffett
6/63	**Maria Elena**...Los Indios Tabajaras
	Marianne
3/57	Hilltoppers
4/57	Terry Gilkyson & The Easy Riders
15/65	**Marie**...Bachelors
4/61	**(Marie's the Name) His Latest Flame**...Elvis Presley
31/59	**Marina**...Rocco Granata
36/63	**Marlena**...Four Seasons
28/69	**Marrakesh Express**...Crosby, Stills & Nash
40/79	**Married Men**...Bette Midler
16/63	**Martian Hop**...Ran-Dells
39/62	**Mary Ann Regrets**...Burl Ives
28/72	**Mary Had A Little Lamb**...Wings
27/67	**Mary In The Morning**...Al Martino
14/94	**Mary Jane's Last Dance**...Tom Petty
26/59	**Mary Lou**...Ronnie Hawkins
12/56	**Mary's Boy Child**...Harry Belafonte
39/62	**Mary's Little Lamb**...James Darren
23/87	**Mary's Prayer**...Danny Wilson
2/62	**Mashed Potato Time**...Dee Dee Sharp
	Massachusetts ..see: (Lights Went Out In)
5/80	**Master Blaster (Jammin')**...Stevie Wonder
18/68	**Master Jack**...Four Jacks & A Jill

POS/YR	RECORD TITLE/ARTIST
33/73	**Master Of Eyes**...Aretha Franklin
3/92	**Masterpiece**...Atlantic Starr
7/73	**Masterpiece**...Temptations
20/64	**Matador, The**...Major Lance
17/64	**Matchbox**...Beatles
2/85	**Material Girl**...Madonna
10/86	**Matter Of Trust**...Billy Joel
39/69	**May I**...Bill Deal
15/65	**May The Bird Of Paradise Fly Up Your Nose**..."Little" Jimmy Dickens
11/59	**May You Always**...McGuire Sisters
	Maybe
15/58	Chantels
29/70	Three Degrees
17/58	**Maybe Baby**...Crickets
14/64	**Maybe I Know**...Lesley Gore
22/79	**Maybe I'm A Fool**...Eddie Money
10/77	**Maybe I'm Amazed**...Wings
20/71	**Maybe Tomorrow**...Jackson 5
	Maybellene
5/55	Chuck Berry
12/64	Johnny Rivers
15/74	**Me And Baby Brother**...War
	Me And Bobby McGee
1/71	Janis Joplin
40/72	Jerry Lee Lewis
22/72	**Me And Julio Down By The Schoolyard**...Paul Simon
1/72	**Me And Mrs. Jones**...Billy Paul
34/71	**Me And My Arrow**...Nilsson
5/71	**Me And You And A Dog Named Boo**...Lobo
34/89	**Me Myself And I**...De La Soul
26/89	**Me So Horny**...2 Live Crew
40/81	**Me (Without You)**...Andy Gibb
5/63	**Mean Woman Blues**...Roy Orbison
12/63	**Mecca**...Gene Pitney
	"Medic" Theme ..see: Blue Star
22/69	**Medicine Man**...Buchanan Brothers
1/81	**Medley**...Stars on 45
11/87	**Meet Me Half Way**...Kenny Loggins
33/94	**(Meet) The Flintstones**...B.C. 52's
2/66	**Mellow Yellow**...Donovan
5/57	**Melodie D'Amour (Melody of Love)**...Ames Brothers

POS/YR	RECORD TITLE/ARTIST
	Melody Of Love
2/55	Billy Vaughn
3/55	Four Aces
8/55	David Carroll
19/55	Frank Sinatra & Ray Anthony
30/55	Leo Diamond
35/69	**Memories**...Elvis Presley
	Memories Are Made Of This
1/56	Dean Martin
5/56	Gale Storm
	Memories Of You
22/55	Four Coins
20/56	Benny Goodman Trio/Rosemary Clooney
39/83	**Memory**...Barry Manilow
	Memphis
5/63	Lonnie Mack
2/64	Johnny Rivers
33/67	**Memphis Soul Stew**...King Curtis
	Men ..also see: Theme From The
33/68	**Men Are Gettin' Scarce**...Joe Tex
6/66	**Men In My Little Girl's Life**...Mike Douglas
27/69	**Mendocino**...Sir Douglas Quintet
29/95	**Mental Picture**...Jon Secada
14/90	**Mentirosa**...Mellow Man Ace
2/88	**Mercedes Boy**...Pebbles
30/69	**Mercy**...Ohio Express
35/64	**Mercy, Mercy**...Don Covay
	Mercy Mercy Me (The Ecology)
4/71	Marvin Gaye
16/91	Robert Palmer (medley)
	Mercy, Mercy, Mercy
5/67	Buckinghams
11/67	"Cannonball" Adderley
32/60	**Mess Of Blues**...Elvis Presley
8/66	**Message To Michael**...Dionne Warwick
5/85	**Method Of Modern Love**...Daryl Hall/John Oates
16/58	**Mexican Hat Rock**...Applejacks
7/61	**Mexico**...Bob Moore
1/85	**Miami Vice Theme**...Jan Hammer
1/61	**Michael**...Highwaymen
18/66	**Michelle**...David & Jonathan
1/82	**Mickey**...Toni Basil
8/63	**Mickey's Monkey**...Miracles
19/84	**Middle Of The Road**...Pretenders
6/74	**Midnight At The Oasis**...Maria Muldaur
5/87	**Midnight Blue**...Lou Gramm
6/75	**Midnight Blue**...Melissa Manchester
5/68	**Midnight Confessions**...Grass Roots

POS/YR	RECORD TITLE/ARTIST
10/70	**Midnight Cowboy**...Ferrante & Teicher
	Midnight Hour ..see: In The
2/62	**Midnight In Moscow**...Kenny Ball
10/64	**Midnight Mary**...Joey Powers
	Midnight Rider
27/72	Joe Cocker
19/74	Gregg Allman
24/80	**Midnight Rocks**...Al Stewart
	Midnight Special
16/60	Paul Evans
20/65	Johnny Rivers
35/59	**Midnight Stroll**...Revels
1/73	**Midnight Train To Georgia**...Gladys Knight & The Pips
28/79	**Midnight Wind**...John Stewart
34/71	**Mighty Clouds Of Joy**...B.J. Thomas
38/59	**Mighty Good**...Ricky Nelson
20/74	**Mighty Love**...Spinners
29/74	**Mighty Mighty**...Earth, Wind & Fire
10/68	**Mighty Quinn (Quinn The Eskimo)**...Manfred Mann
12/91	**Miles Away**...Winger
33/64	**Miller's Cave**...Bobby Bare
	Million To One
5/60	Jimmy Charles
23/73	Donny Osmond
	Millionaire ..see: (How To Be A)
26/69	**Mind, Body and Soul**...Flaming Ember
18/73	**Mind Games**...John Lennon
23/92	**Mind Playing Tricks On Me**...Geto Boys
38/69	**Minotaur, The**...Dick Hyman
14/79	**Minute By Minute**...Doobie Brothers
9/91	**Miracle**...Whitney Houston
12/90	**Miracle**...Jon Bon Jovi
18/56	**Miracle Of Love**...Eileen Rodgers
3/75	**Miracles**...Jefferson Starship
40/83	**Miracles**...Stacy Lattisaw
10/67	**Mirage**...Tommy James & the Shondells
30/83	**Mirror Man**...Human League
8/82	**Mirror, Mirror**...Diana Ross
22/73	**Misdemeanor**...Foster Sylvers
20/95	**Misery**...Soul Asylum
38/95	**Mishale**...Andru Donalds
10/85	**Misled**...Kool & The Gang
23/94	**Misled**...Celine Dion
5/84	**Miss Me Blind**...Culture Club
14/81	**Miss Sun**...Boz Scaggs
1/78	**Miss You**...Rolling Stones
39/94	**Miss You In A Heartbeat**...Def Leppard

POS/YR	RECORD TITLE/ARTIST
7/89	**Miss You Like Crazy**...Natalie Cole
1/89	**Miss You Much**...Janet Jackson
29/88	**Missed Opportunity**...Daryl Hall/John Oates
2/96	**Missing**...Everything But The Girl
1/84	**Missing You**...John Waite
10/85	**Missing You**...Diana Ross
23/82	**Missing You**...Dan Fogelberg
29/61	**Missing You**...Ray Peterson
12/92	**Missing You Now**...Michael Bolton Feat. Kenny G
7/60	**Mission Bell**...Donnie Brooks
14/86	**Missionary Man**...Eurythmics
32/70	**Mississippi**...John Phillips
21/70	**Mississippi Queen**...Mountain
33/85	**Mistake No. 3**...Culture Club
	Mister ..see: **Mr.**
	Misty
12/59	Johnny Mathis
21/63	Lloyd Price
14/75	Ray Stevens
3/76	**Misty Blue**...Dorothy Moore
14/80	**Misunderstanding**...Genesis
5/89	**Mixed Emotions**...Rolling Stones
37/64	**Mixed-Up, Shook-Up, Girl**...Patty & The Emblems
4/94	**Mmm Mmm Mmm Mmm**...Crash Test Dummies
32/58	**Mocking Bird, The**...Four Lads
	Mockingbird
7/63	Inez Foxx (with Charlie Foxx)
5/74	Carly Simon & James Taylor
20/61	**Model Girl**...Johnny Mastro
22/84	**Modern Day Delilah**...Van Stephenson
18/81	**Modern Girl**...Sheena Easton
14/83	**Modern Love**...David Bowie
10/86	**Modern Woman**...Billy Joel
21/65	**Mohair Sam**...Charlie Rich
	Molly-O ..see: **Man With The Golden Arm**
2/55	**Moments To Remember**...Four Lads
	Mona Lisa
25/59	Carl Mann
29/59	Conway Twitty
1/66	**Monday, Monday**...Mama's & The Papa's
13/73	**Money**...Pink Floyd
27/85	**Money Changes Everything**...Cyndi Lauper
23/92	**Money Don't Matter 2 Night**...Prince & The New Power Generation
1/85	**Money For Nothing**...Dire Straits

POS/YR	RECORD TITLE/ARTIST
9/76	**Money Honey**...Bay City Rollers
	Money (That's what I want)
23/60	Barrett Strong
16/64	Kingsmen
20/56	**Money Tree**...Margaret Whiting
28/86	**Money$ Too Tight (To Mention)**...Simply Red
23/91	**Moneytalks**...AC/DC **(also see: Dirty Cash)**
1/88	**Monkey**...George Michael
8/63	**Monkey Time**...Major Lance
39/70	**Monster**...Steppenwolf
	Monster Mash
1/62	Bobby "Boris" Pickett
10/73	Bobby "Boris" Pickett
30/62	**Monsters' Holiday**...Bobby "Boris" Pickett
8/70	**Montego Bay**...Bobby Bloom
15/68	**Monterey**...Animals
	Mony Mony
3/68	Tommy James & The Shondells
1/87	Billy Idol
31/77	**Moody Blue**...Elvis Presley
1/61	**Moody River**...Pat Boone
24/69	**Moody Woman**...Jerry Butler
	Moon River
11/61	Jerry Butler
11/61	Henry Mancini
30/71	**Moon Shadow**...Cat Stevens
28/58	**Moon Talk**...Perry Como
38/69	**Moonflight**...Vik Venus
	Moonglow and Theme From "Picnic"
1/56	Morris Stoloff
4/56	George Cates
13/56	McGuire Sisters (Picnic)
3/76	**Moonlight Feels Right**...Starbuck
3/57	**Moonlight Gambler**...Frankie Laine
	Moonlight Swim
24/57	Tony Perkins
37/57	Nick Noble
23/87	**Moonlighting (Theme)**...Al Jarreau
4/56	**More**...Perry Como
8/63	**More**...Kai Winding
17/93	**More And More**...Captain Hollywood Project
	(More I Love You) ..see: **Lo Mucho Que Te Quiero**
16/66	**More I See You**...Chris Montez
	More Love
23/67	Miracles
10/80	Kim Carnes
17/61	**More Money For You And Me**...Four Preps

POS/YR	RECORD TITLE/ARTIST
4/76	**More, More, More**...Andrea True Connection
5/76	**More Than A Feeling**...Boston
32/78	**More Than A Woman**...Tavares
14/91	**More Than Ever**...Nelson
2/80	**More Than I Can Say**...Leo Sayer
34/82	**More Than Just The Two Of Us**...Sneaker
1/91	**More Than Words**...Extreme
2/90	**More Than Words Can Say**...Alias
18/89	**More Than You Know**...Martika
12/69	**More Today Than Yesterday**...Spiral Starecase
13/59	**Morgen**...Ivo Robic
	Moritat ..see: Mack The Knife
21/83	**Mornin'**...Jarreau
14/75	**Mornin' Beautiful**...Dawn
1/73	**Morning After**...Maureen McGovern
24/79	**Morning Dance**...Spyro Gyra
17/69	**Morning Girl**...Neon Philharmonic
6/72	**Morning Has Broken**...Cat Stevens
	Morning Side Of The Mountain
27/59	Tommy Edwards
8/75	Donny & Marie Osmond
1/81	**Morning Train (Nine To Five)**...Sheena Easton
1/73	**Most Beautiful Girl**...Charlie Rich
3/94	**Most Beautiful Girl In The World**...Prince
14/55	**Most Of All**...Don Cornell
38/71	**Most Of All**...B.J. Thomas
27/62	**Most People Get Married**...Patti Page
31/56	**Mostly Martha**...Crew Cuts
4/72	**Mother And Child Reunion**...Paul Simon
37/71	**Mother Freedom**...Bread
1/61	**Mother-In-Law**...Ernie K-Doe
11/69	**Mother Popcorn**...James Brown
8/66	**Mothers Little Helper**...Rolling Stones
27/86	**Mothers Talk**...Tears For Fears
12/72	**Motorcycle Mama**...Sailcat
36/87	**Motortown**...Kane Gang
10/91	**Motown Song**...Rod Stewart (with The Temptations)
3/91	**Motownphilly**...Boyz II Men
	Mountain Of Love
21/60	Harold Dorman
9/64	Johnny Rivers
2/61	**Mountain's High**...Dick & DeeDee
23/86	**Mountains**...Prince
38/92	**Move Any Mountain (Progen 91)**...Shamen
12/86	**Move Away**...Culture Club

POS/YR	RECORD TITLE/ARTIST
31/69	**Move Over**...Steppenwolf
6/92	**Move This**...Technotronic featuring Ya Kid K
	Move Two Mountains ..see: (You've Got To)
14/76	**Movin'**...Brass Construction
19/75	**Movin' On**...Bad Company
17/78	**Movin' Out (Anthony's Song)**...Billy Joel
34/94	**Moving On Up**...M People
16/63	**Mr. Bass Man**...Johnny Cymbal
2/71	**Mr. Big Stuff**...Jean Knight
1/59	**Mr. Blue**...Fleetwoods
35/78	**Mr. Blue Sky**...Electric Light Orchestra
9/71	**Mr. Bojangles**...Nitty Gritty Dirt Band
28/68	**Mr. Businessman**...Ray Stevens
38/72	**Mr. Can't You See**...Buffy Sainte-Marie
1/60	**Mr. Custer**...Larry Verne
17/66	**Mr. Dieingly Sad**...Critters
	Mr. Dream Merchant ..see: Dream Merchant
4/75	**Mr. Jaws**...Dickie Goodman
6/57	**Mr. Lee**...Bobbettes
1/64	**Mr. Lonely**...Bobby Vinton
40/92	**Mr. Loverman**...Shabba Ranks
21/60	**Mr. Lucky**...Henry Mancini
3/83	**Mr. Roboto**...Styx
37/81	**Mr. Sandman**...Emmylou Harris
36/66	**Mr. Spaceman**...Byrds
18/69	**Mr. Sun, Mr. Moon**...Paul Revere & The Raiders
1/65	**Mr. Tambourine Man**...Byrds
12/85	**Mr. Telephone Man**...New Edition
17/94	**Mr. Vain**...Culture Beat
6/93	**Mr. Wendal**...Arrested Development
	Mr. Wonderful
13/56	Sarah Vaughan
14/56	Peggy Lee
18/56	Teddi King
1/65	**Mrs. Brown You've Got A Lovely Daughter**...Herman's Hermits
	Mrs. Robinson
1/68	Simon & Garfunkel
37/69	Booker T. & The M.G.'s
	Muddy Water ..see: (I Washed My Hands In)
	Muhammad Ali ..see: Black Superman
5/60	**Mule Skinner Blues**...Fendermen
30/62	**Multiplication**...Bobby Darin
39/59	**Mummy, The**...Bob McFadden & Dor
39/82	**Murphy's Law**...Cheri
10/82	**Muscles**...Diana Ross
39/67	**Museum**...Herman's Hermits

POS/YR	RECORD TITLE/ARTIST
1/66	**My Love**...Petula Clark
1/73	**My Love**...Paul McCartney & Wings
5/83	**My Love**...Lionel Richie
16/65	**My Love, Forgive Me**...Robert Goulet
21/90	**My Love Is A Fire**...Donny Osmond
28/95	**My Love Is For Real**...Paula Abdul
2/92	**My Lovin' (You're Never Gonna Get It)**...En Vogue
13/67	**My Mammy**...Happenings
9/73	**My Maria**...B.W. Stevenson
26/59	**My Melancholy Baby**...Tommy Edwards
3/74	**My Melody Of Love**...Bobby Vinton
19/74	**My Mistake (Was To Love You)**...Diana Ross & Marvin Gaye
39/81	**My Mother's Eyes**...Bette Midler
16/73	**My Music**...Loggins & Messina
10/90	**My, My, My**...Johnny Gill
20/91	**My Name Is Not Susan**...Whitney Houston
36/92	**My Name Is Prince**...Prince & The New Power Generation
37/84	**My Oh My**...Slade
	My One Sin
24/55	Nat "King" Cole
28/57	Four Coins
	My Own True Love
33/59	Jimmy Clanton
13/62	Duprees
21/57	**My Personal Possession**...Nat "King" Cole/Four Knights
14/69	**My Pledge Of Love**...Joe Jeffrey Group
1/56	**My Prayer**...Platters
1/89	**My Prerogative**...Bobby Brown
1/79	**My Sharona**...Knack
F/75	**My Ship**...Tavares
30/91	**My Side Of The Bed**...Susanna Hoffs
31/69	**My Song**...Aretha Franklin
	My Special Angel
7/57	Bobby Helms
7/68	Vogues
16/63	**My Summer Love**...Ruby & The Romantics
	My Sweet Lady
17/74	Cliff DeYoung
32/77	John Denver
1/70	**My Sweet Lord**...George Harrison
29/74	**My Thang**...James Brown
39/83	**My Town**...Michael Stanley Band
32/65	**My Town, My Guy And Me**...Lesley Gore
31/56	**My Treasure**...Hilltoppers
22/63	**My True Confession**...Brook Benton

POS/YR	RECORD TITLE/ARTIST
3/58	**My True Love**...Jack Scott
3/61	**My True Story**...Jive Five
	My Way
27/69	Frank Sinatra
22/77	Elvis Presley
9/69	**My Whole World Ended (The Moment You Left Me)**...David Ruffin
24/63	**My Whole World Is Falling Down**...Brenda Lee
12/59	**My Wish Came True**...Elvis Presley
16/72	**My World**...Bee Gees
5/66	**My World Is Empty Without You**...Supremes
9/92	**Mysterious Ways**...U2
24/85	**Mystery Lady**...Billy Ocean
33/65	**Mystic Eyes**...Them

N

POS/YR	RECORD TITLE/ARTIST
	Na Na Hey Hey Kiss Him Goodbye
1/69	Steam
12/87	Nylons
8/76	**Nadia's Theme (The Young And The Restless)**...Barry DeVorzon & Perry Botkin, Jr.
23/64	**Nadine (Is It You?)**...Chuck Berry
25/61	**"Nag"**...Halos
5/96	**Name**...Goo Goo Dolls
3/65	**Name Game**...Shirley Ellis
12/78	**Name Of The Game**...Abba
8/67	**Nashville Cats**...Lovin' Spoonful
3/86	**Nasty**...Janet Jackson
16/71	**Nathan Jones**...Supremes
21/78	**Native New Yorker**...Odyssey
38/60	**Natural Born Lover**...Fats Domino
10/73	**Natural High**...Bloodstone
17/71	**Natural Man**...Lou Rawls
8/67	**Natural Woman**...Aretha Franklin
40/68	**Naturally Stoned**...Avant-Garde
40/61	**Nature Boy**...Bobby Darin
3/88	**Naughty Girls (Need Love Too)**...Samantha Fox
	Naughty Lady Of Shady Lane
3/55	Ames Brothers
17/55	Archie Bleyer
23/85	**Naughty Naughty**...John Parr
6/64	**Navy Blue**...Diane Renay
22/70	**Neanderthal Man**...Hotlegs

POS/YR	RECORD TITLE/ARTIST
10/58	**Near You**...Roger Williams
40/58	**Nee Nee Na Na Na Na Nu Nu**...Dicky Doo & The Don'ts
11/74	**Need To Be**...Jim Weatherly
31/64	**Need To Belong**...Jerry Butler
25/58	**Need You**...Donnie Owens
1/88	**Need You Tonight**...INXS
	Needles And Pins
13/64	Searchers
37/86	Tom Petty/Stevie Nicks
2/73	**Neither One Of Us (Wants To Be The First To Say Goodbye)**...Gladys Knight & The Pips
	Nel Blu Dipinto Di Blu ..see: Volare
24/67	**Neon Rainbow**...Box Tops
6/85	**Neutron Dance**...Pointer Sisters
4/85	**Never**...Heart
21/93	**Never A Time**...Genesis
20/86	**Never As Good As The First Time**...Sade
6/59	**Never Be Anyone Else But You**...Ricky Nelson
15/80	**Never Be The Same**...Christopher Cross
28/82	**Never Been In Love**...Randy Meisner
5/72	**Never Been To Spain**...Three Dog Night
	Never Can Say Goodbye
2/71	Jackson 5
22/71	Isaac Hayes
9/75	Gloria Gaynor
13/71	**Never Ending Song Of Love**...Delaney & Bonnie & Friends
17/85	**Never Ending Story**...Limahl
F/94	**Never Forget You**...Mariah Carey
20/68	**Never Give You Up**...Jerry Butler
11/76	**Never Gonna Fall In Love Again**...Eric Carmen
1/88	**Never Gonna Give You Up**...Rick Astley
17/91	**Never Gonna Let You Down**...Surface
4/83	**Never Gonna Let You Go**...Sergio Mendes
26/70	**Never Had A Dream Come True**...Stevie Wonder
15/94	**Never Keeping Secrets**...Babyface
28/88	**Never Knew Love Like This**...Alexander O'Neal/Cherrelle
6/80	**Never Knew Love Like This Before**...Stephanie Mills
29/75	**Never Let Her Go**...David Gates
27/87	**Never Let Me Down**...David Bowie
5/94	**Never Lie**...Immature

POS/YR	RECORD TITLE/ARTIST
	Never My Love
2/67	Association
12/71	5th Dimension
7/74	Blue Swede
7/74	**Never, Never Gonna Give Ya Up**...Barry White
	Never On Sunday
19/60	Don Costa
13/61	Chordettes
30/93	**Never Should've Let You Go**...Hi-Five
3/85	**Never Surrender**...Corey Hart
7/88	**Never Tear Us Apart**...INXS
33/81	**Never Too Much**...Luther Vandross
22/56	**Never Turn Back**...Al Hibbler
	New ..also see: Nu
27/95	**New Age Girl**...Deadeye Dick
17/85	**New Attitude**...Patti LaBelle
37/64	**New Girl In School**...Jan & Dean
1/77	**New Kid In Town**...Eagles
	New Lovers ..see: (Welcome)
36/63	**New Mexican Rose**...Four Seasons
10/84	**New Moon On Monday**...Duran Duran
6/60	**New Orleans**...U.S. Bonds
39/80	**New Romance (It's A Mystery)**...Spider
3/88	**New Sensation**...INXS
27/84	**New Song**...Howard Jones
21/82	**New World Man**...Rush
13/79	**New York Groove**...Ace Frehley
14/67	**New York Mining Disaster 1941**...Bee Gees
	New York, New York ..see: Theme From
27/77	**New York, You Got Me Dancing**...Andrea True Connection
32/65	**New York's A Lonely Town**...Trade Winds
5/62	**Next Door To An Angel**...Neil Sedaka
17/67	**Next Plane To London**...Rose Garden
F/70	**Next Step Is Love**...Elvis Presley
1/86	**Next Time I Fall**...Peter Cetera w/Amy Grant
37/82	**Nice Girls**...Eye To Eye
30/76	**Nice 'N' Naasty**...Salsoul Orchestra
4/72	**Nice To Be With You**...Gallery
29/90	**Nicety**...Michel'le
35/72	**Nickel Song**...Melanie
39/81	**Nicole**...Point Blank
4/60	**Night**...Jackie Wilson (also see: Nite)
1/74	**Night Chicago Died**...Paper Lace
1/78	**Night Fever**...Bee Gees
3/63	**Night Has A Thousand Eyes**...Bobby Vee

POS/YR	RECORD TITLE/ARTIST
34/85	**Night Is Still Young**...Billy Joel
11/56	**Night Lights**...Nat "King" Cole
4/77	**Night Moves**...Bob Seger
28/86	**Night Moves**...Marilyn Martin
6/81	**Night Owls**...Little River Band
1/73	**Night The Lights Went Out In Georgia**...Vicki Lawrence
3/71	**Night They Drove Old Dixie Down**...Joan Baez
30/66	**Night Time**...Strangeloves
36/88	**Nightime**...Pretty Poison
35/62	**Night Train**...James Brown
33/84	**Nightbird**...Stevie Nicks/Sandy Stewart
9/75	**Nightingale**...Carole King
15/88	**Nightmare On My Street**...DJ Jazzy Jeff & The Fresh Prince
10/76	**Nights Are Forever Without You**...England Dan & John Ford Coley
2/72	**Nights In White Satin**...Moody Blues
24/91	**Nights Like This**...After 7
7/75	**Nights On Broadway**...Bee Gees
3/85	**Nightshift**...Commodores
23/67	**Niki Hoeky**...P.J. Proby
7/86	**Nikita**...Elton John
1/81	**9 To 5**...Dolly Parton
15/85	**19**...Paul Hardcastle
2/66	**19th Nervous Breakdown**...Rolling Stones
1/66	**96 Tears**...? (Question Mark) & The Mysterians
7/67	**98.6**...Keith
26/80	**99**...Toto
2/84	**99 Luftballons**...Nena
11/57	**Ninety-Nine Ways**...Tab Hunter
23/56	**Ninety Nine Years (Dead Or Alive)**...Guy Mitchell
33/71	**1900 Yesterday**...Liz Damon's Orient Express
12/83	****1999****...Prince
7/88	**Nite And Day**...Al B. Sure!
	Nitty Gritty
8/64	Shirley Ellis
19/69	Gladys Knight & The Pips
	No Arms Can Ever Hold You
23/55	Georgie Shaw
26/55	Pat Boone
27/65	Bachelors
39/74	**No Charge**...Melba Montgomery
23/58	**No Chemise, Please**...Gerry Granahan
22/86	**No Easy Way Out**...Robert Tepper
	No Gettin' Over Me ..see: (There's)

POS/YR	RECORD TITLE/ARTIST
40/60	**No If's - No And's**...Lloyd Price
34/85	**No Lookin' Back**...Michael McDonald
16/71	**No Love At All**...B.J. Thomas
21/58	**No Love (But Your Love)**...Johnny Mathis
8/70	**No Matter What**...Badfinger
3/66	**No Matter What Shape (Your Stomach's In)**...T-Bones
31/69	**No Matter What Sign You Are**...Supremes
35/67	**No Milk Today**...Herman's Hermits
33/93	**No Mistakes**...Patty Smyth
	No More
6/55	DeJohn Sisters
17/55	McGuire Sisters
23/95	**No More "I Love You's"**...Annie Lennox
7/90	**No More Lies**...Michel'le
6/84	**No More Lonely Nights**...Paul McCartney
25/73	**No More Mr. Nice Guy**...Alice Cooper
17/89	**No More Rhyme**...Debbie Gibson
1/79	**No More Tears (Enough Is Enough)**...Barbra Streisand/Donna Summer
23/84	**No More Words**...Berlin
13/90	**No Myth**...Michael Penn
23/80	**No Night So Long**...Dionne Warwick
3/75	**No No Song**...Ringo Starr
	No, Not Much!
2/56	Four Lads
34/69	Vogues
	No One
34/61	Connie Francis
21/63	Ray Charles
4/86	**No One Is To Blame**...Howard Jones
19/58	**No One Knows**...Dion & The Belmonts
36/72	**No One To Depend On**...Santana (also see: Mentirosa)
28/93	**No Ordinary Love**...Sade
	No Other Arms ..also see: No Arms Can Ever Hold You
27/59	**No Other Arms, No Other Lips**...Chordettes
10/64	**No Particular Place To Go**...Chuck Berry
20/93	**No Rain**...Blind Melon
29/81	**No Reply At All**...Genesis
12/92	**No Son Of Mine**...Genesis
F/70	**No Sugar Tonight**...Guess Who
14/79	**No Tell Lover**...Chicago
5/70	**No Time**...Guess Who
33/83	**No Time For Talk**...Christopher Cross
23/84	**No Way Out**...Jefferson Starship
15/82	**Nobody**...Sylvia
8/68	**Nobody But Me**...Human Beinz

POS/YR	RECORD TITLE/ARTIST
21/59	**Nobody But You**...Dee Clark
40/69	**Nobody But You Babe**...Clarence Reid
2/77	**Nobody Does It Better**...Carly Simon
12/64	**Nobody I Know**...Peter & Gordon
30/60	**Nobody Loves Me Like You**...Flamingos
18/82	**Nobody Said It Was Easy**...Le Roux
5/84	**Nobody Told Me**...John Lennon
29/73	**Nobody Wants You When You're Down And Out**...Bobby Womack
21/81	**Nobody Wins**...Elton John
8/88	**Nobody's Fool**...Kenny Loggins
13/87	**Nobody's Fool**...Cinderella
39/59	**Nola**...Billy Williams
32/94	**None Of Your Business**...Salt-N-Pepa
3/62	**Norman**...Sue Thompson
4/60	**North To Alaska**...Johnny Horton
34/85	**Not Enough Love In The World**...Don Henley
28/92	**Not Enough Time**...INXS
26/88	**Not Just Another Girl**...Ivan Neville
12/63	**Not Me**...Orlons
16/60	**Not One Minute More**...Della Reese
25/65	**Not The Lovin' Kind**...Dino, Desi & Billy
34/92	**Not The Only One**...Bonnie Raitt
	Nothin' ..also see: Nuthin' & Nuttin'
10/86	**Nothin' At All**...Heart
6/88	**Nothin' But A Good Time**...Poison
19/93	**Nothin' My Love Can't Fix**...Joey Lawrence
39/90	**Nothin' To Hide**...Poco
	Nothin' Yet ..see: (We Ain't Got)
29/92	**Nothing Broken But My Heart**...Celine Dion
34/69	**Nothing But A Heartache**...Flirtations
11/65	**Nothing But Heartaches**...Supremes
12/62	**Nothing Can Change This Love**...Sam Cooke
18/65	**Nothing Can Stop Me**...Gene Chandler
1/90	**Nothing Compares 2 U**...Sinéad O'Connor
34/92	**Nothing Else Matters**...Metallica
	Nothing For Xmas ..see: Nuttin'
1/74	**Nothing From Nothing**...Billy Preston
12/87	**Nothing's Gonna Change My Love For You**...Glenn Medeiros
1/87	**Nothing's Gonna Stop Us Now**...Starship
20/66	**Nothing's Too Good For My Baby**...Stevie Wonder
21/90	**Notice Me**...Nikki
2/87	**Notorious**...Duran Duran

POS/YR	RECORD TITLE/ARTIST
38/87	**Notorious**...Loverboy
3/92	**November Rain**...Guns N' Roses
25/58	**Now And For Always**...George Hamilton IV
7/94	**Now and Forever**...Richard Marx
	(Now And Then There's) A ..see: Fool Such As I
11/91	**Now That We Found Love**...Heavy D. & The Boyz
3/66	**Nowhere Man**...Beatles
8/65	**Nowhere To Run**...Martha & The Vandellas
26/92	**Nu Nu**...Lidell Townsell & M.T.F.
9/75	**#9 Dream**...John Lennon
22/73	**Nutbush City Limits**...Ike & Tina Turner
2/93	**Nuthin' But A "G" Thang**...Dr. Dre
23/62	**Nutrocker**...B. Bumble & The Stingers
40/94	**Nuttin' But Love**...Heavy D & The Boyz
	Nuttin' For Christmas
6/55	Art Mooney/Barry Gordon
20/55	Joe Ward
21/55	Ricky Zahnd
36/55	Fontane Sisters

POS/YR	RECORD TITLE/ARTIST
10/60	**O Dio Mio**...Annette
6/91	**O.P.P.**...Naughty By Nature
25/85	**Object Of My Desire**...Starpoint
38/94	**Objects In The Rear View Mirror May Appear Closer Than They Are**...Meat Loaf
35/84	**Obscene Phone Caller**...Rockwell
6/85	**Obsession**...Animotion
	Ode To Billie Joe
1/67	Bobbie Gentry
28/67	Kingpins
10/80	**Off The Wall**...Michael Jackson
	Oh ..also see: O
3/73	**Oh, Babe, What Would You Say?**...Hurricane Smith
23/64	**Oh Baby Don't You Weep**...James Brown
10/58	**Oh, Boy!**...Crickets
9/59	**Oh! Carol**...Neil Sedaka
15/78	**Oh! Darling**...Robin Gibb
20/90	**Oh Father**...Madonna
	Oh Girl
1/72	Chi-Lites
8/90	Paul Young
39/85	**Oh Girl**...Boy Meets Girl

POS/YR	RECORD TITLE/ARTIST
4/69	**Oh Happy Day** Edwin Hawkins' Singers
40/70	Glen Campbell
12/66	**Oh How Happy**...Shades Of Blue
5/58	**Oh Julie** Crescendos
23/58	Sammy Salvo
38/82	**Oh Julie**...Barry Manilow
33/73	**Oh La De Da**...Staple Singers
34/60	**Oh, Little One**...Jack Scott
7/58	**Oh Lonesome Me**...Don Gibson
22/70	**Oh Me Oh My (I'm A Fool For You Baby)**...Lulu
5/74	**Oh My My**...Ringo Starr
4/81	**Oh No**...Commodores
24/65	**Oh No Not My Baby**...Maxine Brown
7/58	**Oh-Oh, I'm Falling In Love Again**...Jimmie Rodgers
29/86	**Oh, People**...Patti LaBelle
1/64	**Oh, Pretty Woman** Roy Orbison
12/82	Van Halen
1/85	**Oh Sheila**...Ready For The World
3/84	**Oh Sherrie**...Steve Perry
22/55	**Oh! Susanna**...Singing Dogs
10/74	**Oh Very Young**...Cat Stevens
30/79	**Oh Well**...Rockets
10/69	**Oh, What A Night**...Dells **(also see: December, 1963)**
24/78	**Oh What A Night For Dancing**...Barry White
F/71	**Oh Woman Oh Why**...Paul McCartney
39/66	**Oh Yeah**...Shadows Of Knight
14/70	**Ohio**...Crosby, Stills, Nash & Young
3/57	**Old Cape Cod**...Patti Page
5/75	**Old Days**...Chicago
20/80	**Old-Fashion Love**...Commodores
37/77	**Old Fashioned Boy (You're The One)**...Stallion
4/71	**Old Fashioned Love Song**...Three Dog Night
5/60	**Old Lamplighter**...Browns
25/60	**Ol' MacDonald**...Frank Sinatra
31/72	**Old Man**...Neil Young
10/85	**Old Man Down The Road**...John Fogerty
34/56	**Old Philosopher**...Eddie Lawrence
5/62	**Old Rivers**...Walter Brennan
F/95	**Old School**...2 Pac
	Old Schoolyard ..see: (Remember The Days Of The)

POS/YR	RECORD TITLE/ARTIST
15/81	**Old Songs**...Barry Manilow
28/79	**Old Time Rock & Roll**...Bob Seger
25/61	**Ole Buttermilk Sky**...Bill Black's Combo
11/67	**On A Carousel**...Hollies
39/92	**On A Sunday Afternoon**...Lighter Shade Of Brown
5/74	**On And On**...Gladys Knight & The Pips
11/77	**On And On**...Stephen Bishop **(also see: And On And On)**
1/94	**On Bended Knee**...Boyz II Men
9/63	**On Broadway** Drifters
7/78	George Benson
38/56	**On London Bridge**...Jo Stafford
1/86	**On My Own**...Patti LaBelle & Michael McDonald
20/57	**On My Word Of Honor**...Platters
2/89	**On Our Own**...Bobby Brown
7/84	**On The Dark Side**...John Cafferty
26/83	**On The Loose**...Saga
5/80	**On The Radio**...Donna Summer
4/61	**On The Rebound**...Floyd Cramer
16/68	**On The Road Again**...Canned Heat
20/80	**On The Road Again**...Willie Nelson
38/78	**On The Shelf**...Donny & Marie
4/56	**On The Street Where You Live** Vic Damone
18/56	Eddie Fisher
28/64	Andy Williams
27/82	**On The Way To The Sky**...Neil Diamond
27/91	**On The Way Up**...Elisa Fiorillo
29/82	**On The Wings Of Love**...Jeffrey Osborne
14/63	**On Top Of Spaghetti**...Tom Glazer
5/89	**Once Bitten Twice Shy**...Great White
11/61	**Once In Awhile**...Chimes
19/64	**Once Upon A Time**...Marvin Gaye & Mary Wells
26/61	**Once Upon A Time**...Rochell & The Candles
10/75	**Once You Get Started**...Rufus Feat. Chaka Khan
23/72	**Once You Understand**...Think
5/69	**One**...Three Dog Night
7/89	**One**...Bee Gees
9/92	**One, The**...Elton John
10/92	**One**...U2
35/89	**One**...Metallica
10/91	**One And Only**...Chesney Hawkes
18/90	**One And Only Man**...Steve Winwood
1/71	**One Bad Apple**...Osmonds

POS/YR	RECORD TITLE/ARTIST
11/63	One Broken Heart For Sale...Elvis Presley
37/74	One Day At A Time...Marilyn Sellars
34/65	One Dyin' And A Buryin'...Roger Miller
	One Eyed Jacks ..see: Love Theme From
	One Fine Day
5/63	Chiffons
12/80	Carole King
24/71	One Fine Morning...Lighthouse
38/87	One For The Mockingbird...Cutting Crew
28/88	One Good Reason...Paul Carrack
4/88	One Good Woman...Peter Cetera
13/66	One Has My Name (The Other Has My Heart)...Barry Young
10/87	One Heartbeat...Smokey Robinson
11/74	One Hell Of A Woman...Mac Davis
28/86	One Hit (To The Body)...Rolling Stones
11/94	100% Pure Love...Crystal Waters
14/82	One Hundred Ways...Quincy Jones/James Ingram
9/87	One I Love...R.E.M.
20/57	One In A Million...Platters
37/84	One In A Million...Romantics
9/80	One In A Million You...Larry Graham
14/65	One Kiss For Old Times' Sake...Ronnie Dove
13/93	One Last Cry...Brian McKnight
35/79	One Last Kiss...J. Geils Band
2/70	One Less Bell To Answer...5th Dimension
37/73	One Less Set Of Footsteps...Jim Croce
19/85	One Lonely Night...REO Speedwagon
25/76	One Love In My Lifetime...Diana Ross
19/71	One Man Band...Three Dog Night
28/73	One Man Band (Plays All Alone)...Ronnie Dyson
7/75	One Man Woman/One Woman Man...Paul Anka/Odia Coates
8/61	One Mint Julep...Ray Charles
5/88	One Moment In Time...Whitney Houston
15/72	One Monkey Don't Stop No Show...Honey Cone
2/95	One More Chance/Stay With Me...Notorious B.I.G.
29/66	One More Heartache...Marvin Gaye
1/85	One More Night...Phil Collins
	One More Sunrise ..see: Morgen
32/65	One More Time...Ray Charles Singers
1/88	One More Try...George Michael
1/91	One More Try...Timmy -T-
28/78	One Nation Under A Groove...Funkadelic

POS/YR	RECORD TITLE/ARTIST
4/58	One Night...Elvis Presley
3/85	One Night In Bangkok...Murray Head
13/85	One Night Love Affair...Bryan Adams
11/73	One Of A Kind (Love Affair)...Spinners
15/85	One Of The Living...Tina Turner
1/75	One Of These Nights...Eagles
4/96	One Of Us...Joan Osborne
31/60	One Of Us (Will Weep Tonight)...Patti Page
7/83	One On One...Daryl Hall & John Oates
	One On One, Love Theme From ..see: My Fair Share
29/76	One Piece At A Time...Johnny Cash
24/81	One Step Closer...Doobie Brothers
22/86	One Step Closer To You...Gavin Christopher
13/88	One Step Up...Bruce Springsteen
	One Summer Night
7/58	Danleers
22/61	Diamonds
1/95	One Sweet Day...Mariah Carey & Boyz II Men
1/81	One That You Love...Air Supply
30/83	One Thing...INXS
4/83	One Thing Leads To Another...Fixx
	One Tin Soldier (The Legend Of Billy Jack)
34/70	Original Caste
26/71	Coven
10/71	One Toke Over The Line...Brewer & Shipley
9/61	One Track Mind...Bobby Lewis
40/80	One-Trick Pony...Paul Simon
2/65	1-2-3...Len Barry
3/88	1-2-3...Gloria Estefan & Miami Sound Machine
5/68	1, 2, 3, Red Light...1910 Fruitgum Company
24/79	One Way Or Another...Blondie
8/62	One Who Really Loves You...Mary Wells
22/93	One Woman...Jade
15/82	One You Love...Glenn Frey
36/80	Only A Lonely Heart Sees...Felix Cavaliere
25/63	Only In America...Jay & The Americans
4/87	Only In My Dreams...Debbie Gibson
2/62	Only Love Can Break A Heart...Gene Pitney
33/70	Only Love Can Break Your Heart...Neil Young
28/76	Only Love Is Real...Carole King
33/57	Only One Love...George Hamilton IV

POS/YR	RECORD TITLE/ARTIST
	Only Sixteen
28/59	Sam Cooke
6/76	Dr. Hook
24/78	**Only The Good Die Young**...Billy Joel
2/60	**Only The Lonely**...Roy Orbison
9/82	**Only The Lonely**...Motels
4/69	**Only The Strong Survive**...Jerry Butler
9/85	**Only The Young**...Journey
17/82	**Only Time Will Tell**...Asia
28/91	**Only Time Will Tell**...Nelson
6/95	**Only Wanna Be With You**...Hootie & The Blowfish
34/84	**Only When You Leave**...Spandau Ballet
12/75	**Only Women**...Alice Cooper
4/75	**Only Yesterday**...Carpenters
	Only You
5/55	Platters
8/55	Hilltoppers
9/59	Franck Pourcel's French Fiddles
6/75	Ringo Starr
20/71	**Only You Know And I Know**...Delaney & Bonnie
F/75	**Oo-Wee**...Ringo Starr
23/65	**Oo Wee Baby, I Love You**...Fred Hughes
21/92	**Oochie Coochie**...MC Brains
34/67	**Oogum Boogum Song**...Brenton Wood
25/73	**Ooh Baby**...Gilbert O'Sullivan
	Ooh Baby Baby
16/65	Miracles
7/79	Linda Ronstadt
	O-o-h Child
8/70	5 Stairsteps
27/93	Dino
	(also see: Keep Ya Head Up)
10/90	**Ooh La La (I Can't Get Over You)**...Perfect Gentlemen
31/58	**Ooh! My Soul**...Little Richard
36/85	**Ooh Ooh Song**...Pat Benatar
28/60	**Ooh Poo Pah Doo**...Jessie Hill
35/90	**Ooops Up**...Snap!
2/82	**Open Arms**...Journey
10/67	**Open Letter To My Teenage Son**...Victor Lundberg
27/66	**Open The Door To Your Heart**...Darrell Banks
8/55	**Open Up Your Heart (And Let The Sunshine In)**...Cowboy Church Sunday School
1/87	**Open Your Heart**...Madonna
18/85	**Operator**...Midnight Star

POS/YR	RECORD TITLE/ARTIST
22/75	**Operator**...Manhattan Transfer
17/72	**Operator (That's Not the Way it Feels)**...Jim Croce
10/86	**Opportunities (Let's Make Lots Of Money)**...Pet Shop Boys
1/90	**Opposites Attract**...Paula Abdul
13/66	**Opus 17 (Don't You Worry 'Bout Me)**...4 Seasons
3/93	**Ordinary World**...Duran Duran
24/89	**Orinoco Flow (Sail Away)**...Enya
11/83	**Other Guy**...Little River Band
31/67	**Other Man's Grass Is Always Greener**...Petula Clark
22/90	**Other Side**...Aerosmith
4/82	**Other Woman**...Ray Parker Jr.
	Our Day Will Come
1/63	Ruby & The Romantics
11/75	Frankie Valli
7/83	**Our House**...Madness
30/70	**Our House**...Crosby, Stills, Nash & Young
20/81	**Our Lips Are Sealed**...Go-Go's
10/78	**Our Love**...Natalie Cole
	(Our Love Affair) ..see: Affair To Remember
9/78	**(Our Love) Don't Throw It All Away**...Andy Gibb
9/63	**Our Winter Love**...Bill Pursell
39/67	**Out & About**...Tommy Boyce & Bobby Hart
19/80	**Out Here On My Own**...Irene Cara
15/70	**Out In The Country**...Three Dog Night
3/64	**Out Of Limits**...Marketts
37/86	**Out Of Mind Out Of Sight**...Models
24/63	**Out Of My Mind**...Johnny Tillotson
24/64	**Out Of Sight**...James Brown
23/56	**Out Of Sight, Out Of Mind**...Five Keys
3/88	**Out Of The Blue**...Debbie Gibson
17/73	**Out Of The Question**...Gilbert O'Sullivan
1/84	**Out Of Touch**...Daryl Hall/John Oates
21/82	**Out Of Work**...Gary U.S. Bonds
2/72	**Outa-Space**...Billy Preston
28/60	**Outside My Window**...Fleetwoods
34/74	**Outside Woman**...Bloodstone
1/65	**Over And Over**...Dave Clark Five
20/76	**Over My Head**...Fleetwood Mac
	Over The Mountain; Across The Sea
8/57	Johnnie & Joe
21/63	Bobby Vinton
16/60	**Over The Rainbow**...Demensions
13/66	**Over Under Sideways Down**...Yardbirds

POS/YR	RECORD TITLE/ARTIST
7/68	**Over You**...Gary Puckett & The Union Gap
24/86	**Overjoyed**...Stevie Wonder
3/83	**Overkill**...Men At Work
18/74	**Overnight Sensation (Hit Record)**...Raspberries
16/70	**Overture From Tommy (A Rock Opera)**...Assembled Multitude
1/84	**Owner Of A Lonely Heart**...Yes (also see: Tic-Tac-Toe)
13/71	**Oye Como Va**...Santana

P

POS/YR	RECORD TITLE/ARTIST
10/64	**P.S. I Love You**...Beatles
8/62	**P.T. 109**...Jimmy Dean
10/83	**P.Y.T. (Pretty Young Thing)**...Michael Jackson
9/82	**Pac-Man Fever**...Buckner & Garcia
13/58	**Padre**...Toni Arden
1/66	**Paint It, Black**...Rolling Stones
	Paint Me A Picture ..see: (You Don't Have To)
34/74	**Painted Ladies**...Ian Thomas
15/63	**Painted, Tainted Rose**...Al Martino
	Paladin ..see: Ballad Of
3/62	**Palisades Park**...Freddy Cannon
26/76	**Paloma Blanca**...George Baker Selection
22/88	**Pamela**...Toto
13/84	**Panama**...Van Halen
35/66	**Pandora's Golden Heebie Jeebies**...Association
1/86	**Papa Don't Preach**...Madonna
31/74	**Papa Don't Take No Mess**...James Brown (also see: That's The Way Love Goes)
	Papa Joe's ..see: (Down At)
1/72	**Papa Was A Rollin' Stone**...Temptations
	Papa's Got A Brand New Bag
8/65	James Brown
21/69	Otis Redding
34/67	**Paper Cup**...5th Dimension
28/92	**Paper Doll**...PM Dawn
9/87	**Paper In Fire**...John Cougar Mellencamp
	Paper Roses
5/60	Anita Bryant
5/73	Marie Osmond
23/65	**Paper Tiger**...Sue Thompson
1/66	**Paperback Writer**...Beatles
32/82	**Paperlate**...Genesis

POS/YR	RECORD TITLE/ARTIST
16/88	**Paradise**...Sade
39/78	**Paradise By The Dashboard Light**...Meat Loaf
5/89	**Paradise City**...Guns N' Roses
34/86	**Paranoimia**...Art Of Noise with Max Headroom
12/88	**Parents Just Don't Understand**...D.J. Jazzy Jeff & The Fresh Prince
38/58	**Part Of Me**...Jimmy Clanton
31/75	**Part Of The Plan**...Dan Fogelberg
19/63	**Part Time Love**...Little Johnny Taylor
22/75	**Part Time Love**...Gladys Knight & The Pips
22/78	**Part-Time Love**...Elton John
1/85	**Part-Time Lover**...Stevie Wonder
2/85	**Party All The Time**...Eddie Murphy
	Party Doll
1/57	Buddy Knox
5/57	Steve Lawrence
5/62	**Party Lights**...Claudine Clark
34/81	**Party's Over (Hopelessly In Love)**...Journey
18/89	**Partyman**...Prince
10/83	**Pass The Dutchie**...Musical Youth
	P.A.S.S.I.O.N.
2/91	Rythm Syndicate
5/81	**Passion**...Rod Stewart
12/67	**Pata Pata**...Miriam Makeba
F/70	**Patch It Up**...Elvis Presley
4/70	**Patches**...Clarence Carter
6/62	**Patches**...Dickey Lee
4/89	**Patience**...Guns N' Roses
1/58	**Patricia**...Perez Prado
13/71	**Pay To The Piper**...Chairmen Of The Board
28/67	**Pay You Back With Interest**...Hollies
26/74	**Payback, The**...James Brown (also see: Can't You See)
3/85	**Nightshift**...Commodores
39/68	**Paying The Cost To Be The Boss**...B.B. King
11/90	**Peace In Our Time**...Eddie Money
	Peace In The Valley ..see: (There'll Be)
38/77	**Peace Of Mind**...Boston
31/75	**Peace Pipe**...B.T. Express
7/71	**Peace Train**...Cat Stevens
32/70	**Peace Will Come (According To Plan)**...Melanie
12/73	**Peaceful**...Helen Reddy
22/73	**Peaceful Easy Feeling**...Eagles
36/65	**Peaches "N" Cream**...Ikettes
20/61	**Peanut Butter**...Marathons

POS/YR	RECORD TITLE/ARTIST
22/57	**Peanuts**...Little Joe & The Thrillers
28/59	**Peek-A-Boo**...Cadillacs
11/78	**Peg**...Steely Dan
3/57	**Peggy Sue**...Buddy Holly
18/64	**Penetration**...Pyramids
24/60	**Pennies From Heaven**...Skyliners
33/82	**Penny For Your Thoughts**...Tavares
1/67	**Penny Lane**...Beatles
8/84	**Penny Lover**...Lionel Richie
	People
5/64	Barbra Streisand
39/68	Tymes
13/85	**People Are People**...Depeche Mode
35/91	**People Are Still Having Sex**...LaTour
12/67	**People Are Strange**...Doors
8/92	**People Everyday**...Arrested Development
14/65	**People Get Ready**...Impressions
1/68	**People Got To Be Free**...Rascals
22/74	**People Gotta Move**...Gino Vannelli
40/77	**People In Love**...10cc
25/72	**People Make The World Go Round**...Stylistics
23/79	**People Of The South Wind**...Kansas
12/64	**People Say**...Dixie Cups
18/61	**"Pepe"**...Duane Eddy
5/63	**Pepino The Italian Mouse**...Lou Monte
14/55	**Pepper-Hot Baby**...Jaye P. Morgan
1/62	**Peppermint Twist**...Joey Dee & the Starliters
10/62	**Percolator (Twist)**...Billy Joe & The Checkmates
11/85	**Perfect Way**...Scritti Politti
3/88	**Perfect World**...Huey Lewis & The News
15/60	**Perfidia**...Ventures
28/90	**Personal Jesus**...Depeche Mode
2/59	**Personality**...Lloyd Price
19/82	**Personally**...Karla Bonoff
	Peter Gunn
8/59	Ray Anthony
27/60	Duane Eddy
5/59	**Petite Fleur**...Chris Barber's Jazz Band
16/56	**Petticoats Of Portugal**...Dick Jacobs
1/75	**Philadelphia Freedom**...Elton John Band
26/58	**Philadelphia U.S.A.**...Nu Tornados
32/66	**Phoenix Love Theme (Senza Fine)**...Brass Ring
1/73	**Photograph**...Ringo Starr
12/83	**Photograph**...Def Leppard
1/81	**Physical**...Olivia Newton-John
6/88	**Piano In The Dark**...Brenda Russell

POS/YR	RECORD TITLE/ARTIST
25/74	**Piano Man**...Billy Joel
1/75	**Pick Up The Pieces**...AWB
27/68	**Pickin' Wild Mountain Berries**...Peggy Scott & Jo Jo Benson
	Picnic ..see: Moonglow
12/68	**Pictures Of Matchstick Men**...Status Quo
7/91	**Piece Of My Heart**...Tara Kemp
12/68	**Piece Of My Heart**...Big Brother & The Holding Company
19/73	**Pieces Of April**...Three Dog Night
31/83	**Pieces Of Ice**...Diana Ross
4/66	**Pied Piper**...Crispian St. Peters
	Pillow ..see: (Lay Your Head On My)
3/73	**Pillow Talk**...Sylvia
13/80	**Pilot Of The Airwaves**...Charlie Dore
	(Pina Colada Song) ..see: Escape
	Pinball Wizard
19/69	Who
29/73	New Seekers (medley)
11/60	**Pineapple Princess**...Annette
5/88	**Pink Cadillac**...Natalie Cole
8/84	**Pink Houses**...John Cougar Mellencamp
31/64	**Pink Panther Theme**...Henry Mancini
3/59	**Pink Shoe Laces**...Dodie Stevens
	Piove ..see: Ciao, Ciao Bambina
4/63	**Pipeline**...Chantay's
9/66	**Place In The Sun**...Stevie Wonder
6/91	**Place In This World**...Michael W. Smith
34/94	**Place Where You Belong**...Shai
38/59	**Plain Jane**...Bobby Darin
19/55	**Plantation Boogie**...Lenny Dee
40/73	**Plastic Man**...Temptations
11/72	**Play Me**...Neil Diamond
6/55	**Play Me Hearts And Flowers (I Wanna Cry)**...Johnny Desmond
33/74	**Play Something Sweet (Brickyard Blues)**...Three Dog Night
	Play That Funky Music
1/76	Wild Cherry
4/91	Vanilla Ice
17/82	**Play The Game Tonight**...Kansas
36/94	**Playaz Club**...Rappin' 4-Tay
7/62	**Playboy**...Marvelettes
17/68	**Playboy**...Gene & Debbe
13/95	**Player's Anthem**...Junior M.A.F.I.A.
37/94	**Player's Ball**...OutKast
10/91	**Playground**...Another Bad Creation
2/73	**Playground In My Mind**...Clint Holmes
21/57	**Playing For Keeps**...Elvis Presley

POS/YR	RECORD TITLE/ARTIST
F/55	**Playmates**...Fontane Sisters
3/67	**Pleasant Valley Sunday**...Monkees
18/78	**Please Come Home For Christmas**...Eagles
5/74	**Please Come To Boston**...Dave Loggins
15/62	**Please Don't Ask About Barbara**...Bobby Vee
	Please Don't Go
1/80	K.C. & The Sunshine Band
6/92	K.W.S.
39/61	**Please Don't Go**...Ral Donner
10/88	**Please Don't Go Girl**...New Kids On The Block
24/79	**Please Don't Leave**...Lauren Wood
31/63	**Please Don't Talk To The Lifeguard**...Diane Ray
7/93	**Please Forgive Me**...Bryan Adams
8/60	**Please Help Me, I'm Falling**...Hank Locklin (also see: I Can't Help You)
	Please Love Me Forever
12/61	Cathy Jean & The Roommates
6/67	Bobby Vinton
3/75	**Please Mr. Please**...Olivia Newton-John
	Please Mr. Postman
1/61	Marvelettes
1/75	Carpenters
11/59	**Please Mr. Sun**...Tommy Edwards
3/64	**Please Please Me**...Beatles
	(Please Please Please) ..see: Dunkie Butt
26/68	**Please Return Your Love To Me**...Temptations
14/61	**Please Stay**...Drifters
28/66	**Please Tell Me Why**...Dave Clark Five
20/61	**Please Tell Me Why**...Jackie Wilson
14/87	**Pleasure Principle**...Janet Jackson
	Pledge Of Love
12/57	Ken Copeland
25/57	Mitchell Torok
	Pledging My Love
17/55	Johnny Ace
17/55	Teresa Brewer
34/62	**Pocketful Of Miracles**...Frank Sinatra
2/60	**Poetry In Motion**...Johnny Tillotson
5/75	**Poetry Man**...Phoebe Snow
37/70	**Point It Out**...Miracles
28/78	**Point Of Know Return**...Kansas
5/87	**Point Of No Return**...Expose
21/62	**Point Of No Return**...Gene McDaniels
28/86	**Point Of No Return**...Nu Shooz
3/90	**Poison**...Bell Biv DeVoe
7/89	**Poison**...Alice Cooper

POS/YR	RECORD TITLE/ARTIST
25/83	**Poison Arrow**...ABC
7/59	**Poison Ivy**...Coasters
15/90	**Policy Of Truth**...Depeche Mode
24/84	**Politics Of Dancing**...Re-Flex
8/69	**Polk Salad Annie**...Tony Joe White
	Pomp & Circumstance ..see: Graduation Song
1/61	**Pony Time**...Chubby Checker
17/58	**Poor Boy**...Royaltones
24/57	**Poor Boy**...Elvis Presley
38/62	**Poor Fool**...Ike & Tina Turner
22/59	**Poor Jenny**...Everly Brothers
1/58	**Poor Little Fool**...Ricky Nelson
27/63	**Poor Little Rich Girl**...Steve Lawrence
14/57	**Poor Man's Roses (Or A Rich Man's Gold)**...Patti Page
33/81	**Poor Man's Son**...Survivor
	Poor People Of Paris
1/56	Les Baxter
17/56	Lawrence Welk
19/56	Russ Morgan
31/78	**Poor Poor Pitiful Me**...Linda Ronstadt
1/66	**Poor Side Of Town**...Johnny Rivers
35/82	**Pop Goes The Movies**...Meco
29/91	**Pop Goes The Weasel**...3rd Bass
20/88	**Pop Goes The World**...Men Without Hats
7/85	**Pop Life**...Prince
1/79	**Pop Muzik**...M
35/62	**Pop Pop Pop-Pie**...Sherrys
15/89	**Pop Singer**...John Cougar Mellencamp
24/72	**Pop That Thang**...Isley Brothers
9/72	**Popcorn**...Hot Butter
30/69	**Popcorn, The**...James Brown
14/55	**Popcorn Song**...Cliffie Stone
10/62	**Popeye (The Hitchhiker)**...Chubby Checker
21/66	**Popsicle**...Jan & Dean
3/64	**Popsicles And Icicles**...Murmaids
20/56	**Port Au Prince**...Nelson Riddle
	Portrait Of My Love
9/61	Steve Lawrence
36/67	Tokens
19/56	**Portuguese Washerwomen**...Joe "Fingers" Carr
	Poseidon Adventure ..see: Morning After
7/65	**Positively 4th Street**...Bob Dylan
21/90	**Possession**...Bad English
30/85	**Possession Obsession**...Daryl Hall/John Oates
2/88	**Pour Some Sugar On Me**...Def Leppard

POS/YR	RECORD TITLE/ARTIST
2/90	**Power, The**...Snap!
24/78	**Power Of Gold**...Dan Fogelberg/Tim Weisberg
1/85	**Power Of Love**...Huey Lewis & The News
4/91	**Power Of Love (medley)**...Luther Vandross
11/72	**Power Of Love**...Joe Simon
	Power Of Love
26/88	Laura Branigan
1/94	Celine Dion
11/71	**Power To The People**...John Lennon
35/91	**Power Windows**...Billy Falcon
18/94	**Practice What You Preach**...Barry White
2/90	**Pray**...M.C. Hammer
21/94	**Prayer For The Dying**...Seal
1/90	**Praying For Time**...George Michael
3/72	**Precious And Few**...Climax
19/79	**Precious Love**...Bob Welch
30/71	**Precious, Precious**...Jackie Moore
22/81	**Precious To Me**...Phil Seymour
21/86	**Press**...Paul McCartney
20/82	**Pressure**...Billy Joel
	Pretty Baby ..see: (It's Been A Long Time)
15/67	**Pretty Ballerina**...Left Banke
9/60	**Pretty Blue Eyes**...Steve Lawrence
29/66	**Pretty Flamingo**...Manfred Mann
25/95	**Pretty Girl**...Jon B.
39/79	**Pretty Girls**...Melissa Manchester
36/59	**Pretty Girls Everywhere**...Eugene Church
7/61	**Pretty Little Angel Eyes**...Curtis Lee
25/65	**Pretty Little Baby**...Marvin Gaye
15/63	**Pretty Paper**...Roy Orbison
	Pretty Woman ..see: Oh, Pretty Woman
5/90	**Price Of Love**...Bad English
10/63	**Pride And Joy**...Marvin Gaye
33/84	**Pride (In The Name Of Love)**...U2
34/84	**Prime Time**...Alan Parsons Project
8/59	**Primrose Lane**...Jerry Wallace
30/61	**Princess**...Frank Gari
37/65	**Princess In Rags**...Gene Pitney
33/90	**Principal's Office**...Young M.C.
20/56	**Priscilla**...Eddie Cooley
30/89	**Prisoner, The**...Howard Jones **(also see: Love Theme From Eyes Of Laura Mars)**
18/63	**Prisoner Of Love**...James Brown
27/78	**Prisoner Of Your Love**...Player
7/85	**Private Dancer**...Tina Turner
1/81	**Private Eyes**...Daryl Hall & John Oates

POS/YR	RECORD TITLE/ARTIST
2/58	**Problems**...Everly Brothers
11/88	**Promise, The**...When In Rome
40/88	**Promise Me**...Cover Girls
17/58	**Promise Me, Love**...Andy Williams
1/91	**Promise Of A New Day**...Paula Abdul
14/74	**Promised Land**...Elvis Presley
9/79	**Promises**...Eric Clapton
38/81	**Promises In The Dark**...Pat Benatar
11/83	**Promises, Promises**...Naked Eyes
19/68	**Promises, Promises**...Dionne Warwick
29/63	**Proud**...Johnny Crawford
	Proud Mary
2/69	Creedence Clearwater Revival
4/71	Ike & Tina Turner
22/75	**Proud One**...Osmonds
	Proud Ones ..see: Theme From
33/78	**Prove It All Night**...Bruce Springsteen
7/88	**Prove Your Love**...Taylor Dayne
7/70	**Psychedelic Shack**...Temptations
5/66	**Psychotic Reaction**...Count Five
31/67	**Pucker Up Buttercup**...Jr. Walker & The All Stars
2/63	**Puff (The Magic Dragon)**...Peter, Paul & Mary
2/90	**Pump Up The Jam**...Technotronic
13/88	**Pump Up The Volume**...M/A/R/R/S
26/94	**Pumps And A Bump**...Hammer
20/62	**Punish Her**...Bobby Vee
	Puppet Man
24/70	5th Dimension
26/71	Tom Jones
14/65	**Puppet On A String**...Elvis Presley
	Puppy Love
2/60	Paul Anka
3/72	Donny Osmond
38/64	**Puppy Love**...Barbara Lewis
31/90	**Pure**...Lightning Seeds
1/58	**Purple People Eater**...Sheb Wooley
2/84	**Purple Rain**...Prince
27/62	**Push And Kick**...Mark Valentino
	Push And Pull ..see: (Do The)
19/88	**Push It**...Salt-N-Pepa
36/67	**Pushin' Too Hard**...Seeds
25/63	**Pushover**...Etta James
17/58	**Pussy Cat**...Ames Brothers
8/58	**Put A Light In The Window**...Four Lads
	Put A Little Love In Your Heart
4/69	Jackie DeShannon
9/89	Annie Lennox & Al Green

POS/YR	RECORD TITLE/ARTIST
32/58	**Put A Ring On My Finger**...Les Paul & Mary Ford
40/83	**Put It In A Magazine**...Sonny Charles
2/71	**Put Your Hand In The Hand**...Ocean
10/74	**Put Your Hands Together**...O'Jays
2/59	**Put Your Head On My Shoulder**...Paul Anka
27/89	**Put Your Mouth On Me**...Eddie Murphy
4/83	**Puttin' On The Ritz**...Taco

Q

38/93	**Quality Time**...Hi-Five
1/61	**Quarter To Three**...U.S. Bonds
2/56	**Que Sera, Sera (Whatever Will Be, Will Be)**...Doris Day
2/81	**Queen Of Hearts**...Juice Newton
40/76	**Queen Of My Soul**...Average White Band
34/83	**Queen Of The Broken Hearts**...Loverboy
9/58	**Queen Of The Hop**...Bobby Darin
12/65	**Queen Of The House**...Jody Miller **(also see: King Of The Road)**
39/57	**Queen Of The Senior Prom**...Mills Brothers
13/69	**Quentin's Theme**...Charles Randolph Grean Sounde
19/60	**Question**...Lloyd Price
21/70	**Question**...Moody Blues
37/68	**Question Of Temperature**...Balloon Farm
24/71	**Questions 67 And 68**...Chicago
25/68	**Quick Joey Small (Run Joey Run)**...Kasenetz-Katz Singing Orchestral Circus
8/64	**Quicksand**...Martha & The Vandellas
4/59	**Quiet Village**...Martin Denny
27/61	**Quite A Party**...Fireballs

R

15/65	**Race Is On**...Jack Jones
13/74	**Radar Love**...Golden Earring
16/84	**Radio Ga-Ga**...Queen
35/89	**Radio Romance**...Tiffany
28/85	**Radioactive**...Firm
1/64	**Rag Doll**...4 Seasons
17/88	**Rag Doll**...Aerosmith
F/71	**Rags To Riches**...Elvis Presley

POS/YR	RECORD TITLE/ARTIST
16/59	**Ragtime Cowboy Joe**...Chipmunks
9/86	**Rain, The**...Oran "Juice" Jones
14/93	**Rain**...Madonna
23/66	**Rain**...Beatles
19/71	**Rain Dance**...Guess Who
10/66	**Rain On The Roof**...Lovin' Spoonful
21/86	**Rain On The Scarecrow**...John Cougar Mellencamp
12/62	**Rain Rain Go Away**...Bobby Vinton
2/67	**Rain, The Park & Other Things**...Cowsills
4/57	**Rainbow**...Russ Hamilton
25/79	**Rainbow Connection**...Kermit (Jim Henson)
2/61	**Raindrops**...Dee Clark
1/70	**Raindrops Keep Fallin' On My Head**...B.J. Thomas
34/61	**Rainin' In My Heart**...Slim Harpo
31/66	**Rains Came**...Sir Douglas Quintet
26/75	**Rainy Day People**...Gordon Lightfoot
2/66	**Rainy Day Women #12 & 35**...Bob Dylan
2/71	**Rainy Days And Mondays**...Carpenters
4/70	**Rainy Night In Georgia**...Brook Benton
29/61	**Ram-Bunk-Shush**...Ventures
21/61	**Rama Lama Ding Dong**...Edsels
17/69	**Ramblin' Gamblin' Man**...Bob Seger System
2/73	**Ramblin Man**...Allman Brothers Band
2/62	**Ramblin' Rose**...Nat King Cole
27/58	**Ramrod**...Duane Eddy
2/70	**Rapper, The**...Jaggerz
36/80	**Rapper's Delight**...Sugarhill Gang
1/81	**Rapture**...Blondie
2/85	**Raspberry Beret**...Prince
	Raunchy
2/57	Bill Justis
4/57	Ernie Freeman
10/57	Billy Vaughn
37/58	**Rave On**...Buddy Holly
23/59	**Raw-Hide**...Link Wray
24/69	**Ray Of Hope**...Rascals
15/55	**Razzle-Dazzle**...Bill Haley
20/70	**Reach Out And Touch (Somebody's Hand)**...Diana Ross
20/64	**Reach Out For Me**...Dionne Warwick
	Reach Out I'll Be There
1/66	Four Tops
29/71	Diana Ross
10/68	**Reach Out Of The Darkness**...Friend & Lover
18/84	**Read 'Em And Weep**...Barry Manilow
26/75	**Ready**...Cat Stevens

POS/YR	RECORD TITLE/ARTIST
7/90	**Ready Or Not**...After 7
35/69	**Ready Or Not Here I Come (Can't Hide From Love)**...Delfonics
11/78	**Ready To Take A Chance Again**...Barry Manilow
2/89	**Real Love**...Jody Watley
5/80	**Real Love**...Doobie Brothers
7/92	**Real Love**...Mary J. Blige
24/91	**Real Love**...Bob Seger
4/91	**Real, Real, Real**...Jesus Jones
16/81	**Really Wanna Know You**...Gary Wright
	Reaper, The ..see: (Don't Fear)
19/93	**Reason To Believe**...Rod Stewart (with Ronnie Wood)
6/58	**Rebel-'Rouser**...Duane Eddy
15/93	**Rebirth Of Slick (Cool Like Dat)**...Digable Planets
28/69	**Reconsider Me**...Johnny Adams
37/66	**Recovery**...Fontella Bass
2/95	**Red Light Special**...TLC
	Red Red Wine
34/84	UB40
1/88	UB40
5/59	**Red River Rock**...Johnny & The Hurricanes
37/59	**Red River Rose**...Ames Brothers
	Red Roses For A Blue Lady
10/65	Vic Dana
11/65	Bert Kaempfert
23/65	Wayne Newton
2/66	**Red Rubber Ball**...Cyrkle
	Red Sails In The Sunset
36/60	Platters
35/63	Fats Domino
	Reelin' And Rockin'
23/65	Dave Clark Five
27/73	Chuck Berry
11/73	**Reeling In The Years**...Steely Dan
2/67	**Reflections**...Supremes
10/70	**Reflections Of My Life**...Marmalade
1/84	**Reflex, The**...Duran Duran
15/80	**Refugee**...Tom Petty
28/93	**Regret**...New Order
2/94	**Regulate**...Warren G. & Nate Dogg
10/85	**Relax**...Frankie Goes To Hollywood
39/73	**Relay, The**...Who
1/90	**Release Me**...Wilson Phillips
	Release Me
8/62	Esther Phillips
4/67	Engelbert Humperdinck
39/63	**Remember Diana**...Paul Anka

POS/YR	RECORD TITLE/ARTIST
16/71	**Remember Me**...Diana Ross
26/64	**Remember Me**...Rita Pavone
32/65	**(Remember Me) I'm The One Who Loves You**...Dean Martin
33/77	**(Remember The Days Of The) Old Schoolyard**...Cat Stevens
36/84	**Remember The Nights**...Motels
3/92	**Remember The Time**...Michael Jackson
24/63	**Remember Then**...Earls
5/64	**Remember (Walkin' in the Sand)**...Shangri-Las
25/75	**Remember What I Told You To Forget**...Tavares
6/57	**Remember You're Mine**...Pat Boone
3/78	**Reminiscing**...Little River Band
26/75	**Rendezvous**...Hudson Brothers
16/79	**Renegade**...Styx
39/76	**Renegade**...Michael Murphey
4/65	**Rescue Me**...Fontella Bass
9/91	**Rescue Me**...Madonna
	Respect
35/65	Otis Redding
1/67	Aretha Franklin
	Respect Yourself
12/71	Staple Singers
5/87	Bruce Willis
15/66	**Respectable**...Outsiders
35/92	**Restless Heart**...Peter Cetera
	Resurrection Shuffle
38/71	Tom Jones
40/71	Ashton, Gardner & Dyke
15/67	**Return Of The Red Baron**...Royal Guardsmen
4/94	**Return To Innocence**...Enigma
4/58	**Return To Me**...Dean Martin
2/62	**Return To Sender**...Elvis Presley
	Reuben ..see: Ruben
1/79	**Reunited**...Peaches & Herb
25/59	**Reveille Rock**...Johnny & The Hurricanes
15/62	**Revenge**...Brook Benton
8/63	**Reverend Mr. Black**...Kingston Trio
12/68	**Revolution**...Beatles
16/66	**Rhapsody In The Rain**...Lou Christie
11/76	**Rhiannon (Will You Ever Win)**...Fleetwood Mac
1/75	**Rhinestone Cowboy**...Glen Campbell
24/64	**Rhythm**...Major Lance
5/93	**Rhythm Is A Dancer**...Snap!
5/87	**Rhythm Is Gonna Get You**...Gloria Estefan & Miami Sound Machine

POS/YR	RECORD TITLE/ARTIST
F/55	**Rhythm 'N' Blues (Mama's Got The Rhythm - Papa's Got The Blues)** ...McGuire Sisters
2/90	**Rhythm Nation**...Janet Jackson
40/88	**Rhythm Of Love**...Yes
5/91	**Rhythm Of My Heart**...Rod Stewart
3/85	**Rhythm Of The Night**...DeBarge
11/95	**Rhythm Of The Night**...Corona
3/63	**Rhythm Of The Rain**...Cascades
1/77	**Rich Girl**...Daryl Hall & John Oates
7/91	**Rico Suave**...Gerardo
5/62	**Ride!**...Dee Dee Sharp
25/65	**Ride Away**...Roy Orbison
4/70	**Ride Captain Ride**...Blues Image
23/75	**Ride 'Em Cowboy**...Paul Davis
2/80	**Ride Like The Wind**...Christopher Cross
37/67	**Ride, Ride, Ride**...Brenda Lee
16/64	**Ride The Wild Surf**...Jan & Dean
38/91	**Ride The Wind**...Poison
28/65	**Ride Your Pony**...Lee Dorsey
	Riders In The Sky ..see: (Ghost)
14/71	**Riders On The Storm**...Doors
2/76	**Right Back Where We Started From**...Maxine Nightingale
29/84	**Right By Your Side**...Eurythmics
12/78	**Right Down The Line**...Gerry Rafferty
2/91	**Right Here, Right Now**...Jesus Jones
1/89	**Right Here Waiting**...Richard Marx
2/93	**Right Here/Human Nature**...SWV-Sisters With Voices
14/93	**Right Kind Of Love**...Jeremy Jordan
23/71	**Right On The Tip Of My Tongue**...Brenda & The Tabulations
7/87	**Right On Track**...Breakfast Club
	Right Or Wrong
29/61	Wanda Jackson
14/64	Ronnie Dove
9/73	**Right Place Wrong Time**...Dr. John
27/87	**Right Thing**...Simply Red
17/73	**Right Thing To Do**...Carly Simon
6/77	**Right Time Of The Night**...Jennifer Warnes
4/74	**Rikki Don't Lose That Number**...Steely Dan
32/59	**Ring-A-Ling-A-Lario**...Jimmie Rodgers
33/65	**Ring Dang Doo**...Sam The Sham & The Pharaohs
	Ring My Bell
1/79	Anita Ward
20/91	D.J. Jazzy Jeff & The Fresh Prince
F/57	**Ring My Phone**...Tommy Sands

POS/YR	RECORD TITLE/ARTIST
17/63	**Ring Of Fire**...Johnny Cash
31/72	**Ring The Living Bell**...Melanie
1/64	**Ringo**...Lorne Greene
17/71	**Rings**...Cymarron
10/62	**Rinky Dink**...Baby Cortez
14/83	**Rio**...Duran Duran
	Rip It Up
17/56	Little Richard
25/56	Bill Haley
36/64	**Rip Van Winkle**...Devotions
1/79	**Rise**...Herb Alpert
38/88	**Ritual**...Dan Reed Network
14/71	**River Deep - Mountain High**...Supremes & Four Tops
31/69	**River Is Wide**...Grassroots
	River Kwai March ..see: March From
3/93	**River Of Dreams**...Billy Joel
33/74	**River's Risin'**...Edgar Winter
30/78	**Rivers Of Babylon**...Boney M
	Road Runner ..see: (I'm A)
3/90	**Roam**...B-52's
25/59	**Robbin' The Cradle**...Tony Bellus
16/56	**R-O-C-K**...Bill Haley
23/55	**Rock-A-Beatin' Boogie**...Bill Haley
10/57	**Rock-A-Billy**...Guy Mitchell
	Rock-A-Bye Your Baby With A Dixie Melody
10/56	Jerry Lewis
37/61	Aretha Franklin
23/62	**Rock-A-Hula Baby ("Twist" Special)**...Elvis Presley
23/89	**Rock And A Hard Place**...Rolling Stones
	Rock And Roll ..also see: Rock 'N' Roll, Rockin' Roll
7/72	**Rock And Roll**...Gary Glitter
12/76	**Rock And Roll All Nite**...Kiss (Live)
	Rock And Roll Dreams Come Through
32/81	Jim Steinman
13/94	Meat Loaf
20/85	**Rock And Roll Girls**...John Fogerty
3/74	**Rock And Roll Heaven**...Righteous Brothers
23/74	**Rock And Roll, Hoochie Koo**...Rick Derringer
19/58	**Rock And Roll Is Here To Stay**...Danny & The Juniors
28/76	**Rock And Roll Love Letter**...Bay City Rollers
15/72	**Rock And Roll Lullaby**...B.J. Thomas

POS/YR	RECORD TITLE/ARTIST
	Rock And Roll Music
8/57	Chuck Berry
5/76	Beach Boys
1/56	**Rock And Roll Waltz**...Kay Starr
	Rock Around The Clock
1/55	Bill Haley
39/74	Bill Haley
2/86	**R.O.C.K. In The U.S.A.**...John Cougar Mellencamp
8/56	**Rock Island Line**...Lonnie Donegan
13/55	**Rock Love**...Fontane Sisters
10/69	**Rock Me**...Steppenwolf
1/86	**Rock Me Amadeus**...Falco
34/64	**Rock Me Baby**...B.B. King
38/72	**Rock Me Baby**...David Cassidy
1/74	**Rock Me Gently**...Andy Kim
18/85	**Rock Me Tonight (For Old Times Sake)**...Freddie Jackson
15/84	**Rock Me Tonite**...Billy Squier
	Rock 'N' Roll ..also see: Rock And Roll, Rockin' Roll
13/79	**Rock 'N' Roll Fantasy**...Bad Company
30/78	**Rock 'N' Roll Fantasy**...Kinks
15/75	**Rock N' Roll (I Gave You The Best Years Of My Life)**...Mac Davis
19/83	**Rock 'N' Roll Is King**...ELO
29/72	**Rock 'N Roll Soul**...Grand Funk Railroad
16/83	**Rock Of Ages**...Def Leppard
22/88	**Rock Of Life**...Rick Springfield
	Rock On
5/74	David Essex
1/89	Michael Damian
36/56	**Rock Right**...Georgia Gibbs
7/87	**Rock Steady**...Whispers
9/71	**Rock Steady**...Aretha Franklin
1/74	**Rock The Boat**...Hues Corporation
8/83	**Rock The Casbah**...Clash
30/87	**Rock The Night**...Europe
9/82	**Rock This Town**...Stray Cats
7/89	**Rock Wit'cha**...Bobby Brown
1/80	**Rock With You**...Michael Jackson
25/84	**Rock You Like A Hurricane**...Scorpions
1/74	**Rock Your Baby**...George McCrae
17/57	**Rock Your Little Baby To Sleep**...Buddy Knox
38/59	**Rocka-Conga**...Applejacks
12/89	**Rocket**...Def Leppard
6/72	**Rocket Man**...Elton John
39/78	**Rocket Ride**...Kiss

POS/YR	RECORD TITLE/ARTIST
6/88	**Rocket 2 U**...Jets
10/75	**Rockford Files**...Mike Post
27/75	**Rockin' All Over The World**...John Fogerty
14/60	**Rockin' Around The Christmas Tree**...Brenda Lee
25/85	**Rockin' At Midnight**...Honeydrippers
9/75	**Rockin' Chair**...Gwen McCrae
7/60	**Rockin' Good Way (To Mess Around And Fall In Love)**...Dinah Washington & Brook Benton
22/60	**Rockin' Little Angel**...Ray Smith
1/76	**Rockin' Me**...Steve Miller
6/73	**Rockin' Pneumonia And The Boogie Woogie Flu**...Johnny Rivers
	Rockin' Robin
2/58	Bobby Day
2/72	Michael Jackson
	Rockin' Roll ..also see: Rock And Roll, Rock 'N' Roll
14/73	**Rockin' Roll Baby**...Stylistics
18/74	**Rockin' Soul**...Hues Corporation
9/75	**Rocky**...Austin Roberts
9/73	**Rocky Mountain High**...John Denver
23/73	**Rocky Mountain Way**...Joe Walsh
	Rocky, Theme From ..see: Gonna Fly Now
30/79	**Rolene**...Moon Martin
27/83	**Roll Me Away**...Bob Seger
14/75	**Roll On Down The Highway**...Bachman-Turner Overdrive
29/56	**Roll Over Beethoven**...Chuck Berry
10/95	**Roll To Me**...Del Amitri
1/88	**Roll With It**...Steve Winwood
34/79	**Roller**...April Wine
13/55	**Rollin' Stone**...Fontane Sisters
26/84	**Romancing The Stone**...Eddy Grant
1/91	**Romantic**...Karyn White
6/90	**Romeo**...Dino
27/92	**Romeo & Juliet**...Stacy Earl (Feat. The Wild Pair) **(also see: Love Theme, & (Just Like)**
11/80	**Romeo's Tune**...Steve Forbert
3/89	**Roni**...Bobby Brown
6/64	**Ronnie**...4 Seasons
17/90	**Room At The Top**...Adam Ant
9/89	**Room To Move**...Animotion
16/89	**Rooms On Fire**...Stevie Nicks
2/82	**Rosanna**...Toto
3/80	**Rose, The**...Bette Midler

POS/YR	RECORD TITLE/ARTIST
6/56	**Rose And A Baby Ruth**...George Hamilton IV
3/71	**Rose Garden**...Lynn Anderson (also see: I Beg Your Pardon)
	Roses And Roses ..see: And Roses
1/62	**Roses Are Red (My Love)**...Bobby Vinton
24/57	**Rosie Lee**...Mello-Tones
30/80	**Rotation**...Herb Alpert
22/86	**Rough Boy**...ZZ Top
1/57	**Round And Round**...Perry Como
12/84	**Round And Round**...Ratt
12/91	**Round And Round**...Tevin Campbell
21/65	**Round Every Corner**...Petula Clark
13/72	**Roundabout**...Yes
30/62	**Route 66 Theme**...Nelson Riddle
37/82	**Route 101**...Herb Alpert
32/79	**Roxanne**...Police
16/74	**Rub It In**...Billy "Crash" Craddock
3/90	**Rub You The Right Way**...Johnny Gill
6/61	**Rubber Ball**...Bobby Vee
37/79	**Rubber Biscuit**...Blues Brothers
16/70	**Rubber Duckie**...Ernie (Jim Henson)
2/76	**Rubberband Man**...Spinners
F/70	**Rubberneckin'**...Elvis Presley
26/69	**Ruben James**...Kenny Rogers & The First Edition
28/60	**Ruby**...Ray Charles
18/62	**Ruby Ann**...Marty Robbins
	Ruby Baby
2/63	Dion
33/75	Billy "Crash" Craddock
6/69	**Ruby, Don't Take Your Love To Town**...Kenny Rogers & The First Edition
30/60	**Ruby Duby Du**...Tobin Mathews & Co.
	(Ruby Red Dress) ..see: Leave Me Alone
1/67	**Ruby Tuesday**...Rolling Stones
21/60	**Rudolph The Red Nosed Reindeer**...Chipmunks
34/56	**Rudy's Rock**...Bill Haley
35/93	**RuffNeck**...MC Lyte
16/58	**Rumble**...Link Wray
28/86	**Rumbleseat**...John Cougar Mellencamp
8/86	**Rumors**...Timex Social Club
12/62	**Rumors**...Johnny Crawford
2/92	**Rump Shaker**...Wreckx-N-Effect
8/95	**Run-Around**...Blues Traveler
23/60	**Runaround**...Fleetwoods
28/61	**Runaround**...Regents
3/95	**Run Away**...Real McCoy

POS/YR	RECORD TITLE/ARTIST
1/61	**Runaway**...Del Shannon
3/95	**Runaway**...Janet Jackson
12/78	**Runaway**...Jefferson Starship
39/84	**Runaway**...Bon Jovi
6/69	**Run Away Child, Running Wild**...Temptations
12/65	**Run, Baby Run (Back Into My Arms)**...Newbeats
33/78	**Run For Home**...Lindisfarne
18/82	**Run For The Roses**...Dan Fogelberg
4/75	**Run Joey Run**...David Geddes
36/60	**Run Red Run**...Coasters
25/66	**Run, Run, Look And See**...Brian Hyland
27/72	**Run Run Run**...Jo Jo Gunne
20/84	**Run Runaway**...Slade
28/60	**Run Samson Run**...Neil Sedaka
F/70	**Run Through The Jungle**...Creedence Clearwater Revival
2/61	**Run To Him**...Bobby Vee
16/72	**Run To Me**...Bee Gees
6/85	**Run To You**...Bryan Adams
31/93	**Run To You**...Whitney Houston
	Runaround Sue
1/61	Dion
13/78	Leif Garrett
5/93	**Runaway Train**...Soul Asylum
22/84	**Runner**...Manfred Mann's Earth Band
23/72	**Runnin' Away**...Sly & The Family Stone
23/89	**Runnin' Down A Dream**...Tom Petty
18/91	**Running Back To You**...Vanessa Williams
1/60	**Running Bear**...Johnny Preston
11/78	**Running On Empty**...Jackson Browne
1/61	**Running Scared**...Roy Orbison
30/85	**Running Up That Hill**...Kate Bush
7/84	**Running With The Night**...Lionel Richie
39/72	**Runway, The**...Grass Roots
32/91	**Rush**...Big Audio Dynamite II
9/88	**Rush Hour**...Jane Wiedlin
1/91	**Rush, Rush**...Paula Abdul
16/86	**Russians**...Sting
33/65	**Rusty Bells**...Brenda Lee

S

POS/YR	RECORD TITLE/ARTIST
15/75	**S.O.S.**...Abba
39/66	**S.Y.S.L.J.F.M. (The Letter Song)**...Joe Tex
20/61	**Sacred**...Castells

POS/YR	RECORD TITLE/ARTIST
13/89	**Sacred Emotion**...Donny Osmond
18/90	**Sacrifice**...Elton John
1/79	**Sad Eyes**...Robert John
29/60	**Sad Mood**...Sam Cooke
5/61	**Sad Movies (Make Me Cry)**...Sue Thompson
27/65	**Sad, Sad Girl**...Barbara Mason
5/84	**Sad Songs (Say So Much)**...Elton John
14/75	**Sad Sweet Dreamer**...Sweet Sensation
5/91	**Sadeness**...Enigma
3/83	**Safety Dance**...Men Without Hats
6/94	**Said I Loved You...But I Lied**...Michael Bolton
5/58	**Sail Along Silvery Moon**...Billy Vaughn
	(Sail Away) ..see: Orinoco Flow
4/79	**Sail On**...Commodores
1/80	**Sailing**...Christopher Cross
5/60	**Sailor (Your Home Is The Sea)**...Lolita
	Saint ..see: St.
	Saints Rock 'N Roll ..see: When The Saints Go Marchin' In
17/75	**Sally G**...Paul McCartney
2/63	**Sally, Go 'Round The Roses**...Jaynetts
36/83	**Salt In My Tears**...Martin Briley
20/77	**Sam**...Olivia Newton-John
9/81	**Same Old Lang Syne**...Dan Fogelberg
13/55	**Same Old Saturday Night**...Frank Sinatra
16/60	**Same One**...Brook Benton
8/61	**San Antonio Rose**...Floyd Cramer
9/67	**San Franciscan Nights**...Animals
4/67	**San Francisco (Be Sure To Wear Flowers In Your Hair)**...Scott McKenzie
14/86	**Sanctify Yourself**...Simple Minds
23/55	**Sand And The Sea**...Nat "King" Cole
15/60	**Sandy**...Larry Hall
21/63	**Sandy**...Dion
27/66	**Sandy**...Ronny & The Daytonas
32/57	**Santa And The Satellite**...Buchanan & Goodman
23/62	**Santa Claus Is Coming To Town**...4 Seasons
1/86	**Sara**...Starship
7/80	**Sara**...Fleetwood Mac
4/76	**Sara Smile**...Daryl Hall & John Oates
39/80	**(Sartorial Eloquence) Don't Ya Wanna Play This Game No More?**...Elton John
23/66	**Satin Pillows**...Bobby Vinton
28/73	**Satin Sheets**...Jeanne Pruett
22/75	**Satin Soul**...Love Unlimited Orchestra

POS/YR	RECORD TITLE/ARTIST
	Satisfaction ..see: (I Can't Get No)
1/89	**Satisfied**...Richard Marx
39/66	**Satisfied Mind**...Bobby Hebb
3/72	**Saturday In The Park**...Chicago
26/86	**Saturday Love**...Cherrelle with Alexander O'Neal
28/71	**Saturday Morning Confusion**...Bobby Russell
1/76	**Saturday Night**...Bay City Rollers
29/63	**Saturday Night**...New Christy Minstrels
35/79	**Saturdaynight**...Herman Brood
21/77	**Saturday Nite**...Earth, Wind & Fire
18/64	**Saturday Night At The Movies**...Drifters
27/75	**Saturday Night Special**...Lynyrd Skynyrd
34/79	**Saturday Night, Sunday Morning**...Thelma Houston
12/73	**Saturday Night's Alright For Fighting**...Elton John
25/81	**Sausalito Summernight**...Diesel
34/80	**Savannah Nights**...Tom Johnston
16/85	**Save A Prayer**...Duran Duran
22/77	**Save It For A Rainy Day**...Stephen Bishop
10/64	**Save It For Me**...4 Seasons
33/90	**Save Me**...Fleetwood Mac
15/91	**Save Some Love**...Keedy
1/92	**Save The Best For Last**...Vanessa Williams
27/70	**Save The Country**...5th Dimension
	Save The Last Dance For Me
1/60	Drifters
18/74	DeFranco Family
	(also see: I'll Save The Last Dance)
37/92	**Save Up All Your Tears**...Cher
2/65	**Save Your Heart For Me**...Gary Lewis & The Playboys
27/76	**Save Your Kisses For Me**...Brotherhood Of Man
37/61	**Saved**...LaVern Baker
20/83	**Saved By Zero**...Fixx
1/85	**Saving All My Love For You**...Whitney Houston
4/93	**Saving Forever For You**...Shanice
21/90	**Say A Prayer**...Breathe
17/81	**Say Goodbye To Hollywood**...Billy Joel
3/73	**Say, Has Anybody Seen My Sweet Gypsy Rose**...Dawn
21/66	**Say I Am (What I Am)**...Tommy James & The Shondells
27/88	**Say It Again**...Jermaine Stewart
2/83	**Say It Isn't So**...Daryl Hall - John Oates

POS/YR	RECORD TITLE/ARTIST
10/68	**Say It Loud - I'm Black And I'm Proud**...James Brown
20/59	**Say Man**...Bo Diddley
1/83	**Say Say Say**...Paul McCartney & Michael Jackson
22/65	**Say Something Funny**...Patty Duke
32/81	**Say What**...Jesse Winchester
40/64	**Say You**...Ronnie Dove
11/76	**Say You Love Me**...Fleetwood Mac
1/85	**Say You, Say Me**...Lionel Richie
6/88	**Say You Will**...Foreigner
20/81	**Say You'll Be Mine**...Christopher Cross
15/77	**Say You'll Stay Until Tomorrow**...Tom Jones
39/65	**(Say) You're My Girl**...Roy Orbison
21/85	**Say You're Wrong**...Julian Lennon
31/88	**Sayin' Sorry (Don't Make It Right)**...Denise Lopez
	Scarborough Fair
11/68	Simon & Garfunkel
16/68	Sergio Mendes & Brasil '66
13/59	**Scarlet Ribbons (For Her Hair)**...Browns
33/75	**School Boy Crush**...AWB **(also see: Ain't 2 Proud 2 Beg)**
3/57	**School Day**...Chuck Berry
28/61	**School Is In**...Gary (U.S.) Bonds
5/61	**School Is Out**...Gary (U.S.) Bonds
7/72	**School's Out**...Alice Cooper
6/72	**Scorpio**...Dennis Coffey
5/95	**Scream**...Michael Jackson & Janet Jackson
20/87	**Se La**...Lionel Richie
	Se Si Bon ..see: Whispering
14/59	**Sea Cruise**...Frankie Ford
21/61	**Sea Of Heartbreak**...Don Gibson
	Sea Of Love
2/59	Phil Phillips With The Twilights
33/82	Del Shannon
3/85	Honeydrippers
	Sealed With A Kiss
3/62	Brian Hyland
19/68	Gary Lewis & The Playboys
19/72	Bobby Vinton
4/85	**Search Is Over**...Survivor
3/57	**Searchin'**...Coasters
	Searchin' So Long ..see: (I've Been)
27/66	**Searching For My Love**...Bobby Moore
1/88	**Seasons Change**...Expose
1/74	**Seasons In The Sun**...Terry Jacks
38/69	**Seattle**...Perry Como
34/74	**Second Avenue**...Garfunkel

POS/YR	RECORD TITLE/ARTIST
6/89	**Second Chance**...Thirty Eight Special
40/56	**Second Fiddle**...Kay Starr
7/62	**Second Hand Love**...Connie Francis
32/66	**Second Hand Rose**...Barbra Streisand
39/85	**Second Nature**...Dan Hartman
8/80	**Second Time Around**...Shalamar
3/94	**Secret**...Madonna
18/58	**Secret, The**...Gordon MacRae
3/66	**Secret Agent Man**...Johnny Rivers
31/90	**Secret Garden (Sweet Seduction Suite)**...Quincy Jones/Al B. Sure!/James Ingram/El DeBarge/Barry White
	Secret Love
29/66	Billy Stewart
20/75	Freddy Fender
3/86	**Secret Lovers**...Atlantic Starr
6/89	**Secret Rendezvous**...Karyn White
19/86	**Secret Separation**...Fixx
3/58	**Secretly**...Jimmie Rodgers
35/68	**Security**...Etta James
28/80	**Seduction, The**...James Last Band
27/69	**See**...Rascals
	See Me, Feel Me
12/70	Who
29/73	New Seekers (medley)
25/56	**See Saw**...Moonglows
14/68	**See Saw**...Aretha Franklin
	See See ..see: C.C.
9/64	**See The Funny Little Clown**...Bobby Goldsboro
40/91	**See The Lights**...Simple Minds
	See You In September
23/59	Tempos
3/66	Happenings
6/56	**See You Later, Alligator**...Bill Haley
4/84	**Self Control**...Laura Branigan
11/64	**Selfish One**...Jackie Ross
6/57	**Send For Me**...Nat "King" Cole
23/83	**Send Her My Love**...Journey
	Send In The Clowns
36/75	Judy Collins
19/77	Judy Collins
	Send Me An Angel
29/84	Real Life
26/89	Real Life ('89)
13/63	**Send Me Some Lovin'**...Sam Cooke
	Send Me The Pillow You Dream On
17/62	Johnny Tillotson
22/65	Dean Martin
4/79	**Send One Your Love**...Stevie Wonder

POS/YR	RECORD TITLE/ARTIST
5/90	**Sending All My Love**...Linear
40/94	**Sending My Love**...Zhane
4/91	**Sensitivity**...Ralph Tresvant
27/95	**Sentimental**...Deborah Cox
8/78	**Sentimental Lady**...Bob Welch
8/85	**Sentimental Street**...Night Ranger
	(Senza Fine) ..see: Phoenix Love Theme
1/85	**Separate Lives**...Phil Collins & Marilyn Martin
20/73	**Separate Ways**...Elvis Presley
8/83	**Separate Ways (Worlds Apart)**...Journey
8/79	**September**...Earth, Wind & Fire
23/61	**September In The Rain**...Dinah Washington
17/80	**September Morn'**...Neil Diamond
23/80	**Sequel**...Harry Chapin
21/87	**Serious**...Donna Allen
13/78	**Serpentine Fire**...Earth, Wind & Fire
1/91	**Set Adrift On Memory Bliss**...PM Dawn
23/65	**Set Me Free**...Kinks
27/80	**Set Me Free**...Utopia
6/91	**Set The Night To Music**...Roberta Flack with Maxi Priest
26/96	**Set U Free**...Planet Soul
7/93	**7**...Prince & The New Power Generation
33/66	**7 And 7 Is**...Love
21/81	**Seven Bridges Road**...Eagles
27/62	**Seven Day Weekend**...Gary (US) Bonds
	Seven Days
17/56	Dorothy Collins
18/56	Crew Cuts
30/58	**"7-11" (Mambo No. 5)**...Gone All Stars
9/59	**(Seven Little Girls) Sitting In The Back Seat**...Paul Evans
14/67	**7 Rooms Of Gloom**...Four Tops
19/87	**Seven Wonders**...Fleetwood Mac
22/81	**Seven Year Ache**...Rosanne Cash
7/65	**Seventh Son**...Johnny Rivers
	Seventeen
3/55	Fontane Sisters
5/55	Boyd Bennett
18/55	Rusty Draper
26/89	**Seventeen**...Winger
36/84	**17**...Rick James
F/94	**70's Love Groove**...Janet Jackson
28/86	**Sex As A Weapon**...Pat Benatar
15/70	**Sex Machine**...James Brown
20/93	**Sex Me**...R. Kelly
3/83	**Sexual Healing**...Marvin Gaye
	Sexy + 17 ..see: (She's)

POS/YR	RECORD TITLE/ARTIST
5/80	**Sexy Eyes**...Dr. Hook
20/84	**Sexy Girl**...Glenn Frey
17/74	**Sexy Mama**...Moments (also see: It Was A Good Day)
12/65	**Sha La La**...Manfred Mann
7/74	**Sha-La-La (Make Me Happy)**...Al Green
1/78	**Shadow Dancing**...Andy Gibb
25/79	**Shadows In The Moonlight**...Anne Murray
13/82	**Shadows Of The Night**...Pat Benatar
19/62	**Shadrack**...Brook Benton
	Shaft ..see: Theme From
38/64	**Shaggy Dog**...Mickey Lee Lane
7/65	**Shake**...Sam Cooke
25/67	**Shake A Tail Feather**...James & Bobby Purify
29/65	**Shake And Fingerpop**...Jr. Walker & The All Stars
28/89	**Shake For The Sheik**...Escape Club
13/79	**Shake It**...Ian Matthews
4/82	**Shake It Up**...Cars
18/66	**Shake Me, Wake Me (When It's Over)**...Four Tops
31/67	**Shake, Rattle & Roll**...Arthur Conley
33/63	**Shake! Shake! Shake!**...Jackie Wilson
1/76	**(Shake, Shake, Shake) Shake Your Booty**...KC & The Sunshine Band
1/87	**Shake You Down**...Gregory Abbott
7/79	**Shake Your Body (Down To The Ground)**...Jacksons
5/79	**Shake Your Groove Thing**...Peaches & Herb
4/87	**Shake Your Love**...Debbie Gibson
23/77	**Shake Your Rump To The Funk**...Bar-Kays
1/87	**Shakedown**...Bob Seger
31/79	**Shakedown Cruise**...Jay Ferguson
26/75	**Shakey Ground**...Temptations
22/65	**Shakin' All Over**...Guess Who?
3/73	**Shambala**...Three Dog Night
	Shame
9/78	Evelyn "Champagne" King
28/94	Zhane'
21/85	**Shame**...Motels
23/62	**Shame On Me**...Bobby Bare
2/83	**Shame On The Moon**...Bob Seger
29/68	**Shame, Shame**...Magic Lanterns
12/75	**Shame, Shame, Shame**...Shirley (& Company)
31/82	**Shanghai Breezes**...John Denver

POS/YR	RECORD TITLE/ARTIST
	Shangri-La
11/57	Four Coins
15/64	Robert Maxwell
27/64	Vic Dana
6/76	**Shannon**...Henry Gross
22/68	**Shape Of Things To Come**...Max Frost
11/66	**Shapes Of Things**...Yardbirds
10/70	**Share The Land**...Guess Who
	Share Your Love With Me
13/69	Aretha Franklin
14/81	Kenny Rogers
6/79	**Sharing The Night Together**...Dr. Hook
15/62	**Sharing You**...Bobby Vee
31/79	**Shattered**...Rolling Stones
2/88	**Shattered Dreams**...Johnny Hates Jazz
30/75	**Shaving Cream**...Benny Bell
23/70	**She**...Tommy James & The Shondells
1/90	**She Ain't Worth It**...Glenn Medeiros & Bobby Brown
5/79	**She Believes In Me**...Kenny Rogers
33/70	**She Belongs To Me**...Rick Nelson
5/83	**She Blinded Me With Science**...Thomas Dolby
3/84	**She Bop**...Cyndi Lauper
30/70	**She Came In Through The Bathroom Window**...Joe Cocker
19/62	**She Can't Find Her Keys**...Paul Petersen
	She Comes To Me ..see: (When She Needs Good Lovin')
5/62	**She Cried**...Jay & The Americans
23/77	**She Did It**...Eric Carmen
1/89	**She Drives Me Crazy**...Fine Young Cannibals
27/67	**She Is Still A Mystery**...Lovin' Spoonful
1/64	**She Loves You**...Beatles
18/59	**She Say (Oom Dooby Doom)**...Diamonds
30/91	**She Talks To Angels**...Black Crowes
F/77	**She Thinks I Still Care**...Elvis Presley
	She Understands Me
31/64	Johnny Tillotson
40/66	Bobby Vinton (Dum-De-Da)
6/89	**She Wants To Dance With Me**...Rick Astley
27/58	**She Was Only Seventeen (He Was One Year More)**...Marty Robbins
30/89	**She Won't Talk To Me**...Luther Vandross
3/83	**She Works Hard For The Money**...Donna Summer
3/67	**She'd Rather Be With Me**...Turtles
22/81	**She's A Bad Mama Jama (She's Built, She's Stacked)**...Carl Carlton

POS/YR	RECORD TITLE/ARTIST
10/83	**She's A Beauty**...Tubes
5/63	**She's A Fool**...Lesley Gore
16/68	**She's A Heartbreaker**...Gene Pitney
2/71	**She's A Lady**...Tom Jones
25/68	**She's A Rainbow**...Rolling Stones
4/64	**She's A Woman**...Beatles
13/65	**She's About A Mover**...Sir Douglas Quintet
39/71	**She's All I Got**...Freddie North
17/78	**She's Always A Woman**...Billy Joel
18/62	**She's Everything (I Wanted You To Be)**...Ral Donner
7/76	**She's Gone**...Daryl Hall & John Oates
23/82	**She's Got A Way**...Billy Joel
14/62	**She's Got You**...Patsy Cline
3/66	**She's Just My Style**...Gary Lewis & The Playboys
3/88	**She's Like The Wind**...Patrick Swayze/Wendy Fraser
15/68	**She's Lookin' Good**...Wilson Pickett
21/84	**She's Mine**...Steve Perry
14/67	**She's My Girl**...Turtles
38/58	**She's Neat**...Dale Wright
11/71	**She's Not Just Another Woman**...8th Day
	She's Not There
2/64	Zombies
27/77	Santana
5/62	**She's Not You**...Elvis Presley
10/80	**She's Out Of My Life**...Michael Jackson
5/92	**She's Playing Hard To Get**...Hi-Five
5/83	**(She's) Sexy + 17**...Stray Cats
26/80	**She's So Cold**...Rolling Stones
33/64	**She's The One**...Chartbusters
1/62	**Sheila**...Tommy Roe
36/91	**Shelter Me**...Cinderella
17/64	**Shelter Of Your Arms**...Sammy Davis Jr.
1/62	**Sherry**...4 Seasons
	Shifting, Whispering Sands
3/55	Rusty Draper
5/55	Billy Vaughn
24/70	**Shilo**...Neil Diamond
	Shimmy Shimmy ..see: (I Do The)
24/60	**Shimmy, Shimmy, Ko-Ko-Bop**...Little Anthony & The Imperials
11/94	**Shine**...Collective Soul
8/79	**Shine A Little Love**...Electric Light Orchestra
40/81	**Shine On**...L.T.D.
37/84	**Shine Shine**...Barry Gibb
11/74	**Shinin' On**...Grand Funk

POS/YR	RECORD TITLE/ARTIST
1/75	**Shining Star**...Earth, Wind & Fire
5/80	**Shining Star**...Manhattans
10/91	**Shiny Happy People**...R.E.M.
27/87	**Ship Of Fools (Save Me From Tomorrow)**...World Party
9/79	**Ships**...Barry Manilow
10/57	**Shish-Kebab**...Ralph Marterie
29/83	**Shock The Monkey**...Peter Gabriel
18/75	**Shoeshine Boy**...Eddie Kendricks
	Shoo ..also see: Shu
9/68	**Shoo-Be-Doo-Be-Doo-Da-Day**...Stevie Wonder
4/93	**Shoop**...Salt-N-Pepa
	(Shoop Shoop) ..see: Exhale
	Shoop Shoop Song (It's In His Kiss)
6/64	Betty Everett
33/91	Cher
31/68	**Shoot'em Up, Baby**...Andy Kim
	Shop Around
2/61	Miracles
4/76	Captain & Tennille
14/95	**Short Dick Man**...20 Fingers featuring Gillette
5/57	**Short Fat Fannie**...Larry Williams
2/78	**Short People**...Randy Newman
3/58	**Short Shorts**...Royal Teens
4/65	**Shotgun**...Jr. Walker & The All Stars
13/82	**Should I Do It**...Pointer Sisters
3/87	**Should've Known Better**...Richard Marx
19/80	**Should've Never Let You Go**...Neil Sedaka & Dara Sedaka
29/89	**Shoulder To Cry On**...Tommy Page
1/85	**Shout**...Tears For Fears
6/62	**Shout**...Joey Dee & The Starliters
31/76	**Shout It Out Loud**...Kiss
6/62	**Shout! Shout! (Knock Yourself Out)**...Ernie Maresca
1/74	**Show And Tell**...Al Wilson
28/84	**Show Me**...Pretenders
35/67	**Show Me**...Joe Tex
5/93	**Show Me Love**...Robin S
3/91	**Show Me The Way**...Styx
6/76	**Show Me The Way**...Peter Frampton
4/74	**Show Must Go On**...Three Dog Night
37/85	**Show Some Respect**...Tina Turner
28/77	**Show You The Way To Go**...Jacksons
5/89	**Shower Me With Your Love**...Surface
22/76	**Shower The People**...James Taylor

POS/YR	RECORD TITLE/ARTIST
38/75	**(Shu-Doo-Pa-Poo-Poop) Love Being Your Fool**...Travis Wammack
32/61	**Shu Rah**...Fats Domino
23/63	**Shut Down**...Beach Boys
24/63	**Shutters And Boards**...Jerry Wallace
13/95	**Shy Guy**...Diana King
22/58	**Sick And Tired**...Fats Domino
8/74	**Sideshow**...Blue Magic
25/64	**Sidewalk Surfin'**...Jan & Dean
18/86	**Sidewalk Talk**...Jellybean
1/94	**Sign, The**...Ace Of Base
32/84	**Sign Of Fire**...Fixx
3/87	**Sign 'O' The Times**...Prince
11/66	**Sign Of The Times**...Petula Clark
4/88	**Sign Your Name**...Terence Trent D'Arby
	Signed, Sealed, Delivered I'm Yours
3/70	Stevie Wonder
18/77	Peter Frampton
	Signs
3/71	Five Man Electrical Band
8/91	Tesla
11/67	**Silence Is Golden**...Tremeloes
9/91	**Silent Lucidity**...Queensryche
31/92	**Silent Prayer**...Shanice featuring Johnny Gill
6/86	**Silent Running (On Dangerous Ground)**...Mike + The Mechanics
13/89	**Silhouette**...Kenny G
	Silhouettes
3/57	Rays
10/57	Diamonds
5/65	Herman's Hermits
1/76	**Silly Love Songs**...Wings
25/70	**Silver Bird**...Mark Lindsay
20/55	**Silver Dollar**...Teresa Brewer
38/76	**Silver Star**...Four Seasons
20/62	**Silver Threads And Golden Needles**...Springfields
4/68	**Simon Says**...1910 Fruitgum Co.
30/93	**Simple Life**...Elton John
2/88	**Simply Irresistible**...Robert Palmer
	Since I Don't Have You
12/59	Skyliners
23/81	Don McLean
4/63	**Since I Fell For You**...Lenny Welch
17/65	**Since I Lost My Baby**...Temptations
	Since I Met You Baby
12/56	Ivory Joe Hunter
34/57	Mindy Carson
32/67	**Since You Showed Me How To Be Happy**...Jackie Wilson

POS/YR	RECORD TITLE/ARTIST
31/87	**Since You've Been Gone**...Outfield
38/59	**Since You've Been Gone**...Clyde McPhatter
	(also see: Sweet Sweet Baby)
	Sincerely
1/55	McGuire Sisters
20/55	Moonglow's
14/89	**Sincerely Yours**...Sweet Sensation
3/73	**Sing**...Carpenters
5/76	**Sing A Song**...Earth, Wind & Fire
24/58	**Sing Boy Sing**...Tommy Sands
	Singing The Blues
1/56	Guy Mitchell
17/56	Marty Robbins
12/66	**Single Girl**...Sandy Posey
3/60	**Sink The Bismarck**...Johnny Horton
1/77	**Sir Duke**...Stevie Wonder
5/84	**Sister Christian**...Night Ranger
1/75	**Sister Golden Hair**...America
24/74	**Sister Mary Elephant (Shudd-Up!)**...Cheech & Chong
18/85	**Sisters Are Doin' It For Themselves**...Eurythmics & Aretha Franklin
36/67	**Sit Down, I Think I Love You**...Mojo Men
37/71	**Sit Yourself Down**...Stephen Stills
	Sittin' In The Balcony
18/57	Eddie Cochran
38/57	Johnny Dee
19/90	**Sittin' In The Lap Of Luxury**...Louie Louie
	(Sittin' On) The Dock Of The Bay
1/68	Otis Redding
11/88	Michael Bolton
16/73	**Sitting**...Cat Stevens
27/83	**Sitting At The Wheel**...Moody Blues
24/65	**Sitting In The Park**...Billy Stewart
32/63	**Six Days On The Road**...Dave Dudley
40/93	**Six Feet Deep**...Geto Boys
28/59	**Six Nights A Week**...Crests
18/67	**Six O'Clock**...Lovin' Spoonful
13/66	**634-5789 (Soulsville, U.S.A.)**...Wilson Pickett
	(also see: Beechwood 4-5789)
2/59	**16 Candles**...Crests
3/60	**Sixteen Reasons**...Connie Stevens
	Sixteen Tons
1/55	"Tennessee" Ernie Ford
17/55	Johnny Desmond
6/82	**'65 Love Affair**...Paul Davis
19/87	**Skeletons**...Stevie Wonder
	Skillz ..see: (I Know I Got)
13/74	**Skin Tight**...Ohio Players

POS/YR	RECORD TITLE/ARTIST
39/87	**Skin Trade**...Duran Duran
10/67	**Skinny Legs And All**...Joe Tex
22/58	**Skinny Minnie**...Bill Haley
25/68	**Skip A Rope**...Henson Cargill
3/75	**Sky High**...Jigsaw
14/68	**Sky Pilot**...Animals
4/93	**Slam**...Onyx
35/64	**Slaughter On Tenth Avenue**...Ventures
1/86	**Sledgehammer**...Peter Gabriel
	(also see: Pop Goes The Weasel)
13/60	**Sleep**...Little Willie John
1/59	**Sleep Walk**...Santo & Johnny
8/85	**Sleeping Bag**...ZZ Top
	Sleeping Beauty ..see: To A
32/93	**Sleeping Satellite**...Tasmin Archer
32/77	**Slide**...Slave
6/68	**Slip Away**...Clarence Carter
5/78	**Slip Slidin' Away**...Paul Simon
33/56	**Slipin' And Slidin'**...Little Richard
19/75	**Slippery When Wet**...Commodores
16/72	**Slippin' Into Darkness**...War
39/83	**Slipping Away**...Dave Edmunds
3/66	**Sloop John B**...Beach Boys
33/93	**Slow And Sexy**...Shabba Ranks feat. Johnny Gill
20/77	**Slow Dancin' Don't Turn Me On**...Addrisi Bros.
10/77	**Slow Dancing (Swayin' To The Music)**...Johnny Rivers
25/64	**Slow Down**...Beatles
34/77	**Slowdown**...John Miles
2/81	**Slow Hand**...Pointer Sisters
18/92	**Slow Motion**...Color Me Badd
20/76	**Slow Ride**...Foghat
3/62	**Slow Twistin'**...Chubby Checker (with Dee Dee Sharp)
	Slow Walk
17/56	Sil Austin
26/57	Bill Doggett
30/70	**Sly, Slick, And The Wicked**...Lost Generation
F/71	**Smackwater Jack**...Carole King
29/72	**Small Beginnings**...Flash
21/62	**Small Sad Sam**...Phil McLean
6/85	**Small Town**...John Cougar Mellencamp
20/59	**Small World**...Johnny Mathis
25/88	**Small World**...Huey Lewis & The News
35/92	**Smells Like Nirvana**..."Weird Al" Yankovic
6/92	**Smells Like Teen Spirit**...Nirvana

POS/YR	RECORD TITLE/ARTIST
5/69	**Smile A Little Smile For Me**...Flying Machine
34/83	**Smile Has Left Your Eyes**...Asia
21/55	**Smiles**...Crazy Otto
3/71	**Smiling Faces Sometimes**...Undisputed Truth
9/77	**Smoke From A Distant Fire**...Sanford/Townsend Band
	Smoke Gets In Your Eyes
1/59	Platters
27/73	Blue Haze
4/73	**Smoke On The Water**...Deep Purple
17/60	**Smokie**...Bill Black's Combo
	Smokin' In The Boy's Room
3/74	Brownsville Station
16/85	Mötley Crüe
22/87	**Smoking Gun**...Robert Cray Band
24/81	**Smoky Mountain Rain**...Ronnie Milsap
12/62	**Smoky Places**...Corsairs
7/89	**Smooth Criminal**...Michael Jackson
5/85	**Smooth Operator**...Sade
12/85	**Smuggler's Blues**...Glenn Frey
27/68	**Snake, The**...Al Wilson
8/62	**Snap Your Fingers**...Joe Henderson
31/69	**Snatching It Back**...Clarence Carter
F/75	**Snookeroo**...Ringo Starr
2/66	**Snoopy Vs. The Red Baron**...Royal Guardsmen **(also see: Return Of The Red Baron)**
8/70	**Snowbird**...Anne Murray
3/89	**So Alive**...Love & Rockets
31/93	**So Alone**...Men At Large
23/84	**So Bad**...Paul McCartney
11/90	**So Close**...Daryl Hall/John Oates
38/59	**So Close**...Brook Benton
40/83	**So Close**...Diana Ross
1/88	**So Emotional**...Whitney Houston
14/71	**So Far Away**...Carole King
19/86	**So Far Away**...Dire Straits
11/59	**So Fine**...Fiestas
30/79	**So Good, So Right**...Brenda Russell
36/69	**So Good Together**...Andy Kim
39/69	**So I Can Love You**...Emotions
26/85	**So In Love**...Orchestral Manoeuvres In The Dark
7/77	**So In To You**...Atlanta Rhythm Section
28/61	**So Long Baby**...Del Shannon
6/59	**So Many Ways**...Brook Benton

POS/YR	RECORD TITLE/ARTIST
	So Much In Love
1/63	Tymes
5/94	All-4-One
2/57	**So Rare**...Jimmy Dorsey
7/60	**So Sad (To Watch Good Love Go Bad)**...Everly Brothers
21/62	**So This Is Love**...Castells
17/73	**So Very Hard To Go**...Tower Of Power
30/83	**So Wrong**...Patrick Simmons
21/74	**So You Are A Star**...Hudson Brothers
29/67	**So You Want To Be A Rock 'N' Roll Star**...Byrds
31/77	**So You Win Again**...Hot Chocolate
14/67	**Society's Child (Baby I've Been Thinking)**...Janis Ian
6/67	**Sock It To Me-Baby!**...Mitch Ryder & The Detroit Wheels
35/57	**Soft**...Bill Doggett
	Soft Summer Breeze
11/56	Eddie Heywood
34/56	Diamonds
27/64	**Softly, As I Leave You**...Frank Sinatra
F/55	**Softly, Softly**...Jaye P. Morgan
29/72	**Softly Whispering I Love You**...English Congregation
1/62	**Soldier Boy**...Shirelles
2/89	**Soldier Of Love**...Donny Osmond
12/85	**Solid**...Ashford & Simpson
7/83	**Solitaire**...Laura Branigan
17/75	**Solitaire**...Carpenters
21/70	**Solitary Man**...Neil Diamond
34/64	**Some Day We're Gonna Love Again**...Searchers
36/81	**Some Days Are Diamonds (Some Days Are Stone)**...John Denver
13/65	**Some Enchanted Evening**...Jay & The Americans
	Some Guys Have All The Luck
39/73	Persuaders
10/84	Rod Stewart
37/59	**Some Kind-A Earthquake**...Duane Eddy
26/83	**Some Kind Of Friend**...Barry Manilow
10/88	**Some Kind Of Lover**...Jody Watley
3/75	**Some Kind Of Wonderful**...Grand Funk
32/61	**Some Kind Of Wonderful**...Drifters
6/85	**Some Like It Hot**...Power Station
18/85	**Some Things Are Better Left Unsaid**...Daryl Hall/John Oates
30/68	**Some Things You Never Get Used To**...Supremes

POS/YR	RECORD TITLE/ARTIST
25/55	**Song Of The Barefoot Contessa**...Hugo Winterhalter
11/55	**Song Of The Dreamer**...Eddie Fisher
29/79	**Song On The Radio**...Al Stewart
1/72	**Song Sung Blue**...Neil Diamond
4/87	**Songbird**...Kenny G
25/78	**Songbird**...Barbra Streisand
30/70	**Soolaimon (African Trilogy II)**...Neil Diamond
21/96	**Soon As I Get Home**...Faith Evans
9/71	**Sooner Or Later**...Grass Roots
34/69	**Sophisticated Cissy**...Meters
25/76	**Sophisticated Lady (She's A Different Lady)**...Natalie Cole
2/59	**Sorry (I Ran All the Way Home)**...Impalas
6/76	**Sorry Seems To Be The Hardest Word**...Elton John
	Soul And Inspiration ..see: (You're My)
27/87	**Soul City**...Partland Brothers
	(Soul Coaxing) ..see: Ame Caline
18/69	**Soul Deep**...Box Tops
17/67	**Soul Finger**...Bar-Kays
20/85	**Soul Kiss**...Olivia Newton-John
17/68	**Soul-Limbo**...Booker T. & The M.G.'s
35/73	**Soul Makossa**...Manu Dibango
	Soul Man
2/67	Sam & Dave
14/79	Blues Brothers
29/71	**Soul Power**...James Brown
17/89	**Soul Provider**...Michael Bolton
23/68	**Soul Serenade**...Willie Mitchell
37/73	**Soul Song**...Joe Stampley
22/93	**Soul To Squeeze**...Red Hot Chili Peppers
17/62	**Soul Twist**...King Curtis
3/69	**Soulful Strut**...Young-Holt Unlimited
23/83	**Souls**...Rick Springfield
37/69	**Soulshake**...Peggy Scott & Jo Jo Benson
	(Soulsville, U.S.A.) ..see: 634-5789
36/67	**Sound Of Love**...Five Americans
33/91	**Sound Of Your Voice**...38 Special
1/66	**Sounds Of Silence**...Simon & Garfunkel
3/63	**South Street**...Orlons
29/75	**South's Gonna Do It**...Charlie Daniels Band
18/82	**Southern Cross**...Crosby, Stills & Nash
1/77	**Southern Nights**...Glen Campbell
15/64	**Southtown, U.S.A.**...Dixiebelles
2/89	**Sowing The Seeds Of Love**...Tears For Fears
30/83	**Space Age Love Song**...Flock Of Seagulls

POS/YR	RECORD TITLE/ARTIST
15/73	**Space Oddity**...David Bowie
4/73	**Space Race**...Billy Preston
23/72	**Spaceman**...Nilsson
40/85	**Spanish Eddie**...Laura Branigan
15/66	**Spanish Eyes**...Al Martino
27/66	**Spanish Flea**...Herb Alpert
	Spanish Harlem
10/61	Ben E. King
2/71	Aretha Franklin
31/62	**Spanish Lace**...Gene McDaniels
	(Speak Softly Love) ..see: Love Theme From The Godfather
14/72	**Speak To The Sky**...Rick Springfield
38/69	**Special Delivery**...1910 Fruitgum Co.
5/80	**Special Lady**...Ray, Goodman, & Brown
26/68	**Special Occasion**...Miracles
17/56	**Speedoo**...Cadillacs
6/62	**Speedy Gonzales**...Pat Boone
39/91	**Spend My Life**...Slaughter
32/92	**Spending My Time**...Roxette
40/83	**Spice Of Life**...Manhattan Transfer
3/74	**Spiders & Snakes**...Jim Stafford
7/86	**Spies Like Us**...Paul McCartney
3/70	**Spill The Wine**...Eric Burdon & War
2/69	**Spinning Wheel**...Blood, Sweat & Tears (also see: Slow Motion)
40/66	**Spinout**...Elvis Presley
23/70	**Spirit In The Dark**...Aretha Franklin
40/77	**Spirit In The Night**...Manfred Mann's Earth Band
3/70	**Spirit In The Sky**...Norman Greenbaum
35/75	**Spirit Of The Boogie**...Kool & The Gang
11/82	**Spirits In The Material World**...Police
3/58	**Splish Splash**...Bobby Darin
	Spooky
3/68	Classics IV
17/79	Atlanta Rhythm Section
39/77	**Spring Rain**...Silvetti
37/76	**Springtime Mama**...Henry Gross
16/88	**Spy In The House Of Love**...Was (Not Was)
16/76	**Squeeze Box**...Who
1/85	**St. Elmo's Fire (Man In Motion)**...John Parr (also see: Love Theme From)
13/56	**St. Therese Of The Roses**...Billy Ward & His Dominoes
21/86	**Stages**...ZZ Top

POS/YR	RECORD TITLE/ARTIST
	Stagger Lee
1/59	Lloyd Price
22/67	Wilson Pickett
25/71	Tommy Roe
9/60	**Stairway To Heaven**...Neil Sedaka
6/89	**Stand**...R.E.M.
22/69	**Stand!**...Sly & The Family Stone
5/83	**Stand Back**...Stevie Nicks
	Stand By Me
4/61	Ben E. King
12/67	Spyder Turner
20/75	John Lennon
22/80	Mickey Gilley
9/86	Ben E. King
	(also see: I'll Be There)
	Stand By Your Man
19/69	Tammy Wynette
24/70	Candi Staton
10/77	**Stand Tall**...Burton Cummings
34/93	**Stand Up (Kick Love Into Motion)**...Def Leppard
37/74	**Standing At The End Of The Line**...Lobo
6/67	**Standing In The Shadows Of Love**...Four Tops
	Standing On The Corner
3/56	Four Lads
22/56	Dean Martin
29/74	**Star**...Stealers Wheel
39/74	**Star Baby**...Guess Who
	Star Is Born ..see: Love Theme From A
20/91	**Star Spangled Banner**...Whitney Houston
	Star Wars Theme
1/77	Meco
10/77	John Williams
25/60	**Starbright**...Johnny Mathis
	Stardust
12/57	Billy Ward & His Dominoes
32/64	Nino Tempo & April Stevens
28/82	**Stars on 45 III**...Stars On
	(also see: Medley)
2/81	**Start Me Up**...Rolling Stones
9/57	**Start Movin' (In My Direction)**...Sal Mineo
19/72	**Starting All Over Again**...Mel & Tim
	Starting Over ..see: (Just Like)
36/80	**Starting Over Again**...Dolly Parton
3/84	**State Of Shock**...Jacksons
22/85	**State Of The Heart**...Rick Springfield
	Stay
1/60	Maurice Williams
16/64	4 Seasons
20/78	Jackson Browne

POS/YR	RECORD TITLE/ARTIST
4/92	**Stay**...Shakespear's Sister
19/94	**Stay**...Eternal
38/78	**Stay**...Rufus/Chaka Khan
7/71	**Stay Awhile**...Bells
38/64	**Stay Awhile**...Dusty Springfield
1/94	**Stay (I Missed You)**...Lisa Loeb & Nine Stories
10/68	**Stay In My Corner**...Dells
16/84	**Stay The Night**...Chicago
24/87	**Stay The Night**...Benjamin Orr
17/72	**Stay With Me**...Faces
30/84	**Stay With Me Tonight**...Jeffrey Osborne
1/78	**Stayin' Alive**...Bee Gees
33/61	**Stayin' In**...Bobby Vee
22/88	**Staying Together**...Debbie Gibson
37/81	**Staying With It**...Firefall
	Steal Away
17/64	Jimmy Hughes
37/70	Johnnie Taylor
6/80	**Steal Away**...Robbie Dupree
25/81	**Steal The Night**...Stevie Woods
32/93	**Steam**...Peter Gabriel
17/73	**Steamroller Blues**...Elvis Presley
39/90	**Steamy Windows**...Tina Turner
13/62	**Steel Guitar And A Glass Of Wine**...Paul Anka
1/90	**Step By Step**...New Kids On The Block
5/81	**Step By Step**...Eddie Rabbitt
14/60	**Step By Step**...Crests
37/73	**Step By Step**...Joe Simon
24/67	**Step Out Of Your Mind**...American Breed
39/78	**Steppin' In A Slide Zone**...Moody Blues
6/82	**Steppin' Out**...Joe Jackson
36/76	**Steppin' Out**...Neil Sedaka
7/74	**Steppin' Out (Gonna Boogie Tonight)**...Tony Orlando & Dawn
	Steppin' Stone ..see: (I'm Not Your)
35/63	**Stewball**...Peter, Paul & Mary
32/86	**Stick Around**...Julian Lennon
25/61	**Stick Shift**...Duals
11/71	**Stick-Up**...Honey Cone
40/60	**Sticks And Stones**...Ray Charles
1/79	**Still**...Commodores
8/63	**Still**...Bill Anderson
40/76	**Still Crazy After All These Years**...Paul Simon
	Still In Love ..see: Can'tcha Say (You Believe In Me)

POS/YR	RECORD TITLE/ARTIST
22/82	**Still In Saigon**...Charlie Daniels Band
28/81	**Still Right Here In My Heart**...Pure Prairie League
5/76	**Still The One**...Orleans
4/78	**Still The Same**...Bob Seger
19/82	**Still They Ride**...Journey
11/70	**Still Water (Love)**...Four Tops
12/73	**Stir It Up**...Johnny Nash
7/80	**Stomp!**...Brothers Johnson
36/78	**Stone Blue**...Foghat
40/82	**Stone Cold**...Rainbow
34/91	**Stone Cold Gentleman**...Ralph Tresvant
10/87	**Stone Love**...Kool & The Gang
7/70	**Stoned Love**...Supremes
30/73	**Stoned Out Of My Mind**...Chi-Lites
3/68	**Stoned Soul Picnic**...5th Dimension
14/71	**Stones**...Neil Diamond
6/71	**Stoney End**...Barbra Streisand
2/58	**Stood Up**...Ricky Nelson
9/74	**Stop And Smell The Roses**...Mac Davis
8/64	**Stop And Think It Over**...Dale & Grace
3/81	**Stop Draggin' My Heart Around**...Stevie Nicks (with Tom Petty)
	Stop! In The Name Of Love
1/65	Supremes
29/83	Hollies
39/71	**Stop, Look, Listen (To Your Heart)**...Stylistics
7/66	**Stop Stop Stop**...Hollies
36/62	**Stop The Music**...Shirelles
26/71	**Stop The War Now**...Edwin Starr
34/62	**Stop The Wedding**...Etta James
15/87	**Stop To Love**...Luther Vandross
	Stormy
5/68	Classics IV
32/79	Santana
23/71	**Story In Your Eyes**...Moody Blues
15/58	**Story Of My Life**...Marty Robbins
16/61	**Story Of My Love**...Paul Anka
28/59	**Story Of My Love**...Conway Twitty
16/55	**Story Untold**...Crew-Cuts
10/83	**Straight From The Heart**...Bryan Adams
39/81	**Straight From The Heart**...Allman Brothers Band
36/68	**Straight Life**...Bobby Goldsboro
15/78	**Straight On**...Heart
29/74	**Straight Shootin' Woman**...Steppenwolf
1/89	**Straight Up**...Paula Abdul
13/90	**Stranded**...Heart

POS/YR	RECORD TITLE/ARTIST
	Stranded In The Jungle
15/56	Cadets
18/56	Jayhawks
39/56	Gadabouts
21/88	**Strange But True**...Times Two
14/76	**Strange Magic**...Electric Light Orchestra
11/78	**Strange Way**...Firefall
23/83	**Stranger In My House**...Ronnie Milsap
30/65	**Stranger In Town**...Del Shannon
30/84	**Stranger In Town**...Toto
	Stranger On The Shore
1/62	Mr. Acker Bilk
38/62	Andy Williams
1/66	**Strangers In The Night**...Frank Sinatra
8/67	**Strawberry Fields Forever**...Beatles
5/77	**Strawberry Letter 23**...Brothers Johnson
39/68	**Strawberry Shortcake**...Jay & The Techniques
3/83	**Stray Cat Strut**...Stray Cats
1/74	**Streak, The**...Ray Stevens
30/78	**Street Corner Serenade**...Wet Willie
36/79	**Street Life**...Crusaders
12/91	**Street Of Dreams**...Nia Peeples
27/76	**Street Singin'**...Lady Flash
9/94	**Streets Of Philadelphia**...Bruce Springsteen
8/91	**Strike It Up**...Black Box
	String Along
39/60	Fabian
25/63	Rick Nelson
1/62	**Stripper, The**...David Rose
17/81	**Stroke, The**...Billy Squier
3/94	**Stroke You Up**...Changing Faces
4/58	**Stroll, The**...Diamonds
5/95	**Strong Enough**...Sheryl Crow
30/81	**Stronger Than Before**...Carole Bayer Sager
40/84	**Strung Out**...Steve Perry
7/84	**Strut**...Sheena Easton
22/75	**Struttin'**...Billy Preston
6/73	**Stuck In The Middle With You**...Stealers Wheel
1/60	**Stuck On You**...Elvis Presley
3/84	**Stuck On You**...Lionel Richie
1/86	**Stuck With You**...Huey Lewis & the News
21/78	**Stuff Like That**...Quincy Jones
4/79	**Stumblin' In**...Suzi Quatro & Chris Norman
14/58	**Stupid Cupid**...Connie Francis
18/72	**Suavecito**...Malo
39/65	**Subterranean Homesick Blues**...Bob Dylan
16/64	**Such A Night**...Elvis Presley

POS/YR	RECORD TITLE/ARTIST
26/79	**Such A Woman**...Tycoon
11/65	**(Such An) Easy Question**...Elvis Presley
4/85	**Suddenly**...Billy Ocean
20/81	**Suddenly**...Olivia Newton-John & Cliff Richard
9/83	**Suddenly Last Summer**...Motels
	Suddenly There's A Valley
9/55	Gogi Grant
13/55	Jo Stafford
20/55	Julius LaRosa
37/74	**Sugar Baby Love**...Rubettes
10/72	**Sugar Daddy**...Jackson 5
28/89	**Sugar Daddy**...Thompson Twins
36/84	**Sugar Don't Bite**...Sam Harris
32/65	**Sugar Dumpling**...Sam Cooke
35/87	**Sugar Free**...Wa Wa Nee
25/95	**Sugar Hill**...AZ The Visualiza
30/64	**Sugar Lips**...Al Hirt
5/58	**Sugar Moon**...Pat Boone
22/69	**Sugar On Sunday**...Clique
1/63	**Sugar Shack**...Jimmy Gilmer/Fireballs
	Sugar, Sugar
1/69	Archies
25/70	Wilson Pickett
5/66	**Sugar Town**...Nancy Sinatra
9/85	**Sugar Walls**...Sheena Easton
1/58	**Sugartime**...McGuire Sisters
9/90	**Suicide Blonde**...INXS
21/69	**Suite: Judy Blue Eyes**...Crosby, Stills & Nash
	Sukiyaki
1/63	Kyu Sakamoto
3/81	Taste Of Honey
8/95	4 P.M. (For Positive Music) **(also see: Ask Of You)**
4/79	**Sultans Of Swing**...Dire Straits
7/76	**Summer**...War
6/72	**Summer Breeze**...Seals & Crofts
1/66	**Summer In The City**...Lovin' Spoonful
F/75	**Summer Madness**...Kool & The Gang **(also see: Somethin' 4 Da Honeyz, & Summertime)**
	Summer Night ..see: Song For A
5/78	**Summer Nights**...John Travolta & Olivia Newton-John
24/65	**Summer Nights**...Marianne Faithfull
	Summer Of '42 ..see: Theme From
5/85	**Summer Of '69**...Bryan Adams
	Summer Place ..see: Theme From A
14/68	**Summer Rain**...Johnny Rivers

POS/YR	RECORD TITLE/ARTIST
30/90	**Summer Rain**...Belinda Carlisle
26/66	**Summer Samba (So Nice)**...Walter Wanderley
33/71	**Summer Sand**...Dawn
30/60	**Summer Set**...Monty Kelly
7/64	**Summer Song**...Chad & Jeremy
21/73	**Summer (The First Time)**...Bobby Goldsboro
	Summer Time ..see: In The Summertime
25/66	**Summer Wind**...Frank Sinatra
11/60	**Summer's Gone**...Paul Anka
10/66	**Summertime**...Billy Stewart
4/91	**Summertime**...D.J. Jazzy Jeff & The Fresh Prince
	Summertime Blues
8/58	Eddie Cochran
14/68	Blue Cheer
27/70	Who
F/58	**Summertime Lies**...Four Preps
	Summertime, Summertime
26/58	Jamies
38/62	Jamies
13/66	**Sun Ain't Gonna Shine (Anymore)**...Walker Bros.
20/86	**Sun Always Shines On T.V.**...A-Ha
38/85	**Sun City**...Artists United Against Apartheid
18/65	**Sunday And Me**...Jay & The Americans
31/67	**Sunday For Tea**...Peter & Gordon
	Sunday Mornin'
30/68	Spanky & Our Gang
35/69	Oliver
9/67	**Sunday Will Never Be The Same**...Spanky & Our Gang
1/74	**Sundown**...Gordon Lightfoot
39/77	**Sunflower**...Glen Campbell
7/84	**Sunglasses At Night**...Corey Hart
2/66	**Sunny**...Bobby Hebb
14/66	**Sunny Afternoon**...Kinks
34/72	**Sunny Days**...Lighthouse
34/76	**Sunrise**...Eric Carmen
22/85	**Sunset Grill**...Don Henley
4/72	**Sunshine**...Jonathan Edwards
23/89	**Sunshine**...Dino
20/67	**Sunshine Girl**...Parade
13/65	**Sunshine, Lollipops And Rainbows**...Lesley Gore
5/68	**Sunshine Of Your Love**...Cream
1/74	**Sunshine On My Shoulders**...John Denver
1/66	**Sunshine Superman**...Donovan

POS/YR	RECORD TITLE/ARTIST
13/70	**Super Bad**...James Brown
31/73	**Super Fly Meets Shaft**...John & Ernest
16/81	**Super Freak**...Rick James **(also see: U Can't Touch This)**
8/73	**Superfly**...Curtis Mayfield **(also see: Freddie's Dead)**
26/79	**Superman**...Herbie Mann
5/75	**Supernatural Thing**...Ben E. King
30/88	**Supersonic**...J.J. Fad
2/71	**Superstar**...Carpenters
35/76	**Superstar**...Paul Davis
14/71	**Superstar - Jesus Christ Superstar**...Murray Head
18/71	**Superstar (Remember How You Got Where You Are)**...Temptations
1/73	**Superstition**...Stevie Wonder
31/88	**Superstitious**...Europe
8/89	**Superwoman**...Karyn White
33/72	**Superwoman (Where Were You When I Needed You)**...Stevie Wonder
16/74	**Sure As I'm Sittin' Here**...Three Dog Night
9/66	**Sure Gonna Miss Her**...Gary Lewis & The Playboys
1/63	**Surf City**...Jan & Dean
7/63	**Surfer Girl**...Beach Boys
31/62	**Surfer's Stomp**...Mar-Kets
4/64	**Surfin' Bird**...Trashmen
14/62	**Surfin' Safari**...Beach Boys
	Surfin' U.S.A.
3/63	Beach Boys
36/74	Beach Boys
20/77	Leif Garrett
1/61	**Surrender**...Elvis Presley
38/71	**Surrender**...Diana Ross
6/89	**Surrender To Me**...Ann Wilson & Robin Zander
11/68	**Susan**...Buckinghams
	Susie Darlin'
5/58	Robin Luke
35/62	Tommy Roe
3/64	**Suspicion**...Terry Stafford
13/79	**Suspicions**...Eddie Rabbitt
1/69	**Suspicious Minds**...Elvis Presley
1/85	**Sussudio**...Phil Collins
17/86	**Suzanne**...Journey
	Suzie-Q
27/57	Dale Hawkins
11/68	Creedence Clearwater Revival
39/73	**Swamp Witch**...Jim Stafford
F/55	**Swanee**...Jaye P. Morgan

POS/YR	RECORD TITLE/ARTIST
34/57	**Swanee River Rock (Talkin' 'Bout That River)**...Ray Charles
	S.W.A.T. ..see: Theme From
14/60	**Sway**...Bobby Rydell
6/75	**Swearin' To God**...Frankie Valli
16/93	**Sweat (A La La La La Long)**...Inner Circle
	Sweet And Gentle
10/55	Alan Dale
12/55	Georgia Gibbs
7/71	**Sweet And Innocent**...Donny Osmond
19/81	**Sweet Baby**...Stanley Clarke/George Duke
13/68	**Sweet Blindness**...5th Dimension
4/69	**Sweet Caroline (Good Times Never Seemed So Good)**...Neil Diamond
7/69	**Sweet Cherry Wine**...Tommy James & The Shondells
1/88	**Sweet Child O' Mine**...Guns N' Roses
8/71	**Sweet City Woman**...Stampeders
28/69	**Sweet Cream Ladies, Forward March**...Box Tops
5/82	**Sweet Dreams**...Air Supply
15/66	**Sweet Dreams**...Tommy McLain
1/83	**Sweet Dreams (Are Made of This)**...Eurythmics
36/75	**Sweet Emotion**...Aerosmith
7/86	**Sweet Freedom**...Michael McDonald
6/71	**Sweet Hitch-Hiker**...Creedence Clearwater Revival
8/74	**Sweet Home Alabama**...Lynyrd Skynyrd
	Sweet Inspiration
18/68	Sweet Inspirations
37/72	Barbra Streisand (medley)
17/78	**Sweet Life**...Paul Davis
2/58	**Sweet Little Sixteen**...Chuck Berry
5/76	**Sweet Love**...Commodores
8/86	**Sweet Love**...Anita Baker
36/79	**Sweet Lui-Louise**...Ironhorse
7/71	**Sweet Mary**...Wadsworth Mansion
40/75	**Sweet Maxine**...Doobie Brothers
4/60	**Sweet Nothin's**...Brenda Lee
7/56	**Sweet Old Fashioned Girl**...Teresa Brewer
8/66	**Sweet Pea**...Tommy Roe
27/94	**Sweet Potatoe Pie**...Domino
9/72	**Sweet Seasons**...Carole King
20/87	**Sweet Sixteen**...Billy Idol
2/67	**Sweet Soul Music**...Arthur Conley
33/75	**Sweet Sticky Thing**...Ohio Players
13/75	**Sweet Surrender**...John Denver
15/72	**Sweet Surrender**...Bread

POS/YR	RECORD TITLE/ARTIST
5/68	**(Sweet Sweet Baby) Since You've Been Gone**...Aretha Franklin
10/66	**Sweet Talkin' Guy**...Chiffons
17/78	**Sweet Talkin' Woman**...Electric Light Orchestra
	Sweet Thing
5/76	Rufus Feat. Chaka Khan
28/93	Mary J. Blige
26/82	**Sweet Time**...REO Speedwagon
33/73	**Sweet Understanding Love**...Four Tops
40/64	**Sweet William**...Millie Small
29/66	**Sweet Woman Like You**...Joe Tex
9/59	**Sweeter Than You**...Ricky Nelson
18/95	**Sweetest Days**...Vanessa Williams
5/86	**Sweetest Taboo**...Sade
7/82	**Sweetest Thing (I've Ever Known)**...Juice Newton
32/67	**Sweetest Thing This Side Of Heaven**...Chris Bartley
10/81	**Sweetheart**...Franke & The Knockouts
16/61	**Sweets For My Sweet**...Drifters
19/84	**Swept Away**...Diana Ross
11/90	**Swing The Mood (medley)**...Jive Bunny & the Mastermixers
39/60	**Swingin' On A Rainbow**...Frankie Avalon
13/62	**Swingin' Safari**...Billy Vaughn
5/60	**Swingin' School**...Bobby Rydell
23/58	**Swingin' Shepherd Blues**...Moe Koffman Quartette
38/63	**Swinging On A Star**...Big Dee Irwin/Little Eva
17/77	**Swingtown**...Steve Miller Band
26/61	**Switch-A-Roo**...Hank Ballard
5/72	**Sylvia's Mother**...Dr. Hook
38/88	**Symptoms Of True Love**...Tracie Spencer
16/83	**Synchronicity II**...Police
37/76	**(System Of) Doctor Tarr And Professor Fether**...Alan Parsons Project

T

POS/YR	RECORD TITLE/ARTIST
30/92	**T.L.C.**...Linear
24/60	**T.L.C. Tender Love And Care**...Jimmie Rodgers
1/74	**TSOP (The Sound Of Philadelphia)**...MFSB featuring The Three Degrees
23/60	**Ta Ta**...Clyde McPhatter
8/82	**Tainted Love**...Soft Cell

POS/YR	RECORD TITLE/ARTIST
1/95	**Take A Bow**...Madonna
3/78	**Take A Chance On Me**...Abba
2/69	**Take A Letter Maria**...R.B. Greaves
15/80	**Take A Little Rhythm**...Ali Thomson
30/72	**Take A Look Around**...Temptations
16/59	**Take A Message To Mary**...Everly Brothers
20/69	**Take Care Of Your Homework**...Johnnie Taylor
25/61	**Take Five**...Dave Brubeck Quartet
	Take Good Care Of Her
7/61	Adam Wade
F/74	Elvis Presley
	Take Good Care Of My Baby
1/61	Bobby Vee
33/68	Bobby Vinton
10/82	**Take It Away**...Paul McCartney
12/72	**Take It Easy**...Eagles
24/86	**Take It Easy**...Andy Taylor
10/82	**Take It Easy On Me**...Little River Band
33/76	**Take It Like A Man**...Bachman-Turner Overdrive
5/81	**Take It On The Run**...REO Speedwagon
4/76	**Take It To The Limit**...Eagles
16/65	**Take Me Back**...Little Anthony & The Imperials
18/82	**Take Me Down**...Alabama
38/68	**Take Me For A Little While**...Vanilla Fudge
7/86	**Take Me Home**...Phil Collins
8/79	**Take Me Home**...Cher
2/71	**Take Me Home, Country Roads**...John Denver
4/86	**Take Me Home Tonight**...Eddie Money
11/75	**Take Me In Your Arms (Rock Me)**...Doobie Brothers
14/83	**Take Me To Heart**...Quarterflash
26/79	**Take Me To The River**...Talking Heads
25/85	**Take Me With U**...Prince
1/86	**Take My Breath Away**...Berlin
17/81	**Take My Heart (You Can Have It If You Want It)**...Kool & The Gang
16/82	**Take Off**...Bob & Doug McKenzie
1/85	**Take On Me**...A-Ha
10/79	**Take The Long Way Home**...Supertramp
11/76	**Take The Money And Run**...Steve Miller
8/63	**Take These Chains From My Heart**...Ray Charles
20/92	**Take This Heart**...Richard Marx
29/92	**Take Time**...Chris Walker
11/68	**Take Time To Know Her**...Percy Sledge

POS/YR	RECORD TITLE/ARTIST
3/80	**Take Your Time (Do It Right)**...S.O.S. Band
32/86	**Taken In**...Mike + The Mechanics
12/74	**Takin' Care Of Business**...Bachman-Turner Overdrive
13/76	**Takin' It To The Streets**...Doobie Brothers
7/64	**Talk Back Trembling Lips**...Johnny Tillotson
9/87	**Talk Dirty To Me**...Poison
19/89	**Talk It Over**...Grayson Hugh
15/67	**Talk Talk**...Music Machine
34/60	**Talk That Talk**...Jackie Wilson
4/86	**Talk To Me**...Stevie Nicks
21/87	**Talk To Me**...Chico DeBarge
38/59	**Talk To Me**...Frank Sinatra
	Talk To Me, Talk To Me
20/58	Little Willie John
11/63	Sunny & The Sunglows
15/57	**Talkin' To The Blues**...Jim Lowe
12/64	**Talking About My Baby**...Impressions
3/84	**Talking In Your Sleep**...Romantics
18/78	**Talking In Your Sleep**...Crystal Gayle
27/72	**Talking Loud And Saying Nothing**...James Brown
25/88	**Tall Cool One**...Robert Plant
	Tall Cool One
36/59	Wailers
38/64	Wailers
	Tall Oak Tree ..see: (There Was A)
7/59	**Tall Paul**...Annette
6/59	**Tallahassee Lassie**...Freddy Cannon
	Tammy
1/57	Debbie Reynolds
5/57	Ames Brothers
18/76	**Tangerine**...Salsoul Orchestra
31/75	**Tangled Up In Blue**...Bob Dylan
34/68	**Tapioca Tundra**...Monkees
38/66	**Tar And Cement**...Verdelle Smith
13/86	**Tarzan Boy**...Baltimora
7/65	**Taste Of Honey**...Herb Alpert
18/72	**Taurus**...Dennis Coffey
24/72	**Taxi**...Harry Chapin
7/58	**Tea For Two**...Tommy Dorsey Orchestra (Cha Cha)
25/62	**Teach Me Tonight**...George Maharis
16/70	**Teach Your Children**...Crosby, Stills, Nash & Young
21/58	**Teacher, Teacher**...Johnny Mathis
25/84	**Teacher Teacher**...38 Special
31/61	**Tear, A**...Gene McDaniels
23/59	**Tear Drop**...Santo & Johnny

POS/YR	RECORD TITLE/ARTIST
20/57	**Tear Drops**...Lee Andrews & the Hearts
5/56	**Tear Fell**...Teresa Brewer
15/76	**Tear The Roof Off The Sucker (Give Up The Funk)**...Parliament **(also see: We Want The Funk)**
37/84	**Tears**...John Waite
20/64	**Tears And Roses**...Al Martino
2/92	**Tears In Heaven**...Eric Clapton
1/70	**Tears Of A Clown**...Miracles
4/58	**Tears On My Pillow**...Little Anthony & The Imperials
39/59	**Teasin'**...Quaker City Boys
17/60	**Teddy**...Connie Francis
40/76	**Teddy Bear**...Red Sovine **(also see: Let Me Be Your)**
32/73	**Teddy Bear Song**...Barbara Fairchild
	Teen Age ..also see: Teenage
2/57	**Teen-Age Crush**...Tommy Sands
5/62	**Teen Age Idol**...Rick Nelson
	Teen Age Prayer
6/56	Gale Storm
19/56	Gloria Mann
1/60	**Teen Angel**...Mark Dinning
4/59	**Teen Beat**...Sandy Nelson
29/59	**Teen Commandments**...Paul Anka-Geo. Hamilton IV-Johnny Nash
	Teenage Queen ..see: Ballad Of
5/59	**Teenager In Love**...Dion & The Belmonts
2/57	**Teenager's Romance**...Ricky Nelson
9/83	**Telefone (Long Distance Love Affair)**...Sheena Easton
7/77	**Telephone Line**...Electric Light Orchestra
18/77	**Telephone Man**...Meri Wilson
1/83	**Tell Her About It**...Billy Joel
	Tell Her No
6/65	Zombies
27/83	Juice Newton
40/73	**Tell Her She's Lovely**...El Chicano
4/63	**Tell Him**...Exciters
8/59	**Tell Him No**...Travis & Bob
17/70	**Tell It All Brother**...Kenny Rogers & The First Edition
	Tell It Like It Is
2/67	Aaron Neville
8/81	Heart
33/64	**Tell It On The Mountain**...Peter, Paul & Mary
7/88	**Tell It To My Heart**...Taylor Dayne
10/67	**Tell It To The Rain**...4 Seasons
7/60	**Tell Laura I Love Her**...Ray Peterson

POS/YR	RECORD TITLE/ARTIST
23/68	**Tell Mama**...Etta James
5/95	**Tell Me**...Groove Theory
22/62	**Tell Me**...Dick & DeeDee
21/74	**Tell Me A Lie**...Sami Jo
31/90	**Tell Me Something**...Indecent Obsession
3/74	**Tell Me Something Good**...Rufus
37/67	**Tell Me To My Face**...Keith
33/82	**Tell Me Tomorrow**...Smokey Robinson
6/92	**Tell Me What You Want Me To Do**...Tevin Campbell
31/95	**Tell Me When**...Human League
9/90	**Tell Me Why**...Expose
13/64	**Tell Me Why**...Bobby Vinton
18/61	**Tell Me Why**...Belmonts
33/66	**Tell Me Why**...Elvis Presley
24/64	**Tell Me (You're Coming Back)**...Rolling Stones
1/62	**Telstar**...Tornadoes
39/70	**Temma Harbour**...Mary Hopkin
39/91	**Temple Of Love**...Harriet
6/91	**Temptation**...Corina
27/61	**Temptation**...Everly Brothers
15/71	**Temptation Eyes**...Grass Roots
22/58	**Ten Commandments Of Love**...Harvey & The Moonglows **(also see: Teen Commandments)**
38/84	**10-9-8**...Face To Face
25/83	**Tender Is The Night**...Jackson Browne
10/86	**Tender Love**...Force M.D.'s
	Tender, Love and Care ..see: T.L.C.
14/90	**Tender Lover**...Babyface
	Tender Trap ..see: (Love Is)
31/85	**Tender Years**...John Cafferty
31/61	**Tenderly**...Bert Kaempfert
27/85	**Tenderness**...General Public
6/92	**Tennessee**...Arrested Development
23/70	**Tennessee Bird Walk**...Jack Blanchard & Misty Morgan
35/64	**Tennessee Waltz**...Sam Cooke
	Tequila
1/58	Champs
20/58	Eddie Platt
	Testify ..see: (I Wanna)
1/75	**Thank God I'm A Country Boy**...John Denver
22/78	**Thank God It's Friday**...Love & Kisses
21/95	**Thank You**...Boyz II Men
1/70	**Thank You (Falettinme Be Mice Elf Agin)**...Sly & The Family Stone

POS/YR	RECORD TITLE/ARTIST
25/78	**Thank You For Being A Friend**...Andrew Gold
35/64	**Thank You Girl**...Beatles
16/59	**Thank You Pretty Baby**...Brook Benton
32/88	**Thanks For My Child**...Cheryl Pepsii Riley
37/74	**Thanks For Saving My Life**...Billy Paul
16/87	**That Ain't Love**...REO Speedwagon
4/82	**That Girl**...Stevie Wonder
22/80	**That Girl Could Sing**...Jackson Browne
	(That Kiss!) ..see: Eso Beso
6/73	**That Lady**...Isley Brothers
20/64	**That Lucky Old Sun**...Ray Charles
	That Old Black Magic
13/55	Sammy Davis, Jr.
18/58	Louis Prima & Keely Smith
21/61	Bobby Rydell
21/81	**That Old Song**...Ray Parker Jr. & Raydio
28/62	**That Stranger Used To Be My Girl**...Trade Martin
12/63	**That Sunday, That Summer**...Nat King Cole
20/86	**That Was Then, This Is Now**...Mickey Dolenz & Peter Tork
12/85	**That Was Yesterday**...Foreigner
	That'll Be The Day
1/57	Crickets
11/76	Linda Ronstadt
6/84	**That's All!**...Genesis
17/56	**That's All**..."Tennessee" Ernie Ford
3/55	**That's All I Want From You**...Jaye P. Morgan
16/56	**That's All There Is To That**...Nat "King" Cole/Four Knights
6/60	**That's All You Gotta Do**...Brenda Lee
40/63	**That's How Heartaches Are Made**...Baby Washington
39/58	**That's How Much I Love You**...Pat Boone
31/61	**That's It-I Quit-I'm Movin' On**...Sam Cooke
4/66	**That's Life**...Frank Sinatra
28/83	**That's Love**...Jim Capaldi
9/62	**That's Old Fashioned (That's The Way Love Should Be)**...Everly Brothers
3/77	**That's Rock 'N' Roll**...Shaun Cassidy
16/89	**That's The Way**...Katrina & The Waves
12/64	**That's The Way Boys Are**...Lesley Gore
27/72	**That's The Way I Feel About Cha**...Bobby Womack
1/75	**That's The Way (I Like It)**...KC & The Sunshine Band
10/71	**That's The Way I've Always Heard It Should Be**...Carly Simon
1/93	**That's The Way Love Goes**...Janet Jackson

POS/YR	RECORD TITLE/ARTIST
7/69	That's The Way Love Is...Marvin Gaye
33/63	That's The Way Love Is...Bobby Bland
12/75	That's The Way Of The World...Earth, Wind & Fire
1/86	That's What Friends Are For...Dionne & Friends
27/61	That's What Girls Are Made For...Spinners
18/93	That's What Love Can Do...Boy Krazy
19/87	That's What Love Is All About...Michael Bolton
7/91	That's What Love Is For...Amy Grant
35/64	That's What Love Is Made Of...Miracles
27/75	That's When The Music Takes Me...Neil Sedaka
29/70	That's Where I Went Wrong...Poppy Family
27/76	That's Where The Happy People Go...Trammps
13/59	That's Why (I Love You So)...Jackie Wilson
35/60	Theme For Young Lovers...Percy Faith
	Theme From A Summer Place
1/60	Percy Faith
16/65	Lettermen
28/62	Theme From Ben Casey...Valjean
18/73	Theme From Cleopatra Jones...Joe Simon
	Theme From Close Encounters
13/78	John Williams
25/78	Meco
39/61	Theme From Dixie...Duane Eddy
10/62	Theme From Dr. Kildare (Three Stars Will Shine Tonight)...Richard Chamberlain
	Theme From Exorcist ..see: Tubular Bells
2/81	Theme From Greatest American Hero (Believe It Or Not)...Joey Scarbury
10/81	Theme From Hill Street Blues...Mike Post
32/75	Theme From Jaws (Main Title)...John Williams
	Theme From Love Story
9/71	Andy Williams (Where Do I Begin)
13/71	Henry Mancini
31/71	Francis Lai
25/82	(Theme From) Magnum P.I....Mike Post
1/76	Theme From Mahogany (Do You Know Where You're Going To)...Diana Ross
	Theme from Moonlighting ..see: Moonlighting
32/80	Theme From New York, New York...Frank Sinatra
	Theme From Picnic ..see: Moonglow
	Theme From Pink Panther ..see: Pink Panther Theme

POS/YR	RECORD TITLE/ARTIST
	Theme From Rocky ..see: Gonna Fly Now
1/71	Theme From Shaft...Isaac Hayes
21/71	Theme From Summer Of '42...Peter Nero
	Theme From Superfly ..see: Freddie's Dead
1/76	Theme From S.W.A.T....Rhythm Heritage
10/60	Theme From The Apartment...Ferrante & Teicher
21/80	Theme From The Dukes Of Hazzard (Good Ol' Boys)...Waylon Jennings
	Theme From The Man With The Golden Arm ..see: Man With The Golden Arm
38/72	Theme From The Men...Isaac Hayes
39/56	Theme From The Proud Ones...Nelson Riddle
	Theme From The Three Penny Opera ..see: Mack The Knife
27/60	Theme From The Unforgiven (The Need For Love)...Don Costa
2/68	Theme From Valley Of The Dolls...Dionne Warwick
21/78	Theme From Which Way Is Up...Stargard
35/78	Themes From The Wizard Of Oz...Meco
1/74	Then Came You...Dionne Warwicke & Spinners
6/63	Then He Kissed Me...Crystals
	Then You Can Tell Me Goodbye
6/67	Casinos
27/76	Glen Campbell (medley)
34/75	There Goes Another Love Song...Outlaws
	There Goes My Baby
2/59	Drifters
21/84	Donna Summer
	There Goes My Everything
20/67	Engelbert Humperdinck
F/71	Elvis Presley
19/58	There Goes My Heart...Joni James
1/64	There! I've Said It Again...Bobby Vinton
20/68	There Is...Dells
11/67	There Is A Mountain...Donovan
	(There Is Love) ..see: Wedding Song
32/73	There It Is...Tyrone Davis
33/59	There Must Be A Way...Joni James
22/85	There Must Be An Angel (Playing With My Heart)...Eurythmics
26/61	There She Goes...Jerry Wallace
23/60	(There Was A) Tall Oak Tree...Dorsey Burnette
36/68	There Was A Time...James Brown
31/92	There Will Never Be Another Tonight...Bryan Adams

POS/YR	RECORD TITLE/ARTIST
3/67	**This Is My Song**...Petula Clark
32/85	**This Is Not America**...David Bowie/Pat Metheny Group
21/90	**This Is The Right Time**...Lisa Stansfield
18/87	**This Is The Time**...Billy Joel
39/77	**This Is The Way That I Feel**...Marie Osmond
15/95	**This Lil' Game We Play**...Subway featuring 702
32/65	**This Little Bird**...Marianne Faithfull
11/81	**This Little Girl**...Gary U.S. Bonds
21/63	**This Little Girl**...Dion
26/58	**This Little Girl Of Mine**...Everly Brothers
24/58	**This Little Girl's Gone Rockin'**...Ruth Brown
	This Magic Moment
16/60	Drifters
6/69	Jay & The Americans
33/82	**This Man Is Mine**...Heart
10/76	**This Masquerade**...George Benson
19/79	**This Night Won't Last Forever**...Michael Johnson
	This Old Heart Of Mine
12/66	Isley Brothers
10/90	Rod Stewart (with Ronald Isley)
7/89	**This One's For The Children**...New Kids On The Block
29/76	**This One's For You**...Barry Manilow
20/59	**This Should Go On Forever**...Rod Bernard
25/77	**This Song**...George Harrison
6/61	**This Time**...Troy Shondell
24/83	**This Time**...Bryan Adams
27/80	**This Time**...John Cougar
7/89	**This Time I Know It's For Real**...Donna Summer
10/78	**This Time I'm In It For Love**...Player
1/92	**This Used To Be My Playground**...Madonna
6/75	**This Will Be**...Natalie Cole
23/84	**This Woman**...Kenny Rogers
38/72	**This World**...Staple Singers
6/63	**Those Lazy-Hazy-Crazy Days Of Summer**...Nat King Cole
9/61	**Those Oldies But Goodies (Remind Me Of You)**...Little Caesar & The Romans
2/68	**Those Were The Days**...Mary Hopkin
13/65	**Thou Shalt Not Steal**...Dick & DeeDee
13/92	**Thought I'd Died And Gone To Heaven**...Bryan Adams

POS/YR	RECORD TITLE/ARTIST
3/60	**Thousand Stars**...Kathy Young with The Innocents
5/91	**3 A.M. Eternal**...KLF
	Three Bells
1/59	Browns
23/59	Dick Flood
35/61	**Three Hearts In A Tangle**...Roy Drusky
24/67	**Three Little Fishes (medley)**...Mitch Ryder & The Detroit Wheels
17/93	**Three Little Pigs**...Green Jelly
15/60	**Three Nights A Week**...Fats Domino
33/65	**Three O'Clock In The Morning**...Bert Kaempfert
	Three Penny Opera ..see: Mack The Knife
36/74	**Three Ring Circus**...Blue Magic
11/59	**Three Stars**...Tommy Dee
	(Three Stars Will Shine Tonight) ..see: Theme From Dr. Kildare
1/78	**Three Times A Lady**...Commodores
19/80	**Three Times In Love**...Tommy James
28/64	**Three Window Coupe**...Rip Chords
15/70	**Thrill Is Gone**...B.B. King
4/84	**Thriller**...Michael Jackson
16/89	**Through The Storm**...Aretha Franklin & Elton John
13/82	**Through The Years**...Kenny Rogers
4/86	**Throwing It All Away**...Genesis
22/94	**thuggish-ruggish-Bone**...Bone Thugs-N-Harmony
17/72	**Thunder And Lightning**...Chi Coltrane
38/77	**Thunder In My Heart**...Leo Sayer
9/78	**Thunder Island**...Jay Ferguson
25/66	**Thunderball**...Tom Jones
14/90	**Tic-Tac-Toe**...Kyper
1/65	**Ticket To Ride**...Beatles
1/81	**Tide Is High**...Blondie
1/73	**Tie A Yellow Ribbon Round The Ole Oak Tree**...Dawn
3/63	**Tie Me Kangaroo Down, Sport**...Rolf Harris
38/83	**Tied Up**...Olivia Newton-John
37/60	**Ties That Bind**...Brook Benton
3/59	**Tiger**...Fabian
11/72	**Tight Rope**...Leon Russell
1/68	**Tighten Up**...Archie Bell
7/70	**Tighter, Tighter**...Alive & Kicking
12/59	**Tijuana Jail**...Kingston Trio
38/66	**Tijuana Taxi**...Herb Alpert
4/59	**('Til) I Kissed You**...Everly Brothers

POS/YR	RECORD TITLE/ARTIST
29/85	**'Til My Baby Comes Home**...Luther Vandross
32/75	**Til The World Ends**...Three Dog Night
31/95	**'Til You Do Me Right**...After 7
	Till
22/57	Roger Williams
14/62	Angels
27/68	Vogues
26/62	**Till Death Do Us Part**...Bob Braun
25/88	**Till I Loved You**...Barbra Streisand & Don Johnson
20/63	**Till Then**...Classics
30/59	**Till There Was You**...Anita Bryant
14/96	**Time**...Hootie & The Blowfish
15/81	**Time**...Alan Parsons Project
1/84	**Time After Time**...Cyndi Lauper
40/90	**Time After Time**...Timmy -T-
36/66	**Time After Time**...Chris Montez
23/93	**Time And Chance**...Color Me Badd
30/60	**Time And The River**...Nat King Cole
26/88	**Time And Tide**...Basia
2/83	**Time (Clock Of The Heart)**...Culture Club
32/90	**Time For Letting Go**...Jude Cole
32/74	**Time For Livin'**...Sly & The Family Stone
39/68	**Time For Livin'**...Association
	(Time For Us) ..see: Love Theme From Romeo & Juliet
11/68	**Time Has Come Today**...Chambers Brothers
1/73	**Time In A Bottle**...Jim Croce
6/64	**Time Is On My Side**...Rolling Stones
6/69	**Time Is Tight**...Booker T. & The M.G.'s
15/81	**Time Is Time**...Andy Gibb
7/91	**Time, Love And Tenderness**...Michael Bolton
	Time Of My Life ..see: (I've Had)
3/69	**Time Of The Season**...Zombies
22/81	**Time Out Of Mind**...Steely Dan
7/78	**Time Passages**...Al Stewart
33/73	**Time To Get Down**...O'Jays
	Time To Love-A Time To Cry ..see: Petite Fleur
18/84	**Time Will Reveal**...DeBarge
5/66	**Time Won't Let Me**...Outsiders
7/76	**Times Of Your Life**...Paul Anka
17/71	**Timothy**...Buoys
4/74	**Tin Man**...America
5/55	**Tina Marie**...Perry Como
17/68	**Tip-Toe Thru' The Tulips With Me**...Tiny Tim
11/71	**Tired Of Being Alone**...Al Green

POS/YR	RECORD TITLE/ARTIST
8/80	**Tired Of Toein' The Line**...Rocky Burnette
6/65	**Tired Of Waiting For You**...Kinks
	To ..also see: Too
26/62	**To A Sleeping Beauty**...Jimmy Dean
5/84	**To All The Girls I've Loved Before**...Julio Iglesias & Willie Nelson
6/86	**To Be A Lover**...Billy Idol
22/58	**To Be Loved**...Jackie Wilson
1/92	**To Be With You**...Mr. Big
21/60	**To Each His Own**...Platters
29/68	**To Give (The Reason I Live)**...Frankie Valli
	To Know You (Him) Is To Love You (Him)
1/58	Teddy Bears
24/65	Peter & Gordon
34/69	Bobby Vinton
38/73	**To Know You Is To Love You**...B.B. King
	To Love Somebody
17/67	Bee Gees
11/92	Michael Bolton
1/67	**To Sir With Love**...Lulu
35/69	**To Susan On The West Coast Waiting**...Donovan
25/57	**To The Aisle**...Five Satins
17/75	**To The Door Of The Sun (Alle Porte Del Sole)**...Al Martino
25/56	**To The Ends Of The Earth**...Nat "King" Cole
27/56	**To You, My Love**...Nick Noble
20/71	**Toast And Marmalade For Tea**...Tin Tin
14/64	**Tobacco Road**...Nashville Teens
17/64	**Today**...New Christy Minstrels
39/63	**(Today I Met) The Boy I'm Gonna Marry**...Darlene Love
23/76	**Today's The Day**...America
6/61	**Together**...Connie Francis
18/81	**Together**...Tierra
19/66	**Together Again**...Ray Charles
1/88	**Together Forever**...Rick Astley
35/91	**Together Forever**...Lisette Melendez
37/72	**Together Let's Find Love**...5th Dimension
26/60	**Togetherness**...Frankie Avalon
20/63	**Tom Cat**...Rooftop Singers
1/58	**Tom Dooley**...Kingston Trio
5/90	**Tom's Diner**...D.N.A. Feat. Suzanne Vega
29/59	**Tomboy**...Perry Como
23/68	**Tomorrow**...Strawberry Alarm Clock
26/86	**Tomorrow Doesn't Matter Tonight**...Starship
39/88	**Tomorrow People**...Ziggy Marley/Melody Makers

POS/YR	RECORD TITLE/ARTIST
7/90	**Tonight**...New Kids On The Block
8/61	**Tonight**...Ferrante & Teicher
13/84	**Tonight**...Kool & The Gang
26/61	**Tonight (Could Be The Night)**...Velvets
16/83	**Tonight, I Celebrate My Love**...Peabo Bryson/Roberta Flack
15/61	**Tonight I Fell In Love**...Tokens
20/82	**Tonight I'm Yours (Don't Hurt Me)**...Rod Stewart
13/61	**Tonight My Love, Tonight**...Paul Anka
7/86	**Tonight She Comes**...Cars
3/87	**Tonight, Tonight, Tonight**...Genesis
	Tonight You Belong To Me
4/56	Patience & Prudence
15/56	Lawrence Welk with The Lennon Sisters
28/65	**Tonight's The Night**...Solomon Burke
39/60	**Tonight's The Night**...Shirelles
1/76	**Tonight's The Night (Gonna Be Alright)**...Rod Stewart
12/96	**Tonite's Tha Night**...Kris Kross
38/92	**Too Blind To See It**...Kym Sims
4/69	**Too Busy Thinking About My Baby**...Marvin Gaye
39/56	**Too Close For Comfort**...Eydie Gorme
10/92	**Too Funky**...George Michael
	Too Hot
5/80	Kool & The Gang
24/96	Coolio
24/78	**Too Hot Ta Trot**...Commodores
5/85	**Too Late For Goodbyes**...Julian Lennon
12/90	**Too Late To Say Goodbye**...Richard Marx
2/72	**Too Late To Turn Back Now**...Cornelius Brothers & Sister Rose
5/92	**2 Legit 2 Quit**...Hammer
	Too Many Fish In The Sea
25/65	Marvelettes
24/67	Mitch Ryder & The Detroit Wheels (medley)
13/65	**Too Many Rivers**...Brenda Lee
8/91	**Too Many Walls**...Cathy Dennis
1/57	**Too Much**...Elvis Presley
1/79	**Too Much Heaven**...Bee Gees
35/67	**Too Much Of Nothing**...Peter, Paul & Mary
37/92	**Too Much Passion**...Smithereens
19/68	**Too Much Talk**...Paul Revere & The Raiders
30/60	**Too Much Tequila**...Champs
9/81	**Too Much Time On My Hands**...Styx
1/78	**Too Much, Too Little, Too Late**...Johnny Mathis/Deniece Williams

POS/YR	RECORD TITLE/ARTIST
5/83	**Too Shy**...Kajagoogoo
40/81	**Too Tight**...Con Funk Shun
13/69	**Too Weak To Fight**...Clarence Carter
13/72	**Too Young**...Donny Osmond
21/56	**Too Young To Go Steady**...Nat "King" Cole
30/78	**Took The Last Train**...David Gates
8/95	**Tootsee Roll**...69 Boyz
1/73	**Top Of The World**...Carpenters
27/91	**Top Of The World**...Van Halen
27/58	**Topsy I**...Cozy Cole
3/58	**Topsy II**...Cozy Cole
	Torero
18/58	Renato Carosone
21/58	Julius LaRosa
1/77	**Torn Between Two Lovers**...Mary MacGregor
39/59	**Torquay**...Fireballs
17/84	**Torture**...Jacksons
20/62	**Torture**...Kris Jensen
1/61	**Tossin' And Turnin'**...Bobby Lewis
	Total Eclipse Of The Heart
1/83	Bonnie Tyler
2/95	Nicki French
23/74	**Touch A Hand, Make A Friend**...Staple Singers
37/80	**Touch And Go**...Cars
3/69	**Touch Me**...Doors
19/74	**Touch Me**...Fancy
2/91	**Touch Me (All Night Long)**...Cathy Dennis
4/87	**Touch Me (I Want Your Body)**...Samantha Fox
1/73	**Touch Me In The Morning**...Diana Ross
16/81	**Touch Me When We're Dancing**...Carpenters
9/87	**Touch Of Grey**...Grateful Dead
	Touch The Wind ..see: Eres Tu
	Tough ..also see: Tuff
22/85	**Tough All Over**...John Cafferty
5/61	**Tower Of Strength**...Gene McDaniels
13/62	**Town Without Pity**...Gene Pitney
1/89	**Toy Soldiers**...Martika
24/56	**Tra La La**...Georgia Gibbs
35/64	**Tra La La La Suzy**...Dean & Jean
2/69	**Traces**...Classics IV
	Tracks Of My Tears
16/65	Miracles
10/67	Johnny Rivers
25/76	Linda Ronstadt
9/69	**Tracy**...Cuff Links

POS/YR	RECORD TITLE/ARTIST
13/60	Tracy's Theme...Spencer Ross
1/79	Tragedy...Bee Gees
	Tragedy
5/59	Thomas Wayne
10/61	Fleetwoods
39/85	Tragedy...John Hunter
23/80	Train In Vain (Stand By Me)...Clash
36/60	Train Of Love...Annette
27/74	Train Of Thought...Cher
38/79	Train, Train...Blackfoot
22/66	Trains And Boats And Planes...Dionne Warwick
26/67	Tramp...Otis & Carla
38/75	Trampled Under Foot...Led Zeppelin
8/56	Transfusion...Nervous Norvus
35/61	Transistor Sister...Freddy Cannon
13/71	Trapped By A Thing Called Love...Denise LaSalle
2/70	Travelin' Band...Creedence Clearwater Revival
1/61	Travelin' Man...Ricky Nelson
32/67	Travlin' Man...Stevie Wonder
16/56	Treasure Of Love...Clyde McPhatter
26/58	Treasure Of Your Love...Eileen Rodgers
3/71	Treat Her Like A Lady...Cornelius Brothers & Sister Rose
2/65	Treat Her Right...Roy Head
18/57	Treat Me Nice...Elvis Presley
18/81	Treat Me Right...Pat Benatar
18/94	Tremor Christ...Pearl Jam
29/61	Triangle...Janie Grant
25/57	Tricky...Ralph Marterie
6/72	Troglodyte (Cave Man)...Jimmy Castor Bunch
9/82	Trouble...Lindsey Buckingham
35/75	T-R-O-U-B-L-E...Elvis Presley
35/88	Trouble...Nia Peeples
20/60	Trouble In Paradise...Crests
33/63	Trouble Is My Middle Name...Bobby Vinton
7/73	Trouble Man...Marvin Gaye
4/83	True...Spandau Ballet **(also see: Set Adrift On Memory Bliss)**
3/86	True Blue...Madonna
40/90	True Blue Love...Lou Gramm
1/86	True Colors...Cyndi Lauper
32/87	True Faith...New Order
35/69	True Grit...Glen Campbell

POS/YR	RECORD TITLE/ARTIST
	True Love
3/56	Bing Crosby & Grace Kelly
15/56	Jane Powell
13/88	True Love...Glenn Frey
21/63	True Love Never Runs Smooth...Gene Pitney
	True Love, True Love ..see: (If You Cry)
14/65	True Love Ways...Peter & Gordon
1/82	Truly...Lionel Richie
30/61	Trust In Me...Etta James
28/91	Truth, The...TAMI Show
23/69	Try A Little Kindness...Glen Campbell
	Try A Little Tenderness
25/67	Otis Redding
29/69	Three Dog Night
23/83	Try Again...Champaign
15/64	Try It Baby...Marvin Gaye
33/58	Try The Impossible...Lee Andrews & The Hearts
12/66	Try Too Hard...Dave Clark Five
10/76	Tryin' To Get The Feeling Again...Barry Manilow
5/81	Tryin' To Live My Life Without You...Bob Seger
10/77	Tryin' To Love Two...William Bell
15/74	Trying To Hold On To My Woman...Lamont Dozier
40/70	Trying To Make A Fool Of Me...Delfonics
7/74	Tubular Bells...Mike Oldfield
32/59	Tucumcari...Jimmie Rodgers
24/68	Tuesday Afternoon (Forever Afternoon)...Moody Blues
17/62	Tuff...Ace Cannon
10/86	Tuff Enuff...Fabulous Thunderbirds
30/80	Tulsa Time...Eric Clapton
	Tumbling Dice
7/72	Rolling Stones
32/78	Linda Ronstadt
30/58	Tumbling Tumbleweeds...Billy Vaughn
9/88	Tunnel Of Love...Bruce Springsteen
27/64	Turn Around...Dick & DeeDee
7/68	Turn Around, Look At Me...Vogues
3/70	Turn Back The Hands Of Time...Tyrone Davis
16/66	Turn-Down Day...Cyrkle
9/59	Turn Me Loose...Fabian
35/81	Turn Me Loose...Loverboy
28/62	Turn On Your Love Light...Bobby Bland

POS/YR	RECORD TITLE/ARTIST
	Turn The Beat Around
10/76	Vicki Sue Robinson
13/94	Gloria Estefan
13/78	**Turn To Stone**...Electric Light Orchestra
32/84	**Turn To You**...Go-Go's
1/65	**Turn! Turn! Turn!**...Byrds
29/85	**Turn Up The Radio**...Autograph
5/82	**Turn Your Love Around**...George Benson
36/80	**Turning Japanese**...Vapors
13/90	**Turtle Power!**...Partners In Kryme
36/58	**Turvy II**...Cozy Cole
20/75	**Tush**...ZZ Top
8/79	**Tusk**...Fleetwood Mac
	Tutti' Frutti
12/56	Pat Boone
17/56	Little Richard
	Tweedlee Dee
2/55	Georgia Gibbs
14/55	LaVern Baker
	Twelfth Of Never
9/57	Johnny Mathis
8/73	Donny Osmond
20/67	**Twelve Thirty (Young Girls Are Coming To The Canyon)**...Mamas & The Papas
15/63	**Twenty Miles**...Chubby Checker
31/64	**20-75**...Willie Mitchell
17/63	**Twenty Four Hours From Tulsa**...Gene Pitney
6/69	**Twenty-Five Miles**...Edwin Starr
4/70	**25 Or 6 To 4**...Chicago
2/58	**26 Miles (Santa Catalina)**...Four Preps
38/81	**Twilight**...ELO
1/58	**Twilight Time**...Platters
31/88	**Twilight World**...Swing Out Sister
10/83	**Twilight Zone**...Golden Earring
30/80	**Twilight Zone/Twilight Tone**...Manhattan Transfer
14/65	**Twine Time**...Alvin Cash & The Crawlers
39/66	**Twinkle Toes**...Roy Orbison
	Twist, The
1/60	Chubby Checker
28/60	Hank Ballard
1/62	Chubby Checker
16/88	Fat Boys/Chubby Checker (Yo, Twist!) **(also see: Percolator)**
	Twist And Shout
17/62	Isley Brothers
2/64	Beatles
23/86	Beatles
26/62	**Twist-Her**...Bill Black's Combo

POS/YR	RECORD TITLE/ARTIST
25/63	**Twist It Up**...Chubby Checker
5/84	**Twist Of Fate**...Olivia Newton-John
	("Twist" Special) ..see: Rock-A-Hula Baby
9/62	**Twist, Twist Senora**...Gary "U.S." Bonds
22/62	**Twistin' Matilda**...Jimmy Soul
34/62	**Twistin' Postman**...Marvelettes
9/62	**Twistin' The Night Away**...Sam Cooke
27/60	**Twistin' U.S.A.**....Danny & The Juniors
	Twistin' White Silver Sands ..see: White Silver Sands
17/59	**Twixt Twelve And Twenty**...Pat Boone
11/56	**Two Different Worlds**...Don Rondo
16/71	**Two Divided By Love**...Grass Roots
19/78	**Two Doors Down**...Dolly Parton
6/63	**Two Faces Have I**...Lou Christie
33/75	**Two Fine People**...Cat Stevens
1/89	**Two Hearts**...Phil Collins
16/55	**Two Hearts**...Pat Boone
40/81	**Two Hearts**...Stephanie Mills/Teddy Pendergrass
F/55	**Two Hound Dogs**...Bill Haley
38/83	**Two Less Lonely People In The World**...Air Supply
31/68	**Two Little Kids**...Peaches & Herb
18/55	**Two Lost Souls**...Perry Como & Jaye P. Morgan
7/63	**Two Lovers**...Mary Wells
10/88	**Two Occasions**...Deele
3/86	**Two Of Hearts**...Stacey Q
11/78	**Two Out Of Three Ain't Bad**...Meat Loaf
30/87	**Two People**...Tina Turner
30/80	**Two Places At The Same Time**...Ray Parker Jr. & Raydio
7/93	**Two Princes**...Spin Doctors
38/84	**Two Sides Of Love**...Sammy Hagar
12/93	**Two Steps Behind**...Def Leppard
	2001 Space Odyssey ..see: Also Sprach Zarathustra
22/78	**Two Tickets To Paradise**...Eddie Money
32/63	**Two Tickets To Paradise**...Brook Benton
2/90	**Two To Make It Right**...Seduction
2/86	**Typical Male**...Tina Turner

POS/YR	RECORD TITLE/ARTIST

U

U ..see: You

POS/YR	RECORD TITLE/ARTIST
28/68	**U.S. Male**...Elvis Presley
14/59	**Uh! Oh!**...Nutty Squirrels (Part 2)
16/92	**Uhh Ahh**...Boyz II Men
5/64	**Um, Um, Um, Um, Um, Um**...Major Lance
1/91	**Unbelievable**...EMF
F/94	**Unbelievable**...Notorious B.I.G.
9/62	**Unchain My Heart**...Ray Charles
	Unchained Melody
1/55	Les Baxter
3/55	Al Hibbler
6/55	Roy Hamilton
29/55	June Valli
4/65	Righteous Brothers
13/90	Righteous Brothers
19/90	Righteous Brothers
1/71	**Uncle Albert/Admiral Halsey**...Paul & Linda McCartney
29/82	**Under Pressure**...Queen & David Bowie **(also see: Ice Ice Baby)**
4/64	**Under The Boardwalk**...Drifters
2/92	**Under The Bridge**...Red Hot Chili Peppers
24/88	**Under The Milky Way**...Church
35/66	**Under Your Spell Again**...Johnny Rivers
1/77	**Undercover Angel**...Alan O'Day
9/83	**Undercover Of The Night**...Rolling Stones
35/64	**Understand Your Man**...Johnny Cash
8/94	**Understanding**...Xscape
17/85	**Understanding**...Bob Seger
22/69	**Undun**...Guess Who
9/73	**Uneasy Rider**...Charlie Daniels
	Unforgettable
17/59	Dinah Washington
14/91	Natalie Cole with Nat "King" Cole
35/92	**Unforgiven, The**...Metallica **(also see: Theme From The)**
33/70	**Ungena Za Ulimwengu (Unite The World)**...Temptations
7/68	**Unicorn, The**...Irish Rovers
24/76	**Union Man**...Cate Bros.
3/83	**Union Of The Snake**...Duran Duran
13/70	**United We Stand**...Brotherhood Of Man
23/94	**U.N.I.T.Y.**....Queen Latifah
39/68	**Unknown Soldier**...Doors
3/90	**Unskinny Bop**...Poison
40/72	**Until It's Time For You To Go**...Elvis Presley

POS/YR	RECORD TITLE/ARTIST
3/74	**Until You Come Back To Me (That's What I'm Gonna Do)**...Aretha Franklin
26/92	**Until Your Love Comes Back Around**...RTZ
	Up A Lazy River ..see: Lazy River
27/90	**Up All Night**...Slaughter
4/70	**Up Around The Bend**...Creedence Clearwater Revival
16/75	**Up In A Puff Of Smoke**...Polly Brown
25/70	**Up On Cripple Creek**...Band
	Up On The Roof
5/63	Drifters
28/79	James Taylor
10/70	**Up The Ladder To The Roof**...Supremes
7/67	**Up-Up And Away**...5th Dimension
1/82	**Up Where We Belong**...Joe Cocker & Jennifer Warnes
22/67	**Ups And Downs**...Paul Revere & The Raiders
1/80	**Upside Down**...Diana Ross
3/66	**Uptight (Everything's Alright)**...Stevie Wonder **(also see: Little Ole Man)**
13/62	**Uptown**...Crystals
25/77	**Uptown Festival (Motown Medley)**...Shalamar
3/83	**Uptown Girl**...Billy Joel
4/81	**Urgent**...Foreigner
2/72	**Use Me**...Bill Withers
4/78	**Use Ta Be My Girl**...O'Jays
34/65	**Use Your Head**...Mary Wells
27/61	**Utopia**...Frank Gari

V

POS/YR	RECORD TITLE/ARTIST
8/82	**Vacation**...Go-Go's
9/62	**Vacation**...Connie Francis
9/87	**Valerie**...Steve Winwood
3/68	**Valleri**...Monkees
32/82	**Valley Girl**...Frank Zappa
8/57	**Valley Of Tears**...Fats Domino
	Valley Of The Dolls ..see: Theme From
5/88	**Valley Road**...Bruce Hornsby & The Range
9/85	**Valotte**...Julian Lennon
2/70	**Vehicle**...Ides Of March
35/86	**Velcro Fly**...ZZ Top
8/72	**Ventura Highway**...America
1/59	**Venus**...Frankie Avalon

POS/YR	RECORD TITLE/ARTIST
	Venus
1/70	Shocking Blue
1/86	Bananarama
12/75	**Venus And Mars Rock Show**...Wings
7/62	**Venus In Blue Jeans**...Jimmy Clanton
19/89	**Veronica**...Elvis Costello
23/58	**Very Precious Love**...Ames Brothers
31/93	**Very Special**...Big Daddy Kane
	Very Special Love
20/58	Debbie Reynolds
23/58	Johnny Nash
11/74	**Very Special Love Song**...Charlie Rich
26/64	**Very Thought Of You**...Rick Nelson
16/92	**Vibeology**...Paula Abdul
31/79	**Victim Of Love**...Elton John
32/87	**Victim Of Love**...Bryan Adams
10/87	**Victory**...Kool & The Gang
40/79	**Video Killed The Radio Star**...Buggles
18/86	**Vienna Calling**...Falco
1/85	**View To A Kill**...Duran Duran
22/62	**Village Of Love**...Nathaniel Mayer
7/60	**Village Of St. Bernadette**...Andy Williams
12/72	**Vincent**...Don McLean
1/90	**Vision Of Love**...Mariah Carey
29/64	**Viva Las Vegas**...Elvis Presley
28/70	**Viva Tirado**...El Chicano
1/90	**Vogue**...Madonna
15/81	**Voice**...Moody Blues
32/80	**Voices**...Cheap Trick
8/85	**Voices Carry**...'til tuesday
25/89	**Voices Of Babylon**...Outfield
11/91	**Voices That Care**...Voices That Care
	Volare (Nel Blu Dipinto Di Blu)
1/58	Domenico Modugno
12/58	Dean Martin
4/60	Bobby Rydell
33/75	Al Martino
27/65	**Voodoo Woman**...Bobby Goldsboro
29/85	**Vox Humana**...Kenny Loggins
29/82	**Voyeur**...Kim Carnes

W

POS/YR	RECORD TITLE/ARTIST
36/74	**WOLD**...Harry Chapin
40/67	**Wack Wack**...Young Holt Trio
	Wade In The Water
19/66	Ramsey Lewis
37/67	Herb Alpert

POS/YR	RECORD TITLE/ARTIST
2/62	**Wah Watusi**...Orlons
	(also see: El Watusi, & Watusi)
8/88	**Wait**...White Lion
37/61	**Wait A Minute**...Coasters
23/57	**Wait And See**...Fats Domino
18/80	**Wait For Me**...Daryl Hall & John Oates
37/60	**Wait For Me**...Playmates
26/63	**Wait Til' My Bobby Gets Home**...Darlene Love
18/58	**Waitin' In School**...Ricky Nelson
19/81	**Waiting**...Tom Petty
2/81	**Waiting For A Girl Like You**...Foreigner
5/88	**Waiting For A Star To Fall**...Boy Meets Girl
13/91	**Waiting For Love**...Alias
27/91	**Waiting For That Day**...George Michael
13/82	**Waiting On A Friend**...Rolling Stones
1/84	**Wake Me Up Before You Go-Go**...Wham!
	Wake The Town And Tell The People
5/55	Les Baxter
13/55	Mindy Carson
12/76	**Wake Up Everybody**...Harold Melvin & The Blue Notes
	Wake Up Little Susie
1/57	Everly Brothers
27/82	Simon & Garfunkel
39/85	**Wake Up (Next To You)**...Graham Parker
7/58	**Walk, The**...Jimmy McCracklin
12/70	**Walk A Mile In My Shoes**...Joe South
23/65	**Walk Away**...Matt Monro
36/80	**Walk Away**...Donna Summer
9/76	**Walk Away From Love**...David Ruffin
	Walk Away Renee
5/66	Left Banke
14/68	Four Tops
	Walk Don't Run
2/60	Ventures
8/64	Ventures ('64)
10/56	**Walk Hand In Hand**...Tony Martin
12/65	**Walk In The Black Forest**...Horst Jankowski
1/63	**Walk Like A Man**...4 Seasons
19/74	**Walk Like A Man**...Grand Funk
1/86	**Walk Like An Egyptian**...Bangles
7/86	**Walk Of Life**...Dire Straits
5/61	**Walk On By**...Leroy Van Dyke
	Walk On By
6/64	Dionne Warwick
30/69	Isaac Hayes
18/93	**Walk On The Ocean**...Toad The Wet Sprocket
16/73	**Walk On The Wild Side**...Lou Reed
	(also see: Wildside)

POS/YR	RECORD TITLE/ARTIST
21/62	**Walk On The Wild Side**...Jimmy Smith
9/88	**Walk On Water**...Eddie Money
17/72	**Walk On Water**...Neil Diamond
7/61	**Walk Right Back**...Everly Brothers
1/63	**Walk Right In**...Rooftop Singers
7/89	**Walk The Dinosaur**...Was (Not Was)
	Walk This Way
10/77	Aerosmith
4/86	Run-D.M.C.
28/91	**Walk Through Fire**...Bad Company
12/57	**Walkin' After Midnight**...Patsy Cline
	Walkin' In The Rain
23/64	Ronettes
19/70	Jay & The Americans
14/72	**Walkin' In The Rain With The One I Love**...Love Unlimited
	Walkin' In The Sand ..see: Remember
37/67	**Walkin' In The Sunshine**...Roger Miller
12/63	**Walkin' Miracle**...Essex
22/66	**Walkin' My Cat Named Dog**...Norma Tanega
26/63	**Walking Proud**...Steve Lawrence
29/58	**Walking Along**...Diamonds
9/89	**Walking Away**...Information Society
11/87	**Walking Down Your Street**...Bangles
13/91	**Walking In Memphis**...Marc Cohn
6/75	**Walking In Rhythm**...Blackbyrds
18/84	**Walking On A Thin Line**...Huey Lewis & the News
14/92	**Walking On Broken Glass**...Annie Lennox
9/85	**Walking On Sunshine**...Katrina & The Waves
10/63	**Walking The Dog**...Rufus Thomas
	Walking The Floor ..see: I'm Walking
6/60	**Walking To New Orleans**...Fats Domino
32/80	**Walks Like A Lady**...Journey
2/62	**Wanderer, The**...Dion
3/80	**Wanderer, The**...Donna Summer
5/83	**Wanna Be Startin' Somethin'**...Michael Jackson
28/93	**Wannagirl**...Jeremy Jordan
1/71	**Want Ads**...Honey Cone
7/87	**Wanted Dead Or Alive**...Bon Jovi
38/56	**Wanting You**...Roger Williams
	War
1/70	Edwin Starr
8/86	Bruce Springsteen
17/84	**War Song**...Culture Club
17/66	**Warm And Tender Love**...Percy Sledge

POS/YR	RECORD TITLE/ARTIST
13/92	**Warm It Up**...Kris Kross
39/78	**Warm Ride**...Rare Earth
25/62	**Warmed Over Kisses (Left Over Love)**...Brian Hyland
F/95	**Warning**...Notorious B.I.G.
7/84	**Warrior, The**...Scandal
24/90	**Was It Nothing At All**...Michael Damian
2/63	**Washington Square**...Village Stompers
37/81	**Wasn't That A Party**...Rovers
8/75	**Wasted Days And Wasted Nights**...Freddy Fender
9/82	**Wasted On The Way**...Crosby, Stills & Nash
40/79	**Watch Out For Lucy**...Eric Clapton
30/67	**Watch The Flowers Grow**...4 Seasons
11/71	**Watching Scotty Grow**...Bobby Goldsboro
10/81	**Watching The Wheels**...John Lennon
40/61	**Water Boy**...Don Shirley Trio
2/95	**Water Runs Dry**...Boyz II Men
1/95	**Waterfalls**...TLC
4/59	**Waterloo**...Stonewall Jackson
6/74	**Waterloo**...Abba
10/63	**Watermelon Man**...Mongo Santamaria Band
25/61	**Watusi, The**...Vibrations **(also see: El Watusi, & Wah Watusi)**
18/77	**Way Down**...Elvis Presley
3/60	**Way Down Yonder In New Orleans**...Freddie Cannon
40/83	**Way He Makes Me Feel**...Barbra Streisand
12/92	**Way I Feel About You**...Karyn White
24/78	**Way I Feel Tonight**...Bay City Rollers
35/59	**Way I Walk**...Jack Scott
4/75	**Way I Want To Touch You**...Captain & Tennille
1/86	**Way It Is**...Bruce Hornsby & The Range
7/72	**Way Of Love**...Cher
20/94	**Way She Loves Me**...Richard Marx
	Way That You Love Me ..see: (It's Just)
	Way We Were
1/74	Barbra Streisand
11/75	Gladys Knight & The Pips (medley)
	Way You Do The Things You Do
11/64	Temptations
20/78	Rita Coolidge
20/85	Daryl Hall John Oates/David Ruffin/Eddie Kendrick (medley)
6/90	UB40
13/61	**Way You Look Tonight**...Lettermen
7/89	**Way You Love Me**...Karyn White
1/88	**Way You Make Me Feel**...Michael Jackson

POS/YR	RECORD TITLE/ARTIST
24/58	Ways Of A Woman In Love...Johnny Cash
	Wayward Wind
1/56	Gogi Grant
28/56	Tex Ritter
5/67	(We Ain't Got) Nothin' Yet...Blues Magoos
	(We All Shine On) ..see: Instant Karma
14/88	We All Sleep Alone...Cher
2/79	We Are Family...Sister Sledge
4/78	We Are The Champions...Queen
1/85	We Are The World...USA for Africa
25/84	We Are The Young...Dan Hartman
5/85	We Belong...Pat Benatar
32/58	We Belong Together...Robert & Johnny
1/85	We Built This City...Starship
21/68	We Can Fly...Cowsills
	We Can Work It Out
1/66	Beatles
13/71	Stevie Wonder
8/90	We Can't Go Wrong...Cover Girls
36/76	We Can't Hide It Anymore...Larry Santos
35/87	We Connect...Stacey Q
1/89	We Didn't Start The Fire...Billy Joel
5/86	We Don't Have To Take Our Clothes Off...Jermaine Stewart
2/85	We Don't Need Another Hero (Thunderdome)...Tina Turner
7/80	We Don't Talk Anymore...Cliff Richard
20/92	We Got A Love Thang...Ce Ce Peniston
6/59	We Got Love...Bobby Rydell
35/69	We Got More Soul...Dyke & The Blazers
2/82	We Got The Beat...Go-Go's
13/65	We Gotta Get Out Of This Place...Animals
20/71	We Gotta Get You A Woman...Runt
12/77	We Just Disagree...Dave Mason
27/80	We Live For Love...Pat Benatar
39/64	We Love You Beatles...Carefrees
21/73	We May Never Pass This Way (Again)...Seals & Crofts
22/83	We Two...Little River Band
16/91	We Want The Funk...Gerardo
31/80	We Were Meant To Be Lovers...Photoglo
7/87	We'll Be Together...Sting
9/78	We'll Never Have To Say Goodbye Again...England Dan & John Ford Coley
4/64	We'll Sing In The Sunshine...Gale Garnett
14/68	We're A Winner...Impressions
7/77	We're All Alone...Rita Coolidge
35/90	We're All In The Same Gang...West Coast Rap All-Stars
1/73	We're An American Band...Grand Funk
40/72	We're Free...Beverly Bremers
34/74	We're Getting Careless With Our Love...Johnnie Taylor
	(We're Gonna) ..see: Rock Around The Clock
25/65	We're Gonna Make It...Little Milton
15/81	We're In This Love Together...Al Jarreau
21/84	We're Not Gonna Take It...Twisted Sister
9/87	We're Ready...Boston
25/72	We've Got To Get It On Again...Addrisi Brothers
	We've Got Tonite
13/79	Bob Seger
6/83	Kenny Rogers & Sheena Easton
2/70	We've Only Just Begun...Carpenters
1/93	Weak...SWV (Sisters With Voices)
F/57	Wear My Ring...Gene Vincent
2/58	Wear My Ring Around Your Neck...Elvis Presley
23/67	Wear Your Love Like Heaven...Donovan
32/56	Weary Blues...McGuire Sisters & Lawrence Welk
10/65	Wedding, The...Julie Rogers
1/69	Wedding Bell Blues...5th Dimension
	Wedding Bells ..see: (I'm Always Hearing)
24/71	Wedding Song (There Is Love)...Paul Stookey (also see: Down The Aisle)
35/58	Week End...Kingsmen
29/79	Weekend...Wet Willie
10/77	Weekend In New England...Barry Manilow
19/69	Weight, The...Aretha Franklin
1/76	Welcome Back...John Sebastian
22/62	Welcome Home Baby...Shirelles
18/60	(Welcome) New Lovers...Pat Boone
24/83	Welcome To Heartlight...Kenny Loggins
37/86	Welcome To The Boomtown...David & David
7/88	Welcome To The Jungle...Guns N' Roses
29/61	Well. I Told You...Chantels
13/66	Well Respected Man...Kinks
21/78	Werewolves Of London...Warren Zevon
1/86	West End Girls...Pet Shop Boys
37/62	West Of The Wall...Toni Fisher
24/70	Westbound #9...Flaming Ember
8/58	Western Movies...Olympics
5/67	Western Union...Five Americans
24/63	Wham!...Lonnie Mack

POS/YR	RECORD TITLE/ARTIST
16/76	**Wham Bam**...Silver
F/95	**What, The**...Notorious B.I.G. & Method Man
	What A Beautiful World ..see: I.G.Y.
	What A Diff'rence A Day Makes
8/59	Dinah Washington
20/75	Esther Phillips
	What A Feeling ..see: Flashdance
1/79	**What A Fool Believes**...Doobie Brothers
22/61	**What A Party**...Fats Domino
22/61	**What A Price**...Fats Domino
33/61	**What A Surprise**...Johnny Maestro
31/67	**What A Woman In Love Won't Do**...Sandy Posey
32/88	**What A Wonderful World**...Louis Armstrong
	(also see: Wonderful World)
10/85	**What About Love?**...Heart
26/86	**What About Love**...'til tuesday
15/84	**What About Me?**...Kenny Rogers/Kim Carnes/James Ingram
29/83	**What About Me**...Moving Pictures
7/92	**What About Your Friends**...TLC
39/72	**What Am I Crying For?**...Classics IV
35/83	**What Am I Gonna Do (I'm So In Love With You)**...Rod Stewart
8/75	**What Am I Gonna Do With You**...Barry White
	What Am I Living For
9/58	Chuck Willis
26/60	Conway Twitty
14/81	**What Are We Doin' In Love**...Dottie West with Kenny Rogers
39/71	**What Are You Doing Sunday**...Dawn
	What Becomes Of The Brokenhearted
7/66	Jimmy Ruffin
22/92	Paul Young
	What Cha ..also see: What You, and Whatcha
22/79	**What Cha Gonna Do With My Lovin'**...Stephanie Mills
38/65	**What Color (Is A Man)**...Bobby Vinton
19/91	**What Comes Naturally**...Sheena Easton
4/69	**What Does It Take (To Win Your Love)**...Jr. Walker & The All Stars
2/88	**What Have I Done To Deserve This?**...Pet Shop Boys/Dusty Springfield
29/65	**What Have They Done To The Rain**...Searchers
4/86	**What Have You Done For Me Lately**...Janet Jackson

POS/YR	RECORD TITLE/ARTIST
7/89	**What I Am**...Edie Brickell & New Bohemians
28/89	**What I Like About You**...Michael Morales
39/84	**(What) In The Name Of Love**...Naked Eyes
5/60	**What In The World's Come Over You**...Jack Scott
10/71	**What Is Life**...George Harrison
11/93	**What Is Love**...Haddaway
15/59	**What Is Love?**...Playmates
33/84	**What Is Love?**...Howard Jones
19/70	**What Is Truth**...Johnny Cash
9/90	**What It Takes**...Aerosmith
10/81	**What Kind Of Fool**...Barbra Streisand & Barry Gibb
17/62	**What Kind Of Fool Am I**...Sammy Davis Jr.
21/82	**What Kind Of Fool Am I**...Rick Springfield
	What Kind Of Fool Do You Think I Am
9/64	Tams
23/69	Bill Deal
18/62	**What Kind Of Love Is This**...Joey Dee & The Starliters
5/90	**What Kind Of Man Would I Be?**...Chicago
40/65	**What Now**...Gene Chandler
	What Now My Love
14/66	Sonny & Cher
24/66	Herb Alpert
30/67	Mitch Ryder
	What The World Needs Now Is Love
7/65	Jackie DeShannon
8/71	Tom Clay (medley)
9/63	**What Will Mary Say**...Johnny Mathis
	What You ..also see: Whatcha
8/89	**What You Don't Know**...Expose
13/87	**What You Get Is What You See**...Tina Turner
5/86	**What You Need**...INXS
24/88	**What You See Is What You Get**...Brenda K. Starr
	(also see: Whatcha See Is Whatcha Get)
9/79	**What You Won't Do For Love**...Bobby Caldwell
	What'd I Say
6/59	Ray Charles
30/61	Jerry Lee Lewis
24/62	Bobby Darin
21/64	Elvis Presley
	What's ..also see: Wot's
12/62	**What's A Matter Baby**...Timi Yuro
29/64	**What's Easy For Two Is So Hard For One**...Mary Wells
19/82	**What's Forever For**...Michael Murphey

POS/YR	RECORD TITLE/ARTIST
	What's Going On
2/71	Marvin Gaye
12/87	Cyndi Lauper
	(also see: Six Feet Deep)
1/84	**What's Love Got To Do With It**...Tina Turner
8/94	**What's My Name?**...Snoop Doggy Dogg
3/65	**What's New Pussycat?**...Tom Jones
3/88	**What's On Your Mind (Pure Energy)**...Information Society
35/62	**What's So Good About Good-by**...Miracles
21/94	**What's The Frequency, Kenneth?**...R.E.M.
17/64	**What's The Matter With You Baby**...Marvin Gaye & Mary Wells
20/69	**What's The Use Of Breaking Up**...Jerry Butler
14/93	**What's Up**...4 Non Blondes
39/93	**What's Up Doc? (Can We Rock?)**...Fu-Schnickens with Shaquille O'Neal
7/62	**What's Your Name**...Don & Juan
13/78	**What's Your Name**...Lynyrd Skynyrd
	Whatcha ..also see: What You
6/77	**Whatcha Gonna Do**...Pablo Cruise
9/71	**Whatcha See Is Whatcha Get**...Dramatics
	(also see: What You See Is What You Get)
1/74	**Whatever Gets You Thru The Night**...John Lennon
	Whatever Lola Wants
6/55	Sarah Vaughan
12/55	Dinah Shore
	(Whatever Will Be, Will Be) ..see: Que Sera, Sera
38/74	**Whatever You Got, I Want**...Jackson 5
3/94	**Whatta Man**...Salt 'N' Pepa with En Vogue
26/66	**Wheel Of Hurt**...Margaret Whiting
	Wheels
3/61	String-A-Longs
28/61	Billy Vaughn
5/58	**When**...Kalin Twins
	When A Man Loves A Woman
1/66	Percy Sledge
35/80	Bette Midler
1/91	Michael Bolton
27/82	**When All Is Said And Done**...Abba
4/94	**When Can I See You**...Babyface
1/84	**When Doves Cry**...Prince
	(also see: Pray)
30/82	**When He Shines**...Sheena Easton
18/69	**When I Die**...Motherlode

POS/YR	RECORD TITLE/ARTIST
	When I Fall In Love
7/62	Lettermen
23/93	Celine Dion & Clive Griffin
9/64	**When I Grow Up (To Be A Man)**...Beach Boys
8/92	**When I Look Into Your Eyes**...Firehouse
10/89	**When I Looked At Him**...Expose
1/77	**When I Need You**...Leo Sayer
29/57	**When I See You**...Fats Domino
1/89	**When I See You Smile**...Bad English
1/86	**When I Think Of You**...Janet Jackson
20/80	**When I Wanted You**...Barry Manilow
15/67	**When I Was Young**...Animals
7/90	**When I'm Back On My Feet Again**...Michael Bolton
25/65	**When I'm Gone**...Brenda Holloway
1/89	**When I'm With You**...Sheriff
5/88	**When It's Love**...Van Halen
26/82	**When It's Over**...Loverboy
18/66	**When Liking Turns To Loving**...Ronnie Dove
19/56	**When My Blue Moon Turns To Gold Again**...Elvis Presley
14/56	**When My Dreamboat Comes Home**...Fats Domino
28/62	**When My Little Girl Is Smiling**...Drifters
11/93	**When She Cries**...Restless Heart
37/66	**(When She Needs Good Lovin') She Comes To Me**...Chicago Loop
11/81	**When She Was My Girl**...Four Tops
5/87	**When Smokey Sings**...ABC
10/62	**When The Boy In Your Arms (Is The Boy In Your Heart)**...Connie Francis
19/58	**When The Boys Talk About The Girls**...Valerie Carr
3/89	**When The Children Cry**...White Lion
2/86	**When The Going Gets Tough, The Tough Get Going**...Billy Ocean
14/86	**When The Heart Rules The Mind**...GTR
37/83	**When The Lights Go Out**...Naked Eyes
23/64	**When The Lovelight Starts Shining Through His Eyes**...Supremes
11/90	**When The Night Comes**...Joe Cocker
18/56	**When The Saints Go Marching In**...Bill Haley
	When The White Lilacs Bloom Again
12/56	Helmut Zacharias
18/56	Billy Vaughn
40/56	Florian Zabach
38/94	**When We Dance**...Sting

POS/YR	RECORD TITLE/ARTIST
10/61	**When We Get Married**...Dreamlovers
36/88	**When We Kiss**...Bardeux
23/88	**When We Was Fab**...George Harrison
	When Will I Be Loved
8/60	Everly Brothers
2/75	Linda Ronstadt
2/74	**When Will I See You Again**...Three Degrees
14/84	**When You Close Your Eyes**...Night Ranger
33/56	**When You Dance**...Turbans
32/72	**When You Say Love**...Sonny & Cher
35/64	**When You Walk In The Room**...Searchers
30/60	**When You Wish Upon A Star**...Dion & The Belmonts
9/71	**When You're Hot, You're Hot**...Jerry Reed
6/79	**When You're In Love With A Beautiful Woman**...Dr. Hook
23/67	**When You're Young And In Love**...Marvelettes
35/85	**When Your Heart Is Weak**...Cock Robin
39/64	**Whenever He Holds You**...Bobby Goldsboro
5/78	**Whenever I Call You "Friend"**...Kenny Loggins
38/76	**Whenever I'm Away From You**...John Travolta
32/60	**Where Are You**...Frankie Avalon
36/62	**Where Are You**...Dinah Washington
10/89	**Where Are You Now?**...Jimmy Harnen W/Synch
	Where Did Our Love Go
1/64	Supremes
15/71	Donnie Elbert
33/71	**Where Did They Go, Lord**...Elvis Presley
1/88	**Where Do Broken Hearts Go**...Whitney Houston
	(Where Do I Begin) ..see: Theme From Love Story
38/86	**Where Do The Children Go**...Hooters
25/65	**Where Do You Go**...Cher
4/91	**Where Does My Heart Beat Now**...Celine Dion
	Where Have All The Flowers Gone
21/62	Kingston Trio
26/65	Johnny Rivers
5/72	**Where Is The Love**...Roberta Flack & Donny Hathaway
3/60	**Where Or When**...Dion & The Belmonts
28/73	**Where Peaceful Waters Flow**...Gladys Knight & The Pips
	Where The Action Is ..see: Action
4/61	**Where The Boys Are**...Connie Francis

POS/YR	RECORD TITLE/ARTIST
13/87	**Where The Streets Have No Name**...U2
23/59	**Where Were You (On Our Wedding Day)?**...Lloyd Price
28/66	**Where Were You When I Needed You**...Grass Roots
23/79	**Where Were You When I Was Falling In Love**...Lobo
21/67	**Where Will The Words Come From**...Gary Lewis & The Playboys
20/92	**Where You Goin' Now**...Damn Yankees
	Where You Lead
40/71	Barbra Streisand
37/72	Barbra Streisand (medley)
26/69	**Where's The Playground Susie**...Glen Campbell
	Which Way Is Up ..see: Theme From
2/70	**Which Way You Goin' Billy?**...Poppy Family
7/81	**While You See A Chance**...Steve Winwood
6/90	**Whip Appeal**...Babyface
14/80	**Whip It**...Devo
28/83	**Whirly Girl**...Oxo
37/84	**Whisper To A Scream (Birds Fly)**...Icicle Works
	Whispering
11/64	Nino Tempo & April Stevens
27/77	Dr. Buzzard's Original "Savannah" Band
9/57	**Whispering Bells**...Dell-Vikings
11/66	**Whispers (Gettin' Louder)**...Jackie Wilson
	White Christmas
7/55	Bing Crosby
34/57	Bing Crosby
26/60	Bing Crosby
12/61	Bing Crosby
38/62	Bing Crosby
26/84	**White Horse**...Laid Back
19/76	**White Knight**...Cledus Maggard
28/72	**White Lies, Blue Eyes**...Bullet
9/64	**White On White**...Danny Williams
8/67	**White Rabbit**...Jefferson Airplane
6/68	**White Room**...Cream
	White Silver Sands
7/57	Don Rondo
18/57	Owen Bradley Quintet
22/57	Dave Gardner
9/60	Bill Black's Combo
2/57	**White Sport Coat (And A Pink Carnation)**...Marty Robbins
36/83	**White Wedding**...Billy Idol
5/67	**Whiter Shade Of Pale**...Procol Harum
21/66	**Who Am I**...Petula Clark

POS/YR	RECORD TITLE/ARTIST
14/78	**Who Are You**...Who
8/95	**Who Can I Run To?**...Xscape
33/64	**Who Can I Turn To**...Tony Bennett
1/82	**Who Can It Be Now?**...Men At Work
15/89	**Who Do You Give Your Love To?**...Michael Morales
25/64	**Who Do You Love**...Sapphires
15/74	**Who Do You Think You Are**...Bo Donaldson & The Heywoods
40/81	**Who Do You Think You're Foolin'**...Donna Summer
16/87	**Who Found Who**...Jellybean/Elisa Fiorillo
33/68	**Who Is Gonna Love Me?**...Dionne Warwick
14/93	**Who Is It**...Michael Jackson
3/75	**Who Loves You**...Four Seasons
9/57	**Who Needs You**...Four Lads
7/61	**Who Put The Bomp (In The Bomp, Bomp, Bomp)**...Barry Mann
16/84	**Who Wears These Shoes?**...Elton John
19/68	**Who Will Answer?**...Ed Ames
7/87	**Who Will You Run To**...Heart
18/76	**Who'd She Coo?**...Ohio Players
29/80	**Who'll Be The Fool Tonight**...Larsen-Feiten Band
34/65	**Who'll Be The Next In Line**...Kinks
F/70	**Who'll Stop The Rain**...Creedence Clearwater Revival
4/81	**Who's Crying Now**...Journey
35/92	**Who's Gonna Ride Your Wild Horses**...U2
6/85	**Who's Holding Donna Now**...DeBarge
27/73	**Who's In The Strawberry Patch With Sally**...Dawn
3/86	**Who's Johnny**...El DeBarge
	Who's Making Love
5/68	Johnnie Taylor
39/81	Blues Brothers
	Who's Sorry Now
4/58	Connie Francis
40/75	Marie Osmond
1/87	**Who's That Girl**...Madonna
21/84	**Who's That Girl?**...Eurythmics
40/70	**Who's Your Baby?**...Archies
7/85	**Who's Zoomin' Who**...Aretha Franklin
22/77	**Whodunit**...Tavares
3/57	**Whole Lot Of Shakin' Going On**...Jerry Lee Lewis
4/70	**Whole Lotta Love**...Led Zeppelin
6/59	**Whole Lotta Loving**...Fats Domino
1/93	**Whole New World (Aladdin's Theme)**...Peabo Bryson & Regina Belle

POS/YR	RECORD TITLE/ARTIST
9/90	**Whole Wide World**...A'Me Lorain
2/93	**Whoomp! (There It Is)**...Tag Team
11/93	**Whoot, There It Is**...95 South
	Why
1/59	Frankie Avalon
13/72	Donny Osmond
34/92	**Why**...Annie Lennox
5/57	**Why Baby Why**...Pat Boone
33/85	**Why Can't I Have You**...Cars
	Why Can't I Touch You ..see: (If You Let Me Make Love To You Then)
3/86	**Why Can't This Be Love**...Van Halen
6/75	**Why Can't We Be Friends?**...War
3/73	**Why Can't We Live Together**...Timmy Thomas
	Why Do Fools Fall In Love
6/56	Teenagers Feat. Frankie Lymon
9/56	Gale Storm
12/56	Diamonds
7/81	Diana Ross
38/63	**Why Do Lovers Break Each Other's Heart?**...Bob B. Soxx & The Blue Jeans
10/58	**Why Don't They Understand**...George Hamilton IV
37/63	**Why Don't You Believe Me**...Duprees
13/83	**Why Me?**...Irene Cara
16/73	**Why Me**...Kris Kristofferson
26/80	**Why Me**...Styx
18/80	**Why Not Me**...Fred Knoblock
39/87	**Why You Treat Me So Bad**...Club Nouveau
3/69	**Wichita Lineman**...Glen Campbell
6/91	**Wicked Game**...Chris Isaak
15/90	**Wiggle It**...2 In A Room
22/63	**Wiggle Wobble**...Les Cooper
33/63	**Wild!**...Dee Dee Sharp
2/84	**Wild Boys**...Duran Duran
29/56	**Wild Cherry**...Don Cherry
31/67	**Wild Honey**...Beach Boys
28/71	**Wild Horses**...Rolling Stones
26/61	**Wild In The Country**...Elvis Presley
22/57	**Wild Is The Wind**...Johnny Mathis
	Wild Night
28/71	Van Morrison
3/94	John Mellencamp/Me'Shell Ndegéocello
2/60	**Wild One**...Bobby Rydell
34/65	**Wild One**...Martha & The Vandellas
	Wild Thing
1/66	Troggs
20/67	Senator Bobby
14/74	Fancy

POS/YR	RECORD TITLE/ARTIST
2/89	**Wild Thing**...Tone Lōc
8/63	**Wild Weekend**...Rebels
25/86	**Wild Wild Life**...Talking Heads
1/88	**Wild, Wild West**...Escape Club
34/90	**Wild Women Do**...Natalie Cole
	Wild World
11/71	Cat Stevens
25/89	Maxi Priest
27/93	Mr. Big
3/75	**Wildfire**...Michael Murphey
9/73	**Wildflower**...Skylark
10/91	**Wildside**...Marky Mark & The Funky Bunch
17/63	**Wildwood Days**...Bobby Rydell
7/74	**Wildwood Weed**...Jim Stafford
1/73	**Will It Go Round In Circles**...Billy Preston
32/69	**Will You Be Staying After Sunday**...Peppermint Rainbow
7/93	**Will You Be There**...Michael Jackson
39/94	**Will You Be There (In The Morning)**...Heart
	Will You Love Me Tomorrow
1/61	Shirelles
24/68	4 Seasons
39/78	Dave Mason
19/92	**Will You Marry Me?**...Paula Abdul
3/87	**Will You Still Love Me?**...Chicago
	Willie And The Hand Jive
9/58	Johnny Otis Show
26/74	Eric Clapton
26/94	**Willing To Forgive**...Aretha Franklin
15/65	**Willow Weep For Me**...Chad & Jeremy
22/58	**Win Your Love For Me**...Sam Cooke
1/66	**Winchester Cathedral**...New Vaudeville Band
1/89	**Wind Beneath My Wings**...Bette Midler
4/91	**Wind Of Change**...Scorpions
31/69	**Windmills Of Your Mind**...Dusty Springfield
32/67	**Windows Of The World**...Dionne Warwick
38/83	**Winds Of Change**...Jefferson Starship
1/67	**Windy**...Association
12/61	**Wings Of A Dove**...Ferlin Husky
8/81	**Winner Takes It All**...Abba
21/76	**Winners And Losers**...Hamilton, Joe Frank & Reynolds
17/81	**Winning**...Santana
16/70	**Winter World Of Love**...Engelbert Humperdinck

POS/YR	RECORD TITLE/ARTIST
	Wipe Out
2/63	Surfaris
16/66	Surfaris
12/87	Fat Boys (with The Beach Boys)
35/57	**Wisdom Of A Fool**...Five Keys
17/64	**Wish Someone Would Care**...Irma Thomas
38/67	**Wish You Didn't Have To Go**...James & Bobby Purify
6/64	**Wishin' And Hopin'**...Dusty Springfield
18/58	**Wishing For Your Love**...Voxpoppers
26/83	**Wishing (If I Had A Photograph Of You)**...Flock Of Seagulls
9/92	**Wishing On A Star**...Cover Girls
1/88	**Wishing Well**...Terence Trent D'Arby
11/74	**Wishing You Were Here**...Chicago
1/58	**Witch Doctor**...David Seville
21/72	**Witch Queen Of New Orleans**...Redbone
6/58	**Witchcraft**...Frank Sinatra
32/63	**Witchcraft**...Elvis Presley
9/72	**Witchy Woman**...Eagles
29/66	**With A Girl Like You**...Troggs
1/78	**With A Little Luck**...Wings
15/57	**With All My Heart**...Jodie Sands
5/89	**With Every Beat Of My Heart**...Taylor Dayne
39/59	**With Open Arms**...Jane Morgan
1/87	**With Or Without You**...U2
35/69	**With Pen In Hand**...Vikki Carr
21/59	**With The Wind And The Rain In Your Hair**...Pat Boone
27/65	**With These Hands**...Tom Jones
14/67	**With This Ring**...Platters
14/91	**With You**...Tony Terry
4/80	**With You I'm Born Again**...Billy Preston & Syreeta
30/57	**With You On My Mind**...Nat "King" Cole
12/76	**With Your Love**...Jefferson Starship
28/58	**With Your Love**...Jack Scott
	Without Love (There Is Nothing)
19/57	Clyde McPhatter
29/63	Ray Charles
5/70	Tom Jones
	Without You
1/72	Nilsson
3/94	Mariah Carey
7/61	**Without You**...Johnny Tillotson
8/90	**Without You**...Mötley Crüe **(also see: Love Will Never Do)**
24/82	**Without You (Not Another Lonely Night)**...Franke & The Knockouts

POS/YR	RECORD TITLE/ARTIST
20/80	**Without Your Love**...Roger Daltrey
38/87	**Without Your Love**...Toto
14/64	**Wives And Lovers**...Jack Jones
	Wizard Of Oz ..see: Themes From The
40/75	**Wolf Creek Pass**...C.W. McCall
6/62	**Wolverton Mountain**...Claude King
	(also see: I'm The Girl On)
2/81	**Woman**...John Lennon
14/66	**Woman**...Peter & Gordon
15/60	**Woman, A Lover, A Friend**...Jackie Wilson
36/90	**Woman In Chains**...Tears For Fears
1/80	**Woman In Love**...Barbra Streisand
	Woman In Love
14/55	Four Aces
19/55	Frankie Laine
33/83	**Woman In Me**...Donna Summer
24/83	**Woman In You**...Bee Gees
4/81	**Woman Needs Love (Just Like You Do)**...Ray Parker Jr. & Raydio
22/74	**Woman To Woman**...Shirley Brown
4/68	**Woman, Woman**...Union Gap feat. Gary Puckett
29/65	**Woman's Got Soul**...Impressions
36/71	**Women's Love Rights**...Laura Lee
15/71	**Won't Get Fooled Again**...Who
19/60	**Won't You Come Home Bill Bailey**...Bobby Darin
11/61	**Wonder Like You**...Rick Nelson
	Wonder Of You
25/59	Ray Peterson
9/70	Elvis Presley
39/95	**Wonderful**...Adam Ant
22/62	**Wonderful Dream**...Majors
14/63	**Wonderful Summer**...Robin Ward
4/58	**Wonderful Time Up There**...Pat Boone
16/78	**Wonderful Tonight**...Eric Clapton
	Wonderful! Wonderful!
14/57	Johnny Mathis
7/63	Tymes
	(also see: Wun'erful, Wun'erful)
	Wonderful World
12/60	Sam Cooke
4/65	Herman's Hermits
17/78	Art Garfunkel with James Taylor & Paul Simon
	(also see: What A)
25/70	**Wonderful World, Beautiful People**...Jimmy Cliff
40/59	**Wonderful You**...Jimmie Rodgers
12/57	**Wondering**...Patti Page

POS/YR	RECORD TITLE/ARTIST
21/80	**Wondering Where The Lions Are**...Bruce Cockburn
25/80	**Wonderland**...Commodores
	Wonderland By Night
1/61	Bert Kaempfert
15/61	Louis Prima
18/61	Anita Bryant
16/59	**Woo-Hoo**...Rock-A-Teens
	Woo Woo Song ..see: You Should Be Mine
1/61	**Wooden Heart**...Joe Dowell
	Woodstock
11/70	Crosby, Stills, Nash & Young
23/71	Matthews' Southern Comfort
2/65	**Wooly Bully**...Sam The Sham & the Pharaohs
19/88	**Word In Spanish**...Elton John
6/86	**Word Up**...Cameo
11/67	**Words**...Monkees
15/68	**Words**...Bee Gees
5/86	**Words Get In The Way**...Miami Sound Machine
5/67	**Words Of Love**...Mamas & The Papas
13/57	**Words Of Love**...Diamonds
18/66	**Work Song**...Herb Alpert
32/74	**Workin' At The Car Wash Blues**...Jim Croce
33/62	**Workin' For The Man**...Roy Orbison
20/69	**Workin' On A Groovy Thing**...5th Dimension
29/82	**Working For The Weekend**...Loverboy
8/66	**Working In The Coal Mine**...Lee Dorsey
	Working My Way Back To You
9/66	4 Seasons
2/80	Spinners (medley)
33/63	**Workout Stevie, Workout**...Little Stevie Wonder
37/69	**World**...James Brown
19/96	**World I Know**...Collective Soul
7/73	**World Is A Ghetto**...War
19/65	**World Of Our Own**...Seekers
21/58	**World Outside**...Four Coins
30/67	**World We Knew (Over And Over)**...Frank Sinatra
1/64	**World Without Love**...Peter & Gordon
37/64	**Worried Guy**...Johnny Tillotson
20/59	**Worried Man**...Kingston Trio
3/69	**Worst That Could Happen**...Brooklyn Bridge
10/87	**Wot's It To Ya**...Robbie Nevil
5/85	**Would I Lie To You?**...Eurythmics
13/92	**Would I Lie To You?**...Charles & Eddie

POS/YR	RECORD TITLE/ARTIST
8/66	**Wouldn't It Be Nice**...Beach Boys
38/81	**Wrack My Brain**...Ringo Starr
20/85	**Wrap Her Up**...Elton John
8/84	**Wrapped Around Your Finger**...Police
2/76	**Wreck Of The Edmund Fitzgerald**...Gordon Lightfoot
	Wringle Wrangle
12/57	Fess Parker
33/57	Bill Hayes
5/61	**Writing On The Wall**...Adam Wade
16/91	**Written All Over Your Face**...Rude Boys
34/64	**Wrong For Each Other**...Andy Williams
32/57	**Wun'erful, Wun'erful!**...Stan Freberg

8/80	**Xanadu**...Olivia Newton-John/Electric Light Orchestra

POS/YR	RECORD TITLE/ARTIST
2/79	**Y.M.C.A.**....Village People
7/61	**Ya Ya**...Lee Dorsey
19/84	**Yah Mo B There**...James Ingram (with Michael McDonald)
35/63	**Yakety Sax**...Boots Randolph
1/58	**Yakety Yak**...Coasters
16/86	**Yankee Rose**...David Lee Roth
32/88	**Yeah, Yeah, Yeah**...Judson Spence
8/77	**Year Of The Cat**...Al Stewart
35/80	**Years**...Wayne Newton
37/61	**Years From Now**...Jackie Wilson
21/65	**Yeh, Yeh**...Georgie Fame
25/67	**Yellow Balloon**...Yellow Balloon
4/61	**Yellow Bird**...Arthur Lyman Group
23/70	**Yellow River**...Christie
	Yellow Rose Of Texas
1/55	Mitch Miller
3/55	Johnny Desmond
16/55	Stan Freberg
2/66	**Yellow Submarine**...Beatles
30/59	**"Yep!"**...Duane Eddy
	Yes, I'm Ready
5/65	Barbara Mason
2/80	Teri DeSario with K.C.
34/60	**Yes Sir, That's My Baby**...Ricky Nelson

POS/YR	RECORD TITLE/ARTIST
12/57	**Yes Tonight, Josephine**...Johnnie Ray
11/73	**Yes We Can Can**...Pointer Sisters
31/68	**Yester Love**...Miracles
7/69	**Yester-Me, Yester-You, Yesterday**...Stevie Wonder
	Yesterday
1/65	Beatles
25/67	Ray Charles
2/73	**Yesterday Once More**...Carpenters
19/69	**Yesterday, When I Was Young**...Roy Clark
21/64	**Yesterday's Gone**...Chad & Jeremy
11/82	**Yesterday's Songs**...Neil Diamond
3/71	**Yo-Yo**...Osmonds
8/60	**Yogi**...Ivy Three
20/75	**You**...George Harrison
21/58	**You**...Aquatones
25/78	**You**...Rita Coolidge
34/68	**You**...Marvin Gaye
1/74	**You Ain't Seen Nothing Yet**...Bachman-Turner Overdrive
12/61	**You Always Hurt The One You Love**...Clarence Henry
7/83	**You And I**...Eddie Rabbitt with Crystal Gayle
13/78	**You And I**...Rick James
9/77	**You And Me**...Alice Cooper
F/70	**You And Me**...Aretha Franklin
9/74	**You And Me Against The World**...Helen Reddy
4/83	**You Are**...Lionel Richie
9/72	**You Are Everything**...Stylistics
26/62	**You Are Mine**...Frankie Avalon
7/58	**You Are My Destiny**...Paul Anka
12/85	**You Are My Lady**...Freddie Jackson
6/55	**You Are My Love**...Joni James
27/76	**You Are My Starship**...Norman Connors
7/62	**You Are My Sunshine**...Ray Charles
1/95	**You Are Not Alone**...Michael Jackson
5/75	**You Are So Beautiful**...Joe Cocker
17/87	**You Are The Girl**...Cars
25/61	**You Are The Only One**...Ricky Nelson
1/73	**You Are The Sunshine Of My Life**...Stevie Wonder
9/76	**You Are The Woman**...Firefall
20/66	**You Baby**...Turtles
29/86	**You Be Illin'**...Run-D.M.C.
9/62	**You Beat Me To The Punch**...Mary Wells
6/78	**You Belong To Me**...Carly Simon
7/62	**You Belong To Me**...Duprees

POS/YR	RECORD TITLE/ARTIST
2/85	**You Belong To The City**...Glenn Frey
37/59	**You Better Know It**...Jackie Wilson
24/62	**You Better Move On**...Arthur Alexander
20/66	**You Better Run**...Young Rascals
9/67	**You Better Sit Down Kids**...Cher
29/94	**You Better Wait**...Steve Perry
18/81	**You Better You Bet**...Who
23/87	**You Can Call Me Al**...Paul Simon
6/61	**You Can Depend On Me**...Brenda Lee
37/79	**You Can Do It**...Dobie Gray
8/82	**You Can Do Magic**...America
	You Can Have Her
12/61	Roy Hamilton
34/74	Sam Neely
36/58	**You Can Make It If You Try**...Gene Allison
18/63	**You Can Never Stop Me Loving You**...Johnny Tillotson
9/79	**You Can't Change That**...Raydio
14/90	**You Can't Deny It**...Lisa Stansfield
15/84	**You Can't Get What You Want (Till You Know What You Want)**...Joe Jackson
	You Can't Hurry Love
1/66	Supremes
10/83	Phil Collins
36/91	**You Can't Play With My Yo-Yo**...Yo-Yo
40/66	**You Can't Roller Skate In A Buffalo Herd**...Roger Miller
20/56	**You Can't Run Away From It**...Four Aces
	You Can't Sit Down
29/61	Philip Upchurch Combo
3/63	Dovells
8/90	**U Can't Touch This**...M.C. Hammer
12/77	**You Can't Turn Me Off (In The Middle Of Turning Me On)**...High Inergy
12/58	**You Cheated**...Shields
29/91	**You Could Be Mine**...Guns N' Roses
32/72	**You Could Have Been A Lady**...April Wine
15/82	**You Could Have Been With Me**...Sheena Easton
32/81	**You Could Take My Heart Away**...Silver Condor
7/79	**You Decorated My Life**...Kenny Rogers
10/66	**You Didn't Have To Be So Nice**...Lovin' Spoonful
1/78	**You Don't Bring Me Flowers**...Barbra Streisand & Neil Diamond
3/63	**You Don't Have To Be A Baby To Cry**...Caravelles
1/77	**You Don't Have To Be A Star**...Marilyn McCoo & Billy Davis, Jr.

POS/YR	RECORD TITLE/ARTIST
14/91	**You Don't Have To Go Home Tonight**...Triplets
15/66	**(You Don't Have To) Paint Me A Picture**...Gary Lewis & The Playboys
	You Don't Have To Say You Love Me
4/66	Dusty Springfield
11/70	Elvis Presley
20/88	**You Don't Know**...Scarlett & Black
11/64	**(You Don't Know) How Glad I Am**...Nancy Wilson
13/95	**You Don't Know How It Feels**...Tom Petty
	You Don't Know Me
14/56	Jerry Vale
2/62	Ray Charles
4/61	**You Don't Know What You've Got (Until You Lose It)**...Ral Donner
8/72	**You Don't Mess Around With Jim**...Jim Croce
10/57	**You Don't Owe Me A Thing**...Johnnie Ray
2/64	**You Don't Own Me**...Lesley Gore
16/82	**You Don't Want Me Anymore**...Steel Breeze
31/82	**You Dropped A Bomb On Me**...Gap Band
24/69	**You Gave Me A Mountain**...Frankie Laine
3/85	**You Give Good Love**...Whitney Houston
1/86	**You Give Love A Bad Name**...Bon Jovi
38/79	**You Gonna Make Me Love Somebody Else**...Jones Girls
	You Got It
9/89	Roy Orbison
33/95	Bonnie Raitt
3/87	**You Got It All**...Jets
3/89	**You Got It (The Right Stuff)**...New Kids On The Block
20/83	**You Got Lucky**...Tom Petty
2/87	**U Got The Look**...Prince
11/74	**You Got The Love**...Rufus feat. Chaka Khan
18/67	**You Got To Me**...Neil Diamond
	You Got What It Takes
10/60	Marv Johnson
7/67	Dave Clark Five
40/69	**You Got Yours And I'll Get Mine**...Delfonics
5/95	**You Gotta Be**...Des'ree
7/87	**(You Gotta) Fight For Your Right (To Party!)**...Beastie Boys
1/74	**You Haven't Done Nothin**...Stevie Wonder **(also see: Pop Goes The Weasel)**
24/69	**You, I**...Rugbys

POS/YR	RECORD TITLE/ARTIST
	You Keep Me Hangin' On
1/66	Supremes
6/68	Vanilla Fudge
1/87	Kim Wilde
25/68	**(You Keep Me) Hangin' On**...Joe Simon
38/82	**You Keep Runnin' Away**...38 Special
19/67	**You Keep Running Away**...Four Tops
30/94	**You Know How We Do It**...Ice Cube
17/86	**You Know I Love You...Don't You?**...Howard Jones
35/80	**You Know That I Love You**...Santana
12/67	**You Know What I Mean**...Turtles
32/92	**You Lied To Me**...Cathy Dennis
1/77	**You Light Up My Life**...Debby Boone
12/74	**You Little Trustmaker**...Tymes
22/63	**You Lost The Sweetest Boy**...Mary Wells
10/77	**You Made Me Believe In Magic**...Bay City Rollers
9/77	**You Make Loving Fun**...Fleetwood Mac
2/74	**You Make Me Feel Brand New**...Stylistics
1/77	**You Make Me Feel Like Dancing**...Leo Sayer
36/79	**You Make Me Feel (Mighty Real)**...Sylvester
5/81	**You Make My Dreams**...Daryl Hall & John Oates
7/80	**You May Be Right**...Billy Joel
17/60	**You Mean Everything To Me**...Neil Sedaka
7/94	**You Mean The World To Me**...Toni Braxton
35/68	**You Met Your Match**...Stevie Wonder
7/84	**You Might Think**...Cars
15/64	**You Must Believe Me**...Impressions
	You Must Have Been A Beautiful Baby
5/61	Bobby Darin
35/67	Dave Clark Five
40/79	**You Need A Woman Tonight**...Captain & Tennille
11/58	**You Need Hands**...Eydie Gorme
25/70	**You Need Love Like I Do (Don't You)**...Gladys Knight & The Pips
1/78	**You Needed Me**...Anne Murray
14/64	**You Never Can Tell**...Chuck Berry
10/78	**You Never Done It Like That**...Captain & Tennille
3/72	**You Ought To Be With Me**...Al Green
	You Really Got A Hold On Me ..see: You've Really
	You Really Got Me
7/64	Kinks
36/78	Van Halen

POS/YR	RECORD TITLE/ARTIST
27/65	**You Really Know How To Hurt A Guy**...Jan & Dean
29/92	**You Remind Me**...Mary J. Blige
4/95	**You Remind Me Of Something**...R. Kelly
37/81	**You Saved My Soul**...Burton Cummings
	You Send Me
1/57	Sam Cooke
8/57	Teresa Brewer
33/94	**U Send Me Swingin'**...Mint Condition
3/76	**You Sexy Thing**...Hot Chocolate
35/80	**You Shook Me All Night Long**...AC/DC
1/76	**You Should Be Dancing**...Bee Gees
13/86	**You Should Be Mine (The Woo Woo Song)**...Jeffrey Osborne
39/64	**You Should Have Seen The Way He Looked At Me**...Dixie Cups
5/82	**You Should Hear How She Talks About You**...Melissa Manchester
F/57	**You Shouldn't Do That**...Sal Mineo
6/69	**You Showed Me**...Turtles
11/85	**You Spin Me Round (Like A Record)**...Dead Or Alive
10/79	**You Take My Breath Away**...Rex Smith
3/60	**You Talk Too Much**...Joe Jones
38/65	**You Tell Me Why**...Beau Brummels
38/92	**You Think You Know Her**...Cause & Effect
40/79	**You Thrill Me**...Exile
39/79	**You Took The Words Right Out Of My Mouth**...Meat Loaf
8/65	**You Turn Me On**...Ian Whitcomb
25/73	**You Turn Me On, I'm A Radio**...Joni Mitchell
24/95	**You Used To Love Me**...Faith
36/72	**You Want It, You Got It**...Detroit Emeralds
8/94	**You Want This**...Janet Jackson
13/72	**You Wear It Well**...Rod Stewart
12/60	**(You Were Made For) All My Love**...Jackie Wilson
21/65	**You Were Made For Me**...Freddie & The Dreamers
27/58	**You Were Made For Me**...Sam Cooke
21/59	**You Were Mine**...Fireflies
	You Were On My Mind
3/65	We Five
36/67	Crispian St. Peters
30/65	**You Were Only Fooling (While I Was Falling In Love)**...Vic Damone
28/94	**U Will Know**...B.M.U. (Black Men United)
22/62	**You Win Again**...Fats Domino
8/74	**You Won't See Me**...Anne Murray

POS/YR	RECORD TITLE/ARTIST
20/92	**You Won't See Me Cry**...Wilson Phillips
22/65	**You'd Better Come Home**...Petula Clark
14/80	**You'll Accomp'ny Me**...Bob Seger
	You'll Lose A Good Thing
8/62	Barbara Lynn
32/76	Freddy Fender
2/76	**You'll Never Find Another Love Like Mine**...Lou Rawls
	You'll Never Get To Heaven (If You Break My Heart)
34/64	Dionne Warwick
23/73	Stylistics
11/56	**You'll Never Never Know**...Platters
34/64	**You'll Never Walk Alone**...Patti LaBelle & Her Blue Belles
6/95	**You'll See**...Madonna
	You're ..also see: Your
18/86	**You're A Friend Of Mine**...Clarence Clemons & Jackson Browne
36/78	**You're A Part Of Me**...Gene Cotton with Kim Carnes
12/73	**You're A Special Part Of Me**...Diana Ross & Marvin Gaye
15/64	**You're A Wonderful One**...Marvin Gaye
	You're All I Need To Get By
7/68	Marvin Gaye & Tammi Terrell
19/71	Aretha Franklin
34/75	Dawn
3/95	Method Man feat. Mary J. Blige (medley)
28/91	**You're Amazing**...Robert Palmer
25/57	**You're Cheatin' Yourself (If You're Cheatin' On Me)**...Frank Sinatra
35/83	**You're Driving Me Out Of My Mind**...Little River Band
39/66	**(You're Gonna) Hurt Yourself**...Frankie Valli
34/59	**You're Gonna Miss Me**...Connie Francis
1/74	**(You're) Having My Baby**...Paul Anka
1/91	**You're In Love**...Wilson Phillips
4/78	**You're In My Heart (The Final Acclaim)**...Rod Stewart
16/76	**You're My Best Friend**...Queen
6/67	**You're My Everything**...Temptations
27/81	**You're My Girl**...Franke & The Knockouts
	You're My Girl ..see: (Say)
14/57	**You're My One And Only Love**...Ricky Nelson
23/89	**You're My One And Only (True Love)**...Seduction
	(You're My) Soul And Inspiration
1/66	Righteous Brothers
38/78	Donny & Marie

POS/YR	RECORD TITLE/ARTIST
	You're My World
26/64	Cilla Black
18/77	Helen Reddy
	(You're Never Gonna Get It) ..see: My Lovin'
1/75	**You're No Good**...Linda Ronstadt
25/65	**You're Nobody Till Somebody Loves You**...Dean Martin
10/89	**You're Not Alone**...Chicago
9/85	**You're Only Human (Second Wind)**...Billy Joel
7/79	**You're Only Lonely**...J.D. Souther
	You're Sixteen
8/60	Johnny Burnette
1/74	Ringo Starr
17/59	**You're So Fine**...Falcons
1/73	**You're So Vain**...Carly Simon
29/72	**You're Still A Young Man**...Tower Of Power
34/80	**You're Supposed To Keep Your Love For Me**...Jermaine Jackson
3/63	**(You're the) Devil In Disguise**...Elvis Presley
2/75	**You're The First, The Last, My Everything**...Barry White
3/85	**You're The Inspiration**...Chicago
18/78	**You're The Love**...Seals & Crofts
F/58	**You're The Nearest Thing To Heaven**...Johnny Cash
4/65	**You're The One**...Vogues
22/70	**You're The One**...Little Sister
1/78	**You're The One That I Want**...John Travolta & Olivia Newton-John
	You're The Only Woman (You & I)
13/80	Ambrosia
36/90	Brat Pack
11/61	**You're The Reason**...Bobby Edwards
3/63	**You're The Reason I'm Living**...Bobby Darin
33/66	**You've Been Cheatin'**...Impressions
36/65	**You've Been In Love Too Long**...Martha & The Vandellas
	(You've Got) ..see: Personality
	You've Got A Friend
1/71	James Taylor
29/71	Roberta Flack & Donny Hathaway
38/70	**(You've Got Me) Dangling On A String**...Chairmen Of The Board
33/77	**You've Got Me Runnin'**...Gene Cotton
4/56	**(You've Got) The Magic Touch**...Platters
28/71	**You've Got To Crawl (Before You Walk)**...8th Day

POS/YR	RECORD TITLE/ARTIST
10/65	**You've Got To Hide Your Love Away**...Silkie
20/60	**(You've Got To) Move Two Mountains**...Marv Johnson
	(You've Got What It Takes) ..see: Baby
7/65	**You've Got Your Troubles**...Fortunes
	You've Lost That Lovin' Feelin'
1/65	Righteous Brothers
16/69	Dionne Warwick
12/80	Daryl Hall & John Oates
	You've Made Me So Very Happy
39/67	Brenda Holloway
2/69	Blood, Sweat & Tears
22/73	**You've Never Been This Far Before**...Conway Twitty
8/63	**You've Really Got A Hold On Me**...Miracles
25/55	**Young Abe Lincoln**...Don Cornell
28/75	**Young Americans**...David Bowie
17/63	**Young And In Love**...Dick & DeeDee
	Young And The Restless ..see: Nadia's Theme
23/58	**Young And Warm And Wonderful**...Tony Bennett
	Young Blood
8/57	Coasters
20/76	Bad Company
40/79	**Young Blood**...Rickie Lee Jones
12/60	**Young Emotions**...Ricky Nelson
2/68	**Young Girl**...Union Gap feat. Gary Puckett
20/76	**Young Hearts Run Free**...Candi Staton
	Young Love
1/57	Tab Hunter
1/57	Sonny James
17/57	Crew-Cuts
25/73	Donny Osmond
38/82	**Young Love**...Air Supply
6/63	**Young Lovers**...Paul & Paula (also see: Theme For)
5/81	**Young Turks**...Rod Stewart
5/62	**Young World**...Rick Nelson
	Your ..also see: You're
17/90	**Your Baby Never Looked Good In Blue**...Expose
13/94	**Your Body's Callin'**...R. Kelly
24/75	**Your Bulldog Drinks Champagne**...Jim Stafford
29/62	**Your Cheating Heart**...Ray Charles
34/61	**Your Friends**...Dee Clark
18/69	**Your Good Thing (Is About To End)**...Lou Rawls

POS/YR	RECORD TITLE/ARTIST
33/82	**Your Imagination**...Daryl Hall & John Oates
6/86	**Your Love**...Outfield
15/77	**Your Love**...Marilyn McCoo & Billy Davis Jr.
38/75	**Your Love**...Graham Central Station
13/83	**Your Love Is Driving Me Crazy**...Sammy Hagar
	(Your Love Keeps Lifting Me) Higher And Higher
6/67	Jackie Wilson
2/77	Rita Coolidge
24/61	**Your Ma Said You Cried In Your Sleep Last Night**...Kenny Dino
	Your Mama Don't Dance
4/73	Loggins & Messina
10/89	Poison
40/71	**Your Move**...Yes
14/62	**Your Nose Is Gonna Grow**...Johnny Crawford
40/63	**Your Old Stand By**...Mary Wells
40/61	**Your One And Only Love**...Jackie Wilson
28/63	**Your Other Love**...Connie Francis
5/67	**Your Precious Love**...Marvin Gaye & Tammi Terrell (also see: For Your Precious Love)
20/77	**Your Smiling Face**...James Taylor
8/71	**Your Song**...Elton John
40/71	**Your Time To Cry**...Joe Simon
33/67	**Your Unchanging Love**...Marvin Gaye
32/63	**Your Used To Be**...Brenda Lee
20/57	**Your Wild Heart**...Joy Layne
9/86	**Your Wildest Dreams**...Moody Blues
	(Yowsah, Yowsah, Yowsah) ..see: Dance, Dance, Dance
4/68	**Yummy Yummy Yummy**...Ohio Express

Z

POS/YR	RECORD TITLE/ARTIST
8/63	**Zip-A-Dee Doo-Dah**...Bob B. Soxx & The Blue Jeans
36/67	**Zip Code**...Five Americans
16/57	**Zip Zip**...Diamonds
11/66	**Zorba The Greek**...Herb Alpert
17/58	**Zorro**...Chordettes

THE RECORD HOLDERS

TOP ARTIST AND RECORD ACHIEVEMENTS

TOP 100 SINGLES 1955-1995*

PK YR	WKS CHR	WKS T40	WKS T10	WKS @ #1	TITLE...ARTIST
95	20+	20+	19	16	1. One Sweet Day...Mariah Carey & Boyz II Men
94	33	31	22	14	2. I'll Make Love To You...Boyz II Men
92	26	24	16	14	3. I Will Always Love You...Whitney Houston
92	32	28	19	13	4. End of the Road...Boyz II Men
56	28	23	21	11	5. Don't Be Cruel/Hound Dog...Elvis Presley
94	30	26	18	11	6. I Swear...All-4-One
55	26	26	20	10	7. Cherry Pink And Apple Blossom White...Perez "Prez" Prado
55	21	21	18	10	8. Sincerely...The McGuire Sisters
56	26	22	17	10	9. Singing The Blues...Guy Mitchell
81	26	21	15	10	10. Physical...Olivia Newton-John
77	25	21	14	10	11. You Light Up My Life...Debby Boone
59	26	22	16	9	12. Mack The Knife...Bobby Darin
57	30	22	15	9	13. All Shook Up...Elvis Presley
81	26	20	14	9	14. Bette Davis Eyes...Kim Carnes
68	19	19	14	9	15. Hey Jude...The Beatles
81	27	19	13	9	16. Endless Love...Diana Ross & Lionel Richie
60	21	17	12	9	17. The Theme From "A Summer Place"...Percy Faith
55	38	25	19	8	18. (We're Gonna) Rock Around The Clock...Bill Haley & His Comets
95	25	23	16	8	19. Fantasy...Mariah Carey
56	37	22	16	8	20. The Wayward Wind...Gogi Grant
55	22	19	16	8	21. Sixteen Tons..."Tennessee" Ernie Ford
56	27	22	15	8	22. Heartbreak Hotel...Elvis Presley
93	29	26	14	8	23. Dreamlover...Mariah Carey
93	23	20	14	8	24. That's The Way Love Goes...Janet Jackson
83	22	20	13	8	25. Every Breath You Take...The Police
92	21	18	13	8	26. Jump...Kris Kross
78	20	18	13	8	27. Night Fever...Bee Gees
76	23	17	11	8	28. Tonight's The Night (Gonna Be Alright)...Rod Stewart
95	34	28	18	7	29. Waterfalls...TLC
57	34	24	17	7	30. Love Letters In The Sand...Pat Boone
95	30	27	15	7	31. Take A Bow...Madonna
93	29	23	15	7	32. Can't Help Falling In Love...UB40
57	27	19	15	7	33. Jailhouse Rock...Elvis Presley
95	29	24	14	7	34. This Is How We Do It...Montell Jordan
57	25	18	14	7	35. (Let Me Be Your) Teddy Bear...Elvis Presley
93	25	19	13	7	36. Informer...Snow
78	25	19	12	7	37. Shadow Dancing...Andy Gibb

PK YR	WKS CHR	WKS T40	WKS T10	WKS @ #1		TITLE...ARTIST
58	21	18	12	7	38.	At The Hop...Danny & The Juniors
61	23	17	12	7	39.	Tossin' And Turnin'...Bobby Lewis
82	20	16	12	7	40.	I Love Rock 'N Roll...Joan Jett & The Blackhearts
82	19	15	12	7	41.	Ebony And Ivory...Paul McCartney with Stevie Wonder
64	15	14	12	7	42.	I Want To Hold Your Hand...The Beatles
66	15	13	12	7	43.	I'm A Believer...The Monkees
83	24	17	11	7	44.	Billie Jean...Michael Jackson
68	15	15	11	7	45.	I Heard It Through The Grapevine...Marvin Gaye
91	22	17	10	7	46.	(Everything I Do) I Do It For You...Bryan Adams
91	20	15	10	7	47.	Black Or White...Michael Jackson
94	41	33	21	6	48.	The Sign...Ace Of Base
94	27	25	17	6	49.	On Bended Knee...Boyz II Men
55	21	21	17	6	50.	Love Is A Many-Splendored Thing...Four Aces
56	25	20	16	6	51.	Rock And Roll Waltz...Kay Starr
56	24	20	16	6	52.	The Poor People Of Paris...Les Baxter
55	19	19	16	6	53.	The Yellow Rose Of Texas...Mitch Miller
78	25	19	15	6	54.	Le Freak...Chic
56	24	19	15	6	55.	Memories Are Made Of This...Dean Martin
82	25	18	15	6	56.	Eye Of The Tiger...Survivor
83	25	20	14	6	57.	Flashdance...What A Feeling...Irene Cara
57	26	19	14	6	58.	April Love...Pat Boone
80	25	19	13	6	59.	Lady...Kenny Rogers
83	22	18	13	6	60.	Say Say Say...Paul McCartney And Michael Jackson
59	21	18	13	6	61.	The Battle Of New Orleans...Johnny Horton
57	21	17	13	6	62.	Young Love...Tab Hunter
82	25	20	12	6	63.	Centerfold...The J. Geils Band
80	25	19	12	6	64.	Call Me...Blondie
58	22	19	12	6	65.	It's All In The Game...Tommy Edwards
79	22	16	12	6	66.	My Sharona...The Knack
69	17	16	11	6	67.	Aquarius/Let The Sunshine In (The Flesh Failures) ...The 5th Dimension
72	18	15	11	6	68.	The First Time Ever I Saw Your Face...Roberta Flack
72	18	15	11	6	69.	Alone Again (Naturally)...Gilbert O'Sullivan
71	17	15	11	6	70.	Joy To The World...Three Dog Night
60	16	14	11	6	71.	Are You Lonesome To-night?...Elvis Presley
58	14	14	10	6	72.	The Purple People Eater...Sheb Wooley
70	14	13	10	6	73.	Bridge Over Troubled Water...Simon & Garfunkel
84	19	14	9	6	74.	Like A Virgin...Madonna
69	13	12	9	6	75.	In The Year 2525 (Exordium & Terminus)...Zager & Evans
57	31	23	16	5	76.	Tammy...Debbie Reynolds
55	20	20	16	5	77.	The Ballad Of Davy Crockett...Bill Hayes
92	28	24	15	5	78.	Baby Got Back...Sir Mix-A-Lot

PK YR	WKS CHR	WKS T40	WKS T10	WKS @ #1	TITLE...ARTIST
56	23	19	15	5	79. Love Me Tender...Elvis Presley
56	23	20	14	5	80. My Prayer...The Platters
80	22	19	14	5	81. (Just Like) Starting Over...John Lennon
93	22	18	14	5	82. I'd Do Anything For Love (But I Won't Do That)...Meat Loaf
92	27	23	13	5	83. Save The Best For Last...Vanessa Williams
95	24	20	12	5	84. Have You Ever Really Loved A Woman?...Bryan Adams
77	23	17	12	5	85. Best Of My Love...Emotions
58	19	16	12	5	86. All I Have To Do Is Dream...The Everly Brothers
84	21	16	11	5	87. When Doves Cry...Prince
60	20	16	11	5	88. It's Now Or Never...Elvis Presley
58	19	16	11	5	89. Tequila...The Champs
70	16	16	11	5	90. I'll Be There...The Jackson 5
76	19	15	11	5	91. Silly Love Songs...Wings
71	17	15	11	5	92. Maggie May...Rod Stewart
62	18	14	11	5	93. I Can't Stop Loving You...Ray Charles
58	20	16	10	5	94. Don't...Elvis Presley
84	21	15	10	5	95. Jump...Van Halen
79	20	15	10	5	96. Bad Girls...Donna Summer
68	18	15	10	5	97. Love Is Blue...Paul Mauriat
71	17	15	10	5	98. It's Too Late...Carole King
59	17	14	10	5	99. Venus...Frankie Avalon
62	16	14	10	5	100. Big Girls Don't Cry...The 4 Seasons

+ still charted as of 4/13/96

*Ranking period includes all #1 hits which peaked as of December 30, 1995.

PK YR: Year record reached its peak position

WKS CHR: Total weeks charted in the Top 100

WKS T40: Total weeks charted in the Top 40

WKS T10: Total weeks charted in the Top 10

WKS @ #1: Total weeks record held the #1 position

Records are ranked according to the number of weeks they held the #1 position.
Ties are broken in the following order:
1. Total weeks in the Top 10
2. Total weeks in the Top 40
3. Total weeks charted in the Top 100

TOP 100 ARTISTS 1955-1995

	ARTIST	POINTS
1.	ELVIS PRESLEY ●	8,002
2.	THE BEATLES ●	4,549
▲ 3.	ELTON JOHN	4,103
4.	STEVIE WONDER	3,685
▲ 5.	MICHAEL JACKSON	3,256
▲ 6.	MADONNA	3,255
7.	THE ROLLING STONES ●	3,123
8.	PAUL McCARTNEY/WINGS ●	2,978
9.	PAT BOONE	2,827
10.	ARETHA FRANKLIN	2,771
11.	THE SUPREMES ●	2,735
12.	MARVIN GAYE ●	2,716
13.	THE TEMPTATIONS ● ● ●	2,533
14.	CHICAGO ●	2,520
▲ 15.	ROD STEWART	2,508
16.	BEE GEES	2,456
17.	RICKY NELSON ●	2,451
18.	THE BEACH BOYS ●	2,448
19.	NEIL DIAMOND	2,407
▲ 20.	PRINCE	2,393
21.	JAMES BROWN	2,341
▲ 22.	JANET JACKSON	2,324
23.	THE 4 SEASONS	2,305
24.	DARYL HALL & JOHN OATES	2,291
25.	CONNIE FRANCIS	2,285
26.	BILLY JOEL	2,283
27.	OLIVIA NEWTON-JOHN	2,212
28.	FATS DOMINO	2,194
29.	PAUL ANKA	2,192
▲ 30.	WHITNEY HOUSTON	2,120

	ARTIST	POINTS
▲ 31.	MARIAH CAREY	2,112+
32.	GEORGE MICHAEL/WHAM!	2,100
33.	DIANA ROSS	2,069
34.	RAY CHARLES	2,029
35.	DIONNE WARWICK	1,979
36.	THE EVERLY BROTHERS	1,976
37.	BOBBY VINTON	1,956
38.	PERRY COMO	1,944
39.	KENNY ROGERS/FIRST EDITION	1,925
40.	BRENDA LEE	1,883
41.	FRANK SINATRA	1,823
42.	THE JACKSON 5/JACKSONS	1,808
43.	PHIL COLLINS	1,797
44.	GLADYS KNIGHT & THE PIPS	1,791
45.	THE MIRACLES ●	1,735
46.	DONNA SUMMER	1,718
47.	SAM COOKE ●	1,717
48.	CARPENTERS ●	1,687
49.	BARRY MANILOW	1,664
50.	NAT "KING" COLE ●	1,650
▲ 51.	BRYAN ADAMS	1,646
52.	ANDY WILLIAMS	1,638
53.	BARBRA STREISAND	1,595
54.	THE PLATTERS ● ● ●	1,583
55.	CHUBBY CHECKER	1,580
56.	THREE DOG NIGHT	1,580
▲ 57.	BOYZ II MEN	1,560+
58.	BOBBY DARIN ●	1,540
59.	FOUR TOPS	1,527
60.	JOHN COUGAR MELLENCAMP	1,525

ARTIST	POINTS		ARTIST	POINTS
61. ROY ORBISON ●	1,522		81. COMMODORES	1,250
62. LIONEL RICHIE	1,514		82. SIMON & GARFUNKEL	1,247
63. BROOK BENTON ●	1,499		83. GLORIA ESTEFAN/	
64. CHER	1,487		MIAMI SOUND MACHINE	1,244
65. KOOL & THE GANG	1,486		84. SPINNERS ●	1,243
66. LINDA RONSTADT	1,481		85. GLEN CAMPBELL	1,237
67. NEIL SEDAKA	1,446		86. JEFFERSON AIRPLANE/STARSHIP ●	1,237
68. DION/DION & THE BELMONTS	1,444		87. ELECTRIC LIGHT ORCHESTRA	1,211
69. THE 5TH DIMENSION	1,390		88. BRUCE SPRINGSTEEN	1,211
70. HEART	1,363		▲ 89. RICHARD MARX	1,201
			90. BOBBY RYDELL	1,200
▲ 71. BON JOVI	1,359			
72. JACKIE WILSON ●	1,336		91. TOMMY JAMES/SHONDELLS	1,198
73. EAGLES	1,333		92. JOHN DENVER	1,170
74. HUEY LEWIS & THE NEWS	1,332		93. HERB ALPERT/TIJUANA BRASS	1,169
75. BOB SEGER	1,311		94. POINTER SISTERS	1,160
76. HERMAN'S HERMITS ●	1,305		95. JOHNNY RIVERS	1,159
77. DURAN DURAN	1,294		96. TOM JONES	1,153
78. FOREIGNER	1,278		▲ 97. GENESIS	1,147
79. JOHNNY MATHIS	1,276		98. RICK SPRINGFIELD	1,126
80. FLEETWOOD MAC	1,252		99. DAVE CLARK FIVE	1,125
			100. STYX	1,111

SYMBOLS

    ▲ = Hot Artist (at least five Top 40 hits from 1991 through 1995)

    ● = Deceased (solo artist or key member of a group)

    + = Subject to change since a title that peaked in 1995 by this artist
        is still charted in the Top 40 as of the 4/13/96 cut-off date.

POINT SYSTEM

Points are awarded according to the following formula:

1. Each artist's charted singles are given points based on their highest charted position:

    #1 = 100 points for its first week at #1, plus 10 points for each additional week at #1

    #2 = 90 points for its first week at #2, plus 5 points for each additional week at #2

    #3 = 80 points for its first week at #3, plus 3 points for each additional week at #3

    #4-5 = 70 points

    #6-10 = 60 points

    #11-20 = 50 points

    #21-30 = 45 points

    #31-40 = 40 points

2. Total Top 40 weeks charted are added in.

When two artists combine for a hit record, such as Aretha Franklin and George Michael, the full point value is given to both artists. Duos, such as Simon & Garfunkel, Hall & Oates, and Loggins & Messina are considered regular recording teams, and their points are not shared by either artist individually.

TOP ARTISTS BY DECADE

ARTIST	POINTS
FIFTIES ('55-'59)	
1. ELVIS PRESLEY	3,314
2. PAT BOONE	2,447
3. PERRY COMO	1,583
4. FATS DOMINO	1,384
5. RICKY NELSON	1,363
6. THE PLATTERS	1,220
7. NAT "KING" COLE	1,153
8. THE EVERLY BROTHERS	1,049
9. FRANK SINATRA	1,013
10. THE McGUIRE SISTERS	974
11. THE FOUR LADS	901
12. JOHNNY MATHIS	884
13. BILL HALEY & HIS COMETS	878
14. THE DIAMONDS	856
15. PATTI PAGE	838
16. PAUL ANKA	805
17. JIMMIE RODGERS	775
18. TERESA BREWER	719
19. CONNIE FRANCIS	700
20. FRANKIE AVALON	679
21. ANDY WILLIAMS	677
22. THE FONTANE SISTERS	674
23. CHUCK BERRY	626
24. BILLY VAUGHN	606
25. THE AMES BROTHERS	599

ARTIST	POINTS
SIXTIES ('60-'69)	
1. THE BEATLES	4,115
2. ELVIS PRESLEY	3,410
3. THE SUPREMES	2,281
4. THE 4 SEASONS	1,963
5. THE BEACH BOYS	1,887
6. BRENDA LEE	1,883
7. RAY CHARLES	1,732
8. MARVIN GAYE	1,721
9. BOBBY VINTON	1,705
10. CONNIE FRANCIS	1,585
11. THE TEMPTATIONS	1,564
12. THE ROLLING STONES	1,489
13. CHUBBY CHECKER	1,480
14. ROY ORBISON	1,451
15. THE MIRACLES	1,331
16. JAMES BROWN	1,326
17. HERMAN'S HERMITS	1,305
18. DION	1,207
19. SAM COOKE	1,166
20. ARETHA FRANKLIN	1,153
21. DIONNE WARWICK	1,138
22. DAVE CLARK FIVE	1,125
23. STEVIE WONDER	1,124
24. BROOK BENTON	1,091
25. BOBBY RYDELL	1,067

ARTIST	POINTS
SEVENTIES ('70-'79)	
1. PAUL McCARTNEY/WINGS	2,015
2. ELTON JOHN	2,011
3. BEE GEES	1,824
4. CARPENTERS	1,629
5. THE JACKSON 5/JACKSONS	1,541
6. STEVIE WONDER	1,462
7. CHICAGO	1,460
8. THREE DOG NIGHT	1,295
9. OLIVIA NEWTON-JOHN	1,255
10. NEIL DIAMOND	1,242
11. ELVIS PRESLEY	1,228
12. BARRY MANILOW	1,141
13. EAGLES	1,094
14. JOHN DENVER	1,081
15. DIANA ROSS	1,080
16. TONY ORLANDO & DAWN	1,068
17. DONNA SUMMER	1,066
18. GLADYS KNIGHT & THE PIPS	1,045
19. HELEN REDDY	1,023
20. ROD STEWART	978
21. BARBRA STREISAND	967
22. ARETHA FRANKLIN	959
23. EARTH, WIND & FIRE	938
24. JAMES BROWN	934
25. AL GREEN	916

ARTIST	POINTS
EIGHTIES ('80-'89)	
1. MICHAEL JACKSON	1,939
2. MADONNA	1,863
3. DARYL HALL & JOHN OATES	1,796
4. PRINCE	1,669
5. GEORGE MICHAEL/WHAM!	1,631
6. LIONEL RICHIE	1,460
7. BILLY JOEL	1,442
8. ELTON JOHN	1,416
9. PHIL COLLINS	1,379
10. JOHN COUGAR MELLENCAMP	1,255
11. HUEY LEWIS & THE NEWS	1,222
12. KOOL & THE GANG	1,190
13. DURAN DURAN	1,114
14. KENNY ROGERS	1,111
15. WHITNEY HOUSTON	1,104
16. STEVIE WONDER	1,099
17. RICK SPRINGFIELD	1,067
18. JOURNEY	1,041
19. DIANA ROSS	989
20. BRUCE SPRINGSTEEN	976
21. PAUL McCARTNEY	963
22. OLIVIA NEWTON-JOHN	957
23. AIR SUPPLY	946
24. BILLY OCEAN	940
25. CHICAGO	936

ARTIST	POINTS
NINETIES ('90-'95)	
1. MARIAH CAREY	2,112+
2. JANET JACKSON	1,640
3. BOYZ II MEN	1,560+
4. MADONNA	1,392
5. WHITNEY HOUSTON	1,016+
6. MICHAEL BOLTON	914
7. TLC	899
8. BRYAN ADAMS	844
9. MICHAEL JACKSON	795
10. PRINCE	724
11. ROD STEWART	721
12. ELTON JOHN	676
13. COLOR ME BADD	662
14. CELINE DION	645
15. PAULA ABDUL	642
16. EN VOGUE	638
17. WILSON PHILLIPS	607
18. AMY GRANT	553
19. ROXETTE	545
20. ACE OF BASE	537
21. BABYFACE	534
22. VANESSA WILLIAMS	533
23. BON JOVI	518
24. TONI BRAXTON	487
25. M.C. HAMMER	472

+ thru 4/13/96

TOP 40 ARTIST ACHIEVEMENTS

ARTIST	TOTAL
MOST CHARTED SINGLES	
1. ELVIS PRESLEY	114
2. ELTON JOHN	56
3. THE BEATLES	51
4. STEVIE WONDER	46
5. ARETHA FRANKLIN	44
6. JAMES BROWN	44
7. THE ROLLING STONES	41
8. MARVIN GAYE	40
9. PAT BOONE	38
10. THE TEMPTATIONS	38
11. NEIL DIAMOND	38
12. PAUL McCARTNEY/WINGS	37
13. FATS DOMINO	37
14. RICKY NELSON	36
15. THE BEACH BOYS	36
16. MICHAEL JACKSON	35
17. CHICAGO	35
18. CONNIE FRANCIS	35
19. MADONNA	33
20. THE SUPREMES	33
21. ROD STEWART	33
22. BILLY JOEL	33
23. PAUL ANKA	33
24. RAY CHARLES	33
25. THE 4 SEASONS	31
26. DIONNE WARWICK	31
27. BOBBY VINTON	31

ARTIST	TOTAL
MOST TOP 10 SINGLES	
1. ELVIS PRESLEY	38
2. THE BEATLES	34
3. MADONNA	29
4. STEVIE WONDER	28
5. MICHAEL JACKSON	27
6. ELTON JOHN	26
7. THE ROLLING STONES	23
8. PAUL McCARTNEY/WINGS	22
9. JANET JACKSON	21
10. THE SUPREMES	20
11. CHICAGO	20
12. RICKY NELSON	19
13. PRINCE	19
14. GEORGE MICHAEL/WHAM!	19
15. PAT BOONE	18
16. MARVIN GAYE	18
17. ARETHA FRANKLIN	17
18. WHITNEY HOUSTON	17
19. THE TEMPTATIONS	16
20. ROD STEWART	16
21. DARYL HALL & JOHN OATES	16
22. CONNIE FRANCIS	16
23. BEE GEES	15
24. THE BEACH BOYS	15
25. THE 4 SEASONS	15
26. OLIVIA NEWTON-JOHN	15
27. THE EVERLY BROTHERS	15

ARTIST	TOTAL
MOST #1 SINGLES	
1. THE BEATLES	20
2. ELVIS PRESLEY	18
3. MICHAEL JACKSON	13
4. THE SUPREMES	12
5. MADONNA	11
6. WHITNEY HOUSTON	11
7. STEVIE WONDER	10
8. GEORGE MICHAEL/WHAM!	10
9. MARIAH CAREY	10
10. PAUL McCARTNEY/WINGS	9
11. BEE GEES	9
12. ELTON JOHN	8
13. THE ROLLING STONES	8
14. JANET JACKSON	7
15. PHIL COLLINS	7
16. PAT BOONE	6
17. DARYL HALL & JOHN OATES	6
18. DIANA ROSS	6
19. PAULA ABDUL	6
20. PRINCE	5
21. THE 4 SEASONS	5
22. OLIVIA NEWTON-JOHN	5
23. BARBRA STREISAND	5
24. LIONEL RICHIE	5
25. BON JOVI	5
26. EAGLES	5
27. KC & THE SUNSHINE BAND	5

ARTIST	TOTAL
MOST WEEKS HELD #1 POSITION	
1. ELVIS PRESLEY	80
2. THE BEATLES	59
3. MARIAH CAREY	52
4. BOYZ II MEN	49
5. MICHAEL JACKSON	37
6. WHITNEY HOUSTON	31
7. PAUL McCARTNEY/WINGS	30
8. MADONNA	28
9. BEE GEES	27
10. STEVIE WONDER	25
11. GEORGE MICHAEL/WHAM!	23
12. THE SUPREMES	22
13. PAT BOONE	21
14. JANET JACKSON	21
15. LIONEL RICHIE	21
16. ELTON JOHN	20
17. ROD STEWART	20
18. DIANA ROSS	20
19. THE 4 SEASONS	18
20. OLIVIA NEWTON-JOHN	18
21. THE ROLLING STONES	17
22. BRYAN ADAMS	17
23. THE EVERLY BROTHERS	15
24. PHIL COLLINS	15
25. PAULA ABDUL	15
26. DARYL HALL & JOHN OATES	14
27. THE McGUIRE SISTERS	14

TOP SINGLES BY DECADE

PK YR	WKS CHR	WKS T40	WKS T10	WKS @ #1	TITLE...ARTIST
					FIFTIES ('55–'59)
56	28	23	21	11	1. Don't Be Cruel/Hound Dog...Elvis Presley
55	26	26	20	10	2. Cherry Pink And Apple Blossom White...Perez "Prez" Prado
55	21	21	18	10	3. Sincerely...The McGuire Sisters
56	26	22	17	10	4. Singing The Blues...Guy Mitchell
59	26	22	16	9	5. Mack The Knife...Bobby Darin
57	30	22	15	9	6. All Shook Up...Elvis Presley
55	24	24	19	8	7. (We're Gonna) Rock Around The Clock ...Bill Haley & His Comets
56	28	22	16	8	8. The Wayward Wind...Gogi Grant
55	22	19	16	8	9. Sixteen Tons..."Tennessee" Ernie Ford
56	27	22	15	8	10. Heartbreak Hotel...Elvis Presley
57	34	24	17	7	11. Love Letters In The Sand...Pat Boone
57	27	19	15	7	12. Jailhouse Rock...Elvis Presley
57	25	18	14	7	13. (Let Me Be Your) Teddy Bear...Elvis Presley
58	21	18	12	7	14. At The Hop...Danny & The Juniors
55	21	21	17	6	15. Love Is A Many-Splendored Thing...Four Aces
56	25	20	16	6	16. Rock And Roll Waltz...Kay Starr
56	24	20	16	6	17. The Poor People Of Paris...Les Baxter
55	19	19	16	6	18. The Yellow Rose Of Texas...Mitch Miller
56	24	19	15	6	19. Memories Are Made Of This...Dean Martin
57	26	19	14	6	20. April Love...Pat Boone
59	21	18	13	6	21. The Battle Of New Orleans...Johnny Horton
57	21	17	13	6	22. Young Love...Tab Hunter
58	22	19	12	6	23. It's All In The Game...Tommy Edwards
58	14	14	10	6	24. The Purple People Eater...Sheb Wooley
57	31	23	16	5	25. Tammy...Debbie Reynolds
					SIXTIES ('60–'69)
68	19	19	14	9	1. Hey Jude...The Beatles
60	21	17	12	9	2. The Theme From "A Summer Place"...Percy Faith
61	23	17	12	7	3. Tossin' And Turnin'...Bobby Lewis
64	15	14	12	7	4. I Want To Hold Your Hand...The Beatles
66	15	13	12	7	5. I'm A Believer...The Monkees
68	15	15	11	7	6. I Heard It Through The Grapevine...Marvin Gaye
69	17	16	11	6	7. Aquarius/Let The Sunshine In (The Flesh Failures) ...The 5th Dimension
60	16	14	11	6	8. Are You Lonesome To-night?...Elvis Presley
69	13	12	9	6	9. In The Year 2525 (Exordium & Terminus)...Zager & Evans
60	20	16	11	5	10. It's Now Or Never...Elvis Presley
62	18	14	11	5	11. I Can't Stop Loving You...Ray Charles
68	18	15	10	5	12. Love Is Blue...Paul Mauriat
62	16	14	10	5	13. Big Girls Don't Cry...The 4 Seasons

PK YR	WKS CHR	WKS T40	WKS T10	WKS @ #1	TITLE...ARTIST
61	16	13	10	5	14. Big Bad John...Jimmy Dean
63	15	13	10	5	15. Sugar Shack...Jimmy Gilmer & The Fireballs
68	15	13	10	5	16. Honey...Bobby Goldsboro
67	17	15	9	5	17. To Sir With Love...Lulu
60	17	13	9	5	18. Cathy's Clown...The Everly Brothers
68	14	13	9	5	19. People Got To Be Free...The Rascals
69	12	12	9	5	20. Get Back...The Beatles with Billy Preston
66	13	11	9	5	21. The Ballad Of The Green Berets...SSgt Barry Sadler
62	14	12	7	5	22. Sherry...The 4 Seasons
64	10	9	6	5	23. Can't Buy Me Love...The Beatles
69	22	18	12	4	24. Sugar, Sugar...The Archies
68	16	14	11	4	25. (Sittin' On) The Dock Of The Bay...Otis Redding

SEVENTIES ('70-'79)

PK YR	WKS CHR	WKS T40	WKS T10	WKS @ #1	TITLE...ARTIST
77	25	21	14	10	1. You Light Up My Life...Debby Boone
78	20	18	13	8	2. Night Fever...Bee Gees
76	23	17	11	8	3. Tonight's The Night (Gonna Be Alright)...Rod Stewart
78	25	19	12	7	4. Shadow Dancing...Andy Gibb
78	25	19	15	6	5. Le Freak...Chic
79	22	16	12	6	6. My Sharona...The Knack
72	18	15	11	6	7. The First Time Ever I Saw Your Face...Roberta Flack
72	18	15	11	6	8. Alone Again (Naturally)...Gilbert O'Sullivan
71	17	15	11	6	9. Joy To The World...Three Dog Night
70	14	13	10	6	10. Bridge Over Troubled Water...Simon & Garfunkel
77	23	17	12	5	11. Best Of My Love...Emotions
70	16	16	11	5	12. I'll Be There...The Jackson 5
76	19	15	11	5	13. Silly Love Songs...Wings
71	17	15	11	5	14. Maggie May...Rod Stewart
79	20	15	10	5	15. Bad Girls...Donna Summer
71	17	15	10	5	16. It's Too Late...Carole King
73	16	13	9	5	17. Killing Me Softly With His Song...Roberta Flack
71	15	12	9	5	18. One Bad Apple...The Osmonds
77	31	23	16	4	19. I Just Want To Be Your Everything...Andy Gibb
78	27	22	13	4	20. Stayin' Alive...Bee Gees
70	22	19	13	4	21. Raindrops Keep Fallin' On My Head...B.J. Thomas
79	21	18	12	4	22. Da Ya Think I'm Sexy?...Rod Stewart
78	23	17	12	4	23. Kiss You All Over...Exile
73	23	17	11	4	24. Tie A Yellow Ribbon Round The Ole Oak Tree ...Dawn Featuring Tony Orlando
72	19	17	11	4	25. American Pie - Parts I & II...Don McLean

EIGHTIES ('80-'89)

PK YR	WKS CHR	WKS T40	WKS T10	WKS @ #1	TITLE...ARTIST
81	26	21	15	10	1. Physical...Olivia Newton-John
81	26	20	14	9	2. Bette Davis Eyes...Kim Carnes
81	27	19	13	9	3. Endless Love...Diana Ross & Lionel Richie

PK YR	WKS CHR	WKS T40	WKS T10	WKS @ #1	TITLE...ARTIST
83	22	20	13	8	4. Every Breath You Take...The Police
82	20	16	12	7	5. I Love Rock 'N Roll...Joan Jett & The Blackhearts
82	19	15	12	7	6. Ebony And Ivory...Paul McCartney with Stevie Wonder
83	24	17	11	7	7. Billie Jean...Michael Jackson
82	25	18	15	6	8. Eye Of The Tiger...Survivor
83	25	20	14	6	9. Flashdance...What A Feeling...Irene Cara
80	25	19	13	6	10. Lady...Kenny Rogers
83	22	18	13	6	11. Say Say Say...Paul McCartney And Michael Jackson
82	25	20	12	6	12. Centerfold...The J. Geils Band
80	25	19	12	6	13. Call Me...Blondie
84	19	14	9	6	14. Like A Virgin...Madonna
80	22	19	14	5	15. (Just Like) Starting Over...John Lennon
84	21	16	11	5	16. When Doves Cry...Prince
84	21	15	10	5	17. Jump...Van Halen
80	29	17	14	4	18. Upside Down...Diana Ross
83	24	17	13	4	19. All Night Long (All Night)...Lionel Richie
82	23	17	13	4	20. Maneater...Daryl Hall & John Oates
80	25	19	12	4	21. Another Brick In The Wall (Part II)...Pink Floyd
80	22	17	12	4	22. Crazy Little Thing Called Love...Queen
83	29	18	11	4	23. Total Eclipse Of The Heart...Bonnie Tyler
83	25	19	10	4	24. Down Under...Men At Work
86	23	17	10	4	25. That's What Friends Are For...Dionne & Friends
					NINETIES ('90-'95)
95	20+	20+	19	16	1. One Sweet Day...Mariah Carey & Boyz II Men
94	33	31	22	14	2. I'll Make Love To You...Boyz II Men
92	26	24	16	14	3. I Will Always Love You...Whitney Houston
92	32	28	19	13	4. End of the Road...Boyz II Men
94	30	26	18	11	5. I Swear...All-4-One
95	25	23	16	8	6. Fantasy...Mariah Carey
93	29	26	14	8	7. Dreamlover...Mariah Carey
93	23	20	14	8	8. That's The Way Love Goes...Janet Jackson
92	21	18	13	8	9. Jump...Kris Kross
95	34	28	18	7	10. Waterfalls...TLC
95	30	27	15	7	11. Take A Bow...Madonna
93	29	23	15	7	12. Can't Help Falling In Love...UB40
95	29	24	14	7	13. This Is How We Do It...Montell Jordan
93	25	19	13	7	14. Informer...Snow
91	22	17	10	7	15. (Everything I Do) I Do It For You...Bryan Adams
91	20	15	10	7	16. Black Or White...Michael Jackson
94	41	33	21	6	17. The Sign...Ace Of Base
94	27	25	17	6	18. On Bended Knee...Boyz II Men
92	28	24	15	5	19. Baby Got Back...Sir Mix-A-Lot
93	22	18	14	5	20. I'd Do Anything For Love (But I Won't Do That)...Meat Loaf
92	27	23	13	5	21. Save The Best For Last...Vanessa Williams
95	24	20	12	5	22. Have You Ever Really Loved A Woman?...Bryan Adams
91	19	15	9	5	23. Rush, Rush...Paula Abdul
95	32	29	20	4	24. Creep...TLC
94	33	26	16	4	25. The Power Of Love...Celine Dion

+ thru 4/13/96

#1 SINGLES LISTED CHRONOLOGICALLY 1955-1995

For the years 1955 through 1958 (when *Billboard* published more than one weekly pop chart) special columns are used to show the weeks each #1 record spent on each of the various pop charts.

The date shown is the earliest date that a record hit #1 on any of the pop charts. The weeks column (next to date) lists the total weeks at #1, from whichever chart it achieved its highest total. This total is not a combined total from the various pop charts.

Because of the multiple charts used in our research, some dates are duplicated, as certain #1 hits may have peaked on the same week on different charts. *Billboard* also showed ties at #1 on some of these charts; therefore, the total weeks for each year may calculate out to more than 52.

Lines are drawn in on the charts column to show when any of the four pop charts were not published.

See the introduction of this book for more details about researching the four pop charts.

DATE: Date record first hit the #1 position
WKS: Total weeks record held the #1 position
  ↕ Indicates record hit #1, dropped down, then returned to the #1 spot
  * Consensus #1 record—hit #1 on all pop charts published ('55–'58)

CHARTS COLUMN:
  BS Best Sellers
  JY Jockey
  JB Juke Box
  TP Top 100
  HT Hot 100

870 records have hit the #1 position on *Billboard*'s pop charts from 1955 through December 30, 1995. "The Twist," even though it hit #1 in 1960 and again in 1962, is counted only once. There have been 804 #1 records since the Hot 100 chart began in 1958.

Billboard has not published an issue for the last week of the year since 1976. For the years 1976 through 1991, *Billboard* considered the charts listed in the last published issue of the year to be "frozen" and all chart positions remained the same for the unpublished week. This frozen chart data is included in our tabulations. Since 1992, *Billboard* has compiled a Pop chart for the last week of the year, even though an issue is not published. This chart is only available through *Billboard*'s computerized information network (BIN) or by mail. Our tabulations include this unpublished chart data.

DATE	WKS	RECORD TITLE	ARTIST	BS	JY	JB	TP
		1955					
1/01	4	* 1. Let Me Go Lover	Joan Weber	2	4↕	4	6
2/05	3	2. Hearts Of Stone	The Fontane Sisters	1	6	3	6
2/12	10	* 3. Sincerely	The McGuire Sisters	6	10	7	6
3/26	5	* 4. The Ballad Of Davy Crockett	Bill Hayes	5	3	3	6
4/30	10	* 5. Cherry Pink And Apple Blossom White	Perez "Prez" Prado	10	6↕	8	6
5/14	3	6. Dance With Me Henry (Wallflower)	Georgia Gibbs	6	6	3	6
5/14	2 ↕	7. Unchained Melody	Les Baxter	6	2↕	6	6
7/09	8	* 8. (We're Gonna) Rock Around The Clock	Bill Haley & His Comets	8	6↕	7	6
7/09	2 ↕	9. Learnin' The Blues	Frank Sinatra	6	2↕	6	6
9/03	6	* 10. The Yellow Rose Of Texas	Mitch Miller	6↕	6	6	6
9/17	2	11. Ain't That A Shame	Pat Boone	6	6	2	6
10/08	6	* 12. Love Is A Many-Splendored Thing	Four Aces	2↕	6	3	3
10/29	4	13. Autumn Leaves	Roger Williams	4	6	6	6
		11/12/55: BILLBOARD'S "TOP 100" CHART DEBUTS.					
11/26	8	* 14. Sixteen Tons	"Tennessee" Ernie Ford	7	6	8	6

DATE	WKS			RECORD TITLE	ARTIST	CHARTS			
						BS	JY	JB	TP
				1956					
1/07	6	*	1.	Memories Are Made Of This	Dean Martin	5	6	4	5
2/18	6	*	2.	Rock And Roll Waltz	Kay Starr	1	1	6	4
2/18	2		3.	The Great Pretender	The Platters	6	2	1	2
2/25	4		4.	Lisbon Antigua	Nelson Riddle	4	2↕	6	6
3/17	6	*	5.	The Poor People Of Paris	Les Baxter	4	6↕	3	6
4/21	8	*	6.	Heartbreak Hotel	Elvis Presley	8	3	8	7
5/05	1		7.	Hot Diggity (Dog Ziggity Boom)	Perry Como	6	1	6	6
6/02	3		8.	Moonglow and Theme From "Picnic"	Morris Stoloff	6	3	6	6
6/16	8	*	9.	The Wayward Wind	Gogi Grant	6	8	4	7
7/28	4		10.	I Almost Lost My Mind	Pat Boone	6	6	4	2
7/28	1		11.	I Want You, I Need You, I Love You	Elvis Presley	1	6	6	6
8/04	5	*	12.	My Prayer	The Platters	2	3	1	5
8/18	11	*	13.	Don't Be Cruel/					
			14.	Hound Dog	Elvis Presley	11	8	11	7
11/3	5	*	15.	Love Me Tender	Elvis Presley	5	5	1	4↕
11/3	3		16.	The Green Door	Jim Lowe	6	6	3	3
12/8	10	*	17.	Singing The Blues	Guy Mitchell	9	9	10	9
				1957					
2/09	3		1.	Too Much	Elvis Presley	3	6	1	6
2/09	1		2.	Don't Forbid Me	Pat Boone	6	6	1	1
2/09	1		3.	Young Love	Sonny James	6	1	6	6
2/16	6	*	4.	Young Love	Tab Hunter	4	6	5↕	6
3/30	3		5.	Butterfly	Andy Williams	6	2	6	3
3/30	1		6.	Party Doll	Buddy Knox & The Rhythm Orchids	1	6	6	6
4/06	2		7.	Round And Round	Perry Como	1	2	6	1
4/13	9		8.	All Shook Up	Elvis Presley	8	7	9	8
4/13	2	*	9.	Butterfly	Charlie Gracie	6	6	2	6
6/03	7	*	10.	Love Letters In The Sand	Pat Boone	5	7	6	5
				6/17/57: BILLBOARD TERMINATES "JUKE BOX" CHART.					
7/08	7	*	11.	Let Me Be Your) Teddy Bear	Elvis Presley	7	3		7
8/19	5	*	12.	Tammy	Debbie Reynolds	3↕	5		5
9/09	1		13.	Diana	Paul Anka	1	6		6
9/23	4	*	14.	Honeycomb	Jimmie Rodgers	2	4		2
9/23	1		15.	That'll Be The Day	The Crickets	1	6		6
10/14	4	*	16.	Wake Up Little Susie	The Everly Brothers	1	4		2
10/21	7↕	*	17.	Jailhouse Rock	Elvis Presley	7↕	2		6
10/21	1		18.	Chances Are	Johnny Mathis	6	1		6
12/02	3	*	19.	You Send Me	Sam Cooke	2	1		3
12/16	6	*	20.	April Love	Pat Boone	2	6		1
				1958					
1/06	7	*	1.	At The Hop	Danny & The Juniors	5	3		7
2/10	5	*	2.	Don't	Elvis Presley	5	1		1
2/17	4		3.	Sugartime	The McGuire Sisters	6	4		6
2/24	2		4.	Get A Job	The Silhouettes	6	6		2

DATE	WKS		RECORD TITLE	ARTIST	CHARTS			
					BS	JY	TP	HT
3/17	5	* 5.	Tequila	The Champs	5	2		5
3/24	1	6.	Catch A Falling Star	Perry Como	6	1		6
4/14	4	7.	He's Got The Whole World (In His Hands)	Laurie London	6	4		6
4/21	1	* 8.	Twilight Time	The Platters	1	1		1
4/28	3	9.	Witch Doctor	David Seville	2	6		3
5/12	5	* 10.	All I Have To Do Is Dream	The Everly Brothers	4	5		3
6/09	6	* 11.	The Purple People Eater	Sheb Wooley	6	4		6
7/21	2	12.	Hard Headed Woman	Elvis Presley	2	1		6
7/21	1	13.	Yakety Yak	The Coasters	6	6		1

7/28/58: BILLBOARD TERMINATES
THE "JOCKEYS" AND "TOP 100" CHARTS.

DATE	WKS		RECORD TITLE	ARTIST	BS	JY	TP	HT
7/28	1	14.	Patricia	Perez Prado	6	1	1	

8/4/58: BILLBOARD'S "HOT 100" CHART DEBUTS.

DATE	WKS		RECORD TITLE	ARTIST	BS	JY	TP	HT
8/04	2	* 15.	Poor Little Fool	Ricky Nelson	2			2
8/18	5 ↕	* 16.	Nel Blu Dipinto Di Blu (Volare)	Domenico Modugno	5↕			5↕
8/25	1	17.	Little Star	The Elegants	6			1
8/25	1	18.	Bird Dog	The Everly Brothers	1			6
9/29	6	* 19.	It's All In The Game	Tommy Edwards	3			6

10/13/58: BILLBOARD TERMINATES "BEST SELLERS" CHART;
"HOT 100" CHART USED EXCLUSIVELY FROM HERE ON.

DATE	WKS		RECORD TITLE	ARTIST	BS	JY	TP	HT
11/10	2 ↕	20.	It's Only Make Believe	Conway Twitty				2↕
11/17	1	21.	Tom Dooley	The Kingston Trio				1
12/01	3	22.	To Know Him, Is To Love Him	The Teddy Bears				3
12/22	4	23.	The Chipmunk Song	The Chipmunks				4

DATE	WKS		RECORD TITLE	ARTIST
			1959	
1/19	3	1.	Smoke Gets In Your Eyes	The Platters
2/09	4	2.	Stagger Lee	Lloyd Price
3/09	5	3.	Venus	Frankie Avalon
4/13	4	4.	Come Softly To Me	Fleetwoods
5/11	1	5.	The Happy Organ	Dave "Baby" Cortez
5/18	2	6.	Kansas City	Wilbert Harrison
6/01	6	7.	The Battle Of New Orleans	Johnny Horton
7/13	4	8.	Lonely Boy	Paul Anka
8/10	2	9.	A Big Hunk O' Love	Elvis Presley
8/24	4	10.	The Three Bells	The Browns
9/21	2	11.	Sleep Walk	Santo & Johnny
10/05	9 ↕	12.	Mack The Knife	Bobby Darin
11/16	1	13.	Mr. Blue	The Fleetwoods
12/14	2	14.	Heartaches By The Number	Guy Mitchell
12/28	1	15.	Why	Frankie Avalon

DATE	WKS	RECORD TITLE	ARTIST

1960

1/04	2	1. El Paso	Marty Robbins
1/18	3	2. Running Bear	Johnny Preston
2/08	2	3. Teen Angel	Mark Dinning
2/22	9	4. The Theme From "A Summer Place"	Percy Faith
4/25	4	5. Stuck On You	Elvis Presley
5/23	5	6. Cathy's Clown	The Everly Brothers
6/27	2	7. Everybody's Somebody's Fool	Connie Francis
7/11	1	8. Alley-Oop	Hollywood Argyles
7/18	3	9. I'm Sorry	Brenda Lee
8/08	1	10. Itsy Bitsy Teenie Weenie Yellow Polkadot Bikini	Brian Hyland
8/15	5	11. It's Now Or Never	Elvis Presley

RE-ENTERED #1 POSITION IN 1962 FOR 2 MORE WEEKS

9/19	1	12. The Twist	Chubby Checker
9/26	2	13. My Heart Has A Mind Of Its Own	Connie Francis
10/10	1	14. Mr. Custer	Larry Verne
10/17	3 ↕	15. Save The Last Dance For Me	The Drifters
10/24	1	16. I Want To Be Wanted	Brenda Lee
11/14	1	17. Georgia On My Mind	Ray Charles
11/21	1	18. Stay	Maurice Williams & The Zodiacs
11/28	6	19. Are You Lonesome To-night?	Elvis Presley

1961

1/09	3	1. Wonderland By Night	Bert Kaempfert
1/30	2	2. Will You Love Me Tomorrow	The Shirelles
2/13	2	3. Calcutta	Lawrence Welk
2/27	3	4. Pony Time	Chubby Checker
3/20	2	5. Surrender	Elvis Presley
4/03	3	6. Blue Moon	The Marcels
4/24	4	7. Runaway	Del Shannon
5/22	1	8. Mother-In-Law	Ernie K-Doe
5/29	2 ↕	9. Travelin' Man	Ricky Nelson
6/05	1	10. Running Scared	Roy Orbison
6/19	1	11. Moody River	Pat Boone
6/26	2	12. Quarter To Three	U.S. Bonds
7/10	7	13. Tossin' And Turnin'	Bobby Lewis
8/28	1	14. Wooden Heart	Joe Dowell
9/04	2	15. Michael	The Highwaymen
9/18	3	16. Take Good Care Of My Baby	Bobby Vee
10/09	2	17. Hit The Road Jack	Ray Charles
10/23	2	18. Runaround Sue	Dion
11/06	5	19. Big Bad John	Jimmy Dean
12/11	1	20. Please Mr. Postman	The Marvelettes
12/18	3	21. The Lion Sleeps Tonight	The Tokens

1962

| 1/13 | 2 | 1. The Twist | Chubby Checker |

FIRST ENTERED #1 POSITION IN 1960 FOR 1 WEEK

DATE	WKS		RECORD TITLE	ARTIST
1/27	3	2.	Peppermint Twist - Part I	Joey Dee & the Starliters
2/17	3	3.	Duke Of Earl	Gene Chandler
3/10	3	4.	Hey! Baby	Bruce Channel
3/31	1	5.	Don't Break The Heart That Loves You	Connie Francis
4/07	2	6.	Johnny Angel	Shelley Fabares
4/21	2	7.	Good Luck Charm	Elvis Presley
5/05	3	8.	Soldier Boy	The Shirelles
5/26	1	9.	Stranger On The Shore	Mr. Acker Bilk
6/02	5	10.	I Can't Stop Loving You	Ray Charles
7/07	1	11.	The Stripper	David Rose
7/14	4	12.	Roses Are Red (My Love)	Bobby Vinton
8/11	2	13.	Breaking Up Is Hard To Do	Neil Sedaka
8/25	1	14.	The Loco-Motion	Little Eva
9/01	2	15.	Sheila	Tommy Roe
9/15	5	16.	Sherry	The 4 Seasons
10/20	2	17.	Monster Mash	Bobby "Boris" Pickett & The Crypt-Kickers
11/03	2	18.	He's A Rebel	The Crystals
11/17	5	19.	Big Girls Don't Cry	The 4 Seasons
12/22	3	20.	Telstar	The Tornadoes

1963

DATE	WKS		RECORD TITLE	ARTIST
1/12	2	1.	Go Away Little Girl	Steve Lawrence
1/26	2	2.	Walk Right In	The Rooftop Singers
2/09	3	3.	Hey Paula	Paul & Paula
3/02	3	4.	Walk Like A Man	The 4 Seasons
3/23	1	5.	Our Day Will Come	Ruby & The Romantics
3/30	4	6.	He's So Fine	The Chiffons
4/27	3	7.	I Will Follow Him	Little Peggy March
5/18	2	8.	If You Wanna Be Happy	Jimmy Soul
6/01	2	9.	It's My Party	Lesley Gore
6/15	3	10.	Sukiyaki	Kyu Sakamoto
7/06	2	11.	Easier Said Than Done	The Essex
7/20	2	12.	Surf City	Jan & Dean
8/03	1	13.	So Much In Love	The Tymes
8/10	3	14.	Fingertips - Pt 2	Little Stevie Wonder
8/31	3	15.	My Boyfriend's Back	The Angels
9/21	3	16.	Blue Velvet	Bobby Vinton
10/12	5	17.	Sugar Shack	Jimmy Gilmer & The Fireballs
11/16	1	18.	Deep Purple	Nino Tempo & April Stevens
11/23	2	19.	I'm Leaving It Up To You	Dale & Grace
12/07	4	20.	Dominique	The Singing Nun

1964

DATE	WKS		RECORD TITLE	ARTIST
1/04	4	1.	There! I've Said It Again	Bobby Vinton
2/01	7	2.	I Want To Hold Your Hand	The Beatles
3/21	2	3.	She Loves You	The Beatles
4/04	5	4.	Can't Buy Me Love	The Beatles
5/09	1	5.	Hello, Dolly!	Louis Armstrong
5/16	2	6.	My Guy	Mary Wells
5/30	1	7.	Love Me Do	The Beatles
6/06	3	8.	Chapel Of Love	The Dixie Cups
6/27	1	9.	A World Without Love	Peter & Gordon
7/04	2	10.	I Get Around	The Beach Boys

DATE	WKS		RECORD TITLE	ARTIST
7/18	2	11.	Rag Doll	The 4 Seasons
8/01	2	12.	A Hard Day's Night	The Beatles
8/15	1	13.	Everybody Loves Somebody	Dean Martin
8/22	2	14.	Where Did Our Love Go	The Supremes
9/05	3	15.	The House Of The Rising Sun	The Animals
9/26	3	16.	Oh, Pretty Woman	Roy Orbison
10/17	2	17.	Do Wah Diddy Diddy	Manfred Mann
10/31	4	18.	Baby Love	The Supremes
11/28	1	19.	Leader Of The Pack	The Shangri-Las
12/05	1	20.	Ringo	Lorne Greene
12/12	1	21.	Mr. Lonely	Bobby Vinton
12/19	2 ↕	22.	Come See About Me	The Supremes
12/26	3	23.	I Feel Fine	The Beatles

1965

DATE	WKS		RECORD TITLE	ARTIST
1/23	2	1.	Downtown	Petula Clark
2/06	2	2.	You've Lost That Lovin' Feelin'	The Righteous Brothers
2/20	2	3.	This Diamond Ring	Gary Lewis & The Playboys
3/06	1	4.	My Girl	The Temptations
3/13	2	5.	Eight Days A Week	The Beatles
3/27	2	6.	Stop! In The Name Of Love	The Supremes
4/10	2	7.	I'm Telling You Now	Freddie & The Dreamers
4/24	1	8.	Game Of Love	Wayne Fontana & The Mindbenders
5/01	3	9.	Mrs. Brown You've Got A Lovely Daughter	Herman's Hermits
5/22	1	10.	Ticket To Ride	The Beatles
5/29	2	11.	Help Me, Rhonda	The Beach Boys
6/12	1	12.	Back In My Arms Again	The Supremes
6/19	2 ↕	13.	I Can't Help Myself	Four Tops
6/26	1	14.	Mr. Tambourine Man	The Byrds
7/10	4	15.	(I Can't Get No) Satisfaction	The Rolling Stones
8/07	1	16.	I'm Henry VIII, I Am	Herman's Hermits
8/14	3	17.	I Got You Babe	Sonny & Cher
9/04	3	18.	Help!	The Beatles
9/25	1	19.	Eve Of Destruction	Barry McGuire
10/02	1	20.	Hang On Sloopy	The McCoys
10/09	4	21.	Yesterday	The Beatles
11/06	2	22.	Get Off Of My Cloud	The Rolling Stones
11/20	2	23.	I Hear A Symphony	The Supremes
12/04	3	24.	Turn! Turn! Turn! (To Everything There Is A Season)	The Byrds
12/25	1	25.	Over And Over	The Dave Clark Five

1966

DATE	WKS		RECORD TITLE	ARTIST
1/01	2 ↕	1.	The Sounds Of Silence	Simon & Garfunkel
1/08	3 ↕	2.	We Can Work It Out	The Beatles
2/05	2	3.	My Love	Petula Clark
2/19	1	4.	Lightnin' Strikes	Lou Christie
2/26	1	5.	These Boots Are Made For Walkin'	Nancy Sinatra
3/05	5	6.	The Ballad Of The Green Berets	SSgt. Barry Sadler
4/09	3	7.	(You're My) Soul And Inspiration	The Righteous Brothers
4/30	1	8.	Good Lovin'	The Young Rascals
5/07	3	9.	Monday, Monday	The Mama's & The Papa's
5/28	2	10.	When A Man Loves A Woman	Percy Sledge
6/11	2	11.	Paint It, Black	The Rolling Stones

DATE	WKS		RECORD TITLE	ARTIST
6/25	2 ↕	12.	Paperback Writer	The Beatles
7/02	1	13.	Strangers In The Night	Frank Sinatra
7/16	2	14.	Hanky Panky	Tommy James & The Shondells
7/30	2	15.	Wild Thing	The Troggs
8/13	3	16.	Summer In The City	The Lovin' Spoonful
9/03	1	17.	Sunshine Superman	Donovan
9/10	2	18.	You Can't Hurry Love	The Supremes
9/24	3	19.	Cherish	The Association
10/15	2	20.	Reach Out I'll Be There	Four Tops
10/29	1	21.	96 Tears	? & The Mysterians
11/05	1	22.	Last Train To Clarksville	The Monkees
11/12	1	23.	Poor Side Of Town	Johnny Rivers
11/19	2	24.	You Keep Me Hangin' On	The Supremes
12/03	3 ↕	25.	Winchester Cathedral	The New Vaudeville Band
12/10	1	26.	Good Vibrations	The Beach Boys
12/31	7	27.	I'm A Believer	The Monkees

1967

DATE	WKS		RECORD TITLE	ARTIST
2/18	2	1.	Kind Of A Drag	The Buckinghams
3/04	1	2.	Ruby Tuesday	The Rolling Stones
3/11	1	3.	Love Is Here And Now You're Gone	The Supremes
3/18	1	4.	Penny Lane	The Beatles
3/25	3	5.	Happy Together	The Turtles
4/15	4	6.	Somethin' Stupid	Nancy Sinatra & Frank Sinatra
5/13	1	7.	The Happening	The Supremes
5/20	4 ↕	8.	Groovin'	The Young Rascals
6/03	2	9.	Respect	Aretha Franklin
7/01	4	10.	Windy	The Association
7/29	3	11.	Light My Fire	The Doors
8/19	1	12.	All You Need Is Love	The Beatles
8/26	4	13.	Ode To Billie Joe	Bobbie Gentry
9/23	4	14.	The Letter	The Box Tops
10/21	5	15.	To Sir With Love	Lulu
11/25	1	16.	Incense And Peppermints	Strawberry Alarm Clock
12/02	4	17.	Daydream Believer	The Monkees
12/30	3	18.	Hello Goodbye	The Beatles

1968

DATE	WKS		RECORD TITLE	ARTIST
1/20	2	1.	Judy In Disguise (With Glasses)	John Fred & His Playboy Band
2/03	1	2.	Green Tambourine	The Lemon Pipers
2/10	5	3.	Love Is Blue	Paul Mauriat
3/16	4	4.	(Sittin' On) The Dock Of The Bay	Otis Redding
4/13	5	5.	Honey	Bobby Goldsboro
5/18	2	6.	Tighten Up	Archie Bell & The Drells
6/01	3	7.	Mrs. Robinson	Simon & Garfunkel
6/22	4	8.	This Guy's In Love With You	Herb Alpert
7/20	2	9.	Grazing In The Grass	Hugh Masekela
8/03	2	10.	Hello, I Love You	The Doors
8/17	5	11.	People Got To Be Free	The Rascals
9/21	1	12.	Harper Valley P.T.A.	Jeannie C. Riley
9/28	9	13.	Hey Jude	The Beatles
11/30	2	14.	Love Child	Diana Ross & The Supremes
12/14	7	15.	I Heard It Through The Grapevine	Marvin Gaye

DATE	WKS		RECORD TITLE	ARTIST
			1969	
2/01	2	1.	Crimson And Clover	Tommy James & The Shondells
2/15	4	2.	Everyday People	Sly & The Family Stone
3/15	4	3.	Dizzy	Tommy Roe
4/12	6	4.	Aquarius/Let The Sunshine In (The Flesh Failures)	The 5th Dimension
5/24	5	5.	Get Back	The Beatles with Billy Preston
6/28	2	6.	Love Theme From Romeo & Juliet	Henry Mancini
7/12	6	7.	In The Year 2525 (Exordium & Terminus)	Zager & Evans
8/23	4	8.	Honky Tonk Women	The Rolling Stones
9/20	4	9.	Sugar, Sugar	The Archies
10/18	2	10.	I Can't Get Next To You	The Temptations
11/01	1	11.	Suspicious Minds	Elvis Presley
11/08	3	12.	Wedding Bell Blues	The 5th Dimension
11/29	1	13.	Come Together	The Beatles
12/06	2	14.	Na Na Hey Hey Kiss Him Goodbye	Steam
12/20	1	15.	Leaving On A Jet Plane	Peter, Paul & Mary
12/27	1	16.	Someday We'll Be Together	Diana Ross & The Supremes
			1970	
1/03	4	1.	Raindrops Keep Fallin' On My Head	B.J. Thomas
1/31	1	2.	I Want You Back	The Jackson 5
2/07	1	3.	Venus	The Shocking Blue
2/14	2	4.	Thank You (Falettinme Be Mice Elf Agin)	Sly & The Family Stone
2/28	6	5.	Bridge Over Troubled Water	Simon & Garfunkel
4/11	2	6.	Let It Be	The Beatles
4/25	2	7.	ABC	The Jackson 5
5/09	3	8.	American Woman	The Guess Who
5/30	2	9.	Everything Is Beautiful	Ray Stevens
6/13	2	10.	The Long And Winding Road	The Beatles
6/27	2	11.	The Love You Save	The Jackson 5
7/11	2	12.	Mama Told Me (Not To Come)	Three Dog Night
7/25	4	13.	(They Long To Be) Close To You	Carpenters
8/22	1	14.	Make It With You	Bread
8/29	3	15.	War	Edwin Starr
9/19	3	16.	Ain't No Mountain High Enough	Diana Ross
10/10	1	17.	Cracklin' Rosie	Neil Diamond
10/17	5	18.	I'll Be There	The Jackson 5
11/21	3	19.	I Think I Love You	The Partridge Family
12/12	2	20.	The Tears Of A Clown	Smokey Robinson & The Miracles
12/26	4	21.	My Sweet Lord	George Harrison
			1971	
1/23	3	1.	Knock Three Times	Dawn
2/13	5	2.	One Bad Apple	The Osmonds
3/20	2	3.	Me And Bobby McGee	Janis Joplin
4/03	2	4.	Just My Imagination (Running Away With Me)	The Temptations
4/17	6	5.	Joy To The World	Three Dog Night
5/29	2	6.	Brown Sugar	The Rolling Stones
6/12	1	7.	Want Ads	The Honey Cone
6/19	5	8.	It's Too Late	Carole King
7/24	1	9.	Indian Reservation	Raiders
7/31	1	10.	You've Got A Friend	James Taylor

DATE	WKS		RECORD TITLE	ARTIST
8/07	4	11.	How Can You Mend A Broken Heart	The Bee Gees
9/04	1	12.	Uncle Albert/Admiral Halsey	Paul & Linda McCartney
9/11	3	13.	Go Away Little Girl	Donny Osmond
10/2	5	14.	Maggie May	Rod Stewart
11/06	2	15.	Gypsys, Tramps & Thieves	Cher
11/20	2	16.	Theme From Shaft	Isaac Hayes
12/04	3	17.	Family Affair	Sly & The Family Stone
12/25	3	18.	Brand New Key	Melanie

1972

DATE	WKS		RECORD TITLE	ARTIST
1/15	4	1.	American Pie - Parts I & II	Don McLean
2/12	1	2.	Let's Stay Together	Al Green
2/19	4	3.	Without You	Nilsson
3/18	1	4.	Heart Of Gold	Neil Young
3/25	3	5.	A Horse With No Name	America
4/15	6	6.	The First Time Ever I Saw Your Face	Roberta Flack
5/27	1	7.	Oh Girl	Chi-Lites
6/03	1	8.	I'll Take You There	The Staple Singers
6/10	3	9.	The Candy Man	Sammy Davis, Jr.
7/01	1	10.	Song Sung Blue	Neil Diamond
7/08	3	11.	Lean On Me	Bill Withers
7/29	6 ↕	12.	Alone Again (Naturally)	Gilbert O'Sullivan
8/26	1	13.	Brandy (You're A Fine Girl)	Looking Glass
9/16	1	14.	Black & White	Three Dog Night
9/23	3	15.	Baby Don't Get Hooked On Me	Mac Davis
10/14	1	16.	Ben	Michael Jackson
10/21	2	17.	My Ding-A-Ling	Chuck Berry
11/04	4	18.	I Can See Clearly Now	Johnny Nash
12/02	1	19.	Papa Was A Rollin' Stone	The Temptations
12/09	1	20.	I Am Woman	Helen Reddy
12/16	3	21.	Me And Mrs. Jones	Billy Paul

1973

DATE	WKS		RECORD TITLE	ARTIST
1/06	3	1.	You're So Vain	Carly Simon
1/27	1	2.	Superstition	Stevie Wonder
2/03	3	3.	Crocodile Rock	Elton John
2/24	5 ↕	4.	Killing Me Softly With His Song	Roberta Flack
3/24	1	5.	Love Train	O'Jays
4/07	2	6.	The Night The Lights Went Out In Georgia	Vicki Lawrence
4/21	4	7.	Tie A Yellow Ribbon Round The Ole Oak Tree	Dawn Featuring Tony Orlando
5/19	1	8.	You Are The Sunshine Of My Life	Stevie Wonder
5/26	1	9.	Frankenstein	The Edgar Winter Group
6/02	4	10.	My Love	Paul McCartney & Wings
6/30	1	11.	Give Me Love - (Give Me Peace On Earth)	George Harrison
7/07	2	12.	Will It Go Round In Circles	Billy Preston
7/21	2	13.	Bad, Bad Leroy Brown	Jim Croce
8/04	2	14.	The Morning After	Maureen McGovern
8/18	1	15.	Touch Me In The Morning	Diana Ross
8/25	2	16.	Brother Louie	Stories
9/08	2 ↕	17.	Let's Get It On	Marvin Gaye
9/15	1	18.	Delta Dawn	Helen Reddy
9/29	1	19.	We're An American Band	Grand Funk
10/06	2	20.	Half-Breed	Cher
10/20	1	21.	Angie	The Rolling Stones

DATE	WKS		RECORD TITLE	ARTIST
10/27	2	22.	Midnight Train To Georgia	Gladys Knight & The Pips
11/10	2	23.	Keep On Truckin' (Part 1)	Eddie Kendricks
11/24	1	24.	Photograph	Ringo Starr
12/01	2	25.	Top Of The World	Carpenters
12/15	2	26.	The Most Beautiful Girl	Charlie Rich
12/29	2	27.	Time In A Bottle	Jim Croce

1974

DATE	WKS		RECORD TITLE	ARTIST
1/12	1	1.	The Joker	Steve Miller Band
1/19	1	2.	Show And Tell	Al Wilson
1/26	1	3.	You're Sixteen	Ringo Starr
2/02	3 ↕	4.	The Way We Were	Barbra Streisand
2/09	1	5.	Love's Theme	Love Unlimited Orchestra
3/02	3	6.	Seasons In The Sun	Terry Jacks
3/23	1	7.	Dark Lady	Cher
3/30	1	8.	Sunshine On My Shoulders	John Denver
4/06	1	9.	Hooked On A Feeling	Blue Swede
4/13	1	10.	Bennie And The Jets	Elton John
4/20	2	11.	TSOP (The Sound Of Philadelphia)	MFSB featuring The Three Degrees
5/04	2	12.	The Loco-Motion	Grand Funk
5/18	3	13.	The Streak	Ray Stevens
6/08	1	14.	Band On The Run	Paul McCartney & Wings
6/15	2	15.	Billy, Don't Be A Hero	Bo Donaldson & The Heywoods
6/29	1	16.	Sundown	Gordon Lightfoot
7/06	1	17.	Rock The Boat	The Hues Corporation
7/13	2	18.	Rock Your Baby	George McCrae
7/27	2	19.	Annie's Song	John Denver
8/10	1	20.	Feel Like Makin' Love	Roberta Flack
8/17	1	21.	The Night Chicago Died	Paper Lace
8/24	3	22.	(You're) Having My Baby	Paul Anka
9/14	1	23.	I Shot The Sheriff	Eric Clapton
9/21	1	24.	Can't Get Enough Of Your Love, Babe	Barry White
9/28	1	25.	Rock Me Gently	Andy Kim
10/05	2	26.	I Honestly Love You	Olivia Newton-John
10/19	1	27.	Nothing From Nothing	Billy Preston
10/26	1	28.	Then Came You	Dionne Warwicke & Spinners
11/02	1	29.	You Haven't Done Nothin	Stevie Wonder
11/09	1	30.	You Ain't Seen Nothing Yet	Bachman-Turner Overdrive
11/16	1	31.	Whatever Gets You Thru The Night	John Lennon/Plastic Ono Band
11/23	2	32.	I Can Help	Billy Swan
12/07	2	33.	Kung Fu Fighting	Carl Douglas
12/21	1	34.	Cat's In The Cradle	Harry Chapin
12/28	1	35.	Angie Baby	Helen Reddy

1975

DATE	WKS		RECORD TITLE	ARTIST
1/04	2	1.	Lucy In The Sky With Diamonds	Elton John
1/18	1	2.	Mandy	Barry Manilow
1/25	1	3.	Please Mr. Postman	Carpenters
2/01	1	4.	Laughter In The Rain	Neil Sedaka
2/08	1	5.	Fire	Ohio Players
2/15	1	6.	You're No Good	Linda Ronstadt
2/22	1	7.	Pick Up The Pieces	AWB
3/01	1	8.	Best Of My Love	Eagles
3/08	1	9.	Have You Never Been Mellow	Olivia Newton-John

DATE	WKS		RECORD TITLE	ARTIST
3/15	1	10.	Black Water	The Doobie Brothers
3/22	1	11.	My Eyes Adored You	Frankie Valli
3/29	1	12.	Lady Marmalade	LaBelle
4/05	1	13.	Lovin' You	Minnie Riperton
4/12	2	14.	Philadelphia Freedom	The Elton John Band
4/26	1	15.	(Hey Won't You Play) Another Somebody Done Somebody Wrong Song	B.J. Thomas
5/03	3	16.	He Don't Love You (Like I Love You)	Tony Orlando & Dawn
5/24	1	17.	Shining Star	Earth, Wind & Fire
5/31	1	18.	Before The Next Teardrop Falls	Freddy Fender
6/07	1	19.	Thank God I'm A Country Boy	John Denver
6/14	1	20.	Sister Golden Hair	America
6/21	4	21.	Love Will Keep Us Together	The Captain & Tennille
7/19	1	22.	Listen To What The Man Said	Wings
7/26	1	23.	The Hustle	Van McCoy/The Soul City Symphony
8/02	1	24.	One Of These Nights	Eagles
8/09	2	25.	Jive Talkin'	Bee Gees
8/23	1	26.	Fallin' In Love	Hamilton, Joe Frank & Reynolds
8/30	1	27.	Get Down Tonight	K.C. & The Sunshine Band
9/06	2	28.	Rhinestone Cowboy	Glen Campbell
9/20	2 ↕	29.	Fame	David Bowie
9/27	1	30.	I'm Sorry	John Denver
10/11	3	31.	Bad Blood	Neil Sedaka
11/01	3	32.	Island Girl	Elton John
11/22	2 ↕	33.	That's The Way (I Like It)	KC & The Sunshine Band
11/29	3	34.	Fly, Robin, Fly	Silver Convention
12/27	1	35.	Let's Do It Again	The Staple Singers

1976

DATE	WKS		RECORD TITLE	ARTIST
1/03	1	1.	Saturday Night	Bay City Rollers
1/10	1	2.	Convoy	C.W. McCall
1/17	1	3.	I Write The Songs	Barry Manilow
1/24	1	4.	Theme From Mahogany (Do You Know Where You're Going to)	Diana Ross
1/31	1	5.	Love Rollercoaster	Ohio Players
2/07	3	6.	50 Ways To Leave Your Lover	Paul Simon
2/28	1	7.	Theme From S.W.A.T.	Rhythm Heritage
3/06	1	8.	Love Machine (Part 1)	The Miracles
3/13	3	9.	December, 1963 (Oh, What a Night)	The Four Seasons
4/03	4	10.	Disco Lady	Johnnie Taylor
5/01	1	11.	Let Your Love Flow	Bellamy Brothers
5/08	1	12.	Welcome Back	John Sebastian
5/15	1	13.	Boogie Fever	Sylvers
5/22	5 ↕	14.	Silly Love Songs	Wings
5/29	2	15.	Love Hangover	Diana Ross
7/10	2	16.	Afternoon Delight	Starland Vocal Band
7/24	2	17.	Kiss And Say Goodbye	Manhattans
8/07	4	18.	Don't Go Breaking My Heart	Elton John & Kiki Dee
9/04	1	19.	You Should Be Dancing	Bee Gees
9/11	1	20.	(Shake, Shake, Shake) Shake Your Booty	KC & The Sunshine Band
9/18	3	21.	Play That Funky Music	Wild Cherry
10/09	1	22.	A Fifth Of Beethoven	Walter Murphy & The Big Apple Band
10/16	1	23.	Disco Duck (Part 1)	Rick Dees & His Cast Of Idiots

DATE	WKS		RECORD TITLE	ARTIST
10/23	2	24.	If You Leave Me Now	Chicago
11/06	1	25.	Rock'n Me	Steve Miller
11/13	8	26.	Tonight's The Night (Gonna Be Alright)	Rod Stewart

1977

DATE	WKS		RECORD TITLE	ARTIST
1/08	1	1.	You Don't Have To Be A Star (To Be In My Show)	Marilyn McCoo & Billy Davis, Jr.
1/15	1	2.	You Make Me Feel Like Dancing	Leo Sayer
1/22	1	3.	I Wish	Stevie Wonder
1/29	1	4.	Car Wash	Rose Royce
2/05	2	5.	Torn Between Two Lovers	Mary MacGregor
2/19	1	6.	Blinded By The Light	Manfred Mann's Earth Band
2/26	1	7.	New Kid In Town	Eagles
3/05	3	8.	Love Theme From "A Star Is Born" (Evergreen)	Barbra Streisand
3/26	2	9.	Rich Girl	Daryl Hall & John Oates
4/09	1	10.	Dancing Queen	Abba
4/16	1	11.	Don't Give Up On Us	David Soul
4/23	1	12.	Don't Leave Me This Way	Thelma Houston
4/30	1	13.	Southern Nights	Glen Campbell
5/07	1	14.	Hotel California	Eagles
5/14	1	15.	When I Need You	Leo Sayer
5/21	3	16.	Sir Duke	Stevie Wonder
6/11	1	17.	I'm Your Boogie Man	KC & The Sunshine Band
6/18	1	18.	Dreams	Fleetwood Mac
6/25	1	19.	Got To Give It Up (Pt. I)	Marvin Gaye
7/02	1	20.	Gonna Fly Now	Bill Conti
7/09	1	21.	Undercover Angel	Alan O'Day
7/16	1	22.	Da Doo Ron Ron	Shaun Cassidy
7/23	1	23.	Looks Like We Made It	Barry Manilow
7/30	4 ↕	24.	I Just Want To Be Your Everything	Andy Gibb
8/20	5 ↕	25.	Best Of My Love	Emotions
10/01	2	26.	Star Wars Theme/Cantina Band	Meco
10/15	10	27.	You Light Up My Life	Debby Boone
12/24	3	28.	How Deep Is Your Love	Bee Gees

1978

DATE	WKS		RECORD TITLE	ARTIST
1/14	3	1.	Baby Come Back	Player
2/04	4	2.	Stayin' Alive	Bee Gees
3/04	2	3.	(Love Is) Thicker Than Water	Andy Gibb
3/18	8	4.	Night Fever	Bee Gees
5/13	1	5.	If I Can't Have You	Yvonne Elliman
5/20	2	6.	With A Little Luck	Wings
6/03	1	7.	Too Much, Too Little, Too Late	Johnny Mathis/Deniece Williams
6/10	1	8.	You're The One That I Want	John Travolta & Olivia Newton-John
6/17	7	9.	Shadow Dancing	Andy Gibb
8/05	1	10.	Miss You	The Rolling Stones
8/12	2	11.	Three Times A Lady	Commodores
8/26	2	12.	Grease	Frankie Valli
9/09	3	13.	Boogie Oogie Oogie	A Taste Of Honey
9/30	4	14.	Kiss You All Over	Exile
10/28	1	15.	Hot Child In The City	Nick Gilder
11/04	1	16.	You Needed Me	Anne Murray
11/11	3	17.	MacArthur Park	Donna Summer

DATE	WKS		RECORD TITLE	ARTIST
12/02	2 ↕	18.	You Don't Bring Me Flowers	Barbra Streisand & Neil Diamond
12/09	6 ↕	19.	Le Freak	Chic

1979

DATE	WKS		RECORD TITLE	ARTIST
1/06	2	1.	Too Much Heaven	Bee Gees
2/10	4	2.	Da Ya Think I'm Sexy?	Rod Stewart
3/10	3 ↕	3.	I Will Survive	Gloria Gaynor
3/24	2	4.	Tragedy	Bee Gees
4/14	1	5.	What A Fool Believes	The Doobie Brothers
4/21	1	6.	Knock On Wood	Amii Stewart
4/28	1	7.	Heart Of Glass	Blondie
5/05	4	8.	Reunited	Peaches & Herb
6/02	3 ↕	9.	Hot Stuff	Donna Summer
6/09	1	10.	Love You Inside Out	Bee Gees
6/30	2	11.	Ring My Bell	Anita Ward
7/14	5	12.	Bad Girls	Donna Summer
8/18	1	13.	Good Times	Chic
8/25	6	14.	My Sharona	The Knack
10/06	1	15.	Sad Eyes	Robert John
10/13	1	16.	Don't Stop 'Til You Get Enough	Michael Jackson
10/20	2	17.	Rise	Herb Alpert
11/03	1	18.	Pop Muzik	M
11/10	1	19.	Heartache Tonight	Eagles
11/17	1	20.	Still	Commodores
11/24	2	21.	No More Tears (Enough Is Enough)	Barbra Streisand/Donna Summer
12/08	2	22.	Babe	Styx
12/22	3 ↕	23.	Escape (The Pina Colada Song)	Rupert Holmes

1980

DATE	WKS		RECORD TITLE	ARTIST
1/05	1	1.	Please Don't Go	K.C. & The Sunshine Band
1/19	4	2.	Rock With You	Michael Jackson
2/16	1	3.	Do That To Me One More Time	The Captain & Tennille
2/23	4	4.	Crazy Little Thing Called Love	Queen
3/22	4	5.	Another Brick In The Wall (Part II)	Pink Floyd
4/19	6	6.	Call Me	Blondie
5/31	4	7.	Funkytown	Lipps, Inc.
6/28	3	8.	Coming Up (Live at Glasgow)	Paul McCartney & Wings
7/19	2	9.	It's Still Rock And Roll To Me	Billy Joel
8/02	4	10.	Magic	Olivia Newton-John
8/30	1	11.	Sailing	Christopher Cross
9/06	4	12.	Upside Down	Diana Ross
10/4	3	13.	Another One Bites The Dust	Queen
10/25	3	14.	Woman In Love	Barbra Streisand
11/15	6	15.	Lady	Kenny Rogers
12/27	5	16.	(Just Like) Starting Over	John Lennon

1981

DATE	WKS		RECORD TITLE	ARTIST
1/31	1	1.	The Tide Is High	Blondie
2/07	2	2.	Celebration	Kool & The Gang
2/21	2 ↕	3.	9 To 5	Dolly Parton
2/28	2	4.	I Love A Rainy Night	Eddie Rabbitt
3/21	1	5.	Keep On Loving You	REO Speedwagon
3/28	2	6.	Rapture	Blondie

DATE	WKS		RECORD TITLE	ARTIST
4/11	3	7.	Kiss On My List	Daryl Hall & John Oates
5/02	2	8.	Morning Train (Nine To Five)	Sheena Easton
5/16	9 ↕	9.	Bette Davis Eyes	Kim Carnes
6/20	1	10.	Medley: Intro "Venus"	Stars on 45
7/25	1	11.	The One That You Love	Air Supply
8/01	2	12.	Jessie's Girl	Rick Springfield
8/15	9	13.	Endless Love	Diana Ross & Lionel Richie
10/17	3	14.	Arthur's Theme (Best That You Can Do)	Christopher Cross
11/07	2	15.	Private Eyes	Daryl Hall & John Oates
11/21	10	16.	Physical	Olivia Newton-John

1982

DATE	WKS		RECORD TITLE	ARTIST
1/30	1	1.	I Can't Go For That (No Can Do)	Daryl Hall & John Oates
2/06	6	2.	Centerfold	The J. Geils Band
3/20	7	3.	I Love Rock 'N Roll	Joan Jett & The Blackhearts
5/08	1	4.	Chariots Of Fire - Titles	Vangelis
5/15	7	5.	Ebony And Ivory	Paul McCartney with Stevie Wonder
7/03	3	6.	Don't You Want Me	The Human League
7/24	6	7.	Eye Of The Tiger	Survivor
9/04	2 ↕	8.	Abracadabra	The Steve Miller Band
9/11	2	9.	Hard To Say I'm Sorry	Chicago
10/02	4	10.	Jack & Diane	John Cougar
10/30	1	11.	Who Can It Be Now?	Men At Work
11/06	3	12.	Up Where We Belong	Joe Cocker & Jennifer Warnes
11/27	2	13.	Truly	Lionel Richie
12/11	1	14.	Mickey	Toni Basil
12/18	4	15.	Maneater	Daryl Hall & John Oates

1983

DATE	WKS		RECORD TITLE	ARTIST
1/15	4 ↕	1.	Down Under	Men At Work
2/05	1	2.	Africa	Toto
2/19	2	3.	Baby, Come To Me	Patti Austin with James Ingram
3/05	7	4.	Billie Jean	Michael Jackson
4/23	1	5.	Come On Eileen	Dexys Midnight Runners
4/30	3	6.	Beat It	Michael Jackson
5/21	1	7.	Let's Dance	David Bowie
5/28	6	8.	Flashdance...What A Feeling	Irene Cara
7/09	8	9.	Every Breath You Take	The Police
9/03	1	10.	Sweet Dreams (Are Made of This)	Eurythmics
9/10	2	11.	Maniac	Michael Sembello
9/24	1	12.	Tell Her About It	Billy Joel
10/01	4	13.	Total Eclipse Of The Heart	Bonnie Tyler
10/29	2	14.	Islands In The Stream	Kenny Rogers with Dolly Parton
11/12	4	15.	All Night Long (All Night)	Lionel Richie
12/10	6	16.	Say Say Say	Paul McCartney & Michael Jackson

1984

DATE	WKS		RECORD TITLE	ARTIST
1/21	2	1.	Owner Of A Lonely Heart	Yes
2/04	3	2.	Karma Chameleon	Culture Club
2/25	5	3.	Jump	Van Halen
3/31	3	4.	Footloose	Kenny Loggins
4/21	3	5.	Against All Odds (Take A Look At Me Now)	Phil Collins

DATE	WKS		RECORD TITLE	ARTIST
5/12	2	6.	Hello	Lionel Richie
5/26	2	7.	Let's Hear It For The Boy	Deniece Williams
6/09	2	8.	Time After Time	Cyndi Lauper
6/23	2	9.	The Reflex	Duran Duran
7/07	5	10.	When Doves Cry	Prince
8/11	3	11.	Ghostbusters	Ray Parker Jr.
9/01	3	12.	What's Love Got To Do With It	Tina Turner
9/22	1	13.	Missing You	John Waite
9/29	2	14.	Let's Go Crazy	Prince & the Revolution
10/13	3	15.	I Just Called To Say I Love You	Stevie Wonder
11/03	2	16.	Caribbean Queen (No More Love On The Run)	Billy Ocean
11/17	3	17.	Wake Me Up Before You Go-Go	Wham!
12/08	2	18.	Out Of Touch	Daryl Hall & John Oates
12/22	6	19.	Like A Virgin	Madonna

1985

DATE	WKS		RECORD TITLE	ARTIST
2/02	2	1.	I Want To Know What Love Is	Foreigner
2/16	3	2.	Careless Whisper	Wham! Featuring George Michael
3/09	3	3.	Can't Fight This Feeling	REO Speedwagon
3/30	2	4.	One More Night	Phil Collins
4/13	4	5.	We Are The World	USA for Africa
5/11	1	6.	Crazy For You	Madonna
5/18	1	7.	Don't You (Forget About Me)	Simple Minds
5/25	2	8.	Everything She Wants	Wham!
6/08	2	9.	Everybody Wants To Rule The World	Tears For Fears
6/22	2	10.	Heaven	Bryan Adams
7/06	1	11.	Sussudio	Phil Collins
7/13	2	12.	A View To A Kill	Duran Duran
7/27	1	13.	Everytime You Go Away	Paul Young
8/03	3	14.	Shout	Tears For Fears
8/24	2	15.	The Power Of Love	Huey Lewis & the News
9/07	2	16.	St. Elmo's Fire (Man In Motion)	John Parr
9/21	3	17.	Money For Nothing	Dire Straits
10/12	1	18.	Oh Sheila	Ready For The World
10/19	1	19.	Take On Me	a-ha
10/26	1	20.	Saving All My Love For You	Whitney Houston
11/02	1	21.	Part-Time Lover	Stevie Wonder
11/09	1	22.	Miami Vice Theme	Jan Hammer
11/16	2	23.	We Built This City	Starship
11/30	1	24.	Separate Lives	Phil Collins & Marilyn Martin
12/07	2	25.	Broken Wings	Mr. Mister
12/21	4	26.	Say You, Say Me	Lionel Richie

1986

DATE	WKS		RECORD TITLE	ARTIST
1/18	4	1.	That's What Friends Are For	Dionne & Friends
2/15	2	2.	How Will I Know	Whitney Houston
3/01	2	3.	Kyrie	Mr. Mister
3/15	1	4.	Sara	Starship
3/22	1	5.	These Dreams	Heart
3/29	3	6.	Rock Me Amadeus	Falco
4/19	2	7.	Kiss	Prince & The Revolution
5/03	1	8.	Addicted To Love	Robert Palmer
5/10	1	9.	West End Girls	Pet Shop Boys
5/17	3	10.	Greatest Love Of All	Whitney Houston

DATE	WKS		RECORD TITLE	ARTIST
6/07	1	11.	Live To Tell	Madonna
6/14	3	12.	On My Own	Patti LaBelle & Michael McDonald
7/05	1	13.	There'll Be Sad Songs (To Make You Cry)	Billy Ocean
7/12	1	14.	Holding Back The Years	Simply Red
7/19	1	15.	Invisible Touch	Genesis
7/26	1	16.	Sledgehammer	Peter Gabriel
8/02	2	17.	Glory Of Love	Peter Cetera
8/16	2	18.	Papa Don't Preach	Madonna
8/30	1	19.	Higher Love	Steve Winwood
9/06	1	20.	Venus	Bananarama
9/13	1	21.	Take My Breath Away	Berlin
9/20	3	22.	Stuck With You	Huey Lewis & the News
10/11	2	23.	When I Think Of You	Janet Jackson
10/25	2	24.	True Colors	Cyndi Lauper
11/08	2	25.	Amanda	Boston
11/22	1	26.	Human	Human League
11/29	1	27.	You Give Love A Bad Name	Bon Jovi
12/06	1	28.	The Next Time I Fall	Peter Cetera w/Amy Grant
12/13	1	29.	The Way It Is	Bruce Hornsby & The Range
12/20	4	30.	Walk Like An Egyptian	Bangles

1987

DATE	WKS		RECORD TITLE	ARTIST
1/17	1	1.	Shake You Down	Gregory Abbott
1/24	2	2.	At This Moment	Billy Vera & The Beaters
2/07	1	3.	Open Your Heart	Madonna
2/14	4	4.	Livin' On A Prayer	Bon Jovi
3/14	1	5.	Jacob's Ladder	Huey Lewis & the News
3/21	2	6.	Lean On Me	Club Nouveau
4/04	2	7.	Nothing's Gonna Stop Us Now	Starship
4/18	2	8.	I Knew You Were Waiting (For Me)	Aretha Franklin & George Michael
5/02	2	9.	(I Just) Died In Your Arms	Cutting Crew
5/16	3	10.	With Or Without You	U2
6/06	1	11.	You Keep Me Hangin' On	Kim Wilde
6/13	1	12.	Always	Atlantic Starr
6/20	1	13.	Head To Toe	Lisa Lisa & Cult Jam
6/27	2	14.	I Wanna Dance With Somebody (Who Loves Me)	Whitney Houston
7/11	3	15.	Alone	Heart
8/01	1	16.	Shakedown	Bob Seger
8/08	2	17.	I Still Haven't Found What I'm Looking For	U2
8/22	1	18.	Who's That Girl	Madonna
8/29	3	19.	La Bamba	Los Lobos
9/19	1	20.	I Just Can't Stop Loving You	Michael Jackson
9/26	2	21.	Didn't We Almost Have It All	Whitney Houston
10/10	1	22.	Here I Go Again	Whitesnake
10/17	1	23.	Lost In Emotion	Lisa Lisa & Cult Jam
10/24	2	24.	Bad	Michael Jackson
11/07	2	25.	I Think We're Alone Now	Tiffany
11/21	1	26.	Mony Mony "Live"	Billy Idol
11/28	1	27.	(I've Had) The Time Of My Life	Bill Medley & Jennifer Warnes
12/05	1	28.	Heaven Is A Place On Earth	Belinda Carlisle
12/12	4	29.	Faith	George Michael

DATE	WKS	RECORD TITLE	ARTIST
		1988	
1/09	1	1. So Emotional	Whitney Houston
1/16	1	2. Got My Mind Set On You	George Harrison
1/23	1	3. The Way You Make Me Feel	Michael Jackson
1/30	1	4. Need You Tonight	INXS
2/06	2	5. Could've Been	Tiffany
2/20	1	6. Seasons Change	Expose
2/27	2	7. Father Figure	George Michael
3/12	2	8. Never Gonna Give You Up	Rick Astley
3/26	2	9. Man In The Mirror	Michael Jackson
4/09	2	10. Get Outta My Dreams, Get Into My Car	Billy Ocean
4/23	2	11. Where Do Broken Hearts Go	Whitney Houston
5/07	1	12. Wishing Well	Terence Trent D'Arby
5/14	2	13. Anything For You	Gloria Estefan & Miami Sound Machine
5/28	3	14. One More Try	George Michael
6/18	1	15. Together Forever	Rick Astley
6/25	1	16. Foolish Beat	Debbie Gibson
7/02	1	17. Dirty Diana	Michael Jackson
7/09	2	18. The Flame	Cheap Trick
7/23	1	19. Hold On To The Nights	Richard Marx
7/30	4	20. Roll With It	Steve Winwood
8/27	2	21. Monkey	George Michael
9/10	2	22. Sweet Child O' Mine	Guns N' Roses
9/24	2	23. Don't Worry Be Happy	Bobby McFerrin
10/08	1	24. Love Bites	Def Leppard
10/15	1	25. Red Red Wine	UB40
10/22	2	26. Groovy Kind Of Love	Phil Collins
11/05	1	27. Kokomo	The Beach Boys
11/12	1	28. Wild, Wild West	The Escape Club
11/19	2	29. Bad Medicine	Bon Jovi
12/03	1	30. Baby, I Love Your Way/Freebird Medley (Free Baby)	Will To Power
12/10	2	31. Look Away	Chicago
12/24	3	32. Every Rose Has Its Thorn	Poison
		1989	
1/14	1	1. My Prerogative	Bobby Brown
1/21	2	2. Two Hearts	Phil Collins
2/04	1	3. When I'm With You	Sheriff
2/11	3	4. Straight Up	Paula Abdul
3/04	3	5. Lost In Your Eyes	Debbie Gibson
3/25	1	6. The Living Years	Mike & The Mechanics
4/01	1	7. Eternal Flame	Bangles
4/08	1	8. The Look	Roxette
4/15	1	9. She Drives Me Crazy	Fine Young Cannibals
4/22	3	10. Like A Prayer	Madonna
5/13	1	11. I'll Be There For You	Bon Jovi
5/20	2	12. Forever Your Girl	Paula Abdul
6/03	1	13. Rock On	Michael Damian
6/10	1	14. Wind Beneath My Wings	Bette Midler
6/17	1	15. I'll Be Loving You (Forever)	New Kids On The Block
6/24	1	16. Satisfied	Richard Marx
7/01	1	17. Baby Don't Forget My Number	Milli Vanilli

DATE	WKS		RECORD TITLE	ARTIST
7/08	1	18.	Good Thing	Fine Young Cannibals
7/15	1	19.	If You Don't Know Me By Now	Simply Red
7/22	2	20.	Toy Soldiers	Martika
8/05	1	21.	Batdance	Prince
8/12	3	22.	Right Here Waiting	Richard Marx
9/02	1	23.	Cold Hearted	Paula Abdul
9/09	1	24.	Hangin' Tough	New Kids On The Block
9/16	1	25.	Don't Wanna Lose You	Gloria Estefan
9/23	2	26.	Girl I'm Gonna Miss You	Milli Vanilli
10/07	4	27.	Miss You Much	Janet Jackson
11/04	1	28.	Listen To Your Heart	Roxette
11/11	2	29.	When I See You Smile	Bad English
11/25	2	30.	Blame It On The Rain	Milli Vanilli
12/09	2	31.	We Didn't Start The Fire	Billy Joel
12/23	4	32.	Another Day In Paradise	Phil Collins

1990

DATE	WKS		RECORD TITLE	ARTIST
1/20	3	1.	How Am I Supposed To Live Without You	Michael Bolton
2/10	3	2.	Opposites Attract	Paula Abdul with The Wild Pair
3/03	3	3.	Escapade	Janet Jackson
3/24	2	4.	Black Velvet	Alannah Myles
4/07	1	5.	Love Will Lead You Back	Taylor Dayne
4/14	1	6.	I'll Be Your Everything	Tommy Page
4/21	4	7.	Nothing Compares 2 U	Sinead O'Connor
5/19	3	8.	Vogue	Madonna
6/09	1	9.	Hold On	Wilson Phillips
6/16	2	10.	It Must Have Been Love	Roxette
6/30	3	11.	Step By Step	New Kids On The Block
7/21	2	12.	She Ain't Worth It	Glenn Medeiros Feat. Bobby Brown
8/04	4	13.	Vision Of Love	Mariah Carey
9/01	1	14.	If Wishes Came True	Sweet Sensation
9/08	1	15.	Blaze Of Glory	Jon Bon Jovi
9/15	2	16.	Release Me	Wilson Phillips
9/29	1	17.	(Can't Live Without Your) Love And Affection	Nelson
10/06	1	18.	Close To You	Maxi Priest
10/13	1	19.	Praying For Time	George Michael
10/20	1	20.	I Don't Have The Heart	James Ingram
10/27	1	21.	Black Cat	Janet Jackson
11/03	1	22.	Ice Ice Baby	Vanilla Ice
11/10	3	23.	Love Takes Time	Mariah Carey
12/01	1	24.	I'm Your Baby Tonight	Whitney Houston
12/08	4	25.	Because I Love You (The Postman Song)	Stevie B

1991

DATE	WKS		RECORD TITLE	ARTIST
1/05	2	1.	Justify My Love	Madonna
1/19	1	2.	Love Will Never Do (Without You)	Janet Jackson
1/26	2	3.	The First Time	Surface
2/09	2	4.	Gonna Make You Sweat (Everybody Dance Now)	C & C Music Factory Featuring Freedom Williams
2/23	2	5.	All The Man That I Need	Whitney Houston
3/09	2	6.	Someday	Mariah Carey
3/23	1	7.	One More Try	Timmy -T-

DATE	WKS		RECORD TITLE	ARTIST
3/30	2	8.	Coming Out Of The Dark	Gloria Estefan
4/13	1	9.	I've Been Thinking About You	Londonbeat
4/20	1	10.	You're In Love	Wilson Phillips
4/27	2	11.	Baby Baby	Amy Grant
5/11	1	12.	Joyride	Roxette
5/18	1	13.	I Like The Way (The Kissing Game)	Hi-Five
5/25	2	14.	I Don't Wanna Cry	Mariah Carey
6/08	1	15.	More Than Words	Extreme
6/15	5	16.	Rush, Rush	Paula Abdul
7/20	1	17.	Unbelievable	EMF
7/27	7	18.	(Everything I Do) I Do It For You	Bryan Adams
9/14	1	19.	The Promise Of A New Day	Paula Abdul
9/21	2	20.	I Adore Mi Amor	Color Me Badd
10/05	1	21.	Good Vibrations	Marky Mark & The Funky Bunch Featuring Loleatta Holloway
10/12	3	22.	Emotions	Mariah Carey
11/02	1	23.	Romantic	Karyn White
11/09	2	24.	Cream	Prince And The N.P.G.
11/23	1	25.	When A Man Loves A Woman	Michael Bolton

**11/30/91: BILLBOARD BEGINS COMPILING "HOT 100"
FROM DATA PROVIDED BY BDS AND SOUNDSCAN.**

DATE	WKS		RECORD TITLE	ARTIST
11/30	1	26.	Set Adrift On Memory Bliss	PM Dawn
12/07	7	27.	Black Or White	Michael Jackson

1992

DATE	WKS		RECORD TITLE	ARTIST
1/25	1	1.	All 4 Love	Color Me Badd
2/01	1	2.	Don't Let The Sun Go Down On Me	George Michael/Elton John
2/08	3	3.	I'm Too Sexy	R*S*F (Right Said Fred)
2/29	3	4.	To Be With You	Mr. Big
3/21	5	5.	Save The Best For Last	Vanessa Williams
4/25	8	6.	Jump	Kris Kross
6/20	2	7.	I'll Be There	Mariah Carey
7/04	5	8.	Baby Got Back	Sir Mix-A-Lot
8/08	1	9.	This Used To Be My Playground	Madonna
8/15	13	10.	End of the Road	Boyz II Men
11/14	2	11.	How Do You Talk To An Angel	The Heights
11/28	14	12.	I Will Always Love You	Whitney Houston

1993

DATE	WKS		RECORD TITLE	ARTIST
3/06	1	1.	A Whole New World (Aladdin's Theme)	Peabo Bryson & Regina Belle
3/13	7	2.	Informer	Snow
5/01	2	3.	Freak Me	Silk
5/15	8	4.	That's The Way Love Goes	Janet Jackson
7/10	2	5.	Weak	SWV (Sisters With Voices)
7/24	7	6.	Can't Help Falling In Love	UB40
9/11	8	7.	Dreamlover	Mariah Carey
11/06	5	8.	I'd Do Anything For Love (But I Won't Do That)	Meat Loaf
12/11	2	9.	Again	Janet Jackson
12/25	4	10.	Hero	Mariah Carey

DATE	WKS		RECORD TITLE	ARTIST
			1994	
1/22	3	1.	All For Love	Bryan Adams/Rod Stewart/Sting
2/12	4	2.	The Power Of Love	Celine Dion
3/12	6 ↕	3.	The Sign	Ace Of Base
4/09	4	4.	Bump N' Grind	R. Kelly
5/21	11	5.	I Swear	All-4-One
8/06	3	6.	Stay (I Missed You)	Lisa Loeb & Nine Stories
8/27	14	7.	I'll Make Love To You	Boyz II Men
12/03	6 ↕	8.	On Bended Knee	Boyz II Men
12/17	2	9.	Here Comes The Hotstepper	Ini Kamoze
			1995	
1/28	4	1.	Creep	TLC
2/25	7	2.	Take A Bow	Madonna
4/15	7	3.	This Is How We Do It	Montell Jordan
6/03	5	4.	Have You Ever Really Loved Woman	Bryan Adams
7/08	7	5.	Waterfalls	TLC
8/26	1	6.	Kiss From A Rose	Seal
9/02	1	7.	You Are Not Alone	Michael Jackson
9/09	3	8.	Gangstas Paradise	Coolio Featuring L.V.
9/30	8	9.	Fantasy	Mariah Carey
11/25	1	10.	Exhale (Shoop Shoop)	Whitney Houston
12/02	16	11.	One Sweet Day	Mariah Carey & Boyz II Men

ALL THE HITS THAT EVER CHARTED!

Only Joel Whitburn's Record Research Books List Every Record To Appear On Every Major Billboard Chart.

Each book lists every record's significant chart data, such as peak position, debut date, peak date, weeks charted, label, record number and much more, all conveniently arranged for fast, easy reference. Most books also feature artist biographies, record notes, RIAA Platinum/Gold Record certifications, top artist and record achievements, all-time artist and record rankings, a chronological listing of all #1 hits, and additional in-depth chart information.

TOP POP SINGLES 1955–1993 — Over 20,000 Pop singles — every "Hot 100" hit — arranged by artist. 912 pages. $74.95 Hardcover/$64.95 Softcover.

POP ANNUAL 1955–1994 — A year-by-year ranking, based on chart performance, of over 20,000 Pop hits. 880 pages. $69.95 Hardcover/ $59.95 Softcover.

POP HITS 1940–1954 — Compiled strictly from *Billboard* and divided into artist-by-artist and year-by-year sections. 414 pages. Hardcover. $44.95.

POP MEMORIES 1890–1954 — An artist-by-artist, title-by-title chronicle of the 65 formative years of recorded popular music. 660 pages. Hardcover. $59.95.

TOP POP ALBUMS 1955–1992 — Over 17,000 albums that ever appeared on *Billboard's* Pop albums charts, listed by artist. 976 pages. Hardcover. $54.95.

TOP POP ALBUM TRACKS 1955–1992 — An alphabetical index of every song track from every charted pop album. 544 pages. Hardcover. $34.95.

TOP 10 CHARTS 1958–1995 — A complete listing of each weekly Top 10 chart from every "Hot 100" chart, and more! 732 pages. Softcover. $49.95

ROCK TRACKS — Two artist-by-artist listings of all the titles that appeared on *Billboard's* "Album Rock Tracks," and "Modern Rock Tracks" from 1981-1995. 288 pages. Softcover. $34.95.

BUBBLING UNDER THE HOT 100 1959–1985 — All the hits from *Billboard's* unique "Bubbling Under" chart, listed by artist. 384 pages. Hardcover. $34.95.

BILLBOARD HOT 100/POP SINGLES CHARTS:
THE EIGHTIES 1980–1989
THE SEVENTIES 1970–1979
THE SIXTIES 1960–1969
THE FIFTIES 1955–1959
> Four complete collections of the actual weekly "Hot 100" charts from each decade, reproduced in black-and-white at 70% of original size. Over 550 pages each. Deluxe Hardcover. $79.95 each.

BILLBOARD POP ALBUM CHARTS 1965–1969 — Every weekly *Billboard* Pop albums chart, shown in its entirety, from 1965 through 1969. All charts reproduced in black-and-white at 70% of original size. 496 pages. Deluxe Hardcover. $59.95.

TOP COUNTRY SINGLES 1944–1993 — An artist-by-artist listing of every "Country" single ever charted. 624 pages. Hardcover. $59.95.

TOP R&B SINGLES 1942–1995 — Every "Soul," "Black," and "Rhythm & Blues" charted single, listed by artist. 704 pages. Hardcover. $64.95.

TOP ADULT CONTEMPORARY 1961–1993 — Lists, artist by artist, the complete history of *Billboard's* "Easy Listening" and "Adult Contemporary" charts. 368 pages. Hardcover. $39.95.

MUSIC YEARBOOKS 1995/1994/1993/1992/1991/ 1990 — Yearly comprehensive reviews of *Billboard's* major charts. Various page lengths. Softcover. $29.95 to $34.95 each.

For complete book descriptions and ordering information, call, write, fax or e-mail today.

RECORD RESEARCH INC.
P.O. Box 200
Menomonee Falls, WI 53052-0200 U.S.A.
Phone: 414-251-5408 / Fax: 414-251-9452
Web Site: http://www.recordresearch.com / E-mail: record@execpc.com